Interact with your textbook

→ **each book in the complete series offers free teaching and learning solutions online**

www.oxfordtextbooks.co.uk/orc/c

complete: law solution

 online resource centre
www.oxfordtextbooks.co.uk/orc/abass2e/

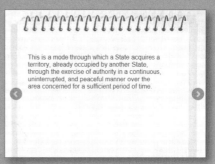

This is a mode through which a State acquires a territory, already occupied by another State, through the exercise of authority in a continuous, uninterrupted, and peaceful manner over the area concerned for a sufficient period of time.

For lecturers

→ A test bank of multiple choice questions

For students

→ Appendices
→ Guidance on answering discussion questions
→ Flashcard glossary
→ Web links

See the **Guide to the Online Resource Centre** on p. viii for full details.

complete

International Law

Text, Cases, and Materials

Second edition

Ademola Abass

LLM (Cantab), PhD (Nottingham)
Fellow of the Cambridge Commonwealth Society
Adjunct Professor of International Law
University of Leuven, Belgium

OXFORD
UNIVERSITY PRESS

Great Clarendon Street, Oxford, OX2 6DP,
United Kingdom

Oxford University Press is a department of the University of Oxford.
It furthers the University's objective of excellence in research, scholarship,
and education by publishing worldwide. Oxford is a registered trade mark of
Oxford University Press in the UK and in certain other countries

1st edition 2012

Impression: 4

Published in the United States of America by Oxford University Press
198 Madison Avenue, New York, NY 10016, United States of America

British Library Cataloguing in Publication Data
Data available

Library of Congress Control Number: 2014934001

ISBN 978–0–19–967907–2

Printed in Great Britain by
Ashford Colour Press Ltd, Gosport, Hampshire

To my son, Kobi

Guide to using the book

Complete International Law: Text, Cases, and Materials is complemented by a number of features which are designed to enrich your learning and provide additional support as you progress through your international law module. This guide highlights the various features to help you to get the most out of your textbook.

● **United Kingdom v. Iceland** [1973] ICJ REP 3 [The **Fisheries Jurisdiction Cases**]

Iceland claimed the authority to extend its fishing zone unilaterally from twe
cal miles. It gave notice of its intention to the UK in 1971, but went ahead
the zone despite the UK's objection. This notice was in accordance with the
between Iceland and the UK to the effect that the former would not extend
without giving the latter at least six months' notice. The 1961 agreement was
exchange of notes between the two countries, which also entitled the two co
jurisdiction on the Court if a dispute arose between the two. The UK conten

Cases and materials

Cases play a pivotal role in shaping international law, so it is important to read first-hand reports in order to fully understand the subject. This book includes extracts from a wide range of cases, legislation, and academic material which complement and illustrate the text.

Learning objectives

This chapter will help you to:

• learn in brief the historical development of international l
• understand the meaning and concept of 'international lav
• appreciate the nature, basis, and function of international

Learning objectives

Each chapter begins with a bulleted outline of the key concepts which you should understand by the end of the chapter.

thinking points

• For how long, and by how many States, should a us
  be regarded as a rule of customary international law
• If State practice consists in what States do or say, wha
  from doing as a matter of legal obligation?

Thinking points

Why was a particular decision reached in a certain case? Is the law on this point logical and coherent? Thinking points draw out these issues and help you to stop and reflect on these questions.

KEY POINTS

• 'Sources of law' are vital for establishing the val

• Sources of law may be formal or material, althou
  'formal', in its real connotation, can be applied

• There are no law-making institutions in interna

Key points

Key points provide a commentary on cases and emphasize the essential points of law.

Conclusion

State responsibility refers to the liability of States for
breaches or violations of international obligations. Such
out of recognized rules of general international law. Th
between States, or between States and the nationals o
legal or juristic persons. We have noted the rules rela
by States on the international plane and instance

Chapter conclusions

The central points and concepts covered in each chapter
are distilled into conclusions at the end of chapters. These
reinforce your understanding and can be used for quick
revision.

Key cases

- *Botswana v. Namibia* (1999) ICJ Rep 1045 (the *Kasikil*
- *Cameroon v. Nigeria; Equatorial Guinea Intervening (2
  Maritime Boundary between Cameroon and Nigeria)*
- *Conditions of Admission of a State Membership in the
  (1957) ICJ Rep 57 (the Condition of Admissions C*

Key cases

A list of key cases is provided at the end of each chapter.

Questions

Self-test questions

1 Explain the terms 'monism' and 'dualism'.

2 What obligations do States incur under international treaties concern
tion of international law?

3 Distinguish between 'transformed' and 'untransformed' treaties.

4 What does 'incorporation' mean?

Self-test questions

Self-test questions at the end of chapters help you to recap
the topic covered and encourage you to test your understanding of the law.

Discussion questions

1 'The International Court of Justice cannot review t
Nations.' With reference to case law, consider to w
practice of the Court.

2 What is legal personality in relation to internationa
mined in international law?

Discussion questions

Discussion questions at the end of each chapter help you
to develop analytical and problem-solving skills.

Assessment question

Teletoys, a company registered in Candoma, entered into
State Department with 500 plasma units during the reign
the military junta overthrew the democratic government
it until it was overthrown in 2008 by another military ju
brought an action against Rutamu, following the refusal
Teletoys money due under the contract. Roué's governr

Assessment questions

Assessment questions provide examples of the types of
problem and essay questions you will encounter in the
exams.

Further reading

Bardonnet, D., 'Les frontières terrestres et la relativité de leu
(1976) 153 Recueil des cours de l'Académie de Droit Intern

Crawford, J., *The Creation of States in International Law* (2nd
2006)

Grant, T. D., 'Defining statehood: the Montevideo Conven

Further reading

Selected further reading is included at the end of each
chapter to provide a springboard for further study.

Guide to the Online Resource Centre

The Online Resource Centre that accompanies this book provides students and lecturers with ready-to-use learning resources. They are free of charge, and are designed to complement the book and maximize the teaching and learning experience.

www.oxfordtextbooks.co.uk/orc/abass2e/

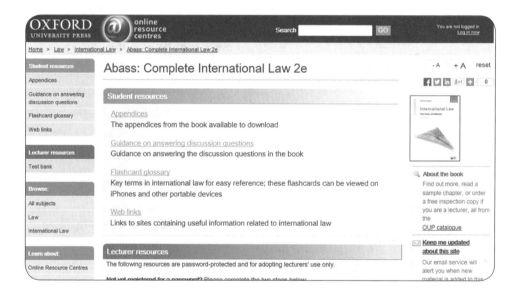

For students

These resources are available to all, enabling students to get the most from their textbook; no registration or password required.

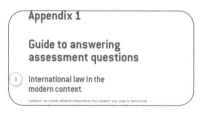

Appendices

The appendices from the book are available to download. These include guides to answering assessment and discussion questions.

Discussion Questions and Answers

Chapter 1: International law in modern context

1. To what extent is the assertion that international law is not law a true reflection of international law?

Start with the reasoning as to why international law was not originally thought of as a distinct field of law. Highlight the linkage between international law and politics in the thinking at the time. What were the original uses of teaching international law and who was it aimed at? What was the focus of the study? How was international law thought of by judges at the time? Recall the attitude of the English courts and judges and any famous sayings in this aspect. Explain the evolution of international law into the area known today. Emphasize the absence of enforcement mechanisms in

Guidance on answering discussion questions

Advice from the author on how to approach the end-of-chapter exam-style questions which appear in the book.

Abass: Complete International Law, 2nd edition Flashcards

Instructions: Click on the card to flip it, use the navigational arrow buttons to view the previous/next cards, and the links below for additional functionality.

Condomium

Flashcard glossary

Test your knowledge of the key terminology used in international law.

Chapter 01

For a definition of international law:
http://www.globalization101.org/index.php?file=issue&pass1=subs&id=232
http://www.wisegeek.com/what-is-international-law.htm

For a short history of international law:
http://www.globalization101.org/index.php?file=issue&pass1=subs&id=232
http://legalhistoryblog.blogspot.com/2009/12/history-of-international-law.html

For the distinction between Public international Law and Private international law:
http://www.law.cornell.edu/wex/international_law

For a survey of international law:

Web links

Annotated links to useful websites enable you to click straight through to reliable sources of information and efficiently direct your online study.

For lecturers

These resources are password-protected for adopting lecturers to assist in their teaching. Registering is easy: click on 'Lecturer resources' on the Online Resource Centre and complete a simple registration form which allows you to choose you own username and password.

International law regulates the relationship between which of the following? Please select all that apply.

☐ a. States and States
☐ b. Individuals and individuals
☐ c. Nationals and foreigners within a State
☐ d. States and their subjects

General Feedback
International law regulates how States interact with each other as well as governing the relationship between a State and its subjects within its own territory and externally. It does not regulate the behaviour of individuals towards each other, which is the area of municipal/domestic law.
Section reference Section 1

Test bank

A fully customizable test bank of a range of different types of questions including multiple response, multiple choice, fill-in-the-blank, and true-false, with answers and feedback to test your students.

Preface

Much has happened in the world since the publication of the first edition of this book in 2012. In that short period, the Arab Spring revolution blew away governments in Libya, Tunisia, and Egypt, but met a darker fate in Syria where the government and armed opposition have subjected ordinary Syrians to a colossal humanitarian disaster. On a more cheerful note, the International Law Commission concluded its work on the responsibility of international organizations, while the International Criminal Court (ICC) continues to make progress in holding leaders of countries accountable for violations of international crimes. At the expiration of the first phase of the Kyoto Protocol in December 2012, States recommitted themselves to reducing greenhouse gases (GHG) for another seven years (2013–2020). The second edition of this book attempts to reflect some of the changes that have taken place over the past three years.

I have tried as much as space permitted to reflect the suggestions and recommendations made by students and colleagues from literally across the world, and I am grateful for the professional insights and judgements of the anonymous reviewers for Oxford University Press. I very much hope that in the new chapters on international humanitarian law and the law of immunity, in the expanded chapters of international economic law and the law of treaties, in the reworked chapters on collective security and international organizations, in updating every single chapter of the book, in restructuring and reordering some chapters, and in tightening and easing the language in specific places, your efforts and words of encouragement have not fallen on deaf ears.

I thank Dominique Mystris for received assistance, and Ilias Bantekas for advice on some of the chapters. The understanding and perseverance of the Oxford University Press team, especially Carol Barber, are fundamental to the completion of this edition. To my wife and kid, as ever, thanks for your love.

AA

Brussels

2014

New to this edition

- Two new chapters—on immunity and international humanitarian law
- Expanded chapters on the law of treaties and international economic law
- Complete reworking of the chapter on collective security law
- Discussion of the responsibility of international organizations
- Inclusion of the post-Kyoto regulation in the international environmental law chapter
- Analysis of the procedural concerns raised by the first case to be decided by the ICC, *Thomas Lubanga*, and an assessment of its impact on the development of war crimes elements: *actus reus* and *mens rea*

Contents

Contents

Contents

xviii

Table of cases

Table of statutes of the international courts

Page references in **bold** indicate that the text is reproduced in full

Table of treaties and conventions

Page references in **bold** indicate that the text is reproduced in full

Table of other documents

1

International law in the modern context

Learning objectives

This chapter will help you to:

- learn in brief the historical development of international law;
- understand the meaning and concept of 'international law';
- appreciate the nature, basis, and function of international law; and
- understand the modern context of international law.

Introduction

Not long ago, international law was regarded as unserious, unenforceable, and something of a 'non-law' discipline. It meant little or nothing then to refer to oneself or be referred to as an 'international lawyer'. International law was regarded as politics dressed in the language of the law—a sentiment also reflected in academia. In most countries, university curricula did not include 'international law' until around the late 1970s. Academic writers rarely wrote about international law, and the few who did so wrote mainly for the benefit of officials of foreign ministries and diplomats, who were mostly concerned with issues relating to consular relations and the protection of aliens in their countries. The rather cynical attitude of most countries towards international law was aptly captured by a famous English adage 'English Law is law, foreign law is fact, and international law is fiction' (restated in A Contributor (1995) 54 CLJ 230.

In the last fifty years, however, international law has witnessed a radical transformation. Not only is it the fastest growing of any legal discipline today, it is perhaps the most fashionable of all legal disciplines for law students to pursue. From its relative obscurity as a discipline developed mainly for the convenience of States and of which 'the great majority of the lawyers of all states [knew] little or nothing', as Oppenheim once put it (see 'The Science of International Law: Its Task and Method' (1908) 2 AJIL 313, 323), international law has grown into the most effective weapon for preserving global peace and security. Today, international law regulates not only how States behave towards one another, but also how States deal with their own subjects, especially concerning the protection of human rights, even within a State's own territory. This chapter provides a concise discussion of what international law is all about. It analyses the basis, nature, and ramifications of international law, and considers how international law has become such a powerful tool for regulating interstate relations, and how its rules and principles are now applied across civilizations, religions, and cultures all over the world.

1.1 A brief history of international law: a distinction between the 'origin' and 'documentation' of international law

There is an extensive literature on the history and development of international law. However, 'history' depends on who is telling it, for what purpose, and for the benefit of which audience. For example, it is customary for most textbook writers to begin chronicling the origin of international law by referring to developments in Western society. Some writers say that international law, properly so called, *began* with the conclusion of the Peace of Westphalia in 1648, which ended the Thirty Years War in Europe. Some locate the birth of international law in the post-Renaissance period or the classical era in Europe. Other accounts have provided more or less recent narratives than these dates.

One common trend in most historical accounts of the origin of international law is the tendency for writers to confuse the period when the *formal documentation* of international law began with when international law, as a distinct legal field, emerged. These are two remarkably different issues that must not be confused. It is important to distinguish between saying that international law, as *used in modern times*, began to *grow* from the second half of the Middle Ages, and saying that international law actually *began* in the Middle Ages.

In Robert Jennings and Arthur Watts (eds), *Oppenheim's International Law, Vol. 1: Peace* (9th edn, London/New York: Longman, 1996), p. 4, it is stated that:

> As a *systematised body* of rules [international law] owes much to the Dutch jurist Hugo Grotius, whose work, *De jure belli ac pacis libri tres*, appeared in 1625, and became a foundation of later development. [Emphasis added]

This is a widely accepted view of when international law started to be properly *documented and systematized in contrast to when it actually emerged*. It is important to maintain this type of distinction, in order to ensure the accuracy of historical analysis.

For many reasons it is difficult to speculate when international law was actually born. For instance, the Chinese are among the various peoples credited with inventing the art of writing, even if it was perfected elsewhere. Nonetheless, the various Chinese languages were not accessible to a great part of the world until fairly recently. In this situation, how can one be sure what the early Chinese scholars wrote about international law or State relations, or if they wrote on the subject at all.

Another difficulty is the question of who documented international law and what parameters were used in determining what constituted international law. Until the twentieth century, the standard for measuring acceptability of civilization was mainly Western. In the *Institutes of the Law of Nations* (1884), James Lorimer classified China as 'barbarous'. In the first edition of his *International Law: A Treatise*, Vol. 1 (London: Longman: 1905), pp. 32–34, Oppenheim ranked European States as number 1, American States, Liberia, and Haiti as number 2, Turkey number 3, Japan number 4, and Persia, Siam, China, Korea, and Abyssinia as number 5. He specifically pronounced that countries in the lower category have not raised their civilization to the level of the Western States. In 1955, H. Lauterpacht (ed.), *Oppenheim's International Law: A Treatise, Vol. 1: Peace* (8th edn, London: Longman, 1955), p. 49, the author added India and Pakistan to the fourth category and removed Korea and Persia from the fifth.

Perhaps this classification reflects the personal opinions of individual authors. However, such opinions significantly affect how the contributions made by others are regarded. (For general discussion, see Xue Hanqin, *Chinese Contemporary Perspectives of International Law. History, Culture, and International Law*, 355 Recueil des cours (Hague Academy of International Law, 2012); Sundhya Pahuja, *Decolonising International Law* (Cambridge: Cambridge University Press, 2011).

Authoritative international legal scholars have also shown that the general belief that Hugo Grotius's work was the first *proper* documentation of international law was inaccurate.

According to Jennings and Watts (1996, see section 1.1):

> Although he is rightly called the father of the law of nature as well as the law of nations, he has *created neither the one nor the other*. Long before Grotius, the opinion was generally prevalent that above the positive law which had grown up by custom or by legislation there was in existence another law which had its roots in human reason and was therefore called the 'law of nature'. [Emphasis added]

One major problem with attempting to put a specific date on the origin of international law is that most of what became international law principles already existed among primitive nations long before documentation started. An example is the principle of good faith.

In his book *Histories* (trans. A. de Sélincourt, Harmondsworth: Penguin, 1954), Herodotus, the ancient Greek historian, recorded the early transactions that took place between certain North African tribes. These early transactions, for the most part, constituted a practice whereby commodities were sold between two tribes without as much as an exchange of words. The Carthaginians, who inhabited several cities from the Gulf of Tunis to present-day Tunisia around 1 BC, would arrive in ships, offload their goods onto the beach, send a smoke signal, and then retire. The other tribes would come, inspect the goods, and deposit a sum in gold that they deemed a fair price for the goods. The Carthaginians would return, inspect the gold, and, if satisfied, would take the payment and depart; if not, they would leave both the gold and goods untouched until the other tribe deposited a fair price. This is what Herodotus described in his work as 'silent trading'—but see also Stephen Neff, 'A short history of international law' in Malcolm Evans (ed.), *International Law* (3rd edn, Oxford: Oxford University Press, 2010), at p. 4.

It may be too optimistic to regard this episode as international law proper. Nonetheless, the narrative indicated the evolution of the doctrine of *good faith* amongst 'nations', even if this primitive form did not exactly correspond to the *pacta sunt servanda*. As we will see in Chapter 3 dealing with the law of treaties, this well-established principle of international law enjoins States to implement faithfully those obligations that they assume under international law.

The various instances recalled earlier show the need to be cautious when dealing with historical accounts of the origin of international law. However, by distinguishing the 'origin' of international law from its 'documentation', as Oppenheim did in the previous quotation, we avoid making hasty and often ill-founded conclusions about the 'inception' of international law.

There is little academic benefit to derive from seeking the 'origin' of international law. As such, this book seeks to understand the 'meaning', 'basis', 'nature', and the 'modern context' of international law. Understanding these topics will be of greater benefit to those who are new to the subject than would be an attempt to establish the origin of international law—at least until such time as, as Oppenheim hoped in 'The Science of International Law: Its Task and Method' (1908) 2 AJIL 313, 317:

> The master-historian, to whose appearance we look forward, will in especial have to bring to light the part certain states have played in the victorious development of certain rules and what were the economic, political, humanitarian, religious, and other interests which have helped to establish the present rules of international law.

thinking points

- Why is it difficult to render accurately a historical account of the origin of international law?
- What should be the focus of any account of how and why international law began?
- What is the importance of Hugo Grotius's early work on the development of international law?

1.2 The meaning and concept of international law

1.2.1 What is 'international law'?

'International law' was believed to have been coined by the British philosopher Jeremy Bentham in 1789, who described it as 'that branch of jurisprudence . . . [exclusively concerned with] mutual transactions between sovereign as such'. (See Jeremy Bentham, *An Introduction to the Principles of Morals and Legislation* ([1789] ed Burns and Hart, London: Athlone Press, 1970), p. 297.) This definition embodies the notion of international law in the classical era when the subject was regarded as applying only to States.

During this time, however, some writers believed that international law applied to entities other than States. William Blackstone, an eminent English jurist, was of the view that apart from applying to interstate relations international law also applied to individuals so that the subject applies to 'intercourse which must frequently occur between two or more independent states, and the individuals belonging to each' (W. Blackstone, *Commentaries on the Laws of England* (1st edn, Oxford: Clarendon Press, 1765–69), Book IV, p. 66).

Most modern writers tend to define international law as a body of rules and principles applicable only to States. Let us consider some examples.

According to Clive Parry, 'The function of law in the international community' in M. Sørensen (ed.), *Manual of Public International Law* (London: Macmillan, 1968), p. 1:

> 'International law' is a strict term of art, connoting that system of law whose primary function it is to regulate the relations of states with one another.

Section 101 of the Restatement of the Law (Third), Foreign Relations Law of the United States, provides that:

> International Law, as used in this Restatement, consists of rules and principles of general application dealing with the conduct of states and of international organizations and with their relations inter se, as well as with some of their relations with persons, whether natural or juridical.

And the *Oxford Dictionary* defines 'international law' as:

> the law of nations, under which nations are regarded as individual members of a common polity, bound by a common rule of agreement or custom; opposed to *municipal law*, the rules binding in local jurisdictions. [Emphasis added]

It is nowadays both problematic and outdated to define international law as only applying to States. International law was so defined when it applied only to the relations among nations. If we go back—perhaps to the late nineteenth century, when the proper documentation of international law began—it is obvious that States created international law, through customs that were common in their relation with one another. From this customary practice, States began to record the rules and principles that they wanted to apply in their relations with one another. The first modern type of such records was the 1856 Declaration of Paris, concluded in an effort to end the Crimean War. States were thus the only subjects of international law at these early stages, because they alone were capable of applying its rules and principles, and it was only to them that international law could be applied. For this reason, as we will see in Chapter 4, States remain the most important subjects of international law, making it some-what accurate to continue to describe international law as the 'law of nations'.

By the twentieth century, international law application opened wider. Following the International Court of Justice's Advisory Opinion in the *Reparation for Injuries* case—that international organizations have their own legal personality—they became fully recognized as international law subjects. Even then, Hersch Lauterpacht, who was a great campaigner for the recognition of individuals as subjects of international law, still wrote in 1947 that 'As a rule, the subjects of the rights and duties arising from the Law of Nations are States solely and exclusively' (H. Lauterpacht (ed.), *International Law: A Treatise* (6th edn, London: Longman, 1947), p. 19).

As we will see in Chapter 4, in addition to international organizations, international law now applies to human beings in certain circumstances. International organizations can apply the rules and principles of international law, which can also be applied to them. It is possible to argue that since international organizations consist of States, a definition of international law as applying to 'States' invariably includes international organizations. However, as we will see in Chapter 5, international organizations are legal persons and subjects of international law and, as such, they can be distinguished from the individual States that compose them.

A similar opinion was expressed in *Akehurst's Modern Introduction to International Law* (7th rev'd edn, ed Peter Malanczuk, London: Routledge, 1997), in which Akehurst noted that, during the years between the two World Wars, writers had no difficulty defining 'international law' as the law governing the relations between States. However, he said (at p. 1) that this definition:

> did not reflect the reality even at that time. The Holy See, although not a State, was recognized to have international legal personality, and so, for certain purposes, were insurgents and some forerunners of modern international organizations. Since the inter-war period, the matter has become more complicated due to both the expansion of the scope of international law into new areas and the emergence of actors other than states on the international plane, such as inter-governmental organizations established by states, non-governmental organizations created by private individuals, transnational companies, individuals and groups, including minorities and indigenous peoples.

The extension of international law definition to cover entities other than States must be handled with caution. While international law can be applied to or against natural persons—for example, under the Rome Statute of the International Criminal Court (see Chapter 16)—human beings cannot apply international law in the same way that States and international organizations can. Thus, despite the fact that certain categories of human being (including diplomats, staff of international organizations, among others) enjoy some international rights and privileges that ordinary people do not, they cannot appear before the International Court of Justice (ICJ), or conclude treaties on their own behalf, although they can do so as State officials. Furthermore, individuals cannot open diplomatic missions (embassies, high commissions, etc.) in foreign countries, no matter how important they may be. Therefore we need to be cautious when we describe individuals as 'subjects' of international law for the purpose of defining international law. In truth, they are international law subjects only because international law can be applied to them under given circumstances; they cannot apply the rules of international law in their own relations, and, as such, are not on the same platform as States and international organizations as subjects of international law.

Nevertheless, it is no longer correct to continue to define international law as rules that apply to States alone, even if States remain the most important subjects of international law. Thus, in light of the shortcomings in the various existing definitions of international law, we propose to define international law, for the purpose of this book, as:

> a body of rules and principles, contained in various sources, including treaties and customs, which the subjects of international law have accepted as binding on them either in their relations with one another per se, or in those with other juristic or natural persons.

This definition is distinguishable from most of the existing definitions in many ways:

- it recognizes that international law applies to entities *other* than States;
- it lists the main sources of international law—treaties and customs—but is not limited to these;
- it reveals that the authority of international law derives mainly from the *acceptance* of its binding force by its subjects; and
- it demonstrates that international law does not regulate only the relations of one State with another, but also governs the relations of States with humans and juristic persons (whether nationals or foreigners).

thinking points

- *Explain the meaning of international law as the 'laws of nations'.*
- *List which entities other than States may apply international law and those to which international law may apply.*
- *To what extent does the proposed definition of international law improve upon or detract from other definitions of international law with which you are familiar?*

1.2.2 Public and private international law: a distinction

As a concept, we use the phrase 'international law' rather loosely to refer to two distinct areas of a legal discipline. On the one hand, when we say 'international law', we may mean 'public international law'—that is, the law of nations, which, as discussed previously, concerns relations among subjects of international law.

example

Let us suppose that two fictional States, Candoma and Rutamu, regularly conduct relations with each other and that they each have an embassy on the other's territory. Thus the exchange of diplomatic officials between these countries, the conclusion of treaties regulating the treatment of nationals of one visiting the territory of the other, the adoption of rules and principles for dealing with the commercial enterprises of one country carrying on business in the other, and so on, are all matters for public international law. This is because such matters involve the application of certain rules and principles of international law to the two States. The rules and principles are 'public' because neither State can claim *ownership* of them; rather, they are rules agreed upon by both Candoma and Rutamu alone, or in conjunction with other States.

On the other hand, when we say 'international law', we may, in fact, mean 'private international law', otherwise called 'conflict of laws'. This is a branch of international law that deals with relations between individuals or legal persons, such as corporations, in which the laws of more than one State may be applied. Private international law, or conflict of laws, concerns rules developed by States to deal with such matters as transactions involving private nationals of one State and another State, which may contain some foreign elements.

example

Let us imagine that X and Y are Candoman citizens who married in Candoma, but live in Rutamu. Their children were born in Rutamu and they carry on business activities in that country. In a divorce proceeding between X and Y instituted in a Rutamuan court, the resolution of issues concerning the custody of their children, the distribution of property owned by the couple, and the disposition of their resources will involve a consideration of the law of Candoma, under which the couple were married, and that of Rutamu, under which their children were born and under which they and their children reside, and under which they practise their business. It is the interaction of the laws of Candoma and Rutamu, and the consequences arising therefrom, that are referred to as 'conflict of laws', or 'private international law'.

NOTE Although the laws of two States (Candoma and Rutamu) are involved in the divorce proceedings between X and Y, the case is not *actually* between these two States. Rather, the case is about how Candoman nationals who, despite having married in Candoma, must have their marriage dissolved in their country of domicile, Rutamu, which, nevertheless, must consider how Candoman law deals with certain issues arising in the proceedings.

Distinguishing between 'public' and 'private' international law does not imply that these two aspects of international law are always mutually exclusive, or that they operate independently of each other at all times. On the contrary, there are circumstances in which certain aspects of these two 'international laws' interrelate, and in which one may be relevant in determining whether a breach of the other has occurred.

In Jennings and Watts (1996, see section 1.1), at p. 7, it was said that:

> Although the rules of private international law are part of the internal law of the state concerned, they may also have the character of public international law where they are embodied

in treaties. Where this happens the failure of a state party to the treaty to observe the rule of private international law prescribed in it will lay it open to proceedings for breach of an international obligation owed another party. Even where the rules of private international law cannot themselves be considered as rules of public international law, their application by a state as part of its internal law may directly involve the rights and obligations of the state as a matter of public international law, for example where the matter concerns the property of alien or the extent of the state's jurisdiction.

This is a very important observation. Indeed, situations may arise in which failure to apply the rules of private international law may be regarded as a breach of public international law. As will be seen in Chapter 3, States accept certain private international law rules as governing their international relations and such rules may involve private international law issues. Therefore if a State fails to apply a private international law rule embodied in a treaty to which it is a party, that failure may be considered to be a breach of an international obligation agreed upon by the two States, which, in effect, constitutes a breach of public international law.

thinking points

- *Distinguish between 'public' and 'private' international law.*
- *Are public and private international laws mutually exclusive?*
- *Name one circumstance under which the failure to apply a private international law rule can give rise to a breach of public international law.*

9

1.2.3 General, regional, and particular international law

Aside from the distinction between public and private international law, a further categorization (although not a distinction as such) can be made in the operations of public international law. While there is a general body of rules and principles that makes up public international law, the operation of these rules and principles may sometimes vary. Generally speaking, international law rules may operate globally, but they may also be restricted to specific regions of the world. Usually, international law applies to a vast majority of States all over the world; nonetheless, there are certain rules that are peculiar to particular regions of the world. Thus we often speak of 'general' international law and 'regional' international law in respect of the universal or regional application of international law.

The basis of the distinction between 'general' and 'regional' international law lies mainly in the scope of the application of international legal rules, as well as the number of States involved. General international law usually applies to a greater majority of States in *all regions* of the world. Regional international law may also apply to a considerable number of States (although they are usually fewer than those involved in 'general international law'), but the States are usually located within a single region of the world.

Whereas the rule prohibiting the threat or use of force by States (see Chapter 10) is an example of general international law, because it applies to all States regardless of the region in which they are located, the 'Estrada' doctrine, which concerns the 'recognition of States' (see Chapter 4), originated from and initially operated only in Latin America. However, more

States elsewhere have now adopted the doctrine. Another example of regional international law can be seen in the requirements set for new entities aspiring to become States in Europe, under European Union law, in addition to fulfilling the criteria of statehood under the 1933 Montevideo Convention. These new rules apply only in Europe (see Chapter 4).

It is also possible to describe some rules of public international law as 'particular international law'. This refers mainly to rules that are accepted by only a few States, but which are not confined to a particular region of the world. Such a rule is not 'regional international law', since the few States that subscribe to it are not necessarily confined to the same region (in which case, it would be 'regional international law' notwithstanding the small number of States). Thus referring to such a rule instead as 'particular international law' accurately represents the fact that it applies only to a few States, unrelated to their geographical location.

The bulk of international legal rules are applied on a universal basis. Examples of such rules can be found in eminent international treaties such as the Charter of the United Nations (UN Charter) and various human rights treaties—especially the International Covenant on Civil and Political Rights (ICCPR) and the International Covenant on Economic, Social and Cultural Rights (ICESCR). In addition, general international law rules can be found in such specific legal regimes as the 1948 Convention on the Prevention and Punishment of the Crime of Genocide (the Genocide Convention).

Although 'regional' or 'particular' international laws are subservient to general international law, there are occasions when regional or particular international law obligations clash with general international law obligations. In order to avoid such situations, general international law often regulates the relations between itself and its subcategories (see Chapter 2).

Article 103 of the UN Charter provides: 'In the event of a conflict between the obligations of the Members of the United Nations under the present Charter and their obligations under any other international agreement, their obligations under the present Charter shall prevail.'

This provision relates specifically to the obligations of UN member States under *any other* international agreements, but such *other* international agreements include those that apply either among a few States or in a particular region. The other obligations of the UN member States over which their Charter obligations take precedence might be obligations under general international law (outside those of the UN Charter), regional international law, or particular international law. This means that even within the class of general international law, the obligations assumed by States under the UN Charter (which embodies general international law) are superior to their obligations under other agreements, which may also embody general international law.

Further, Article 53 of the 1969 Vienna Convention on the Law of Treaties (VCLT) states that:

A treaty is void if, at the time of its conclusion, it conflicts with a peremptory norm of general international law. For the purposes of the present Convention, a peremptory norm of general international law is a norm accepted and recognized by the international community of States as a whole as a norm from which no derogation is permitted and which can be modified only by a subsequent norm of general international law having the same character.

As will be discussed fully in Chapter 2, a peremptory norm—otherwise called *ius* (or *jus*) *cogens*—is widely regarded as the most fundamental norm of the international community, breach of which shakes the very foundation of human civilization. Examples of such norms include the prohibition of the slave trade, genocide, and the use of force by States. Peremptory norms are therefore rules of general international law and may not be contradicted by any other rule, whether regional or particular international law. However, a peremptory norm may be replaced by another norm of international law having a similar character, pursuant to the provisions of Article 64 VCLT.

'Regional' and 'particular' international laws are not as popular today as they were in the past. This is partly because almost all States are now members of the United Nations, and partly because the existence of regional customs are being successfully challenged before the ICJ (see Chapter 2). In a fast globalizing world where States are constantly expanding their areas of cooperation, it is becoming increasingly difficult for a few States to claim that they accept customs or rules not open to the vast majority of States.

KEY POINTS

thinking point
Distinguish between 'general', 'regional', and 'particular' international law.

- 'General international law' means a body of rules and principles of international law that applies among a vast majority of States.

- 'Regional international law' refers to the rules and principles of international law that apply to States within a particular region of the world (for example, the Estrada doctrine).

- 'Particular international law' refers to the rules or principles of international law applicable to a few States regardless of where they are located.

- The use of both 'regional' and 'particular' international law has decreased considerably in modern times.

- It is often very difficult for States to prove the existence of a regional or particular custom, especially in matters involving States that are not located within the same region.

 (1.3)

The nature of international law: theories

Across generations, legal scholars, philosophers, thinkers, and political scientists have propounded various theories about the nature of international law in order to better understand its functions, characteristics, and limitations. The most important and influential of these are the naturalist, the positivist, and the Grotian schools. This does not constitute an exhaustive list, but are only three of the many schools of thought that put forward different theories about the nature of law and through which the nature of international law may be better understood.

1.3.1 Naturalism

According to naturalism, there is a law of nature that applies to States just as such law applies to individuals. In proposing that *a law of nature* applies to States and individuals, the naturalists oppose the idea that States *voluntarily*, in their conduct with one another, should be bound by laws that they either make themselves or which they observe by custom. Consequently, naturalists believe that all other types of law—including those that are man-made—must conform to a higher (natural) law. Some eminent members of the naturalist schools included Pufendorf, Hobbes (who would later become a positivist), Rutherford, and Barbeyrac.

In *The Concept of Law* (Oxford: Oxford University Press, 2nd ed 1994), p. 186, H. L. A. Hart, who was actually a positivist, agreed that:

> there are certain principles of human conduct, awaiting discovery by human reason, with which manmade law must conform if it is to be valid.

In a nutshell, natural law theory proposes that it is the same law of nature that regulates human conduct that also regulates States in their conduct with one another. It posits that while States, like humans, may make other laws by themselves, such laws must conform to the law of nature in order to be valid. Nonetheless, because the naturalists do not accept that States make the laws that bind them in their conduct with one another, they attracted the title 'deniers of the Laws of Nations'—that is, they were seen to reject international law.

1.3.2 Positivism

Opposed to the natural law theory is the concept of positivism, a term believed to have been coined in the 1830s by French social philosopher August Comte. Comte used the term *positivism* to mean something 'scientific' and 'objective', as opposed to something deduced through some religious or speculative means.

However, before discussing positivism as a theory on the nature of international law, we need to remind ourselves that, as a concept, positivism is capable of a wide range of things. In this regard, we can speak broadly of three branches of positivism. According to A. P. d'Entrèves, *Natural Law* (2nd rev'd edn, London: Hutchins & Co., 1970), p. 175, these are:

- imperativism;
- normativism; and
- legal realism.

Although the last two branches have some broad relations to the theory of law, it is 'imperativism' with which we are mainly concerned here. Imperativism captures the whole essence of positivism, in that it conveys the notion that the law is a command of a 'sovereign' endorsed by the habitual obedience of his or her subjects—a theory generally credited to English legal philosopher John Austin.

Positivists reject the notion of some 'higher' or 'natural' law to which all man-made laws (positive laws) must conform before they can be valid. For the positivists, States are bound only by those laws that are either man-made (such as treaties) or which derive through customs and are issued by a sovereign. In short, positivism is based on the idea that the law is the command of an uncommanded commander.

1.3.3 Grotianism

The third theoretical school is the Grotian perspective, or 'Grotianism'. As noted previously, Hugo Grotius is credited as being the 'father of international law'. It is not surprising therefore that this eminent international lawyer has a whole school of legal theory dedicated to his name.

The Grotians occupy a middle position between the naturalists and the positivists, regarding neither natural law nor positive law as having any more or any less character than the other. Hugo Grotius saw a possibility of harmonizing the various schools.

In *De Jure Praedae* (*The Law of Prize*) (1868), Grotius speaks of the need to systematize:

> That body of law…which is concerned with the mutual relations among states or rulers of states, whether derived from nature, or established by divine ordinances or having its origin in custom or tacit agreement…[and to the importance of] a knowledge of treaties of alliance, conventions, and understandings of peoples, kings and sovereign nations…in short, of the whole law of war and peace.

In *The Anarchical Society*: *A Study of the Order of the World Politics* (London: Macmillan, 1977), p. 27, Hedley Bull observes that the Grotians:

> View international law politics as taking place within an international society [in which] states are bound not only by rules of prudence or expediency but also by imperatives of morality and law.

(See also H. Bull, 'The Grotian conception of international society' in H. Butterfield and M. Wight (eds), *Diplomatic Investigations* (Cambridge, MA: Harvard University Press, 1968), pp. 51–73.)

Clive Parry (1968, see section 1.2.1), at p. 26, sums up the main tenets of the Grotian theory of international law to the effect that it attributes 'equal weight to what states actually do, to habit and custom and to the course of dealing between parties, which contribute significantly to whatever system of law; and no less to what states are—or what they must do because of their nature'.

In summary, international law, like municipal law, is regarded as having transcendental, as well as mundane, origins. States agree to be bound by international law when they sign treaties and enter into different types of agreement, and when their practice indicates such agreement. In addition, States are regarded as being bound by certain norms and tenets, such as peremptory norms, not necessarily based on any agreement, but based on the nature of the norms themselves. Grotianism therefore provides a more comprehensive understanding of the basis of international law and its binding nature as law.

thinking points

- *Distinguish between 'naturalism' and 'positivism'.*
- *What does 'Grotianism' stand for? How can it be differentiated from naturalism and positivism?*
- *In your opinion, which of the theories do you think best represents international law and why?*

1.4 The relationship of theories of law with international law

As will have been noticed, the various theories considered previously relate to 'law' in general and not only to international law in particular. This raises the question: how do the theories relate to public international law?

The relevance of these theories to international law manifests in their subtle influences on the various aspects of international law rather than a single, dominant effect. For example, the relationship between international law and municipal or domestic law, which is usually expressed as a contest between monism and dualism (see Chapter 9), can be properly understood only against a sound appreciation of the theories. Whether one believes that international law is superior to domestic law (monism), or that the two are indeed separate and function as such (dualism), depends partly on to what theoretical view of law one subscribes.

Generally speaking, the influence of the above theories on international law today is much less than it was when the discipline began to be systematized. Nonetheless, Grotianism has proved to be the most enduring of all of the theories, especially after the Second World War. The development of a strong international human rights system after the war meant that laws could not simply be viewed as the 'command of an uncommanded commander', nor could it be sharply divorced from morality, as positivists want us to believe. Today, a soldier cannot hope to escape liability for committing heinous crimes during an armed conflict by simply stating that he or she is authorized by his or her superior commander. International law makes efforts nowadays to ensure that every soldier is aware of the laws of war, and that all soldiers behave according to these laws and not simply according to the whims of their commanders. In addition, the idea of the absolute sovereignty of the State as an 'uncommanded commander' in the international forum is being challenged by the development of instances in which international law will, in a sense, pierce the veil of sovereignty and punish offenders for crimes committed in their territory, as will be seen in our discussion of international criminal law. All of these developments in international law have led to a sharp decline in positivism, just as the role played by law in the modern society has equally reduced the efficacy of the belief that some higher (natural) law is all that matters.

KEY POINTS

- The relevance of 'theory' to international law generally declined after the Second World War, due partly to the development of international human rights.

- The impact of 'theory' on international law can be seen in its influence on specific aspects of international law rather than as an overall effect.

1.5 The basis of international law: consent

In any given society, laws are made by certain institutions. In democratic societies, laws are made by the legislature, known by different names in different countries. In the UK, for example, the 'Parliament' is divided into the 'House of Commons' and the 'House of Lords'; in the USA, the federal legislature is called 'Congress'; in Nigeria, it is the 'National Assembly', comprising the 'Senate' and the 'House of Representatives'; and in Israel and Russia, they are called 'Knesset' and 'Duma', respectively.

In contrast to domestic legal systems, international law does not have law-making institutions. Hence, man-made laws, in the sense of legislative enactments or Acts of Parliament, do not form the basis of the international legal system; rather, international law is based principally on the consent of those States that agree to be bound by it. It is only when States accept to form international law that international law can exist. How States consent to the formation of international law can, however, vary. States may explicitly agree to set out the rules of international law that they wish to apply and to be applied to them in their relations, and this can be done in treaties or conventions; such an agreement can also emerge from the customary practices of States. These two modes (treaty and custom) are discussed in Chapter 2.

The origin of 'consent' as the basis of international law is both ancient and modern. It is believed that consensual international law emanated from the practice of the Roman Empire. Thus Clive Parry (1968, see section 1.2.1), at p. 17, notes that:

> The *ius gentium* of the Romans—that amalgam of the laws of all the peoples of the empire . . . having been received over much of the European continent after the Renaissance, constituted an actually operative common system of law providing a basis ready made for international law.

Obviously, consent as a basis of international law was influenced by developments within domestic legal systems, but it took a while before these domestic developments actually registered a meaningful impact on international law.

As Reisman observes in 'Sovereignty and human rights in contemporary international law' (1990) 84 AJIL 866, 867:

> It took the formal international system time to register these profound changes. Another century beset by imperialism, colonialism and fascism was to pass, but by the end of the Second World War, popular sovereignty was rooted as one of the fundamental postulates of political legitimacy. Article 1 of the UN Charter established as one of the purposes of the United Nations, to develop friendly relations between States, not on any terms, but 'based on respect for the principles of equal rights and self-determination of peoples'.

It does not follow, however, that *every* State must give its consent before international law can be established. According to Oppenheim (1908, see section 1.1), at n. 14:

> The 'common consent' cannot mean, of course, that all states must at all times expressly consent to every part of the body of rules constituting international law, for such common consent

could never in practice be established. The membership of the international community is constantly changing; and the attitude of individual members who may come and go must be seen in the context of that of the international community as a whole, while dissent from a particular rule is not to be taken as withdrawal of consent to the system as a whole.

John Duggard notes, in *International Law: A South African Perspective* (3rd edn, Cape Town: Juta & Co. Ltd, 2008), at p. 14:

While the notions of justice and the values of legal idealism associated with natural laws form the foundation of much of contemporary international law, particularly the promotion of human rights and the right of self-determination, it cannot be denied that for many states consent remains the basis of their participation in the international community.

As will be seen in Chapter 2, in the case of customs what is required is that a great majority of States gives their consent; in that way the custom comes to be regarded as international law. With treaties, the rule is different: only States that consent to a treaty can be bound by the rules contained in that treaty, subject to notable exceptions. (See also Fernando R. Teson, 'Interdependence, consent, and the basis of international obligation' (1989) *Proceedings of the Annual Meeting of the American Society of International Law*, 5–8 April, pp. 558–566, and Wilfred C. Jenks, 'The challenge of universality' (1959) *Proceedings of the Annual Meeting of the American Society of International Law*, 30 April–2 May, pp. 85–98; Anthony Carty, 'Critical international law: recent trends in the theory of international law' (1991) 2 EJIL 66.)

KEY POINTS

- State consent is the basis of international law.
- Consent as the basis of international law was inspired by developments in domestic law in Europe and the USA.
- State consent does not imply that all States must give their consent at all times for the purpose of establishing international law; the consent of the majority of States is sufficient.

1.5.1 The limits to State consent as the basis for international law

There are instances in which State consent is precluded. These include situations concerning a special class of norms and with regard to some existing customs. We will now consider some examples of these instances.

Consent versus peremptory norm

While State consent is crucial to the formation of international law, there are certain aspects of international law in relation to which State consent is practically irrelevant. Once a norm is categorized as a peremptory norm (that is, the most fundamental in the hierarchy of norms), States cannot consensually derogate from such a norm (see Article 53 VCLT). A State cannot, for example, consent to the commission of the crime of genocide on its territory simply because it has not ratified the 1948 Genocide Convention; neither can a State, in present times, permit slave trade on its territory for any reason. The proscription of genocide and slavery are now widely regarded as peremptory norms by States, because they are so fundamental to the existence of humankind that a disturbance of them threatens that very foundation. A State cannot also claim that its internationally wrongful act which violates a peremptory norm is precluded by consent. (See Article 26 of the International Law Articles on State Responsibility for Internationally Wrongful Acts, 2001.)

Nevertheless, the fact that only a few crimes belong to the category of peremptory norms demonstrates that it is only for *extraordinary* reasons that State consent can be precluded from operating on international law. Outside these norms, there are no other instances in which State consent is precluded as being the basis of international law. State consent is so powerful that, as we will see in Chapter 13, when States create international law, their consent is even needed before they can be held responsible for its breach. If a State does not accept that the ICJ, for example, should adjudicate a case involving the State's breach of an international obligation that it owes to another State, then there is little that can be done in terms of holding it legally liable. This is one of the main reasons why international law is frequently seen as 'no law', since everything seems to depend on the wishes of States. It is, in other words, considered to have no independent or objective regime of sanctions against recalcitrant States. But, as we shall see later, this is not a true picture of the nature of international law. (See generally Anthony D'Amato, 'It's a bird, it's a plane, it's jus cogens' (1990–91) 6 Conn JIL 1.)

Consent and pre-existing customs

It is often the case that a State accepts the existence of a particular custom in international law. Naturally, this means that the State practises the custom and is bound by it. The question is: what happens to that consent if the State breaks up into several other States? This question is important because, generally speaking, 'new' States are not afforded the opportunity to exercise choice over whether or not they accept that custom. This has led some writers to deny that consent is the basis of international law, since, although such new States have not been given an opportunity to express their consent in respect of such customs, they are nonetheless automatically bound by it.

In an ideal world, it would be desirable for every State to consent to every rule of international law, but this is unrealistic in the modern context in which events occur at an exponential pace. The fact that new States do not have the opportunity to consent to old customs does not *ipso facto* mean that their consent is irrelevant. It does suggest, however, that while consent is the basis of international law, it is not itself sufficient for the purpose of formulation and development of the rules and principles of international law. As John Duggard (2008, see section 1.5) notes, at p. 14:

> Consent, on its own, however fails to provide an explanation for the rules and principles that comprise international law. Third World States, for instance, have at no time expressly consented to the rules that shaped international law before they attained independence. Indeed, as consent becomes more difficult to obtain for the creation of new rules of law, consensus in the form of majority decision-making is increasingly adopted.

As will be seen in Chapter 2, if a number of (new) States begin to depart from the existing custom, this raises significant doubt as to the validity and sustainability of that custom in the long run. Also, a new State can be presumed to have accepted a pre-existing customary rule if such rule relates, for example, to a peremptory norm. The specific consent of that new State will be irrelevant, since the customary rule regarding the peremptory status of a norm derives not by virtue of State consent, but from the fact of the prescient status that the international community has accorded to that norm. Lastly, to argue that State consent is not the basis of international law only because consent appears assailable on a particular occasion is to stretch the relevance of exceptions to breaking point.

thinking points

- *What are the possible exceptions to State consent as the basis of international law?*
- *Do you agree that the fact that new States are not given the opportunity to confirm or reject old customs undermines State consent as the basis of international law?*
- *What are 'peremptory norms' and why are they excluded from the reach of State consent?*

1.6 The functions of international law

So far we have considered a brief history, the nature, and the basis of international law, but these do not tell us what international law actually *does*. After all, if we were to ask what functions domestic law performs, we could come up with scores of answers. We might say, for example, that domestic law regulates the relations between people and the State; we might even say that it is a code of conduct that spells out the duties and responsibilities of everyone who lives within a State, including those entrusted with the responsibility for running the State or conducting its affairs. Clearly, these kinds of function make it possible for people to empower specific individuals—legislators—to make laws on their behalf. However, since, as stated previously, the international legal system does not have traditional law-making institutions as such, does it then mean that we cannot expect international law to function in a manner similar to municipal law?

The question what function international law performs has exercised the minds of legal scholars for many years. This is a tricky question because, as observed earlier, international law used to be considered as irrelevant. In 1968, Richard Falk gave as his main reason for investigating the relevance of international law that it was part of a larger effort of 'liberating the discipline of international law from a sense of its own futility' (see Richard A. Falk, 'The relevance of political context to the nature and functioning of international law: an intermediate view' in Karl W. Deutsch and Stanley Hoffmann (eds), *The Relevance of International Law* (Cambridge, MA: Schenkman, 1968), at p. 142).

International law performs many functions, and these include encouraging friendly relations among States, outlawing wars among nations, and promoting the peaceful resolution of disputes among nations. The most fundamental of these is the maintenance of international peace and security among States. This rather sacred function is also underscored by the United Nations.

One of the objectives of the organization, contained in Article 1 of the UN Charter, is:

> To maintain international peace and security, and to that end: to take effective collective measures for the prevention and removal of threats to the peace, and for the suppression of acts of aggression or other breaches of the peace, and to bring about by peaceful means, and

> in conformity with the principles of justice and international law, adjustment or settlement of international disputes or situations which might lead to a breach of the peace;

According to C. Tomuschat, in 'International law: ensuring the survival of mankind on the eve of a new century' (1999) 23 Recueil des Cours 1, 23, international law:

> has a general function to fulfil, namely to safeguard international peace, security, and justice in relations between States.

However, expressing the core function of international law as the maintenance of international peace and security neither answers the practical question of how this can be achieved—especially where the need to maintain peace and security conflicts with the attainment of justice—nor explains what the terms used mean in reality. In his chapter 'What is international law for?' in Evans (2010, see section 1.1), p. 32, Martti Koskenniemi rightly queries:

> What do 'peace', 'security', or 'justice' really mean? As soon as such words are defined more closely, disagreement emerges. To say that international law aims at peace *between States* is perhaps already to have narrowed down its scope unacceptably. Surely, as Tomuschat [1999, above] asks at p. 33, it must also seek to advance 'human rights as well as the rule of law domestically inside States for the benefit of human beings'? But what if advancing human rights would call for the destruction of an unjust peace?

There is a whole generation of writings on the so-called 'peace versus justice' tension to which Koskenniemi (in Evans, 2010, above) alludes, but this is not our concern. It suffices to note that, originally, international law was not as concerned with the justice of a situation as it was with the maintenance of peace and security. However, this approach has changed, partly because of the increasing pressure that international law imposes on States to ensure that they do justice while pursuing peace and security. For example, it is now common for a State that has experienced civil war or an authoritarian regime to seek to do justice by confronting its past. This mechanism—nowadays referred to as 'transitional justice'—is a process by which post-conflict societies attempt to understand the ills and shortcomings of the past that led to the collapse of the rule of law, so as to devise strategies for how best to address these issues as they build new societies. Transitional justice has featured in post-apartheid South Africa, and post-conflict Liberia and Sierra Leone, as well as post-authoritarian Cambodia.

Another important function of international law is the settlement of disputes among States. With regard to this function, international law does not operate with the same strength or prediction as domestic law. This is entirely due to the consensual basis of international law, as explained previously, and the topic is discussed fully in Chapter 13.

H. L. A. Hart (2nd edn, 1994, see section 1.3.1), at p. 214, underscores this weakness in international law by observing that:

> International law not only lacks the secondary rules of change and adjudication which provide for legislature and courts, but also a unifying rule of recognition specifying 'sources' of law and providing general criteria for the identification of its rules.

While it is true that international law lacks institutions such as legislatures and courts, the view that international law lacks unifying rules of recognition specifying sources is open to challenge. In 'Wicked heresies or legitimate perspectives? Theory and international law', in Evans (2010, see section 1.1), at p. 64, Iain Scobbie did challenge Hart on this point:

This view was wrong when Hart first expressed it in 1961. Despite criticism, whether on the grounds of inadequacy or inept drafting, it is generally accepted that Article 38 of the Statute of the International Court of Justice provides at least a starting place for the enumeration of the sources of international law and thus functions as a 'rule of recognition' for the international legal system, should one wish to adopt a Hartian analysis.

The category of the functions performed by international law is not closed. It is important that, when engaged in an inquiry into the function of international law, legal scholars should endeavour to be as creative and flexible as possible, and not be over preoccupied by ideas expressed by others.

In 'International law: content and function—a review' (1967) 11 J Confl Res 504, Anthony D'Amato, remarked about a writer's over reliance on other people's views:

> From the writer's point of view, therefore, the possibility of a self-fulfilling prophecy exists. This possibility in turn encourages the writer to incorporate, to a greater or lesser extent, her own ideas of what the law should be into her account of existing international rules. Nor should we be surprised that legal writers invariably do this. For they are, primarily, jurists and not political scientists; they have no particular commitment to scientific detachment, but rather were attracted to their subject for motives such as patriotism, humanitarianism, morality, or merely a passion for 'tidying up' the disparate assortment of available international legal rules.

If one accepts this proposition, it is possible to find a great number of other functions that international law could be said to perform, depending on one's understanding of the subject matter and the context in which international law operates. Anne-Marie Slaughter Burley noted that in 1992 the task of liberating international law from its own futility 'appears to have been accomplished. International legal rules, procedures and organizations are more visible and arguably more effective than at any time since 1945' (see Anne-Marie Slaughter Burley, 'International law and international relations theory: a dual agenda' (1983) 87 AJIL 205.

---

thinking points

- *Summarize the main functions of international law.*
- *To what extent is justice important when international law seeks to maintain peace and security?*
- *Do you agree with Hart's view of the function of international law with regards to the identification of its rules?*

1.7 What next in international law?

Despite its phenomenal popularity in the last fifty years or so, some still doubt that international law is 'law' properly so called. This view derives from a belief that international law is either entirely unenforceable—for example, where a State refuses to give its consent to adjudication before the ICJ or any other international tribunal—or that it is not enforceable against powerful countries. It is true, as we have discussed previously, that States need to give their consent before the ICJ can adjudicate a matter involving them; thus there is no compulsory jurisdiction, as such, under international law.

Also, there is no denying that the current structure of international law does not make it possible for its enforcement against powerful States. It is idealistic to expect that international law can be enforced as easily against the likes of the USA, the UK, Russia, France, and China as it can against weak and poor States. As we will see later in the book, these rich and powerful States are the five permanent members of the UN Security Council (known as the 'P5') and they enjoy a special status based on their possession of the veto power—that is, a negative vote that each can cast in a decision of the Security Council involving them or any other State. The implication of the vote is to nullify or render it impossible to pass a Security Council resolution in the event of dissent by any of the P5. Therefore the fact that the structure of the system created by the UN Charter creates a distinction between the permanent Security Council members and all other States undermines the effectiveness of international law. To many observers, if all States are equal according to one provision of the UN Charter, certainly those that wield the veto are more equal than others.

The overwhelming sense of frustration about the Orwellian nature of the current international legal order has continued to haunt several generations of international law students. The dilemma for students of international law can be illustrated by the exchange between some international law students on a popular website called 'Answerbag', available at http://www.answerbag.com/q_view/1682. An anonymous writer called 'agnostic' posed the question: 'Is "international law" true law?' on the website, to which several people—apparently mostly international law students—responded. On 12 April 2009, 'little bear' responded: 'I bloody hope so, considering I just dedicated 50+ hours of my life studying it.' And 'firebrand' responded: 'Yes, it is—although not all countries abide by the laws.'

Mapping the future of international law, therefore, invites us to create a fine balance between the question posed by 'agnostic' and the answer provided by 'firebrand'. In reconciling agnostic's doubt and firebrand's reassurance, it must be said that international law is often judged by its failures rather than by its successes. For every single instance in which international law is unable to enforce its measures against powerful States, either for reasons of the veto of or lack of capacity to do so, there are several instances in which international law succeeds: when you post a letter in England to France, when you ship an item from Albania to Swaziland, there is international law present, accompanying the post and the freight, guiding all hands that come into contact with the chattels regarding what they can and cannot do with the items; when you sleep in your house and listen to the droning sound of aeroplanes flying overhead, international law ensures that no alien planes invade your country's territory. It is only in recognizing that international law does far more good than is recognized that we can assure 'little bear' that the fifty-plus hours that he or she dedicated to studying the discipline were well worth it.

 # Conclusion

International law has grown significantly in recent times. From the 1990s, international law made considerable progress, especially in the areas of collective security, human rights, international criminal law, international economic law, and international environmental law, to mention but a few. The UN Security Council was able to authorize an enforcement action against Iraq when it invaded Kuwait in 1990, a feat that the same institution was unable to achieve in the first forty-five years of the United Nations. Government officials, including heads of State, are no longer able to commit heinous crimes against their nationals, or foreigners, and hide under diplomatic immunity (see Chapter 16). More and more States now take the human rights of their peoples more seriously than they did during the first forty-five years of the UN Charter. Many Arab countries, which have long experienced dictatorship and autocratic regimes, are currently undergoing monumental revolution; in the cases of Egypt, Tunisia, and Libya, that revolution has already led to the replacement of governments. In the Ivory Coast, the United Nations and some of its member States assisted Ivorians in realizing their democratic aspirations by forcing out Laurent Gbagbo from the office that he refused to vacate after suffering defeat in democratic elections.

Nonetheless, there remains significant room for improvement. As international law becomes more assertive in the modern context, more areas emerge in which improvements are required. The future of international law lies notably in how much it is able to harness the general goodwill that it continues to enjoy among the majority of States to the benefit of humankind.

Questions

Self-test questions

1 Define 'international law'.

2 Explain the difference between 'public' and 'private' international law.

3 What are 'general international law', 'regional international law', and 'particular international law'?

4 What functions does international law perform?

5 Distinguish naturalism, positivism, and Grotianism.

6 What is the basis of international law and is this enough for the purpose of international law development?

7 Under what circumstances may consent, as a basis of international law, be varied?

Discussion questions

1 To what extent is the assertion that international law is not law a true reflection of international law?

2 'Without consent, there can be no international law. Consent is the beginning and end of international law.' Discuss.

3 Outline the various theories of law and discuss what relevance these have to international law.

4 'International law is international law. The use of the terms "private" and "public" to describe international law is a matter of personal preference with no practical consequences.' Do you agree?

5 'Understanding positivism, naturalism, and Grotianism as theoretical foundations of law says nothing about the foundation of international law.' Discuss.

6 'The future of international law is precarious.' Evaluate this assertion.

Assessment question

Candoma* has recently obtained independence from Rutamu* and, eager to demonstrate that it is now a State in its own right, decides to join the UN. However, the newly elected president of the country is concerned that since Candoma was not a State when the UN was established, it took no part in establishing the rules and principles contained in the UN Charter, which it must accept upon becoming a member of the organization. The opposition party, which lost the election that brought in the new government, is mounting a vociferous campaign against Candoma joining the UN. Among several arguments that the opposition is making are: that international law, which the UN will administer, is no law at all; that it privileges rich and powerful nations; that since international law has no enforcement mechanisms, States will freely violate it, rendering Candoma open to violations without remedy; and that if Candoma does not join the UN, it has no responsibility to respect international law. As an international law student in a prestigious Candoman university currently on internship with the Foreign Affairs Ministry, the minister has asked you to prepare a counter-argument that might be presented when he debates the issues with a representative of the opposition party live on television.

Outline the argument that you would suggest.

Note that both Candoma and Rutamu are fictional States. They will appear in assessment questions throughout the book.

Key case

- *Trendtex Trading Corporation v. Central Bank of Nigeria* [1977] 2 WLR 356

Further reading

Coplin, W. D., *The Functions of International Law* (Chicago, IL: University of Chicago Press, 1965)

Duggard, J., *International Law: A South African Perspective* (3rd edn, Cape Town: Juta & Co. Ltd, 2008)

Franck, T., *Fairness in International Law and Institutions* (Oxford: Oxford University Press, 1995)

Hart, H. L. A., *The Concept of Law* (Oxford: Oxford University Press, 2nd ed. 1994)

Higgins, R., *Problems and Process: International Law and How We Use It* (Oxford: Oxford University Press, 2004)

Jennings, R. and Watts, A. (eds), *Oppenheim's International Law, Vol. 1: Peace* (9th edn, London/New York: Longman, 1996)

Kadduri, M., *War and Peace in the Law of Islam* (Baltimore, MD: Johns Hopkins University Press, 1955)

Kelsen, H., *Principles of International Law* (New York: Rinehart & Co., 1952)

Neff, S., 'A short history of international law' in M. Evans (ed.), *International Law* (3rd edn, Oxford: Oxford University Press, 2010), p. 3

Oppenheim, L., 'The Science of International Law: Its Task and Method' (1908) 2 AJIL 313

Parry, C., 'The function of law in the international community' in M. Sørensen (ed.), *Manual of Public International Law* (London: Macmillan, 1968), p. 1

Schwarzenberger, G., *The Inductive Approach to International Law* (London: Stevens, 1965)

2

Sources of international law

Learning objectives

This chapter will help you to:

- identify the sources of international law;
- understand different theories about sources of international law;
- appreciate whether there are sources of international law other than those explicitly mentioned in the Statute of the International Court of Justice (ICJ Statute);
- recognize how these sources relate to one another; and
- evaluate whether there is a hierarchy among the sources of international law.

Introduction

International law derives from several sources, which vary greatly in terms of their typologies and significance. Unlike domestic law, the primary and most distinctive source of which is the laws made by parliaments, international law does not derive from national parliaments. There are no law-makers for international law; rather, international law consists mostly in agreements freely entered into by States to regulate their relations with one another, in various norms and usages, in which States have voluntarily participated and agreed carry the force of law in their relations with one another (customs), in the judgments given by the International Court of Justice (ICJ), and in the teachings of the most qualified academics of all nations, among others. However, despite the relative clarity with which Article 38 of the ICJ Statute lists the sources of international law, several theories and controversies surround how these sources evolve and whether there is a hierarchy among them, as well as their impact on States. While it is common to regard the sources listed in the ICJ Statute as the only sources of international law, this chapter will consider whether there might be other sources outside this list.

2.1 What does the phrase 'sources of law' mean?

In most parts of the world, there are national bodies for making laws for the people. Such bodies are usually established by the constitution of each country and are known by various names. In addition to the provisions of the constitution, the laws made by such bodies constitute the source of laws for that country.

This is not the case with international law. There is no law-making body for international law. It is therefore not possible to seek the source of international law by looking into laws made by some legislators as is common with States.

Nonetheless, to have a source is to have a basis for determining the origin and legality of a system. In legal parlance, we use the phrase 'source of law' to refer to something specific and technical. It generally means the authority by which legal rules derive their force.

2.2 'Formal', 'material', and 'functional' sources of law

A distinction is usually made between 'formal' and 'material' sources of law, and between these two, on the one hand, and 'functional' sources of law, on the other hand. We are concerned here with *formal* sources of law. This refers to 'sources of law' in the technical sense and refers to from where the law derives its force. An example of this is the 'sources of international law', which we will consider shortly. The 'material' sources of law deal with the historical evolution of a particular law, as opposed to from *where* the law derives its force. Examples include morality and reason. Both the 'formal' and 'material' sources of law differ from the 'functional' sources of law, which merely refer to places where laws might be found, such as libraries, journals, manuals, and so on.

It is doubtful whether we can apply the term 'formal' to international law as we can to domestic law. As noted previously, in domestic legal systems laws are made by some specific institutions of the State, depending on the type of governmental arrangement in that country. Thus, in democratic countries such as the UK, the USA, Australia, and Canada, laws are made by their parliaments. When we therefore speak of 'formal' sources' of law in these countries, we mean their parliaments. These are the bodies from which laws in these countries derive their force. Even in undemocratic countries, such as countries under military rule, it is still possible to locate a formal source of law. There is no equivalent of these national law-making bodies in the international legal system.

KEY POINTS

- 'Sources of law' are vital for establishing the validity of legal rules.

- Sources of law may be formal or material, although it is uncertain whether the term 'formal', in its real connotation, can be applied to international law.

- There are no law-making institutions in international law.

What are the sources of international law?

2.3

Article 38(1) of the ICJ Statute provides that:

> 1. The Court, whose function is to decide in accordance with international law such disputes as are submitted to it, shall apply:
>   (a) International conventions, whether general or particular, establishing rules expressly recognized by the contesting states;
>   (b) International custom, as evidence of general practice accepted as law;
>   (c) The general principles of law recognized by civilized nations;
>   (d) Subject to the provisions of Article 59, judicial decisions and the teachings of the most highly qualified publicists of the various nations, as subsidiary means for the determination of rules of law.
> 2. This provision shall not prejudice the power of the Court to decide a case *ex aequo et bono*, if the parties agree thereto.

This Article concerns two issues. First, the provision in Article 38(1)(a)–(d) contains certain instruments that the ICJ may apply when dealing with disputes submitted to it. Secondly, Article 38(2) gives the Court the power to disregard any of those instruments if parties to a conflict agree to that effect. So this means that if the parties to a dispute before the ICJ both (or all) agree to do so, they can ask the Court not to apply any of the elements listed in Article 38(1)(a)–(d) to their case. If the Court accepts this advice, it is said that it has acted *ex aequo et bono*—that is, it has ignored the rules created by the sources listed in Article 38. We will return to this more fully later.

2.3.1 Article 38(1) as sources of international law

The word 'sources' is not used in Article 38(1) to describe those elements that the Court must apply to disputes. Nor does Article 38 directly ask the ICJ to treat these elements as sources, although they are now commonly referred to as such. This then raises the question why the provisions of Article 38(1) are regarded as 'sources of international law'.

The universal acceptance of the elements listed in Article 38(1) as the sources of international law is due to many reasons. According to Article 92 of the Charter of the United Nations (the UN Charter), the ICJ is the principal judicial organ of the United Nations. Once a State becomes a member of that organization, it automatically becomes a member of the ICJ. Therefore, since the job of the Court is to settle disputes among the UN members (which are its own members as well), it is important that the Court applies the rules of international law—as found in the sources listed in Article 38(1).

Furthermore, even before the establishment of the ICJ, most international tribunals had always applied international law rules to disputes between States. Thus, all that Article 38(1) does is to ensure that the ICJ continues in this well-known international practice. According to Brierly, *The Law of Nations* (Oxford: Clarendon Press, 1963), p. 56, Article 38(1):

> is a text of the highest authority, and we may fairly assume that it expresses the duty of any tribunal which is called upon to administer international law.

An important question to ask is whether Article 38(1) contains *all* of the sources of international law. Two interpretations are possible.

- On the one hand, we can regard Article 38(1) as exhaustive—that is, complete—so that no other source can be added to it. As Georg Schwarzenberger noted in *International Law*, Vol. 1 (3rd edn, London: Stevens and Sons Ltd, 1957), at pp. 26–27, 'the significance of this enumeration lies in its exclusiveness'.

- On the other hand, we can regard Article 38(1) as incomplete, so that it is possible to add new sources to those listed in that Article.

thinking point
Why is Article 38(1) regarded as constituting sources of international law?

It does not really matter which interpretation of Article 38(1) one accepts. What is important is that any additions to the sources expressly mentioned in Article 38(1) must be proved as constituting a source.

2.4 Treaties

The first source referred to in Article 38(1) of the ICJ Statute is 'conventions, whether general or particular, establishing rules expressly recognized by the contesting states'. As a term of international law, 'conventions' are more commonly referred to as 'treaties', but we must be careful not to confuse the two senses in which the word 'convention' itself can be used: it may also be used to refer to the gathering of people for some general discussion or deliberations.

Imagine that representatives of rail workers in all countries decide to hold an annual meeting in a country chosen for that purpose. Such a gathering may be called the 'World Railway Workers Annual Convention', but this is not a 'convention' in the same sense as would constitute a treaty, because it merely refers to a meeting or assembly of people. The fact that each national delegate to the Railway Convention may, in fact, be representing his or her individual country does not make the outcome of the meeting a treaty.

Article 2 of the 1969 Vienna Convention on the Law of Treaties (VCLT) defines a 'treaty' as:

…an international agreement concluded between States in written form and governed by international law, whether embodied in a single instrument or in two or more related instruments and whatever its particular designation.

Treaties are also sometimes called 'protocols', 'pacts', 'general Acts', 'accords', 'statutes', 'declarations', 'charters', and 'covenants'. Treaties are the most certain, popular, and important source of international law. They are created by the deliberate acts of two or more States (known as the 'signatories', or 'State parties') coming together and writing down their agreements (and also disagreements) over specific issues and the rights deriving from such, as well as the obligations attaching thereto. In other words, a treaty contains certain obligations that a State undertakes to perform in return for certain rights.

Let us assume that there are two States, Candoma and Rutamu. Representatives of these States meet at a beach resort called Colo in Candoma to discuss the migration of their nationals. These two States then sign an agreement exempting their nationals from visa requirements when visiting the other country. Let us also assume that this 'visa-free' agreement will be effective during the summer of every year, for twenty years. Both States may decide to refer to this agreement as the 'Colo Summer Treaty' (or 'CST', for short).

The objective of the CST is to remove travel restrictions on nationals of parties to the treaty. The time element of the CST is specific: no national of either State requires a travel visa to the other country during the summer period. The treaty will expire twenty years after its entry into force.

Treaties exist mainly in written form, although there is no rule that says that all of the provisions of a treaty must be contained in a single document; there may, in fact, be several volumes of a treaty. The provisions of a treaty can be amended, reduced, or added to by means of a lesser treaty. For example, the signatories to the CST in the above example may decide to extend the number of years during which their nationals will travel visa-free and they could do this by signing a document amending the relevant provision of the original treaty. This additional document is usually called a 'protocol'.

But if, in the course of amending the CST, the representatives of both States were to exchange several letters on the proposed amendment, this series of exchanges, although written down, would be neither a treaty nor a protocol; they would simply be diplomatic exchanges, which are no more than courteous letters or correspondences. Such letters or correspondences do not establish the type of international obligations that treaties or protocols establish.

KEY POINTS

- A treaty is an international agreement between two or more States, written and contained in one or several volumes, consisting of certain rights and obligations of the parties.

- Treaties are the most stable source of international law.

- Treaties are known by other names such as 'conventions', 'protocols', 'pacts', 'agreements', and 'charters'.

- A protocol, which is a subsequent supplement to a treaty, can be used to amend a treaty.

2.4.1 Types of treaty: law-making treaties and contractual treaties

Article 38(1)(a) talks about conventions, whether 'general or particular'. This phrase thus raises the question of whether all treaties are equal, as far as their ability to constitute a source of international law is concerned.

A distinction is usually made between 'law-making treaties' and 'contract treaties', when determining the ability of treaties to constitute a source of international law. A 'law-making treaty' can be defined as an agreement through which several States declare their understanding of the law on a particular subject. Law-making treaties can thus be used to lay down new rules to govern the future conduct of the ratifying States. They can also be used to terminate the operation of some rules that are already in existence (Brierly, 1963, p. 58, see section 2.3.1). 'Contract treaties', meanwhile, are agreements concluded by a few States—usually two States—relating to common and shared interests between those States.

It is commonly believed that only treaties that are ratified by a great number of States can establish general international law. Conversely, contract treaties do not create general international law; at most, they create only 'particular' international law, since they apply only to a few States. Even then, some writers believe that there is no such thing as 'particular international law'.

According to G. G. Fitzmaurice, 'Some problems regarding the formal sources of international law' (1958) 9 Symbolae Verzijl 153:

> . . . the attempts which have been made to ascribe a law-making character to *all* treaties irrespective of the character of their content or the number of the parties to them, by postulating that some treaties create 'particular' international law and others 'general', is of extremely dubious validity. There is really no such thing as 'particular' international treaty law, though there are particular international treaty rights and obligations.

The use of the terms 'general' and 'particular' international law to distinguish between law-making treaties and contract treaties is problematic. First, those who seek to distinguish between the two sometimes rely on the analogy of national laws. They argue that a treaty is to be regarded as law-creating only if it creates the kind of obligations that national laws create for people. They also state that such treaties must apply to all people and for a long period of time. Therefore, since contract treaties are more like commercial transactions between a few States, they do not meet these criteria and cannot create law.

Secondly, it is often said that for a treaty to be law-creating a great number of States must accept it—that is, that it is only when a treaty is signed by many States that it can said to create general international law.

However, both views have been criticized by Michael Akehurst, 'Custom as a source of international law' (1974–75) 47 BYBIL 1, 37. Accordingly:

> the analogy between national statutes and law-making treaties is misleading for two reasons. First, in national systems of law anyone who is contractually competent (i.e. anyone who is sane and not a minor) can enter into a contract, but parliamentary legislation is passed by a small group of people. In international law, any state can enter into a treaty, including a law-making treaty. Secondly, in national systems of law contracts create rights and duties only for the contracting parties, who are very few in number, whereas statutes of national law apply to a very large number of people. In international law all treaties, including law-making treaties, apply only to states which agree to them. Normally the parties to a law-making treaty are more numerous than the parties to a 'contract-treaty', but there is no reason why this should always be so.

Practically, the real distinction between a 'law-making treaty' and a 'contract treaty' is one of content. Some treaties are neither solely 'law-creating treaties' nor 'contract treaties', because they contain features of both, and it is possible to have a treaty signed by many States, but which creates only contractual obligations for parties, rather than establishes international rules.

Nonetheless, there might be some sense in maintaining a distinction between 'law-making treaties' and 'contract treaties'. For example, a contract treaty is more likely to be terminated by the outbreak of war between the parties than a law-making treaty. This is because there are always so few parties to contract treaties and the substance of such treaties is usually not particularly normative.

In light of the possibility of overlap between law-making treaties and contract treaties, it does not seem very helpful to regard law-making treaties as the only treaties that are a source of international law; it is better to regard all treaties as a source of international law. After all, as we shall see in Chapter 3 dealing specifically with treaties, the law of treaties applies to both types of treaty. For similar conclusions, see also Akehurst (1974–75, earlier in this section) at 38, Ian Brownlie, *Principles of Public International Law* (6th edn, Oxford: Oxford University Press, 2003), pp. 13–14, and Malcolm N. Shaw, *International Law* (6th edn, Cambridge: Cambridge University Press, 2008), pp. 88–89.

What seems to be the most important consideration in determining what type of treaty constitutes a source of international law is the consent of States to be bound by it. In their joint dissenting opinion to the ICJ's *Advisory Opinion (Reservations to the Genocide Convention)* (1951) ICJ Rep 15, 31–32, Judges Guerrero, McNair, Read, and Hsu Mo said that:

> The circumstance that this activity is often described as 'legislative' or 'quasi-legislative', must not obscure the fact that the legal basis of these conventions, and the essential thing that brings them into force, is the common consent of the parties.

Clearly, these judges lay emphasis on the consent of parties to a treaty, rather than the number of such parties, in determining whether such a treaty can be regarded as law-creating.

KEY POINTS

- The distinction between general and particular treaties lies first and foremost in the number of intended parties upon which the treaty is to operate, and the nature of obligations contained in the treaty.

- Contract treaties operate on far fewer States (hence they are called 'particular') than law-creating treaties, which operate on a greater number of States (hence 'general').

- The fulfilment of the main objective of a particular treaty will terminate the treaty, whereas law-making treaties create a more general norm for the future.

- It is sometimes difficult to distinguish between the two types of treaty with regard to their ability to constitute a source of international law, because they often overlap.

2.4.2 Who is bound by the terms of a treaty?

Only parties to a treaty are bound by it.

Anthony D'Amato, 'Thrashing customary international law' (1985) 81 AJIL 81, notes that:

> [a] treaty is obviously not equivalent to custom; it binds *only* the parties, and binds them only according to the enforcement provisions contained in the treaty itself. However, rules in treaties reach beyond the parties because a treaty itself constitutes state practice.

● *Federal Republic of Germany v. The Netherlands* (1969) ICJ REP 3 (THE *North Sea Continental Shelf Cases*)

The main issue for determination in this case concerned the delineation of the North Sea continental shelf involving the Netherlands, the Federal Republic of Germany, and Denmark. The Netherlands and Germany concluded two bilateral agreements in 1964, while Denmark and Germany concluded two agreements in 1965. The question that arose for the Court's determination was whether some rules of the 1958 Geneva Convention on the Continental Shelf applied to non-parties to that convention. Netherlands and Denmark argued that Article 6 of the Convention, dealing with equidistance, applied to non-parties to that Convention by virtue of that provision having become a rule of customary international law.

Held: By a majority of eleven votes to six, that this Convention did not apply to non-parties.

KEY POINT Note that, in *North Sea Continental Shelf*, the Court accepted that treaty provisions can become rules of customary international law that will be binding on non-parties to the treaty. The only condition to be met is that the treaty must be fundamentally norm-creating in character, such as could be regarded as forming the basis of a general rule of law (see *North Sea Continental Shelf* at 42).

2.4.3 The registration of treaties

Prior to the establishment of the United Nations, treaties were not readily accessible. Treaties were collected and published mainly by individuals who were interested in undertaking such tasks. The most important treaty collections dated back to the efforts of G. F. von De Martens in 1771, and these collections were published under various titles until the outbreak of the Second World War in 1939.

Article 102 of the UN Charter obligates UN member States to register treaties concluded by them with the UN Secretary-General. Thus it is now much easier to locate treaties and there are almost 50,000 treaties currently registered with the UN. While most treaties are multilateral (that is, treaties between more than two nations), some are bilateral (that is, treaties between two States).

Customs

Article 38(1)(b) of the ICJ Statute refers to international custom as evidence of general practice accepted as law.

In everyday conversations, we use the word 'custom' casually. We often ask others questions, such as 'Is it customary to leave a tip?' after we have been served in a restaurant and we are about to pay our bill. Sometimes, dignitaries visiting foreign countries perform some acts so regularly that it can be said that it is 'their custom' to do so: the late Pope John Paul II, for example, had the remarkable habit of kissing the ground of any country that he visited upon disembarking from the aircraft, and it is habitual for the Queen of England to shake people's hands wearing a pair of gloves. The question is: when we speak of 'custom' in international law, do we mean such ordinary habits as these?

The answer to this question is both 'yes' and 'no'. It is 'yes' because for a thing to become custom in international law, it requires a degree of consistency in its occurrence; it is 'no' because international law custom requires much more in terms of duration, consistency, prevalence, and expectation. Unlike the mere habits of individuals described above, international customs are not observed as and when States feel like it. Once customs are established, they must *always* be observed and non-observance would attract sanctions. For example, the head of State of a country being visited by Pope John Paul II could not sue the Vatican (the Papal State) if the Pope were to refuse to kiss the ground on his visit to that country; nor could England be sanctioned if the Queen were to decide to take off her gloves when shaking the hands of the citizens of a foreign State. The Pope's and the Queen's habits are matters of individual choice, not matters of legal obligation.

Thus the difference between the ordinary and the technical senses in which we use the word 'custom' is clear. In the ordinary sense, States simply act in certain ways as a matter of habit:

there is no expectation that they will always do so, nor are they bound to do so; acting, or refusing to act, in those habitual ways does not create any legal obligations for the States in question. In the technical sense, however, custom involves legal obligations.

2.5.1 'Custom' in international law/customary international law

According to §102(2) of the Restatement of the Law (Third), Foreign Relations Law of the United States, published by the American Law Institute in 1987:

> Customary international law results from a general and consistent practice of states followed by them from a sense of legal obligation.

While this is a useful description, it must be emphasized that there is no universally acceptable definition of 'customary law'. It is important always to remember that an international custom is an act done, or omitted to be done, by States in circumstances in which such an act or omission is regarded as having legal effects on all States that recognize it.

Therefore an international custom is more than a mere habit or usage. A legal custom carries with it specific obligations and is so-called in international law if participating States are aware that such an obligation exists, a violation of which could attract sanctions. For example, it is an international custom that a State will not generally prosecute foreign diplomats under its own laws: customarily, an offending diplomat is sent back to his or her home country by the host State. It is also customary that a ship flies its national flag while at sea. There is no custom in international law if a usage does not create legal obligations. An act or omission is not a custom if States do not *feel* that they are bound by law to follow it.

As observed by Brierly (1963, see section 2.3.1), p. 59:

> Custom in its legal sense means something more than mere habit or usage; it is a usage felt by those who follow it to be an obligatory one. There must be present a feeling that, if the usage is departed from, some form of sanction probably, or at any rate ought to, fall on the transgressor.

KEY POINTS

- A custom is distinguished from a mere usage because, unlike usages, custom involves legal obligations.

- International custom can arise through acts or omissions.

2.5.2 The criteria for determining customs: State practice and *opinio juris*

Article 38(1) of the ICJ Statute lays down two criteria for proving the existence of custom in international law:

(a) general practice; and

(b) the acceptance of this practice as *law*.

For there to be custom in international law, it is necessary that a usage is generally *practised* by States. Also, that *practice* must be accepted by those and other States as creating a legal obligation. Therefore, in order to determine custom, we need to look at *how* States regularly behave in respect of an issue or a situation. Thus *State practice* can be objectively determined. All we have to do is to look at a series of actions and reactions by a State towards a given situation.

The second criterion is much more complicated. To determine how States *feel* about a practice is to inquire into the psychological being of States. What this criterion requires is that we look into the *mind* of a State and discern whether it accepts a particular practice as constituting a legal obligation. The problem with this rather subjective criterion is that it is often difficult to understand how a single human mind works, let alone the mind of a State, comprising millions of individuals. A State is an abstract entity, operated by thousands of officials with millions of motives.

In the international legal discourse, these two criteria are commonly referred to as 'State practice' and *opinio juris sive neccesitatis*, or *opinio juris* for short. Some of the most important cases of the ICJ have dealt with these criteria.

● *Colombia v. Peru* (1950) ICJ REP 266 (The *Asylum Case*)

Following a failed attempt to overthrow the government of Peru in 1948, the coup leader, Mr Haya de la Torre, was granted refuge in the Colombian embassy in Lima, the capital of Peru. Colombia then attempted to fly the rebel out of Peru, but the Peruvian government refused to allow him passage. Colombia claimed before the ICJ that, as the asylum-granting nation, it was entitled, under a regional custom in Latin America, to qualify the offence for the purpose of the asylum.

Held:

The parties which rely on a custom of *this kind* must prove that this custom is established in such a manner that it has become *binding* on the other party. The Colombian Government must prove that the rule invoked by it is in accordance with a constant and uniform usage practised by States in question in such a manner that it has become binding on the other Party. [Emphasis added]

● *Federal Republic of Germany v. Denmark, Federal Republic of Germany v. The Netherlands* (1969) ICJ REP 3 (The *North Sea Continental Shelf Cases*)

For the facts, see section 2.4.2.

Held:

...not only must the act concerned amount to a settled practice, but they must also be such, or be carried out in such a way, as to be evidence of a belief that this practice is rendered obligatory by the existence of a rule of law requiring it. The need for such a belief, i.e., the existence of a subjective element, is implicit in the very notion of the *opinio juris sive necessitatis*.

● *The Scotia* 14 WALL (81 US) 170 (1872), US SUPREME COURT

This case was an interesting early example of customary international law.

A collision occurred between an American sailing vessel, *The Berkshire*, and a British steamer, *The Scotia*. A British law of 1863 and an 1864 US Act had both established that ships should carry coloured, not white lights when sailing on the high seas. Nearly all of the maritime nations worldwide had adopted these regulations before the end of 1864, including both countries. On the fateful day, *The Berkshire* had displayed only white lights. The American owners of *The Berkshire* had argued that the regulation requiring their ships to carry coloured lights was a domestic regulation and that not conforming to it should not excuse the loss or damage caused to their ships by British vessels.

It was held that *The Scotia* had complied with all of the rules concerning lights display and movement in accordance with the *custom* at that time.

In a very interesting passage about the evolution of custom, the Court said, at 188, that:

> This is not giving to the statutes of any nation extraterritorial effect. It is not treating them as general maritime laws, but it is recognition of the historical fact that by *common consent of mankind*, these rules have been acquiesced in as of *general obligation*. [Emphasis added]

The Court made it clear it was not elevating the law of Britain or the USA regarding the colour of lights that ships should display at that time into a universal law, but was recognizing a practice that the majority of the maritime States at the relevant time had accepted as giving rise to a general obligation.

As noted by Gerhard von Glahn, *Law among Nations: An Introduction to Public International Law* (7th edn, New York: Longman, 1996), p. 15:

> The court reasoned that, although no single country can change the law of the sea, when navigational rules *established by two states* (in this case, the US and UK) had been widely accepted by virtually every maritime state, and accepted as obligatory by more than 30 of the world's principal maritime nations, 'those rules have become part of the law of sea, a usage has been changed into a legal custom, and the rules in question were the law at the place and time the collision occurred'. [Emphasis added]

. . . .

● *Nicaragua v. United States (Merits)* (1986) ICJ Rep 14 (*Military and Paramilitary Activities in and against Nicaragua*, or The *Nicaragua Case*)

The Court said (at [184]) that:

> The mere fact that States declare their recognition of certain rules is not sufficient for the Court to consider these as being part of customary international law, and as applicable as such to those States. Bound as it is by Article 38 of its Statute to apply, *inter alia*, international custom 'as evidence of a general practice accepted as law', the Court may not disregard the essential role played by general practice. Where two States agree to incorporate a particular rule in a treaty, their agreement suffices to make that rule a legal one, binding upon them; but in the field of customary international law, the shared view of the Parties as to the content of what they regard as the rule is not enough. The Court must satisfy itself that the existence of the rule in the *opinio juris* of States is confirmed by practice.

KEY POINTS

- State practice and *opinio juris* are the two ingredients of customary international law. Both criteria must be proved in order to establish that a custom exists in international law.

- In the *Asylum Case*, the Court accepted that a custom could be established between a few States. This is called 'regional' or 'particular' custom.

- All States against which a regional custom is claimed *must* have accepted it. By comparison, not all States have to accept general custom; a majority of States will suffice.

- *The Scotia* established that an international custom could develop through domestic law, provided that the generality or majority of States have accepted it as creating a general obligation for them.

Determining what constitutes State practice

The ICJ Statute requires customs to be established through general practice. As noted earlier, this means the general practice of States. But as Mark Janis has rightly pointed out in *An Introduction to International Law* (4th edn, New York: Aspen, 2003), p. 44: 'The determination of customary international law is more an art than a scientific method.' So given that States engage daily in countless activities and say many things through various means and avenues, how is the relevant State practice to be discerned from the plethora of what is available?

State practice is a total sum of how States behave in respect of a particular issue or situation. To establish State practice, one needs to look at a combination of many things. The easiest point at which to start is to consider what States do. Nothing could be more assuring of State practice on any given subject than how a State acts in relation to that issue. However, apart from what States *do*, it is also important to look at what States *say*. What States say about an issue can be seen in comments made by State officials in newspapers, official publications, and from statements made in the parliament and at conferences. We can also look into historical records, and listen to radio and television interviews of government officials. By what States say, we can easily infer the position of the State on that particular issue, such as whether it considers itself under an obligation to act in a particular manner.

According to Akehurst (1974–75, see section 2.4.1), State practice is:

> any act or statement by a State from which views about customary law can be inferred; it includes physical acts, claims, declarations *in abstracto* (such as General Assembly resolutions), national judgments and omissions.

As stated in §103(a) of the US Third Restatement:

> For customary law the 'best evidence' is the proof of state practice, ordinarily by reference to official documents and other indications of governmental action.

According to Brownlie (2003, see section 2.4.1), p. 6:

> The material sources of custom are very numerous and include the following: diplomatic correspondence, policy statements, press releases, the opinions of official legal advisers, official manuals on legal questions, e.g. manuals of military law, executive decisions and practices, orders to naval forces etc., comments by governments on drafts produced by the International Law Commission, state legislation, international and national judicial decisions, recitals in treaties and other international instruments, a pattern of treaties in the same form, the practice of international organs, and resolutions relating to legal questions in the United Nations General Assembly.

However, it should be pointed out that most States would rarely publish the majority of the materials that disclose their practice of international law issues. Exchanges between government officials, either of the same State or different States, can be very sensitive. Such exchanges are never made public at the relevant time and are usually labelled 'classified'. A classified document often proves to be the most revealing of a State's position on an issue. But since most 'classified' documents will only be accessible to the public either after the concerned issue is no longer of any significance or after a new government has come to power, their value as State practice can be problematic.

For how long should State practice have existed?

thinking point
What is State practice and how can this best be determined from the numerous things done and said by States?

In order to constitute a customary rule of international law, how long should States have practised a usage?

A habitual act or omission that will constitute custom does not need to have existed for a very long period of time. While some reasonable length of time certainly helps in establishing the profile of a custom, especially in terms of its stability and consistency, it is not required that the custom has existed from time immemorial. A long practice is not necessary; in fact, the customary rules relating to airspace and the continental shelf have emerged from fairly recent practice.

What is important is that, no matter how long or how short the period for which a rule has existed, it must have been practised consistently by a generality of States. 'Generality', in this context, means a great number of States, not all of them. In most of the cases in which it decided on State practice, the ICJ did not emphasize the time element in State practice.

According to Akehurst (1974–75, see section 2.4.1), p. 53:

> as regards the quantity of practice needed to create a customary rule, the number of States participating is more important than the frequency or duration of the practice. Even a practice followed by a few States, on a few occasions and for a short period of time, can create a customary rule, provided there is no practice which conflicts with the rule.

● ***Federal Republic of Germany v. Denmark, Federal Republic of Germany v. The Netherlands*** [1969] ICJ REP 3 (The ***North Sea Continental Shelf Cases***)

See the facts in section 2.4.2.

In this case, the ICJ said:

> Although the passage of only a short period of time is not necessarily, or of itself, a bar to the formulation of a new customary international law on the basis of what was originally a purely conventional rule, an indispensable requirement would be that within the period in question, short though it might be, State practice, including that of States whose interests are specially affected, should have been both extensive and virtually uniform in the sense of the provision invoked;—and should moreover have occurred in such a way as to show a general recognition that a rule of law or legal obligation is involved.

See also *UK v. Norway* (1951) ICJ Rep 116 (the *Anglo-Norwegian Fisheries Case*).

KEY POINTS

- State practice is the aggregate of how States behave in relation to a particular issue.

- Time, per se, is not the essence of custom, but it helps if the custom in question has existed for a reasonable length of time.

- It is more important that *many* States practise a particular custom and that they do so consistently.

Consistency of State practice

. . . .

● *Colombia v. Peru* (1950) ICJ REP 266 (The *Asylum Case*)

For the facts, see earlier in this section.

In this case, the ICJ offered what is generally considered to be the leading statement on the issue of consistency of State practice:

> The party which relies on a custom … must prove that this custom is established in such a manner that it has become binding on the other party. The Colombian Government must prove that the rule invoked by it is in accordance with a *constant and uniform* usage practised by States in question, and that this usage is the expression of a right appertaining to the States granting asylum and a duty incumbent on the territorial State. This follows from Article 38 of the Statute of the Court, which refers to international custom 'as evidence of a general practice accepted by law'.
>
> The facts brought to the knowledge of the Court disclose so much *uncertainty and contradiction*, so much *fluctuation and discrepancy* in the exercise of diplomatic asylum and in the official views expressed on different occasions; there has been so much inconsistency in the rapid succession of conventions on asylum, ratified by some States and rejected by others, and the practice has been so much influenced by considerations of political expediency in the various cases, that it is not possible to discern in all of this any constant and uniform usage accepted as law with regard to the alleged rule of unilateral and definitive qualification of the offence. [Emphasis added]

. . . .

● *United Kingdom v. Iceland* (1973) ICJ REP 3 (The *Fisheries Jurisdiction Case*)

In their joint opinion, Judges Forster, Bengzon, Jiménez de Aréchaga, Nagendra Singh, and Ruda stated that:

> Another essential requirement for the practice of States to acquire the status of customary law is that such State practice must be *common*, *consistent* and *concordant*. The contradiction in the practice of States or inconsistent conduct, particularly emanating from these very States which are said to be following or establishing the custom, would prevent the emergence of a rule of customary law. [Emphasis added]

. . . .

● *United Kingdom v. Norway* (1951) ICJ REP 116 (The *Anglo-Norwegian Fisheries Case*)

In this case, however, the Court said (at 116) that:

> a small degree of inconsistency does not prevent the creation of a customary rule although in such cases the rule in question probably needs to be supported by a large amount of practice, in order to outweigh the conflicting practice in question.

KEY POINTS

- In the *Asylum Case*, the Court emphasized *constancy* and uniformity of practice in order to prove custom.

- The presence of *fluctuations* and *discrepancies* in State practice can adversely affect the usage in question, no matter how many States are involved in the practice, although a small degree of inconsistency will not normally prevent the creation of customary rules.

Can omission constitute State practice?

In our definition of 'custom', we refer not only to acts, but also to omissions. This implies that it is not only what States say or do, but also what they *omit* to say or do that can constitute custom. It is possible that a State may refrain from doing a thing because it believes that it has a legal obligation not to do that thing. If that happens, then, in those circumstances, that omission can constitute a custom provided that other States expect it so to act. A good example of omission is perhaps that provided in Article 2(4) of the UN Charter, which enjoins States not to use, or threaten to use, force against other States in their international relations. As will be seen in Chapter 10 concerning the law of the use of force, most States and international legal scholars regard this prohibition as evidence of customary international law—a view that the ICJ endorsed in the *Nicaragua Case*.

thinking points

- *For how long, and by how many States, should a usage have been practised before it can be regarded as a rule of customary international law?*
- *If State practice consists in what States do or say, what is the position of what States refrain from doing as a matter of legal obligation?*

Opinio juris

Opinio juris was first formulated by French writer Francois Gény as an effort to differentiate legal custom from mere social usage (Shaw, 2008, p. 71, see section 2.4.1, citing Gény, *Méthode d'Interprétation et Sources en Droit Privé Positif*, 1899, para. 10). *Opinio juris* has been variously defined by writers. Some see it as a 'conviction felt by states that a certain form of conduct is required by international law' (*Akehurst's Modern Introduction to International Law* (7th rev'd edn, ed. Peter Malanczuk, London: Routledge, 1997), p. 44; Brierly (1963, see section 2.3.1) thought of it as the recognition by States of a certain practice as 'obligatory' (p. 60).

Irrespective of how it is described, what is crucial is that *opinio juris* is a psychological element which deals with how States *feel* about a practice. It invites us to look not only at what States do in relation to one another, but also to understand *why* they do it. And this is what makes it extremely difficult to know what *opinio juris* is in most instances. However, how far a State's behaviour can be subjected to psychoanalysis is doubtful. As Akehurst has observed (1997, above), at p. 44:

> There is something artificial about trying to analyse the psychology of collective entities such as states. Indeed, the modern tendency is not to look for direct evidence of a state's psychological convictions, but to infer *opinio iuris* indirectly from the actual behaviour of states. Thus, official statements are not required; *opinio iuris* may be gathered from acts or omissions.

● **Federal Republic of Germany v. Denmark, Federal Republic of Germany v. The Netherlands** (1969) ICJ REP 3 (The **North Sea Continental Shelf Cases**)

In this case, Judge Sørensen said, in his dissenting opinion (at 128), that:

> ...I do not find it necessary to go into the question of the *opinio juris*. This is a problem of legal doctrine which may cause great difficulties in international adjudication. In view of the manner in which international relations are conducted, there may be numerous cases in which it is practically impossible for one government to produce conclusive evidence of the motives which have prompted the action and policy of other governments.

● **Federal Republic of Germany v. Denmark, Federal Republic of Germany v. The Netherlands** (1969) ICJ REP 3 (The **North Sea Continental Shelf Cases**)

Judge Tanaka gave a similar dissenting opinion when he said (at 176) that:

> Next so far as the qualitative factor *opinio juris sive necessitatis* is concerned, it is extremely difficult to get evidence of its existence in concrete cases. This factor, relating to international motivation and being of a psychological nature, cannot be ascertained very easily, particularly when diverse legislative and executive organs of a government participate in an internal process of decision-making in respect of ratification or other State acts.

● **France v. Turkey** (1927) PCIJ SER. A, NO. 10 (The **SS Lotus Case**)

A French merchant ship collided with a Turkish merchant ship on the high seas, leading to the death of several people on the Turkish ship. Turkey claimed that the collision occurred through the negligence of a French officer, Lieutenant Demons. Both Turkey and France claimed that they had jurisdiction to try the offender. Although the jurisdiction of France over its accused national was not in question, the main issue before the Court was whether Turkey had the right to try the French officer. Turkey claimed that there was a permissive rule of general international law entitling it to try the culprit, whereas France claimed that Turkey was under a duty not to try the French officer.

Held: Turkey had jurisdiction to try the French national. The Permanent Court of International Justice (PCIJ) stated (at 18) that:

> (1) ...although there are very few instances in which states in the position that Turkey found itself had prosecuted foreign nationals, other states had not opposed or objected to such prosecution;
> (2) ...even though most states in Turkey's position had refrained from prosecuting foreign nationals in these circumstances, there was no evidence that they have done so out of a legal obligation.

In a very important passage, the PCIJ stated (at 28) that:

> Even if the rarity of the judicial decisions to be found among the reported cases were sufficient to prove in point of fact the circumstances alleged by the Agent for the French Government, it would merely show that States had often, in practice, abstained from instituting criminal proceedings, and not that they recognized themselves as being obliged to do so; for only if such abstention were based on their being conscious of a duty to abstain would it be possible to speak of an international custom. The alleged fact does not allow one to infer that States have been conscious of having such a duty; on the other hand ... there are other circumstances calculated to show that the contrary is true.

> The States concerned must therefore feel that they are conforming to what amounts to a legal obligation. The frequency, or even habitual character of the acts is not in itself enough. There are many international acts e.g. in the field of ceremonial and protocol, which are performed almost invariably, but which are motivated only by considerations of courtesy, convenience or tradition, and not by any sense of legal duty.

Clearly, this statement shows that, as with State practice, an omission to act may also constitute *opinio juris* provided that States believe that they have a legal obligation to refrain from doing the act and do not merely abstain for lack of interest in doing the act.

KEY POINTS

- *Opinio juris* is the psychological element underscoring States' belief that they are under a legal obligation to do, or to refrain from doing, an act.

- In the *SS Lotus Case*, the PCIJ stated that a mere act of omission for its own sake does not constitute a customary rule; only an omission based on a belief that there is a legal obligation to refrain constitutes a customary rule.

The implication of the two statements in *SS Lotus* was that the Court accepted that absence of objection to a practice would evidence custom if it were to manifest *opinio juris*. But it did not regard mere absence of any reaction to be of the same effect.

Ascertaining **opinio juris**: the difference between what States say and do

As noted earlier, what States say and do are both important in determining State practice. The question is: how do we determine whether States regard a practice as constituting *opinio juris*?

The tendency in international law it to emphasize what States believe as evidence of *opinio juris*. This belief is mostly obtained from what States do. This approach may sometimes mean that States have to believe that something is already law even *before* that thing has become such.

Determining *opinio juris* from what States *believe* can be very tricky. For example, some States may believe that something is law, while other States may not challenge this belief; the result is that a new rule will emerge, despite the fact that not all of the States concerned may realize this, which departs from their own *beliefs* on the same, or similar, issues.

To expect States to believe that a State practice is law *before* it has become law is paradoxical. To become law, a customary rule has to be evidenced in practice. If States therefore *believe* that a usage is already law, then their practice plays no role in that formation process. Clearly, the problem of what States *believe* arose mainly from looking at what States *do*. But attempting to obtain *opinio juris* only from what States do is problematic: most developing countries express their beliefs on many issues, but fail to act on them. This may be due to the fact that these are relatively poor and uninfluential States.

Before the UN Charter prohibited the use of force, most of the powerful and influential States would use military force against other States to demonstrate the existence of a particular customary rule. The fact that smaller and poor States did not act in a similar way does not mean that they *believed* that the attitude of their powerful counterparts constituted *opinio juris*—they may, in fact, have believed the opposite—but with no equally effective ability to demonstrate their own understanding of the rule, their true belief would be lost in silence.

The problem arising from determining *opinio juris* from what States do can be solved if we also look at what States say. Fortunately, the emergence of modern communication techniques and improvements in diplomatic relations have now shifted emphasis from States' physical actions to milder gestures. As Zemanek notes in 'What is "State practice" and who makes it?' in Ulrich Beyerlin, Michael Bothe, Rainer Hofmann, and Ernst-Ulrich Petersmann (eds), *Recht zwischen Umbruch und Bewahrung: Völkerrecht, Europarecht, Staatsrecht—Festschrift für Rudolf Bernhardt* (Berlin: Springer, 1995), at p. 306:

> The beloved 'real' acts become less frequent because international law, and the Charter of the UN in particular, place more and more restraints on States in this respect. And what formerly was confined to diplomatic notes is now often transmitted via new forms of communication, mainly for reasons of domestic or international policy. The present information society forces governments which seek the widest possible support for their stance to resort to publicity.

O. Schachter, 'New custom: power, *opinio juris* and contrary practice' in J. Makarczyk (ed.), *Theory of International Law at the Threshold of the 21st Century* (The Hague: Kluwer Law International, 1996), pp. 531–532, underscores the problem with *opinio juris* thus:

> The fact that governments do not always practice what they preach comes as no surprise; indeed, we would be surprised if they did, at least in some areas. Still...we lawyers are called upon to determine whether a putative rule of customary law meets the requirements of general and consistent practice followed by States from a sense of legal obligation. The latter requirement—*opinio juris sive necessitatis*—calls for a belief by States that the practice in question is obligatory by virtue of a rule of law requiring it. In the words of an International Court of Justice judgment, 'Not only must the acts concerned amount to a settled practice, they must also be such, or be carried out in such a way, as to be evidence of a belief that this practice is rendered obligatory by the existence of a rule of law requiring it'. As this passage indicates, custom begins with 'acts' that become a 'settled practice;' that practice may then give rise to the belief that it had become obligatory.

The above extracts show that States act in a way that, by consistency and uniformity, becomes practice. It is after these acts are developed into practice that we can conclude that the States consider them obligatory. Nevertheless, the latter point remains difficult to prove.

The general view about how *opinio juris* is established became a controversial issue in the *Nicaragua Case* (see earlier in this section). In delivering its judgment, the ICJ first established the *opinio juris* on the prohibition of force, in the unanimous acceptance of relevant UN General Assembly resolutions that defined aggression. After that, the Court then declared that it 'must satisfy itself that the existence of the rule in the *opinio juris* of States is confirmed by practice'. Clearly, the Court reversed the order of things. As we discussed earlier, when proving custom we must first look at the general practice of States: if there is consistent, prevalent, general practice, then the first criterion is met. Next, we look at whether those States feel that the practice creates a legal obligation. So, the order is: state practice; then *opinio juris*. In *Nicaragua*, the ICJ first established *opinio juris*, before finding State practice. It is a logic that many writers have heavily criticized.

Aside from applying reverse logic in *Nicaragua*, the ICJ also inferred *opinio juris* on the basis of States' unanimous acceptance of the UN General Assembly resolutions touching on the concerned rule. This approach has also been widely criticized.

According to Anthony D'Amato (1985, see section 2.4.2), p. 101:

> The Court thus completely misunderstands customary law. First, a customary rule arises out of state practice; it is not necessarily to be found in UN resolutions and other majoritarian political documents. Second, *opinio juris* has nothing to do with 'acceptance' of rules in such documents. Rather, *opinio juris* is a psychological element associated with the formation of a customary rule as a characterization of state practice ... If voting for a UN resolution means investing it with *opinio juris*, then the latter has no independent content; one may simply apply the UN resolution as it is and mislabel it 'customary law.' Finally, instead of beginning with state practice, the Court ends with it.

A more generally acceptable view is that UN General Assembly resolutions are not law-creating, even if they reflect the law.

. . . .

● *SEDCO Inc v. National Iranian Oil Company and the Islamic Republic of Iran* CASE NO. ITL 59-129-3, THE HAGUE, 27 MARCH 1986

Chamber Three of the Iran–US Claims Tribunal confirmed that:

> General Assembly resolutions were not binding on states and could not be considered evidence of customary law, although they might reflect such law when there existed virtual unanimity in their adoption.

A decade earlier, the USA had expressed the view to the Sixth (Legal) Committee of the General Assembly (11 November 1977) that:

> ... [the General] Assembly is not a law-making body. Its resolutions, in the ordinary course, do not enact, formulate or alter international law, progressively or regressively. In the exceptional cases in which a General Assembly resolution may contribute to the development of international law, it can do so only if the resolution gains virtually universal support, if the Members of the General Assembly share a lawmaking or law-declaring intent—and if the content of that resolution is reflected in general state practice.

According to Erik Suy, UN legal counsel during the time at which the USA presented its view on UN General Assembly resolutions:

> The General Assembly's authority is limited to the adoption of resolutions. These are mere recommendations having no legally binding force for member states. Solemn declarations adopted either unanimously or by consensus have no different status, although their moral and political impact will be an important factor in guiding national policies. Declarations frequently contain reference to existing rules of international law. They do not create, but merely restate and endorse them. Other principles contained in such declarations may appear to be the new statement of legal rules. But the mere fact that they are adopted does not confer any specific and automatic authority.

KEY POINTS

- What States say is as important as what they do in relation to State practice. It will be misleading to refer only to what States do when determining customary international law.

- It is inappropriate to seek *opinio juris* mainly from UN General Assembly resolutions (or the resolutions of any other body, for that matter).

- UN resolutions may reflect international law, especially when they are unanimously accepted. But they do not constitute the law.

2.5.3 Regional custom

Can there be regional customs? In other words, can certain customary rules of international law be applicable only in certain regions of the world?

● *Colombia v. Peru* (1950) ICJ REP 266 (The *Asylum Case*)

See the facts in section 2.5.2.

In this case, the ICJ was confronted with the question of whether a regional custom existed in Latin America with respect to protecting political offenders. The Court did not dispute that such a custom might indeed exist, but insisted that the existence of such a custom must be proved by the State alleging it and accepted by *all* States against which it is claimed.

Held: The Court did not find that Colombia had proved this convincingly. The Court said (at 266) that:

> . . . even if it could be supposed that such a custom existed between certain Latin-American States only, it could not be invoked against Peru which, far from having by its attitude adhered to it, has, on the contrary, repudiated it by refraining from ratifying the Montevideo Conventions of 1933 and 1939, which were the first to include a rule concerning the qualification of the offence in matters of diplomatic asylum.

It must be noted that, when alleging the existence of regional custom, the standard of proof required is usually higher than in cases in which a general custom is alleged. In proving general customary rules, what is required is that the majority of participating States accept the rule as *opinio juris*.

● *Portugal v. India* (1960) ICJ REP 6 (The *Rights of Passage over Indian Territory Case*)

Portugal alleged that India had prevented it from exercising a sovereign right over two enclaves of its territory, Dadra and Nagar-Aveli, located in the Indian peninsula and surrounded by India. Portugal supported this claim by stating that a custom to that effect existed between it and India. India, on the other hand, claimed that no local custom could be established between only two States.

Held:

> It is difficult to see why the number of states between which a local custom may be established on the basis of long continued practice between two States accepted by them as regulating their relations should not form the basis of mutual rights and obligations between the two states.

The above case shows that custom is about practice and intention, as opposed to the number of parties involved. As long as the State parties involved continue to behave in a particular manner, and it can be inferred by their acts or omissions that they recognize that legal rights and obligations flow from such practice, then they can be said to have established customary law as between or among themselves.

KEY POINTS

- There can be customs that apply only to certain regions of the world.

- As few as two States in a region can form a regional custom.

- Regional customs do not establish a general rule of law, but apply only to the States of the region of its application.

- The standard of proving regional custom is usually much higher than that of proving general custom.

2.5.4 Persistent objector

Are customary rules binding on all States? Put differently, under what circumstances can a State not be bound by a rule of customary international law?

The answer to this question is to be found in the 'persistent objector' rule. Simply put, a persistent objector is a State that does not accept that the practice of a particular usage by other States creates a legal obligation for it. Therefore, the persistent objector constitutes an exception to the general rule that not all States have to consent to a particular custom for it to be enforceable against them.

As was noted earlier, for usages to become customary international rules, only a *majority* of States have to consent to it; those States that do not consent to that rule must specifically object to it. If any of those States reject that rule, then that State becomes an 'objector' and if that objection is constant, then the State is said to be a 'persistent objector'.

The persistent objector does not dispute the existence of the customary rule concerned; rather, what it objects to is that the customary rule binds or applies to it. The persistent objector does not keep silent: it resists and speaks out against a usage so vehemently and frequently that it will be unreasonable to ignore its objection and to expect it to be bound by the custom into which the usage later emerges.

. . . .

● *United Kingdom v. Norway* (1951) ICJ Rep 116 (The *Anglo-Norwegian Fisheries Case*)

See the facts in section 2.5.2.

This is the leading judicial authority on the persistent objector rule. One of the main issues before the Court was whether the traditional system of delineation practised by most coastal States applied to Norway, which had always applied a straight baseline rule constructed by the Norwegian government for measuring its fishery zone.

Held:

> The general toleration of foreign States with regard to the Norwegian practice is an unchallenged fact. For a period of more than 60 years the United Kingdom Government itself in no way contested it...even before the dispute arose, this method had been consolidated by a constant and sufficiently long practice, in the face of which the attitude of governments bears witness to the fact that they did not consider it to be contrary to international law.

In this case, the Court held that several States, including the UK, had accepted the Norwegian practice of using the straight baseline measurement without any objection for as many as sixty years. In other words, if the UK—or any other State—had any objection to the Norwegian measurement, it ought not to have allowed the practice to go on for so long without challenge. On the contrary, the Norwegian practice was allowed to consolidate as a customary rule before any objection was made to it. To be implied from this, therefore, is that objection to a rule should be made before the rule becomes a custom.

According to §102 of the Restatement of the Law (Third), Foreign Relations Law of the United States, it is said that:

> ...in principle a state that indicates its dissent from a practice while the law is still in the process of development is not bound by that rule even after it matures. Historically, such dissent and consequent exemption from a principle that became customary law has been rare.

As Gerhard von Glahn (1996, see section 2.5.2), observes at p. 15:

> ...any country objecting to the usage may state its objections from the beginning and refuse to follow the example of others who assent to the practice in question. When the usage changes into a legal custom at a later date, the objecting nation is not bound by the new rule.

The rationale for encouraging States to commence their objections right from the start of the evolution of a custom is to provide their objection with credibility. Certainly, a State stands a much better chance of resisting a custom if it can show that its objection did not simply start overnight. Thus the State must prove that it did not start objecting only *after* the usage had fully evolved into a rule of customary international law.

thinking point

What is the rationale for the ICJ decision in Anglo-Norwegian Fisheries, and how does this relate to the principle that objection to a customary rule should be made before the evolution of the rule into a full custom?

The arguments against the persistent objector rule

There are many arguments against the persistent objector rule. At the extreme, it is often said that there is no such thing as a 'persistent objector' in international law.

According to Charney, 'The persistent objector rule and the development of customary international law' (1985) 56 BYBIL 1:

> it might be wise to conclude that regardless of one's theory of international law, the persistent objector rule has no legitimate basis in the international legal system. Not only is the rule hard to reconcile with the current theories of international law, but evidence which might be produced to support the rule is weak indeed.

Charney's argument is based on the role played by the 'societal context' in which States find themselves in their acceptance or rejection of customs. For him, States do not have free will in accepting or rejecting a *binding rule* of international law. They are shaped by the society and, according to Charney, it is this societal context that is the source of States' obligation to conform to rules of international law. Hence, for him, their consent is irrelevant.

This argument is littered with loopholes. If States play no role in the evolution of customs—assuming that only the 'societal context' performs that role, as Charney argues—they certainly do not lose their right to object to those in the formation of which they have not partaken. The very fact that a State does not participate in the formation of a customary rule should make its objection to it a lot easier.

It may be that it is difficult for a State to remain permanently a persistent objector to a rule; no doubt a persistent objector can be influenced by other States to abandon its position. However, this does not mean that the State has no right to object to a usage in the first place.

As Brownlie (2003, see section 2.4.1) notes (p. 11):

> The way in which, as a matter of practice, custom resolves itself into a question of special relations is illustrated further by the rule that a state may contract out of a custom in the process of formation. Evidence of objection must be clear and there is probably a presumption of acceptance which is to be rebutted. Whatever the theoretical underpinnings of the principle, it is well recognized by international tribunals, and in the practice of states. Given the majoritarian tendency of international relations the principle is likely to have increased prominence.

Also, a State may not be able to object to some kinds of international norm. An example is a peremptory norm of international law: the most fundamental norms of international law, from which no derogation is permitted, except by a norm of similar character (see the *Namibia Advisory Opinion* (1971) ICJ Rep 16).

It must be pointed out, however, that the objection of one State to a usage, if successful, does not prevent that usage from becoming a customary rule, as has long been recognized by the ICJ.

. . . .

● *Ethiopia v. South Africa; Liberia v. South Africa (Second Phase)* (1966) ICJ Rep 291 (The *South West Africa Cases*)

In his dissenting opinion, Judge Tanaka considered whether the objection of one State prevents a practice from maturing into a custom. According to him:

> . . . the answer must be in the negative for the reason that Article 38, paragraph 1(b), of the Statute does not exclude the possibility of a few dissidents for the purpose of the creation of a customary international law and that the contrary view of a particular State or States would result in the permission of obstruction by veto, which could not have been expected by the legislator who drafted the said Article.

KEY POINTS

- To make a viable claim of persistent objection, a State needs to have been objecting right from the moment at which the particular rule starts evolving. The State should not wait for the practice to mature before expressing its objection.

- Subsequent maturation of a usage into custom does not invalidate a persistent objection, provided that it began before that stage of maturation.

- The position of a persistent objector may be undermined by pressure from other States and subsequent developments in the international environment.

- A persistent objector's case is helped by the acquiescence of other States to such objection.

- The objection by one State, even if successful, does not prevent the objected rule from becoming a custom for other States.

- Article 38(1) of the ICJ Statute does not exclude the possibility of a persistent objector.

2.6 General principles of law

The third source of international law listed in Article 38(1) is 'the general principles of law recognized by civilized nations'.

The phrase 'civilized nations' was previously used to describe States with well-developed legal systems that could cater for complex relations amongst nations. For example, in *Petroleum Development Ltd v. Sheikh of Abu Dhabi* (1951) 18 ILR 144 (the *Abu Dhabi Arbitration*), the arbitrator found that the law of Abu Dhabi contained no legal principles that could be applied to modern commercial instruments, and could not therefore be applied to oil concessions. However, the phrase often implied a more general distinction between developed and undeveloped States, and was used during the colonial era to distinguish between colonial governments and the colonized peoples. Thus, in ancient times, only general principles of law developed and practised by 'civilized nations' qualified as a source of international law. However, following the formation of the United Nations, the phrase 'civilized nations' has been replaced by 'peace-loving nations' under Article 4 of the UN Charter. All nations are now considered 'civilized'.

As a source of international law, the 'general principles of law recognized by civilized nations' was inserted into the ICJ Statute in order to enable the Court to decide disputes in circumstances in which neither treaties nor custom provide guidance or solutions regarding a particular claim. This kind of situation, in which the Court would be forced to declare a case inadmissible due to lack of applicable law, is known as *non liquet*.

2.6.1 General principles of *which* law?

What does the phase 'the general principles of law' actually mean? Does it refer to 'general principles of *international* law' or 'general principles of *municipal* law'? When we seek to adopt a particular qualification to the 'law' referred to, that provision becomes ambiguous.

It is possible to interpret this phrase as referring to principles of municipal law, if we take into consideration the state of international relations at the time when the ICJ Statute was drafted. The ICJ Statute was originally drafted for the use of the PCIJ. The Statute was drafted at a time when it was unclear whether anything other than treaties and customs governed the international legal relations of States. Thus it is safe to assume that 'the general principles of law' referred to by the Statute means those principles that are mainly derived from principles of municipal law. The rationale for this position is that even if nothing other than treaty and custom were to play any role in States' relations during the time at which the Statute was drafted, there could be no doubt that the legal systems of individual States contained certain principles known to other systems and which could be justly applied to disputes between States.

In *International Law: A Treatise, Vol. 1: Peace* (8th edn, ed. H. Lauterpacht, London: Longmans, 1955), p. 29, Oppenheim states that:

> the intention is to authorize the Court to apply the general principles of municipal jurisprudence, in particular of private law, in so far as they are applicable to relations of States.

It does not mean, however, that international tribunals will, like robots, simply take principles common to domestic legal systems and apply them to cases. As Brownlie (2003, see section 2.4.1) has pointed out:

> ...it would be incorrect to assume that tribunals have in practice adopted a mechanical system of borrowing from domestic law after a census of domestic systems. What has happened is that international tribunals have employed elements of legal reasoning and private law analogies in order to make the law of nations a viable system for application in a judicial process...An international tribunal chooses, edits, and adapts elements from better developed systems: the result is a new element of international law the content of which is influenced historically and logically by domestic law.

The ICJ has ruled on several occasions that 'general principles of law' means 'principles of national law'.

● ***Advisory Opinion Concerning the International Status of South West Africa*** (1950) ICJ Rep 133 (The ***South West Africa Cases***)

Judge McNair said:

> ...international law has recruited and continues to recruit many of its rules and institutions from private systems of law, Article 38(1)(c) of the Statute of the Court bears witness that this process is still active...the way in which international law borrows from this source is not by means of importing private law institutions 'lock, stock and barrel', ready-made and fully equipped with a set of rules. It would be difficult to reconcile such a process with the application of the 'general principles of law'. In my own opinion, the true duty of the international tribunals in this matter is to regard any features or terminology which are reminiscent of the rules and institutions of private law as an indication of policy and principles rather than as directly importing these rules and institutions.

● ***Portugal v. India*** (1960) ICJ Rep 6 (The ***Rights of Passage over Indian Territory Case***)

See the facts in section 2.5.3.

Portugal contended that general principles of law supported its claim that it had a right of passage from the coast to its enclaves of territories. It supported its argument by demonstrating that a comparative study of various legal provisions of many States tended to support what can be called 'rights of way of necessity' (see 10 *et seq*).

● ***Tunisia v. Libya*** (1981) ICJ Rep 1 (The ***Continental Shelf Case***)

This case primarily concerned Tunisia and Libya, and Malta had petitioned the Court, under Article 62 of the ICJ Statute, to intervene in the case. In justification of its application, Malta referred to a comparative law study to justify the principle of intervention in judicial proceedings in many national legal systems.

The second possible interpretation of the phrase 'general principles of law' is that it means general principles of international law. One argument in favour of this interpretation is that Article 38(1) addresses international courts and tribunals, not domestic ones. Therefore the principles are those applied by its addressees.

The problem with the second interpretation is that not all general principles applied in international judicial practice are derived from domestic legal systems; further, not all such principles have attained international recognition. As Akehurst notes (1997, see section 2.5.2), p. 49:

> some are based on 'natural justice' common to all legal systems (such as the principle of good faith, estoppel and proportionality), others simply apply logic familiar to lawyers (such as the rules *lex specialis derogate legi generali, lex posterior derogate legi priori*), and another category is related to 'the specific nature of the international community', as expressed in the principle of *ius cogens*. Therefore, a real transplantation of the domestic law principles to the international level is limited to a number of procedural rules, such as the right to a fair hearing… denial of justice, or the exhaustion of local remedies, and some substantive principles, such as prescription and liability for fault.

However, there is no reason why the phrase 'general principles of law' should mean 'either' national 'or' international law. Nothing says that we cannot generously interpret the phrase to mean principles of *both* domestic and international law. In fact, since the reason for including the phrase in the Statute was to ensure that the Court did not run out of applicable principles, then the suggested flexible interpretation advances that purpose.

KEY POINTS

- The phrase 'general principles of law' refers to either general principles of international law or general principles of national law, or both.

- It can be difficult to determine what general principles of law are, given that not all principles applied in international law derive from domestic legal systems.

2.6.2 *Ex aequo et bono* and equity

Ex aequo et bono is a Latin phrase that loosely translates as 'according to what is right and good', or 'according to equity and good conscience'. It implies the principles of fairness in the same way as equity is used in some domestic systems. In the UK, for example, the courts will, in the exercise of their discretion, apply equitable principles where a strict application of legal rules might cause injustice. Thus, under most domestic systems, there is a clear distinction between equitable and legal rules, and courts do not require the consent of parties to a dispute to apply them.

Ex aequo et bono empowers parties to a dispute to authorize the ICJ to disregard all other sources of international law in dealing with their dispute, and do what is just and fair. The first condition of *ex aequo et bono* is that parties to a dispute must agree to it. Unlike under domestic systems, the Court cannot apply the principle discretionally.

Judge Hudson stated in *Netherlands v. Belgium* (1937) PCIJ Ser. A/B, No. 70 (the *River Meuse Case*), at 76–77, that international law does not distinguish between equity and law. Equitable principles are far more elaborate and go beyond what *ex aequo et bono* encapsulates, but this is not an issue worthy of considering here (see Michael Akehurst, 'Equity and general international law' (1976) 25 ICLQ 801).

The question is: in the absence of agreement by the parties that the Court deal with their case *ex aequo et bono*, can it apply equity?

● **Burkina Faso v. Mali** (1985) ICJ REP 6 (The **Frontier Dispute Case**)

In this case, the Court held that it:

> cannot apply *ex aequo et bono* principle to this case since the parties have not agreed to that effect. Also, that since the parties have not entrusted the Court with the task of carrying out an adjustment of their respective interests, it must also dismiss any possibility of resorting to equity...

But the Court did not rule out applying equity in a limited sense and only if such 'constitutes a method of interpretation of the law in force'.

● **India v. Pakistan** (1968) 50 ILR 2 (The **Rann of Kutch Arbitration**)

Similarly, in this case, the ad hoc tribunal stated that (at 18):

> equity forms part of international law; therefore the Parties are free to present and develop their cases with reliance on principles of equity [although an] International tribunal will have the wider power to adjudicate a case *ex aequo et bono*, and thus go outside the bounds of law, only if such power has been conferred on it by mutual agreement between the Parties.

● **Federal Republic of Germany v. Denmark, Federal Republic of Germany v. The Netherlands** (1969) ICJ REP 3 (The **North Sea Continental Shelf Cases**)

See the facts in section 2.4.2.

In this case, the ICJ directed a delimitation of the continental shelf between Germany, the Netherlands, and Denmark 'in accordance with equitable principles' (at 3).

● **Tunisia v. Libya** (1981) ICJ REP 1 (The **Continental Shelf Case**)

See the facts in section 2.6.1.

In this case, the ICJ declared that:

> it is bound to apply the equitable principles as part of international law, and to balance up the various considerations which it regards as relevant in order to produce an equitable result. While it is clear that no rigid rules exist as to the exact weight to be attached to each element in the case, this is very far from being an exercise of discretion or conciliation; nor is it an operation of distributive justice.

Although the ICJ Statute did not provide for equity, some important international treaties have now expressly incorporated the rule into their systems. Article 59 of the 1982 UN Convention on the Law of the Sea (UNCLOS III) expressly provides that conflicts between coastal and other States, concerning their exclusive economic zones (EEZs), are to be resolved on the basis of equity. A similar provision is also contained in Article 5 of the 1997 Law of the Non-Navigational Uses of International Watercourses (see UN Doc. A/49/10, 1994, pp. 197, 218 *et seq*).

thinking points

- *Do you think that equity and* ex aequo et bono *mean the same thing, and apply to the same situations?*
- *Explain the ICJ's approach to whether or not it could apply equity in disputes in which parties have not asked it to decide* ex aequo et bono.

2.6.3 Other commonly applied general principles of law: reparation, *res judicata*, and *pacta sunt servanda*

Aside from equity, the ICJ (as well as other international tribunals) has applied other general principles of law to disputes among States.

● *Germany v. Poland* (1928) PCIJ Ser. A, No. 17 (The *Chorzów Factory Case*)

In this case, the Court said (at 29) that:

It is a principle of international law, and even a general conception of law, that any breach of an engagement involves an obligation to make reparation.

● *Effect of Awards of Compensation Made by the UN Administrative Tribunal Advisory Opinion* (1954) ICJ Rep 47 (The *Administrative Tribunal Opinion*)

The case concerned the dismissal of some employees of the UN Secretariat. On the question of whether the UN General Assembly can refuse to effectuate the awards made by the tribunal in favour of the dismissed staff, it was held that:

According to a well-established and generally recognised principle of law, a judgment rendered by a judicial body is *res judicata* and has binding force between the parties to the dispute.

● *Argentina v. Chile* (1994) 113 ILR 1 (The *Laguna del Desierto Case*)

The tribunal stated (at 43) that:

A judgment having the authority of *res judicata* is judicially binding on the Parties to the dispute. This is a fundamental principle of law of nations repeatedly invoked in the jurisprudence, which regards the authority of *res judicata* as a universal and absolute principle of international law.

● *AMCO Asia Corporation v. Republic of Indonesia* (1982) 89 ILR 366

The tribunal applied an even less common principle of law. It stated (at 504) that:

the full compensation of prejudice, by awarding to the injured party the *damnum emergens* and *lucrum cessans* is a principle common to the main systems of municipal law, and therefore, a general principle of law which may be considered as a source of international law.

The last general principle to be considered is *pacta sunt servanda*. This is the principle that obligates States to discharge their treaty obligations in good faith. It is perhaps the most important principle in the law of treaties, since the whole essence of States agreeing to a treaty rests on their readiness to act in good faith.

Although the principle of *pacta sunt servanda* is a principle of general international law, in the sense that it owes its existence to customary international law, it has now been formally codified by the UN Charter and the VCLT. Article 2(2) of the Charter states that:

> All Members, in order to ensure to all of them the rights and benefits resulting from membership, shall fulfil in good faith the obligations assumed by them in accordance with the present Charter.

● **Australia v. France** (1973) ICJ REP 99 (The **Nuclear Test Cases**)

In this case, the ICJ stated (at [46]) that:

> One of the basic principles governing the creation and performance of legal obligations, whatever their sources, is the principle of good faith. Trust and confidence are inherent in international cooperation, in particular in an age when this cooperation in many fields is becoming increasingly essential. Just as the very rule of *pacta sunt servanda* in the law of treaties is based on good faith, so also is the binding character of an international obligation assumed by unilateral obligations.

2.6.4 When will the ICJ not apply general principles of law?

The fact that the ICJ recognizes a principle as common to most domestic legal systems does not mean that it will invariably apply it. As noted previously, with regard to equity, the Court or tribunal will not simply apply a general principle, no matter how well or widely accepted it is; much depends on the facts and circumstances of individual cases.

In practice, international tribunals show a great deal of discretion in whether or not to apply general principles. Indeed, there have been many situations in which they refused to apply general principles of law. Examples of these include most decisions relating to the acquisition of territory. International tribunals have hardly followed domestic rules in dealing with such cases.

Similarly, international tribunals have not considered changes in domestic law in establishing rules concerning the effect of duress on treaties. In *Great Britain v. United States of America* (1910) Hague Court Rep 141 (the *North Atlantic Coast Fisheries Case*), 'the tribunal considered the concept of servitude and then refused to apply it' (Brownlie, 2003, p. 16, see section 2.4.1).

● **United States v. Italy** (1989) ICJ REP 15 (The **Elettronica Sicula SPA Case** OR **ELSI Case**)

The USA brought a claim against Italy in respect of an investment dispute. The Court had the opportunity to proclaim on the applicability of the well-known general principle, estoppel. Italy had objected to the USA bringing the action before the ICJ on the basis that the two US companies involved, which owned a 100 per cent interest in the company based in Italy, had not exhausted local remedies in Italy. In response, the USA claimed that since Italy did not raise the local remedies claim in its earlier response to the USA, Italy's silence in those circumstances constituted estoppel, meaning that once Italy had kept silence, it had waived its objection.

Commenting on this point, the Court stated (at 44) that:

> ...although it cannot be excluded that an estoppel could in certain circumstances arise from a silence when something ought to have been said, there are obvious difficulties in constructing an estoppel from a mere failure to mention a matter at a particular point in somewhat desultory diplomatic exchanges.

KEY POINTS

- The fact that a principle is common to most domestic systems does not mean that the Court will always apply it.

- The Courts are not bound to apply general principles of law just because such principles have been raised by one of the parties to the case.

Judicial decisions

Article 38(1)(d) of the ICJ Statute lists judicial decisions as one of the two subsidiary sources to which the Court might resort when dealing with a dispute.

In resorting to judicial decisions, the Court is limited by Article 59 of its Statute, which states that, 'the decision of the Court has no binding force except between the parties and in respect of that particular case'. This implies that the doctrine of *stare decisis*—the famous common law doctrine that obliges courts to follow their own previous decisions—does not apply to the ICJ. Thus, while the ICJ is not prevented from applying its existing decisions to a new case before it, by virtue of Article 59, those previous decisions do not bind the Court. However, since judges do not make law, judicial decisions cannot be strictly regarded as a source of international law, although they are authoritative evidence of the state of the law. Judicial decisions are regarded as a 'subsidiary' source because they can only be used to reinforce principal sources. A subsidiary source is not self-sufficient; it must be combined with another source or used only in the absence of substantial sources.

Although Article 38(1) does not explicitly include domestic judicial decisions, it seems plausible to assert that decisions of domestic courts are well within the contemplation of the provision. National courts have been considerably influential in establishing international rules such as those on diplomatic immunity and human rights.

The writings of publicists

Article 38(1)(d) of the ICJ Statute provides that the Court consider the teachings of the most qualified publicists of various nations.

As a subsidiary means, the writings of publicists generally show evidence of the law. However, some works have had significant influence on the development of international law. For example, from time immemorial States had claimed the right to explore areas adjacent to their territorial seas—but it was Gilbert who introduced the concept of the 'contiguous zone' as a means of discussing the validity of their claims (see Chapter 6 on territory and the law of the sea). Also, the majority of international legal scholars acknowledge the decisive impact of Grotius, Vattel, and Gentili, on the various aspects of international law, especially between the sixteenth and eighteenth centuries.

The influence of writers as a subsidiary source of international law has declined remarkably in recent times. Reasons for this decline include the rise of State sovereignty and the considerable role of custom and treaties. Moreover, one could also point to the impact of some significant historical developments late in the twentieth century. The end of colonialism, for example, showed that most former colonial States regard some aspects of international law to be one-sided. Post-colonial States largely perceived international law as a discipline that was developed by the imperial powers and that the predominantly Western writers did not reflect their aspirations. One of the legal developments most criticized by former colonial States was the general prohibition of the use of force. Former colonial States argued for an exception whereby force could be used to depose colonial governments. Other challenged developments include the agitation by minorities for a right to secede from a State. Thus, post-colonial writers constantly expressed the view that some aspects of international law were developed by Western writers to protect their own governments.

Regardless of the merits or demerits of the above claims, there is no doubt that the end of colonialism and the emergence of new writers from the former colonies affected the strong influence previously associated with the teachings of publicists. Furthermore, the increasing pluralization of international law cultures and orientations now make the determination of the teachings of highly qualified publicists far more difficult to ascertain.

2.9 The relationship between sources of international law

Whatever sources the ICJ might want to consider in the determination of a dispute submitted to it, the Court has to deal with two issues on the relationship of the sources. First, there might be an issue arising as to which source is to be applied by the Court, where there is a rule that is common to both treaty and custom as sources of international law. The second issue is whether there is a hierarchy between all of the sources listed in Article 38(1), since they appear in a particular order. We will now consider these two issues separately.

2.9.1 The relationship between customs and treaties

The relationship between customs and treaties is marked out for discussion separately from the general question of the hierarchy of sources (see section 2.9.2), because they are the two most important of the five sources listed in Article 38(1) of the ICJ Statute. In addition, it is clear that Article 38(1) prioritizes custom and treaties as the principal sources, since treaties embody rules 'recognized by the contesting states', and customs are 'evidence of a general practice accepted as law' by those States.

The relationship between customs and treaties, as sources of international law, is a very intricate one. This is because one influences the other: one is reflective of, or is subsumed by, the other.

According to Hugh Thirlway, 'The source of international law' in Malcolm Evans (ed.), *International Law* (3rd edn, Oxford: Oxford University Press, 2010), at pp. 111–112:

> ... the treaty in itself creates certain rights and obligations which are not of a customary nature; but if a number of States make a habit of concluding treaties containing standard provisions, then this may, in suitable circumstances, be taken to show that they recognize the existence of a custom requiring them to do so. The difficulty is of course that it can also be argued that the very fact that States have recourse to treaties to establish certain rules shows that they consider that those rules would not be applicable if no treaty were concluded, ie, that there is *no* customary rule of that nature ... as a result of the parallel existence of treaties and customs as sources of international law, the same question may be governed simultaneously by a treaty, as regards the relationship between the parties to the treaty, and by customary rules, as regards the relationships between non-parties, or between a party to the treaty and non-party.

R. Baxter, 'Multilateral treaties as evidence of customary international law' (1965) 41 BYBIL 275, 298 *et seq*, lays out the main issue between sources and treaties:

> If reliance is to be placed on a multilateral treaty as evidence of customary international law, it is first necessary to establish whether the treaty was intended to be declaratory of existing customary international law or constitutive of the new law. The silence of the treaty, which may necessitate resort to the *travaux préparatoires*, can make this a task of great difficulty.
>
> If it can be established that a treaty that purports to be declaratory of international law actually lays down new law ... the impact of the treaty may be weakened. It nevertheless remains that if a State declares that what is apparently a new law is actually part of the existing law, that very assertion counts in favour of the rule's incorporation into customary international law.

A treaty is said to be declaratory of customary international law if it merely recognizes the existence of the custom that it codifies. Conversely, a treaty is constitutive of customary international law if it gives birth to that custom afresh. Thus, what Baxter's statement above implies is that we first have to establish what a treaty does to custom. If it is established that the treaty is merely declaratory of the custom, then this affects the strength of the treaty for obvious reasons.

....

● *Federal Republic of Germany v. Denmark, Federal Republic of Germany v. The Netherlands* (1969) ICJ REP 3 (The *North Sea Continental Shelf Cases*)

See section 2.4.2 for the facts.

The Court identified three occasions on which the creation or existence of customary rules might impact on treaty provisions. These are namely:

(a) where treaties are merely declaratory of the concerned customary rule;

(b) where a treaty consists of rules and principles which are reflected in the practice of States, but which are not recognized as custom before the treaty itself has been adopted;

(c) a situation may arise whereby, after the adoption of a treaty, States, which are not party to the treaty, accept all or certain provisions of the treaty as applying to them, and that such may then constitute State practice, leading to the development of a customary rule.

The Court accepted that some provisions of the 1958 Geneva Convention on the Continental Shelf fell under the first category, although the Court did not accept that this included Article 6, which was the provision in contention in the case. Where this last situation arises, however, the Court requires the evidence that such a norm is of a significant status.

● ***Nicaragua v. United States (Merits)*** (1986) ICJ REP 14 (***Military and Paramilitary Activities in and against Nicaragua***, or The ***Nicaragua Case***)

In this case, the ICJ was confronted with a slightly different question about the relationship between treaties and customs. The pertinent argument to which the Court was to respond here was made by the USA that the Court:

> should refrain from applying the rules of customary international law because they have been 'subsumed' and 'supervened' by those of international treaty law, and especially those of the United Nations Charter. Thus the United States apparently takes the view that the existence of principles in the United Nations Charter precludes the possibility that similar rules might exist independently in customary international law, either because existing customary rules had been incorporated into the Charter, or because the Charter influenced the later adoption of customary rules with a corresponding content.

The Court said (at [177]) that:

> ...even if customary norm and the treaty norm were to have exactly the same content, this would not be a reason for the Court to hold that the incorporation of the customary norm into treaty-law must deprive the customary norm of its application as distinct from that of treaty norm. The existence of identical rules in international treaty law and customary law has been clearly recognized by the Court in the *North Sea Continental Shelf* cases.

Thus the Court rejected the US argument that because the rules contained in the UN Charter exactly matched those that existed under customary international law, the rules in the Charter had overtaken customary rules, so that the latter could not be applied against the USA. The Court proceeded to lay down the rationale for its ruling:

> There are a number of reasons for considering that, even if two norms belonging to two sources of international law appear identical in content, and even if the States in question are bound by these rules both on the level of treaty-law and on that of customary international law, these norms retain a separate existence. This is so from the standpoint of their applicability. In a legal dispute affecting two States, one of them may argue that the applicability of a treaty rule to its own conduct depends on the other State's conduct in respect of the application of other rules, on other subjects also included in the same treaty ... But if the two rules in question also exist as rules of customary international law, the failure of the one State to apply the one rule does not justify the other State in declining to apply the other rule. Rules which are identical in treaty law and customary international law are also distinguishable by reference to methods of interpretation and application. A State may accept a rule contained in a treaty not simply because it favours the application of the rule itself, but also because the treaty establishes what that State regards as desirable institutions or mechanisms to ensure implementation of the rule. Thus, if that rule parallels a rule of customary international law, two rules of the same content are subject to separate treatment as regards the organs competent to verify their implementation, depending on whether they are customary or treaty rules ...

In the above passage from the *Nicaragua Case*, the ICJ gave two grounds to justify the existence of parallel rules in treaty law and customary international law.

(a) It stated that where a rule exists only in treaty law, parties may base the applicability of the treaty to them on the applicability of the treaty to other parties.

example

Candoma may subscribe to a rule on fishing that is contained in a treaty, whereas Rutamu subscribes to a rule on ship lighting that is also contained in the treaty. In a dispute between the two States, Candoma may then insist that for the rule on ship lighting, contained in that same treaty, to apply to its conduct, the rule on fishing in that same treaty must be applied to Rutamu's conduct.

NOTE The only instance in which this first approach will not apply is if the two rules in question (that is, on fishing and ship lighting in the example above) both exist under customary international law. In that case, the failure by one State to apply one rule does not absolve the other from applying the other rule. This is simply because, unless the State declining to apply the other rule is a persistent objector, both States would have been bound by the customary rules. The reason why they are not so bound with regards to the treaty rules is that, since treaties are entered into in good faith, one party's reliance on the application of the provisions of a treaty to another party will depend on that party's readiness to abide by the treaty. There is no corresponding rule in the application of customary rules, by which States are bound by the existence of the rule in State practice, regardless of the behaviour of other States.

(b) The second rationale for the Court's decision in the *Nicaragua Case* is much more straightforward. The Court was of the opinion that the fact that a State ratifies a treaty does not necessarily evidence its acceptance of the treaty rules, but that such a move might have been motivated by the simple reason that the treaty establishes an enforcement mechanism. A clear example is that although there is a prohibition of the use of force by States in customary international law, until the UN Charter there was no international institutional mechanism for enforcing that rule against defaulters. Therefore the fact that a State subscribes to the Charter rule prohibiting the use of force does not prevent that State from still accepting a parallel rule in customary international law. In that situation, it may be a matter of convenience that the State ratifies the treaty; it may not be because it prefers the rules contained in the treaty to those of customary international law.

KEY POINTS

thinking point
Is it of any significance to recognize the parallel existence of a rule in treaty law and customary international law?

- A treaty can be declaratory of customs, meaning that the treaty confirms the existence of customs, or it can be constitutive, meaning that it formulates the new custom. Treaties are mostly silent on whether they are declaratory or constitutive, thus making this question rather difficult to determine.

- A treaty can crystallize a customary rule. This means that a treaty supports an evolving customary rule into full maturation.

- The fact that a treaty incorporates a customary rule does not prevent the application of such a customary rule.

2.9.2 Hierarchy of sources: are all sources equal—or are some more equal than others?

In what order must the Court apply the sources of international law to a dispute?

The answer to this question appears deceptively straightforward. Looking at the structure of Article 38(1) of the ICJ Statute, it is tempting to conclude that the sources are to be applied in their order of appearance. This is even more the case because Article 38(1) seems to subordinate some sources to others by the use of the phrase 'subsidiary means' in describing some of the sources.

Yet there is evidence that, when that provision was being drafted, the Advisory Committee of Jurists rejected a proposal to the effect that the sources listed should be considered by the Court 'in the undermentioned order' (see PCIJ Advisory Committee of Jurists, *Procés Verbaux of the Proceedings of the Committee*, 16 June–24 July, LN Publications, 1920). This implies that the sources were *not* intended to rank in the order of their appearance in Article 38(1).

The issue for consideration here is not that of the intricate relationship between customs and treaties, as discussed earlier, but that of which of the two is given priority before the Court.

In general, if the issue relates to applicable rules in several treaties, this is easy to deal with. The Court will normally apply the principles of *lex specialis derogate legi generali* and *lex posterior derogate legi priori*, meaning that the 'special rule overrides the general rule' and the 'later rule overrides the earlier rule', respectively. However, matters are not as simple when considering a choice of application between two species of sources. As Thirlway (2010, see section 2.9.1) noted at p. 114:

> It will normally be the case that a treaty is *lex specialis*, and as such prevails over any inconsistent rules of customary international law, or at least such as existed at the time of the conclusion of the treaty. It has to be presumed that the parties to the treaty were aware of the existing customary rule, and decided to provide otherwise in their treaty precisely in order to exclude the customary rule.

Certainly, where a State that alleges that a treaty rule overtakes a customary rule adduces evidence that it was aware of the existing customary rule before ratifying the treaty and that, in ratifying the treaty, it accepted the supremacy of the treaty rule, Thirlway's presumption will be applicable.

However, where neither of the disputing States makes such a claim, then the presumption that a State that ratifies a treaty intends its provision to overtake the customary rules flies in the face of the ICJ's reasoning in the *Nicaragua Case*. In that case, the Court held that a State may ratify a treaty for many reasons, none of which may be an acceptance of the superiority of the ratified treaty over customary rules.

The situation is far more complex where, rather than a treaty, it is the rule of customary international law that arises after the conclusion of a treaty and becomes *lex specialis* (the special law) on the same issue governed by the treaty.

> **example**
>
> Let us recall our example of the Colo Summer Treaty (CST) that we gave earlier in this chapter. This treaty entitles nationals of the two States to visit the other's countries without visas during the summer period of any given year. Let us imagine that, after the treaty has entered into force, citizens of the two parties to the treaty begin to visit each other's countries for several weeks *after* the summer period has ended, and that, in doing so, they will simply give notice of their impending visit to the Home Affairs ministry of the other country. In addition to this, these citizens also develop several specific practices, relating to their visits, which are neither contemplated by, nor provided for, in the treaty. No one protests against any of these practices.

In the situation given in the example, these later developments would constitute *lex specialis*—that is, special rules governing the visits of these nationals. The question is whether it is the specific customary developments or the general regulation contained in the treaty that will prevail?

In answering this question, Thirlway (2010, see section 2.9.1) states, at p. 133, that:

> If the new customary norm is one accepted as *jus cogens*, then according to the Vienna Convention on the Law of Treaties, not merely is any inconsistent provision in the treaty over-ridden, but 'any existing treaty which is in conflict with that norm becomes void and terminates ... [but where] the new norm is not of ... [*jus cogens*] nature ... [then] if the parties to the treaty have themselves contributed to the development of the new customary rule by acting inconsistently with the treaty, or have adopted the customary practice in their relations after the rule has become established, then the situation may be analysed as in effect a modification (or even perhaps an interpretation) of the treaty.

However, where none (or only some) of the parties to the treaty have participated in the new customary rule, then the situation will be dealt with by the provision of Article 41 VCLT concerning the amendment of multilateral treaties.

Thus, where a treaty is adopted before a custom arises and the latter develops into a *jus cogens* rule, the latter prevails over that treaty and any other treaties inconsistent with that norm. This is because a rule of *jus cogens*, according to Article 53 VCLT, is a peremptory norm of general international law, which can only be derogated from or modified by norms of a similar character. A peremptory norm is considered to be the most fundamental norm in the international society, the violation of which threatens the very essence of our civilization. An example is often given of the use of force by States.

Akehurst's view (1997, see section 2.5.2) seems to differ from that of Thirlway. Whereas Thirlway accords priority to treaties (on the basis that they are specifically concluded by States to take priority over customs), Akehurst expressed a different opinion. According to him (at p. 56), when:

> ... treaties and customs are of equal authority; the earlier in time prevails. This conforms to the general maxim of *lex posterior derogate legi priori* (the later law repeals an earlier law). However, in deciding possible conflicts between treaties and customs, two other principles

must be observed, namely *lex posterior generalis non derogate priori speciali* (a later law, general in nature, does not repeal an earlier law which is more special in nature) and *lex specialis derogate legi generali* (a special law prevails over a general law).

KEY POINTS

- Article 38(1) does not explicitly instruct that there is hierarchy among the sources. There is historical evidence to suggest that a hierarchy is not intended even if the Article uses a language of subordinating some sources to the others.

- Treaties and customs are the most important sources of international law.

- The principles concerning the time in which treaties are adopted govern the priority order of the rules contained in them when there is a conflict.

- If a treaty rule provides for a specific issue that is also subject to a general provision of another treaty, the specific rule prevails.

---

thinking points

- *Do you think that there is a hierarchy among the various sources of international law listed under Article 38(1) of the ICJ Statute?*

- *Do you believe that although all sources of international law are equal, some are more equal than others?*

 2.10

Are there other sources of international law?

It is often said that Article 38(1) of the ICJ Statute contains a complete list of sources, although it has also been suggested that other sources might be added to those listed in that Article. This debate will surely continue. However, certain developments have impacted on international law so much that we cannot ignore their potential as sources of international law. We consider the most important of these in the following sections.

2.10.1 International organizations

International organizations constitute a distinct potential source of international law, especially in light of the explicit reference by the ICJ to the resolutions of the UN General Assembly in the *Nicaragua Case* (see section 2.5.2). However, it is extremely doubtful that the ICJ intended to refer to those General Assembly resolutions in the technical sense of a source of law. If it did, the extensive criticism that the Court's ruling received in that case surely undermined the campaign for elevating the General Assembly to the level of a law-creating institution.

That is not to say, however, that international organizations do not have some effect on the development of international legal norms. As the ICJ said in its 1996 *Advisory Opinion on the Legality of the Threat or Use of Nuclear Weapons*, with regards to the various General Assembly resolutions adopted in 1961, condemning the use of such weapons:

> General Assembly resolutions, even if they are not binding, may sometimes have normative value. They can, in certain circumstances, provide evidence important for establishing the existence of a rule of law or the emergence of an *opinio juris*. To establish whether this is true of a given General Assembly resolution, it is necessary to look at its content and the conditions of its adoption; it is also necessary to see whether an *opinio juris* exists as to its normative character. Or a series of resolutions may show the gradual evolution of the *opinio juris* required for the establishment of a new rule.

The approach of States regarding the impact of UN General Assembly resolutions on the formation of law has already been noted earlier. What is left to observe is that there is a strong probability that the resolutions of the Assembly will continue to play a considerable role in the development of international law.

2.10.2 Soft law

The place of soft law in the development of international law is rather interesting. Soft law refers to a bundle of non-binding legal instruments, voluntarily assumed by States, on the expectation that the soft obligations that those instruments create will mature into hard law in the future. The law of treaties does not govern soft laws, since they are not real law; and because they do not definitively represent States' positions on any issue, soft laws neither generate State practice nor *opinio juris*.

Whilst States experiment with soft laws, they are not expected to shoulder any responsibility towards obligations contained therein although they enjoy the full support of the institutions or bodies promoting the laws.

example

The doctrine of soft law can be compared to the position of a person who wishes to buy a car. This person may decide first to test-run the car, with a view to making a full purchase if, after the test, he or she is convinced of the advantages that the car would confer. A generous motor dealer, eager to win a new customer, may gently encourage this person by allowing him or her to take the car for a series of test drives. In the test-drive period, it is understood that the test-driver incurs no liability towards the car or its dealer. Until the test-driver decides to buy the car, he or she reserves the right to turn up one day, after yet another test drive, and declare: 'Thanks, the car is good—but I am not ready to make a purchase just yet.'

Certain international instruments are regarded as creating soft law due to the sheer number of States that have ratified them, and the importance attached to the norms and ideas they promote. Prominent among these include the 1992 Rio Declaration on Environment and Development, the 1975 Helsinki Final Act of the Conference on Security and Cooperation in Europe, and the 1978 Bonn Declaration on International Terrorism.

Although soft laws do not create any legal obligation, they exact pressure on States—so much so that it is not considered wise to ignore them. As Sir Robert Jennings observed in his contribution to the *Cambridge–Tilburg Law Lectures* (3rd series, Boston, MA/Deventer: Kluwer Law International, 1983), pp. 3–32:

Recommendations may not make laws, but you would hesitate to advise a government that it may, therefore, ignore them, even in a legal argument.

And as Van Hoof said in *Rethinking the Sources of International Law* (Deventer: Kluwer Law Publishing, 1983), pp. 187–189, the importance of soft laws is that they:

> Map out the legal implications of legally non-binding instruments, in particular also their relations with full-fledged legal rules. This job . . . is extremely useful, as in international law, because of the lack of formal organizational structure, 'soft law' rules play a more prominent role than in national legal systems and are likely to do so also in the future.

However, some writers have cautioned against soft law. As Sztucki states in 'Reflections on international "soft law" ' in Lars Hjerner, Jan Ramberg, Ove Bring, and Said Mahmoudi (eds), *Festskrift till Lars Hjerner: Studies in International Law* (Stockholm: Norstedts, 1990), pp. 550–551:

> . . . the term [soft law] is inadequate and misleading. There are two levels or 'species' of law— something is law or is not law . . . the concept is counterproductive or even dangerous. On the other hand, it creates illusory expectations of (perhaps even insistence on) compliance with what no one is obliged to comply; and on the other hand, it exposes binding legal norms for risks of neglect, and international law as a whole for risks of erosion, by blurring the threshold between what is legally binding and what is not.

But despite occasional criticisms, a great majority of writers welcome soft law. Soft laws allow for the opportunity to nudge sceptical States gently, over a period of time, towards assuming responsibility for obligations to which they ordinarily would not want to sign up. This is a method much preferred to pressuring States to immediately sign up to treaties which they may refuse to perform or withdraw from at the earliest opportunity.

 # Conclusion

The 'sources of international law' is one of the most important topics of public international law with which a student, especially one new to the discipline, must immediately grapple. The various themes and sub-themes covered in this chapter—treaties, customs, general principles of law, judicial decisions, writings, international organizations—form the bulk of the substance in the topics to be discussed in several of the subsequent chapters. 'Sources of international law' provides international law with validity. It answers such questions as: from where is international law derived, and through which processes? It shows, to a reasonable extent, how States behave towards one another in relation to new and emerging norms, as well as in relation to settled conduct.

However, deciding which source is to apply in a case and tracking the relationship between some of the sources, such as treaty and customs, are as tricky as indeed it is to determine whether there is a hierarchy among the sources and, if there is, what the practical importance of this is.

Article 38(1) of the ICJ Statute provides an invaluable list of sources of international law. However, as we have seen, it is difficult to regard the list as exhaustive. The evolution of 'soft laws', as well as the practice of international organizations, continues to enrich and expand the sources of international law.

? Questions

Self-test questions

1 What is 'custom'?

2 What are the sources of international law?

3 Explain the persistent objector rule.

4 What does the phrase *opinio juris* imply and how is it determined?

5 What constitutes State practice?

6 Define 'treaty' and briefly outline its main features.

7 Suggest other possible sources of international law.

8 Distinguish between soft law and hard law.

Discussion questions

1 Discuss State practice and *opinio juris* as the twin requirements for establishing the existence of custom.

2 'There is no hierarchy among the sources of customary international law listed in Article 38(1) of the ICJ Statute. It is, in fact, nothing but an exercise in futility to attempt to justify a ranking of some sort among these sources.' To what extent does this statement represent the true nature of the provisions contained in Article 38(1) of the ICJ Statute?

3 Critically examine the assertion that the relationship between treaty and custom, as sources of international law, is too complex to make any sense.

4 ' "Consistency" is an essential element of State practice. Once there is a slight digression from a usage, it destroys its chances of ever becoming a custom.' Discuss.

5 ' "The general principles of law recognized by civilized nations" means general principles of international law.' Critically examine this statement.

6 'The persistent objector is nothing but a daydreamer whose claim is of no consequence in international law.' Discuss.

Assessment question

Candoma and Rutamu are two neighbouring coastal States along which the river Hope runs. Hope is densely populated by a rare fish that is of high commercial value. From time immemorial, both States have fished in this river without any problem. But, due to the narrowness of the river, the States developed a system whereby whenever one State was fishing, the other would wait a distance away until the first had left. On one particular occasion, a vessel from Candoma was fishing when a vessel from Rutamu approached. The latter vessel refused to halt. Instead, it progressed until it got entangled at the mouth of the river Hope. Unaware, the captain of the Candoman vessel collided with the Rutamuan vessel, killing three members of his crew, although there were no casualties aboard the Rutamuan vessel. When the Rutamuan vessel reached Candoman shores, the Candoman revolutionary guard promptly arrested the vessel's captain for trial in Candoma. Rutamu objected to this proposed trial and claimed, in objection to Candoma, that there was no breach of any 'waiting' custom between it and Candoma. Rutamu also claimed that it actually objected once to that 'stupid culture' by writing to Candoma.

Advise the parties.

Key cases

- *Colombia v. Peru* (1950) ICJ Rep 266 (the *Asylum Case*)
- *Federal Republic of Germany v. Denmark, Federal Republic of Germany v. The Netherlands* (1969) ICJ Rep 3 (the *North Sea Continental Shelf Cases*)
- *France v. Turkey* (1927) PCIJ Ser. A, No. 10 (the *SS Lotus Case*)
- *Nicaragua v. United States (Merits)* (1986) ICJ Rep 14 (*Military and Paramilitary Activities in and against Nicaragua* or the *Nicaragua Case*)
- *United Kingdom v. Norway* (1951) ICJ Rep 116 (the *Anglo-Norwegian Fisheries Case*)

Further reading

Akehurst, M., 'Custom as a source of international law' (1974–75) 47 BYBIL 1

Charney, J., 'The persistent objector rule and the development of customary international law' (1985) 56 BYBIL 1

Cheng, B., '*Opinio juris*: a key concept in international law that is much misunderstood' in S. Yee and W. Tieya (eds), *International Law in the Post-Cold War World* (London: Routledge, 2001), p. 56

McNair, A., 'General principles of law recognised by civilised nations' (1957) 33 BYBIL 1

Sloan, B., 'The binding force of a recommendation of the General Assembly of the United Nations' (1948) 25 BYBIL 1

The law of treaties

Learning objectives

This chapter will help you to:

- understand what treaties are and their importance in States' relations;
- appreciate the various types of treaty and their nature;
- understand the rules governing the various aspects of treaties;
- understand the various provisions of the Vienna Convention on the Law of Treaties (VCLT);
- appreciate current cases on several aspects of treaties; and
- understand how treaties are made, avoided, reserved against, and terminated.

Introduction

In Chapter 2, we discussed the several sources of international law and noted that treaties are the most important of these sources. For many reasons, treaties are the most widely used international instruments through which States and other international law subjects conduct relations with one another. This chapter discusses what treaties are, how they are made and terminated, and what functions they perform. These issues will be discussed in light of the provisions of the 1969 VCLT, which embodies most of the rules governing the various aspects of treaties, such as the interpretation, validity, reservation, and termination of treaties.

 3.1

General issues: the definition, scope, and nature of treaties

3.1.1 Defining a 'treaty'

Article 2(a) VCLT defines a 'treaty' as:

> an international agreement concluded between States in written form and governed by international law, whether embodied in a single instrument or in two or more related instruments and whatever its particular designation.

Treaties are usually concluded by two or more States, being subjects of international law, and not by subjects of national law, such as human beings and companies. States are the most important subjects of international law and mostly interrelate through treaties. It is almost unimaginable for States to transfer territories to one another, send international criminals across their frontiers, partition boundaries, and settle international disputes without the instrument of treaties.

However, apart from States, there are other subjects of international law, such as international organizations, which can conclude treaties with one another or with States. A famous example of a treaty concluded between an international organization and a state is the 1947 United Nations Headquarters Agreement between the United Nations and the USA. But, as we shall see later, international organizations are generally exempted from the scope of the VCLT—with certain exceptions.

Treaties can be referred to alternatively as 'declarations', 'protocols', 'instruments', 'conventions', and 'agreements', amongst other things.

The scope of the Vienna Convention on the Law of Treaties

3.2

The VCLT is the foremost instrument on the law governing treaties and it limits its scope to certain classes of agreement, which can be deduced from its provisions. This section will discuss the types of agreement that the Convention covers.

3.2.1 Treaties concluded between or among States (Articles 1–3)

Article 1 VCLT states that 'the present Convention applies only to treaties between States'. This restriction is further confirmed by the explicit reference to 'agreement concluded between States' in Article 2.

While Articles 1 and 2 limit the VCLT to 'States', it does not mean that treaties concluded by States with other subjects of international law have no legal effect. Article 3 states that:

> the fact that the present Convention does not apply to international agreements concluded between States and *other* subjects of international law or between such other subjects of international law, or to international agreements not in written form, shall not affect the legal force of such agreements. [Emphasis added]

Thus, while agreements concluded by entities such as international organizations, either between themselves or with States, are not governed by the VCLT, they are nonetheless valid under international law.

3.2.2 Constitutive treaties and treaties adopted within international organizations (Article 5)

Article 3 VCLT excludes international organizations and other subjects of international law from the scope of the Convention. Nonetheless, by Article 5, the VCLT applies to two types of treaty concluded by such organizations: treaties that establish international organizations, and treaties concluded *within* (not between) such organizations. A clarification of these distinctions is important, since the Convention does not generally apply to treaties concluded by international organizations, either *between* themselves or *with* States.

An international organization is usually formed by a group of States that sign up to a treaty to that effect. This founding treaty is variously referred to as a 'constituent instrument', 'constitutive Act', 'pact', or 'charter'. Regardless of the different terminologies, what these treaties do is establish an international organization. Examples of constitutive treaties include the Charter of the United Nations Organization (the UN Charter, adopted in 1945), the 1948 Charter establishing the Organization of American States (the OAS Charter), and the Constitutive Act of the African Union (the AU Act, adopted in 2000). But, as is obvious from the foregoing, the word 'constituting' or 'constitutive' need not appear in the title of a treaty that establishes an international organization. They are called *constitutive* treaties because they are the main treaties that *establish* international organizations and the term need not necessarily be part of their designation or description.

Once established, international organizations can adopt other treaties, which mainly regulate the relations of member States and of that organization. Like the constitutive treaty, these subsequent treaties must be signed by the members of the organization. However, unlike the constitutive treaties, which apply between the organizations and *other* subjects of international law (since they bring the organization into existence and establish the legal personality of that organization), treaties adopted by international organizations to regulate the conduct of members vis-à-vis the organization apply solely *within* that organization. Such treaties do not involve the participation of non-members or any other outsider. It is this kind of treaty, and the constitutive kind, that is governed by Article 5 VCLT, and is thus not excluded by the provisions of Articles 1–3.

Since the adoption of its Charter (which is its constitutive treaty), the United Nations has adopted many other treaties, declarations, conventions—such as the Genocide Convention and the UN Convention on the Law of the Sea (UNCLOS)—which apply among UN member States. Thus, whereas the Headquarters Agreement between the United Nations and the USA is not covered by the VCLT (being an agreement concluded by an international organization and a State, and thus excluded by Article 3 VCLT), UNCLOS and the Genocide Convention fall under Article 5 VCLT as treaties adopted *within* the organization.

3.2.3 Obligations of other international law subjects under general international law (Article 3(b))

Another interesting point worth mentioning in the provision of Article 3 VCLT is that, under certain circumstances, the Convention could apply to subjects of international law other than States. According to Article 3(b), nothing in the Convention affects the application to such international law subjects:

> of any of the rules set forth in the present Convention to which they would be subject under international law independently of the Convention.

The implication of this statement is that there might be rules to which international organizations, in their relations with one another or with States, could be subject, outside the Convention. Where such rules are also codified by the Convention, they will be applicable to agreements concluded by those organizations *if and only if* those rules exist under other general or customary international law to which the organization would ordinarily be subject.

A combined reading of Articles 1 and 3(b) thus means that whereas the rules of international law, which are codified by the Convention, do not generally apply to agreements concluded between international organizations or between them and States, such rules will apply if they exist elsewhere. Therefore, if certain international rules contained in the Convention are also found to exist in other international agreements to which the subject of international law in question is subject, then such rules will apply to those subjects of international law.

An example of the rule referred to in Article 3(b) would be customary international law rules on the peremptory norm (*jus cogens*). Peremptory norms are regarded as applicable to *all* subjects of international law, regardless of whether or not those entities sign up to the specific conventions prohibiting those norms. Article 53 VCLT codifies the rule relating to *jus cogens*. But the fact that the VCLT does not generally apply to international organizations does not prevent the application of the rule in Article 53 to them, since international customary law already makes the same rule codified in Article 53 VCLT applicable independent of the VCLT.

3.2.4 Treaties involving at least two States and international organizations (Article 3(c))

The VCLT does not apply to international agreements concluded by States with other subjects of international law as parties, or oral agreements, or agreements between other subjects of international law *per se*.

Nonetheless, the Convention applies as between States, which are parties to an international agreement to which other subjects of international law are also parties, provided that the concerned agreement is a multilateral treaty (Article 3(c)).

Thus at least *two States* must be party to such a multilateral treaty, in addition to *other* subjects of international law. Hence, Article 3(c) does not apply to a bilateral agreement between one State and a non-State subject of international law, or a multilateral agreement with *only one* State even if there are two or more international organizations because, in that case, the criterion of 'relations of States as between themselves' laid down in Article 3(c) will not be met.

KEY POINTS

thinking point
Distinguish between treaties concluded between subjects of international law and those concluded within them. Which of the two is not covered by the VCLT?

- States are the only subjects of international law to which the definition of treaties under the VCLT applies.

- The VCLT does not generally apply to treaties concluded between international organizations, or between them and States, except in specific circumstances.

- The VCLT applies to multilateral treaties provided that there are at least two States involved, and one or more other subjects of international law.

- The rules of the VCLT will apply to other subjects of international law if such rules already apply to them under general international law.

3.3 The nature of treaties

Treaties are usually written, and contained in a single document, although it is possible to have a treaty that is contained in several documents or volumes. The fact that treaties are written makes them a more predictable and better defined source of international law than customs.

Treaties are easily referable. Unlike customs, it is unnecessary to establish treaty validity formally through State practice. The mere fact that States or international organizations consciously agree to treaty obligations dispenses with any need to seek secondary validation of those obligations. However, subsequent practice, where available, can enhance the legitimacy of a treaty.

It is possible that, after a treaty enters into force, its provisions remain unimplemented for several years. Such late application does not affect the validity of that treaty, provided that, at the time that its provisions are eventually implemented, the treaty is still in force for the parties that conclude it. A good example is the North Atlantic Treaty adopted in 1949, which established the North Atlantic Treaty Organization (NATO). Article 5 of this treaty obligates every NATO member State to consider an attack on a member of that organization to be an attack on all of its members, so that members can take individual or joint military action to repel such attacks. The first time that NATO would implement this obligation was in 2001 when, following terrorist attacks on the USA, it called on its members to join the USA in self-defence action against Afghanistan, a State that was linked with Al Qaeda, the terrorist organization that admitted responsibility for the attack against the USA. There was a fifty-year gap between the entry into force of the treaty and the implementation of its core obligation—which is not to say that NATO had been inactive during the period between its establishment and the 2001 attacks.

There are no prescriptions under general international law or the VCLT about the shape that a treaty can take. There is no template for treaties, and no technical form or format is inherently good or bad. Some treaties can be lengthy, while some can be very short. Some treaties can be negotiated over a long period, while some may have a relatively short passage. It took the United Nations almost twenty years to negotiate UNCLOS, compared to the 1937 Nyon Agreement, which was negotiated and agreed in just four days.

In drafting a treaty, it is important that parties must have the intention to create legal relations between themselves. It is the intention to create legal relations that makes the treaty a valid and important source of international law. States often make statements to support political causes or objectives, with no intention that such public display of solidarity should create legal obligations for them. It is very common for States to make declarations, especially at international public fora such as the UN General Assembly, in respect of events in other States or general issues affecting the international community, without intending legal consequences to arise from such statements.

It must be noted that while parties to treaties (sometimes called 'member States', 'State parties', or 'contracting parties')—be they States, international organizations, or other subjects of international law—are at liberty to determine the nature, format, and shape of their treaties, they do not have unlimited freedom to determine the temporal application of a treaty. Whereas contracting parties can decide that a treaty that they conclude on a given date is to apply to issues occurring from that date, or any other stipulated time thereafter, they may generally not decide that such a treaty operates on transactions concluded prior to the inception of that treaty. This is a general rule against retrospective, or retroactive, laws.

Treaties are generally not retroactive in effect. The simple rationale for this is that a treaty is a piece of legislation and it is inappropriate to penalize States' conduct in hindsight. Otherwise, contracting parties may become liable for breaches that were not illegal at the time that they were committed. A clear example of this is that the Rome Statute of the International Criminal Court (ICC) does not apply to crimes committed before 1 July 2002, the day on which the treaty entered into force for the contracting parties.

Article 4 VCLT provides that the Convention applies only to treaties concluded after its entry into force.

thinking points

- *In what form can a treaty appear and how lengthy should a treaty be in order for it to be valid?*
- *Of what relevance is the intention to create legal relations among States in treaty formation?*
- *Why are treaties generally not retroactive, and what exemption, if any, is there to this rule?*

3.3.1 Determining what constitutes a treaty

One problem that often arises as a result of the lack of direct instruction, in the VCLT, on how a treaty may be constituted is determining what constitutes a treaty. This problem sometimes arises when a party to a discussion, a conference, or some other form of formal meetings assumes that the resulting communiqué or declaration constitutes a treaty between it and others.

International tribunals have always applied an 'objectivity test' to decide whether a treaty exists whenever parties disagree about the effect of international documents. In most disputes involving the effects of communiqués or declarations adopted at a meeting, tribunals will often look at two things in order to decide whether such communiqués or declarations constitute a treaty:

(a) the particular facts and circumstances of the case; and

(b) whether the concerned communiqué or declaration is duly registered, as required under international law for treaties to be effective.

. . . .

● *Qatar v. Bahrain* (1994) ICJ REP 112 (*Maritime Delimitation and Territorial Questions between Qatar and Bahrain*) (*Jurisdiction and Admissibility*)

This case involves a long territorial dispute between Qatar and Bahrain. During a Saudi-brokered negotiation, both States signed several documents, including two important ones in 1987 and 1990. The latter document comprised the minutes of the consultation between the two States, detailing what they had agreed on, including some agreements that they had reached in 1987. Principal amongst those previous agreements was that if peaceful negotiation between them were to fail, either State may apply to the International Court of Justice (ICJ) for settlement. Consequently, following failure of the Saudi intervention, Qatar instituted a proceeding before the ICJ on 8 July 1991. Bahrain challenged the Court's jurisdiction on the basis, inter alia, that the 1990 Minutes did not constitute a legally binding instrument.

The Court held that:

> The Parties agree that the exchanges of letters of December 1987 constitute an international agreement with binding force in their mutual relations...the Court would observe, in the first place, that international agreements may take a number of forms and be given a diversity of names...furthermore, as the Court said, in a case concerning a joint communiqué, 'it knows of no rule of international law which might preclude a joint communiqué from constituting an international agreement to submit a dispute to arbitration or judicial settlement' (*Aegean Sea Continental Shelf, I. C. J. Reports 1978*, p. 39, para. 96). In order to ascertain whether an agreement of that kind has been concluded, 'the Court must have regard above all to its actual terms and to the particular

circumstances in which it was drawn up'...the 1990 Minutes include a reaffirmation of obligations previously entered into; they entrust King Fahd with the task of attempting to find a solution to the dispute during a period of six months; and, lastly, they address the circumstances under which the Court could be seised after May 1991. Accordingly, and contrary to the contentions of Bahrain, the Minutes are not a simple record of a meeting, similar to those drawn up within the framework of the Tripartite Committee; they do not merely give an account of discussions and summarize points of agreement and disagreement. They enumerate the commitments to which the Parties have consented. They thus create rights and obligations in international law for the Parties. They constitute an international agreement.

This statement by the Court in *Qatar v. Bahrain* underscores two principles:

- that it is possible, as in this case, for an international agreement to arise from minutes of a meeting and from communiqués issued at the end of a meeting between States and, by logical extension, other international law subjects; and

- that the Court will have regard to all of the 'actual terms' and to the 'particular circumstances' in which the agreement in question is drawn up.

However, care must be taken not to confuse the rationale for the Court's decision in this case with a generalization that *all* communiqués and minutes of meetings constitute international agreements. It is clear from its reference to 'actual terms' and 'particular circumstances' that the Court did not intend to lay down such a general theory. The Court's decision was based on very specific facts and circumstances, which may not be present in other cases. Both Qatar and Bahrain had agreed to a set of issues and courses of action in previous binding documents (such as the 1987 one). All that the 1990 Minutes did was merely restate these agreements, therefore having the same validity as the previous agreements.

- ● *Ethiopia v. South Africa; Liberia v. South Africa (Preliminary Objections)* (1962) ICJ Rep 319 (The *South West Africa Cases*)

The case arose out of a system of international governance—the mandate system—that emerged after the First World War. Under Article 119 of the Treaty of Versailles of 28 June 1919, Germany renounced all rights and titles over overseas possessions in favour of the Principal Allied and Associated Powers. The Allied Powers, shortly before the signature of the Treaty of Peace, agreed to allocate those German-renounced overseas territories as mandates to certain Allied States that had already occupied them. South West Africa (present-day Namibia) was allocated to the UK under the agreement, which was to be administered by South Africa on behalf of the UK. Liberia and Ethiopia instituted an action before the Permanent Court of International Justice (PCIJ) alleging, among other things, that South Africa severally violated the terms of the mandate entrusted to it. Central to this challenge was the question of whether the mandate was a treaty between the mandate (South Africa) and the League of Nations and its members. Although South Africa had all along treated the mandate as a treaty, it modified its objection and later submitted (at 327) that:

...the Mandate for South West Africa *has never been, or at any rate* is since the dissolution of the League of Nations no longer, a 'treaty or convention in force' within the meaning of Article 37 of the Statute of the Court. [Emphasis added]

It was held by the Court (at 330), that the mandate—in fact and in law—is an international agreement having the character of a treaty or convention. The preamble of the mandate itself shows this character. The agreement referred to therein was effected by a decision of the Principal Allied and Associated Powers, including the UK, taken on 7 May 1919 to confer a 'Mandate for the Territory on His Britannic Majesty' and by the confirmation of its acceptance on 9 May 1919 by the Union of South Africa.

As seen above, the Court accepted mandates as treaties. Nevertheless, it is important to understand the role played by certain facts, which guided the Court towards this conclusion. South Africa had claimed, during its objection, that the mandate was of no greater effect than the resolutions of the League of Nations. The Court conceded that the mandate took the form of a Council resolution, but argued (at 330) that:

> obviously it was of a different character. It cannot be correctly regarded as embodying only an executive action in pursuance of the Covenant.

Another factor that might have weakened South Africa's case was perhaps the fact that, up until the question of the characteristics of the mandate arose in the case, it had treated the mandate as a treaty. Therefore, the Court was not too pleased when, for obvious reasons, South Africa made a U-turn on its position, suddenly pleading that mandates were not treaties. Thus, in addition to the nature of the mandate, the conduct of the parties vis-à-vis the instrument concerned is a crucial factor in determining whether, on the authority of this case, mandates constitute treaties under international law.

KEY POINTS

- Communiqués or any other records of meetings can be regarded as treaties if they establish rights and obligations, and if parties clearly intend them to constitute a binding agreement between them.

- A mandate is a trust-like power under which the administration of a territory is entrusted to the care of another entity on behalf of the international community.

- The administrator of a mandate owes certain obligations towards the mandate territory and such obligations are usually set out in the instrument that creates the mandate. Depending on the circumstances, these instruments may be regarded as treaties.

Despite its readiness to accept that communiqués and minutes may constitute international agreements in certain circumstances, the Court decisively rejected stretching such flexibility to contractual agreements between companies and States.

● *United Kingdom v. Iran* [1952] ICJ REP 93 (The *Anglo-Iranian Oil Company Case*)

In 1932, Iran cancelled a concessionary contract that it had with D'Arcy, a British company. Following its failure to make Iran reverse its decision, the UK took the matter to the League Council. Both countries decided to withdraw the matter from the League in February 1933 and, following another round of negotiations, Iran and D'Arcy signed a new concessionary agreement on 29 April 1933. In 1951, Iran nationalized the company. The UK argued that Iran's measure violated the 1933 Convention between the Imperial Government of Persia and the Anglo-Persian Oil Company Ltd. The UK also argued (at 111–112) that:

the agreement signed by the Iranian Government with the Anglo-Persian Oil Company on April 29th, 1933, has a double character, the character of being at once a concessionary contract between the Iranian Government and the Company and a treaty between the two Governments. It is further argued by the United Kingdom that even if the settlement reached in 1933 only amounted to a tacit or an implied agreement, it must be considered to be within the meaning of the term 'treaties or conventions' contained in the Iranian Declaration.

The Court held (at 111–112) that it could not:

accept the view that the contract signed between the Iranian Government and the Anglo-Persian Oil Company has a double character. It is nothing more than a concessionary contract between a government and a foreign corporation...Under the contract the Iranian Government cannot claim from the United Kingdom Government any rights which it may claim from the Company, nor can it be called upon to perform towards the United Kingdom Government any obligations which it is bound to perform towards the Company. The document bearing the signatures of the representatives of the Iranian Government and the Company has a single purpose: the purpose of regulating the relations between that Government and the Company in regard to the concession. It does not regulate in any way the relations between the two Governments.

It is clear from this passage that the Court was mindful not to confuse an agreement between Iran and a British company with an agreement between Iran and the UK. The 1933 Convention was an agreement between Iran and the British company. Thus, insofar as neither Iran nor the UK could have applied it to each other, it did not constitute a treaty between the two States.

. . . .

● *United Kingdom v. Iceland* [1973] ICJ REP 3 [The *Fisheries Jurisdiction Cases*]

Iceland claimed the authority to extend its fishing zone unilaterally from twelve to fifty nautical miles. It gave notice of its intention to the UK in 1971, but went ahead with extending the zone despite the UK's objection. This notice was in accordance with the 1961 agreement between Iceland and the UK to the effect that the former would not extend its fishing zone without giving the latter at least six months' notice. The 1961 agreement was contained in an exchange of notes between the two countries, which also entitled the two countries to confer jurisdiction on the Court if a dispute arose between the two. The UK contended (at 6) that:

for the purposes of Article 36(1) of the Statute of the Court, the Exchange of Notes of 11 March, 1961, constitutes a treaty or convention in force, and a submission by both parties to the jurisdiction of the Court in case of a dispute in relation to a claim by Iceland to extend its fisheries jurisdiction beyond the limits agreed in that Exchange of Notes.

On the question whether the Optional Protocol under Article 36(1) of the ICJ Statute constituted a treaty, the Court stated that 'It should be observed at the outset that the compromissory clause has a bilateral character' (at 16). Thus, the Court regarded the 1961 exchange of notes between Iceland and the UK as constituting a treaty. (See the Court's statement at 17 *et seq.*)

Care must be taken not to confuse the Court's reasoning in *Fisheries Jurisdiction*, in which it attached a treaty status to an Optional Clause, with that in *Anglo-Iranian Oil Co.*, in which the ICJ rejected a similar declaration. In the latter case, the Court rejected the argument of the UK because the contract in question was not between Iran and the UK, but between Iran and a company. The Court stated that since the UK was not privy to the contract and could not be requested to undertake obligations under it by Iran, it could not argue that the contract created obligations between that country and Iran. The UK's argument in *Anglo-Iranian Oil Co.* fell apart mainly because it attempted to create a double-character status for the contract such that the contract would not only bind Iran and D'Arcy, but also Iran and the UK. The Court confined itself to the fact that the issue at hand had to do with a contract between a company and a State; the Court did not deny in that case that, under certain circumstances, 'unilateral declarations' of a certain nature could constitute treaties.

In contrast, the Court's *ratio* in *Fisheries Jurisdiction* was different. Here, what was in question was not particularly the issue of the Optional Clause, but the effect of a compromise clause forming the very basis of the optional clauses between the UK and Iceland. The agreement as to the circumstances of the optional clause was contained in the 1961 agreement, which was a product of a bilateral negotiation between the two countries. Hence, while optional clauses may have a unilateral character, the compromissory clause, which was the issue in this case, has a bilateral character.

A compromissory clause is basically a dispute resolution arrangement, usually provided for in international agreements between two or more parties, by which they refer disputes among them to the ICJ. Compromissory clauses are not as popular nowadays, given that most treaties now provide for their own dispute settlement mechanisms, which are often arbitrations.

thinking points

- *Is there any difference between the approaches taken by the Courts in* Qatar v. Bahrain *and the* South West Africa Cases *as to the status of communiqués and mandates under international law?*
- *What is the rationale for the ICJ's refusal to regard the agreement between Iran and the British company D'Arcy as a treaty?*
- *In view of the Court's decision in* the Fisheries Jurisdiction Case, *in what circumstances may unilateral declarations constitute a treaty between parties?*

3.3.2 Must all international agreements be registered to constitute treaties?

● ***Ethiopia v. South Africa; Liberia v. South Africa (Preliminary Objections)*** (1962) ICJ REP 319 (The ***South West Africa Cases***)

See section 3.3.1 for the facts.

South Africa contended that its mandate over Namibia did not constitute a treaty, since the mandate was not registered in accordance with Article 18 of the Covenant of the League of Nations. The Court rejected this argument on two grounds. It is true that Article 18 states 'No such treaty or international engagement shall be binding until so registered'. Nonetheless, the Court stated that:

> if the Mandate was *ab initio* null and void on the ground of non-registration it would follow that the Respondent has not and has never had a legal title for its administration of the territory of South West Africa; it would therefore be impossible for it to maintain that it has had such a title up to the discovery of this ground of nullity.

However, Article 13 of the League Covenant provided only for registration of 'every treaty or international engagement entered into *hereafter* by any Member of the League'. The Court noted that the word 'hereafter':

> meant after 10 January 1920 when the Covenant took effect, whereas the Mandate for South West Africa, as stated in the preamble of the instrument, had actually been conferred on and accepted by the Union of South Africa more than seven months earlier on 7–9 May 1919; and its terms had been provisionally agreed upon between the Principal Allied and Associated Powers and the Mandatory, in August 1919.

The Court also considered the purpose for which registration is required. According to the Court (at 332):

> Article 18, designed to secure *publicity and avoid secret treaties*, could not apply in the same way in respect of treaties to which the League of Nations itself was one of the Parties as in respect of treaties concluded among individual Member States. The Mandate for South West Africa, like all the other Mandates, is an international instrument of an institutional character, to which the League of Nations, represented by the Council, was itself a Party. It is the implementation of an institution in which all the Member States are interested as such. The procedure to give the necessary publicity to the Mandates including the one under consideration was applied in view of their special character, and in any event they were published in the *Official Journal* of the League of Nations.

The Court accepts that a treaty can be invalidated on the ground of non-registration. However, in the *South West Africa Cases* this consequence was avoided on several grounds. First, if the treaty in question had been void from the start for non-registration, as South Africa claimed, then that would mean that South Africa did not have any validity in relation to Namibia at all. Secondly, registration applied only to treaties adopted after the League Covenant. Thus, since the South African mandate was adopted *before* the Covenant of the League, Article 13 did not apply to it. But suppose that the South African mandate had been adopted *after* the Covenant: would non-registration have invalidated the mandate?

In the previous extract, the Court answered this question by explaining that the reason for requiring registration of treaties was to ensure publicity and avoid incidents of secret treaties. The Court noted that since the concerned mandate involved the League of Nations as a participant, non-registration (even if Article 13 did not save the mandate) would not have been detrimental to its validity. In the Court's view, the League's participation in the mandate meant that there would be adequate publicity (hence, no secrecy involved). In any case, publicity for the treaty was achieved by its publication in the Official Journal of the League. Again, the question that this reasoning raises is this: what if the League had not been involved in this mandate and the South African mandate had not subsequently been published in the League's Official Journal?

● *Qatar v. Bahrain* (1994) ICJ REP 112 (*Maritime Delimitation and Territorial Questions between Qatar and Bahrain*) (*Jurisdiction and Admissibility*)

The Court went on to clarify the precise effect of non-registration of treaties in this case, in which it said that:

> an international agreement or treaty that has not been registered with the Secretariat of the United Nations may not, according to the provisions of Article 102 of the Charter, be invoked by the parties before any organ of the United Nations. *Non registration or late registration, on the other hand,*

does not have any consequence for the actual validity of the agreement, which remains no less binding upon the parties. The Court therefore cannot infer from the fact that Qatar did not apply for registration of the 1990 Minutes until six months after they were signed that Qatar considered, in December 1990, that those Minutes did not constitute an international agreement. [Emphasis added]

The Court's statement accords with the provision of Article 102 of the UN Charter, which is to the effect that:

1. Every treaty and every international agreement entered into by any Member of the United Nations after the present Charter comes into force shall as soon as possible be registered with the Secretariat and published by it.
2. No party to any such treaty or international agreement which has not been registered in accordance with the provisions of paragraph 1 of this Article may invoke that treaty or agreement before any organ of the United Nations.

There are two effects of non-registration of treaties. First, such a treaty cannot be pleaded by any UN member State before an organ of the United Nations. This means that UN member States are free to plead the treaty either between themselves in a dispute not brought before a UN organ or in any other respect. Secondly, non-registration of treaties has no effect whatsoever between non-UN member States. In other words, the provision of Article 102 of the UN Charter applies only to UN member States. Non-UN members are under no obligation to register their treaties.

thinking points

*   *When must treaties be registered according to Article 102 of the UN Charter?*
*   *What is the effect, if any, of non-registration of treaties under international law?*
*   *List the grounds upon which, despite non-registration, the ICJ held that the South African mandate in Namibia was valid.*
*   *Do you think that it makes sense to distinguish between treaties that consist only of State parties and those that involve international organizations, such as the United Nations, in determining the effect of non-registration?*

3.3.3 The VCLT and oral treaties

From the previous discussion it might seem that there is no such thing as an oral treaty. The concept of oral treaties would appear to be anomalous, given that a treaty is said to be such mainly because it exists in written form and can be independently verified regardless of statements from the parties to the agreement. As a matter of legal analysis, the idea of an oral treaty seems to stem from the provision of Article 3 VCLT. That Article states that the non-applicability of the VCLT to 'international agreements not in written form' shall not affect the legal force of such agreements. Certainly, there are many international agreements that are not in written form. An example is customary international law, which may be regarded as consisting of international agreements, to the extent of its acceptance by States in their practice and *opinio juris* (see Chapter 2).

The provision of Article 3 must thus be taken to refer to international agreements, such as customs, which are not governed by the VCLT. After all, the Convention does not purport to codify all international customs and other unwritten international agreements that were in existence in 1969.

The phrase 'international agreements' appearing in Article 3 VCLT cannot be taken to mean 'treaties', but must mean other forms of agreement. It would be odd, to say the least, to state that the 1969 VCLT recognizes oral treaties, even if it clearly does not govern such, or that there can be oral treaties as such, for the obvious reasons stated previously.

3.3.4 The VCLT and customary international law

The nature of the relationship between the VCLT and customary international law is extremely important. The issue revolves around the two main tasks of the International Law Commission (ILC), which drafted the VCLT, and which is responsible for the 'codification' and 'development' of international law.

In context, to 'codify' is to reduce existing customary rules and general international law to a treaty obligation in a written form. To engage in the 'progressive development of international law' is to track emerging rules and principles of international law, and reflect them in treaties. The question that arises in respect of the VCLT is twofold: which of the Convention provisions codify customary international law, and which provisions merely reflect a progressive development of international law?

The answers to these questions are not always easy, because the Convention offers no guidance. Yet answering this question is extremely important in one principal respect. As stated earlier, the VCLT applies to States that are parties to it, but since the Convention is not retroactive, it does not apply to treaties concluded by such States before it entered into force (Article 4 VCLT). However, the Convention may apply to States that are not parties to it, and to treaties concluded before the Convention, if its provisions contain rules that reflect customary international law.

The ICJ has applied the rules of the VCLT to non-parties where the rules codify customary international law. Such rules include those on a fundamental change of circumstances (Article 62) and material breach (Article 60).

. . . .

● *Libyan Arab Jamahiriya v. Chad (Judgment)* [1994] ICJ Rep 21 [The *Territorial Dispute Case*]

Libya and Chad submitted a boundary dispute to the ICJ. The Court was confronted with the interpretation of various treaties that concerned the case, but which were concluded prior to the VCLT. On the applicability of the VCLT rules on the interpretation of treaties, the Court held (at [41]) that:

> The Court would recall that, *in accordance with customary international law, reflected in Article 31 of the 1969 Vienna Convention on the Law of Treaties*, a treaty must be interpreted in good faith in accordance with the ordinary meaning to be given to its terms in their context and in the light of its object and purpose. Interpretation must be based above all upon the text of the treaty. As a supplementary measure recourse may be had to means of interpretation such as the preparatory work of the treaty and the circumstances of its conclusion. [Emphasis added]

The Court would again follow this trend two years later.

• **Islamic Republic of Iran v. United States of America (Preliminary Objections)** (1996) ICJ REP 803 (The **Oil Platforms Case**)

Iran filed a suit against the USA on 2 November 1992 in respect of a dispute (at 805):

> aris[ing] out of the attack [on] and destruction of three offshore oil production complexes, owned and operated for commercial purposes by the National Iranian Oil Company, by several warships of the United States Navy on 19 October 1987 and 18 April 1988, respectively.

On the question of interpreting the 1955 Treaty of Amity, Economic Relations and Consular Rights between the USA and Iran, which Iran alleged was breached by US actions, the Court reiterated its statement in the *Territorial Dispute Case* (see earlier in this section) to the effect that the VCLT rules of interpretation codified customary international rules on the matter, which were applicable to the case.

The Court has also applied this principle to instances in which disputing States were not parties to the VCLT.

• **Botswana v. Namibia** (1999) ICJ REP 1045 (The **Kasikili/Sedudu Island Case**)

In 1996, Botswana and Namibia submitted a dispute to the ICJ and asked the Court (at 1049):

> to determine the boundary between Namibia and Botswana around Kasikili/Sedudu Island on the basis of the Treaty of 1 July 1890 between Great Britain and Germany respecting the spheres of influence of the two countries in Africa and the applicable principles of international law.

Central to the case before the Court was the interpretation of the 1890 Treaty. Given that neither Botswana nor Namibia was party to the VCLT, the Court could not automatically apply the rules of that Convention relating to interpretation of treaty to the case.

Nevertheless, it was held (at 1059) that:

> As regards the interpretation of that Treaty, the Court notes that neither Botswana nor Namibia are parties to the Vienna Convention on the Law of Treaties of 23 May 1969, but that both of them consider that Article 31 of the Vienna Convention is applicable inasmuch as it reflects customary international law.

See also *Hungary v. Slovakia* (1997) ICJ Rep 7 (the *Gabčíkovo-Nagymaros Project Case*) and *Indonesia v. Malaysia* (2002) ICJ Rep 625 (the *Case concerning Sovereignty over Palau Ligitan and Palau Sipadan*).

Although all of the above cases relate to situations in which the Convention has codified some customary international rules, there are other rules that are regarded as merely reflecting progressive development and not codifying customary international law.

KEY POINTS

- The relationship between the VCLT and customary international law is important, because it helps to determine when the Convention may apply to non-parties and to treaties concluded prior to the Convention despite the non-retroactivity rule in Article 4.

81

- The VCLT and customary international law are linked by codification of customary rules, while the former may also contain a reflection of progressive developments.

3.3.5 Making a treaty (Articles 6–18 VCLT)

There are no hard-and-fast rules as to how, where, and when to make a treaty. It is entirely up to the negotiating States to decide the venue, time, and manner in which they want their negotiation to take place. The VCLT does not deal with such issues, apparently in recognition of the sovereign rights of States to decide such matters.

However, the Convention governs such issues as the capacity and authority to conclude a treaty, the competence to sign a treaty on behalf of States, the modalities for expressing consent to be bound by a treaty, and the ratification of treaties. These are issues dealt with under the various provisions of Part II, Section 1 (Articles 6–18) of the VCLT. However, before going any further it is important to distinguish briefly the various terms used to describe States in this section.

A 'negotiating State' means a State that takes part in the drawing up and adoption of the text of the treaty (Article 2(e)), whereas a 'contracting State' is a State that has consented to be bound by a treaty, whether or not the treaty has entered into force (Article 2(f)). It is possible that a State may take part in the negotiation of a treaty, but decide not to be bound by it. Occasionally, a State that has taken part in the negotiation of a treaty and has signed up to be bound by it may change its position before the treaty enters into force. The USA decided to withdraw its signature to the Rome ICC Statute after having taken part in the negotiation and having already consented to be bound by the treaty.

3.3.6 The authority to conclude a treaty

Article 6 VCLT provides that 'Every State possesses the capacity to conclude treaties'. Since they are not human beings, States are usually represented by several hundreds, or even thousands, of officials in their relations with one another.

Article 7(1) states that a person can represent a State only:

> for the purpose of adopting or authenticating the text of a treaty or expressing the consent to be bound by a treaty if (a) he produces appropriate full powers; or (b) it appears from the practice of the States concerned or from other circumstances that their intention was to consider that person as representing the State for such purposes and to dispense with full powers.

Clearly, Article 7(1) recognizes two categories of person that might represent States: those who have 'full powers', and those whom negotiating States generally regard as having the competence to represent their State even though they do not have full powers.

Article 2(c) VCLT defines 'full powers' as:

> a document emanating from the competent authority of a State designating a person or persons to represent the State for negotiating, adopting or authenticating the text of a treaty, for expressing the consent of the State to be bound by a treaty, or for accomplishing any other act with respect to a treaty.

It is obvious from this provision that 'full powers' is a very important authority, since it applies to everything—from negotiating a treaty to expressing the consent to be bound by it. Having said that, full powers must be distinguished from 'credentials', which are no more than documents submitted by a State in respect of the officials representing it at an international conference. Such credentials authorize the State delegates only to adopt the text of the treaty and sign its Final Act on behalf of the State (see Malgosia Fitzmaurice, 'The practical working of the law of treaties' in Malcolm Evans (ed.), *International Law* (3rd edn, Oxford: Oxford University Press, 2010), p. 172).

However, apart from those who are exempted from providing full powers under Article 7(1), there is another class of State functionary that is not required to provide full powers before they can attend to any of the previously listed functions on behalf of their States. These are, according to Article 7(2)(a):

- heads of State and government, who can undertake *all* of the tasks listed under Article 2(c) VCLT;
- heads of diplomatic missions, under Article 7(2)(b), who can represent their States only to the extent of *adopting* treaties between their States and the States to which they are accredited; and
- representatives accredited by States to an international conference or to an international organization or one of its organs, for the purpose of adopting the text of a treaty in that conference, organization, or organ (Article 7(2)(c)).

The principle that heads of State and government can represent their States without providing full powers has been confirmed by the ICJ in a few cases.

● *Bosnia and Herzegovina v. Serbia and Montenegro* (1996) ICJ Rep 595 (*Case concerning the Application of the Convention on the Prevention and Punishment of the Crime of Genocide*)

In this case Bosnia and Herzegovina claimed that Yugoslavia (Serbia and Montenegro) violated some provisions of the Genocide Convention. In its objection to the admissibility of the case by the Court, Yugoslavia contended (at 612–622), among other things, that the application was inadmissible because 'Mr. Alija Izetbegović was not serving as President of the Republic . . . at the time at which he granted the authorization to initiate proceedings' and that authorization was granted in violation of certain rules of domestic law of fundamental significance.

Yugoslavia likewise contended that Mr Izetbegović was not even acting legally at that time as President.

On the question of the competence of the President to act on behalf of the State, it was held that:

> The Court does not, in order to rule on that objection, have to consider the provisions of domestic law which were invoked in the course of the proceedings either in support of or in opposition to that objection. According to international law, there is no doubt that every Head of State is presumed to be able to act on behalf of the State in its international relations.

The Court recently affirmed this principle.

● *Cameroon v. Nigeria; Equatorial Guinea Intervening* (2002) ICJ Rep 303 (*Land and Maritime Boundary between Cameroon and Nigeria*)

In 1994, Cameroon brought an action against Nigeria concerning sovereignty over an area, known as the 'Bakassi Peninsula', adjoining the two countries. One of the issues before the

Court was the validity of an agreement signed by the heads of State of the two countries on 1 June 1975 at Maroua, Cameroon. Nigeria had argued that the Maroua agreement could not be regarded as binding because the agreement was never approved by the Supreme Military Council, which was Nigeria's highest governing body at the relevant time.

It was held (at 265) that:

> Heads of State ... are considered as representing their State for the purpose of performing all acts relating to the conclusion of a treaty.

3.3.7 *Ex post facto* authority to conclude a treaty (Article 8 VCLT)

Persons who have no authority under Article 7 to conclude a treaty on behalf of a State often act as such. This does not divest the treaty of legal effect. According to Article 8 VCLT:

> An Act relating to the conclusion of a treaty performed by a person who cannot be considered under Article 7 as authorized to represent a State for that purpose is without effect unless afterwards confirmed by that State.

Thus the effect of such an illegal act depends on whether or not the concerned State subsequently confirms the act. A State may explicitly confirm the act (for example, by making a formal declaration to that effect) or implicitly (for example, by further dealing with the document as though it is a legitimate instrument). In either scenario, the State shall be deemed to have authorized the illegal act *ex post facto*. However, if the State does not adopt the act, then the treaty is without any legal effect on the State.

KEY POINTS

- Only those who possess full powers, or those who appear from the practice of the concerned State and other circumstances to represent that State, may validly ratify a treaty on behalf of the State.
- Heads of State are presumed to have the authority to deal with any aspects of treaties on behalf of their countries.
- A State can validate the act of an authorized person to conclude a treaty on its behalf. This is called *ex post facto* authority and is governed by Article 8 VCLT.

3.3.8 Adoption, consent, and entry into force (Articles 9–15 VCLT)

Adoption

Procedurally, once a treaty has been concluded, its texts must be formally adopted. Adoption of a treaty takes place, according to Article 9 VCLT, 'by the consent of all the States participating in its drawing up' or, if the treaty is that of an international organization, then by a two-thirds majority vote of all of its members, unless the same majority decides to apply a different rule.

The adoption of a treaty does not necessarily mean that everyone accepts the adopted text as the only authentic text. Treaties exist in various languages and this is especially so for treaties of international organizations such as the UN Charter. Thus Article 10 VCLT provides for the establishment of the text of a treaty 'as authentic and definitive'. Participating States may agree on this during negotiation or at any time thereafter, although it is also possible to authenticate the text of a treaty through the Final Act of a conference incorporating the text. For example, Article 111 of the UN Charter specifically states that the Charter's authentic texts appear in five languages: English; Chinese; French; Russian; and Spanish.

Consent

The consent to be bound by a treaty and its entry into force are two sides of the same coin. However, before a treaty can enter into force, it is necessary that parties to it give their consent to be bound by it. A treaty does not automatically bind a State simply because it signs it, unless the treaty or State specifically says that it does. Consent to a treaty can be expressed in several ways, depending on what the parties decide and what they write down in the treaty as guidelines. The most common forms of consent to treaties include signature, ratification, accession, and exchange of instruments.

According to Article 12(1), a State may be bound by a treaty upon its representative signing that treaty if:

(a) the treaty so provides;

(b) the negotiating States agree that signature should have that effect; and

(c) that is the intention of States, as disclosed by their representatives in the exercise of their full power during negotiation.

Where any of the above modes applies, a signature is deemed to have been appended to a treaty once the representatives initialize the treaty, or there has been a referendum that the treaty shall be so signed (Article 13 VCLT). Often, a treaty may simply provide that it becomes binding on States once the treaty has been exchanged between the State parties. This mode can be established by the treaty itself providing for it or by the parties otherwise agreeing that this is the mode that they prefer (Article 13 VCLT).

Article 14 VCLT provides that a treaty can become binding through ratification either because:

(a) the treaty so stipulates;

(b) parties otherwise agree;

(c) the representatives of States sign the treaty, but subject to ratification; or

(d) the concerned State intends to sign a treaty, but subject to ratification disclosed on the full powers of its representatives.

Ratification is a process whereby a State, which has already signed a treaty, ultimately accepts to be bound by it. Ratification provides an interlude between the signing of a treaty and the expression of an intention to be bound by it. During this lull, new facts may have emerged since a State signed the treaty, or the State may become aware of facts previously unknown to it that have serious implications for its being bound by the treaty.

example

A good example of the use of ratification can be seen in the controversy that trailed the Intermediate-Range Nuclear Forces (INF) Treaty, signed by the USA in 1988. Although already adopted by the Senate Foreign Relations Committee, the treaty faced serious problems when it was laid before the US Senate for ratification due to the lack of agreement over terms used in the treaty, such as the meaning of 'weapons', and also because of concerns about its potential impact on future military developments in the USA.

In practice, what constitutes ratification is a matter of great variation among States. In the UK, there is no formal requirement for ratification, since treaties are usually concluded by the Crown. Nevertheless, treaties concluded by the Crown may be placed before the Parliament for up to twenty-one days for inspection and information under the so-called 'Ponsonby Rule', a twentieth-century rule proposed by Mr Arthur Ponsonby, then Under-Secretary of State for Foreign Affairs in Labour's first government.

The Ponsonby Rule was originally intended to afford anyone the opportunity to raise concerns and request clarifications in respect of a treaty already signed, prior to its ratification by the Parliament. However, due to considerations that ratification would be an expensive and laborious process for Parliament, it was never put into practice. The Rule thus became a mere constitutional convention that serves little purpose, since the treaty being inspected would have been signed by the government and, given that there is no ratification necessary, would already have entered into force in the UK before being inspected.

It should be noted that the *Constitutional Reform and Governance Act 2010 (Ratification of Treaties)* has effected certain changes to the Ponsonby Rule. This Act 'gives legal effect to a vote against ratification in the Commons or Lords. It prevents the Government from moving immediately to ratify a treaty if either House votes against ratification.' The full extent of the changes brought by the Act can be found in Part 2 of the Act. In the USA, a treaty concluded on behalf of the government must be passed by at least a two-thirds majority of the Senate. But the US President can also make 'executive agreements', which are binding international agreements and which do not require approval by any other organ of the US government.

thinking points

- *In what manner may consent be given to a treaty?*
- *What is the purpose of a treaty already signed by the UK being presented to Parliament under the 'Ponsonby Rule'?*

The relationship between signature and ratification as modes of consent

Signing and ratifying a treaty are two different things, but they often mingle. Generally speaking, when States intend to subject a treaty to ratification after signing it, they will expressly say so, except if the treaty provides for ratification. However, this is not always the case, because situations do arise in which one State, having signed a treaty, genuinely or disingenuously believes that it has indicated its intention to subject the treaty to ratification.

● **Cameroon v. Nigeria; Equatorial Guinea Intervening** (2002) ICJ Rep 303 (*Land and Maritime Boundary between Cameroon and Nigeria*)

The ICJ had to deal with this issue in *Cameroon v. Nigeria*, in which Nigeria argued that the Maroua agreement, signed by the Nigerian and Cameroonian heads of State in 1975, was not a binding instrument because it was never ratified by the Nigerian government as required by the country's constitution.

As a matter of law, this argument is weak. Article 46 VCLT provides that:

> [a] State may not invoke the fact that its consent to be bound by a treaty has been expressed in violation of a provision of its internal law regarding competence to conclude treaties as invalidating its consent unless that violation was manifest and concerned a rule of its internal law of fundamental importance.

Clearly, this provision negates Nigeria's argument, since it is a matter of internal law for the head of State to comply with the country's constitution, unless the act of such head of State or other official constitutes a manifest violation of the country's law of fundamental importance. Nigeria also argued that the provision of Article 46, which prevents States from relying on violations of their internal laws regarding the competence to conclude a treaty, allows such a plea where the violation complained about was 'manifest and concerned a rule of internal law of fundamental importance'. According to Article 46(2):

> [a] violation is manifest if it would be objectively evident to any State conducting itself in the matter in accordance with normal practice and in good faith.

Thus, as far as Nigeria was concerned, the violation committed by its head of State in signing the Maroua agreement was manifest and fundamental, and Cameroon should have seen this clearly from a series of events. Hence, Nigeria argued (at [258]) that:

> Cameroon, according to an objective test based upon the provisions of the Vienna Convention, either knew or, conducting itself in a normally prudent manner, should have known that the Head of State of Nigeria did not have the authority to make legally binding commitments without referring back to the Nigerian Government—at that time the Supreme Military Council—and that it should therefore have been 'objectively evident' to Cameroon, within the meaning of Article 46, paragraph 2, of the Vienna Convention on the Law of Treaties that the Head of State of Nigeria did not have unrestricted authority.

The Court accepted that, indeed, where a violation is manifest and fundamental, then a State can plead its internal law in respect of authority to conclude treaties on its behalf. The Court then reviewed the various circumstances that Nigeria claimed ought to have demonstrated to Cameroon (or ought to have put the latter on notice) that Nigeria's head of State did not have the authority to conclude the treaty on its behalf. The Court rejected the evidence provided by Nigeria to show that there was sufficient communication to Cameroon. The Court said (at [265]) that:

> a limitation of a Head of State's capacity in this respect is not manifest in the sense of Article 46, paragraph 2, unless at least properly publicized. This is particularly so because Heads of State belong to the group of persons who, in accordance with Article 7, paragraph 2, of the Convention '[i]n virtue of their functions and without having to produce full powers' are considered as representing their State.

The nature of treaties

87

The Court ruled (at [266]) that:

> there is no general legal obligation for States to keep themselves informed of legislative and constitutional developments in other States which are or may become important for the international relations of these States.

The process of ratification is therefore based on the domestic law of a State, and the onus is on that State to ensure that the process is duly followed, especially where such requirement is not expressly stated to the other contracting party, which is not expected to be versed in the domestic law of another State.

Accession

A State that did not take part in the negotiation of a treaty may become party to it through accession. Accession, which is also known as 'adherence' and 'adhesion', is possible where a treaty explicitly provides for such or, absent that, if parties to the treaty agree to such. Regardless of how it is achieved, once a State accedes to a treaty the effect is as if the State has, in fact, taken part in its negotiation and has ratified the treaty. Despite the distinction between the various modes of consenting to treaties, the reality of international relations often makes demarcation impossible. The practice has become quite common, especially with the United Nations and other major international organizations, of opening up treaties for signing, ratification, or accession, all at the same time. Obviously, this may give the impression that these are identical processes but, as we have seen previously, nothing could be further from the truth.

Entry into force

The manner and date on which a treaty will enter into force depend on what is stated in the treaty or otherwise agreed by the State parties. In practice, it is normal for a treaty to specify a particular date upon which it will enter into force. In most bilateral treaties, entry into force occurs upon the signing or ratification of the treaty.

However, it is also often the case that a treaty will stipulate the happening of an event as the relevant date upon which it enters into force. This mode is commonly used in the case of multilateral treaties. Given the huge number of States usually involved in multilateral treaties—for example, treaties of international organizations such as the UN—it is impractical to stipulate ratification or signature of all member States as the relevant date. Several States that participate in the negotiation of multilateral treaties may not immediately ratify them—or may not even ratify them at all—making it extremely difficult to achieve a consensus date on which *all* States will have achieved ratification. The usual practice in this case is for the treaty to provide that it will enter into force once a given number of States have ratified it. The Rome ICC Statute, which was signed in 1998, for example, entered into force on 1 July 2002 upon the ratification of sixty State parties.

thinking points

- *How would you distinguish between 'signing' and 'ratifying' a treaty, and what is the importance of this distinction?*
- *What are 'full powers' and why are they important?*
- *Under what circumstance(s) may a State plead violation of its internal laws regarding the authority to conclude a treaty on its behalf?*
- *What are the modes for consenting to a treaty?*

3.4 Procedural obligations of treaties

Every party to a treaty accepts two types of obligation under the treaty: the substantive obligations and the procedural obligations. The substantive obligations are embodied in the various provisions of the treaty dealing with the essential issues that the treaty covers. For example, a substantive obligation of the UN Charter is that UN member States will not threaten or use force against one another in their international relations (Article 2(4)). This is substantive because it is of essence to the objectives of the treaty.

The VCLT does not deal with substantive treaty obligations since these are matters peculiar to individual treaties. The only exception to this is *jus cogens*, which are otherwise known as peremptory norms of international law. Although these constitute a substantive obligation, their status is of such fundamental importance to all treaties as to exclude them, by virtue of Article 53 VCLT, from the whims of individual treaties.

The VCLT deals with procedural treaty obligations, which are obligations relating to practice and procedure. These obligations in the VCLT include those that govern how to interpret, modify, reserve, invalidate, and terminate treaties. They are obligations that generically apply to all treaties regardless of type.

3.5 The reservation of treaties

3.5.1 The general rule and rationale

A State may accept to be bound by a treaty, but not by *all* of its provisions. In practice, what States will often do, if they do not accept certain obligations of a treaty although they accept others, is to enter 'reservations' when they accept a treaty. It is 'turning a *prix fixe* menu *à la carte*' (Edward T. Swaine, 'Reserving' (2006) 31(2) Yale JIL 357).

Article 2 VCLT defines a 'reservation' as:

> a unilateral statement, however phrased or named, made by a State, when signing, ratifying, accepting, approving or acceding to a treaty, where it purports to exclude or modify the legal effect of certain provisions of the treaty in their application to that State.

Article 19(1) of the Convention determines the types of reservation that States might formulate thus:

> a State may, when ratifying, acceding, approving or acceding to a treaty, formulate a reservation unless:
> (a) the reservation is prohibited by the treaty;
> (b) the treaty provides that only specified reservations, which do not include the reservations in question, may be made; or
> (c) in cases not falling under sub-paragraphs (a) and (b), the reservation is incompatible with the object and purpose of the treaty.

This provision shows that a State may not formulate three types of reservation: reservations prohibited by the treaty itself; reservations not envisaged by the treaty; and reservations that, although do not fall into the above categories, are nonetheless incompatible with the object and purpose of the treaty. Examples of prohibited reservations are rare, but are provided in Article 1 of the League of Nations Covenant, Article 120 of the Rome ICC Statute, and Article 26(1) of the Basel Convention on the Control of Transboundary Movements of Hazardous Wastes and their Disposal.

Article 19(1)(a) cases are straightforward, since that provision of the VCLT expressly prohibits reservations—but two complications can arise from its application. First, far from being explicit, some prohibitions falling under that article may be ambiguous. For example, paragraph 14 of the Final Act of the 1961 Geneva Conference, which adopted the European Convention on International Commercial Arbitration, states that:

> the delegations taking part in the negotiation of the Convention...declare that their respective countries do not intend to make any reservations to the Convention.

Aside from this prohibition not being categorical, the declaration by which State parties manifested the intention was made in an instrument separate from the treaty. As Professor Alain Pellet observed (UN Doc. A/CN.4/558, 1 June 2005, para. 28):

> in a case of this type, it could seem that reservations are not strictly speaking prohibited, but that if a State formulates a reservation, the other Parties must, logically, object to it.

Secondly, the prohibition under Article 19(a) may be partial, and may simply relate to some of the provisions of the treaty and not to the whole treaty itself. Although this is rare, examples include clauses listing the provisions of the treaty to which reservations are not permitted. Article 42 of the 1951 Convention Relating to the Status of Refugees and Article 26 of the 1972 International Convention for Safe Containers of the International Maritime Organization are examples of partial prohibition of reservations.

Article 19(b) is the converse of Article 19(a) in that it permits reservations to be formulated only if the treaty expressly specifies such reservations. In a way, this seems to duplicate Article 19(a) since, by explicitly specifying what reservations can be formulated, Article 19(b) seems implicitly to prohibit other reservations. Examples of treaties specifying provisions that can be reserved, pursuant to Article 19(b), include Article 12 of the 1958 Geneva Convention on the Continental Shelf, which states that:

> at the time of signature, ratification or accession, any State may make reservations to Articles of the Convention other than to Articles 1 to 3 inclusive.

Although this treaty does not specify what reservations can be formulated against the three Articles, it did specify which Articles can be reserved against.

A better example of cases falling under Article 19(b) are the instances in which a treaty actually specifies the reservations that can be formulated. Article 39 of the General Act of Arbitration provides a significant example:

1. ...a Party, in acceding to the present General Act, may make his acceptance conditional upon the reservations exhaustively enumerated in the following paragraph. These reservations must be indicated at the time of accession.

2. These reservations may be such as to exclude from the procedure described in the present Act:

   (a) Disputes arising out of facts prior to the accession either of the Party making the reservation or of any other Party with whom the said party may have a dispute;

   (b) Disputes concerning questions which by international law are solely within the domestic jurisdiction of States;

   (c) Disputes concerning particular cases or clearly specified subject matters, such as territorial status, or disputes falling within clearly defined categories.

● *Greece v. Turkey* (1978) ICJ REP 28 (The *Aegean Sea Continental Shelf Case*)

In this case, the ICJ stated (at [55]) that:

> When a multilateral treaty thus provides in advance for the making only of particular, designated categories of reservations, there is clearly a high probability, if not an actual presumption, that reservations made in terms used in the treaty are intended to relate to the corresponding categories in the treaty.

Since Article 19(1)(c) deals with the wider issue of incompatibility of reservations, we will deal with it later.

Reservations may be used to reject, modify, or amend treaty obligations unilaterally, in the sense that they are often made by individual States without input from others. The need for reservation can arise where a State disagrees on the meaning of specific words or terms contained in a treaty. It is practically impossible to expect several States (sometimes more than 100), which are parties to a multilateral treaty, to negotiate every definition, legal term, word, or phrase in the treaty until consensus is achieved. Consensus of this nature may never be achieved in multilateral treaties, hence the usefulness of reservations. The USA reserved against the 1989 UN Convention on the Rights of the Child (CRC) on the basis that it disagreed with the legal definition of a 'child' under the Convention.

Reservations might also be warranted when certain treaty obligations are irreconcilable with a State's religious or cultural principles and practices, as is often common with States that officially endorse particular religions. An example is the 1979 UN Convention on the Elimination of Discrimination against Women (CEDAW). Many Islamic States reserved against some provisions of this treaty because their substantive obligations are incompatible with Islamic doctrines and practices, such as in matters relating to women and inheritance.

Reservation is mainly a feature of multilateral treaties. There is usually no reservation in bilateral treaties, because if a disagreement arises in the negotiation of a bilateral treaty, the two States involved will be expected to negotiate the divisive terms until a compromise is reached. A reservation by one of the two State parties to a bilateral treaty would effectively render the treaty unadoptable. Since the agreement of the two States is essential to conclude a bilateral treaty, a reservation by one or both States would render the obligation in question unenforceable.

KEY POINTS

- A State can formulate its own reservations, except in cases in which a treaty prohibits reservations, specifies the types of reservation permitted under that treaty, or in which the reservation is incompatible with the object and purpose of that treaty.

- Reservations are normally used in multilateral treaties, but not in bilateral treaties.

3.5.2 The principles guiding reservation

International law has three approaches to regulating States' relations to reservations:

- the reservation could be rejected if not endorsed by all parties (the absolute integrity approach);
- it could be accepted to bind only those that accept it (the universality approach); or
- it could be rejected if found to be incompatible with the object of the treaty (the consistency test).

When a State enters a reservation, three questions may arise. First, what is the effect of that reservation on States that have not made the same reservation? Secondly, what is the effect of the reservation as between the reserving State and the States that object to it? Finally, what is the effect of the reservation between the reserving State and others that make different reservations under the treaty? International law deals with these questions through the above-named three approaches.

The absolute integrity approach

'Absolute integrity' is the classical approach to reservations, under which once a State makes a reservation, all other State parties to the concerned treaty must *accept* that reservation, otherwise the reserving State ceases to be a party to that treaty. The absolute integrity approach is based on the consideration that, in order to protect the integrity of a treaty, it is important that *all* State parties must have exactly the same obligations under the treaty. This approach was dominant during the League of Nations years, although there was a general inconsistency in State practice during this time. The League Secretariat and, subsequently, the UN Secretary-General—who is the depository of treaties—embraced the absolute integrity approach.

The universality approach

Despite general inconsistency of State practice as per the effect of reservations during the League era, members of the Pan American Union (PAU) adopted a different approach from that followed by the League. The PAU's rather flexible approach emphasized involving as many States as possible in a treaty. Thus, whenever a State made a reservation that was rejected by others, the PAU did not exclude such a reserving State, as is the case under the 'absolute integrity' approach; rather, the treaty would be made applicable as between the reserving State and those that did not object to the reservation. A universal participation of States in treaties was therefore prioritized above the integrity of treaty obligations. The common consequence of the 'universality' approach was that States were allowed to pick and choose what obligations they accepted or rejected, while remaining parties to treaties even after they had made substantial reservations.

The compatibility test

The third approach was borne out of the controversy that trailed the adoption of the Convention on the Prevention and Punishment of the Crime of Genocide (the Genocide Convention) by the UN General Assembly in 1948. The Genocide Convention contains no provision permitting or prohibiting reservations, therefore making Article 19(a) and (b) VCLT inapplicable to its provisions (see earlier).

Many States capitalized on the silence of the Genocide Convention in this regard and reserved widely against it. This alarmed the General Assembly, which then requested the opinion of the ICJ (being the principal judicial organ of the United Nations) on the matter. Specifically, the ICJ was asked whether a State that has made a reservation to a treaty can be party to that treaty, and if the affirmative were the case, what the effect of such reservations would be on States that accepted or rejected the reservation.

● ***Reservations to the Convention on the Prevention and Punishment of the Crime of Genocide Advisory Opinion*** [1951] ICJ REP 15

In its judgment, the ICJ held (at 29) that:

> a State which has made and maintained a reservation which has been objected to by one or more of the parties to the Convention *but not by others*, can be regarded as being a party to the Convention if the reservation *is compatible* with the object and purpose of the Convention; otherwise, that State cannot be regarded as being a party to the Convention. [Emphasis added]

The Court obviously followed the PAU's flexible approach, which encouraged universal participation in treaties. However, two points must be noted in the Court's judgment: a reserving State will be regarded as party to the treaty only if *some*, and not all, other parties object (just as with the PAU practice), and if the reservation itself is *compatible* with the object of the treaty—a condition that was not present in the PAU practice. As the Court said (at 30):

> if a party to the Convention objects to a reservation which it considers to be incompatible with the object and purpose of the Convention, it can in fact consider that the reserving State is not a party to the Convention . . . [but] if, on the other hand, a party accepts the reservation as being compatible with the object and purpose of the Convention, it can in fact consider that the reserving State is a party to the Convention . . .

As Professor Waldock stated in the 'Fourth Report on the Law of Treaties' (1962) 2 YBILC 3, 65–66, the 'compatibility' test is the least objectionable solution, although it is by no means ideal. The compatibility test is by far the most subjective approach, since it is not always easy to tell which reservation is or is not compatible with a treaty, except where the treaty is clear on such issues. For example, some treaties do not permit reservations because the obligations that they contain are so fundamental as to be endangered by any reservation whatsoever. Examples of these include the UN Charter and the ICC Statute. There are instances, however, in which treaties may not prohibit reservations, but it would appear that certain reservations are incompatible with the obligations that they embody. The International Covenant on Civil and Political Rights (ICCPR) is one such treaty. The silence of the Covenant, as well as its First

Optional Protocol, on reservations has led several States to reserve against some of its provisions; in some cases, these provisions contain very fundamental obligations.

In its general comment on the effect of reservations made to the ICCPR (UN Doc. CCPR/C/21/ Rev.1/Add.6, General Comment No. 24, para. 7, 4 November 1994), the UN Human Rights Committee stated that:

> In an instrument which articulates very many civil and political rights, each of the many Articles, and indeed their interplay, secures the objectives of the Covenant. The object and purpose of the Covenant is to create legally binding standards for human rights by defining certain civil and political rights and placing them in a framework of obligations which are legally binding for those States which ratify; and to provide efficacious supervisory machinery for the obligations undertaken.

The thrust of this statement is that one may not always identify a specific provision of a treaty that embodies its object and purpose. In treaties that are concerned with establishing 'standards', such as the ICCPR, the object and purpose is often embedded in the entire provisions of the treaty, so that each provision is an integral part of the whole and the soul of the treaty inheres crucially in the interplay of all of its provisions.

Notwithstanding this poignant observation, the Human Rights Committee did identify that:

> Reservations that offend peremptory norms would not be compatible with the object and purpose of the Covenant...provisions in the Covenant that represent customary international law...when they have the character of peremptory norms may not be the subject of reservations. Accordingly, a State may not reserve the right to engage in slavery, to torture, to subject persons to cruel, inhuman or degrading treatment or punishment, to arbitrarily deprive persons of their lives, to arbitrarily arrest and detain persons, to deny freedom of thought, conscience and religion, to presume a person guilty unless he proves his innocence, to execute pregnant women or children, to permit the advocacy of national, racial or religious hatred, to deny to persons of marriageable age the right to marry, or to deny to minorities the right to enjoy their own culture, profess their own religion, or use their own language.

The ILC initially rejected the compatibility test in 1951 on the basis that it was too subjective to serve as a useful guide. Instead, it opted for the absolute integrity test, so that every single member of a treaty must accept a reservation for such reservation to be effective. The ILC objection was overturned in 1952, when the UN General Assembly instructed the UN Secretary-General to defer to the ICJ's opinion in the Genocide Convention: after all, the Court is the principal judicial organ of the UN and it does not bode well for its decisions to be ignored or undermined by other UN organs. The ILC implemented this directive in 1962.

As noted earlier, the compatibility test has now been endorsed by Article 19(c) VCLT.

thinking points

- *Explain the different approaches of international law to the effects of reservation on treaty obligations.*
- *What is the merit of the approach adopted by the PAU and how does this approach differ from that followed by the ICJ in the Reservations to the Genocide Convention Advisory Opinion?*
- *What is the effect of reservation against (a) parties that have not made any reservation all, (b) parties that make different reservations, and (c) parties that object totally to the reservation?*

3.5.3 The consequences of incompatible reservations

A very important question is: what happens once a tribunal determines that a reservation is incompatible with a treaty? Does that reservation contaminate the obligation or position of the reserving party in respect of the whole treaty or only in part, or do the reservation and the unreserved parts of the treaty coexist harmoniously so that their waters run side by side without ever mingling?

- **Belilos v. Switzerland** Application No. 10328/83 (1988) 10 EHRR 466

Marlène Belilos, a Swiss national, brought an action before the European Court of Human Rights (ECtHR). The facts arose from a public demonstration that took place in Lausanne on 4 April 1981. Belilos, who was a student at that time, was indicted by the Lausanne Police Board for having taken part in an unauthorized demonstration and was issued a fine, in her absence, of 200 Swiss francs (CHF). She appealed against this decision and claimed, inter alia, that the decision was incompatible with Article 6 of the European Convention on Human Rights (ECHR), which enshrines the right to a hearing by an independent and impartial tribunal established by law, and that the reservations made when Switzerland acceded to the Convention did not allow an administrative authority, where it was an agency of the executive that was judge in its own cause, to determine a criminal charge. Switzerland had formulated two reservations and two interpretative declarations when ratifying the Convention, and the particular declaration in question, which Belilos complained was breached, states that:

> the Swiss Federal Council considers that the guarantee of fair trial in Art. 6, paragraph 1 (art. 6–1), of the Convention, in the determination of ... any criminal charge against the person in question is intended solely to ensure ultimate control by the judiciary over the acts or decisions of the public authorities relating to ... the determination of such a charge.

The bone of contention was the impact of this declaration on Article 64 ECHR, which prohibits reservations of a general character.

It was held (at [60]) that:

> the declaration in question does not satisfy two of the requirements of Article 64 ... of the Convention, with the result that it must be held to be invalid. At the same time, it is beyond doubt that Switzerland is, and regards itself as, bound by the Convention irrespective of the validity of the declaration.

Clearly, the European Court treated the incompatible reservation as severable from the ECHR, with the consequence that Switzerland remained bound by the Treaty.

- **Loizidou v. Turkey (Preliminary Objections)** Application No. 15318/89 (1995) 20 EHRR 99

The applicant was a Cypriot national who complained that Turkish forces prevented her from enjoying her property located in Kyrenia, Northern Cyprus, which was under Turkish occupation. In relation to this, Loizidou participated in a protest march organized by Greek Cypriot women to encourage Greek Cypriot refugees to return home. The applicant was arrested by the Turkish police and was detained for ten hours, prompting her complaint that her rights were violated. The main issue before the ECtHR was to determine the validity of a reservation formulated by Turkey in accepting the ECHR.

On 22 January 1990, Turkey formulated the following reservation pursuant to Article 46 of the European Convention:

> The Government of the Republic of Turkey acting in accordance with Article 46 ... of the European Convention for the Protection of Human Rights and Fundamental Freedoms, hereby recognises as compulsory ipso facto and without special agreement the jurisdiction of the European Court of Human Rights in all matters concerning the interpretation and application of the Convention which relate to the exercise of jurisdiction within the meaning of Article 1 ... of the Convention, performed within the boundaries of the national territory of the Republic of Turkey ...

By this reservation, Turkey had purported to limit the jurisdiction of the ECtHR to matters occurring within Turkey. The facts of the incidence in the present case happened in Turkish overseas territory.

Turkey argued that the ECtHR lacked competence to consider the merits of the case on the grounds that the matters complained of did not fall within Turkish jurisdiction, but within that of the Turkish Republic of Northern Cyprus (TRNC). It also argued that it was entirely consistent with international law practice that its reservation excluded the Court from dealing with matters occurring outside Turkey.

The Court considered the object and purpose of the ECHR, and held (at [77]–[79]) that:

> in the Court's view, the existence of such a restrictive clause governing reservations suggests that States could not qualify their acceptance of the optional clauses thereby effectively excluding areas of their law and practice within their 'jurisdiction' from supervision by the Convention institutions. The inequality between Contracting States which the permissibility of such qualified acceptances might create would, moreover, run counter to the aim, as expressed in the Preamble to the Convention, to achieve greater unity in the maintenance and further realisation of human rights ...

This reveals the intention of the European institutions to encourage a uniform applicability of rules to State parties, particularly relating to the maintenance of human rights. Consequently, the ECtHR declared that:

> taking into consideration the character of the Convention, the ordinary meaning of Articles 25 and 46 ... in their context and in the light of their object and purpose and the practice of Contracting Parties, the Court concludes that the restrictions *ratione loci* attached to Turkey's Article 25 and Article 46 ... declarations are invalid.

Thus, as with *Belilos*, the Court rejected the incompatible reservation as invalid and hence severable from the acceptance of the Convention by the concerned State.

These cases indicate that some courts regard the effect of offensive reservations as severable from a treaty, and not affecting the validity of the treaty. However, the approach of the International Court of Justice (ICJ) has not been as clear-cut.

. . . .

● *France v. Norway* (1957) ICJ REP 19 (The *Norwegian Loans Case*)

France, which had accepted the ICJ's jurisdiction but with the reservation that the Court could not try any matter falling within its domestic jurisdiction, brought an action against Norway. Although Norway had made no such reservation to its own acceptance of the Court's jurisdiction, it had invoked the French reservation on the basis of reciprocity.

The Court held that since the French reservation precluded the Court from trying the matter, then it could not entertain the French action against Norway since Norway's invocation of the French reservation would be deemed to have reserved against the Court's jurisdiction by virtue of reciprocity (see pp. 23–24).

It should be noted that the Court did not pronounce directly on the validity of the reservation made by France unlike the European Courts discussed previously. Since neither France nor Norway challenged the validity of that reservation, the Court seemed to accept it as valid. However, the Court noted, 'the French Declaration accepted the Court's jurisdiction [although] within narrower limits than the Norwegian's Declaration' (see p. 23). Thus, the Court accepted both the French Declaration and its reservations as valid.

Several ICJ judges in this case accepted that the Court had no jurisdiction but rejected its basing its decision on the French reservation. (See Judges Quintana at 28 and Badawi at 29–33.) Judges Lauterpacht (at 35–36), Basdevant (at 78), and Read (at 86), also rejected the Court's rationale holding, in effect, that the reservation was invalid. Judge Lauterpacht in particular held that the French reservation was not only invalid, but its effect was to render the entire French Declaration accepting the Court's jurisdiction null and void so that in effect France had actually not accepted the Court's jurisdiction (at 57–59).

● *Switzerland v. United States* (1957) ICJ REP 105 (The *Interhandel Case*) (*Interim Measures*).

The USA, which had made a reservation precluding the Court from trying cases falling under its domestic jurisdiction, was sued by Switzerland. The USA invoked the reservation but the Court, once again, did not consider the effect of the reservation but confirmed, on other grounds, that it had prima facie jurisdiction in the case.

Judge Lauterpacht once again affirmed the position he expressed in the *Norwegian Loan Case*. He concluded that the reservation formed an essential part of the Declaration to accept the Court's jurisdiction and therefore cannot be separated from it so as to leave the remaining part of the Declaration valid. Thus, the reservation contaminated the whole declaration rendering it null and void.

KEY POINT While some courts treat incompatible reservations as severable so that the reserving party is still bound by the treaty, some, like the ICJ, believe such reservations render the entire treaty null and void.

3.5.4 The acceptance of, and objection to, reservations

Having considered the principles guiding reservations, mainly in terms of the relations between a reserving State and the treaty itself, we now turn to discuss the wider implications of reservations. The issues here include matters such as situations in which reservations are authorized by a treaty, the position when the object and purpose of a treaty necessitates acceptance of reservations by all parties, and the situation in which reservations are made against provisions of constituent treaties of organizations. The provisions of Article 20(1)–(5) VCLT deal with these situations—although some provisions are more apt and exact than others.

Expressly authorized reservations

With regard to a reservation that is expressly authorized by a treaty, Article 20(1) states that such a reservation 'does not require any subsequent acceptance by other parties unless the treaty so provides'. However, according to Article 20(2):

> when it appears from the limited number of the negotiating States and the object and purpose of a treaty that the application of the treaty in its entirety between all the parties is an essential condition of the consent of each one to be bound by the treaty, a reservation requires acceptance by all the parties.

From this provision, it is clear that where the object and purpose of a treaty, in addition to the limited number of parties that negotiate it, clearly indicate that the application of the treaty in its entirety to *all* members is an essential condition of the consent of each State to be bound by the treaty, *then a reservation requires acceptance by all parties to the treaty.*

There are two points worth mentioning in light of the provisions of Article 20(2). First, the State parties to the treaty in question should be limited, which gives the impression that the treaties concerned here are exclusive. These could include disarmament treaties, such as the 1995 Treaty on Non-Proliferation of Nuclear Weapons (NPT). Secondly, application of the treaty obligations to all members is crucial to achieving the object and purpose of the treaty.

Reservations against constituent treaties

Article 20(3) is equally straightforward:

> When a treaty is a constituent instrument of an international organization and unless it otherwise provides, a reservation requires the acceptance of the competent organ of that organization.

Here, a reservation to a constituent treaty of an organization must be accepted by all of the competent organs of that organization.

Situations outside Article 20(2) and (3)

Article 20(4) VCLT governs the relations of other State parties to the reservations made by some parties to that treaty. According to this provision:

> In cases not falling under the preceding paragraphs and unless the treaty otherwise provides:
> (a) acceptance by another contracting State of a reservation constitutes the reserving State a party to the treaty in relation to that other State if or when the treaty is in force for those States;
> (b) an objection by another contracting State to a reservation does not preclude the entry into force of a treaty as between the objecting and reserving State unless a contrary intention is definitely expressed by the objecting State;
> (c) an act expressing a State's consent to be bound by the treaty and containing a reservation is effective as soon as at least one other contacting State has accepted the reservation.

Under Article 20(4)(a), if a State party accepts a reservation made by another State party, that acceptance means that the reserving State is party to the treaty with respect to the accepting State(s), unless the contrary is intended. Under Article 20(4)(b), if a State objects to the reservation, that objection has no effect on the operation of the treaty regarding the reserving and objecting States, except if the objecting State specifically refuses that the treaty binds it vis-à-vis the reserving State, in which case the treaty will be in force between the objecting State and other parties to the treaty except the reserving State. Therefore, under Article 20(4)(b), the fact that the objecting State does not want the treaty to be in force between it and the reserving State cannot be implied from its objection; that consequence has to be specifically stated by the objecting State.

Article 20(4)(c) deals with the time at which acceptance by one State of another's reservation to a treaty enjoining both of them comes into effect.

thinking points

- *What is the impact of accepting a reservation on parties to the treaty?*
- *What is the impact of rejecting a reservation on the relationship between the reserving and objecting parties vis-à-vis the treaty?*

3.5.5 The effects of reservation and objections vis-à-vis treaty obligations

What are the effects of reservations and objections to reservations in relation to the other obligations contained in the treaty?

Article 21(1) VCLT states that:

> A reservation established with regard to another party in accordance with Articles 19, 20, and 23:
> (a) modifies for the reserving State in its relations with that other party the provisions of the treaty to which the reservations relates to the extent of the reservation; and
> (b) modifies those provisions to the same extent for that other party in relations with the reserving State.

These provisions operate on the basis of reciprocity, in that the State accepting the reservation is entitled to rely on that reservation in its dealings with the reserving State as though it has itself taken out the same reservation.

Libya made a reservation to the 1961 Vienna Convention on Diplomatic Relations, which permitted Libya to search diplomatic bags with the consent of the State concerned. The fact that the UK did not object to this reservation entitled the UK also to search Libya's diplomatic bags as though the UK had made similar reservations.

However, where reservations are objected to, Article 21(2) states that the 'reservation does not modify the provisions of the treaty for the other parties to the treaty inter se'. This means that other parties will carry on, as between themselves, as though there were no reservations against the provisions that have modified the relations between the reserving and accepting States. But under Article 21(3):

when a State objecting to a reservation has not opposed the entry into force of the treaty between itself and the reserving State, the provisions to which the reservation relates do not apply as between the two States to the extent of the reservation.

The difference between Article 21(2) and (3) can be demonstrated as follows.

example

Suppose that State A has formulated a reservation that excludes the application of Article 100 of Y Treaty to itself, which reservation State B has accepted. Article 21(2) entitles States B, C, D, and E to continue to deal with themselves in respect of all of the Articles of that treaty, including Article 100. Of course, the reservation has modified the relations between States A and B in respect of Article 100.

However, let us suppose that when State A formulates its reservation against Article 100 of Y Treaty, States B, C, and D oppose the entry into force of Y Treaty altogether between them and State A. State E objects to the reservation to Article 100, but does not oppose Treaty Y entering into force between it and State A. In that case, between States A and E, Treaty Y will be in force without the reserved provisions.

. . . .

● *United Kingdom v. France* (1977) 18 UNRIAA 3 (The ***Anglo-French Continental Shelf Arbitration***)

In this case, the Permanent Court of Arbitration (PCA) stated (at 42) that:

> The combined effect of the French reservations and their rejection by the United Kingdom is neither to render Article 6 [of the 1958 Geneva Convention on the Continental Shelf] inapplicable *in toto* as the French Republic contends, nor to render it applicable as the United Kingdom primarily contends. It is to render the Article inapplicable as between the two countries to the extent of the reservations.

thinking points

- *How do reservations affect the obligations contained in a treaty?*
- *Explain the difference between the effect of a reservation of a treaty on the relations among member States and the effect of a reservation on the treaty obligations themselves.*

3.6 The interpretation of treaties

The interpretation of treaties is one of the most controversial issues in international law. The plainest provisions of a treaty, on which States agree when drafting the treaty, will often generate huge controversy when it comes to applying the treaty. Reasons for this include the fact that the implementation of a treaty can have a serious impact on, and implications for, the national interests of parties to the treaty.

Article 31 VCLT provides that:

> (1) A treaty shall be interpreted in good faith in accordance with the ordinary meaning to be given to the terms of the treaty in their context and in light of its object and purpose.

(2) The context for the purpose of the interpretation of a treaty shall comprise, in addition to the text, including its preamble and annexes:

    (a) any agreement relating to the treaty which was made between all the parties in connection with the conclusion of the treaty;

    (b) any instrument which was made by one or more parties in connexion with the conclusion of the treaty and accepted by other parties as an instrument related to the treaty;

(3) There shall be taken into account, together with the context:

    (a) any subsequent agreement between the parties regarding the interpretation of or the application of its provisions;

    (b) any subsequent practice in the application of the treaty which establishes the agreement of the parties regarding its interpretation;

    (c) any relevant rules of international law applicable in the relations between the parties.

(4) A special meaning shall be given to a term if it is established that the parties so intended.

International law recognizes three approaches to treaty interpretation: the 'literal', or 'textual', approach; the 'intention of the parties' approach; and the 'object and purpose' (that is, teleological) approach. To a large extent, these various approaches are enshrined in Article 31 VCLT, which reflects the customary international law rules on interpretation of treaties.

3.6.1 The 'literal', or 'textual', approach

Article 31 embodies the fundamental rule of treaty interpretation, which enjoins that treaties are to be interpreted in light of the ordinary meaning of their provisions. The Article further states that the ordinary meaning of terms used in treaties must be determined by reference to the 'context' and the 'object and purpose' of that treaty.

As listed in Article 31(2)(a) and (b), and (3)(a)–(e), the 'context' of a treaty includes any agreements or instruments made between the parties and so accepted by them as related to the *conclusion* of the treaty, and any subsequent agreements or practice regarded by the parties as relating to the *interpretation* of the treaty, as well as any relevant rules of international law accepted by the parties as applicable to them. The distinction between the 'agreements' and 'instruments' referred to under Article 31(2)(a) and (b), and those under Article 31(3)(a) and (b), is that while the former concern the 'conclusion' of the treaty, the latter relate to the 'interpretation'.

In practice, what constitutes the 'ordinary' meaning' of a treaty term has proven to be just as elusive as what constitutes agreements, instruments, or subsequent practice developed by States towards treaty interpretation.

Let us now consider some aids contained in the wording of Article 31.

'Natural and ordinary meaning'

. . . .

● *Competence of the General Assembly for the Admission of a State to the United Nations Advisory Opinion* [1950] ICJ REP 4

The UN General Assembly asked the ICJ (at 5) whether:

the admission of a State to membership in the United Nations, pursuant to Article 4, paragraph 2, of the Charter, [can] be effected by a decision of the General Assembly when the Security Council has made no recommendation for admission by reason of the candidate failing to obtain the requisite majority or of the negative vote of a permanent Member upon a resolution so to recommend.

The Court stated (at 8) that:

the first duty of a tribunal which is called upon to interpret and apply the provisions of a treaty, is to endeavour to give effect to them in their natural and ordinary meaning in the context in which they occur. If the relevant words in their natural and ordinary meaning make sense in their context, that is an end of the matter.

Relying on the decision of the PCIJ in *Polish Postal Service in Danzig Advisory Opinion* (1925) PCIJ Ser. B, No. 11, the Court further stated that:

It is a cardinal principle of interpretation that words must be interpreted in the sense which they would normally have in their context, unless such interpretation would lead to something unreasonable or absurd.

. . . .

● *Conditions of Admission of a State Membership in the United Nations Advisory Opinion* [1957] ICJ REP 57 (The *Condition of Admissions Case*)

Similarly in this case, the General Assembly sought the opinion of the ICJ, in respect of Article 4 of the UN Charter, whether:

a Member of the United Nations which is called upon, in virtue of Article 4 of the Charter, to pronounce itself by its vote, either in the Security Council or in the General Assembly, on the admission of a State to membership in the United Nations, is juridically entitled to make its consent to the admission dependent on conditions not expressly provided by paragraph I of the said Article? In particular, can such a Member, while it recognizes the conditions set forth in that provision to be fulfilled by the State concerned, subject its affirmative vote to the additional condition that other States be admitted to membership in the United Nations together with that State?

The Court stated (at 62–63), that:

the natural meaning of the words used leads to the conclusion that these conditions constitute an exhaustive enumeration and are not merely stated by way of guidance or example . . . To warrant an interpretation other than that which ensues from the natural meaning of the words, a decisive reason would be required which has not been established . . . If the authors of the Charter had meant to leave Members free to import into the application of this provision considerations extraneous to the conditions laid down therein, they would undoubtedly have adopted a different wording.

. . . .

● *Constitution of the Maritime Safety Committee of the Inter-Governmental Maritime Consultative Organization Advisory Opinion* [1960] ICJ REP 150 (The *IMCO Case*)

The Secretary General of the IMCO requested the ICJ's opinion as to whether the Maritime Safety Committee of the IMCO, in not electing Liberia and Panama to the Committee, exercised its electoral power in accordance with the provisions of Article 28(a) of the 1948 Convention for the Establishment of the Inter-Governmental Maritime Consultative Organization. The main issue for the Court to determine was how to interpret the provision of Article 28(a) of the Convention that established the IMCO, which states that the assembly of the organization shall elect the fourteen members of the Maritime Safety Committee, eight of which must be the largest ship-owning nations in the organization.

The Court ruled (at 159–160) that:

> The words of Article 28 (a) must be read in their natural and ordinary meaning, in the sense which they would normally have in their context. It is only if, when this is done, the words of the Article are ambiguous in any way that resort need be had to other methods of construction.

But the fact that the text of a treaty is clear to the naked eye does not mean that it is entirely free from controversy.

● **United States v. Alvarez-Machain** 504 US 655 (1992), US Supreme Court

The defendant, a Mexican national, was kidnapped in Mexico and brought to trial in the USA. The US Supreme Court applied the provision of an extradition treaty between the USA and Mexico, and held that the USA had jurisdiction to try the criminal despite his forcible capture. In support of the USA was the fact that the concerned treaty did not prohibit the forcible capture of citizens of State parties.

In the above case, the US Supreme Court's application of the ordinary meaning of the text of the treaty in question was controversial. The fact that a treaty does not prohibit abduction does not mean that a State may forcibly enforce its jurisdiction on the territory of another State (see Chapter 7 on jurisdiction). Further, the US courts have departed from such cases as *United States v. Rauscher* 119 US 407 (1886) in many cases whenever defendants were brought into the USA through means that violate international law.

'Context'

The 'context' within which the ordinary meaning of a treaty is to be construed includes the preamble, annexes of the treaty, and the other materials listed previously. However, in practice, the Court does not distinguish between agreements and instruments related to conclusions, and those that relate to interpretation of treaties. It treats all as some part of an attempt to interpret treaties in light of their ordinary meaning.

See *United States v. Mexico* (1911) 5 AJIL 785 (the *Chamizal Arbitration*), which held subsequent practice to be crucial. However, in the *Kasikili/Sedudu Island Case* (see section 3.3.4), the ICJ adopted a strict view to rejecting such practice on the basis that the instrument was no more than a unilateral act of Botswana, since the action, which involved reports prepared by Botswana on its frontier with Namibia, was not known in the latter country, but was an internal matter for the former. Similarly, in *Indonesia v. Malaysia* (2002) ICJ Rep 625 (the *Pulau Ligitan/Pulau Sipadan Case*), the Court rejected the Pulaus' reliance on a map as an agreement on the basis that such was never accepted by Malaysia's previous regime as an agreement.

However, if the ordinary meaning of a treaty will lead to absurdity, Article 32 allows States to resort to supplementary means of interpretation, such as the use of the historical documents concerning the negotiation of the treaty—*travaux préparatoires*. But as the ICJ confirmed in the *Application of the Interim Accord of 13 September 1995 (the former Yugoslav Republic Macedonia v. Greece)*, (2011) I. C. J. Reports, 644, where the ordinary meaning is clear from the texts of a treaty, supplementary means would not be used to alter this.

Generally speaking, the literal interpretation of treaties should clearly reveal the intention of parties. As the Court stated in the *IMCO Case* (see section 3.6.1):

> the words of the Article 'of which not less than eight shall be the largest ship-owning nations' have a mandatory and imperative sense and precisely carry out *the intention* of the framers of the Convention. [Emphasis added]

However, occasions do arise on which literal interpretation seems to be at variance with the actual intention of parties to treaties. In such a case, the Court will often jettison the ordinary meaning of words used in treaties and attempt to discover the actual intent of the parties.

. . . .

● *Golder v. United Kingdom* [1975] 1 EHRR 524

In the first case in which the UK appeared before the ECtHR as a defendant, an application was made by Golder, a UK citizen, to the European Commission, complaining of violation of his rights under Article 6(1) ECHR. Mr Golder was serving a fifteen-year prison term in the UK for armed robbery. While in jail, a disturbance broke out one day, and he was implicated in the incident by the evidence of a prison officer, but another warden stated that Golder was not involved. Although he was not eventually charged, Mr Golder petitioned the Commission that the negative entries entered in his file as a result of the disturbance prejudiced his chances for parole. The question in this case was whether Golder had a right under the ECHR to access the Court under Article 6(1).

The UK said that Golder did not. In support of its argument, the UK relied on a comparison of the contested provision with Articles 5(4) and 13 ECHR to argue that if access to the court were intended by Article 6(1), then the provision would have said so, as was the case with Articles 5 and 13, and also that, were that to be the case, then the express provision of that access in the latter provisions would be superfluous.

The Court distinguished the premises of Article 6(1) from Articles 5(4) and 13 ECHR, and after analysis of other relevant cases, held that Article 6(1) guaranteed access to the Court. In coming to this conclusion, the ECtHR said that, in interpreting the provisions of a treaty, the Court does not substitute its own interpretation for the text, but interprets the treaty in light of the 'object and purpose' of the treaty, as manifested by the parties themselves.

The Court said (at [34]) that:

> the most significant passage in the Preamble to the European Convention is the signatory Governments declaring that they are resolved, as the Governments of European countries which are like-minded and have a common heritage of political traditions, ideals, freedom and the rule of law, to take the first steps for the collective enforcement of certain of the Rights stated in the Universal Declaration of 10 December 1948.

The Court stated (at [36]) that:

> This is not an extensive interpretation forcing new obligations on the Contracting States: it is based on the very terms of the first sentence of Article 6 para. 1 (art. 6–1) read in its context and having regard to the object and purpose of the Convention, a lawmaking treaty.

● **Constitution of the Maritime Safety Committee of the Inter-Governmental Maritime Consultative Organization Advisory Opinion** (1960) ICJ Rep 150 (The *IMCO Case*)

In this case, the ICJ also stated (at 159–160), that:

> the words of Article 28 (a) must be read in their natural and ordinary meaning, in the sense which they would normally have in their context. *It is only if, when this is done, the words of the Article are ambiguous in any way that resort need be had to other methods of construction.* [Emphasis added]

thinking points

- List the various approaches to the interpretation of treaties in international law.
- When may parties to a treaty abandon the literal interpretation of the treaty for other forms of interpretation?

3.7 Invalid treaties

Although States are free to enter into contracts based on their own terms and conditions, there are certain instances in which such treaties entered into by States will be declared invalid. The circumstances under which a treaty would be declared invalid are discussed in the following sections.

3.7.1 Treaties consented to inconsistently with the internal law of a State

We noted earlier, in relation to the power of State officials to conclude treaties on behalf of their States, that a State may not rely on its internal law in justifying non-performance of international obligations. Therefore a treaty is still valid even if a State's consent to be bound is expressed in violation of its internal laws governing competence to conclude treaties. The only exception to that rule is if the violation in question is manifest and concerns an internal law of fundamental importance. We have already discussed attempts by States to rely on their internal laws (Nigeria, in *Cameroon v. Nigeria*, see section 3.3.6) and we have also discussed what 'manifest' means in that context. Thus a treaty is generally valid under Article 46 VCLT except in cases of manifest reliance on an internal law of fundamental significance. The question of fundamentality of a rule of internal law of States is a question of fact.

3.7.2 Error, fraud, corruption, and coercion of State representatives

Aside from the manifest inconsistency with determining fundamental internal rules, other circumstances that may render an otherwise valid treaty invalid include error (Article 48), fraud (Article 49), corruption of a State representative (Article 50), and coercion of a State representative (Article 52).

Article 52 also renders invalid a treaty procured by the threat or use of force in violation of the principles of international law embodied in the UN Charter. This provision obviously follows the general prohibition of the use or threat of force by Article 2(4) of that treaty. It is worth mentioning that, prior to the adoption of the 1928 Kellogg–Briand Pact, there was no prohibition on the use or threat of force (see Chapter 10). This implies that a treaty procured through either the use or threat of war was as good as a treaty procured through other normal means. This, however, changed during the interwar years, and more forcefully with the adoption of the UN Charter.

The attempt by many weak and former colonies to extend the meaning of 'force' in this context to include economic force, such as sanctions, did not succeed. The rationale for this attempt lay in the desire of such States to ensure that it is not only when powerful States use military forces against them that they can be held accountable, but also when they impose sanctions on them. Surely, sanctions imposed by an economically powerful State on a poor State would be expected to have a more devastating effect on the will and free choices of the poor State than, say, a military attack by a poor State on a more powerful State? Nonetheless, this proposal was rejected during the negotiation of the UN Charter, so that only military force may invalidate a treaty.

3.7.3 Peremptory norms

Article 53 renders invalid treaties that, when concluded, conflict with a peremptory norm of general international law. As already explained, these are a special class of international obligations in respect of which derogation is not permitted. It is also believed that States cannot generally derogate from a peremptory norm by consent. An example of a peremptory norm, according to most international lawyers, is the prohibition of the use or threat of force, which is contained in the UN Charter. It is thought that States cannot conclude a treaty that permits the use of force among themselves.

3.8 The termination and suspension of treaties

Once concluded, the performance of treaty obligations is not at the mercy of a State's whim, so that if a State simply does not feel like observing its obligations, it may terminate the treaty. Far from it being capricious, a State's obligation under a treaty is to be performed in good faith (Article 26 VCLT). Thus, instances of termination presuppose that a State has done everything possible to ensure performance, but has no choice other than to terminate.

Termination can be voluntary or automatic. A voluntary or consensual termination happens where State parties to a treaty decide to bring the treaty to an end. An automatic termination arises where an act of one State automatically ends a treaty, except otherwise provided by the treaty or agreed by those parties.

3.8.1 Termination by treaty provisions and consent

Article 54 VCLT states that:

> the termination of a treaty or the withdrawal of a party may take place (a) in conformity with the provision of the treaty (b) at any time, by consent of all parties.

It must be noted that it is possible that all of the parties to a treaty generally regard the treaty as no longer in force. This certainly can be implied from the general conduct of State parties towards the obligations that they assume under the treaty. For example, although Article 107 of the UN Charter entitles UN members to use force against former enemy States—that is, Germany and the States that supported it during the Second World War—all UN members regard this obligation as outdated, partly because all of those former enemy States are now UN members.

3.8.2 Denunciation

To denounce a treaty is to avow publicly that one is no longer bound by the treaty. Article 56 VCLT thus provides that:

> (1) A treaty which contains no provision regarding its termination and which does not provide for denunciation or withdrawal is not subject to denunciation or withdrawal unless:
>   (a) it is established that the parties intended to admit the possibility of denunciation or withdrawal; or
>   (b) a right of denunciation or withdrawal may be implied by the nature of the treaty.
> (2) A Party shall give not less than twelve months' notice of its intention to denounce or withdraw from a treaty under paragraph 1.

An example of this provision can be observed in the withdrawal of North Korea from the 1970 NPT in March 1993. It appears that withdrawal and denunciation have exactly the same effect as termination of the treaty, in respect of the denouncing or withdrawing State. Such denunciation or withdrawal cannot be implied, especially if the class of treaty is so special that withdrawal from, or denunciation of, it goes to the very root of all parties' agreement to be bound by it in the first place, as is the case with the NPT.

Article 56(2) provides that a withdrawing or denouncing State must give twelve months' notice to other parties to the treaty. In the case of North Korea, it declared an 'automatic and immediate effectuation of its withdrawal from the NPT'. Thus no notice was served.

3.8.3 Material breach

Under Article 60 VCLT:

> 1. A material breach of a bilateral treaty by one of the parties entitles the other to invoke the breach as a ground for terminating the treaty or suspending its operation in whole or in part.
> 2. A material breach of a multilateral treaty by one of the parties entitles:

(a) The other parties by unanimous agreement to suspend the operation of the treaty in whole or in part or to terminate it either;

    (i) in the relations between themselves and the defaulting State, or

    (ii) as between all the parties

(b) a party specifically affected by the breach to invoke it as a ground for suspending the operation of the treaty in whole or in part in the relations between itself and the defaulting State;

(c) any party than the defaulting State to invoke the breach as a ground for suspending the operation of the treaty in whole or in part with respect to itself if the treaty is of such a character that a material breach of its provision by one party radically changes the position of every party with respect to the further performance of its obligations under the treaty.

According to Article 60(3), a material breach is:

(a) a repudiation of a treaty not sanctioned by the present Convention; or

(b) the violation of a provision essential to the accomplishment of the object or purpose of the treaty.

The provisions concerning material breach are very important for many reasons. They set out the fact that mere breach of a condition, even if it is material, does not automatically result in the suspension or termination of an obligation by another party to a treaty, except in respect of those treaties the fulfilment of which depends on every party performing the obligation contained therein. A material breach of such, according to Article 60(c), entitles other parties to the treaty to suspend the performance of the breached obligation. However, this is dangerous: for example, should all other parties to the NPT suspend or terminate the treaty simply because North Korea has withdrawn from it? The obvious answer is 'no', because that presupposes serious danger of nuclear proliferation. However, should other States continue to abide by the NPT when one State has withdrawn from it, taking into consideration the possibility that other States will follow suit?

A few points need to be made about material breach. A State party to a treaty cannot rely on the previous conduct of its counterpart under another treaty to justify its own action.

● **Hungary v. Slovakia** (1997) ICJ REP 7 (The **Gabčíkovo-Nagymaros Project Case**)

In this case, the ICJ rejected Hungary's argument that its behaviour under the treaty between it and Czechoslovakia was dictated by the conduct of the latter under other agreements.

The Court held (at [106]) that:

it is only material breach of the treaty itself, by a State party to that treaty, which entitles the other party to rely on it as a ground for terminating the treaty.

3.8.4 Termination by supervening events

Article 61(1) entitles parties to a treaty to terminate it if circumstances occurring after the conclusion of the treaty make performance impossible as a result of a permanent disappearance or destruction of an object indispensable for the execution of the treaty. It must be pointed out that the impossibility concerned here has to be permanent for it to amount to a ground for termination; temporary impossibilities can lead only to suspension, with the hope of resumption of obligation once the situation normalizes. Under Article 61(2), where a party contributes to the occurrence of the impossibility that leads to non-performance, that party cannot rely on the impossibility to justify termination, withdrawal, or suspension from the treaty.

. . . .

● *Hungary v. Slovakia* (1997) ICJ Rep 7 (The *Gabčíkovo-Nagymaros Project Case*)

Hungary argued that the essential object of the 1977 treaty between it and Czechoslovakia—a joint economic investment—had become impossible to perform due to some environmental constraints.

The ICJ said that if, indeed, this was the case, it was because of Hungary's own failure to perform its own part of the contract and therefore that country could not rely on it as a ground for termination.

3.8.5 Fundamental change of circumstances (*rebus sic stantibus*)

A *rebus sic stantibus* situation arises where a fundamental change occurs which alters the original intention of parties to a treaty to the extent that performance will be totally useless in the circumstances. An invocation of a fundamental change, according to Article 62, terminates a treaty. However, such a fundamental change must relate specifically to the essential basis of the States' consent to the treaty. In the *Fisheries Jurisdiction Cases* (see section 3.3.1), the ICJ stated that the rule about fundamental change in Article 62 reflects customary international law. Hence, in the *Gabčíkovo-Nagymaros Project Case*, the ICJ refused Hungary's argument about the change in the circumstance, since the change in the environment conditions complained of by Hungary would not radically alter the original intention of the parties to the 1977 treaty.

👁 Conclusion

This chapter discussed the various rules relating to the making of treaties. It analysed various VCLT rules relating to interpretation, reservation, and termination of treaties. It considered many principal cases and judicial pronouncements, as well as important academic works on various aspects of the law of treaties. The law of treaties remains one of the most significant contributions of international law. While most of the aspects of treaty law covered in this chapter are also dealt with under customary international law, the fact still remains that the VCLT provides incomparable stability as far as clarity and certainty are concerned.

? Questions

Self-test questions

1 What is a 'treaty'?

2 Explain the term 'reservation'.

3 Distinguish between 'multilateral' and 'bilateral' treaties, and confirm which of them is (or are) covered by Article 3(b) VCLT.

4 Explain the rule that a State cannot plead its internal law as excuse for non-performance of an international obligation. Does this rule permit any exception?

5 Under what circumstances may a treaty be terminated? Explain two such circumstances.

6 What is meant by the 'object' and 'purpose' of a treaty in relation to its interpretation?

7 List the various approaches of international law to dealing with reservations to a treaty. In your opinion, which is (or are) more effective than the others?

8 What is a 'material breach' of a treaty?

Discussion questions

1 'A State party to a treaty may enter into any reservation against the provisions of the treaty without any consequence to other parties.' Discuss.

2 'A reservation to a treaty provision does not affect the remaining obligations of the treaty.' Critically examine this statement.

3 'If a head of State signs a treaty on behalf of his or her country in excess of or without the authority of his or her country's governing body, such treaty shall be void for inconsistency with the domestic law of the country.' Discuss.

4 What do you understand by the term 'reservation' and in respect of what provisions can a reservation be made?

5 'International organizations are not governed by the VCLT and, to that extent, treaties concluded by them are not a concern of international law.' Do you agree?

6 'The distinction between treaties concluded within organizations and between organizations is a semantic nonsense, and has no implications on the applicability of the VCLT on international organizations as subjects of international law.' Discuss.

Assessment question

General Roué is the current head of State of Rutamu. At a State banquet recently held in honour of the outgoing Candoman ambassador to Rutamu, the Candoman foreign minister presented General Roué with a document, neatly bound in a folder, saying to him: 'Your Excellency, this is the text of the treaty negotiated by your country with mine in respect of the disputed peninsular. Would your Excellency wish to append your signature so that the treaty will enter into force immediately, as agreed by your foreign minister and myself without any further delay?'

General Roué, a well-known alcoholic and philanderer, signed the treaty while distracted by two young women, one of whom held a large bottle of vodka and the other of whom held a glass—apparently for the General. A couple of days after the party, the Rutamuan foreign affairs minister complained to his Candoman counterpart that General Roué had signed the treaty without the authority of the Rutamuan Supreme Military Council, the highest governing body of the country, and that the General was both drunk and distracted when he signed. He also complained that, in fact, the text of the treaty that the General signed that day differed slightly from what was previously agreed. The minister argued that therefore Rutamu was not bound by the act of signing.

Advise the parties.

Key cases

- *Botswana v. Namibia* (1999) ICJ Rep 1045 (the *Kasikili/Sedudu Island Case*)
- *Cameroon v. Nigeria; Equatorial Guinea Intervening* (2002) ICJ Rep 303 (*Land and Maritime Boundary between Cameroon and Nigeria*)
- *Conditions of Admission of a State Membership in the United Nations Advisory Opinion* (1957) ICJ Rep 57 (the *Condition of Admissions Case*)
- *Golder v. United Kingdom* [1975] 1 EHRR 524
- *Hungary v. Slovakia* (1997) ICJ Rep 7 (the *Gabčíkovo-Nagymaros Project Case*)
- *Loizidou v. Turkey (Preliminary Objections)* Application No. 15318/89 (1995) 20 EHRR 99
- *Reservations to the Convention on the Prevention and Punishment of the Crime of Genocide Advisory Opinion* (1951) ICJ Rep 15
- *United Kingdom v. Iceland* (1973) ICJ Rep 3 (the *Fisheries Jurisdiction Cases*)

 # Further reading

Aust, A., *Modern Treaty Law and Practice* (2nd edn, Cambridge: Cambridge University Press, 2007)

Cannizzaro, E. (ed.), *The Law of Treaties beyond the Vienna Convention* (Oxford: Oxford University Press, 2011)

Fitzmaurice, M., 'The practical working of the law of treaties' in M. Evans (ed.), *International Law* (3rd edn, Oxford: Oxford University Press, 2010), p. 172

Fitzmaurice, M. and Elias, O., *Contemporary Issues in the Law of Treaties* (Utrecht: Eleven International Publishing, 2005)

Sinclair, Sir I., *The Vienna Convention on the Law of Treaties* (Manchester: Manchester University Press, 1984)

4

Statehood and recognition in international law

Learning objectives

This chapter will help you to:

- understand statehood in international law;
- learn how entities become States in international law;
- appreciate attributes of States and other subjects of international law;
- study recognition of States and government; and
- grapple with the various theories about recognition of States and government.

Introduction

Traditionally, international law applied only to States. This was mainly because States create international law, either through treaties or customs. It is not surprising, then, that during the early stages of its development international law regarded only States as its subjects. However, just as contemporary developments widened the scope of international law, so also have they expanded the category of its subjects to include international organizations and, in some cases, human beings. Nonetheless it is still possible to differentiate between various subjects of international law. In the *Case concerning Reparation for Injuries Suffered in the Service of the United Nations* (1949) ICJ Rep 178, the ICJ said that 'the subjects of law in any legal system are not necessarily identical in their nature or in the extent of their rights, and their nature depends upon the needs of the community'.

This chapter examines States as a subject of international law and discusses the recognition of States and government under international law. International organizations, which are other important subject of international law, are dealt with in the next chapter.

4.1 Legal personality of States

It is important to emphasize at the outset that although 'legal personality' is a generic concept, it applies variously to subjects of international law and attracts different consequences. For instance, while there is a general sense of what 'legal personality' means, the implications of this concept for States differ from the implications for international organizations. Therefore, while a definition of 'legal personality' may mean the same to both States and international organizations, the operation of the concept by States and international organizations varies. The following discussion thus focuses mainly on the general aspects of legal personality as applicable to States as international law subjects. However, the discussion of such issues as legal personality in this chapter does not foreclose a consideration of their particular application to international organizations in the next chapter.

4.1.1 Definition of legal personality

'Legal personality' per se refers to the substance of a juristic person; it connotes someone who can act legally, one who can sue or be sued in law. Thus, an 'international legal person' is 'someone' who is capable of being a subject and object of international law; that is to say, someone who can apply international law, and against whom international law can be applied. This definition applies to all subjects of international law, although, as already noted, the rights, duties, and obligations attaching to subjects vary considerably according to different subjects.

As stated in D. P. O'Connell, *International Law* (2nd edn, London: Stevens, 1970), p. 80:

> it is clear that the word 'person' is used to refer to one who is a legal actor, but that is of no assistance in ascertaining who or what is competent to act. Only the rules of law can determine this,

and they may select different entities and endow them with different legal functions, so that it is a mistake to suppose that by merely describing an entity as a legal 'person' one is formulating its capacities in law . . .

Often, subjects of international law are described in term of persons who have certain rights and duties. However, this description is somewhat problematic, because these rights accrue to an entity by virtue of its being a subject of international law, and it does not actually define *what* the entity is. It is therefore more appropriate to define a subject of international law with regard to the application of international law. This definition is independent of what the specific features of such entities are, which can only be revealed upon further investigation.

In Robert Jennings and Arthur Watts (eds), *Oppenheim's International Law, Vol. 1: Peace* (9th edn, London/New York: Longman, 1996), p. 119, an international legal person is defined as:

> One who possesses legal personality in international law, meaning one who is a subject of international law *so as itself to* enjoy rights, duties or powers established in international law, and generally, the capacity to act on the international plane either directly, or through another state (as in the case of a protected state). [Emphasis added]

This is a better definition for many reasons. First, it avoids the pitfall of defining international legal persons as those who *have* certain rights and powers. As we observed earlier, these are features that an entity derives by virtue of being an international legal person. Therefore, to describe an international legal person as one that is a subject of international law *so as to itself enjoy rights* recognizes that the enjoyment of the right is a consequence of being an international legal person. Secondly, Jennings and Watts' definition recognizes that international legal persons possess some capacities, and that they can act either by themselves or through another State.

In Max Sørensen (ed.), *Manual of International Law* (London: Macmillan, 1968), Nkambo Mugerwa said, at p. 249, that:

> To be a subject of law, or to be a legal person within the rules of that system implies three essential elements. First, a subject has duties, thereby incurring responsibility for any behaviour at variance with that prescribed by the system. Second, a subject is capable of claiming the benefit of rights. This is more than being a beneficiary of a right since a considerable number of rules may serve the interest of groups of individuals who do not have a legal claim to the benefit conferred by the particular rules. Third, a subject possesses the capacity to enter into contractual or other legal relations with other legal persons recognized by the particular system of law.

4.2 The status of international legal persons

Subjects of international law are distinguished by their capacity to engage exclusively in certain matters and endeavours. International legal capacity is therefore the ability to conduct affairs of or under international law. These capacities are several, and may include the ability to enter into international contracts, to sign and ratify treaties, to sue or be sued before international courts and tribunals, and to impose punishments in the form of sanctions against those who violate international law. In the case of international organizations, it includes capacity to operate on the territory of member States (see Chapter 5).

In exercising their competencies, international legal persons are often protected against interferences such as the arrest and prosecution of their representatives, to ensure that, as subjects of international law, they are able to execute their mandate without fear or favour. (See Chapter 8 on immunity.)

● **Reparation for Injuries Suffered in the Service of the United Nations Advisory Opinion** (1949) ICJ REP 174 (The **Reparation for Injuries Case**)

In this case, the ICJ said (at 183) that:

> In order that the agent may perform his duties satisfactorily, he must feel that this protection is assured to him by the Organization, and that he may count on it. To ensure the independence of the agent, and, consequently, the independent action of the Organization itself, it is essential that in performing his duties he need not have to rely on any other protection than that of the Organization...

Thus international legal persons enjoy diplomatic immunity, which is conferred on their official representatives—that is, exemption from any form of prosecution when performing their official duties. Also, such officials are often exempted from paying taxes to the States within which they operate.

International persons are also entitled to express their views and opinions on any matter in the course of their duties without being liable to the libellous laws of any country.

● **Applicability of Article VI, Section 22, of the Convention on the Privileges and Immunities of the United Nations Advisory Opinion** (1989) ICJ REP 177 (The **Mazilu Case**)

In this case, the ICJ was confronted with interpreting the provision of the 1946 UN Convention on the Privileges and Rights of the United Nations. The relevant provision is Article 22, which provides that:

> experts...performing missions for the United Nations shall be accorded such privileges and immunities as are necessary for the independent exercise of their functions during the period of their missions, including time spent on journeys in connection with their missions. In particular they shall be accorded: *(b)* in respect of words spoken or written and acts done by them in the course of the performance of their mission, immunity from legal process of every kind. This immunity from legal process shall continue to be accorded notwithstanding that the persons concerned are no longer employed on missions for the United Nations.

The Court said (at [47]) that:

> the purpose of Section 22 is ... evident, namely, to enable the United Nations to entrust missions to persons who do not have the status of an official of the Organization, and to guarantee them 'such privileges and immunities as are necessary for the independent exercise of their functions' ... The essence of the matter lies not in their administrative position but in the nature of their mission.

● **Advisory Opinion on the Difference Relating to Immunity from Legal Process of a Special Rapporteur of the Commission of Human Rights** (1999) ICJ REP 62

The UN Special Rapporteur on the Commission on Human Rights on the Independence of Judges and Lawyers, Dato' Param Cumaraswamy, gave an interview to a British magazine,

International Commercial Litigation, in 1995. Two commercial companies in Malaysia brought a libel suit against Mr Cumaraswamy on the ground that his interview defamed them. The critical issue here was whether the Special Rapporteur was immune from prosecution by Malaysia. Once again, the relevant issue was the meaning of Article 22 of the 1946 Convention (see the previous extract).

The Court held that Mr Cumaraswamy made the statement in his capacity as a UN Special Rapporteur and that, as such, he was entitled to immunity under Article 22 of the 1946 Convention.

As stated previously, international legal persons have many powers, and enjoy many rights and privileges. However, they also have many obligations attached to their position as subjects of international law. For example, States regularly incur treaty obligations towards other States, their own citizens, or citizens of other States. Some obligations imposed on States are even considered to be peremptory norms, which, as we recall from Chapter 2 and other chapters, are norms from which States may not derogate. Thus States have an obligation not to use or threaten force against other States under Article 2(4) of the Charter of the United Nations (UN Charter).

It is also widely believed that, in addition to peremptory norms, States enter into obligations not only with one another, but also with the rest of the international community. The concept of *obligatio erga omnes* covers this type of situation, which involves an obligation 'amongst all'. It is believed that *erga omnes* obligations create a contract between a State and the rest of the international community. While peremptory norms may not be derogated from, obligations *erga omnes* do not have this level of rigidity.

While the concept of *obligatio erga omnes* is quite controversial among international lawyers, the fact that there is the possibility of such an open-ended obligation imposed on States shows the enormity of obligations that attach to States by virtue of their being subjects of international law.

KEY POINTS

- An international legal person is an entity who can apply international law and to which international law can be applied.

- International law subjects enjoy several rights and privileges, and possess certain powers, such as the capacity to enter into relations with other subjects of international law.

- The rights, powers, and privileges of a subject of international law vary according to the subject and the rights, duties, and obligations in question.

 ## 4.3 States as a subject of international law

States are the most important subjects of international law. However, what constitutes a State is often controversial, and the question whether an entity has become a State for the purpose of international law is often tainted by political considerations. It is therefore necessary to lay down the foundation of States in international law leaving the question as to whether it is recognized as such to different considerations.

4.3.1 The criteria for statehood

States are the primary and, as stated earlier, the most important subjects of international law. However, while understanding what an entity requires in order to become a State is not as straightforward, determining the criteria of statehood is of particular importance. First, there may be many entities within a single territory claiming to be autonomous *States*. For example, during a civil war or other form of national uprising, breakaway parts of an existing State may describe themselves as States and may even sometimes be recognized as such by their sympathizers. Often, an existing State collapses, or, as is sometimes said, 'fails'.

example

Following a violent conflict in Somalia in the 1990s, the Somali State collapsed. The rule of law broke down; the legitimate government was sacked by the rebel insurgency. The physical entity called 'Somalia' splintered into various parts.

The same example can be given of the former Socialist Federal Republic of Yugoslavia (SFRY). Following a civil war in the 1990s, SFRY broke into as many as six States, with each claiming autonomy and the competence to represent the old State. The remains of the old SFRY, the Federal Republic of Yugoslavia (FRY), also known as Serbia and Montenegro, claimed that it had succeeded the old SFRY.

It may even be that a State does not disintegrate in terms of physically breaking into several parts, but that issues still arise as to the status of the State as a subject of international law.

example

Due to a severe civil war that broke out in Liberia in 1989, the then legitimate government of the country was restricted to the capital city, Monrovia, while the rebel groups controlled the remaining parts (constituting 98 per cent of the country).

In cases such as these, it is necessary to be able to recognize and distinguish a State, as a subject of international law, from the several other entities that may exist within the same territory alongside the State.

The criteria, or the required conditions, that an entity must meet before it can be regarded as a State in international law are listed in an international treaty. Article 1(1) of the 1933 Montevideo Convention on Rights and Duties of States provides that:

> The state as a person of international law should possess the following qualifications: (a) a permanent population; (b) a defined territory; (c) government; and (d) capacity to enter into relations with the other states.

Before delving into a discussion of the Montevideo criteria for statehood, it is important to deal briefly with the meaning of 'State' in international law.

The meaning of 'State' under international law

It should be noted that when we speak of 'a State' in international law, we do not refer to the component units of a country or federating States. According to Article 1(2) of the

Montevideo Convention, for example, 'the federal state shall constitute a sole person in the eyes of international law'.

When used to refer to a country, the term 'State' can be used in two different senses, depending on the constitutional arrangement of the country. First, 'State' may refer to countries such as the UK, the USA, Australia, Ghana, Nigeria, Tonga, Indonesia, etc. Thus, 'State', used in this sense, refers to the single entity otherwise known as a country.

However, within such 'States', as mentioned above, it is possible to have 'lesser' entities also referred to as States. For example, the USA and Nigeria operate a constitutional arrangement known as 'federalism', which entails the sharing of governmental powers between a central authority and component federating units. Under a federal constitutional arrangement, the central, or federal, government, which usually sits in the capital (Washington DC in the USA; Abuja in Nigeria), exercises governmental powers over all items assigned to it under the constitution, which may cover issues such as currency, defence, foreign affairs, the armed forces, and so on.

The 'State' that is referred to in the Montevideo Convention is the *federal unit*, such as the USA, Nigeria, Tonga, the UK, and Ghana, not the federating States or component units, even if the former usually exercise power from capitals such as Washington DC, Abuja, Nuku'alofa, London, and Accra, which are also component units of the State.

The criteria for statehood contained in the Montevideo Convention provide important guidelines for identifying entities that may be considered subjects of international law and, as we will see later in this chapter, provide States with some of the guidelines for State recognition. We will discuss these criteria in the following sections.

KEY POINT The Montevideo Convention does not apply to component or federating units, such as New York or Abuja, which make up a country. Countries are represented on the international plane by the central or federal unit, not their individual component units, which may also be called States.

A permanent population

For an entity to be regarded as a State in international law, it must have a permanent population. Two things are implied in this criterion: 'population' and 'permanence'. A State's population can be enormous and run into several millions, a billion, or even more, as with China and India, or it may consist of a few thousand, as with Nauru, which, at independence in 1968 when it became a State, had only 8,042 inhabitants.

By 'permanent population', it does not mean that a State's population must be non-transitory or non-migratory, or rooted in a specific space within that State forever; rather, the term implies that the organic population of a State must be distinguishable, by virtue of its identity, culture, and customs, from other peoples who may be present in the State, such as foreigners. Thus a State cannot solely be composed of foreigners. This criterion therefore requires the existence of a core people who belong permanently to that State in terms of citizenship or nationality.

Therefore, a State may consist of *fixed* and *nomadic* populations. The Fulanis, an ethnic group found mostly in West and Central Africa (Nigeria, Niger, and Chad) have nomadic tribes among them. These people move from one part of their country to another mainly for commercial purposes: they are pastoralists, and the need to graze their cattle all year round requires that they move and make temporary homes wherever they find enough grazing land and water. Often, nomads move across two or more countries, as is the case with the Fulanis. Nevertheless, wherever these people may move to, and no matter how frequent their movement might be, they are part of the permanent population of their country of origin and are not excluded by the criterion of permanence in the Montevideo Convention, because their *belonging* can usually be traced to their country of citizenship.

● *Case concerning Western Sahara Advisory Opinion* (1975) Icj Rep 12 (The *Western Sahara Case*)

The Court affirmed that nomads could constitute a population. In relation to the people of Sahara, who were mostly nomads, the Court noted (at 63–64), that:

> the tribes, in their migrations, had grazing pastures, cultivated lands, and wells or water-holes in both territories, and their burial grounds in one or other territory. These basic elements of the nomads' way of life, as stated earlier in this Opinion, were in some measure the subject of tribal rights, and their use was in general regulated by customs . . . the nomadic peoples of the Shinguitti country should, in the view of the Court, be considered as having in the relevant period possessed rights, including some rights relating to the lands through which they migrated.

How many people may form a State?

There is no requirement in the Montevideo Convention for any given number as the absolute minimum for the purpose of forming a State. Thus, in theory, any number of people can form a State, insofar as all other requisite conditions of the Convention are met by the entity claiming statehood.

self-determination
The ability of a people to govern themselves, a process that must be preceded by the people being able to form an independent State.

In 1974, the UN Committee 24 conducted an inquiry into the issue of **self-determination**. The Committee Report (UN Doc. A/9623/Add 5, 1974, Part III, pp. 6–7) revealed that the United Nations was concerned about the small size of the populations of the non-self-governing States when it considered their quest for self-determination. However, it seems that the UN is not as concerned today about the size of populations seeking to form States as it was before.

In the *Report of the Special Committee with Regard to the Implementation of the Declaration on the Granting of Independence to Colonial and People* (General Assembly, Official Records Sixty-First Session Supplement No. 23, A/61/23, 2006), the UN Committee 24 said, in relation to Anguilla, Bermuda, the British Virgin Islands, the Cayman Islands, Guam, Montserrat, Pitcairn, Saint Helena, the Turks and Caicos Islands, and the United States Virgin Islands, that it:

> will continue to pay attention to the specific problems of the remaining Non-Self-Governing Territories . . . without any prejudice to territorial size, geographical location, size of population or natural resources . . .

It is clear from this statement that the smallness of a people's population may not prevent their transition to statehood under international law, despite this undoubtedly making such a State more vulnerable to a number of uncertainties. What seems to be paramount is that the people comply with the relevant provisions of the UN Charter, in addition to the specific requirements of the Montevideo Convention.

thinking points

- *Explain what a 'permanent population' means under the Montevideo Convention.*
- *How relevant is the size of the population of an entity in order for it to qualify as a State?*
- *Do you think that a country composed only of nomadic people can be said to have a permanent population under the Montevideo Convention?*

A defined territory

The Montevideo Convention also requires a defined territory for the existence of a State, recognizable as such under international law. But what does a 'defined territory' mean? Does it mean that the territory of the aspiring entity (or 'putative State', as the entity aiming to become a State is often called) must have all of its frontiers or boundaries totally settled, so that no aspects of such territory are subject to controversy or litigation by the time of its becoming a State?

A territory is, amongst other things, a geographical expression that refers to a space, whether solid land, terrestrial, or marine. The vast land of the Sahara desert is as much a territory, in the sense of space, as the Atlantic ocean. Thus, in addition to its physical land asset, a State claims as its territory its waters and airspace. Therefore, in speaking about a 'defined territory' as a requirement of statehood, we mean the land, sea, and airspace of a State, over which the State possesses and exercises control.

However, what composes a territory does not answer the question of what a 'defined territory' means, for the purpose of statehood. A 'defined territory' means a territory that is reasonably ascertainable. It simply means that it should be possible that if they were to be asked where the territory of the State lies, those of its citizens who desire self-determination would be able to respond: 'From this pillar to this pole—although we are still uncertain about how far deep in or spread out our territory goes vis-à-vis our neighbours.'

In the *Official Records of the 385th Meeting of the UN Security Council* (UN Doc. S/PV.385, 17 November 1948) related to the admission of Israel to the membership of the United Nations, Mr El-Khouri, the Syrian delegate to the UN, made some interesting observations concerning Israel becoming a State, with regard to the requirement of a defined territory. He noted that, for there to be a State, 'the first qualification is that it should have a defined territory which is not *contested* by other States'.

In the *Official Records of the 383th Meeting of the UN Security Council* (UN Doc. S/PV.383, 2 December 1948), on the same subject, Phillip Jessup, a member of the US delegation to the UN, stated that:

> the reason for the rule that one of the necessary attributes of a state is that it shall possess territory is that one cannot contemplate a state as a kind of disembodied spirit.

In order to be a 'defined territory', it is not necessary that all of the frontiers of the aspiring State are free from controversy. Most of the Israeli territory was bitterly contested by its Arab neighbours at the time it became a State in 1948.

• **Federal Republic of Germany v. Denmark; Federal Republic of Germany v. Netherlands** (1969) ICJ REP 3 (The **North Sea Continental Shelf Cases**)

In this case, the ICJ said (at 33) that:

> there is for instance no rule that the land frontiers of a State must be fully delimited and defined, and often in various places and for long periods they are not, as is shown by the case of the entry of Albania into the League of Nations.

The ICJ had cited the opinion of the Permanent Court of International Justice (PCIJ) in *Monastery of Saint-Naoum Advisory Opinion* (1924) PCIJ Ser. B, No. 9, in coming to this conclusion.

• **Deutsche Continental Gas-Gesellschaft v. Polish State** (1929–30) 5 AD 11

In this case, it was said also that what was important was not so much evidence of a fully defined territory, but rather that:

> in order to say that a state exists and can be recognised as such…it is enough that… [its] territory has a sufficient consistency, even though its boundaries have not yet been accurately delimited.

However, an artificial creation will not constitute a defined territory under the Montevideo Convention.

• **Re Duchy of Sealand** (1978) 80 ILR 683

In this case, an island, the Duchy of Sealand, was originally erected as an anti-aircraft platform used by the UK. The platform was erected eight miles outside the UK territorial waters, but was attached to the seabed by concrete pillars. The UK abandoned the platform after the Second World War, but it became occupied in 1967 by a former British Army officer, who proclaimed the establishment of the Duchy. The plaintiff, who held the title of Foreign Secretary and President of the State Council of the so-called Duchy of Sealand, brought an action for a declaration that, as one of 106 persons who had acquired the citizenship of the 'Duchy', he had lost his citizenship of the Federal Republic of Germany.

The German Bundesverwaltungsgericht (Federal Administrative Court) found that the case was admissible, but unfounded. The court said (at 685) that:

> international law required three essential attributes for Statehood. The State must have a territory, a people and a government. At least two of these requirements were absent in the case of the 'Duchy'. Territory must consist in a natural segment of the earth's surface. *An artificial island, albeit connected to the earth's surface, did not satisfy this criterion.* Whilst size was irrelevant, in order to constitute a people the group of persons in question must form a cohesive vibrant community. An association whose common purpose covered merely commercial and tax affairs was insufficient. [Emphasis added]

KEY POINTS

• A defined territory does not imply that the frontiers of an entity aspiring to become a State should be free from dispute or controversy. All that matters is that there is an ascertainable territory.

- For the purpose of statehood, the size of a territory is irrelevant.

- An artificial creation will not suffice to satisfy the requirement of a 'defined territory' under the Montevideo Convention (see *Duchy of Sealand*).

Government

An aspiring State must also have a sovereign government. This is a very important requirement because it is only when a people are self-governing that they can be said to constitute a State under international law.

However, the Montevideo Convention does not specify any particular type of government for the purpose of statehood. While most States today desire to have democratic governments, 'democracy' is not a requirement of statehood under international law. Thus, the Kingdom of Saudi Arabia is considered a State, despite the fact that its leaders are not chosen in a popular election and are not subject to periodic elections as common in democracies. Also, States ruled by military juntas are nonetheless States in international law. What is critical is that these States have fully functional governments.

· ·

● *Case concerning Western Sahara Advisory Opinion* [1975] ICJ REP 12 [The *Western Sahara Case*]

The ICJ stated (at 43–44) that:

> No rule of international law, in the view of the Court, requires the structure of a State to follow any particular pattern, as is evident from the diversity of forms of State found in the world today.

Moreover, the occurrence of frequent coups d'état, or revolutions, does not affect statehood in the eyes of international law.

· ·

● *Italy v. Venezuela* [1903] RIAA VOL. X 499 [The *Sambaggio Claim*]

In a dispute between Italy and Venezuela over the rights of Italian nationals resident in the latter, Italy asked the arbitrator to regard Venezuela as a lesser State in international law, given the fact that it has suffered many revolutions and that it was generally characterized by ill governance.

The arbitrator rejected the Italian argument (at 523–524).

For the purpose of statehood, a government does not have to operate from within its State. Circumstances do sometimes compel governments to operate from exile.

example

In 1990, the government of the Kuwaiti State fled into exile in Saudi Arabia and ruled from there, following the Iraqi attack on Kuwait.
  Similarly, the Tejan Kabbah-led government in Sierra Leone fled into exile in Guinea in 1997 after its overthrow by a military junta.

However, regardless of where it operates from, the government must be effective, legitimate, and, more importantly, independent. It is only when a government can exercise total control over its territory that it can be said truly to be a government in the language of the Montevideo Convention.

However, a State does not lose its statehood just because it relies on another financially, or because it seeks financial aid from other States to bail it out of trouble. In modern society, States, no matter how economically buoyant, must interact with other States and will sometimes require the assistance of other States or international institutions. Following the global economic crisis of 2007–8, several European States, such as Greece, Portugal, and Ireland, had to fall back on financial bailouts from such bodies as the International Monetary Fund (IMF) and help from individual States.

In *International Law: A South African Perspective* (3rd edn, Cape Town: Juta and Co. Ltd, 2006), John Duggard argues, at p. 84, that:

> The fact that a government receives substantial financial aid from another state would not in itself appear to affect its formal independence. This fact, together with other indication of dependence, however, may provide evidence of a lack of independence. This is one of the reasons given by the UK for its refusal to recognize Bophuthatswana.

KEY POINTS

- There are no prescribed forms of government for the purpose of the Montevideo Convention.

- The fact that a State is subject to frequent revolutions does not make it a lesser State under international law.

- Dependence on other States for financial or other support does not necessarily affect statehood.

Having considered the criteria for statehood under the Montevideo Convention, it is important to examine other features and capacities that have been useful in determining the existence of statehood under international law.

Capacity to enter into relations with other States

The capacity of a State to enter into relations with other States is one of the most important features of statehood and, in many respects, it distinguishes a State from other subjects of international law, such as individual persons. The capacity to enter into foreign relations with other States is the strongest certification of State sovereignty.

As John Duggard (2006, see earlier in this section) observes at p. 84:

> the capacity of a state to enter into relations with other states is a consequence of independence. If an entity is subject to the authority of another state in the handling of its foreign affairs, it fails to meet this requirement and cannot be described as an independent state.

● *Netherlands v. United States* [1928] 2 RIAA 829 [The *Island of Palmas Arbitration*]

The USA and the Netherlands disputed the ownership of the Island of Palmas in the East Indies. The Permanent Court of Arbitration (PCA) said (at 839) that:

> Sovereignty in the relations between States *signifies independence*. Independence in regard to a portion of the globe *is the right to exercise therein, to the exclusion of any other State, the functions of a State*. The

development of the national organisation of States during the last few centuries and, as a corollary, the development of international law, have established this principle of the exclusive competence of the State in regard to its own territory in such a way as to make it the point of departure in settling most questions that concern international relations. [Emphasis added]

As noted by Hersch Lauterpacht, *International Law: Collected Papers* (Cambridge: Cambridge University Press, 1975), at p. 487:

> The first condition of statehood is that there must exist a government actually independent of that of any other state ... If a community, after having detached itself from the parent state, were to become, legally or actually, a satellite of another, it would not be fulfilling the primary conditions of independence and would not accordingly be entitled to recognition as a state.

States have the capacity to enter into diverse relations with other States and, by necessary implication, other subjects of international law. A State is able therefore to conduct commercial business with other entities, to conclude treaties, to exchange diplomats, and to adjudicate its matters before international fora with other subjects of international law. The scope of relations that a State has capacity to enter into vis-à-vis other States is indeed wide, which is why States continue to occupy the position as the primary subjects of international law.

4.3.2 Are the Montevideo criteria exhaustive?

It is doubtful that the criteria listed in this Article are meant to be exhaustive. From the ordinary reading of Article 1, that the State as a person 'should possess the following qualifications ...', it is highly unlikely that the intention here was to set these criteria in stone. Drafters of international legal treaties have customarily adopted the imperative 'shall' whenever they intend a set of conditions to be final and exhaustive.

It seems more appropriate to view the Montevideo criteria of statehood as mere benchmarks, or common denominators. Therefore it is possible that, in practice, other criteria may be required by international law before an entity can attain statehood, even if it meets all of the Montevideo criteria.

In 'Security Council Resolutions on Rhodesia' (1964–65) 41 BYBIL 102, Fawcett, one of the earliest proponents of the view that the Montevideo criteria are not exhaustive, stated that:

> But to the traditional criteria for the recognition of a regime as a new state must now be added the requirement that it shall not be based upon a systematic denial in its territory of certain civil and political rights, including in particular the right of every citizen to participate in the government of his country, directly or through representatives elected by regular, equal and secret suffrage. This principle was affirmed in the case of Rhodesia by the virtually unanimous condemnation of the unilateral declaration of independence by the world community, and by universal withholding of recognition of the new regime which was a consequence.

While this is an interesting view, we must be cautious in accepting it as an article of faith. In the South Rhodesia (now Zimbabwe) situation referred to in the above quote, the entity was still under the colonial administration of Britain when a white minority in South Rhodesia unilaterally declared its independence from Britain. Thus the question of accepting the statehood of South Rhodesia was inseparably bound with the issue of recognizing the new government.

Looking at the example of apartheid South Africa, it is clear that a State may not fail the test of statehood simply because its government is based on morally indefensible practices, such as violation of human rights and exclusion from political participation (as in South Rhodesia) or on a formal policy of racial segregation (as in South Africa). At best, the government of such a State might suffer non-recognition, as happened with South Africa, which is a separate and distinct matter from recognition of statehood per se, to be discussed later in this chapter.

A good example of situations in which such 'new requirements' of statehood, as were proposed by Fawcett, were applied to deny statehood was in the European zone after the collapse of Yugoslavia, as seen in the following section.

4.3.3 The European Union, the Badinter Arbitration Committee, and the Montevideo Convention: an example of the flexible interpretation of statehood criteria

Following the collapse of the Socialist Federal Republic of Yugoslavia (SFRY) in the 1990s, the then European Community (EC) set up an Arbitration Commission of the Conference on Yugoslavia, on 27 August 1991, headed by Robert Badinter, then President of the French Constitutional Council, to advise the EC on legal issues arising from the break-up of the SFRY. On 16 December 1991, EC members adopted a set of guidelines that would apply to entities wishing to be recognized as States by the Community.

In its Declaration on the Guidelines on the Recognition of New States in Eastern Europe and in the Soviet Union of 16 December 1991, the EC listed the following new conditions that must be fulfilled by new States from Eastern Europe and the former Soviet Republic:

- respect for the provisions of the UN Charter and the commitments subscribed to in the Final Act of Helsinki and in the Charter of Paris, especially with regard to the rule of law, democracy, and human rights;

- guarantees for the rights of ethnic and national groups and minorities in accordance with the commitments subscribed to in the framework of the Commission on Security and Cooperation in Europe (the Helsinki Commission, or the CSCE);

- respect for the inviolability of all frontiers, which can only be changed by peaceful means and by common agreement;

- acceptance of all relevant commitments with regard to disarmament and nuclear non-proliferation, as well as to security and regional stability; and

- commitment to settle by agreement, including where appropriate by recourse to arbitration, all questions concerning State succession and regional disputes.

Several members of the collapsed SFRY applied for their statehood to be recognized by the Community. In its Opinions 4, 5, and 6 on the applications by Bosnia and Herzegovina, Croatia, and Macedonia, respectively, the Commission:

- decided that Bosnia and Herzegovina should not be recognized at the time, because it had not yet held a referendum on independence;

- decided that Croatia's independence should not be recognized, because the new Croatian Constitution did not incorporate the protections for minorities required, which prompted the Croatian President to write to Robert Badinter, giving assurances that this deficit would be remedied, after which Croatia was accordingly recognized; and

- recommended that the EC accept the request of Macedonia, because it had given the necessary guarantees that it would respect human rights, and international peace and security.

The above example is particularly interesting, because none of the new conditions adopted are provided for in the Montevideo Convention. Also, some of the concerned States had already been recognized by other States at the time: Germany unilaterally recognized Croatia in 1991, for example, whereas the EC did not do so until January 1992. (Note that there are theories governing the relationship between recognition and statehood, which will be discussed later.)

The European situation provides a perfect example of the application of the Fawcett requirements. Whereas the States concerned were previously members of a confederation of the SFRY, they were independent States at the time of disintegration and met all of the criteria of Montevideo. Consequently, as far as the formal criteria were concerned, they were bona fide States in international law, and the Badinter Arbitration Committee recognized this fact.

Some writers have argued that the new conditions for the recognition of States proposed by Fawcett (1964–65, see section 4.3.2) and adopted by the EC in 1991 were not intended to have any more effect than to regulate diplomatic relations among member States (see, for example, Marc Weller, 'The international response to the dissolution of the Socialist Federal Republic of Yugoslavia' (1992) 86 AJIL 569, 588 and 604). Nonetheless, the manner in which the (now) European Union (EU) has applied the conditions so far, as seen in those cases that we have considered previously, demonstrates that the conditions form the basis upon which the EC bestowed the status on Croatia, Macedonia, and Bosnia and Herzegovina of States within the Community. All of these States already met the Montevideo criteria before they were asked to fulfil the additional conditions.

Since the concerned States were already recognized by the EC before they joined the United Nations, it is impossible to determine whether the UN would have accepted their application for membership if they had applied *prior* to their recognition by the Community. Nevertheless, it seems unlikely that the UN would have declined the application of any of these States on the basis that they had not fulfilled the EC criteria for recognizing States, although they had met the Montevideo criteria. It is possible that the States in question did consider that their application to the UN would have a greater chance of success if they were first recognized by the EC, many members of which hold very powerful positions in the UN, such as France, Russia, and the UK, all which are permanent members of the UN Security Council.

The safe conclusion to reach on this issue is that whereas the Montevideo Convention established the general criteria for statehood, it does not preclude entities such as regional organizations from adding conditions that embody values shared by their member States as new requirements for admitting new States into their membership. But, so far, the UN as a universal organization has not denied statehood to a State that has met the Montevideo criteria, but not the new requirements. Until the UN does this, the new requirements proposed by Fawcett (1964–65, see section 4.3.2) and applied by the then EC should be regarded purely as complementary to the Montevideo criteria.

It is important to mention briefly the unilateral declarations of independence by such entities as Somaliland (1991), Abkhazia (2008), and Kosovo (2008). These three entities were parts of independent States of Somalia, Georgia, and Serbia and Montenegro prior to the outbreak of civil war or armed conflicts in those countries. While Abkhazia is recognized by only a handful of States—Russia, Venezuela, Nicaragua, and Nauru—no single State recognizes Somaliland. Also, neither the UN nor the ICJ has pronounced yet on the two cases.

However, the situation is different with Kosovo.

. . . .

● *Accordance with International Law of the Unilateral Declaration of Independence in Respect of Kosovo, Advisory Opinion* (2010) ICJ REP 403 (The *Kosovo Case*)

Following Kosovo's unilateral declaration in 2008, Serbia and Montenegro, the State of which Kosovo formed part until then, decided to challenge the validity of Kosovo's independence before the ICJ.

The question before the Court was whether the unilateral declaration of independence by Kosovo was in accordance with international law. The Court said (at [84]) that the 'declaration of independence of 17 February 2008 did not violate general international law'.

It is difficult to draw any hard conclusions from the Court's judgment in the *Kosovo Case*. The Court did not go into whether Kosovo met the criteria of statehood, because this was not part of the question asked to it. The main relevance of the Court's judgment in *Kosovo* from our perspective is that it ruled that unilateral declarations of independence are not prohibited by international law. This is crucial because the capacity to enter into legal relations is a consequence of independence; hence, whether a State acquires its independence legally or illegally has a direct impact on its capacity to enter into relations with other States.

thinking points

- *Explain the difference between the criteria of statehood under the Montevideo Convention and the EU requirements.*
- *What forms of government satisfy the third requirement of the Montevideo Convention on statehood?*
- *What are 'artificial islands' and why are they not regarded as territory for the purpose of statehood?*

4.4 Lesser States and special territories

Apart from fully fledged States (independent States), which are covered by the Montevideo Convention, there are certain entities that, although they look like States and enjoy a special status under international law, are not international law subjects within the meaning of the Montevideo Convention. They cannot apply to be recognized as States; nor can they enjoy the rights and privileges available to States under the Montevideo Convention. Such lesser States include condominiums, the Holy See and the Vatican City, free cities, colonies, protected States, and protectorates.

4.4.1 Condominiums

A 'condominium' exists where two or more States jointly exercise political power over an entity, usually through the agencies of local administrations. A good example of a condominium is the New Hebrides, a group of islands in the South Pacific established in 1902 by Britain and France. The condominium was under Anglo-French administration until both States agreed to grant its independence; it became the sovereign State of Vanuatu in 1980. Some of the regular features of condominiums include the use of multiple languages by its inhabitants (each State usually administers its section of the condominium in its own language), and the fact that administrations consist of foreign and local personnel.

4.4.2 Free cities

A 'free city' exists where an entity is virtually a State under international law except that it lacks sovereignty (or independence), which, as we recall from earlier, is the most important criterion of statehood. Free cities have fixed territories, populations, and some autonomy.

. . . .

● *Free City of Danzig and the International Labour Organization (ILO) Advisory Opinion* (1930) PCIJ Ser. B, No. 18

The Free City of Danzig is a semi-autonomous entity created in 1920 under the 1919 Treaty of Versailles. Historically, Danzig was part of the German Empire. Following the First World War, the League of Nations ordered that Danzig be separated from Germany and Poland. At the outbreak of the Second World War, the Free City of Danzig decided to join Germany (which had invaded Poland). However, following the invasion of Germany by the Soviets in 1945, Danzig was put under Polish administration by the Allied States under the Potsdam Agreement, where it remained until 1990, when it was fully assimilated into Poland following the unification of Germany.

The question before the PCIJ was whether the Free City of Danzig could join the ILO. Commenting on the issue of capacity to enter into relations with States, the PCIJ stated (at 13) that:

> It is now common ground between Poland and the Free City that the rights of Poland as regards the conduct of the foreign relations of the Free City are not absolute. The Polish Government is not entitled to impose a policy on the Free City nor to take any step in connection with the foreign relations of the Free City, against its will. On the other hand, the Free City cannot call upon Poland to take any step in connection with the foreign relations of the Free City which are opposed to her own policy … The result is that, as regards the foreign relations of the Free City, neither Poland nor the Free City are completely masters of the situation …

Clearly, the fact that the Free City of Danzig was not completely responsible for the conduct of its foreign relations, even if it had a considerable say in this, means that it was not a State under the Montevideo Convention.

4.4.3 International territories, mandates, and trusteeships

An 'international territory' exists where an entity remains part of a bona fide State, but also enjoys special protection under international law. For example, between 1924 and 1939, the Memel Territory enjoyed a special status under international law even though, at this time, it formed part of Lithuania. Often, such a territory will be administered directly by an international organization under an arrangement called a 'trusteeship', as was the case with the City of Jerusalem under the mandate of the League of Nations, although the agreement was itself never implemented. After the First World War, the League established a series of 'mandates' whereby certain territories that were formerly under the control of Germany were taken away and entrusted to the care of other Allied Powers to administer on behalf of the international community represented by the League of Nations. Upon the dissolution of the League, all remaining mandate territories were placed under the trusteeship of the United Nations. The only exception was South West Africa (Namibia), which, as we will recall from the *South West Africa Cases* discussed in earlier chapters, remained under South African authority in defiance of the UN Security Council resolution, until it obtained its independence in 1990.

There are, therefore, no more *trust* territories, and because the UN Charter recognizes the equality and sovereignty of States, placing a State under a trust to prepare it for independence is no longer an acceptable practice in modern international law and relations. However, there are *international* territories, which are territories administered by an international organization on behalf of the international community, in order to prepare the entity for independence. Recent examples include the United Nations' transitional administration in Cambodia (UNTAC) and the transitional administration in East Timor. Still, there remain controversies as to the legality of the exercise of such capacity by the United Nations.

4.4.4 Colonies and protectorates

One of the black spots of international relations was the practice by which powerful States subjugate the will of weak States and entities, under various pretexts, in the name of 'civilizing' them. An extreme form of this dominion is what was widely called 'colonialism'. A colonial power used persuasion or brutal force to subjugate the territory that it wished to colonize, and subsequently administered it either entirely by itself and its people, or through a system that featured personnel of the colonial territory.

The end product of colonialism is the obtaining of the status of independence by the colonized peoples, usually through political campaign, sometimes backed by insurgency. On rare occasions, independence resulted from negotiations between the colonial power and the colonized peoples, derogatorily referred to as 'natives'.

A 'protectorate' exists where a territory is protected by a military power in return for obligations imposed upon the protected territory, and where the protector exercises foreign relations on behalf of the protectorate. An example of a British protectorate in Africa was the Protectorate of Southern Nigeria, which was extremely crucial to the British, because it was a coastal entity with considerable wealth, such as rubber, which was often a subject of dispute between the UK and other entities (see HC Deb, 3 September 1895, vol. 36, col. 1549).

KEY POINTS

- Condominiums, mandates, and international territories enjoy a special status under international law, but are not States within the meaning of the Montevideo Convention and are usually referred to as 'lesser States'.

- Although lesser States meet certain Montevideo criteria (such as territory and population), they often lack political sovereignty or independence and hence cannot be regarded as bona fide States under the Convention.

International organizations

As subjects of international law, international organizations are a special breed. They are established by States, and usually are as powerful and relevant as the establishing States wish them to be. The general principle is that an international organization cannot be more powerful than the States that establish it. However, this principle is now of limited usage considering the development of a special class of international organizations generally referred to as 'supranational organizations'. These bodies often have considerable powers vis-à-vis the States that establish them and have a special status under international law.

As will be recalled from the discussion of cases such as Reparation for Injuries (see section 4.2), issues concerning the status of international organizations as subjects of international law include whether they have distinct rights, enjoy immunities, and so on.

Individuals

We noted at the beginning of this chapter that international law traditionally applied to States. Consequently, States have zealously asserted their sovereignty over matters within their domestic jurisdiction and have shielded such from the reach of international law. Most especially, States have exclusively applied their laws to their citizens, and to everyone else present within their territory. However, between the First and the Second World Wars, the international community began contemplating the possibility of applying international law to individuals, and making human beings subjects of international law in certain respects.

● **Case Concerning Jurisdiction of the Courts in Danzig Advisory Opinion** [1928] PCIJ SER. B, No. 15

The advisory opinion of the PCIJ was requested as to whether an international agreement between Poland and the Free City of Danzig (Beamtenabkommen):

> form part of series of provisions governing the legal relationship between the Polish Railways Administration and the Danzig officials.

Although the Court stated that, according to a well-established principle of international law, an international agreement cannot create rights and obligations for private individuals, it emphasized (at 17) that:

> It cannot be disputed that the very object of an international agreement, according to the intention of the contracting Parties, may be the adoption by the Parties of some definite rules creating

> individual rights and obligations and enforceable by the national court. That there is such an intention in the present case can be established by reference to the terms of the *Beamtenabkommen*.

Obviously, the Court in this case had contemplated the possibility of a treaty creating an exception to the general rule that international agreements do not apply to individuals. It must be noted, however, that this exception is not one that can merely be inferred from the conduct of the parties; rather, an agreement to apply international law to individuals must specifically be provided for by the treaty between the parties—one that provides that the terms of the agreement apply to individuals.

Since the bold step undertaken by the PCIJ in the *Danzig Case*, international law has developed more assertively towards regarding the individual as a subject, although this first started in the area of international criminal law, before spreading into human rights. For example, the charter and the judgment of the Nuremberg Tribunal (which tried the Nazi officials and their collaborators) made it very clear that individuals could be held responsible for *international* crimes. In its judgment, the Nuremberg Tribunal explicitly recognized that individuals could be punished for violations of international law. (See Chapter 16.)

In US Office of Chief of Counsel for the Prosecution of Axis Criminality, *Nazi Conspiracy and Aggression: Opinion and Judgment* (Washington DC: US GPO, 1947), p. 53, the Nuremberg Tribunal is reported as stating that:

> crimes against international law are committed by men, not by abstract entities, and only by punishing individuals who commit such crimes can the provisions of international law be enforced.

Article 3 of the Draft Code of Crimes against the Peace and Security of Mankind (1996) 2 ILCYB 13, 22, states that:

> An individual who is responsible for a crime against the peace and security of mankind shall be liable to punishment. The punishment shall be commensurate with the character and gravity of the crime.

The foundation laid by the Nuremberg trials was consolidated when, following a brutal war in the Balkans in 1993 and genocide in Rwanda in 1994, the UN Security Council established the International Criminal Tribunal for the Former Yugoslavia (ICTY) and the International Criminal Tribunal for Rwanda (ICTR). As will be seen later, in Chapter 16 dealing with international criminal law, the adoption in 1998 of the Rome Statute establishing the International Criminal Court (ICC) and the entry into force of the ICC Statute in 2002 crystallized the criminal responsibility of individuals under international law.

Since the 1948 Universal Declaration of Human Rights (UDHR), human rights have transformed from a system that applied only to States and imposed on them the obligation to protect the civil liberties of their citizens to one that now empowers individuals, in their capacity as human beings, to bring claims against States. Although not every human rights instrument provides for individual enforcement of human rights, notable groundbreakers include:

- the Eleventh Protocol to the 1950 European Convention on Human Rights (ECHR), adopted in 1998, changed the basis for individual applications under the Convention from an optional one - in which an applicant's State must permit the application under Article 25 of the Convention - to a mandatory one under the new Article 34.

- the Inter-American Commission on Human Rights, established on the basis of the 1948 Charter of the Organization of American States (OAS) (see Articles 26 and 32–41 of the Commission's Regulations);
- the 1948 American Declaration of the Rights and Duties of Man (see Articles 44–47);
- the 1969 American Convention on Human Rights; and
- the 2008 Protocol on the Statute of the African Court of Justice and Human Rights.

Article 44 of the 1969 American Convention on Human Rights states that:

> Any person or group of persons, or any nongovernmental entity legally recognized in one or more member states of the Organization, may lodge petitions with the Commission containing denunciations or complaints of violation of this Convention by a State Party.

● *Karen Atala Riffo v. Chile* Case No. P-1271-04 (2010), Inter-American Commission on Human Rights (The *Atala Case*)

In this case, the Commission ruled in favour of a Chilean lesbian mother in a case concerning the custody of her children, following a divorce from her husband. Although Karen Atala had retained the custody of her three children upon divorce on the basis of a mutual agreement with her ex-husband, the latter brought an action for custody upon discovering that Atala was a lesbian. In this high-profile case, the Chilean Supreme Court stripped Atala of her right to custody, prompting her to seek vindication before the Commission.

On 17 April 2010, the Commission ruled in favour of Atala and pronounced that she was entitled to live free from discrimination. The Commission stated that discrimination against a parent in a child-custody dispute because of his or her sexual orientation violates the American Convention on Human Rights.

What is important about the *Atala Case* is that it was the first time the Commission had reviewed a gay rights case, overruling a supreme court in the process and firmly establishing the right of individuals in international law.

Article 30(f) of the Statute of the African Court of Justice and Human Rights lists as entities that may also bring a case to the African Court:

> Individuals or relevant Non-Governmental Organizations accredited to the African Union or to its organs, subject to the provisions of Article 8 of the Protocol.

thinking points

- *To what extent can an individual be a subject of international law?*
- *Is there any difference between individuals and States as subjects of international law?*
- *Define an 'international organization'.*

Having considered the subjects of international law, we now turn to discuss recognition. This is a very important topic that, as we will see, forms the other side of the subject of international law, in that whereas criteria of statehood tell us how States emerge, recognition show us how already existing States deal with *new* States and governments.

4.7 The recognition of States and governments

4.7.1 The rationale for recognition

A State may exist legally because it meets all of the criteria of the Montevideo Convention, but that does not mean other States accept its existence or want to have any relationship with it. A State may physically exist but if other States do not recognize its government, certain fundamental consequences will follow as regards its relations with other States. Recognition applies not only to States, but also to governments, so that a new State would have to be recognized by other States in order for them to deal with it, and a new government—particularly one that comes into power by unconstitutional means—would have to be recognized by other States for it to deal with them. Even democratically elected governments may be refused recognition, as was the case with the popular election of Hamas in the parliamentary elections of the Palestinian territories, which the US government refused to recognize.

With regard to the recognition of States, a new State may emerge by breaking away from an old State (Eritrea from Ethiopia), or through the dissolution of a former State (the former Soviet Union). Recognition of government is usually, but not always, necessary when a new government assumes power in a country by unconstitutional means (for example, by coup d'état). In any of these situations, it may be necessary for States to grant or withhold recognition from the new State or government.

Recognition is a rather difficult subject because, as noted by Nkambo Murgewa, 'Subjects of international law' in M. Sørensen (ed.), *Manual of Public International Law* (London: Macmillan, 1968), at p. 267:

> Recognition, or the withholding of recognition, is often used as a political instrument to express approval or disapproval of a new state or government or a territorial change. The opinions expressed on behalf of a new state or government as to the legal nature and effects of recognition are therefore not devoid of ambiguity, and international legal doctrine is divided on certain central issues.

4.7.2 The recognition of States

The existence of a State as a subject of international law is complete upon fulfilling the legal criteria contained in the Montevideo Convention, but the political acknowledgement of the existence of a State is a question of recognition.

In the *Dictionnaire de la Terminologie du Droit International* (Paris: Sirey, 1960), pp. 509 and 511, the recognition of a new State is defined as:

> a unilateral act by which one or more states declare, or tacitly admit, that they consider a political unit which exists in fact and considers itself to be a state, as a state having the rights and duties which flow from statehood.

See also Murgewa (1968, section 4.7.1), at p. 267.

thinking point
What is the rationale for recognition?

133

The effects of recognition

Article 3 of the Montevideo Convention states that:

> The political existence of the state is independent of recognition by the other states. Even before recognition the state has the right to defend its integrity and independence, to provide for its conservation and prosperity, and consequently to organize itself as it sees fit, to legislate upon its interests, administer its services, and to define the jurisdiction and competence of its courts.
>
> The exercise of these rights has no other limitation than the exercise of the rights of other states according to international law.

A similar provision is found in Article 9 of the OAS Charter, adopted in Bogotá in 1948.

When dealing with recognition of States, the important issue to consider is not whether a State has attained statehood—this is a question solely for international law to decide—but whether the rights and obligation of a new State depend on its recognition by others. In other words, is recognition a mere political act, as denoted by the Article 3 provision in the previous extract, or a legal requirement, so that legal consequences arise from non-recognition?

International law attempts to answer this question by postulating two theories of the effects of recognition: the declaratory theory and the constitutive theory.

The declaratory theory

Under the 'declaratory' theory, the recognition of one State by another is a mere political act that does not confirm the statehood of the recognized State. In other words, recognition is legally inconsequential and is merely a political gesture. Thus a State becomes a State upon fulfilling the Montevideo criteria. If another State later declares that it recognizes that State as a State, the effect of this declaration is that the former is ready to conduct international relations with the latter. However, under the declaratory theory, the recognized State was a bona fide State before that recognition by virtue of its fulfilling the Montevideo criteria and could legally conduct business with other States. The declaratory theory holds that recognition is a mere political act by means of which a State formally signifies that it recognizes another; a declaration of recognition does not confer statehood upon a State, but merely declares the existence of an already constituted statehood.

The declaratory theory conforms to the traditional notion of statehood in international law. In classical international law, States did not require validation of their existence by others. As Pufendorf stated in *De Jure Naturae et Gentium, Bk VII* (1688), ch. 3, §9, para. 689, cited in Crawford, *The Creation of States in International Law* (2nd edn, Oxford: Oxford University Press, 2006), at p. 13:

> Just as a king owes his sovereignty and majesty to no one outside his realm, so he needs not obtain the consent and approval of other kings or states, before he may carry himself like a king and be regarded as such ... it would entail an injury for the sovereignty of such a king to be called in question by a foreigner.

Also, according to J. Saalfeld, *Handbuch des positiven Völkerrechts* (Lausanne: University of Lausanne, 1833), p. 26, cited in Crawford (2006, above), p. 13:

... in order to consider the sovereignty of a State as complete in the law of nations, there is no need for its recognition by foreign powers; though the latter may appear useful, the *de facto* existence of sovereignty is sufficient.

Explaining the basis of the declaratory theory, (Jennings and Watts, 1996, see section 4.1.1) notes, at p. 129, that:

Although in practice recognition is necessary to enable every new state to enter into official intercourse with other states, theoretically every new state becomes, according to this view, a member of the international community *ipso facto* by its rising into existence; recognition is thus viewed as purely declaratory or confirmatory in nature, supplying only the necessary evidence of the fact of a new state's existence.

KEY POINTS

- The declaratory theory proposes that recognition is merely a political act and that a State is a State once it fulfils the criteria for statehood, hence recognition only declares this state of affairs.

- The act of recognition is different from the fulfilment of criteria for statehood.

The constitutive theory

According to 'constitutive' theory, a State is a State only if it is recognized as such by existing States. This is a positivist view of international law. As we will recall from Chapter 1, the basis of positivism is that international law is founded upon State consent; hence international law *becomes* or *ceases* only with State consent. The creation of new States creates new obligations for already existing States, such as whether or not they should deal with it. Consequently, those States for which these new obligations are created must decide whether they recognize the new State or not. Hence it is only when existing States recognize the new State that the latter exists. The fact that the new State has all of the attributes required by international law and fulfils all of the Montevideo criteria is irrelevant.

Jennings and Watts, 1996, section 4.1.1, p. 129, notes that:

... it is a rule of international law that no new state has a right as against other states to be recognised by them; that no state has a duty to recognise a new state; that a new state before its recognition cannot claim any right which a member of the international community has against other members; and that it is recognition which constitutes the new state as a member of the international community.

Supporting the constitutive theory, Hersch Lauterpacht, *Recognition in International Law* (New York: AMS Press, 1978), pp. 55 *et seq*, restated in Crawford (2006, see earlier in this section), p. 20, states that:

The full international personality of rising communities ... cannot be automatic ... as its ascertainment requires the prior determination of difficult circumstance of facts and law, there must be someone to perform that task. In the absence of a preferable solution, such as the setting up of an impartial international organ to perform that function, the latter must be fulfilled by States already existing. The valid objection is not against the fact of their discharging it, but against their carrying it out as a matter of arbitrary policy as distinguished from legal policy.

The constitutive theory has been challenged. James Crawford (2006, above) noted that the argument of the constitutive theorists does not generally apply to international law. According to him (at p. 20), while the determination that the legality of a State's conduct often involves 'difficult circumstances of facts and law' (to which Lauterpacht alludes in his quote), 'it has never been suggested that the views of particular States are constitutive'. Consequently, Crawford notes that:

> If individual States were free to determine the legal status or consequences of particular situations and to do so *definitely*, international law would be reduced to a form of imperfect communications, a system of registering the assent or dissent of individual States without any prospect of resolution. Yet it is, and should be more than this—a system with the potential for resolving problems, not merely expressing them. [Emphasis added]

Jennings and Watts, 1996, see section 4.1.1, expresses a view that is midway between those who think recognition is totally irrelevant to the creation of statehood (declaratory theory) and those who posit that recognition in fact constitutes statehood (constitutive theory). He states, at p. 133, that:

> Recognition, while declaratory of an existing fact, is constitutive in its nature, *at least so far as concerns relations with the recognising states.* It marks the beginning of effective enjoyment of the international rights and duties of the recognised community. [Emphasis added]

Indeed, there have been several instances in which recognition was constitutive—that is, in which a State was only deemed to be a State, at least by the recognizing States—only after recognition has been bestowed.

example

While several States recognized the Republic of Korea (South Korea) before it joined the United Nations, only Communist countries first recognized North Korea and this did not change for a long time until after other (non-)Communist States also recognized it, despite the fact that it met all of the Montevideo criteria.

Similarly, most Western nations did not recognize the German Democratic Republic (GDR), created in 1949 by the Soviet Union following the creation of the Federal Republic of Germany (FRG) by Britain, France, and the USA. Although the latter States recognized the FRG in 1955, it was not until 1973 that Britain recognized the GDR—and that took place only following the signing of the 1972 General Relations Treaty between the FRG and the GDR. Most Western powers regarded the GDR as a dependant of the (then) Soviet Republic and therefore lacking in sovereignty, which is the foremost criterion of the Montevideo Convention.

● *International Registration of Trademark (Germany) Case* (1959) 28 ILR 82, FEDERAL SUPREME COURT OF THE FRG

A question arose whether the FRG could protect a trademark that originated in the GDR. The Federal Supreme Court of the FRG ruled that the trademark could not be protected because the GDR was not recognized by the FRG at the relevant time. The Court emphasized that non-recognition is detrimental to statehood.

The *Trademark Case* reinforces the basis of the constitutive theory: a State may exist under international law, but that does not impose an obligation on other States to recognize it. Therefore, if there is no obligation to recognize the statehood of an entity, then the non-recognizing State may disregard issues concerning the non-recognized State within its internal legal system. The decision of the FRG court might have been different had the case involved international law issues such as an incident on the high seas or a boundary dispute. In that instance, regardless of the position of the FRG regarding the statehood of the GDR, the court would have had to deal with the matter within the parameters of international law, since, in the eyes of international law, the GDR was an international legal person. This is why Jennings and Watts, 1996, see section 4.1.1, said that recognition performs some constitutive function *relative to the recognizing States*. We will say more about this later when we consider how municipal law deals with recognition.

The problems of the constitutive theory

In addition to James Crawford's critique of the constitutive theory already noted earlier, there are a few other problems concerning the theory. First, to allow the existence of a State to be dependent on recognition by other States, as the constitutive theory represents, means that a new State exists without its rights and privileges vis-à-vis those States until recognition is granted. This clearly negates the principle of equality of States in international law and renders the relevant provisions of the Montevideo Convention, which have become customary international law, somewhat useless.

Secondly, it is difficult to lay down trite rules concerning the number of States required before an entity can be recognized as a State in international law. Does a State have to be recognized by specific States, or does it need to be recognized by all, or the majority of, other States before it can be deemed to be a State? The fact that State practice does not disclose any specific rules of ascertaining the requisite number of States for the purpose of recognizing a new State makes the constitutive theory a speculative, and therefore dangerous, theory.

Thirdly, it is generally accepted that recognition is more of a political than a legal act. This explains why, for example, despite the fact that a State is not recognized, its territory cannot be appropriated by others, and non-recognizing States cannot use force against it. Thus it seems odd that a State that is, in law, a State will not be treated *fully* as such until political recognition is accorded it.

Fourthly, it is difficult to understand what motivates recognition or non-recognition of States. Recognition is subjective and mostly depends on individual States, as distinct from the collective interests of non-recognizing States. Therefore, to give to States the sacred task of according recognition to other States is to allow the collective interest to be subordinated to the whims of a few States.

. . . .

● ***Bosnia and Herzegovina v. Serbia and Montenegro*** (2007) ICJ REP 91 (***Case Concerning the Application of the Convention on the Prevention and Punishment of the Crime of Genocide***)

In this case, Al-Khasawneh, the Vice President of the Court, noted that when considering statehood there is a 'relativism inherent in the constitutive theory of recognition [which] itself prevents the drawing of any firm inferences'.

It is difficult to separate clinically the two theories from statehood. There is no doubt that the declaratory theory accords more with international law, whereas the constitutive theory underscores the political reality of statehood. State practice has not helped matters as such, because

States tend to shift either way. While we may choose to discard constitutive theory, the case of the several breakaway States from the former SFRY, which all desperately sought recognition despite having met the Montevideo criteria, seems to strengthen the constitutive theory of recognition. Certainly if these States believed, as the declaratory theorists and orthodox international law want us to believe, that recognition is merely confirmatory, then they would not have bothered so much with recognition, having met the Montevideo criteria. But they not only sought recognition, they also did so as though their very existence depended on it.

That notwithstanding, we must be careful not to equate the quest for recognition by the former SFRY States with an affirmation of the constitutive theory. The craving of those States for recognition took place within a specific context: they needed recognition by the EU, because they intended to become members of that organization. Hence it might, indeed, have been nothing more than a political calculation on their part that if they were recognized by the EU at inception, that would pave the way for joining the organization later.

thinking points

- *Explain the constitutive theory.*
- *To what extent do you think the constitutive theory differs from the declaratory theory?*
- *What are the problems of the constitutive theory?*
- *In no more than five sentences, summarize why you prefer one theory to the other.*

4.7.3 The recognition of governments

As stated previously, the recognition of States is different from the recognition of governments. Whereas the recognition of a State automatically affects the recognition of its government, the non-recognition of a government does not generally affect the recognition of a State. Thus a State can be recognized even though its government is not, but a government cannot be recognized in the absence of a recognized State.

General approaches to the recognition of governments

Generally speaking, it is possible to speak of three approaches to the recognition of governments. First is recognition based on factual circumstances of the new government, in which case an existing government recognizes a new government simply because the latter is in effective control of a State, regardless of the method through which it came to power. This approach is not generally concerned with judging the legality of a new government, although it may occasionally do so. Prior to the First World War, the UK adopted this approach, but it insisted on evidence that the new government met with popular approval by its own people. It later abandoned this requirement, but reinstated it when it refused to recognize the Albanian government in 1924.

Following a revolution in Hungary in 1956, the UK Under-Secretary of State for Foreign Affairs declared the basis of the UK's recognition of the Kadar government thus:

> Her Majesty's Government have never taken any special step to recognise the Kadar Government [but it has continued] to maintain a diplomatic mission [in Hungary] and to accept a Hungarian mission in London. Generally speaking, Her Majesty's Government's policy in the matter of recognition of governments is to face facts and acknowledge de facto a government which has

effective control of the territory within its jurisdiction, and of the inhabitants within the territory. Such de facto recognition does not constitute a judgment on the legality of the government concerned, still less does it imply approval of it.

The second approach to recognition is when a new government is subjectively approved on the basis of the legality of its ascendance to power. Thus a government that comes to power through revolutionary or other unconstitutional means may not be recognized. A perfect example of this happened between 1907 and 1923, when five Central American republics concluded a treaty that embodied the 'Tobar doctrine' through which they collectively agreed not to recognize any government that came to power through revolution 'so long as the freely elected representatives of the people have not constitutionally reorganised the country' (see (1908) 2 AJIL Supp 229; (1923) AJIL Supp 118).

However, due to the perception that this subjective approach encouraged interference by powerful States in the internal affairs of smaller States, Genaro Estrada, the Mexican Foreign Minister, proposed the 'Estrada doctrine' in 1930. Principally, this doctrine rejected recognition based on a consideration of the legality of a government and altogether rejected formal declarations of recognition of governments. In 1977 and 1980, the USA and the UK respectively ended issuing formal declarations of recognition of governments. It must be noted, however, that this does not imply that the USA abandoned applying the legality test to recognition of governments when it impliedly recognizes them.

Degree of recognition: de facto and de jure recognition

International lawyers often speak about *types* of recognition when discussing recognition of governments. They distinguish between 'de facto recognition' and 'de jure recognition', the intention being to express the degree of recognition granted by one government to another. While de facto recognition is a complete recognition of the authority of a government, de jure recognition refers to a recognition that is inchoate, usually pending the acquisition of full and effective control and powers by the government seeking recognition. There is a lot of controversy surrounding the *real* difference between both types of recognition, especially when it becomes necessary to identify the type of recognition being adopted by a particular State in practice. We can speak of a de facto government (a government that exists in fact and is in effective control of a State) or a de jure government (a government that exists in law, but is not in effective control of a State).

example

The Candoman government may choose both to recognize a new government that has just taken power through a coup d'état in Rutamu and has effective control of the country, and to deal with the overthrown democratic government of Rutamu now conducting its business in exile. Candoma may deal with the new military junta, for example, in order to protect the Candoman business interests inside Rutamu over which the new government has effective control. However, the representative of Candoma to the United Nations may still be engaged in conducting international affairs with the representative of the exiled Rutamu government, which is the only one that sits in the UN General Assembly.

In such a scenario, it is possible to speak of the varying degrees of recognition: Candoma recognizes the de facto government established by the junta for the purpose of the internal affairs of Rutamu; it recognizes the de jure authority of the government in exile for the purpose of international law.

Jennings and Watts, 1996, see section 4.1.1, notes at p. 155 that the terms de facto and de jure:

> are convenient but elliptical: the terms *de jure* or *de facto* qualify the state of government recognised rather than the act of recognition itself... The distinction between *de jure* and *de facto* is in essence that the former is the fullest kind of recognition while the latter is a lesser degree of recognition, taking account on a provisional basis of present realities. Thus *de facto* recognition takes place when, in the view of the recognising state, the new authority, although actually independent and wielding effective power in the territory under its control, has not acquired sufficient stability or does not as yet offer prospects of complying with other requirements of recognition.

● *Luther v. Sagor* [1921] 3 KB 532

In this case, Bankes LJ distinguished between de facto and de jure recognition (at 543) thus:

> A de jure government is one which in the opinion of the person using the phrase ought to possess the powers of sovereignty, though at the time it may be deprived of them. A de facto government is one which is really in possession of them, although the possession may be wrongful or precarious.

This distinction between the types of government and the types of recognition is important because States usually grant de jure recognition to the de jure government and de facto recognition to the de facto government—but the reverse may be the case, in that the de facto leader has established a very strong authority backed by legitimacy. De facto recognition usually consists in acts that are not conclusive, such as representing the State at the inauguration of another country's head, while de jure recognition includes such conclusive acts as the exchange of diplomats. The distinction between de facto and de jure governments was much stronger prior to 1980, in which year the UK formally abandoned it.

4.7.4 The recognition of States and governments under municipal law

As a matter of practice, most States make formal declarations on recognition. In the UK, the Foreign and Commonwealth Office (FCO) used to issue certificates of declaration, at the request of British courts, stating categorically whether Her Majesty's Government recognized a State or government or not, and if it did, to what extent.

● *The Gagara* [1919] FOL 2; [1919] ANNUAL DIGEST 1919–22, CASE NO. 25; [1919] P 95

The question arose as to whether the UK recognized the new government in Estonia. The FCO stated that:

> for the time being provisionally, and with all necessary reservations as to the future, [Her Majesty's Government] recognised the Estonian National Council as the *de facto*, independent body, and accordingly has received a certain gentleman as the formal representative of the provisional Government.

● *Hesperides Hotels Ltd v. Aegean Turkish Holidays Ltd* [1978] 1 QB 205

In contrast, in this case, the FCO stated that the British government:

> Do[es] not recognize the administration established under the name of the 'Turkish Federated State of Cyprus' [and] do[es] not recognise such administration as being the government of an independent *de facto* sovereign state.

In general, the distinction made by the UK between de facto and de jure was constantly mis-understood by those who simply treated the UK's de facto recognition as recognition per se. This led the UK to abandon the issuance of formal declarations in 1980, resorting to implicit recognition. The discontinuance of formal declarations left British courts in a confused state since, prior to 1980, they had exclusively relied on the FCO's guidance on whether they should recognize acts of foreign governments that may come before English courts.

● *Gur Corp. v. Trust Bank of Africa* [1986] 3 WLR 583

An English court was faced with determining whether the 'government of Ceskei' was a sovereign government that could bring claims in an English court. As usual, the court sought guidance from the FCO, but the latter stated that recognition was now being granted implicitly. The court declined to recognize the government based on an inference that it made from the FCO's response (which did not state categorically that the government did not recognize the Ceskei government) and by relying on the decision in the earlier case *Carl Zeiss* (see the following section), on recognition of States.

The recognition of States

● *Carl Zeiss Stiftung v. Rayner and Keeler Ltd* [1965] 1 ALL ER 300

The English Court of Appeal had to determine the validity of a title to property originating from the GDR at a time when the latter was unrecognized by the UK. Lord Diplock stated that although the English conflict-of-law rules (private international law) provided for the application of foreign rules under certain circumstances, this was only when such rules are made (at 318):

> By or on the authority of those persons who are recognised by the Government of the United Kingdom as being the sovereign Government of the place where the thing happened.

Although this seemed a sound application of the principle of recognition by the British munici-pal legal system, the application of private international law rules to recognition was capable of rendering relations among ordinary persons within unrecognized States such as the GDR useless and devoid of legal meaning.

● *Carl Zeiss Stiftung v. Rayner and Keeler Ltd (No. 2)* [1967] 1 AC 853

On appeal from the above case, the defendants claimed that the plaintiff had no *locus standi* to bring an action against them, because, according to the defendants, the laws that created the plaintiff were those of an unrecognized State. If the House of Lords were to be consistent, it would accept this claim and decide the case alongside the decision in the lower court, dis-cussed above. The Lords did not; instead, they reversed the decision and allowed the appeal.

The House of Lords did not cite the hardship inherent in the application of private international law rules to recognition as the basis for reversing the decision (see later). Nonetheless, their Lordships clearly appreciated the severe hardship that a strict application of the non-recognition principle (such as that in the first *Carl Zeiss* case) brought upon ordinary human beings.

According to Lord Reid (at 907), strictly applying the non-recognition principle means that:

> We must not only disregard all new laws and decrees made by the German Democratic Republic or its Government, but we must also disregard all executive and judicial acts as invalid. The result would be far reaching. Trade with the Eastern zone of Germany is not discouraged, but the incorporation of every company in East Germany under any new law made by the German Democratic Republic or by the official act of any official appointed by its Government would have to be regarded as a nullity so that any such company could neither sue nor be sued in this country. Any civil marriage under any such new law or owing its validity to the acts of any such official would also have to be treated as a nullity so that we should have to regard the children as illegitimate; and the same would apply to divorces and all manners of judicial decisions whether in family or commercial questions. That would affect not only the status of persons formerly domiciled in East Germany but also in this country the devolution of which depended on the German law.

Lord Wilberforce, while accepting that the GDR was not recognized by the UK, was prepared to consider (at 955) whether:

> Where private rights, or acts of everyday occurrence, or perfunctory acts of administration are concerned the courts may, in the interests of justice and common sense, where no consideration of public policy to the contrary has to prevail, give recognition to the actual facts or realities found to exist in the territory in question.

It must be noted, however, that this was a chance remark (*obiter dictum*) by the Lords, which did not form part of the *ratio decidendi* (the reasons for the decision).

Instead of taking the bold step suggested by Lord Wilberforce, the House of Lords chose to decide the case on the basis of a **legal fiction**: that since the GDR was a creation of the (then) Soviet Republic and since the UK recognized that State, acts done by the GDR were therefore acts of the Soviet Republic and could be accepted by the English courts. This was clearly a practical solution (to avoid a strict application of the non-recognition principle), but one predicated upon deeply flawed legal reasoning—especially since the UK did not officially recognize the GDR until 1973. Obviously, the fact that the British government had not recognized the GDR at that time, but the court had, presented an incoherent approach from the UK.

legal fiction

A creation or assumption of facts by a court that allows it to apply legal rules or principles that are not necessarily designed to be used in that way or for that purpose. It is an attempt by the courts to provide for situations to which existing rules do not aptly cater.

● *Adams v. Adams (Attorney-General Intervening)* [1971] P 188

In this case, an English court refused to recognize a divorce already granted by a South Rhodesian court on the basis that Britain did not recognize South Rhodesia as a sovereign State. Hence there was no recognition of its government.

● **Hesperides Hotels v. Aegean Holidays Ltd** [1978] 1 ALL ER 277

The plaintiff in this case brought an action for trespass in respect of two hotels owned by him, but which, following the 1974 Turkish invasion of Cyprus, fell into the hands of some Turkish Cypriots. The Court of Appeal rejected the claim on the basis that, since the UK did not recognize the Turkish Republic of Northern Cyprus (TRNC), it had no jurisdiction to hear the case.

Interestingly, Lord Denning, like Lord Wilberforce in *Carl Zeiss* before him, favoured a more flexible approach towards the application of the non-recognition principle. His Lordship stated (at 283) that:

> If it were necessary...I would unhesitatingly hold that the Courts of this country can recognise the laws or acts of a body which is in effective control of a territory even though it has not been recognised by Her Majesty's Government de jure or de facto: at any rate, in regard to the laws which regulate the day-to-day affairs of the people, such as their marriages, their divorces, their leases, their occupations, and so forth; and furthermore that the Courts can receive evidence of the state of affairs so as to see whether the body is in effective control or not.

● **Emin v. Yeldag (Attorney-General and Secretary of State for Foreign and Commonwealth Affairs intervening)** [2002] 1 FLR 956

In this case, the British courts finally took the bull by the horns. The issue before the court was whether a divorce granted by the TRNC was valid before an English court. As may be recalled from the previous case, the TRNC was not recognized by the UK and an application of the non-recognition principle to a similar case had led to the non-recognition of a divorce granted by the TRNC (see *B v. B* [2000] 2 FLR 707).

However, the court accepted the argument that administrative acts constituted an exception to the principle of non-recognition. In coming to this decision, Justice Sumner stated that the judge in *B v. B* would have decided the same way had he had the benefit of the full argument. He also distinguished *Yeldag* from *Resat Caglar* [1996] STC (SCD) 150; [1996] 1 LRC 526, which, although also involved the TRNC, primarily concerned the immunity of the latter before the English courts and not administrative acts, such as divorce, as dealt with in *Emin v. Yeldag* and *B v. B*.

It is clear, from the above, that the British courts have found a way in which to sidestep the recognition of States by the British government, by distinguishing between the types of case in question. This is because recognition is such a political act that there are no laid-down criteria to guide States in the exercise of their right to recognize other States. Therefore, the courts have restricted the application of municipal law to issues bordering on recognition by applying the laws of unrecognized States to acts regarding personal transactions of individuals, as distinct from acts and transactions of such unrecognized States.

KEY POINTS

- The UK no longer issues formal declarations for recognition, but now grants recognition implicitly.

- The English courts have largely abandoned the strict application of non-recognition rules to cases concerning administrative acts of unrecognized States, such as divorce.

143

- The flexible approaches adopted by Lord Wilberforce and Lord Denning eventually prevailed upon the adoption of legal fiction by English courts to avoid the hardship of applying private international law rules to recognition.

The recognition of governments

As we have seen in the previous section, English courts usually disregard acts done in unrecognized States, other than administrative acts. However, the consequences of unrecognized governments before English courts are many and severe. Faced with termination of formal declarations of recognition by the FCO, the English courts have had to devise their own means of determining when foreign governments will or will not enjoy immunity in an English court, can sue or be sued, and will or will not be entitled to recover property before English courts.

● *The Arantzazu Mendi* [1939] AC 256

The issue before an English court was the validity of a requisitioning order. The ship, then owned by the defendant and in a London port, was requisitioned by the Nationalist government, which ruled the Basque region of Spain following a civil war, in 1938. The question was whether the Nationalist government ruled over a sovereign State. The FCO answered affirmatively and declared that the Nationalist government enjoyed immunity before the English courts.

An unrecognized government cannot sue or be sued in an English court. This was held in *City of Berne v. Bank of England* (1804) 9 Ves 347. In addition, it should be noted that the laws of unrecognized governments are inapplicable before the English courts.

● *Luther v. Sagor* [1921] 3 KB 532 (*Luther's Case*)

The defendant bought some timber from the government of the Soviet Union. The plaintiff claimed ownership of the timber on the basis that it owned the factory from which the timber came before its nationalization by the new Soviet government in 1919, and that since the UK did not recognize the latter, the nationalization decree should not be recognized by the court.

The court held in favour of the plaintiff.

However, this decision was revised on appeal because, in the interim, the UK recognized the Soviet Republic and that recognition was deemed to be retroactive (see section 4.7.6 for a discussion of retroactive recognition). It must be pointed out, however, that the Court of Appeal noted that the decision in the court of first instance was correct.

● *Haile Selassie v. Cable and Wireless Ltd (No. 2)* [1939] 1 CH 182

Emperor Haile Selassie entered into a contract with the defendant to supply wireless transmission between Abyssinia (now Ethiopia) and the UK. This was shortly before Abyssinia was invaded and annexed by Italy in 1935 and 1936, respectively. The plaintiff brought an action to recover money due under the contract. The question for the court was whether the fact that the UK recognized the de facto authority of Italy prevented the plaintiff, whose de jure authority the UK also recognized, from bringing the action. The defendant had relied on *Luther's Case* to argue that only the de facto government could bring the action to recover the sum.

It was held that, since Abyssinia was recognized as the de jure authority, it could bring an action to recover the sum, despite the fact that the UK recognized the de facto authority of Italy.

Distinguishing this case from *Luther*, Bennet J said (at 190) that:

> ...the only point established by [*Luther*] is that where the Government of this country has recognised that some foreign Government is de facto governing some foreign territory, the law of England will regard the acts of the de facto Government in that territory as valid and treat them with all the respect due to the acts of a duly recognised foreign sovereign state...It was not suggested in that case nor was anything said in it which supports the view that on or in consequence of such recognition a title to property in this country vests in the de facto Government and in that a title vested in a displaced Government is divested...[t]he present case is not concerned with the validity of acts in relation to persons or property in Ethiopia. It is concerned with the title to a chose in action—a debt, recoverable in England.

While the case was on appeal, the British government recognized the de jure authority of Italy over Abyssinia. Consequently, the Court of Appeal held that Ethiopia could not bring an action for the sum.

. . . .

● *Republic of Somalia v. Woodhouse Drake and Carey (Suisse) SA* [1993] QB 54

A similar, but distinguishable, situation arose when the government of Somalia entered into a contract with the defendant to deliver rice cargo to Somalia. Before delivery, the government was overthrown in a civil war and replaced by a provisional government. The latter brought an action to recover funds due under the contract. The question for the English court was whether the provisional government could bring an action before the English court.

(It must be noted that there was no government in effective control of Somalia at this time and the British government had no dealings whatsoever with the provisional government.)

Hobhouse J laid down some guidelines (at 68) to help him to decide whether or not the court should recognize the provisional government—namely:

1. whether the plaintiffs were the constitutional government of the state;
2. the degree, nature and stability of administrative control, if any, that the plaintiffs maintained over the territory of the state;
3. whether Her Majesty's Government had any dealings with the provisional government, and, if so, what were the nature and extent of those dealings; and
4. the extent of the international recognition afforded by the world community to the government of the state.

The provisional government failed to satisfy these conditions and the action failed.

. . . .

● *Sierra Leone Telecommunications Co. Ltd v. Barclays plc* [1998] 2 ALL ER 821

The question for the court to decide was whether it should entertain a request by Sierratel to disregard the mandate issued by the overthrown and exiled government of Tejan Kabbah concerning Sierra Leone accounts held at Barclays Bank in London. At this time, the British government still recognized the exiled government of Tejan Kabbah as the de jure authority in Sierra Leone and the international community opinion was strongly in favour of the restoration of that democratic regime. The Sierra Leonean Ambassador to the UK, who owed allegiance to Kabbah's government, brought an action that Barclays Bank should maintain the original mandate.

The court applied the 'Hobhouse criteria' (see the previous case) and came to the conclusion that the new military junta could not be regarded as the government of Sierra Leone.

Obviously, this decision was motivated by the preponderance of international opinion and the fact that the UK was not dealing with the new government. In reality, the military junta was in effective (hence de facto) control of Sierra Leone at the relevant time.

The Hobhouse criteria fill a gap in the principle of recognition in the UK and may yet become the guiding principle for determining when English *courts* may or may not recognize foreign governments. It is clear that, for now, these criteria demonstrate that the courts are able to decide recognition issues independently, without deference to the executive arm of the government. The danger, however, remains that the courts and the State occasionally work at cross purposes on recognition, as *Carl Zeiss (No. 2)* reminds us.

thinking points

- *Summarize the effects on non-recognition of government within a municipal legal system.*
- *How do English courts attempt to resolve the confusion created by the termination of formal declarations of recognition by the FCO?*
- *Is there a distinction between the administrative acts of a State or government, involving individuals, and the executive acts, involving the State, as represented by the government?*
- *Distinguish Haile Selassie v. Cable and Wireless Ltd from Republic of Somalia v. Woodhouse Drake and Carey.*

4.7.5 The reality of recognition and non-recognition in the present world

The consequences of non-recognition vary. When a new State is not recognized, the consequences of this depend on the reasons for non-recognition, who is not recognizing it, the status of the unrecognizing State in the community of nations, how many States do not recognize the new State, and the fora in which non-recognition applies. In other words, there are no hard-and-fast rules for determining the consequences of non-recognition of States.

Non-recognition of a new State by a vast majority of existing States

Where a new State is not recognized by a vast majority of existing States, the fact of non-recognition can hamper its enjoyment of certain rights under international law. For example, such a State may not be admitted as a member of the United Nations, even though it has already met the criteria of the Montevideo Convention. This is not because the new State is not, in fact, a State in international law—it certainly is—but because there remains such a strong mix of law and politics in the creation of new States that the efficacy of law is rendered dependent, to a reasonable extent, on political realities. Israel was recognized by several States at a time when there was a huge controversy about its territory. On the contrary, the German Democratic Republic and North Korea were not recognized for many years after their creation, even though they met the Montevideo criteria.

Irrespective of whether a new State is or not recognized, provided that it meets the Montevideo criteria, certain fundamentals never change. First, non-recognition does not imply that the existing States can treat the territory of the new State as *terra nullius* (that is, 'no-man's-land').

Thus far, recognition plays a crucial role, at least between the recognizing and recognized States. While non-recognition does not mean that a new State has no rights under international law, it means that, as between it and the unrecognizing State, such rights do not exist since the latter does not recognize its existence. As Jennings and Watts, 1996, see section 4.1.1, notes at p. 133:

> Recognition, while declaratory of an existing fact, is constitutive in its nature, at least so far as concerns relations with the recognising state. It marks the beginning of the effective enjoyment of the international rights and duties of the recognised community.

However, the fact that, under international law, States have no obligation to recognize new States (see later) affects the relevance of the declaratory theory to a considerable extent. Also, non-recognition of a State does not affect its own internal order, such as, for example, the validity of its own law within its territory, nor does it mean that the State ceases to exist. What is mainly affected is the level of the State's relations with other States and how existing States deal with it. This is particularly so if the new State is party to a treaty to which a non-recognizing State is also a party (see, for example, *Zalcmanis v. United States* (1959) ILR 28, 95; *Re Nepogodin Estate* (1955) ILR 22, 90; *Re Eng's Estate* (1964) ILR 35, 235).

KEY POINTS

- Even if a State fulfils the Montevideo criteria of statehood, its non-recognition by a vast majority of existing States can seriously hamper its international relations.

- Non-recognition of a State does not rob it of certain fundamentals such as the ability to keep its territory. Non-recognizing States cannot treat the territory of an unrecognized State as *terra nullius*.

4.7.6 The time of recognition

There are no prescriptions about when recognition can be bestowed on a State. Generally, the time at which recognition is conferred depends on the circumstances surrounding the emergence of a State or government. The recognition of a State that achieves independence after a period of colonization may be quicker than that of a State that breaks away from an existing State. Presumably, there will be less controversy about the status of the former than the latter. For example, most African States that emerged from colonialism were recognized almost immediately and admitted to UN membership without problems. The recognition of the States that split from the former SFRY—Croatia, Macedonia, Bosnia and Herzegovina, Serbia, and Montenegro, etc.—took a much longer period due to the controversy surrounding their breakaway and their territories, and also due to the additional criteria that were imposed by the then EC before these States could be admitted (see discussion in section 4.3.3).

Premature recognition

Despite the fact that no definite rules govern when recognition may be granted, it is problematic if recognition is bestowed prematurely or, as it is often expressed, 'precipitately'. According to Jennings and Watts, 1996, see section 4.1.1, at p. 144:

The recognition of Israel by the United States on 14 May 1948 has been regarded as precipitate. It was granted on the same day that the Israeli Act of Independence became effective, notwithstanding that the existence of the State of Israel was not by then firmly established.

The UK declined to recognize Israel immediately. It argued that to recognize Israel so quickly would be 'a positive act of favouring one side' (see HC Deb, 10 June 1948, vol. 451, cols. 2664–6).

Where a State bestows recognition on its former colony, it cannot later complain that an earlier recognition of that colony by third States is precipitate. Thus while the French recognition of the USA in 1778, following the latter's breakaway from Britain, was originally regarded as premature, the fact that Britain then recognized the USA in 1792 prevented it from later claiming that the French recognition was precipitate.

Similarly, where a colony declares its independence by breaking away from its parent State, the fact that the parent State is unable to reverse the situation may lead to the recognition of the new State even before the parent body offers such recognition. Thus, following the Bangladeshi declaration of independence from Pakistan in 1971, several States recognized the Bangladeshi State before Pakistan eventually did so in 1974. Also, although several States had refused to recognize the declaration of independence by many South American colonies from Spain, the fact that the latter was unable to reclaim these colonies led other States, such as the USA and the UK, to recognize these new States.

thinking points

- *When should recognition be granted or bestowed on a new State?*
- *What does the phrase 'precipitate recognition' mean and can you give two examples of this?*

Retroactive recognition

Granted that there is no specific time prescription for the recognition of States and governments, the question is: what is the effect of recognition bestowed on the new government on acts done by the previous government or by the State prior to the commencement of its regime?

As a matter of practice, recognition is retroactive. This means that, once bestowed, recognition dates back to the time at which the State or the government first came into existence. This clearly causes a problem for the declaratory theory, which, as explained previously, implies that recognition is merely confirmatory of a State or government.

As Lauterpacht said in 'Recognition of States in international law' (1944) 53 Yale LJ 385, 440:

> Recognition is retroactive in the meaning that, once granted, it dates back to the actual commencement of the activities of the recognized authority with regard to international rights and duties and, in particular, with regard to the recognition by foreign courts of the validity of its internal acts. *That principle is obviously an embarrassment for the declaratory view.* For if a State is a subject of international rights and duties as soon as it 'exists,' then there is no necessity for a special judicial doctrine sanctioning the validity of those rights and duties *ab initio*. [Emphasis added]

However, we should note that the retroactivity of recognition is a matter of convenience; it is not a principle of international law. Otherwise, it would be almost impossible for States to conduct business with one another if they were under the perpetual fear that activities conducted with one government, prior to its recognition, may yet be regarded as illegal by courts after recognition is bestowed. The need to avoid this unnecessary obstruction in State relations has been repeatedly emphasized, especially by the US Supreme Court.

. . . .

● *United States v. Belmont* 301 US 324 (1937)

On behalf of the US Supreme Court, Justice Sutherland stated (at 203) that:

> ...the conduct of foreign relations is committed by the Constitution to the political departments of the Federal Government; that the propriety of the exercise of that power is not open to judicial inquiry; and that recognition of a foreign sovereign conclusively binds the courts and is retroactive and validates all actions and conduct of the government so recognized from the commencement of its existence.

. . . .

● *United States v. Pink* 315 US 203 (1942)

Similarly, in this case, the US Supreme Court said (at 230) that:

> Recognition is not always absolute; it is sometimes conditional...Power to remove such obstacles to full recognition as settlement of claims of our nationals...certainly is a modest implied power of the President who is the 'sole organ of the federal government in the field of international relations.'...Effectiveness in handling the delicate problems of foreign relations requires no less. Unless...such a power exists, the power of recognition might be thwarted or seriously diluted. No such obstacle can be placed in the way of rehabilitation of relations between this country and another nation, unless the historic conception of the powers and responsibilities of the President in the conduct of foreign affairs...is to be drastically revised... *We would usurp the executive function if we held that that decision was not final and conclusive in the courts*. [Emphasis added]

Furthermore, it must be noted that the retroactivity of recognition relates only to acts done within the authority of the concerned State or government prior to its recognition, not acts done ultra vires (that is, in excess of its authority). Also, recognition does not affect the validity of acts of a previously recognized government after such recognition has been withdrawn.

Note that the retroactivity of recognition applies only to acts done by a State or government within its own country, prior to recognition; it does not affect the validity of acts done by a previously recognized government, as the following case makes clear.

. . . .

● *Guaranty Trust Company v. United States* 304 US 126 (1938)

The Imperial Russian Government opened an account at a New York bank, the Guaranty Trust Company, in 1916, but the government was overthrown on 5 July 1917 and replaced by the Provisional Government of Russia, which was recognized by the USA on 12 July 1917. On 17 November 1917, the Provisional Government of Russia was overthrown and replaced by the Union of the Soviet Socialist Republics (USSR). The USA recognized the USSR in 1933, in which year the USSR government assigned all monies due to it from Guaranty Trust and American nationals to the US government. The USA brought an action against the bank to recover the money. The bank brought the current action to dismiss the claim by the USA.

The USA argued that its recognition of the USSR in 1933 operated retroactively and that it nullified rights acquired in the USA in consequence of its prior recognition of the Provisional Government. In effect, it would mean that the rights acquired by American nationals from their transactions with the Russian Provisional Government (which the USA recognized at the time) were invalid, since the proper government recognized from 1917 would have been the USSR by the operation of retroactivity.

The US Supreme Court rejected this argument. It stated (at 141) that to treat the recognition of the USSR as operating to invalidate all of the legal consequences of the prior recognition by the USA of the Provisional Government and its representatives, as though such recognition had never been accorded:

> ignores the distinction between the effect of our recognition of a foreign government with respect to its acts within its own territory prior to recognition, and the effect upon previous transactions consummated here between its predecessor and our own nationals. The one operates only to validate to a limited extent acts of a de facto government which, by virtue of the recognition, has become a government de jure. But it does not follow that recognition renders of no effect transactions here with a prior recognized government in conformity to the declared policy of our own Government.

The facts of this case show that where acts are conducted by a recognized de facto government, such acts will not be nullified by the subsequent recognition of another government. The USA wanted its recognition of the USSR to be retroactive to nullify transactions entered into with the recognized Provisional Government. The Court rejected this position.

Note that retroactive recognition dates back to transactions entered into from the inception of the government in question and not to transactions with other duly recognized governments, so as to nullify the latter. Therefore, for retroaction to apply, the transaction should have been with the government that is subsequently recognized.

Also, as stated earlier, retroactive recognition applies only to acts done by a government within its sphere of authority and control, and not to acts done ultra vires its authority prior to recognition.

• **Boguslawski v. Gdynia-Ameryka Linie** [1950] 1 KB 157

The Polish government, which was already established in Warsaw (the 'Warsaw government'), but was at the material time exiled in London, entered into an agreement with some Polish employees on 3 July 1945 that it would pay them some sums of money if they were to leave their employment. Meanwhile, on 28 June 1945, the Provisional Polish Government of National Unity was established in Lubin, Poland (the 'Lubin government'), and was recognized by Her Majesty's Government from midnight of 5–6 July 1945, thus ending the previous recognition of the Warsaw government on that date. The plaintiffs left the defendants' employment, based in London, and claimed three months' salary from 5 July 1945 based on the agreement that they had with the Warsaw government dated 3 July 1945.

The defendants argued that since the British government recognized the Lubin government on 5 July 1945, the recognition was retroactive so that it went back to 28 June 1945, when the Lubin government was formed. As such, the purported agreement with the Warsaw government was illegal, since only the Lubin government could represent Poland as from 28 June.

The court held that since the British recognition accorded to the Warsaw government lasted until 5–6 July 1945, the 3 July agreement remained valid. The court also held that while it was true that the British recognition of the Lubin government meant that the latter had been in existence since 28 June 1945, it was not in control of the activities carried out outside Poland, such as the agreement that was reached in London. Until that time, it was the Warsaw government that was in charge of such matters.

4.7.7 Is there a duty to recognize in international law?

The question of whether there is a duty to recognize in international law is fundamental to the determination of the effect of recognition. If there is a duty to recognize, then logically it means that recognition will be legally consequential, so that non-recognition of a new State implies serious legal and not merely political consequences. A duty to recognize will imply that the existence of a State depends on other States performing that duty, regardless of whether the new State has met the formal criteria for statehood.

The opinions of writers are divided on this issue. According to Lauterpacht (1978, see section 4.7.2), p. 6:

> In the absence of an international organ competent to ascertain and authoritatively to declare the presence of full international personality, states already established fulfil that function in their capacity as organs of international law. In thus acting they administer the law of nations.

Clearly, Lauterpacht believed that the duty to recognize exists. Indeed, the UK laid down the criteria for recognition thus (HC Deb, 29 February 1984, vol. 55, col. 226):

> The criteria which normally apply for the recognition of a state are that it should have, and seem likely to continue to have, a clearly defined territory with a population, a Government who are able of themselves to exercise effective control of that territory and independence in their external relations. There are, however, exceptional cases when other factors, including relevant United Nations resolutions, may have to be taken into account.

The attitude of the USA on the question of whether there is a duty to recognize was stated in (1976) US Digest 19–20, to the effect that:

> International law does not require a state to recognize another entity as a state; it is a matter for the judgement of each state whether an entity merits recognition as a state. In reaching this judgment, the United States has traditionally looked to the establishment of certain facts. These facts include effective control over a clearly-defined territory and population; an organized governmental administration of that territory; and a capacity to act effectively to conduct foreign relations and to fulfil international obligations. The United States has also taken into account whether the entity in question has attracted the recognition of the international community of states.

State practice has been uneven as far as applying the Montevideo criteria for the purpose of recognition. While the USA refused to recognize Cuba in 1875, due to the absence of an effective government, it recognized Albania in 1919, despite that country's not having an effective government; while it recognized Algeria as a State in 1962, it did not recognize the Algerian government until three months later (see J. B. Moore and F. Wharton, *A Digest of International Law* (Washington DC: GPO, 1906), eight vols; M. M. Whiteman, *Digest of International Law* (Washington DC: GPO, 1963–73) fifteen vols).

There is little support for the view that there is a duty to recognize in international law. Views such as that expressed by Lauterpacht (see earlier) have been increasingly challenged by other writers, including those who favour the constitutive theory.

Thus in 'Some thoughts on the doctrine of recognition in international law' (1934) 47 Harv L Rev 776, 780, Sir John Fischer Williams noted that:

> The Members of the Family [of Nations], acting in the absence of a central authority, when they admit to membership, have a duty to act as in discharge of a duty to the Family and therefore upon some general principle, not in a merely selfish and arbitrary interest [but when it comes to recognition] each State cannot be conceived as doing more than declaring its own policy.

This statement suggests that even if existing States discharge some duty to admit new members into the family of nations (a point that resonates with the constitutive theory), as far as recognition is concerned, each State does no more than merely declare its own policy. Hence (ibid.):

> ...it is also clear that the nature of the act of each State cannot be creative in the sense of making a new international person, but must be limited to a declaration that it personally accepts the fact that a new international person has come into being.

Regardless of whether or not there is a duty to recognize in international law, it must always be borne in mind that, once recognized, a State cannot subsequently cease to exist, even if it is without a government, except under exceptional circumstances such as the breaking up of the State into several new States. As Jennings and Watts, 1996, see section 4.1.1, at p. 131, puts it:

> Once recognised as a state, its government may go near to disappearing without necessarily affecting the state's continued existence, as may happen during a civil war; similarly, in 1945, Germany was virtually without a government (as opposed to the authorities of the occupying powers) but was still regarded as continuing as a state... The UK recognises no government in Kampuchea (Cambodia), but still acknowledges its continuation as a state.

example

During the Liberian civil war, the government of Samuel Doe, the legitimate government of Liberia when the war broke out in 1989, was later confined to the capital city, Monrovia, while the rebel forces of the Charles Taylor-led National Patriotic Front of Liberia (NPFL) controlled nearly 98 per cent of the country. Nonetheless, Liberia was still widely regarded as a State in international law and was so dealt with by other States.

● **Great Britain v. Costa Rica** (1923) 1 RIAA 369 (The **Tinoco Arbitration**)

The dispute arose from the nullification of acts of the Tinoco government by a government that overthrew Tinoco's administration in 1919. The UK, which did not recognize the de facto government of Tinoco while it was in power, made a claim against the new government in Costa Rica regarding commercial matters concerning British subjects. The new Costa Rican government objected, amongst other things, on the ground that since the UK did not recognize the Tinoco government, it could not bring an action for claims due under that government.

Arbitrator Taft disagreed. He stated (at 382) that:

> Here the executive of Great Britain takes the position that the Tinoco government which it did not recognize, was nevertheless a *de facto* government that could create rights in British subjects which it now seeks to protect. Of course, as already emphasized, its failure to recognize the *de facto* government can be used against it as evidence to disprove the character it now attributes to that government, but this does not bar it from changing its position. Should a case arise in one of its

own courts after it has changed its position, doubtless that court would feel it incumbent upon it to note the change in its further rulings.

In effect, the UK's non-recognition of the Tinoco government, although evidence that that government did not meet universal approval, did not prevent it from bringing a claim against the government.

Conclusion

States constitute the most important subjects of international law. However, as we have seen, they are not the only subjects of international law; international organizations are also subjects of international law, and have grown considerably in status and importance in recent years. Under certain circumstances, human persons can also be regarded as subjects of international law, even if only for the enjoyment and enforcement of specific rights and privileges. Under the European Convention on Human Rights and the Protocol relating to the establishment of the African Court for Human Rights and Justice, individuals can bring actions against States before international tribunals.

We have also seen that the criteria for statehood, laid down in the Montevideo Convention, are by no means exhaustive of what communities, such as the EU, may ask of their prospective members.

When a new State has emerged—by fulfilling the Montevideo criteria and whatever additional conditions there may be—it is important that it is recognized by other States. Whether such recognition is merely declaratory or constitutes the essence of the State is always debatable. What is certain is that recognition is not entirely devoid of content. If nothing more, it gives a State a better basis upon which to enjoy its international rights and to interrelate with other States. A recognized State is, therefore, a solid international legal person, fully capable of enforcing its rights as guaranteed under international law, just as a government that is recognized is able to represent its State both in foreign courts and international fora. It is thus clear that recognition of States contributes to their capacity as subjects of international law, making both subjects inextricably interlinked. They are, indeed, two sides of the same coin.

Questions

Self-test questions

1 What are the criteria for statehood under the Montevideo Convention?

2 List the 'new requirements' of statehood adopted by the European Community in 1991.

3 List the subjects of international law.

4 Explain the terms 'declaratory theory' and 'constitutive theory'.

5 What does the 'Estrada doctrine' imply?

6 How do you understand the term 'recognition'?

7 When must recognition be granted?

8 Explain the term 'retroactive recognition'.

Discussion questions

1 'The criteria for statehood under the Montevideo Convention are exhaustive and do not permit any additional criteria or practices to be added.' Discuss.

2 'A "defined territory" means a territory free from controversy or dispute.' To what extent does this assertion reflect the understanding of 'defined territory' under the Montevideo Convention?

3 What is the relationship between the Montevideo criteria of statehood and the 'new requirements' proposed by Fawcett (1964–65, see section 4.3.2) and adopted by the European Community in 1991?

4 'Retroactive recognition is a matter of convenience in State relations; it is not a principle of international law.' Discuss.

5 'There is no duty of recognition in international law.' Discuss.

Assessment question

Teletoys, a company registered in Candoma, entered into a contract in 2003 to supply Rutamu's State Department with 500 plasma units during the reign of General Blast in Rutamu. Although the military junta overthrew the democratic government in 2005, Candoma never recognized it until it was overthrown in 2008 by another military junta led by General Roué. Teletoys has brought an action against Rutamu, following the refusal of General Roué's government to pay Teletoys money due under the contract. Roué's government argues that since Candoma never recognized Blast's government, it cannot bring an action against it.

Advise Teletoys.

 # Key cases

- *Emin v. Yeldag (Attorney-General and Secretary of State for Foreign and Commonwealth Affairs intervening)* [2002] 1 FLR 956

- *Great Britain v. Costa Rica* (1923) 1 RIAA 369 (the *Tinoco Arbitration*)

- *Guaranty Trust Company v. United States* 304 US 126 (1938)

- *International Registration of Trademark (Germany) Case* (1959) 28 ILR 82

- *Karen Atala Riffo v. Chile* Case No. P-1271-04 (2010), Inter-American Commission on Human Rights (the *Atala Case*)

- *Netherlands v. United States* (1928) 2 RIAA 829 (the *Island of Palmas Arbitration*)

- *Opinion on the Difference Relating to Immunity from Legal Process of a Special Rapporteur of the Commission of Human Rights* (1999) ICJ Rep 62

- *Republic of Somalia v. Woodhouse Drake and Carey (Suisse) SA* [1992] 3 WLR 744

- *Sierra Leone Telecommunications Co. Ltd v. Barclays plc* [1998] 2 All ER 821

Further reading

Bardonnet, D., 'Les frontières terrestres et la relativité de leur tracé: problèmes juridiques choisis' (1976) 153 Recueil des cours de l'Académie de Droit International de La Haye 9

Crawford, J., *The Creation of States in International Law* (2nd edn, Oxford: Oxford University Press, 2006)

Grant, T. D., 'Defining statehood: the Montevideo Convention and its discontents' (1999) 37(2) Colum J Transnat'l L 403

Hillgruber, C., 'The admission of new States to the international community' (1998) 9 EJIL 491

John, F. (ed.), *International Legal Personality* (Farnham: Ashgate, 2009)

Lauterpacht, H., 'Recognition of States in international law' (1944) 53(3) Yale LJ 385

Orakhelashvili, A., 'The position of the individual in international law' (2001) 31 Cal W Int'l LJ 241

Rama-Montaldo, M., 'International legal personality and implied powers of international organizations' (1970) 44 BYBIL 111

Schwebel, M. S., 'Mini-States and a more effective United Nations' (1973) 67 AJIL 108

International organizations

Introduction

International organizations are a very important feature of international law. Not only are they important as subjects of international law (see Chapter 4), but they are also very important players on the international plane. However, unlike States, international organizations have not always been part of the international legal system: they are more or less late arrivals on the scene, and their emergence was not primarily for the purpose for which they are popular today. This chapter will discuss the origin, types, roles, functions, powers, and limitations of international organizations.

5.1 Origins: from the Congress of Vienna to the League of Nations

The origin of international organizations dates back to the second half of the nineteenth century. As seen in Chapter 4, traditional international law mainly concerned States and, under that system, States functioned largely as individual entities, with international law (or the 'law of nations', as it was then called) regulating their relations with one another.

According to Inis Claude, *Swords into Plowshares* (3rd edn, London: University of London Press, 1964), while the emergence of States as sovereign entities in the seventeenth and eighteenth centuries was crucial, the preconditions for the creation of international organizations were not met during those centuries. For example, there was little contact between States and generally there was no perceived need for institutionalized mechanisms to manage international relations. In essence, the international legal system that prevailed in the seventeenth and eighteenth centuries was one in which, according to Richard Falk 'a decentralized control by sovereign States' provided the basis for a horizontal international order critical for the subsequent development of international organizations: 'The interplay of Westphalia and Charter conceptions of international legal order' in Cyril E. Black and Richard A. Falk (eds), *The Future of the International Legal Order, Vol. I: Trends and Patterns* (Princeton, NJ: Princeton University Press, 1969), at p. 69.

The Congress of Vienna, held between 1814 and 1815 after the devastation of the Napoleonic wars aimed to reorganize Europe and ensure that peace and security prevailed in the continent thereafter. It was at this Congress that the idea of a 'Concert of Europe', which had been expressed in the 1814 Treaty of Chaumont Europe, took a firm foothold.

The Congress of Vienna established a system of international organizations as they are known today. The Final Act of the Congress, for instance, made no provisions for any regular meeting of the Congress (a significant feature of the procedure of international organizations).

In their chapter 'International organization' in B. Bouckaert and G. De Geest (eds), *Encyclopedia of Law and Economics, Vol. I: The History and Methodology of Law and Economics* (Cheltenham: Edward Elgar, 2000), p. 692, Alexander Thompson and Duncan Snidal note (at p. 694) that the Congress of Vienna:

Created a more systematic and institutionalized approach to managing issues of war and peace in the international system. The principal innovation at Vienna was that representatives of states should meet at regular intervals—not just in the wake of war—to discuss diplomatic issues. Accordingly, four major peacetime conferences were held between 1815 and 1822.

Two factors undermined the Congress's ability to deal with the challenges of late eighteenth-century Europe: first, the Congress was reactive in its operation and, secondly, the nature of post-Napoleonic War challenges in Europe.

There were no regular but only sporadic meetings tailored towards specific occurrences.

However, in the nineteenth century more concrete steps emerged towards the establishment of international organizations, with the creation of many unions, starting with the establishment of the Central Commission for the Navigation of the Rhine by the littoral States of the Rhine, in 1815 in Vienna.

According to Abdullah El-Erian, 'The historical development of international institutions' in Max Sørensen (ed.), *Manual of Public International Law* (London: Macmillan, 1968), at p. 59:

> The decisive step forward in international organizations in, the nineteenth century was undoubtedly the creation of the Telegraph and Postal Unions in 1865 and 1874. The International Telegraph Union was created by the Paris Telegraph Convention of 1865, and with the establishment in 1868 of the International Bureau of Telegraph Administrations, the Telegraph Union became the first truly international organization of states with a permanent secretariat.

Aside from establishing permanent structures, the unions also inspired important changes in the direction of international law at the time. For example, prior to this time, it was the practice amongst States that a treaty or convention could be changed only on the basis of a unanimous decision of all of the parties to it (known as the 'unanimity' rule). However, early international organizations altered this position and the 'majority rule' was gradually introduced into the international legal system.

In *International Law: Chiefly as Interpreted and Applied by the United States* (2nd edn, Boston, MA: Little, Brown and Co., 1947, vol I), C. C. Hyde states, at p. 131, that the unions had a more general influence on the growth of international law, especially by increasing the awareness:

> of potentialities of international organizations as a means of furthering an interest common to numerous states without detriment to that of any concerned.

In 1919, the League of Nations was established as a first truly international organization with a permanent structure with an Assembly, an Executive Council, and a Secretariat (Article 2, League Covenant).

KEY POINTS

- International organizations emerged around the middle of the nineteenth century, starting with the Congress of Vienna, and began to take shape, later that century, with the establishment of international unions.

- The Congress of Vienna made significant contributions to the evolution of international organizations.

- The unions which emerged after the Napoleonic wars established structures such as secretariats and bureaus which distinguished them from the Congress of Vienna.

5.2 Definitions

International organizations are of various types and they perform widely differing functions, thus making a single definition almost impossible.

In his 'Report on the law of treaties' (1956) 2 ILCYB 108, Gerald Fitzmaurice defines 'international organizations' as:

> A collectivity of States established by treaty, with a constitution and common organs, having a personality distinct from that of its member-States, and being a subject of international law with treaty-making capacity.

P. Reuter and J. Combacau, *Institutions et Relations Internationals* (3rd edn, Paris: PUF, 1985), p. 278 (also quoted in (1985) 2 ILCYB 106), define an 'international organization' as:

> An entity which has been set up by a means of a treaty concluded by States to engage in co-operation in a particular field and which has its own organs that are responsible for engaging in independent activities.

These definitions contain several limitations. They seem to give the impression that international organizations are established only by States and must be established by treaty. This is not always the case. International organizations may also be established by non-State entities, which do not conclude treaties, and may be established by States through other instruments, such as resolutions and declarations. A better definition is offered by the International Law Commission (ILC) which, in Article 2 of its Draft Articles on the Responsibility of International Organizations states that:

> For the purposes of the present draft Articles, the term 'international organization' refers to an organization established by a treaty or other instrument governed by international law and possessing its own international legal personality. International organizations may include as members, in addition to States, other entities.

In the *Statement of the Chairman of the Drafting Committee* (Mr James L. Kateka; UN Doc. A/CN.4/L.632, 4 June 2003, also found at (2003) ILC Rep 38), the ILC explains that:

> As regards the mode of establishment, an 'international organization' falling within the scope of this topic should be established by a 'treaty' or 'other instrument' governed by international law. The general view in the Drafting Committee was that an international organization covered by these articles should be created by some form of an *act under international law*, clearly expressing *the consent* of the parties … The word 'treaty' is defined, broadly, in article 2, paragraph (1)(a) of the Vienna Convention on the Law of Treaties. The same definition was repeated in article 2, paragraph (1)(a) of the 1986 Vienna Convention on the Law of Treaties between States and International Organizations or between International Organizations.

This is, indeed, a very important clarification, because it explains the criteria for distinguishing international organizations from other types of organization that, although *international* as well, do not fall under the purview of this chapter, such as international non-governmental organizations (NGOs) or international corporations.

> **thinking points**
>
> • *How would you define 'international organizations'?*
> • *Distinguish between the ILC definition of international organizations and the definitions offered by other writers, such as Fitzmaurice, and Reuter and Combacau.*
> • *What is the highlight of the elaboration of the ILC definition?*

5.3 Classification: international (governmental) organizations, international (non-governmental) organizations, and international public corporations

Whenever we say 'international organization', we may mean broadly one of three things:

• public intergovernmental organizations which, as the name suggests, are composed of States (represented by governments);

• private international organizations (also known as NGOs); or

• international public corporations (IPCs).

The United Nations consists of States, was established by a treaty (the Charter of the United Nations, or UN Charter), and was founded under international law. Therefore it is a public international organization (that is, an intergovernmental organization), the type referred to in the ILC definition and with which we are concerned in this chapter.

In contrast, the International Committee of the Red Cross (ICRC) is a private international organization, or international NGO. It was founded by an individual, Henry Dunant, in 1863, does not have States as members (although it operates *within* several States), was not established by a treaty, and, although it now implements international law mandates (such as international humanitarian law), it was not established under international law.

Finally, IPCs, according to W. Friedman ('International public corporations' (1943) 6(4) MLR 185) 'are corporate bodies established for purposes of international government but constituted as commercial corporations'. Former US President, Franklin Roosevelt, in his message to the US Congress in 1933, aptly described IPCs as clothed 'with the power of government, but possessed of the flexibility and initiative of a private enterprise' (restated in Friedman, at p. 186).

In general, the major distinctions between intergovernmental organizations, international NGOs, and IPCs can summarized as in Table 5.1.

Table 5.1

Typologies of international organizations

Public international organizations	Private international non-governmental organizations (NGOs)	International public corporations (IPCs)
Set up and composed generally and predominantly, but not always, by States	Usually no State members	Set up by States, but not composed of States as members
Composed mostly of States as members	Largely set up by individuals or associations of individuals	Mainly corporate in nature and set up for commercial interests
Usually possess constitutions or treaties, or constitutive instruments	No constitutions or treaties, only articles of association	Have independent identity, but controlled by State organs such as parliaments
Have organs that are separate from member States	Have no independent organs	Have no separate organs
Created under international law	Mostly established under domestic law	Established under domestic law, although meant to operate internationally

Despite these differences, there are certain commonalities between public and private international organizations. For example, each may have its headquarters in a single country and branches in other countries. Hence, the United Nations has its headquarters in the USA, but has branches in Switzerland and Kenya, which are effectively operational seats of some of its programmes. Likewise, the ICRC has its headquarters in one State, Switzerland, but has many branches (or 'chapters', as they are sometimes called) in several States. In this regard, IPCs differ from the other two types of international organization, because they usually have their offices in one country, although they might operate in several locations.

thinking points

- *What is the importance of the criteria established in the ILC definition of international organizations and how does it help you to understand what these entities are?*
- *What are the major distinctions between intergovernmental organizations and international NGOs?*

5.3.1 'Open' and 'closed' international organizations

While public international organizations are different from NGOs and IPCs, not all public international organizations are the same. We can further distinguish between public international organizations on the basis of whether they are 'open' or 'closed'. An open international organization is a universal organization, meaning that its membership is open to all States. A 'closed' organization is one the membership of which is restricted to certain regions or States.

In his 'First Report to the ILC on Relations between States and Inter-Governmental Organizations' (1963) 2 BYBIL 162, El-Erian clarifies thus:

A universal organization is one which includes in its membership all the States of the world. This is not the case of any past or present international organization yet. Thus, it may be more accurate to use the terms 'universalist' suggested by Schwarzenberger or 'of potentially universal character' used in the treatise of Oppenheim. The French term 'à avocation universelle' conveys the same meaning as these two terms, which is that while the organization is not completely universal, it tends towards that direction. This was partially the case of the League of Nations and is, in a much broader sense, the case of the United Nations especially after 1955, and the specialized agencies.

The United Nations is the closest organization in existence to an open, or universal, organization, but since there are States that are yet to become members, it cannot be described exactly so, but rather as a *universalist* organization. However, 'openness' does not mean the absence of strict membership criteria.

Regarding closed international organizations, H. G. Schermers, *International Institutional Law* (Leiden: A. W. Sijthoff, 1980), p. 23, writes that:

> In contrast to universal organizations there are organizations which aim at membership from a closed group of States. No members are admitted from outside of the group. We shall denominate these organizations as 'closed' organizations, to emphasize their closed membership... There are three types of closed organizations: regional organizations, organizations of States with a common background, such as language or common political system, and closed functional organizations.

Examples of closed organizations include the European Union, the African Union, the Organization of American States (OAS), the Arab League, and so on. These organizations restrict their membership based on criteria, including a geographical area, usually set out in their founding treaties—that is, the treaties or constitutions establishing them.

5.4 Features of international organizations

As already noted, international organizations are of different kinds and are usually formed for different purposes. Nevertheless, there are certain general features that can be identified as being necessary for the existence and operation of any international organization, including:

- membership;
- a constitutive instrument;
- legal personality; and
- privileges and immunities.

5.4.1 Legal personality

It will be recalled that the ILC definition of 'international organizations' provided earlier refers to their legal personality. This is one of the most important features of international organizations, because they are established in order to carry out certain functions for which they must possess certain capacities. It is thus necessary that, for them to be 'operative', international organizations must possess legal personality. The questions is what is 'legal personality' and what are its consequences in international law?

The phrase 'legal personality' is sometimes used to refer to the 'juristic person', 'juridical person', or *personne morale*. Instead of definitions, most writers and States tend rather to describe what they understand by the term.

The Spanish *Còdigo Civil* (Civil Code), Lib. I, Tit. II, ss 35–9, defines the 'juristic person' as:

> 1. Corporations, associations and organizations of a public nature recognized by the law. Their personality begins from the very instant in which they have been formally established in accordance with the provision of the law.

Legal personality thus refers to the qualifying status of an entity which implies its existence within a particular sphere and indicates certain functions and capacities, or rights and duties, that would enable it to operate within that sphere. A legal person is a recognized entity. The recognition is strictly legal, and not natural, and is to be defined by law, since that is what establishes it.

As Amerasinghe notes in *Principles of the Institutional Law of International Organizations* (2nd edn, Cambridge: Cambridge University Press, 2005), at p. 68:

> Without personality an organization would not be able to appear in its own right in legal proceedings, whether at the international or non international level. There would also not be a single international person as such having the capacity in its own right to have rights, obligations and powers, whether implied or expressed, both at the international level and at the non-international level. Such rights, obligations and powers would be vested collectively in all the creating states, which may not have been the intention behind the creation of the organization, and also could create unnecessary practical problems, particularly in the area of responsibility, both active and passive.

Due to the absence of its definition in the treaties of international organization, legal personality has proved to be controversial, in terms of its significance, notwithstanding that almost all treaties obligate member States to recognize the personality of the institution on their territory.

In order better to understand the status of international organizations, it is necessary to consider how these organizations derive their personality.

5.4.2 Theoretical approaches to determining the legal personality of international organizations

There are two approaches to understanding how international organizations derive their personality: the 'inductive' approach and the 'objective' approach.

The 'inductive' approach

Under this approach, the legal personality of international organizations is to be implied in the capacities, rights, and privileges conferred on them in their constituent instruments, by members of the organization.

Manuel Rama-Montaldo, 'International legal personality and implied powers of international organizations' (1970) 44 BYBIL 111, 112, notes that:

> The inductive approach starts from the basis of the existence of certain rights and duties expressly conferred upon international organizations, and derives from these particular rights and duties a general international personality. Those who adopt this approach generally link it with the foundation of the personality on the will of States concerned either expressed or implied in the constituent instruments. For this approach, personality becomes a point of arrival rather than a point of departure.

Obviously, under the inductive approach, the legal personality of international organizations derives from the generous act of their member States that confers such powers on international organizations through their constituent instruments.

. . . .

● *Reparation for Injuries Suffered in the Service of the United Nations Advisory Opinion (Pleadings, Oral Arguments, Documents)* (1949) ICJ REP 174 (The *Reparations Case*)

At 116, Gerald Fitzmaurice, representing the UK, stressed the importance:

> [w]hich the Government of the United Kingdom attaches to the principle that the constitutive instrument setting up an organization, and containing its constitution, must be the primary source of any conclusion as to the status, capacities and powers of the organizations concerned. It would, in the opinion of the United Kingdom Government, be as dangerous as it would be unsound to ascribe to international organizations, a status, capacities or powers not provided for or to be inferred from their constitutive instruments, except in so far as may result from clearly applicable, universal, and recognized principles of general law.

In the same vein, the United Nations confirmed, during the oral hearing of the case, that its personality derived from the UN Charter, as conferred by its member States (Statement by Mr Feller, Counsel for the Secretary-General of the United Nations at the Public Sittings of 7 and 8 March 1949).

In summing up the position of the United Nations on the question of its personality, Counsel for the Secretary-General of the United Nations stated (at 70) that:

> The United Nations *possesses* international juridical personality conferred upon it by the States which created it; that incidental to such personality the United Nations possesses the procedural capacity to present an international claim; and that as a consequence of its personality the United Nations possesses certain substantive rights under international law. [Emphasis added]

The 'objective' approach

In contrast to the inductive approach is the objective approach which holds that legal personality derives not from the constituent treaties of international organizations as a generous act of member States, but on the basis of international organizations fulfilling certain objective criteria.

According to Rama-Montaldo (1970, see the previous section), at 112:

> Once the existence of these prerequisites is confirmed, the legal personality of the international organization is established. Although the objective elements are said to be found in the constitutive instrument of the organization, those who adopt this approach normally tend to consider

that the foundation of the personality *is not the will of the States but is to be discovered in general international law*. In other words, it is the international legal order which automatically ascribes personality to an entity fulfilling certain conditions. [Emphasis added]

In 'International personality of intergovernmental organizations: do their capacities really depend upon their constitutions?' (1964) 4 IJIL 1, F. Seyersted argues that an international convention is not:

> the crucial test ... of international personality. International organizations, like States, come into being on the basis of general international law when certain criteria exist, and these necessary criteria do not include convention.

One criticism of the objective approach is its failure to show State practice supports that the legal personality of international organizations derives from customary international law.

The difference between the 'inductive' approach and the 'objective' approach became a subject of much academic debate after the International Court of Justice (ICJ), for the first time, decided on the question of the international legal personality of international organizations in the *Reparations Case*.

. . . .

● *Reparation for Injuries Suffered in the Service of the United Nations Advisory Opinion* (1949) ICJ REP 174 (The *Reparations Case*)

A UN diplomat, Count Folke Bernadotte, was murdered in Jerusalem by a Jewish group. Israel was then not a UN member. The UN General Assembly requested the opinion of the ICJ as to whether the UN had the capacity to bring an action against Israel for reparation for the loss of its staff. The question by the General Assembly did not specifically request the ICJ to discuss the issue of international legal personality.

However, the Court said it was important to determine first whether the UN had international legal personality. The Court held (at 179) that:

> It must be acknowledged that its Members, by entrusting certain functions to it, with the attendant duties and responsibilities, have clothed it with the competence required to enable those functions to be effectively discharged. The Organization was intended to exercise and enjoy, and is in fact exercising and enjoying, functions and rights which can only be explained on the basis of the possession of a large measure of international personality and the capacity to operate upon an international plane. It is at present the supreme type of international organization, and it could not carry out the intentions of its founders if it was devoid of international personality.

Accordingly, the basis for the legal personality of international organizations can be explained from different perspectives, but there is no question that such institutions possess legal personality.

KEY POINTS

- The inductive approach and objective approach are the two theoretical approaches to determining the legal personality of international organizations.

- Proponents of the 'objective personality' approach fail to justify their viewpoint in customary international law.

5.4.3 The impact of the Court's opinion on the inductive–objective debate

Despite not specifically referring to a particular approach, the ICJ statement in the *Reparations Case* can be viewed as endorsing both schools of thoughts to legal personality. By affirming that the UN member States *entrusted* it with certain functions and 'clothed it with the competence required to enable those functions to be effectively discharged', the Court seemingly approved the inductive approach, while its specific reference to the 'objective international personality' at p. 18 strongly tilts its opinion in favour of that approach.

However, many proponents of the inductive school disagree with the ICJ's reference to the objective approach.

> In the *Reparation for Injuries* ... the International Court of Justice pronounced the *objective* international personality of the United Nations. While some international lawyers accepted this statement, the United Nations being a very special case, the *majority* attacked it. The prevailing doctrine is that international organizations, unlike states, do not come into existence directly by international law, as soon as certain facts, determined by international law, are present, but must be created by treaty, which is not binding on non-member states. Hence they have international personality only in so far as the treaty confers it on them; it is only this treaty, which forms their constitution, which delegates to them such powers as they may exercise; unlike states, they are not original, necessary, but derived subjects of international law; not general, but limited subjects with no objective personality, and therefore need recognition, which in this case, has constitutive effect, by non-member states. The prevailing doctrine can invoke many dicta of the Court in the ... advisory opinion. [Emphasis added] (Josef L. Kunz, 'Review of Seyersted, "Objective international personality of intergovernmental organisations: do their capacities really depend upon their constitution"' (1964) 58(4) AJIL 1042, 1042)

It may be argued the fact that advocates of both schools draw support for their viewpoints from the same judgment suggest the two approaches may not be irreconcilable. If one agrees that States create international organizations and allocate to them functions they can undertake only if they possess international legal personality, then one agrees that international organizations have international legal personality by virtue of international law (objective) to carry out their member States' intention as conferred by the constituent instruments (inductive). Other writers have amplified this view.

> The two views ... appear *prima facie* to be opposed. In fact, they may, or rather should, be reconciled. On the one hand, the Member States are the founding fathers of the institution. It means that their will, as expressed in the constituent treaty, cannot be easily disregarded. But the treaties establishing international organizations are often prudent on the question of personality and, except in a few instances, are silent or limit themselves to the recognition of a capacity in the municipal law of Member States. In this context, it is necessary to scrutinize the context of the constituent treaty to assess whether an international personality may be substantiated by, or deducted from, actual rights and obligations conferred to the organization ... by saying that, we do not endorse a subjective approach based solely on the will of the drafters of the treaty. On the contrary, an assessment based on the provisions of the constituent treaty may also be described as an objective test. Once a treaty is concluded, it leads its own life. States are not free to lay down the law; their acts and conducts do not escape the consequences to be drawn from

them by international law. (Philippe Gautier, 'The *Reparation for Injuries Case* revisited: the personality of the European Union' in J. A. Frowein (ed.), *Max Planck Yearbook of International Law* (The Hague: Kluwer Law International, 2000), p. 331)

thinking points

- *How reconcilable are the two approaches to determining the legal personality of international organizations?*
- *Which of the approaches did the ICJ adopt in* the Reparations Case?
- *What is the impact of the opinion of the Court in* the Reparations Case *on the debates about approaches to the legal personality of international organizations?*

5.5 The operation of legal personality

International organizations are conferred with legal personality mainly to enable them to operate on member States' territories (see Chapter 8 on immunity). Thus while they are international bodies, international organizations will often have to function within domestic systems. The following section therefore discusses how members and non-member States of international organizations deal with the question of legal personality.

5.5.1 Legal personality under domestic law

Article 104 of the UN Charter provides that:

> The Organization shall enjoy *in the territory* of each of its Members such legal capacity as may be necessary for the exercise of its functions and the fulfilment of its purposes. [Emphasis added]

Article 105 of the UN Charter concerning immunities also takes the same approach:

> The Organization shall enjoy in the territory of each of its Members such privileges and immunities as are necessary for the fulfilment of its purposes.

Also, Article 335 (ex Article 282 TEC) of the Treaty on the Functioning of the European Union (TFEU) provides that:

> In each of the Member States, the Union shall enjoy the most extensive legal capacity accorded to legal persons under their laws[.]

It must be noted that in all of these provisions, what the constituent treaties of the organizations require member States to accord them is legal capacity, not legal personality.

In the case of the UN, the reason for explicitly obligating member States to accord the organization legal capacity (not personality) on their territory was explained in *The Report to the [US] President on the Results of the San Francisco Conference* (Department of State Publication 349, Conference Series 270, 26 June 1945) thus:

It is apparent that an organization like the United Nations which *will have offices and employees, will purchase supplies, and presumably rent or purchase office space*, must have the legal capacity to enter into contracts, to take title to real and personal property and to appear in court (although its position as a defendant is protected by Article 105). The purpose of Article 104 is to make clear that the organization has the legal capacity ... The need for such a provision was discussed and rediscussed at the conferences dealing with those organizations and it has been the conclusion that for some states at least it is helpful to have such a provision included in the Charter to remove any doubt. It is the national law of each country which determines whether a particular body or organization which is not set up as a corporation under the law of that country will have legal capacity. *National laws vary greatly on this matter; in some instances Article 104 may be unnecessary, in some cases it may need to be supplemented by legislation, and in others it may operate of its own force to confer the necessary status.* The simple text adopted, using the same criterion as that applied in the case of privileges and immunities under Article 105, should be ample to take care of the actual needs of the Organization. [Emphasis added]

As is apparent from the above passage, UN member States must accord the organization legal capacity:

(a) in order to avoid doubt about the status of the organization;

(b) because, since the organization was not formed under the law of the concerned State, as national corporations are, it is the responsibility of the State to confer such capacity on it; and

(c) because it is only with the possession of legal capacity under the domestic law of a State that an international organization may enter into contracts, possess property, and carry out other activities listed in the above passage.

However, not every commentator agrees that it should be left to States to confer legal capacity on international organizations.

C. W. Jenks, in 'The legal personality of international organizations' (1945) 22 BYBIL 267, 270, notes that:

The legal capacity of public international organizations, like that of individual foreign States, derives from public international law; municipal legislation may be necessary to secure effective recognition of this capacity for municipal purposes, but the function of such legislation is declaratory and not constitutive; it is compatible with the declaratory function of such legislation that it should prescribe any conditions which may be thought appropriate for the exercise within the jurisdiction of the State concerned of legal personality attributed to the organization in question by an international constituent or by customary international law.

Clearly, Jenks was of the opinion that, rather than States, it is international law that has the responsibility of conferring legal capacity on international organizations, just as it confers it on States before other States. Therefore, if domestic law purports to confer legal capacity on international organizations, as Article 104 of the UN Charter apparently obligates States to do, such a law would be merely declaratory. It will be recalled from Chapter 4 that a law is declaratory if it is regarded as merely confirming what already exists.

... it is as inherently fantastic as it is destructive of any international legal order to regard the existence and extent of legal personality provided for in the constituent instrument of an international organization as being derived from, dependent upon, and limited by, the constitution and laws of its individuals member States. (Jenks, above, at 271)

thinking points

- *Distinguish between 'legal personality' and 'legal capacity'.*
- *What does it mean to say that the conferral of legal capacity on international organizations to operate on the territory of their member States is merely declaratory?*

5.5.2 The recognition of legal personality by non-member States

A case involving an international organization may come before the national court of a State that is not a member of that organization. Such a case may involve the State itself, its nationals, or other national interests. Whether the courts of that State will have jurisdiction to deal with the case depends largely on whether, in the first place, the State recognizes the personality of that organization.

Furthermore, since international organizations have an objective personality the personality of international organizations does not depend on States, but on their fulfilling certain prerequisites. The question, then, is whether such objective personality, being generally derived independently of States, binds non-member States of an organization.

● *Reparation for Injuries Suffered in the Service of the United Nations Advisory Opinion* (1949) ICJ REP 174 (The *Reparations Case*)

The Court considered whether Israel, against which the UN had brought the action, could object on the basis that it was not a member of the UN at the relevant time. In other words, since Israel was not a member of the UN, was it under any obligation to recognize the legal personality of the UN to bring an action against it?

In response to this question, the Court said (at 185) that:

> the Court's opinion is that fifty States, representing the vast majority of the members of the international community, had the power, in conformity with international law, to bring into being an entity possessing objective international personality, and not merely personality recognized by them alone, together with capacity to bring international claims.

This statement seems to imply that when fifty States established the UN in 1945, they did not intend the organization's objective personality to bind only those States. By implication, the Court decided that non-member States are bound to recognize the organization as well. However, the Court did not justify its statement.

In *Principles of Public International Law* (7th edn, Oxford: Oxford University Press, 2008), Ian Brownlie observed, at p. 689, that:

> In the ... case the International Court, with little elaboration, regarded the power to bring claims against non-members of the United Nations as a sort of corollary of the power to do so in respect of member states. The Court produced a statement which represents an assertion of political and constitutional fact rather than a reasoned conclusion.

However, with recognizing the legal personality of international organizations there is a distinction to be made between member and non-member States of the UN. As Amerasinghe has noted (2005, see section 5.4.1), at p. 76:

> Even where the constituent instrument of an organization does not expressly provide for legal personality in national law, member states are probably under an obligation to recognize such personality in their national legal systems. Such an obligation is an implied one arising from the relationship between members and organizations and from the principle of good faith. As for non-member states, *there is probably no such obligation* per se (even *though … the international personality of organization may be objective*). The problem is that there is no legal nexus between the non-member states and organization *and it cannot be assumed that there is a general customary rule* of international law requiring such recognition of personality in national legal systems. [Emphasis added]

The relationship between international organizations and non-member States, therefore, is one of continuing debate and discussion. While the legal personality of the organization may be recognized objectively on the international plane, with domestic recognition, issues relating to domestic law apply and the status of the organization should depend on the approach of the domestic law in question, as well as the relationship of the State in question with the organization.

thinking points

- *Of what relevance is the legal personality of international organizations to non-member States?*
- *How did the ICJ rationalize the relations of legal personality to non-member States of international organizations?*
- *Explain why it is important to understand how non-member States of international organizations recognize the personality of the latter.*

A rather interesting question, then, is: if international organizations have an objective personality and there is no customary international law principle that such personality must be recognized by *all* States, how do States recognize the personality of organizations of which they are not members? Note that this question is different from the question of *whether* non-member States should recognize the personality of international organizations.

The general principle of law guiding the relationship of States to treaties to which they are not party is laid down in Article 34 of the 1969 Vienna Convention on the Law of Treaties (VCLT). This Article states that 'a treaty does not create either obligations or rights for a third State without its consent'. The only exception to this is contained in Article 2(6) of the UN Charter, which states that:

> The Organization shall ensure that States which are not members of the United Nations act in accordance with the Principles so far as may be necessary for the maintenance of international peace and security.

But as Brownlie (2008, p. 689, see earlier in this section) has noted:

> This exception rests on the special character of the United Nations as an organization concerned primarily with the maintenance of peace and security in the world and including in its membership the great powers as well as the vast majority of states.

From practice, it has emerged that there are at least three ways in which non-members can recognize the legal personality of such organizations:

(a) through headquarters (or seat) agreements;

(b) by means of conflict-of-law (or private international) rules; and

(c) by non-member States taking unequivocal measures, with the effect of recognizing the organization.

These are illustrated by the following examples.

The headquarters agreement

. . . .

● *Centre pour le Développement Industrie (CDI) v. X* (1992) ACTUALITÉS DU DROIT 1377, TRIBUNAL CIVIL BRUXELLES

The CDI, an international organization established within the framework of the Lomé Convention concerning the EU and seventy Afro, Caribbean and Pacific (ACP) countries, had its headquarters in Belgium. It was set up mainly to promote partnership between ACP and European companies, in such areas as financial, technical, and commercial activities, among others. The defendant, who worked for CDI as a marketing adviser, had his contract terminated. He sought, and obtained, a substantial arbitral award from CDI which, in turn, sued him in Belgium to annul the award and also to stop the enforcement order that he had obtained from a lower court in Belgium. The defendant argued that CDI had no legal personality in Belgium and therefore could not sue in its courts.

It was held that the legal personality of the CDI was explicitly recognized in the headquarters agreement that it concluded with Belgium and also as a result of the automatic legal personality of the UN.

See also *In Re Poncet* (1948) 15 ILR 346, in which Switzerland, which at the relevant time was not a member of the UN, allowed the latter to defend an action on the basis of the headquarters agreement that it had with the UN.

The comity of nations and conflict-of-law rule

. . . .

● *Arab Monetary Fund v. Hashim (No. 3)* [1991] 2 AC 114

In 1976, twenty Arab States and Palestine entered into an agreement to create a monetary fund, with headquarters in Abu Dhabi. In 1985, the fund brought criminal proceedings in Switzerland against H, its former director-general, claiming that large sums belonging to it had been paid into the personal accounts of H and his wife at the Geneva branch of its bankers. The defendants applied to strike out the action on the ground that the fund was not an entity recognized under English law. The judge concluded that, ignoring the 1976 agreement, the fund was to be regarded as a foreign juridical personality constituted as a *persona ficta* under the law of the United Arab Emirates (UAE) and, as such, recognized under the common law conflict rules. He accordingly held that the Fund had capacity to sue in the English courts and dismissed the applications.

The Court of Appeal, by a majority, allowed the appeals by the defendants. Upon further appeal, the House of Lords, overruling the Court of Appeal and restoring Hoffmann J's decision in the lower court, held (at 114–115):

> that by the *comity of nations* the courts of the United Kingdom recognised a corporate body created by the laws of a foreign state recognised by the Crown, as the U.A.E. was; that the U.A.E. federal decree had conferred legal personality on the fund and created a corporate body that the English courts could and should recognise as entitled to sue; and that the fact that the fund had been incorporated not only in the U.A.E. but also in the other signatory states did not prevent that result. [Emphasis added]

It must be pointed out that, in allowing the Arab Monetary Fund (AMF) to sue in an English court, despite the fact that the Fund had no legal personality in the UK, the House of Lords relied on *conflict-of-law* rules, the principle of comity, and also the presence of certain *unequivocal measures* of the UK towards such entities as the AMF. But since this book is not concerned with private international law, it is not necessary to take this any further.

Unequivocal measures

Unequivocal measures are measures or steps which manifest a person's or body's acceptance to act or behave in a particular manner towards another notwithstanding the absence of any formal agreement between the two parties to act or behave in that specific manner. An example of the UK taking *unequivocal measures* towards recognizing the Fund's legal personality prior to the above case was recorded in the 1978 British Yearbook of International Law, pp. 346–348. The Bank of England had sought Her Majesty's advice about the status of:

> banks and other financial entities set up by a group of foreign sovereign states by a treaty (to which the United Kingdom is not a party), empowering them, expressly or by implication, to engage in banking, financial or other trading activities in member and non-member states and conferring on them, by virtue of the treaty, any related agreements and any necessary implementing legislation, legal personality in one or more states outside the UK, and, in particular, under the law of one or more member states or the state wherein the entity concerned has its seat or permanent location.

In response, the Foreign and Commonwealth Office (FCO) said that:

> In these circumstances, and on the assumption that the entity concerned enjoys, under its constitutive instrument or instruments and under the law of one or more member states or the state wherein it has its seat or permanent location, legal personality and capacity to engage in transactions of the type concerned governed by the law of a non-member state, the Foreign and Commonwealth Office, as the branch of the executive responsible for the conduct of foreign relations, would be *willing officially to acknowledge that the entity concerned enjoyed such legal personality and capacity*, and to state this. [Emphasis added]

● *Westland Helicopters Ltd & ors v. Arab Organization for Industrialization*
(1987) 80 ILR 622

The Arab Organization for Industrialization (AOI) was established by treaty between four Arab States in 1975, with significant assets to produce an Arab arms industry. The treaty made AOI independent of the laws of participating States. As a result of the 1978 Egyptian–Israeli peace treaty, other Arab States agreed to sanctions against Egypt, at a time when contracts had been made with Westland Helicopters. Three Gulf States party to AOI purported to terminate the activities of AOI. Egypt denied the effectiveness of such termination, because AOI was incorporated in Egypt which, by a 1979 decree, changed the constitution of AOI and declared that Egyptians would conduct the affairs of the organization, to be known as AOI 1979. Westland Helicopters brought this action for compensation from AOI, although Egypt maintained that by virtue of its 1979 decree, AOI continued in existence. Westland Helicopters obtained an arbitration award in its favour against AOI. The Cairo-based AOI 1979 claimed to intervene, in order to challenge the award, on the basis that it was the same organization as AOI. AOI 1979 claimed that the constitution and representation of AOI were governed by Egyptian law and continued by the 1979 decree. Westland Helicopters disputed the *locus standi* of AOI 1979.

The implication of Egypt's argument was that the activities of the old and new AOI were governed by Egyptian law. The Court rejected this argument, and said (at 304) that:

> It is ... difficult to conceive of a course more obviously contrary ... to the comity of nations than the imposition as the governing law by the English courts of the domestic law of any one such member state, whether or not the seat of the organisation. To do so would be (a) at least potentially an affront to all the other member states whose domestic law was necessarily to be ignored and (b) inconsistent with a widely accepted principle of public international law to which member states would be likely to adhere, namely that an international organisation is a creature exclusively of public international law ... If in such a case there were to be imposed a rule of English domestic conflicts law that such a treaty provision were to yield to the domestic law of the seat state, that would involve the application to issues likely to affect the member states of a body of law which they had expressly agreed was to be inapplicable. Such a rule would be eccentric by comparison with the approach of other states to the same matter and would be contrary to the comity of nations inasmuch as it would involve ignoring the express terms of the treaty ...

And (at 313) the Court continued:

> Having concluded that the proper law governing the constitution of A.O.I. is public international law and further that the intervener is unable to prove in the English courts that under that body of law it is the same entity as A.O.I., I reject the intervener's submission that in these courts it has standing to set aside the order of Clarke J. of 9 July 1993 giving leave to enforce the award against A.O.I. as a judgment.

KEY POINTS

- Non-member States of international organizations can recognize their legal personality by: (a) concluding headquarters (or seat) agreements with them, such as that which exists between Switzerland and the UN; (b) application of the principle of *comity of nations*; and (c) taking certain measures that amount to recognizing the legal personality of the organization.

- *Westland Helicopters* is particularly important because it firmly established that it is the principles of international law, not those of national law, that govern the constitution and activities of international organizations.

- *Arab Monetary Fund* is authority for establishing that: (a) where an international organization is established in a foreign country recognized by the UK, the UK will recognize the personality of the organization; and (b) by the principle of comity of nations and conflict-of-law rules, once an international organization has been established by one State and is recognized by other States, the UK will recognize the legal personality of such an organization.

thinking points

- *What is the relevance of Article 34 VCLT to the recognition of legal personality by non-members of international organizations?*
- *Is there any exception to the rule in Article 34 VCLT?*
- *Explain the following terms: 'headquarters agreements'; 'comity of nations'; and 'conflict-of-law rules'. How do these apply to legal personality?*

5.5.3 The consequences of legal personality

That international organizations possess legal personality does not explain the consequences thereof. Legal personality is nothing but a quality and suggests only that the organization is a juristic person, which can sue and be sued in its own name.

In *Law-Making by International Organizations* (Stockholm: Norstedt, 1965), p. 21, Ingrid Deter said that:

> ...the concept of personality does not say anything about the qualities of the person: it may be a State, it may be an organization, it may perhaps even be an individual. The fact that, for example, an organization has international personality does not indicate that it will enjoy any particular rights.

D. P. O'Connell, *International Law, Vol. 1* (2nd edn, London: Stevens, 1970), p. 109, notes that:

> It is a mistake to jump to the conclusion that an organization has personality and then to deduce specific capacities from an *a priori* conception of the concomitants of personality. The correct approach is to equate personality with capacities and to inquire what capacities are functionally implied in the entities concerned.

The singularly most undeniable effect of legal personality is that it sets the organization apart from its member States.

. . . .

● *J. H. Rayner (Mincing Lane) Ltd v. Department of Trade and Industry & ors and related appeals* (1989) 5 BCC 872, HL

In this case, Lord Oliver said (at 897) that:

> the effect of the grant of the legal capacities of a body corporate was that in UK law, the ITC...was invested with a legal personality distinct from its members, *with the consequence that, when it entered into engagements, it and not the membership was the contracting party.* [Emphasis added]

The manner in which the courts and writers have generally dealt with the consequences of legal personality of international organizations leads to the identification of two sets of consequences: the capacity to exercise certain powers; and the enjoyment of certain rights and privileges.

The capacity to exercise powers

In addition to having a separate identity from that of member States, international organizations, which possess legal personality, have certain capacities, including the capacity to bring international claims in their own right, to conclude treaties, to bear full responsibility for non-performance or breach of international obligations, and to take decisions relevant to their sphere of operation, among others. Also, by virtue of their possessing legal personality, some (but not all) international organizations enjoy certain immunities and privileges different from the general capacities, which will be discussed separately.

Express powers

The constituent treaties of international organizations usually list the specific powers that they can exercise. These powers are usually linked to the purposes and objectives for which specific international organizations are established and may cover a wide range of activities. A perfect example of express power is found in the UN Charter, Article 1 of which provides that the purposes of the United Nations are:

> To maintain international peace and security, *and to that end: to take effective collective measures* for the prevention and removal of threats to the peace, and for the suppression of acts of aggression or other breaches of the peace, and to bring about by peaceful means, and in conformity with the principles of justice and international law, adjustment or settlement of international disputes or situations which might lead to a breach of the peace…[Emphasis added]

Here, one of the purposes of the UN is to 'maintain international peace and security'. But the Charter does not stop there: it goes on to confer the UN with the specific power that it needs to accomplish this purpose. Hence, the statement 'to that end, to take effective collective measures…'.

Often, international organizations are given the capacity to make treaties and enter into treaties with third parties. For example, it is envisaged that the UN will have to conclude several treaties bringing its specialized agencies into existence.

Article 57(1) of the UN Charter states that:

> The various specialized agencies, established by intergovernmental agreement and having wide international responsibilities, as defined in their basic instruments, in economic, social, cultural, educational, health, and related fields, shall be brought into relationship with the United Nations in accordance with the provisions of Article 63.

Article 63 provides that:

> The Economic and Social Council may enter into agreements with any of the agencies referred to in Article 57, defining the terms on which the agency concerned shall be brought into relationship with the United Nations. Such agreements shall be subject to approval by the General Assembly.

These two provisions show that the UN may conclude agreements (treaties, conventions, etc.) to establish its specialized agencies. Also, such powers can relate to the seat of international organizations. For example, the 1949 Statute of the Council of Europe envisages the conclusion of such a treaty with France.

Article 42(b) of the 1949 Statute reads:

> The members undertake as soon as possible to enter into agreement for the purpose of fulfilling the provisions of paragraph a above. For this purpose the Committee of Ministers shall recommend to the governments of members the acceptance of an agreement defining the privileges and

> immunities to be granted in the territories of all members. In addition, a special agreement shall be concluded with the Government of the French Republic defining the privileges and immunities which the Council shall enjoy at its seat.

As seen, international organizations enjoy great freedom in exercising powers; however, the treaty-making power is not unlimited. It is possible, for example, that the organization itself has mechanisms for controlling such treaties. Hence, in Article 63 of the UN Charter, any treaty concluded by the UN concerning the creation of its specialized agencies must be approved by the UN General Assembly.

The process of control is even more rigorous under the Treaty on the Functioning of the European Union (TEU) and the validity of the exercise of such power in any situation may be subject to judicial determination.

Article 218(11) TEU (ex Article 300(6) TEC) provides:

> A Member State, the European Parliament, the Council or the Commission *may obtain the opinion of the Court of Justice* as to whether an agreement envisaged is *compatible* with the Treaties. Where the opinion of the Court is adverse, the agreement envisaged may not enter into force unless it is amended or the Treaties are revised. [Emphasis added]

Clearly, the aim of this Article is to ensure that international organizations do not conclude treaties that are inconsistent with their own constituent treaties or any other treaties already ratified by them. But, more importantly, it is to ensure that whatever treaties an international organization concludes are reconcilable with the purposes and objectives of the organization.

Implied powers

In the vast majority of cases and as seen in the previous examples, the treaty-making powers of international organizations are expressed in their constituent treaties. Nonetheless, international organizations often encounter situations in respect of which their treaties contain no provisions at all. Such situations could, in fact, relate to treaty-making, immunities and privileges, deployment of troops, and so on. In those circumstances, such organizations will often have to invoke what is generally referred to as the 'implied powers' doctrine. Under this doctrine, an international organization is able to assume powers that are not explicitly provided for in its treaty, but are also not forbidden, in order to discharge its functions.

In *The International Status of the United Nations* (London: Stevens & Sons Ltd, 1961), Guenter Weissberg states, at p. 203, that:

> The execution of an objective by means not specifically listed in the Charter increases the capabilities of the Organization. An application of a particular function often leads to the exercise of additional new functions, which may be of greater relevance than the original purposes. Yet it must be realised that these are derivative powers.

● *Reparation for Injuries Suffered in the Service of the United Nations Advisory Opinion* (1949) ICJ REP 174 (The *Reparations Case*)

The ICJ was confronted with determining whether the UN had the capacity to bring an international claim against a State responsible for causing injury to the UN and to a UN staff member. The Court stated (at 180) that:

...the rights and duties of an entity such as the Organization must depend upon its purposes and functions as *specified* or *implied* in its constituent documents and developed in practice...and the Court concludes that the Members have endowed the Organization with *capacity* to bring international claims when necessitated by the discharge of its functions. [Emphasis added]

In determining whether the UN has powers in its Charter to deal with the claims, the Court divided the issue into two: first, it considered whether the UN could claim for damages caused to *itself*; and, secondly, it looked at whether it can claim for injury caused to its *agents*.

As per the UN claim in respect of itself, the Court said (at 180) that:

The question is concerned solely with the *reparation of damage caused to the Organization* when one of its agents suffers injury at the same time. *It cannot be doubted that the Organization has the capacity to bring an international claim against one of its Members which has caused injury to it by a breach of its international obligations towards it.* The damage specified in Question 1 (a) means exclusively damage caused to the interests of the Organization itself, to its administrative machine, to its property and assets, and to the interests of which it is the guardian. It is clear that the Organization has the capacity to bring a claim for this damage. [Emphasis added]

Clearly, the Court accepted that the UN had the capacity to bring a claim against any of its member States that has caused it injury.

Although there is no specific provision to the effect that the UN can bring an international claim when it is injured, the Court implied this capacity from the personality of the UN. As it said (at 179):

It is difficult to see how such a convention could operate except upon the international plane and as between parties possessing international personality. In the opinion of the Court, the Organization was intended to exercise and enjoy, and is in fact exercising and enjoying, functions and rights which can only be explained on the basis of the possession of large measures of international personality and the capacity to operate on the international plane.

With regard to the second question before the Court—that is, whether the 'United Nations...has the capacity to bring an international claim...in respect of the damage caused...*to the victim* or to persons entitled through him'—the Court implied the power of the UN to do so. It said (at 182) that:

The Charter does not expressly confer upon the Organization the capacity to include, in its claim for reparation, *damage caused to the victim* or to persons entitled through him. The Court must therefore begin by enquiring whether the provisions of the Charter concerning the functions of the Organization, and the part played by its agents in the performance of those functions, imply for the Organization power to afford its agents the limited protection that would consist in the bringing of a claim on their behalf for reparation for damage suffered in such circumstances. Under international law, *the Organization must be deemed to have those powers which, though not expressly provided in the Charter, are conferred upon it by necessary implication as being essential* to the performance of its duties. [Emphasis added]

thinking points

- *Give examples of express capacities of international organizations.*
- *Explain the basis upon which the Court in* the Reparations Case *accepted that the UN can bring international claims against States that cause it injury.*
- *Is there any limit to the power of international organizations to make treaties or to enter into agreements?*

In cases after *Reparations*, the ICJ adapted the implied power theory to situations ranging from the setting up of administrative tribunals by the UN to the authorization of peacekeeping operations by the UN General Assembly.

- ● *Effects of Award of Compensation made by the UN Administrative Tribunal Advisory Opinion* (1954) ICJ Rep 47

In this case, the question before the Court was whether the UN General Assembly could refuse to give effect to the decisions of the UN Administrative Tribunal on the termination of UN staff contracts without their consent.

The Court stated (at 57) that:

> The Charter contains no provision which authorizes any of the principal organs of the United Nations to adjudicate upon these disputes, and Article 105 secures for the United Nations jurisdictional immunities in national courts. It would, in the opinion of the Court, hardly be consistent with the expressed aim of the Charter to promote freedom and justice for individuals and with the constant preoccupation of the United Nations Organization to promote this aim that it should afford no judicial or arbitral remedy to its own staff for the settlement of any disputes which may arise between it and them. In these circumstances, the Court finds that the power to establish a tribunal, to do justice as between the Organization and the staff members, was essential to ensure the efficient working of the Secretariat, and to give effect to the paramount consideration of securing the highest standards of efficiency, competence and integrity. *Capacity to do this arises by necessary intendment out of the Charter.* [Emphasis added]

- ● *Certain Expenses of the United Nations Advisory Opinion* (1962) ICJ Rep 151

In this case (at 168) the Court said that:

> when the Organization takes action which warrants the assertion that it was appropriate for the fulfilment of one of the stated purposes of the United Nations, the presumption is that such action is not *ultra vires* the Organization.

thinking points

- On what basis would the Court infer the implied power doctrine in favour of an international organization?
- What difference, if any, is there between the UN suing for injuries caused to it and those caused to its personnel?
- In what situations has the ICJ applied the implied power doctrine?

The rather liberal attitude of the ICJ regarding the implied power doctrine, revealed by the various instances in which it has invoked the doctrine, has led to some writers cautioning against using the theory as an excuse for attributing undue powers to international organizations.

According to Ian Brownlie (2008, see section 5.5.2), at pp. 686–687:

> Judicial interpretation may lead to expansion of the competence of an organization if resort be had to the teleological principle according to which action in accordance with the stated purposes of an organization is *intra vires* or at least is presumed to be … Obviously the judicial power of appreciation is wide, and the principles enunciated *in this fashion may be used as a cloak for extensive legislation*. The process of interpretation cannot be subordinated to arbitrary

devices . . . Particular care should be taken to avoid an automatic implication, from the very fact of legal personality, of particular powers, such as the power to make treaties with third states or the power to delegate powers. [Emphasis added]

● **Reparation for Injuries Suffered in the Service of the United Nations Advisory Opinion** (1949) ICJ REP 174 [The **Reparations Case**]

Brownlie's caution reflected the dissenting opinion of Hackworth J in this case. Although Hackworth J did not seem to reject the 'implied theory' altogether, he denied its application to this particular case when he said (at 198):

> There can be no gainsaying the fact that the Organization is one of delegated and enumerated powers. It is to be presumed that such powers as the Member States desired to confer upon it are stated either in the Charter or in complementary agreements concluded by them. Powers not expressed cannot freely be implied. Implied powers flow from a grant of expressed powers, and are limited to those that are 'necessary' to the exercise of powers expressly granted. No necessity for the exercise of the power here in question has been shown to exist.

According to Hackworth J, powers can be implied only if there are expressed powers. This would mean, in practice, that international organizations can extend only powers that already exist by virtue of express provisions of their treaties, so that where no power is stated at all, none can be implied.

More recently, some international organizations have limited the scope of what can be implied in their functioning. For example, the 1994 Agreement Relating to the Implementation of Part XI of the United Nations Convention on the Law of the Sea (UNCLOS) (1982), in delimiting the powers of the International Seabed Authority (ISA), states that:

> . . . The powers and functions of the Authority shall be *those expressly conferred upon it by the Convention*. The Authority shall have such incidental powers, consistent with the Convention, as are implicit in, and necessary for, the exercise of those powers and functions with respect to activities in the Area. [Emphasis added]

Obviously, the ISA cannot always resort to implied powers in order to deal with situations with which it may be confronted. Its ability to imply powers depends on whether what is to be implied is necessary with respect to its activities and such must be consistent with its Convention, so the provision may be somewhat redundant.

thinking points

- *What are the consequences of legal personality?*
- *Explain the meaning of 'implied powers'? How has the ICJ applied its application?*
- *Explain what is meant by 'express powers'. On what basis do international organizations derive their express powers?*
- *With regard to the Agreement between the Swiss Federal Council and the International Labour Organization Concerning the Legal Status of the [ILO] in Switzerland and the Reparations Case, how did the Court understand the principle of 'essentiality' in relation to implied powers?*
- *In what ways do international organizations now attempt to limit what can be implied with regard to the powers of international organizations?*

Powers to make decisions

As a result of possessing legal personality, international organizations are also able to take decisions regarding their own internal working and concerning their activities on the international plane. Although the decision-making powers of international organizations are either expressed in their constituent treaties or implied, and therefore fall under the general powers discussed earlier, separate treatment of the issue is required, because of the consequences of such decisions—especially for third States (non-member States).

A first important point to note is that international organizations can take binding decisions in respect of their members. For example, Article 25 of the UN Charter provides that:

> The Members of the United Nations agree to accept and carry out the decisions of the Security Council in accordance with the present Charter.

Article 4(h) of the Constitutive Act of the African Union provides for:

> The right of the Union to intervene in a Member State *pursuant to a decision of the Assembly* in respect of grave circumstances, namely war crimes, genocide and crimes against humanity. [Emphasis added]

Article 14 of the Inter-American Democratic Charter of the OAS states that:

> Member states agree to review periodically the actions adopted and carried out by the Organization to promote dialogue, cooperation for integral development, and the fight against poverty in the Hemisphere, *and to take the appropriate measures* to further these objectives. [Emphasis added]

Aside from binding decisions, international organizations are also able to make recommendations to their member States. The difference is that while decisions of the UN Security Council under Article 25 are binding on UN member States, its *recommendations* made under Article 39 are not.

Article 39 of the UN Charter states that:

> The Security Council shall determine the existence of any threat to the peace, breach of the peace, or act of aggression and shall make *recommendations*, or decide what measures shall be taken in accordance with Articles 41 and 42, to maintain or restore international peace and security.

Considering that international organizations do not possess law-making powers, the power to make non-binding decisions, such as recommendations, is very important. Some non-binding decisions can take the form of declarations. These are regarded as soft laws—that is, a bundle of norms that may later evolve into binding legal obligations for member States. Furthermore, although, generally speaking, recommendations are not binding, it is expected that States will implement them in good faith, therefore attracting some legal significance to them.

● *Grimaldi v. Fonds des Maladies Professionnelles* Case C-322/88 [1989] ECR 4407 (The *Grimaldi Case*)

In this case, the European Court was confronted with a determination of the effect of two recommendations of the European Community.

Mr Grimaldi, who worked in Belgium from 1953 to 1980, suffered an occupational disease in relation to which he brought a claim. His employer decided that since the disease was not one of those listed in the Belgian schedule of occupational diseases, he had no claim. In a subsequent action that Grimaldi brought before a tribunal, it was held that while the disease was indeed not one of the listed ones, it formed part of a list of diseases that a European directive recommended that member States should implement.

On the status of this recommendation, the Court said (at [18]) that:

> it must be stressed that the measures in question [recommendatory measures] cannot therefore be regarded as having no legal effect. The national courts are bound to take recommendations into consideration in order to decide disputes submitted to them, in particular where they cast light on the interpretation of national measures adopted in order to implement them or where they are designed to supplement binding Community provisions.

Inherent powers

Aside from express and implied powers, international organizations also possess inherent powers. Inherent powers are powers which accrue to international organizations by virtue of their possessing legal personality. But what constitutes the inherent powers of international organizations, much as with domestic institutions like courts or legislators, is not always easy to determine. This is because unlike express powers, inherent powers are not usually written into constitutions or treaties, even if they are believed to form part of the purpose for which the constitution or treaty exists. Therefore, entities which claim inherent powers over anything often have to infer such from their being, that is from the very purpose of their existence.

There is also a lack of early engagement by writers with the inherent powers doctrine, with the most attention devoted to implied powers with which inherent powers is often confused. In *Common Law of International Organizations* (Leiden: Martinus Nijhoff Publishers, 2008), Finn Seyersted states (at p. 31) that:

> Even the International Court of Justice used the doctrine of 'implied powers' in its advisory opinions of 1949 and 1954—until it in 1962 turned to the contrary principle of inherent powers submitted to the judges by the present writer. However, the majority of writers never discovered this turnaround; they still stick to the false point of departure and then escaped via 'implied' powers.

Inherent power: definition and distinction from implied powers

Inherent powers has been defined, in relation to the US inherent presidential powers, as 'a general class of power which are neither expressly stated in the constitution nor delegated by the Congress' (L. Fisher, President and Congress (1972), p. 32, restated in Erwin Chemerinsky, 'Controlling inherent presidential powers: providing a framework for judicial review' (1983) 56 Southern California L Rev 863, 866).

Inherent powers is often confused with implied powers. In 'The inherent power of the judiciary' (1935) 11(2) Indiana LJ, p. 116, Henry M. Dowling describes the US courts' attempt to deal with a range of cases over which the constitution did not ascribe explicit powers to them (pp. 119–120) thus:

> While the courts thus freely use the term 'inherent power,' they do not always define it ... it may mean the right of the court to act in a matter left untouched by the legislature ... *Or, again, the term*

may connote what is essential to the existence, dignity and functions of the court as a constitutional tribunal and from the very fact that it is a court, in which case the power may be described either as 'implied,' 'essential,' 'incidental' or 'inherent;' always understanding that it is a necessary adjunct to such courts as the constitution has seen fit to create. *It is in this latter sense that we shall use the term, as such is the meaning usually attached to it by the courts.* [Emphasis added]

Clearly this statement equates 'inherent powers' with 'implied powers'. Inherent powers are different from implied powers in that whereas with regard to the latter an entity claims that power in order to be able to perform the functions for which it is established, inherent powers form part of the essence of that entity's existence. Thus, in a sense implied powers enable an entity to achieve its goals, and those goals can be expressly stated in the treaty of an international organization or inherent in it.

example

The President of Candoma is the head of State and Commander in Chief of Armed Forces of Candoma. The constitution enumerates the powers of the president as (a) to ensure the security of the country and citizens, (b) to represent Candoma in all transactions with other countries, and (c) to take necessary steps to defend the country. These are the only powers found in the Candoman Constitution. Rutamu declares a war against Candoma and the latter's president, seeing that his country's army is poorly equipped, calls on friendly States to send their troops as reinforcements. The power to do this would be deemed 'inherent'—that is, innate in the very purpose of the office of the president as the Commander in Chief of Armed Forces of Candoma. This is inherent power. However, if the Candoman president decides to delegate the responsibility for managing the war against Rutamu to a Committee he or she sets up for that purpose (and which committee is also provided for by the constitution), then the power to delegate is implied. The power to delegate does not form part of the reasons for the office of the president as the Commander in Chief. However, it is a power that will help the president to achieve the purpose of his or her office, which is defending the country against enemies.

KEY POINTS

- International organizations can make both binding decisions and recommendations.

- Recommendations are often implemented in good faith and thus attract some serious legal consequences.

- International organizations have various powers both in relation to their internal administration and external relations.

5.5.4 'Beyond power' (ultra vires) decisions

A decision taken by an organization may be within its powers (intra vires) but not necessarily valid in relation to third parties. Conversely, a decision taken by an international organization may be valid externally, but in breach of its own procedural regulations. In addition, since international organizations can imply powers that are not expressly provided for by their treaties, determining what is intra vires is not always straightforward.

A logical question is: if an organization takes a decision that is ultra vires, does it mean that the decision is void *ab initio* (that is, void from the beginning), so that it is of no legal consequence whatsoever, or is it only merely voidable, in which case it stands as good unless and until otherwise avoided?

Before considering these issues, let us first examine how to determine the legality of decisions made by international organizations.

Determining the legality of international organizations' decisions

Treaties of most international organizations do not explicitly empower members to challenge or judicially review decisions of international organizations. One of the few exceptions is the TEU.

According to Article 19(3)(b) TEU:

> The Court of Justice of the European Union shall, in accordance with the treaties give preliminary rulings, at the request of courts or tribunals of the Member States, on the interpretation of Union law or the validity of acts adopted by the institutions.

The right of member States to challenge decisions of international organizations is widely recognized as derived from the consensual nature of international law, and the duty of every member State of an international organization to ensure consistency between the works of the organization and its purposes and objectives.

. . . .

● *Certain Expenses of the United Nations Advisory Opinion* [1962] ICJ REP 151

In this case, in his dissenting opinion Judge Bustamante stated (at 304) that:

> When, in the Opinion of one of the Member States, a mistake of interpretation has been made or there has even been an infringement of the Charter, there is a right to challenge the resolution in which the error has been noted for the purpose of determining whether or not it departed from the Charter.

Academic writers have echoed this view. According to Ebere Osieke, 'The legal validity of ultra vires decisions of international organizations' (1983) 77 AJIL 239:

> The right of member states in these cases appear to derive from the consensual nature of the constitution concerned. Because they are international treaties, each party possesses an inherent right to supervise their implementation to ensure that the organizations do not adopt decisions that would be incompatible with their objects and purposes, or that would be detrimental to the interests of the member states in excess of what they had accepted as the basis for membership.

The UN Charter does not contain a provision comparable to that of the EU quoted above. However, under Article 96, the UN, or its specialized agencies, can request an advisory opinion of the ICJ. In practice, the Court has taken advantage of this process to determine the legality of UN Security Council decisions in some circumstances.

. . . .

● *Legal Consequences for States of the Continued Presence of South Africa in Namibia (South West Africa) notwithstanding Security Council Resolution 276 (1970) Advisory Opinion* [1971] ICJ REP 16 (The *Namibia Advisory Opinion*)

Following the termination of South Africa's mandate over South West Africa (now Namibia), and South Africa's refusal to vacate that country, the question was asked to the ICJ of the consequences of South Africa's continued presence in Namibia. It must be pointed out that the Court was not directly asked about the validity of the UN General Assembly and Security Council resolutions in this case.

At [89] of its judgment, the Court acknowledged that it:

> does not possess powers of judicial review or appeal in respect of the decisions taken by the United Nations organs concerned. The question of the validity or conformity with the Charter of General Assembly resolution 2145 (XXI) or of related Security Council resolutions does not form the subject of the request for advisory opinion.

But despite this outright denial of review power, the Court went on to pronounce that:

> in the exercise of its judicial function and since objections have been advanced, the Court, in the course of its reasoning, will consider these objections before determining any legal consequences arising from those resolutions.

At [95], the Court pronounced on the validity of the relevant resolution:

> The resolution in question is therefore to be viewed as the exercise of the right to terminate a relationship in case of a deliberate and persistent violation of obligations which destroys the very object and purpose of that relationship.

● *Certain Expenses of the United Nations Advisory Opinion* (1962) ICJ Rep 151

The UN General Assembly requested the ICJ to consider whether certain expenses incurred by the UN in its operations in Congo and Egypt constituted UN expenses within the meaning of Article 17 of the UN Charter. One interesting point in this case was that France had proposed an amendment to the request made to the Court by the General Assembly. The effect of the amendment was that the Court should also decide whether the expenditures were 'decided in conformity with provisions of the Charter'. This effectively requested a review of the expenses decisions. The General Assembly rejected the amendment.

Nonetheless, the Court stated (at 157) that:

> The rejection of the French amendment does not constitute a directive to the Court to exclude from its consideration the question whether certain expenditures were 'decided on in conformity with the Charter', if the Court finds such consideration appropriate. It is not to be assumed that the General Assembly would thus seek to fetter or hamper the Court in the discharge of its judicial functions; the Court must have full liberty to consider all relevant data available to it in forming an opinion on a question posed to it for an advisory opinion.

The Court's reference to 'if the Court finds such consideration appropriate' implies that it is up to the Court to decide whether or not to exercise power of judicial review.

KEY POINTS

- Most treaties of international organizations do not provide for members to challenge decisions of international organizations or mechanisms for the judicial review of such decisions (but see the TEU).

- The power of States to challenge decisions of international organizations derives from the consensual nature of international law.

- In practice, the ICJ has quietly reviewed some decisions of UN organs, especially those contained in recommendatory resolutions, and when giving advisory opinions.

The effects of ultra vires acts of international organizations

There are two opposing views about the effect of ultra vires acts in international law. On the one hand, some view such acts as devoid of all legal effects. In *Certain Expenses*, Judge Morrelli, said (at 222) that since international law does not have the concept of 'voidability', which, in domestic law, means that an act is valid until avoided, then acts of international organizations can either be valid or invalid; there is nothing in between. On the other hand, however, it has been said that ultra vires acts of international organizations are good until avoided.

There is considerable debate about these opposing views. However, what is important to note is that some organizations have removed doubts about the status of ultra vires acts from their functioning. Some international organizations' treaties now preserve the initial actions of organizations or institutions until the power of such organizations or institutions to perform such actions has been nullified by the appropriate process.

Article 7(3) of the 1919 ILO Constitution, as amended by the Instrument of Amendment of 1972, which entered into force on 1 November 1974, states that:

> The Governing Body shall, as occasion requires, determine which are the Members of the Organization of chief industrial importance and shall make rules to ensure that all questions relating to the selection of the Members of chief industrial importance are considered by an impartial committee before being decided by the Governing Body. Any appeal made by a Member from the declaration of the Governing Body as to which are the Members of chief industrial importance shall be decided by the Conference, *but an appeal to the Conference shall not suspend the application of the declaration until such time as the Conference decides the appeal.* [Emphasis added]

Similarly, Article 264 TEU (ex Article 231 TEC) provides:

> If the action [challenging the legality of an act] is well founded, the Court of Justice of the European Union shall declare the act concerned to be void. However, the Court shall if it considers this necessary, state *which of the effects of the act which it has declared void shall be considered as definitive.* [Emphasis added]

Thus while it is fairly clear that an illegal act shall be declared void, the Court of Justice of the European Union reserves for itself the discretion to exclude some effects of the acts from being permanently void.

According to Osieke (1983, see earlier in this section), at 245:

> The non attribution of absolute nullity to the substantive *ultra vires* acts of international organiza-tions . . . would appear to be justified by the special character of the decisions of international organizations. Many of their decisions, such as those relating to admission of new members or the creation of committees or subsidiary organs, very often become effective immediately after adoption, and it would be unrealistic to maintain that all the actions taken by the organiza-tion and its organs, as well as third parties, should be considered as absolute nullities on the basis of the subsequent invalidation of the substantive decision by a review body. The fact that these acts are only voidable may not be entirely satisfactory, but the alternative would lead to uncertainties and chaos, which would weaken the effectiveness of international organizations.

A possible solution may be to suspend the implementation of decisions against which objections have been made until the matter is decided by the review body.

Article 86 of the Convention on International Civil Aviation, signed at Chicago on 7 December 1944 (the Chicago Convention), states that:

> *Unless the Council decides otherwise* any decision by the Council on whether an international airline is operating in conformity with the provisions of this Convention *shall remain in effect* unless reversed on appeal. On any other matter, decisions of the Council shall, if appealed from, *be suspended until the appeal is decided*... [Emphasis added]

It must be pointed out that only the substantive acts that are ultra vires attract nullification. 'Substantive acts' are those that touch on the core activities of the organization, such as appointment of members, setting up of committees, and so on. In contrast, 'procedural acts', such as acts undertaken by an element of an international organization that is not constitutionally empowered to so act, are not necessarily void. This is a mere procedural ultra vires and the widely accepted view is that such is not void. This certainly has been the attitude of the ICJ in those cases in which procedural irregularity occurs.

● *Certain Expenses of the United Nations Advisory Opinion* [1962] ICJ REP 151

One of the grounds of the complaint was that the action in respect of which the contested expenses were incurred was authorized by the UN General Assembly, an organ that the UN Security Council complained was not *constitutionally empowered* to authorize such missions.

As seen earlier, the Court held that the expenses themselves, since they were incurred pursuant to UN activities, were UN expenses. However, on the issue of the expenses being incurred in an operation supposedly authorized by an incompetent organ of the UN, the Court said (at 168) that:

> If it is agreed that the action in question is within the scope of the functions of the Organization but it is alleged that it has been initiated or carried out in a manner not in conformity with the division of functions among the several organs which the Charter prescribes, one moves to the internal plane, to the internal structure of the Organization. If the action was taken by the wrong organ, it was irregular as a matter of that internal structure, but this would not necessarily mean that the expense incurred was not an expense of the Organization. Both national and international law contemplate cases in which the body corporate or politic may be bound, as to third parties, by an *ultra vires* act of an agent.

● *India v. Pakistan* [1972] ICJ REP 69 (*Appeal Relating to the Jurisdiction of the International Civil Aviation Organization [ICAO] Council*)

In this case, the Court had to deal with a matter that arose from an appeal by India against a decision of an aviation matter between India and Pakistan by the ICAO Council. While India was prepared to admit that the ICAO Council had jurisdiction over the matter, it complained, however, that the ICAO process 'was vitiated by various procedural irregularities and should accordingly, on that ground alone, be declared null and void' (at [44]).

The Court held (at 69–70), that:

> Since the Court holds that the Council did and does have jurisdiction, then, if there were in fact procedural irregularities, the position would be that the Council would have reached the right conclusion in the wrong way. Nevertheless, it would have reached the right conclusion.

thinking points

- *What does the term 'ultra vires' mean?*
- *What are the justifications for proposing that ultra vires acts should be void ab initio?*
- *What are the grounds for positing that ultra vires acts should be voidable?*
- *Explain the difference between 'substantive' and 'procedural' irregularities with regard to ultra vires acts.*

Accountability of international organizations

Closely related to the issue of ultra vires is the accountability of international organizations. While ultra vires concerns whether the act of an organization is within its constitutional authority, accountability deals with holding international organizations responsible for all their acts. As will be seen in Chapter 18 dealing with international economic law, for example, the accountability of the World Bank involves ensuring that the projects funded by the Bank are implemented in accordance with its policies and procedures. Similarly, holding the UN accountable for its actions entails that the activities of its organs, such as the Security Council, are carried out in a way consistent with the core values, purposes, and principles of the Charter.

The quest for accountability of international organizations attained seriousness only when the ILC decided to focus on the responsibility of international organizations in 2000. This was a year before the ILC adopted its Articles on States Responsibility for Internationally Wrongful Acts (ARSIWA) on which it spent almost fifty years (see Chapter 13).

However, this does not mean that there was no attempt of some sort at the international plane to focus on the accountability of international organizations much earlier. In 1996, the International Law Association (ILA), a community of international legal scholars, established a Committee on the Accountability of International Organizations. (See the Final Report of the Committee adopted by the ILA's 71st Conference in Berlin, Germany, 16–21 August 2004, Report of the International Law Association Committee on Accountability of International Organizations, available at http://www.ila-hq.org/en/committees/index.cfm/cid/9.)

It should be emphasized that the ILA is only an academic community, not a UN body like the ILC responsible for the codification of international law. Hence, while the ILA's work on international law might be intellectually beneficial and perhaps serve as reference points on areas of international law that are worthy of attention, such works do not bind States or international organizations, and play no formal role whatsoever in the codification of international law.

Ironically, the major reason for the ILC's slow take on the responsibility of international organizations is the latter's legal personality. The ILC's initial approach to responsibility was that since international organizations possess their own personality, they could not bear responsibility for their member States' actions. However, the ILC Rapporteur for State Responsibility, James Crawford, abandoned the idea that State responsibility implies only the 'responsibility of one state to another state'. (See James Crawford, *International Law as an Open System* (London: Cameron May, 2002), p. 29.) From this moment, it became apparent that:

> The legal personality of international organizations could no longer be seen as a démarche for member states to avoid joint and several responsibility for their conduct.... It is now clear that the legal personality of international organizations entails a responsibility for their conduct.
> (Eisuke Suzuki and Suresh Nanwani, 'Responsibility of international organizations: the accountability mechanisms of multilateral development banks' (2005) 27 Mich JIL 177, 179)

In 2011, the ILC adopted its Draft Articles on the Responsibility of International Organizations (DARIO). (See *Yearbook of the International Law Commission, 2011*, vol. II, Part Two; see also http://legal.un.org/ilc/texts/instruments/english/draft%20articles/9_11_2011.pdf.)

While DARIO is not a treaty, ILC articles are very important documents which are expected to become the principal authority on their areas of focus. A clear example is the ARSIWA, discussed in Chapter 13.

DARIO contains several provisions that are geared towards ensuring that international organizations are accountable for their acts whether they perform these acts directly or act through the agency of others, in conjunction with their member States, or jointly with other organizations. While a full discussion of the provisions of DARIO is beyond the scope of this book, it is worthwhile enumerating some of the cogent rules.

Article 6 DARIO states that:

> The conduct of an organ or agent of an international organization in the performance of functions of that organ or agent shall be considered an act of that organization under international law, whatever position the organ or agent holds in respect of the organization.

This provision is extremely important in ensuring that an international organization does not avoid liability for its action by stating that the offending conduct was carried out by its agents. A typical scenario where this provision will apply is a situation where troops from member States of international organizations commit internationally unlawful acts while serving as part of a mission led by that organization. What is required in order to hold the organization responsible in this scenario, according to Article 7, is that the 'organ of a State or an organ or agent of an international organization . . . is placed at the disposal of another international organization [which] exercises effective control over that conduct'.

In the *Behrami* case (*Behrami v. France, Saramati v. France* Joined Application Nos 71412/01 and 78166/01 (2007)), the European Court of Human Rights construed 'effective control' in terms of 'ultimate authority and control'. The Court attributed to the UN the responsibility of acts committed by the NATO-led KFOR (a non-UN organ) but which entity was placed under the UN mission in Kosovo. The Court's reasoning was that the UN Security Council retained ultimate control of command for the KFOR mission even if the day-to-day command and control lay with NATO.

Article 9 DARIO recognizes that conduct which is 'not attributable to an international organization under articles 6 to 8 shall nevertheless be considered an act of that organization under international law if and to the extent that the organization acknowledges and adopts the conduct in question as its own.'

example

Candoma deploys its troops to Rutamu to perform peacekeeping operation therein. Some time later, the World Organization for Peace (WOP), an organization to which Candoma and Rutamu belong, decides to send in an international peacekeeping force to take over the mission by Candoma. WOP acknowledges the misconduct committed by the Candoman troops prior to its arrival. Under these circumstances, that misconduct would be deemed to have been committed by WOP for which it will be held accountable. However, what constitutes acknowledgement will vary from case to case and the entire circumstances of each situation will be crucial.

Other instances in which international organizations may be held responsible include where an international organization aids or assist a State or an international organization to commit an internationally wrongful act with the knowledge that the act is wrongful, and provided the act would be wrongful if committed by the organization itself (Article 14 DARIO).

5.6 Privileges and immunity

International organizations enjoy certain privileges and immunities in order to enable them to function without undue interference from their member States and guarantee their international status. The types of privilege and immunity enjoyed by international organizations vary according to the purposes and objectives for which such organizations are established, and according to the environment in which they operate. As a topic immunity is fully considered in Chapter 8. As such, some general aspects of immunity, for example jurisdictional immunity, which is fully discussed in that chapter, will be exempted from the discussion here. This section only discusses aspects of immunity that are peculiar to international organizations or that arguably have particular application to international organizations.

5.6.1 Sources of privileges and immunities of international organizations

Generally speaking, the privileges and immunities of international organizations can arise from three sources:

- treaties;
- customary international law; and
- bilateral agreements between organizations and States.

Treaties as a source of privileges and immunities

It is common for constituent treaties of international organizations to provide for their privileges and immunities—although, with the exception of a few, such constitutions only contain general provisions on immunities.

Article 105 of the UN Charter provides that:

> The Organization shall enjoy in the territory of each of its Members such privileges and immunities as are necessary for the fulfilment of its purposes.

The Protocol Annexed to the Treaties Establishing the European Community and the European Atomic Energy Community Protocol (No. 36) on the Privileges and Immunities of the European Communities (1965) provides that:

> The High Contracting Parties, considering that, in accordance with Article 28 of the Treaty establishing a Single Council and a Single Commission of the European Communities, these Communities and the European Investment Bank shall enjoy in the territories of the Member States such privileges and immunities as are necessary for the performance of their tasks.

Article 103 of the OAS Charter provides that:

> The Organization of American States shall enjoy in the territory of each Member such legal capacity, privileges and immunities as are necessary for the exercise of its functions and the accomplishment of its purposes.

Whereas constituent treaties provide for general privileges and immunities, international organizations conclude multilateral treaties, which specifically detail the privileges and immunities that they enjoy. Examples include the 1946 General Convention on the Privileges and Immunities of the United Nations (the UN Immunities Convention), the General Convention on the Privileges and Immunities of the Specialized Agencies, and the Agreement on Privileges and Immunities of the Organization of American States.

Bilateral agreements as a source of privileges and immunities

In addition to constituent instruments and multilateral conventions, bilateral agreements that international organizations usually conclude with their host States—generally known as 'headquarters agreements', or 'seat agreements'—also confer certain privileges and immunities on such organizations, as the following example will show.

example

> The Agreement between the United Nations and the United States regarding the Headquarters of the United Nations, signed at Lake Success on 26 June 1947 (the UN Headquarter Agreement with the USA), covers a number of issues ranging from communication assets (§4), to the passage of UN personnel and officials into and out of the USA.
>
> It should be noted that, except where such laws are inconsistent with the 1946 UN Immunities Convention, US law applies in the district of the UN Headquarters (§7).

An international organization that does not have a headquarters agreement with a particular State, but desires to conduct a specific operation within that State, may conclude other types of bilateral agreement, such as a status of force agreement (SOFA) or status of mission agreement (SOMA), governing the relations between the organization and a State hosting its peacekeeping operation or other type of mission. The UN adopted a model SOFA in 1990, which today serves as a template for several other organizations.

Customary international law as a source regarding privileges and immunities

The fact that treaties do not provide for privileges and immunities of international organizations is not fatal. Indeed, courts have inferred privileges and immunities of international organizations from customary international law.

. . . .

● ***Z.M. v. Permanent Delegation of the League of Arab States to the United Nations*** (1993) 116 ILR 643

In this case, the Swiss Labour Court said (at 647) that:

> customary international law recognize[s] that international organizations, whether universal or regional, enjoy absolute jurisdictional immunity ... [t]his privilege arises from ... the purposes and functions assigned to international organizations as [t]hey can only carry out their tasks if they are beyond censure.

5.6.2 The nature of privileges and immunities accruing to international organizations

International organizations enjoy four types of immunity:

- immunity from prosecution or jurisdiction (jurisdictional immunity);
- inviolability of premises;
- freedom of communication; and
- immunity relating to financial matters.

'Jurisdictional immunity' means that an international organization cannot be subject to the judicial processes of its host State. This allows the organization to function independently and without fear of judicial harassment on the territory of its host State. Hence, such judicial processes as courts summons, seizure of property, etc. do not normally apply to international organizations, except where the concerned organization has waived its rights. The same applies to officials of international organizations, although, as will be seen later, certain exceptions apply.

The scope of jurisdictional immunity of international organizations

According to Article 2(2) of the 1946 UN Immunities Convention:

> The United Nations, its property and assets wherever located and by whomsoever held, shall enjoy immunity from every form of legal process except insofar as in any particular case it has expressly waived its immunity. It is, however, understood that no waiver of immunity shall extend to any measure of execution.

Article 5(18)(a) states that:

> Officials of the United Nations shall be immune from legal process in respect of words spoken or written and all acts performed by them in their official capacity.

This immunity can be waived only by the Secretary-General, and where the alleged offender is the Secretary-General, the UN Security Council shall exercise the waiver.

Article 5 (20) provides that:

> Privileges and immunities are granted to officials in the interests of the United Nations and not for the personal benefit of the individuals themselves. The Secretary-General shall have the right and the duty to waive the immunity of any official in any case where, in his opinion, the immunity would impede the course of justice and can be waived without prejudice to the interests of the United Nations. In the case of the Secretary-General, the Security Council shall have the right to waive immunity.

The fact that prosecution is possible only where there has been a waiver implies that the immunity of international organizations is absolute. Consequently, many people have clamoured for a restriction of the immunity of international organizations. Unlike States, international organizations do not have their own courts in which they can be sued. This means that, in disputes between international organizations and private individuals relating to torts, contracts, and so on, all that is available to an aggrieved party is an internal dispute settlement arrangement, which is often inadequate. It has also been pointed out that, since there is considerable uncertainty about the precise nature of the human rights obligations of the UN, the need for access to justice by wronged persons must be balanced against the organization's absolute immunity.

example UN personnel have sometimes been implicated in allegations of sexual exploitation and abuse of the people whom they are meant to protect, as alleged in the Democratic Republic of Congo (DRC), Sierra Leone, and Liberia. The absolute immunity of UN officials means that such officials cannot be tried for their alleged crimes and that the victims are inevitably condemned to whatever administrative procedures the UN might apply to its erring officials.

Approaches towards restricting jurisdictional immunity

There have been attempts to control the jurisdictional immunity of international organizations through treaties and national laws, as well as through judicial interventions.

Treaties

Article VII(3) of the Articles of Agreement of the International Bank for Reconstruction and Development (IBRD), as amended effective 16 February 1989, provides that:

Actions may be brought against the Bank only in a court of competent jurisdiction in the territories of a member in which the Bank has an office, has appointed an agent for the purpose of accepting service or notice of process, or has issued or guaranteed securities.

. . . .

● *Lutcher SA e Papel Candor v. Inter-American Development Bank* [1967] 42 ILR 138

The plaintiff, who obtained some loan facilities from the Inter-American Development Bank (IDB), brought an action to restrain the Bank from granting loan facilities to its competitor. Although the US Court of Appeals dismissed the suit for lack of a cause of action, the court ruled that the Bank was not entitled to immunity.

The provision involved here was similar to Article VII(3) of the IBRD Articles of Agreement. Therefore this decision implies that the scope of jurisdictional immunity of such organizations may not necessarily be confined to the causes of action listed in their treaties.

See also Article 52 of the Agreement Establishing the African Development Bank (6th edn, June 2002) and Article 274 TEU (ex Article 240 TEC).

Judicial intervention

States have also attempted to restrict the jurisdictional immunity of international organizations through judicial intervention—that is, through national courts developing case law, which narrows the scope of jurisdictional immunity available to international organizations.

Judicial intervention consists of two distinct forms. First, several national courts now distinguish between acts done by international organizations in their personal capacity (*jure gestionis*) and those done in their official capacity (*jure imperii*), excluding from jurisdiction only the latter category. The argument is that the immunity of international organizations is functional and should therefore be available only with regard to acts done in their *sovereign* capacity. (See Chapter 8 for a discussion.)

Secondly, national courts now seek to balance the immunity of international organizations with the constitutional guarantees of access to justice for individuals.

. . . .

● *Giovani Porru v. Food and Agriculture Organization* (1969) UNJY 238 (**Summary**)

A former UN Food and Agriculture Organization (FAO) employee brought an action against the organization for employment-related compensation. Although it dismissed the action, an Italian court of first instance said (at 238–239) that there was:

> '[N]o rule of customary international law under which foreign States and subjects of international law in general are to be considered as immune from the jurisdiction of another State. Such immunity could only be recognized with regards to public law activities, i.e., in the case of an international organization, with regard to the activities by which it pursues the specific purposes (*uti imperii*) but not with regard to private law activities where the organization acts on equal footing with private individuals (*uti privatus*).'

. . . .

● *Mrs C v. The Intergovernmental Committee of the European Migration (ICEM)* DECISION OF 7 JUNE 1973, COUR DE CASSATION

Similarly, in this case the plaintiff, a former employee of ICEM, brought an action against the organization for terminal emoluments. The court of first instance denied immunity to ICEM on the basis of a distinction between private and personal acts. On appeal, ICEM argued that it was not subject to this distinction. The Cour de Cassation rejected this argument and applied the distinction.

Although, on appeal, the court applied the distinction, it held that ICEM was entitled to immunity because:

> Acts which an organization arranges in its internal structure, including the rules laid down by it in respect of the employment relationship with the staff, were manifestation of the organization's power under international law ... [and] ... the provisions and measures adopted by ICEM, also in so far as they regarded terminal emoluments, were governed by the organization's systems of rules; they were consequently not subject to the Italian legal system and were exempt from the jurisdiction of the Italian courts ...

. . . .

● *UNFAO v. Instituto Nazionale di Previdenze per I Dirigenti di Aziende Industriali (INPDAI)* (1982) UNJY 234 (SUMMARY)

In this case, the Italian Court of Cassation, speaking about international organizations, emphasized that:

> irrespective of their public or private character, whenever they act in the private law domain, they place themselves on the same footing as private persons with whom they had entered into contracts, and thus forwent the right to act as sovereign bodies that were not subject to the sovereignty of others.

The attempt to restrict the immunity of international organizations has also been emphatic in the practice of the USA. In 1952, the acting legal adviser to the State Department, Jack B. Tate, wrote a letter (known as the 'Tate Letter') to the acting US Attorney-General, in which he stated that:

> According to the newer or restrictive theory of sovereign immunity, the immunity of the sovereign is recognized with regard to sovereign or public acts (*jure imperii*) of a state, but not

with respect to private acts (*jure gestionis*)... [T]he Department feels that the widespread and increasing practice on the part of governments of engaging in commercial activities makes necessary a practice which will enable persons doing business with them to have their rights determined in the courts. For these reasons it will hereafter be the Department's policy to follow the restrictive theory of sovereign immunity in the consideration of requests of foreign governments for a grant of sovereign immunity.

- -

● *Dupree Associate Inc. v. OAS* (1977) 63 ILR 92

The US District Court of Columbia considered the immunity extended to the OAS under the US International Organizations Immunities Act (IOIA). Taking into consideration the US policy shift towards restricting the immunity of international organizations, the court held that the IOIA immunities extended to the OAS only as far as such immunities are enjoyed by foreign States.

The rationale behind restricting the immunity of international organizations was set out by the Dutch Supreme Court in *A.S. v. Iran – United States Claims Tribunal*, Supreme Court (Hooge Raad) of the Netherlands, 20 December 1985, [1994] ILR 327, 329; According to the Court: On the one hand there is the interest of the international organization having a guarantee that it will be able to perform its tasks independently and free from interference under all circumstances; on the other there is the interest of the other party in having its dispute with an international organization dealt with and decided by an independent and impartial judicial body.

In 'In the Shadow of Waite and Kennedy, The Jurisdictional Immunity of International Organizations, The Individual's Right of Access to the Courts and Administrative Tribunals as Alternative Means of Dispute Settlement', *International Organizations Law Review* 1: 59–110, 2004, August Reinisch and Ulf Andreas Weber observe, at pp. 64–65 that:

> In the quest for an appropriate immunity standard for international organizations, the paramount underlying rationale of functional immunity, the protection of the independent functioning of the organization, should be kept in mind. It has been observed that this purpose should be balanced against the equally cogent demand of protecting the interests of potential litigants in having a possibility to pursue their claims against an international organization before an independent judicial or quasi-judicial body.

The denial of absolute immunity to international organizations, based upon a distinction between private and sovereign acts, has been attacked by jurists.

According to Amerasinghe (2005, see section 5.4.1), at p. 322:

> There is some difficulty in attributing to an organization the power to act *iure imperii*. To assume that the distinction has relevance to organizations is to assimilate them to states which is inappropriate. Their basis of immunity is not the same as for states. The test is whether an immunity from jurisdiction is necessary for the fulfilment of the organization's function and purposes. To answer that question a reference to whether the organization was, in respect of the subject matter of litigation, acting *iure imperii* or *iure gestionis* is irrelevant.

Access to the courts

The need to strike a balance between the absolute immunity of international organizations and access to courts is particularly important in cases in which international organizations do not have alternative dispute resolution (ADR) arrangements. The constitutions of most States, as well as the constituent instruments of some international organizations, guarantee access to justice by wronged citizens.

Article 6(1) of the European Convention on Human Rights (ECHR) provides that:

> In the determination of his civil rights and obligations or of any criminal charge against him, everyone is entitled to a fair and public hearing within a reasonable time by an independent and impartial tribunal established by law.

Article 8(29) of the 1946 UN Immunities Convention provides that:

> The United Nations shall make provisions for appropriate modes of settlement of: (a) disputes arising out of contracts or other disputes of a private law character to which the United Nations is a party; (b) disputes involving any official of the United Nations who by reason of his official position enjoys immunity, if immunity has not been waived by the Secretary-General.

In line with this provision, the UN has established some tribunals, such as administrative tribunals, which have very limited scope.

As Jan Wouters and Pierre Schmitt, *Challenging Acts of Other United Nations' Organs, Subsidiary Organs and Officials* (Leuven Centre for Global Governance Studies Working Paper No. 49, April 2010), p. 4, have observed:

> No independent and impartial international court has been established before which private individuals can file claims against the UN. An individual claimant who wants to challenge an act of the UN has often no real other option than to seek a remedy before national courts. As a consequence, individuals are dependent on the will and ability of domestic courts to decide on their case.

For similar views, see *Urban v. United Nations* 768 F2d 1497, 1500 (DC Cir., 1985), in which the DC Court of Appeals recognized that a 'court must take great care not to "unduly impair" [a litigant's] constitutional right of access to the courts'.

. . . .

● ***Radicopoulos v. United Nations Relief and Works Agency (UNRWA)*** (1957), REPORTED IN THE ANNUAL REPORT OF THE DIRECTOR OF UNRWA (1958) 13 UN GAOR SUPP (No. 14) 41 (UN Doc. A/391)

A former employee of UNRWA brought an action before an Egyptian court against the organization for dismissal pay. UNRWA argued that the plaintiff could avail himself of an internal remedy, a course of action taken by the plaintiff.

In a subsequent suit brought by the plaintiff before the UN Administrative Tribunal, the tribunal confirmed that national courts have no jurisdiction for claims directed against UN subsidiary organs.

. . . .

● ***People v. Mark S. Weiner*** 378 NYS 2D 966 (1976), CRIMINAL COURT OF THE CITY OF NEW YORK

In this case, however, the plaintiff brought before the Criminal Court of New York an action for assault and harassment against a UN official. The court admitted the claim and stated that it had jurisdiction in the case. In anticipation of a UN counterclaim for immunity, the court held that the UN would not be so entitled, because, according to the court (at [19]), such immunity would be:

Nonetheless, in other cases, such as *Abdi Hosh Askir v. Boutros Boutros-Ghali, Joseph E. Connor et al.* 933 F Supp 368 (SDNY, 1996), concerning a claim by a Somali for compensation for the alleged unlawful taking of his possession by the UN in Mogadishu, and *Boimah v. United Nations General Assembly* 664 F Supp 69 (EDNY, 1987), in which the plaintiff claimed that he was denied permanent employment by the UN based on his race and nationality, the US courts dismissed the suits on the basis of immunity of the UN. The bone of contention in most of these cases is whether the organization in question has effective ADR mechanisms.

● ***African Development Bank v. Haas*** (2005) Journal des Tribunaux 454, French Cour de Cassation

In this case, the French Cour de Cassation rejected the immunity claim of the African Development Bank, on the ground that the Bank had not put in place a tribunal that could handle the dispute.

● ***Waite and Kennedy v. Germany; Beer and Regan v. Germany*** Application No. 26083/94 (1999) 30 EHRR 261

In an industrial dispute case that went on appeal to the European Court of Justice, the Court said (at [68]) that:

● ***Mothers of Srebrenica et al. v. State of the Netherlands and United Nations*** Case No. District Court 07-2973 (30 March 2010)

In June 1995, during the war in the former Yugoslavia, some 7,600 male Muslim inhabitants of Srebrenica were murdered by Bosnian Serb forces. Although a small Dutch contingent forming part of the UN Protection Forces (UNPROFOR) had been deployed to protect the area, the troops had proved unable to stop the genocide. In 2007, a group calling itself 'Mothers of Srebrenica' brought an action for compensation against the UN in the Dutch District Court at The Hague on the ground that the UN had failed in its responsibility to protect the people.

The District Court dismissed the claim on the basis that the UN enjoyed absolute immunity.

An appeal to the Dutch Court of Appeal was equally dismissed.

It is important, however, to note in this case that the Dutch courts relied mainly on the jurisprudence of the European Court of Human Rights (ECtHR) in the *Behrami* case *(Behrami v. France, Saramati v. France*, Joined Application Nos. 71412/01 and 78166/01 (2007)), in which the Court decided that the ECHR should not impede the effective implementation of UN mandates. Consequently, the Court held that States contributing troops to the UN could not be held liable for acts and omissions of their troops in missions authorized by the UN Security Council.

Curiously, the Dutch District Court did not consider whether an alternative remedy was available within the UN system that the applicants might use. In fact, in this case, the Court was not influenced at all by the jurisprudence of the European Court on such matters, which was relied on by the plaintiffs.

5.6.3 The inviolability of premises and archives

The treaties of most international organizations almost invariably provide for the inviolability of their premises and archives.

Section 9 of the UN Headquarters Agreement provides that:

> The Headquarters district shall be inviolable. Federal, State or local officers or officials of the United States, whether administrative, judicial, military or police, shall not enter the headquarters district to perform any official duty therein except with the consent of and under conditions agreed to by the Secretary-General.

Article 2(3) of the 1946 UN Immunities Convention states that:

> The premises of the United Nations shall be inviolable. The property and assets of the United Nations, wherever located and by whomsoever held, shall be immune from search, requisition, confiscation, expropriation and any other form of interference, whether by executive, administrative, judicial or legislative action.

Section 2(4) of the Convention provides that:

> The archives of the United Nations, and in general all documents belonging to it or held by it, shall be inviolable wherever located.

Treaties of other international organizations contain similar provisions, although in cases of financial institutions, there are some variations. For example, Article VII(5) of the IBRD Articles of Agreement states that:

> Property and assets of the Bank, wherever located and by whomsoever held, shall be immune from search, requisition, confiscation, expropriation or any other form of seizure by executive or legislative action.

Similarly, Article IX(4) of the Articles of Agreement of the International Monetary Fund (IMF) provides that:

> Property and assets of the Fund, wherever located and by whomsoever held, shall be immune from search, requisition, confiscation, expropriation, or any other form of seizure by executive or legislative action.

It should be pointed out that these provisions do not use the word 'inviolable' per se, which is a much stricter word than the phrase 'immune from search' adopted by these provisions. This indicates that these provisions are meant to operate differently from 'inviolability', which is an absolute term. The fact that the provisions limit immune activities to legislative and executive actions supports this view.

It must be noted that it is not only documents belonging to these organizations that are inviolable, but *all* documents held by them. The implication of this is that documents that do not belong to the respective organizations are also immune, provided that such documents are in the custody of the organization.

Provisions relating to the inviolability of property and archives of international organizations have given rise to some problems in practice. As has been mentioned previously, international organizations are not sovereign entities and, as such, they do not have their own bodies of laws such that apply to day-to-day transactions. This means that if their premises are to be absolutely immune against member States—especially host States—then a situation might arise in which wrongs might be suffered without remedies. However, as we will recall from earlier, although §9 of the UN Headquarters Agreement establishes the inviolability of UN premises, this is subject to the consent of the UN Secretary-General. Also, it is clear under §7(b) of the UN Headquarters Agreement that it is the local laws of the USA that apply within the UN premises.

. . . .

● *Maclaine Watson & Co. v. International Tin Council (No. 2)* [1989] Сн 286

In this case, the English Court of Appeal was confronted with a question of whether it was appropriate that Millett J, in the High Court, granted an order for the plaintiffs to disclose all assets of the International Tin Council (ITC) both within and outside the UK. The relevant facts of the case were that the plaintiffs obtained an arbitral award against the ITC, following the collapse of the latter and its inability to discharge its obligations towards the plaintiffs. The plaintiffs had then brought an action asking the court to compel representatives of the ITC to disclose the locations of all of their company's assets in order to satisfy the arbitral award.

The Court of Appeal confirmed the judgment of Millett J in the lower court and held that, under the circumstances of the case, the archives of the ITC did not enjoy immunity since the organization did not enjoy immunity in matters concerning arbitration.

The Court of Appeal stated (at p. 307) that:

> The order made by Millett J. and now unanimously affirmed by this court forms part of the process of enforcement in relation to which the I.T.C. has no immunity whatever. That order does not violate the official archives of the I.T.C. nor any other immunity in respect whereof the I.T.C. is entitled to raise any objection. In our view, this order should stand without qualification.

◉ Conclusion

International organizations are, without doubt, very important actors in the international sphere. They have become a major instrument through which States monitor and regulate their affairs and relations with one another, and by which they establish rules to govern their activities on a wider scale than treaties and agreements would so govern. The features of such organizations are not categorically set in stone but, based on more than a century of experience and observation, certain features can be said to be necessary for the establishment of such organizations or for their claim to such a status.

We have noted that the personality of such organizations implies certain rights and responsibilities, and that such personality may or may not be recognized by third parties, depending on the circumstances of the case. The capacity of organizations that flows from their personality also differs from organization to organization, and certain capacities may be listed as being essential, and therefore imperative for the execution of the organization's functions.

In addition to its capacity, which flows from its personality, an international organization is usually entitled to privileges and immunities, which may be spelt out by law, be it treaty or statute, and may be restricted in practice. These privileges and immunities are not always absolute, and the courts in different jurisdictions have sought, over time, to strike a balance between the immunity of organizations and citizens' rights of access to the courts.

International organizations continue to metamorphose as their role in international relations becomes more defined, and recent trends in peace and security operations, as well as international adjudication, have required a more nuanced understanding of the position of such organizations in international relations between States, between States and individuals, and between such organizations vis-à-vis their relationships with other organizations, with States, and with individuals.

Questions

Self-test questions

1 Define 'international organizations'.

2 What types of international organization are there?

3 List the features of international organizations.

4 List the consequences of legal personality.

5 What is 'capacity' of international organizations?

6 What is your understanding of 'legal personality'?

7 Who determines whether the acts of international organizations can be reviewed judicially?

8 What does 'ultra vires' mean?

Discussion questions

1 'The International Court of Justice cannot review the decisions of organs of the United Nations.' With reference to case law, consider to what extent this statement reflects the practice of the Court.

2 What is legal personality in relation to international organizations and how is this determined in international law?

3 'There are many ways in which non-members of international organizations can recognize the legal personality of such organizations.' Discuss this assertion, with reference to decided cases.

4 What are the legal consequences of ultra vires decisions of international organizations?

Assessment question

'To say that an international organization has legal personality is to mean nothing more than that an international organization is a person of its own. There are no consequences of such legal personality. It is nothing more than a nicety.'

Discuss.

Key cases

- *Arab Monetary Fund v. Hashim* (No. 3) [1991] 2 AC 114
- *Effects of Award of Compensation made by the UN Administrative Tribunal* (1954) ICJ Rep 47
- *Grimaldi v. Fonds des Maladies Professionnelles* Case C-322/88 [1989] ECR 4407 (the *Grimaldi Case*)
- *J. H. Rayner (Mincing Lane) Ltd v. Department of Trade and Industry & ors; related appeals* (1989) 5 BCC 872
- *Legal Consequences for States of the Continued Presence of South Africa in Namibia (South West Africa) notwithstanding Security Council Resolution 276 (1970)* (1971) ICJ Rep 16 (the *Namibia Advisory Opinion*)
- *Westland Helicopters Ltd & ors v. Arab Organization for Industrialization* (1987) 80 ILR 622

Further reading

Allen, Sir C., 'Status and capacity' (1930) 46 LQR 277

Brownlie, I., *Principles of International Law* (7th edn, Oxford: Oxford University Press, 2008)

Graefrath, M., 'Leave to the court what belongs to the court: the *Libyan Case*' (1993) 4 EJIL 184

Jenks, C. W., 'The legal personality of international organizations' (1945) 22 BYBIL 267

O'Connell, D. P., *International Law, Vol. 1* (London: Stevens, 1970)

Rama-Montaldo, M., 'International legal personality and implied powers of international organizations' (1970) 44 BYBIL 111

Seyersted, F., 'International personality of intergovernmental organizations: do their capacities really depend upon their constitutions?' (1964) 4 IJIL 1

Wellens, K., 'Fragmentation of international law and establishing an accountability regime for international organizations: the role of judiciary in closing the gap' (2003–4) 25 Mich JIL 1159

Wessel, R. A., 'The international legal status of the European Union' (1997) 2 EFA Rev 109

6

Territory and the law of the sea

Learning objectives

This chapter will help you to:

- understand how States acquire territory in international law;
- appreciate the rules and principles relating to the acquisition of territory;
- study modern developments in the acquisition of territory;
- learn the rules governing the law of the sea; and
- analyse how States exercise rights on the sea.

Introduction

As will be seen in the next chapter, every State has jurisdiction over its territory. A State's territory consists of its land mass, contiguous seas, and some areas of its air and outer space. In addition to their contiguous seas, States also exercise certain rights over the high seas—the mass body of waters owned not by any single State, but by all of humankind. States exercise absolute control over their territories except where part of the territory, be it land, sea, or space, is subject to temporary control by the international community. For example, the UN Security Council may create a 'no-fly' zone within a State in order to protect civilians against their governments, as did Security Council Resolution 1973 concerning Libya on 17 March 2011. This chapter will discuss territory, with specific reference to a State's land mass, and also the law of the sea, considering that the sea is part of a State's territory. However, the chapter is not concerned with the air or outer space, which forms part of a State's territory. Since the manner in which States acquire territory and exercise jurisdiction over their waters often raises serious questions in international law, this chapter focuses on analysing international law rules and principles governing the acquisition of territory by States, as well as the law of the sea.

6.1 The modes of acquiring territory

There are at least four ways through which a State can acquire territory. These are namely by occupation, by prescription, by cession, and by accretion. Prior to the emergence of the United Nations, States could also acquire territory through conquest or annexation by war. However, the UN Charter has now prohibited the use of force by States, and even though States may still use force in self-defence (Article 51), this does not entitle States to keep captured territory as their property.

6.2 Occupation and prescription

Occupation and prescription are the two most common modes of acquiring territory, though these methods have declined considerably in modern times. While these modes share some similarities in that they each concern States unilaterally acquiring territory rather than being granted the territory by another State, there are notable differences between them.

Occupation occurs when a State exercises sovereign rights over a previously unoccupied or 'virgin' territory. Generally speaking, a State may only occupy a territory that is considered *terra nullius* (that is, 'no-man's-land'), but where a territory previously occupied by another State has been abandoned, such can also be a subject of occupation. 'Prescription' occurs when a State exercises sovereignty over a territory that belongs to another sovereign with the latter's acquiescence. Therefore a State claiming acquisition by prescription must demonstrate that its acquisition is *effective* and has cancelled out the previous ownership in all respects.

We shall return later to prescriptive acquisition; now we shall consider the rules governing occupation.

6.2.1 Occupation

. . . .

● *Netherlands v. United States of America* (1928) 2 RIAA 829 (The *Island of Palmas Case*)

In 1898, Spain ceded to the USA the Philippine Islands, which included the Island of Palmas (or Miangas, as it was called by the Netherlands). In 1906, an American General visited the Island of Palmas, but found the Dutch flag flying on the territory.

The Court had to determine whether the island belonged to the USA or the Netherlands. To do this, it was important for the arbitrator first to consider whether Spain 'occupied' the disputed territory at the time it gave it to the USA.

It was held that the island belonged to the Netherlands. Even if the island did originally belong to Spain, the latter did not exercise 'effective occupation' over the island so as to have displaced Dutch sovereignty at the time that the island was ceded to the USA.

Judge Huber said (at 838) that:

> If a dispute arises as to the sovereignty over a portion of territory, it is customary to examine which of the States claiming sovereignty possesses a title— cession, conquest, occupation, etc.—*superior* to that which the other State might possibly bring forward against it. However, if the contestation is based on the fact that the other Party has actually *displayed* sovereignty, it cannot be sufficient to establish the title by which territorial sovereignty was validly acquired at a certain moment; it must also be shown that the territorial sovereignty *has continued to exist and did exist at the moment which for the decision of the dispute must be considered as critical*. This demonstration consists in the actual display of State activities, such as belongs only to the territorial sovereign … It seems therefore natural that an element which is essential for the constitution of sovereignty should not be lacking in its continuation … The growing insistence with which international law, ever since the middle of the 18th century, has demanded that the occupation shall be effective would be inconceivable, if effectiveness were required only for the act of acquisition and not equally for the maintenance of the right. [Emphasis added]

Upon a consideration of the facts and evidence before the arbitration, he held (at 846) that:

> No act of occupation nor, except as to a recent period, any exercise of sovereignty at Palmas by Spain has been alleged. But even admitting that the Spanish title still existed as inchoate in 1898 and must be considered as included in the cession under Article III of the Treaty of Paris, an inchoate title could not prevail over the *continuous and peaceful display* of authority by another State; *for such display may prevail even over a prior, definitive title put forward by another State*. [Emphasis added]

The jurisprudence of Judge Huber in *Island of Palmas* is rich on the international law requirements for the acquisition of territory by occupation and thus merits a fuller analysis.

In summary, in respect of the *Island of Palmas*, Arbitrator Huber based his decision on: effective occupation; critical date; and intertemporal laws. We will now discuss these criteria or requirements for a valid occupation. (See Daniel-Erasmus Khan, 'Max Huber as arbitrator: the *Palmas (Miangas)* case and other arbitrations' (2007) 18(1) EJIL 145.)

Effective exercise of sovereignty

For acquisition by occupation to be valid, it is important that the claiming State must demonstrate that it maintains not only nominal, but also 'effective' sovereignty over the territory. What constitutes 'effectiveness' is fluid and varies from circumstance to circumstance, but it seems that the size of the territory is a crucial factor.

● *Indonesia v. Malaysia* (2002) ICJ REP 625 (The *Pulau Ligitan and Pulau Sipadan Case*)

In this case, the International Court of Justice (ICJ) said (at [134]), that:

> in the case of very small islands which are uninhabited or not permanently inhabited—like Ligitan and Sipadan, which have been of little economic importance (at least until recently)—*effectivités* will indeed generally be scarce.

● *Eritrea v. Yemen* (1998) 114 ILR 14

The arbitral tribunal said, at 71 ([239]), that:

> The factual evidence of '*effectivités*' presented to the Tribunal by both parties is voluminous in quantity but is sparse in useful content. This is doubtless owing to the *inhospitability* of the Islands themselves and the relative *meagreness* of their human history. The *modern international law of the acquisition* (or attribution) of territory generally requires that there be: an intentional display of power and authority over the territory, by the exercise of jurisdiction and state functions, on a continuous and peaceful basis. The latter two criteria are tempered to suit the nature of the territory and the size of its population, if any. [Emphasis added]

KEY POINTS

- Acquisition by occupation may occur on a territory that has never been occupied by any human or sovereign (*terra nullius*), or which is inhabited by humans who are not organized for the purpose of administering themselves (see later in the chapter on this latter point).

- Occupation must be complemented by effective exercise of sovereignty. How much control a sovereign must demonstrate over a territory depends on the size and nature of the territory itself.

'Effectiveness' thus helps to determine who among disputing parties has a stronger title to territory, as well as constituting notice to all other sovereigns that a territory is now under new control.

● *Netherlands v. United States of America* (1928) 2 RIAA 829 (The *Island of Palmas Case*)

As the Court said in this case (at 845–846):

> International law in the 19th century…laid down the principle that occupation, to constitute a claim to territorial sovereignty, must be effective, that is, offer certain guarantees to other States and their nationals…discovery alone, without any subsequent act, cannot at the present time suffice to prove sovereignty over the Island of Palmas (or Miangas).

● **Norway v. Denmark** (1933) PCIJ SER. A/B, No. 53 (The **Legal Status of Eastern Greenland Case**)

In 1931, Norway proclaimed that it was 'taking possession' of Eastern Greenland, forming part of the Greenland Island. Denmark, which had colonies in other parts of the island, requested the Permanent Court of International Justice (PCIJ) to declare the Norwegian Declaration, which purported to occupy the whole of Greenland, invalid. Denmark had argued that its title over the disputed territory was 'founded on the peaceful and continuous display of state authority over the Island' (at 45).

The Court said (at 45–46) that:

> a claim to sovereignty based not upon some particular act or title such as a treaty of cession but merely upon continued display of authority, involves two elements each of which must be shown to exist: the *intention* and *will* to act as sovereign, and some *actual exercise* or *display* of such authority... [Emphasis added]

Applying the test of 'intention and will' to act as sovereign, and 'actual exercise of display' of such authority, the Court found that Denmark fulfilled these criteria through making laws to regulate such activities as fishing and hunting, and also giving access to the island to British and French nationals (at 62–63). Hence, judgment was given for Denmark.

● **Indonesia v. Malaysia** (2002) ICJ REP 625 (The **Pulau Ligitan and Pulau Sipadan Case**)

Indonesia and Malaysia disputed title to the islands of Pulau Ligitan and Pulau Sipadan. Both parties claimed to have exercised effective sovereignty, and that they also derived authority from the actions of previous sovereigns over the disputed areas, the Netherlands and Britain. The Court found that none of these previous sovereigns passed on a valid title to either of the claimants and had to decide the case principally with reference to effective occupation.

Each party provided evidence of the effective measures they took in relation to the disputed areas including fishing, administration, usage of the areas for passage by their naval forces, and preservation of items such as turtles, among others (at 130).

On the whole, the Court found Indonesia's measures over the disputed areas to consist largely in acts of private individuals and not official acts such as making law and regulating activities in the areas, whereas Malaysia, as with Britain from which it derived its authority, exercised legislative, administrative, and quasi-judicial acts which, though few in numbers, were diverse in character (at 132). The Court ruled in favour of Malaysia.

The Court's approach in this case was thus consistent with the jurisprudence of the PCIJ in the *Legal Status of Eastern Greenland*, in which the earlier Court had also relied heavily on the legislation on hunting and fishing, and the admission of British and French nationals into certain trading privileges by Denmark (at 62–63).

thinking points

- What does the phrase 'effective occupation' mean and what role, if any, does it play in disputes concerning title to territory?
- What constitutes 'effectivités' and how do the courts determine which effectivités carry more weight than others in resolving disputes over sovereignty?
- What are the main reasons given by the ICJ for requiring parties who claim acquisition of territory by occupation to prove effectiveness?

The critical date

Another important criterion that the Court has consistently applied in determining the validity of title to territory is the critical date. This is the date on which the dispute between the parties crystallizes and which is generally determinative of their rights (see L. F. E. Goldie, 'The critical date' (1963) 12 ICLQ 1251 and D. H. N. Johnson, 'Acquisitive prescription in international law' (1950) 27 BYBIL 332).

Gerald Fitzmaurice, 'The law and procedure of the International Court of Justice, 1951–54: points of substantive law—part II' (1955–56) 32 BYBIL 20, recapping his statement as the representative of the UK in the *Minquiers* case (see later in this section), states that:

> . . . the theory of the critical date involves that . . . whatever was the position at the date determined to be the critical date, such is still the position now. Whatever were the rights of the Parties then, those are still the rights of the Parties now. If one of them then had sovereignty, it has it now, or it is deemed to have it . . . The whole point, the whole *raison d'être*, of the critical date is, in effect, that time is deemed to stop at that date. Nothing that happens afterwards can operate to change the situation that then existed. Whatever the situation was, it is deemed in law still to exist; and the rights of the Parties are governed by it.

We should be careful, however, not to confuse the critical date with the date on which a dispute is born. For, as Fitzmaurice has observed (1955–56, above, 24–5):

> This moment, however—which is the critical one—is clearly not that at which the dispute was born—even when the dispute can be said to have had its birth at any definite moment, which is seldom the case: the critical moment is, normally, not the date when the dispute was born, but that on which it crystallised into a concrete issue.

International and national courts have applied the critical date to many cases involving territorial disputes.

● *Netherlands v. United States of America* (1928) 2 RIAA 829 (The *Island of Palmas Case*)

See earlier in this section for the facts.

In this case, the Court laid down the rule concerning the critical date (at 845) thus:

> Both Parties are also agreed that a juridical fact must be appreciated in the light of the law contemporary with it, and not of the law in force at the time when a dispute in regard to it arises or falls to be settled. The effect of discovery by Spain is therefore to be determined by the rules of international law in force in the first half of the 16th century—or (To take the earliest date) in the first quarter of it.

● *Indonesia v. Malaysia* (2002) ICJ REP 625 (The *Pulau Ligitan and Pulau Sipadan Case*)

In this case, the Court said (at [135]) that:

> it cannot take into consideration acts having taken place after the date on which the dispute between the Parties crystallized unless such acts are a normal continuation of prior acts and are not undertaken for the purpose of improving the legal position of the Party which relies on them . . .

KEY POINTS

- The critical date is the date on which the dispute between the parties crystallizes and after which acts done cannot be accepted as relevant to the validity of the contested title.

- The main object of the critical date is to ensure that disputes are decided as equitably as possible and with regard to all relevant circumstances of the case.

- Only when acts that occur after the critical date do not improve the positions of the parties can they be considered.

However, some observers have argued that just as the Court should not take into account events that occur after the crystallization of a dispute—that is, after the critical date has arisen—neither should it set the critical date too early in the history of the dispute.

● *United Kingdom v. France* (1953) ICJ REP 47 (The *Minquiers and Ecrehos Case*)

The UK and France had a dispute over title to the Ecrehos and Minquiers Islets. The islets previously formed part of the Duchy of Normandy. The main issue for the Court to determine was the date that the dispute crystallized. France argued that it should be 2 August 1839, being the date on which the Fisheries Convention demarcated exclusive fishery zones within the Bay of Granville; the UK proposed 29 December 1950 which was the date when a Special Agreement between the two States was concluded. If the Court accepted the French proposal, it meant that all acts occurring after 1839 would be disregarded, and if it accepted the British proposal, all acts occurring until 1950 would be accepted.

The Court did not make a formal determination of the critical date, but it accepted activities that occurred after 1839 because, as it stated (at p. 59), such activities were not calculated to improve the legal position of France.

For the view that the 'critical date' doctrine can be extended to cover areas of international law other than territorial disputes, see Goldie (1963, see earlier in this section), at 1267. See also *Romania v. Ukraine* (2009) ICJ Rep 1 (the *Case Concerning Maritime Delimitation in the Black Sea*).

thinking points

- *What is the 'critical date'? Explain its relevance to the settlement of territorial disputes.*
- *What view of the critical date did the Court form in* Minquiers *and why did it form that view?*
- *Explain the term 'crystallization' in relation to the critical date.*
- *Summarize the arguments of Gerald Fitzmaurice in* Minquiers *as to why the Court should be flexible in setting critical dates.*

The current state of occupation in international law

It is important to say a few words on the current position of international law regarding occupation, especially on the occupation of the so-called *terra nullius*. As will be recalled, *terra nullius* was broadly defined by States at the early stages of modern international law, especially when slavery and colonialism were rampant as international practices of the most powerful States in the world. At these historical moments, most places regarded as *terra nullius*—that is, as 'no-man's-land'—were actually occupied by peoples, but still considered unoccupied under international law, since these peoples were often considered to be barbarians and savages, incapable of forming cohesive social and political systems comparable to those in Western States.

As early as 1830, the eminent English jurist, Sir William Blackstone, had challenged the legality or justifiability of treating inhabited territories as *terra nullius* simply because the way of life of the habitants differed from that of the colonizers.

In his *Commentaries on the Laws of England* (17th edn, London: Sweet & Maxwell, 1830), Book II, ch. 1, p. 7, Blackstone welcomed the practice of European countries sending colonizers off to discover new habitations, but noted that:

> so long as it was confined to the stocking and cultivation of desert uninhabited countries, it kept strictly within the limits of the law of nature. But how far the seising on countries already peopled, and driving out or massacring the innocent and defenceless natives, merely because they differed from their invaders in language, in religion, in customs, in government, or in colour; how far such a conduct was consonant to nature, to reason, or to christianity, deserved well to be considered by those, who have rendered their names immortal by thus civilizing mankind.

Thus there has been a growing tendency for courts to reject inhabited territories as *terra nullius*.

In 1884, Spain colonized Western Sahara (otherwise known as 'Rio de Oro', and 'Sakiet El Hamra'). This territory was inhabited largely by nomadic Saharan tribes and was rich in phosphate. The UN General Assembly adopted Resolution 1514 in 1966, which, inter alia:

> *Invites* the administering Power to determine at the earliest possible date, in conformity with the aspirations of the indigenous people of Spanish Sahara and in consultation with the Governments of Mauritania and Morocco and any other interested Party, the procedures for the holding of a referendum under United Nations auspices with a view to enabling the indigenous population of the Territory to exercise freely its right to self-determination.

. . . .

● *Western Sahara Advisory Opinion* (1975) ICJ REP 12

Faced with Spain's recalcitrance, the General Assembly requested an advisory opinion from the ICJ to determine whether Western Sahara was *terra nullius* at the time of its colonization by Spain, and, if this question was answered in the negative, to determine the relation of Morocco and Mauritania, which had competing claims to the territory.

The Court held (at [81]) that:

> In the present instance, the information furnished to the Court shows that at the time of colonization Western Sahara was inhabited by peoples which, if nomadic, *were socially and politically organized in tribes and under chiefs competent to represent them*. It also shows that, in colonizing Western Sahara, Spain did not proceed on the basis that it was establishing its sovereignty over *terrae nullius*. In its Royal Order of 26 December 1884, far from treating the case as one of occupation of *terra nullius*, Spain proclaimed that the King was taking the Rio de Oro under his protection on the basis of agreements which had been entered into with the chiefs of the local tribes: the Order referred expressly

> to 'the documents which the independent tribes of this part of the coast' had 'signed with the representative of the Sociedad Española de Africanistas', and announced that the King had confirmed 'the deeds of adherence' to Spain. [Emphasis added]

In order for the Court to arrive at this conclusion, it stated categorically (at [56]) that it:

> ... must take into consideration the changes which have occurred in the supervening half-century, and its interpretation cannot remain unaffected by the subsequent development of law, through the Charter of the United Nations and by way of customary law.

Although this was the first instance in which the Court had held that an inhabited territory was not *terra nullius*, it must be noted that it was able to rule as such only because there was evidence that the inhabitants of the Western Sahara, at the time at which Spain colonized them, were well organized and, as Spain also indicated in the Order that it concluded with the tribal chief, independent. The contribution of this case to the development of the modern view on *terra nullius* is therefore limited. It was not until seventeen years later, in *Mabo v. Queensland (No. 2) (Mabo No. 2)* [1992] HCA 23; (1992) 175 CLR 1, that an Australian court would make the most radical departure from the concept. However, since *Mabo No. 2* deals more with the land tenure system, it is not necessary that it is considered here.

Intertemporal law

Another criterion used by the PCIJ in the *Island of Palmas Case* to determine the validity of title of territories acquired by occupation or prescription is intertemporal law.

Georg Schwarzenberger, in *International Law, Vol. I: International Law as Applied by International Courts and Tribunals* (London: Stevens, 1957), pp. 21–24, defines 'intertemporal law' as the 'determination of international law at successive periods in their application of a particular case'.

. . . .

● *Netherlands v. United States of America* [1928] 2 RIAA 829 (The *Island of Palmas Case*)

Speaking about the intertemporal law, Judge Huber said (at 845) that:

> ... a juridical fact must be appreciated in the light of the law contemporary with it, and not of the law in force at the time when a dispute in regard to it arises or falls to be settled.

Intertemporal law is the law that is in force at the time when the juridical facts pertaining to a particular dispute arise, in contradistinction to the law that is in force at the time that the dispute itself arises, which is the critical date. The purpose of intertemporal law, as formulated by Judge Huber, is to ensure that the legal consideration of juridical facts takes cognizance of the currency of law at any given time.

. . . .

● *Cameroon v. Nigeria* [2002] ICJ Rep 331 (The *Land and Maritime Boundary between Cameroon and Nigeria Case*)

In a case involving Cameroon and Nigeria disputing title to the Bakassi Peninsula, an oil-rich peninsula situated in the hollow of the Gulf of Guinea, the ICJ had to determine the effect of an 1884 treaty by which Britain undertook to protect Nigeria. Nigeria had argued that in light of Britain's obligation under this treaty, which was only to protect Nigeria, it had no other powers and could not have ceded the disputed territory to Germany, through which Cameroon now claimed as successor.

Commenting on the effect of the 1884 treaty, the Court said (at 345) that:

> … in territories that were not *terra nullius*, but were inhabited by tribes or people having a social and political organization, agreements concluded with local rulers … were regarded as derivative roots of title … Even if this mode of acquisition does not reflect current international law, the principle of intertemporal law requires that the *legal consequences of the treaties* concluded at that time in the Niger delta be given effect today, in the present dispute.

The trouble with intertemporal law

● *Netherlands v. United States of America* [1928] 2 RIAA 829 [The *Island of Palmas Case*]

The USA had argued that the relevant law to determine the validity of the disputed land should be the law in force when Spain ceded the territory to USA. The Netherlands had argued (at p. 839) that title to territory cannot be determined by reference to a single moment, but in accordance also with subsequent laws.

In response Judge Huber formulated the intertemporal rule, as noted earlier, but added (at 831) that:

> … as regards the question which of different legal systems prevailing at successive periods is to be applied in a particular case (The so-called intertemporal law), a distinction must be made between the *creation* of rights and the *existence* of rights. The same principle which subjects the act creative of a right to the law in force at the time the right arises, demands that the existence of the right, in other words its continued manifestation, shall follow the conditions required by the evolution of law. [Emphasis added]

The implication of this statement is that a title that is valid at the time that a State acquires a territory—for example, by occupation—may be lost if the State does not continuously maintain the title in accordance with the evolution of the law.

Several scholars have challenged this view.

In 'The *Palmas Island Arbitration*' (1928) 22 AJIL 735, 740, Philip Jessup observes that the original hypothesis upon which Judge Huber based his decision:

> … is the *original* existence of sovereignty or title by discovery. If it once existed, the question of abandonment would be pertinent, especially since the new rule of international law is said to have arisen only in the nineteenth century and the Dutch claims antedated this period. One must assume the meaning to be that abandonment is irrelevant because the original sovereignty (under the hypothesis) ceased to exist by virtue of the principle of 'intertemporal law.' [Emphasis in original]

Put simply, most writers agree with Judge Huber on the point that title to territory must be evaluated in accordance with the law existing at the time of its creation. However, they reject the second condition, which is that such acts must be continuously maintained *after* creation according to the evolving law because this condition is retroactive in nature. By this condition titles that were valid when they were created will become invalid by subsequent law regardless of whether the previous owner ever abandoned such title. This, obviously, is a dangerous proposition. As Jessup noted, at 740:

> Such a retroactive effect of law would be highly disturbing. Every state would constantly be under the necessity of examining its title to each portion of its territory in order to determine whether a change in the law had necessitated, as it were, a reacquisition. If such a principle were applied to private law and private titles, the result would be chaos.

While the fear expressed by Jessup in this statement appears well founded, it is highly unlikely for valid titles to become invalidated by subsequent events.

In 'The doctrine of intertemporal law' (1980) 74 AJIL 285, 286, T. O. Elias argues that:

> There is little doubt that, in theory, this fear is justified, although in practice other principles of interpretation and application of intertemporal law such as acquiescence, prescription, desuetude, and the rule against nonretroactivity of treaty provisions would operate to make it impossible for the second element of the doctrine to work injustices.

See also Rosalyn Higgins, 'Some observations on the inter-temporal rules in international law' in Jerzy Makarczyk (ed.), *Theory of International Law at the Threshold of the Twenty-First Century* (The Hague: Kluwer Law International, 1996), p. 173.

---

thinking points

- *Define 'intertemporal law'.*
- *Distinguish between intertemporal law and the critical date theory.*
- *Explain the practical significance of intertemporal law.*

6.2.2 Acquisition by prescription

As briefly stated previously, when a State acquires title over a territory that is already occupied by another State, the former is said to acquire the territory by prescription insofar as it can prove that the previous occupier acquiesced to the subsequent title. Thus prescription, if successful, can displace original titles to territory.

Definition

D. H. N. Johnson (1950, see section 6.2.1), at 353, states that:

> 'Acquisitive prescription' is the means by which, under international law, legal recognition is given to the right of a state to exercise sovereignty over land or sea territory in cases where that state has, in fact, exercised its authority in a continuous, uninterrupted, and peaceful manner over the area concerned for a sufficient period of time, provided that all other interested and affected states (in the case of land territory the previous possessor, in the case of sea territory neighbouring states and other states whose maritime interests are affected) have acquiesced in this exercise of authority.

This definition is very useful, because it encompasses the various conditions that must be met before a territory can be acquired by prescription. Before dealing with these conditions, it is necessary first to distinguish between the various ways in which the term 'prescription' may be used in international law, because our discussion here is limited to 'acquisitive prescription', as defined by Johnson.

The term prescription may mean 'extinctive prescription', which is similar to 'limitation' under the English law. As explained by Johnson (ibid.):

> In this sense prescription means that, if State A has an international claim against State B which it fails to bring before an international tribunal within a reasonable time, then the international tribunal before which the claim is eventually brought may reject it. This doctrine is subject to the rule that the failure to present the claim must be due to the negligence or laches of the claimant party and not due to the obstruction of the defendant party.

This is not the sense of the prescription that we intend to discuss here.

Prescription may alternatively mean 'acquisitive prescription'. Johnson explains, at 332, that:

> In addition to the rule that claims not prosecuted within a reasonable time must be held to have lapsed, all legal systems have found it no less necessary to have a doctrine whereby legal validity can be given to titles to property that are either originally invalid or whose original validity it is impossible to prove.

According to W. E. Hall and A. Pearce Higgins, *A Treatise on International Law* (8th edn, Oxford: Clarendon Press, 1924), p. 143:

> Title by prescription arises out of a long-continued possession, where no original source or proprietary right can be shown to exist, or where possession in the first instance being wrongful, the legitimate proprietor has neglected to assert his right or has been unable to do so.

6.2.3 Conditions for acquisitive prescription

Certain conditions govern the validity of acquisitive prescription—namely:

(a) possession must be exercised *à titre de souverain*;

(b) possession must be 'peaceful and uninterrupted'; and

(c) possession must exist for 'a reasonable length of time'.

Possession *à titre de souverain*

Possession *à titre de souverain* implies that a State that claims acquisition by prescription must act, with regard to the concerned territory, absolutely and without recognition or deference to the sovereignty of any other State over the same territory. Logically, if a State claiming acquisitive prescription acknowledges the sovereignty of another State over that territory, then the acquiescence of the other State, which is a necessary requirement of acquisitive prescription, is lacking (see also Johnson, 1950, at 333, see section 6.2.1). For a State to fulfil the criterion of possession *à titre de souverain*, it must manifest the intention and display the authority to do so. What constitutes a manifestation of these elements varies from case to case.

● *Malaysia v. Singapore* (2008) ICJ Rep 12 (*Case Concerning Sovereignty over Pedra Branca/ Pulau Batu Puteh*)

A dispute arose between Malaysia and Singapore over title to sovereignty over Pedra Branca/ Pulau Batu Puteh, Middle Rocks, and South Ledge. Each State claimed it undertook various activities concerning the disputed territory which it believed constituted possession *à titre de souverain*. Singapore put forward such acts as investigating shipwrecks on the island, maintaining and operating a lighthouse, etc.

The Court said (at [239]) that:

> This Singaporean conduct is to be seen as conduct *à titre de souverain*. The permission granted or not granted by Singapore to Malaysian officials was not simply about the maintenance and operation of the lighthouse and in particular its protection. Singapore's decisions in these cases related to the survey by Malaysian officials of the waters surrounding the island. The conduct of Singapore in giving permission for these visits does give significant support to Singapore's claim to sovereignty over Pedra Branca/Pulau Batu Puteh.

Possession must be peaceful and uninterrupted

Peaceful and uninterrupted possession requires that there is no active opposition by the State that has original title to the territory to such activities by another State as impinge on its title. In other words, the State with the original title must acquiesce to the claim. Acquiescence occurs when a State is silent in the face of acts done by another State against which it should have protested. Thus where a State with original title to a territory chooses to do nothing while another State takes steps that are either inconsistent with or derogate from the former's sovereignty, then that State shall be presumed to have acquiesced to the claim of the other State.

● *Malaysia v. Singapore* (2008) ICJ Rep 12 (*Case Concerning Sovereignty over Pedra Branca/Pulau Puteh*)

The Court said (at [121]) that:

> Under certain circumstances, sovereignty over territory might pass as a result of the failure of the State which has sovereignty to respond to conduct *à titre de souverain* of the other State or, as Judge Huber put it in the *Island of Palmas* case, to concrete manifestations of the display of territorial sovereignty by the other State (*Island of Palmas Case (Netherlands/United States of America)*, Award of 4 April 1928, *RIAA*, Vol. II, (1949) p. 839). Such manifestations of the display of sovereignty may call for a response if they are not to be opposable to the State in question. The absence of reaction may well amount to acquiescence.

However, a State with original title does not have to protest where the acts of the latter claimant do not warrant any response.

● *Canada v. United States of America (Judgment)* (1984) ICJ Rep 305 (*Delimitation of the Maritime Boundary in the Gulf of Maine Area*)

The Court said (at [130]): 'Thus there is no peaceful and uninterrupted possession where there is protest.'

● *Mexico v. United States* (1911) 11 RIAA 309 (The *Chamizal Arbitration*)

A dispute arose between the USA and Mexico over Chamizal tract. The USA argued that its claim by prescription arose by virtue of 'undisturbed, uninterrupted, and unchallenged possession of the territory since the treaty of 1848' (at 317). The tribunal rejected this argument.

The Arbitral Panel said (at 328) that:

> Upon the evidence adduced it is impossible to hold that the possession of El Chamizal by the United States was undisturbed, uninterrupted, and unchallenged from the date of the treaty [*sic*] of the creation of a competent tribunal to decide the question, the Chamizal case was first presented. On the contrary, it may be said that the physical possession taken by citizens of the United States and the political control exercised by the local and Federal Governments, have been constantly challenged and questioned by the Republic of Mexico, through its accredited diplomatic agents.

What constitutes valid protests against claims of acquisitive prescription varies from case to case, although it is possible to formulate certain fundamental principles. First, considering that Article 2(4) of the UN Charter has prohibited the use of force, acquisitive prescription cannot be maintained by force even if the territory was originally procured by that means; conversely, a State cannot be expected to mount a valid resistance only by forceful means. Under classical international law, protests were regarded to be effective only if they were accompanied by the use of force. However, given that the tendency of modern international law is to encourage peaceful resolution of conflicts among States, recourse to international courts and tribunals will be treated as effective protests against claims of acquisitive prescription.

Possession must exist for a reasonable length of time

For it to be valid, prescriptive acquisition must exist for a reasonable length of time. This is an important requirement because even scholars who do not accept acquisitive prescription agree that immemorial possession constitutes a valid title to territory. Thus Grotius, in *De Jure Belli ac Pacis*, Book ii, ch. iv, §1, conceded that:

> since time beyond the memory of man is morally, as it were infinite, a silence for such a time will always suffice to establish derelict, except where there are very strong reasons on the other side.

However, it is difficult to specify what constitutes a 'reasonable time' for the purpose of acquisitive prescription. Writers have formulated various tests. For Grotius (ibid., restated in Johnson, 1950, at 336, see section 6.2.1), it has to be at least 100 years, for:

> time beyond the memory of man [was not very different from a century] … because the common term of a human life is a hundred years, which commonly included three generations of men.

Obviously, it is problematic to accept this formulation in light of improvements in modern medicine and life expectancies of peoples across various civilizations.

6.3 Cession and accretion

Cession and accretion are two other ways in which States may acquire territory in international law. Cession occurs when a previous owner of a territory transfers it to another who becomes the new owner and it is usually accomplished by agreements. Cession was a major means of establishing colonialism in Africa: several colonial powers concluded agreements with local rulers for the transfer of all or parts of their territories to the imperial powers. Cession was also a common feature of agreements terminating wars. It must be noted, however, that since cession concerns the transfer of title from one owner to another, such a transaction is subject to the principle *nemo dat quod non habet* (that is, no one can give what he or she does not have). In other words, the transferring State cannot confer on the new owner any better title than that which it possesses. Hence, cession does not cure a defect in the title to the territory being transferred.

Accretion takes place when, due to a shift in land mass, land that previously belonged to a State becomes attached to another State. Accretion is really not so much a case of a State deliberately acquiring territory as it is a State's territory being extended through an act of nature. As a means of acquiring territory, accretion is both rare and contentious.

Other modes of territory acquisition include 'avulsion', and 'annexation' (or 'conquest'). Avulsion is a sudden change in the course of land or water brought about by violent activities of nature, such as floods, storms, and volcanic eruptions.

6.4 The law of the sea

As briefly indicated previously, a State's territory does not comprise only its land mass, but also includes its waters. However, whereas a State has an absolute jurisdiction over its land mass, this is not the case with its seas. The jurisdiction of a State over the sea is subject to various rules and principles. Furthermore, there is an area of sea—usually called the 'high seas'—over which no individual State has jurisdiction. In addition to all of these, recent developments in international law, especially within the law of the sea, have further affected areas of the sea over which States previously exercised 'absolute' jurisdiction.

In this part of the chapter, we will examine the regulation of the sea as part of a State's territory. The focus here is not to discuss the law of the sea exhaustively—which can never be accomplished in a work of this nature; rather, we will discuss how the regulation of the sea emerged in modern times and consider the various areas of the sea over which a State may exercise its jurisdiction, as well as discussing certain fundamental challenges militating against a full implementation of the law of the sea.

6.4.1 The regulation of the sea in modern times

Despite the widely held belief that in ancient times the sea was free for all and belonged to no one, early historians recorded the attempt, first by the Roman Caesar, and then others kings and emperors to regulate the sea (see Percy Thomas Fenn, 'Origin of the theory of territorial waters' (1926) 20 AJIL 465).

The increasing assertion by States of rights over the sea led Albericus Gentilis, in his appreciation of the Dutch/Spanish dispute, to state in his book *Hispanicae Advocationis* (Amstelodami: Libri duo, 1661), p. 32, that territory included land and the sea.

Gentilis' formulation inspired seventeenth-century scholars to seek to understand whether the sea could be subject to the sovereignty of any nation as part of its territory—a discourse that fascinated several eminent authorities of international law, such as Grotius.

The emergence of the cannon rule (the three-mile rule)

One of the earliest issues confronted by States in their desire to regulate the sea is the extent to which a State ought to exercise its jurisdiction over the sea. On the one hand are States, such as the Netherlands, inspired by Hugo Grotius's 1609 work *Mare Liberum* (*The Free Sea*), which claimed that the sea belonged to all nations and should be explored limitlessly. Grotius thus laid the ground for the Dutch to use superior naval power to break any State's monopoly over the sea. On the other hand are States, such as England which vigorously opposed the 'free for all' principle of the Dutch, claiming total dominion over its seas. This English stance was endorsed by William Welwod, the Scottish jurist credited with formulating the first law of the sea in the English language in the 1613 *An Abridgement of All Sea-Lawes*, to which Grotius would respond in 1615.

Scholars coming several centuries after Welwod also maintained that England indeed possessed sovereignty over its territorial waters, tracing such claims as far back as the thirteenth century.

● ***The King v. Oldsworth*** (1637) (Restated in Hale, DE JURE MARIS, Hargrave MS. No. 97, p. 381 At p. 397)

The Court held that:

> As the King is supreme upon the land, so he is upon the sea, and all the land was originally in the Crown, and therefore so is the sea, and the ungranted lands left derelict by the sea's recession: For, as the land was in the King when it was parcel of the sea; now, when it is made parcel of the dry land, it shall not be taken from him.

The English reinforced their position in 1651 with the adoption of the Navigation Act which forbade any goods to enter the country except on English ships, leading to the first Anglo–Dutch War of 1652–54.

In his work *De Dominio Maris* (1702), Cornelius Bynkershoek proposed a link between maritime dominion and the distance over which a State's cannon range could effectively protect it, as a way of solving the problem. This became universally adopted and developed into the 'three-mile rule'.

In *Classics of International Law* (Carnegie Endowment Series, New York: Oxford University Press, 1923), p. 17, James Brown Scott stated that:

> In the days of Bynkershoek, a cannon carried approximately three miles; hence the statement that a nation may occupy and exercise ownership over waters three miles within low water mark. This was the solution proposed by the young publicist; this was the solution accepted by the nations; this is the solution still obtaining, unless modified by express consent.

However, some writers have argued that Bynkershoek never intended his formulation as a three-mile rule he was credited with since he did not mention a three-mile rule but refers instead to the limit of a cannon shot, a practice already common in maritime wars at the time. In any case, it was also doubted if any cannon existed in Bynkershoek's time or soon thereafter that had a range of three miles. (See Wydham L. Walker, 'Territorial waters: the cannon shot rule' (1945) 22 BYBIL 210, 210.)

There is no doubt, however, that Bynkershoek popularized the cannon rule theory, or that the majority of States indeed accepted and applied it until much later times, as was manifested in several cases that arose from the war against France, which started the War of the League of Augsburg.

The period between the eighteenth and early twentieth centuries witnessed a consolidation in the theory that States exercised sovereignty over their territorial waters to the extent that there was very little dissent from scholars.

D. P. O'Connell, 'The juridical nature of the territorial sea' (1971) 45 BYBIL 303, 343, states that:

> After 1900 the controversy about the juridical nature of the territorial sea waned, and scarcely any author took issue with the notion that the territorial sea is subject to sovereignty. Of the fifty-three writers whose work has been examined in the period 1900–25, when codifiers almost unanimously referred to sovereignty over the territorial sea, thirty support that principle, sixteen appear to oppose it or echo the later nineteenth-century writers who argued for limited jurisdiction, and seven give no indication of their views.

KEY POINTS

- The division between those who argued for jurisdiction over the territorial sea and those opposed to it was motivated by security considerations (those who supported jurisdiction) and commercial interests, or interests in freedom of navigation (those opposed to jurisdiction). Neither interest was motivated by a desire for objective regulation of the sea.

- The cannon rule was the precursor of the three-mile rule. It basically posits that a State's coastal waters over which it could exercise jurisdiction extend only as far as the reach of its cannon.

- Bynkershoek was credited with being the originator of the cannon rule, although the more accurate description is that he merely popularized the already existing rule.

6.5 The codification of the law of the sea: 1930

By the twentieth century, many practices concerning the regulation of the sea had become well established. These include the acceptance of the three-mile rule as the correct measurement of the territorial sea of a State; accepting the territorial sea as forming part of a coastal State's territory and over which it has exclusive jurisdiction; and the recognition that some States preferred to measure their territorial seas differently.

It was also generally accepted that the high seas belonged to all States, with none able to exercise jurisdiction over it.

However, developments in science, the increase in commercial activities on the sea, and the desire by many States to have greater access to areas of the sea that were categorized as part of the territorial waters of coastal States or their exclusive fisheries zones (EFZs), brought tension amongst States. Several States campaigned for the extension of the three-mile rule, as well as for limits on such areas previously regarded as the exclusive economic zones (EEZs) of coastal States.

In 1930, the Conference for the Codification of International Law, held at The Hague, became the first attempt to codify international law in general. Among other things the conference established a Commission on the Territorial Waters to examine various issues of concern among States regarding the law of the sea. The conference proved to be of little success. It faced many challenges, such as the difficult nature of the subject matter, the divergent interests of participating States, and the disparity of States' views on the breadth of territorial water, all of which hindered its progress. (See Jesse S. Reeves, 'The codification of the law of territorial waters' (1930) 24 AJIL 486.)

Particularly frustrating at the conference was the disagreement between States which wanted greater navigational rights with minimum interference by coastal States and coastal States that wanted to reserve the largest possible areas of their waters as EFZs for their nationals. According to Whittemore Boggs, 'Delimitation of the territorial sea: the method of delimitation proposed by the delegation of the United States at The Hague Conference for the Codification of International Law' (1930) 24 AJIL 541, 542, since international law already recognized the rule whereby:

> only the nationals of the coastal state may fish in its territorial waters, there is a tendency, on the part of states whose coastal waters are good for fishing purposes, to delimit their own territorial waters in such a way as to acquire the largest possible area of territorial sea.

It must be noted, however, that despite the non-agreement on the breadth of the territorial sea, the traditional three-nautical mile rule appeared to have survived the conference.

According to Gilbert Gidel, then considered the greatest living authority on the law of the sea (see C. H. M. Waldock, 'The *Anglo-Norwegian Fisheries Case*' (1951) 28 BYBIL 114), the effect of the failure of the conference to agree on the breadth of the territorial sea was to leave the three-mile limit as a universally accepted minimum and the validity of larger claims dependent on the consent of other States (see Gidel (1934) 2 Recueil des Cours de l'Académie de Droit International 180).

thinking points

- *What factors militated against the success of the 1930 Commission on the Territorial Waters?*
- *Explain the divergent nature of States' interests regarding such matters as the breadth of the sea and the EFZs during the 1930 Hague Conference.*
- *To what extent do you think the divergent interests of States over the breadth of the territorial sea undermined the work of the Territorial Waters Commission?*

6.6 The 1958 and 1960 UN Conference on the Law of the Sea (UNCLOS I and II)

In 1956, the United Nations held its first Conference on the Law of the Sea (UNCLOS I) in Geneva and the second, UNCLOS II, in Paris in 1960. UNCLOS I resulted in the conclusion of four Conventions (the Geneva Conventions) on the Law of the Sea in 1958:

- the Convention on the Territorial Seas and Contiguous Zone (the Territorial Seas Convention), entered into force 10 September 1964;
- the Convention on the Continental Shelf (the Continental Shelf Convention), entered into force 10 June 1964;

- the Convention on the High Seas (the High Seas Convention), entered into force 30 September 1962; and

- the Convention on Fishing Conservation of Living Resources of the High Seas (the Fishing Conservation Convention), entered into force 20 March 1966.

Unlike the 1930 conference, UNCLOS I was considered a success, even if it left several issues of concern unanswered. For example, the conference introduced a new topic altogether—the **continental shelf**—into the law of the sea. Although discussion around the continental shelf had always formed part of the concern of international lawyers, it was not until US President Harry Truman's proclamation of 28 September 1945 that it began to attract major attention.

continental shelf

This term refers to the seabed and subsoil of a State.

According to President Harry S Truman, Proclamation 2667 'Policy of the United States With Respect to the Natural Resources of the Subsoil and Sea Bed of the Continental Shelf' 10 Fed Reg 12303 (28 September 1945). (restated in J. A. C. Gutteridge, 'The 1958 Geneva Convention on the Continental Shelf' (1959) 35 BYBIL 102, 103):

> The Government of the United States regards the natural resources of the subsoil and the sea-bed of the continental shelf beneath the High Seas but contiguous to the coasts of the United States as appertaining to the United States [and] subject to its jurisdiction and control.

It needs to be pointed out that the notion of the continental shelf had been known to States and scholars long before Truman's proclamation. Gutteridge (1959, above) traced the origin of claims over the continental shelf to the days of Vattel and asserted that the first international agreement on the continental shelf, even if it was not so described in the concerned agreement, was between the UK and Venezuela in 1942.

Another innovation of UNCLOS I was the Fishing Conservation Convention. However, this did not enjoy the support of many States.

KEY POINTS

- The 1956 UN Conference on the Law of the Sea led to the adoption of four conventions, two of which addressed new areas regarding the continental shelf and fishing management.

- The US President Truman's 1945 Proclamation popularized the idea of the continental shelf and made it a subject of specific formulation in the 1958 Convention on the Continental Shelf.

Like its predecessor, UNCLOS I left many issues unresolved, the most important of which was the breadth of the territorial waters. Ingeniously, UNCLOS II attempted to solve the problem by proposing a system whereby States would be allowed to fish within a belt outside their territorial water instead of advocating an extension of the territorial water itself, as favoured by some States. The ICJ favoured, and experimented with, this approach.

● **Federal Republic of Germany v. Denmark, Federal Republic of Germany v. The Netherlands** [1969] ICJ Rep 3 (The **North Sea Continental Shelf Cases**)

A dispute arose between Germany and Denmark, and between Germany and the Netherlands, regarding the application of the equidistance principle in delimiting undelimited areas of the continental shelf adjacent to the parties. On the question of how to measure which parts of the shelf belonged to a coastal State, the Netherlands and Denmark argued (at [39]) that only those parts of the shelf closer to a coastal State than to any point of another coastal State could be so regarded. Although the Court accepted this argument, it noted (at [40]) that such a measurement does not apply at all times and there may be instances when a different measurement will be applied.

●●

● *United Kingdom v. Iceland (Merits)* (1974) ICJ REP 3 (The *Fisheries Jurisdiction Case*)

In 1952, Iceland extended its territorial waters from three to four nautical miles; in 1958, it extended its EFZ to a twelve-mile limit. It then sought (at [24]):

> ...a recognition of Iceland's right to the entire continental shelf area in conformity with the policy adopted by the Law of 1948, concerning the Scientific Conservation of the Continental Shelf Fisheries and that fishery limits of less than 12 miles from base-lines around the country are out of the question.

Iceland had claimed that where a nation is overwhelmingly dependent upon fisheries, it should be lawful to take special measures and to decide a further extension of the EFZ for meeting the needs of such a nation.

The Court stated (at [62]) that:

> The concept of preferential rights is not compatible with the exclusion of all fishing activities of other States. A coastal State entitled to preferential rights is not free, unilaterally and according to its own uncontrolled discretion, to determine the extent of those rights. The characterization of the coastal State's rights as preferential implies a certain priority, but cannot imply the extinction of the concurrent rights of other States and particularly of a State which, like the Applicant, have for many years been engaged in fishing in the waters in question, such fishing activity being important to the economy of the country concerned. The coastal State has to take into account and pay regard to the position of such other States, particularly when they have established an economic dependence on the same fishing grounds. Accordingly, the fact that Iceland is entitled to claim preferential rights does not suffice to justify its claim unilaterally to exclude the Applicant's fishing vessels from all fishing activity in the waters beyond the limits agreed to in the 1961 Exchange of Notes.

thinking points

- *Explain one major contribution of UNCLOS II to the law of the sea.*
- *What approach did the ICJ take in* North Sea Continental Shelf *and* Fisheries Jurisdiction *as regards coastal States' claims to fishing rights beyond their territorial waters?*
- *How did the Court attempt to balance the recognition and concession of 'preferential rights' to needy and desirous coastal States and the rights of other States? (You may need to read the two cases discussed previously again in order to appreciate fully the Court's jurisprudence on this important issue. Pay particular attention to the fact that the Court did not favour any unilateral or arbitrary recourse to exercising preferential rights by coastal States fishing beyond their territorial waters or contiguous zones.)*

Despite its efforts, UNCLOS II left many issues unresolved. For example, States continued to extend their EFZs arbitrarily beyond their territorial waters and the contiguous zone recognized by the 1958 Convention. This development further reduced the demarcation between the territorial sea, in respect of which States have exclusive jurisdiction, and the high seas, in respect of which all States have access. Certainly, the more seaward States expanded their fishing seabeds (as seen in the Icelandic attempt), the fewer the areas of the high seas available to other States to explore. In 1967, the Maltese Ambassador to the United Nations summed up the view of most States towards the brazen attempt to shrink the high seas by declaring that seabed resources lying outside the jurisdiction of coastal States are a 'common heritage of mankind' that must be available to all nations. It was inevitable, therefore, that the UN would return, one more time, to consider all of the outstanding issues unresolved by UNCLOS II, as well as to deal with newly emergent ones. This fell to the 1982 United Nations Convention on the Law of the Sea (UNCLOS III). In order to appreciate this convention fully, it is important briefly to revisit its particular and peculiar negotiation and adoption history.

The 1982 UN Convention on the Law of the Sea (UNCLOS III)

6.7.1 UNCLOS III in context

The 1982 UNCLOS was negotiated over a nine-year period (between 1974 and 1982). The negotiation was tense and difficult. States had conflicting interests, and there were many problems carried over from the 1958 conventions, as well as new issues with which to deal.

UNCLOS contains 320 Articles. Its attempt to capture all issues from the past and the future makes it the most comprehensive effort to date by the international community to find solutions to the many problems of the law of the sea.

In Verbatim Records (1982) 17 Third United Nations Conference on the Law of the Sea, Official Records, 191st Plenary Meeting, at 111, the representative of Denmark to UNCLOS III observes that:

> This is a unique event in the history of international law. The Convention on the Law of the Sea is the most comprehensive treaty ever drafted. It is a modern constitution for the uses of the ocean. It deals with all conceivable peaceful human activities in an area larger than 70 per cent of the surface of the globe. It has been worked out by the largest Conference in the history of the United Nations. The results embodied in the 320 articles and related annexes and resolutions reflect a willingness to cooperate and to accept compromise solutions.

UNCLOS III entered into force on 16 November 1994, with all of its provisions being adopted without a vote. Nonetheless, Part XI of UNCLOS III dealing mainly with the continental shelf regime almost proved fatal to the convention. Although the USA had already taken a stance on this issue in 1945 (see earlier), the USA, as with Germany and the UK, ultimately rejected the convention while the majority of the developing States voted for the convention. (See the statement of Ambassador James L. Malone to the Plenary Meeting on 30 April 1982 (reported at (1983) 19 Weekly Comp Pres Doc 383).)

In principle, the negative votes of the USA and other major, powerful States did not prevent the convention from entering into force on 16 November 1994, following the deposition of sixty ratifications, as required under Article 308. Nevertheless, the non-participation of such powerful, advanced States was certain to undermine the convention seriously. In order to avert this potential disaster, which would probably have killed off the convention at birth, the UN orchestrated a process that resulted in the adoption of the so-called New York Implementation Agreement in 1996—in undisguised terms, no more than a conciliatory gesture towards the USA and its allies. The strategy worked. Many more States accepted the convention, including Germany and the UK, which had previously voted against it; the USA, however, remains a non-party to the 1982 UNCLOS.

Currently, there are over 160 member States of UNCLOS and almost as many States have ratified the 1996 Implementation Agreement. UNCLOS covers a wide array of issues, both new to the law of the sea and carried forth from previous efforts. In the following section, we consider some of the key provisions of the convention relevant for our purpose. These include: the EEZs; the rights of archipelagic States'; the right of landlocked States (that is, States without seas); the conservation of marine resources; the control of marine pollution; the peculiar problem of States with crooked and unstraight waterlines; and, of course, the regime of the high seas.

KEY POINTS

- UNCLOS III is the most comprehensive attempt at regulating the law of the sea to date. It was negotiated over the course of nine years and contains 320 Articles.

- The USA's refusal to ratify UNCLOS III is primarily due to the provision of Part XI of the convention dealing with the regulation of the seabed and subsoil (the continental shelf). Although the UN attempted, by the so-called 1996 Implementation Agreement, to meet some of the concerns of the USA and other developed States about the continental shelf regime, the USA still did not accept the convention.

- UNCLOS III provides for some new developments, such as provisions relating to the exclusive economic zone and landlocked States.

6.7.2 UNCLOS III and the territorial sea

Article 2 UNCLOS III provides that:

> (1) The sovereignty of a coastal State extends beyond its land and internal waters and, in the case of an archipelagic State, its archipelagic waters, to an adjacent belt of sea, described as the territorial sea.
>
> (2) This sovereignty extends to the airspace over the territorial sea as well as to its bed and subsoil.
>
> (3) The sovereignty over the territorial sea is subject to this Convention and to other rules of international law.

This provision is important and uncontroversial. That the territorial sea of a State extends beyond its land mass and internal waters has never really been in doubt, and reflects customary international law on the matter. As a matter of fact, it does not seem that a State may only accept its territorial waters by choice: it is clear that international law imposes obligations and rights on coastal States in respect of their territorial waters.

. . . .

● *Norway v. Sweden* (1909) HAGUE REPORTS 121 (The *Grisbadarna Case*)

In this case, Judge Arnold MacNair said (at 127) that:

> International Law does not say to a State: 'You are entitled to claim territorial waters if you want them'. No maritime state can refuse them. International law imposes upon a maritime State certain obligations and confers upon it certain rights arising out of the sovereignty which it exercises over its maritime territory.

Aside from determining the coastal State's territorial sea, UNCLOS III also succeeded in prescribing the width of such sea as twelve nautical miles. It will be recalled that this was not possible in 1958 due to disagreement among States.

According to Article 3 UNCLOS III:

> Every State has the right to establish the breadth of its territorial sea up to a limit not exceeding 12 nautical miles measured from baselines determined in accordance with this Convention.

This Article clearly establishes twelve miles as the maximum width for a State's territorial sea. Nonetheless, while the majority of States apply the twelve-mile rule, some Latin American countries apply up to 200 miles.

Delimitation of the 'territorial sea'

Determining what waters form part of a State's territorial sea is not the same as how such waters are to be measured. In customary international law, the appropriate measurement of a State's territorial waters has always been in accordance with a formula, now codified in Article 5 UNCLOS III:

> Except where otherwise provided in this Convention, the normal baseline for measuring the breadth of the territorial sea is the low-water line along the coast as marked on large-scale charts officially recognized by the coastal State.

While the majority of States abide by this rule, some find it impossible to comply with this rule due to the crooked and unsuitable nature of their coastline. Where this has been the case, the ICJ has shown accepted different measuring methods from affected States.

● **United Kingdom v. Norway** (1951) ICJ REP 116 (The **Anglo Norwegian Fisheries Case**)

Due to the presence of islands and rocks along its coast, Norway measured its territorial sea not only from the low-water mark as customary, but also from straight baseline incorporating 'drying rocks' both above water and low-water tide. By so doing, Norway was able to enclose within its territorial sea parts of the high seas that would have normally been open to other States had it adopted the traditional low-water line alone. Norway justified adopting this measurement method on many grounds, including the survival of its population living in those difficult areas which the Court agreed with.

Regarding Norway's departure from the usual measurement method, the Court stated (at 128–129) that:

> Where a coast is deeply indented and cut into…the baseline becomes independent of the low-water mark, and can only be determined by means of geometric construction. In such circumstances the line of the low-water mark can no longer be put forward as a rule requiring the coast line to be followed in all its sinuosities. Nor can one characterise as an exception to the rule the very many derogations which would be necessitated by such a rugged coast; the rule would disappear under the exceptions. Such a coast, viewed as a whole, calls for the application of a different method; that is the method of baselines which, within reasonable limits, may depart from the physical line of the coast.

It is interesting to note that rather than treating Norway's departure as an exception to the rule, the Court treated it as a new rule altogether. Otherwise, if the Court would have to treat every derogation as an exception, then the rule itself will eventually disappear altogether.

However, not everyone is happy with the Court's creative approach in this case.

Waldock (1951, see section 6.5), at 167, sums up his concerns with the Court's decision thus:

(a) The Court has made some very important pronouncements on general international law apparently against the weight both of state practice and juristic opinion without adequately explaining why it rejected all the former authority or how it felt able to present its own conclusions as rules of international law binding upon states.

(b) The Court has made important findings on disputed issues of fact without so much as a passing reference to what sometimes appear to be obstinate facts in the opposing case.

Similarly, D. H. N. Johnson, 'The *Anglo-Norwegian Fisheries Case*' (1952) 11 ICLQ 145, 155–156, writes that:

There is no doubt that the Court rejected the coastline rule as a rule binding on Norway. What is less clear is whether the Court intended to reject the coast-line rule as a rule of international law altogether. It might be inferred, from the emphasis placed on the peculiarities of the coast of northern Norway, that the Court had no such intention. Yet, when the judgment is examined closely, the conclusion is inescapable that it was the Court's intention to reject the coast-line rule as a general rule of law, but that, in view of the very great authority in favour of that rule, it felt impelled to effect the change in a somewhat oblique fashion . . .

Nonetheless, the Court's approach in the *Anglo Norwegian Fisheries Case* has now been incorporated into the UNCLOS. Article 7(1) UNCLOS III provides that:

In localities where the coastline is deeply indented and cut into, or if there is a fringe of islands along the coast in its immediate vicinity, the method of straight baselines joining appropriate points may be employed in drawing the baseline from which the breadth of the territorial sea is measured.

This provision virtually mirrored the Court's judgment in the *Anglo Norwegian Fisheries Case* which was decided before any of the UNCLOS conventions took place. The only condition attached to the new rule is according to Article 7(4) UNCLOS III, that:

Straight baselines shall not be drawn to and from low-tide elevations, unless lighthouses or similar installations which are permanently above sea level have been built on them or except in circumstances where the drawing of baselines to and from such elevations has received general international recognition.

Also, under Article 7(5) UNCLOS III, the use of baselines must take into consideration the economic interests of the particular region, and under Article 7(6):

The system of straight baselines may not be applied by a State in such a manner as to cut off the territorial sea of another State from the High Seas or an exclusive economic zone.

thinking points

- *On what basis did the ICJ accept the delimitation of the Norwegian territorial sea using the baseline method instead of the customary low-water mark rule considering that the former is well known to customary international law?*

- *Summarize the criticisms of the ICJ's decision in* Anglo Norwegian Fisheries *by Waldock and Johnson. (You are advised to read the full articles to be able to grasp the arguments fully and to answer this question comfortably.)*

- *List the grounds put forward by Norway in justifying its derogation from the low-water mark rule.*

- *What is the status of the baseline method adopted by Norway in measuring its territorial sea under current international law?*

6.7.3 UNCLOS III and the continental shelf

Article 1(1) UNCLOS III defines 'the sea-bed and ocean floor and subsoil thereof, beyond the limits of national jurisdiction'. But as Edwin Egede notes, in 'The outer limit of the continental shelf: African States and the 1982 Law of the Sea Convention' (2004) 35 Ocean Dev & Int'l L 157, 157:

> Prior to the [1982 UNCLOS], the determination of the legal outer limit of the continental shelf depended on the rather vague exploitability provisions of the 1958 Geneva Convention on the Continental Shelf, adopted at a time when the possibility of deep seabed mining was very remote.

There was doubt that prior to the 1958 convention, State practice on the continental shelf constituted customary international law.

Joseph L. Kunz, 'Continental shelf and international law: confusion and abuse' (1956) 50 AJIL 828, 832, for example, wrote that:

> We may conclude: the doctrine of the continental shelf . . . is not yet a norm of general international law; but in view of the practice of a number of states, the lack of protests, and the general consent of writers . . . it can be considered as a new norm of general customary international law . . . there is a clear tendency towards the coming into existence of this new norm . . .

That every State is entitled to explore its continental shelf is not in question, but such exploration must be carried out in collaboration with a concerned coastal State—a fact to which the 1945 Truman Proclamation referred when it stated that the USA regards:

> the natural resources of the subsoil and seabed of the continental shelf beneath the High Seas but contiguous to the coasts of the US as appertaining to the US, subject to its jurisdiction and control.

But such declarations, as made by President Truman and many others, did not affect the right of a coastal State to explore its continental shelf, as has been recognized by the ICJ.

. . . .

● *Federal Republic of Germany v. Denmark, Federal Republic of Germany v. The Netherlands* (1969) ICJ REP 3 (The *North Sea Continental Shelf Cases*)

The Federal Republic of Germany (FRG), Denmark, and the Netherlands entered into a series of agreements regarding the delimitation of their continental shelves. Due to the inability of the parties to agree on how to delimit certain parts of the continental shelf adjoining them, they referred the dispute to the ICJ to decide, inter alia:

> what principles and rules of international law are applicable to the delimitation as between the Parties of the areas of the continental shelf in the North Sea which appertain to each of them beyond the partial boundary determined by . . . the Convention of 1 December 1964.

Rejecting the argument made by the FRG that it was entitled to 'a just and equitable share' of the contested undelineated shelf area, the Court said (at [19]) that:

> . . . the right of the coastal State in respect of the area of the continental shelf that constitutes a natural prolongation of its land territory into and under the sea exists *ipso facto* and *ab initio*, by virtue of its sovereignty over the land, and as an extension of it in an exercise of sovereign rights for the purpose of exploring the seabed and exploring its natural resources. In short, there is an inherent right. In order to exercise it, no special legal process has to be gone through, nor have any special legal acts to be performed. Its existence can be declared . . . but does not have to be constituted. Furthermore, the right does not depend on its being exercised . . . it is 'exclusive' in the sense that if the coastal State does not choose to explore or exploit the areas of shelf appertaining to it, that is its own affairs, but no one else may do so without its express consent.

It is important to note that the fact that a coastal State is entitled to explore its continental shelf does not necessarily mean that it is free to foray into the outer limit of its continental shelf. This is especially so because it is possible—and indeed has been found to be so in many cases, particularly in Latin America—that the seabed of a coastal State extends beyond its continental shelf. It must be recalled that the 1958 Continental Shelf Convention recognizes that the continental shelf lies beyond the territorial sea (Article 1) and that it extends well into the maximum reach of a coastal State's exploratory capabilities. The problem with this formulation is twofold: it clearly outpaced technological developments of the time by subjecting the legal regime of the continental shelf to instability, based on technological anticipation; and, with hindsight, the formulation contradicted the very idea espoused in the 1960s that designated the seabed as a 'common heritage of mankind'. This latter problem especially concerns States the continental shelves of which do not 'naturally' extend beyond their territorial sea. Such States nonetheless wanted to be able to explore their continental shelf. As such, they called for a measurement of the continental shelf to be made from baselines of the territorial waters regardless of the nature of their seabed.

As seen in its statement quoted earlier (at [19]) of its judgment in *North Sea Continental Shelf*), the ICJ attempted to resolve the divergence between the formulation of the continental shelf by the 1958 Continental Shelf Convention as an unlimited prolongation of the territorial sea and the idea that the seabed belongs to all, by construing the continental shelf as a 'natural prolongation' of the territorial sea. However, this does not help States the continental shelves of which do not form a natural extension of their territorial sea.

The challenges of UNCLOS III with the continental shelf regime were many. First, the USA, which had always supported a territorial sea of three nautical miles, wanted UNCLOS III to maintain that extent. However, if this would prove impossible because of agitation for a wider limit, then the USA was prepared to accept a maximum of twelve nautical miles, if coupled with a guaranteed freedom of transit through all maritime straits. Obviously, the wider the area of territorial State claimed by a State, the more the area it could claim as its continental shelf.

The US stance over the extension of the territorial sea beyond the three, or a maximum of twelve, nautical miles had to be reconciled with the desires of developing nations in Africa and Latin America in particular. These two regions wanted much wider EFZs and EEZs, thereby favouring a much wider continental shelf of up to 200 miles. Clearly, the wider and deeper the area of the sea and the seabed and subsoil for which States pushed, the greater their opportunity and the fewer areas of the high seas remained open to all. The view of the Latin American countries was summed up in opinion gathered in Peru, the then leading fishing nation in the world, by certain scholars.

Arthur D. Martinez, for example, in his article 'The Third United Nations Conference on the Law of the Sea: prospects, expectations and realities' (1975–76) 7 J Mar L & Com 253, 261–262, wrote that:

> The Peruvian message to the developing countries around the world, would seem to be as follows: Utilize the resources of the adjacent sea for purposes of nutrition and development. Peru has made considerable progress in this regard, and other coastal nations have the potential to do the same. In order to realize such progress or success, however, it will be necessary to extend your territorial waters jurisdiction beyond the customary 3 miles. Together we must insist that marine resources to a distance of at least 200 miles are *national* property, and denounce as outdated and unjust the customary notion that no one owns the resources of the sea beyond 3 miles; such a law benefits only those nations which have the technological capability, capital and distant water fleets to sail around the world in search of the best fishing zones. If these nations are allowed to exploit the fisheries close to our shores, they will in due time cause their depletion. It is time to take a firm stand against this indiscriminate and voracious activity.

African States also supported the 200-nautical-mile position, but objected to any extension beyond that, except where such extension would be coupled or traded off with a financial contribution by the State so extending to the International Seabed Authority (ISA) from mineral resources derived from areas beyond 200 miles (see UNCLOS III, Official Records, Vol. II, p. 161, at para. 17).

UNCLOS III endorsed the 200-mile limit and the position that an extension beyond 200 miles must be cushioned by financial payments made to the ISA.

Article 76 provides that:

> (1) The continental shelf of a coastal State comprises the sea-bed and subsoil of the submarine areas that extend beyond its territorial sea throughout the natural prolongation of its land territory to the outer edge of the continental margin, or to a distance of 200 nautical miles from the baselines from which the breadth of the territorial sea is measured where the outer edge of the continental margin does not extend up to that distance.
>
> ...
>
> (5) The fixed points comprising the line of the outer limits of the continental shelf of the sea-bed, drawn in accordance with paragraph 4(a)(i) and (ii), either shall not exceed 350 nautical miles...

Thus, as far as the measurement of the outer limit of the continental shelf is concerned—which, as discussed previously, had become a seriously thorny issue since 1958—UNCLOS III 'resolved' the issue by using a rather complex formula to strike a balance: rather than limiting the continental shelf to the extent of the 'natural prolongation' of a State's territorial sea, as espoused by the ICJ in *North Sea Continental Shelf*, Article 76 links that natural prolongation to the 'outer edge' of the 'continental margin' or, alternatively, to a distance of 200 miles from the baselines from which the territorial water of a State is measured. In this way, it matters less whether or not a State's continental shelf naturally extends beyond its territorial sea insofar as it extends to the outer edge of the continental margin.

Obviously, Article 76 entitles States to extend their continental shelf up to a maximum of 350 miles (150 miles more than the African States had favoured) or 100 miles from the point at which the depth of its water is 2,500 metres. However, the condition proposed by African States for such an extension was equally met by the convention.

Article 82(1) UNCLOS III states that:

> The coastal State shall make payments or contributions in kind in respect of the exploitation of the nonliving resources of the continental shelf beyond the 200 nautical miles from the baselines from which the breadth of the territorial sea is measured.

It must be noted that States must submit details of their continental shelves that extend beyond 200 miles to the Commission on the Limits of the Continental Shelf, established under Article 76(8) UNCLOS III. The Commission is tasked with the responsibility of making recommendations to States, which shall then use these recommendations to delimit their continental shelves definitely. Several States have already submitted details to the Commission, although not as many as might have been hoped. The recommendations of the Commission are not made public, making public scrutiny of its modus operandi virtually impossible.

thinking points

- *To what extent did the provisions of UNCLOS III strive to meet the concerns of various States concerning the continental shelf?*
- *How would you summarize the nature of contention between the USA and countries from Latin America and Africa over the measurement of the continental shelf?*
- *What condition(s) must be fulfilled before a State can extend its continental shelf beyond 200 nautical miles?*

6.7.4 Exclusive fishing zones and exclusive economic zones

Prior to the 1958 UNCLOS, several States had begun claiming an expansive area of water—much wider than the customarily recognized breadth of the territorial sea—as their EFZs. This practice was more rampant amongst Latin American countries which, by 1940, had become acutely concerned by the extensive whaling activities carried out in the waters in their region by several Western States. As a result, Latin American countries began to proclaim EFZs of up to 200 nautical miles.

The historical rationale for the claim of 200 nautical miles was neatly summed up by Ann L. Hollick in 'The origin of 200-mile offshore zones' (1977) 71 AJIL 494, 495, who explains that:

> On June 23, 1947, Chile became the first country to claim a 200-mile zone, when it proclaimed national sovereignty over the continental shelf off its coasts and islands and over the seas above the shelf to a distance of 200 miles. The considerations motivating Chile's claim were several. Chilean business interests were seeking such a measure to protect their new off-shore

operations. Chilean legal specialists, on behalf of these interests, thought that a 200-mile claim was consistent with the security zone adopted in the 1939 Declaration of Panama. And the distinction in the claim between the continental shelf and the superjacent waters was added to strengthen Chile's assertion that the claim followed the precedent set by the United States in the Truman Proclamations of September 28, 1945.

On 17 February 1956, the Inter-American Council of Jurists adopted Resolution XIII, popularly referred to as the Principles of Mexico on the Juridical Regime of the Sea as Applicable to the Expression of the Juridical Conscience of the Continent and as Applicable between the American States. Paragraph A of the Principles states that:

> The distance of three miles as the limit of the territorial waters is insufficient, and does not constitute a rule of general international law . . . Each State is competent to establish its territorial waters within reasonable limits, taking into account geographical, geological, and biological factors, as well as the economic needs of its population, and its security and defense.

Paragraph C provides that:

> Coastal States have, in addition, the right of exclusive exploitation of species closely related to the coast, the life of the country, or the needs of the coastal population.

(Both paragraphs are restated in Kunz, 1956, at 847, see section 6.7.3.)

In seeking EFZs, the Latin American countries were chiefly motivated by what they perceived as the ineffective international protection of whales. Many States then began to claim up to twelve nautical miles as their EFZs. Neither UNCLOS I nor II led to the establishment of such, although there was evidence that several States continued to claim the twelve-mile EFZ. There was initial resistance by other States but, by 1974, the ICJ itself had recognized the legality of the twelve-mile EFZ.

. . . .

● *United Kingdom v. Iceland (Merits)* [1974] ICJ REP 3 [The *Fisheries Jurisdiction Case*]

The Court said (at [53]) that:

> In recent years the question of extending the coastal State's fisheries jurisdiction has come to the forefront. The Court is aware that a number of States has asserted an extension of fishery limits. The Court is also aware of present endeavours, pursued under the auspices of the United Nations, to achieve a third Conference on the Law of the Sea the further codification and progressive development of this branch of the law, as it is of various proposals and preparatory documents produced in this framework, which must be regarded as manifestation of the views and opinions of individual States and as vehicles of their aspirations . . .

By the time of UNCLOS III, the claimed EFZ of twelve nautical miles had dovetailed into the wider assertion by Latin American States to exercise sovereign rights over all living and non-living things (hence, not only fish) over a single zone of 200 miles. This was then regarded as an EEZ.

Article 55 UNCLOS III provides that:

> The exclusive economic zone is an area beyond and adjacent to the territorial sea, subject to the specific legal regime established in this Part [Part V], under which the rights and jurisdiction of the coastal State and the rights and freedoms of other States are governed by the relevant provisions of this Convention.

Article 57 provides that:

> The exclusive economic zone shall not extend beyond 200 nautical miles from the baselines from which the breadth of the territorial sea is measured.

These provisions clearly codified customary law on the EEZ and have been so recognized by the ICJ in several cases.

● **Libyan Arab Jamahiriya v. Malta (Judgment)** (1985) ICJ REP 13 (The *Continental Shelf Case*)

Libya and Malta disagreed over the interpretation of Article 76 UNCLOS III concerning the 'distance principle'. Although both agreed that the provision related to the EEZ, while Malta argued that the rules of customary international law apply to EEZs (see [31]), Libya contested the point (at [32]).

On this point, the Court said (at [34]) that:

> It is in the Court's view incontestable that, apart from those provisions, the institution of the exclusive economic zone, with its rule on entitlement by reason of distance, is shown by the practice of States to have become part of customary international law.

● **Denmark v. Norway (Judgment)** (1993) ICJ REP 38 (*Maritime Delimitation in the Area between Greenland and Jan Mayen*)

Accepting the Norwegian claim to a 200-mile EFZ, the Court said (at [47]) that:

> Regarding the law applicable to the delimitation of the fishery zone, there appears to be no decision of an international tribunal that has been concerned only with a fishery zone . . . the question was raised during the hearings of the relationship of such zones to the concept of the exclusive economic zone . . . Whatever that relationship may be, the Court takes note that the Parties adopt in this respect the same position, in that they see no objections, for the settlement of the present dispute, to the boundary of the fishery zones being determined by the law governing the boundary of the exclusive economic zone, which is customary international law . . .

Although the Court was uncertain about the relationship between the EFZ and EEZ—except to affirm that the acceptance of the 200 nautical mile EEZ applies also to EFZs—it was categorical about the nature of the relationship between the EEZ and the continental shelf.

● **Libyan Arab Jamahiriya v. Malta (Judgment)** (1985) ICJ REP 13 (The *Continental Shelf Case*)

The Court said (at [33]) that:

> As the 1982 Convention demonstrates, the two institutions—continental shelf and exclusive economic zone—are linked together in modern law. Since the rights enjoyed by a State over its continental shelf would also be possessed by it over the sea-bed and subsoil of any exclusive economic zone which it might proclaim, one of the relevant circumstances to be taken into account for the delimitation of the continental shelf of a State is the legally permissible extent of the exclusive economic zone appertaining to that same State. This does not mean that the concept of the continental shelf had been absorbed by that of the exclusive economic zone; it does however signify

that greater importance must be attributed to elements, such as distance from coast, which are common to both concepts.

Also (at [34]) the Court further noted that:

> Although the institution of the continental shelf and the exclusive economic zone are different and distinct, the rights which the exclusive economic zone entails over the sea-bed of the zone are defined by reference to the regime laid down for the continental shelf. Although there can be a continental shelf where there is no exclusive economic zone, there cannot be an exclusive economic zone without a corresponding continental shelf.

KEY POINTS

- The exclusive economic zone (EEZ) developed from the exclusive fishing zone (EFZ) in order to mitigate the unsustainable manner in which whaling was being carried out by several States.

- The EEZ crystallized from the EFZ and was directly legislated upon by UNCLOS. However, UNCLOS III does not mention the EFZ.

- The EEZ is today a single zone of 200 miles, which includes the continental shelf, although the latter does not have to include an EEZ.

- The EEZ exists under customary international law.

6.7.5 The 'high seas' and their particular problems

The high seas are open to all States and are widely regarded as the common heritage of mankind. This means that no State can exercise jurisdiction over the high seas and any claim of sovereignty over the high seas is invalid (Article 89 UNCLOS III).

As noted by Joseph Kunz (1956, see section 6.7.3), at 828:

> The principle of the freedom of the High Seas is today a fully valid fundamental rule *jus cogentis*.
> The High Seas—*res omnium communis*, not *res nullius* —cannot in whole or in part be under the sovereignty of any state or group of states.

As we have observed earlier, the extension to the territorial sea and the establishment of the various exclusive resource zones by coastal States have a direct impact on the high seas: the wider a State's territorial sea and resource zones, the narrower the high seas.

Article 87(1) UNCLOS III lists the freedoms of the high seas as the freedoms of navigation, of overflight, to lay submarine cables and pipelines, to construct artificial islands and other installations permitted under international law, and of fishing. In general, the high seas are to be used only for peaceful purposes (Article 88), although what constitutes 'peaceful purposes' is not defined. However, during the 1982 conference (see Official Records, 67th Plenary Meeting, 1976, p. 56, para. 2), the representative of Ecuador expressed the view held by many developing countries that:

> the use of the ocean space for peaceful purposes, must mean complete demilitarization and the exclusion from it of all military activities.

This view is opposed to the one expressed by—and since the conference, the practice of—most Western nations. At the conference (Official Records, above, p. 62, para. 81), the USA stated that:

> The term 'peaceful purpose' did not, of course, preclude military activities generally. The United States had consistently held that the conduct of military activities for peaceful purposes was in full accord with the Charter of the United Nations and the principle of international law. Any specific limitation on military activities would require the negotiation of a detailed arms control agreement.

This position has been endorsed by a 2005 United Nations Secretary-General Report (UN Doc. A/40/535, 40 GAOR), at para. 178, which states that:

> Military activities which are consistent with the principles of international law embodied in the Charter of the United Nations, in particular, with Article 2, paragraph 4, and Article 51, are not prohibited by the Convention on the Law of the Sea ... [and that] in the exercise of the right of collective self-defense it is clear that parties to [collective] security arrangements may use force upon the High Seas, within the limits prescribed by international law, to protect their armed forces, public vessels or aircraft.

Similarly, the UK regards the testing of rockets and weapons as compatible with Article 88 (see (1978) 49 BYBIL 397).

6.7.6 Jurisdiction on the high seas

The fact that the high seas are open to all States poses two major problems: it raises concerns about the jurisdiction over ships duly registered in one State, but which commit crimes against ships of another State, or within another State's territorial waters; and it raises concerns over how to police the high seas against inimical activities by ocean thieves (pirates), drug traffickers, those engaged in slavery, those using the high seas to traffic weapons of mass destruction, and so on.

With regard to the status of ships travelling on the high seas, Article 94(1) UNCLOS III provides that:

> Every State shall effectively exercise its jurisdiction and control in administrative, technical and social matters over ships flying its flag.

The nationality of ships is governed by rigorous principles of international law, such as the existence of a 'genuine link' between the ship and the State in which it is registered. The reality, however, is that this provision is often difficult to enforce. The 'flag of convenience' syndrome—the practice whereby ships register under the laws of States of their choice, rather than those with which they are genuinely linked—makes the application of the international law criterion of 'genuine link' almost impossible to achieve. Ships flying 'flags of convenience' seldom, if ever, berth at the ports of their registered States, hence making it impossible for the latter to enforce its law against them for crimes committed on the high seas, where they desire to so prosecute (which is not always the case).

The fact that not many States are keen to enforce their jurisdiction against ships registered under their laws led to UNCLOS III providing for several exceptions to the rule that only the State of registration of a ship has jurisdiction over it. Thus there are instances in which international law permits other States and, in fact, international organizations to enforce international law on the high seas.

6.7.7 The high seas and international security

Article 110(1) UNCLOS III states that:

> 1. Except where acts of interference derive from powers conferred by treaty, a warship which encounters on the High Seas a foreign ship, other than a ship entitled to complete immunity in accordance with articles 95 and 96, is not justified in boarding it unless there is reasonable ground for suspecting that:
>   (a) ship is engaged in piracy;
>   (b) the ship is engaged in the slave trade;
>   (c) the ship is engaged in unauthorized broadcasting and the flag State of the warship has jurisdiction under article 109;
>   (d) ship is without nationality; or
>   (e) flying a foreign flag or refusing to show its flag, the ship is, in reality, of the same nationality as the warship.

Piracy is the oldest crime in international law, and is subject to universal jurisdiction, meaning that any State can prosecute those involved in acts of piracy regardless of the nationality of the criminals or where the crime is committed. Unfortunately, the definition of 'piracy' adopted in Article 101(a) UNCLOS III is rather limited, because it concerns only:

> any illegal acts of violence or detention, or any act of depredation, committed for private ends by the crew or the passengers of a private ship or a private aircraft.

Similarly, slavery, which is now commonly regarded as one of the most abhorrent international law crimes and is arguably *jus cogens*, is included in the crimes that attract the right to visit a foreign ship on the high seas. However, UNCLOS III does not empower the arrest of ships suspected of engaging in slavery; rather, the obligation imposed on States, by virtue of Article 99, is to:

> take effective measures to prevent and punish the transport of slaves in ships authorized to fly its flag and to prevent the unlawful use of its flag for that purpose. Any slave taking refuge on board any ship, whatever its flag, shall *ipso facto* be free.

This is, indeed, a puzzling provision. It would have been thought that, considering the explosion in human trafficking, especially of women and children, UNCLOS III would incorporate a more robust regime against slavery than at present. Clearly, insofar as a State, the ship of which is on the high seas at the same time as a slave-trafficking ship, is not itself involved in the activity and the other ship is not registered under its laws, then that State does not have any obligation under UNCLOS III to arrest, or even disturb, the passage of the other ship.

However, if a slave is lucky enough to escape from the slave-trading ship and seek refuge on the State's ship, that slave shall by that very act be free. In plain language, it can be argued that UNCLOS III recognizes, *but does not prohibit*, the slave trade.

Conclusion

The law and principles concerning territory in international law are both well established and dynamic. Territory is important to States and is by far the greatest area over which a State can confirm its sovereignty. The methods for acquiring territories have much altered, as indeed have the various perceptions of the basis for occupying territory in international law. Whether one refers to 'territory' in terms of land mass or the sea, the same principle of sovereignty applies to both, although the law of the sea attracts much more technical regulation than land, apparently for reasons of the nature of the subject matter. The ICJ, as well as arbitral tribunals, plays a considerable role in resolving disputes among States over territory—and, indeed, a great number of the disputes adjudicated by the Court or other tribunals arise as a result of one form of issue focusing on territory or another, since sovereignty, the greatest preserve of the State in international law, is usually tied to territory. But beyond this role, the Court also engages in law-making in its handling of territorial disputes between States. As we have seen, as a convention born of a conference, UNCLOS III attempts to regulate virtually all aspects of the international law of the sea, but unfortunately misses the opportunity to stamp its authority on such appalling crimes as slavery.

Questions

Self-test questions

1 What do you understand by the term 'territory' in international law?

2 What elements comprise a State's territory?

3 Explain the 'cannon rule'.

4 Define 'territorial water'.

5 What do you understand by the phrase 'intertemporal law'?

6 Explain 'acquisition by prescription'.

7 What are the 'continental shelf', an 'exclusive economic zone', and the 'high seas'?

8 What are the forms of acquisition of territory in international law?

Discussion questions

1 'A State that first physically occupies a territory retains sovereignty over it forever.' To what extent is this statement true of the acquisition of territory in international law?

2 '*Terra nullius* is no-man's-land. It is a wasteland that is not occupied by any human, or which is occupied by tribes of barbarians and savages, and, as such, it is open for occupation by the first civilized State to arrive on the scene.' Discuss.

3 'Judicial determination of what constitutes *effectivities* for the purpose of ascertaining the validity of territorial sovereignty is a precise and succinct exercise.' Discuss.

4 'The breadth of the territorial sea is the sole problem that undermined the work of the Territorial Waters Commission during the 1930 Conference on the Codification of International Law.' Discuss.

5 To what extent did UNCLOS I and II contribute to the development of the law of the sea?

6 What are the high and low points of UNCLOS III?

Assessment question

'The State that is the first to occupy a territory physically retains sovereignty and control over that territory at all times, regardless of what it does thereafter and of whether it takes any further measure in respect of the territory. Once a State has proclaimed its sovereignty over a territory, such sovereignty cannot be assailed by any other State under any circumstances.'

Critically analyse this statement, with reference to the acquisition of territory under international law.

Key cases

- *Indonesia v. Malaysia* (2002) ICJ Rep 625 (the *Pulau Ligitan and Pulau Sipadan Case*)
- *King, The v. Oldsworth* (1637)
- *Libyan Arab Jamahiriya v. Malta* (1985) ICJ Rep 13 (the *Continental Shelf Case*)
- *Mabo v. Queensland (No. 2)* [1992] HCA 23; (1992) 175 CLR 1 (*Mabo No. 2*)
- *Netherlands v. United States of America* (1928) 2 RIAA 829 (the *Island of Palmas Case*)
- *Norway v. Denmark* (1933) PCIJ Ser. A/B, No. 53 (the *Legal Status of Eastern Greenland Case*)
- *United Kingdom v. Iceland (Merits)* (1974) ICJ Rep 3 (the *Fisheries Jurisdiction Case*)
- *United Kingdom v. Norway* (1951) ICJ Rep 116 (the *Anglo Norwegian Fisheries Case*)
- *Western Sahara Advisory Opinion* (1975) ICJ Rep 12

# Further reading

Caminos, H. and Molito, M. R., 'Progressive development of international law and the package deal' (1985) 79 AJIL 871

Johnson, D. H. N., 'The *Anglo-Norwegian Fisheries Case*' (1952) 11 ICLQ 145

Martinez, A. D., 'The Third United Nations Conference on the Law of the Sea: prospects, expectations and realities' (1975–76) 7 J Mar L & Com 253

Waldock, C. H. M., 'The *Anglo-Norwegian Fisheries Case*' (1951) 28 BYBIL 114

Jurisdiction

Learning objectives

This chapter will help you to:

- understand the various meanings of 'jurisdiction';
- appreciate the various ways in which States exercise their jurisdiction and the implications of these for other States;
- recognize the various issues concerning the exercise of jurisdiction by States in international law;
- understand the limits on States' jurisdiction in international law; and
- deal with emerging and contemporary issues in jurisdiction.

Introduction

Jurisdiction is the foundation of the internal order of every State. It is the assertion of a State's sovereignty over the making of law, the enforcement of law, and the adjudication of legal issues within, and sometimes outside, its territory. Since international legal order involves the operation of the internal orders of all States, jurisdiction plays the most fundamental role in shaping both orders.

As a term of art, 'jurisdiction' is capable of several meanings. The term may be used in a general sense to denote the 'scope', or 'reach', of a thing or an activity; it may also be used in a technical sense to imply the competence of a court or tribunal to try a case or deal with a dispute, criminal or civil, before it. This chapter does not deal with the technical use of jurisdiction (which is dealt with in Chapter 16 concerning international criminal law); rather, this chapter is mainly concerned with jurisdiction in the general sense. It discusses the bases upon which a State exercises its jurisdiction either to legislate or to prescribe laws for all entities, human or otherwise, present on its territory, or to enforce its own laws in relation to foreigners within and outside its territory.

7.1 The meaning and nature of jurisdiction

When non-lawyers use 'jurisdiction' in a sentence such as 'the drug money has been taken out of the French jurisdiction by the cartel', jurisdiction is understood by the speakers simply to mean 'the money has been taken out of France'. The lay speaker or listener does not fully comprehend what the court, the police, and the French Parliament have to do with the given situation. Jurisdiction, in this sense, means nothing more than national space. But if a lawyer addresses the same sentence to another lawyer, a plethora of possible interpretations opens up. The statement could mean 'the money has been taken out of France, so that its parliament cannot legislate on it', or '. . . so that the French police cannot retrieve it', or '. . . so that French courts will be unable to adjudicate cases arising from it'. In this sense, jurisdiction goes well beyond a mere consideration of geographical space. However, the lawyer's mind does not stop there: it ponders whether France can legislate on the money taken outside its jurisdiction; it considers whether the French police can chase the money *outside* France and retrieve it *extraterritorially*. The lawyer's mind wonders how French courts might be able to try the cartel *in absentia* if there is no treaty of extradition between France and the State to which the cartel has fled. Used in this scenario, jurisdiction involves so many issues giving rise to several considerations and options.

. . . .

● *Lipohar v. The Queen* [1999] 200 CLR 485

Judges Gaudron, Gummow, and Hayne stated (at [78]) that:

> The term 'jurisdiction' here, as elsewhere, gives rise to difficulty. It is a generic term . . . It is used in a variety of senses, some relating to geography, some to persons and procedures, others to constitutional and judicial structures and powers.

See also *Baxter v. Commissioners of Taxation (NSW)* (1907) 4 CLR 1087, 1142, in which Isaacs J stated that jurisdiction can be used in a variety of senses.

Every State exercises three types of jurisdiction:

- a State may make laws covering everyone and everything within its territory (prescriptive or legislative jurisdiction);
- it may try anyone within its territory (adjudicatory jurisdiction); and
- it may enforce its laws against anyone that contravenes them, through acts such as seizure (enforcement jurisdiction).

But a State's ability to exercise any of these jurisdictions depends on factors such as the nature of the action involved (criminal or civil), and the person or object against whom or which the State proceeds (whether these are nationals, human or companies, or foreigners, present within or outside its territory).

Often the exercise of jurisdiction by States may run into conflict with the right of other States to exercise jurisdiction on the same issue. When such a problem arises, jurisdictional conflicts between States are resolved through the application of international law rules, which are either codified by treaties or generally accepted by States as customary international law rules.

There are five principles governing the exercise of jurisdiction by States—namely, the nationality, territoriality, universality, passive personality, and protective principles. These principles (or 'bases', as they are sometimes called) vary considerably in terms of the importance accorded them by States, but the territoriality principle is by far the most established (and applied) jurisdictional basis in international law. Nevertheless, this principle often clashes with other jurisdictional principles. Thus in the 1988 *Lockerbie* incident, in which an American airliner was bombed by two Libyan nationals over Lockerbie in Scotland, France claimed jurisdiction on the basis that most of the victims of the bombing were its nationals (nationality of victims), a jurisdictional claim that was also open to the USA, being the national State of the airline involved. Libya, the national State of the alleged perpetrators, was also entitled to a jurisdictional claim on this front.

As will be seen in this chapter, modern developments in State relations have necessitated a re-evaluation of how we treat these principles in international law. This is true of the territorial principle and also the enforcement jurisdiction of a State. For example, regarding the latter, international law strongly supports the principle that a State may not forcibly seize its nationals or foreign nationals wanted in connection with a crime from the territory of another State without the latter's consent or acquiescence. However, recent developments in international criminal law have posed serious challenges to this principle, so that while it may yet be irresponsible or premature to advocate total rejection of that rule, it is certainly reasonable to question its absolute application in the modern-day context.

It must be noted that the jurisdictional principles and their various dimensions considered in this chapter relate solely to criminal, not civil, jurisdiction of States. International law does not limit States' jurisdiction in civil law matters, and there is nothing stopping a State from extending its law in civil matters to another State through conflict-of-law rules (private international law). This is so because, unlike criminal law, civil law is usually tied to the rights of the parties that arise from personal claims not tied to the public sphere.

KEY POINTS

- 'Jurisdiction' can be used in a general or technical sense.

- There are three types of jurisdiction that a State can exercise: prescriptive; adjudicatory; and enforcement.

- Jurisdiction refers to the right of a State to make, apply, and enforce its laws to a particular situation.

- The five recognized bases for the exercise of criminal jurisdiction by States can be classified under the territoriality principle, the nationality principle, the protective principle, the universality principle, and the passive personality principle.

- The strongest and most recognized principle for the exercise of criminal jurisdiction by States is the territoriality principle.

Let us now examine the various jurisdictional principles of international law, and, in particular, consider modern developments that have affected the fundamental premises of these principles and their application.

7.2 The territoriality principle

The territorial principle entitles a State to exercise jurisdiction over everything and everyone found on its territory, except those that are excluded under treaties or customary international law, such as diplomatic embassies or high commissions of foreign States. For example, Article 22 of the 1961 Vienna Convention on Diplomatic Relations makes such missions inviolable and provides that authorities of their host States may not enter them without the consent of the head of the mission. Thus, while the Indian High Commission in London is not an Indian sovereign territory as such, it enjoys a special status vis-à-vis the right of the UK authorities. Without the consent of the Indian High Commissioner, the UK cannot exercise its jurisdiction on the premises, such as to serve court notices, or to search for or arrest an offender present within the embassy. (See Chapter 8 on immunity.)

Aside from making law covering people and things on its territory, a State may also enforce its laws, as well as prosecute matters arising from breaches of such laws, against any individuals, whether its nationals or foreigners, or any entities such as companies present on its territory. The right of a State to exercise territorial jurisdiction is essential, and it is considered that such right is absolute and unassailable. In fact, it would be right to assert that the territoriality principle is the most visible way through which a State demonstrates its sovereignty.

. . . .

● *Compania Naviera Vascongado v. Steamship Cristina* [1938] AC 485

A ship, *Cristina*, belonging to the appellant Spanish company, set sail from Spain and docked at the port of Cardiff in the UK. While at sea, but before arriving at Cardiff, the Spanish government requested that it be arrested upon arrival at Cardiff by the British authorities. In an action by the appellants for release of the ship, the Spanish government objected, claiming that the action amounted to trying a sovereign State.

It was held that a foreign sovereign State could not be subject to trial, directly or indirectly, without its consent. Hence, the claim brought by the appellants was set aside.

Clearly, the British court in this case had treated the ship as a territory of Spain. The territory of a State comprises not only its physical land mass, its seas, or its airspace, but also moving objects such as ships belonging to or registered in the State, although the latter is subject to different regulation under the law of the sea (see Chapter 6).

7.2.1 The test of territorial jurisdiction

It is not always exact for a State to determine when it possesses an exclusive territorial jurisdiction. Much depends on the circumstances of a crime committed on its territory.

Where a crime commences and ends on the territory of a particular State, there is no problem with that State claiming jurisdiction.

example

If a rebel group within Rutamu plans to hit the Rutamuan government, and bombs several government buildings and private houses of certain government officials in Rutamu, Rutamu's territorial jurisdiction in these circumstances is absolute and unquestionable.

However, suppose that the rebel group planned the crime in Rutamu but, other than bombing Rutamuan government buildings, it also bombed targets in Candoma, a neighbouring State that has sympathy for the Rutamuan government. Clearly, in this case, the crime took place on the territory of *two* States.

The occurrence of the above kind of scenario is becoming more frequent, especially with regard to transborder crimes such as terrorism and financial crimes.

example

The Lockerbie incident, mentioned earlier, concerned the bombing of a Pan American commercial plane over Lockerbie, in Scotland, in 1988. It was believed that the bombs that exploded in the airliner were loaded in Malta (meaning that part of the crime was committed there), although the explosion itself took place in the airspace of Scotland.

In this scenario, it is clear that the crime was committed on the territory of more than one State, albeit partly in each. In this example, as with the previous example, the crucial question is: which States, as between Rutamu and Candoma, on the one hand, and Malta and Scotland, on the other, have territorial jurisdiction?

States, through their practice, have developed certain formulae for resolving such jurisdictional contests. In addition, academic writers have also put forward several theories aiming to help States to determine when they may be able to exercise territorial jurisdiction in a situation that could result in conflict between States.

Broadly speaking, there are the 'objective' and 'subjective' tests of territoriality. Early attempts to resolve jurisdictional conflicts as between two States claiming that the same crime occurred on their territories, as seen in the previous examples, failed to produce a clear and logical solution. While some writers preferred to confer jurisdiction in such instances on States within the territory of which the crime was initiated, others preferred the State in which the crime was completed. However, the unsatisfactory nature of this solution, mainly because of its illogicality, was noted by Michael Akehurst in his seminal article on jurisdiction 'Jurisdiction in international law' (1972–73) 46 BYBIL 145, 152, thus:

> But the arguments were so evenly matched that it was eventually realized that there was no logical reason for preferring the claims of one State over the claim of the other; and the only alternative to granting jurisdiction to neither State (which would have led to intolerable results) was to grant jurisdiction to both States... Logically a State should be able to claim jurisdiction only if the offence has been committed, in part or in whole, in its territory; it must prove that a constituent element of the offence occurred in its territory. This is the formulation adopted in the *Lotus* case, by the Harvard Research Draft Convention on Jurisdiction with respect to Crime, by Article 18 of the American Law Institute's *Restatement of Foreign Relations Law*, by the criminal codes of many countries and by many judicial decisions in common law countries and elsewhere.

From this statement, it is clear that the issue for determination is as between the objective and subjective tests of jurisdiction. We consider these theories in turn.

The objective test

Under the objective test, a State is able to exercise jurisdiction if an offence is completed on its territory, regardless of where the offence is initiated. It is generally considered that the *SS Lotus Case* is the judicial authority for this test.

....

● *France v. Turkey* (1927) PCIJ Ser. A, No. 10 (The *SS Lotus Case*)

See the facts in Chapter 2.

In that case, the Permanent Court of International Justice (PCIJ) stated (at 23) that:

> offences, the authors of which at the moment of commission are in the territory of another State, are nevertheless to be regarded as having been committed in the national territory, if one of the constituent elements of the offence, and more especially its effects, have taken place there.

In 'Venue and the ambit of criminal law' (1965) 81 LQR 518, Glanville Williams described the objective test as the 'terminatory theory' of jurisdiction, in contrast to the 'initiatory theory' (the subjective test). Accordingly, he said, at 518, that:

> The argument in favour of the terminatory theory of jurisdiction is that the State where the last element of the crime occurs is presumably the sufferer from it, and therefore has the greatest interest in prosecuting it.

The objective test, or terminatory theory, has a long history under English law, as seen in the following cases.

....

● *R v. Ellis* (1899) 1 QB 1

The defendant, who carried on business in the county of Durham, obtained goods on credit in that county from a traveller by means of false representations made by the defendant in Glasgow, in which place they carried on business.

It was held by Hawkins, Wills, and Bruce JJ (at 230) that:

> the offence was properly triable in the county of Durham on the ground that the offence consisted in obtaining the goods, and not in making the false pretences whereby they might be obtained, and that therefore an English Court has jurisdiction to try a charge of obtaining goods by false pretences where the goods have been obtained within the jurisdiction of the Court dealing with the charge, although the false representations may have been made beyond the jurisdiction of the English Courts.

See also *R v. Harden* [1963] 1 QB 8, which was decided to similar effect.

As seen from these cases, the rationale for the objective test is that the crime is completed in the State asserting jurisdiction. However, while it may be unproblematic in some cases to determine precisely where a crime is completed, precise determination is not always possible.

. . . .

● *R v. Blythe* (1895) 1 CCC 263, BC SC

The defendant, who was in Canada, wrote a letter to a girl under the age of 16, who was in the USA, persuading her to leave her father and come to him in Canada. The girl accepted. The man was tried in Canada.

It was held that:

> the defendant could not be tried in Canada of taking an underage girl because the offence was wholly committed out of the jurisdiction when the girl left her father's household in consequence of the persuasion.

As far as the court was concerned in this case, the crime was committed in the USA when the girl left her father to come to Canada. This seems sensible in that, although the letter was written in Canada, the crime was completed only when the girl, then in the USA, accepted to leave. One could have argued that the crime was indeed completed once the letter was posted in Canada.

The cases of *Ellis* and *Harden* (discussed previously) were decided on the basis of where the letter was written. But whereas those decisions seem sensible within the rules concerning commercial engagements, the same would have been difficult in the context of the facts of *Blythe*. It would have been extremely illogical to argue that the crime was committed when the invitation letter was dropped in the post.

The subjective test

A State can exercise territorial jurisdiction over a crime that commences on its territory, regardless of whether the crime is actually completed on its territory or elsewhere. What is important under this test is that the crime is *initiated* on the territory of the State claiming jurisdiction—that is, that the commission of the crime began there. In the Lockerbie incident mentioned earlier, an application of the subjective test would entitle Malta (upon proof that the bombs were loaded into the plane in that country) to exercise territorial jurisdiction; it would be irrelevant that the explosion did not occur there.

The rationale for this exercise of subjective territorial jurisdiction rests mainly on the fact that one constituent element of the crime itself took place there.

> **example**
>
> A Maltese law forbids the loading of dangerous items onto an aircraft for whatever reason, especially for the purpose of causing harm either to the aircraft, its passengers, or both. Most national laws and international instruments concerning aviation prohibit practices such as loading dangerous items on an aircraft. There are several international legislative instruments focusing on causing acts of terrorism against an aircraft. Thus loading bombs in Malta will be deemed to be a constituent element of the crime itself.

The subjective test of territoriality is important, particularly in respect of transnational or trans-border crimes such as money laundering and terrorism.

. . . .

● *R v. Treacy* [1971] AC 537

The appellant, while on the Isle of Wight, posted a letter written by him and addressed to a Mrs X in West Germany, demanding money with menaces. The letter was received by Mrs X in West Germany and the appellant was charged with blackmail, contrary to section 21 of the Theft Act 1968.

It was held by the House of Lords (at 558) that:

> the offence of blackmail had been committed by the appellant in that he had made a demand when he had written and posted the letter to Mrs. X.

In this case, the Law Lords had established English jurisdiction on the basis of the place where the crime was initiated.

A strict application of the subjective test can be illogical and counterproductive.

. . . .

● *Director of Public Prosecutions v. Doot* [1973] AC 807

The respondents, US citizens, had, by an agreement made abroad, imported cannabis resin into England, with the object of re-exporting it from there to the USA. No part of the agreement was made in England. At their trial, the appellants had claimed that the English courts had no jurisdiction given that the crime was completed when the agreement was reached abroad. The trial court rejected this claim and convicted them.

The Appeal Court, however, quashed the conviction, holding that the English courts had no jurisdiction to try the offence charged, since the essence of the offence was the agreement between the respondents to do the unlawful act, the offence was complete when the agreement had been made, and the agreement had been made abroad. The Crown appealed to the House of Lords.

It was held that the conviction was correct and the appeal was allowed. The House of Lords ruled (at 827) that:

> . . . agreement made outside the jurisdiction of the English courts to commit an unlawful act within the jurisdiction was a conspiracy which would be tried in England if the agreement was subsequently performed, *wholly* or *in part*, in England. Although the crime of conspiracy was complete once the agreement had been made, nevertheless, the conspiratorial agreement remained in being until terminated by completion of its performance or by abandonment; accordingly where acts were committed in England in performance of the agreement that would suffice to show the existence of a conspiracy within the jurisdiction triable by the English courts. It followed that the crime of conspiracy had been committed by respondents in England.

It is clear that the Court of Appeal, in quashing the conviction, had endorsed the subjective test—that is, a basis on where the crime was initiated—whereas the House of Lords had seemingly applied the objective test—that is, a basis on the place where the crime was completed. Clearly, an application of the subjective test in the circumstances of this case would have produced an absurd result—that it did not matter that the conspiracy to commit a crime continued in England, from where the criminals intended to export the contraband to the USA. It would have sufficed, using the subjective test, that the original agreement was not made in the UK. However, one must recognize the peculiarity of this case, which is that although the agreement to commit the crime was originally entered into abroad and the items imported into the UK, the conspiracy still continued since the items were to be shipped to the USA as a continuation of the crime.

The practical utility of the subjective theory, as a tool for avoiding the uncertainties that often surround the objective theory, has been recognized for nearly 150 years.

thinking points

- *Explain the difference between the 'objective' and the 'subjective' tests of jurisdiction.*
- *Which of the tests of territorial jurisdiction is more suitable for transborder crimes and why?*
- *Distinguish* Ellis *and* Harden *from* Blythe. *Which one do you think is a better decision and why?*

7.3 The 'effect' doctrine

Objective territorial jurisdiction has often been stretched to include not only where the crime is completed, but where its *effect* is actually felt. The main difference between objective territoriality and the effect doctrine is as follows. In objective territoriality, a State in which a crime is completed asserts jurisdiction on the basis that one of the 'constituent elements' of the crime—commission—took place on its territory. Under the 'effect doctrine', none of the 'constituent elements' of the crime took place in the territory of the State that is asserting jurisdiction; rather, it is only the effect of a crime, which is planned and executed elsewhere, that is felt on its territory. Let us illustrate the distinction.

example

A and B, both nationals of Candoma, plan in Candoma to rob a bank in Rutamu. Later, they travel to Rutamu, where they commit the crime. Rutamu can claim jurisdiction on the basis of the objective test, since the crime was actually *committed* on its territory.

Now suppose that when A and B plan in Candoma to rob a bank, they decide to rob a bank in Candoma. All of the shareholders of the bank live in Rutamu and, as a result of the robbery, many of them become insolvent. The question is: does Rutamu have jurisdiction?

If we apply objective personality to this question, Rutamu would have no jurisdiction, because neither the planning of the crime nor the actual commission of the crime took place on its territory. However, Rutamu will be able to assert jurisdiction only because the *effect* of the crime that was committed in Candoma was felt on its territory. This is the essence of the 'effect doctrine'.

'Effect doctrine' jurisdiction is possible only because there is no requirement that a constituent element of a crime occurs on the territory of the State asserting that jurisdiction. In fact, it is because of the absence of such an element that recourse is had to the 'effect doctrine'. If either the planning of the crime or its actual commission takes place on the territory of a State, then it will assert the objective or subjective territorial principle.

The effect doctrine was developed by the USA through the adoption in 1890 of the Sherman Antitrust Act. The Act was intended to prevent business cartels outside the USA from collusions and monopoly, which may harm the US market. Thus antitrust law in the USA is what is known in Europe as 'competition law'.

Section 402 of the Restatement of the Law (Third), Foreign Relations Law of the United States states that:

> a state has jurisdiction to prescribe law with respect to . . . (c) conduct outside its territory that has or is intended to have substantial effect within its territory.

Since the Sherman Antitrust Act, US courts have asserted jurisdiction over crimes planned and committed elsewhere, but which produce effects on US territory.

. . . .

● *Hartford Fire Insurance Co. v. California* 509 US 764 (1993)

Several British insurance companies colluded to pressurize US insurers into abandoning certain insurance policies, which were beneficial to customers but financially detrimental to the undertakers. The appellants argued that the USA had no jurisdiction on many grounds, including that some US laws explicitly excluded them from being sued. The trial court accepted this argument, but the Court of Appeals rejected it.

In an appeal to the Supreme Court, it was held that the Sherman Antitrust Act applied. In his opinion, Justice Souter stated (at 796) that:

> it is well established by now that the Sherman Act applies to foreign conduct that was meant to produce and did in fact produce some substantial effect in the United States.

It should also be pointed out that even if the offending act is lawful where it is committed, this does not prevent the application of the effect doctrine. Hence, in the *Hartford Insurance* case, the US Supreme Court rejected the plea of the appellants that the reinsurers' conduct was lawful in the UK.

According to the US Restatement (Third), Foreign Relations Law, §415(j):

> The fact that conduct is lawful in the state in which it took place will not, of itself, bar application of the United States antitrust laws, even where the foreign state has a strong policy to permit or encourage such conduct.

However, the assertion of jurisdiction by the USA on the basis of the effect doctrine did not meet with instant, unanimous approval by all States. In fact, certain European States, as well as the European Court of Justice (ECJ), have remained more sceptical than welcoming of the assertion of jurisdiction by the USA over offences that are neither planned nor executed on its territory. In most cases that have come before the courts of these States and the ECJ, the objective territorial principle has been applied where, arguably, the effect doctrine seems more reasonable.

● **A. Ahlström Osakeyhtiö and others v. Commission of the European Communities,** Joined cases C-89/85, C-104/85, C-114/85, C-116/85, C-117/85 and C-125/85 to C-129/85, [1993] ECR I-1307, European Court of Justice (The *European Wood Pulp Case*)

A cartel of manufacturers located outside the European market colluded on price-fixing for customers in the (then) European Community. At their trial, they challenged the jurisdiction of the ECJ, arguing that the alleged crime had taken place outside the Community.

The Court studiously avoided discussing the effect of this offence on the basis of jurisdiction. Instead, the Court held that since the offence was 'implemented' in Europe, it actually *occurred* in the European market. See also Stephen Weatherill and Paul Beaumont, *EU Law* (London: Penguin, 1999), p. 812.

Thus, as observed by Dieter Lange and John Byron Sandage, 'The *Wood Pulp Decision* and its implications for the scope of EC competition law' (1989) 26 CML Rev 157, the Court used a 'fiction that there was some quasi-territorial basis for jurisdiction'. Clearly, in this case, the ECJ had preferred using the objective territoriality principle in a rather strained way to adopting the more appropriate effect doctrine.

Also, in cases concerning the Internet, the courts have generally tended to apply the objective personality principle rather than the effect doctrine.

● **LICRA v. Yahoo!** ORDONNANCE DE RÉFÉRÉ, RENDERED 22 MAY 2000, TRIBUNAL DE GRANDE INSTANCE DE PARIS, NO. RG: 00/05308, 00/05309 (The *Yahoo! Auctions Case*); SEE ALSO (2001) 1(3) EBLR 11

Two French anti-Semitism organizations, Ligue contre le Racisme et l'Antisémitisme (LICRA) and Union des Étudiants juifs de France (UEJF), brought an action against Yahoo! US, Yahoo! France, and a French firm. The substance of their case was that Yahoo! allowed the auction of Nazi memorabilia on its website, which was accessible to French citizens. It was not in dispute that the organization was based in the USA, that the website was homed there, and that none of the acts had been committed in France. The only link to France was that the website was accessible to people in France. Under Article R645-1 of the French Code Penal (Penal Code), the wearing or public exhibition of Nazi-related items is a crime.

The Tribunal de Grande Instance (the Superior Court) in Paris held that it had jurisdiction. According to the Court:

> By permitting [anti-Semitic] objects to be viewed in France and allowing surfers located in France to participate in such a display of items for sale, the Company Yahoo! Inc. is therefore committing a wrong in the territory of France, a wrong whose unintentional character is averred but which has *caused damage* to be suffered by LICRA and UEJF, both of whom are dedicated to combating all forms of promotion of Nazism in France. [Emphasis added]

A similar decision was held by the German Landsgericht (LG) in *Tolben* (LG Mannheim, 10 November 1999, 5 KLs 503 Js 9551/99), in which certain online writing of an Australian on the subject of Auschwitz was alleged to have caused offence in Germany.

Although the courts did not expressly state that they applied the objective principle in these cases, this could be inferred from several of their statements. For example, the court in *Tolben* said that the result of the publication produced a result that 'is an element' of the alleged offence.

Thus, in a nutshell, effective doctrine applies where:

(a) offences are planned and committed in one State, but the 'effect' is felt in another State;

(b) none of the constituent elements of the crime, whether the planning or the commission, takes place on the territory of the State asserting the 'effect doctrine' jurisdiction; and

(c) it is irrelevant that the offending conduct is lawful in the State in which it is executed.

See further:

• *Rio Tinto Zinc Corp. v. Westinghouse Electric Corp.* [1978] 1 All ER 434, HL;

• *Grecor Ltd v. Commission of the European Communities* Case T-102/96 [1999] ECR II-0753, [89]–[92];

• *Dow Jones & Co. Inc. v. Gutnick* [2002] HCA 56; and

• *Graduate Management Admission Council v. Raju* 241 F Supp 2d 589 (ED Va, 2003), in which the sale by someone in India of dubious post-graduate record examinations (GREs) to US customers on the Internet was regarded as falling under US antitrust law.

As a way of preventing that 'slippery slope' into which the use of the effect doctrine can fall, towards which *Raju* seems to point, Akehurst (1972–73, see section 7.2.1) suggested confining the effect doctrine only to countries in which the primary effect of a crime is felt. It should be pointed out that §402 of the US Restatement (Third), Foreign Relations Law (see earlier in this section) affords jurisdiction only to States that feel the substantial effect on their territory.

thinking points

• *Distinguish the 'effect doctrine' from the objective territoriality principle.*

• *Summarize the main element of the 'effect doctrine' and how this doctrine differs from the two other tests of territorial jurisdiction.*

• *How would you describe the attitude of the ECJ and some European courts to the effect doctrine?*

7.4 The nationality principle

A State may exercise jurisdiction not only on its nationals within its territory, but also on its nationals who are abroad. The nationality principle is perhaps the least controversial basis of jurisdiction.

Under this principle, a State may extend its jurisdiction over its nationals beyond its territory. Nationality principle will generally be applied where, for example, the State of abode of a criminal refuses to prosecute a crime committed by that person, either because the offence committed is not a crime under its own law or simply for lack of interest in that matter. Sometimes, the national State requires that the conduct in question is also a crime in the place where it is committed (the *lex loci*), while other States simply restrict prosecution on the basis of nationality to the most severe crimes in respect of which foreign States may require them to prosecute their nationals. However, this is not a requirement of international law (Akehurst, 1972–73, at 156, see section 7.2.1).

In most countries, a person can become a national either because he or she is born in that country (*jus soli*), or because his or her parents were born in that country (*jus sanguinis*). But a person may also acquire nationality through naturalization, such as if he or she has fulfilled nationality requirements of the concerned State. Sometimes, the renunciation of one's nationality is a condition for obtaining another State's nationality, although it is possible for one to hold dual nationality, where this is permitted by both States. But dual nationality often comes with a caution: a dual national of the UK and another country is not protected by British law against that other State. This caution is often written into the national passport for the general awareness of all concerned.

Dual nationality must also be distinguished from cases that, although they confer certain benefits on foreign nationals, do not amount to dual nationality. For example, in 2006 India launched a programme called 'Overseas Citizens of India' (OCI). While those who carry the OCI cards are conferred with Indian visas on a somewhat permanent basis, they are not Indian nationals and, as such, cannot enjoy the benefits that accrue to Indian nationals, nor can they be subject to the national jurisdiction of India under the nationality principle. As a matter of legal certainty, India does not permit dual nationality.

The legal requirements for becoming a national of a State are usually laid down by the domestic law of that State. International law generally stays out of this. However, the validity of the nationality of a person can be contested in international law, in matters of diplomatic protection of that person by the State the nationality of which he or she claims. This was laid down in *Nottebohm*.

● *Liechtenstein v. Guatemala (Second Phase) (Judgment)* (1955) ICJ Rep 4 (The *Nottebohm Case*)

See the facts in Chapter 9.

In this case, the principle was laid down (at 20–23) that:

> Nationality is within the domestic jurisdiction of the State, which entitles, by its own legislation, the rules relating to the acquisition of its nationality ... But on the other hand, a State cannot claim that the rules it has laid down are entitled to recognition by another State unless it has acted in conformity with the general aim of making the nationality granted accord with an effective link between the State and the individual.

A particular use of the nationality principle is to prevent a situation in which a national of one State seeks to circumvent that State's laws forbidding certain acts by going to commit such acts in countries in which the acts are not illegal. The 'doctrine of evasion' is variously known as in France as *fraude à la loi*, in Spain as *fraude de ley*, in Italy as *violazione di norme di legge*, and in Germany as *Rechtswidrige Umgehung eines Gesetzes*. Under the doctrine, a national of one State cannot avoid the laws of that State that forbid members of the same family from marrying by simply travelling to another country that does not prohibit such practices.

● *Princess Bauffremont Affair* CIV 18 March 1878, S.78.1.193, French Cour de Cassation

This case, decided by the French Cour de Cassation, highlights this doctrine.

A French princess sought to circumvent a French law concerning divorce by obtaining German citizenship. Although she was able to divorce as a German citizen in Germany, the divorce was not recognized in France and was a nullity under French law.

The nationality principle has been found to be particularly useful in child trafficking cases. Instances abound, for example, of tourists abusing and sexually exploiting children in developing countries in which most of these crimes are either not criminalized, or in which the possibility of prosecution is generally lax. In the End Child Prostitution, Child Pornography, Child Sex Tourism and Trafficking in Children for Sexual Purposes (EC-PAT) European Enforcement Group study entitled *Extraterritorial Jurisdiction as a Tool to Combat Sexual Exploitation of Children* (Amsterdam: European Commission, 1999), it was found that the nationality principle was a very effective tool for prosecuting culprits in their home countries.

Recent developments in international criminal law have had some effect on the nationality principle. The use of the principle in respect of serious crimes has been increased by the appearance of the *aut dedere aut judicare* principle in several multilateral treaties. This principle obligates parties to such treaties to prosecute offenders present within their territories, or to extradite them for prosecution. Furthermore, the unwillingness or inability of a State to prosecute its nationals only now serves to empower the International Criminal Court (ICC) Prosecutor to prosecute them himself, pursuant to the complementarity principle under Article 19 of the Statute of the International Criminal Court (the ICC Statute). Also, the fact that the UN Security Council can, under Article 13 of the ICC Statute, refer any criminal to the ICC, regardless of whether such a person is from a State party to the Statute or not, has evidently bolstered States' determination to ensure that they prosecute crimes committed by their nationals either at home or abroad (see Chapter 16).

KEY POINTS

- States are only responsible for setting the criteria for determining the nationality of their citizens.

- International law may contest the validity of nationality conferred by a State in a case involving the diplomatic protection of people.

7.5 The protective principle

Often, acts done by foreigners abroad may harm or threaten the vital interests of other States. Such acts usually include espionage activities against a country or broadcasting dangerous propaganda against a country. Sometime around the nineteenth century, States began to assert 'protective' jurisdiction over acts by their own and foreign nationals, committed abroad, which threaten or harm them. After the initial resistance by States to this jurisdictional basis, the protective principle became more popular from the 1960s, when a plethora of cases based on this principle surged in the USA.

According to §33 of the US Restatement (Second), Foreign Relations Law of 1965, the protective principle gives a country the:

> jurisdiction to prescribe a rule of law attaching legal consequences to conduct outside its territory that threatens its security as a state or the operation of its governmental functions, provided the conduct is generally recognized as a crime under the law of states that have reasonably developed legal systems.

It must be noted that this principle is different from the 'effect doctrine' discussed earlier in that there is no requirement that the effect of the offence be felt on the territory of the State asserting jurisdiction. What is required is that the *interest* of that State, its security or functioning, wherever these may be located, are *threatened* by the crime.

Articles 7 and 8 of the 1935 Harvard Research Draft Convention on Jurisdiction with respect to Crime (1935 Supp) 29 AJIL 435, 543, lists crimes against 'the security, territorial integrity or political independence' of a State and crimes against the 'seals, currency, instruments of credits, stamps, passport, public documents' issued by States as some areas over which a State can claim protective jurisdiction.

● **United States v. Zehe** 601 F Supp 196 (D Mass., 1985)

The US government brought this criminal prosecution under the Espionage Act, 18 USC §§792–799, against Alfred Zehe, an East German citizen, for alleged acts of espionage against the USA committed in Mexico and the German Democratic Republic (GDR). Zehe moved for dismissal of the indictment, contending that the Act failed to confer jurisdiction over acts of espionage committed outside US territorial boundaries by persons who are not US citizens.

It was held that the USA had jurisdiction over acts committed abroad, either by its own or foreign nationals, which threaten its security.

The Court reasoned (at 197) that, in previous similar cases:

> ...the courts expressly relied upon the nature of the offenses, and not just upon the citizenship of the defendants, in order to apply other criminal statutes extraterritorially to citizens.

There is no doubt that the protective principle of jurisdiction can be a useful tool in the hands of States when sensibly applied. However, the variety of issues over which States now assert the protective principle are dubious and tend to undermine its integrity. For example, both the USA and Germany have claimed protective principle jurisdiction over cases involving the selling and importing of cannabis (marijuana) into the two countries, respectively.

● **United States v. Gonzales** 77 F2d 931 (11th Cir., 1985)

In this case, the USA justified the interception of a Honduran vessel, off the coast of Florida, which had a huge quantity of marijuana as its cargo, in contravention of the US High Seas Act.

There are many still less convincing uses of the protective principle. Several historical examples can be found of instances in which German courts convicted foreigners who had sexual intercourse with German girls on the ground that the act threatened the racial purity of the German nation.

thinking points

- Is there any difference between the 'effect doctrine' and the 'protective principle'?
- What is the basis for the exercise of jurisdiction under the protective principle?

7.6 The universality principle

It is generally accepted in international law that the impact of certain crimes transcends the jurisdiction of any single State. When committed, such crimes invite the jurisdiction of any State. A State may exercise universal jurisdiction over crimes which are neither committed against it, nor are committed by or against its own nationals.

As stated in §404 of the US Restatement (Third), Foreign Relations Law:

> a State has jurisdiction to define and prescribe punishment for certain offenses recognized by the community of nations as of universal concern, such as piracy, slave trade, attacks on or hijacking of aircraft, genocide, war crimes, and perhaps certain acts of terrorism.

Unlike the other jurisdictional bases, there is no requirement of a link between the person who commits a 'universal' crime, the effect of the crime, or the place where it is committed and the State that claims universal jurisdiction. What is important is that the *nature* of the crime is such that it is of universal concern.

The crime of *piracy jure gentium* has been recognized as the crime of universal jurisdiction par excellence from time immemorial. When piracy occurs on the high seas, it poses a danger to all States. No single State's jurisdiction covers the high seas; hence, pirates constantly prey on this somewhat 'lawless' zone to wreak havoc on vessels. From 2007, for example, there has been an upsurge in the menace of piratical attacks off the coast of Somalia. In some cases, fatalities have occurred.

● ***Re Piracy Jure Gentium*** [1934] AC 586

In 1931, a number of armed Chinese nationals cruising in two Chinese boats on the high seas pursued and attacked a Chinese cargo vessel. The cargo vessel attempted to escape. Following an intensive chase, a steamship intervened and arrested the culprits.

The main question before the Court in this case was whether an accused person may be convicted of piracy in circumstances in which no robbery has occurred. The Full Court of Hong Kong held that robbery was necessary to support a conviction of piracy and, in the result, the accused persons were acquitted.

Although the decision of the Hong Kong court was final, the Privy Council had pronounced on the nature of piracy and jurisdiction (at 589) stating that:

> ...whereas according to international law the criminal jurisdiction of municipal law is ordinarily restricted to crimes committed on its territorial waters or its own ships, and to crimes by its own nationals wherever committed, it is also recognised as extending to piracy committed on the High Seas by any national on any ship, because a person guilty of such piracy *has placed himself beyond the protection of any State. He is no longer a national, but hostis humani generis and as such he is justiciable by any State anywhere*. [Emphasis added]

In coming to this conclusion, the Council had partly relied on the authoritative work of Hugo Grotius (1583–1645), *De jure Belli et Pacis*, vol. 2, cap. 20, s. 40.

Until recently, it was thought that universal jurisdiction applied only to piracy. However, increasing attempts have been made, especially since the adoption of the four Geneva Conventions in 1949, to extend universal jurisdiction over crimes that were previously considered to belong to the municipal jurisdiction of individual States. Consequently, it is now being claimed that universal jurisdiction exists in respect of war crimes, crimes against humanity, and genocide.

Advocates of universal jurisdiction often rely on *SS Lotus* for support.

● ***France v. Turkey*** (1927) PCIJ Ser. A, No. 10 (The ***SS Lotus Case***)

See Chapter 2 for the facts of this case.

In this case, the PCIJ famously stated (at 46) that:

> It does not, however, follow that international law prohibits a State from exercising jurisdiction in its own territory, in respect of any case which relates to acts which have taken place abroad... Such a view would only be tenable if international law contained a general prohibition to States to extend the application of their laws and the jurisdiction of their courts to persons, property and acts outside their territory, and if, as an exception to this general prohibition, it allowed States to do so in certain specific cases. But this is certainly not the case under international law as it stands at present. *Far from laying down a general prohibition to the effect that States may not extend the application of their laws and the jurisdiction of their courts to persons, property and acts outside their territory, it leaves them in this respect a wide measure of discretion which is only limited in certain cases by prohibitive rules; as regards other cases, every State remains free to adopt the principles which it regards as best and most suitable.* [Emphasis added]

It is often said that the PCIJ recognized universal jurisdiction in this statement. This assertion has not gone unchallenged, and it is noteworthy that the International Court of Justice (ICJ) has not endorsed the PCIJ's statement.

. . . .

● *Democratic Republic of Congo v. Belgium* (2000) ICJ Rep 182 (The *Arrest Warrant Case*)

In their separate opinion in this case, Judges Higgins, Kooijmans, and Buergenthal said (at 78) that:

> And those States and academic writers who claim the right to act unilaterally to assert a universal criminal jurisdiction over persons committing such acts, invoke the concept of acting as 'agents for the international community'. This vertical notion of the authority of action is significantly different from the horizontal system of international law envisaged in the '*Lotus*' case.

Notwithstanding the controversy surrounding its status, universal jurisdiction has been asserted by many States—and often over crimes that were committed prior to the existence of the claiming States.

. . . .

● *State of Israel v. Adolf Eichmann* Criminal Case 40/61 (1960), Israeli Supreme Court (The *Trial of Adolf Eichmann*), reported in (1968) 36 ILR 5 (DC) 340

Adolf Eichmann was a Nazi officer who was in charge of implementing the Nazi 'Final Solution' against Jews during the Second World War. The Final Solution was a euphemism for the intention of Hitler to exterminate Jews across Europe. Following the defeat of the Nazis, Eichmann escaped and lived for several years in Argentina under the assumed name 'Ricardo Klement'. In 1960, Eichmann was captured by the Israeli intelligence service, Mossad, and smuggled to Israel where, following his trial and conviction, he was executed by hanging in May 1962.

Eichmann raised several defences against his trial, including that Israel had no jurisdiction since he was not an Israeli and the crimes were not committed in Israel, which State did not exist at the time of the crimes. The crimes were committed during the Second World War (1939–45), whereas Israel came into existence as a nation only from 1948. Finally, Eichmann claimed that since the legal base for prosecution was created after the alleged crimes were committed, this made the law retroactive.

The Israeli Supreme Court convicted Eichmann on all fifteen counts, holding effectively that the nature of the crimes of which Eichmann was accused justified the extraterritorial jurisdiction of Israel. This was one of the earliest applications of the universal jurisdiction principle.

More recently, universal jurisdiction has been asserted in respect of human rights violations. The basis of this extension is often that some human rights have become *erga omnes* obligations (that is, contracts enforceable even by non-parties) and that their violators are no longer only people subject to the ordinary jurisdictions of their States, but are also enemies of mankind.

· ·

● *Filártiga v. Peña-Irala* 630 F. 2D 876 (2nd Cir., 1980)

The suit was brought by an alien residing in the USA against a former official of Paraguay, then visiting the USA. The complaint alleged torture of the plaintiff's brother, leading to his death.

It was held (at 879) that deliberate torture perpetrated by a person invested with official authority was a violation of customary law, supporting the jurisdiction of the district courts over 'a civil action by an alien for a tort only, committed in violation of the law of nations' (see 28 USC §1350). The court further declared that 'indeed, for purposes of civil liability, the torturer has become like the pirate and slave trader before him *hostis humani generis*, an enemy of all mankind' (at 890). The court found that torture perpetrated by a person invested with official authority violates universally accepted human rights norms, regardless of the nationality of the parties. Whenever an alleged torturer is found and served with process by an alien within US territory, §1350 applies and provides federal jurisdiction.

It seems, however, that the increasingly proactive approach of States towards universal jurisdiction is partly due to the emergence of multilateral treaties, many of which not only forbid certain crimes, but also encourage States to ensure that they are prosecuted if committed on their territory, or otherwise that those responsible should be extradited to other countries. Examples of these treaties include the 1948 UN Convention on the Prevention and Punishment of Genocide (the Genocide Convention), the 1984 UN Convention against Torture and other Cruel, Inhuman and Degrading Treatment or Punishment (the Torture Convention), and the 1973 International Convention on the Suppression and Punishment of the Crime of Apartheid.

However, while some of these conventions have been rightly described as the 'quintessential human rights treaty'—especially if one recalls the devastating nature of crimes that they seek to abolish—controversy remains as to whether the conventions actually advocate universal jurisdiction. In other words, can any State seize anyone indicted for genocide, for example, and prosecute them, whether or not the criminal is their national, is on their territory, or has committed the crime against the seizing State and its nationals?

Article VI of the Genocide Convention states that:

> Persons charged with genocide or any of the other acts enumerated in Article III shall be tried by a competent tribunal of the State in the territory of which the act was committed, or by such international penal tribunal as may have jurisdiction with respect to those Contracting Parties which shall have accepted its jurisdiction.

Clearly, the obligation contained in the above provision is for States to assert their territorial jurisdiction over the crime of genocide. However, the provision does not affect the right of a State to exercise criminal jurisdiction on its own nationals for acts committed outside the State.

Article 49 of the First Geneva Convention, Article 50 of the Second Geneva Convention, Article 129 of the Third Geneva Convention, and Article 146 of the Fourth Geneva Convention, all of 12 August 1949, provide:

> Each High Contracting Party shall be under the obligation to search for persons alleged to have committed, or to have ordered to be committed, grave breaches, and shall bring such persons, regardless of their nationality, before its own courts. It may also, if it prefers, and in accordance with

the provisions of its own legislation, hand such persons over for trial to another High Contracting Party concerned, provided such High Contracting Party has made out a *prima facie* case.

But, as stated earlier, this kind of provision—which encourages States to prosecute or to extradite criminals to foreign countries—has now become a regular feature of many multilateral treaties, but has not been generally accepted as conferring universal jurisdiction.

The Genocide Convention, as with other conventions that obligate States to prohibit heinous crimes on their territory, does not make any explicit provision for universal jurisdiction, despite occasional arguments to the contrary. Certainly, there is a remarkable difference between an obligation to prohibit and prosecute a crime committed on one's territory, or to extradite the criminal to a foreign country, and an assumption of a universal jurisdiction over such crimes by *all* States. Even the US Restatement (Third), which lists some of these offences as attracting universal jurisdiction, relies solely on customary international law for support. Yet there is no agreement in customary international law as to the validity of universal jurisdiction over these crimes, nor has the ICJ made any pronouncement on such matters, even when it has had the rare opportunity to do so.

. . . .

● *Democratic Republic of Congo v. Belgium* (2000) ICJ REP 182 (The *Arrest Warrant Case*)

Belgium had issued an international arrest warrant against the then serving Foreign Minister of the Democratic Republic of Congo Mr Yerodia Ndombasi for committing crimes punishable in Belgium under the Law of 16 June 1993 concerning the Punishment of Grave Breaches of the International Geneva Conventions of 12 August 1949 and of Protocols I and II of 8 June 1977 Additional Thereto, as amended by the Law of 19 February 1999 concerning the Punishment of Serious Violations of International Humanitarian Law. Belgium claimed universal jurisdiction to prosecute the alleged crimes. In its response, the Congo argued, inter alia, that the universal jurisdiction that the Belgian State attributed to itself under Article 7 of the law in question constituted a violation of the principle that a State may not exercise its authority on the territory of another State, and of the principle of sovereign equality among all members of the United Nations.

In its judgment, the Court did not pronounce on whether or not Belgium was right in claiming universal jurisdiction, but instead decided the case in favour of the Congo on the basis that the arrest warrant violated the immunity of the accused person.

Nevertheless, in their separate opinions, Judges Higgins, Kooijmans, and Buergenthal went on to review several domestic legislations of many States, and found (at 69) that:

Save for the Belgian legislation of 10 February 1999, national legislation, whether in fulfilment of international treaty obligations to make certain international crimes offences also in national law, or otherwise, does not suggest a universal jurisdiction over these offences. Various examples typify the more qualified practice. The Australian War Crimes Act of 1945, as amended in 1988, provides for the prosecution in Australia of crimes committed between 1 September 1939 and 8 May 1945 by persons who were Australian citizens or residents at the time of being charged with the offences (Arts. 9 and 11). The United Kingdom War Crimes Act of 1991 enables proceedings to be brought for murder, manslaughter or culpable homicide, committed between 1 September 1935 and 5 June 1945, in a place that was part of Germany or under German occupation, and in circumstances where the accused was at the time, or has become, a British citizen or resident of the United Kingdom. The statutory jurisdiction provided for by France, Germany and (in even broader terms) the Netherlands, refer for their jurisdictional basis to the jurisdictional provisions in those international treaties to which the legislation was intended to give effect.

The judges also reviewed instances in which States have asserted universal jurisdiction, as in the US cases of *United States v. Yunis* 681 F Supp 896 (DDC, 1988) and *United States v. Bin Laden* 92 F Supp 2d 225 (SDNY, 2000). On balance, the three judges concluded (at 80) that universal jurisdiction exists, although it must be exercised with great caution, and with safeguards:

> There cannot be an obligation to extradite someone you choose not to try unless that person is within your reach. National legislation, enacted to give effect to these treaties, quite naturally also may make mention of the necessity of the presence of the accused. These sensible realities are critical for the obligatory exercise of *aut dedere aut prosequi* jurisdiction, but cannot be interpreted *a contrario* so as to exclude a voluntary exercise of a universal jurisdiction.

Persuasive as the statement of the three judges might be, it must be remembered that it did not form part of the judgment of the Court, which remained silent on the issue of universal jurisdiction. Thus it must be concluded that there is no final word on whether States can assert universal jurisdiction over such matters falling outside piracy, which does not attract any controversy whatsoever.

In 2003, Belgium abolished its universal jurisdiction laws; it now asserts its jurisdiction over international crimes only when committed by those primarily resident in Belgium.

thinking points

- *On what basis may a State exercise universal jurisdiction?*
- *What is the main requirement of universal jurisdiction?*
- *On what basis did the ICJ decide that Belgium did not have jurisdiction in* Arrest Warrant *and how did the reaction to this case affect the prospect of universal jurisdiction?*

7.7 The passive personality principle

The passive personality principle allows a State to prosecute a foreigner whose act abroad affects a national of that State. This jurisdictional principle resembles the 'effect doctrine' in that the 'act' concerned is committed abroad. But whereas with the 'effect doctrine' the impact of the act is *actually* felt by the State claiming jurisdiction, only the nationals of the States need be harmed under the passive personality principle. The 'effect doctrine' attaches to the territorial jurisdiction of the State claiming it. For example, the effect of a bomb launched from one State across a border is felt in the State in which the bomb landed and detonated. On the contrary, the passive personality principle arises where an act done abroad injures the nationals (and not the territory or those present on the territory) of another State, thereby attaching to the nationality principle, but in a reverse manner. This is an interesting principle, the historical basis of which is discussed later, and which remains somewhat controversial, so that it was not included as one of the principles for exercising jurisdiction in the 1935 Harvard Research Draft Convention on Criminal Jurisdiction.

● *United States v. Cutting* 70 US 441, 3 WALL 441 (1866) (The *Cutting Case*)

Mr Cutting, an American, published in the USA some libellous materials about Mr Barayd, a Mexican diplomat. Mr Cutting was arrested, upon entering Mexico, imprisoned, and charged with libel under a novel jurisdictional heading now known as the 'passive personality principle'. Although Mr Cutting was eventually released, following high-powered representation made by the USA and guarantees that Mr Cutting would not bring a civil claim for damages against Mexico, the incident became extremely important for the jurisdictional principle that it was thought to have established.

As US President Grover Cleveland put it in his address to Congress in 1886 (reported in Department of State, 'Report on extraterritorial crime and the *Cutting Case*' (1887) Foreign Relations of the United States 751), the *Cutting Case*:

> disclosed a claim of jurisdiction by Mexico novel in our history, whereby any offense committed anywhere by a foreigner, penal in the place of its commission, and of which a Mexican is the object, may, if the offender be found in Mexico, be there tried and punished in conformity with Mexican laws.

The reaction of the USA to the assertion of extraterritorial jurisdiction (in the form of the passive personality principle) by Mexico should be understood in the context of its ancient reluctance to extend jurisdiction beyond its territory.

....

● *Forley Bros v. Filardo* 336 US 281 (1949)

This US approach is reiterated in the much-quoted rule of presumption against extraterritoriality laid down in this case (at 285) thus:

> it is a longstanding principle of American law that legislation of Congress unless a contrary intent appears, is meant to apply only within the territorial jurisdiction of the United States.

....

● *EEOC v. Arabian American Oil Co. (Aramco); EEOC v. Arabian American Oil Co. (Aramco)* 449 US 248 (1991)

As Chief Justice Rehnquist noted in this case, the presumption against extraterritoriality:

> serves to protect against unintended clashes between our laws and those of other nations which could result in international discord.

For many years, the only permissible exception to this rule under the US legal system was the US Trademark Act (the Lanham Act), which protected trademarks and upon which the Supreme Court decided *Steele v. Bulova Watch Co.* 344 US 280 (1952).

The *Cutting Case* is regarded as the *locus classicus* of the passive personality principle.

Be that as it may, the USA had cause to resist the passive personality principle on several occasions. In 1975, it vehemently opposed the assertion of jurisdiction by Greece over US nationals for injuring some Greek nationals in a car accident in Greece (see (1975) Digest of United States Practice in International Law 339). Also, in 1989, the USA opposed extraterritorial jurisdiction in a case involving the murder of its national in Korea (see the Letter of Assistant Secretary of State Janet G. Mullins, 26 December 1989, criticizing the passive personality principle, reprinted in (1991) 137 Cong Rec S4750, statement of Senators Thurmond and Hollings).

Nevertheless, initial resistance has given way to a friendlier approach to the passive personality principle. In 1989, the USA abducted the then President of Panama Manuel Noriega and brought him to the USA to try him on alleged drug-related charges. In doing so, the USA also relied partly on the principle in *Yunis* (see section 7.6).

As Michael Hirst, 'Jurisdiction over cross-frontier' (1981) 97 LQR 80, confirms, the UK, meanwhile, has always reserved extraterritorial jurisdiction for the most exceptional cases.

KEY POINTS

- Passive personality derives from the nationality of the injured person.

- Its application remains somewhat controversial, and it is not included in the 1935 Harvard Research Draft Convention on Criminal Jurisdiction.

7.7.1 The test of the passive personality principle

As mentioned earlier, the passive personality principle is available to a State the nationals of which have been victims of crimes committed abroad. This is what distinguishes the passive personality principle from the nationality principle, in which nationals are the perpetrators of the crimes in question. The important question to ask for the passive personality principle is: is it enough that a State's nationals are victims of a crime committed abroad, or must a State prove something more before it can exercise the passive personality principle of jurisdiction? Spain attempted to provide an answer to this question in two cases.

. . . .

● *Sentencia del Tribunal Supremo sobre el caso Guatemala por Genocidio Appeal* ROLL 115/2000, CASE 331/99, FILE 162/2000 (TRIBUNAL SUPREMO, SECOND PENAL CHAMBER, 25 FEBRUARY 2003) (The *Guatemala Genocide Case*)

In 1999, several non-governmental organizations (NGOs), human rights organizations, and certain individuals, principally from Guatemala and Spain, brought an action in a Spanish court concerning some grave criminal acts allegedly perpetrated by certain officials of Guatemala against the parties represented by the applicants. According to the claimants, the acts, which were said to have taken place in Guatemala between 1978 and 1990, constituted the crimes of genocide, terrorism, and torture. The victims of the alleged genocide were the Mayan indigenous population of Guatemala, while some Spanish nationals were also said to have suffered torture and death.

It was held that passive personality did not apply, despite the fact that some Spaniards were victims of the crimes committed in Guatemala. In explaining its refusal to apply the principle, Spain attempted to lay down the test by which the passive personality principle should be applied.

According to the Tribuno Supremo (the Spanish Supreme Tribunal):

> the minimum relevance of national interest exists when the act with which the national interest connects reaches a meaning equivalent to that which is recognized by other acts which, according to the internal law and to treaties, gives rise to the application of the remaining criteria of extraterritorial criminal jurisdiction.

The tribunal reasoned that:

> the link should be considered *in direct relation to the crime used as a basis for finding jurisdiction and not for other crimes*, even though they appear related to it, for only in this way may such jurisdiction be found. In this manner, the existence of a connection to the crime or certain crimes does not authorize the extension of jurisdiction to other different crimes, for which no links appears. [Emphasis added]

The implication of this reasoning on the passive personality principle is twofold. First, there must be the 'national interest' at stake in order for the protective principle to apply. This national interest is mainly in the form of the victims of the crime being nationals of the State exercising or seeking to exercise jurisdiction.

Secondly, even where this first criterion exists, there is a further requirement that the crime complained about must be the same one that forms the basis of the jurisdiction.

In this case, only one requirement was met: that some of the victims were Spanish nationals. The crime complained about in the case was genocide, which was not suffered by the Spaniards, but committed against Guatemalans. Since the national interest must be affected by the *specific* crime forming the basis of jurisdiction, there was no link between the crime and Spanish national interest.

Within a few years of this decision, Spain had the opportunity to apply the test laid down in *Guatemala Genocide*.

. . . .

● *Sentencias del Tribunal Supremo español en el case del Gral. Chinelo Hernán Julio Brady Roche* SENTENCIA NO: 319/2004 (The *General Hernán Rochie Case*)

On 8 March 2004, the case came before the court, as with *Guatemala Genocide*, on appeal from the Audiencia Nacional. The facts before the court in the present case concerned the crime of torture, allegedly committed against Spanish nationals by the accused person, a Chilean general and former Defence Minister, General Hernán Julio Brady Roche. In line with its jurisprudence in *Guatemala Genocide*, the Audiencia Nacional declined jurisdiction over the claims, causing the widow of Spanish diplomat Don Carmelo Soria to appeal to the Supreme Court. Don Carmelo, who was in Chile at the end of the 1936–39 Spanish Civil War, was kidnapped on 14 July 1976, and his body, showing signs of torture, was later found in Santiago.

It was held that Spanish courts have jurisdiction over the crimes alleged in this case. In explaining the basis for its decision, the court referred to its reasoning in *Guatemala Genocide*. In particular, the court singled out the *link* between the alleged *crimes* and Spanish national interests (thus subscribing to the passive personality principle), as well as the nature of the crime (torture), which, it thought, justified the application of the universality principle.

One notorious problem with the passive personality principle is that it promotes jurisdictional conflicts, especially if the act complained about is also a crime in the place of commission.

example

Certainly, if A, being a national of Rutamu, resides in Candoma and was killed by B, a national of Candoma, Candoma would want to exercise territorial or nationality jurisdiction over B, while, as seen previously, Rutamu may want to exercise its passive personality principle as well over B.

It is possible that passive personality is attractive where the national States of alleged criminals are unwilling to prosecute their nationals. If this is the case, the fact that such serious crimes as those over which a State may want to assert its passive personality are now subject to prohibition under the ICC Statute may be a solace or compromise. Failure by one State to prosecute its nationals does not end the matter, because Article 17 of the ICC Statute compels the Court, through its prosecutor, to try the case.

Furthermore, as Glanville Williams (1965, see section 7.2.1) noted, at 518:

> In any case, modern States are well aware that it is their common interest to suppress crime, so that there is generally little reason to fear that the State where the offender physically acts will remain passive, even if the ill effect is not felt within its own borders.

KEY POINTS

- 'National interest' is the essential element in order for States to exercise the passive personality principle.

- There must be a link between the national interest of a State claiming the passive personality principle and the crime forming the basis of that jurisdiction.

7.8 Problems of illegal enforcement jurisdiction

International law is categorical about how a State can enforce its own laws in respect of criminals in other States. Where a criminal wanted by one State is present on the territory of another State, the most traditional and acceptable means of retrieving such person is a class of conventions known as 'extradition treaties'. These treaties are usually bilateral in nature (that is, between two States), although there are also examples of multilateral extradition treaties. Where there is no extradition treaty between two States, then the advance consent or acquiescence of a State in which a criminal is present is required before the claiming State can enter and seize the culprit.

The reality of international relations, however, is that these two processes are not always followed. A State that does not have an extradition treaty with another State may want to seize a person present on that State's territory with the full knowledge that the other State may not cooperate. This is usually the case if the culprit has committed a crime on behalf of his or her home State, for example, in which case it is to be expected that his or her home State will not easily give him or her up. Sometimes, it is simply because the host State of the criminal benefits commercially from the presence of that criminal and may not want to extradite him or her. These instances are in addition to the fact that extradition treaties themselves can be extremely complicated and, since time is often of the essence in prosecution, following a full extradition process may take too long, thus defeating the whole purpose. Hence, most States—especially those without an extradition treaty—will seek to circumvent the process by 'invading' the territorial integrity of the host State and forcibly taking out the offenders, in the hope that, after the act, diplomatic gestures and overtures will resolve the serious diplomatic dispute that is bound to follow.

Illegal enforcement of one State's jurisdiction against another is not infrequent in contemporary society. Famous cases include Israel's forcible abduction from Argentina of Adolf Eichmann (see section 7.6). It was said, however, that Argentina acquiesced in this act.

example

In 1984, the UK did not acquiesce in the botched attempt to extradite Alhaji Umaru Diko, Nigerian Minister for Transportation and head of the Presidential Task Force on Rice from 1979 to 1983. The culprit, Diko, was wanted by the Nigerian military government in connection with the alleged embezzlement of several billion naira (NGN, the national currency) from the national coffers. He was drugged by agents procured by the Nigerian government and put in a crate labelled 'diplomatic bag' to be flown to Nigeria.

Although this mission was not accomplished (because the drug wore off and he drew the attention of officials at Stansted airport), this attempt by Nigeria to enforce its jurisdiction on British soil, even though in respect of its own national, attracted serious repercussions.

But this failure begs the bigger question: what is the status, under international law, of a criminal who is abducted from another State's territory? Does the fact of abduction mean that the courts of the abducting State will decline jurisdiction? Can the culprit challenge his or her subsequent trial on the basis of being procured in violation of international law?

Approaches differ and, in reality, as much will depend on the importance of the criminal to the capturing State as it will on the nature of the government in power in that State. For example, in *Eichmann*, Israel tendered an apology to Argentina, but the Israeli courts did not decline jurisdiction. It is possible that the significance of the prosecution of that criminal to the State of Israel was an overriding factor, although it is possible that, at the relevant time, Israeli domestic law did not forbid such exercise of jurisdiction. Although international law frowns upon the violation of territorial integrity of States, it does not penalize the jurisdiction that results therefrom. Consequently, the subsequent Israeli trial of Eichmann did not violate international law rules on jurisdiction, even if the manner in which the State captured the culprit undoubtedly did. Usually, diplomatic means are employed to rectify the wrong, as was done in *Eichmann*.

The approach in the UK is different. In general, British courts would decline jurisdiction if a criminal were to be procured in violation of international law.

. . . .

● *R v. Horseferry Road Magistrates' Court, ex p Bennett* [1994] 1 AC 42

The defendant, a citizen of New Zealand, who was alleged to have committed certain crimes in England, was traced to South Africa by the English police, and forcibly returned to England. There was no extradition treaty between the two countries and, although special arrangements could be made for extradition in a particular case under section 15 of the Extradition Act 1989, no such proceedings were taken. The defendant claimed that he had been kidnapped from the Republic of South Africa as a result of collusion between the South African and British police, and returned to England, where he was arrested and brought before a magistrates' court to be committed to the Crown Court for trial.

The defendant sought an adjournment to enable him to challenge the court's jurisdiction. The application was refused, and he was committed for trial.

He sought judicial review of the magistrates' court's decision. The Court of the Queen's Bench Division, refusing the application, held that the English courts had no power to inquire into the circumstances under which a person appearing before them had been brought within the jurisdiction.

The defendant appealed to the House of Lords, which allowed the appeal and held (at 42) that:

> where a defendant in a criminal matter had been brought back to the United Kingdom in disregard of available extradition process and in breach of international law and the laws of the state where the defendant had been found, the courts in the United Kingdom should take cognisance of those circumstances and refuse to try the defendant; and that, accordingly, the High Court, in the exercise of its supervisory jurisdiction, had power to inquire into the circumstances by which a person had been brought within the jurisdiction and, if satisfied that there had been a disregard of extradition procedures, it might stay the prosecution as an abuse of process and order the release of the defendant.

The USA's original approach was directly opposed to that of the UK. Thus, in *Ker v. Illinois* 119 US 436 (1886), the principle was laid down that a criminal abducted from abroad cannot challenge his or her abduction as contrary to the US Constitution. However, this approach has now changed, and the practice is now for the USA to decline jurisdiction over criminals forcibly taken from overseas, as held in *Frisbie v. Collins* 342 US 519 (1952).

Nevertheless, the USA had to rethink its position in a later case rather than simply follow *Ker* and *Frisbie*.

● *United States v. Toscanino* 500 F. 2D 267 (2nd Cir., 1974)

In this case, the court decided to consider carefully whether it should simply disregard the accused's plea of illegal procurement from abroad in light of executive lawlessness and also in light of the fact that the territorial integrity of the host State had been violated.

After a comprehensive review, the court said (at 275) that:

> Faced with a conflict between the two concepts of due process, the one being the restricted version found in Ker–Frisbie and the other the expanded and enlightened interpretation expressed in more recent decisions of the Supreme Court, we are persuaded that to the extent that the two are in conflict, the Ker–Frisbie version must yield. *Accordingly we view due process as now requiring a court to divest itself of jurisdiction over the person of a defendant where it has been acquired as the result of the Government's deliberate, unnecessary and unreasonable invasion of the accused's constitutional rights.* This conclusion represents but an extension of the well-recognized power of federal courts in the civil context to decline to exercise jurisdiction over a defendant whose presence has been secured by force or fraud. [Emphasis added]

This trend mirrors the earlier statement of Justice Holmes, in *Silverthorne Lumber Co. v. United States* 251 US 385 (1920), that to allow the US government to benefit illegally from seized evidence 'reduces the Fourth Amendment to a form of words'.

In South Africa, the matter is not as clear-cut. Much depends on the circumstances of the kidnap and also, particularly, on whether the kidnapped person is officially arrested by the South African authorities.

● *Abrahams v. Minister of Justice* 1963 (4) SA 542

The applicant applied for habeas corpus on the ground that he was abducted from Bechuanaland (as Botswana was then known) by members of the South African police and taken to Gobabis in South West Africa (now Namibia), where he was duly arrested.

It was held, relying on the authority of *R v. Robertson* 1912 TPD 10 and *R v. Officer Commanding Depot Battalion, Colchester, ex p Elliot* [1947] 1 All ER 373, that where a lawful arrest took place *within a State's own borders*, the circumstances under which the accused was brought into the State were irrelevant.

. . . .

● *Nduli & ors v. Minister of Justice* 1978 (1) SA 893 (A)

In this case, the accused persons were abducted from Swaziland by members of the South African police in breach of orders from their commanding officer.

It was held that the South African State was not responsible and, accordingly, there was no violation of international law. Consequently, the trial court was not deprived of its competence to try the accused.

As with the USA, the South African courts had to rethink their position a few years after *Nduli*.

. . . .

● *State v. Ebrahim* (1991) 31 ILM 888

The accused, a member of the military wing of the African National Congress (ANC), was jailed for a period in South Africa, later released, but then confined to an area. He escaped to Swaziland, from where he was abducted by agents of the South African government. He was arrested by South African authorities upon being brought within the South African borders. He challenged his trial on the basis of his illegal abduction.

The trial judge followed *Nduli* to find jurisdiction.

On appeal, it was held that the lower court erred in applying *Nduli*, since the South African authorities were not responsible for the abduction of the culprit in that case; in the present case, the South African authorities *were* responsible.

It is instructive that, in coming to its decision in *Ebrahim*, the South African Supreme Court had referred to several decisions of US courts, including *United States v. Archer* 486 F.2d 670 (2nd Cir., 1973) and the following case.

. . . .

● *Olmstead v. United States* 277 US 438 (1928)

In this case, it was said (at 484–485) that:

> Decency, security and liberty alike demand that Government officials shall be subjected to the same rules of conduct that are commands to the citizen. In a government of laws, existence of the Government will be imperilled if it fails to observe the law scrupulously. Our Government is the potent, the omnipresent teacher. For good or for ill, it teaches the whole people by its example. Crime is contagious. If the Government becomes a lawbreaker, it breeds contempt for law; it invites every man to become a law unto himself; it invites anarchy. To declare that in the administration of the criminal law the end justifies the means—to declare that the Government may commit crimes in order to secure the conviction of a private criminal—would bring terrible retribution. Against that pernicious doctrine this Court should resolutely set its face.

It should be noted that the courts of different countries base their decisions whether or not to exercise jurisdiction on different reasons. While the English courts seem to rely on international law and the comity of nations, the US courts, and the South African courts by association, refer to their domestic criminal or constitutional law. Nevertheless, whatever the reason given by the courts, international law does not provide legal rules on this particular matter; it is safe to assume that the State from which an alleged criminal is abducted can bring an action for violation of territorial sovereignty.

So far, in the absence of an international law pronouncement on the matter, it remains within the realm of domestic institutions to regulate their own affairs in this matter.

thinking points

- *By what legal means may a State request the transfer to it of a criminal living in another State?*
- *Where a criminal is not legally obtained from the territory of a State to face trial in another State, will the unlawful obtainment of that criminal by the latter State be fatal to the jurisdiction by the courts of the erring country?*

Conclusion

The various types of jurisdiction that a State can exercise depend on the circumstances involved in a case. As has been shown, several developments in the contemporary world order have affected the way in which States exercise jurisdiction, especially in the prescription of their laws. While it is true that States have a collective interest in ensuring that crimes are suppressed and violations are punished, one cannot overlook the possibility of certain States shielding their officials from prosecution, either within their countries or overseas. In such cases, the passive personality principle might become very useful.

As has also been seen, the use of the nationality principle is particularly suitable for protecting children, just as the effect doctrine can be a very potent tool in ensuring that those who plan abroad to injure people and objects in the territory of another State do not escape for lack of jurisdiction by the affected State.

It has also been shown that asserting jurisdiction is one thing, but enforcing it is another. Whether a State is able to enforce its jurisdiction in another State's territory depends on the relations between the two States. Self-help measures, such as forcible seizure and kidnappings, are often practised when legal arrangements for enforcing jurisdiction are not available. However, such measures are debilitating to international peace and not generally good for interstate relations, as shown by the *Eichmann* and *Umaru Dikko* cases.

It is almost impossible to lay down definitive rules to govern States' relations in respect of jurisdiction, especially where there is the possibility of conflict, such as between the territorial jurisdiction and the extraterritorial jurisdiction (for example, the nationality or protective principle). Much will come down to amicable understanding and the spirit of comity among nations.

Questions

Self-test questions

1 Explain the term 'jurisdiction'.

2 What requirement do States have to meet before they can exercise subjective territorial jurisdiction?

3 Distinguish between the nationality principle and the protective principle.

4 In what circumstances will a State exercise the passive personality principle?

5 What do you understand by 'universal jurisdiction'?

6 When will enforcement jurisdiction be illegal?

7 What is the territoriality principle?

8 Explain the phrase 'the effect doctrine'.

Discussion questions

1 'A State may exercise its territorial jurisdiction once a crime is committed on its territory, regardless of where the crime starts or ends.' Discuss.

2 'The "effect doctrine" and the "protective principle" are so similar that there is no point in treating them separately.' Critically examine this statement.

3 'A State can exercise universal jurisdiction over any crime committed abroad.' Assess the validity of this statement.

4 'Once a State's national has been injured abroad, that State has an unquestionable right to exercise jurisdiction on the basis of the passive personality principle.' Discuss.

5 'The forcible capturing of a criminal from an overseas territory is irrelevant to his or her subsequent prosecution in the capturing State.' Critically examine this statement.

6 'Jurisdiction is a generic term and can mean different things in different circumstances.' Discuss.

Assessment question

John, a citizen of Candoma who lives and works in Rutamu, killed Dan, a citizen of Rutamu, when a fight broke out between them over an alleged car theft. Rutamuan police promptly arrested John and put him in jail pending trial. In connivance with a prison warden, John escaped and fled home to Candoma. The Candoman government, headed by John's uncle, decided not to prosecute him and, despite repeated requests from Rutamu to extradite the accused, Candoma refused. In a spontaneous street demonstration in Rutamu, five Candoman citizens were injured and hospitalized. In a further bid to scare Candoma and to pressure it into surrendering the culprit, members of the Rutamuan armed forces fired a few shots across the territory, which hit targets in Candoma—but still the State refused to extradite its national. After six months of waiting in vain, Rutamu sent ten members of its secret services into Candoma at night to abduct the culprit. This action angered Candoma, which decided to commence proceedings before the International Court of Justice complaining of the violation of its territorial integrity by Rutamu.

Advise the State parties.

Key cases

- *Democratic Republic of Congo v. Belgium* (2000) ICJ Rep 182 (the *Arrest Warrant Case*)
- *France v. Turkey* (1927) PCIJ Ser. A, No. 10 (the *SS Lotus Case*)

- *R v. Ellis* (1899) 1 QB 1
- *R. v. Treacy* [1971] AC 537
- *United States v. Zehe* 601 F Supp 196 (D Mass., 1985)

# Further reading

Akehurst, M., 'Jurisdiction in international law' (1972–73) 46 BYBIL 46

Cameron, I., *The Protective Principle of International Jurisdiction* (Aldershot/Brookfield, VT: Dartmouth, 1994)

Hist, M., 'Jurisdiction over cross-frontier' (1981) 97 LQR 80

Jennings, R., 'Extraterritorial jurisdiction and the United States antitrust laws' (1957) 33 BYBIL 146

Meesen, K. M. (ed.), *Extraterritorial Jurisdiction in Theory and Practice* (The Hague: Kluwer Law International, 1996)

Molenaar, E. J., *Coastal State Jurisdiction over Vessel-Source Pollution* (The Hague/Boston/London: Kluwer Law International, 1998)

Rijken, C., *Trafficking in Persons: Prosecution from a European Perspective* (The Hague: T. M. C. Asser Press, 2003)

Watson, G. R., 'The passive personality principle' (1993) 28 Texas Int'l LJ 1

Williams, G., 'Venue and the ambit of criminal law' (1965) 81 LQR 518

8

Immunity

Learning objectives

This chapter will help you to:

- understand the meaning of 'immunity' and the various senses in which we use the term in international law;

- appreciate the principles governing immunity of States and those applying to certain cadres of individuals representing States;

- recognize the different circumstances in which immunity can be waived, or in which those otherwise entitled may lose their immunity;

- understand the modern dynamics of immunity, especially as it relates to States officials and high-level functionaries of States.

Introduction

Immunity refers to an international law principle which prevents the courts of one State from exercising jurisdiction over another State or certain of its officials. We said in the last chapter that every State is entitled to exercise jurisdiction over all things present on its territory. The principle of immunity constitutes an exception to that rule. International law obligates every State to accord immunity to another State and its diplomatic staff, and failure to do so often leads to international responsibility (see Chapter 9). This chapter discusses the law, principles, application, and limitations thereto, of immunity.

8.1 The nature of immunity

Immunity creates a procedural bar to the adjudication of a suit before a domestic or international court, over which such a court will normally have jurisdiction. It does not matter whether the suit is of a civil or criminal character. The effect of immunity is not to extinguish the person's liability under domestic or international law, but to prevent the court in question from entertaining the suit.

To the extent that it operates to prevent a court from exercising jurisdiction, immunity shares some similarity with non-justiciability, a principle which also concerns the inability of the court to try cases in certain circumstances. However, the 'inability to try a case' is the only similarity between 'immunity' and 'non-justiciability', as the terms differ significantly both in terms of their rationale and the legal consequences thereof.

Immunity relates to a situation in which a court, which has jurisdiction over the subject matter of a case, is prevented from trying it on the basis of the *identity* of the litigant involved.

> For example, Salome, a citizen of Candoma who lives in Rutamu where he works as a diplomat representing Candoma, drives his car while drunk, and kills Jalo, a citizen of Rutamu. In Rutamu, drink-driving is a serious offence. While Rutamuan courts have jurisdiction over the subject matter of the crime (drink-driving), they are prevented from trying it mainly because of the identity of Salome. Being a diplomat, Salome falls into the category of individuals who, by virtue of their special status, cannot be tried by countries where they represent their States.

Non-justiciability, on the other hand, relates to situations in which it is the subject matter before the court, not the identity of the culprit, that prevents the court from trying a case. An example of a case that is non-justiciable as opposed to falling under immunity is the UK case of *Buck v Attorney-General*, in which six Sierra Leonean nationals sought to challenge the validity of the Sierra Leone Constitution by claiming the Order in Council by which the constitution was established went beyond the powers which the 1887 British Settlement Act conferred. So, the subject matter here is the 'validity' of a country's constitution which some of its nationals wanted the British court to determine. As explained by Harman LJ:

> These courts [the UK courts] cannot, in my view, make a declaration impugning the validity of the constitution of a foreign or independent state, at any rate where that is the object of the action. This may be put as a matter of international comity, or upon the ground of effectiveness. No relief effective in this country or anywhere else is sought by the action. Any declaration which the court might make may be ignored with impunity by the independent country into whose affairs it pretends to pry, and I am of opinion that it would be not only improper, but contrary to law in those circumstances to make such a declaration as is here sought. Even if, however, I thought that we could, I should still think that we should not make such a declaration which would amount to an unwarrantable interference in the affairs of an independent member of the British Commonwealth.
> [*Buck and ors v. Attorney-General* [1965] Ch 745, 768]

Thus, here, the court could not entertain the subject matter of the case primarily because, as it reasoned, such would be interfering in the affairs of other States, and also because whatever decisions it makes on such a matter would not be enforceable in that country. The issue here has nothing to do with the identity of those involved in the case, but rather on the nature of the subject matter. There are instances, however, in which English courts might be able to adjudicate cases involving the validity of foreign constitutions, but since 'non-justiciability' is not our concern in this chapter, there is no need to take the matter any further.

The law on immunity is one of the areas of international law in which customary law shapes the majority of contemporary practices and domestic laws, obligations, and principles. Indeed, in the absence of a generic treaty on immunities, the relevant law is found mostly in domestic statutes and relevant case law, both international and domestic. This is not to say that there have not been initiatives to conclude treaties on this subject. The 1961 Vienna Convention on Diplomatic Relations, the 1963 Vienna Convention on Consular Relation, and the 1948 General Convention on the Privileges and Immunities of Specialized Agencies are important examples of treaties governing various aspects of immunity.

KEY POINTS

- Immunity prevents a court from trying cases involving States or certain individuals who enjoy special status under international law.

- Immunity can apply to States or certain categories of individuals.

- Immunity is different from non-justiciability in that the former relates to the court's inability to try a case due to the identity of the culprit while the latter relates to inability to try a case due to the subject matter before the court.

The question to ask is: why do States confer immunity on one another? Why should Candoman courts not be able to try crimes committed by Rutamu against it? Why should Rutamuan courts not be able to try crimes committed by Candoman diplomats?

8.2 The rationale behind immunity

There are several reasons for the existence of immunity, but it is only necessary to enumerate a few of these here.

8.2.1 Equality of States

International law generally regards States as equal. This implies that no State can sit in judgement over another, which will be the case if one State were to subject another to its jurisdiction.

. . . .

● *The Schooner Exchange v. MacFaddon* 11 US 116 (1912)

An American ship, which was improperly seized by Napoleon of France, had sailed to an American port where the previous owners brought a claim to repossess it. The US Supreme Court rejected the claim, despite acknowledging that the ship had been improperly seized by Napoleon in the first place.

Marshall Ch. J, delivering the judgment of the US Supreme Court, had laid down the principle (at p. 137) that:

> The jurisdiction of the nation within its own territory is necessarily exclusive and absolute. It is susceptible of no limitation not imposed by itself. Any restriction upon it, deriving validity from an external source, would imply a diminution of its sovereignty to the extent of the restriction, and an investment of that sovereignty to the same extent in that power which could impose such restriction.

The Court then went on to state that:

> The world being composed of distinct sovereignties, possessing *equal rights and equal* independence, whose mutual benefit is promoted by intercourse with each other, and by an interchange of those good offices which humanity dictates and its wants require, all sovereigns *have consented to a relaxation in practice*, in cases under certain peculiar circumstances, of that absolute and complete jurisdiction within their respective territories which sovereignty confers. [Emphasis added]

Thus clearly immunity arises in recognition of the equality of States, secured by the waiver of the absolute jurisdiction each State has over all within its territory.

. . . .

● *Union of India and another v. Bilash Chand Jain and anr* (2001) 3 CALLT 352 HC

A Calcutta High Court relied on these provisions and the Diplomatic Relations (Convention Act) 1972 to reject an application to try the former Socialist Republic of Romania in India for an unsettled debt for services rendered to a certain Ice Chimica.

Justice Chattopadhyay, referring to an earlier judgment by Justice Sabyasachl Mukherji, said (at para. 17) that:

> the root of diplomatic immunity lies in the principle that, one equal cannot have jurisdiction over another equal. In other words, in the international field the States of Romania and India are both sovereign. Thus according to the strict theory of sovereignty neither the State of India nor the Courts of India can pronounce upon the State of Romania.

. . . .

● *Jurisdictional Immunities of the State (Germany v. Italy; Greece intervening)* (2012)
   ICJ REP 99

At p. 117, para. 37:

> Germany requests the Court ... to find that Italy has failed to respect the jurisdictional immunity which Germany enjoys under international law by allowing civil claims to be brought against it in

the Italian courts, seeking reparation for injuries caused by violations of international humanitarian law committed by the German Reich during the Second World War.

The Court held Italy to be in breach (at para. 57):

> The Court considers that the rule of State immunity … derives from the principle of sovereign equality of States, which, as Article 2, paragraph 1, of the Charter of the United Nations makes clear, is one of the fundamental principles of the international legal order … Exceptions to the immunity of the State represent a departure from the principle of sovereign equality. Immunity may represent a departure from the principle of territorial sovereignty and the jurisdiction which flows from it.

8.2.2 Necessity of interstate relations

Aside from the question of equality, it is arguable that immunity developed as a necessity of interstate relations. The nature of interactions among States in the modern world makes it almost impracticable for the engine of that relation to be kept alive if those responsible for representing the interest of Candoma in Rutamu and of Rutamu in Candoma are to operate with the eternal fear that their activities, no matter how big or small, will be subjected to the jurisdiction of their host States.

example

> Practically speaking, the detention and trial of several staff of the Candoma Embassy, including the country's ambassador to Rutamu, for failure to obey traffic regulation and penalty charges in Rutamu, will most likely affect the speed with which the Candoman embassy in Rutamu will grant visas to nationals of Rutamu who may wish to visit Candoma, or process work permits for its businessmen and women.

It was in testimony to the practice amongst States to exclude foreign States and diplomats on their territory from domestic prosecution, that the law of immunity developed. In the *Jurisdictional Immunities* case (see section 8.2.1), the International Court of Justice (ICJ) observed (at p. 123, para. 56) that:

> the rule of State immunity had been adopted as a general rule of customary international law solidly rooted in the current practice of States.

8.2.3 Unenforceability of judgments against foreign States

It is a fundamental reality of international relations that judgments against acts of foreign States may not be enforceable against that State. It is one thing for Candoma to breach the laws of Rutamu, but it is another for Rutamu to seek to enforce judgments arising from that case against Candoma. Whereas foreign judgments are generally enforceable in most ordinary cases, enforcing judgments against foreign States will have to cross the hurdle of immunity. The issue of enforceability of judgment against foreign States is so sensitive that in countries like India it is important for the operation of the law that any Indian individual or enterprise that wishes to enforce judgment against a foreign State in India first seeks the permission of the State.

In India, a private citizen who desires to sue a foreign government is required by law to meet two distinct criteria of Section 86 Sub-section of the 1956 Code of Civil Procedure (Amendment) Act of India. The first, Section 86(1), deals with permission to institute a proceeding: 'No foreign State may be sued in any Court otherwise competent to try the suit except with the consent of the Central Government Certified in writing by a Secretary to that Government'. The second, Section 86(3), regards permission to enforce judgment: 'Except with the consent of the Central Government certified in writing by a Secretary to that Government, no decree shall be executed against the property of any foreign State.'

In the UK, the State Immunity Act 1978 provides at section 3(1) that 'A State is not immune as respective proceedings relating to— (a) a commercial transaction entered into by the State'. However, this is not the only thing that has to be proved before English courts will permit the enforcement of a foreign judgment.

● *NML Capital Ltd v. Republic of Argentina* [2011] UKSC 31

The Supreme Court held (at [15]) that in order for a foreign judgment to be enforced by English courts:

> The Plaintiff had to establish that a number of conditions were satisfied in order to claim successfully on the foreign judgment. In particular, he had to establish that the foreign court had had jurisdiction over the defendant in accordance with the English rules of private international law and the judgment had to be final and conclusive on the merits.

In other words, where a foreign State would have been entitled to immunity in the substantive case, the English court would not grant an application to enforce the judgment in the UK. The court also spoke about conditions such as whether the enforcement proceedings related to the proceedings relating to the transaction that gave rise to the award for the purposes of section 3(1)(a) of the State Immunity Act.

● *AIC Ltd v. Central Government of Nigeria* [2003] EWHC 1357 (QB)

Stanley Burnton J stated (at [24]):

> In my judgment, the proceedings resulting from an application to register a judgment relate not to the transaction or transactions underlying the original judgment, but to that judgment. The issues in such proceedings are concerned essentially with the question of whether the original judgment was regular or not.

See also *Svenska Petroleum Exploration AB v. Government of the Republic of Lithuania (No. 2)* [2005] EWHC 2437 (Comm).

What these cases disclose is that there is an enormous burden of proof that those claiming to enforce jurisdiction against foreign States have to discharge.

thinking points

- *Enumerate the rationale behind State immunity.*
- *To what extent do you think these rationale make sense?*

State immunity

State immunity is concerned with conduct attributed to the State or with assets belonging to a State, as opposed to conduct attributed solely to an individual acting as an agent of a State (in which case the State also bears civil responsibility). This form of immunity stems from the concept of State sovereignty and equality, and the associated principle that it is not possible for another State to pass judgment in court on the acts of another State. It is with this rationale that the law on State immunity has developed. It has helped to shape the approaches taken and explains, at times, why both national and international courts have taken a strict approach when determining if an immunity stands. This was confirmed by the US Supreme Court in the *Schooner Exchange* case (see Judge Marshall's statement in section 8.2.1).

The US Supreme Court's emphasis on the notion of consent of the State itself being required before an immunity can be set aside by another State's court is a principle as old as immunity itself. This giving of consent is known as a waiver, whereby the immunity is set aside enabling prosecution. A State can waive immunity for the State itself or for individuals.

8.3.1 Approaches to State immunity

There are two approaches to State immunity; absolute and restrictive immunity. Absolute immunity prevents any proceedings from being heard before a court against another State's actions or conduct, whereas restrictive immunity enables non-sovereign acts to be tried before another State's courts. In essence, absolute immunity is applicable to pure acts of sovereigns, also known as acts *jure imperii*, in contradistinction from commercial acts of sovereigns, also known as *jure gestionis*. Absolute immunity developed when States acted solely in respect of sovereign matters, or acts that were essentially public in nature and concerned the State. As Lord Denning put it in *Trendtex* (see section 8.4.1) (at p. 366):

> A century ago no sovereign state engaged in commercial activities. It kept to the traditional functions of a sovereign—to maintain law and order—to conduct foreign affairs—and to see to the defence of the country. It was in those days that England—with most other countries—adopted the rule of absolute immunity. It was adopted because it was considered to be the rule of international law at that time.

example

> If Candoma orders cement from Rutamu to use in building military barracks in Candoma, or if it impounds a Rutamuan ship which is berthed in one of the Candoman ports, such acts are acts of sovereignty in that they are public acts by a sovereign deriving from the essence of the State as a sovereign. These are acts called *jure imperii* and attract absolute immunity, and it is with this approach to immunity that the law on State immunity commenced.

Sir Hersch Lauterpacht noted that even by 1951, many European countries had abandoned the doctrine of absolute immunity and adopted that of restrictive immunity (see 'The problem of jurisdictional immunities of foreign states' (1951) 28 BYBIL 220).

example

Today, Candoma regularly imports furniture items for the offices of its civil servants, engages in selling its petroleum resources to Rutamu, and imports notebooks from Rutamu for the use of students in Candoma. While these latter were acts done by the sovereign State of Candoma, they are not sovereign acts in themselves in that they are not acts which only sovereigns could carry out. They are acts open to private individuals. While the Candoman civil servants are no doubt employees of the government, the procurement of furniture for their apartments and offices from Rutamu, either from the State of Rutamu or individual suppliers in Rutamu, are acts that private ordinary individuals of any State could do. They are not sovereign acts such as impounding a Rutamuan ship. No private individual could do this.

Absolute immunity exempts acts of sovereign Candoma from the jurisdiction of Rutamu.

As commercial interaction between States grew, as shown in the example of Candoma importing commercial items from Rutamu, some States still applied only absolute immunity to such transactions. Thus, in our examples should Candoma refuse to pay for the items it imported for its civil servants, it would be entitled to absolute immunity in the Rutamuan courts. Clearly, this disadvantages the Rutamuan nationals who sold the goods to Candoma since they are left without the protection of their own laws.

example

Meanwhile, Candoma, in its own transactions with Rutamu, began to distinguish between sovereign acts and acts of a private nature. Hence, when a Rutamuan national sells some furniture items to Candoma to build hospitals or houses for its civil servants and Candoma fails to honour the terms, Candoma allows its own nationals to sue Rutamu before the courts in Candoma. This puts Rutamu in a bad spot since, in the same circumstances as described previously, it is unable to protect its own citizen because it recognizes the absolute immunity of Candoma before its own courts. In the earlier example, the Candoman court was able to try Rutamu in an action brought by the Candoman citizen because Candoma believes that when a State engages in acts of a purely commercial nature, which any private individual could have conducted, such acts are precluded from immunity. Thus, for Candoma, immunity is no longer absolute for all purposes, but could be restrictive where the nature of the transaction is purely commercial and private. In other words, such acts are *jure gestionis*.

As has been explained, restrictive immunity:

> relies on the distinction between *acta jure imperii* (acts of government) and *acta jure gestionis* (acts of a commercial or private law nature). It is now more or less generally accepted that states can be sued for the latter, although it is not always clear what falls under this exception. (Simon de Smet, 'The immunity of heads of state in US courts after the decision of the International Court of Justice' (2003) 72 Nordic JIL 313, 315)

The basis of restrictive immunity thus lies in the realization that:

> during this century [the twentieth century] the individual states have to an increasing extent and in more or less outspoken forms come to act as trading partners. It is a natural consequence of such a development that the rules on state immunity have had to undergo changes. In a situation where states so to speak have taken over the functions which were previously left to private legal subjects it has been found unreasonable if states were not to act on all fours

with such individual legal subjects. (Gören Melander, 'Waiver of immunity' (1976) 45 Nordisk Tidsskrift for Int'l Ret 22, 26)

In the *Victory Transport Inc. v. Comisaria General* (see section 8.4.1) the US Court explained that:

> The purpose of the restrictive theory of sovereign immunity is to try to accommodate the interest of individuals doing business with foreign governments in having their legal rights determined by the courts, with the interest of foreign governments in being free to perform certain political acts without undergoing the embarrassment or hindrance of defending the propriety of such acts before foreign courts.

8.3.2 State immunity: the law and practice

A survey of State practice and provisions of some international treaties and instruments on immunity reveals that the restrictive immunity approach has become the preferred choice, although it is by no means subject to universal acceptance. While most European countries, North America, and some African countries have endorsed restrictive immunity, many States are yet to do so. For instance, China still applies absolute immunity.

● *Democratic Republic of the Congo v. FG Hemisphere Associates LLC* FACV Nos 5, 6 & 7 of 2010, HONG KONG COURT OF FINAL APPEAL

FG Hemisphere Associates (FGH), a company which specializes in the recovery of sovereign debt, sought to recover funds from the Democratic Republic of Congo (the DRC) due from the construction of a hydro-electric facility undertaken by a Yugoslavian company, Energoinvest, in the 1980s. FGH sought to enforce two arbitration awards in Hong Kong against fees due to the Congo by China Railway Group. The DRC successfully challenged the suit on the ground that it enjoyed immunity. The Hong Kong Court of Appeal overturned that decision on the basis that Hong Kong recognized the doctrine of restrictive (as opposed to absolute) sovereign immunity. The DRC then appealed to the Hong Kong Court of Final Appeal (CFA).

It was held that the DRC was entitled to immunity.

The majority of the CFA said that, although Hong Kong practised restrictive immunity and enjoyed judicial autonomy from China, articles 13 and 19 of the Basic Law provides that the Chinese Central Government shall be responsible for foreign affairs relating to Hong Kong and that the Hong Kong courts have no jurisdiction over '*acts of state such as defence and foreign affairs*'. They held that, since China applies a doctrine of absolute sovereign immunity, so must Hong Kong lest '*a divergent state immunity policy [between Hong Kong and China] embarrass and prejudice the State in its conduct of foreign affairs.*'

(See James Rogers, 'Sovereign immunity absolute in Hong Kong', July 2011, available at http://www.nortonrosefulbright.com/knowledge/publications/94487/sovereign-immunity-absolute-in-hong-kong. See also Yilin Ding, 'Absolute, restrictive, or something more: did Beijing choose the right type of sovereign immunity for Hong Kong' (2010) 26(2) Emory Int'l L Rev 997.)

Recent studies reveal that while restrictive immunity has become more and more popular, there is still some reluctance among several States to sign up to it. As Pierre-Hugues Verdier and Erik Voeten argue in their draft paper, 'How does customary international law change? The case of state immunity', at pp. 12–13 (working paper 2014):

> Other countries such as the Netherlands, Austria, Germany and France also adopted restrictive immunity. The trend, however, played itself out slowly and was far from universal. In particular, the USSR and China became increasingly vocal in protesting exercises of jurisdiction against them and resisted UN efforts to codify restrictive immunity. (Boguslavsky 1979; Osakwe 1982; Memorandum Presented by Mr. Nikolai A. Ushakov, UN Doc. A/CN.4/371 (1983).) Some Third World countries also resisted restrictive immunity. The UK and Commonwealth states were also holdouts, until the former adopted restrictive immunity in 1977. The trend then accelerated substantially from 1980 to 2000. In 2011, seventy-five of the 118 countries in our study practised restrictive immunity.

8.3.3 The International Law Commission's approach to immunity

The International Law Commission (ILC), mandated by a UN General Assembly resolution (GA Res. 32/151, 19 December 1977), conducted an in-depth study bringing together the law on State territorial jurisdiction with foreign State sovereignty. The result of this work was the 1991 Draft Articles on Jurisdictional Immunities of States and Their Property. Following a further Ad Hoc Committee established in 2000, the General Assembly adopted the 2004 UN Convention on Jurisdictional Immunities of States and Their Property (GA Res. 53/86, 16 December 2004) which reflects the 1991 Draft Articles. The 2004 UN Convention adopted a restrictive approach with Article 5 and Article 10:

> A state enjoys immunity, in respect of itself and its property, from the jurisdiction of the courts of another State subject to the provisions of the present Convention. (Article 5)
>
> If a State engages in a commercial transaction with a foreign natural or juridical person and, by virtue of the applicable rules of private international law, differences relating to the commercial transaction fall within the jurisdiction of a court of another State, the State cannot invoke immunity from that jurisdiction in a proceeding arising out of that commercial transaction. (Article 10(1))

The 2004 UN Convention only envisions State immunity as applying to official acts by the removal of commercial activity from the scope of immunity. The 1972 European Convention on State Immunity took a similar approach, and achieved this by:

> Taking into account the fact that there is in international law a tendency to restrict the cases in which a State may claim immunity before foreign courts;
>
> Desiring to establish in their mutual relations common rules relating to the scope of the immunity of one State from the jurisdiction of the courts of another State, and designed to ensure compliance with judgments given against another State;
>
> (Preamble to the 1972 European Convention on State Immunity)

The 1972 European Convention then goes on to list the situations in which immunity will not be applied or set aside and the scope of State immunity through Articles 1–15.

The 2004 UN Convention, whilst not yet in force, has come to be considered as reflective of international consensus as States that have traditionally taken the absolute immunity approach have signed, but not ratified, the 2004 UN Convention. As stated previously, China does not accept the restrictive immunity approach and the Hong Kong Court of Final Appeal made this clear in the *DRC v. FG Hemisphere* case:

> The Convention [2004 UN Convention] has no binding force on China, and moreover it cannot be the basis of assessing China's principled position on relevant issues. After signature of the Convention, the position of China in maintaining absolute immunity has not been changed, and has never applied or recognized the so-called principle or theory of 'restrictive immunity'. [*DRC v FG Hemisphere Associates LLC*, Hong Kong Court of Final Appeal, judgment of 8 June 2011, §202]

thinking points

- *Distinguish between absolute and restrictive sovereignty.*
- *How can you explain the rationale behind the difference?*

8.4 Distinguishing between absolute and restrictive immunity

Immunity is a fundamental aspect of international law and State relations and any claim that a State is not entitled to it, except in situations where the State has waived its immunity (see later), must be founded on credible grounds. As said earlier, a generic ground for denying immunity to States is if the transaction concerned in a case is of a commercial, and not of a sovereign, nature. Yet, telling whether an act is sovereign or commercial for the purpose of immunity is not an exact science, and State practice has thrown up such a babble of decisions that it is stretching credulity too thin to say that it is easy to calibrate the variables.

In an effort to remove this uncertainty, some treaties and domestic legislation specifically enumerate the kind of transactions considered to be commercial in nature and therefore not a sovereign act. The problem with this approach is the impracticability of establishing whether or not the lists are exhaustive, whether there is scope for expanding the lists, and whether or not they provide enough discretion for the courts to consider the true nature of an act of State or its conduct. Courts have also developed some tests to guide them in determining when a transaction is either a sovereign act or a commercial act. While these tests vary in their usefulness and acceptability, they have so far proved to be widely used. We will now consider what these tests are and how they have worked in practice.

8.4.1 Purpose of the transaction

In determining whether a foreign State's act is *jure imperii* or *jure gestionis* many States often look at the purpose for which a sovereign commercial act is done. The rationale behind the 'purpose' test is that if a sovereign government engages in a commercial transaction, which any ordinary private person can undertake, we should look at the purpose served by that transaction. If the purpose is to serve a State or public function, as opposed to private ones, then such should still attract immunity. In other words, the act is commercial, which normally puts its immunity in jeopardy, but the purpose is public and thus sovereign. Then the absolute immunity, not the restrictive one, applies in such a situation.

The 2004 UN Convention endorses this approach:

> In determining whether a contract or transaction is a 'commercial transaction' under paragraph 1(c) reference should be made primarily to the nature of the contract or transaction, but its purpose should also be taken into account if the parties to the contract or transaction have so agreed, or if, in the practice of the State of the forum, that purpose is relevant to determining the non-commercial character of the contract or transaction. (Article 2(2))

● **Union of India and anr v. Bilash Chand Jain** (2001) 3 CALLT 352 HC

An Indian company sought to recover a debt due from the Socialist Republic of Romania. Romania claimed immunity. The court considered the distinction between absolute immunity and restrictive immunity, and applied the 'purpose' test. It stated (at [26]) that:

> Whenever and wherever a foreign State either acting by itself or through its agents or instrumentalities engages in ordinary or commercial transactions with parties or persons of another State, in all such cases, the sovereign comes down from his high pedestal. The sovereign engages in businesses and commerce and subjects itself to the ordinary incidents of commerce and industry and attempts at profit makings. In such cases there will be disputes, and resolution of disputes, and the necessity of the consequent satisfaction of the rights and liabilities arising either in favour of or against the foreign sovereign. The foreign sovereign might well have to sue in a foreign Court and might equally will be sued in a foreign Court. No principle of international amity or the maintenance of dignity of an international sovereign in the modern days requires that the Courts of law stay their hands against a foreign sovereign only because he is a foreign sovereign.

The court found that the restrictive theory of immunity prevented Romania from claiming immunity in this case. In coming to this conclusion, the court reasoned (at [27] and [28]) that:

> The transactions in which the foreign sovereign has got involved are to be examined. If on such examination it appears that the sovereign has been dealing in the matters in question as a sovereign, and not as an ordinary participator in the matters in issue, if the dignity of the sovereign has been maintained as such and at a level not accessible to persons below the rank of absolute sovereignty, then and in that event, the Courts will not touch, those matters, or embarrass the sovereign.
> If, however, this cannot be established, and it will be a difficult task to establish this in ordinary commercial matters, then the Courts will happily go ahead and it is the duty of the Central Secretariat to let them go ahead happily.

As for the purpose of the transaction, the court said (at [30]) that:

> we find not a whiff or smell of sovereignty in the transactions brought before the Court. The plaintiff wanted agency commission. *This was for boosting up the business of the State of Romania*. Thus in these matters the State of Romania remained a sovereign no doubt but it was not doing a classical prototype sovereign job. [Emphasis added]

Clearly, the court admitted that the transaction itself was a sovereign act but the purpose which it served was not sovereign.

As useful as the 'purpose' test might seem in helping the court to determine instances of restrictive sovereignty, not every State is happy with it. The UK, for instance, does not think the purpose test is necessary at all.

....

● *Trendtex Trading Corp. v. Central Bank of Nigeria* [1977] 2 WLR 356

In July 1975, the Central Bank of Nigeria (CBN) ordered some cement from London to build government barracks. Due to congestion at the Lagos port, the ship could not discharge its cargo and the cement went into demurrage. The Bank declined to make payments claimed for the price and for demurrage. Nigeria had argued that it was entitled to immunity since the purpose of the commercial transaction was to buy cement to build government barracks. This implied that this was an act *jure imperii* attracting absolute immunity.

It was held that Nigeria was liable. The court said that the purpose of the transaction should not matter. On behalf of the court, Lord Denning rationalized the 'purpose' test (at 370) thus:

> It was suggested that the original contracts for cement were made by the Ministry of Defence of Nigeria: and that the cement was for the building of barracks for the army. On this account it was said that the contracts of purchase were acts of a governmental nature, *jure imperii*, and not of a commercial nature, *jure gestionis*. They were like a contract of purchase of boots for the army. *But I do not think this should affect the question of immunity*. If a government department goes into the market places of the world and buys boots or cement—as a commercial transaction—that government department should be subject to all the rules of the market place. *The seller is not concerned with the purpose to which the purchaser intends to put the goods*. [Emphasis added]

....

● *I Congreso del Partido* [1981] 2 ALL ER 1064

The House of Lords ruled that the 'purpose' test is not enough. Lord Wilberforce said that:

> in considering, under the restrictive theory whether state immunity should be granted or not, the court must consider the whole context in which the claim against the state is made, with a view to deciding whether the relevant act(s) upon which the claim is based, should, in that context, be considered as fairly within an area of activity, trading or commercial, or otherwise of a private law character, in which the state has chosen to engage, or whether the relevant act(s) should be considered as having been done outside that area, and within the sphere of governmental or sovereign activity.

....

● *Holland v Lampen Wolfe* [2000] 1 WLR 1573

The House of Lords said that:

> In the present case the context is all important. The overall context was that of the provision of educational services to military personnel and their families stationed on a U.S. base overseas. The maintenance of the base itself was plainly a sovereign activity ... this looks about as imperial an activity as could be imagined. But that is not enough to determine the issue.
>
> At first sight, the writing of a memorandum by a civilian educational services officer in relation to an educational programme provided by civilian staff employed by a university seems far removed from the kind of act that would ordinarily be characterised as something done *iure imperii*. But regard must be had to the place where the programme was being provided and to the persons by whom it was being provided and who it was designed to benefit—where did it happen and whom did it involve? The provision of the programme on the base at Menwith Hill was designed to serve the needs of U.S. personnel on the base, and it was provided by U.S. citizens who were working there on behalf of a U.S. university. The whole activity was designed as part of the process of maintaining forces and associated civilians on the base by U.S. personnel to serve the needs of the U.S. military authorities. The memorandum was written on the base in response to complaints which are alleged to have been made by U.S. servicemen about the behaviour of the appellant, who is also a U.S. citizen, while she was working there. On these facts the acts of the respondent seem to me to fall well within the area of sovereign activity.

. . . .

● *Claim Against the Empire of Iran* [1963] 45 ILR 57

The German Federal Constitutional Court said (at 81) that purpose alone is insufficient to distinguish between *jure imperii* and *jure gestionis*.

> As a means for determining the distinction between acts *jure imperii* and *jure gestionis* one should rather refer to the nature of the state transaction or the resulting legal relationships, and not to the motive or purpose of the state activity. It thus depends upon whether the foreign state has acted in exercise of its sovereign authority, that is in public law, or like a private person, that is in private law.

Perhaps, the most persuasive reason for the reluctance of many States to accept the 'purpose' test as the sole criterion for distinction between *jure imperii* and *jure gestionis* was expressed in the following case.

. . . .

● *Victory Transport Inc. v. Comisaria General De Abastecimientos y Transportes* 336 F2D 354 [1964]

Spain ordered some shipment of wheat from the USA. The consignment was shipped to Spain, but the ship sustained damage due to its size when it unloaded at a Spanish port that was considered unsuitable for its size. When Spain refused to pay for damages or submit itself for arbitration, the plaintiff applied for an order before a US court to compel arbitration and to serve notices on the defendant in its Madrid office. Spain objected on the basis of immunity.

The court held that Spain was liable, and that the act involved was *jus gestionis*. On the relevance of the 'purpose' test in distinguishing between absolute immunity and restrictive immunity, the court said (at 360) that:

> Others have looked to the purpose of the transaction, categorizing as *jure imperii* all activities in which the object of performance is public in character. But this test is even more unsatisfactory, for conceptually the modern sovereign always acts for a public purpose.

Implied in this statement is that if we accept that a commercial act by a sovereign could be regarded as a sovereign act on the basis that it is for a public and not private purpose, then we might as well conclude that every single commercial transaction by a sovereign will be for public purposes and thus still qualify them for absolute immunity.

thinking points

- *Explain the purpose test.*
- *On what basis did the UK court reject the purpose test in* Trendtex?
- *What does* I Congreso del Partido *add to the 'purpose' test?*

8.4.2 Nature of the transaction

The more widely acceptable test is to consider the nature of the transaction. In situations where a government body or institution engages in acts that are more commercial in nature, State immunity is unlikely to apply, as it serves no official State purpose other than in its commercial dealings. This was the approach adopted by the UK court in *Trendtex* (see section 8.4.1). In addition to Lord Denning's statement quoted previously, the learned judge also said (at 370) that:

> There is another answer. Trendtex here are not suing on the contracts of purchase. They are claiming on the letter of credit which is an entirely separate contract. It was a straightforward commercial transaction. The letter of credit was issued in London through a London bank in the ordinary course of commercial dealings. It is completely within the territorial jurisdiction of our courts. I do not think it is open to the Government of Nigeria to claim sovereign immunity in respect of it . . .

Here the UK court distinguished between the purpose for which the goods were bought from the nature of the transaction. The mere fact that goods are purchased by a State or one of its organs does not automatically mean it will be an act of State. Through analysing the nature of the transaction it is possible to reflect a fuller picture of the type of conduct undertaken and prevent many commercial acts from having State immunity applied unnecessarily. This is particularly relevant in today's globalized marketplace. If it were the case that the commercial acts of a State were subject to immunity there would be a disincentive for companies and individuals to contract with State bodies and organs as they would have no recourse to the courts should there be any legal issues which arise; be it lack of payment or breach of contract.

The intricacy of the 'nature' test emerges more sharply in the following case.

● *Roy v. South Africa*, 2013 ONSC 4633

The plaintiff had been employed by the High Commission for South Africa in Ottawa since 1988; first as an administrative clerk, then as a consular clerk and most recently as assistant consular for immigration. In the latter senior role, she was responsible for the intake and processing of all visa and permit applications, diplomatic protocol, maintenance orders, pension and outstanding revenue matters, custom declarations, birth, marriage and death certificate processing, email inquiries, and personal interviews. Due to consolidation of various consular services from Ottawa to Toronto, the plaintiff's employment was terminated in 2010. The plaintiff sued for wrongful dismissal and issued a statement of claim on April 4, 2012.

The question before the court was whether South Africa was entitled to immunity since, by virtue of section 3 of the State Immunity Act of Canada, 'a foreign state is immune from the jurisdiction of any court in Canada'. Section 5 of the Act provides an exception to this immunity 'in any proceedings that relate to any commercial activity of the foreign state.'

The court reviewed a long line of similar cases and came to the conclusion that South Africa was not entitled to immunity because the act complained of by the plaintiff was not one of a sovereign but of a commercial nature. Justice Tranmer (at [56]) said:

> I find that the allegation that the plaintiff was targeted for termination because of illness does not touch on any sovereign affair of the Republic of South Africa, but rather is an employee issue most closely related to commercial activity. The same can be said for the reason given for the termination, namely that immigration and consular services have been largely consolidated.

Here, the court found that sacking an employee for reasons of illness and due to consolidation of the embassy functions and officers were commercial acts, not sovereign acts.

KEY POINTS

- It is important to look at the nature, not just the purpose, of a commercial act.

- *Roy v. South Africa* shows that a sovereign act may be commercial in nature.

8.4.3 Subject matter

As said earlier, the practice has developed of specifically enumerating the subject matter of transactions that will be considered commercial acts in treaties and domestic laws. For example, the 2004 UN Convention provides some guidance as to what constitutes a commercial transaction:

'commercial transaction' means:

(i) any commercial contract or transaction for the sale of goods or supply of services;

(iii) any contract for a loan or other transaction of a financial nature, including any obligation of guarantee or of indemnity in respect of any such loan or transaction;

(iii) any other contract or transaction of a commercial, industrial, trading or professional nature, but not including a contract of employment of persons. (Article 1(c))

The US courts have taken a similar approach in determining certain acts that will be considered exclusively sovereign in nature.

● *Victory Transport Incorporation v Comisaria General de Abastecimientos y Transportes* 336 F2D 354 (2ND CIR., 1964)

The Court said (at 361) that:

Since the State Department's failure or refusal to suggest immunity is significant, we are disposed to deny a claim of sovereign immunity that has not been 'recognized and allowed' by the State Department unless it is plain that the activity in question falls within one of the categories of strictly political or public acts about which sovereigns have traditionally been quite sensitive. Such acts are generally limited to the following categories:

(1) internal administrative acts, such as expulsion of an alien.

(2) legislative acts, such as nationalization.

(3) acts concerning the armed forces.

(4) acts concerning diplomatic activity.

(5) public loans.

We do not think that the restrictive theory adopted by the State Department requires sacrificing the interests of private litigants to international comity in other than these limited categories. Should diplomacy require enlargement of these categories, the State Department can file a suggestion of immunity with the court. Should diplomacy require contraction of these categories, the State Department can issue a new or clarifying policy pronouncement.

The US court has taken a proactive approach in providing guidance as to what it will consider as a sovereign act based upon the subject matter. These categories are somewhat vague and further clarity would be beneficial. As seen in the judgment, the court calls on the State Department to provide further guidance should it wish to change or extend these categories.

thinking points

- *Explain what the 'subject matter' test involves.*
- *What did the court suggest doing in the* Victory Transport case *when the State is silent on providing guidance on transactions that are commercial?*
- *Identify the weaknesses in the 'subject matter' test.*

8.4.4 Two-stage contextual approach

A further approach was adopted by the UK House of Lords in the *I Congreso del Partido* case. Here, the House of Lords required two tests to be satisfied before the act would be considered private and therefore not subject to State immunity. First, the initial act had to be capable of being concluded by a citizen and, finally, the act under dispute also needed to be a private law act possible for a citizen to conclude:

> When therefore a claim is brought against a state ... and state immunity is claimed, it is necessary to consider what is the relevant act which forms the basis of the claim: is this, under the old terminology, an act 'jure gestionis' or is it an act 'jure imperii': is it ... a 'private act' or is it a 'sovereign or public act,' a private act meaning in this context an act of a private law character such as a private citizen might have entered into? It is upon this point that the arguments in these appeals is focussed. (*I Congreso del Partido* [1981] 3 WLR 328, 262)
>
> Even cases based upon the plain absolute rule might involve similar problems ... Under the 'restrictive' theory the court has first to characterise the activity into which the defendant state has entered. Having done this, and (assumedly) found it to be of a commercial, or private law, character, it may take the view that contractual breaches ... fall within the same sphere of activity. It should then be for the defendant state to make a case ... that the act complained of is outside that sphere, and within that of sovereign action. (*I Congreso del Partido* [1981] 3 WLR 328, 265)
>
> The conclusion which emerges is that in considering, under the 'restrictive' theory whether state immunity should be granted or not, the court must consider the whole context in which the claim against the state is made, with a view to deciding whether the relevant act(s) upon which the claim is based, should, in that context, be considered as fairly within an area of activity, trading or commercial, or otherwise of a private law character, in which the state has chosen to engage, or whether the relevant act(s) should be considered as having been done outside that area, and within the sphere of governmental or sovereign activity. (*I Congreso del Partido* [1981] 3 WLR 328, 267)

This approach was followed by the Canadian Supreme Court and provides a good illustration of the two-stage contextual approach being applied. The Canadian court held that despite the fact that the nature of the transaction, being an employment contract, was considered commercial the context in which it was adopted was sovereign, as it related to Canadian employees on a US military base within Canadian territory. (See *United States v. The Public Service Alliance of Canada* (1993) 32 ILM 1.) It appears that such an approach provides a broad discretion to be applied while truly distinguishing the kind of act/conduct undertaken. Yet it may also provide opportunities for courts to interpret the context widely and thus increase the scope of State immunity.

KEY POINT The 'two-stage contextual' test involves determining twice the nature of the commercial act involved, first the initial act and then, second, the act that gives rise to the case.

8.4.5 Third party being directed by States?

Courts have also had to consider what happens in situations where a State directs a non-State body to do something. Will this come under a governmental act or not? The UK is of the view that this is not a government act.

> It is apparent from Lord Wilberforce's statement of principle that the ultimate test of what constitutes an act *jure imperii* is whether the act in question is of its own character a governmental act, as opposed to an act which any private citizen can perform. It follows that, in the case of acts done by a separate entity, it is not enough that the entity should have acted on the directions of the state, because such an act need not possess the character of a governmental act. To attract immunity under section 14(2), therefore, what is done by the separate entity must be something which possesses that character. An example of such an act performed by a separate entity is to be found in *Arango v. Guzman Travel Advisors Corporation* (1980) 621 F.2d 1371 in which Dominicana (the national airline of the Dominican Republic), faced with a claim by a passenger in respect of inconvenience suffered in 'involuntary rerouting,' was held entitled to plead sovereign immunity under the United States Foreign Sovereign Immunities Act 1976, on the ground that it was impressed into service, by Dominican immigration officials acting pursuant to the country's laws, to perform the functions which led to the rerouting of the plaintiff. Reavley J., delivering the judgment of the court, said, at p. 1379:
>
> > 'Dominicana acted merely as an arm or agent of the Dominican government in carrying out this assigned role, and, as such, is entitled to the same immunity from any liability arising *from that governmental function* as would inure to the government, itself.' (Emphasis supplied.)
>
> But where an act done by a separate entity of the state on the directions of the state does not possess the character of a governmental act, the entity will not be entitled to state immunity, though it may be able to invoke a substantive defence such as force majeure despite the fact that it is an entity of the state: see, e.g., *C. Czarnikow Ltd. v. Centrala Handlu Zagranicznego Rolimpex* [1979] A.C. 351. Likewise, in the absence of such character, the mere fact that the purpose or motive of the act was to serve the purposes of the state will not be sufficient to enable the separate entity to claim immunity under section 14(2) of the Act. (*Kuwait Airways Corp. v. Iraqi Airways Co.* [1995] 1 WLR 1147, 1160)

The focus here is on the character of the act undertaken and whether or not it was governmental. The purpose of the act being governmental will not be enough to have immunity applied to it and thus characterized as a governmental act.

8.5 International crimes and State immunity

Despite the recent trend of domestic courts determining that State immunity does not bar them from hearing cases related to civil torts brought for violations of international law or war crimes, the ICJ has since ruled that States cannot be sued before domestic courts under the law of tort for acts committed by their armed forces as well as for enforcement of judgments in foreign courts related to reparations. It is important to note, however, that this does not affect the law of immunity for individuals being held criminally liable for international law violations and war crimes. In a 2012 decision the ICJ stated that:

> State practice in the form of judicial decisions supports the proposition that State immunity for *acta jure imperii* continues to extend to civil proceedings for acts occasioning death, personal injury or damage to property committed by the armed forces and other organs of a State in the conduct of

armed conflict, even if the relevant acts take place on the territory of the forum State. That practice is accompanied by opinio juris, as demonstrated by the positions taken by States and the jurisprudence of a number of national courts which have made clear that they considered that customary international law required immunity. The almost complete absence of contrary jurisprudence is also significant, as is the absence of any statements by States in connection with the work of the International Law Commission regarding State immunity and the adoption of the United Nations Convention or, so far as the Court has been able to discover, in any other context asserting that customary international law does not require immunity in such cases.

In light of the foregoing, the Court considers that customary international law continues to require that a State be accorded immunity in proceedings for torts allegedly committed on the territory of another State by its armed forces and other organs of State in the course of conducting an armed conflict. That conclusion is confirmed by the judgments of the European Court of Human Rights to which the Court has referred. (*Jurisdictional Immunities of the State (Germany v. Italy: Greece intervening)* (Judgment) February 2012, 77–78)

It is worth mentioning that while the 2004 UN Convention provides for the exclusion of commercial acts from State immunity, this restriction on State immunity has not gone so far as to cover human rights and international humanitarian law, which has been claimed as being intentional on the drafters' part.

> It is true that the long-term erosion of state immunity in civil cases leading to the adoption of the Convention has largely been in the field of private international law matters, such as commercial contracts and torts involving insurable conduct, such as car accidents. However, the drafters had the opportunity, which they twice rejected, apart from a handful of possible narrow exceptions, to accept proposals reflecting developments in the field of human rights and international humanitarian law. (Christopher Hall, 'UN Convention on State Immunity: The Need for a Human Rights Protocol' (2006) 55 ICLQ 411, 412)

8.6 Individual immunity

Having considered State immunity, let us now look at the position of individual State officials and at the level of immunity afforded to them. Within this section we will be referring to State officials, be they heads of State, ministers, or any other government official. Diplomats and consular staff will be dealt with in a separate section later. It may not automatically be clear why there is a distinction made between State immunity and the immunity of heads of State given that they tend to be the ultimate decision-maker for the State. But if you take into account the background and rationale for the different immunities a clearer understanding of the distinction is possible. As:

> The immunity of the Head of State derives from the sovereign immunity of the state in that the Head of State represents the state and personally manifests the independent will of the state. It is sometimes even said that the Head of State embodies the state for the international community. Nevertheless, the state and its constitutional rulers are two separate legal entities and, formally speaking, it is perfectly feasible to sue the state but not the Head of State and vice versa. Therefore, although both sovereign immunity and Head of State immunity are based on the same premise, in modem international law the two legal regimes are clearly distinct. (De Smet, 2003, at 316, see section 8.3.1)

As already mentioned, other State officials' actions are also subject to immunity. Once again, customary international law is the main source in order to understand and define the scope of this immunity. The ICJ in the *DRC v. Belgium* case confirmed this when it held:

> These conventions [the Vienna Convention on Diplomatic Relations, the 1963 Vienna Convention on Consular Relations, and the 1969 New York Convention on Special Missions], provide useful guidance on certain aspects of the question of immunities. They do not, however, contain any provision specifically defining the immunities enjoyed by Ministers for Foreign Affairs. It is consequently on the basis of customary international law that the Court must decide the questions relating to the immunities of such Ministers raised in the present case. (*Case Concerning the Arrest Warrant of II April 2000 (Democratic Republic of the Congo v. Belgium)*, 14 February 2002, 52)

Given the scope and type of the work State officials undertake and the different nature of their roles, international law has developed two distinct forms of individual immunity. This is in recognition of the importance of immunity and the different position of officials and their State function. These are known as immunity *ratione materiae* (functional immunity) and immunity *ratione personae* (personal immunity).

8.6.1 *Ratione materiae* (functional immunity)

Functional immunity is that, immunity which is dependent upon the function of the act in question. Where it is linked to a State's function then the individual's actions will fall under the protection of immunity. Given the nature of the immunity it applies to all State officials when acting in an official capacity and will come to an end only when the State in question waives it. Functional immunity has close links to State immunity, as seen in the 2004 UN Convention where the meaning of 'State' includes:

> Representatives of the State acting in that capacity (Article 2(1)(b)(iv))

Arguably, one of the main reasons for this position is to prevent a situation where State immunity applies but the individual who undertakes the legitimate State action is prosecuted instead. Immunity *ratione materiae* covers those acts which are official or governmental in form undertaken by individuals. It is the individual who is afforded immunity from prosecution based upon the official act itself. It is not granted to the individual due to their status but rather to cover the act in question. This is done to minimize interference by States in another State's internal matters. This immunity will apply even after the individual has left their position, as it attaches to the act not the individual.

As the majority of the law on this area is from customary international law the practice of States need to be looked at, and to do this domestic legislation and case law is the starting point.

The UK has enacted the State Immunity Act 1978 and their courts have had numerous instances in which it has been considered. In helping to clarify the scope of immunity *ratione materiae* as it applies under the Immunity Act, the Court of Appeal held:

> The protection afforded by the Act of 1978 to States would be undermined if employees, officers or (as one authority puts it) 'functionaries' could be sued as individuals for matters of State conduct in respect of which the State they were serving had immunity. Section 14(1) must be read as affording individual employee or officer of a foreign State protection under the same cloak as protects the State itself. (*Propend Finance v. Sing* (1997) 111 ILR 611, 669)

● *Jones v. Ministry of Interior for the Kingdom of Saudi Arabia and ors* [2006] UKHL 26

The UK House of Lords reaffirmed this notion in a civil claim against Saudi Arabian officials, and Saudi Arabia as a State, for torture.

The claimants alleged that while in Saudi Arabia they had been subjected to systematic torture and were seeking a claim against the Saudi Arabian Kingdom and individuals of the police and Ministry of Interior. Lord Bingham thought (at [13]) that:

> certain conclusions (taking the pleadings at face value) are inescapable: (1) that all the individual defendants were at the material times acting or purporting to act as servants or agents of the Kingdom; (2) that their acts were accordingly attributable to the Kingdom; (3) that no distinction is to be made between the claim against the Kingdom and the claim against the personal defendants; and (4) that none of these claims falls within any of the exceptions specified in the 1978 Act. Save in the special context of torture, I do not understand the claimants to challenge these conclusions, as evidenced by their acquiescence in the dismissal of their claims not based on torture. On a straightforward application of the 1978 Act, it would follow that the Kingdom's claim to immunity for itself and its servants or agents should succeed, since this is not one of those exceptional cases, specified in Part 1 of the 1978 Act, in which a state is not immune, and therefore the general rule of immunity prevails. It is not suggested that the Act is in any relevant respect ambiguous or obscure: it is, as Ward LJ observed in *Al-Adsani v Government of Kuwait (No 2)* (1996) 107 ILR 536, 549, 'as plain as plain can be'. In the ordinary way, the duty of the English court is therefore to apply the plain terms of the domestic statute. Inviting the House to do otherwise, the claimants contend, as they must, that to apply the 1978 Act according to its natural meaning and tenor by upholding the Kingdom's claim to immunity for itself and the individual defendants would be incompatible with the claimants' well-established right of access to a court implied into article 6 of the European Convention on Human Rights. To recognise the claimants' Convention right, the House is accordingly asked by the claimants to interpret the 1978 Act under section 3 of the Human Rights Act 1998 in a manner which would require or permit immunity to be refused to the Kingdom and the individual defendants in respect of the torture claims, or, if that is not possible, to make a declaration of incompatibility under section 4.

In this instance, the House of Lords upheld the immunity and prevented the claims from being heard by the court. This judgment has been criticized as ultimately using immunity to result in impunity for the individuals involved due to the lack of their being held to account by Saudi Arabia. This notion of impunity is explored further below.

● *Al-Adsani v. United Kingdom* (2001) 34 EHRR 273 (The *Al-Adsani Case*)

The European Court of Human Rights was presented with an opportunity to consider how the immunity *ratione materiae* of a State agent impacts the right to a fair trial, if at all. In this instance, a Kuwait government agent was held by the UK court to come under immunity in relation to alleged acts of torture. The European Court held that the two principles did not conflict due to their different objectives and an individual's human rights were not disproportionately affected by the immunity.

The effect of immunity *ratione materiae* is such that:

> the official will remain immune for acts committed in his or her official capacity, even after leaving office. This is sometimes referred to as a form of residual immunity. (De Smet, 2003, at 320, see section 8.3.1)

While it may not seem desirable in all instances that State officials' immunity is upheld, the alternative is equally, if not more, undesirable, since:

States value the principle of non-interference and sovereignty highly, and are unlikely to place their official conduct before another's court to be judged. The mere fact that immunity is in place does not necessarily mean that the individual who committed a crime, whether domestic or international in nature, will get away with it. Immunity is not the same thing as impunity, and it will be seen later just how States and the international community are trying to ensure this.

8.6.2 *Ratione personae* (personal immunity)

This type of immunity is distinctly different from *ratione materiae* as the nature of the act being official or not is irrelevant, it is as a result of the individual's status that immunity is applied. The number of officials afforded such broad immunity is limited. It tends to be heads of State, heads of government, ambassadors, and foreign ministers and lasts for the duration of the individual's tenure in office. The ICJ made it clear that it is not just heads of State who enjoy this kind of immunity, foreign ministers and other equivalent ministers are also entitled. They also explain that the rationale for applying this immunity centres on ensuring that the individuals are able to fulfil their official functions.

. . . .

● *Case Concerning the Arrest Warrant of 11 April 2000 (Democratic Republic of Congo v. Belgium)* (2002) ICJ REP 3 (The *Arrest Warrant Case*)

According to the Court (at 53–54):

In customary international law, the immunities accorded to Ministers for Foreign Affairs are not granted for their personal benefit, but to ensure the effective performance of their functions on behalf of their respective States. In order to determine the extent of these immunities, the Court must therefore first consider the nature of the functions exercised by a Minister for Foreign Affairs. He or she is in charge of his or her Government's diplomatic activities and generally acts as its representative in international negotiations and intergovernmental meetings. Ambassadors and other diplomatic agents carry out their duties under his or her authority. His or her acts may bind the State represented, and there is a presumption that a Minister for Foreign Affairs, simply by virtue of that office, has full powers to act on behalf of the State (see, for example, Article 7, paragraph 2(u), of the 1969 Vienna Convention on the Law of Treaties). In the performance of these functions, he or she is frequently required to travel internationally, and thus must be in a position freely to do so whenever the need should arise. He or she must also be in constant communication with the Government, and with its diplomatic missions around the world, and be capable at any time of communicating with representatives of other States. The Court further observes that a Minister for Foreign Affairs, responsible for the conduct of his or her State's relations with all other States, occupies a position such that, like the Head of State or the Head of Government, he or she is recognized under international law as representative of the State solely by virtue of his or her office. He or she does not have to present letters of credence: to the contrary, it is generally the Minister who determines the authority to be conferred upon diplomatic agents and countersigns their letters of credence. Finally, it is to the Minister for Foreign Affairs that chargés d'affaires are accredited.

The Court accordingly concludes that the functions of a Minister for Foreign Affairs are such that, throughout the duration of his or her office, he or she when abroad enjoys full immunity from criminal jurisdiction and inviolability. That immunity and that inviolability protect the individual concerned against any act of authority of another State which would hinder him or her in the performance of his or her duties.

Nevertheless, the ICJ's finding has been criticized for extending the scope of individuals covered by immunity *ratione personae*:

> without reference to any supporting state practice that absolute immunity ratione personae also applies to foreign ministers because they are responsible for the international relations of the state and '[in] the performance of these functions, he or she is frequently required to travel internationally, and thus must be in a position freely to do so whenever the need should arise.'
>
> Although basing this type of immunity on the fact that the official concerned is charged with international functions would conform with the rationale for such immunity, it would considerably extend the range of officials entitled to it. The current state of international affairs requires a very wide range of officials (senior and junior) to travel in the exercise of their functions. (Dapo Akande, 'International Law Immunities and the International Criminal Court' (2004) 98 AJIL 407, 412)

Akande raises very valid concerns over the vast number of government officials, who undertake international duties, and its erosion of the exclusivity of immunity *ratione personae*. However, it is unlikely that courts will find all these individuals subject to this immunity. This is particularly the case when for certain situations and functions it may be more appropriate to apply the law of immunity for diplomatic and other special missions (considered later).

Immunity *ratione personae* is applied strictly by courts and upheld, in general, regardless of the situation. There is no distinction made between the substance of the act being commercial or an act of State. This form of immunity covers all acts of a personal and official capacity. The seriousness of the alleged crime does not necessarily present an exception to applying the immunity. (The effect of international courts and international crimes on immunity *ratione personae* is explored in subsequent sections later.) A good illustration of this is the case against Fidel Castro brought before the Spanish courts. Following Spain's implementation of the 1985 Fundamental Law of the Judiciary (Ley Organica del Poder Judicial) the courts were able to apply universal jurisdiction for serious crimes, and a case was brought to try Fidel Castro for torture while he was still in office. Spain would later restrict its claims to crimes with which it has solid jurisdictional links. However, due to immunity *ratione personae* the Spanish court was prevented from hearing the case. The reasoning, as explained by Cassese, is based upon personal immunity:

> The *Audiencia Nacional* held that the Spanish Court could not exercise its criminal jurisdiction, as provided for in Article 23 of the Law on the Judicial Power, for the crimes attributable to Fidel Castro. He was an incumbent head of state, and therefore the provisions of Article 23 could not be applied to him because they were not applicable to heads of states, ambassadors etc. in office, who thus enjoyed immunity from prosecution on the strength of international rules to which Article 21 (2) of the same Law referred (this provision envisages an exception to the exercise of Spanish jurisdiction in the case of 'immunity from jurisdiction or execution provided for in the rules of public international law'). See Legal Grounds nos. 1–4. The Court also stated that its legal finding was not inconsistent with its ruling in *Pinochet*, because Pinochet was a former head of state, and hence no longer enjoyed immunity from jurisdiction (see Legal Ground No. 5). (Antonio Cassese, 'When may senior state officials be tried for international crimes? Some comments on the *Congo v Belgium* case' (2002) 13(4) EJIL 853, 860–861, fn 21)

Individuals who enjoy personal immunity are entitled to functional immunity upon leaving office. This is applied in the same way as for any other official, predominately applying to official acts. Despite universal acceptance of immunity *ratione personae*, challenges to it are beginning to appear when related to international crimes and high-ranking government officials. The main method the courts have used to reconcile this kind of immunity with international crimes and the pursuit of justice is through reaffirming the time limit applicable to immunity *ratione personae*.

● *R v. Bow Street Metropolitan Stipendiary Magistrate and ors, ex p Pinochet Ugarte (Amnesty International and others intervening (No. 3)* [1999] 2 ALL ER 97

The UK House of Lords was faced with the question of what happens after an individual is no longer in office or is deposed. The *Pinochet* case was a result of a Spanish-issued arrest warrant through Interpol for the former Chilean dictator Augusto Pinochet. The Spanish courts were seeking to prosecute Pinochet for torture and crimes against humanity. Pinochet was in the UK at the time receiving medical treatment and Spain was seeking his extradition. The argument put forward by Pinochet's side was that due to him being head of State at the time of the alleged crime, he was covered by immunity *ratione personae*. Ultimately it was held that Pinochet was not entitled to immunity, but he was never extradited due to the Home Secretary halting the extradition proceedings. The House of Lords set out their understanding of immunity *ratione personae* under international law (at 202) as follows:

> The position of the ambassador is covered by the Vienna Convention on Diplomatic Relations (1961). After providing for immunity from arrest (article 29) and from criminal and civil jurisdiction (article 31), article 39(1) provides that the ambassador's privileges shall be enjoyed from the moment he takes up post; and paragraph (2) provides:
>
> > 'When the functions of a person enjoying privileges and immunities have come to an end, such privileges and immunities shall normally cease at the moment when he leaves the country, or on expiry of a reasonable period in which to do so, but shall subsist until that time, even in case of armed conflict. However, with respect to acts performed by such a person in the exercise of his functions as a member of the mission, immunity shall continue to subsist.'
>
> The continuing partial immunity of the ambassador after leaving post is of a different kind from that enjoyed *ratione personae* while he was in post. Since he is no longer the representative of the foreign state he merits no particular privileges or immunities as a person. However in order to preserve the integrity of the activities of the foreign state during the period when he was ambassador, it is necessary to provide that immunity is afforded to his official acts during his tenure in post. If this were not done the sovereign immunity of the state could be evaded by calling in question acts done during the previous ambassador's time. Accordingly under article 39(2) the ambassador, like any other official of the state, enjoys immunity in relation to his official acts done while he was an official. This limited immunity, *ratione materiae*, is to be contrasted with the former immunity ratione personae which gave complete immunity to all activities whether public or private.

8.6.3 Heads of State and other top government officials' position in terms of international crimes

Heads of State and other high-ranking officials have been afforded the widest possible immunity of ratione personae. Yet as already evident from the previous discussion, there are certain instances where it may seem unjust to apply immunity when related to international crimes. In theory, this is not problematic as a case can potentially be brought following their removal from office either in their own State or by another State. However, this is not always a desirable alternative or even possible. This is particularly undesirable when the crimes are ongoing. Once again, there are distinctions to be made between immunity *ratione personae* and *ratione materiae*.

Ratione personae

In terms of *ratione personae* the case law seems to be pretty consistent in upholding the official's immunity. The French Cour de Cassation upheld the applicability of immunity for sitting heads of State regardless of the crime in question. The case brought against the then sitting head of Libya Gaddafi related to a terrorist attack explosion on a plane in 1989 over Chad. The French Cour de Cassation:

> ...considered the general principles of international law. International custom precludes Heads of State in office from being the subject of proceedings before the criminal courts of a foreign State, in the absence of specific provisions to the contrary binding on the parties concerned...
>
> In upholding the order of the examining magistrate that it was appropriate to initiate proceedings, notwithstanding the contrary arguments of the Ministère public, the judges in the Court of Appeal considered that, whilst the immunity of foreign Heads of State was still recognized by the international community, including France, no immunity could cover complicity in the destruction of property as a result of an explosion causing death and involving a terrorist undertaking.
>
> [This court considers] however, that in giving this ruling, when in the current state of international law the alleged crime, however serious, did not constitute one of the exceptions to the principle of the jurisdictional immunity of foreign Heads of State in office, the Chambre d'accusation of the Court of Appeal misconstrued the above-mentioned principle. (*Gaddafi* case (2001) 125 ILR 490)

Here the French court refers to exceptions to the principle of jurisdictional immunity but does not go on to define what would fall under the exception. They are clear in their finding that terrorist attacks and their resulting deaths do not exclude immunity *ratione personae* from applying.

The UK House of Lords in *Pinochet* also came to the same conclusion in relation to sitting heads of State in that the:

> immunity enjoyed by a head of state in power and an ambassador in post is a complete immunity attaching to the person of the head of state or ambassador and rendering him immune from all actions or prosecutions whether or not they relate to matters done for the benefit of the state. Such immunity is said to be granted ratione personae. (*R v Bow Street Metropolitan Stipendiary Magistrate and ors, ex p Pinochet Ugarte (Amnesty International and others intervening (No. 3)* [1999] 2 All ER 97, 201–202)

It is not only national courts that uphold immunity *ratione personae* even when related to international crimes.

● **Case Concerning the Arrest Warrant of 11 April 2000 (Democratic Republic of Congo v. Belgium)** (2002) ICJ REP 3 (The *Arrest Warrant Case*)

See also section 8.6.2.

The ICJ considered Belgium's argument that 'immunities accorded to incumbent Ministers for Foreign Affairs can in no case protect them where they are suspected of having committed war crimes or crimes against humanity'. The Court said (at 58) that it had:

> carefully examined State practice, including national legislation and those few decisions of national higher courts, such as the House of Lords or the French Court of Cassation. It has been unable to deduce from this practice that there exists under customary international law any form of exception to the rule according immunity from criminal jurisdiction and inviolability to incumbent Ministers for Foreign Affairs, where they are suspected of having committed war crimes or crimes against humanity.
>
> The Court has also examined the rules concerning the immunity or criminal responsibility of persons having an official capacity contained in the legal instruments creating international criminal tribunals, and which are specifically applicable to the latter . . . It finds that these rules likewise do not enable it to conclude that any such an exception exists in customary international law in regard to national courts.
>
> Finally, none of the decisions of the Nuremberg and Tokyo international military tribunals, or of the International Criminal Tribunal for the former Yugoslavia, cited by Belgium deal with the question of the immunities of incumbent Ministers for Foreign Affairs before national courts where they are accused of having committed war crimes or crimes against humanity. The Court accordingly notes that those decisions are in no way at variance with the findings it has reached above.
>
> In view of the foregoing, the Court accordingly cannot accept Belgium's argument in this regard.

Interestingly the ICJ made sure to clarify that the corollary of immunity *ratione personae* is not impunity. The immunity does not excuse the individual for their actions and the Court set out (at 61) instances where immunity would not be a hurdle to prosecution:

> The Court emphasizes, however, that the immunity from jurisdiction enjoyed by incumbent Ministers for Foreign Affairs does not mean that they enjoy impunity in respect of any crimes they might have committed, irrespective of their gravity. Immunity from criminal jurisdiction and individual criminal responsibility are quite separate concepts. While jurisdictional immunity is procedural in nature, criminal responsibility is a question of substantive law. Jurisdictional immunity may well bar prosecution for a certain period or for certain offences; it cannot exonerate the person to whom it applies from all criminal responsibility.
>
> Accordingly, the immunities enjoyed under International law by an incumbent or former Minister for Foreign Affairs do not represent a bar to criminal prosecution in certain circumstances.
>
> First, such persons enjoy no criminal immunity under international law in their own countries, and may thus be tried by those countries' courts in accordance with the relevant rules of domestic law.
>
> Secondly, they will cease to enjoy immunity from foreign jurisdiction if the State which they represent or have represented decides to waive that immunity.
>
> Thirdly, after a person ceases to hold the office of Minister for Foreign Affairs, he or she will no longer enjoy all of the immunities accorded by international law in other States . . .
>
> Fourthly, an incumbent or former Minister for Foreign Affairs may be subject to criminal proceedings before certain international criminal courts, where they have jurisdiction.

While this approach seems to be consistent with State practice, there have been initiatives which seek to remove immunity for international crimes even for sitting heads of State. With the:

> Resolution on Head of State Immunity, the Institut de Droit International accepted that former Heads of State remain immune for crimes committed in the exercise of their official function, but the text expressly provides that 'he or she may be prosecuted and tried when the acts alleged constitute a crime under international law, or when they are performed exclusively to

satisfy a personal interest, or when they constitute a misappropriation of the State's assets and resources. (De Smet, 2003, at 318, fn 28, see section 8.3.1)

Ratione materiae

Now looking at immunity *ratione materiae* it seems that State practice only applies this to official acts, even those of heads of State and other high-ranking officials. One only needs to look at the ICJ's decision in the *Arrest Warrant* case, the French court in the *Gaddafi* case, and the UK House of Lords in the *Pinochet* case. They clearly limit the application of immunity for international crimes when considered as part of an official/State act where immunity *ratione materiae* is in question. As stated:

> even though serving or former state officials are generally entitled to immunity ratione materiae in relation to their official acts, such immunity from foreign domestic criminal jurisdiction does not exist when the person is charged with an international crime. There have been a significant number of domestic prosecutions of officials of foreign states for international crimes. (Akande, 2004, at 413, see section 8.6.2)

When put in the context of the rationale for immunity *ratione materiae*, it is easier to see why international crimes are likely to be an exception when it comes to official acts. Such acts cannot be considered as an official act, or one to which the rationale for applying the immunity can apply. This has been expressed by Lord Millett's decision in the *Pinochet* case. His was of the view that:

> Immunity ratione materiae is very different. This is a subject matter immunity. It operates to prevent the official and governmental acts of one state from being called into question in proceedings before the courts of another, and only incidentally confers immunity on the individual. It is therefore a narrower immunity but it is more widely available. It is available to former heads of state and heads of diplomatic missions, and any one whose conduct in the exercise of the authority of the state is afterwards called into question, whether he acted as head of government, government minister, military commander or chief of police, or subordinate public official. The immunity is the same whatever the rank of the office-holder. This too is common ground. It is an immunity from the civil and criminal jurisdiction of foreign national courts but only in respect of governmental or official acts. The exercise of authority by the military and security forces of the state is the paradigm example of such conduct. The immunity finds its rationale in the equality of sovereign states and the doctrine of non-interference in the internal affairs of other states ... The immunity is sometimes also justified by the need to prevent the serving head of state or diplomat from being inhibited in the performance of his official duties by fear of the consequences after he has ceased to hold office. This last basis can hardly be prayed in aid to support the availability of the immunity in respect of criminal activities prohibited by international law. (*R v Bow Street Metropolitan Stipendiary Magistrate and ors, ex p Pinochet Ugarte [Amnesty International and others intervening (No. 3)* [1999] 2 All ER 97, 269)

In their Joint Separate Opinion in the *Arrest Warrant Case*, Judges Higgins, Kooijmans, and Buergenthal (at p. 85) also consider the extent to which there appears to be an exception in international crimes for applying immunity *ratione materiae*. They held:

> Nonetheless, that immunity prevails only as long as the Minister is in office and continues to shield him or her after that time only for 'official' acts. It is now increasingly claimed in the literature ... that serious international crimes cannot be regarded as official acts because they are neither normal State functions nor functions that a State alone (in contrast to an individual) can perform (Goff, J. (as he then was) and Lord Wilberforce articulated this test in the case of *Io Congreso del Partido* (1978) QB 500 at 528 and (1983) AC 244 at 268, respectively). This view is underscored by the

increasing realization that State-related motives are not the proper test for determining what constitutes public state acts. The same view is gradually also finding expression in State practice, as evidenced in judicial decisions and opinions. (For an early example, see the judgment of the Israel Supreme Court in the Eichmann case; Supreme Court, 29 May 1962, 36 International Law Reports, p. 312.) See also the speeches of Lords Hutton and Phillips of Worth Matravers in R. v. Bartle and the Commissioner of Police for the Metropolis and Others, ex parte Pinochet ('Pinochet III'); and of Lords Steyn and Nicholls of Birkenhead in 'Pinochet I', as well as the judgment of the Court of Appeal of Amsterdam in the Bouterse case (Gerechtshof Amsterdam, 20 November 2000, para. 4.2.)

thinking points

- *Explain the difference between immunity* ratione materiae *and immunity* ratione personae.
- *Does immunity apply to international crimes of heads of States?*
- *Which class of officials enjoys functional immunity?*

8.7 Immunities before international tribunals and courts

So, where does this leave heads of States and other officials when it comes to international crimes? This question has become increasingly relevant with the establishment of international criminal tribunals and courts, many of which expressly exclude immunity in their constitutional instruments. The first instances of such an explicitly provided for provision was in the Nuremberg and Tokyo Tribunals:

> The official position of defendants, whether as Heads of State or responsible officials in Government Departments, shall not be considered as freeing them from responsibility or mitigating punishment. (Article 7 of the Charter of the International Criminal Tribunal of Nuremberg)
>
> Neither the official position, at any time, of an accused, nor the fact that an accused acted pursuant to order of his government or of a superior shall, of itself, be sufficient to free such accused from responsibility for any crime with which he is charged, but such circumstances may be considered in mitigation of punishment if the Tribunal determines that justice so requires. (Article 6 of the Charter of the Tokyo Tribunal)

Identical provisions appear under Article 7(2) of the Statute of the International Criminal Tribunal for the Former Yugoslavia (ICTY) and Article 6(2) of the Statute for the International Criminal Tribunal for Rwanda (ICTR):

> The official position of any accused person, whether as Head of State or Government or as a responsible Government official, shall not relieve such person of criminal responsibility nor mitigate punishment.

A strikingly similar provision is in Article 6(2) of the Statute of the Special Court for Sierra Leone:

> The official position of any accused persons, whether as Head of State or Government or as a responsible government official, shall not relieve such person of criminal responsibility nor mitigate punishment

This exclusion of immunity is easier to reconcile with the UN-established tribunals and hybrid courts based upon the powers of the Security Council under Chapter VII of the UN Charter. As a consequence of a Chapter VII resolution, it is possible for all UN member States to displace immunity in relation to cooperation with these tribunals and courts in terms of arresting, detaining, and transferring those individuals to which immunity would otherwise be afforded. However, this has not always met with compliance.

The most recent treaty provision excluding immunity as a barrier to prosecution is contained in the Statute of the International Criminal Court under Article 27:

> 1. This Statute shall apply equally to all persons without any distinction based on official capacity. In particular, official capacity as a Head of State or Government, a member of a Government or parliament, an elected representative or a government official shall in no case exempt a person from criminal responsibility under this Statute, nor shall it, in and of itself, constitute a ground for reduction of sentence.
> 2. Immunities or special procedural rules which may attach to the official capacity of a person, whether under national or international law, shall not bar the Court from exercising its jurisdiction over such a person.

This provision is not like the earlier Allied Powers or UN-established tribunals and courts. The International Criminal Court (ICC) is an independent international court established by treaty. The concept of consent comes into play since for States to be subject to the ICC they need to agree to such through joining the Court, or through situations that have been referred to the ICC by the UN Security Council subject to a Chapter VII decision. The rationale for the removal of immunity is said to come from the explicit waiver of immunities by those State parties to the ICC's Statute, therefore this is in line with customary international law. The position when the immunity relates to a third party not a member of the ICC is less clear. The arrest warrant which was issued by the ICC's Prosecutor for sitting Sudanese President Omar Al Bashir was the first time the ICC Trial Chamber had to determine the effect of immunity *ratione personae* of a non-State party for the ICC. In this situation, the Trial Chamber held:

> Finally, in relation to the jurisdiction ratione personae, the Chamber considers that, insofar as the Darfur situation has been referred to the Court by the Security Council, acting pursuant to article 13(b) of the Statute, the present case falls within the jurisdiction of the Court despite the fact that it refers to the alleged criminal liability of a national of a State that is not party to the Statute, for crimes which have been allegedly committed in the territory of a State not party to the Statute.
>
> Furthermore, in light of the materials presented by the Prosecution in support of the Prosecution Application, and without prejudice to a further determination of the matter pursuant to article 19 of the Statute, the Chamber considers that the current position of Omar Al Bashir as Head of a state which is not a party to the Statute, has no effect on the Court's jurisdiction over the present case.
>
> The Chamber reaches this conclusion on the basis of the four following considerations. First, the Chamber notes that, according to the Preamble of the Statute, one of the core goals of the Statute is to put an end to impunity for the perpetrators of the most serious crimes of concern to the international community as a whole, which 'must not go unpunished'.
>
> Second, the Chamber observes that, in order to achieve this goal, article 27(1) and (2) of the Statute provide for the following core principles:
>
> (i) 'This Statute shall apply equally to all persons without any distinction based on official capacity;'
> (ii) '[...] official capacity as a Head of State or Government, a member of Government or parliament, an elected representative or a government official shall in no case exempt a person from criminal responsibility under this Statute, nor shall it, in and of itself, constitute a ground for reduction of sentence;' and

> (iii) 'Immunities or special procedural rules which may attach to the official capacity of a person, whether under national or international law, shall not bar the Court from exercising its jurisdiction over such a person.'
>
> Third, the consistent case law of the Chamber on the applicable law before the Court has held that, according to article 21 of the Statute, those other sources of law provided for in paragraphs (I) (b) and (I)(c) of article 21 of the Statute, can only be resorted to when the following two conditions are met: (i) there is a lacuna in the written law contained in the Statute, the Elements of Crimes and the Rules; and (ii) such lacuna cannot be filled by the application of the criteria of interpretation provided in articles 31 and 32 of the Vienna Convention on the Law of the Treaties and article 21(3) of the Statute.
>
> Fourth, as the Chamber has recently highlighted in its 5 February 2009 'Decision on Application under Rule 103', by referring the Darfur situation to the Court, pursuant to article 13(b) of the Statute, the Security Council of the United Nations has also accepted that the investigation into the said situation, as well as any prosecution arising therefrom, will take place in accordance with the statutory framework provided for in the Statute, the Elements of Crimes and the Rules as a whole. (*The Prosecutor v. Omar Hassan Ahmad Al Bashir* (Decision on the Prosecution's Application for a Warrant of Arrest against Omar Hassan Ahmad Al Bashir), 4 March 2009, Case No. ICC-02/05-01/09, 40–45)

thinking point
Is there any difference between the provision of the ICC Statute and those of the ICTY and ICTR regarding immunity?

However, this does not mean that States have complied with the ICC's ruling. Many instances have occurred where a State party to the ICC has not arrested President Omar Al Bashir despite its obligations under the ICC Statute. Typically, the defence for violating the obligation is based upon immunity of sitting heads of State. One thing has become very clear, while States and international courts and tribunals may be willing to state their commitment to removing immunity for international crimes, at the very least for immunity *ratione materiae*, it cannot be said that there is always the political will when it comes down to it.

8.8 Diplomatic and consular immunities

The final area to consider is the immunities afforded to diplomatic and consular missions and personnel. Laws and principles related to diplomacy go back thousands of years and are influenced from a broad spectrum of cultures and customs. The practice of sending diplomats and envoys goes back to ancient times:

> The formal sending of envoys as representatives of nation States may be traced back to the practice of the Greek cities. The ambassadors sent between the members of the Amphictyonic League were not professional diplomats, and their missions were invariably ad hoc, but choice for the task was regarded as a high honour and those appointed were selected for their ability to present a case effectively, being by profession usually orators or actors.... Both heralds, the earliest kind of envoy, and ambassadors of all varieties were universally regarded as inviolable.
>
> The instances of breach of the rule were rare and seem always to have been followed by terrible reprisals—for the outrage committed at Athens and Sparta on the Persian envoys of Darius two Spartan nobles offered their lives in expiation to Xerxes. But he replied that as he blamed them for breaking the laws of all mankind he would not break them himself ... the basis for this inviolability was purely religious. The reprisals took place not because any legal right

of the envoy or of his sending State was believed to have been violated but because the act constituted a sacrilege to be avenged. (Eileen Young, 'The development of the law of diplomatic relations' (1964) 40 BYBIL 141)

Over time the practice and customs amongst States developed into what we know today as the law relating to diplomacy and it is within this that the scope of immunities developed:

By the end of the seventeenth century the broad outlines of the law of diplomatic relations had emerged as a result of three hundred years of State practice, and the controversial areas, such as the granting of asylum in the embassy and the position of the suite, were also evident. The law, however, was entirely customary and very much subject to political considerations, although these tended to have the effect of extending immunity for fear of reprisals, particularly where the head of legation was concerned. (Ibid., at 157)

It was only with the 1961 Vienna Convention on Diplomatic Relations that any real efforts at codifying this area were attempted. It is with:

The recent entry into force of the Vienna Convention on Diplomatic Relations marks the evolution to maturity of a branch of international law which derives from customs in existence three thousand years ago. (Ibid., at 141)

This was swiftly followed by the 1963 Vienna Convention on Consular Relations and the 1969 UN Convention on Special Missions. The rationale for extending immunity to diplomats and consular staff is generally accepted to be based upon the functional necessity theory. In order for officials and diplomatic and consular missions to perform their functions fully immunities are applied. These follow the same distinctions as discussed earlier in relation to immunity *ratione materiae* and *ratione personae*. Diplomatic agents are afforded immunity *ratione personae* pursuant to Article 31 of the Vienna Convention on Diplomatic Relations which sets out the scope of diplomats' immunity:

1. A diplomatic agent shall enjoy immunity from the criminal jurisdiction of the receiving State. He shall also enjoy immunity from its civil and administrative jurisdiction, except in the case of:
   (a) a real action relating to private immovable property situated in the territory of the receiving State, unless he holds it on behalf of the sending State for the purposes of the mission;
   (b) an action relating to succession in which the diplomatic agent is involved as executor, administrator, heir or legatee as a private person and not on behalf of the sending State;
   (c) an action relating to any professional or commercial activity exercised by the diplomatic agent in the receiving State outside his official functions.
2. A diplomatic agent is not obliged to give evidence as a witness.
3. No measures of execution may be taken in respect of a diplomatic agent except in the cases coming under sub-paragraphs (a), (b) and (c) of paragraph 1 of this Article, and provided that the measures concerned can be taken without infringing the inviolability of his person or of his residence.

The basis of diplomatic relations is founded on consent:

The establishment of diplomatic relations between States, and of permanent diplomatic missions, takes place by mutual consent. (Article 2 Vienna Declaration on Diplomatic Relations)

And it is through this notion of consent whereby immunity can also be restricted. It is possible for the sending State to waive the diplomat's immunity as per Article 32:

1. The immunity from jurisdiction of diplomatic agents and of persons enjoying immunity under Article 37 may be waived by the sending State.
2. Waiver must always be express.
3. The initiation of proceedings by a diplomatic agent of by a person enjoying immunity from jurisdiction under Article 37 shall preclude him from invoking immunity from jurisdiction in respect of any counter-claim directly connected with the principal claim.
4. Waiver of immunity from jurisdiction in respect of civil or administrative proceedings shall not be held to imply waiver of immunity in respect of the execution of the judgment, for which a separate waiver shall be necessary.

NOTE Article 32(4) requires a further waiver for enforcing judgments separate from the initial waiver to enable the host State's court to hear the case. This double requirement could result in situations in which a diplomat has had a ruling made against them but it is not possible to enforce it unless specifically provided for under a separate waiver.

The Vienna Convention provides for distinction to be made between family members of diplomatic agents, general administrative and technical staff, service staff, and individual staff of the mission personnel in terms of applying immunity and what level of immunity. Immunities will only apply provided the individual in question is not a national of the receiving State, a very logical and fair limitation as it should not be possible for an individual to be outside the jurisdiction of their State of nationality when in its territory. These distinctions are enumerated as follows:

1. The members of the family of a diplomatic agent forming part of his household shall, if they are not nationals of the receiving State, enjoy the privileges and immunities specified in Articles 29 to 36.
2. Members of the administrative and technical staff of the mission, together with members of their families forming part of their respective households, shall, if they are not nationals of or permanently resident in the receiving State, enjoy the privileges and immunities specified in Articles 29 to 35, except that the immunity from civil and administrative jurisdiction of the receiving State specified in paragraph 1 of Article 31 shall not extend to acts performed outside the course of their duties. They shall also enjoy the privileges specified in Article 36, paragraph 1, in respect of articles imported at the time of first installation.
3. Members of the service staff of the mission who are not nationals of or permanently resident in the receiving State shall enjoy immunity in respect of acts performed in the course of their duties, exemption from dues and taxes on the emoluments they receive by reason of their employment and the exemption contained in Article 33.
4. Private servants of members of the mission shall, if they are not nationals of or permanently resident in the receiving State, be exempt from dues and taxes on the emoluments they receive by reason of their employment. In other respects, they may enjoy privileges and immunities only to the extent admitted by the receiving State. However, the receiving State must exercise its jurisdiction over those persons in such a manner as not to interfere unduly with the performance of the functions of the mission. (Article 37)

In situations where a diplomatic agent is a national of the receiving State, they are only afforded immunity *ratione materiae* applying a restrictive approach—that is,. only for official acts:

> Except insofar as additional privileges and immunities may be granted by the receiving State, a diplomatic agent who is a national of or permanently resident in that State shall enjoy only immunity from jurisdiction, and inviolability, in respect of official acts performed in the exercise of his functions. (Article 38)

Generally the immunities of diplomats are while they are in the receiving State, as it relates to the relationship and dealings between the sending and receiving States. However, it is possible to extend these immunities to third States in limited situations, mainly while in transit:

> If a diplomatic agent passes through or is in the territory of a third State, which has granted him a passport visa if such visa was necessary, while proceeding to take up or to return to his post, or when returning to his own country, the third State shall accord him inviolability and such other Immunities as may be required to ensure his transit or return. The same shall apply in the case of any members of his family enjoying privileges and immunities who are accompanying the diplomatic agent, or travelling separately to join him or to return to their country. (Article 40)

All those individuals afforded immunity under this area are obligated to refrain from participating in illegal activities and to uphold the laws and regulations of the receiving State:

> Without prejudice to their privileges and immunities, it is the duty of all persons enjoying such privileges and immunities to respect the laws and regulations of the receiving State. They also have a duty not to interfere in the internal affairs of that State. (Article 41)

Similar concepts and principles are applied to consular staff, however, only in terms of immunity *ratione materiae*. This is due to the purpose of consular missions and their staff. They are established to promote and protect the interests of the sending State, so perform more administrative and technical work as opposed to political. Generally, consular staff cannot be detained unless it is for grave crimes or pursuant to a competent judicial finding. This again is down to the realization:

> that the purpose of such privileges and immunities is not to benefit individuals but to ensure the efficient performance of functions by consular posts on behalf of their respective States (Preamble to the 1964 Vienna Convention on Consular Relations)

KEY POINTS

- Consular and diplomatic immunity arises out of functional necessity.
- Diplomatic immunity applies to family members except if such are nationals of receiving States.
- Diplomatic immunity applies during the service of the holders.

8.9 Diplomatic missions

It is not just diplomatic agents and associated individuals afforded immunity. The diplomatic mission and its premises are considered to be inviolable. This is not as commonly perceived to be a result of the mission premises being treated as if it is the territory of the State in question. Instead it comes down to the functional necessity theory; it enables the diplomatic mission to fulfil its purpose and prevents interference from other States in accordance with sovereignty and equality. This principle of inviolability is stipulated in Article 22 of the Vienna Convention on Diplomatic Relations 1961:

1. The premises of the mission shall be inviolable. The agents of the receiving State may not enter them, except with the consent of the head of the mission.
2. The receiving State is under a special duty to take all appropriate steps to protect the premises of the mission against any intrusion or damage and to prevent any disturbance of the peace of the mission or impairment of its dignity.
3. The premises of the mission, their furnishings and other property thereon and the means of transport of the mission shall be immune from search, requisition, attachment or execution.

Conclusion

The law of immunity is one of the most fundamental areas of international law. The development of international law in modern times, especially since the end of the Second World War, has influenced the fast transformation in this area of law. As commercial interaction amongst nations grew, as accountability of heads of State and other high office holders increased, so also have the various laws governing immunity of these officials altered. Gone were the days when States claimed absolute immunity for every kind of action they undertook and every transaction conducted with foreign governments and nationals. However, as the cases have shown, some aspects of immunity law have remained relatively untouched by the exponential changes. A head of State may still not be held accountable for acts undertaken in his official capacity while in office except where his or her State has waived its immunity under such treaties as the Rome Statute of the International Criminal Court.

Questions

Self-test questions

1 What is a immunity?

2 Explain the terms '*jure imperii*' and '*jure gestionis*'.

3 Distinguish between 'immunity *ratione personae*' and 'immunity *ratione materiae*'.

4 Enumerate the various tests for distinguishing between absolute immunity and restrictive immunity.

5 Under what circumstances will a State lose its absolute immunity?

6 What is meant by the term 'diplomatic immunity'?

7 Explain 'functional immunity'.

8 To whom does diplomatic immunity apply?

Discussion questions

1 'A State which enters into commercial transactions with foreign nationals loses its absolute immunity in international law.' Discuss.

2 'The "purpose" for which a State conducts a commercial transaction is of no relevance whatsoever in deciding whether it enjoys immunity.' Critically examine this statement.

3 'If a head of State authorizes his country's army to commit war crimes, he can be sued for these crimes.' To what extent is this statement true?

4 'The various tests for deciding whether an act is a sovereign act or is commercial, for the purpose of immunity are the same and utterly useless.' Assess this statement.

5 Distinguish between immunity *ratione personae* and immunity *ratione materiae* in relation to international crimes.

6 'As far as enjoying diplomatic immunity is concerned, once a diplomat always a diplomat.' Discuss.

Assessment question

The Ministry of Defence of Candoma ordered boots for its armed forces from Rutamu. The ship which brought in the goods from Rutamu experiences difficulty when it arrives at the port in Candoma due to ongoing construction work in parts of the port. The goods entered into demurrage. The Rutamuan shipping company asked for payment, but Candoma refused. The company sued Candoma before a Rutamuan court, asking the court to grant its application to seize some property belonging to Candoma in Rutamu. Candoma argued that the court has no jurisdiction on the basis of immunity.

Advise the parties.

 # Key cases

- *Case Concerning the Arrest Warrant of 11 April 2000 (Democratic Republic of Congo v. Belgium)* (2002) ICJ Rep 3, 53–54) (the *Arrest Warrant Case*)

- *Democratic Republic of the Congo v. FG Hemisphere Associates LLC* FACV Nos 5, 6, & 7 of 2010, Hong Kong Court of Final Appeal

- *Al-Adsani v. United Kingdom* (2001) 34 EHRR 273 (the *Al-Adsani Case*)

- *Victory Transport Inc. v. Comisaria General De Abastecimientos y Transpertos* 336 F.2d 354 (2nd Cir., 1964)
- *I Congreso del Partido* [1981] 2 All ER 1064
- *Trendtex Trading Corp. v. Central Bank of Nigeria* [1977] 2 WLR 356
- *Roy v. South Africa*, 2013 ONSC 4633

 # Further reading

Akande, D., 'International law immunities and the International Criminal Court' (2004) 98 AJIL 407

De Smet, S., 'The immunity of heads of state in US courts after the decision of the International Court of Justice' (2003) 72 Nordic JIL 313

Hall, C., 'UN Convention on State Immunity: the need for a human rights protocol' (2006) 55 ICLQ 411

Lauterpacht, H., 'The problem of jurisdictional immunities of foreign states' (1951) 28 BYBIL 220

Melander, G., 'Waiver of immunity' (1976) 45 Nordisk Tidsskrift for International Ret 22

Young, E., 'The development of the law of diplomatic relations' (1964) 40 BYBIL 141

International law and municipal law

Learning objectives

This chapter will help you to:

- understand the nature of the relations between international law and municipal law;

- appreciate the current dynamics of this relationship;

- recognize the various implications of international legal issues in municipal legal systems and vice versa;

- follow current developments in the relations between the two legal regimes;

- appreciate what drives States' attitudes towards international law; and

- understand how modern developments have impacted on the relationship.

Introduction

International law is traditionally concerned with the relations among States. Relations between individuals, no matter how wealthy and influential, or between individuals and companies, or between companies, are matters usually dealt with by municipal law. However, more recently, international law has deeply penetrated into municipal law. The gap between international and municipal legal regimes has considerably narrowed. Today, individuals contest the legality of international arrests and detentions before national courts, and challenge their own governments' actions before international and regional courts. As Harold Koh explains, in 'Why do nations obey international law?' (1997) Yale LJ 2599, 2605:

> the law of nations was thought to embrace private as well as public, domestic as well as transborder transactions to encompass not simply the law of states, but also the law between 'states' and individuals.

This chapter considers the various contours of the relations between international law and municipal law.

9.1 International and municipal law: what relationship?

Writers have put forward several theories to explain the relationship between international law and municipal law. The two most well known of such theories are monism and dualism. Although these theories are often applied to several aspects of international and domestic law, the focus in this chapter is on using these two theories to try to explain the relationship between international and municipal legal systems. Thus particular attention will be paid to how these theories have influenced certain developments in the relationship.

9.1.1 Monism

According to monism, or the monist theory, international law and municipal law form one and the same legal order. Both systems are two sides of the same coin, so that the adjectives 'international' and 'municipal' describe only the various aspects to which this single, unified legal regime applies.

 example

In *Kadic v. Karadzic* 70 F.3d 232 (2nd Cir., 1995), the US Court of Appeals noted that a private person might be liable for breach of customary international law while remedies for such a breach are available under the US Alien Tort Claim Act (ATCA). Here, then, is an example of both international and domestic law applying to the same breach, but in different aspects.

However, the fundamental basis of monism is not that co-occurrence is, as explained, possible between international and municipal laws; rather, the issue is what happens when both conflict, as they often do.

The ultimate argument of monists, in response to this question, is that international law is superior to national law and that, where there is a conflict between the two, the former prevails. This, in essence, is the soul of monism. Thus while monism recognizes the coexistence of international law and municipal law, it affirms the superiority of the former to the latter.

The basis for privileging international law over municipal law can be explained in practical terms. It may be dangerous, for example, to entrust only States with the responsibility to protect peoples' human rights. States are often the worst violators of human rights. In developing countries, for instance, most constitutions provide for the protection of such rights and for redress when these are breached. However, citizens whose rights are violated by their governments may often find it difficult to seek redress in domestic courts, which are often controlled by the same government. Even in Western societies where respect for human rights is better observed and the judiciary is more independent, States may become heavy-handed in dealing with human rights during national emergencies such as terrorist threats or attacks. In these cases, international courts such as the European Court of Human Rights become the ultimate guarantors of human rights (see Chapter 19).

KEY POINTS

- Monism acknowledges the coexistence of international law and municipal law, and views them as two sides of the same coin.

- The soul of monism is that where there is a conflict between international law and municipal law, the former prevails.

9.1.2 Dualism

Dualists believe that international law and municipal law operate in different areas, and do not belong to same realm. Dualism also rejects the notion that international law is superior to municipal law. They contend that national courts are bound to apply international law to a case before them *only* if national constitutions allow them to do so and not simply because international law is better trusted than, or superior to, municipal law.

The dualists see the relationship between the two as a matter of practicality, not hierarchy. They believe that international law is indebted to municipal law and can deny international law some of its privileges, such as those that international law confers on individuals within a State. For example, despite the fact that many treaties forbid States from detaining people for longer than the time permitted under their constitutions, States still frequently restrict people's freedoms especially in times of emergency, such as terror attacks.

9.1.3 Is there really a conflict between the two theories?

There is difference and tension between international law and municipal law, but it does seem that the significance of the theoretical difference has been exaggerated by legal scholars.

In practice, States hardly ever claim that they act under one theory or another or that these theories influence their behaviour.

According to Gerald Fitzmaurice ('The general principles of international law considered from the standpoint of the rule of law' (1957-II) 92 Recueil des Cours 1, 71):

> the entire monist–dualist controversy is unreal, artificial and strictly beside the point, because it assumes something that has to exist for there to be a controversy at all—and which in fact does not exist—namely a *common field* in which the two legal orders under discussion both simultaneously have their spheres or activity. [Emphasis added]

Rather than dwelling on theories, it is better to try to understand the nature of the relationship between international law and domestic law. Thus, one needs to look at four basic areas:

(a) What is the attitude of international law to domestic law?

(b) How does international law become part of municipal law?

(c) How do municipal legal systems deal with international law in all aspects of their operation, such as questions of applicability, priority, and coordination?

(d) What new developments have impacted the relations between international and municipal laws?

In relation to question (d), we will particularly consider how entities within States that were not previously concerned with international law have now become international law actors, while still maintaining their private identity.

thinking points

- *Distinguish 'monism' from 'dualism'.*
- *Is the difference between monism and dualism of any consequence in the practice of States with regard to the relations between international law and municipal law?*
- *What possible third theory might be able to explain the relations between international and municipal laws?*

9.2 Municipal law issues under international law

International law and municipal law interrelate in many areas and this relation has continued to expand in modern times. In the following section, we consider some of the most important areas of such interrelation.

9.2.1 A State cannot rely on municipal law in justification of non-performance of international obligations

International law has certain expectations of municipal law, and lays those expectations out in clear and concise language. It determines its own primacy vis-à-vis municipal law, although it does not invalidate the latter.

Article 27 of the Vienna Convention on the Law of Treaties (VCLT) lays down the general principle governing the approach of international law to municipal law. It provides that:

> A party may not invoke the provision of its internal law as justification for its failure to perform a treaty. This rule is without prejudice to Article 46.

This provision is important in two principal respects: first, it dictates the relations between international law and municipal law in the context of treaty law, since it refers to 'a party' to a treaty; and, secondly, it recognizes one exception under which a State may plead its internal law to justify non-fulfilment of international obligations assumed under a treaty.

This is the limitation contained in Article 46 VCLT:

> 1. A State may not invoke the fact that its consent to be bound by a treaty has been expressed in violation of a provision of its internal law regarding competence to conclude treaties as invalidating its consent unless that violation was manifest and concerned a rule of its internal law of fundamental importance.
> 2. A violation is manifest if it would be objectively evident to any State conducting itself in the matter in accordance with normal practice and in good faith.

Article 27 thus sets the standard for international law's general approach to municipal law, while laying out, at the same time, the only basis upon which international law will accept derogation from that standard. Viewed from this angle, international law is a yardstick not for measuring the validity of municipal laws as they apply *within* a State, but for determining the validity of municipal laws that govern the same obligations as international law.

● **Advisory Opinion on the Interpretation of the Convention between Greece and Bulgaria Respecting Reciprocal Emigration, Signed at Neuilly-Sur-Seine on 27 November 1919** (1930) PCIJ SER. B, No. 17 (The **Greco-Bulgarian Communities Case**)

The President of the Greco-Bulgarian Mixed Commission requested, through the League of Nations, an advisory opinion of the Permanent Court of International Justice (PCIJ) on the interpretation of some clauses of the Greco-Bulgarian Convention relating to communities. One of the questions before the Court (at 32) was:

> If the application of the Convention of Neuilly is at variance with provisions of internal law in force in the territory of one of the two Signatory Powers, which of the conflicting provisions should be preferred—that of the law or that of the convention?

The Court stated (at 32) that:

> it is a generally accepted principle of international law that in the relations between powers which are contracting Parties to a treaty, the provision of municipal law cannot prevail over those of the treaty.

● **Treatment of Polish Nationals and Other Persons of Polish Origin or Speech in the Danzig Territory Advisory Opinion** (1932) PCIJ SER. A/B, No. 44 (**Polish Nationals in Danzig**)

Similarly in this case, the PCIJ stated (at 24) that:

> It should however be observed that ... a State cannot adduce as against another State its own constitution with a view to evading obligations incumbent upon it under international law or treaties in force.

KEY POINT A State cannot invoke the provisions of its own law to excuse non-performance of its international obligation. The only exception to this rule is Article 46 VCLT.

9.2.2 Disputes arising solely from municipal law: private individuals versus States

International tribunals deal daily with many issues concerning municipal legal systems. Such issues include questions about disputes between States and private individuals, questions regarding the nationality of individuals, and so on and so forth. Often, these tribunals have to determine their competence to adjudicate matters not only involving questions of international law, which they are entitled to deal with, but also those concerning the private interests of individuals under municipal law.

● *Case Concerning the Payment of Various Serbian Loans Issued in France* (1929) PCIJ SER. A, No. 20–1 (The *Serbian Loans Case*)

The issue before the Court was a matter concerning loans between Serbia and some private individuals in France. The Serb-Slovene-Croat State issued some loans to French citizens. A dispute arose regarding the loans and the French citizens called on their government to take up their case. Although the Serb-Slovene-Croat State did not object to France's intervention on behalf of its citizens, it did maintain that the process that it had adopted with regard to serving notices concerning the loan was in order.

Under Article 14 of the League Covenant, the PCIJ could only decide issues between two States. The present case concerned the dispute between Serbia and individuals in France, not France itself. This meant that the Court first had to determine its own competence to deal with the case (at 16).

The hurdle that the Court had to cross in order for it to be able to exercise jurisdiction in the case, which, it admitted, apparently fell within the municipal legal system, was the principle that it had laid down in its previous judgments in *Greece v. United Kingdom* (1924) PCIJ Ser. A, No. 2 (the *Mavrommatis Palestine Concessions*) and *Germany v. Poland* (1927) PCIJ Ser. A, No. 13 (*Interpretation of Judgments Nos 7 and 8; the Chorzów Factory Case*). In both cases, the Court had laid down the principle that when a State takes up a case on behalf of its nationals before international tribunals, a State is asserting its own rights—that is, its right to ensure, in the person of its subjects, respect for the rules of international law. Accordingly, in all of the cases in which the Court has had to deal with private interests, the State's claim has been based upon an alleged breach of an international agreement.

Evidently, the facts of the two earlier cases were different from those of the present case because, as the Court noted (at 18):

> The controversy submitted to the Court in the present case, on the contrary, solely relates to the existence and extent of certain obligations which the Serbian State is alleged to have assumed in respect of the holders of certain loans. *It therefore is exclusively concerned with relations between the borrowing States and private persons*, that is to say relations which are, in themselves, within the domain of municipal law. [Emphasis added]

Having distinguished the facts of the two cases from the instant case, the Court proceeded to lay down the basis upon which it felt international law could address an issue that, prima facie, was within the municipal legal system. The Court said (at 18) that:

> It is however to be noted that the question whether the manner in which the Serb-Croat-Slovene Government is conducting the service of its loans is in accordance with the obligation accepted by it, is no longer merely the subject of a controversy between the Government and its creditors. When the holders of the Serbian loans, considering that their rights were being disregarded, appealed to the French Government, the latter intervened on their behalf with the Serb-Croat-Slovene Government. Diplomatic negotiation followed: but whatever took place during these negotiations, it is common ground that the Serbia-Slovene-Croatia Government did not reject the intervention of the French Government, but contended that the service of the loan was being affected by it in full conformity with obligations resulting from the contract. This view however was not shared by the Government of the French Republic. As from this point, there exists between the two Governments a difference of opinion, which though fundamentally identical with the controversy already existing between the Serbia-Croatia-Slovene and its creditors, is distinct therefrom; for it is between the Government of the Serbia-Croatia-Slovene Kingdom and that of the French Republic, the latter acting in the exercise of its right to protect its nationals. It is this difference of opinions between the two Governments and not the dispute between the Serb-Croatia-Slovene Government and the French holders of the loans, which is submitted by the Special Agreement to the Court.

Thus the PCIJ could not bring itself to apply municipal law as between individuals and States, but when such issues have been transformed to international issues as between two States, then the jurisdiction of the Court would be correctly exercised. What these cases show is that international courts will apply international law and determine issues of international law between two States, regardless of the manner in which the legal issues arose.

thinking points

- *Under what circumstances will the International Court of Justice entertain a case involving a State and individual persons?*
- *How did the PCIJ distinguish between the* Mavrommatis Palestine Concessions *and the* Serbian Loans Case *with regard to its jurisdiction to try the latter?*

9.2.3 Issues arising from the exercise of municipal law: nationality of individual persons

The International Court of Justice (ICJ) has also applied the principle formulated in *Mavrommatis Palestine Concessions* and *Interpretation of Judgment Nos. 7 and 8* (see section 9.2.2) in cases concerning the question of nationality. Generally speaking, international law leaves the question of nationality of a person to be determined by the municipal law of States. This is because a State is the competent authority that can determine who is or is not its national; international law does not intrude into that sphere of responsibility.

In *Exchange of Greek and Turkish Populations Advisory Opinion* (1925) PCIJ Ser. B, No. 10, the Court said (at 20) that 'the national status of a person belonging to a State can only be based on the law of that State'.

See also A. McNair, *Law of Treaties* (2nd edn, Oxford: Clarendon Press, 1961), p. 100.

However, while a State is free to determine who are its nationals, it may not prescribe that its own rules of nationality must bind other States, nor can it dictate the effect of its domestic rules on the international plane.

. . . .

● *Liechtenstein v. Guatemala (Second Phase)* [1955] ICJ Rep 4 (The *Nottebohm Case*)

Nottebohm, who was a German national, had lived in Guatemala since 1905, where he had the centre of his business, until 1943. However, in 1939, he applied for naturalization in Liechtenstein, a place where one of his brothers lived and which he had always visited prior to the application. His application was successful. Liechtenstein brought the present claim on behalf of Nottebohm, whose property had been nationalized by Guatemala. Liechtenstein claimed that since it had duly granted its citizenship to Nottebohm, it had every right to represent him in the case against Guatemala. The principal question before the Court was whether Guatemala was obligated to recognize Nottebohm's citizenship as conferred by Liechtenstein.

The Court held (at 20–23) that:

> Nationality is within the domestic jurisdiction of the State, which entitles, by its own legislation, the rules relating to the acquisition of its nationality. But the issue which the Court must decide is not one which pertains to the legal system of Liechtenstein; to exercise protection is to place oneself on the plane of international law…when two States have conferred their nationality upon the same individual, on the same person and this situation is no longer confined within the limits of the domestic jurisdiction of one of these States but extends to the international field, international arbitrators or Courts of third States which are called upon to deal with this situation would allow the contradiction to subsist if they confine themselves to the view that nationality is exclusively within the domestic jurisdiction of the State. In order to resolve the conflict they have, on the contrary, sought to ascertain whether nationality has been conferred in circumstances such as to give rise to an obligation on the part of the respondent State to recognize the effect of nationality…
>
> …the character thus recognized on the international level as pertaining to nationality is in no way inconsistent with the fact that international law leaves it to each State to lay down the rules governing the grant of its own nationality… [b]ut on the other hand, a State cannot claim that the rules it has laid down are entitled to recognition by another State unless it has acted in conformity with the general aim of making the nationality granted accord with an effective link between the State and the individual.

thinking point
What is the principle regarding a State representing its nationals before an international court or tribunal?

The above quote from the decision of the Court in the *Nottebohm Case* clearly shows that matters of municipal jurisdiction may become relevant upon the international plane, in which case they do not remain exclusively within the domestic or municipal realm but become matters involving international persons and institutions. Where a question of international law (such as the link between a person and a State in a case in which the latter brings an international action to protect the former) arises from questions of municipal law (such as the grant of citizenship), such matters cease to be exclusively municipal.

9.2.4 Conflicts between international law and municipal law: the duty to fulfil international obligations in good faith

In international law, States must implement their international obligations in good faith. This principle, known as *pacta sunt servanda*, is one principal expectation that international law has of municipal law. This principle is most useful in two instances. Where there is conflict between international and municipal law, the rule is that the latter prevail. Where a State is unsure about how to interpret or implement international law vis-à-vis it own law, the rule is that the State must act in good faith and bring its internal law into conformity with its international obligations.

As the PCIJ said in the *Exchange of Greek and Turkish Populations Advisory Opinion* (1925) PCIJ Ser. B, No. 10, at 20, the principle:

> is self-evident, according to which a State which has contracted valid international obligations is bound to make in its legislation such modifications as may be necessary with a view to ensure the fulfilment of the obligations undertaken.

The Declaration on Rights and Duties of States, which was prepared by the International Law Commission and approved by the UN General Assembly in 1949, laid down the guidelines in its Article 13 thus:

> Every State has a duty to carry out in good faith its obligations arising from treaties and other sources of international law, and it may not invoke its provisions in its constitutions or its laws as an excuse for failure to perform this duty.

In addition to non-performance of obligations, a State may not also rely on its internal law to limit the scope of its international obligations, as confirmed in the *Free Zones of Upper Savoy and the District of Gex Advisory Opinion* (1932) PCIJ Ser. A/B, No. 46 (the *Free Zones Case*).

However, it is not for international law to decide for States how to avoid conflicts between their laws and international laws. Only States are entitled to decide this. Nevertheless, States sometimes fail to ensure avoidance of such conflicts and such instances have been known to generate tension between the two systems.

● ***Germany v. United States of America (Merits)*** (2001) ICJ Rep 466 (The *LaGrand Case*)

Two brothers, Karl and Walter LaGrand, German nationals who had resided permanently in the USA since childhood, were arrested in 1982 in Arizona for their involvement in an attempted bank robbery, in the course of which the bank manager was killed and another bank employee seriously injured. In 1984, an Arizona court convicted both brothers of murder in the first degree and sentenced them to death. The LaGrands being German nationals, the 1963 Vienna Convention on Consular Relations required the competent authorities of the USA to inform them without delay of their right to communicate with the German diplomatic consulate. The USA acknowledged that this did not occur.

Karl LaGrand was executed on 24 February 1999. On 2 March 1999, the day before the scheduled date of execution of Walter LaGrand, Germany brought the case to the ICJ. On 3 March 1999, the Court made an order indicating provisional measures stating, inter alia, that the USA should take all measures at its disposal to ensure that Walter LaGrand was not executed, pending a final decision of the Court. On that same day, Walter LaGrand was executed.

Germany alleged, among other things, that the failure of the USA to inform the LaGrand brothers of their right to contact the German authorities 'prevented Germany from exercising its rights under Art. 36(1)(a) and (c) of the Convention'. The main issue before the Court, in relation to our purpose here, was the claim by Germany that the failure of the USA to notify the LaGrand brothers of their rights under the Convention was a breach of its international obligation.

At [80] of the judgment, Germany argued that under Art. 36(2) VCLT:

> the United States is under an obligation to ensure that its municipal 'laws and regulations … enable full effect to be given to the purposes for which the rights accorded under this Article are intended' [and that it] is in breach of this obligation by upholding rules of domestic law which make it impossible to successfully raise a violation of the right to consular notification in proceedings subsequent to a conviction of a defendant by a jury …

The USA rejected this submission, claiming that a US procedural default rule, concerning the distribution of responsibilities between US federal and State courts, prevented it from applying the Convention.

On the effect of the 'procedural default' rule, which prevented the USA from complying with its obligation under the Convention, the Court said (at [90]–[91]) that:

> a distinction must be drawn between that rule as such and its specific application in the present case. In itself, the rule does not violate Article 36 of the Vienna Convention. The problem arises when the procedural default rule does not allow the detained individual to challenge a conviction and sentence by claiming, in reliance on Article 36, paragraph 1, of the Convention, that the competent national authorities failed to comply with their obligation to provide the requisite consular information 'without delay', thus preventing the person from seeking and obtaining consular assistance from the sending State. In this case, Germany had the right at the request of the LaGrands 'to arrange for [their] legal representation' and was eventually able to provide some assistance to that effect. By that time, however, because of the failure of the American authorities to comply with their obligation under Article 36, paragraph 1 (b), the procedural default rule prevented counsel for the LaGrands to effectively challenge their convictions and sentences other than on United States constitutional grounds. As a result … the procedural default rule prevented [US courts] from attaching any legal significance to the fact … that the violation of the rights set forth in Article 36, paragraph 1, prevented Germany, in a timely fashion, from retaining private counsel for [the LaGrands] and otherwise assisting in their defence as provided for by the Convention. Under these circumstances, the procedural default rule had the effect of preventing 'full effect [from being] given to the purposes for which the rights accorded under this Article are intended', and thus violated paragraph 2 of Article 36.

The facts of the above case and the decision of the Court present a clear example of the rule that a State cannot rely on its domestic law as a justification for violating its international law obligations. While the Court would usually not look into the value of the particular domestic law in question, or into whether it was properly or improperly exercised, it will consider the effect of the exercise of such domestic law on the country's international law obligation.

KEY POINTS

- In the *LaGrand Case*, the Court accepted that the issue regarding the distribution of responsibilities between federal and State courts in the USA, with respect to the 'procedural default' rule, is a matter for municipal law. However, if this distribution of responsibilities affects fulfilment of international obligations, that is a question for international law to resolve.

- An international court or tribunal does not intrude into municipal law simply because it exercises its jurisdiction in respect of the implementation of a municipal law that affects compliance of a State with its international obligations.

● *Mexico v. United States of America* (2004) ICJ REP 12 (The *Case Concerning Avena and Other Mexican Nationals*)

Mexico brought an action before the ICJ in respect of fifty-two of its nationals, all of whom were on death row in the USA for various charges. Mexico alleged, as with the *LaGrand Case*, that the USA violated the 1963 Vienna Convention on Consular Relations when it failed to inform the nationals of their right under the Convention. The USA raised similar objections to that which it raised in *LaGrand* and as in that case argued that the Court 'has no jurisdiction to review appropriateness of sentences in criminal cases, and even less to determine guilt or innocence, matters which only a court of criminal appeal could go into (at 33).

Mexico had specifically asked the Court to comment on the whole US criminal justice system on the basis of the 'procedural default' rule.

After considering the circumstances of the case, the Court stated (at 30) that:

> its jurisdiction in the present case has been invoked under the Vienna Convention and Optional Protocol to determine the nature and extent of the obligations undertaken by the United States towards Mexico by becoming party to that Convention. If and so far as the Court may find that the obligations accepted by the parties to the Vienna Convention *included commitments as to the conduct of their municipal courts in relation to the nationals of other parties, then in order to ascertain whether there have been breaches of the Convention, the Court must be able to examine the actions of those courts in the light of international law.* [Emphasis added]

It must be noted that, in *LaGrand*, the Court had called on the USA to revisit its procedural default rule and ensure that its implementation did not affect its fulfilment of its obligation under the Vienna Convention. In *Avena*, the Court found that the USA had not done this—a default that was partly responsible for the case brought against it by Mexico.

On the question of what remedy would be adequate to accommodate the operation of a municipal law rule that consistently made compliance with an international obligation impossible, the Court rejected the undertaking by the USA to give an advance apology for the recurrence of such problem, as was warranted by the 'procedural default' rule in both *LaGrand* and *Avena*. The Court stated (at [121] of the judgment) that its task is:

> to determine what would be adequate reparation for the violations of Article 36. It should be clear from what has been observed above that the internationally wrongful acts committed by the United States were the failure of its competent authorities to inform the Mexican nationals concerned, to notify Mexican consular posts and to enable Mexico to provide consular assistance. It follows that the remedy to make good these violations should consist in an obligation on the United States to permit review and reconsideration of these nationals' cases by the United States courts . . . with a view to ascertaining whether in each case the violation of Article 36 committed by the competent authorities caused actual prejudice to the defendant in the process of administration of criminal justice.

In essence, the Court in *Avena* refused to allow the USA to give an advance apology as a remedy for its repeated application of the domestic rule that caused it constantly to fail to implement its obligation under the Vienna Convention on Consular Relations.

The point of interest here is that whereas a State is entitled to prescribe remedies for wrongs suffered within its legal system, when such a wrong arises as a result of non-performance of international obligations due to the application of domestic rules, then that State will not be allowed to use its domestic rule to trump international law.

The attitude of international law to municipal law—in the context of the two cases discussed—was for international law to regard the pertinent municipal law as inconsistent with its rules. In neither of the cases did the Court challenge the validity of the domestic law involved; all that the Court was concerned with was to hold that the implementation of that municipal law prevented the USA from fulfilling its international obligations to both Germany and Mexico under the Convention.

As a matter of law, a general failure to bring municipal law into conformity with obligations under international law, whether these are treaty or customary obligations, does not constitute a breach. A breach occurs when failure to observe an obligation occurs on a particular occasion. In other words, the existence of the errant municipal law rule does not constitute a breach of international law, but rather the country's violation of international law obligations on the basis of such an errant rule is the actual breach.

It must also be pointed out that, in the cases discussed, the Court did not impose a solution on the municipal legal system: it did not instruct the US courts on what to do. What the Court insisted on was that whatever measures or remedies the USA adopted in response to the problem must be adequate and must remove the problem as it related to the fulfilment of an international obligation. The Court said quite clearly that a mere apology tendered by the USA in advance to countries in respect of which it may violate its obligations under the Vienna Convention on Consular Relations would be inadequate.

In response to the Court's stance in those cases, the USA reviewed all the cases of Mexicans on death row in respect of which Mexico brought the claim. However, perhaps in a retaliatory measure, the USA went on to withdraw its acceptance of the Optional Protocol to the Vienna Convention on the Settlement of Disputes, thereby terminating the Court's jurisdiction over such matters.

thinking points

- *What was the position of the ICJ towards the US application of its 'procedural default' rule vis-à-vis the country's treaty obligation in the 1963 Vienna Convention on Consular Relations?*
- *What remedy would be sufficient for a State to take in order to avert the constant violation of its international obligation by virtue of applying its municipal laws?*

9.3 International legal issues before municipal legal systems

International law issues before municipal legal systems are intricate and diverse. They range from how international law becomes part of national law, to how international legal matters are dealt with by municipal courts, and also how national authorities, such as the parliament, deal with international law. Perhaps, of all of these matters, the most engaging relate to the reception of international law by municipal law and the consideration of international legal matters before municipal courts.

The issue of international law before municipal courts is not as simple as the issue of municipal law before international law, which, as we discussed earlier, is partly regulated by international law itself and guided by a set of uniform rules. What is certain is that before municipal courts, particularly in the UK and most of the Commonwealth, international law, once ascertained, enjoys the status of law. This means that it does not require any formal proof for its establishment. This is unlike the status of foreign laws before English courts, which, unless specifically proved in evidence, remain only facts.

9.3.1 The reception of international law by municipal law

While international law enjoys a certain status before municipal courts, that does not mean that, upon ascertainment, all international legal rules automatically become part of the municipal law of a given country. This is partly due to the fact that international law itself is not a single body of law, but that which, in a traditional classification, consists mainly of treaty rules and customary rules, as well as general principles of law. And, as we discussed in Chapter 3, the processes for making treaties are radically different from the ways in which customary rules evolve—although one could mature into the other, just as one could influence the working of the other.

Further, international law deals with very different issues from those dealt with by municipal laws. Thus when States ratify treaties, such treaties often need to be reconciled, realigned, or synchronized with the ordinary law or constitutional laws of individual countries, which might be at variance with the obligations assumed under treaties. Therefore it is essential that the effect of international law within municipal legal systems is subject to specific consideration and processes by municipal authorities, lest the lamb of municipal law swallows the beast of international law.

There are many theories surrounding the process through which international law becomes part of municipal law. However, much depends on whether the international legal rules in question are customary rules or treaty obligations. The two most considered doctrines through which municipal law receives international law are called 'transformation' and 'incorporation', which we will discuss in the following sections.

9.3.2 Incorporation and transformation

. . . .

● *Trendtex Trading Corp. v. Central Bank of Nigeria* [1977] 1 QB 529

Lord Denning explained (at 553–554) the premises of the two doctrines as follows:

> One school of thought holds to the doctrine of incorporation. It says that the rules of international law are incorporated into English law automatically and considered to be part of English law unless they are in conflict with an Act of Parliament. The other school of thought holds to the doctrine of transformation. It says that the rules of international law are not to be considered as part of English law except in so far as they have been already adopted and made part of our law by the decisions of the judges, or by Act of Parliament, or long established customs. The difference is vital when you are faced with a change in the rules of international law. Under the doctrine of incorporation, when the rules of international law change, our English law changes with them. But, under the doctrine of transformation the English law does not change. It is bound by precedent. It is bound down to those rules of international law which have been accepted and adopted in the past. It cannot develop as international law develops.

As noted previously, when we speak of the process through which international law becomes part of municipal law we mean a process through which either treaties or customary rules become part of municipal law. In other words, how an international legal rule becomes part of a municipal legal system depends on whether the rule is a customary or treaty rule. And as Lord Denning indicates, each model of transmitting international law has a different and decisive effect on the municipal law of the recipient State.

9.3.3 Customs: the receipt of international law on the basis of incorporation

In most common law countries, the doctrine of incorporation is regarded as the vehicle through which customary rules become part of the municipal legal system. What this means is that once a customary rule has been certified as such, there is no need for an Act of Parliament to be introduced or for formal proof to be tendered before that rule can be recognized as forming part of the municipal legal system. Thus, once a customary rule is incorporated into the municipal system, it effectively alters that system, which must conform to the new rules of international law.

The doctrine of incorporation has been known to the English legal system for almost 300 years and has found acceptance among several judicial authorities. The origin of this doctrine is commonly credited to the often-quoted dictum of Lord Talbot in *Buvot v. Barbuit* (1736) 3 Burr 2016, taken down by a young William Murray (who was counsel in the case) and adopted by him in 1764 (when he had become Lord Mansfield CJ), in *Triquet v. Bath* (1764) 3 Burr 1478.

Lord Talbot had declared in *Barbuit* that:

> the law of nations in its full extent was part of the law of England ... that the law of nations was to be collected from the practice of different nations and the authority of writers.

In support of his proposition, Lord Talbot had relied on the authorities of Grotius, Barbeyrac, Binkershoek, Wiquefort, and so on, there being at that time no English writer of eminence on the subject.

Aside from its endorsement by Lord Mansfield in *Triquet v. Bath* in 1764, several renowned judicial and academic authorities adopted Lord Talbot's dictum during the years that followed. Principal among endorsing judges was Lord Lyndhurst who, in the House of Lords in 1853, with the concurrence of all his colleagues, declared that 'the law of nations, according to the decision of our greatest judges, is part of the law of England', as reported by Sir George Cornwall Lewis, *Lewis on Foreign Jurisdiction* (London: J. W. Parker and Son, 1859), pp. 66–67.

In *West Rand Gold Mining Co. v. R* (1905) 2 KB 391 (*West Rand*), the court stated that convincing evidence would be required to prove that the custom:

> was of such a nature, and has been so generally and widely accepted that it can hardly be supposed that any civilized state would repudiate it.

As will be recalled from Chapter 2, this follows from what needs to be proved before accepting certain norms as constituting customs in international law.

The relatively easy process of incorporating customary rules into municipal law, in comparison with the cumbersome transformation of treaties, owes much to the existence of many advantages enjoyed by customary rules of international law, which are not present in relation to the transformation of treaties into municipal law. To start with, there is no tension or division between different organs of government in respect of competence to deal with customary rules of international law, thereby guaranteeing a rather straightforward approach when compared to that of treaties. It will be recalled that treaties are concluded in many countries either by the parliament acting without significant input of the executive, or by the latter with minimum input from the parliament.

In fact, in countries such as the USA, the President is able to conclude certain treaties without any reference to Congress whatsoever. One undesirable consequence of the division of labour between various arms of government, in relation to concluding treaties, is that it may occasion a situation in which an organ of government, which is not traditionally responsible for making laws for the country, is able to conclude a treaty—which, in effect, may be law-making—without the concurrence or participation of the law-making organ as the parliament. This explains why although the Queen of England signs treaties on behalf of the British government, such treaties will have no effect *within* the country until they have been transformed specifically by Acts of Parliament. In this way, the possibility that the Queen might inadvertently make law for the country is averted. Thus, in a transformation scenario, it is often necessary for the entire structure of a government to know what is contained in a treaty before it can be transformed into the municipal law of the land.

In contrast, a country has a choice whether to accept a customary rule or persistently to object to it upon its formation. If it chooses the former, that rule will be regarded as incorporated into its law; if the latter, however, provided that the rule is generally accepted by the majority of other States (see Chapter 2), it is automatically incorporated into the municipal law. It does not depend upon a particular organ of the government to determine whether a country accepts or objects to a customary rule, and there is no need for laying eligible customs before any organ of the government, as with the 'Ponsonby Rule' in the UK.

When may customary rules not be incorporated into municipal law?

Despite the comparable ease of incorporating customary rules into municipal laws, there are circumstances under which a customary rule may not be automatically incorporated, or may not be incorporated at all, into municipal laws. First, the relevant customary rule must not be inconsistent with an existing Act of Parliament; otherwise, there will be no incorporation at all. Secondly, in certain countries, some customary rules must be specifically transformed into law by Acts of Parliament; this means that incorporation is possible only through transformation of the rules by Acts of Parliament. An example of this is the incorporation of international law crimes.

Let us now consider the situations under which custom will not be incorporated automatically or will not be incorporated at all.

Inconsistency with a municipal law

. . . .
● *Mortensen v. Peters* (1906) 8F (JC) 93, Scottish Court of Justiciary

The Danish master of a Norwegian steam trawler was prosecuted for using a particular method of fishing in the Moray Firth. He argued that although the statute banning the method would have caught a British fisherman, it should be construed as impliedly excepting all foreigners fishing from foreign vessels outside the territorial jurisdiction of the British Crown.

The court held that the defence failed. Lord Salvesen said that it could scarcely be supposed that the British Parliament should pass legislation placing British fishermen under a disability that did not extend to foreigners:

> I think it was a just observation of the Solicitor General that, if legislation of this nature had been proposed, and the words inserted which the Dean of Faculty maintained were implied, it would never have been submitted by a responsible minister or have received the approval of Parliament.

● *Polites v. Commonwealth* (1945) 70 CLR 60, High Court of Australia

The issue arose for the first time in this case, in which the Australian court had to consider the status of customary rules in Australia. In the course of his judgment, William J stated that customary international law:

> when it has been established to the satisfaction of the court, is recognised and acted upon as part of . . . municipal law so far as it is not inconsistent with rules enacted by statutes or finally declared by courts.

Incorporation of customary international crimes: the so-called attempt to abandon incorporation for transformation in the UK

In the UK, it is not in doubt that customary rules are incorporated into municipal law, provided that they are not inconsistent with Acts of Parliament. Thus customary international law forms part of UK law (*Trendtex*, see section 9.3.2). However, some writers have suggested that there was an attempt, at a point in the development of incorporation theory, when it might have been abandoned in favour of transformation. Support for this view was drawn from a much-quoted statement of Cockburn J in the following case.

● *R v. Keyn* (1876) 2 Ex D 63

This case arose from an incident in which *The Franconia*, a German ship, collided with a British ship, sinking the latter and killing its passengers. The German captain was sued for manslaughter in the UK. The question before the court was whether it had jurisdiction to try the matter.

It was held that there was no jurisdiction. Cockburn CJ stated (at 203) that:

> Nor, in my opinion, would the clearest proof of unanimous assent on the part of other nations be sufficient to authorize the tribunals of this country to apply, without an Act of Parliament, what would practically amount to a new law. In so doing we should be unjustifiably usurping the province of the legislature. The assent of nations is doubtless sufficient to give the power of parliamentary legislation in a matter otherwise within the sphere of international law; but it would be powerless to confer without such legislation a jurisdiction beyond and unknown to the law, such as that now insisted on, a jurisdiction over foreigners in foreign ships on a portion of the high seas.

Several writers interpret this statement as suggesting that the court moved away from incorporation in favour of the transformation of customary rules. For example, Malcolm Shaw, *International Law* (6th edn, Cambridge: Cambridge University Press, 2008), at p. 107, said that *West Rand* (see earlier in this section) 'showed a further blurring of the distinction between the incorporation and transformation theories'.

But really it seems that the interpretations accorded to Cockburn CJ's statement in *R v. Keyn* by writers was much wider than his Lordship had intended and what, as will be seen shortly, a careful analysis of the statement seems to indicate.

It seems that all Cockburn CJ attempted to do in *R v. Keyn* was:

(a) to make a stronger case for incorporation of customary rules; and

(b) to limit the scope of *the* customary rules that can be regarded as *automatically* incorporated into the municipal law of the UK.

On the first point, Ian Brownlie, in *Principles of International Law* (7th edn, Oxford: Oxford University Press, 2008), p. 43, rightly observes that:

> the elements of 'transformation' in the judgment of Cockburn, CJ, are entirely *compatible with the doctrine of incorporation if it is seen that he was concerned with the proof of the rules of international law*: if the evidence is inconclusive and the issue affects the liberty of persons, then assent by the legislature of the forum is needed to supplement the evidence. Yet as a general condition he does not require express assent or a functional transformation by Act of Parliament. [Emphasis added]

On the second point, it is clear that what his Lordship advocated *against* was the incorporation of *all* rules of customary international law into the UK domestic legal system. He clearly argued that the 'assent of nations' (which obviously enables treaties, as well as customs) is 'powerless to confer without such legislation a *jurisdiction* beyond what is known to the law'. Thus Cockburn CJ intended to exclude from being incorporated into the English municipal laws *'jurisdiction beyond and unknown to the law'*. Certainly, customary international law does not only deal with issues of jurisdiction. The question therefore is: what is 'jurisdiction beyond and unknown to the law' of the UK, which Cockburn CJ precluded from the incorporation doctrine? The answer, it seems, has come from both the UK and Australia.

. . . .

● *R v. Jones* [2006] UKHL 16

In March 2003, the appellants, Margaret Jones and Paul Milling, broke into the Royal Air Force (RAF) base at Fairford in Gloucestershire and caused damage to fuel tankers and bomb trailers. They had conspired together to do so. A little later, the appellants Toby Olditch and Philip Pritchard, conspired together to cause criminal damage at the base. On 18 March 2003, they had in their possession articles that they intended to use to destroy or damage the runway at the base and aircraft belonging to the United States Air Force (USAF). On the same date, 18 March 2003, the appellant Josh Richards attempted to set fire to an aircraft at the base belonging to the USAF. He had with him on that date articles that he intended to use to destroy or damage such aircraft. Also on that date, he caused damage to a perimeter fence at the base.

In their case, the 'Fairford appellants' had argued, inter alia, that:

> crimes recognised in customary international law are, without the need for any domestic statute or judicial decision, *recognised and enforced by the domestic law of England and Wales*. [Emphasis added]

In support of their arguments, the appellants relied mainly on the authorities of Blackstone, who listed 'principal offences against the law of nations, animadverted on as such by the municipal laws of England' (see Bk IV, ch. 5, p. 68).

Lord Bingham undertook a comprehensive review of those customary international law crimes, and held (at [23]) that:

> I would accordingly accept that a crime recognised in customary international law may be assimilated into the domestic criminal law of this country. The appellants, however, go further and contend that that result follows automatically. The authorities, as I read them, *do not support that proposition*. Lord Cockburn CJ rejected it in *R v. Keyn* (1876) 2 Ex D 63, 203. [Emphasis added]

Lord Bingham had killed the proverbial two birds with one stone in this judgment. On the one hand, he accepted that it is possible that a crime recognized by customary international law may be assimilated (incorporated) into the law of the UK, which means that he did not generally attempt to replace incorporation with transformation. On the other hand, he stated that incorporation does not *automatically* apply to *customary crimes*, which means that he advocated transformation only in respect of certain customary rules—namely, customary crimes. What is more important is that Lord Bingham had supported his second view with the same statement of Cockburn CJ that gave birth to the rather strained interpretation.

In support of his position in the above case, Lord Bingham had relied on *Nulyarimma v. Thompson*, a very interesting Australian case that clarified that country's position on the relations between customary rules and municipal law. But before delving into *Nulyarimma*, it is instructive to consider briefly what the position was in Australia before the case was decided in 1999.

Prior to *Nulyarimma*, the relation of customary international law and municipal law in Australia was somewhat hazy. Although, in *Mabo v. Queensland (No. 2)* (1992) 175 CLR 42, it was said that international law, including treaties and customary laws, is a 'legitimate and important influence on the development of the common law, especially when international law declares the existence of universal human rights', the exact nature of this relationship was not clear.

See also *Polites v. Commonwealth* (earlier in this section).

. . . .

● *Chow Hung Ching v. R* (1948) 77 CLR 449

In this case, however, Dixon J stated *obiter* that 'international law is not a part of, but is one of the sources of, English law'. In the same case, Latham CJ noted that:

> International law is not as such part of the law of Australia . . . but a universally recognised principle of international law would be applied by our courts.

. . . .

● *Nulyarimma v. Thompson* (1999) 96 FCR 153 www.hrlc.org.au/files/FZAYZKX1XJ/Customary International Law in Australia.DOC (pp. 2–4).

The applicants brought this case against the respondents, some officials of the federal government, alleging that they had acted unlawfully by declining to proceed with an application by Australia to place the lands of the Arabunna people on the World Heritage List, and through the formulation of the government's Ten-Point Plan and support for the Native Title Amendment Act 1998. The appellants claimed that, as a result of the conduct of the respondents, the latter had committed acts of genocide, in breach of customary international law. The respondents argued that the application did not give rise to any reasonable cause of action known to Australian law.

The question before the court was not whether Australia recognized the crime of genocide: Australia certainly does and is a signatory to the 1948 UN Convention on the Prevention and Punishment of the Crime of Genocide (the Genocide Convention). The main issue was whether genocide, as a crime under customary international law, forms part of Australian municipal law so that it can lead to a right of action before its domestic courts.

The court held (at 2–3) that the customary crime of genocide does not form part of the Australian law. According to Wilcox J (at 20):

> … it is one thing to say Australia has an international legal obligation to prosecute or extradite a genocide suspect found within its territory, and that the Commonwealth Parliament may legislate to ensure that obligation is fulfilled; *it is another thing to say that, without legislation to that effect, such a person may be put on trial for genocide before an Australian court*. If this were the position, it would lead to the curious result that an international obligation incurred pursuant to customary law has greater domestic consequences than an obligation incurred, expressly and voluntarily, by Australia signing and ratifying an international convention. Ratification of a convention does not directly affect Australian domestic law unless and until implementing legislation is enacted. This seems to be the position even where the ratification has received Parliamentary approval, as in the case of the Genocide Convention. [Emphasis added]

In a similar vein, Whitlam J said (at 52) that:

> … Even if it be accepted that customary international law is part of the common law, *no one has identified a rule of customary international law to this effect: that courts in common law countries have jurisdiction in respect of those international crimes over which States may exercise universal jurisdiction*. Universal jurisdiction conferred by the principles of international law is a component of sovereignty [*Polyukhovich* per Toohey J at 661], and the way in which sovereignty is exercised will depend on each common law country's peculiar constitutional arrangements. [Emphasis added]

But the rationale for the view expressed by Wilcox J is suspect, considering that he drew support from the rather unrelated statements of Mason CJ and Deane J in *Minister for Immigration and Ethnic Affairs v. Teoh* (1995) HCA 20; (1995) 183 CLR 273, 286–287, in which their Lordships said that:

> It is well established that the provisions of an international treaty to which Australia is a party do not form part of Australian law unless those provisions have been validly incorporated into our municipal law by statute. This principle has its foundation in the proposition that in our constitutional system the making and ratification of treaties fall within the province of the Executive in the exercise of its prerogative power whereas the making and the alteration of the law fall within the province of Parliament, not the Executive. So, a treaty which has not been incorporated into our municipal law cannot operate as a direct source of individual rights and obligations under that law.

This statement related to treaties, not customary international law, which was in issue in *Nulyarimma*.

The third judge in *Nulyarimma*, Merkel J, however, disagreed with his colleagues. In his view, customary international law is a source of domestic law, so that it forms part of the municipal law of Australia, and this includes customary international law crimes. However, the judge formulated some six principles to guide the adoption of customary rules into the municipal legal system.

Although one may find Merkel J's statement more persuasive, the effect of the majority judgment in *Nulyarimma* is that Australia does not accept the automatic incorporation of customary crimes, although the country accepts the incorporation doctrine in general. This, it is submitted, is exactly what Cockburn CJ also attempted to do in *R v. Keyn*—that is, while Cockburn CJ accepted the incorporation of customary rules in general, he objected to the automatic incorporation of such in respect of jurisdiction over certain crimes.

Later cases in Australia have confirmed the judgment in *Nulyarimma*.

● **Thorpe v. Kennett** (1999) VSC 442

Warren J, in the Victorian Supreme Court, adopted the judgments of Wilcox and Whitlam JJ in *Nulyarimma*, and declined to regard genocide as incorporated as a criminal offence in Victoria unless the Parliament enacted specific legislation.

● **Sumner v. United Kingdom of Great Britain & ors** [2000] SASC 456, SUPREME COURT OF SOUTH AUSTRALIA, 27 OCTOBER 1999

Nyland J, in the South Australian Supreme Court, followed *Nulyarimma*, finding (particularly at [27] *et seq*) that:

> notwithstanding the fact that both customary international law and international conventions may ... have some influence upon the common law, in the case of the crime of genocide there is no scope for such development. [See 'Blake Dawson Waldron'.]

With respect to other common law jurisdictions of note, the situation with regard to the relations between customary international law and the common law is unsettled. In Canada, for example, this issue is yet to be considered by the Canadian Supreme Court. However, in *Bouzari v. Iran (Islamic Republic)* [2002] OJ No. 1624, in the Ontario Superior Court of Justice, Swinton J, stated (*obiter* at [39]) that 'customary rules of international law are directly incorporated into Canadian domestic law unless ousted by contrary legislation'. Notably, the decision was not unanimous and the dissenting judgments were vigorous. Further, the decision did not touch on the issue of customary international crimes in particular. The New Zealand courts have not had the opportunity to consider whether customary international law forms part of domestic law.

thinking points

- *Explain the difference between incorporation and transformation, and explain the benefits of one over the other, if any.*
- *When will customary international law rules not be incorporated into the municipal legal system?*
- *What is the ratio for the decision in* Nulyarimma *and to what extent does this decision mirror the practice in the UK?*

Stare decisis

It is often said that a customary rule cannot be incorporated if it will conflict with a decision of a higher court of the land. This is the English doctrine of *stare decisis*, a common law doctrine applicable by most common law countries. By this doctrine, a decision of a higher court is binding on a lower court and the lower court can depart from that decision only by distinguishing facts of a case before it from those before the higher court or if the higher court overrules itself. The question then is whether the doctrine of *stare decisis* should be applied to the relations between customary rules and the English legal system. If it applies, it will mean that a court in England will not accept a customary rule if that rule is inconsistent with a decision of a higher court.

If one subscribes to the position of Merkel J in *Nulyarimma*, then the answer would be in the affirmative: if there is a judgment of a higher court against a customary rule, such customary rule cannot be recognized by a lower court, even in the absence of a statute. In that case, since judgments of the courts constitute part of common law and since the judgments of higher courts cannot be derogated from by lower courts, except in the circumstances identified above, then the customary rule is inconsistent with the law of the land.

However, the position is not so certain in England. The initial approach of the English courts to the issue was enunciated in *Chung Chi Cheung v. The King* [1939] AC 160. In that case, Lord Atkins stated that a rule will be adopted or received into, and so become a source of, domestic law if it is 'not inconsistent with rules enacted by statutes or finally declared by [the courts]'. The use of 'or' suggests that a customary rule can be inconsistent either with a statute or a declaration of the court. But this subjugating incorporation of customary rules to the principle of *stare decisis* or common law in general has been criticized by several authorities. For some judges, what constitutes common law is fluid and does not reflect the democratic processes that Acts of Parliament undoubtedly reflect.

The statement of Laws J in *R v. Lord Chancellor, ex p Witham* [1998] QB 575, 581D, is apt here:

> In the unwritten legal order of the British state, at a time when the common law continues to accord a legislative supremacy to Parliament, the notion of a constitutional right can in my judgment inhere only in this proposition, that the right in question cannot be abrogated by the state save by specific provision in an Act of Parliament, or by regulations whose vires in main legislation specifically confers the power to abrogate. General words will not suffice. And any such rights will be creatures of the common law, since their existence would not be the consequence of the democratic political process but would be logically prior to it.

However, it seems that the English courts might not apply the doctrine of *stare decisis* where the previous decision in question is obsolete, as regards the development of international law.

. . . .

● *Trendtex Trading Corporation v. Central Bank of Nigeria* [1977] 1 QB 529

Lord Denning (at 578–579) said, regarding the application of the doctrine of *stare decisis*, that:

> Seeing that the rules of international law have changed—and do change—and that the courts have given effect to the changes without any Act of Parliament, it follows to my mind inexorably that the rules of international law, as existing from time to time, do form part of our English law. It follows, too, that a decision of this court—as to what was the ruling of international law 50 or 60 years ago—is not binding on this court today. *International law knows no rule of* stare decisis. If this court today is satisfied that the rule of international law on a subject has changed from what it was 50 or 60 years ago, it can give effect to that change—and apply the change in our English law—without waiting for the House of Lords to do it. [Emphasis added]

The above decision shows that where a doctrine of international law has been applied by the courts, the courts will not be bound to follow that decision where the rule of international law has changed.

The transformation of treaties into municipal law

In Chapter 3 we noted that treaties are the most stable source of international law, since they mostly evolve through the conscious efforts of States to write down, in black and white, obligations by which they wish to be bound and which they intend to share with other States.

However, the processes by which States ratify treaties, in terms of the State entities having political authority for such a task, differ from one State to another, and this has differing consequences for the effect of a treaty within that State and the modality through which the treaty becomes part of the relevant State law.

In the UK, for example, a treaty is ratified by the Queen upon the advice of the Prime Minister—but only after the treaty has been laid before the Parliament for twenty-one days under the 'Ponsonby Rule' (as amended, see Chapter 3). Thus, except for the Ponsonby requirement, the UK Parliament would normally have no direct involvement in the making of a treaty. If this treaty were to be incorporated directly into domestic law, one possible consequence that might result is that the Queen would be empowered to alter domestic law, constituting in real terms, making a new law for the country. Without doubt, the possibility of the monarch 'making' or altering the laws of the UK runs contrary to the concept of parliamentary sovereignty that is the bedrock of the British political system.

Thus while a treaty duly ratified by the Queen may automatically become effective in the international relations of the UK with other States—that is, without the need for further measures from the UK government—this is not so with regard to the effectiveness of the same treaty under British municipal law. This is especially so for treaties that affect the private rights of British citizens.

. . . .

● ***The Parlement Belge*** (1879) 4 PD 129

A case arose from an action brought in 1878 by owners of a steam tug *Daring* against owners of a steamship, *The Parlement Belge*, for a sum of money due from a collision between the two vessels in 1878, near Dover. The owners of *The Parlement Belge* claimed that the ship enjoyed immunity, being property of the King of Belgium, and that there was a convention between the latter and the Queen of England that placed *The Parlement Belge* in the category of war ships, thereby entitled to immunity. There was no doubt that there was indeed a convention. But the issue was whether, in the absence of the convention being transformed into English domestic law by an Act of Parliament, the convention formed part of English law.

The court held (per Sir Robert Phillimore) that the convention could not be regarded as having become part of English law in the absence of an Act of Parliament to that effect. His Lordship relied heavily on the authoritative writing of *William Blackstone*, which stated that the only type of conventions that do not require transformation by Acts of Parliament before becoming part of the English law are war-related treaties, such as the 1856 Declaration of Paris. The basis of this is that such treaties do not deprive British subjects of their private rights.

Sir Robert Phillimore also relied on the writing of Chancellor Kent (Kent's Comm. Vol. i., 1873, p. 166) thus:

> Treaties of peace, when made by the competent power, are obligatory upon the whole nation. If the treaty requires the payment of money to carry into effect, and the money cannot be raised but by an Act of the legislature, the treaty is morally obligatory upon the legislature to pass the law, and to refuse it would be a breach of public faith.

Although the judgment of Sir Robert Phillimore was overturned on appeal, on the basis that the relief sought existed in customary international law, the rationale of the decision concerning the relations of treaties with the domestic law of England stands.

● *Maclaine Watson v. Department of Trade* [1990] 2 AC 418, House of Lords

Lord Oliver stated (at 500) that:

> as a matter of the constitutional law of the United Kingdom, the royal prerogative, whilst it embraces the making of treaties, does not extend to altering the law or conferring rights on individuals or depriving individuals of rights which they enjoy in domestic law without the intervention of Parliament. Treaties, as it is sometimes expressed, are not self-executing. Quite simply, a treaty is not part of English law unless and until it has been incorporated into the law by legislation.

9.4.1 Transformed and untransformed treaties and municipal courts

There are many issues that arise concerning the relations of treaties, whether transformed or untransformed, before municipal courts. It must be noted that although a treaty has to be transformed—that is, adopted by an Act of Parliament in England—before it can be of any effect *within* the country, untransformed treaties are not devoid of legal effects as per the international relations between the UK and other countries.

Untransformed treaties and rights of State parties before the court

A treaty that has not been transformed into the municipal law of England is not justiciable in its courts. This means that matters arising from untransformed treaties cannot form the basis of actions before the UK municipal courts. As laid down in *Cook v. Sprigg* [1899] AC 572, 578, and confirmed in the *Tin Council Cases*:

> It is axiomatic that municipal courts have not and cannot have the competence to adjudicate upon or to enforce the rights arising out of transactions entered into by independent sovereign states between themselves on the plane of international law. That was firmly established by this House in *Cook v. Sprigg* [1899] A.C. 572, 578, and was succinctly and convincingly expressed in the opinion of the Privy Council delivered by Lord Kingsdown in *Secretary of State in Council of India v. Kamachee Boye Sahaba* [1859] 13 Moo. P.C.C. 22, 75 …

● *J. H. Rayner (Mincing Lane) Ltd v. Department of Trade and Industry* [1990] 2 AC 418 (The *Tin Council Cases*)

The International Tin Council (ITC) was an international organization established by treaty in 1956 and was constituted by the Sixth International Tin Agreement (ITA6) made between a number of States, including the UK. Under ITA6, its functions were to adjust world production and consumption of tin, and to prevent excessive fluctuation in the price of tin. Although ITA6 was never made part of the law of England, the ITC had its headquarters and principal office in London, pursuant to another agreement. The ITC was recognized under English law by the International Tin Council (Immunities and Privileges) Order 1972, SI 1072/120. The Order endowed the ITC, for all relevant purposes of English law, with the legal character and status and legal capacities of a corporate body, which enabled it to contract under the name ITC. The Order granted certain immunities to the ITC.

The case arose from a suit brought by certain banks to which the ITC owed money for the enforcement of a judgment that they obtained at arbitration. The relevant issue before the court was whether it could recognize and allow an untransformed treaty to be the basis for a claim in the English court.

It was held that:

> ...the Crown's power to conclude treaties with other sovereign states was an exercise of the Royal Prerogative...but that the Royal Prerogative did not extend to altering domestic law or rights of individuals without the intervention of Parliament and a treaty was not part of English law unless and until it had been incorporated into it by legislation

Lord Templeman, on behalf of their Lordships, said (at 476) that:

> [a] treaty to which Her Majesty's Government is a party does not alter the laws of the United Kingdom. A treaty may be incorporated into and alter the laws of the United Kingdom by means of legislation. Except to the extent that a treaty becomes incorporated into the laws of the United Kingdom by statute, the courts of the United Kingdom have no power to enforce treaty rights and obligations at the behest of a sovereign government or at the behest of a private individual.

An interesting question that follows from the non-justiciable status of an untransformed treaty is whether such treaties can be referred to at all before municipal courts. On this point, opinions vary.

● **J. H. Rayner (Mincing Lane) Ltd v. Department of Trade and Industry** [1990] 2 AC 418
(The *Tin Council Cases*)

Lord Oliver stated that an untransformed treaty could not be referenced by the UK courts. According to his Lordship (at 500 *et seq*):

> Treaties, as it is sometimes expressed, are not self-executing. Quite simply, a treaty is not part of English law unless and until it has been incorporated into the law by legislation. So far as individuals are concerned, it is *res inter alios acta* from which they cannot derive rights and by which they cannot be deprived of rights or subjected to obligations; and it is outside the purview of the court not only because it is made in the conduct of foreign relations, which are a prerogative of the Crown, but also because, as a source of rights and obligations, it is irrelevant.

But his Lordship was happy to reference transformed treaties. According to Lord Oliver, the propositions that an untransformed treaty is outside the purview of the court:

> ...do not involve as a corollary that the court must never look at or construe a treaty. Where, for instance, a treaty is directly incorporated into English law by Act of the legislature, its terms become subject to the interpretative jurisdiction of the court in the same way as any other Act of the legislature. *Fothergill v. Monarch Airlines Ltd.* [1981] A.C. 251 is a recent example.

His Lordship then went on to state several examples of when a transformed treaty may be referenced by English courts:

> it is well established that where a statute is enacted in order to give effect to the United Kingdom's obligations under a treaty, the terms of the treaty may have to be considered and, if necessary, construed in order to resolve any ambiguity or obscurity as to the meaning or scope of the statute. Clearly, also, where parties have entered into a domestic contract in which they have chosen to incorporate the terms of the treaty, the court may be called upon to interpret the treaty for the purposes of ascertaining the rights and obligations of the parties under their contract. Further cases in which the court may not only be empowered but required to adjudicate upon the meaning or scope of the terms of an international treaty arise where domestic legislation, although not incorporating the treaty, nevertheless requires, either expressly or by necessary implication, resort to be had to its terms for the purpose of construing the legislation (as in *Zoernsch v. Waldock* [1964] 1 W.L.R. 675) or the very rare case in which the exercise of the Royal Prerogative directly effects an extension or contraction of the jurisdiction without the constitutional need for internal legislation, as in *Post Office v. Estuary Radio Ltd*. [1968] 2 Q.B. 740.

From the above, it is clear that untransformed treaties cannot be referenced, while transformed ones can be for particular purposes, some of which were listed by Lord Oliver.

It must be pointed out that the rather strict approach of Lord Oliver, by which an untransformed treaty must not be referenced at all, is contrary to that of Kerr and Nourse LJJ who, in the Court of Appeal, had shown a greater flexibility towards untransformed treaties. As far as the two Lord Justices were concerned, since the British Parliament, in its Order-in-Council, had referred to the ITC, nothing prevented their referring to the treaty.

Lord Oliver rejected the approach by Kerr and Nourse LJJ, and treated their rationale for referring to an untransformed treaty—the supposed reference to it by the Parliament—as mistaken. According to Lord Oliver (at 511):

> As regards the references [by the Parliament] to the treaty provisions, these are made *for the very limited purposes of defining the official activities of the I.T.C.* and the inter-governmental organisations whose representatives are qualified for the immunities conferred by the Order. It cannot be deduced from this that Parliament was opening the door for the reception into English law of all the terms of the treaty and the creation, *sub silentio*, of rights and duties not grounded upon domestic law but created solely by the treaty provisions. [Emphasis added]

Lord Oliver clearly distinguished between a general blanketing of references to untransformed treaties. Thus an untransformed treaty can be referenced where, as in the *Tin Council Cases*, it is for defining the official representatives of an organization, as well as others entitled to immunity under the treaty, which is a matter of international law. This reference, however, must not extend to identifying the rights of those people before the court. It is doubtful, for example, whether a court in England can use untransformed treaties to identify and determine the constitution of an organization on the basis that such an exercise avails the court of evidence of certain facts. This was the approach taken by Coleman J in *Westland Helicopters Ltd v. Arab Organization for Industrialization* [1992] 2 All ER 387.

9.4.2 Untransformed treaties and foreign companies before English courts

Another issue that arises before the courts in relation to untransformed treaties is the fate of foreign companies before the English courts. The issue is an interesting one. As already noted, an untransformed treaty cannot form the basis for identifying the rights of State parties before the English courts, simply because such a treaty has not been made part of English municipal law. But a situation could arise in which an international organization, which is formed under that treaty and incorporated in a country with which the UK enjoys full diplomatic relations, appears before the English courts. The question here is: should the UK recognize the organization that is formed under the treaty, which remains untransformed in the UK, but is transformed in the national State of that organization, which State has diplomatic relations with the UK?

· ·

● *Arab Monetary Fund v. Hashim (No. 3)* [1991] 2 AC 114

Part of the issue before the English courts in this case was the status of the Arab Monetary Fund (AMF) before English courts. The AMF was established under an international treaty to which the UK was not a party; hence, the treaty was not transformed into UK law. However, the Fund was incorporated under the laws of the United Arab Emirates (UAE) with which the UK had a diplomatic relationship. On the question as to the status of the Fund before the English courts, the House of Lords held that the Fund, being an international organization established under a treaty not recognized by UK law, had no legal existence under the laws of the UK. However, curiously, their Lordships accepted that, since the Fund had a separate legal entity under UAE law and the UK had diplomatic relations with the UAE, then the Fund would be recognized to that effect under UK law.

It is worth noting that the House of Lords applied private international law rules (that is, conflict-of-law rules) in order to recognize the Fund under UK law.

While some writers have questioned the Lords' decision in the above case not to apply the same conflict-of-law rule to the Fund as it would to an international law creation, the fact of the matter is that private international law rules and public international law rules work differently. Therefore, the fact that a juristic entity fails to be recognized under UK law on the plausible basis that it was established under a treaty not transformed in the UK does not preclude such an entity from enjoying a certain status before the UK courts under a different legal category, such as conflict of laws.

KEY POINTS

- An English court may not use an untransformed treaty as the basis for identifying the individual rights of parties to that treaty.

- An English court may make reference to an untransformed treaty for specific purposes, as identified by Lord Oliver in the *Tin Council Cases*.

- Where the public international law rules governing a particular situation cannot be applied by the courts, the courts may resort to the application of private international law (conflict of law) rules.

9.4.3 Treaty versus municipal law: the question of superiority

Does a treaty take precedence over the municipal laws of the land upon transformation? Put differently: as between domestic laws and treaty obligations, which takes precedence? This question is different from that considered previously, which dealt with the obligation of State parties to a treaty to ensure that their own laws do not hinder them from implementing the treaty; the current question deals with the status between treaty and domestic laws.

The approach of States to the above-formulated question depends on their legal traditions. Generally speaking, the UK and most of the common law countries follow a system whereby municipal laws are construed in a way that does not contradict treaty obligations. However, where a subsequent Act of Parliament negates such a treaty, then the Act takes precedence since, in that case, the new law is regarded as an effective amendment or repeal of the treaty obligations.

In countries following the civil law traditions, however, the issue is addressed differently. In many of such countries, treaties enjoy equal status with municipal law, while in others, treaties are even regarded as superior to municipal law. This latter position is an endorsement of monism, although this is not so explicitly stated by the constitutions of the relevant countries.

In the Netherlands, the 1983 Constitution clearly places treaties above the municipal laws. According to Article 94, the relevant provision:

> Statutory regulations in force within the Kingdom shall not be applicable if such application is in conflict with provisions of treaties or of resolutions by international institutions that are binding on all persons.

Despite the fact that this provision clearly places treaties above Dutch national laws, there are many controls that national institutions can exercise over the process. To start with, according to Article 91(3) of the Constitution:

> Any provisions of a treaty that conflict with the Constitution or which lead to conflicts with it may be approved by the Parliament only if at least two-thirds of the votes cast are in favour.

It is obvious from this provision that a treaty that conflicts with the Dutch Constitution can be passed only by a two-thirds majority of the Parliament. This is a serious and effective constitutional constraint to ensure that a treaty that, in fact, conflicts with the Dutch Constitution will not be allowed to become part of the law of the land. Furthermore, it is important that all treaties—including those exempted from approval under article 91(1), as well as resolutions of international organizations—are published before they can be regarded as binding.

The situation is quite similar in Germany, as far as the status of treaties vis-à-vis municipal law is concerned. By virtue of Article 25 of the Grundgesetz (GG), or 'Basic Law':

> the general rules of international law shall be an integral part of federal law. They shall take precedence over the laws and directly create rights and duties for the inhabitants of the federal territory.

But here is where the comparison ends, because, according to Article 59(1), it is the President of Germany who is responsible for concluding treaties with foreign States. However, under Article 59(2):

> treaties that regulate the political relations of the Federation or relate to subjects of federal legislation shall require the consent or participation, in the form of a federal law, of the bodies responsible in such a case for the enactment of federal law.

This provision also applies to executive agreements.

However, unlike the situation in the Netherlands, the Bundesverfassungsgericht (BVerfG, the German Federal Constitutional Court) has enormous powers in determining the relations between the German municipal law and treaties, a power that the court used effectively in the attempt by Germany to sign up to the 1993 Maastricht Treaty of the European Union.

Of the common law countries—most of the practices of which resemble those of the UK—the US approach is remarkably different. In the USA, the President is empowered by the Constitution to conclude treaties, acting with the advice and consent of the Senate, two-thirds of which are expected to support the treaty. The treaty, with the law of the USA, constitutes part of the supreme laws of the land, binding both federal and State authorities. This means that once the US President concludes treaties, those treaties automatically become part of US law without transformation.

The fact that treaties enjoy virtually the same status as the municipal laws of the USA means that a treaty may alter the position of an existing domestic law; conversely, new legislation made by Congress takes precedence over a treaty.

Conclusion

The relationship between municipal law and international law is constantly evolving. Whereas, in its early days, international law dealt mainly with relations between States, modern developments have extended its scope to the extent that international law now deals not only with its own relations with municipal entities, but also governs matters concerning private entities within States. Nowadays, activities of non-State entities, such as non-governmental organizations (NGOs) and civil society organizations (CSOs), significantly impact on the relations between municipal and international law, just as it is now possible for international law to deal directly with individual human rights issues in domestic legal systems, as did the ICJ in the *LaGrand Case*.

It should be noted that the theoretical approach to the status of international law within municipal legal systems, as well as the relationship between international and municipal law, depends on the approach adopted by the State in question. The practice of some of the civil law countries discussed previously lends credence to the monist school, while the common law countries present shifting positions, but mostly embrace the dualist position. For the latter countries, the municipal institutions guard the realm of municipal law jealously, not easily introducing or welcoming the application of 'externally' produced rules.

Nevertheless, regardless of what theoretical approach one adopts, it can safely be said that international tribunals will usually apply international law, and municipal tribunals, municipal law. This means that when municipal tribunals acknowledge and apply international law, it is usually to the extent that such international law is regarded as part of the municipal legal system and therefore law. This probably tilts the balance in favour of the dualist school of thought, since each system can be said to operate within its own realm, bringing in rules from the other realm when they become duly applicable 'at home'.

Questions

Self-test questions

1 Explain the terms 'monism' and 'dualism'.

2 What obligations do States incur under international treaties concerning the implementation of international law?

3 Distinguish between 'transformed' and 'untransformed' treaties.

4 What does 'incorporation' mean?

5 Explain what is meant by the 'Ponsonby Rule'?

6 In what circumstance(s) would the doctrine of *stare decisis* not apply to international issues before municipal courts?

7 Why is the consent of the British Parliament necessary for treaties concluded by the Queen?

8 Explain the transformation theory.

Discussion questions

1 'Incorporation and transformation are two modalities for adopting international law into the municipal legal system.' Discuss.

2 'A State cannot rely on its internal law as justification for not performing its international obligations.' Critically examine this statement.

3 To what extent do dualism and monism explain how States relate to international law?

4 'An untransformed treaty has no recognition whatsoever before the English courts.' Discuss.

5 With the aid of decided cases, discuss the circumstances in which a customary international law rule may not be transformed into municipal law.

6 'Treaties are equal with municipal laws once transformed.' To what extent is this statement true?

Assessment question

Dale and Francis are twin brothers who were nationals of the State of Rutamu. In 2000, they relocated with their family to the Federal Republic of Candoma, following the posting of their father to the country as the director of the Candoma office of the National Bank of Rutamu. In 2008, while on a night out with their mates, a brawl broke out, during the course of which, while attempting to protect his brother, Dale seriously injured a person who later died in hospital. The State of Andoma (one of the federating States of Candoma) held Dale in solitary confinement, allowing him no contact with anyone, and told him nothing about his legal entitlements and rights. He was later convicted by that State for murder and was sentenced to death.

Dale has appealed to the Federal Supreme Court of Candoma—as the highest court for the whole country—alleging, among other things, the violation of his rights under the Vienna Convention on Consular Relations.

Advise Dale.

Key cases

- *Germany v. United States of America (Merits)* (2001) ICJ Rep 466 (the *LaGrand Case*)
- *R v. Keyn* (1876) 2 Ex D 63
- *Nulyarimma v. Thompson* (1999) 96 FCR 153
- *Parlement Belge, The* (1879) 4 PD 129
- *R v. Jones* [2006] UKHL 16
- *Trendtex Trading Corp. v. Central Bank of Nigeria* [1977] 1 QB 529

Further reading

Akehurst's Modern Introduction to International Law (rev'd edn, ed. P. Malanczuk, 7th edn, London: Routledge, 1997)

Denza, E., 'The relationship between international and national law' in M. Evans (ed.), *International Law* (3rd edn, Oxford: Oxford University Press, 2010), p. 411

Fitzmaurice, G., 'The general principles of international law considered from the standpoint of the rule of law' (1957-II) 92 Recueil des Cours 92

Nijman, J. and Nollkaemper, A. (eds), *New Perspectives on the Divide between National and International Law* (Oxford: Oxford University Press, 2007)

White, R., 'When is a British protected person not a British protected person?' (1974) 23 ICLQ 866

10

The law of use of force

Learning objectives

This chapter will help you to:

- understand international law rules on the use of force;

- recognize the factors that can make the application of these rules difficult;

- appreciate the changing nature of international legal rules on the use of force;

- understand developments by regional organizations that seriously impact on international legal rules on the use of force by States;

- understand the latest developments in this area following several terrorist attacks in the world; and

- consider seriously whether the current rules are adequate or there is need for substantial legal reform in this area.

Introduction

Under international law, States can neither threaten to use force nor use force in their international relations. This rule is found in Article 2(4) of the UN Charter, and is widely regarded as a peremptory norm. As we said in Chapter 2, a peremptory norm is a norm from which States cannot depart (see also Article 53 of the Vienna Convention on the Law of Treaties, VCLT). So the prohibition of the threat or use of force is the most important obligation of States under international law, which seeks, for the most part, to maintain and promote international peace and security. However, despite this prohibition, States continue, to this day, to threaten to use and use force against one another. As we will see later, the UN Charter permits States to use force in certain instances, but States have continued to use force in circumstances not provided for under the Charter. Perhaps this is a way of alleging that the Charter rules are not enough. An example of this is so-called humanitarian intervention, which is referred to in this chapter, but more fully developed in Chapter 11. Other important questions include whether the prohibited 'force' should continue to mean only *military* force. Also, how should States deal with the fact that the Charter rules do not prohibit or regulate the use of force by non-State entities such as terrorist organizations, especially when such force is applied against States?

Before the advent of the United Nations in 1945, States were free to decide whether or not to wage war against one another. There was no strict regulation on the use of force by States; the only form of restraint on States was a moral consideration relating to whether the war was 'just' or not—that is, whether the war would fulfil certain philosophical, religious, and ethical requirements. Further, there was no objective system of determining what was 'just' or 'unjust'; hence, the 'regulation' of the use of force during this period was unpredictable. Consequently, States waged brutal wars against one another without legal constraints, until the outbreak of the First World War in 1914.

10.1 The League of Nations and the Kellogg–Briand Pact

Towards the end of the First World War in 1918, the international community (that is, the majority of States in existence at that time) began to look for ways in which to regulate the use of force by States. This resulted in the establishment of the League of Nations in 1919. The treaty that established the League was the Covenant of the League of Nations, which was signed and ratified by most of the States in existence at the time. As you may recall from previous chapters, this Covenant was a multilateral treaty, since it was ratified by more than two States.

The 1919 League Covenant did not really prohibit the use of force by States. Article 10 provides that:

> The Members of the League undertake to respect and preserve as against external aggression the territorial integrity and existing political independence of all Members of the League. In case of any such aggression or in case of any threat or danger of such aggression the Council shall advise upon the means by which this obligation shall be fulfilled.

This provision does two things. First, it encourages States not to attack one another. Note that this is not a prohibition, but a mere encouragement not to do something. In fact, it is clear from the words of that provision that States might easily disregard this advice. Secondly, the rule states that if a State is attacked it must seek advice from the Executive Council of the League on what to do. The Council was the highest decision-making body of the League.

So, on this point, important questions would be: how long should an attacked State wait for the Council to act, and what exactly can the Council do?

Article 12 of the Covenant provides that:

> The Members of the League agree that, if there should arise between them any dispute likely to lead to a rupture they will submit the matter either to arbitration or judicial settlement or to enquiry by the Council, and they agree in no case to resort to war until three months after the award by the arbitrators or the judicial decision, or the report by the Council. In any case under this Article the award of the arbitrators or the judicial decision shall be made within a reasonable time, and the report of the Council shall be made within six months after the submission of the dispute.

example

If Candoma attacks Rutamu, Rutamu must not respond by force. Instead, it should inform the Executive Council immediately and wait for the Council to act, or submit the issue to a judicial body. If Rutamu submits the dispute to an arbitration or judicial body, it must wait for at least three months after the decision by the arbitral tribunal, but there is no time stipulated in which the tribunal must give its decision, only that it must do so within a reasonable time. But if Rutamu submits to the League Council, then the waiting time is six months. Whichever way, Rutamu must do nothing during the waiting period.

It is obvious that a State that has been attacked by another is unlikely to wait that long for a settlement—and it is easy to imagine what the attacking State might do in the meantime.

KEY POINTS

- Until the start of the twentieth century, there was no regulation of the use of force under general international law.

- The League of Nations was the first attempt made at regulating the use of force.

In 1928, a further attempt was made at regulating the use of force by States. The Kellogg–Briand Pact, which is still in force today, was adopted on 27 August 1928 by fifteen States. At its peak, there were sixty-three signatories to the Pact. The Pact, which was named after its authors, US Secretary of State Frank B. Kellogg and French Foreign Minister Aristide Briand, attempted to prohibit war and to compel States to settle their disputes only peacefully.

Article 1 of 1928 Kellogg–Briand Pact states that:

> The High Contracting Parties solemnly declare in the names of their respective peoples that they *condemn* recourse to war for the solution of international controversies, and *renounce* it, as an instrument of national policy in their relations with one another.

Again, we do not see prohibition here. 'Renouncing' an activity is not the same as 'prohibiting' it. We could renounce something today, but resume doing it occasionally without any serious consequences to ourselves. Notice also that the Pact renounced only *war*, meaning that actions that are considered less than war are not illegal. Additionally, there was no penalty against States that breached the Pact. It was no surprise, therefore, that the Pact proved ineffective in restraining States from using force.

10.1.1 Why the League Covenant and the Kellogg–Briand Pact failed to prohibit force

The reasons why the League Covenant and the 1928 Pact failed to prohibit the use of force can be summarized as follows.

(a) The Covenant and the Pact did not prohibit the use of force, but merely put pressure on States not to resort to it.

(b) None of the treaties provided State parties with the right of self-defence.

(c) There were no sanctions against defaulters. Therefore, State parties to the treaties did not feel any significant pressure to respect the rules.

(d) Not all States participated in the League or the Pact. The USA never joined the League, despite signing up to its Covenant, and the (then) Soviet Union never signed the Kellogg–Briand Pact and was expelled from it. Without the simultaneous participation of these two powerful States in any effort to regulate the use of force at that time, it would be impossible to achieve the desired results.

thinking points

- *What is the significance of the renunciation of war, as distinct from the prohibition of use of force, by the 1928 Kellogg–Briand Pact?*
- *Why do you think the League Covenant and the Kellogg–Briand Pact failed to regulate effectively the use of force by States?*
- *How was the use of force regulated prior to 1919?*

10.2 The UN Charter and the prohibition of the use and threat of force

The single most important subject of concern during the conferences that led to the establishment of the United Nations was how to regulate the use of force by States. As seen previously, States used force freely against one another, leading to disastrous consequences. Therefore it is not surprising that the regulation of the use of force, under the UN regime would be fundamentally different from the previous regimes discussed earlier.

Article 2(4) of the Charter of the United Nations (the UN Charter) provides that:

> All Members shall refrain in their international relations from the threat or use of force against the territorial integrity or political independence of any State, or in any manner inconsistent with the Purposes of the United Nations.

There are at least three ways in which this provision differs from the League Covenant and the Kellogg–Briand Pact. First, Article 2(4) *prohibits* force and does not only encourage States to renounce war. Note the use of 'shall refrain' in that provision: this is a command, not a plea. Secondly, in addition to actual force, Article 2(4) also prohibits the *threat* of force. This was the first time that this had been done. Thirdly, Article 2(4) prohibits not only war, but also *any* use of force.

Article 2(4) is loaded with substance, which has arguably made it the most controversial provision of the UN Charter. For example, it prohibits the threat or use of force by States in their 'international relations'. Can it not be argued that this means that States can use force in their *internal* relations, such as against rebel groups? The Article seems to forbid only force directed *against* the 'territorial integrity' or 'political independence' of a State. So does this mean that States can threaten or use force that is not against the 'territorial integrity or political independence' of other States? What do these phrases mean anyway? And when is a use or threat of force not 'inconsistent with the Purposes of the United Nations'?

To answer these questions, we need to analyse the meaning and implication of the various terms contained in Article 2(4), starting with the meaning of 'force'.

10.2.1 The meaning of 'force' under Article 2(4)

There is controversy about the meaning of 'force' under Article 2(4). This debate arose mainly because the adjective 'armed' does not appear before 'force' in that provision, whereas in other provisions, such as Articles 41 and 46, the phrase 'armed force' is used. (See R. D. Kearney and R. E. Dalton, 'The treaty on treaties' (1970) 64 AJIL 495.) The question is thus whether Article 2(4) envisages other types of force, such as economic sanctions, in addition to armed force.

The general understanding among writers and States is that only military force is prohibited by Article 2(4). Those who support this position give two main reasons. First, they argue that since the UN itself was formed in response to the tragedy of the Second World War, the force referred to in the provision means the kind of force employed in that war, which was mainly military force. As Dinstein argues, 'when studied in context, the term "force" in Article 2(4) must denote armed—or military—force. Psychological or economic pressure (including economic boycott) as such does not come within the purview of the article, unless coupled with the use or at least the threat of force' (Y. Dinstein, *War, Aggression and Self Defence* (Cambridge: Cambridge University Press, 2011); see also A. Randelzhofer, 'Article 2(4)' in B. Simma et al. (eds), *The Charter of the United Nations: A Commentary* (Oxford: Oxford University Press, 2012)). Secondly, the history of the negotiation of the UN supports this view. When the formation of the UN was being discussed at a conference in San Francisco in the USA, some States had proposed that economic aggression be prohibited. However, this proposal was rejected by the majority of other participants. The latter argued that since States were generally free to choose whether or not to trade with one another, refusal by one State to trade with another should not be considered a violation of international law. Consequently, only military force was prohibited in 1945 and there is no good reason to believe that this position has changed today.

However, although only military force is still regarded as being the object of prohibition under Article 2(4), the United Nations has made it clear that economic aggression is unacceptable where such is used to coerce States.

The UN General Assembly's Declaration on Principles of International Law Friendly Relations and Cooperation among States in Accordance with the Charter of the United Nations, confirmed by General Assembly Resolution 2625(XXV) of 24 October 1970 (the Friendly Relations Resolution), provides that:

> No State may use or encourage the use of economic political or any other type of measures to coerce another State in order to obtain from it the subordination of the exercise of its sovereign rights and to secure from it advantages of any kind.

thinking points

- *What kind of force is referred to in Article 2(4) of the UN Charter?*
- *What other kind of force was considered during the negotiation of the Charter and why was it not included in the Article 2(4) meaning of 'force'?*

KEY POINTS

- Article 2(4) prohibits the threat or use of force.

- Article 2(4) is regarded as a rule of *jus cogens*, or a peremptory norm from which no derogation is permitted except by a norm of similar character.

- Article 2(4) prohibits not only war, but also any kind of use of (military) force.

10.2.2 'Threats of force'

In addition to actual force, Article 2(4) prohibits the 'threat of force'. What constitutes a *threat* of force?

A threat of force is 'a form of coercion' (R. Sadurska, 'Threats of force' (1988) 82 AJIL 239, 241).

> If Candoma assembles several thousand of its troops along its border with Rutamu and points its armoured tanks towards that State, this will seem to be a serious threat against Rutamu.
>
> If Candoma verbally threatens to 'wipe Rutamu off the face of the earth' or to 'reduce it to rubble', this may also be a threat, depending on the circumstances under which the threat is made.

There is no requirement under international law that a State must have the capability to deliver its threat, or that a threat is coupled with any concrete demand before such a threat can be considered unlawful. A threat is unlawful under Article 2(4) if the threatened force would be illegal when used. An illegal threat can beget only an unlawful force and vice versa. For example, if an attacked State is threatening to retaliate, the threat is lawful because the force, if used, would be in self-defence.

In State practice, the issue of threats has been of very little significance because States do not generally go about threatening one another. Nonetheless, the International Court of Justice (ICJ) has had the opportunity to deal with the issue of threats.

. . . .

● *The Legality of the Threat or Use of Nuclear Weapons Advisory Opinion* [1996] ICJ REP 226

On 19 December 1995, the UN General Assembly requested the Court to give its opinion on an issue contained in UN General Assembly Resolution 49/75K, adopted on 15 December 1994. The question was whether the threat or use of nuclear weapons was in any circumstance permissible.

The ICJ answered this question by looking at the relationship between the use of force and the threat of force. The Court said (at 246) that:

> Whether a signalled intention to use force if certain events occur is or is not a 'threat' within Article 2, paragraph 4, of the Charter depends upon various factors. *If the envisaged use of force is itself unlawful, the stated readiness to use it would be a threat prohibited under Article 2, paragraph 4.* Thus it would be illegal for a State to threaten force to secure territory from another State, or to cause it to follow or not follow certain political or economic paths. The notions of 'threat' and 'use' of force under Article 2, paragraph 4, of the Charter stand together in the sense that if the use of force itself in a given case is illegal—for whatever reason—the threat to use such force will likewise be illegal. In short, if it is to be lawful, the declared readiness of a State to use force must be a use of force that is in conformity with the Charter. For the rest, no State—whether or not it defended the policy of deterrence—suggested to the Court that it would be lawful to threaten to use force if the use of force contemplated would be illegal. [Emphasis added]

The statement of the Court here was to the effect that the lawfulness of a threat depended on the lawfulness of the use of force itself.

> In 2013, the USA threatened to use force against the Syrian government. However, such a threat was unlawful because the use of force would have been without the Security Council's authorization.

KEY POINTS

- A threat is legal only if the actual force that it threatens is legal.

- Deterrence does not justify a threat or make it legal.

10.2.3 'Refrain in their international relations'

As we said earlier, this phrase seems to imply that only use of force by one State against another is prohibited, not force used by a State within its territory. The reason for the limitation under this provision can be given as the principle of sovereignty and territorial integrity, which States continue to guard jealously. Neither States nor the United Nations are allowed to interfere in the internal affairs of other States, and this has been a time-honoured principle of international law. However, contemporary international law sees the reliance on sovereignty shifting in favour of other critical principles, such as those relating to human rights and self-determination. In fact, States often argue that since Article 2(4) of the UN Charter concerns only 'international relations' of States, they are free to use force to resolve problems within their territory. (See Oscar Schachter, 'Sovereignty and threats to peace' in Thomas G. Weiss (ed.), *Collective Security in a Changing World* (Boulder: CO: Lynn Rienner, 1993.)

example

Argentina took this position when it attacked the Falkland Islands in 1982, in an attempt to reclaim the territory from the UK (see (1982) UNYB 1320).

Iraq under Saddam Hussein similarly attempted to justify its invasion of Kuwait in 1990 on the basis that Kuwait was historically part of Iraq (see (1991) UNYB 167, 169 *et seq*).

At various times, Nigeria and Cameroon claimed that they were justified in using force on the Bakassi Peninsular, a disputed oil-rich area adjoining both countries, over which both States claimed ownership.

So can use of force by States within their territory be legal?

There are several problems with the arguments proffered by States in favour of using force within their territories. First, as far as the UN Charter is concerned, States should settle their disputes peacefully. It is no good defence that a State uses force only within its own territory. There is ample evidence to suggest that using force within one's territory could have as much of an impact, or an even worse impact, on a whole region than that of one State attacking another.

example

The civil war in Syria, which started in 2011, has lasted much longer—and caused greater suffering to civilians—than, for example, the invasion of Kuwait by Iraq in 1990.

Also, whenever States argue that they use force only to deal with internal problems, they automatically assume that such use of force is legal and that disputes can be purely domestic. In fact, Article 2(7) of the UN Charter forbids the UN to interfere in matters occurring within the domestic jurisdiction of its member States. Several authors have, however, criticized this provision. For Kelsen, the 'domestic jurisdiction' is 'erroneous' because 'there is no matter that cannot be regulated by a rule of customary or contractual international law, and if a matter is regulated by a rule of international law, it is no longer...within the domestic jurisdiction of the state concerned' (Hans Kelsen, 'Limitations on the functions of the United Nations' (1945–46) 55 Yale LJ 997). Akehurst shared the same view (Michael Akehurst, *Modern Introduction to International Law* (7th edn, London: Routledge, 1997). The correct stance, therefore, seems to be that the use of force by States to suppress those seeking equal rights and self-determination, for example, is unlawful. Even the UN General Assembly has noted the unacceptability of such actions. In its 1970 Friendly Relations Resolution, it stated, at operative paragraph 8, that:

> Every State has the duty to refrain from any forcible action which deprives peoples referred to in the elaboration of the principle of equal rights and self-determination of their right to self-determination and freedom and independence.

Another problem with the argument for use of force internally is that whenever States argue for the use of force to deal with internal matters, they assume that it is always possible to characterize conflicts as *either* internal *or* international. Yet, as the Bosnia and Herzegovina conflict of the 1990s demonstrates, such matters are not always that simple. (See Marc Weller, 'The international response to the dissolution of the Socialist Federal Republic of Yugoslavia' (1992) 86(3) AJIL 569; M. E. Brown (ed.), *The International Dimensions of Internal Conflict*, Cambridge, MA: MIT Press, 1996.)

Similarly, by using force to capture a territory, a State assumes that the territory is, in law, its own. Thus the claims by the UK and Argentina over the Falkland Islands, India and Pakistan over Kashmir, and Nigeria and Cameroon over Bakassi all overlooked the important fact that, at the time that such force was used, none of these States had *undisputed* title to the concerned territory. Indeed, international law prohibits the use of force in respect of boundaries.

The UN General Assembly has also commented on this position in its 1970 Friendly Relations Resolution, at operative paragraph 5:

> Every State has the duty to refrain from the threat or use of force to violate the existing international boundaries of any State or as a means of solving international disputes, including territorial disputes and problems concerning frontiers of States.

On the whole, it will be problematic to argue that a State that is forbidden from using force in its international relations is then free to use force against its own citizens.

It must be noted that General Assembly resolutions are not binding on UN member States, because they do not have the same legal effect as Security Council resolutions. However, some resolutions of the General Assembly may become customary international law (see Chapter 2) and the Friendly Relations Resolution is an example of such. Therefore the prohibition of the use of force internally may be cited as a rule of customary law, since it is not expressly provided for under the UN Charter.

thinking points

- *Under what circumstances does Article 2(4) of the UN Charter prohibit the use of force and why?*
- *What are the arguments against those who think that Article 2(4) prohibits force used only in external relations of States?*

10.2.4 'Territorial integrity and political independence'

This is probably the most controversial phrase found in Article 2(4) of the UN Charter. Basically, there are two broad views on how to interpret the phrase.

Some writers argue that the prohibition in Article 2(4) should be interpreted narrowly, so that more cases will fall within the realm of legality, while others think that it should be interpreted as widely as possible, so that fewer cases will be considered legal under the provision. A narrow interpretation (or the 'permissive view', as it is sometimes called), in the present context, implies that any use of force that does not result in a permanent loss of any part of a State's territory does not violate its territorial integrity. (See A. D'Amato, *International Law: Process and Prospect* (Dobbs Ferry, NY: Transnational Law Publishers, 1987), pp. 58–59.) A broad interpretation suggests that the purpose of the phrase is not to narrow the scope of the prohibited force; rather, it is an assurance that the threat or use of force will not be permitted under any circumstances, except as allowed by the Charter. (See J. Stone, *Aggression and World Order: A Critique of the United Nations Theories of Aggression* (Berkeley, CA: University of California Press, 1958), p. 43.) According to Dinstein, 'if the injunction against resort to force in international relations is confined to specific situations affecting only the territorial integrity and the political independence of States, a legion of loopholes will inevitably be left open' (2011, p. 82, see section 10.2.1).

In practice, interpreting this phrase has arisen mainly whenever States use force to rescue their nationals from abroad, use **force for democracy** in other countries, or use force to prevent humanitarian tragedies. As we shall see later, none of these instances is explicitly recognized by the UN Charter as constituting lawful use of force, no matter how charitable the motive might appear. (See E. Suzuki, 'Self-determination and world public order: community response to territorial separation' (1975–76) 16 Va JIL 779.)

. . . .

force for democracy

This is the claim that a State can use force to install a democratic government in another State to replace a government that it considers totalitarian and undemocratic. One of the most recent examples of this is the 2003 US invasion of Iraq, which was, among other things, expected to promote the installation of a democratic government in that country.

. . . .

H. Lauterpacht, *Oppenheim's International Law, Vol. II* (7th edn, London: Longmans, 1952), p. 154:

> Neither is the obligation not to resort to force or threat of force limited by the words 'against the territorial integrity or political independence'. Territorial integrity, especially where coupled with political independence is synonymous with territorial inviolability. Thus a State would be acting in breach of its obligations under the Charter if it were to invade or commit an act of force within the territory of another State, in anticipation of an alleged impending attack or in order to obtain redress, without the intention of interfering permanently with the territorial integrity of that State. The prohibition of paragraph 4 is absolute except with regard to the use of force in fulfilment of the obligations to give effect to the Charter or in pursuance of action in self-defence consistent with the provisions of Articles 51 of the Charter.

It is obvious from this statement that Oppenheim believes that the prohibition in Article 2(4) is absolute. No motive could justify any unlawful intervention except the use of force to fulfil the Charter obligation or self-defence.

Some other writers, however, believe that not all unauthorized use of force on a State's territory are illegal: see, for example, W. Friedmann, 'Conference proceedings' in R. Lillich (ed.), *Humanitarian Intervention and the United Nations* (Charlottesville, VA: University Press of Virginia, 1973), p. 115. According to this view, an intervention that is not legally justifiable may be morally condonable.

In his chapter 'Humanitarian intervention' in J. N. Moore (ed.), *Law and Civil War in the Modern World* (Baltimore, MD: Johns Hopkins University Press, 1974), at p. 225, Professor Ian Brownlie states that such an intervention would 'make a fine basis for a political plea in mitigation in parliament, U.N. organs, and regional organizations'.

It is submitted that there is a serious danger in attempting to justify an illegal use of force on the ground of morality. What is moral to one State may be immoral to another. So, using moral arguments in this circumstance will bring nothing but chaos to Article 2(4).

J. R. D'Angelo, 'Resort to force by states to protect nationals: the US rescue mission to Iran and its legality under international law' (1981) 21 Va JIL 485, 491, states that a mitigation doctrine in this context measures State action by moral rather than legal standards, thus subverting the already limited normative content of international law.

State practice on territorial integrity and political independence

Let us now consider some examples in which States have used force, and of how scholars view such actions with regard to the 'territorial integrity and political independence' of the States in which the force was used. We will consider these cases under certain categories, based on the justifications proffered by the States that resorted to the use of force. It should be reiterated, however, that the rule against the use of force is not absolute, because States may lawfully use force in self-defence or where the UN Security Council has so authorized. An example of a case in which self-defence has been raised as a justification for the use of force is Tanzania's 1979 invasion of Idi Amin's Uganda. Most of the cases mentioned here do not fall within any of these categories, but whether or not they are considered illegal will depend on the interpretation of Article 2(4) adopted.

Regime change, protection of one's nationals, and humanitarian interventions

States have often attempted to justify forceful intervention in other States in order to promote democracy. This incidence is often referred to as 'regime change'—the 'overthrow' or foreign assistance in the overthrow of a country's government. Other reasons include to rescue their own nationals from foreign lands, or to protect citizens of a country from serious violations of their rights and repression by their governments (so-called 'humanitarian intervention'). The section below focuses on whether these uses of force constitute violations of the territorial integrity or political independence of the concerned States. While we consider the use of force to rescue one's nationals in foreign lands and regime change here briefly, the discussion of humanitarian intervention is dealt with in Chapter 12.

Regime change

In 1989, the USA invaded Panama citing as its principal justification the need to replace the country's dictatorial regime. George Bush's Administration announced that Panama had declared 'a state of war with the United States and publicly threatened the lives of Americans

343

in Panama' (see Statement of the President, 20 December 1989, Office of the Press Secretary to the White House). The President also said (in his 3 January 1990 Statement) that the US invasion of Panama was:

> to safeguard the lives of American citizens, to help restore democracy, to protect the integrity of the Panama Canal Treaties, and to bring General Manuel Noriega to justice.

Vietnam's 1978 overthrow of the Pol Pot regime in Cambodia and the USA/UK 2003 unilateral attack on Iraq were both partly based on the need to end the brutal and repressive regimes in those countries. (See Chapter 11.)

Following a popular uprising against Colonel Gaddafi's regime and the violent reaction by the latter in 2011, the UN Security Council adopted Resolution 1973, which, authorized the creation of a **no-fly zone** in Libya in order to protect Libyans from aerial assault by forces loyal to head of State Colonel Gaddafi's regime. The resolution also called on States and regional organizations to take 'all necessary measures' to ensure the protection of civilians. While the resolution did not authorize the overthrow of the Gaddafi government, key members of NATO, the USA, the UK, and France—which spearheaded the enforcement of the mandate— had openly canvassed the replacement of the regime. (See Chapter 11.)

....

no-fly zone

A part, or the whole, of a country's airspace that is cordoned off either to that country's aircraft and/or to those of foreign countries.

....

Rescue/protection of own national abroad

In 1976, Israel forcibly freed its nationals taken hostage by hijackers at Entebbe Airport in Uganda. In 1983, the USA deployed its troops to Grenada, apparently to protect American medical students caught up in the country's turmoil. A State may also act to protect its interests, such as its property within the territory of another State or its vessels in another State's territorial waters, although such attacks may be termed 'reprisals' when the incident involves a prior attack on such interests. In 1946, the UK deployed its naval ships to sweep the Corfu Channel for evidence, following an attack on its ships in Albanian waters.

The interests that a country seeks to protect may not be so direct, because they may be political or economic interests, which will lead the country to support armed groups within another country as opposed to perpetrating the attack itself. Between 1979 and 1988, the Soviet Union used force in Afghanistan in support of one political faction in the country against another. In the US attack of Nicaragua, the former provided support to armed groups within the latter State.

What is important to note is that, in all of these cases, force was used *without* the authority of the UN Security Council, and not in self-defence. The question is: did such use of force violate the territorial integrity or political independence of Grenada, Nicaragua, and the former Yugoslavia?

Many American writers do not think so. They argue that using force to protect nationals abroad, as the USA claimed it had done in Grenada and Panama, did not violate the territorial integrity or political independence of States. According to this view, the USA did not attempt to reduce the size of Panamanian or Grenadian territory physically or to change their governments. In fact, some American writers argue that the 'territorial integrity or political independence' of States should not be respected if they oppress their citizens. As far as these writers are concerned, respecting the territorial integrity and political independence of oppressive States is comparable to the nineteenth-century American courts' practice which, despite recognizing that husbands abused their wives, sometimes held that 'A man's home is his castle'. Anthony

D'Amato, 'The invasion of Panama was a lawful response to tyranny' (1990) 84 AJIL 516, 517, adopted this reasoning to justify the US invasion of Panama:

> The citizens of Panama were as powerless against Noriega and his henchmen as the 19th-century American wives were against physically stronger husbands. In describing Noriega's rule, we should discard loaded words like 'governments', 'legitimate', 'authority', 'army', 'police', and so forth. These words only serve to dull our senses against the reality of power by begging the very question that is the subject of the present debate—whether Panama's boarders should be treated as an exclusive reservation of 'domestic jurisdiction' to Noriega or whether those borders should be permeable for some purposes.

However, there are those who believe that these justifications border on morality, and can lead only to the erosion of international law. In 'The customary international law doctrine of humanitarian intervention: its current validity under the UN Charter' (1974) Cal W Int'l LJ 203, 249, Jean-Pierre Fonteyne argues that:

> [morally justifying the use of force to rescue one's nationals from another country] ... could only encourage States to run the risk, break the law, invoke some vague, plausible, higher motive, and hope that the world community will fail to censor their conduct. In the long run such a situation must inevitably lead to an increasing authority deflation of international law in general, and of the Charter in particular. If States can 'acceptably' break the law for humanitarian reasons, why should it not be equally so to violate it for other, perhaps morally less commendable motives as well?

In 'Humanitarian intervention: a reply to Ian Brownlie and a plea for constructive alternatives' in J. N. Moore (1974, see earlier in this section), p. 229, Richard Lillich argues, at p. 241:

> Unless one relies exclusively upon Article 51 to justify the protection of nationals ... any rationale allowing interventions to protect nationals also authorizes humanitarian interventions generally.

From these statements, we can conclude that any use of force that is not permitted under the UN Charter is illegal. It is irrelevant whether such an action is morally sound or not.

thinking points

- *Based on these statements, what are the disagreements between the different approaches to interpreting the phrase 'territorial integrity or political independence'?*
- *Does Professor D'Amato favour or oppose a narrow interpretation of 'territorial integrity or political independence'?*
- *Should territorial integrity be equated with the physical size of a territory?*

The ICJ has pronounced on what constitutes the 'territorial integrity and political independence' of a State, and what actions violate them.

● *Albania v. United Kingdom (Merits)* [1949] ICJ REP 4 (The *Corfu Channel Case*)

Albania brought a claim before the ICJ that the UK had violated its sovereignty by mining its waters without its authority. The action complained about by Albania became necessary following the destruction of certain UK ships on 22 October 1946, in Albanian waters that had

345

been mined either by Albania or with its knowledge. The UK argued before the Court that its subsequent act of sweeping Albania waters—code-named 'Operation Retail'—was necessary as an act of self-protection or self-help.

The Court held (at [35]) that:

> The Court cannot accept this defence either. Between independent States, respect for territorial sovereignty is an essential foundation of international relations. The Court recognizes that the Albanian Governments' complete failure to carry out its duties after the explosions, and the dilatory nature of its diplomatic notes, are extenuating circumstances for the action of the United Kingdom Government. But to ensure respect for international law, of which it is the organ, the Court must declare that the action of the British Navy constituted a violation of Albanian sovereignty.

Clearly, the Court was of the view that no amount of wrongdoing by one State can justify the use of force on its territory by another, except, of course, as permitted by the Charter.

Practice shows that whenever States use force against other States, they tend to prefer to seek political, rather than legal, explanations for their acts. This perhaps demonstrates that, despite their posturing, States do not always believe that the use of force on the territory of other States outside the Charter rule is legal or consistent with the purposes of the UN.

In 1956, France and the UK invaded Egypt, following a dispute over the Suez Canal. Prior to the invasion, the legal adviser to the British Foreign Office, Gerald Fitzmaurice, had advised the UK government against using force against Egypt. The British government ignored this advice. In his memoirs of the crisis, *No End of a Lesson: The Story of Suez* (London: Constable, 1967), p. 95, Sir Anthony Nutting, at the time Parliamentary Under-Secretary of State at the Foreign Office, recalled the attitude of then British Prime Minister Anthony Eden, during a meeting that Eden called to discuss the issue with his Cabinet:

> I was to represent the Foreign Secretary, until he should arrive in person. Meanwhile I was to consult only two Senior Foreign Office officials. My suggestion that at least the Foreign Office Legal Adviser, Sir Gerald Fitzmaurice, should be brought in on a matter which involved taking law into our own hands met with the flattest negatives. 'Fitz is the last person I want consulted', Eden retorted. 'The lawyers are always against our doing anything. For God's sake, keep them out of it. This is a political affair.'

Similarly, following the US invasion of Panama in 1989, President Bush declared that the USA had 'used its resources in a manner consistent with political, diplomatic and moral principles'. No reference was made to legal principles in that statement.

The real danger in all of this is that academic writers often subscribe to political justifications of illegal actions. Professor D'Amato (1990, see earlier in this section) argued that we should 'discard loaded words like "governments", "legitimate", "authority", "army", "police", and so forth', when referring to Noriega's regime. According to him, 'these words only serve to dull our senses against the reality of power'.

D'Amato also argues, at p. 520, that:

> There is no doubt that under our present understanding of international law the use of military force for the purpose of territorial aggrandizement or colonialism violates customary

international law. Nor is there any doubt that such use of force would not count as humanitarian intervention even if appropriately disguised at the time—rather, it would be regarded as pure aggression. I submit that the core intent of Article 2(4) was to secure these understandings. Accordingly, the U.S. forcible intervention in Panama did not violate Article 2(4) because the United States did not act against the 'territorial integrity' of Panama; there was never an intent to annex part or all of Panamanian territory, and hence the intervention left the territorial integrity of Panama intact. Nor was the use of force directed against the 'political independence' of Panama: the United States did not intend to, and has not, [*sic*] colonialized, annexed or incorporated Panama. Before and after the intervention, Panama was and remains an independent nation.

Obviously, Professor D'Amato interpreted the phrase 'territorial integrity and political independence' quite literally. Hence, according to the learned scholar, unless an intervention physically reduces the territory of a State or results in a change of government, then use of force against such a State cannot be regarded as violating Article 2(4).

It is difficult to accept Professor D'Amato's view. To argue that the territorial integrity of a State is violated only if an action reduces its size is to undermine seriously Article 2(4) of the UN Charter. It is irrelevant that, as a matter of fact, the USA did not reduce the size of either State by an inch.

In State practice, since the emergence of the UN in 1945 no single claim of territory by force has succeeded and only a handful of States have claimed territory by force. Most uses of force—for example, Israel against Uganda, Tanzania against Uganda, the Soviet Union against Afghanistan, and India against Bangladesh—did not involve any claim over territory. The reason is simple: Article 2(4) does not permit States to use force to claim territory.

Another problem with Professor D'Amato's interpretation is that it curiously overlooks the undercurrents of politics. How many States would declare, in advance of an invasion, that they were attacking another State because it had failed to act in the manner that they had wanted it to? Certainly, if one were to follow D'Amato's reasoning, then the ICJ would never have found the USA liable for undermining the political independence of Nicaragua. Yet, the USA, acting through its agents, was very much involved in an unlawful attempt to overthrow the government of that country.

On balance, it seems appropriate to conclude that State practice better supports the view that the phrase 'territorial integrity and political independence' was not inserted in the Charter to exempt some categories of the use of force from the Article 2(4) prohibition. This view has been confirmed by the 1970 Friendly Relations Declaration, operative paragraph 23, which states that:

> ...No State or group of States has the right to intervene, directly or indirectly, for any reasons whatever, in the internal or external affairs of any other State. Consequently armed interventions and all other forms of interference or attempted threats against the personality of the State or against its political, economic and cultural elements, are in violation of international law.

There is no doubt that the reference to 'any reasons whatever' is broad enough to cover such motives as humanitarian interventions, protection of one's nationals, and any other reasons on which a State may want to rely as a justification for the use of force against another State.

10.2.5 'Inconsistent with the purposes of the United Nations'

The last phrase to consider under Article 2(4) of the UN Charter is that which says that force cannot be used in 'any other manner inconsistent with the Purposes of the United Nations'. States and writers sometimes argue that the use of force to protect human rights or prevent humanitarian tragedies is not inconsistent with the purposes of the UN. Supporters of this view argue that, since one of the core purposes of the United Nations is to prevent humanitarian tragedies, using force to prevent a State from violating its citizens' rights or destroying their lives is perfectly consistent with Article 2(4).

Nonetheless, the 'force for good' theory, as we can call arguments in support of UN purposes, has been severely criticized. According to some writers, since the Charter does not recognize humanitarian intervention, such action is illegal except when authorized by the Security Council. In other words, humanitarian intervention can become a pretext for meddling in the internal affairs of other States. (See the next chapter for a discussion of humanitarian intervention.)

It is true that the UN Charter does not prohibit actions that are consistent with the purpose of the UN, but does this mean that such actions are lawful under Article 2(4)?

Sir Gerald Fitzmaurice, restated in Geoffrey Martson, 'Armed intervention in the 1956 Suez Canal crisis: the legal advice tendered to the British government' (1988) 37 ICLQ 1, advised the British government that:

> In any case it is a logical fallacy to argue that, because the Charter prohibits the use of force in a manner inconsistent with the purposes of the United Nations, this involves an implication that the use of force would be legitimate in order to achieve one of those purposes. This is rather like arguing that, because it is one of the purposes of English law that people should receive their due legal rights, they are therefore entitled to assert those rights by force. The fallacy of this would speedily become apparent to anyone who proceeds to try it on.

KEY POINTS

- 'Territorial integrity or political independence' and 'inconsistent with the Purposes of the United Nations' were inserted into the Charter not to narrow the circumstances of prohibited force, but to strengthen the assurance that force will not be used in any instance except as permitted by the Charter.

- The UN Charter does not recognize humanitarian intervention and force for democracy.

10.3 Exceptions to the prohibition of the use of force

Despite the strict prohibition against the use of force under Article 2(4), the Charter permits certain exceptions to the rule. We need first to understand that Article 2(4) prohibits only **unilateral use of force** or force not used in self-defence.

unilateral use of force

The use of force by one or more States without the authorization of relevant international bodies, such as the UN Security Council. Thus use of force by a single State against another is not unilateral if it is authorized by a relevant authority. What makes use of force unilateral is not the number of States that use it, but whether or not it is authorized.

The UN Charter provides for three exceptions to the prohibition on the use of force:

- use of force in self-defence (Article 51);
- use of force authorized by the UN Security Council, commonly called 'collective security' (Chapter VII), at which we will look in the next chapter; and
- use of force against former enemy States (Article 107).

When the UN Charter was adopted, Germany, Italy, and Japan were regarded as former enemy States because they fought against the rest of the world during the Second World War instigated by the German aggression on various European countries. Article 107 permits a UN member State to attack one of the former enemy States if the UN member State believed that the former enemy was renewing its policy of aggression. However, since all former enemy States are now UN members, Article 107 is regarded as a dead provision.

This leaves us with two exceptions to Article 2(4): self-defence and collective security. While we will deal with self-defence in the following section, we will consider collective security in Chapter 11, because it concerns the powers of the UN Security Council to maintain international peace and security.

10.3.1 Self-defence

Article 51 of the UN Charter provides that:

> Nothing in the present Charter shall impair the inherent right of individual or collective self-defence if an armed attack occurs against a Member of the United Nations, until the Security Council has taken measures necessary to maintain International peace and security. Measures taken by members in the exercise of this right of self-defence shall be immediately reported to the Security Council and shall not in any way affect the authority and responsibility of the Security Council under the present Charter to take at any time such action as it deems necessary in order to maintain or restore international peace and security.

According to this provision, States that have suffered armed attacks can defend themselves either *individually* or *collectively*—that is, an attacked State can call on other States to help to defend it against the attackers. It must be noted that the Charter did not create this right, but merely recognized its existence, hence the phrase 'inherent right'. The right of self-defence is innate in the State by virtue of it being a sovereign entity.

It is important to understand the origins of Article 51 in order to appreciate the provision properly. During the San Francisco Conference, several proposals for the Charter were put forward. However, Article 51 was not originally part of the proposed Charter. The original proposal was that all powers to authorize force and to defend States should be given to the Security Council. However, members of the Inter-American System (IAS) attending the Conference were not happy with this position. The IAS was deeply troubled by not knowing what to do if any of its members were attacked by a State and the Security Council was unable to respond as anticipated under Chapter VII of the Charter (see Chapter 11). To guarantee its survival, the IAS therefore requested that the UN Charter explicitly recognize its right to act, without waiting for the Security Council.

If the UN had acceded to the IAS's request, it would have created a dangerous precedent for the coherence of its regulation of the use of force. Certainly, other organizations may have wanted to make similar requests. However, if it had ignored the IAS's request altogether, this would have meant that the UN was insensitive to the genuine plight of small and weak States right from its inception. So, as a compromise, Article 51 was inserted in the Charter, under which if a State is attacked, it can defend itself—but only *until* the Security Council has taken those measures prescribed in Article 51.

10.3.2 Interpreting the conditional elements in Article 51

Considerable disagreement remains, among States and writers, on interpreting the various elements of Article 51. These include: what constitutes an 'armed attack'; whether a State threatened with nuclear weapons should wait until it has been attacked before acting, or act pre-emptively; and whether attacks by non-State entities, such as terrorist organizations, fall within the purview of that provision since Article 51 does not specify from where the attack must have come, but only against who the attack must have been directed—that is, UN member States. Other contested issues include who may determine whether the measures taken by the Security Council are enough to truncate the rights of self-defence, and whether a State is able to continue to act in self-defence after the Security Council has taken those measures.

10.3.3 The meaning of 'armed attack'

The Charter does not define the term 'armed attack'. Nonetheless, it is generally believed that an armed attack occurs when the *regular* forces of one State attack the territory of another, be it by land, sea, or airspace. But this raises the question whether an armed attack can be levelled only by the regular forces of a State.

● ***Nicaragua v. United States of America*** (1986) ICJ REP 14 (The ***Military and Paramilitary Activities in and against Nicaragua Case***, or the ***Nicaragua Case***)

Nicaragua claimed before the ICJ that the USA, through American personnel and foreigners working for the USA, undertook activities that Nicaragua considered to be directed against its legitimate government. Nicaragua also claimed that the USA created, financed, and provided logistical support to the Contras, a Nicaraguan insurgent group. In its counterclaim, the USA stated that its action was in collective self-defence of El Salvador, Honduras, and Costa Rica, countries that it claimed Nicaragua had attacked. One of the questions before the Court was whether the activities of the USA complained of by Nicaragua constituted an armed attack.

It was discovered that some of the acts were done not by American military personnel, but by agents such as the Contras' rebel forces, who were supported by the USA. The Court found that the support of the USA for the activities of the Contras took various forms over the years, such as logistical support, the supply of information on the location and movements of the Sandinista troops, the use of sophisticated methods of communication, etc. But the Court said that the evidence did not warrant a finding that the USA gave direct combat support.

The Court held (at [195]) that:

> There appears now to be general agreement on the nature of the acts which can be treated as constituting armed attacks. In particular, it may be considered to be agreed that an armed attack must be understood as including not merely action by regular armed forces across an international border, but also 'the sending by or on behalf of a State of armed bands, groups, irregulars or mercenaries, which carry out acts of armed force against another State of such gravity as to amount to' (*inter alia*) an actual armed attack conducted by regular forces, 'or its substantial involvement therein'. This description, contained in Article 3, paragraph (g), of the Definition of Aggression annexed to General Assembly resolution 3314 (XXIX), may be taken to reflect customary international law. *The Court sees no reason to deny that, in customary law, the prohibition of armed attacks may apply to the sending by a State of armed bands to the territory of another State, if such an operation, because of its scale and effects, would have been classified as an armed attack rather than as a mere frontier incident had it been carried out by regular armed forces.* [Emphasis added]

So, it is obvious that, in this case, the ICJ considered that irregular forces such as armed bands and rebel groups can also level armed attacks against States if they act on behalf of a State. However, on the question of whether merely providing logistical support for irregular forces amounted to armed attacks, the Court said (at [195]) that it:

> does not believe that the concept of 'armed attack' includes ... also assistance to rebels in the form of the provision of weapons or logistical or other support.

KEY POINTS

- According to the ICJ, armed attacks include acts by regular forces of a State beyond its borders, or acts by irregular forces acting on behalf of that State.

- The Court stated that acts such as the provision of weapons and logistical support do not constitute an armed attack.

It is not entirely clear why, despite accepting that acts done by others on behalf of a State can constitute armed attacks if the acts are grave enough, the Court did not accept that measures such as giving weapons, and logistical and financial support, for the same purpose do not constitute armed attacks. Where does the distinction lie?

example

Does this mean that if Candoma supplies weapons to a rebel group intent on destabilizing the government of Rutamu, and gives the group jet fighters, war ships, and accurate satellite maps of Rutamu's military installations, such weapons and logistical support will not constitute an armed attack?

The Court in *Nicaragua* decided that none of these measures constitute an 'armed attack'.

This very strict approach by the Court attracted a strong dissention by one of its judges.

● *Nicaragua v. United States of America* (1986) ICJ REP 14 (The *Military and Paramilitary Activities in and against Nicaragua Case*, or the *Nicaragua Case*)

Sir Robert Jennings (dissenting at 543 *et seq*) believed that:

> It may readily be agreed that the mere provision of arms cannot be said to amount to an armed attack. But the provision of arms may, nevertheless, be a very important element in what might be thought to amount to armed attack, where it is coupled with other kinds of involvement. Accordingly, it seems to me that to say that the provision of arms, coupled with 'logistical or other support' is not armed attack, is going much too far. Logistical support may itself be crucial. According to the dictionary, logistics covers the 'art of moving, lodging, and supplying troops and equipment' (*Concise Oxford English Dictionary*, 7th ed., 1982). If there is added to all this 'other support', it becomes difficult to understand what it is, short of direct attack by a State's own forces, that may not be done apparently without a lawful response in the form of collective self-defence: nor indeed may be responded to at all by the use of force or threat of force, for, to cite the Court again, 'States do not have a right of 'collective' armed response to acts which do not constitute an 'armed attack' (see para. 211).

The basis of Sir Robert Jennings's view must be well understood. He was responding to a general question of *law* as to whether logistical support and financial assistance can constitute armed attacks.

In relation to the question of *fact* as to whether the support given by Nicaragua to El Salvadorian rebels constituted 'armed attack', the learned judge went on to say that:

> ...I remain somewhat doubtful whether the Nicaraguan involvement with Salvadorian rebels has not involved some forms of 'other support' besides the possible provision, whether officially or unofficially, of weapons. There seems to have been perhaps overmuch concentration on the question of the supply, or transit, of arms; as if that were of itself crucial, which it is not.

It is obvious from this statement that the USA failed to plead its case concerning the support given by Nicaragua to El Salvadorian rebels since it withdrew from the case. Nevertheless, Judge Schwebel fully tackled the question of whether providing logistical support to rebels, such as that which Nicaragua gave to the El Salvadorian rebels, could constitute armed attack.

Judge Schwebel, dissenting, quoting from many eminent authorities on international law, summarized the positions (at [155]) as follows:

> As to the Court's conclusions of law to this effect, it may be observed that the Court has taken one position, while I have taken another, which latter position, however, is essentially shared by (a) Nicaragua, (b) the United States, (c) El Salvador, and (d) 40 years of progressive development of the law and of authoritative interpretation of the governing principles of the United Nations Charter. In my view, the Judgment of the Court on the critical question of whether aid to irregulars may be tantamount to an armed attack departs from accepted—and desirable—law. Far from contributing, as so many of the Court's judgments have, to the progressive development of the law, on this question the Court's Judgment implies a regressive development of the law which fails to take account of the realities of the use of force in international relations: realities which have unfortunately plagued the world for years and give every sign of continuing to do so—whether they are recognized by the Court or not. I regret to say that I believe that the Court's Judgment on this profoundly important question may detract as much from the security of States as it does from the state of the law.

Thus Judge Schwebel believed that the Court was wrong in its dealing with the question of whether aid provided by Nicaragua to El Salvadorian rebels constituted an armed attack. In his dissention, in particular at [156], [157], and [228]–[237], the learned judge gave many reasons for his position. He stated (at [156]) that:

> In its Memorial on the merits of the case, Nicaragua set out the accepted law on the question. It applied that law to what it sees as the facts of United States support of the *contras*. But, since Nicaragua, together with Cuba, has participated so pervasively in the organization, training, arming, supplying and command and control of the insurgent forces in El Salvador, its analysis is no less pertinent to the question of whether its actions are tantamount to armed attack upon El Salvador.

He also drew support for his view from the law of State responsibility. He cited (at [157]) the view of the former Special Rapporteur of the International Law Commission (ILC), Judge Roberto Ago, expressed in his Third Report on State Responsibility (1971, Vol. II, Part 1, pp. 263–266)

> The attribution to the State, as a subject of international law, of the conduct of persons who are in fact operating on its behalf or at its instigation is unanimously upheld by the writers on international law who have dealt with this question . . . private persons may be secretly appointed to carry out particular missions or tasks to which the organs of the State prefer not to assign regular State officials; people may be sent as so-called 'volunteers' to help an insurrectional movement in a neighbouring country—and many more examples could be given'.

Many authoritative writers on international law support the view taken by Judge Schwebel. For example, Professor Ian Brownlie, *International Law and the Use of Force by States* (Oxford: Clarendon Press, 1963), p. 361, wrote that:

> there can be little doubt that 'use of force' is commonly understood to imply a military attack, an 'armed attack': by the organized military, naval, or air forces of a state; but the concept in practice and principle has a wider significance . . . governments may act by means of completely 'unofficial' agents, including armed bands, and 'volunteers', or may give aid to groups of insurgents on the territory of another State.

Although Brownlie accepts that sporadic operations by armed groups might not amount to armed attack, he believed (ibid., pp. 278–279) that it would be:

> conceivable that a coordinated and general campaign by powerful bands or irregulars, with obvious or easily proven complicity of a government of a state from which they operate would constitute an 'armed attack'.

Professor Rosalyn Higgins has also supported the position that use of irregulars to carry out armed attacks against another State is, from a functional point of view, a use of force, in her article 'The legal limits to the use of force by sovereign states: United Nations practice' (1961) 37 BYBIL 269, 278. She drew attention to the growing emphasis on indirect uses of force in UN practice. Whereas at San Francisco the focus was on conventional methods of armed attack, as we have seen with the provisions of Article 51, Professor Higgins noted (ibid.) that 'the unhappy events of the last fifteen years' necessitated a substantial re-evaluation of the concept of the use of force. Thus the 'law-making activities' of the UN General Assembly and the ILC in defining and outlawing 'indirect aggression' did not take place *in vacuo*, but arose from a combination of the continuing efforts to define aggression, the Nuremburg Principles, and the stream of incidents confronting the Security Council and the General Assembly (ibid., at 290).

According to A. M. Rifaat, *International Aggression* (Stockholm: Almqvist and Wiksell International, 1979), p. 217, since 1945, States have, with growing frequency, used armed bands and other covert means in an attempt to circumvent the prohibitions of Article 2(4). The learned writer argues that:

> States, while overtly accepting the obligation not to use force in their mutual relations, began to seek other methods of covert pressure in order to pursue their national policies without direct armed confrontation. The incompatibility of the classical external armed aggression with the present rules regulating international relations, led to the development of other methods of covert or indirect aggression.

It is interesting to note that a view similar to Judge Schwebel's position had been advanced by the USA much earlier in the life of the United Nations. In 1947, the US Representative to the UN, in a statement made to the Security Council, reported at (1947) 2 UN SCOR (147th and 148th meetings), 1120–1121, condemned the support provided to guerrillas in Greece thus:

> I do not think that we should interpret narrowly the 'Great Charter' of the United Nations. In modern times, there are many ways in which force can be used by one State against the territorial integrity of another. Invasion by organized armies is not the only means for delivering an attack against a country's independence. Force is effectively used today through devious methods of infiltration, intimidation and subterfuge. But this does not deceive anyone. No intelligent person in possession of the facts can fail to recognize here the use of force, however devious the subterfuge may be. We must recognize what intelligent and informed citizens already know. Yugoslavia, Bulgaria and Albania, in supporting guerrillas in northern Greece, have been using force against the territorial integrity and political independence of Greece. They have in fact been committing acts of the very kind which the United Nations was designed to prevent, and have violated the most important of the basic principles upon which our Organization was founded.

The implication of Judge Schwebel's review of those many great authorities in international law is to demonstrate convincingly that the Court's finding on the relevance of assistance and logistical support to armed attack is at variance with the development of international law. This is significant if we recall from Chapter 2 that the decisions of the ICJ constitute a source of international law. This implies that its decision will have far-reaching effects even if, as in the present case, the majority of States and writers feel otherwise. Happily enough, as will be recalled from Chapter 2, the ICJ is not bound to follow its own previous decision in a similar case (that is, it is not bound by the doctrine of *stare decisis*) and may take a decision contrary to that which it took in *Nicaragua*.

KEY POINTS

- Judge Schwebel, in his dissenting opinion in *Nicaragua*, stated that the Court's decision that logistical support does not constitute armed attack reverses the development of international law in this area.

- The majority of writers and authorities support the position that indirect use of force through armed groups or mercenaries constitutes armed attack.

thinking points

- *On what bases does Judge Schwebel argue that assistance and logistical support to rebels could constitute armed attacks?*
- *Is there any danger in allowing support provided to rebel groups to amount to armed attacks?*
- *What concerns might the ICJ have had that might perhaps have led it to reject the assertion that logistical support provided to rebels could amount to armed attacks?*

10.3.4 'The objects of self-defence': the particular case of terrorist organizations

Article 51 permits only States to take self-defence measures. However, States are not the only entities that can *use* force or cause armed attacks against States. The world has witnessed attacks by non-State entities such as terrorist organizations and rebel groups especially since the September 2001 attacks on the USA.

Article 2(4) does not prohibit States from using force against non-State entities, or non-State entities from using force against one another or against States, although non-State entities cannot defend themselves under Article 51 of the UN Charter when they are attacked by States. However, given the silence of Article 51 on the source of 'armed attacks', the question is whether States can defend themselves on the basis of Article 51 when attacked by non-State entities.

● *Legal Consequences of the Construction of a Wall in the Occupied Palestinian Territory (Palestinian Wall) Advisory Opinion* (2004) ICJ REP 136

The ICJ stated (at 139) that:

> Article 51 of the Charter thus recognizes the existence of an inherent right of self-defence in the case of armed attack by one State against another State. However, Israel does not claim that the attacks against it are imputable to a foreign State.

The Court's explicit linking of self-defence to an attack by a *State* in that sentence could lead to claims that the Court said that *only* attacks caused by States lead to a right of self-defence. The Court noted that Israel did not claim that the attacks against it are *imputable* to a foreign State. The reference to 'imputable' suggests that the Court recognized the right of self-defence against acts done by insurgent or terrorist groups on behalf of a State.

There is nothing in the UN Charter that prevents States from taking self-defence measures against non-State entities. Thus following the attacks on the USA of 11 September 2001 (the '9/11 attacks'), the US government called on NATO member States to assist in defending it against the Al Qaeda group responsible for the attack.

According to Article 5 of the 1949 North Atlantic Treaty:

> The Parties agree that an armed attack against one or more of them in Europe or North America shall be considered an attack against them all and consequently they agree that, if such an armed attack occurs, each of them, in exercise of the right of individual or collective self-defence recognised by Article 51 of the Charter of the United Nations, will assist the Party or Parties so attacked by taking forthwith, individually and in concert with the other Parties, such action as it

> deems necessary, including the use of armed force, to restore and maintain the security of the North Atlantic area.
>
> Any such armed attack and all measures taken as a result thereof shall immediately be reported to the Security Council. Such measures shall be terminated when the Security Council has taken the measures necessary to restore and maintain international peace and security.

Furthermore, the Organization of American States (OAS) equally assisted the USA in self-defence against Al Qaeda. According to Article 28 of the 1948 OAS Charter:

> Every act of aggression by a State against the territorial integrity or the inviolability of the territory or against the sovereignty or political independence of an American State shall be considered an act of aggression against the other American States.

Although self-defence against insurgents or terrorists is permissible, the question remains: on what basis would a State act in self-defence against such groups, such groups not being States?

In order to act in self-defence against a non-State entity, a State against which an armed attack has occurred has two options. First, it might show that although the attack is conducted by a non-State entity, the act is done with the actual or implicit *knowledge* of a State, or that the latter condones the act, or, at the very least, that it acquiesces to the act. Thus, since Al Qaeda operated out of Afghanistan with the proven knowledge and acquiescence of the Taliban government in that country, for the purpose of international law, the terrorist attack on the USA would be deemed to have been committed by Afghanistan.

This customary international rule has been codified by the ILC. Article 11 of the 2001 ILC Articles on the Responsibility of States for Internationally Wrongful Acts, which specifically deals with conduct acknowledged and adopted by a State as its own, provides that:

> Conduct which is not attributable to a State under the preceding articles shall nevertheless be considered an act of that State under international law if and to the extent that the State acknowledges and adopts the conduct in question as its own.

The other basis for acting in self-defence against non-State entities is that since Article 51 limits the exercise of such measures to States, then non-State entities are automatically included in the class of those that can be attacked in self-defence. Thus even if a significant link between Al Qaeda and Afghanistan had not been established, which made the self-defence action of the USA quite straightforward, the USA would have been able to act against the organization on the basis of Article 51 alone.

A different reading of the provisions of Article 51 to limit all actions to States might mean that the UN Charter does not cover situations concerning non-State entities, which would make such matters outside the scope of the Charter and therefore not impute illegality to a State that acts as such against a non-State entity.

However, given that terrorist organizations always have to operate from within States, it is unlikely that States will have problems proving linkages between those groups and their host States. In addition, since terrorist organizations usually have their facilities within the territory of States, it would be impossible for an attacked State to target those facilities without attacking the host State; hence, it is important for the attacked State to establish a link between the terrorist organization and the attack before acting in self-defence.

Perhaps a more useful approach is the one adopted by the African Union Non-Aggression and Common Defence Pact (2005). Article 1(c)(xiii) of this treaty defines 'aggression' or 'attack' as emanating from such a wide group as 'States', 'mercenaries', and 'criminal groups'.

thinking points

- *How does the statement of the ICJ regarding logistical support provided to irregular soldiers sit with the fact that a State can attack another State on the basis of the latter's support or harbouring of a terrorist organization?*
- *Can you explain the basis upon which a State may attack another State for acts committed by a terrorist group operating from within the latter State?*

It should be noted that the fact that a terrorist group is physically present on a State's territory does not necessarily make that State responsible for the activities of that group for the purpose of self-defence. The fact that the State *is* aware, or *ought* to be aware, of the presence of that organization or group on its territory is essential in any attempt to draw a link between the State and the group.

In the USA's case, the USA did not have to prove this formally: there was wide acceptance that Afghanistan shielded Al Qaeda and this was somewhat implicitly endorsed by the UN Security Council in its Resolution 1378 of 14 November 2001:

> *Condemning* the Taliban for allowing Afghanistan to be used as a base for the export of terrorism by the Al-Qaida network and other terrorist groups and for providing safe haven to Usama Bin Laden, Al-Qaida and others associated with them, and in this context supporting the efforts of the Afghan people to replace the Taliban regime,
> *Reaffirming* its strong commitment to the sovereignty, independence, territorial integrity and national unity of Afghanistan,
> *Deeply concerned* by the grave humanitarian situation and the continuing serious violations by the Taliban of human rights and international humanitarian law, . . .

From this resolution, it can be seen that although the Security Council did not specifically authorize the use of force against Afghanistan, the Council did specifically determine that Afghanistan provided a safe haven for Al Qaeda. The Council also noted that the Taliban allowed Afghanistan to be used 'for the export of terrorism by the Al-Qaida network'.

357

KEY POINTS

- Only States may act in self-defence under Article 51 of the UN Charter.

- Article 51 does not specify the entities against which self-defence measures can be taken. Hence, non-State entities, such as terrorist organizations, can be targeted in self-defence.

- It is important that linkages between a State (the host State) and non-State entities that use force against another State (the attacked State) are proved before the attacked State can attack the host State in self-defence.

10.3.5 Anticipatory self-defence

The requirement in Article 51 of the UN Charter that the right of self-defence exists only if an armed attack 'occurs' is a very controversial one. What does 'occurs' mean? Does it mean that States should wait until they have been attacked before defending themselves? What should a State threatened with the use of nuclear weapons do?

Many States and writers argue that when confronted by an overwhelming sense of danger, such as an imminent attack, States cannot afford to wait for an attack to occur before they act. So, some States argue that, in those circumstances, they can act in anticipation of an attack. This is what the notion of 'anticipatory self-defence' implies.

In 1981, Israel attacked the Iraqi nuclear reactor in Osirak and claimed to have acted in self-defence because, it said, Iraq directed its nuclear weapons towards Tel Aviv.

However, the Security Council sharply criticized Israel for this action.

United Nations Security Council Resolution 487 (19 June 1981)

. . . .

The Security Council,

Fully aware of the fact that Iraq has been a party to the Treaty on the Non-Proliferation of Nuclear Weapons since it came into force in 1970, that in accordance with that Treaty Iraq has accepted IAEA safeguards on all its nuclear activities, and that the Agency has testified that these safeguards have been satisfactorily applied to date,

Noting furthermore that Israel has not adhered to the non-proliferation Treaty,

Deeply concerned about the danger to international peace and security created by the premeditated Israeli air attack on Iraqi nuclear installations on 7 June 1981, which could at any time explode the situation in the area, with grave consequences for the vital interests of all States,

Considering that, under the terms of Article 2, paragraph 4, of the Charter of the United Nations: 'All Members shall refrain in their international relations from the threat or use of force against the territorial integrity or political independence of any State, or in any other manner inconsistent with the Purposes of the United Nations,'

1. *Strongly condemns* the military attack by Israel in clear violation of the Charter of the United Nations and the norms of international conduct;

2. *Calls upon* Israel to refrain in the future from any such acts or threats thereof;

3. *Further considers* that the said attack constitutes a serious threat to the entire IAEA safeguards regime which is the foundation of the non-proliferation Treaty;

4. *Fully recognizes* the inalienable sovereign right of Iraq, and all other States, especially the developing countries, to establish programmes of technological and nuclear development to develop their economy and industry for peaceful purposes in accordance with their present and future needs and consistent with the internationally accepted objectives of preventing nuclear weapons proliferation;

5. *Calls upon* Israel urgently to place its nuclear facilities under IAEA safeguards;

6. *Considers* that Iraq is entitled to appropriate redress for the destruction it has suffered, responsibility for which has been acknowledged by Israel; . . .

The UN Charter does not provide for anticipatory self-defence. As a right, this defence originates from the customary international law principles governing self-defence, many of which, as will be seen later, are believed to have survived the Charter.

The customary rules supporting anticipatory self-defence were laid down in the famous 'Caroline Affair' of 1837.

The facts of the Caroline Affair arose from a dispute involving the USA and the UK over some affairs in Canada. In 1837, some Canadians connived with Americans to mount an insurrection against the British authorities, then the colonial powers in Canada. Both rebellions were crushed, but a few rebels managed to escape to the USA, from where they continued their activities. The rebels enlisted the services of the US steamboat, Caroline, which was used for troops and arms mobilization purposes. The British authorities destroyed the boat and pushed her over the Niagara Falls.

In a follow-up series of communications between the US and British authorities over the affair, it fell on British Secretary of State Daniel Webster to justify the British action to the USA. In his seemingly well thought out letter to Special Minister Ashburton (restated in The People v. McLeod 1 Hill 377 (NY Sup Ct, 1841)), he stated that the USA had fulfilled its own duty as per the non-intervention principle and therefore that Britain must justify its action.

He argued that Britain must demonstrate the:

> necessity of self-defence, instant, overwhelming, leaving no choice of means, and no moment for deliberation. It will be for it to show, also, that the local authorities of Canada,—even supposing the necessity of the moment authorized them to enter the territories of the United States at all,—did nothing unreasonable or excessive; since the act justified by the necessity of self-defence, must be limited by that necessity, and kept clearly within it. It must be strewn that admonition or remonstrance to the persons on board the 'Caroline' was impracticable, or would have been unavailing; it must be strewn that daylight could not be waited for; that there could be no attempt at discrimination, between the innocent and the guilty; that it would not have been enough to seize and detain the vessel; but that there was a necessity, present and inevitable, for attacking her, in the darkness of the night, while moored to the shore, and while unarmed men were asleep on board, killing some, and wounding others, and then drawing her into the current, above the cataract, setting her on fire, and, careless to know whether there might not be in her the innocent with the guilty, or the living with the dead, committing her to a fate, which fills the imagination with horror.

KEY POINT A State claiming to have taken action in anticipation of an attack must prove that: (a) there is overwhelming evidence of imminent attack on it; (b) it acts out of necessity; and (c) its action is proportionate.

The question of anticipatory self-defence is particularly important for two reasons. First, Article 51 was not designed with nuclear or biological weapons in mind—that is, the two types of weapon that might be used without troops crossing the border of a country. Furthermore, if the purpose of armed attack is to cause maximum damage to the facilities of another country—especially its military facilities—then we can add technological attacks as another deadly means by which one country can now attack another without visibly crossing its borders.

example

There have been cases in which computer hackers have hacked into the most secretive websites of the intelligence facilities at the US National Aeronautics and Space Administration (NASA). Surely, if this hacking were done with malicious intent (as opposed to misadventure) and serious harm to US military facilities were to occur as a result of infection by a software virus used by the hacker, it would be ridiculous not to regard this as an armed attack.

Secondly, Article 51 did not envisage such phenomena as terrorist organizations becoming one of the most rabid users of force against States. These entities use the most unconventional means in their activities, such as the use of commercial planes by Al Qaeda in its 9/11 attacks.

What these new developments show is that Article 51 has fallen behind contemporary developments in international affairs and technology.

● *Nicaragua v. United States of America* (1986) ICJ Rep 14 (The *Military and Paramilitary Activities in and against Nicaragua Case*, or the *Nicaragua Case*)

At [94], the ICJ declined to comment on anticipatory self-defence, since the issue with which it was confronted with concerned a real attack and not an imaginary one:

> With regard to the characteristics governing the right of self-defence, since the Parties consider the existence of this right to be established as a matter of customary international law, they have concentrated on the conditions governing its use. In view of the circumstances in which the dispute has arisen, *reliance is placed by the Parties only on the right of self-defence in the case of an armed attack which has already occurred, and the issue of the lawfulness of a response to the imminent threat of armed attack has not been raised. Accordingly, the Court expresses no view on that issue.* [Emphasis added]

● *The Legality of the Threat or Use of Nuclear Weapons Advisory Opinion* (1996) ICJ Rep 226

The ICJ was offered the opportunity to pronounce on anticipatory self-defence, especially given the nature of the question posed to the Court. It will be recalled that the main question that the General Assembly asked the Court was whether the possession of nuclear weapons was permitted under international law. Some States argue that the possession of nuclear weapons is clear evidence of the readiness to use them.

The relevance of the nuclear weapons question to anticipatory self-defence is obvious.

example

If Candoma believes that the possession of nuclear weapons by Rutamu is sufficient evidence of the latter's readiness to use them, then Candoma could attack Rutamu in self-defence, in anticipation of the latter's attack.

If we project this hypothesis to contemporary times, then Candoma's argument (in the example above) seems logical; otherwise, the international community's worry about the prospect of a nuclear-armed Iran or North Korea would be senseless. Simply stated, if the international community does not believe that the mere possession of nuclear weapons by either Iran or North Korea is evidence of these countries' readiness to use them, then why the grave concern about the matter?

Unfortunately, the ICJ did not seize the opportunity and failed to consider the issue of anticipatory self-defence at all. This may be because the Court did not feel any particular need to pronounce on the issue, since the question did not arise. After all, even in respect of the specific question asked of the Court, it simply said that a threat is unlawful if the subsequent use of force is illegal—an answer that one might say was far too superficial to satisfy the seriousness of the question posed to the Court.

On the whole, the Court said of the *Dispositif* (at [2E]) that:

> in view of the current state of international law, and of the elements of fact at its disposal, the Court cannot conclude definitively whether the threat or use of nuclear weapons would be lawful or unlawful in an extreme circumstance of self-defence, in which *the very survival of a State* would be at stake. [Emphasis added]

The Court had an ideal opportunity to lay to rest many troubling questions on one of the most vexed issues in international law. Yet, all that the Court did was pontificate on the present state of international law which, in any case, was well known to States and writers. It even concluded that it could say nothing about the question, except *when the very survival of a State would be at stake*. This added condition did not form part of the question asked of the Court. It was no surprise, then, that some members of the Court heavily criticized its pronouncement.

Vice President Schwebel, dissenting, said (at 322) that:

> This is an astounding conclusion to be reached by the International Court of Justice. Despite the fact that its Statute 'forms an integral part' of the United Nations Charter, and despite the comprehensive and categorical terms of Article 2, paragraph 4, and Article 51 of that Charter, the Court concludes on the supreme issue of the threat or use of force of our age that it has no opinion. In 'an extreme circumstance of self-defence, in which the very survival of a State would be at stake', the Court ... has nothing to say.... When it comes to the supreme interests of State, the Court discards the legal progress of the twentieth century, puts aside the provisions of the Charter of the United Nations of which it is 'the principal judicial organ', and proclaims, in terms redolent of *Realpolitik*, its ambivalence about the most important provisions of modern international law. If this was to be its ultimate holding, the Court would have done better to have drawn on its undoubted discretion not to render an opinion at all.

The problem with the Court's attitude is not only that it refused to exercise its discretion to pronounce on this fundamental issue comprehensively, or even adequately, but also that it appears to have given a rather dangerous impression that if a State's survival is threatened, only then may the use of nuclear weapons be lawful. This view was rejected by some of the judges.

Judge Koroma, also dissenting, argued (at 571) that:

> This finding that would appear to suggest that nuclear weapons when used in circumstances of a threat to 'State survival'—a concept invented by the Court—would constitute an exception to the corpus of humanitarian law which applies in all armed conflicts and makes no exception for nuclear weapons. In my considered opinion, the unlawfulness of the use of nuclear weapons is not predicated on the circumstances in which the use takes place, but rather on the unique and established characteristics of those weapons which under any circumstance would violate international law by their use. It is therefore most inappropriate for the Court's finding to have turned on the question of State survival when what is in issue is the lawfulness of nuclear weapons. Such a misconception of the question deprives the Court's finding of any legal basis.

In her dissention, Judge Higgins faulted the Court's approach to the issue principally because the Court chose to answer a question that it was not asked (that is, whether the use of nuclear weapons can be lawful when the *survival* of a State is at stake) and did not answer that which it was asked (that is, whether the possession of nuclear weapons is lawful under international law).

Judge Higgins, dissenting, said (at 583):

> Through this formula of non pronouncement the Court necessarily leaves open the possibility that a use of nuclear weapons contrary to humanitarian law might nonetheless be lawful. This goes beyond anything that was claimed by the nuclear weapon States appearing before the Court, who fully accepted that any lawful threat or use of nuclear weapons would have to comply with both the *jus ad bellum* and the *jus in bello* (see Advisory Opinion, para. 86).

thinking points

- *Read the Court's judgment in* The Legality of the Threat or Use of Nuclear Weapons Advisory Opinion *again and summarize the bases of its decision regarding whether it is permissible in international law to possess nuclear weapons.*
- *Summarize the dissenting opinions of Judges Koroma and Higgins on the Court's treatment of the issue at stake.*
- *Of what relevance is the question about the legality of nuclear weapons to anticipatory self-defence?*

10.3.6 Anticipatory self-defence after 9/11

Despite disagreement among States and writers, developments after the 9/11 terrorist attacks have increased the importance of anticipatory self-defence in international law. These are remarkably different scenarios from when Israel attacked Iraq in 1981. Perhaps not surprisingly, the USA has become the loudest and most assertive claimant to anticipatory self-defence by far, even making it its national security strategy. According to President George W. Bush (as reported in 'President Bush delivers graduation speech at West Point', White House Press Release 20020601–3, 1 June 2002):

> For much of the last century, America's defense relied on the Cold War doctrines of deterrence and containment. In some cases, those strategies still apply. But new threats also require new thinking. Deterrence—the promise of massive retaliation against nations—means nothing against shadowy terrorist networks with no nation or citizens to defend. Containment is not possible when unbalanced dictators with weapons of mass destruction can deliver those weapons on missiles or secretly provide them to terrorist allies.... Our security will require transforming the military you will lead—a military that must be ready to strike at a moment's notice in any dark corner of the world. And our security will require all Americans to be forward-looking and resolute, to be ready for *preemptive* action when necessary to defend our liberty and to defend our lives.

International law is not settled as to whether States have the right to defend themselves in anticipation of an attack. However, what can be said for sure is that there seems to be an increase in the number of States claiming this right. For example, after President George W. Bush characterized North Korea, alongside Iran and Iraq, as part of the 'axis of evil', North

Korea claimed that it could attack the USA if it were to feel threatened by US actions. North Korea had interpreted Bush's statement as a prelude to a US attack.

The UN Security Council has also become more receptive to States acting under Article 51. It can additionally be said that the Council has tacitly endorsed anticipatory self-defence. In a 2001 resolution, it mandated States to act against terrorists in a *proactive* manner:

United Nations Security Council Resolution 1373 (28 September 2001)

. . . .

The Security Council,
  Reaffirming also its unequivocal condemnation of the terrorist attacks which took place in New York, Washington, D.C. and Pennsylvania on 11 September 2001, and expressing its determination to prevent all such acts,

  . . .

2. *Decides also* that all States shall:

  . . .

  (b) Take the necessary steps to prevent the commission of terrorist acts, including by provision of early warning to other States by exchange of information;
  (c) Cooperate, particularly through bilateral and multilateral arrangements and agreements, to *prevent and suppress* terrorist attacks and take action against perpetrators of such acts; . . .

Mandating States to 'Take the necessary steps to prevent the commission of terrorist acts, including by provision of early warning to other States by exchange of information' can be interpreted in many ways. Thus if one State provides an early warning to another State that there is a plan being hatched on its territory, or that of a third State, which is to culminate in an attack against another State, nothing stops the latter from attacking the group hatching the plan. Resolution 1373 seems to support such an action fully.

Paragraph 3(c) also enjoins States to cooperate to 'prevent and suppress' terrorist activities, and this can be read to include anticipatory action that is preventive.

However, the Security Council still requires some evidence (in the form of an early warning) before a State can take action to forestall a terrorist attack. This indicates that anticipatory self-defence must be based on real evidence of an impending attack. Therefore this resolution cannot justify actions based on the pre-emptive doctrine, which is a nebulous doctrine that would allow a State to attack another State not because the latter has an intention to attack it, but because it has a history of violence towards other States.

KEY POINTS

- Anticipatory self-defence has attained a new significance after the 9/11 attacks.

- There is currently considerable support by the Security Council for States acting to forestall terrorist activities.

- A State that wishes to take anticipatory measures against terrorists must demonstrate that there is a plan by the group to attack that State.

10.3.7 'Until the Security Council has taken measures necessary...'

The 'until' clause implies that the right of self-defence is neither a blank cheque nor exist *ad infinitum*. It exists only insofar as the Security Council has not taken the measures prescribed in Article 51. But while the majority of writers believe that only the affected State can determine the sufficiency of the measures taken by the Security Council, there is disagreement about who may determine whether such measures automatically trump the right of self-defence. Bowett argued that measures taken by the Security Council do not suspend the right of self-defence and that a State which has been attacked may exercise its self-defence right even in conflict with the Security Council (Derek Bowett, *Self-Defence in International Law* (Manchester: University of Manchester Press, 1958). However, for Rein Mullerson, the mere placing of an item on the Security Council agenda renders self-defence dormant (Rein Mullerson, Remarks made at the American Society of International Law and the Soviet Association of International Law, Washington DC, 4–6 October 1990). Mullerson's further contended, as did also Franck and Patel, that only if the Security Council is prevented by the veto from functioning that the right could be revived. (See Thomas M. Franck and Faiza Patel, 'UN police action in lieu of war: the old order changeth' (1995) 85 AJIL 63.) Franck and Patel regard the right of self-defence as the 'old war system' created in the Charter as a fall-back when the new police power (Security Council) fails to act. Rostow rejected this view holding, in effect, that an intervention by the Security Council does not trump the right of self-defence (Eugene Rostow, 'Until what? Enforcement action or collective self-defense: can Security Council action suspend the right of self-defence?' (1991) 85(3) AJIL 506). The records of the US government participation at the 1945 San Francisco Conference, which led to the formation of the UN, show that the Administration believed that the right of collective self-defence exists concurrently with the intervention of the Security Council (US Government: 'Minutes of the Thirty-Six Meeting of the United States Delegation, San Francisco', 11 May 1945, 1 *Foreign Relations of the United States* (1945), p. 677). According to Dinstein (see section 10.2.1), and Sir Humphrey Waldock ('The regulation of the use of force by individual states in international law' (1952-II) 81 Recueil des Cours 451), once self-defence right is on course, only an affirmative action by the Security Council can terminate it.

Thus far, there are various views on the exact implication of the 'until' clause and it is futile to pronounce on any as the correct or wrong one. What we must bear in mind are that: the right of self-defence is temporary; that States will hardly ignore measures taken by the Security Council; and that if a State defending itself is a permanent member of the Security Council, it will be expected that such issues concerning adequacy of measures or whether the measures terminate the State's right would have been ironed out before the Security Council will vote on the measures. In practice, such measures have not generated any problem between a self-defending State and the Security Council.

10.3.8 The condition for 'collective self-defence'

● *Nicaragua v. United States of America* [1986] ICJ Rep 14 [The *Military and Paramilitary Activities in and against Nicaragua Case*, or the *Nicaragua Case*]

While pronouncing on what constitutes 'armed attacks', the Court also pronounced (at [195]) on what constitutes '*collective* self-defence' under Article 51:

It is also clear that it is the State which is the victim of an armed attack which must form and declare the view that it has been so attacked. There is no rule in customary international law permitting another State to exercise the right of collective self-defence on the basis of its own assessment of the situation. Where collective self-defence is invoked, it is to be expected that the State for whose benefit this right is used will have declared itself to be the victim of an armed attack.

According to this statement, it is necessary for an attacked State specifically to invite others to defend it. Some writers have argued in favour of this view and the majority of the judges in *Nicaragua* indeed favoured this approach.

The Court concluded (at [199]) that:

At all events, the Court finds that in customary international law, whether of a general kind or that particular to the inter-American legal system, *there is no rule permitting the exercise of collective self-defence in the absence of a request by the State which regards itself as the victim of an armed attack. The Court concludes that the requirement of a request by the State which is the victim of the alleged attack is additional to the requirement that such a State should have declared itself to have been attacked.* [Emphasis added]

The rationale behind this approach seems fairly obvious: formally requesting assistance for collective self-defence removes the danger of third States taking advantage of a situation and intervening in matters that do not directly involve them.

Nonetheless, the requirement seems overly formalistic. Such a requirement is not obvious from the provision of Article 51: an armed attack on a State is an open fact in international law and not a secret act that must be brought to the attention of the public by a formal declaration or request.

Furthermore, the Court's reasoning on this point is open to challenge. The absence of a customary international law rule permitting the exercise of collective self-defence without a specific request to that effect should not imply that the act is itself illegal. Perhaps what the Court should have established is that the practice whereby attacked States regularly make requests to others, as a procedural requirement, is established in customary international law. Had it done so, then non-compliance would be treated as a breach of that law.

Did the USA have to inform its NATO allies formally that it had been attacked in 2001 as a condition for those States supporting its collective self-defence action against Afghanistan and Al Qaeda? Did Kuwait formally invite its allies? Both States probably did so—but only as a matter of courtesy. It cannot mean that, without such a request, there could not have been a valid collective self-defence. There is no evidence of either the USA or Kuwait making the request as a procedural necessity.

In fact, Article 5 of the 1949 North Atlantic Treaty says that an attack on one is an attack on all. Similarly, Article 28 of the OAS Charter states that:

Every act of aggression by a State against the territorial integrity or the inviolability of the territory or against the sovereignty or political independence of an American State shall be considered an act of aggression against the other American States.

thinking point
Having read and understood the previous passages, how would you now define 'collective self-defence' and on what basis can it be exercised?

Neither stipulates that a formal request must be made. It is submitted that these provisions imply that once a NATO or OAS member is attacked, all are deemed attacked. Therefore it would not make any sense, in this instance, to insist that an attacked State must invite all attacked States to defend themselves: why should one then have to report to *itself* that it has been attacked?

The absence of a request for collective self-defence is different from the objection raised by Sir Robert Jennings to the exercise of collective self-defence.

. . . .

● **Nicaragua v. United States of America** (1986) ICJ REP 14 (The **Military and Paramilitary Activities in and against Nicaragua Case**, or the **Nicaragua Case**)

In his dissenting opinion, Sir Robert Jennings stated that collective self-defence was not a right known to customary international law. He even argued that the practice is not supported by a majority of States. Consequently, he stated that each State that intends to support another in collective self-defence must establish its own individual claim under Article 51.

He said (at 545 *et seq*):

> But there is another objection to this way of looking at collective self-defence. It seems to be based almost upon an idea of vicarious defence by champions: that a third State may lawfully come to the aid of an authenticated victim of armed attack provided that the requirements of a declaration of attack and a request for assistance are complied with. But whatever collective self-defence means, it does not mean vicarious defence; for that way the notion is indeed open to abuse. The assisting State is not an authorized champion, permitted under certain conditions to go to the aid of a favoured State. The assisting State surely must, by going to the victim State's assistance, be also, and in *addition* to other requirements, in some measure defending itself. There should even in 'collective self-defence' be some real element of self involved with the notion of defence. This is presumably also the philosophy which underlies mutual security arrangements, such as the system of the Organization of American States, for which indeed Article 51 was specifically designed. By such a system of collective security, the security of each member State is meant to be involved with the security of the others; not merely as a result of a contractual arrangement but by the real consequences of the system and its organization . . .
>
> This, I believe, should not be regarded as a mere contractual arrangement for collective defence—a legal fiction used as a device for arranging for mutual defence—; *it is to be regarded as an organized system of collective security by which the security of each member is made really and truly to have become involved with the security of the others, thus providing a true basis for a system of collective self-defence.* [Emphasis added]

The effect of Sir Robert Jennings's insistence that there is a *real* element of self in each and every State that seeks to defend another collectively is to ensure that self-serving States do not use collective self-defence as a pretext to further their own agendas in the attacked State.

Nonetheless, caution should not be taken too far. We should not insist that unless third States can demonstrate by some direct means that they also have *suffered* or have been threatened by the attack on the State that they intend to defend, the exercise of collective self-defence is inappropriate. This, with respect, is stretching Article 51 too far. Such an approach would defeat the whole purpose of collective self-defence which, rather than being a mere legal fiction, is a significant indication that a collection of States regards the welfare of one as the welfare of all, and danger to one as danger to all, and that 'a collection of States' might mean the entire international community, or the majority of States as represented by the United Nations. If this noble notion would then come to mean, as Sir Robert Jennings's idea suggests, that danger to one is danger to all *only* when *all* can individually show the danger to them from an attack, then the whole idea of collective self-defence (or even collective security, as we will see in the next chapter) does not make sense at all.

In support of his own argument, Sir Robert Jennings relied on a definition of collective self-defence by Lauterpacht (1952, see section 10.2.4), p. 155, which reads thus:

> It will be noted that, in a sense, Article 51 enlarges the right of self-defence as usually understood—and the corresponding right of recourse to force—by authorising both individual and collective self-defence. This means that a Member of the United Nations is permitted to have recourse to action in self-defence not only when it is itself the object of armed attack, but also when such attack is directed against any other State or States whose safety and independence are deemed vital to the safety and independence of the State thus resisting—or participating in forcible resistance to—the aggressor.

Yet this definition is also capable of a different interpretation: that a State may exercise self-defence when an attack is directed against another State, but one that the latter has an obligation to assist. It could also mean that a State may exercise self-defence when an attack occurs against another that may have serious implications for its own security as well. The widest interpretation of this, absurd as it may seem, would be that the threat to one is a threat to international peace and security, and therefore a threat to all. Certainly, it stands the logic of collective self-defence on its head if one were to insist that every State that may wish to assist Kenya, should it decide to respond to the Somalia-based Al Shabib's attack on Nairobi Westgate Mall under Article 51, should demonstrate, as Sir Jennings suggested, that they each were directly affected.

KEY POINT Although the ICJ held in *Nicaragua* that it is necessary for an attacked State to make a request to others for collective self-defence, this is not a legal requirement under Article 51 of the UN Charter.

10.4 Is Article 2(4) sufficient in the modern world?

One last issue to consider briefly in this chapter is the clamour for changes to the structure of the UN Charter. Some writers claim that the 9/11 attacks show that Article 2(4), which applies only to States, has fallen out of step with modern realities. If the threat or use of force is prohibited only amongst States, but not by or amongst non-State entities, then the Charter might have unwittingly left its greatest objective vulnerable.

The provisions of Article 2(4) might indeed have fallen behind a little. But this does not mean that we have to review the Charter; if we do so, there will be some instability in the legal regulation of the use of force. What needs to be done is for the international community to approach Charter provisions with some flexibility. For example, under the Security Council resolutions, greater support has been lent to States to take anticipatory self-defence than perhaps Article 51 embodies. Also, we have shown that it is possible to undertake self-defence actions against terrorist groups. On its own, the ICJ has been able to interpret the provisions of Article 51—especially on whether irregular forces can constitute armed attacks—in more liberal ways than Article 51 suggests. We do not need specifically to change the Charter to incorporate these changes. The institutions of the United Nations must be creative in addressing contemporary issues, so that the widely couched rules of the Charter can be interpreted to cover current trends.

👁 Conclusion

This chapter has dealt with the legal regulation of the use of force. It considered how States and writers deal with the various elements contained in Article 2(4) of the UN Charter. In particular, it analysed the meanings of 'force' and 'territorial integrity and political independence', as well as the use of force in a manner 'inconsistent with the Purposes of the United Nations'. We tried to look into what States, writers, and the ICJ make of these apparently controversial provisions. The use of force is a highly controversial topic of international law, all the more so because of the difference between what the law says and what States do, and also between what writers and the ICJ conceive. But, despite the occasional disagreement and disparity of approaches, there are common grounds. For example, we have seen that Article 2(4) prohibits the use and threat of force, and not only war, unlike its predecessors the 1919 League Covenant and the 1928 Kellogg–Briand Pact. We have also seen that States are limited in their exceptions to the rule: only self-defence and collective security (to be discussed fully in the next chapter) are permitted. Using force for democracy, using force to protect one's own nationals abroad, or using force to prevent humanitarian tragedies are all popular positions, but are not recognized under the UN Charter and, unless they can be supported by peremptory custom, remain illegal.

❓ Questions

Self-test questions

1 What does 'force' mean under Article 2(4) of the UN Charter?

2 Explain the meaning of 'territorial integrity' and of 'political independence'.

3 What do we mean by 'armed attack' under Article 51 of the UN Charter?

4 What is 'anticipatory self-defence'?

5 How did the ICJ define 'threat' in *Nuclear Weapons*?

6 Distinguish 'individual self-defence' from 'collective self-defence'.

Discussion questions

1 'There is no armed attack unless the regular forces of a State attack another State.' Discuss.

2 'To constitute a violation of territorial integrity and political independence of a State, the use of force against that State must reduce the size of its territory and instigate a change of its government.' Critically examine this statement.

3 'Article 2(4) of the UN Charter is an absolute prohibition of the use or threat of force.' Analyse the validity of this statement in light of writers' and States' approaches to interpreting the Article.

4 'An attacked State must make a formal request to others before there can be a right of collective self-defence and it is important that third States willing to help the attacked State must justify their involvement by some measure.' Critically examine this statement, with reference to the ICJ decision in the *Nicaragua Case* and Sir Robert Jennings's dissention.

5 'There is considerable support for anticipatory self-defence in contemporary international society. Even the UN Security Council has lent greater support to this practice in the aftermath of the 9/11 attacks in the USA.' Critically examine this statement, with reference to State practice and particular post-2001 Security Council resolutions.

Assessment question

After a series of border incidents with its neighbour over a piece of land adjoining the two States, Candoma decided to teach Rutamu a 'bitter lesson'. On 1 January 2014, the Candoman president announced on the State television channel, the Candoman Broadcasting Corporation (CBC), that he had decided to put a stop to the endless frictions along its borders—but he did not explain what he meant by that. In the following days, thousands of forces from the Candoman National Army moved to the border shared with Rutamu, taking with them scores of armoured tanks, anti-aircraft guns, and heavy artillery. Brigadier John Safor, director of military intelligence in Rutamu and who was on a private visit to Candoma, happened upon an official memo in that country in which Colonel Ellen Diacrass, the military intelligence adviser to Candoma, advised her government to ensure a total assault on the enemy. The memo did not mention Rutamu by name.

As legal adviser to the Rutamuan Foreign Office, advise your president on what action to take under these circumstances.

Key cases

- *Albania v. United Kingdom (Merits) (Judgment)* (1949) ICJ Rep 4 (the *Corfu Channel Case*)
- *Legal Consequences of the Construction of a Wall in the Occupied Palestinian Territory Advisory Opinion* (2004) ICJ Rep 136 (*Palestinian Wall Advisory Opinion*)
- *Legality of the Threat or Use of Nuclear Weapons Advisory Opinion* (1996) ICJ Rep 226
- *Nicaragua v. United States of America* (1986) ICJ Rep 14 (*Military and Paramilitary Activities in and against Nicaragua*, or the *Nicaragua Case*)

# Further reading

Corten, O., *Le droit contre la guerre* (Paris: Pedone; translated into English as *The Law against War* (Oxford: Hart Publishing, 2010)

Dinstein, Y., *War, Aggression, Self-Defence* (Cambridge: Cambridge University Press, 2011)

Gray, C., *International Law and the Use of Force* (3rd edn, Oxford: Oxford University Press, 2008)

Higgins, R., 'The legal limits to the use of force by sovereign states: United Nations practice' (1961) 37 BYBIL 269

Martson, G., 'Armed intervention in the 1956 Suez Canal Crisis: the legal advice tendered to the British government' (1988) 37 ICLQ 1

Moore, J. N. (ed.), *Law and Civil War in the Modern World* (Baltimore, MD: Johns Hopkins University Press, 1974)

Slaughter, A.-M. and Burke-White, W. W., 'An international constitutional moment' (2002) 43 Harv Int'l LJ 1

Collective security

Learning objectives

This chapter will help you to:

- understand the meaning of 'collective security', 'peacekeeping', and 'humanitarian intervention';

- distinguish between these three concepts, and understand their place in the overall quest for international peace and security;

- appreciate how the UN Security Council works as an important organ charged with the custody of international peace and security;

- understand the efforts of certain regional organizations towards the maintenance of peace and security within their regions;

- recognize the different meanings and implications of actions towards international peace and security;

- understand the latest developments in this area following several terrorist attacks in different parts of the world; and

- consider the adequacy of the current rules in this area and the possible need for substantial legal reform.

Introduction

In Chapter 10, we mentioned that there are three exceptions to the prohibition on the use of force. We discussed one exception (self-defence) and indicated that the second exception, Article 107, is now obsolete. The third exception to the prohibition on the use of force is any action duly authorized by the UN Security Council. These are generally referred to as 'collective security' measures, because they are, simply put, actions taken or authorized by the Security Council, on behalf of the international community, to enforce international law. Although this last exception could have been discussed in the previous chapter alongside self-defence, dealing with it separately here allows it to be understood more clearly, particularly since it embodies the powers of the Security Council and thus offers an opportunity to study the operations of that institution. Similarly, the decision to cover peacekeeping, humanitarian intervention, and responsibility to protect in this chapter instead of the last is based on the fact that it is mostly when collective security under the Security Council fails that recourse is had to humanitarian considerations. Peacekeeping, although mostly used when the Security Council is immobilized by the veto, is often authorized by the Security Council itself as an alternative to collective security measures in situations in which, for example, it is impractical or inappropriate to authorize outright collective security measures. The responsibility to protect, which is the latest arrival of all, is in some ways the international community's response to frequent inaction by the Security Council and the shortcomings of humanitarian intervention. Thus all three themes treated in this chapter are linked to collective security in one way or another.

 11.1 # The meaning of 'collective security'

There is no universally agreed definition of collective security. According to Roland Stromberg, collective security is widely regarded as a slippery idea, which makes it neither a system of the world government nor the old international anarchy ('The idea of collective security' (1956) 17(2) J History of Ideas 250). Nonetheless, there have been several attempts to define collective security, but the idea that the concept embodies the use of force by the international community to deter aggression finds near universal endorsement.

Hans Kelsen believes we speak of collective security when the protection of the rights of States, the reaction against the violation of the law, assumes the character of a collective enforcement action (H. Kelsen, 'Collective security and collective self-defence under the Charter of the United Nations' (1948) 41 AJIL 783). Bourquin argues that collective security entails a far-reaching renunciation by States of the use of armed violence to secure justice for themselves, and to make their will prevail (M. Bourguin, 'General report on the preparatory memoranda submitted to the General Study Conference' in M. Borquin (ed.), *Collective Security:*

A Record of the Seventh and Eighth International Studies Conference, Paris 1934–London 1935 (Paris: International Institute of Intellectual Cooperation, 1936). Robert Butterworth conceives collective security as a general international organization to coordinate and embody the community's response to aggression (R. L. Butterworth, 'Organizing collective security: the UN Charter's Chapter VIII in practice' (1976) 28(2) World Politics 197). In his fascinating 2011 work on the subject, Alexander Orakhelashvili describes collective security as referring to a group of States that unites around a set of common values and principles, and includes, on a permanent basis, the institutional capacity to determine and remedy violation of the values (M. Orakhelashvili, *Collective Security* (Oxford: Oxford University Press, 2011)). For Thompson, the key factor in collective security is the institutional machinery, endowed with the capacity to administer collective security (K. W. Thompson, 'Collective security re-examined' (1954) 47(3) Am Pol Sc Rev 761).

Despite the prevalence of the use of force in these definitions, some authors see collective security as not involved only with the use of force. Robert Kolb, for instance, defines collective security as a system geared to the keeping of the peace and the avoidance of war ('The eternal problem of collective security: from the League of Nations to the United Nations' (2007) 26(4) Refugee Survey Quarterly 220). As we will see later, this definition is important especially in relation to the organization of peacekeeping operations as one of the less violent systems to achieve collective security. (For more definitions, see George Downs (ed.), *Collective Security beyond the Cold War* (Ann Arbor, MI: University of Michigan Press, 1994) and Thomas G. Weiss, *Collective Security in a Changing World* (Boulder, CO: Lynne Rienner, 1993.)

Certain points are worth emphasizing in these definitions. First is the idea of the 'use of preponderant force', which refers to the size or amount of force employed. The word 'over-whelming' is sometimes used to describe the force that is used collectively against a breacher of the peace. However, the word also implies that the 'preponderant' force is used on behalf of, and to enforce the will of, the 'international community'. 'International community' in the present context means all of the nations in the world.

Therefore, for 'preponderant force' to amount to collective security, it is required that it is not only used on behalf of the international community, but is also approved by a competent representative of that community. By this, we mean a body that is recognized as having the legal powers to take decisions on behalf of members of the international community. In the context of collective security, this body is the UN Security Council, which is the most powerful political organ of the United Nations. However, as will be seen later, there may also be organs that are competent to authorize collective security, apart from the Security Council, although this is quite controversial. Under the Charter of the United Nations (UN Charter), collective security is provided for in Articles 39–51, which are contained in Chapter VII. As will be seen in the following analysis, these provisions are critical to the ability of the Security Council to maintain international peace and security; alongside the prohibition of force in Article 2(4), it constitutes the nerve centre of the UN system.

KEY POINTS

- **Collective security is the preponderant use of force to maintain international peace and security. One must bear in mind at all times that collective security must be approved by a competent organ of the international community.**

- **Collective security does not only consist of use of force but involves keeping the peace to prevent aggression.**

11.2 Collective security in a modern world

Before 1914 when the First World War broke out, the world security system was based on a 'balance of power'. Under this system, no State was allowed to possess more military capabilities than others which may enable it to threaten international peace and security. The two World Wars (1914–18, 1939–45) not only shattered that hope, they also brought untold suffering on mankind. The postwar order emphasizes replacing deadly rivalry amongst powerful States with a collective responsibility for managing and responding to threats, a global society where consensus and concessions are promoted, and where dedicated multilateral institutions would play a decisive role in the administration of peace and security. The advent of the League of Nations and the United Nations would have a decisive impact on collective security which, though not perfect, remarkably advances the search for an effective collective security system.

11.3 Collective security under the League of Nations

The League of Nations (LoN) established the first ever effort by an international organization to administer collective security. The League existed between the two World Wars and grew out of the American League Council experiment. (See *Proceedings of the First Annual National Assemblage of the League to Enforce Peace, Washington*, 26–27 May 1916.) It had its headquarters in Geneva, Switzerland and had an Assembly and an Executive Council—Articles 2 and 4 respectively. The League Covenant was shaped by the experiences of the First World War, although its provisions failed to address many fundamental concerns of States. (See D. H. Miller, *The Drafting of the Covenant* (New York: G. P. Putnam, 1928.)

The League experiment failed for many reasons, although the non-participation of the USA in its affairs denied the organization a major means of support and enforcement of its values. (See Henry Noel Brailsford, *A League of Nations* (New York: Macmillan, 1917.) The League Covenant did not prohibit States from the use of force, the most critical factor in any idea of collective security, but only declared wars or threats of war as 'a matter of concern to the whole League' (Article 11 LoN Covenant). The Covenant did not recognize the right of self-defence either. Instead, it obligated member States to submit to a judicial settlement or to the League Council any dispute likely to lead to violence. Such States should also not resort to war for at least three months after an arbitral award or a report by the League Council was given—Article 13. (See T. Conwell-Evans, *The League Council in Action* (Oxford: Oxford University Press, 1929.) Furthermore, as Josef Kunz has noted, the League woefully failed effectively to deal with the issue of regional collective security (Josef L. Kunz, 'The Inter-American system and the United Nations Organization' (1945) 39(4) AJIL 758).

The scope of, and authority for, collective security

From the previous discussion, we have shown that where a number of States come together to use force against another State, this is collective security insofar as that action *is authorized* by the UN Security Council or any other competent representative of the international community. Also, where a *single* State uses force against another, it is collective security *if* that State acts with the authority of the Security Council or any other competent representative of the international community. However, where several States act without relevant authorization, then that action is *unilateral* action. This situation might appear confusing, because even when several States use unauthorized force, we still call it 'unilateral action'. Whether action is unilateral or collective does not depend on the number of States involved, but on *whether or not* the action is authorized by a competent body. Therefore if only one State uses force with the authorization of the Security Council, for example, then that constitutes a collective security action since the State acts on behalf of the international community. However, if fifty States use force without such an authorization, the action is unilateral, because it is not one taken on behalf of the international community.

The definition of collective security stated above is useful but, as we will see shortly, it is limited. On the one hand, the definition is useful because, indeed, when narrowly understood, collective security occurs when a collection of States, or a single State, use(s) force *with the authority of the Security Council*, or any other body empowered to represent the international community, in order to maintain peace and security.

Writers often define 'collective security' with reference to two parameters: that collective security is mainly the 'use of preponderant force'; and that collective security is an action authorized only by the Security Council. These two parameters are problematic.

First, to describe collective security *only* as a 'use of overwhelming force' is too narrow, because such a definition ignores the peaceful element of collective security. One of the main objectives for establishing the United Nations was to ensure that, as far as is possible, States do not go to war with one another. But if this objective is not achievable, then it is expected that States will do all that is necessary to settle their disputes peacefully. In fact, the UN Charter obliges the UN Security Council to assist States in peacefully settling their disputes (see Chapter 14 on the settlement of international disputes) and this is also part of that body's exercise of collective security. As we will see later, the Security Council can authorize the use of force against a State only as a last resort—that is, only after all else has failed. Therefore collective security cannot consist *only* in a measure that is meant to be exercised when all efforts at peaceful settlement have failed.

When we look at the UN Charter, we see that the system of collective security that it contains matches what we have just described—that is, it permits the use of preponderant force only after a failure to settle disputes peacefully. Article 1 of the Charter, which lists the purposes of the United Nations, spells out the organization's *main* objective as being:

> To maintain international peace and security, and to that end: to take effective collective measures for the *prevention* and removal of threats to the peace, and for the suppression of acts of aggression or other breaches of the peace, and to bring about by *peaceful means*, and

in conformity with the principles of justice and international law, adjustment or settlement of international disputes or situations which might lead to a breach of the peace. [Emphasis added]

We noted earlier that the UN Charter does not use the phrase 'collective security'. It is widely accepted, however, that the phrase 'collective measures', which appears in the foregoing provision, means the same thing as 'collective security'. A careful reading of that provision will show that the intention is to make the UN apply 'collective measures' for the *prevention*, as well as *removal*, of threats or acts of aggression. This supports our view expressed earlier that the use of collective security to remove threats or acts of aggression is to be resorted to only after other peaceful measures have failed to *prevent* such threat or acts of aggression. After all, that same provision enjoins the United Nations to bring about the settlement of international disputes by *peaceful means*.

The second problem with definitions of collective security is the reference to actions authorized *only* by the UN Security Council as collective security. This means that if any other entity authorizes such an action, it cannot be regarded as collective security. The problem with this restriction is that regional organizations often claim that they too can authorize collective security actions in their regions. This claim, as we will see later, has been regarded as unlawful, since it is only the Security Council to which the UN Charter gives the power to act on behalf of the international community. Whether the claim of regional organizations is right or wrong is debatable, but the fact remains that some regional organizations still proceed to exercise this authority. Therefore it will be useful to seek to understand State practice in this area in order to determine the current state of international law.

thinking points

- *What is 'collective security' and how many States need to take an action before it can be regarded as a collective security measure?*
- *Who must authorize a collective security action?*

11.5 The United Nations and collective security

The UN Charter, which is the treaty establishing the United Nations, is divided into several chapters, each of which covers an issue relevant to the objectives or operations of the organization. Chapter VII deals with collective security powers, and sets out the various steps that the Security Council will take, from the moment at which international peace and security is threatened or breached, to when the Security Council restores the peace.

Once the international peace is breached, the measures available to the Security Council do not start with the use of preponderant force against the party in breach of the peace; rather, collective security starts with the Security Council taking a series of steps aimed at calming the tension between the States involved in a conflict. These measures are detailed in the provisions of Chapter VII, starting with Article 39 and ending with Article 42. In order to understand how the Security Council facilitates collective security in practice, we will now undertake a brief analysis of each of the provisions and demonstrate the process from start to finish.

11.5.1 Article 39: determining that aggression or threat to, or breach of, peace exists

Whenever there is a problem anywhere in the world, such as the violation of Article 2(4) of the UN Charter by a State, the first thing that the UN Security Council must do is to inform the international community formally that there is such a problem, and that the problem threatens or has breached international peace. In legal language, this is called a 'determination' that there is a threat to peace, breach of the peace, or act of aggression. The Security Council makes this determination by adopting a **resolution**, usually under Chapter VII of the UN Charter.

Article 39, which empowers the Security Council to make a determination, provides that:

> The Security Council shall determine the existence of any threat to the peace, breach of the peace, or act of aggression and shall make recommendations, or decide what measures shall be taken in accordance with Articles 41 and 42, to maintain or restore international peace and security.

Now, let us ask ourselves one question: why must the Security Council make a formal determination under Article 39? After all, when there is a crisis, such as the 1990 Iraqi invasion of Kuwait, there is usually substantial information about the incident provided by different media.

The reason is simple. The power of the Security Council to authorize collective security measures depends on the *nature* of the crisis. If a crisis is purely of an internal nature—that is, if it is happening *inside* the territory of a State—the United Nations *cannot* ordinarily intervene in the matter. This is because, according to Article 2(7) of the UN Charter on non-intervention:

> Nothing contained in the present Charter shall authorize the United Nations to intervene in matters which are essentially within the domestic jurisdiction of any state or shall require the Members to submit such matters to settlement under the present Charter; but this principle shall not prejudice the application of enforcement measures under Chapter VII.

It is obvious from this provision that the UN can intervene in crises occurring inside a State *only* if it (the UN) is taking an enforcement action. An 'enforcement action' is another name for collective security. However, before the UN can take an enforcement action, it must satisfy itself that the crisis occurring inside a State threatens international peace and security. Therefore, by making a formal determination under Article 39, the Security Council fulfils a legal requirement that a crisis is an international one and assures the entire world that it is not meddling in the internal affairs of UN member States. On the issue of whether any dispute can be regarded as purely within the domestic jurisdiction of States so as to preclude the UN from intervening, views differ. Some writers think this is not possible and believe every dispute between two States involves at least one international element. (See Hans Kelsen, 'Limitations on the functions of the United Nations' (1945–46) 55 Yale LJ 997; M. Schröder, 'Non-intervention, the principle of' in R. Bernhardt (ed.), *Encyclopaedia of Public International Law* 7 (Amsterdam: Elsevier, 1984), 619; Michael Akehurst, *Modern Introduction to International Law* (7th edn, London: Routledge, 1997); Oscar Schachter, 'Sovereignty and threats to peace' in Thomas G Weiss (ed.), *Collective Security in a Changing World* (Boulder, CO: Lynn Rienner 1993.)

resolution

A written motion adopted by a deliberative body—in this case, the UN Security Council.

KEY POINT In general, the United Nations cannot intervene in crises occurring inside the territory of its member States. However, it can intervene if such internal matters threaten international peace and security.

The components of Article 39 determination

Normally, a determination by the Security Council under Article 39 should state clearly the exact nature of the crisis to which it is responding—that is, whether the crisis merely threatens international peace and security, or breaches it, or is an act of aggression. However, the Security Council, a political organ, does not like to be seen to be judging UN member States. If the Security Council uses words such as 'aggression' or 'aggressive behaviour' to describe States' behaviour, this may affect its subsequent intervention. Also, States are generally very sensitive to being labelled as aggressors, and they tend not to cooperate with other States and institutions when described in such terms.

So, whenever States commit aggression, such as when Iraq attacked Kuwait in 1990 or when North Korea attacked South Korea in 1950, the Security Council uses gentler words to describe their behaviour.

Let us consider some resolutions that show how the Security Council has described aggression by States.

United Nations Security Council Resolution 84 on the invasion of South Korea by North Korea (1950)

. . . .

The Security Council,
Having determined that the armed attack on the Republic of Korea by forces from North Korea constitutes a breach of the peace, . . .

United Nations Security Council Resolution 660 on the invasion of Kuwait by Iraq (1990)

. . . .

Adopted by the Security Council at its 2932nd meeting, on 2 August 1990

The Security Council,

Alarmed by the invasion of Kuwait on 2 August 1990 by the military forces of Iraq,

Determining that there exists a breach of international peace and security as regards the Iraqi invasion of Kuwait,

Acting under Articles 39 and 40 of the Charter of the United Nations,

1. Condemns the Iraqi invasion of Kuwait; . . .

In neither of these resolutions did the Security Council use the word 'aggression', despite the fact that there were acts of aggression in both cases.

We mentioned earlier that the Security Council avoids name-calling so as not to be seen as judging States. But there is also a legal reason why the Security Council does not use the word 'aggression' as such. Aggression is a very difficult term to define; to refer to certain behaviours as 'aggressive' when the UN Charter does not define the term 'aggression' may pose serious legal problems for the Security Council.

The question to ask is whether the Security Council suffers anything by choosing to describe an action in lesser terms than aggression. As far as collective security is concerned, the answer is 'no'. Whether the Security Council calls an act an 'invasion', a 'breach of peace', or an 'irresponsible act', it will achieve the same purpose, insofar as it is an occurrence that requires it to take collective security action.

It must be noted, however, that while the Security Council does not generally describe the attack of one State by another as 'aggression', it does occasionally use the term to describe other acts committed by the attacking State. For example, when, following its invasion of Kuwait in 1990, Iraq began taking some steps inside Kuwait, the Security Council described these as 'aggressive acts'.

United Nations Security Council Resolution 667 on aggressive acts (1990)

Adopted by the Security Council at its 2940th meeting on 16 September 1990

The Security Council,

Deeply concerned that Iraq, notwithstanding the decisions of the Security Council and the provisions of the Conventions mentioned above, has committed acts of violence against diplomatic missions and their personnel in Kuwait,

Outraged at recent violations by Iraq of diplomatic premises in Kuwait and at the abduction of personnel enjoying diplomatic immunity and foreign nationals who were present in these premises,

Acting under Chapter VII of the Charter of the United Nations,

1. Strongly condemns *aggressive acts* perpetrated by Iraq against diplomatic premises and personnel in Kuwait, including the abduction of foreign nationals who were present in those premises; ... [Emphasis added]

In this resolution, it is obvious that the Security Council is more comfortable describing the lesser acts of Iraq, such as closing diplomatic missions and arresting diplomats within Kuwait, as 'aggressive acts' than the actual invasion of Kuwait by Iraq. This may be because characterizing these later actions as aggression would not be as controversial as characterizing the main attack.

By comparison, the UN General Assembly, another organ of the UN, has been more direct in referring to 'aggressive' behaviour of States. This was particularly so during the Korean crisis in the 1950s.

United Nations General Assembly Resolution 500 (V) of 18 May 1951 Additional Measures to be employed to meet the aggression in Korea

The General Assembly, noting the report of the Additional Measures Committee dated 14 May 1951,

Recalling its resolution 498 (V) of 1 February 1951,

Noting that:

(a) The Additional Measures Committee established by that resolution has considered additional measures to be employed to meet *aggression* in Korea ... [Emphasis added]

Here, the General Assembly used the word 'aggression'. However, in the 1980s and 1990s, the General Assembly also adopted a much gentler approach towards describing States' aggression. Hence, in its response to Iraq's attack on Kuwait in 1990, the General Assembly used words that were similar to those used by the Security Council. As shown in the following resolution responding to the Iraqi attack on Kuwait in 1990, instead of 'aggression', the General Assembly opted for 'invasion'.

> **United Nations General Assembly Resolution 45/170 (1990) The situation of human rights in occupied Kuwait**
>
> ....
>
> The General Assembly,
>
> Guided by the principles embodied in the Charter of the United Nations, the Universal Declaration of Human Rights, the International Covenants on Human Rights and the Geneva Conventions of 12 August 1949,
>
> Aware of its responsibility to promote and encourage respect for human rights and fundamental freedoms for all and resolved to remain vigilant with regard to violations of human rights wherever they occur,
>
> Reaffirming that all Member States have an obligation to promote and protect human rights and fundamental freedoms and to fulfil obligations they have freely undertaken under the various international instruments,
>
> Condemning the *invasion* of Kuwait on 2 August 1990 by the military forces of Iraq...[Emphasis added]

KEY POINTS

- The UN Security Council must make an Article 39 determination before commencing collective security measures under Chapter VII of the UN Charter. This determination is important because it qualifies the matter to which the Security Council is responding as 'international', so as not to bar UN action under any of the Charter provisions such as Article 2(7).

- The Security Council usually adopts terms that are less judgemental in describing the actions of States. This includes not using the word 'aggression', because such words could worsen tension and make political resolution of conflicts more difficult.

thinking points

- *Why must the UN Security Council make a determination under Article 39?*
- *What is the relationship between Article 2(7) and Chapter VII of the UN Charter?*

The meaning of 'threats to peace'

When a State unlawfully attacks another State, it breaches the peace or commits an act of aggression.

example

When Iraq attacked Kuwait in 1990, it committed an unlawful attack. Iraq was not acting in self-defence, because it had not been attacked by Kuwait prior to its own attack. In those circumstances, it was easy for a determination of breach of the peace or acts of aggression to be made.

It is difficult, however, to define what constitutes a 'threat' to international peace and security. When can one say a State has threatened another State and, consequently, international peace and security? This question is important because when the Security Council makes a determination under Article 39, it does so not only in relation to acts of aggression, but it may also make a determination that a 'threat' to the peace has occurred. We will recall that Article 2(4) does not prohibit only the use of force, but also prohibits the threat of force. A threat to use force certainly constitutes a threat to international peace, but there may be other situations, other than a threat of force, that constitute threats to international peace.

A 'threat' is what the Security Council says is a threat, even if common sense dictates otherwise. In the past, the Security Council has determined, quite appropriately, that a massive violation of a people's rights or the repression of a people by their governments (as in Kosovo and Iraq) threatened international peace and security. The Security Council had also determined, in the past, that a rumoured attempt to assassinate former US President George Bush when he visited Kuwait in 1993 was a threat to international peace and security. Some writers have also argued that decisions by oil-rich States not to sell their oil to States they are in dispute with or have certain disagreements with constitute a threat to international peace and security. (See, for instance, Jordan J. Paust and Albert P. Blaustein, 'The Arab oil weapon: a threat to international peace' (1974) 68 AJIL 410.) Some would argue that these latter two categories were of lesser significance than the annihilation of people by their own governments. Nonetheless, such determinations, no matter how seemingly ill-conceived or spurious, are not illegal under Article 39, since the Charter supplies no template for determining what constitutes a 'threat' to international peace and security.

11.5.2 Article 40: provisional measures

Once the Security Council has formally determined that a threat, or breach of peace, or an act of aggression exists, the next thing that it must do is try to reduce the tension between the States concerned. Article 40 of the UN Charter provides that:

In order to prevent an aggravation of the situation, the Security Council may, before making the recommendations or deciding upon the measures provided for in Article 39, call upon the parties concerned to comply with such provisional measures as it deems necessary or desirable. Such provisional measures shall be without prejudice to the rights, claims, or position of the parties concerned. The Security Council shall duly take account of failure to comply with such provisional measures.

The measures referred to in this provision are called *provisional* measures because they are temporary. They are designed basically to give the Security Council the opportunity to deliberate on how best to respond to the conflict and also to give the concerned States the opportunity to rethink their actions.

In practice, the Security Council will often impose the provisional measures in the same resolution in which it makes a determination under Article 39. An example of this is Resolution 660 adopted in 1990, in which the Security Council *condemned* the action of Iraq, on the one hand, and *called* on that country and Kuwait to take steps to resolve the situation and their differences, on the other. The Security Council's instruction to Iraq was that it must immediately withdraw its troops from Kuwait, but it also instructed both countries to begin 'intensive negotiation' for the resolution of their differences. So Articles 39 and 40 are combined here—the Security Council recommending and, at the same time, deciding.

KEY POINTS

- Once the UN Security Council makes a determination, it will usually follow this with provisional measures.

- Provisional measures are intended to enable parties to a conflict to rethink their action and the Security Council to consider how best to proceed.

- The Security Council will often make a determination and impose provisional measures in the same resolution.

11.5.3 The difference between 'recommendations' and 'decisions'

It will have been noticed from the previous discussion that, in Article 39—and, as will be seen, in the remaining parts of Chapter VII—the words 'recommendation' and 'decision' are used in describing steps that the Security Council may take once it has made a determination under Article 39. Is there any difference between the two terms as used in the Charter? The answer to this question is 'yes'.

A *recommendation* made by the Security Council to members of the UN under Chapter VII is, strictly speaking, not binding on UN members. Being a recommendation, it has no force of law. In contrast, a *decision* of the Security Council is an obligation that UN members must implement. This is not merely because it is called a 'decision', but also because Article 25 of the UN Charter states that:

> the Members of the United Nations agree to accept and carry out the *decisions* of the Security Council in accordance with the present Charter. [Emphasis added]

We need to bear this distinction in mind as we go deeper into the remaining parts of Chapter VII.

The types of provisional measure that the Security Council may recommend or decide under Article 40 vary. Usually, the Security Council will simply ask conflicting States to refrain from doing anything that could worsen the situation. However, the Security Council might also request such States to take some specific measures, such as entering into negotiation, with a view to resolving the dispute between them.

What needs to be noted here is that regardless of what provisional measures the Security Council recommends or on which it decides, these do not affect the rights and positions of the concerned States. This means that whether a State has been aggressive towards another is not judged definitively simply because the Security Council asks both States to start discussing their problem. For example, the fact that the Security Council asks the two States to refrain from engaging in further acts that could worsen the situation does not affect the responsibility of the aggressor State to repair the damage that its action has caused to the attacked State. We will see how this works in Chapter 13 dealing with the law of State responsibility. (See David Caron, 'The legitimacy of the collective authority of the Security Council' (1993) 87 AJIL 552; M. C. Wood, 'The interpretation of Security Council resolutions' (1998) Max Planck Yearbook of United Nations Law; O. Schachter, 'The quasi-judicial role of the Security Council and the General Assembly' (1964) 58 AJIL 960; M. Glennon, 'The Constitution and Chapter VII of the United Nations Charter' (1991) 85(1) AJIL 74.)

KEY POINTS

- There are several types of provisional measure. These include asking conflicting States to refrain from worsening the situation, commencing negotiations in order to resolve the dispute, and so on.

- The measure recommended or decided on by the Security Council depends on the particular situation.

11.5.4 Article 41 and non-forcible measures

So far, two steps in the Chapter VII process have been discussed: making a determination and imposing provisional measures on concerned States. Once the Security Council has imposed provisional measures, the road is clear for it to take other measures. The first set of such measures, which do not involve the use of force, are listed in Article 41 of the UN Charter thus:

> The Security Council may decide what measures not involving the use of armed force are to be employed to give effect to its decisions, and it may call upon the Members of the United Nations to apply such measures. These may include complete or partial interruption of economic relations and of rail, sea, air, postal, telegraphic, radio, and other means of communication, and the severance of diplomatic relations.

From this provision, we see clearly that the process seems to have progressed from the Security Council simply trying to cool the tempers of the concerned States to it doing something much stronger. The Security Council will impose Article 41 measures either because it sees that one or all parties to the conflict has, or have, refused to mend their ways or begin negotiations, as it is hoped that they will do under Article 40.

As we recall from the last sentence in Article 40, the Security Council must take account of the failure of the provisional measures before going to Article 41. It would be illogical if the Security Council were to progress to Article 41 when the conflicting States had already complied with its measures under Article 40.

However, practice shows that aggressor States do not usually comply with provisional measures. Examples include North Korea in 1950 and Iraq in 1990. Therefore, following Resolution 660 imposing provisional measures on Iraq and Kuwait, the Security Council imposed **economic sanctions**, pursuant to its Article 41 powers. But it must be noted that, in this situation, sanctions were imposed only on Iraq, being the State that refused to comply with the provisional measures.

. . . .

economic sanctions

Also known as 'trade embargoes', these are measures aimed at preventing States from entering or continuing any commercial activities with a particular State. In the context of collective security, they are usually imposed on an offending State in order to weaken its financial and economic powers, in the hope that this will make the State more readily agreeable to the will of the international community.

. . . .

thinking points

• *Can you reflect on the reasons why the UN Security Council might impose economic sanctions on a State?*

• *What does the Security Council need to take into consideration before imposing economic sanctions on a State after it has already imposed provisional measures?*

One example of a Security Council resolution imposing Article 41 measures (economic sanction) is Resolution 661.

United Nations Security Council Resolution 661 (1990)

. . . .

Adopted by the Security Council at its 2933rd meeting on 6 August 1990

The Security Council,

Reaffirming its resolution 660 (1990) of 2 August 1990,

Deeply concerned that that resolution has not been implemented and that the invasion by Iraq of Kuwait continues with further loss of human life and material destruction,

Determined to bring the invasion and occupation of Kuwait by Iraq to an end and to restore the sovereignty, independence and territorial integrity of Kuwait,

Noting that the legitimate *Government of Kuwait has expressed its readiness* to comply with resolution 660 (1990)...

Acting under Chapter VII of the Charter of the United Nations,

1. *Determines that Iraq so far has failed to comply* with paragraph 2 of resolution 660 (1990) and has usurped the authority of the legitimate Government of Kuwait;

2. Decides, *as a consequence*, to take the following measures to secure compliance of Iraq with paragraph 2 of resolution 660 (1990) and to restore the authority of the legitimate Government of Kuwait;

3. Decides that all States shall prevent:

    (a) The import into their territories of all commodities and products originating in Iraq or Kuwait exported therefrom after the date of the present resolution;

    (b) Any activities by their nationals or in their territories which would promote or are calculated to promote the export or trans-shipment of any commodities or products from Iraq or Kuwait; and any dealings by their nationals or their flag vessels or in their territories in any commodities or products originating in Iraq or Kuwait and exported therefrom after the date of the present resolution, including in particular any transfer of funds to Iraq or Kuwait for the purposes of such activities or dealings;

    (c) The sale or supply by their nationals or from their territories or using their flag vessels of any commodities or products, including weapons or any other military equipment, whether or not originating in their territories but not including supplies intended strictly

> for medical purposes, and, in humanitarian circumstances, foodstuffs, to any person or body in Iraq or Kuwait or to any person or body for the purposes of any business carried on in or operated from Iraq or Kuwait, and any activities by their nationals or in their territories which promote or are calculated to promote such sale or supply of such commodities or products;
>
> 4. Decides that all States shall not make available to the Government of Iraq or to any commercial, industrial or public utility undertaking in Iraq or Kuwait, any funds or any other financial or economic resources and shall prevent their nationals and any persons within their territories from removing from their territories or otherwise making available to that Government or to any such undertaking any such funds or resources and from remitting any other funds to persons or bodies within Iraq or Kuwait, except payments exclusively for strictly medical or humanitarian purposes and, in humanitarian circumstances, foodstuffs; . . . [Emphasis added]

This resolution clearly demonstrates that, in order to impose economic sanctions, following the imposition of provisional measures, the Security Council must determine that:

(a) one, or all, of the parties failed to comply with the provisional measures (and in this case, it stated categorically that Iraq failed to comply with those measures);

(b) it is taking Article 41 measures *as a consequence of the failure* to comply with Article 40 (and it states this in the very first paragraph of that resolution, after which it goes on to list the embargoes imposed on Iraq, which, in actual terms, are addressed to all States to refrain from conducting certain commercial activities with Iraq); and

(c) activities that will enable the sanctioned State to procure food, medicines, and other humanitarian needs for its population are exempted from the sanctions.

An interesting point that we must note here is that because the Security Council commenced punishing Iraq for not complying with Resolution 660, it *rewarded* Kuwait for its compliance with that resolution. Thus, in paragraph 6, the Security Council exempted Kuwait from the sanctions, and called on other States to provide assistance to the legitimate government of Kuwait (in exile) and not the illegitimate government imposed on Kuwait by Iraq.

Another worthwhile point to mention here is that once the Security Council had put these measures in place, it then set up a sanctions committee to monitor how other States were implementing its decisions against Iraq. This is important because the effectiveness of collective security is determined not only by how many sanctions the Security Council is able to impose on those States that breach the peace, but also by how much the Security Council is able to prevent its efforts from being undermined by other States, which, despite the sanctions, may be secretly dealing with the sanctioned State.

When imposed on countries, comprehensive sanctions often hurt the ordinary citizens more than the target government and, as shown by Reisman and Douglas, do not comply with international law standards (W. Michael Reisman and L. Stevick Douglas, 'The applicability of international law standards to the United Nations Economic Sanction Programmes' (1998) 9 EJIL 86). The initial indiscriminate nature of the sanctions imposed on Iraq in 1990, as part of the global efforts to revise its aggression on Kuwait, caused considerable hardship on the populace. This was especially so in the health sector due to restrictions placed on the importation of drugs and so on. As Cortright and Lopez show in their comprehensive treatment of the subject, the concerns about humanitarian implications of sanctions have compelled the Security Council to develop so-called 'smart' or 'targeted' sanctions' (D. Cortright and G. Lopez, *Smart Sanctions: Targeting Economic Statecraft* (New York: Rowman & Littlefield, 2002). 'Smart' or 'targeted' sanctions are aimed specifically at identified officials of the target governments, facilities in the target country, movements of people, financial transactions, and so on, with precise details of items to be excluded from the sanction regime identified.

KEY POINTS

- Article 41 measures consist mainly of economic embargoes, although, as seen in UN Security Council Resolution 661, allowance is given for certain trading activities to take place. Thus States can carry on trading with a sanctioned State in order to enable the latter to obtain food, medicine, and humanitarian needs for its population.

- It is important for the Security Council to take note of the failure of a State to comply with its provisional measures (under Article 40) before imposing sanctions (under Article 41) on it.

11.5.5 Article 42: forcible (enforcement) action on recalcitrant States

So if, after they are imposed, sanctions do not achieve their aims, what next?

Article 42 of the UN Charter answers this question thus:

> Should the Security Council consider that measures provided for in Article 41 would be inadequate or have proved to be inadequate, it may take such action by air, sea, or land forces as may be necessary to maintain or restore international peace and security. Such action may include demonstrations, blockade, and other operations by air, sea, or land forces of Members of the United Nations.

The various measures listed in this provision are what we call 'enforcement actions' or 'collective security measures'. They are mainly designed to bring a State, which has so far failed to comply with Articles 40 and 41 measures, finally to its knees.

We need to pay careful attention to the wording of this provision. It is obvious from the provision that the UN Security Council does not have to impose Article 41 sanctions before imposing the forcible measures in Article 42 on a State. For example, if the Security Council *believes* that imposing Article 41 measures on a State will be inadequate in any event, it may simply proceed to impose Article 42 measures after the provisional measures of Article 40. Accordingly, if the Security Council exercises this option, the process would look something like that shown in Figure 11.1.

The implication of this is that the Security Council simply makes a determination under Article 39, imposes provisional measures under Article 40, then, having considered that economic sanctions, if imposed, would be inadequate, simply moves to impose military measures. In this scenario, there will be no need for a sanctions committee or for the monitoring of the sanctions, since there were no economic sanctions in the first place.

However, the Security Council may decide to impose Article 42 measures after it has first imposed Article 41 sanctions. If it takes this second option, then there will be a full-cycle adoption of collective security measures, as in Figure 11.2.

Figure 11.1

Collective security: short cycle

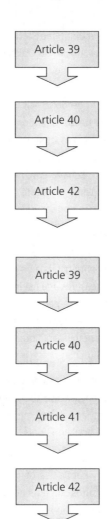

Figure 11.2

Collective security: full cycle

In order to go the full cycle, as Figure 11.2 shows, Article 42 contains a crucial requirement: the Security Council must first determine that the sanctions imposed by Article 41 have proved *inadequate*—that is, the sanctions are either ineffective or simply not adequate to bring about the desired change. This means that, after imposing Article 41 measures, the Security Council is not at liberty to impose forcible measures under Article 42 as a matter of choice. The provisions of the Charter do not permit this. Once it chooses to impose economic sanctions, the Security Council must wait to determine whether or not the sanctions are effective.

KEY POINTS

- The Security Council can impose military measures on a State without first imposing economic sanctions on it if it decides that imposing economic sanctions will not achieve the desired results.

- The Security Council can impose military measures on a State after it has imposed economic sanctions on it.

- If the Security Council decides to impose economic sanctions, then it must wait to see whether or not such sanctions work before imposing military measures.

The reason for requiring the Security Council to show that sanctions have failed before author-izing force under Article 42 is fairly straightforward. The kind of measures contained in Article 42 are not such that they should be imposed with levity: they are the most serious measures available to the international community. If Article 42 measures fail to solve a situation, there is nothing else to be done—at least as far as collective security is concerned. Therefore the Security Council needs to demonstrate to the world that it has no other choice than to employ these measures. It is as though the Security Council is telling the world: 'Look—we imposed provisional measures, but this State failed to comply. We imposed economic measures, but they have failed to have any meaningful impact. So we have no choice other than to use military force against this State in order to reverse the undesirable situation, and to restore international peace and security.'

If the Security Council fails to demonstrate clearly that it indeed allows enough time between imposing economic sanctions on a State and authorizing the use of force against it, this may lead to dissent amongst its own members. Thus when it came to the Security Council author-izing forcible measures against Iraq, following the Resolution 661 economic sanctions, Cuba and Yemen, both non-permanent members of the Security Council at that time, abstained from voting for the measures. They argued that the Security Council did not allow enough time for the economic sanctions to take effect.

If a State behaves in a way that leaves the Security Council with no choice other than to authorize Article 42 measures against it, that State is undoubtedly in trouble. Collective secu-rity measures may involve thousands of foreign troops entering the country, attacking its military facilities, and destroying its defensive powers. These are measures that can be taken using land, sea, and air powers.

The measures that the Security Council can take under Article 42 do not stop at defeat-ing the military capacities of the State in question; the Security Council can also take follow-up measures, such as authorizing a cut in the size of the military of that country, so that it will not be in a position to repeat such unlawful acts, and the Security Council can prescribe the amount of natural resources that the country can sell (and to whom), in order to control how much funds are available to the aggressor government. Collective security measures, at this stage, can be very debilitating and humiliating to a country at the receiving end. This is why they are not to be treated lightly, but with the utmost consideration. The gravity of Article 42 measures is revealed by the fact that, in sixty-five years of the UN's existence, only once has the Security Council authorized these measures (in Iraq in 1990)—and even then some of its members queried its process, although they did not prevent the measures.

Let us consider some instances in which the Security Council has operated collective security.

Collective security action against Iraq: 1991 and 2003

We have referred a few times in the earlier discussion to the attack by Iraq on Kuwait in 1990. In response, the Security Council imposed several measures on Iraq, including a maritime blockade, economic sanctions, and so on (Resolution 661, see section 11.5.4). Nonetheless, Iraq refused to comply. Consequently, the Security Council decided to authorize collective security measures against Iraq. This was done through Resolution 678.

> **United Nations Security Resolution 678 (1990)**
>
> Adopted by the Security Council at its 2963rd meeting on 29 November 1990
>
> The Security Council,
>
> Noting that, despite all efforts by the United Nations, Iraq refuses to comply with its obligation to implement resolution 660 (1990) and the above-mentioned subsequent relevant resolutions, in flagrant contempt of the Security Council,
>
> Determined to secure full compliance with its decisions,
>
> Acting under Chapter VII of the Charter,
>
> 1. Demands that Iraq comply fully with resolution 660 (1990) and all subsequent relevant resolutions, and decides, while maintaining all its decisions, to allow Iraq one final opportunity, as a pause of goodwill, to do so;
>
> 2. Authorizes Member States cooperating with the Government of Kuwait, unless Iraq on or before 15 January 1991 fully implements, as set forth in paragraph 1 above, the above-mentioned resolutions, to use all necessary means to uphold and implement resolution 660 (1990) and all subsequent relevant resolutions and to restore international peace and security in the area.
>
> . . .

The resultant military action against Iraq achieved the most important mandate of Resolution 678: the expulsion of Iraqi troops from Kuwait. The Security Council then adopted Resolution 687, which set out the conditions upon which the Security Council would terminate the collective security measures against Iraq. In other words, the expulsion of Iraqi troops from Kuwait did not formally end the collective security measures against Iraq, hence the need to adopt Resolution 687 for the specific purpose.

In Resolution 687, adopted on 3 April 1991, the Security Council laid out several conditions, the most crucial of which are the provisions contained in paragraphs 12, 13, 33, and 34.

Paragraph 12 forbids Iraq to acquire or develop nuclear weapons, while paragraph 13 empowers the International Atomic Energy Agency (IAEA) to conduct on-site inspections in Iraq in order to verify whether or not Iraq complied with this condition. Paragraph 33 states that, upon Iraq's acceptance of all of the conditions contained in the resolution, and following a formal notification of that acceptance to the UN Secretary-General and the Security Council, a formal ceasefire would be 'effective between Iraq and Kuwait and the Member States cooperating with Kuwait in accordance with Resolution 678 (1990)'. Paragraph 34 of Resolution 687 provides, rather ominously, that the:

> Security Council remain seized of the matter and to take such further steps as may be required for the implementation of the present resolution and to secure peace and security in the region.

ceasefire

The establishment of a truce between conflictual or disputing parties. (See more in section 11.8 on peacekeeping.)

Thus Resolution 687 imposed several conditions, which all form part of collective security, upon which the international community would suspend the military action against Iraq and commence a formal **ceasefire**.

As we observed earlier, the use of Resolution 687 shows clearly that collective security measures may not stop at using force against a country, but may, in fact, include measures aimed at regulating what kinds of weapon it may have and how its military is to be organized henceforth. With regard to Iraq, the international community decided that it should never acquire or develop nuclear weapons.

Tension arose in 2001 between Saddam Hussein's government in Iraq and the IAEA, leading to the expulsion of the latter from Iraq. This action effectively means that Iraq violated one of the core conditions of Resolution 687 (the 'Ceasefire Resolution')—that is, affording unrestricted access to the IAEA officials. The Security Council responded with Resolution 1441 in 2002.

United Nations Security Council Resolution 1441 (2002)

. . . .

Adopted by the Security Council at its 4644th meeting, on 8 November 2002

The Security Council . . .

Acting under Chapter VII of the Charter of the United Nations,

1. *Decides* that Iraq has been and remains in material breach of its obligations under relevant resolutions, including resolution 687 (1991), in particular through Iraq's failure to cooperate with United Nations inspectors and the IAEA, and to complete the actions required under paragraphs 8 to 13 of resolution 687; . . .

. . . .

material breach

This implies a substantial breach or a breach of a fundamental condition.

. . . .

Clearly, the Security Council had formed the view that non-cooperation by Iraq with the IAEA was a **material breach** of Resolution 687.

However, the Security Council did not go as far as to authorize any action against Iraq because of that breach. Instead, it:

2. *Decide[d]* . . . to afford Iraq . . . a final opportunity to comply with its disarmament obligations under relevant resolutions of the Council; and accordingly decides to set up an enhanced inspection regime with the aim of bringing to full and verified completion the disarmament process established by resolution 687 (1991) and subsequent resolutions of the Council; . . .

Nonetheless, in 2003, and after a failed attempt by the UK and USA to obtain a new resolution from the Security Council authorizing collective security action against Iraq, those States decided to act unilaterally—that is, without the authorization of the Security Council.

The invasion of Iraq by a US-led coalition in 2003 proved to be extremely controversial. The UK and USA mounted several defences. As for the USA, it first attempted to justify the action on the basis of self-defence (see Chapter 10). It will be recalled that the USA was attacked by Al Qaeda terrorists on 11 September 2001 (the '9/11 attacks'). The USA argued that Iraq shielded and supported Al Qaeda, and thus made itself a target of a self-defence action by the USA. This argument was unconvincing, because the prevalent opinion of States and scholars then showed that there was no connection between Iraq and the Al Qaeda organization. This might have forced the USA to drop that line of argument and to resort to more generic ones, such as that Iraq had developed weapons of mass destruction (WMDs).

More interestingly, the UK argued that the 2003 action did not require a new authorization by the Security Council. The UK contended that because the suspension of the 1991 action against Iraq was based on the latter's full compliance with the terms of the Ceasefire Resolution, Iraq's refusal to cooperate with the IAEA was a breach. Therefore, the UK argued, once the breach of Resolution 687 had occurred, this automatically resuscitated the authorization to use force contained in Resolution 678 of 1991. However, the fact that both the UK and USA did attempt to secure a new authorization after Resolution 1441 might be interpreted as meaning that the UK did not genuinely believe that no new authorization was required for the 2003 action.

Either way, the legality or otherwise of the 2003 action against Iraq will always remain controversial. What is important to remember is that the actions against Iraq in 1991 and 2003 exemplify collective security in action. However, if one were to subscribe to the argument that the 2003 action was not covered by Resolution 678 of 1991, contrary to the UK's argument, then this would imply that the invasion of Iraq by the coalition forces in 2003 was a unilateral, and not collective security, action, because it was not authorized by the Security Council. Conversely, one might believe (as the UK apparently does) that following the breach of the terms of the Ceasefire Resolution, the Security Council, by adopting Resolution 1441, implicitly brought back Resolution 678 from its grave to reactivate force against Iraq.

thinking points

- *What are the two processes through which the Security Council can move from imposing provisional measures under Article 40 to imposing enforcement action under Article 42? (Refer to Figures 11.1 and 11.2.)*
- *What are 'economic sanctions', and what types of activity are usually exempted by the Security Council from those that it embargoes and why?*
- *Why does the Security Council need to demonstrate that economic sanctions have been ineffective before imposing forcible measures?*
- *Why may the 2003 invasion of Iraq by the US-led coalition not be regarded as a collective security action?*

11.5.6 Article 43 and the envisaged Security Council forces

The questions that we must ask ourselves now are: how does the Security Council intend to effect Article 42 measures? Can the Security Council force States to use force against an aggressor? These questions are important because, with regard to Article 40, only the conflicting States have to comply with the measures of the Security Council, as was the case with Resolution 660. Also, in relation to the imposition of economic sanctions (Article 41), all that must be done is that UN members must stop trading with the sanctioned State, as Resolution 661 directed against Iraq. Up to that point, the forces or personnel of member States are not involved.

However, once Article 42 measures are imposed, it means that the Security Council needs forces, thousands of land soldiers, air force men and women, and naval forces to implement resolutions such as Resolution 678. So where does the Security Council get these forces from?

Article 43 provides an answer to this question:

All Members of the United Nations, in order to contribute to the maintenance of international peace and security, undertake to make available to the Security Council, on its call and in accordance with a special agreement or agreements, armed forces, assistance, and facilities, including rights of passage, necessary for the purpose of maintaining international peace and security.

When the establishment of the UN was being negotiated at San Francisco, one of the most important issues before the conference was how the Security Council would raise its forces for the purpose of collective security.

Several proposals were advanced. One was that each member of the organization should select members of their own national contingents and dedicate them to the Security Council, so that whenever the Security Council needed them, they would be ready to go. This was considered too expensive for most member States, many of which were very poor; hence, to expect them to continue to maintain forces specially dedicated to the Security Council would have been outrageously expensive, especially since the Security Council would not necessarily require these forces frequently. The other proposal was that, instead of dedicating specific members of national forces to the Security Council permanently, it would be more efficient only to earmark such forces—that is, nominally to identify them so that if the need were to arise, they would immediately be deployed. This was the proposal that became Article 43.

Many problems prevented Article 43 from being realized. First, many States required the approval of their domestic legislature before they were able to deploy their troops overseas. Secondly, the existence of deep suspicion among UN members—especially the USA and the Soviet Union—meant that these States could not agree on how to deploy troops, who should command them, on what principles, and so on. All of these matters hampered the realization of Article 43. France is the only country ever to have promised some of its national troops for the Security Council's use.

Due to the failure of the UN Security Council to secure the forces agreed to by UN members under Article 43, whenever it imposes Article 42 measures, the Security Council has always called on the coalition of 'able and willing States', as it did in Resolution 678, 'to use all neces-sary means to restore international peace and security'. This simply means that States should use force against the aggressor.

At first glance, it would appear that there is no difference between the Security Council using its own forces, as originally envisaged under Article 43, and authorizing States to take 'all necessary means', as it did in Resolution 678. In reality, there is one major difference between the two: if States had provided the Security Council with the forces anticipated under Article 43, these would be regarded as the Security Council's own forces. It would therefore mean that the Security Council could obligate those forces to take specific action under Article 42. However, since this is not the case, all that the Security Council can do presently—and all that it did in Iraq in 1990—is recommend 'able and willing' States to take necessary measures.

Because it can recommend only that States take necessary action, this means that the Security Council cannot obligate States to act. Thus States will respond only if they are 'willing' and, of course, 'able' to do so, not because they feel obligated. Also, the Security Council can ask States only to take 'necessary means'; it cannot prescribe any specific means, as it could easily have done with Article 43 forces. In practice, however, a good number of States have always responded to the Security Council's call to act under Article 42.

KEY POINTS

- The Security Council does not have its own forces. Forces are contributed by States that are 'able and willing' to implement Security Council resolutions, as exemplified by Resolution 678. Nevertheless, the Security Council cannot compel States to sup-port its actions.

- Whenever the Security Council asks States to take 'necessary measures' to restore peace and security, this is generally regarded as asking States to use forcible meas-ures under Article 42 to enforce the will of the international community against a State that has breached the peace.

11.6 Regional collective security systems

We noted earlier that the Security Council has overall responsibility for collective security. But we noted too that regional organizations have equally asserted the competence to undertake collective security measures in their own regions.

11.6.1 Collective security under Chapter VIII of the UN Charter

We recall from our discussion in Chapter 10 that, during the San Francisco Conference on the United Nations, the Inter-American System (IAS) was very concerned about the safety of its member States, because all of the powers to use force were concentrated in the Security Council. In order to allay the fear expressed by the IAS, Article 51 (on self-defence) was included in the Charter.

As we also noted in Chapter 10, attacked States are entitled to defend themselves. Article 51 was primarily included to protect regional organizations such as the IAS, which had expressed the fear on behalf of its member States. Of course, when the provision was eventually written down in the Charter, it addressed States and not regional organizations, even if, albeit historically, the provision was primarily for the protection of regional organizations.

It was not only self-defence rights that the Charter gave to regional organizations at San Francisco; the question also arose about what the relationship of the UN should be with regional organizations, as a general issue. This came about because, as noted previously, the IAS was a regional organization already in existence at the birth of the UN. Hence, it was only common sense that the founders of the UN should contemplate the nature of the relationship between the UN, on the one hand, and the IAS and any other regional organization, on the other. Also, the IAS had already organized security arrangements in the Americas before the establishment of the UN. It was therefore important that the UN consider how its own global security arrangement would coexist with that of the IAS and any other regional organizations that might eventually emerge.

11.6.2 Article 52: the peaceful aspect of regional collective security

As with the UN collective security, the need to establish regional collective security on the basis of peaceful settlement of disputes is at the forefront of the regional framework. According to Article 52:

> 1. Nothing in the present Charter precludes the existence of regional arrangements or agencies for dealing with such matters relating to the maintenance of international peace and security as are appropriate for regional action provided that such arrangements or agencies and their activities are consistent with the Purposes and Principles of the United Nations.

2. The Members of the United Nations entering into such arrangements or constituting such agencies shall make every effort to achieve pacific settlement of local disputes through such regional arrangements or by such regional agencies before referring them to the Security Council.

3. The Security Council shall encourage the development of pacific settlement of local disputes through such regional arrangements or by such regional agencies either on the initiative of the states concerned or by reference from the Security Council.

4. This Article in no way impairs the application of Articles 34 and 35.

We will deal more fully with this provision in Chapter 14, which deals with peaceful settlement of disputes. It is enough to observe here that this provision is included in the framework of Chapter VIII, as an emphasis on the point made earlier that the use-of-force element of collective security is designed to be the last resort.

Obviously, Article 52(1) recognizes the existence of regional arrangements or agencies and affirms that they can deal with matters appropriate to their regions. The first thing to note is that this provision uses the phrase regional 'arrangements', or 'agencies', whereas today we more commonly use the term regional 'organizations'. But this should not confuse, because they essentially mean the same thing.

Another important point to make about Article 52(1) is that it speaks of regional organizations dealing with matters 'appropriate to regional actions': what are these? It would seem that this phrase limits regional organizations to dealing only with disputes in their own regions. We need also to point out that a 'region' in this context is not simply determined by a question of geography, but may be based on common interests or any other matter that forms the link among members.

While, in the majority of cases, regional organizations will act only in their own region, nothing stops the Security Council from requesting a regional organization to act outside its region. A clear example of this was when the Security Council asked the European Union to act in the Democratic Republic of Congo (DRC) in 2003. This mission was called 'Operation Artemis' and is discussed by Ademola Abass in, 'Extra-territorial collective security: the European Union and Operation Artemis in Congo' in Martin Trybus and Nigel White (eds), *European Security Law* (Oxford: Oxford University Press, 2007), p. 134.

KEY POINTS

- Regional organizations can settle disputes between their member States peacefully. They do not require the authorization of the Security Council to do this.

- In general, regional organizations can only deal with conflicts within their region. However, the Security Council can authorize regional organizations to act outside their regions (such as Operation Artemis in Congo in 2003).

11.6.3 Article 53: the delegation of collective security to regional organizations

Article 53 of the Charter, which also deals with the role of regional organizations in the maintenance of international peace and security, provides as follows:

1. The Security Council shall, where appropriate, utilize such regional arrangements or agencies for enforcement action under its authority. But no enforcement action shall be taken under regional arrangements or by regional agencies without the authorization of the Security Council, with the exception of measures against any enemy state, as defined in paragraph 2 of this Article, provided for pursuant to Article 107 or in regional arrangements directed against renewal of aggressive policy on the part of any such state, until such time as the Organization may, on request of the Governments concerned, be charged with the responsibility for preventing further aggression by such a state.

2. The term enemy state as used in paragraph 1 of this Article applies to any state which during the Second World War has been an enemy of any signatory of the present Charter.

The opening paragraph of this provision shows the link between the Security Council and regional organizations. It basically entitles the Security Council to delegate its collective security powers to regional organizations to act on its behalf. This seems to be a sensible provision. The UN cannot be expected to deal with all conflicts all over the world, especially if there are regional organizations that are better suited and willing to do the job. Regional organizations are more familiar than the UN with the dynamics of conflicts in their regions. They understand the cultures, values, and circumstances of States and peoples in their regions better than the UN, which usually sits thousands of miles away from the theatre of conflict.

The first point to be noted in Article 53 is that it does two things. First, it says that the Security Council can utilize regional organizations for enforcement action, where appropriate. 'Appropriate' here does not mean the same thing as 'appropriate for regional actions' as we see under Article 52(1), which somehow restricts regional organizations to their regions when they act on their own. 'Appropriate', as used by Article 53(1), means as the Security Council deems fit.

example

It will seem inappropriate for the Security Council to authorize a whole UN mission to stop a minor border dispute between Candoma and Rutamu. It will be more expedient for the Security Council to ask a regional organization, to which both States belong, to go in and do the job. It is only when matters go beyond the capacity of the regional organization that the UN may then authorize a UN mission to step in and take over.

Secondly, Article 53(1) says that regional organizations cannot take enforcement action *without* Security Council authorization. This is sensible since the first leg of that provision says that the Security Council can use regional organizations for these types of action whenever it deems fit. Hence, it would be contradictory if the same provision were to entitle the Security Council to use regional organizations for enforcement actions that regional organizations are empowered to take on their own. In such a scenario, conflict is inevitable. Thus the simple meaning of Article 53(1) is that, on the one hand, the Security Council can use regional organizations for enforcement actions, but that, on the other hand, these organizations cannot take such actions without the authorization of the Security Council.

What are 'enforcement actions' and when must regional organizations seek the authority of the Security Council to take them?

Enforcement action

As we will see later in our discussion on peacekeeping and humanitarian intervention, enforcement action is what distinguishes collective security measures from these two other actions. An enforcement action is directed against those who breach the peace, and when you enforce an action against someone, you do not need their permission to do so; otherwise, it is *not* an enforcement action. Some definitions offered by writers reflect this.

In Jost Delbrück (ed.), *Allocation of Law Enforcement Authority in the International System: Proceeding of an International Symposium of the Kiel Institute of International Law, 23–25 March 1994* (Berlin: Duncker & Humblot, 1995), Fred L. Morrison defines 'enforcement action' (at p. 43) as:

> [A]ny action which would itself be a violation of international law, if taken without either some special justification or without any contemporary consent or acquiescence of the target state.

This definition is useful only to the extent that, nowadays, some States give their consent to relevant organizations to take enforcement action on their territories.

example

The member States of the Economic Community of West African States (ECOWAS) gave their consent to the organization taking enforcement action on their territories by ratifying a protocol. (See Articles 25 and 26 of the ECOWAS *Protocol Relating to the Mechanism for Conflict Prevention, Management, Resolution, Peacekeeping, and Security* (1999) on the conditions for the application and initiation of the Mechanism.) Thus, since all members of ECOWAS have consented to this organization taking enforcement action on their territories, such enforcement actions arguably do not breach international law (see Ademola Abass, 'Consent precluding State responsibility: a critical analysis' (2004) 53(1) ICLQ 211).

This definition is, however, weak, because it misses out the vital element of an enforcement action—that is, the collective authorization of such actions by the Security Council or relevant regional organizations.

The features to look for in enforcement actions are fairly straightforward: is the action authorized by the Security Council, or a regional organization acting under the authority of the Security Council? Is the action directed towards forcing a State to comply with the wish of the international community—particularly to restore international peace and security? Does the action consist of military action, such as the use of military force? If the answers to all of these questions are positive, then the action is most likely an enforcement action.

The only question that may not be easy to answer is whether economic sanctions (which are authorized by the Security Council or relevant regional organizations, directed towards forcing a State to comply with measures set by the international community, and so on) qualify as enforcement action under Article 53(1). This is because a single State or a group of States may, on their own, decide not to trade with one particular State. This, in itself, does not violate international law, and may not necessarily be used to enforce the will of the entire international community.

example

The USA has imposed some economic sanctions against Cuba for more than forty years, but this US action is not to enforce the will of the international community, only that of the USA. Therefore this cannot be seen to be an enforcement action.

thinking points

- *Define 'enforcement action'.*
- *Can regional organizations undertake enforcement actions on their own?*
- *What does it mean to say that the Security Council can utilize regional organizations 'where appropriate'?*

When do regional organizations have to obtain Security Council authorization to take enforcement action?

Article 53(1) requires only that regional organizations obtain Security Council authorization as a condition for taking enforcement action. The provision does not speak of *when* this authorization is to be obtained. Should it be before, during, or after the enforcement action itself?

If the phrase 'but no enforcement action shall be taken without the authorization...' were to be construed literally, this would lead to the conclusion that the Security Council must authorize the action *before* it is taken. In practice, this has not been confirmed. Indeed, what seems to have been usual practice is that regional organizations take enforcement actions first, and *then* go back to the Security Council for its post-action approval.

When ECOWAS deployed its monitoring group (ECOMOG) to Liberia in 1990 to end the civil war in that country, the Security Council gladly welcomed the enforcement action, although it was careful not to refer to the action as enforcement; instead, it simply commended ECOWAS's efforts to resolve the conflict. See Security Council Resolution 866 (S/RES/866, 22 September 1993).

397

The point is that the ECOWAS's action was an enforcement action, since its troops used intense military action to force the rebels out of town. In a normal analysis, this would seem to breach Article 53(1), but in light of the commendatory gesture of the Security Council, it is difficult to argue that regional enforcement action must always be approved in advance. In addition, the fact that conflicts ensue much faster than the pace of Security Council meetings means that it will always be difficult to arrest conflicts until the Security Council has approved a regional enforcement action. Delays are always costly. Hence, reality dictates that, whenever possible, regional organizations act first and seek the approval of the Security Council later. However, such organizations must be conscionable in their action and avoid questionable activities that may make it difficult for the Security Council to approve the action.

KEY POINT Article 53 of the UN Charter does not specify the exact point at which regional organizations that desire to take enforcement actions in respect of their members' disputes must seek the authority of the Security Council. In practice, regional organizations have normally acted first and *then* sought Security Council *endorsement* of their actions.

11.7 The distinction between 'collective security' and 'collective self-defence'

Usually, when we define 'collective security' in the terms suggested earlier, we do not distinguish this concept from 'collective self-defence' (dealt with in Chapter 10). In fact, scholars often confuse the two, since the latter, like collective security, is also the use of force by a collection of States that is sanctioned by the UN Charter. However, in reality, the two are different.

The first major distinction between 'collective security' and 'collective self-defence' is that the latter refers to a system whereby a group of States enters into an alliance for the purpose of using force to resist *external* aggression on any of its members. In the case of the former, States form an alliance in order to *prevent one of their own* members from breaching the peace. That means that, in a collective security system, the collective force is used primarily *internally* against members of the same group, such as the UN, whereas collective self-defence is used to protect a member of the same group, usually from a State or entity outside the group. Yoram Dinstein refers to these internal and external directions of force as 'introverted' and 'extroverted' uses of force (Yoram Dinstein, *War, Aggression and Self-Defence* (5th edn, Cambridge: Cambridge University Press, 2011, p. 303). An example of a collective self-defence organization is the North Atlantic Treaty Organization (NATO).

In 'Assessing the theoretical case against collective security' in Downs (1994, see section 11.1), at pp. 18 *et seq*, George W. Downs and Keisuke Lida state that:

> While the term [collective security] has been used to describe everything from loose alliance systems to any period of history in which wars don't take place, the sine qua non of collective security is collective self regulation: a group of states attempts to reduce security threats by agreeing to collectively punish any member state that violates the system's norms. This internal focus distinguishes it from a typical alliance system, which has a goal of collectively reducing threats that originate from outside its membership.

Another distinction between the two concepts, which derives from this difference, is that whereas collective security requires prior authorization, collective self-defence does not. However, a collective self-defence action could still be the subject of investigation after it has occurred, but a collective security action usually starts with a determination, which provides the basis for legal justification.

example As we discussed in the previous chapter, if Candoma is attacked by Rutamu, Candoma is entitled, under Article 51, to defend itself individually or collectively. But this is only *until* the Security Council has taken measures to maintain international peace and security.

Chapter 11 Collective security

398

This proviso demonstrates that the fact that the attacked State is entitled, under Article 51, to resort to self-defence does not necessarily mean that it cannot be guilty of disrupting international peace and security. It is up to the Security Council to decide guilt when it intervenes. As noted in Chapter 10, despite the fact that Israel attacked and destroyed the Iraqi nuclear reactor in 1981 (in anticipatory self-defence), this did not prevent it from subsequently being condemned by the Security Council.

Although Israel's action did not appear to be well founded on this occasion, it is possible indeed that while a State genuinely believes that it is acting lawfully under Article 51, it may still be condemned by the Security Council at a later stage. Thus there is an element of gambling and uncertainty whenever States act in collective self-defence, especially since States rarely accept that they have been aggressive in the first place. This element of uncertainty is not present in collective security. In a proper collective security operation, the Security Council must authorize the action in the first place; collective security being an action taken not only to defend one or a few States (unlike self-defence), but also on behalf of the international community at large. (See further Hans Kelsen, 'Collective security and collective self-defence under the Charter of the United Nations' (1948) 42 AJIL 783.)

11.8 Peacekeeping

One of the most frequently used phrases in international affairs is 'peacekeeping operations'. Ironically, it is one phrase that is not used in the UN Charter, just like the phrases 'collective security' and 'humanitarian intervention'. However, while the substance of collective security is contained in the Charter, as the previous discussion has shown, the Charter does not explicitly provide for peacekeeping. Nonetheless, peacekeeping operations have become perhaps the most important and common means by which the UN and regional organizations attempt to resolve conflicts among their members. So what is 'peacekeeping'?

Simply put, peacekeeping means 'to keep the peace'. It is a method employed to stop States from fighting by physically separating them from one another.

According to the United Nations, *Peacekeeping Operations: Principles and Guidelines*, 2008, available at http://pbpu.unlb.org/pbps/Library/Capstone_Doctrine_ENG.pdf (known as the 'Capstone Doctrine'), 'peacekeeping' is:

> a technique designed to preserve the peace, however fragile, where fighting has been halted, and to assist in implementing agreements achieved by the peacemakers.

It is obvious from this definition that peacekeeping operations are deployed only when fighting has stopped; hence, peacekeeping aims to prevent an aggravation or renewal of a conflict—although, as will be seen later, this original goal of peacekeeping operations has been much enlarged by new generations of peacekeeping.

Usually, a conflict can be stopped in many ways. Conflicting parties may decide to negotiate a truce (that is, a ceasefire). This could be on a temporary basis, so as to allow them fully to explore ways in which to settle their dispute or to resolve their conflict. A truce can also be inspired or brokered by the intervention of a State not involved in the conflict, or by an eminent person who has strong moral authority within that community, whether regional or global. By whatever means a truce is achieved, the effect is to obtain a brief halt in hostilities. However, it must be noted that when a truce is imposed by an enforcement action (another phrase by which collective security is known), as was the case in relation to UN Security Council Resolution 687 (see section 11.5.5), this is not a ceasefire in the context of peacekeeping, because it is not a truce either voluntarily negotiated by conflictual parties or through the intervention of a third party; rather, it is imposed as a collective security measure.

However, because it is not often practical that fighting parties will themselves call a truce, third States or international organizations such as the UN now frequently assist fighting parties to reach a temporary ceasefire. Once this is done, and with the agreement of parties to the conflict, a peacekeeping mission is then deployed to the concerned country, mainly physically to prevent the parties from starting the conflict again while discussions continue on how to resolve the crisis permanently. Principally, once a ceasefire has been achieved, a peacekeeping mission is first and foremost tasked with ensuring the implementation of the ceasefire.

Peacekeeping was introduced in 1948, when the UN deployed peacekeepers to maintain the ceasefire during the Arab–Israel war. The task of this and many early UN peacekeeping operations was fairly basic or, as it is sometimes expressed, 'traditional'. As the UN itself has noted in the Capstone Doctrine, at p. 21:

> Traditional United Nations peacekeeping operations are deployed as an interim measure to help manage a conflict and create conditions in which the negotiation of a lasting settlement can proceed. The tasks assigned to traditional United Nations peacekeeping operations by the Security Council are essentially military in character and may involve the following: Observation, monitoring and reporting—using static posts, patrols, overflights or other technical means, with the agreement of the parties; Supervision of cease-fire and support to verification mechanisms; Interposition as a buffer and confidence-building measure.

Although peacekeeping was developed by the UN, it is important to state that other international organizations now regularly engage in peacekeeping operations. Additionally, individual States or groups of States have also been known to act as peacekeepers.

KEY POINTS

- A peacekeeping operation is usually deployed into a country after a truce or ceasefire has been reached. Its main function is therefore to help to police the ceasefire.

- Peacekeeping mainly consists of monitoring, observing, reporting, and supervising the ceasefire, and interposing forces between fighting parties.

- Peacekeeping operations can be undertaken by the UN, other international organizations, or individual or groups of States.

11.8.1 The legal requirements of peacekeeping

Regardless of who is undertaking a peacekeeping operation, for it to qualify as such, peacekeeping must fulfil certain criteria—namely: consent; neutrality or impartiality; non-use of force except in defence of peacekeepers; and not influencing the outcome of conflict between parties.

Consent

Peacekeeping must be based on the *consent* of, or invitation by, the host State—that is, the country in which the conflict is taking place. Without such consent or invitation, a peacekeeping mission makes itself an unwelcome guest and one that opens itself to attack by either or both fighting sides.

Consent may take various forms. It could be by the legitimate government of a country, which is experiencing conflict, asking the UN, other organization, or friendly State(s) to intervene in a conflict on its territory or between it and another State.

example

In 1989, a civil war broke out in the West African country of Liberia, when a rebel group levelled attacks on the legitimate government of the country. Then Liberian President Samuel Doe invited the UN to help to restore peace and order in the country; the UN declined. Then UN Secretary-General Javier Pérez de Cuéllar announced that the nature of the conflict in Liberia (civil war) was not a situation in which the UN could intervene. In plain terms, this view was based on Article 2(7) of the UN Charter, which forbids the UN from intervening in matters occurring within the territory of its member States. Since the conflict in Liberia then was a civil war, the UN thought that this prevented its intervention.

The UN's refusal to intervene in Liberia was, however, based on an erroneous application of Article 2(7) of the Charter. This is because that same Article permits the UN to intervene in matters that are occurring in its member States if the Security Council authorizes an action under Chapter VII of the Charter—that is, a collective security measure. Although, strictly speaking, peacekeeping operations do not qualify as collective security, since they do not involve the use of force without the consent of the target State, in fact, nothing in Chapter VII says that the Security Council cannot authorize peacekeeping operations on the basis of that chapter. As will be recalled from our discussion of collective security, Article 40 of the Charter empowers the Security Council to take measures designed to ease the tension between conflictual parties and to prevent the aggravation of the dispute between them which, some might argue, is what peacekeeping is really about. The fact that, since Liberia, the Security Council has authorized countless peacekeeping operations on the basis of Chapter VII and in matters that were essentially within the territory of the concerned States reinforces this point.

Consent must be given by all parties to a conflict for a peacekeeping operation to take place. This is a major challenge to peacekeeping, because there will often be several factions in a conflict.

example

In the Liberian and Sierra Leone crises of 1989–97 and 1997–2000, respectively, there were several rebel factions. In Liberia, ECOWAS decided to deploy its own monitoring group (ECOMOG). However, ECOWAS did not obtain the consent of the Charles Taylor-led National Patriotic Front of Liberia (NPFL). This compromised the integrity of the mission as a peacekeeping mission from the start and it soon became clear, after ECOMOG's deployment, that the mission was anything but peacekeeping.

While, ideally, all parties must give their consent to a peacekeeping mission, the reality is that this is not often practical. However, at the minimum, consent of the government of the State and main rebel faction(s) is crucial before deploying peacekeeping missions.

Impartiality

A peacekeeping mission must remain *neutral and impartial* at all times; a biased or partial peacekeeping mission compromises its integrity and objectivity. This criterion, to some extent, follows from consent.

Once ECOMOG was deployed to Liberia without the consent of the NPFL, the stage seemed already set for its partiality. Even if the mission did not originally mean to be partial, the fact that one of the key parties to the conflict did not invite its intervention meant that ECOMOG had to fight to remain in Liberia. It is not possible to fight a party that is being encouraged to make peace with others; that clearly does not bode well for impartiality.

Use of force only in the defence of peacekeepers

As a general rule, peacekeepers cannot use force against any of the parties to the conflict. However, when they are fired upon or otherwise attacked by any of the parties to the conflict, peacekeepers are permitted to use force to protect themselves.

This criterion is critical to peacekeeping. Unlike collective security, a peacekeeping mission is not tasked with forcing one or both parties to accept peace, nor is it charged with enforcing international law against them; a peacekeeping mission is intended to facilitate and encourage conflictual parties to resolve their dispute amicably.

Not influencing outcome of conflict

A peacekeeper is not a referee or an umpire—that is, it is not charged with judging between conflictual parties. Thus a peacekeeping operation cannot influence the outcome of conflict even in situations in which the peacekeeping organization has its own belief about what the outcome should be. It is up to conflictual parties to decide for themselves how they want their conflict to be resolved.

thinking points
- What are the requirements of peacekeeping?
- When may peacekeepers use force against parties to a conflict?

11.8.2 The legal basis of peacekeeping operations

Notwithstanding the absence of any rules governing peacekeeping in the UN Charter, States have come to accept certain practices as essential features of peacekeeping operations—that is, those criteria outlined previously. Since most States accept these requirements, they are now widely regarded as forming the customary law on peacekeeping. Thus peacekeeping is governed by customary international law. But we must also note that nowadays some regional treaties do provide for peacekeeping operations.

The Constitutive Act of the African Union (the 'AU Act') was adopted in 2002. The AU operates on the basis of many principles, one of which is peacekeeping. Thus Article 4(j) of the AU Act recognizes 'the right of Member States to request intervention from the Union in order to restore peace and security'. This Article formed the basis of the deployment of the AU Mission in Sudan (AMIS) in 2004, to undertake peacekeeping following the outbreak of conflict in Darfur (see Ademola Abass, 'The United Nations, the African Union, and the Darfur crisis: of apology and utopia' (2007) 54 NILR 415).

It needs to be pointed out, however, that while peacekeeping is subject to customary international law, the Security Council has played a major role in developing the law and practice of peacekeeping. For example, it is common nowadays for the Security Council to adopt specific resolutions establishing UN peacekeeping missions under its Chapter VII powers.

As you will recall from our earlier discussion of collective security, we stated that Chapter VII allows the Security Council to use force against recalcitrant States. What does this imply, then, when the Security Council adopts a peacekeeping resolution under Chapter VII?

First, it means that while the UN Charter does not explicitly provide for peacekeeping, the Security Council is subtly bringing it under the Charter rules. Secondly, academic writers often regard peacekeeping as falling under Chapter VI of the UN Charter, which deals with the peaceful settlement of disputes (as we will see in Chapter 14). However, by adopting peacekeeping resolutions under Chapter VII of the UN Charter, the Security Council has been able to upgrade peacekeeping from the 'traditional' model discussed earlier. It is common nowadays to speak about 'peacekeeping with teeth', or 'muscular peacekeeping'. Today, many peacekeeping operations do not simply go into a country and meekly watch parties that have agreed to ceasefires go on the rampage and kill innocent people; 'peacekeeping with teeth', or 'muscular peacekeeping', now enables peacekeepers to *enforce* the peace when the need arises.

11.8.3 The UN and peacekeeping

The UN has had a long history of peacekeeping operations, one of the earliest examples of which is its mission—the United Nations Emergency Force (UNEF)—physically to separate the Egyptian and Israeli troops that were in conflict over the Suez Canal in 1956. However, Egypt later withdrew its consent from UNEF and the mission withdrew. This is a serious lesson for peacekeeping operations: they must withdraw if one of the parties that gave consent subsequently withdraws it.

However, despite having become well practised in peacekeeping operations, the UN sometimes gets it wrong. This is especially so when its missions become involved in the conflict, so that rather than being seen as a solution, they are regarded as part of the problem. Examples of these include missions in Zaire (now the DRC) in 1960–66, in Somalia in 1994, and in the former Yugoslavia in 1990–93. In all of these operations, UN forces became embroiled in the conflicts. Many personnel were taken hostage by parties to the conflicts and, in some cases, peacekeeping personnel were killed. Reasons for this development included issuing the wrong mandates to UN missions and not responding to situations expeditiously enough.

In response to the shortcomings of certain of its missions, therefore, the UN has developed a new generation of peacekeeping missions.

11.8.4 The new generation of peacekeeping

Peacekeeping has undergone tremendous changes since the period during which it first emerged. The transformation to peacekeeping has occurred in two distinct ways: first, in terms of the nature of peacekeeping operations especially regarding the delivery of their mandate— that is, how they fulfil their objective; secondly, in terms of the extent or scope of their mandate.

In the first instance, in relation to the delivery of their mandate, the UN peacekeeping operations have continued to come under the increasing criticism that often the UN deploys peacekeepers to situations in which there is no peace to keep at all.

For example, when the UN deployed peacekeepers to Sierra Leone, the country was still in a state of devastating civil war, with heavy killings and destruction of property taking place. In such a situation, lightly armed peacekeepers are fairly useless and may become bystanders while atrocities are committed against the people whom they are meant to protect. In such a situation, it seems more appropriate that the UN should deploy more muscular peacekeepers—that is, well-armed and better equipped troops, who can use superior weapons to stop atrocities. Such a step will, of course, mean that the mandate cannot be 'traditional' peacekeeping, but will be known instead as 'peace enforcement'. Peace enforcement will be very useful, for example, in situations in which despite having agreed to a ceasefire, one or both of the parties continue to violate the agreement.

In the second instance, in relation to the scope of the peacekeeping mandate, classical or traditional peacekeeping missions, such as those that we discussed previously, were mainly concerned with ensuring compliance by parties to ceasefire agreements and with creating buffer zones between conflictual parties. Once that was achieved, peacekeepers would exit the country. However, modern peacekeeping missions, such as the UN missions in Kosovo and East Timor (now Timor Leste), now perform such tasks as helping affected countries to rebuild their infrastructure, to conduct democratic elections, and to disarm former rebels and fighters and to resettle them among the civilian population.

thinking points

- *What are the key features of peacekeeping operations?*
- *To what extent can it be said that peacekeeping is nothing more than a practice whereby the international community assists warring factions to maintain peace by observing the ceasefire agreement between them?*

11.9 Humanitarian intervention

In our discussion on the use of force in the previous chapter, we noted that States often claim that they can use force against a State that is violating the human rights of its people and brutally suppressing them. Examples of humanitarian intervention include the invasion of India by East Pakistan in 1971, the invasion of Uganda by Tanzania in 1979, the ECOWAS intervention in Liberia in 1990 to 'stop the senseless killings', and the NATO action against Yugoslavia in 1999, for the latter's repression of Albanians in Kosovo. The most recent examples are the 2011 interventions in Ivory Coast and Libya by the international community. Although these two actions were taken apparently to protect civilians from repressive governments (and hence qualify as humanitarian intervention of a type), they are, legally speaking, accommodated within the concept of the responsibility to protect.

One interesting point in instances of humanitarian intervention is that the States involved rarely justify their actions on that basis.

example Tanzania formally claimed to be acting in self-defence against Uganda, while NATO claimed that it took the action in order to ensure that Yugoslavia complied with various Security Council resolutions.

However, we also noted that no matter how sound and morally compelling a State's claim of humanitarian intervention might be, the truth is that the UN Charter does not recognize such a doctrine. This perhaps explains the reluctance of States to rely on that basis officially, despite the fact that international public opinion is often sympathetic towards such interventions, as in Uganda, for example. Even when Vietnam relied on humanitarian intervention as the basis for its invasion of Cambodia in 1978, the majority of States that took part in the Security Council debate on that incident rejected that Vietnam had such a right under international law.

11.9.1 From where do States claim their right of humanitarian intervention?

Without doubt, humanitarian intervention raises one of the most controversial questions in international law, and one that has been resolved neither by academic writing nor by State practice. Humanitarian intervention is a highly sensitive issue, and the arguments of those who support the practice are often as sound and convincing as the contentions of those who oppose it.

So, rather than seeking the legal basis for humanitarian intervention, this section will focus on understanding the arguments for and against the doctrine of humanitarian intervention. After all, whether one agrees that there are legal bases for humanitarian intervention in the UN Charter or general international law, this does not affect the reality that humanitarian intervention continues to take place and seems set in State practice.

11.9.2 Arguments in support of and against humanitarian intervention

In general, States have always claimed that since the core objective of the UN is to save 'succeeding generations from the scourges of war' (see the Preamble to the UN Charter), it is entirely legitimate for them to use force against a State that is violently repressing its own citizens. This argument seems to state that humanitarian intervention is one of those means of helping the UN to realize its objective.

Indeed, stories about the vile atrocities committed by the Pol Pot-led Khmer Rouge regime in Cambodia or the Idi Amin-led government in Uganda against their own people elicit support for this line of justification. These were simply some of the worst cases of human rights violations witnessed anywhere in the world. Interestingly, despite the fact that the world was united in its condemnation of these regimes, the international community was not prepared to accept that the reprehensible acts of those governments gave the right to other States to use force against them.

example

In 1999, NATO forces commenced an aerial bombardment of the then Federal Republic of Yugoslavia (Serbia and Montenegro). This action was taken to halt the brutal repression of the Kosovar Albanian populations of Serbia and Montenegro. Kosovo then formed part of the country, although it enjoyed some autonomy (it declared unilateral independence in 2008). The Security Council was prevented from acting against Yugoslavia by Russia's threat that it would veto any Chapter VII resolution that might authorize collective security measures against that country. NATO's subsequent unilateral invasion of Yugoslavia took place, from a legal point of view, because it was not authorized by the Security Council. The action was not a collective security action and since Yugoslavia did not attack any NATO member State, NATO could not claim that it acted in self-defence.

NATO claimed that it undertook humanitarian intervention in order to ensure that Yugoslavia complied with Security Council resolutions. This was another way of saying that the Security Council failed to enforce its decisions against Yugoslavia.

As with the rationale in Cambodia and Uganda, the majority of States and writers rejected NATO's claim. They argued that no provision of the UN Charter empowers NATO—or any other organization, for that matter—to use force in support of Security Council resolutions, especially when the Security Council itself does not authorize such an action. NATO, on the other hand, claimed that since its North Atlantic Council (NAC), its highest decision-making body, had decided that it should act, such a decision made its action against Yugoslavia legal.

NATO's reliance on the decision of the NAC has been severely criticized. (See Nigel White, 'The legality of bombing in the name of humanity' (2000) 5 JCSL 27.) However, a number of international legal scholars have shown some willingness to accept, or at least an understanding of, the premises of humanitarian intervention and therefore were willing to give NATO the benefit of the doubt for its action against Yugoslavia.

Commenting on NATO's action in 'NATO, the UN and the use of force: legal aspects' (2000) 1 EJIL 22, Professor Bruno Simma noted that although NATO's action breached the UN Charter, 'only a thin red line separates NATO's action in Kosovo from international legality'. He then went on to add that:

> should the Alliance now set out to include breaches of the UN Charter as a regular part of its
> strategic programme for the future, this would have an immeasurably more destructive impact
> on the universal system of collective security embodied in the Charter. To resort to illegality as

an explicit *ultima ratio* for reasons as convincing as those put forward in the Kosovo case is one thing. To turn such an exception into a general policy is quite another.

While Simma agreed that NATO's action was illegal, he contended (at 22) that the Alliance:

> made every effort to get as close to legality as possible by, first, following the thrust of, and linking its efforts to, the Council resolutions which did exist, and, second, characterizing its action as an urgent measure to avert even greater *humanitarian catastrophies* in Kosovo, taken in a state of *humanitarian necessity*. [Emphasis added]

Clearly, for Simma, while NATO's action was illegal for lack of Security Council authorization, it was excusable as a humanitarian intervention among others:

> The lesson which can be drawn from this is that unfortunately there do occur 'hard cases' in which terrible dilemmas must be faced and imperative political and moral considerations may appear *to leave no choice but to act outside the law*. [Emphasis added]

In '*Ex iniuria ius oritur*: are we moving towards international legitimation of forcible humanitarian countermeasures in the world community?' (1999) 10 EJIL 23, Professor Antonio Cassese rejected Simma's viewpoint that only a 'thin red line' separates NATO's action from legality. As far as Cassese was concerned, there is no 'small' breach of the UN Charter.

Nonetheless, on the issue of humanitarian intervention he expressed a similar view to that of Simma. Cassese noted, at 25, that:

> I cannot but add, however, that any person deeply alert to and concerned with human rights must perforce see that important moral values militated for the NATO military action. Admittedly, strategic, geopolitical or ideological motivations may have also contributed to prompting NATO to threaten and then take military action against the FRY. From the angle of law, what primarily counts, however, are the official grounds adduced by NATO countries to justify their resort to force. Their main justification has been that the authorities of FRY had carried out massacres and other gross breaches of human rights as well as mass expulsions of thousands of their citizens belonging to a particular ethnic group, and that this humanitarian catastrophe would most likely destabilize neighbouring countries such as Albania, Bosnia and Herzegovina and the Former Yugoslav Republic of Macedonia, thus constituting a threat to the peace and stability of the region.

The views of those who oppose humanitarian intervention are equally several. First, they argue that humanitarian intervention can become a pretext for a State that has a hidden agenda in the conflict. This is not a view that one can dismiss easily, for, indeed, regional superpowers often intervene in conflicts in their regions in order to promote their own agendas.

The objection to humanitarian intervention, both by States and writers, seems to have prevailed in 2013. Despite the heinous crimes committed by the Al-Assad regime against Syrians in the Syrian civil war, the USA failed to convince the rest of the international community to undertake military action against the regime without Security Council authorization. Even traditional allies of the USA, such as the UK and France could not obtain the approval of their parliaments to support such an action while the US Administration did not formally seek the approval of Congress for the action.

Another reason for opposing humanitarian intervention is that the right transforms the intervener into a judge. This is so because the intervening State decides for itself that the human suffering in another State has reached a level that necessitates its intervention. This is often a very ironic development, especially when governments that are themselves some of the worst violators of the human rights of their citizens insist on intervening in light of similar conditions in another country.

example

Many States and academic writers criticized the Ibrahim Babangida-led government in Nigeria when it decided to intervene in Liberia. At the relevant time, this Nigerian government was one of the most dictatorial regimes in Africa.

Also, the human cost of humanitarian intervention is considerable and raises the question of whether it is worth it at all. In the NATO action against Yugoslavia, thousands of innocent people died, both from NATO bombs and Yugoslav fire in retaliation against those whom NATO sought to protect. In the allied action against Iraq since 2003, the human death toll has been substantial. The question that we can thus ask ourselves is whether the substantial civilian deaths—usually referred to as 'collateral damage', in military terms—make humanitarian intervention worthwhile.

Certainly, there is no shortage of reasons to be suspicious of the motives for why States undertake humanitarian intervention. However, there is very little evidence in State practice to suggest that States generally accept this doctrine. On the contrary, the majority of States always oppose it.

thinking points
- *Define 'humanitarian intervention'.*
- *List the arguments for and against humanitarian intervention.*
- *Should States resort to humanitarian intervention whenever the Security Council fails to act in a given situation?*

 # Responsibility to protect

11.10

The objection to humanitarian intervention created a dilemma for the international community's desire to maintain peace and security. The frequent inaction of the Security Council, whenever conflicts break out, often results in tragic loss of lives, as seen in the nearly one million lives lost in Rwanda in 1994 and several thousand deaths in Syria between 2011 and 2014. Yet, there was deep resentment against the idea that a few States could arrogate to themselves the power to intervene in another State on their own even if to stop a humanitarian catastrophe.

In 2005, the UN General Assembly endorsed the doctrine of responsibility to protect people ('R2P'). (See World Summit Outcome Document UN Doc. A/60/L.1, hereafter WSOD.)

Paragraph 138 of the WSOD provides that (a) every State has a primary responsibility to protect its citizens; (b) the international community has the responsibility to provide assistance to that State in order to enable it to undertake its responsibility towards its people. Paragraph

139 states that should the State fail to protect its own people, the international community has the responsibility to protect the people and may use force if need be, although as a last resort.

The obligation of the international community ingrained by paragraph 139 is not a full solution to the dilemma posed by humanitarian intervention. According to this paragraph, where a State has failed to protect its people, the international community may only use force to protect people 'through the Security Council'. As many writers have suggested, this implies that Security Council authorization is necessary—the same condition required for the legality of humanitarian intervention. However, the former UN Secretary-General, Kofi Annan, has raised some interesting points on this issue in his reports especially in 'Implementing the responsibility to protect: report of the Secretary General (UN Doc. A/63/677, 29 January 2009). (See also Carsten Stahn, 'Responsibility to protect: political rhetoric or emerging legal norm?' (2007) 101(1) AJIL 99.)

11.10.1 Basic distinctions between R2P and humanitarian intervention

There are at least four possible differences between R2P and humanitarian intervention.

1. R2P is based on a clear set of principles, as listed in the previous section. States wishing to undertake R2P must demonstrate that the target State has failed to protect its people, that other States have offered it assistance, and that they—the States taking R2P measures—do so only as a matter of last resort. These principles serve as guidelines, and are likely to lead to tighter use and stronger regulation of R2P than is ever possible with humanitarian intervention.

2. As a principle, R2P was formally presented to States so that they had the opportunity to debate it before endorsing it. This transparent process establishes the legitimacy of the concept unlike humanitarian intervention.

3. R2P can be taken only with the authorization or some kind of approval from the Security Council. The strongest criticism against humanitarian intervention is that it is not authorized by the Security Council. This will not be the case with R2P. However, whether it is a sensible option to base the legality of R2P on Security Council authorization is another question. In 2013, the Security Council failed to authorize military intervention in order to protect Syrians from death and destruction in the country's civil war. It may mean in practice that R2P suffers the same fate as humanitarian intervention.

4. Finally, under the R2P framework force can only be used as a last resort and, in principle, only after the exhaustion of the two principles contained in paragraph 138 WSOD mentioned earlier. Thus there is less likelihood that States will use R2P as a pretext to intervene for other reasons as is quite possible with humanitarian intervention. For instance, in 2013 the USA abandoned its plan to attack the Syrian regime after that government accepted international community assistance to enable it to dismantle its chemical weapons.

In March 2011, the Security Council invoked the R2P doctrine as the basis for its Resolution 1973 (2011) concerning the Libyan crisis. This resolution mandated States and regional organizations 'to take all necessary measures...to protect civilians and civilian populated areas under threat of attack...' from the forces of Colonel Gaddafi's regime.

While there has been controversy about whether Resolution 1973 envisaged a regime change in Libya, the timely action by the Security Council demonstrates that R2P may become an effective collective security system. However, the Security Council's inability decisively to deal with the Syrian crisis warrants a cautious optimism in the utility of the R2P doctrine.

◉ Conclusion

Collective security is written into the UN Charter mainly to provide the world with a better security system. It posits that any breach of that peace will be met with severe punishment. Therefore, in a real sense, collective security is the other side of the coin to the prohibition of the use of force discussed in Chapter 10. One rule says 'do not use force at all, except in self-defence or when authorized by the Security Council', while the other says 'we will act decisively against any violator of that rule on behalf of humankind'.

Nonetheless, as a system for enforcing the prohibition of force, collective security is both effective and problematic. When used in a decisive manner, collective security can be a powerful tool. This was the case when the Security Council led the charge against Saddam Hussein's Iraq after that country attacked Kuwait in 1990 and was used in Libya in 2011. However, when collective security is hindered from functioning because of political considerations, it can be a very useless instrument. The most recent example of collective security failure is the Security Council's failure to stop the Syrian government's onslaught on its own people which has led to thousands of deaths and catastrophic destruction.

❓ Questions

Self-test questions

1 What is 'collective security'?

2 What powers does the UN Security Council have under Article 39 of the UN Charter?

3 Identify the essential features of peacekeeping operations.

4 What is 'humanitarian intervention'?

5 Explain the difference between 'recommendations' and 'decisions' of the UN Security Council.

6 What does 'threat of force' mean?

7 Distinguish between 'collective self-defence' and 'collective security'.

Discussion questions

1 List the stages of the process outlined by the UN Security Council in Articles 39–42.

2 Define 'humanitarian intervention' and explain its main features.

3 'States can use force against each another as long as such force is not against their territorial integrity or political independence.' Critically examine this statement.

4 'The only power that regional organizations have is to settle disputes among their members peacefully.' Evaluate this statement in light of Chapter VIII of the UN Charter.

5 List the differences between humanitarian intervention and the responsibility to protect people (R2P).

Assessment question

In a referendum that the government of the State of Candoma expected to win, 80 per cent of the Agama tribe of Candoma voted for autonomy from the State. Disappointed, the Candoman government immediately declared that the result was unacceptable and that it would announce a new referendum date 'sometime soon'. The Agama tribe began to stage a series of peaceful demonstrations in an attempt to pressure the government into recognizing the result of the referendum and setting a timetable for the tribe's transition to autonomy. The State—which is ruled by the largest ethnic group, the Baraba tribe—cracked down heavily on the Agama people. Anti-riot police were deployed, who charged at protesters with batons and in some cases even shot at them with live ammunition. Women and children were thrown into jail, while men were tortured horrendously in several secret locations. The United Nations decided that the issue of elections was an internal matter and that it therefore could not intervene. This emboldened Candoma, which intensified its violent repression of the Agama people. Rutamu, a State that is traditionally unfriendly towards the Candoman government, decided to send in jet fighters to bomb the Candoman government troops in an attempt to force the government to halt its repression. In the process, Rutamu destroyed the defence facilities of Candoma and destroyed its international airport.

As the legal adviser to Rutamu, you have been called upon by your government to prepare a defence in a suit brought before the International Court of Justice by Candoma. What will be your advice?

 # Further reading

Abass, A., *Regional Organisations and the Development of Collective Security: Beyond Chapter VIII of the UN Charter* (Oxford: Hart Publishing, 2004)

Farrall, J. M., *United Nations Sanctions and the Rule of Law* (Cambridge: Cambridge University Press, 2009)

Gray, C., *International Law and the Use of Force* (3rd edn, Oxford: Oxford University Press, 2008)

Orakhelashvili, A., *Collective Security* (Oxford: Oxford University Press, 2011)

Simma, B., 'NATO, the UN and the use of force: legal aspects' (1999) 10(1) EJIL 1

Weiss, T. (ed.), *Collective Security in a Changing World* (Boulder, CO: Lynne Rienner, 1993)

White, N. D., *Keeping the Peace: The United Nations and the Maintenance of International Peace* (Manchester: Manchester University Press, 1997)

White, N. D., 'The legality of bombing in the name of humanity' (2000) 5(1) J Conflict & Sec L 27

International humanitarian law

Introduction

Wars have been fought since time immemorial and affect every corner of the globe. So it is unsurprising that over time different approaches to conflicts were advocated and implemented. The laws that developed to regulate the conduct of combatants in armed conflict and to minimize its impact on the civilian population is known as the 'laws of war', 'international humanitarian law', or 'the law of armed conflict'. These terms are used interchangeably. The term international humanitarian law (IHL) has gained wide use by academics and civil society; given the purpose of the laws it is easy to see the logic of incorporating 'humanitarian' due to the focus and links with humanitarian concepts and relief work. Militaries, understandably, prefer to use the law of armed conflict, which reflects their perspective and objectives. Regardless of which terminology is adopted the law is still the same, what may skew things is the interpretation and application depending on if it is from a military objective or civilian protection perspective.

But what exactly is IHL and is it really even law?

IHL is not the same as the law on the use of force, which we discussed in Chapter 10. The law of force or *jus ad bellum* concerns the law governing the legality of the use of force in international law. Article 2(4) of the Charter of the United Nations (UN Charter) embodies that law in that it prohibits the use of or threat of force, while other provisions of the UN Charter, such as Chapter VII provide for exceptions to that rule. IHL or the law of armed conflict or *jus in bello* concerns how to conduct war once hostilities break out. It does not deal with whether the use of force is or is not legal, but whether the conduct of the war conforms to the principles of general international law. It is with the latter that this chapter is concerned.

Famously Lauterpacht once described IHL as being an elusive area of law with many questions left unanswered and uncertainties abounding. His view was that:

> If international law is in some ways at the vanishing point of law, the law of war is, perhaps even more conspicuously, at the vanishing point of international law (H. Lauterpacht, 'The problem of revision of the law of war' (1952) 29 BYBIL 382)

Yet this is not to take away from the fact IHL is law just as any other area of international law is considered law. There have been numerous developments and sources to consult which set out and explain the scope of IHL. This is seen from the definition of IHL provided by the International Committee of the Red Cross (ICRC) as the:

> international rules, established by treaties or custom, which are specifically intended to solve humanitarian problems directly arising from international or non-international armed conflicts and which, for humanitarian reasons, limit

the right of parties to a conflict to use the methods and means of warfare of their choice or protect persons and property that are, or may be, affected by conflict. (Yves Sandoz, Christophe Swinarski, and Bruno Zimmermann (eds), *Commentary on the Additional Protocols of 8 June 1977 to the Geneva Conventions of 12 August 1949* (Leiden: Martinus Nijhoff, 1987), p. xxvii)

12.1 Background

It is not uncommon to think international humanitarian law is a relatively new concept with regulation only taking place recently as State interactions became more civilized and less barbaric. However, this is a misconception. There is nothing new in the idea of regulating the conduct of warfare and reducing the damage and effects. Various conceptualizations can be traced back to numerous periods across all nations, religions, and races. Ancient Greece and Rome, the Middle East, China as well as Africa have been found to have had some form of regulated conduct throughout history.

As Diallo reflects:

> many principles expressed in the Geneva Conventions are to be found in the law of war in pre-colonial Africa. It was only after the introduction of slavery and the inroads of colonialism into Africa south of the Sahara that traditional societies began to disintegrate, causing the code of honour to fall into disuse in war. However, the memory of this code of honour is kept alive in the narratives of the storytellers, and the code perhaps could be revived as a means of humanising present-day conflicts. (Y. Diallo, *African Traditions and Humanitarian Law: Similarities and Differences* (Geneva: ICRC, 1976), p. 16)

What is more, despite the fact that most emphasis on the development focuses on European scholars and initiatives with linkages being drawn predominantly from Christianity and occasionally Judeo-Christian traditions, other major religions also contain principles reflected in present day IHL. For instance, the first caliph Abu Bakr (c.632) stipulated:

> The blood of women, children and old people shall not stain your victory. Do not destroy a palm tree, not burn houses and cornfields and do not cut any fruitful tree. You must not slay any flock or herds save for your own subsistence. (*The Law of Armed Conflict: Basic Knowledge* (Geneva: ICRC, 2002), p. 17)

Having now recognized the cross-cultural dimension of IHL concepts and principles, the next relevant step to take is to establish how modern IHL has developed and what the sources are.

KEY POINTS

- IHL regulates the conduct of war.
- IHL has existed for generations across various peoples and cultures.
- IHL is *jus in bello* and deals with the conduct of wars.

12.2 International customary law and the codification of IHL

The conduct of warfare and the associated protections were originally established by customary international law, with few treaties and for those that were they were concluded between few States, thus of little international impact. It was only in the 1800s that the first initiative to set out protection in a legally binding treaty occurred. The experiences of a Swiss national, Henry Dunant, during the 1859 battle of Solferino and his shock at the suffering of those taking part in the battle led to the establishment of the ICRC and impetus for the first Geneva Conference. The result of which was the Geneva Convention of 1864—the Convention for the Amelioration of the Condition of the Wounded in Armies in the Field—through the participation of European and American State governments. It was during this conference, and appearing within the 1864 Geneva Convention, that the white flag with the red cross that has come to represent humanitarian assistance internationally was adopted and is now one of the most recognizable emblems.

Over time, the 1864 Geneva Convention has been replaced by further Geneva Conventions incorporating a wider framework of protection. In 1906 and 1929, protections for the sick, wounded, and prisoners of war were codified. It was not until 1949 that the most comprehensive Geneva Conference took place between April and August, where fifty-nine State delegations and four State observers participated and:

> Its purpose was the revision of the Convention of 1929 for the Amelioration of the Condition of Wounded and Sick in Armies in the Field and of the Convention of 1929 relative to the Treatment of Prisoners of War; the revision of the Tenth Hague Convention of 1907 for the adaptation to Maritime Warfare of the principles of the 'Geneva' Convention of 1906; and the preparation of a new Convention for the Protection of Civilian Persons in Time of War. (Joyce Gutteridge, 'The Geneva Conventions of 1949' (1949) 26 BYBIL 294)

The result of the Diplomatic Conference was the four 1949 Geneva Conventions still applied today. While elaboration on the specifics of the four conventions is beyond this section, an in-depth analysis of certain provisions will be undertaken in subsequent sections of this chapter.

As a supplement to the 1949 Geneva Conventions, three Additional Protocols have been adopted. Their scope is limited by the fact that they only apply to those States that have signed and ratified them (see the section on treaties and the legal consequences of signature and ratification in Chapter 2). Additional Protocol I, adopted in June 1977, covers the Protection of Victims of International Armed Conflicts; Additional Protocol II, also adopted in June 1977, is concerned with the Protection of Victims of Non-International Conflicts; while Additional Protocol III, adopted in December 2005, addresses the Adoption of an Additional Emblem, the red crystal, alongside the red cross and red crescent.

Simultaneous to the Geneva conferences and conventions, other initiatives concerned with the conduct of hostilities and conflict were taking place. In 1856, the Paris Declaration was adopted which covered maritime warfare with ratification open to all States and which was one of the first multilateral treaties of its time to cover IHL. In 1899, the First Hague Peace

Conference took place and culminated in the adoption of three conventions covering land and maritime war, as well as three declarations over the conduct of warfare. It was under the championing of the then Russian Czar Nicholas II that the First Hague Peace Conference took place:

> with the object of seeking the most effective means of ensuring to all peoples the benefits of a lasting and real peace, and, above all, of limiting the progressive development of existing armaments. (Russian note of 30 December 1898/11 January 1899, as quoted in Dietrich Schindler and Jiri Toman (eds), *The Laws of Armed Conflicts: A Collection of Conventions, Resolutions and Other Documents* (Dordrecht: Kluwer Academic Publishers, 1988), p. 49)

Further to this, in 1904 the Hague Convention on hospital ships was adopted. It was not, however, until the Second Hague Peace Conference in 1907 that a huge step forward was taken in the codification and regulation of the conduct of hostilities. In fact:

> no single conference since the Second Hague Peace Conference has succeeded in formulating as many conventions concerning the laws of war, the process of codification continued, with varying degrees of success. (Adam Roberts and Richard Guelff, *Documents on the Laws of War* (3rd edn, Oxford: Oxford University Press, 2000), p. 5)

The 1907 Hague Peace Conference resulted in the adoption of thirteen conventions and one declaration ranging from regulating the opening of hostilities (Convention III), the laws and customs of war on land (Convention IV), to the laying of automatic submarine contact mines (Convention VIII), and finally the Declaration Prohibiting the Discharge of Projectiles and Explosives from Balloons. Further conventions have been adopted regulating the type of weaponry to be used in conflicts; most notably, the 1980 UN Convention on Prohibitions or Restrictions on the Use of Certain Conventional Weapons Which May be Deemed to be Excessively Injurious or to Have Indiscriminate Effects, and the Convention on the Prohibition of the Development, Production, Stockpiling and Use of Chemical Weapons and on Their Destruction. While the Hague Conventions generally cover the regulation of weapons and other forms of military action, the conduct of warfare has also been regulated through minimizing the damage of conflict to cultural property: the 1954 Hague Convention for the Protection of Cultural Property in the Event of Armed Conflict and the 1954 First Protocol for the Protection of Cultural Property in the Event of Armed Conflict.

It can be seen that IHL is separated into two distinct, but complementary, components; the law setting out the protections afforded to those taking part in conflict as well as civilians and other non-participants as established by the Geneva Conventions and the Additional Protocols, and the law governing the conduct and methods of warfare, predominantly regulated by the Hague Conventions and subsequent international conventions. Yet, despite this vast scope of treaty law, there are challenges. Arguably one of the biggest to overcome is the rapid development of technology and weapons; the law is not necessarily able to respond as quickly and, in fact, some of the treaty obligations and regulations may become redundant and obsolete as a result of advancements and the subsequent changing nature of warfare. This does not, however, mean there are no IHL principles that can be applied in such situations. In fact, where treaty law is absent or inadequate it may be possible for customary law to fill the gap.

Customary international law and IHL

Customary international law has played, and continues to play, a huge role in IHL. As already seen, many of today's treaty laws and principles stem from customary law principles and State practice. Within IHL, both customary law and treaty law are applicable. Customary international law plays a dual role when interacting with IHL treaty law, through establishing the embodied law and being created by the treaty law. Some of the conventions already mentioned have come to be regarded as forming part of customary law, most notably Hague Convention IV of 1907 as it applies to land warfare, as recognized by the International Military Tribunal at Nuremberg and reiterated by the UN Secretary-General, who was of the opinion that:

> The part of conventional international humanitarian law which has beyond doubt become part of international customary law is the law applicable in armed conflict as embodied in: the Geneva Conventions of 12 August 1949 for the Protection of War Victims; 3/ the Hague Convention (IV) Respecting the Laws and Customs of War on Land and the Regulations annexed thereto of 18 October 1907; 4/ the Convention on the Prevention and Punishment of the Crime of Genocide of 9 December 1948; 5/ and the Charter of the International Military Tribunal of 8 August 1945.
> (Report of the Secretary-General Pursuant to Paragraph 2 of the Security Council Resolution 808 (UN Doc. S/25704, 3 May 1993, p. 35)

While customary law can be used in certain instances to extend the application of specific treaty law, customary law and its associated principles and rules continued to exist alongside the treaty provisions. It was recognized that customary law in fact applied and contained additional principles and rules to those codified. This can be seen in the adoption of what is known as the Martens Clause. The first enunciation of which is from the 1899 Hague Convention II Preamble:

> Until a more complete code of the laws of war is issued, the high contracting Parties think it right to declare that in cases not included in the Regulations adopted by them, populations and belligerents remain under the protection and empire of the principles of international law, as they result from the usages established between civilized nations, from the laws of humanity, and the requirements of the public conscience.

This concept has been utilized further by the 1949 Geneva Conventions with the position being taken that the Martens Clause concept applies for any party as the denouncing of the convention:

Shall in no way impair the obligations which the Parties to the conflict shall remain bound to fulfil by virtue of the principles of the law of nations, as they result from the usages established among civilized peoples, from the laws of humanity and the dictates of the public conscience.

KEY POINTS Customary international law complements IHL, but also fills the gap when there are no treaty provisions on certain aspects of IHL.

When does an armed conflict occur?

In order for IHL to apply there needs to be an armed conflict. The question, however, exists as to what the meaning of an armed conflict is. There is no one acceptable definition of armed conflict despite the widespread use of the term throughout treaty and customary law. What threshold of violence needs to exist to be considered an armed conflict? There is also a distinction made between an international armed conflict and a non-international armed conflict, or internal armed conflict. As seen in the previous discussion, IHL has developed with different levels of protection and application depending on the type of conflict. One only needs to look at the names of 1949 Geneva Convention Additional Protocols I and II (AP I and AP II) to see this; AP I applies to international conflicts and AP II to non-international conflicts. Thus, in order to answer this question, first we must deal with what an armed conflict is, and then when an international armed conflict can be said to occur.

12.4.1 'Armed conflict'

. . . .

● *Prosecutor v. Duško Tadić,* Decision on the Defence Motion for Interlocutory Appeal on Jurisdiction (Interlocutory Appeal), Case No. IT-94-1-AR72, 2 October 1995 (The *Tadić Case*)

The ICTY stated (at 70) that:

> an armed conflict exists whenever there is a resort to armed force between States or protracted armed violence between governmental authorities and organized armed groups or between such groups within a State.

This definition relates to armed conflicts in general and not to a specific type of conflict. Thus, the definition offers a rather conceptual view of armed conflict, describing when an armed conflict can be said to occur rather than when a specific kind of armed conflict exists.

12.4.2 International armed conflict

Under Common Article 2 of the 1949 Geneva Conventions ('common' in this instance meaning it appears in identical wording and article number throughout all four of the Geneva Conventions) an armed conflict exists in:

All cases of declared war or of any other armed conflict which may arise between two or more of the High Contracting Parties even if the state of war is not recognized by one of them. The Convention shall also apply to all cases of partial or total occupation of the territory of a High Contracting Party, even if the said occupation meets with no armed resistance. (Common Article 2 of the 1949 Geneva Conventions)

By using 'two or more of the High Contracting Parties' this definition automatically limits this type of armed conflict to between States. This is a result of the only entities able to be a High Contracting Party being States. Therefore it is arguably safe to assume that this definition relates to international armed conflicts and is limited in its application to that alone. It may be questioned as to why Common Article 2 uses the terminology 'war' and 'any other armed conflict', yet through looking at the ICRC's commentary on the Geneva Conventions it was merely a tactic to cover situations whereby States had not declared war but hostilities were still taking place which were more than mere police enforcement and could include acts of self-defence.

Subsequent initiatives have extended the definition of an international armed conflict to include:

Armed conflicts in which peoples are fighting against colonial domination and alien occupation and against racist regimes in the exercise of their right to self-determination, as enshrined in the Charter of the United Nations and the Declaration on Principles of International Law concerning Friendly Relations and Co-operation among States in accordance with the Charter of the United Nations. (Additional Protocol I to the 1949 Geneva Conventions, Article 1(4))

While this extends the notion of an international armed conflict to previously conceived internal conflicts, in relation to self-determination conflicts it must be borne in mind that AP 1 has not been ratified by all States and will only apply to those that have. Furthermore, some ratifying States have included statements of understanding in order to limit the application of Article 1(4). In the instance of the UK's Declaration in relation to AP I, the UK was careful to restrict the Additional Protocol from applying to acts of terrorism unless otherwise provided due to the ongoing situation in Northern Ireland at the time and the desire of the UK to prevent IHL being applied in relation to the conflict:

It is the understanding of the United Kingdom that the term 'armed conflict' of itself and in its context denotes a situation of a kind which is not constituted by the commission of ordinary crimes including acts of terrorism whether concerted or in isolation.

The United Kingdom will not, in relation to any situation in which it is itself involved, consider itself bound in consequence of any declaration purporting to be made under paragraph 3 of Article 96 unless the United Kingdom shall have expressly recognised that it has been made by a body which is genuinely an authority representing a people engaged in an armed conflict of the type to which Article 1, paragraph 4, applies. (United Kingdom Declaration 2 July 2002 in relation to Protocol Additional to the Geneva Conventions of 12 August 1949, and relating to the Protection of Victims of International Armed Conflicts (Protocol I), 8 June 1977, available at http://www.icrc.org/ihl/NORM/0A9E03F0F2EE757CC1256402003FB6D2?OpenDocument)

thinking points

- *Define 'armed conflict'.*
- *When does an international armed conflict occur?*
- *What provisions of the Geneva Convention and Additional Protocol define international armed conflicts?*

12.4.3 Non-international armed conflicts

In general international conflicts are subject to more extensive regulation than non-international conflicts. Given the fact that State sovereignty is one of the fundamental principles recognized by public international law and that States traditionally viewed their internal matters as beyond the scope of international law regulation, consensus over the applicable regulation was harder to come by. Nevertheless, consensus was reached. As with international armed conflicts, the Geneva Conventions are sorely lacking in any definition for a non-international armed conflict. The first point of call to consider is Common Article 3 of the Geneva Conventions which takes a negative definitional approach. In essence, Common Article 3 is merely the converse of Common Article 2. Non-international armed conflicts are an:

> armed conflict not of an international character occurring in the territory of one of the High Contracting Parties

While little is developed in this Article, a few points are clear. The armed conflict needs to occur within a High Contracting Party's territory, thus excluding conflicts which extend beyond the territory of one State and spill into other States. By stipulating that it is 'not of an international character' it can be deduced that the armed conflict cannot be between two or more States, therefore some other actor(s) or group must be involved.

With the adoption of the 1977 AP II further guidance as to what constitutes a non-international armed conflict was provided. AP II is supplementary to Common Article 3 and applies to:

> all armed conflicts which are not covered by Article 1 of the Protocol Additional to the Geneva Conventions of 12 August 1949, and relating to the Protection of Victims of International Armed Conflicts (Protocol I) and which take place in the territory of a High Contracting Party between its armed forces and dissident armed forces or other organized armed groups which, under responsible command, exercise such control over a part of its territory as to enable them to carry out sustained and concerted military operations and to implement this Protocol. (Additional Protocol II Article 1(1))

It appears as if AP II provides the catch-all provisions for those armed conflicts not considered international under AP I and the 1949 Geneva Conventions. It requires the actors involved to possess a level of organization and command structure as well as having a degree of control over territory within the State. The rationale for this is to distinguish between an actual internal conflict and lower levels of disturbances which do not require the same level of protection afforded under IHL. This is clearly shown with the explicit exclusion of the following situations from coming under AP II's scope. Article 1(2) states that:

> This Protocol shall not apply to situations of internal disturbances and tensions, such as riots, isolated and sporadic acts of violence and other acts of a similar nature, as not being armed conflicts.

Once again, AP II does not include any definition as to what such internal disturbances and tensions are. The problem with AP II's approach is that through imposing such a high threshold for a non-international armed conflict by requiring the exercise of control over a part of the territory, many situations will fall short. Furthermore, the requirement of 'sustained and concerted military operations' seeks to separate minor rebellions, which have no real impact on the government's control of their territory, and those situations in which rebels or militia succeed in controlling areas of a State. The consequence is that such minor rebellions remain in the domain of an internal matter to which IHL does not apply. This is further compounded by the limited scope of application of AP II due to the small number of State parties. The Inter-American Commission for Human Rights has provided guidance on how to distinguish between tensions, internal disturbances, and non-international armed conflicts. It is said to boil down to the nature of the violence, its intensity, and the organization and coordination of the attacks. The *Tablada Base Case* involved the Argentinean army and a group of attackers who confronted the army at the Tablada Base, with the whole thing lasting thirty hours.

> The Commission came to the conclusion that the incident, despite its brief duration, triggered the application of Common article 3, as well as other rules relevant to the conduct of internal hostilities. What differentiated the events at the Tablada Base from situations of internal disturbances was, according to the Commission, 'the concerted nature of the hostile act undertaken by the attackers, and the nature and level of violence attending the event in question. More particular, the attackers involved carefully planned, coordinated and executed an armed attack, i.e., a military operation, against a quintessential military objective—a military base.' The Commission based its findings on an understanding that the existence of an armed conflict does not require a large scale and generalized hostility or a situation comparable to a civil war in which dissident armed groups exercises control over parts of national territory. (Arne Dahl and Magnus Sanbu, 'The threshold of armed conflict' (2006) 45 Military Law and Laws of War Rev 369, 378)

The importance of State sovereignty and non-intervention has been reinforced in AP II Article 3:

> 1. Nothing in this Protocol shall be invoked for the purpose of affecting the sovereignty of a State or the responsibility of the government, by all legitimate means, to maintain or re-establish law and order in the State or to defend the national unity and territorial integrity of the State.
> 2. Nothing in this Protocol shall be invoked as a justification for intervening, directly or indirectly, for any reason whatever, in the armed conflict or in the internal or external affairs of the High Contracting Party in the territory of which that conflict occurs.

It seems that with this Article AP II is affirming its limited application, the importance of State sovereignty, and trying to prevent any intervention initiatives being based on non-international armed conflicts as defined in this treaty. The focus is on protecting and limiting the effect of the internal armed conflict, and preventing the internationalization of it.

It is clear from the previous discussion that, concerning internal armed conflicts, many questions still remain as to when exactly a conflict can be said to occur. What timescale, if any, is required? What level of suffering and/or death needs to be present? In essence, at what point does the application of IHL start, and also cease, to apply?

It has been suggested that:

> It makes no difference how long the conflict last, or how much slaughter takes place. (Jean S. Pictet, *Geneva Convention for the Amelioration of the Condition of the Wounded and Sick in Armed Forces in the Field: Commentary* (ICRC 1952) 32)

Other international bodies, which have considered the definition and scope of an armed conflict have found:

an armed conflict exists whenever there is a resort to armed force between States or protracted armed violence between governmental authorities and organized armed groups or between such groups within a State. International humanitarian law applies from the initiation of such armed conflicts and extends beyond the cessation of hostilities until a general conclusion of peace is reached; or, in the case of internal conflicts, a peaceful settlement is achieved. Until that moment, international humanitarian law continues to apply in the whole territory of the warring States or, in the case of internal conflicts, the whole territory under the control of a party, whether or not actual combat takes place there. (*Prosecutor v. Duško Tadic´*, Decision on the Defence Motion for Interlocutory Appeal on Jurisdiction (Interlocutory Appeal), Case No. IT-94-1-AR72, 2 October 1995, 70)

The judgment of the International Criminal Tribunal for the former Yugoslavia (ICTY) is helpful as it considers the situation for both an international and non-international armed conflict. Most likely this was due to the nature of the conflict which was taking place in the former Socialist Federal Republic of Yugoslavia, and which encompassed both international and non-international armed conflicts. Ultimately, IHL is applicable from the earliest point possible and extending to the latest possible point.

thinking points

- *Explain non-international armed conflict.*
- *Of what importance is time to characterizing a conflict as non-international?*
- *What are examples of internal armed conflicts?*

423

12.5 Armed conflict classification and the war on terror

Determining the kind of armed conflict taking place has significant legal consequences for those participants and non-participants alike. This is seen most recently with the controversial conflicts in Iraq and Afghanistan on the basis of the so-called 'war on terror'. It is generally accepted that the initial conflict in Afghanistan between October 2001 and June 2002 fell under international armed conflict and the resulting occupation also comes under the IHL law applicable to occupation (see Geneva Convention IV on belligerent occupation). It is the subsequent armed conflict aimed at the 'terrorist' groups which are not a High Contracting Party which causes problems and a lack of consensus:

The underlying argument here is that, to be considered an armed conflict under inter-national law, the conflict must fall within the parameters of either an international or non-international armed conflict, and that a conflict with al Qaeda doesn't fall into either category. Most commentators point to its non-State nature to insist that al Qaeda cannot be a party to an international armed conflict which traditionally refers to conflicts between two or more States. (Natasha Balendra, 'Defining armed conflict' (2007–08) 29 Cardozo L Rev 2461, 2472)

The conflict is not within a territory of the USA so cannot be viewed as a non-international conflict in that respect; furthermore, the territory from which these groups operate is more transnational in nature and it is difficult to reconcile these groups with the established actors of an armed conflict under international law. As the ICRC pointed out:

> it is difficult to see how a loosely connected network of cells-a characterization that is undisputed for the moment-could qualify as a 'party' to the conflict (ICRC, *International Humanitarian Law and the Challenges of Contemporary Armed Conflicts* (2003), p. 19, available at http://www.icrc.org/eng/assets/files/other/IHLcontemp_armedconflicts_FINAL_ANG.pdf)

Without knowing what type of armed conflict is taking place, it is difficult to know what IHL laws and principles to apply. You can end up with situations where one party to a conflict is operating under the assumption that an international armed conflict is the appropriate one, while the other party may determine that neither is the correct approach and therefore consider the situation to fall outside IHL completely, or in certain aspects, and not comply with any IHL laws and principles.

Having considered when an armed conflict exists and associated definitional elements and consequences, attention will now be given to some specific provisions and protections afforded under IHL in order to see the kind of scope this area of law provides.

12.6 Combatants, civilians, and somewhere in between: the principle of distinction

The following definitions and distinctions are relevant for international armed conflicts due to the linked protections and conduct regulations imposed on the groupings.

Traditionally, IHL never included a definition of combatant as it was only ever soldiers who participated in war and usually the battles were not located close to civilian areas. Slowly but surely the concept of a combatant began to appear, as did the use of standard uniforms for armies throughout the seventeenth and eighteenth centuries. Nevertheless, there was no real controversy as to who constituted a combatant. Yet, from the Franco-Prussian War of 1870–71 questions were being raised as to the status of *francs-tireurs* (free-shooters) and the *levée en masse* (mass uprising). The free-shooters were groups or militia who armed themselves independently from the government or military and fought against an invading army. Whereas the mass uprising categorization encompasses civilians who during an invasion spontaneously take up arms against the invading army and become recognized as combatants when they carried arms openly.

While it may seem obvious that anyone who is involved in fighting in the conflict should be classified a combatant, it is not always that straightforward. The fundamental criterion for being a combatant and therefore enjoying the rights of combatants (eg prisoners of war or POW status if captured) is based on taking a direct part in hostilities. (See Nils Melzer, *Interpretive Guidance on the Notion of Direct Participation in Hostilities under International Humanitarian Law*, Geneva: ICRC, 2009.)

In order lawfully to take a direct part in hostilities, one must satisfy the four criteria of Article 4 (A)(2), Geneva Convention III, which are that the person must:

1. be commanded by a person responsible for his subordinates;
2. have a fixed distinctive emblem recognizable at a distance;
3. carry arms openly; and
4. conduct their operations in accordance with the laws and customs of war.

It is irrelevant whether a person is a member of the armed forces, a militia, or a volunteer corps, including such organized resistance movements. What is important is that he or she fulfils these four criteria upon which he or she becomes a lawful combatant. The consequence is that: only combatants can be made the object of attack; only lawful combatants possess the right to be POWs, whereas if a random civilian in occupied territory kills a member of the occupying forces he or she is subject to the criminal laws of the occupying power.

It is important to note that not all military personnel are considered combatants, military medical and religious personnel are considered non-combatants (see Article 33 of the 1949 Geneva Convention III). Subsequent treaty provisions have developed the definition and concept of combatant and non-combatant in relation to POW protection. What they have done is to include certain non-combatants in the same level of protection for combatants recognized as prisoners of war:

A. Prisoners of war, in the sense of the present Convention, are persons belonging to one of the following categories, who have fallen into the power of the enemy:

1) Members of the armed forces of a Party to the conflict as well as members of militias or volunteer corps forming part of such armed forces.

2) Members of other militias and members of other volunteer corps, including those of organized resistance movements, belonging to a Party to the conflict and operating in or outside their own territory, even if this territory is occupied, provided that such militias or volunteer corps, including such organized resistance movements, fulfil the following conditions:

a) that of being commanded by a person responsible for his subordinates;

b) that of having a fixed distinctive sign recognizable at a distance;

c) that of carrying arms openly;

d) that of conducting their operations in accordance with the laws and customs of war.

3) Members of regular armed forces who profess allegiance to a government or an authority not recognized by the Detaining Power.

4) Persons who accompany the armed forces without actually being members thereof, such as civilian members of military aircraft crews, war correspondents, supply contractors, members of labour units or of services responsible for the welfare of the armed forces, provided that they have received authorization from the armed forces which they accompany, who shall provide them for that purpose with an identity card similar to the annexed model.

5) Members of crews, including masters, pilots and apprentices of the merchant marine and the crews of civil aircraft of the Parties to the conflict, who do not benefit by more favourable treatment under any other provisions of international law.

6) Inhabitants of a non-occupied territory who, on the approach of the enemy, spontaneously take up arms to resist the invading forces, without having had time to form themselves into regular armed units, provided they carry arms openly and respect the laws and customs of war (1949 Geneva Convention III Article 4)

The above, however, does not make it explicitly clear who are combatants and non-combatants, merely that they are all to be granted POW protection. Combatants do not need to be part of a recognized State's military or government forces. Following AP I, the armed forces of a State, and therefore combatants, include:

> All organized armed forces, groups and units which are under a command responsible to that Party for the conduct of its subordinates, even if that Party is represented by a government or an authority not recognized by an adverse Party. (Article 43 Additional Protocol I Relating to the Protection of Victims of International Armed Conflicts)

This determination of combatant or belligerent status irrespective of being recognized by the adverse party is a marked improvement for protection of combatants and for civilian alike, as it enables non-State actors, and non-recognized military groups of States to come under the definition. Consideration has also been given to the evolving nature of warfare and the different types of conflict which are subject to IHL. The 1907 Hague Regulations required a fixed distinctive emblem to be worn by belligerents in order to come under IHL's scope, but nowadays this is not always possible or what happens in reality. AP I strives to balance this with the best internationally acceptable approach. The compromise was that:

> In order to promote the protection of the civilian population from the effects of hostilities, combatants are obliged to distinguish themselves from the civilian population while they are engaged in an attack or in a military operation preparatory to an attack. Recognizing, however, that there are situations in armed conflicts where, owing to the nature of the hostilities an armed combatant cannot so distinguish himself, he shall retain his status as a combatant, provided that, in such situations, he carries his arms openly:
>
> a) during each military engagement, and
> b) during such time as he is visible to the adversary while he is engaged in a military deployment preceding the launching of an attack in which he is to participate. (Additional Protocol I Article 44(3).)

The recognition that a combatant can be indistinguishable from a civilian is important and in terms of the criteria set out in Article 44(3) recognized the changing nature of armed conflict and the reality that IHL still applied, as:

> combatants who act in exceptional situations are to comply with the minimum requirements of distinction. The Conference agreed that such exceptional situations could arise in occupied territories and in struggles for self-determination as defined in Article 1(4). (Nissim Bar-Yaacov, 'Some aspects of prisoner-of-war status according to the Geneva Protocol I of 1977' (1985) 20 Israeli L Rev 243, 251)

In fact, this appears to be an acceptance that there will be times when certain combatants do not need to distinguish themselves from civilians at all if related to national liberation movements:

> The representative of the Socialist Republic of Vietnam, Mr. Van Luu, with whom Mr. Aldrich worked out the text of draft Article 42 (final Article 44), declared that under certain conditions the combatants of movements fighting for national and social emancipation were now 'allowed to fight without distinguishing themselves from the civilian population'. They lost the status of prisoners of war only when they did not carry their weapons openly as laid down in para. 3 of the

article. (CDDH/SR. 41, 26 May 1977, para. 56, OR, vol. VI, 153, as quoted in Bar-Yaacov, 1985, at 268, see the previous extract)

The problem with this is that two different standards are applied to regular soldiers and other combatants, when read with the requirements of AP I Article 44(7) that a State's armed forces wear distinctive uniforms:

> This Article is not intended to change the generally accepted practice of States with respect to the wearing of the uniform by combatants assigned to the regular, uniformed armed units of a Party to the conflict

thinking points

- *Distinguish between combatants and non-combatants.*
- *Of what relevance are the four criteria listed under Article 4 (A)(2) Geneva Convention III to fighters?*
- *What categories of non-combatants may enjoy the protection of IHL?*

12.6.1 Civilian

The definition of a civilian is anyone who does not come under the definition of a combatant as discussed in the previous section. Little discussion over this aspect is required. The reasoning for this is likely to be that civilians used to be outside the scope of IHL:

> mainly because the nature of warfare prior to the early twentieth century was such that civilians were rarely subjected to direct attack and specific measures of protection were thus not thought necessary, the experience of 'total war' in various conflicts of the 1930s and 1940s made it clear that development of the law in this direction was urgently required. (David Turns, 'The law of armed conflict' in Malcolm Evans (ed.), *International Law* (3rd edn, Oxford: Oxford University Press, 2010), p. 837)

Civilians have now been afforded a separate convention specifically addressing their protection issues—1949 Geneva Convention IV Relative to the Protection of Civilian Persons in Time of War. It was with Article 4 that civilians were defined:

> Persons protected by the Convention are those who at a given moment and in any manner whatsoever, find themselves, in case of a conflict or occupation, in the hands of persons a Party to the conflict or Occupying Power of which they are not nationals.
> Nationals of a State which is not bound by the Convention are not protected by it. Nationals of a neutral State who find themselves in the territory of a belligerent State, and nationals of a co-belligerent State, shall not be regarded as protected persons while the State of which they are nationals has normal diplomatic representation in the State in whose hands they are.
> The provisions of Part II are, however, wider in application, as defined in Article 13.
> Persons protected by the Geneva Convention for the Amelioration of the Condition of the Wounded and Sick in Armed Forces in the Field of August 12, 1949, or by the Geneva Convention for the Amelioration of the Condition of Wounded, Sick and Shipwrecked Members of Armed Forces at Sea of August 12, 1949 or by the Geneva Convention relative to the Treatment of Prisoners of War of August 12, 1949, shall not be considered as protected persons within the meaning of the present Convention.

Despite the clear distinctions provided for in IHL between a combatant and a non-combatant, this has been greatly called into question given the realities of warfare, where and how it is conducted, and the parties/actors involved:

> In practice, the distinction between combatants and non-combatants cannot be upheld in the face of human distress. War, as it becomes more and more total, practically annuls the differ-ence as to injury and exposure to danger which formerly existed between armed forces and non-combatants. (Max Huber, Address to the Preliminary Red Cross Conference, Geneva, 1946 as cited in Jean Pictet, 'The new Geneva Conventions for the Protection of War Victims' (1951) 45 AJIL 462, 474)

While there is truth in this statement, it does not appreciate the reasoning for the dif-ferent protection and the consequential obligations and implications of the distinctions. The effects of conflict are being felt across a broader range of individuals but the need to distinguish the protections is never more so needed than in complicated and uncertain times.

Of late, a third category has been put forward, that of unlawful combatants. But before a further discussion takes place it should be noted that while many of these arguments are put forward by States, academics, and other commentators, the ICTY has clearly stated:

> There is no gap between the Third and the Fourth Geneva Conventions. If an individual is not entitled to the protections of the Third Convention as a prisoner of war (or of the First or Second Conventions) he or she necessarily falls within the ambit of Convention IV, provided that its arti-cle 4 requirements are satisfied. The Commentary to the Fourth Geneva Convention asserts that; "[e]very person in enemy hands must have some status under international law: he is either a prisoner of war and, as such, covered by the Third Convention, a civilian covered by the Fourth Convention, or again, a member of the medical personnel of the armed forces who is covered by the First Convention. There is no intermediate status; nobody in enemy hands can be outside the law. We feel that this is a satisfactory solution—not only satisfying to the mind, but also, and above all, satisfactory from the humanitarian point of view". (*Prosecutor v. Delalić et al.* Judgment, Case No. IT-96-21-T (16 November 1998) 271 (*Čelebići case*).)

There can hardly be a more bold and accurate statement. When one starts to look closely at many of the arguments made for classifying an individual as an unlawful combatant, it gener-ally has an ulterior motive.

The origin of the term 'unlawful combatant' is traceable to a US Supreme Court ruling in 1942 after German soldiers dressed in civilian clothes were captured by the USA on American territory and brought before a US court. The US Supreme Court took the view that:

> The Laws of War distinguished between combatants and civilians, and between lawful combat-ants and unlawful ones. Lawful combatants are subject to capture and detention as POWs by the opposing military forces. Unlawful combatants are likewise subject to capture and detention, but in addition they are subject to trial and punishment by military tribunals for acts which render their belligerency unlawful. (*Ex parte Quirin* 317 US 1, 3 0-31 (1942))

Yet this ruling and reasoning have been heavily criticized as placing the rationale incorrectly on the determination of an unlawful belligerent status when in fact it was the criminal act in and of itself which led to the criminal prosecution by the US court.

The term unlawful combatant does not appear in any of the four 1949 Geneva Conventions, while AP I is considered by some to have a similar conceptualization with the recognition of 'irregular force'. Even if this specific interpretation of the term 'irregular force' can be equated to unlawful combatant, the fact of its inclusion in AP I no longer means unlawful combatants are outside the scope of IHL as they are recognized belligerents and it would seem that the ICTY's opinion holds true. For those States that are not a party to AP I, there may be stronger legal arguments for unlawful combatant classification but that is still subject to much conjecture.

The term did not come into much discussion again until after the 11 September 2001 attacks on the USA (known as '9/11'). The USA in particular sought to classify Al Qaeda and the Taliban as unlawful combatants in order to remove them from the scope of IHL and the USA refused to afford them protection as prisoners of war; thus enabling indefinite detention in Guantánamo Bay, Cuba. However, this is a hard position to accept when you take into account Article 5 of Geneva Convention III. Under this provision:

> Should any doubt arise as to whether persons having committed a belligerent act and having fallen into the hands of the enemy belong to any of the categories enumerated in Article 4, such persons shall enjoy the protection of the present Convention until such time as their status has been determined by a competent tribunal.

In addition, AP I also provides guidance on situations in doubt as to the status of an individual:

> A person who takes part in hostilities and falls into the power of an adverse Party shall be presumed to be a prisoner of war, and therefore shall be protected by the Third Convention, if he claims the status of prisoner of war, or if he appears to be entitled to such status, or if the Party on which he depends claims such status on his behalf by notification to the detaining Power or to the Protecting Power. Should any doubt arise as to whether any such person is entitled to the status of prisoner of war, he shall continue to have such status and, therefore, to be protected by the Third Convention and this Protocol until such time as his status has been determined by a competent tribunal. (Article 45(1) AP I)

Both under Geneva Convention III and AP I, an individual who has taken part in hostilities or undertaken belligerent acts will be entitled to POW status until a competent tribunal determines their status. Consequently, there is unlikely to be a situation whereby IHL protection does not apply. IHL is clear as to the classification of individuals as well as what protections each are afforded. It would seem, then, that the basis for the USA's argument of unlawful combatants being outside IHL protection is flawed. Even if you accept the US proposed unlawful combatant position, it would seem to fly in the face of the purpose of IHL and all it has managed to achieve by reducing the protections and safeguards:

> Some scholars, the majority of them addressing the issue after the events of 9/11, have opined
> that international law should acknowledge a third category of unlawful or non-privileged com-
> batants who may be considered legitimate targets as well as being subject to criminal pros-
> ecution for their unlawful acts. In contrast, the position of the ICRC is that no such category
> was intended in the basic instruments of IHL and that creating one would blur the distinction
> between combatants and civilians. Eventually, it would endanger the protections accorded to
> civilians and make it more difficult to ensure that they are left out of the scope of those con-
> sidered legitimate targets. (Hilly Moodrick-Even Khen, 'Case note: can we now tell what "direct
> participation in hostilities" is? (2007) 40 Israel L Rev 213, 228)

When it comes to dealing with terrorism, international law, arguably, has not yet caught up with developments in warfare and the types of individual involved. As explained:

> The main difficulty in dealing with terrorism through legal means is the fact that international law is inherently State-oriented. International law has difficulties relating coherently to international organisations or individuals (Shlomy Zachary, 'Between the Geneva Conventions: where do unlawful combatants belong?' (2005) 38 Israel L Rev 378, 388)

This is not to say that international law does not have room for interpreting its provisions to apply to terrorism. In fact, the Inter-American Commission on Human Rights has determined that in terms of taking part in hostilities there can be situations in which terrorist acts and counter-terrorist acts can be of the intensity needed to be considered an armed conflict:

> Although terrorist or counter-terrorist action may give rise to or occur in the context of situations of armed conflict, it must be recalled that the concepts of terrorism and war are distinct. In certain circumstances, terrorist or counter-terrorist actions may involve organized violence of such intensity as to give rise to an armed conflict. Such would be the case, for example, where terrorist or counter-terrorist actions involve resort to armed force between States or low intensity and armed confrontations between a State and a relatively organized armed force or group or between such forces or groups within the territory of a state, which in some cases may take place with the support or connivance of states. In addition to constituting the trigger for an armed conflict, terrorist or counter-terrorist actions may take place as discrete acts within an existing armed conflict. Terrorist violence committed under these circumstances is also subject to international humanitarian law, even if it occurs in territory where combat is not taking place, provided that the incidents are sufficiently linked to the armed conflict. This would clearly be the case, for example, where the terrorist or counter-terrorist acts are committed by agents of a belligerent party against the members or objects of an adverse party. In all circumstances, the specific international humanitarian law norms applicable to terrorist violence will vary depending upon whether they give rise to or take place in the context of a conflict of an international or non-international nature. It is also important to recall that the fact that terrorist acts are perpetrated within the context of an armed conflict does not otherwise affect the legal status of that conflict, although it may, as noted above, render the perpetrator and his or her superior individually criminally responsible for those acts that constitute serious violations of the law and customs of law. (Inter-American Commission on Human Rights, Report on Terrorism and Human Rights (OEA/Ser.L/-V/II. 116 Doc.5 rev. 1 corr., 22 October 2002), p. 73)

Again, it seems that IHL can be interpreted broadly enough to cover the developing situations we presently find the international community is dealing with in terms of conflict and who takes part in hostilities. In addition, the only time in which specific individuals are expressly excluded from such POW protection, and conversely could be argued are outside the scope of IHL, is in the case of mercenaries. Pursuant to AP I :

> A mercenary shall not have the right to be a combatant or a prisoner of war. (Article 47(1) Additional Protocol I)

Therefore, surely if IHL did not intend to apply to certain groups or other categorizations of individuals it would have been provided for. This is even more so the case when you take the

1949 Geneva Convention's negative approach to defining civilians; being those not classified as combatants. With such clear guidance, how can there be room for a third category?

thinking points

- *Explain the situation of the unlawful combatant under IHL.*
- *What dangers are associated with recognition of unlawful combatants?*

12.7 Restricting methods of warfare through the distinction and proportionality and control of weapons

431

Customary international law plays an important role in restricting the conduct of warfare and one of the most fundamental principles upon which this is possible is proportionality and distinction. You will already have come across the concept of proportionality in relation to the use of force, however in this instance what is being referred to is the notion of proportionality in relation to the damage caused (be it to civilians or physical structures) when taking into account the military advantage gained. A phrase you are most likely to have come across before encompasses this principle; collateral damage. What this means in essence is that there is an acceptable level of casualties during times of armed conflict as long as it is not excessive. Furthering this principle is the requirement of distinction. For this, military objects and targets, including combatants, need to be distinguished from civilians and civilian objects. (Yet another reason why it is so important to understand the position on the status of combatants and civilians as discussed previously.) The reasoning for the principles of proportionality and distinction has been explained as:

> Deriv[ing] from the basic principle of the law of armed conflict that belligerents do not have an unlimited choice of means to inflict damage on the enemy. From this principle, and the other basic precept of the law of armed conflict, that the sole object of war is to weaken the military forces of the enemy, developed noncombatant immunity, which in turn dictated the evolution of a theory of proportionality in relation to civilian losses that covers indiscriminate attacks, the greatest threat to noncombatant immunity (Judith Gardam, 'Proportionality and force in international law' (1993) 87 AJIL 391, 402–403)

It is not only customary international law that requires distinction between combatants, military objectives, and civilians and civilians objects. AP I has also included this obligation:

In order to ensure respect for and protection of the civilian population and civilian objects, the Parties to the conflict shall at all times distinguish between the civilian population and combatants and between civilian objects and military objectives and accordingly shall direct their operations only against military objectives. (Additional Protocol I, Article 48.)

Furthermore, there are considered to be three principles which are incorporated into the concept of proportionality and distinction; the principles of military necessity, humanity, and chivalry. The UK Ministry of Defence defines these principles in the following manner:

> 2.2 Military necessity permits a state engaged in an armed conflict to use only that degree and kind of force, not otherwise prohibited by the law of armed conflict, that is required in order to achieve the legitimate purpose of the conflict, namely the complete or partial submission of the enemy at the earliest possible moment with the minimum expenditure of life and resources . . .
>
> 2.4 Humanity forbids the infliction of suffering, injury, or destruction not actually necessary for the accomplishment of legitimate military purposes.
>
> 2.4.1 The principle of humanity is based on the notion that once a military purpose has been achieved, the further infliction of suffering is unnecessary. Thus, if an enemy combatant has been put out of action by being wounded or captured, there is no military purpose to be achieved by continuing to attack him. For the same reason, the principle of humanity confirms the basic immunity of civilian populations and civilian objects from attack because civilians and civilian objects make no contribution to military action.
>
> 2.4.3 The principle of humanity can be found in the Martens Clause in the Preamble to Hague Convention IV 1907. It incorporates the earlier rules of chivalry that opposing combatants were entitled to respect and honour. From this flowed the duty to provide humane treatment to the wounded and those who had become prisoners of war. (United Kingdom Ministry of Defence, *The Joint Service Manual of the Law of Armed Conflict* (Ministry of Defence Joint Service Publication 383, 2004), pp. 21 and 23)

thinking points

- *What do you understand by 'collateral damage'?*
- *What does the principle of proportionality and distinction entail?*

12.8 Civilian objects and military objectives

So how does one determine what a civilian object is? By understanding what constitutes civilian objects and who should not be attacked, an overview as to military objectives comes to light. Under Article 51(2) AP I:

> The civilian population as such, as well as individual civilians, shall not be the object of attack. Acts or threats of violence the primary purpose of which is to spread terror among the civilian population are prohibited.

AP I goes further and prohibits indiscriminate attacks, which are considered to be:

> a) those which are not directed at a specific military objective;
> b) those which employ a method or means of combat which cannot be directed at a specific military objective; or
> c) those which employ a method or means of combat the effects of which cannot be limited as required by this Protocol;

and consequently, in each such case, are of a nature to strike military objectives and civilians or civilian objects without distinction. (Additional Protocol I, Article 51(4).)

Civilian objects and military objectives are also covered by AP I:

In so far as objects are concerned, military objectives are limited to those objects which by their nature, location, purpose or use make an effective contribution to military action and whose total or partial destruction, capture or neutralization, in the circumstances ruling at the time, offers a definite military advantage. (Additional Protocol I Article 52(2))

AP I also provides guidance for those situations where there may be doubt over the classification of a military objective:

In case of doubt whether an object which is normally dedicated to civilian purposes, such as a place of worship, a house or other dwelling or a school, is being used to make an effective contribution to military action, it shall be presumed not to be so used.

While it cannot be forgotten that AP I is not binding on all States, it is useful in helping to identify the kind of situations and objectives that may be applicable when determining whether something is a legitimate target or not during an armed conflict.

One of the biggest challenges in this area is determining whether something is proportional or not. There are no set criteria for determining how many casualties are acceptable or what degree of military advantage would justify the armed action. The real problem comes down to who is interpreting the proportionality. Military personnel are likely to put greater emphasis on the military aims and therefore may be more likely to accept a higher proportion of civilian loss. Whereas non-military individuals are more likely to emphasize the protection of civilians, striving for little to no casualties, with less emphasis and understanding of military objectives:

The key to the dilemma is the subjective nature of assessing proportionality. It requires balancing between two opposing goals: the swift achievement of the military goal with the minimum losses of one's own combatants and the protection of the other party's civilian population. The military are extremely unwilling to see the balance shift from the emphasis on the former (Judith Gardam, 'Proportionality and force in international law' [1993] 87 AJIL 391, 409)

This was the issue the ICTY had to consider when assessing whether the North Atlantic Treaty Organization (NATO) bombing of the Serbian Radio and Television (RTS) building constituted a military target. NATO bombed the building late at night to ensure the least number of civilians would be in the building. The reason for targeting the civilian building was that it was alleged the Serbian forces used this building as their backup communication network. Unfortunately, sixteen civilians died as a result of the bombing and the Serb armed forces were able to utilize another backup from a secret location.

As shown in the ICTY, Final Report to the Prosecutor by the Committee Established to Review the NATO Bombing Campaign Against the Federal Republic of Yugoslavia ((2000) 39 ILM 1257, 78–79), NATO knew that bombing the RTS building was strategically important to the Yugoslav command and control network.

In this instance, the dual use of a civilian building was considered and assessments were made as to the anticipated military advantage which would be achieved by its bombing in relation to the loss of civilian life.

thinking points

- *What may be classified as military objectives?*
- *Under what circumstances will a civilian institution be a legitimate military target?*

12.9 # Regulating weapons

Having looked at the principle of proportionality and distinction, attention will now be turned towards another form of regulating the conduct of warfare, that of the regulation of weapons. It has long been recognized that:

> The only legitimate object which States should endeavour to accomplish during war is to weaken the military forces of the enemy; That for this purpose it is sufficient to disable the greatest possible number of men; That this object would be exceeded by the employment of arms which uselessly aggravate the sufferings of disabled men, or render their death inevitable; That the employment of such arms would, therefore, be contrary to the laws of humanity (The St Petersburg Declaration Renouncing the Use, in Time of War, of Explosive Projectiles Under 400 Grammes Weight, 1868, Preamble)

This principle was included in the 1907 Hague Regulations through its recognition that:

> The right of belligerents to adopt means of injuring the enemy is not unlimited (Article 22 Hague Regulations 1907)

Article 23 of the Hague Regulations goes further in stipulating the kind of weapons prohibited:

> Besides the prohibitions provided by special Conventions, it is especially prohibited
>
> (a) To employ poison or poisoned arms;
>
> (b) To kill or wound treacherously individuals belonging to the hostile nation or army;
>
> (c) To kill or wound an enemy who, having laid down arms, or having no longer means of defence, has surrendered at discretion;
>
> (d) To declare that no quarter will be given;
>
> (e) To employ arms, projectiles, or material of a nature to cause superfluous injury;
>
> (f) To make improper use of a flag of truce, the national flag or military ensigns and uniform of the enemy, as well as the distinctive badges of the Geneva Convention;
>
> (g) To destroy or seize the enemy's property, unless such destruction or seizure be imperatively demanded by the necessities of war.

AP I develops the notion of 'superfluous injury' further and extends the prohibition to cover unnecessary suffering as well:

> It is prohibited to employ weapons, projectiles and material and methods of warfare of a nature to cause superfluous injury or unnecessary suffering. (Article 35(2))

Through regulating the kind of weapons employed during armed conflict, it is hoped to limit the related damage and suffering as much as possible while still accepting that suffering and destruction are not ever going to be completely eradicated from armed conflict due to its very nature and the use of force. It must also be taken into account that while there is general regulation in the form of the above, it remains subjective as to what is considered unnecessary suffering and superfluous injury. It is this subjective element which leads to various interpretations and different applications of IHL and its associated principles. Perhaps as a direct response to this there have been numerous treaties concluded over specific forms of weaponry. Some examples include the 1980 UN Convention on Prohibitions or Restrictions on the Use of Certain Conventional Weapons Which May be Deemed to be Excessively Injurious or to Have Indiscriminate Effects, the 1996 Amended Protocol II on Prohibition or Restriction on the Use of Mines, Booby-Traps and Other Devices, the 1997 Ottawa Convention on the Prohibition of the Use, Stockpiling, Production and Transfer of Anti-Personnel Mines and on their Destruction, and the 2008 Dublin Convention on Cluster Munitions. Protection has also been extended to include the environment by preventing its utilization as a method of warfare through the 1976 UN Convention on the Prohibition of Military or any Other Hostile Use of Environmental Modification Techniques. This includes the practice of modifying the environment as part of a military strategy which has negative long-term effects:

> Each State Party to this Convention undertakes not to engage in military or any other hostile use of environmental modification techniques having widespread, long-lasting or severe effects as the means of destruction, damage or injury to any other State Party. (Article 1(1))

Guidance as to what constitutes such environmental modification techniques is provided in Article 2:

> 'environmental modification techniques' refers to any technique for changing—through the deliberate manipulation of natural processes—the dynamics, composition or structure of the Earth, including its biota, lithosphere, hydrosphere and atmosphere, or of outer space.

435

KEY POINTS

- The 1907 Hague Regulations and many other treaties regulate the choice of weapons to be used in conflicts.

- Additional Protocol I forbids the use of weapons that can cause superfluous injuries and unnecessary suffering.

12.10 The International Committee of the Red Cross and its role

The ICRC is not a United Nations body but an independent international body. Established by five Swiss nationals, Henry Dunant being instrumental, in February 1863 the ICRC was the key player bringing together States at the Geneva Peace Conferences. Originally the ICRC played only a coordinating role that has expanded to include field operations and the ICRC is now regarded as a neutral intermediary providing humanitarian assistance and education. The ICRC is an authoritative body in terms of interpretation of IHL treaties and

State practice, and thus customary international law. It has undertaken in-depth studies on the current state of IHL and customary international law, as well as issues related to combatant status, ongoing conflicts, and the applicable laws. It also tries to help to protect civilians from the effect of armed conflict through the provision of humanitarian aid, while also providing the capacity to train both State and non-State actors in IHL in order to ensure compliance as much as possible. The role of the ICRC is broad, the organization itself describes the legal basis of its functions:

> The four Geneva Conventions and Additional Protocol I confer on the ICRC a specific mandate to act in the event of international armed conflict. In particular, the ICRC has the right to visit prisoners of war and civilian internees. The Conventions also give the ICRC a broad right of initiative.
>
> In non-international armed conflicts, the ICRC enjoys a right of humanitarian initiative recognized by the international community and enshrined in Article 3 common to the four Geneva Conventions.
>
> In the event of internal disturbances and tensions, and in any other situation that warrants humanitarian action, the ICRC also enjoys a right of initiative, which is recognized in the Statutes of the International Red Cross and Red Crescent Movement. Thus, wherever international humanitarian law does not apply, the ICRC may offer its services to governments without that offer constituting interference in the internal affairs of the State concerned. (ICRC Mandate and Mission, available at http://www.icrc.org/eng/who-we-are/mandate/overview-icrc-mandate-mission.htm)

 Conclusion

IHL is a cornerstone of international law. It strives to preserve life and order in times of utter chaos and anarchy. It is unrealistic to expect IHL to eradicate all forms of armed conflict. As with other fields of law, IHL has its own flaws most notably in terms of dealing with the modern forms of warfare and dealing with such issues as distinction between combatants and non-combatants, characterizing conflicts as international or non-international, and in ensuring compliance. Nonetheless, IHL has managed to achieve remarkable feats. States have continued to apply customary law and principles of IHL throughout the ages, and continue to codify new laws and restatements of many of the customs in the form of treaty obligations. Despite the limited application of IHL to non-international conflicts, the sheer fact that there has been a convention that specifically addresses such situations, which before were considered outside international law's scope, cannot be ignored.

Questions

Self test questions

1 Define the law of armed conflict.

2 Distinguish *jus ad bellum* from *jus in bello*.

3 When does an international armed conflict occur and to what extent do the requirements of international armed conflicts differ from internal armed conflicts?

4 What are military objects and objectives?

5 Who are unlawful combatants and what is the stance of IHL on this category?

6 How does IHL regulate the choice of weapons in hostilities?

Discussion questions

1 Customary international law plays a complementary role to IHL. Explain.

2 Trace the development of IHL from 1856 to 1949.

3 Explain the differences, if any, between armed conflict of international character and armed conflicts of non-international character.

4 Discuss the term 'collateral damage'.

5 Explain what you understand by proportionality and distinction.

6 Discuss civilian objects and military objectives.

Assessment question

Sagoe, the Chief of Army Staff of Candoma, is preparing the national army for a possible invasion of Rutamu over a disputed territory. Sagoe, a long-known adversary of Rutamu, has promised to 'give no quarter' to the enemy and utterly and comprehensively destroy them and everything they stand for. To ensure he delivers on his promise, Sagoe has ordered tons of chemical weapons, deadly projectiles, and many more weapons which he boasts will reduce Rutamu to ashes. As an international lawyer in the Ministry of Justice, Sagoe has summoned you and your colleague to deliberate on the impending war and the legality of the weapons he is about to issue to the members of Candoman armed forces.

Advise him.

 # Key cases

- *Prosecutor v. Duško Tadić*, Decision on the Defence Motion for Interlocutory Appeal on Jurisdiction (Interlocutory Appeal), Case No. IT-94-1-AR72, 2 October 1995 (the *Tadić Case*)
- *Prosecutor v. Delalić et al.* (Judgment), Case No. IT-96-21-T, ICTY, 16 November 1998 (the *Čelebići Case*)
- *Ex parte Quirin* 317 US 1 (1942)

# Further reading

Balendra, N., 'Defining armed conflict' (2007–08) 29 Cardozo L Rev 2461, 2472

Bar-Yaacov, N., 'Some aspects of prisoner-of-war status according to the Geneva Protocol I of 1977' (1985) 20 Israeli L Rev 243

Dahl, A. and Sanbu, M., 'The threshold of armed conflict' (2006) 45 Military Law and Laws of War Rev

369

Diallo, Y., *African Traditions and Humanitarian Law: Similarities and Differences* (Geneva: ICRC, 1976)

Gardam, J., 'Proportionality and force in international law' (1993) 87 AJIL 391

Gutteridge, J., 'The Geneva Conventions of 1949' (1949) 26 BYBIL 294

International Committee of the Red Cross, *International Humanitarian Law and the Challenges of Contemporary Armed Conflicts* (Geneva: ICRC, 2003)

Lauterpacht, H., 'The problem of revision of the law of war' (1952) 29 BYBIL 382

Moodrick-Even Khen, H., 'Case note: can we now tell what "direct participation in hostilities" is?' (2007) 40 Israeli L Rev 213

Pictet, J. S., *Geneva Convention for the Amelioration of the Condition of the Wounded and Sick in Armed Forces in the Field: Commentary* (ICRC, 1952), p. 32

Report of the Secretary-General Pursuant to Paragraph 2 of the Security Council Resolution 808 (UN Doc. S/25704, 3 May 1993), p. 35

Roberts, A. and Guelff, R., *Documents on the Laws of War* (3rd edn, Oxford: Oxford University Press, 2000)

Sandoz, Y., Swinarski, C., and Zimmermann, B., (eds), *Commentary on the Additional Protocols of 8 June 1977 to the Geneva Conventions of 12 August 1949* (Leiden: Martinus Nijhoff Publishers, 1987)

Schindler, D. and Torman, J., (eds), *The Laws of Armed Conflicts: A Collection of Conventions, Resolutions and Other Documents* (Dordrecht: Kluwer Academic Publishers, 1988)

Turns, D., 'The law of armed conflict' in M. Evans (ed.), *International Law* (3rd edn, Oxford: Oxford University Press, 2010), p. 837

United Kingdom Ministry of Defence, *The Joint Service Manual of the Law of Armed Conflict* (Ministry of Defence Joint Service Publication 383, 2004)

Zachary, S., 'Between the Geneva Conventions: where do unlawful combatants belong?' (2005) 38 Israel L Rev 378

State responsibility

Learning objectives

This chapter will help you to:

- understand what State responsibility is and its role in State relations;
- appreciate the different theories about State responsibility;
- recognize the rules governing State responsibility and how we apply them;
- learn the various consequences of responsibility; and
- appreciate the various defences against responsibility.

Introduction

States interact with one another on a daily basis. These interactions are governed by several rules of international law, whether established by treaties or custom. These rules consist of obligations, which are commitments undertaken by States to do—or refrain from doing—certain acts in relation to one another. Obligations can be moral, political, legal, or even social.

Nevertheless, in their relations with one another, States frequently breach their international obligations, whether knowingly or inadvertently. When a breach of an international obligation occurs, the offending State is known as the 'responsible State'; the wronged State is known as the 'injured State'. The breach itself is usually referred to as an 'internationally wrongful act'. Thus when a State breaches an international obligation against another State, the responsible State may be liable in international law to the injured State. State responsibility is therefore that aspect of international law which determines whether a State has breached its international obligations, by acts or omissions, the consequences arising as a result, and the circumstances in which responsibility may be excluded.

This chapter will examine the various rules dealing with when State responsibility arises, the consequences of breach of internationally recognized obligations, and defences against such breaches. All of these topics are dealt with by the 2001 International Law Commission Articles for Responsibility of States for Internationally Wrongful Acts.

13.1 The International Law Commission

The International Law Commission (ILC) was set up by the UN General Assembly in 1947 for the 'progressive development of international law and its codification', under Article 1(1) of the Statute of the International Law Commission (the ILC Statute), adopted by the UN General Assembly in Resolution 174(II) of 21 November 1947, as amended by Resolutions 485(V) of 12 December 1950, 984(X) of 3 December 1955, 985(X) of 3 December 1955, and 36/39 of 18 November 1981. In simple terms, the ILC is responsible for developing international law and for systematizing (that is, codifying) its rules. It consists of thirty-four members of recognized competence in international law; the representatives are appointed on their own merit and not as representatives of their States (Article 2(1) ILC Statute).

rapporteur

A technical specialist or an expert on a subject matter, who coordinates all works and activities in respect of such matters on behalf of a larger body.

In 2001, the ILC adopted its draft Articles on Responsibility of States for Internationally Wrongful Acts (ARSIWA). These draft Articles were the culmination of a long, tedious period of negotiation. As once observed by the Commission's first Special **Rapporteur** on State Responsibility, F. V. García Amador, in his 'First Report on International Responsibility' (1956) 2

YBILC 173, 175, para. 6 (UN Doc. A/CN.4/SER.A/1956/Add.1), 'it would be difficult to find a topic beset with greater confusion and uncertainty'.

KEY POINTS

- The ILC is the body responsible for the codification of international law. It comprises members appointed on their own merit, not as representatives of their States.

- The ILC Special Rapporteur on State Responsibility leads the process of developing and organizing the subject on behalf of the Commission.

13.2 Determining the internationally wrongful acts of a State

How do we know that a State has committed an internationally wrongful act? Since States are abstract entities and can do nothing by themselves, *who* can commit such acts on behalf of States? What does it mean, anyway, to say that a State has committed an 'internationally wrongful act'? We will seek, in this section, to answer these questions.

13.2.1 A breach of obligation entailing international responsibility

Part 1 ARSIWA sets out the general principles of State responsibility. As a general principle, a State is liable for its own acts or omissions.

Article 1 provides that 'every internationally wrongful act of a State entails the international responsibility of that State'. This means that once a State breaches its obligations, a series of consequences follow. The following pronunciations of international tribunals illuminate this principle.

....

● *Italy v. France (Preliminary Objections)* [1923] PCIJ SER. A/B, NO. 74 [The *Phosphate in Morocco Case*]

In this case, Morocco, acting with France, monopolized its phosphates to the detriment of Italian nationals interested in the materials. This, according to Italy, breached the obligations that Morocco owed to Italy under a convention in force between the two countries.

Commenting on Morocco's decision to monopolize the phosphate, the Permanent Court of International Justice (PCIJ) said (at 28) that:

> it is in this decision that we should look for the violation of international law—a definitive act which would, by itself, directly involve responsibility. This act being attributable to the State and described as contrary to the treaty right of another State, *international responsibility would be established immediately as between the two States*. [Emphasis added]

• *Great Britain v. Spain* [1925] 2 RIAA 615 [The *Spanish Zone of Morocco Claims*]

In this case (at 641) Judge Huber noted that:

> responsibility is the necessary corollary of a right. All rights of an international character involve international responsibility. *Responsibility results in the duty to make reparation if the obligation in question is not met.* [Emphasis added]

• *Germany v. Poland (Jurisdiction)* [1927] PCIJ Ser. A, No. 9
[The *Chorzów Factory Case*]

The Court declared (at 21) that 'it is a principle of international law that the breach of an engagement involved an obligation to make reparation'.

It must be noted, however, that, in order for a breach to entail responsibility, a State does not necessarily have to do anything. Mere omission to act is as good as performing a wrongful act.

• *United Kingdom v. Albania (Merits)* [1949] ICJ Rep 4 (The *Corfu Channel Case*)

This case arose from the explosion of certain British ships caused by mines in the Corfu Channel inside Albanian waters, on 22 October 1946. Britain argued that Albania failed in its obligation to notify all ships coming through the Corfu Channel, and that, as a result, it was responsible for the act.

The International Court of Justice (ICJ) found that Albania did nothing to notify Britain of the mines and declared (at 23) that 'these grave omissions involve the international responsibility of Albania'.

• *United States v. Mexico* [1931] RIAA 1 [The *Dickson Car Wheel Company Case*]

The USA brought a claim on behalf of a US company, Dickson Car Wheels, against Mexico. The company's rights to supply car wheels to the National Railways (of Mexico) were terminated when a new government in Mexico nationalized the railways. During the proceedings, counsel for the US company referred to the fact that certain persons who might have been able to throw some light on the issue were not called upon to testify.

Commenting on this assertion, the Claims Commission emphasized (at 668) that:

> that *omission* certainly would have been serious in its effect on the international responsibility of the Government of Mexico, if it had been established that the testimony of such persons was so important and decisive that its lack would have caused the failure of the investigation. [Emphasis added]

Unlike in the *Corfu Channel Case*, the omission of the Mexican government to call on a particular witness was not proved to be detrimental to the course of proceedings. Hence, that omission did not amount to the creation of international responsibility, because it did not constitute a breach of an obligation owed by Mexico in those circumstances.

KEY POINTS

- A breach of an international obligation entails an international responsibility of the responsible State.

- Acts and/or omissions can constitute breaches of international obligations that will entail international responsibility.

13.2.2 The conditions necessary for international responsibility

The next question is: how do we know when an internationally unlawful act is committed?

According to Article 2 ARSIWA, internationally wrongful acts arise when an act or omission:

(a) is attributable to the State under international law;

(b) constitutes a breach of an international obligation of the State.

Clearly, from these provisions, two conditions are necessary in order for an act or omission by a State to amount to an internationally unlawful act. First, the act or omission in question must be attributable to a State. This means that such act or omission must be deemed to have been committed by a State—a condition that we will explain shortly. Secondly, the act or omission must be a breach of an international obligation of that State. As already noted, an international obligation can be established between States, either by treaty or by customary international law.

● **United States v. Iran** (1980) ICJ REP 3 (The **Hostage Case**)

The ICJ said (at 28) that, in order to establish the responsibility of Iran:

> first, it must determine how far, legally, the acts in question may be regarded as imputable to the Iranian State. Secondly, it must consider their compatibility or incompatibility with the obligations of Iran under treaties in force or under any other rules of international law that may be applicable.

● **United States v. Mexico** (1931) RIAA 1 (The **Dickson Car Wheel Company Case**)

See section 13.2.1 for the facts.

The Mexico–US General Claims Commission noted (at 678) that:

> Under international law...in order that a State may incur responsibility it is necessary that an unlawful international act be imputed to it, that is, that there exist a violation of a duty imposed by an international juridical standard.

It should be noted that breaches of *international* obligations make a State incur responsibility against another State. International responsibility does not arise if a State breaches an obligation towards its own people, although in some circumstances breaches of obligations owed to one's citizens may lead to a breach of international human rights obligations. International responsibility is usually owed by international persons to one another and can be enforced on the international plane.

Attribution of acts or omissions to States

It is not everyone who is associated with a State that can act on behalf of that State. According to James Crawford, *The International Law Commission's Articles on State Responsibility: Introduction, Text and Commentaries* (Cambridge: Cambridge University Press, 2002; 'the 2002 ILC Commentary'), p. 91, international law avoids attributing the acts or omissions of any and everyone to the State:

> both with a view to limiting the responsibility to conduct which engages the State as an organization, and also as to recognize the autonomy of persons acting on their own account and not at the instigation of public authority.

Articles 4–11 ARSIWA supply a list of entities whose internationally unlawful acts may be attributed to States and under what circumstances—namely:

(a) organs of states;

(b) private individuals; and

(c) insurrectional, or rebel, groups.

The manner and processes by which acts of these entities can be attributed to States vary. While some are direct and explicit, others are less obvious.

13.3.1 Acts of organs of State

Article 4 ARSIWA states that:

> The conduct of any State organ shall be considered an act of that State under international law, whether the organ exercises legislative, executive, judicial or any other functions, whatever position it holds in the organization of the State, and whatever its character as an organ of the central government or of a territorial unit of the State.

States are abstract entities and can function only through human beings. In most democratic States, governmental powers are shared by three organs: the legislature; the executive; and the judiciary. Any internationally unlawful act of officials of any of these organs can therefore be imputed to the State in question.

However, there are circumstances in which internationally unlawful acts of State officials may not be imputed on States. For example, an act or omission committed by a government minister while on holidays may not be attributed to the State.

The rule that State organs can act on behalf of States is well entrenched in international law.

● *Claim of the Salvador Commercial Company* (1902) USFR 838

In this case, the Commission said (at 837) that:

> There can be no doubt...that a State is responsible for the acts of its rulers, whether they belong to the legislative, executive or judicial departments of the government, so far the acts are done in their official capacity.

• *Claims of Italian Nationals Resident in Peru* (1901) 15 RIAA 395

This case concerned injuries suffered by Italian nationals resident in Peru during the Peruvian civil war.

The Arbitral Tribunal noted (at 399) that it is:

> ...a universally recognized principle of international law...that the State is responsible for the violations of the laws of nations committed by its agents.

In order for acts of officials of a State to be imputed to that State, it is important to look at:

(a) the character of the act in question; and

(b) the nature of the function which the official is entrusted to discharge.

There is need to distinguish between private acts and official acts of government officials in order to determine attributability to the State. As illustrated by the following cases, such a distinction cannot always be presumed.

• *Mallén (United Mexican States) v. USA* (1927) 4 RIAA 173

See also Bin Cheng, *General Principles of Law as Applied by Courts and Tribunals* (Cambridge: Cambridge University, 2006), p. 200.

In this case, Deputy Constable Franco of Texas had personal grudges against the Mexican consul, Mallén. On a chance encounter between the two, the Constable assaulted Mallén, locked him up, and fined him US$50.

In a subsequent claim, the Mexican–US General Claims Commission held that the act of Mr Franco could not be imputed to the US government. According to the Commission (at 174):

> The evidence of the assault...clearly indicates a malevolent and unlawful act of a private individual who happened to be an official; not the act of an official.

Almost two months later, while on street patrol in El Paso, Constable Franco once again happened on Mr Mallén. He struck him a blow to the head, threatened him with his pistol, and took him to jail on a charge.

In a claim, the Commission held (at 177) that:

> it is essential to note that...both governments consider Franco's acts as the act of an official on duty...and that the evidence establishes his showing his badge to assert his official capacity. Franco could not have taken Mallén to jail if he had not been acting as a police officer. Though his act would seem to have been a private act of revenge which was disguised, once the first thirst of revenge has been satisfied, as an official act of arrest, the act as a whole can only be considered as the act of an official...

Obviously, the facts of the two scenarios in which Constable Franco struck Mr Mallén were similar. The same individuals were involved; the circumstances were virtually the same. However, the point of distinction in the two instances—and one that was crucial in establishing which of the two acts could be imputed to the US government—was the *nature* and *character* of the act. Clearly, when he committed the first act, Constable Franco had been at leisure: he did not assert his authority and official capacity either by flashing his badge or confronting Mallén with a pistol. He had acted as a private citizen. But when he committed the second act, he was in a patrol car, brandished his badge, and threatened Mallén with his pistol. All of these are acts consistent with his official status as a police officer.

thinking points

- List the two conditions necessary for the act of a State official to be imputed to a State.
- If you understand the point about distinguishing when a State official acts personally and officially, summarize the rationale for the two decisions in Mallén.

The importance of using the *character* and *nature* of the acts or omissions as the criteria for determining what acts are imputable to States also emerges when dealing with acts committed by State officials who may be acting under the guidance of an international organization.

As shown by the following cases from the European Court of Human Rights (ECtHR) and the UK courts, this is more complex than when dealing with acts of such officials vis-à-vis their States.

• •

● **Behrami and Behrami v. France** APPLICATION NO. 71412/01; **Saramati v. France, Germany and Norway** APPLICATION NO. 78166/01 (2007) 45 EHRR 10 (**Behrami and Saramati**)

In the first of these two separate, but merged, cases, Mr Agim Behrami and Mr Bekim Behrami were a father and son of Albanian origin. They lived in the municipality of Mitrovica in Kosovo, Republic of Serbia (prior to Kosovo's declared independence in February 2008). On 11 March 2000, eight boys, including Agim Behrami's children, were injured while playing, by bombs that had been dropped during the North Atlantic Treaty Organization (NATO) bombardment in 1999. The bombs killed Gadaf Behrami and seriously injured Bekim Behrami.

In the second case, Saramati complained of an extrajudicial detention by officers acting on the order of the Kosovo Forces (KFOR) between 13 July 2001 and 26 January 2002. In the consolidated case, the applicants claimed that since the respondent countries, France, Germany, and Norway, were the NATO member States responsible for the sector of operations in which the bomb detonation and Saramati's arrest took place, they were responsible for the acts.

In its decision, the ECtHR concluded (at [151]) that, since the UN Mission in Kosovo (UNMIK) was a subsidiary organ of the United Nations created under Chapter VII of the Charter of the United Nations (the UN Charter), and since KFOR was exercising powers lawfully delegated under Chapter VII by the UN Security Council, their actions were directly attributable to the UN.

Note that, in this case, the Court strongly favoured the fact that UNMIK was authorized by the UN. Consequently, France, Germany, and Norway could not be held responsible for the act, since, as individual States, they were not really in control of what the forces did and how they did it. UNMIK was in overall control of the situation and the acts complained of were therefore imputable to the UN.

However, the attempt to attribute certain acts to the UN, in circumstances that appear similar to those of *Behrami and Saramati*, was rejected by the English House of Lords in the next case.

The appellant, a national of the UK and Iraq, had been held in custody by British troops at detention facilities in Iraq since October 2004. He complained that his detention infringed his rights under Article 5(1) of the European Convention on Human Rights (ECHR), a Convention right also protected in the UK by the Human Rights Act 1998. Following rejection of the claims by the lower courts, Al Jedda appealed to the House of Lords.

Upon appeal and by agreement of the claimant, the British government raised a new issue: that the act in question was attributable to the UN and not the British government. If this argument succeeded, it would mean that the UK had not violated the claimant's Convention rights, as alleged, and that Al Jedda's detention could not be attributed to the UK.

As the House of Lords noted, the UK Secretary of State appeared to have been encouraged by the decision of the Grand Chamber of the ECtHR in *Behrami v. France* (as discussed in the previous case).

In considering whether the case fell within the same category as *Behrami and Saramati*, and consequently whether the unlawful detention of Al Jedda could be attributed to the UN, the House of Lords asked itself a series of questions: were UK forces placed at the disposal of the UN? Did the UN exercise effective control over the conduct of UK forces? Is the specific conduct of the UK forces in detaining the appellant to be attributed to the UN rather than the UK? Did the UN have effective command and control over the conduct of UK forces when they detained the appellant? And were the UK forces part of a UN peacekeeping force in Iraq?

On behalf of the court, Lord Bingham answered these questions in the negative. His Lordship went on to state (at 584) that:

> it has not, to my knowledge, been suggested that the treatment of detainees at Abu Ghraib was attributable to the UN rather than the US. Following UNSCR 1483 in May 2003 the role of the UN was a limited one focused on humanitarian relief and reconstruction, a role strengthened but not fundamentally altered by UNSCR 1511 in October 2003. By UNSCR 1511, and again by UNSCR 1546 in June 2004, *the UN gave the multinational force express authority to take steps to promote security and stability in Iraq, but (adopting the distinction formulated by the European Court in para 43 of its judgment in* Behrami and Saramati) *the Security Council was not delegating its power by empowering the UK to exercise its function but was authorising the UK to carry out functions it could not perform itself.* At no time did the US or the UK disclaim responsibility for the conduct of their forces or the UN accept it. It cannot realistically be said that US and UK forces were under the effective command and control of the UN, or that UK forces were under such command and control when they detained the appellant. [Emphasis added]

When analysing this case vis-à-vis *Behrami and Saramati*, it is important to remember that, in *Al Jedda*, the Law Lords reasoned that, when considering whether an act is attributable to a State or not, much depends on the nature of the official function and the character of the act committed, as already noted, but also on the *circumstances* in which the acts are committed. Here, although the United Nations was involved in the activities in Iraq at the relevant time, just as in *Behrami and Saramati*, the House of Lords emphasized that the UN's involvement was *limited* and *confined* to areas such as humanitarian relief. On the other hand, the UK, like other coalition States, had been given the powers to take direct charge of the situation. Therefore the detention of the claimant by British troops was imputable to the UK and not the UN in those circumstances.

KEY POINTS

- Where officials of a State commit internationally unlawful acts in the course of their duty under the direction and guidance of an international organization, such acts are attributed to the organization and not to the State.

- In addition to the character of the act and the nature of the function of State officials, we must also consider the circumstances under which the acts are committed, especially if there is an involvement of an international organization in the situation.

The status of officials of State organs

Article 4(1) ARSIWA does not distinguish between the status of government officials for the purpose of attributability. It does not matter whether an official is inferior or superior. This is obvious from the phrase 'whatever position it holds in the organization of the State . . .'.

As noted in the 2002 ILC Commentary (see section 13.3), at p. 96:

> Nor is any distinction made at the level of principle between the acts of 'superior' and 'subordinate' officials, provided they are acting in their official capacity . . . No doubt lower level officials may have a more restricted scope of activity and they may not be able to make final decision. But conduct carried out by them in their official capacity is nonetheless attributable to the State for the purpose of Article 4.

This observation reflects the trend that international tribunals have followed for nearly a century.

. . . .

● *United States of America v. Mexico* [1927] 4 RIAA 155 (*Massey*)

In this case, an American citizen was killed by a Mexican in Vera Cruz, Mexico. The killer, Saenz, was apprehended and put in a jail, from where he was unlawfully allowed to escape by a junior prison officer. On evidence, it was not shown that the appropriate officials took any step towards apprehending the accused person.

The State of Mexico rejected responsibility by arguing that the prison officer who facilitated the escape of the accused from prison was a junior officer, whose action could not be imputed to the State.

In response to this argument, Commissioner Nielson said (at 155–157) that:

> When misconduct of any official, whatever his status or rank, results in failure of a State to perform its international obligations, . . . to attempt by some broad classification to make a distinction between some 'minor' or 'petty' officials and other kinds of officials must obviously at times involve practical difficulties. Irrespective of the propriety of attempting to make any such distinction at all, it would seem that in reaching conclusions in any given case with respect to responsibility for acts of public servants, the most important considerations of which account must be taken are the character of the acts alleged to have resulted in injury to persons or to property, or the nature of functions performed whenever a question is raised as to their proper discharge.

. . . .

● *Britain v. Italy* [1954] 14 RIAA 21 (The *Currie Case*)

In this case, a British couple who lived in Italy had their property in that country confiscated by the Prefect of the Province of Milan and the property was badly damaged during the war. Great Britain claimed on behalf of the couple against the Italian government.

The Italian government argued that it was not responsible for all of the damage that occurred to the property, but only for that damage which was expressly mentioned in Article 78(4)(a) and (d) of the Italian Peace Treaty, and that all other losses were due to the neglect of the Milan government, which sequestrated the property.

The Anglo-Italian Conciliation Commission rejected this argument and held (at 24) that:

> in fact, even if one were to accept the interpretation which the Italian Government places upon paragraph 4 *(a)* and 4 *(d)* of the Peace Treaty, the responsibility of the Italian Government would still exist in either case, i.e., whether the sequestrator were able or unable to make arrangements in good time for the necessary repairs to be carried out.

See also *Great Britain v. Venezuela* (1903) 9 RIAA 349.

The character of State organs: regional, federal, or district

Furthermore, the provisions of Article 4(1) ARSIWA do not distinguish between organs of central, regional, and district governments for the purpose of determining international responsibility of a State. This is implied from the phrase 'whatever its characters as an organ of the central government or of a territorial unit of the State'. This provision is particularly important when dealing with federal States, although it applies equally to unitary systems of government, such as in the UK.

In countries with the federal system of government, such as the USA, powers are usually shared between the federal government, which is responsible for the whole country, and the subsidiary governments, which operate within individual sub-entities, usually also called States, and sometimes there are local authorities, which operate at even further sublevels. Normally, due to this power-sharing arrangement, the acts or omissions of the organ of a component unit (a State or local government) do not bind the country.

However, Article 4(1) ARSIWA removes the constitutional distinction between various levels of government in federal States for the purpose of a country incurring responsibility. Thus a breach of an international obligation by the State of New York will be regarded as an act of the US government, just as an internationally unlawful act committed by the Mayor of the London Borough of Hillingdon against another country can be imputed to the UK government. It thus means that international responsibility is an exception to whatever power-sharing constitutional arrangement exists within a State.

In the *Montijo (United States v. Colombia*, award of 26 July 1875), cited in John Bassett Moore, *History and Digest of International Arbitrations to which the United States has been a Party* (Washington: Government Printing Office, 1898), vol 2, 1421, the arbitrator stated, at 1440, that:

> 'a treaty is superior to the constitution, which latter must give way. The constitution of the republic must be adapted to the treaty, not the treaty to the law'.

● *France v. Italy* (1951) 13 RIAA 150 (The *Heirs of the Duc Guise Case*)

In this case, the Franco-Italian Conciliation Commission stated (at 161) that:

> for the purposes of reaching a decision in the present case it matters little that the decree of 29 August 1947 was not enacted by the Italian State but by the region of Sicily. For the Italian State is responsible for implementing the Peace Treaty, notwithstanding the autonomy granted to Sicily in internal relations under the public law of the Italian Republic.

● *France v. Mexico* (1929) 5 RIAA 534 (The *Estate of Hyacinthe Pellat Case*)

In this case, the arbitrator reaffirmed (at 536):

> the principle of international responsibility ... of a federal State for all acts of its separate States which give rise to claims by foreign States ... [which] cannot be denied, not even in cases where the federal Constitution denies the central Government the right of control over the separate States of the right to require them to comply, in their conduct, with the rules of international law.

Clearly, if international law were to have to concern itself with determining whether an act is done by the central, district, or regional unit of a given State, then there would be much uncertainty. It would be all too easy for States to avoid international responsibility by unlawfully acting through their regional or district authorities.

thinking points

- *What status should a State official possess before his or her unlawful act can be attributed to State?*
- *Do you think that it makes sense to allow acts of component units of a country, such as State or regional governments, to be imputable to the State?*

Apparatuses representing the State

Usually, organs of State are the legislative, executive, and judicial arms of the government. However, these three are only the broad categories. In practice, governmental functions are carried out by countless apparatuses and bodies. These include national drug enforcement agencies, private security firms, and so on, to which States often delegate their powers. The acts of such apparatuses are deemed to be acts of their States, even if such bodies do not explicitly fall under any of the three organs of the State.

Article 5 ARSIWA states that:

> The conduct of a person or entity *which is not an organ* of the State under Article 4 but which is empowered by the law of that State to exercise elements of the governmental authority shall be considered an act of the State under international law, provided the person or entity is acting in that capacity in the particular instance. [Emphasis added]

According to the ILC, *Articles on Responsibility of States for Internationally Wrongful Acts* (Cambridge: Cambridge University Press, 2001), also available at http://legal.un.org/ilc/texts/instruments/english/commentaries/9_6_2001.pdf, 'the 2002 ILC Commentary' at p. 100, these apparatuses:

> may include public corporations, semi-public entities, public agencies of various kinds and even, in special cases, private companies, provided that in each case the entity is empowered by the law of the State to exercise functions of a public character normally exercised by State organs, and the conduct of the entity relates to the exercise of the governmental authority concerned. For example, in some countries private security firms may be

contracted to act as prison guards and in that capacity may exercise public powers such as powers of detention and discipline pursuant to a judicial sentence or to prison regulations. Private or State-owned airlines may have delegated to them certain powers in relation to immigration control or quarantine.

The rationale behind this principle is that, since such bodies are empowered by the State, they serve, in a sense, as agents of the State in that capacity and their acts can be imputed to the State. As the German government observed during the 1930 Hague Conference on the Codification of International Law (reported in League of Nations, *Conference for the Codification of International Law: Bases of Discussion for the Conference Drawn up by the Preparatory Committee, Vol. III—Responsibility of States for Damage Caused in their Territory to the Person or Property of Foreigners* (C.75.M.69.1929.V, 1929), p. 90):

> when, by delegation of powers, bodies act in a public capacity, *e.g.*, police an area ... the principles governing the responsibility of the State for its organs apply with equal force. From the point of view of international law, it does not matter whether a State polices a given area with its own police or entrusts this duty, to a greater or less extent, to autonomous bodies.

● *Hyatt International Corp. v. The Government of the Islamic Republic of Iran* (1985) 9 IRAN–US CTR 72

Iran established an autonomous foundation for the purpose of holding property for charitable purposes under close governmental control, having as one of its powers the identification of appropriate property for seizure. On the question concerning the nature of the entity, the tribunal held (at 88–94) that the foundation was a public and not a private entity, and therefore within the tribunal's jurisdiction.

KEY POINTS

parastatal

A government-owned or State-owned corporation, company, or enterprise.

- Acts of government **parastatals**, and sometimes private actors, can be imputed to States even if these entities do not fall under a specific organ of government.

- Every State is entitled to designate its competent organs according to its own laws. However, the standards adopted by the State must conform to international law.

Acts in excess of authority

The various situations considered previously concern instances in which acts of State officials can be imputed to the State in question. One thing common to all of these instances is that, regardless of their status or the level of government for which they work, all of those officials act *within the authority* given to them by their respective States. Those who did not, such as the police officer discussed in the facts of *Mallén* (see earlier in this section), were found to have acted mainly in their private capacity.

Next to be discussed are situations in which State officials, or any other person or entity empowered to act on behalf of a State, act in excess of their authority—that is, ultra vires. Before we go further, it is important to emphasize that acting ultra vires is not the same thing as acting as a private individual. Whereas Constable Franco (in *Mallén*), a State official, acted in his private capacity when he first attacked Mr Mallén, this did not amount to an ultra vires action, because he acted outside his official capacity as a public official and did what he did as a private person.

Article 7 ARSIWA provides that:

> The conduct of an organ of a State or of a person or entity empowered to exercise elements of the governmental authority shall be considered an act of the State under international law if the organ, person or entity acts in that capacity, even if it *exceeds* its authority or contravenes instructions. [Emphasis added]

The rationale for this provision, according to the 2002 ILC Commentary (available at http://legal.un.org/ilc/texts/instruments/english/commentaries/9_6_2001.pdf), at p. 45, is to ensure that:

> The State cannot take refuge behind the notion that, according to the provisions of its internal law or to instructions which may have been given to its organs or agents, their actions or omissions ought not to have occurred or ought to have taken a different form. This is so even where the organ or entity in question has overtly committed unlawful acts under the cover of its official status or has manifestly exceeded its competence. It is so even if other organs of the State have disowned the conduct in question.

The necessity of this rule is based on the notion that to allow a State to claim that its officials act in excess of their authority is to open a Pandora's box. First, how will foreigners determine when a State official is acting *outside* his or her authority? Secondly, will that not make it very easy for States perpetually to commit unlawful acts without taking responsibility for their action? Thirdly, if a State were able to avoid responsibility simply by claiming that its officials acted beyond their authority, would that not negate the provision of Article 3 ARSIWA? This Article states that:

> The characterization of an act of a State as internationally wrongful is governed by international law. Such characterization is not affected by the characterization of the same act as lawful by internal law.

International tribunals have generally followed this principle, as will be shown in the following cases.

. . . .

● ***United States v. Great Britain*** [1924] 6 RIAA 138 (The ***Union Bridge Company Claim***)

Building materials shipped from New York were meant to be delivered to the Orange Free State in South Africa. However, before the ship's arrival, war broke out between Great Britain and the Orange Free State. The materials were wrongfully delivered to the British authorities through the mistake of the duty railway storekeeper.

In a suit to determine whether Britain was responsible, the Commission found that the materials had come into British possession by sheer mistake. Nonetheless, the Commission further ruled (at 141) that:

> it was certainly within the scope of Mr. Harrison's duty as Railway Storekeeper to forward materials by rail, and he did so under instructions which fix liability on His Britannic Majesty's Government. *That liability is not affected either by the fact that he did so under a mistake* as to the character and ownership of the material or that it was a time of pressure and confusion caused by war, or by the fact, which, on the evidence, must be admitted, that there was no intention on the part of the British authorities to appropriate the material in question. [Emphasis added]

Thus a mistake, even if innocent, has no bearing on the international responsibility of a State for ultra vires acts of its officials, provided that they act within their competence.

● *France v. Mexico* (1929) 5 RIAA 516 (The *Caire Case*)

Two Mexican military officers demanded a bribe from a French national, Mr Caire. When he refused to give the bribe the solders took him to a barracks and shot him dead. Mexico argued that although the culprits were its officers, they acted *beyond* their authority and, as such, their act could not be imputed to the State.

The Commission held (at 531) that:

> the two officers, even if they are deemed to have acted outside their competence ... and even if their superiors countermanded an order, have involved the responsibility of the State, since *they acted under cover of their status as officers and used means placed at their disposal on account of that status.* [Emphasis added]

● *Velásquez Rodriguez v. Honduras* (1988) INTER-AM CT HR SER. C, NO. 4

Manfredo Velásquez, a student at the National Autonomous University of Honduras, was arrested without a warrant by members of the Honduran armed forces and then tortured.

One of the questions for the Inter-American Court of Human Rights to determine was whether the acts of Honduras breached the American Convention on Human Rights. The Court answered in the affirmative. The Court said (at 296) that such a conclusion:

> ... is independent of whether the organ or official has contravened provisions of internal law or overstepped the limits of his authority: under international law a State is responsible for the acts of its agents undertaken in their official capacity and for their omissions, even when those agents act outside the sphere of their authority or violate internal law.

453

● *United States v. Mexico* (1926) 4 RIAA 110 (*Youmans' Claim*)

Three Americans worked for a British construction company in Mexico. A dispute arose between one Mexican labourer and his American supervisor over 12 cents. A mob, largely composed of Mexican labourers, attacked the house in which the Americans lived. The Mexican authorities ordered troops to protect the Americans and to dispel the riot. Instead, the troops joined the mob and opened fire, killing the three Americans.

One of the issues before the arbitration was whether Mexico was responsible for the act of its troops since they clearly acted beyond their authority.

Mexico put forward two interesting arguments in order to prove that it was not responsible for the act of the soldiers. First, it recalled a statement made by a subcommittee of the League of Nations Committee of Experts for the Progressive Codification of International Law. In the relevant passage, the subcommittee had said that a State *could not* be held responsible for illegal acts of its officials. Secondly, Mexico relied on a famous statement once made by Umpire Leiber that a State is not responsible for the malicious acts of soldiers committed in their private capacity.

The Commission acknowledged these two statements. However, it distinguished them from the issue raised in the case at hand. On the effect of the League Committee's statement, the Commission noted (at 116) that:

> it seems clear that the passage to which particular attention is called in the Mexican Government's brief is concerned solely with the question of the authority of an officer as defined by domestic law to act for his Government with reference to some particular subject. Clearly it is not intended

by the rule asserted to say that no wrongful act of an official acting in the discharge of duties entrusted to him can impose responsibility on a Government under international law because any such wrongful act must be considered to be 'outside the scope of his competency.' If this were the meaning intended by the rule it would follow that no wrongful acts committed by an official could be considered as acts for which his Government could be held liable.

On the second point, the Commission ruled (at 116) that it could not:

consider...the participation of the soldiers in the murder...acts of soldiers committed in their private capacity when it is clear that at the time of the commission of these acts the men *were on duty under the immediate supervision and in the presence of a commanding officer*. Soldiers inflicting personal injuries or committing wanton destruction or looting always act in disobedience of some rules laid down by superior authority. There could be no liability whatever for such misdeeds if the view were taken that any acts committed by soldiers in contravention of instructions must always be considered as personal acts. [Emphasis added]

Hence, Mexico was held liable for the acts of its soldiers.

KEY POINTS

- As far as the Commission in *Youmans' Claim* was concerned, the statement made by the League Committee referred only to a specific matter within a State and not to a general rule of international law absolving States from responsibility for ultra vires acts of their officials.

- There is a difference between officials who act ultra vires their authority and those who act in their private capacity. States are not responsible for the private acts of their officials.

thinking points

- *What is the difference between State officials acting in a private capacity and acting ultra vires for the purpose of imputing responsibility to States? (Compare Mallén and Youmans.)*
- *Why should a State be responsible for an ultra vires act of its officials?*

So far, we have considered circumstances in which acts of State officials can be imputed to States. We also discussed circumstances in which although a person is a State official, their unlawful act may not be imputed to the State. Now, let us consider when the acts of private individuals—that is, those who are not State officials and who ordinarily cannot act on behalf of the State—can be imputed to States.

13.3.2 Acts of individual persons

As a general rule, acts of private individuals cannot be imputed to States for reasons already explained earlier. However, there are two exceptions to this rule according to the ARSIWA: acts of 'instructed persons' and acts of 'directed (or controlled) persons'.

Article 8 ARSIWA states that:

> The conduct of a person or group of persons shall be considered an act of a State under international law if the person or group of persons is in fact acting *on the instructions* of, or *under the direction or control* of, that State in carrying out the conduct. [Emphasis added]

Thus acts of private individuals can be imputed to States if:

(a) such persons are *instructed* to act by the State; or

(b) such persons, in their actions, are being *directed* or *controlled* by the State.

But what do these terms mean in practice?

Acts of instructed persons

International law has long recognized that conduct of private persons who act under the instruction of a State are imputable to the State, even if such conduct is unlawful.

● *Great Britain v. United States* (1925) 6 RIAA 160 [*Zafiro*]

The claimants in this case were employees of the Manila Shipway Company and lived in the company's houses in a wharf. During a naval battle they fled to safety, leaving their property in charge of Filipino watchmen and Chinese employees of the company. On evidence, it was shown that the claimants' property was looted by, among others, the Chinese crew of a British ship, the *Zafiro*, moored at the company's wharf at the time. The ship was registered as a US vessel and the Chinese crew employed in the US merchant service.

The question before the arbitrator was whether the USA was responsible for the acts of its crew. The USA argued that, since the ship was registered as a merchant ship and not a public ship, its acts were not those of the USA and as such the USA could not be held liable.

In determining this question, the Commission stated (at 163) that:

> we have next to inquire whether at the time of the looting in question the Chinese crew *were under discipline and officered so as to make the United States responsible*, and to consider how far the United States would be chargeable for want of supervision by those who had or should have had the crew in charge under the circumstances. [Emphasis added]

The Commission held that the USA was responsible for the act of the *Zafiro* crew.

● *United States v. Mexico* (1951) 4 RIAA 265 [The *Stephen Case*]

A Mexican guard unlawfully killed an American national, Edward Stephens, on 9 March 1924. The culprit, Lorenzo Valenzuela, was detained by Mexican military authorities, but was later unlawfully discharged by an officer Hermôgenes Ortega. Valenzuela was never apprehended after his escape. Although Ortega was prosecuted and sentenced for the unlawful release of the accused, he was later acquitted by the Supreme Court of Justice of the State of Chihuahua. The USA alleged that Mexico was liable for the unlawful killing by Valenzuela, and for not protecting Stephens, not prosecuting Valenzuela, and not punishing Ortega.

The Commission found that the culprit, Valenzuela, was acting as a private citizen during the time of the murder. When the killing happened, he was part of a guard that was trying to preserve peace during a revolution in the State of Chihuahua.

However, the Commission emphasized that Valenzuela was, at this time, acting *under the direction* of a sergeant who had ordered him to stop the car in which Stephens was travelling. Thus (at 267) the Commission said that:

> Valenzuela when trying to halt the car acted in the line of duty. But holding that these guards were entitled to stop passengers on this road and, if necessary, to use their guns…does not imply that Valenzuela *executed this authorization of the law in the right way*. On the contrary, the use he made of his firearm would seem to have been utterly reckless…Being under the orders of a sergeant, the guards should have halted the car in accordance with his instructions…*Responsibility of a country for acts of soldiers in cases like the present one, in the presence and under the order of a superior, is not doubtful*. Taking account of the conditions existing in Chihuahua then and there, Valenzuela must be considered as, or assimilated to, a soldier. [Emphasis added]

Clearly, in these two cases, acts of private individuals were deemed to be acts of their States regardless of whether the acts in question were pursuant to government activity or not. Thus, in order for the act of a private individual to be imputed to a State, what is important is not that the act itself must be in relation to a government power or activity, but that the individual has been *instructed* to act by the concerned State.

As the ILC observes in its 2002 Commentary (see section 13.3), at p. 47:

> Most commonly, cases of this kind will arise where State organs supplement their own action by recruiting or instigating private persons or groups who act as 'auxiliaries' while remaining outside the official structure of the State. These include, for example, individuals or groups of private individuals who, though not specifically commissioned by the State and not forming part of its police or armed forces, are employed as auxiliaries or are sent as 'volunteers' to neighbouring countries, or who are instructed to carry out particular missions abroad.

KEY POINTS

- The crucial element for the act of an 'instructed person' to be attributed to a State is that such a person is a private individual, but one who acts under the instruction of a State, usually through an official of such State.

- The concerned act does not need to be a governmental act in the sense of being specifically for the benefit of the concerned State.

Acts of directed or controlled persons

The second class of private individuals whose acts can be imputed to States are those whose conduct is not authorized, but is either *directed* or *controlled* by the concerned State. In practice, this model of imputability is trickier than where private individuals are instructed by the State. Unlike the latter case, there is a requirement of 'directing' or 'controlling' of the private individual. The question, then, is: how do we prove that a State *directs* or *controls* the conduct of private individuals, for the purpose of imputability? What degree of direction or control by the State will suffice to make it responsible for acts of private individuals that it has not authorized?

● *Nicaragua v. United States (Merits)* (1986) ICJ Rep 14 (The *Nicaragua Case*)

Nicaragua brought an action against the USA alleging that the latter was supporting insurrection by a Nicaraguan rebel group, the Contras, against the Nicaraguan government. One of the issues confronted by the ICJ was whether the USA was responsible for the violations of humanitarian law committed by the rebel group. In order to answer this question, the Court had to determine whether the USA was in control of the Contras and, if it was, to what degree.

The Court held the USA responsible for the 'planning, direction and support' that it gave to the Contras, but rejected that the USA was responsible for *all* of the conduct of the rebel group. In the Court's analysis, merely supporting the group by providing direction and planning assistance did not, in itself, amount to such degree of control as to warrant US responsibility for all the conduct of the Contras.

According to the Court (at [64]–[65]):

> ... all the forms of United States participation mentioned above, and even the general control by the respondent State over a force with a high degree of dependency on it, would not in themselves mean, without further evidence, that the United States directed or enforced the acts contrary to human rights and humanitarian law alleged by the applicant State. Such act could well be committed by members of the *contras* without the control of the United States. For this conduct to give rise to legal responsibility of the United States, it would in principle have to be proved that that State had *effective control* of the military or paramilitary operations in the course of which the alleged violations were committed. [Emphasis added]

From this statement, it is clear that the Court did not apply a broad or general control test, but rather applied an *effective control* test. While the Court did not precisely define what 'effective control' means in this context, it made it clear that it was a kind of control that was linked *specifically* to the alleged violation complained about by Nicaragua. As far as the Court was concerned, the mere fact that the USA provided a general control to the Contras was not sufficient to hold it responsible for the acts of humanitarian violations; after all, the Court said, the Contras could have committed these acts without the control of the USA.

Does this mean that 'effective control' exists only where the conduct for which a State is to be held responsible would not have been committed without *that* control?

The ICJ answered this question affirmatively in *Nicaragua*—but the Court's approach has been challenged.

● *Prosecutor v. Tadić Case No.* IT-94-1 (1999) 38 ILM 1518

The International Criminal Tribunal for the former Yugoslavia (ICTY) grappled with whether acts of a private individual, Mr Tadić, could be attributed to Yugoslavia.

In determining the requisite degree of control for imputability, the tribunal stated (at 1541) that:

> The requirement of international law for the attribution to States of acts performed by private individuals is that the State exercises control over the individuals. The degree of control may, however, vary according to the factual circumstances of each case. The Appeals Chambers fails to see why in each and every circumstance international law should require a high threshold for the test of control.

457

In *Tadić*, the ICTY applied the *overall* control test, contrary to the ICJ's *effective* control test in *Nicaragua*. What the tribunal was saying, unlike the Court, was that, in determining the responsibility of a State for acts of private individuals, the important question is whether the State is in *overall control* of the person who commits the act; it is not necessary to prove that the State is in *effective* control of the person when the *particular* unlawful act is committed. For the tribunal, it does not make any sense to seek different degrees of control for each and every case, even if we agree that the degree of control that a State may exercise in each case varies according to the facts.

As a matter of analysis, the tribunal's approach appears very persuasive. However, it seems that the tribunal was mistaken in its grounds for rejecting the ICJ's *effective control* test, for one principal reason. In *Nicaragua*, the Court was dealing with a specific issue concerning the imputability of an action to a State; what the ICTY was concerned with in *Tadić* was determining the individual criminal responsibility of persons accused of committing international crimes during the Yugoslavian conflict, not the responsibility of the State, which was the issue in *Nicaragua*. It might be that the difference in the tasks of the Court and the tribunal explains the difference in the approach of these bodies to the issues at hand.

How has the ICJ responded, if at all, to the requisite control test after *Tadić*? In other words, has the Court embraced the more liberal approach of *Tadić* or held on to the restrictive approach in *Nicaragua*?

. . . .

● **Bosnia v. Serbia** (2007) ICJ REP 43 (The **Bosnian Genocide Case**)

The ICJ had to decide whether Serbia was responsible for unlawful acts committed by private groups during the Bosnia and Herzegovina crisis.

The Court said (at 205) that:

> Persons or entities may, for the purposes of international responsibility, be equated with State organs even if that status does not follow from internal law, provided that in fact the persons, groups or entities act in 'complete dependence' on the State, of which they are ultimately merely the instruments.

Bosnia asked the Court specifically to reject the 'effective control' test that it applied in *Nicaragua* in favour of the ICTY 'overall control' in *Tadić*, especially given that the crimes that these groups were alleged to have committed amounted to genocide, for which Bosnia wanted Serbia to be held responsible.

The Court declined. It emphatically stated (at 208) that:

> The particular characteristics of genocide do not justify the Court in departing from the criterion elaborated in... [*Nicaragua v. United Stated of America*]... the rules for attributing alleged internationally wrongful conduct to a State do not vary with the nature of the wrongful act in question...

Obviously, rather than depart from the 'effective control' test that it had laid down in *Nicaragua*, the Court affirmed it in the *Bosnian Genocide Case*. Furthermore, the Court maintained, in a veiled response to the ICTY decision in *Tadić* perhaps, that the rule for determining the imputability of acts to States does not vary with the nature of the act itself which, ironically, seems to be what the ICTY postulated, although applying a different standard. Thus, conclusively, the test for attributing acts of private persons to States remains that of *effective control*.

For an excellent discussion of the issues tackled here, see Antonio Cassese, 'The *Nicaragua* and *Tadić* test revisited in light of the ICJ judgment on genocide in Bosnia' (2007) 18(4) EJIL 649.

thinking points

- *Summarize the difference between acts of instructed persons and acts of directed or controlled persons, with regard to the attributability of international unlawful acts.*
- *Between the ICJ's approach in* Nicaragua *and* Bosnia Genocide *and that of the ICTY in* Tadić, *which do you prefer and why?*
- *Do you think that the test of overall control provides a better solution than that of effective control? Which do you think provides greater stability for the jurisprudence of the ICJ?*

Having dealt with the imputability of private acts to States, we will now move on to other acts that can amount to the international responsibility of States.

13.3.3 Acts done in the absence or default of official authority

In all of the situations considered previously, imputability derives either from a situation in which States authorize, direct, or control individuals or entities, or one in which State organs act on behalf of the State.

However, Article 9 ARSIWA deals with situations in which internationally unlawful acts are carried out in the *absence* or *default* of State officials. According to that provision:

The conduct of a person or group of persons shall be considered an act of a State under international law if the person or groups of persons is in fact exercising elements of governmental authority in the absence or default of official authorities and in circumstances such as to call for the exercise of those elements of authority.

In order to appreciate the situation to which this provision applies, it is important to imagine a series of scenarios. In the situations of revolution, civil war, or general civil disorder in a country, instability may occur; some aspects of government may be absent. Immigration controls, general policing, and the protection of lives and property, for example, may all be affected.

In any such situation, it may fall on ordinary citizens to defend the country, or to run State institutions fully or partially until such time as normalcy returns.

However, in order for conduct carried out during these times to be attributed to States, three elements must be present, as follows.

(a) The conduct in question *must be governmental*.

This means that the conduct must relate solely to governmental functions.

example

When, during a national revolution, certain members of the National Association of House Painters of Candoma decide to repaint all foreign embassies in Candoma in the Candoman national colour, such an act cannot be imputed to the State.

(b) The conduct must be carried out in the *absence* or *default* of official authorities.

For Article 9 ARSIWA to apply, it is not enough that the person(s) in question carry out governmental functions; they must do so in the absence or default of relevant State officials.

interregnum

A situation in which, although all governmental structures are in place, there is no leadership clearly in charge of running the State.

'Absence' denotes a total collapse, or non-existence, of the State function in question—a very rare occurrence in contemporary politics. Somalia is often treated as a collapsed State because there is absence of an effective government, or functional governmental structures and institutions, and this provision might apply.

'Default', however, connotes something lesser than 'absence'. A default case may occur during an **interregnum**, such as the situation in Nigeria in 1966.

example

Following a military coup d'état in Nigeria in 1966, the head of State, Major General Aguiyi Ironsi, was captured. For a few days, the entire nation (other than his capturers) did not know where the head of State was. A new head of State was not appointed, because the nation was in disarray. Effectively, Nigeria was in interregnum until the condition of the head of State was confirmed (he had been killed) and another was appointed.

If civil defence groups had emerged during this time to protect lives and property in the absence of a functional government, or had taken over the task of clearing the immigration status of people entering and departing the country at the time, such governmental activities as might have been performed by these groups would be imputable to Nigeria under Article 9 ARSIWA.

(c) The circumstances must have called for governmental powers to be exercised.

This is a vital element of Article 9. Thus while conduct must relate to governmental authority and be carried out in the absence or default of the relevant government officials, such conduct must fill a vacuum, not the fantasy of the doers—that is, there must be a genuine need for the exercise of governmental authority at that moment.

KEY POINTS

- There are three requisite elements for applying Article 9 ARSIWA: governmental functions; absence or default; and a call for power to be exercised.

- An Article 9 situation is rare, although it may occur from time to time.

13.3.4 Acts of rebel or insurrectional groups

Situations do arise in which groups agitate for governmental powers. These groups may stage a revolution, which may or may not succeed in replacing the government. The Contras in Nicaragua (1984), the Islamic Revolutionary Guard in Iran (1979), the African National Congress during the apartheid regime in South Africa (1960–94), and the National Patriotic Front of Liberia (NPFL; 1989–2003) are all recent examples of insurrectional, or rebel, groups that either succeeded or failed in replacing the governments of their respective countries.

The question is whether the conduct of such groups can be imputed to the State. This query is important for the following reasons. Not all insurrectional groups succeed in gaining control of the State. If they succeed in becoming *the* State, it is natural that they accept responsibility for acts done when they were revolting against the government of the day. However, if they do not succeed, or if they succeed only in controlling *parts* of the State, then a difficult question of imputability of their conduct arises. Rebel groups often direct their activities *against* States. Thus the question is: should States be held responsible for conduct directed against them or, as is often the case, conduct intended to destroy the existing order altogether?

Article 10 ARSIWA addresses the various situations, providing thus:

1. The conduct of an insurrectional movement which becomes the new government of a State shall be considered an act of that State under international law.
2. The conduct of a movement, insurrectional or other, which succeeds in establishing a new State in part of the territory of a pre-existing State or in a territory under its administration shall be considered an act of the new State under international law
3. This article is without prejudice to the attribution to a State of any conduct, however related to that of the movement concerned, which is to be considered an act of that State by virtue of articles 4 to 9.

The general rule is that conduct by insurrectional movements is not imputable to States, mainly because such conduct is generally directed *against* the State. Furthermore, since rebel groups usually operate independently of the State, the State exerts no authority whatsoever over them.

International tribunals have consistently affirmed this principle.

. . . .

● *USA v. Great Britain* [1920] 6 RIAA 42 [The *Home Missionary Society Claim*]

The USA brought an action against the UK for loss of the lives of American missionaries in Sierra Leone. At the relevant time, Sierra Leone was a British protectorate. The British government had imposed a 'hut tax' on the native Sierra Leoneans, which was resisted, leading to several days of revolt.

In response to the US claim that the UK should have known that the imposition of the tax would lead to riots, the Commission held (at 44) that:

it is a well-established principle of international law that no government can be held responsible for the act of rebellious bodies of men committed in violation of its authority, where it is itself guilty of no breach of good faith, or of no negligence in suppressing insurrection.

(See also: *Moore's International Law Digest*, Vol. VI, p. 956, and Vol. VII, p. 957; *Moore's Arbitrations*, pp. 2991–2; *British Answer*, p. 1; and *American Agent's Report*, p. 425.)

● **United States v. Mexico** (1928) 4 RIAA 358 (The **Soli Case**)

The USA claimed from Mexico compensation for cattle allegedly stolen from the ranch of Soli, a US national, by some Mexican insurgent troops during a revolution. Mexico denied liability for the conduct of the revolutionary forces even though its national troops stationed within the locality of the ranch did nothing to prevent the theft.

Commissioner Nielsen relied on the *Home Missionary Case* to hold that Mexico could not be held liable for the conduct of insurgent troops, regardless of whether it was itself not guilty of a breach of good faith, nor of negligence in suppressing insurrection.

At 362, Commissioner Nielsen referred to the opinion of Mr Frank Plumley, the Umpire in *United Kingdom v. Venezuela* (1903), who made reference to the following provision found in a treaty concluded in 1892 between Germany and Colombia, as declaratory of international law:

> [it] is also stipulated between the contracting parties that the German Government will not attempt to hold the Colombian Government responsible, unless there be due want of diligence on the part of the Colombian authorities or their agents, for the injuries, oppressions, or extortions occasioned in time of insurrection or civil war to German subjects in the territory of Colombia, through rebels, or caused by savage tribes beyond the control of the Government.

See also J. H. Ralston and W. T. Sherman Doyle, *Venezuelan Arbitrations of 1903* (Washington DC: GPO, 1904), p. 38.

● **Italy v. Venezuela** (1903) 10 RIAA 499 (The **Sambaggio Case**)

In this case concerning the claim by Italy for damages caused to its nationals during an unsuccessful revolution in Venezuela, the Italy–Venezuela Mixed Claims Commission rejected Italy's claims on the grounds (at 499) that:

> a. revolutionaries are not agents of government, and no natural responsibility exists;
> b. their acts are committed to destroy the government, and no one should be held responsible for acts of an enemy attempting his life;
> c. the revolutionaries were beyond governmental control, and the government cannot be held responsible for injuries committed by those who have escaped its restraints

As explained earlier, where an insurrectional group succeeds, its conduct during its revolutionary phase will be imputed to it as a State. The movement replaces the State, just as the leadership and organization of the movement replace that of the State. Thus it is a matter of common sense that the continuity of the organization of the State by that of the movement translates into imputing conduct of the movement to the new State. Article 10(1) ARSIWA recognizes this rule.

The Preparatory Committee (League of Nations, 1929, see section 13.3.1), p. 108, addressed the question of whether acts of successful revolutionary groups should be attributed to governments. The response by governments, at p. 116, formed the basis of discussion by the Committee thus:

> [a] State is responsible for damage caused to foreigners by an insurrectionist party which has been successful and has become the Government to the same degree as it is responsible for damage caused by acts of Government *de jure* or its officials or troops.

● *Yaeger v. Iran* (1987) 17 Iran–US CTR 92

The claimant, who was expelled by members of the revolutionary guard, was entitled to compensation from the State of Iran. Although the Commission acknowledged that the revolutionary guard was not in charge of Iran at the time that the expulsion was committed, nonetheless its act was attributable to the new State.

● *Shott v. The Republic of Iran* (1987) 16 Iran–US CTR 76

A US national brought an action against Iran. He claimed that he was forced to leave Iran due to direct threats to his person by private individuals during the 1979 revolution in the country.

The Commission agreed that, as a general principle, conduct by the revolutionary guard was imputable to the State of Iran, because the revolution succeeded. However, the particular conduct complained of here was done by private individuals, not by officials of the revolutionary guard; therefore, the State of Iran—which was not being governed by the movement—could not be held responsible for their acts.

The success of a revolutionary movement, which becomes a new State, should not be confused with a situation in which the old State and the revolutionary movement conclude a peace agreement. A peace agreement does not constitute the revolutionary movement into a new State, even if some of its members are incorporated into the existing government. This is an effort to broker peace, not a replacement of the government by the movement. In this scenario, the State cannot be held responsible for the conduct of an insurrectional group, unless it so decides.

KEY POINTS

- As a general rule, conduct of rebel movements is not imputable to States because: (a) such acts are directed against the State; and (b) States have no control over insurrectional groups.

- Conduct of revolutionary movements that become governments is attributable to the new States emerging from the revolutions.

We have seen previously that, under Article 10(1) ARSIWA, where rebel movements succeed in becoming the State, they will be held responsible for conduct during their revolt. Article 10(2) deals with situations in which a rebel movement succeeds, but only in establishing control over parts, not the whole, of the territory. Examples include secession, which is the breaking away of one part of a country from the rest.

example

In 1967, the Eastern Region of Nigeria broke away from the country, adopting instead the name the 'Biafra Republic'.
   In 1960, the Katanga region broke away from the Republic of Zaire (now the Democratic Republic of Congo).

When secession occurs, the rule of continuity of State, explained earlier, means that the new government (which was previously a rebel movement) will be responsible for the acts done in that part of the country that it subsequently administers. But in terms of the conduct of the group in relation to those parts of the country that it did not succeed in controlling, these acts will be treated as under the general rule and such conduct cannot be imputed to the new State.

Nonetheless, upon becoming the new State, some insurrectional groups generously accept responsibility for conduct *directed against them* by the previous government, even though they are under no obligation to do so.

● *Minister of Defence, Namibia v. Mwandinghi* (1992) 2 SA 355

In this case the new government of Namibia accepted responsibility for 'anything done' by the predecessor administration of South Africa (at 360).

thinking points

- *What is the general principle governing imputability of conduct of insurrectional groups to a State?*
- *To what extent can the unlawful acts of a rebel movement that is successful in controlling parts of a State be imputed to the State?*
- *Distinguish between* Shott v. Iran *and* Yaeger v. Iran. *Are you convinced by the Commission's rationale in* Shott?

13.3.5 Attribution by acknowledgement

The final rule to be considered in attributing internationally unlawful acts to States is 'acknowledgement'. The basis of attribution under this heading differs from those discussed earlier, in that it applies to conduct that is not otherwise attributable to States under any other rules.

Article 11 ARSIWA provides that:

Conduct which is not attributable to a State under the preceding articles shall nevertheless be considered an act of that State under international law if and to the extent that the State acknowledges and adopts the conduct in question as its own.

Under this rule, a State decides, on its own, to accept responsibility for an internationally unlawful act for which it is otherwise not liable.

In most cases, conduct attributed to States under this rule will be that of private entities or individuals, although occasionally the conduct of groups can also fall under the category.

● *France v. Greece* (1956) 23 ILR 299 (The *Lighthouses Arbitration*)

The facts of this case relate to a dispute between France and Greece over a concession. At the relevant time, the concession was initiated by Crete, an autonomous entity under the Ottoman Empire.

It was held that Greece was liable on the basis, among others, that it had endorsed the transaction and taken over the island of Crete. The arbitration regarded Greece as a successor to Crete and, having taken over the administration of the lighthouses, treated the concession as its own.

As shown in this case, acknowledgement does not have to be by a formal proclamation; condoning an unlawful act may also constitute sufficient acknowledgement. And where condoning is combined with a formal statement of approval, the evidence of acknowledgement is even stronger.

example

Al Qaeda had been known to operate within the State of Afghanistan under the Taliban regime prior to the 11 September 2001 attacks on the USA (known as '9/11'). Thus the fact that the group operated within Afghanistan led to the imputability of Al Qaeda's acts of terrorism against the USA to Afghanistan.

13.4 Theories of imputability

The next issue to consider is whether it is necessary to prove that a State has been negligent or at fault in order to hold it responsible for an internationally wrongful act. Put differently: is the mere fact that a State has committed an internationally unlawful act sufficient to establish liability, or is it necessary also to establish negligence or fault?

Customary international law recognizes two theories for holding States responsible for internationally unlawful acts. The first, which can be described as a 'strict liability' rule, posits that a State is liable for an internationally unlawful act regardless of its intention. Thus whether the State is negligent, acts in good faith, or intends the act is immaterial; what is important is that an internationally unlawful act has occurred. This is called 'objective responsibility', or 'risk theory'. In opposition to this is the 'subjective responsibility', or 'fault theory', under which a State is responsible for an internationally wrongful act only if it intentionally causes the unlawful act (*dolus*) or if it is negligent in doing so (*culpa*).

13.4.1 The objective responsibility, or risk theory

Most arbitral tribunals and writers lean more favourably towards the principle of objective responsibility.

. . . .

● *France v. Mexico* (1929) 5 RIAA 516 (The *Caire Claim*)

Mexican soldiers killed a French national who had failed to give them a bribe. France brought a claim against Mexico for compensation on behalf of its national. Despite proof that the soldiers operated without orders from their superior, the Commission held Mexico liable for their action.

In considering the liability of Mexico, the Commission applied the objective principle, stating that:

> the doctrine of 'objective responsibility' of the State, that is responsibility for the acts of the officials or organs of a State . . . may devolve upon it even in the absence of any 'fault' of its own . . .

• **Great Britain v. United States of America** [1921] 6 RIAA 57 (**The Jesse**)

US officers boarded British vessels that were hunting for seals in the North Pacific Ocean and searched for sealskins. Failing to find sealskins, the officers seized firearms that they found on the British vessels. There was no agreement between the USA and Great Britain permitting such a search.

The USA conceded that the search by its officers was illegal, but rejected liability on the grounds that the officers had acted in good faith and without fraud.

Affirming the responsibility of the USA, the Commission said (at 59) that:

> It is unquestionable that the United States naval authorities acted bona fide, but though their bona fides might be invoked by the officers in explanation of their conduct to their own Government, its effect is merely to show that their conduct constituted an error in judgment, and any Government is responsible to other Governments for errors, in judgment of its officials purporting to act within the scope of their duties and vested with power to enforce their demands.

• **United States v. Great Britain** [1921] 6 RIAA 60 (**The Argonaut**)

Canada, a British colony at the time, seized some US vessels fishing within a three-mile limit of Canadian waters. By Article 1 of the Treaty of London, concluded with Great Britain on 20 October 1818, the USA renounced all rights in Canadian territorial waters.

The USA brought an action for compensation and argued that its fishermen acted in good faith. The Court rejected the claim. The Commission stated (at 63) that:

> ...the question whether or not, under the circumstances of these cases, taking into consideration the good faith of the fishermen and the exact character of their acts, a proper interpretation and application of the Canadian law was made by the Canadian court is a question of municipal law *and not a question of international law to be decided by this Tribunal*, so far as these cases stand. [Emphasis added]

Thus, as with *The Jesse*, the Court applied the objective responsibility principle. The judgment of the tribunal here shows that where the matter comes before a domestic tribunal, domestic law may determine the basis for, and the level of, responsibility involved in a given case.

13.4.2 Subjective responsibility (fault or negligence)

• **USA v. Great Britain** [1920] 6 RIAA 42 (The **Home Missionary Society Claim**)

See section 13.3.4 for the facts.

The USA argued that the UK was responsible for the loss of American lives and property because, according to the USA (at 43):

> it was within the knowledge of the British Government that this tax was the object of deep native resentment; that in the face of the native danger the British Government wholly *failed to take proper steps for the maintenance of order* and the protection of life and property; that the loss of life and damage to property was the result of this *neglect and failure of duty*, and therefore that it is liable to pay compensation. [Emphasis added]

In its response, the Commission said that a State cannot be held responsible for acts of insurrectional groups without its own fault or negligence (see earlier). In addition, it said (at 44) that:

> the good faith of the British Government cannot be questioned, and as to the conditions prevailing in the Protectorate there is no evidence to support the contention that it failed in its duty to afford adequate protection for life and property.

Clearly, the Commission had relied on the principle of subjective responsibility in coming to these conclusions.

However, we must be careful when interpreting the Commission's statement in *Home Missionary* that a State cannot be held responsible for the conduct of an insurrectional group. As we noted earlier, certain conduct of insurrectional groups is not imputable to States and it was such conduct that was in question in that case. Hence, it is doubtful whether the Commission was actually laying down a general principle of subjective responsibility.

· ·

● *United Kingdom v. Albania* (1949) ICJ REP 4 (The *Corfu Channel Case*)

Two British warships were destroyed by mines in the Corfu Strait, causing the death of forty-four and injuries to forty-two British officers and personnel. One of the grounds for Britain's action for compensation from Albania was that the mines were laid with the knowledge of Albania and that the latter also failed to warn foreign ships of the danger.

The ICJ held that Albania was responsible for the consequences of minelaying. The Court was of the opinion, in accordance with evidence before it, that Albania had knowledge of the mines and failed to warn other States, thereby breaching its international obligation.

In determining the question of the fault or negligence of Albania, the Court leaned favourably towards the subjective responsibility principle.

The Court stated (at 18) that:

> It cannot be concluded from the mere fact of the control exercised by a State over its territory and waters that that State necessarily knew, or ought to have known, of any unlawful act perpetrated therein, nor yet that it necessarily knew, or should have known, the authors. This fact, by itself and apart from other circumstances, neither involves *prima facie* responsibility nor shifts the burden of proof.

Thus, whereas the evidence before the ICJ with regard to Albania's knowledge of the mines led to Albania's responsibility, the Court also considered whether Albania was negligent in its failure to communicate to foreign States the fact that there were mines in its waters.

We must be careful not to confuse 'subjective responsibility' with a State's failure to adopt a particular level of diligence that may be considered desirable in a particular case.

· ·

● *United States v. Mexico* (1926) 4 RIAA 60 (The *Neer Claim*)

A US national working in Mexico was killed by a group of armed Mexicans. The USA brought a claim on behalf of the widow and daughter of the deceased, citing the alleged lackadaisical manner in which the Mexican authorities handled the matter. As far as the USA was concerned, Mexico was liable. Applying objective responsibility, the Commission did not find Mexico liable.

While the Commission accepted that there might have been lapses in the Mexican approach and that different methods could have been adopted, it did not agree that failing to use one

particular method was synonymous with negligence. Consequently, the Commission said (at 61) that, in its view:

> there is a long way between holding that a more active and more efficient course of procedure might have been pursued, on the one hand, and holding that this record presents such lack of diligence and of intelligent investigation as constitutes an international delinquency, on the other hand.

While subjective responsibility demands that the State in question must have incurred liability not only by its act or omission, but also by the manner in which such act or omission occurred, it does not require that the State must have acted in a *particular* way, failing which it would become internationally responsible.

---

thinking points

- *Explain the difference between subjective and objective theories of responsibility. (Consider* Caire, Home Missionary, *and* Corfu Channel *in your answer.)*
- *Which theory do you think States are likely to find more attractive and why?*

13.4.3 The value of theories of responsibility and ARSIWA

There is no provision in ARSIWA that refers to fault theories, although customary international law seems to support both theories discussed. A good approach is perhaps to treat each case on its own merit, instead of looking for a generalized theory of responsibility.

It is both difficult and illusory to seek a single acceptable or dominant theory of responsibility. As James Crawford and Simon Olleson have argued, in their chapter 'The nature and forms of international responsibility' in Malcolm Evans (ed.), *International Law* (3rd edn, Oxford: Oxford University Press, 2010), at p. 465:

> When scholarly debate bogs down around some dichotomy such as 'responsibility for fault'/'objective responsibility', something has almost always gone wrong. Here the problem is one of level of analysis: there is neither a rule that responsibility is always based on fault, nor one that is always independent of it—indeed, there appears to be no presumption either way. This is hardly surprising, in a legal system which has to deal with a wide range of problems and disposes of a limited armoury of techniques. But in any event circumstances alter cases, and it is illusory to seek for a single dominant rule ... everything depends on the specific context and on the content and interpretation of the obligation said to have been breached.

13.5 Enforcing responsibility against delinquent States

When a State commits an internationally unlawful act against aliens, either by injuring their person or property, the question arises as to how the aliens are to seek redress against the responsible States.

13.5.1 The general principle

Under international law, every State is entitled to protect its nationals diplomatically in foreign States. This principle allows a State to take up cases, on behalf of its injured nationals, against responsible States.

● ***Greece v. United Kingdom (Jurisdiction)*** (1924) PCIJ Ser. A, No. 2 (The ***Mavrommantis Palestine Concession Case***)

In this case, the PCIJ stated that when a State takes up the case of its national, the State is 'in reality asserting its own right—its right to ensure, in the person of its subjects, respect for the rules of international law'.

● ***Estonia v. Lithuania (Preliminary Objections)*** (1939) PCIJ Ser. A/B, No. 76, 4 (The ***Panevezys-Saldutiskis Railway Case***)

The Court emphasized the principle laid down in *Mavrommantis* and added (at 16) that:

> This right [of diplomatic protection] is necessarily limited to intervention on behalf of its own nationals because, in the absence of a special agreement, it is the bond of nationality between the State and the individual which alone confers upon the State the right of diplomatic protection, and it is a part of the function of diplomatic protection that the right to take up a claim and to ensure respect for the rules of international law must be envisaged.

A State is under no obligation to take up the claims of its nationals against foreign States. Where a State affords diplomatic protection, however, this does not mean that the amount of compensation to be paid to the injured national will be greater than the extent of the injury suffered.

KEY POINTS

- Every State is entitled to afford diplomatic protection to its nationals against foreign countries.

- In taking up a case involving its nationals against foreign States, a State is regarded as taking up its own case.

13.5.2 The conditions for enforcing State responsibility

It is obvious from the statement of the PCIJ in *Panevezys-Saldutiskis* (in the previous extract) that diplomatic protection is not automatic. Before a State can offer diplomatic protection to its nationals who have been injured by another State, certain conditions must be met. In other words, when a State takes up a claim on behalf of its nationals against a foreign State, the latter may object to the former's diplomatic protection on the basis:

(a) of the nationality of the claimant;

(b) of whether local remedies have been exhausted; and

(c) that there is a waiver of responsibility for the injury in question.

We will now consider these three situations in order.

The nationality of the claimant

Nationality is the first condition for diplomatic protection. In *Panevezys-Saldutiskis*, the PCIJ expressed this criterion as 'the bond of nationality between the State and the individual'. It is up to every State to decide who its nationals are. However, it is the prerogative of international law to decide whether the nationality conferred by a State on a person is sufficient for that State to afford diplomatic protection to that person. Thus, as Professor Borchard clarifies, in (1931) 1 Annuaire de l'Institut de Droit International 277, if a State decides to give diplomatic protection to its national who has been injured by another State:

> it is the duty of the defendant State to look into the question as to whether the individual, on whose behalf the Petition is submitted, is a national of the plaintiff State.

The question of sufficiency of nationality may arise, for example, where an injured person possesses two or more nationalities and the claim in question is against one of the States, or where injury is caused by a third State. In order to understand the intricacies of nationality as a condition for diplomatic protection, let us consider some instances.

Single nationality

Where a foreign national who is injured by a host country possesses the nationality of only one State, then the matter is simple: his or her country of nationality can afford him or her diplomatic protection. This is a straightforward issue, because the nationality of the injured person is not in conflict or competition with any other nationality.

Dual or multiple nationality

Where an individual possesses the nationality of two or more States (that is, has dual or multiple nationality), then questions may arise as to which of the States would be the best to take up his or her claim before a court.

. . . .

● *Italy v. Peru* (1912) 6 AJIL 746, PCA (The *Canevaro Case*)

Italy brought an action against Peru on behalf of Raphael Canevaro, a Peruvian by birth and an Italian by naturalization. Peru objected to the claim on the basis that Canevaro was a Peruvian and that Italy could not take up his case against Peru, and that Canevaro was more strongly linked to Peru, because he stood for election into the Peruvian Senate and represented the country as a consul to the Netherlands.

The Permanent Court of Arbitration (PCA) accepted Peru's claim and held (at 747) that:

> under these circumstances, whatever Raphael Canevaro's status may be in Italy with respect to his nationality, the Government of Peru has the right to consider him as a Peruvian citizen and to deny his status as an Italian claimant.

The *Canevaro Case* was the first in which an international tribunal had considered the issue of dual nationality in the context of diplomatic protection. Although the tribunal had obviously favoured the 'effective nationality' principle, it did not exercise itself too far on the matter.

● *Egypt v. USA* (1932) 2 RIAA 1161 (The *Salem Case*)

The USA brought an action against Egypt on behalf of George Salem, who held US, Egyptian, and Persian nationalities. Egypt objected to the USA giving diplomatic protection to Salem on the bases that he did not have an effective link with the USA and that Salem was a Persian.

The tribunal acknowledged the 'effective nationality' principle, as laid down in the *Canevaro Claim*, but rejected it. The tribunal said (at 1187) that:

> The principle of the so-called 'effective nationality' the Egyptian Government referred to does not seem to be sufficiently established in international law. It was used in the famous *Canevaro* case; but the decision of the Arbitral Tribunal appointed at that time has remained isolated. In spite of the *Canevaro* case, the practice of several governments, for instance the German, is that if two powers are both entitled by international law to treat a person as their national, neither of these powers can raise a claim against the other in the name of such person.

Apparently, the tribunal rejected the 'effective nationality' test that was applied to dual-nationality cases.

Salem involved multiple nationalities of the injured party and the decision of the tribunal to reject the effective nationality test was based on the fact that Egypt had raised the Persian nationality of the injured party in order to defeat the claim of the USA. Thus the case may not be authority for the application of the 'effective nationality' principle to dual-nationality cases, because the *ratio* of the case relates more to multiple nationalities. Therefore the reliance on it by some writers to gauge the approach of international law to the 'effective nationality' principle in dual-nationality cases is suspect.

thinking points

- *What are the conditions governing diplomatic protection?*
- *Distinguish between* Canevaro *and* Salem *on the application of the 'effective nationality' principle.*

● *Liechtenstein v. Guatemala* (1955) ICJ REP 4 (The *Nottebohm Case*)

A German national by birth lived and carried on business for several years in Guatemala. He subsequently obtained the nationality of Liechtenstein. Upon the expropriation of his property by Guatemala during the Second World War, Liechtenstein brought an action on his behalf. Guatemala objected on the basis that Liechtenstein could not bring a claim against Guatemala, which the latter considered as having a stronger link with Nottebohm.

In its judgment, the ICJ did not dispute Nottebohm's Liechtensteiner nationality, nor that every State must recognize that nationality (at 31); rather, the Court said that the Liechtensteiner nationality of Nottebohm must be specifically recognized for the admissibility of its case on behalf of Nottebohm against Guatemala. Thus the Court held that Liechtenstein could not protect Nottebohm, because there was no real and effective link between Nottebohm and Liechtenstein to enable the latter to take up the former's claim before the Court.

As the Court said (at 22 of its judgment):

> International arbitrators have decided in the same way numerous cases of dual nationality, where the question arose with regard to the exercise of protection. They have given their preference to the *real and effective nationality*, that which accorded with the facts, that based on stronger factual ties between the person concerned and one of the States whose nationality is involved. [Emphasis added]

The Court justified the basis of the 'real and effective nationality' test by reference to the writings of publicists and, more importantly, State practice. It said (at 22) that:

> the practice of certain States which refrain from exercising protection in favour of a naturalized person when the latter has in fact, by his prolonged absence, severed his links with what is no longer for him anything but his nominal country, manifests the view of these States that, in order to be capable of being invoked against another State, nationality must correspond with the factual situation.

The Court also said (at 22–23) that this trend is reflected in some bilateral treaties between States:

> A similar view is manifested in the relevant provisions of the bilateral nationality treaties concluded between the United States of America and other States since 1868, such as those sometimes referred to as the Bancroft Treaties, and in the Pan-American Convention, signed at Rio de Janeiro on August 13th, 1906, on the status of naturalized citizens who resume residence in their country of origin.

In this case, the German nationality of Nottebohm was considered a stronger one, since he had never cut his ties to that country and, ever since receiving the citizenship of Liechtenstein, had not sought particularly strong ties with that country. He continued to communicate with his family in Germany and to pursue business interests in that country, having never given up his German citizenship. Although he visited a brother in Liechtenstein regularly, he had no other solid ties to that country.

KEY POINTS

- Nationality must be 'real and effective' in order to be sufficient for diplomatic protection.

- The fact that every State must generally recognize the nationality conferred by one State on a person does not mean that the nationality is sufficient for the admissibility of cases of diplomatic protection.

- Some State practice and bilateral treaties show that a number of States accept the test of real and effective nationality.

The application of the 'real and effective' test of admissibility

The ICJ's clear statement in *Nottebohm* about the 'real and effective' test of nationality has generated enormous controversy among international lawyers. It is clear that the Court's decision in *Nottebohm* was aided by the fact that Nottebohm's Liechtensteiner nationality was considerably weaker than his connection to Germany. However, the Court did not make it clear how the 'effective nationality' principle should apply. The question remains whether the test applies to a State that takes up a case on behalf of its national, whose only nationality is its own, or applies only to dual or multiple nationality cases.

In order to understand how these queries have been dealt with, let us consider some cases that emerged after *Nottebohm*.

● **United States v. Italy** (1955) ILR 443 (The **Mergé Claim**)

In a case involving a dual national of the USA and Italy, the tribunal applied the effective nationality principle to hold that the State with the dominant and more effective nationality was entitled to afford diplomatic protection to its national.

● **Italy v. USA** (1958) ILR 91 (The **Flegenheimer Claim**)

The USA brought a case against Italy on behalf of its national, Flegenheimer, who possessed the nationality of both the USA and Germany. Italy objected to US diplomatic protection of the claimant on the basis that he was more strongly and effectively connected to Germany than the USA.

The Italian–US Conciliation Commission rejected this claim on the basis that the doctrine of effective nationality did not apply because Italy had raised the German nationality of Flegenheimer in order to deny the USA the right to give diplomatic protection to its national.

The tribunal set out the application of the effective nationality principle to different situations (at 150) as follows:

1. Where a person possesses multiple nationalities, one of the States cannot oppose the nationality of the other States. In other words, the nationality of the third State is dismissed and the claimant is treated as a single State national.

2. Where a person is a dual national, then the test of effective nationality applies and the State with the dominant nationality is the one entitled to afford diplomatic protection...the theory of effective or active nationality was established, in the Law of Nations, and above all in international private law, for the purpose of settling conflicts between two national States, or two national laws, regarding persons simultaneously vested with both nationalities, in order to decide which of them is to be dominant...whether that described as nominal, based on legal provisions of a given legal system, or that described as effective or active, equally based on legal provisions of another legal system, but confirmed by elements of fact (domicile, participation in the political life, the center of family and business interests, etc.). It must allow one to make a distinction between two bonds of nationality equally founded in law, which is the stronger and hence the effective one.

3. When a person has a single nationality, the tribunal held that the test of 'effective nationality' does not apply because when a person is vested with only one nationality, which is attributed to him or her either *jure sanguinis* or *jure soli*, or by a valid naturalization entailing the positive loss of the former nationality, the theory of effective nationality cannot be applied without the risk of causing confusion.

However, despite going to great lengths to consider how the 'effective nationality' principle applies to single, dual, and multiple nationalities, the Commission did note (at 148) that it:

is of the opinion that it is doubtful that the International Court of Justice intended to establish a rule of general international law in requiring, in the *Nottebohm Case*, that there must exist an effective link between the person and the State in order that the latter may exercise its right of diplomatic protection on behalf of the former.

Some writers do rely on this statement to support the view that *Flegenheimer* rejected the test of effective nationality in its entirety. This is not a correct reading of the statement. The Commission rejected applying the test to *Flegenheimer* principally because the defendant in that case (Italy) raised the third nationality of Flegenheimer in order to frustrate US diplomatic protection. This brought the decision in line with *Salem*, in which Egypt had equally raised the Persian nationality of Salem to defeat the US claim against Egypt. Clearly, by expressing the view later that the doctrine applies to dual nationality, the Commission in *Flegenheimer* would have decided differently if Italy had simply objected to US diplomatic protection on the basis that the Italian nationality of Flegenheimer was stronger than his US citizenship, because that would have brought the matter in line with *Nottebohm*.

It is thus clear that there is a fair level of certainty about the application of the effective nationality test today than there was previously. The test does not apply to cases involving a single nationality claim because if it were to do so, it may render the injured person Stateless for the purpose of diplomatic protection. Also, it seems clear that, in cases of multiple nationality, a defendant State cannot invoke a third nationality of the claimant against the State affording him or her diplomatic protection. Where there is a clear case of dual nationality, then the State with a stronger and effective nationality is entitled to protect its nationals. What must be avoided—and what seems to have caused the confusion in academic analysis—is an attempt to think about the 'effective nationality' test in terms of a one-size-fits-all requirement. It is not: it applies differently to different claims of nationalities, depending on the number of nationalities involved and the circumstances of each individual case.

KEY POINTS

- *Flegenheimer* clarifies the application of 'effective nationality' to single, dual, and multiple nationality claims.

- The invocation of third nationality by the defendant State (Italy) in *Flegenheimer* was a major factor in the decision of the Commission to reject the application of the 'effective nationality' principle to the case.

---

thinking points

- *Summarize the main findings in* Flegenheimer *with respect to the application of 'effective nationality' to single, dual, and multiple nationality cases.*

- *Compare and contrast* Salem *and* Flegenheimer, *and the relevance of third State nationality to their decisions.*

Diplomatic protection of corporate entities

Like human beings, companies can be injured by the States in which they carry on business. When companies are injured, they too can be given diplomatic protection by their State of nationality, just as can human beings. This is because companies have legal personality and thus are treated as separate and juristic entities, as are the humans that direct and control them. However, it must be pointed out at once that only limited liability companies, being so distinguished from other types of company by the fact of their shareholding, are entitled to diplomatic protection.

Yet determining the nationality of a company for the purpose of diplomatic protection is not as straightforward as determining that of a human being, even when the company is registered in only one State. This is because whereas an injury may occur to a person or to his or her property—in which case, the injury is still considered to be to the person—injury may occur to a company per se or to its shareholders. The nationality of a company may not be the same as the nationality of its shareholders or the majority of such shareholders. The split in the nationality of shareholders and the company may therefore upset the traditional balance of consideration of a company's nationality for the purpose of diplomatic protection.

The general rule

A company is a national of the State in which it is registered or incorporated. However, a company may be registered in a State, but carry on business mostly in another State. The question about which State is entitled to protect the company depends on whether injury is done to the company itself or to its shareholders. Even where injury is done to the company itself, the State in which it is incorporated may not rely merely on the fact of incorporation for the purpose of affording it diplomatic protection. State practice seems to require the State of incorporation also to show evidence of control over the company well and above the mere incidence of incorporation. This seems to be the corporate equivalent of the effective nationality test.

. . . .

● *Enrique Cortes and Company* (1896) (See *Cheshire and North's Private International Law* (11TH EDN, LONDON: BUTTERWORTH), P. 173)

Enrique was registered in England, but had the majority of its shareholders in Colombia. The Colombian shareholders asked the British authorities whether they would be entitled to seek diplomatic protection from England if there were a problem with the company in Colombia.

In response, the British authorities stated that:

> The principle ought not to be recognised that foreigners, by registering themselves here as a limited company, are entitled to claim from her Majesty's Government the protection accorded to British subjects in foreign countries.

It will appear from this statement that, in addition to registration, a State must demonstrate that it has a strong and effective link to a company that it wishes to protect diplomatically. The question, then, is: how have international tribunals understood the 'effective link' doctrine with regard to limited liability companies?

. . . .

● *Belgium v. Spain* (1970) ICJ REP 4 (The *Barcelona Traction, Light and Power Co. Ltd Case*)

> A company was incorporated in Canada in 1911 to supply electricity to Spain, but had majority shareholders in Belgium. In 1948, Spain declared the company bankrupt. Belgium brought an action against Spain, on behalf of its nationals, on the basis that the injury to the company adversely affected its shareholders. Spain objected on the basis that the injury was to the company and not its shareholders, and that, as such, Belgium lacked the legal basis to exercise diplomatic protection of the shareholders against Spain.

The ICJ held that Belgium could not bring an action against Spain. Rejecting the Belgian application, the Court said (at [71]) that:

> In the present case, it is not disputed that the company was incorporated in Canada and has its registered office in that country. The incorporation of the company under the law of Canada was an act of free choice. Not only did the founders of the company seek its incorporation under Canadian law but it has remained under that law for a period of over 50 years. It has maintained in Canada its registered office, its accounts and its share registers. Board meetings were held there for many years; it has been listed in the records of the Canadian tax authorities. Thus a close and permanent connection has been established, fortified by the passage of over half a century. This connection is in no way weakened by the fact that the company engaged from the very outset in commercial activities outside Canada, for that was its declared object. Barcelona Traction's links with Canada are thus manifold.

Obviously, the Court considered 'effective nationality', but concluded that this belonged to Canada, by virtue not only of registration of the company in Canada, but also the activities held there, which included board meetings and paying taxes to Canada over a considerable period. Thus it was Canada, not Belgium, which was entitled to afford diplomatic protection to the company.

To arrive at this conclusion, the Court distinguished between injury done directly to the company and indirect injury that resulted to its shareholders by virtue of the company's situation. In the Court's opinion, indirect injury to the shareholders does not entitle them to diplomatic protection, such as that which Belgium sought on their behalf. As the Court said (at [66]):

> It cannot however, be contended that the corporate entity of the company has ceased to exist, or that it has lost its capacity to take corporate action. It was free to exercise such capacity in the Spanish courts and did in fact do so. It has not become incapable in law of defending its own rights and the interests of the shareholders. In particular, a precarious financial situation cannot be equated with the demise of the corporate entity, which is the hypothesis under consideration: the company's status in law is alone relevant, and not its economic condition, nor even the possibility of its being 'practically defunct'- a description on which argument has been based but which lacks all legal precision. *Only in the event of the legal demise of the company are the shareholders deprived of the possibility of a remedy available through the company; it is only if they became deprived of all such possibility that an independent right of action for them and their government could arise.* [Emphasis added]

It is important to emphasize that the Court did not entirely say that shareholders cannot be protected by their countries of nationality under any circumstances; on the contrary, the Court affirmed this possibility—but only where injury to the company affected the rights of shareholders, such as the rights to attend meetings and vote (see [47]).

KEY POINTS

- Limited liability companies are entitled to diplomatic protection if they suffer injury, but this does not automatically extend to their shareholders.

- Shareholders may be protected diplomatically by their State only where their company has lost all legal ability to take up a claim on their behalf.

Although the Court did not apply the principle of 'effective nationality' in *Barcelona Traction*, it must be noted that this principle was not really in issue; rather, the core of the

Court's decision centred on the distinction between 'injury to a company' and 'injury to its shareholders'.

The Court seemed to think that Canada had a stronger link with the company than Belgium, the country of its majority shareholders. The fact that the Court did not allow the mere evidence of 'genuine link' between Belgium and the company to be the decisive factor in this case helped to avoid the possibility of 'nationality shopping'.

Exceptions to the rule in *Barcelona Traction*

Despite refusing Belgium the opportunity to protect its shareholders diplomatically—and thus laying down the rule that indirect injury to shareholders does not entitle them to diplomatic protection by their State—the ICJ recognized two instances in which this rule may be overridden. At [64], the Court said that the rule will not apply where the company has ceased to exist or to operate altogether, or where its national State lacks capacity to take action by itself.

Clearly, the Court must have considered these exceptions in *Barcelona Traction*, because it observed in the statement quoted earlier that the company had not ceased to exist or operate, even though in dire financial difficulties. It should also be noted that Canada, the national State of the company, did have the capacity to protect it and attempted to do so, but later abandoned its effort.

Thus we must be cautious about citing *Barcelona Traction* as authority for the proposition that the national State of shareholders cannot, under any circumstances, protect them against injury done to the company.

Some countries have now incorporated these exceptions in their law.

The UK's 1985 Rules Regarding the Taking Up of International Claims by Her Majesty's Government (HMG), restated in Colin Warbrick, 'Protection of nationals abroad' (1988) 37(4) ICLQ 1002, 1006, provide thus:

> **Rule III**
> ....
> Where the claimant is a dual national, HMG may take up his claim . . . if the respondent State has, in the circumstances which gave rise to the injury, treated the claimant as a UK national.

> **Rule V**
> ....
> Where a UK national has an interest, as a shareholder or otherwise, in a company incorporated in another State, and the company is injured by the acts of a third State, HMG [may] . . . take up his claim . . . [e]xceptionally . . . where the company is defunct . . .

> **Rule VI**
> ....
> Where a UK national has an interest, as a shareholder or otherwise, in a company incorporated in another State and of which it is therefore a national, and that State injures the company, HMG may intervene to protect the interests of that UK national.

It is clear from Rule III that the UK treats as evidence of the 'effective nationality' principle in dual-nationality cases the fact that the injured person in question had been 'treated . . . as a UK national'. Under Rule VI, it is clear that the UK will intervene in a situation in which the injury to UK nationals, who are shareholders, is caused by the national State of the company, of which such UK nationals are also nationals.

thinking points

- Is the approach adopted by the Court in distinguishing between injury to shareholders and to the company, in order to determine the right of diplomatic protection, practically useful?
- Are there other possible exceptions, in addition to the two posited by the Court in Barcelona Traction, to the rule involving diplomatic protection of shareholders?

Exhaustion of local remedies

A foreign national against whom an internationally unlawful act has occurred must first seek redress in the courts of the responsible State. Without exhausting local remedies, there can be no recourse to international remedies.

The exhaustion of local remedies is a doctrine that seeks to preserve State sovereignty and the notion of equality of States. In international law, every State has sovereignty over all of those present on its territory—and this includes the exercise of jurisdiction over them.

Exhaustion of local remedies thus performs distinct purposes, one of which is to prevent abuse of the legal process and to achieve efficiency.

● ***Panama v. France*** (2000) ITLOS/PV.00/1, 27 January (The ***Camouco Case***)

In his dissenting comment, Judge Anderson said of the purpose of exhaustion of local remedies:

> It must be unprecedented for the same issue to be submitted in quick succession first to a national court of appeal and then to an international tribunal, and for the issue to be actually pending before the two instances at the same time. This situation is surely undesirable and not to be encouraged. It smacks of 'forum hopping' and hardly makes for the efficient administration of justice. An international tribunal can best adjudicate when the national legal system has been used not partially, as here, but completely and exhaustively.

● ***Greece v. United Kingdom*** (1956) 12 RIAA 83 (The ***Ambatielos Arbitration***)

The UK contracted a Greek national to supply ships. A dispute arose from the interpretation of certain terms of the contract. A British court gave a judgment on the case. It was contended that the UK did not release some documents vital to the case. Greece instituted a claim on behalf of Ambatielos in the ICJ. The UK objected to this case on the basis, inter alia, that Ambatielos had not exhausted local remedies in the UK.

The Court held (at 118–119):

> . . . that the State against which an international action is brought for injuries suffered by private individuals has the right to resist such an action if the persons alleged to have been injured have not first exhausted all the remedies available to them under the municipal law of that State. The defendant State has the right to demand that full advantage shall have been taken of all local remedies before the matters in dispute are taken up on the international level by the State of which the persons alleged to have been injured are nationals.

● *Switzerland v. United States* (1959) ICJ REP 6 (The *Interhandel Case*)

Switzerland brought a case on behalf of Interhandel, a Swiss firm that was badly affected when the USA, as a consequence of the Second World War, took certain measures against a German company controlling Interhandel. Although the US Supreme Court held that Switzerland was entitled to appeal a decision by the US Court of Appeals further, Switzerland decided to take the case to the ICJ, which held that Switzerland failed to exhaust local remedies in the USA and as a result could not bring the claim to the ICJ.

It must be noted at once that it is only in respect of injuries done to a foreign national that local remedies must be exhausted, not injuries suffered by the State itself.

example

If Candoma sets fire to Rutamu's embassy in Candoma, Rutamu does not have to exhaust local remedies, but may take the case directly to an international tribunal.

Effective, not useless, local remedies

A claimant is required to exhaust effective, not useless, remedies, as a condition for recourse to international tribunals. Thus if local remedies will be inefficient or unrealistic, one does not have to exhaust them.

According to Professor E. M. Borchard, *Diplomatic Protection of Citizens Abroad* (New York: Banks Law Publishing, 1914), p. 383:

> the rule that local remedies must be exhausted before diplomatic interposition is proper is in its application subject to the important condition that the local remedy is effective in securing redress.

Also, according to *Moore's International Law Digest*, Vol. VI, p. 677: 'A claimant in a foreign State is not required to exhaust justice in such State when there is no justice to exhaust.'

● *Greece v. United Kingdom* (1956) 12 RIAA 83 (The *Ambatielos Arbitration*)

The ICJ said (at 119) that:

> The ineffectiveness of local remedies may result clearly from the municipal law itself. That is the case, for example, when a Court of Appeal is not competent to reconsider the judgment given by a Court of first instance on matters of fact, and when, failing such reconsideration, no redress can be obtained. In such a case there is no doubt that local remedies are ineffective.

● *Finland v. Great Britain* (1934) 3 RIAA 1479 (The *Finnish Vessels Arbitration*)

A dispute arose between Finland and the UK in which the former claimed that the latter failed to pay for the loss of certain Finnish ships used by the UK during the First World War. The British Admiralty Transportation Arbitration Board ruled that the UK was not responsible for the loss of the ships. Finland did not appeal to a higher court, but instead took the matter to international arbitration.

Although the arbitration tribunal agreed with the UK that there was a formal right of appeal open to Finland against the judgment, it said that this was not enough to bring in the local remedies rule. Finland had argued that considering that the available appeal was confined to questions of law—questions that it could not raise due to some technical hindrances—the remaining local remedies were therefore ineffective.

Agreeing with Finland, the tribunal held (at 1543) that:

> the appealable points of law...obviously would have been insufficient to reverse the decision of the Arbitration Board...and that, in consequence, there was no effective remedy against this decision.

Where a State is found to engage in acts calculated to frustrate an applicant's claim, the rule of local remedies will not apply.

● *United States v. Great Britain* (1923) 6 RIAA 120 (The *Robert Brown Case*)

Mr Brown, a US national with an interest in gold, applied for licences to prospect in South Africa. Although his application was duly filed, the government declined to grant him the licences. He challenged the decision in a court and it was upheld. However, the government had removed from office the Chief Justice who decided in favour of Mr Brown and openly threatened judges who refused to comply with the government order.

There was no doubt that a formal appeal was open to Mr Brown, but he refused to use this on the basis that the remedy was useless. In upholding his claim, brought on his behalf by the USA, the arbitration held (at 129) that the circumstances of the case disclosed 'a real denial of justice'.

It must be noted, however, that the local remedies that need to be exhausted are not only court processes, but also other available means of legal protection.

● *Greece v. United Kingdom* (1956) 12 RIAA 83 (The *Ambatielos Arbitration*)

The Court said (at 120) that:

> These 'local remedies' include not only reference to the courts and tribunals, but also the use of the procedural facilities which municipal law makes available to litigants before such courts and tribunals. It is the whole system of legal protection, as provided by municipal law, which must have been put to the test before a State, as the protector of its nationals, can prosecute the claim on the international plane.

The exclusion of diplomatic protection: the Calvo clause

By practice, most contractual agreements between foreign nationals and States now incorporate the 'Calvo clause' (named after its author, Argentine diplomat Carlos Calvo). By this doctrine, a foreign national undertakes to forfeit the right to diplomatic protection by his or her State in respect of internationally unlawful acts suffered in the host State. The effect of the Calvo clause is to give the local courts final jurisdiction in cases involving foreign nationals on a State's territory.

However, some writers have expressed the view that the Calvo clause may not be used to prevent diplomatic protection, but merely to reinforce an obligation for recourse to domestic courts. This reasoning is challengeable. The Calvo clause could not be construed as merely reinforcing recourse to domestic jurisdiction without it being rendered redundant or superfluous: after all, every State has definitive jurisdiction on all persons or entities within its territory, so there is no need for a helping hand from the Calvo clause. Indeed, the Calvo clause has not been invalidated for its attempt to prevent diplomatic protection (see James C. Baker and Lois J. Yoder, 'ICSID and the Calvo clause: a hindrance to foreign direct investment LDCs' (1989–90) 5 Ohio St J Dis Resol 75).

The exclusion of local remedies rule

Unlike the Calvo clause, which mainly seeks to ensure the compulsory (arguably sole) application of local remedies in cases of internationally unlawful acts to foreigners, States may, by agreement, totally exclude local remedies in cases involving their nationals. In such situations, all cases of internationally unlawful acts are referred to international tribunals without first going through local courts. A good example is the US–Iran Claims Tribunal.

KEY POINTS

- It is important for injured parties to seek local remedies before taking up their case with international tribunals.

- Where local remedies are ineffective or useless, they can be dispensed with.

13.5.3 Reparation for injury

When a State causes an injury to another State, the responsible State is liable to make full reparation to the injured State. Under Article 34 ARSIWA, reparation may take the form of restitution, compensation, and satisfaction.

● *Germany v. Poland (Jurisdiction)* (1927) PCIJ Ser. A, No. 9 (The *Chorzów Factory Case*)

The PCIJ stated (at 21) that:

> It is a principle of international law that the breach of an engagement involves an obligation to make reparation in an adequate form. Reparation therefore is the indispensable complement of a failure to apply a convention and there is no necessity for this to be stated in the convention itself.

The Court further noted (at 47) that:

> Reparation must, as far as possible, wipe out all the consequences of the illegal act and re-establish the situation which would, in all probability, have existed if that act had not been committed. Restitution in kind, or, if this is not possible, payment of a sum corresponding to the value which a restitution in kind would bear; the award, if need be, of damages for loss sustained which would not be covered by restitution in kind or payment in place of it—such are the principles which should serve to determine the amount of compensation due for an act contrary to international law.

Restitution (Article 35 ARSIWA)

Restitution involves the restoration of a situation that existed before the wrongful act was committed, provided that this is possible and does not impose a greater burden on the responsible State than compensation.

Restitution in its pure form (*status ante*) is not always possible.

● *France v. Switzerland* (1932) PCIJ Ser. A/B, No. 46 (The ***Free Zones of Upper Savoy and the District of Gex Case***)

In this case, the Court ordered France to withdraw its customs cordon in order to restore Switzerland to its original position.

Compensation (Article 36 ARSIWA)

Compensation is available where the internationally unlawful act actually results in losses. Compensation is not designed to punish or to serve as a deterrent.

● *United States v. Germany* (1923) 7 RIAA 17 (The ***Lusitania Cases***)

On 7 May 1915, a German submarine torpedoed a British ocean liner, *RMS Lusitania*, off the coast of Ireland, resulting in the loss of 128 American lives, despite the fact that the USA was neutral in the then unfolding First World War. In a subsequent arbitration, Germany accepted to pay compensation.

The Umpire stated (at 36) that:

> the legal concept of damages is judicially ascertained compensation for wrong. The compensation must be adequate and balance as near as may be the injury suffered . . . to deny such reparation would be to deny the fundamental principle that there exists a remedy for the direct invasion of every right.

Satisfaction (Article 37 ARSIWA)

A State that causes injury to another may undertake satisfaction—that is, acknowledgement of the breach, an expression of regret, and an offer of apology. Satisfaction will be necessary where restitution or compensation is inadequate.

Satisfaction is often used as reparation for non-material injury.

● *New Zealand v. France* (1987) 26 ILM 1346 (The ***Rainbow Warrior Arbitration***)

In this case, the Court said (at [122]) that:

> There is a long established practice of States and international Courts and Tribunals of using satisfaction as a remedy or form of reparation (in the wide sense) for the breach of an international obligation. This practice relates particularly to the case of moral or legal damage done directly to the State, especially as opposed to the case of damage to persons involving international responsibilities.

Satisfaction may also take the form of declarations by a court that an act was illegal or unlawful. In the *Corfu Channel Case* (see section 3.4.2), the ICJ declared that the mine-sweeping of the Albanian waters by the British Navy, without Albania's authority, was a violation of Albanian sovereignty and illegal. This was held to constitute satisfaction in that case.

 ## 13.6 Circumstances precluding wrongfulness

It is not in every situation in which a State commits an internationally unlawful act against another State that responsibility arises. Just as a human being may have defences for committing crimes, a State may have excuses for committing acts that would be otherwise unlawful. These defences—technically referred to as 'circumstances precluding wrongfulness for internationally unlawful acts'—are contained in Articles 20–25 ARSIWA. They are, namely: consent, self-defence, countermeasures, *force majeure*, distress, and necessity.

13.6.1 Consent (Article 20 ARSIWA)

Under Article 20 ARSIWA, a State may give its consent for another State to commit an act on its territory that would ordinarily be unlawful but for that consent. This is a commonsensical application of the rule *volenti non fit injuria*—translated as 'that to which you have consented, you cannot complain against'.

Consent, under such circumstances, may be express or implied. In determining the validity of consent given by a State for the commission of an internationally wrongful act against it, the question as to who is competent to give the consent on behalf of the State will normally arise. It is important that such a person is duly authorized to give the relevant consent, whether express or implied (see Ademola Abass, 'Consent precluding State responsibility: a critical analysis' (2004) 53 ICLQ 211).

13.6.2 Self-defence (Article 21 ARSIWA)

If an internationally unlawful act occurs while a State is defending itself in accordance with the right recognized under Article 51 of the UN Charter, then the State's responsibility for the internationally unlawful act is precluded. It must be noted that since the UN Charter recognizes both individual and collective self-defence, it thus follows that not only will the State be able to preclude its responsibility for such acts, but also other States involved collectively in the exercise of Article 51 will equally escape liability. (See also the discussion of self-defence in Chapter 10.)

13.6.3 Countermeasures (Article 22 ARSIWA)

Countermeasures are like self-defence, except that, unlike the latter, they do not include the use of force. Hence, if a State imposes sanctions on another State and serious breaches or violations of international obligation result from this, its responsibility is excluded if such an action was exercised as a countermeasure.

13.6.4 *Force majeure* (Article 23 ARSIWA)

Force majeure is the occurrence of an irresistible force or of an unforeseen event beyond the control of the State, making it materially impossible in the circumstances to perform an obligation. Thus the important elements of *force majeure* are 'irresistibility', 'beyond control', and 'unforseeability' of the force or event.

● *France v. Greece* (1956) 23 ILR 299 (The *Lighthouses Arbitration*)

A lighthouse owned by a French company, which was taken over by the Greek government in 1915, was subsequently destroyed by enemy action. The arbitral tribunal rejected the French claim for restoration of the lighthouse on grounds of *force majeure*.

Under Article 23 (2)(a)-(b), where a State could have resisted or foreseen the consequence of its actions, or where such action or any part thereof is due to its own conduct, then it cannot plead *force majeure*.

● *Belgium v. Greece* (1939) PCIJ Ser. A/B, No. 78 (The *Société Commerciale de Belgique Case*)

Greece and Belgium entered into a contract under which the Belgian company would finance the building of some railway facilities in Greece. Greece failed to repay the loans on the ground, among others, that 'it is materially impossible for the Greek Government to execute the awards as formulated' due to the precarious financial situation in which Greece found itself. This, in effect, amounted to a plea of *force majeure* by Greece.

The Court rejected the Greek claim (at 160).

● *New Zealand v. France* (1987) 26 ILM 1346 (The *Rainbow Warrior Arbitration*)

Two Frenchmen who planted explosives on the *Rainbow Warrior*, a vessel belonging to New Zealand, were sentenced to ten years in prison by the New Zealand authorities. However, following arbitration, New Zealand agreed that the men be detained in Hao for three years. In breach of this agreement, and without informing New Zealand, France smuggled one of the men back to France. It claimed that the accused person was in need of urgent medical attention and that this constituted *force majeure*.

The tribunal rejected the argument.

13.6.5 Distress (Article 24 ARSIWA)

A breach of an international obligation may be precluded if a State can show that it had no choice, to save lives, other than to take the course of action resulting in a breach of its international obligation. This is on the basis, however, that the State itself has not contributed to the situation and that the measure that it takes does not create a comparable or greater peril than that which it seeks to avoid.

The defence of distress is most commonly pleaded in relation to aircraft or ships entering other States' airspace and territorial waters, without prior permission, in order to avert disaster. Examples include US planes entering Yugoslav airspace in 1946 and a British ship entering Icelandic territorial waters in 1975, apparently to 'shelter from severe weather, as they have the right to do under customary international law' (see Official Records of the Security

Council, Thirtieth Year, 1866th Meeting, 16 December 1975, para. 24, cited in the 2002 ILC Commentary, p. 79, see section 13.3.1).

13.6.6 Necessity (Article 25 ARSIWA)

In order to plead necessity as a circumstance precluding a wrongful act, a State must:

(a) demonstrate that the offending act was the only way in which it could prevent a grave and imminent peril to an essential interest of the State;

(b) not have contributed to the act; and

(c) not attempt to use the defence in relation to an obligation in respect of which it is not available.

example

In 1967, a Liberian oil tanker, *Torrey Canyon*, capsized off the coast of Cornwall, just outside British territorial waters, spilling large amounts of oil that threatened the English coastline. After various remedial attempts had failed, the British government decided to bomb the ship to burn the remaining oil. This operation was carried out successfully. Britain claimed that the ship posed a great environmental and ecological threat to Britain, and that its destruction was therefore necessary and taken only after all other efforts had failed.

Neither Liberia nor any other State protested against the British action.

• **Hungary v. Slovakia** (1997) ICJ REP 7 (The **Case Concerning the Gabčíkovo-Nagymaros Project**)

Hungary and Slovakia jointly undertook to construct a hydro-electric dam. Hungary abandoned work on the project, on the ground, inter alia, that there were some 'uncertainties' revealed in a study of the project that might lead to serious environmental problems. It then concluded that a 'state of ecological necessity' compelled it to abandon the project (see [40]).

The Court rejected the Hungarian argument. The Court said (at [42]) that:

serious though these uncertainties might have been they could not, alone, establish the objective existence of a 'peril' in the sense of a component element of a state of necessity. The word 'peril' certainly evokes the idea of 'risk': that is precisely what distinguishes 'peril' from material damage. But a state of necessity could not exist without a 'peril' duly established at the relevant point in time: the mere apprehension of a possible 'peril' could not suffice in that respect.

13.7 Peremptory norms: breaches that can never be excused (Article 26 ARSIWA)

There can be no defence against the breach of peremptory norms of international law. As will be recalled from Chapter 2, these are obligations that admit of no derogation, even by consent of States (see Article 53 Vienna Convention on the Law of Treaties, VCLT). The prohibition of the use of force by Article 2(4) of the UN Charter is widely regarded as a peremptory norm of international law.

As the ILC said in its 2002 Commentary (see section 13.3), at p. 85:

> The criteria for identifying peremptory norms of general international law are stringent. Article 53 of the 1969 Vienna Convention requires not merely that the norm in question should meet all the criteria for recognition as a norm of general international law, binding as such, but further that it should be recognized as having a peremptory character by the international community of States as a whole.

Conclusion

State responsibility refers to the liability of States for internationally wrongful acts—that is, breaches or violations of international obligations. Such obligations may arise out of treaties or out of recognized rules of general international law. These rules may relate to the interactions between States, or between States and the nationals of other States, which nationals may be legal or juristic persons. We have noted the rules relating to the representation of nationals by States on the international plane and instances in which such rules will not apply. While ARSIWA explicates many of these rules, some of them, such as the application or interpretation of the 'effective nationality' principle, are left to be determined by courts and tribunals.

While there is a general rule that States will be held responsible for their internationally wrongful acts, there are instances in which such responsibility will not be incurred by an erring State, such as where the consent of the injured State is given for the act and instances of *force majeure*, distress, necessity, self-defence, and countermeasures.

Questions

Self-test questions

1 Explain the term 'State responsibility'.

2 What does the phrase 'internationally wrongful acts' mean?

3 What are the conditions necessary for international responsibility?

4 Distinguish between 'acts of instructed persons' and 'acts of directed or controlled persons'.

5 What is the difference between objective responsibility and risk theories?

6 Explain what is meant by 'exhaustion of local remedies'.

7 Under what circumstances may responsibility for breaches of international obligations be precluded?

Discussion questions

1 Discuss the requirements of lawful expropriation.

2 With reference to relevant cases, explain the basis of the diplomatic protection of nationals.

3 Examine the circumstances precluding internationally wrongful acts.

4 Discuss the 'exhaustion of local remedies' as a condition for diplomatic protection.

5 Discuss the various standards of treatment of aliens.

6 Discuss the various reparations available to an injured State.

Assessment question

In January 2010, Candoma decided to nationalize two companies owned by Mr Dempsey, a national of Rutamu. In a widely televised statement, the Candoman President said that the nationalization was necessary to enable Candoman companies to develop their commercial activities in the areas of production in which the nationalized companies operated. He also said that the nationalization was intended to send a strong message that Candoma would not tolerate insults from its neighbour, Rutamu. It is widely reported that Rutamu recently described the government of Candoma as 'roguish and belonging to the axis of evil'. Mr Dempsey intends to seek remedy from the Candoman courts. However, he is required by law first to obtain the permission of the President of Candoma as a condition for bringing an action against the State.

Advise Mr Dempsey.

Key cases

- *Belgium v. Spain* (1970) ICJ Rep 4 (the *Barcelona Traction Case*)
- *Bosnia v. Serbia* (2007) ICJ Rep 43 (the *Bosnian Genocide Case*)
- *France v. Greece* (1956) 23 ILR 299 (the *Lighthouses Arbitration*)
- *Greece v. United Kingdom (Jurisdiction)* (1924) PCIJ Ser. A, No. 2 (the *Mavrommatis Palestine Concession Case*)
- *New Zealand v. France* (1987) 26 ILM 1346 (the *Rainbow Warrior Arbitration*)
- *United Kingdom v. Albania* (1949) ICJ Rep 4 (the *Corfu Channel Case*)
- *Yaeger v. Iran* (1987) 17 Iran–US CTR 92

Further reading

Amerasinghe, C. F., 'Issues of compensation for the taking of alien property in the light of recent cases and practice' (1992) 41 ICLQ 22

Crawford, J., *State Responsibility. The General Part* (Cambridge: Cambridge University Press, 2013)

Crawford J., Pellet, A., and Olleson, S., *The Law of International Responsibility* (Oxford: Oxford University Press, 2010)

Elagab, O. Y., *The Legality of Counter-Measures in International Law* (Oxford: Oxford University Press, 1988)

Epstein, R. A., *Takings: Private Property under the Power of Eminent Domain* (Cambridge, MA: Harvard University Press, 1985)

Ragazzi, M. (ed.), *International Responsibility Today*: *Essays in Memory of Oscar Schachter* (Leiden/ Boston, MA: Martinus Nijhoff, 2005)

Schachter, O., *International Law in Theory and Practice* (Dordrecht: Martinus Nijhoff, 1991)

White, N. and Abass, A., 'Countermeasures and sanctions' in M. Evans (ed.), *International Law* (3rd edn, Oxford: Oxford University Press, 2010), p. 531

14

The settlement of international disputes

Learning objectives

This chapter will help you to:

- understand the processes for peacefully settling disputes amongst States;
- appreciate the rules concerning the diplomatic settlement of disputes;
- learn the different modalities for settling disputes among States;
- decide what the processes for settling disputes are and recognize how we use them; and
- learn the role of the UN Security Council in peaceful dispute settlement.

Introduction

The settlement of international disputes through peaceful means is central to the international legal order and is one of the principal reasons why the UN exists. Just as human beings, States' daily interaction with one another often gives rise to misunderstandings. As we have seen in Chapters 10 and 11, it is only when States fail to settle their disputes amicably that they resort to force or face collective enforcement by the UN or regional organizations. International law provides States with various means of settling disputes peacefully. The Charter of the United Nations (UN Charter), as well as regional instruments, embodies the rules for settling international disputes. A solid understanding of these processes will enhance students' appreciation of how States deal with such issues as the responsibility for breaching international obligations, which will be considered later in this book. This chapter focuses on the dispute settlement processes that are recognized under the UN Charter. It does not cover regional processes, which are mostly replications of the ones in the UN Charter and only apply to members of specific organizations, unlike the UN one having nearly a global reach. Concentrating on the UN peaceful settlement system allows us to study the special role of the UN Security Council in such processes. Finally, this chapter does not deal with the International Court of Justice (ICJ), a subject that is covered by Chapter 15.

14.1 What is a dispute?

In everyday conversation, the meaning of 'dispute' is taken for granted. When two persons disagree over an issue we say that they are 'in dispute'. When controversy ensues over something, it is said that there is a dispute among those involved.

 example

A car park enforcement officer may place a penalty notice on your car for parking without displaying a valid parking ticket. You may challenge him on the basis that your car has been there for only a couple of minutes and that you simply went into one of the shops to get coins for the ticket machine, in order to obtain a ticket. The enforcement officer may state that he has allowed enough time for you to get a ticket for your car.

In this scenario, a dispute has arisen between the two parties because of their failure to agree on what constituted 'enough time' for the purpose of obtaining a parking ticket. Whether or not you will have to pay the penalty charge will depend on the decision by the local council authority to which you must appeal within a specified period, which will then resolve the dispute in one way or another.

In international law, a 'dispute' has a specific legal meaning and does not refer to all instances of disagreement. Disputes between States may relate to determination of legal rights, interest, duty, or obligations; or to interpretation of treaties; delineation of boundaries; and so on and so forth. However, this does not presuppose that States always agree on when a 'dispute' arises between them, and it is often up to international tribunals, such as the ICJ, to determine the existence of a dispute. As we will see in Chapter 15, without a dispute, the Court cannot adjudicate matters involving States. So, what then is a dispute, and when does it exist?

. . . .

● *Belgium v. Senegal* (2012) ICJ REP 1 (*Question Relating to the Obligation to Prosecute or Extradite*)

Belgium argued that Senegal had an obligation to prosecute Mr Habré, the former President of Chad, who was in asylum in Senegal, and that failing to do that, Senegal should extradite him to Belgium for trial. Belgium contended that Senegal's failure to prosecute or extradite the accused breached Articles 5 and 6 of the Convention against Torture. Senegal argued that there was no dispute between itself and Belgium on the interpretation of the Torture Convention and, as such, the ICJ had no jurisdiction to try the case.

Held (at para. 46) that:

> in order to establish whether a dispute exists, '[i]t must be shown that the claim of one party is positively opposed by the other' [and that] '[w]hether there exists an international dispute is a matter for objective determination'.

. . . .

● *Georgia v. Russian Federation* (*Case Concerning Application of the International Convention on the Elimination of All Forms of Racial Discrimination*) Preliminary Objections, Judgment, 1 April 2011, available at: http://www.icj-cij.org/docket/files/140/16398.pdf; for analysis see Phoebe Okowa, 'The International Court of Justice and the Georgia/Russia Dispute', *Human Rights Law Review* 11:4 (2011), 739–757.

The Court rejected Russia's argument that the word 'dispute' as used by the Convention on Elimination of Racial Discrimination, attracts a narrower meaning than recognized under general international law. The Court affirmed the principle laid down by the Permanent Court of International Justice (PCIJ) in *Greece v. United Kingdom* (1924) PCIJ Ser. A, No. 2 (the *Mavrommatis Palestine Concessions*) that 'A dispute is a disagreement on a point of law or fact, a conflict of legal views or of interests between two persons.' The Court went further to state (at para. 30) that:

> the existence of a dispute may be inferred from the failure of a State to respond to a claim in circumstances where a response is called for. While the existence of a dispute and the undertaking of negotiations are distinct as a matter of principle, the negotiations may help demonstrate the existence of the dispute and delineate its subject matter.

Disputes can relate to either civil or criminal matters, as well as it may affect individuals and States.

. . . .

● *France v. United States of America* (1952) ICJ REP 176 (**Rights of Nationals of the United States of America in Morocco**)

The USA had argued that the word 'dispute' concerned all disputes between the USA and France, France countered that the word 'dispute', in its ordinary and natural sense, should be confined to civil disputes, and that crimes are offences against the State and not disputes between private individuals.

The Court held (at 189) that:

> it is necessary to construe the word 'dispute' as . . . referring both to civil disputes and to criminal disputes, in so far as they relate to breaches of the criminal law . . .

KEY POINTS

- A dispute is a disagreement on points of law or facts—a conflict of legal views or interests.

- At international law, a dispute usually involves subjects of international law, such as States and international organizations.

14.1.1 When does a dispute arise?

Defining a dispute is quite different from determining *when* a dispute arises in international law, and this point is of particular importance. Whereas most international disputes arise directly between States or international organizations, some of these disputes arise between individuals and States.

example

It is possible that a dispute between Candoma and Rutamu might arise from a transaction between Candoma and Mr X, a Rutamuan national. Since Mr X, a human being, cannot sue Candoma before the ICJ, Mr X's case may be taken up by Rutamu, his country. In such a scenario, it is crucial that the Court determines when a dispute arises between Candoma and Rutamu, as it were, in order for the latter to be able to vindicate its citizen's claim before the Court.

The PCIJ and the ICJ had to deal with questions concerning when a dispute arose in the following cases.

. . . .

● ***Greece v. United Kingdom*** (1924) PCIJ Ser. A, No. 2 (The ***Mavrommatis Palestine Concessions***)

Mr Mavrommatis, a Greek national, had performed certain public works in Palestine which, at the time, was under British control. Following a dispute between Mr Mavrommatis and Palestine/Britain, Greece decided to take up the case on behalf of its citizen. Britain objected to the jurisdiction of the PCIJ over the case, on the basis that, under Articles 34 and 36 of the Statute of the Court, only members of the League of Nations could be parties to a suit before the Court; since the case involved a State and a human being, Britain argued that the Court had no jurisdiction.

In order to resolve the challenge to its jurisdiction, the Court first had to decide whether a dispute had arisen between Greece and Britain, as the State then in charge of Palestine.

Having defined a dispute in the terms already stated previously, the Court went ahead to state (at 12) that:

> It is an elementary principle of international law that a State is entitled to protect its subjects, when injured by acts contrary to international law committed by another State, from whom they have been unable to obtain satisfactions through ordinary channels. By taking up the case of one of its subjects and by resorting to diplomatic action or international judicial proceedings on his behalf, a State is in reality asserting its own rights—its right to ensure, in the person of its subjects, respect for the rule of international law.

In this case, the ICJ was asked to determine, on the basis of the Anglo-German Treaty of 1 July 1890 and the rules and principles of international law, the boundary between Namibia and Botswana around Kasikili/Sedudu Island, and the legal status of the island. Each party had indicated to the Court the point it thought marked the disputed boundary.

On the question as to when the dispute arose, it was said (at [27]) that:

> In the Court's opinion, the real dispute between the Parties concerns the location of the main channel where the boundary lies...the Court will therefore proceed first to determine the main channel. In so doing, it will seek to determine the ordinary meaning of the words 'main channel' by reference to the most commonly used criteria in international law and practice, to which the Parties have referred.

From these cases it is clear that the question of when a dispute arises is one of fact, and that the Court will often take the entire circumstances of the disagreement into consideration before deciding on whether a dispute has arisen and when that dispute arose.

It also emerged from the *Kasikili/Sedudu* case that in determining whether a dispute has arisen in any given case, the Court will be guided by, but not confined to, what one or both parties put forward as their own interpretation or understanding of the situation. This is because while it is a question of fact whether or not a dispute has arisen, it is a question of law what constitutes a dispute, and the Court is entitled to determine a question of law, as well as a question of fact, in any case.

thinking points

- *Explain the difference between a dispute and when a dispute arises under international law.*
- *Under what circumstances can a dispute involving a State and an individual person become a dispute between two States?*

14.1.2 'Dispute' distinguished from 'conflict' and 'situation'

Though often used interchangeably with 'situations' or 'conflicts', 'dispute' is distinguishable from these words. A 'situation' exists when there is a complex chain of events and issues giving rise to not one, but several, disputes that are interlinked within a given context, such as the situation between Israel and Palestine. As John Merrills points out, in 'The meaning of dispute settlement' in Malcolm Evans (ed.), *International Law* (2nd edn, Oxford: Oxford University Press, 2006), at pp. 533–534, to describe the Israeli–Palestinian situation as a 'dispute' would be inaccurate, since it is extremely difficult to pinpoint a single issue that is *the* main contention between the two entities. (See also K. K. Koufa, 'International conflictual situations and their peaceful adjustment' (1988) 18 Thesaurus Acroasium 7.)

'Conflict' often denotes a general state of hostility between States and/or other subjects of international law. In a typical conflict scenario, the use of force is sometimes applied, although this is not always the case. A general state of hostility will suffice to manifest a conflict.

14.2 The peaceful settlement of disputes

There are two ways in which States can settle their disputes peacefully. The first is through negotiation, conciliation, mediation, good offices, and inquiry. These are generally referred to as the 'diplomatic' settlement of disputes. None of these methods involves judicial process. The second system consists of arbitration and judicial settlements. Arbitration is peaceful, but distinguishable from the diplomatic processes because it involves some level of judicial activity. Arbitration is therefore a midway point between the diplomatic processes and a full judicial trial by an international court like the ICJ.

An important feature of the diplomatic settlement of disputes is its informality and directness. In fact, the PCIJ recognized its role as that of facilitating the diplomatic means of settling disputes.

● *France v. Switzerland* (1929) PCIJ SER. A, No. 22 (The *Case of the Free Zones of Upper Savoy and the District of Gex*)

The Court said (at 13) that:

> Whereas the judicial settlement of international disputes, with a view to which the Court has been established, is simply an alternative to the direct and friendly settlement of such disputes between Parties; as consequently it is for the Court to facilitate, so far as is compatible with its Statute, such direct and friendly settlement...

As we said earlier, the various processes for settling international disputes under international law have now been incorporated into the UN Charter. Therefore, we will now consider these processes as they are provided for in the Charter, and we will discuss the role of the UN Security Council separately.

14.2.1 Chapter VI of the UN Charter

Chapter VI of the UN Charter recognizes both the diplomatic and judicial processes for settling international disputes amongst States. According to Article 33:

> (1) The parties to any dispute, the continuance of which is likely to endanger the mainte-nance of international peace and security, shall, first of all, seek a solution by negotiation, enquiry, mediation, conciliation, arbitration, judicial settlement, resort to regional agencies or arrangements, or other peaceful means of their own choice.
>
> (2) The Security Council shall, when it deems necessary, call upon the parties to settle their dis-pute by such means.

Article 33(1) imposes an obligation on all States to seek a diplomatic resolution of their disputes, which, as would have been noticed, includes arbitration and judicial settlement. The sense of 'obligation' is confirmed by the use of the word 'shall'.

14.3 Negotiation, inquiry, mediation, good offices, and conciliation

14.3.1 Negotiation

Negotiation is the dispute settlement method most commonly used by States. It is a process whereby disputing parties discuss the various issues of contention between them, either with a view to finding an amicable solution or, at least, to achieving an understanding of their differences. As a dispute settlement technique, negotiation is fast, direct, easy, and flexible. It does not involve extensive formalities and avoids such things as standard operation procedures (SOPs). How, where, and what to negotiate are decisions solely for the disputing States to make. There is no involvement of third parties in negotiation, although it may be motivated or inspired by such parties behind the scenes.

The ICJ has confirmed these liberal attributes of negotiation.

● *Federal Republic of Germany v. Denmark, Federal Republic of Germany v. The Netherlands* (1969) ICJ REP 3 (The *North Sea Continental Shelf Cases*)

The Court said (at [86]) that:

> There is no need to insist upon the fundamental character of this method of settlement, except to point out that it is emphasized by the observable fact that judicial or arbitral settlement is not universally accepted.

● *Greece v. United Kingdom* (1924) PCIJ SER. A, No. 2 (The *Mavrommatis Palestine Concessions*)

The Court said (at 13) that:

> Negotiations do not of necessity always presuppose a more or less lengthy series of notes and despatches; it may suffice that a discussion should have been commenced, and this discussion may have been very short; this will be the case if a deadlock is reached or if finally a point is reached at which one of the Parties definitely declares himself unable, or refuses, to give way, and there can therefore be no doubt that the dispute cannot be settled by diplomatic negotiations. This will also be the case, in certain circumstances, if the conversations between the Governments are only the continuation of previous negotiations between a private individual and a government.

These statements show that what matters in negotiation are the intention and content of negotiation, not procedures or formality.

The principles of negotiation

Being an informal method does not imply that there is no process to negotiations. In fact, negotiation performs better when it is conducted on the basis of some fundamental principles. Although such principles are many, it is worthwhile listing the most important of these in the following sections.

A separation of interest from position

A good negotiation should clearly separate interests from positions. This means that disputing States need to separate what their people want from what they, as States, need in negotiations. The interests of parties do not necessarily mirror their people's positions, and negotiation should always endeavour to put things in proper perspective. A good example of this principle can be seen in the *North Sea Continental Shelf Cases* (see earlier in this section), in which the issue seemed to be more of what and how resources should be allocated, rather than where the boundaries between the parties should be located. By being able to separate interests from positions, negotiation is able to deal with the dispute more effectively and to reach an agreement much sooner.

The application of objective criteria

One of the most difficult aspects of settling international disputes is the application of objective standards and rules. Once disputing parties decide to negotiate, it will be of great advantage for them to agree to a set of objective criteria from the onset. This may logically follow from their being able, sometimes, to separate their positions as States from the interests at stake (such as distribution of wealth or resources from an area of contested boundary) among their people.

Readiness to make concessions

Parties to negotiation will get results more quickly if they show, from the outset, that they are willing to make concessions on some of the most difficult and contentious points. Making concessions does not show weakness; rather, it shows the utmost desire of disputing parties to prioritize finding amicable solutions to problems, instead of maintaining unreasonable positions simply to 'save face'. There is no doubt that parties to negotiations do not want to 'lose face'—that is, they do not want to be considered weak or unable to stand their ground. However, the disadvantages of being unreasonably rigid and uncompromising far outweigh the benefits of kind flexibility and consideration.

The identification of common grounds

While it is useful for disputing parties to make concessions on hard and difficult issues, this can be preceded by an identification of common grounds from the start. By doing so, the parties are able to narrow their disputes to specific issues, and are also able to identify, in advance, on which areas they may need to compromise. This saves the time of the negotiating parties and it allows them to establish a reasonable level of engagement from the start.

thinking point
What are the important principles of negotiation?

Is there an obligation to negotiate?

As mentioned previously, the UN Charter imposes an obligation on States to settle their disputes peacefully, but that obligation does not require that States adopt a particular process. Nevertheless, an important question is: is there an obligation on States to negotiate under general international law? This question is very important given that the ability of the Court to assert its jurisdiction over a case often depends on whether States have negotiated the dispute.

● *Greece v. United Kingdom* (1924) PCIJ SER. A, No. 2 (The *Mavrommatis Palestine Concessions*)

In this case, the PCIJ said (at 15) that:

> it recognises, in fact, that before a dispute can be made the subject of an action at law, its subject matter should have been clearly defined by means of diplomatic negotiations.

Under general international law, there is no obligation that States must negotiate their disputes, although treaties often provide for such an obligation, as seen in the following examples.

Article 283(1) of the 1982 United Nations Convention on the Law of the Sea (UNCLOS III) states that:

> When a dispute arises between State Parties concerning the interpretation or application of this Convention, the parties to the dispute shall proceed expeditiously to an exchange of views regarding its settlement by negotiation or other peaceful means.

Article VIII(2) of the 1959 Antarctic Treaty provides that:

> Without prejudice to the provisions of paragraph 1 of this Article, and pending the adoption of measures in pursuance of subparagraph 1(e) of Article IX, the Contracting Parties concerned in any case of dispute with regard to the exercise of jurisdiction in Antarctica shall immediately consult together with a view to reaching a mutually acceptable solution.

Article 4(3) of the 1994 World Trade Organization (WTO) Agreement states that:

> If a request for consultations is made pursuant to a covered agreement, the Member to which the request is made shall, unless otherwise mutually agreed, reply to the request within 10 days after the date of its receipt and shall enter into consultations in good faith within a period of no more than 30 days after the date of receipt of the request, with a view to reaching a mutually satisfactory solution...

As evident in these three provisions, the degrees to which treaties impose an obligation to negotiate vary. For example, the WTO Agreement and the Antarctic Treaty impose a clear obligation to negotiate on their parties. However, UNCLOS III seems merely to require parties to 'proceed expeditiously to an exchange of views' regarding how the dispute should be resolved by negotiation. Nonetheless, a more generous interpretation could regard the provision as also imposing an obligation to negotiate on State parties.

KEY POINTS

- There is no obligation to negotiate in general international law, but treaties may impose such obligations on State parties.

- The degree to which treaties impose a duty on States to negotiate may vary.

Does an obligation to negotiate imply a duty to agree?

● *Cameroon v. Nigeria* (2002) ICJ Rep 303 (*Land and Maritime Boundary between Cameroon and Nigeria Case*)

Cameroon and Nigeria disputed an area popularly known as the Bakassi Peninsula. With regards to Articles 74 and 83 of UNCLOS III, concerning settlement of boundary disputes by negotiation, Nigeria argued that Cameroon had failed to negotiate a particular area of the boundary with it (Nigeria), and that, as such, the ICJ could not hear the case brought by Cameroon on that point.

The Court held (at 423–424) that:

> Articles 74 and 83 of the United Nations Law of the Sea Convention do not require that delimitation negotiation should be successful; like all similar obligations to negotiate in international law, the negotiations have to be conducted in good faith.
>
> From this provision, it is obvious that the obligation on parties is to negotiate in *good faith*. A party to negotiation cannot insist on agreement. [Emphasis added]

● *Railway Traffic between Poland and Lithuania Advisory Opinion* (1931) PCIJ Ser. A/B, No. 42

This case concerns a dispute between Poland and Lithuania on a railway traffic matter. The League Executive Council recommended that both States enter into direct negotiations. Poland argued that both parties had agreed not only to negotiate, but also to reach an agreement, and that, to that effect, Lithuania had incurred an obligation to open up the Kaisiadorys railway sector to traffic.

On the question of whether there was an obligation to negotiate, the Court held (at 116) that:

> The Court is indeed justified in considering that the engagement incumbent on the two Governments in conformity with the Council's Resolution is not only to enter into negotiation, but also to pursue them as far as possible, with a view to concluding agreements. This point of view appears, moreover, to have been adopted by the Council at its subsequent meetings. *But an obligation to negotiate does not imply an obligation to reach an agreement* ... [Emphasis added]

The PCIJ thus held that there was a duty to negotiate and possibly to reach an agreement. But the Court was more emphatic on the fact that the duty was to negotiate in good faith.

So what does it mean to negotiate in good faith?

● *Federal Republic of Germany v. Denmark, Federal Republic of Germany v. The Netherlands* (1969) ICJ Rep 3 (The *North Sea Continental Shelf Cases*)

The relevant issue in this case concerned negotiating the delimitation of boundaries between disputing parties. According to the Court, when undertaking negotiation of this nature, it is important that parties do so with a view to arriving at an agreement. But, the Court added (at 47):

...such agreement must be arrived at in accordance with *equitable* principles. On a foundation of very general precepts of *justice and good faith*, actual rules of law are here involved ... it is not a question of applying equity simply as a matter of abstract justice, but of applying a rule of law which itself requires the application of equitable principles, in accordance with the ideas which have always underlain the development of the legal régime of the continental shelf in this field, namely:

> the parties are under an obligation to enter into negotiations with a view to arriving at an agreement, and not merely to go through a formal process of negotiation as a sort of prior condition for the automatic application of a certain method of delimitation in the absence of agreement; they are under an obligation so to conduct themselves that the negotiations are meaningful, which will not be the case when either of them insists upon its own position without contemplating any modification of it.

This case is often cited as an authority for the Court, stating that an obligation to negotiate implies an obligation to reach an agreement. This is definitely not so. All the Court said was that once parties agree to negotiate, then they must do so equitably—that is, in fairness and *with a view to arriving at an agreement*. The obligation therefore is to pursue negotiation with the intention of *possibly*, not *mandatorily*, reaching an agreement.

● ***Legality of the Threat or Use of Nuclear Weapons Advisory Opinion*** [1996] ICJ Rep 226

In this case, the ICJ further clarified the requirement of 'good faith negotiation'. The Court was confronted with interpreting Article VI of the Treaty on the Non-Proliferation of Nuclear Weapons, which states that:

> Each of the Parties to the Treaty undertakes to pursue negotiations in good faith on effective measures relating to cessation of the nuclear arms race at an early date and to nuclear disarmament, and on a treaty on general and complete disarmament under strict and effective international control.

Commenting on the nature of this obligation, the Court said (at 263–264) that:

> The legal import of that obligation goes beyond that of a mere obligation of conduct; the obligation involved here is an obligation to achieve a precise result—nuclear disarmament in all its aspects—by adopting a particular course of conduct, namely, the pursuit of negotiations on the matter in good faith.

From the above, it is obvious that where an obligation to negotiate exists, then there is a duty to pursue it in good faith and to reach agreement equitably. What is required is that parties make serious efforts to reach an agreement.

See also *France v. Spain* (1957) 12 RIAA 281; 24 ILR 101 (the *Lake Lanoux Arbitration*), in which the arbitrator said that consultations and negotiations between the two States must be genuine, must comply with the rules of good faith, and must not be mere formalities.

(See C. M. Chinkin, 'The challenge of soft law: development and change in international law' (1989) 38(4) ICLQ 850.)

KEY POINTS

- An obligation to negotiate does not imply an obligation to reach an agreement.

- Negotiation must be carried out in good faith, meaning with the intention to reach an agreement that is acceptable to both parties.

Relationship between negotiation and litigation

What is the relationship between negotiation and litigation—that is, bringing a dispute before a court of law? Can parties to a dispute go to court while pursuing negotiation? Or does negotiation preclude simultaneous resort to the courts?

As a principle of law, negotiation can exist simultaneously with other forms of dispute settlement, including recourse to the courts.

● *Greece v. Turkey* (1978) ICJ REP 3 (The *Aegean Sea Continental Shelf Case*)

One of the issues before the Court was to determine whether a matter is subject to negotiation precludes its trial by the Court.

The Court held (at 12) that:

> Negotiation and judicial settlement are enumerated together in Article 33 of the Charter of the United Nations as means for the peaceful settlement of disputes. The jurisprudence of the Court provides various examples of cases in which negotiations and recourse to judicial settlement have been pursued *pari passu*... Consequently, the fact that negotiations are being actively pursued during the present proceedings is not, legally, any obstacle to the exercise by the Court of its judicial function.

● *Former Yugoslavia Republic of Macedonia v. Greece* (2011) ICJ REP 644

In this case, the Court had to decide whether agreement to negotiate prevented the Court from hearing the case. At paragraph 57, the Court confirmed the principle it laid down in the *Aegean Sea Case* (see earlier in this section).

Where negotiation and judicial settlement are simultaneously pursued, the success of negotiation terminates the judicial process.

● *Pakistan v. India* (1973) ICJ REP 347 (The *Trial of Pakistani Prisoners of War Case*)

Pakistan brought an action against India, claiming that it, Pakistan, had the sovereign right to prosecute 195 Pakistanis who were in the custody of India on charges of genocide. As the case got under way before the Court, Pakistan and India commenced negotiations, which later resulted in an agreed settlement. Pakistan then brought a notice for discontinuation of its case before the Court.

The Court agreed and the case was terminated.

KEY POINTS

- Negotiation can coexist with litigation.

- If negotiation succeeds, then litigation must terminate, because the issue(s) before the Court will usually have been resolved.

- As a general principle, the ICJ expects negotiation to precede litigation.

- There is no guarantee that negotiation will always take place.

The existence of parallel negotiations

Another important issue to consider is whether the fact that parties to a dispute may have commenced negotiation within an international organization, to which they both belong, precludes them from simultaneous recourse to the courts.

● **Nicaragua v. USA** [1986] ICJ Rep 14 [The **Military and Paramilitary Activities in and against Nicaragua Case**]

Nicaragua brought an action against the USA alleging subversive activities by the latter against the former. The USA argued that since the matter raised by Nicaragua was already being dealt with under the Contadora Process, a dispute settlement process established by Latin American countries in 1983, to which Nicaragua is a State party, the Court should not adjudicate it.

The Court held (at 440) that:

> …the Court considers that even the existence of active negotiations in which both parties might be involved should not prevent both the Security Council and the Court from exercising their separate functions under the Charter and the Statute of the Court.

Importantly, the Court also emphasized (at 440) that:

> The Court is unable to accept either that there is any requirement of prior exhaustion of regional negotiating processes as a precondition to seising the Court; or that the existence of the Contadora process constitutes in this case an obstacle to the examination by the Court of the Nicaraguan Application and judicial determination in due course of the submissions of the Parties in the case.

thinking points

- Does an obligation to settle disputes under regional arrangements preclude recourse to the ICJ or the Security Council?
- What is the relationship between negotiation and litigation?
- Explain the ICJ's reasoning in Nicaragua for holding that the Contadora Process does not prevent recourse to the Court or the Security Council.

Are there circumstances in which negotiation will be impossible?

There are situations in which it will be impractical to insist on negotiation even if an obligation to negotiate exists. For example, if one party, or both parties, to a dispute fail(s) or refuse(s) to negotiate, then litigation can commence. Similarly, where there are political hindrances against negotiation, then litigation can arise.

● **Greece v. United Kingdom** [1924] PCIJ Ser. A, No. 2 [The **Mavrommatis Palestine Concessions**]

In this case, the Court said (at 15) that:

> It recognises, in fact, that before a dispute can be made of an action at law, its subject matter should have been clearly defined by means of diplomatic negotiations. Nevertheless, in applying

this rule, the Court cannot disregard, amongst other considerations, the views of the States concerned, who are in the best position to judge as to political reasons which may prevent the settlement of a given dispute by diplomatic negotiation.

Consider the following examples where negotiation was impossible.

Where the nature of the dispute is such that there is no clear party with which to negotiate

. . . .

● *United States Diplomatic and Consular Staff in Tehran Advisory Opinion* (1980) ICJ REP 3 (The *Hostages Case*)

Certain elements of the Iranian Revolutionary Guard took hostage the staff of the US Embassy in Tehran. This was during an insurrection following the overthrow of the Iranian government. In the ensuing confusion, it was unclear who was in charge of the country.

Where one party to a dispute insists on a particular mode or place of negotiation that may make negotiation dispensable

. . . .

● *United Nations Headquarters Agreements Advisory Opinion* (1988) ICJ REP 12

The US government closed the office of the Palestine Liberation Organization (PLO) Observer Mission in New York. The Court held that the UN Secretary-General had tried his utmost to have the parties settle the dispute by negotiation, but that litigation of the dispute in the USA, as the USA insisted, could not be regarded as 'an agreed mode of settlement'.

Where the nature of a dispute is extremely complex—with not only single, but several, causes, spanning many generations—it may also be pragmatically impossible to deal with such a dispute by negotiation. An example is the Israel–Palestine conflict, the cause of which goes back over several decades. The interests at stake, the legal issues in question, and the areas of divergences in this dispute are such that they cannot be dealt with by negotiation. Negotiation thrives where there is relative clarity as to what is to be negotiated.

thinking point
List two circumstances in which negotiation may prove impossible.

KEY POINTS

- Negotiation and litigation can coexist.

- If negotiation succeeds, then litigation must terminate.

14.3.2 Inquiry

Inquiry is another important method of settling international disputes among States and it is different from negotiation in several ways. Inquiry is used, first and foremost, in trying to get to the bottom of the facts of a dispute. It aims at obtaining facts and figures about a dispute. Thus inquiry is more of a process to set the dispute settlement process rolling rather than one that is itself used to settle disputes.

Inquiry is mainly concerned with seeking facts, not the application of the law or legal processes. However, it is possible that inquiry settles the dispute between parties, if the outcome of the investigation is acceptable to all sides.

In a 1991 Resolution and Declaration on fact-finding by the United Nations, the UN General Assembly defined 'inquiry' as:

> Any activity designed to obtain detailed knowledge of the relevant facts of any dispute or situation which the competent United Nations organs need in order to exercise effectively their functions in relation to the maintenance of international peace and security.

Clearly, this definition concerns the use of inquiry and fact-finding missions by UN organs. Nonetheless, the substance of the definition itself—that is, 'to obtain detailed knowledge of the relevant facts about any dispute or situation'—applies to all inquiry and fact-finding missions.

According to Article 9 of the 1899 Convention for the Pacific Settlement of International Disputes (I) and the 1907 Convention for the Pacific Settlement of International Disputes (II), for the Pacific Settlement of International Disputes (hereafter the 'Hague I and II Conventions' discussed in full later):

> In disputes of an *international* nature involving neither honour nor vital interests, and arising from a difference of opinion on points of facts, the Contracting Powers deem it expedient and desirable that the parties *who have not been able to come to an agreement by means of diplomacy*, should, as far as circumstances allow, institute an International Commission of Inquiry, to facilitate a solution of these disputes by elucidating the facts by means of an impartial and conscientious investigation. [Emphasis added]

This provision seems to imply that disputing States should resort to inquiry if they are unable to negotiate a settlement on their own. However, as we will see, practice shows that inquiry can be authorized at any point in a dispute.

Although inquiry has existed for a long time, it became formally recognized by international law following an incident in 1898 that involved a US ship, *USS Maine*, and has come to be known as the '*Maine* Affair' (available at http://www.u-s-history.com/pages/h818.html).

The *USS Maine* was dispatched to the Havana harbour in January 1898, to protect American lives and property in the troubled colony of Cuba. On 15 February, *USS Maine* exploded, killing 260 men aboard. The USA blamed Spain for the act, which resulted in a 144-day war between Spain and the USA. It must be noted that, at the time of this disaster, there was huge tension between Spain and the USA over how Spain was dealing with its colony, Cuba, which was agitating for independence. Cuba was considered strategically important to growing US interests.

Following the blowing-up of the *USS Maine*, the USA set up a commission of inquiry in March 1898 to determine what caused the explosion. Although Spain had specifically requested to participate in the inquiry, the USA insisted that it would conduct the inquiry alone (see *The New York Times*, 'Spain and the *Maine*: a request to take part in the inquiry at Havana declined in Washington', 20 February 1898).

The Inquiry Commission reported that Spain had torpedoed the ship—a decision that was confirmed by another inquiry that took place between 1911 and 1912. Since then, several other inquiries have taken place, with some determining that the explosion was merely an accident not uncommon aboard ships.

Prior to the *Maine* Affair, there had been no international system regulating how inquiry was to be conducted; hence the USA acted under its own laws.

thinking points

- *Define 'inquiry'.*
- *Is inquiry significantly concerned with the legal process?*
- *To what types of dispute may inquiry apply?*

Inquiry and the 1899 and 1907 Hague Conventions

The *Maine* Affair inspired the first Peace Conference held at The Hague in 1899. The Conference adopted the Hague I Convention, which made crucial provisions for the use of inquiry as a dispute settlement method.

According to Article 10 of the 1899 Hague Convention:

> the International Commissions of Inquiry are constituted by special agreement between the parties in conflict...[and] both sides must be heard.

As seen previously, while Article 9 asserts the principal purpose of commission of inquiry to be 'elucidating the facts by means of impartial and conscientious investigation', Article 10 expects all parties to a dispute to be heard by an inquiry. This provision is very important, given that the USA had not allowed Spain to participate in the *Maine* inquiry despite its belief that Spain was responsible for the act.

The 1899 Conference marked the first recognition of inquiry as a dispute settlement process under international law. The 1899 Convention proved considerably useful and was applied to several disputes, the most popular of which was an incident involving Russian and British ships in 1904, known as the Dogger Bank incident.

During a war between Russia and Japan in 1904, the Russian Baltic Fleet mistook some British trawlers at Dogger Bank for an Imperial Japanese Navy force and attacked them killing three British sailors and wounding many. Russia agreed to investigate the matter and, upon accepting responsibility, paid compensation to the victims of the attack. See *Great Britain v. Russia* (1908) 2 AJIL 931 (ICI Report of 26 February 1906) (the *Dogger Bank Case*).

The Dogger Bank inquiry revealed several weaknesses in the provisions of the 1899 Convention. In particular, the Convention made no provision for dealing with procedural issues by an inquiry commission. As a result, the Dogger Bank inquiry spent a great deal of time deciding how it should conduct its affairs.

In 1907, the second Peace Conference at The Hague adopted a convention that substantially improved on the 1899 Convention by including many provisions on matters of procedure (see, in particular, Articles 9–36).

In another significant event in 1960, known as the *Red Crusader* Affair, a Danish frigate stopped and arrested a UK fishing vessel, the *Red Crusader*, leading to a dispute between Denmark and the UK. However, following a proposal by Denmark, both countries agreed to set up a commission of inquiry.

According to the agreement between the two countries (available at http://legal.un.org/riaa/cases/vol_XXIX/521-539.pdf), the Commission was requested:

...to investigate and report to the two Governments:

(i) the facts leading up to the arrest of the British trawler *Red Crusader* on the night of the 29th of May, 1961, including the question whether the *Red Crusader* was fishing, or with her fishing gear not stowed, inside the blue line on the map annexed to the Agreement between the two Governments concerning the regulation of fishing around the Faroe Islands constituted by the Exchange of Notes of the 27th of April, 1959;

(ii) the circumstances of the arrest; and

(iii) the facts and incidents that occurred thereafter before the *Red Crusader* reached Aberdeen.

thinking point
What was the contribution of the Dogger Bank incident to the development of inquiry?

KEY POINTS

• The 1907 Convention remarkably improved upon the 1899 Convention in provisions concerning procedures on inquiry commissions.

• The two Conventions recommend that all parties to disputes should participate in the proceedings of commissions of inquiry.

Treaties and inquiry

Inquiry has become more popular since 1907 and is today widely used by States and international organizations. Bilateral and multilateral treaties now regularly make provisions similar to those of the two Hague Conventions on inquiry. The most famous of these was negotiated in 1913–14 by the US Secretary of State William Jennings Bryan for the 'advancement of peace'. Known as the 'Bryan Treaties', there are forty-eight in all, although very few disputes were ever submitted to them (see http://law.jrank.org/pages/4907/Bryan-Treaties.html).

The Bryan Treaties provide that wherever a dispute arises between State parties, an inquiry commission will review the underlying facts to the dispute and issue reports within a year. Such parties undertake not to resort to hostility while the report is awaited. This tactical delay is aimed at defusing the tension between the parties. (For a critique of the Bryan Treaties, especially with regards to the procedures that they envisaged, see R. M. Easley, 'The imperative case: weakness of arbitration as contemplated in Mr Bryan's treaties', *New York Times*, 11 June 1915.)

While they were rarely used, the most high-profile application of the treaties was to the dispute arising from the assassination of Mr Orlando Letelier, a top Chilean diplomat and political figure, and his US assistant, Ronni Moffit (reported at (1992) 25 RIAA 1). The USA invoked the treaty between it and Chile, which resulted in Chile agreeing to pay compensation to the victims' families, although it denied responsibility for the crime.

International organizations and inquiry

International organizations also make regular use of inquiry in dispute settlements. The Latin American Contadora Process (referred to in section 14.3.1) is clearly an example of a regional arrangement.

There are many ways in which international organizations can use inquiry. First, international organizations can use inquiry to settle disputes *between* their member States.

example

In 2013, following reports of chemical weapons used against civilians in the Syrian crisis, the UN set up an inquiry to investigate the matter although the mandate of this inquiry did not include a finding of guilt or responsibility for the use of the weapons. Nonetheless, the establishment that chemical weapons had been used led to the agreement between the Syrian government and the USA for the dismantling of the chemical weapons possessed by Syria. (See S/RES/2118 (2013).)

Secondly, international organizations can use inquiry in respect of disputes occurring *within* a member State, such as between the government and rebel groups.

example

In 2009, following the war between Israel and the Palestinian armed group, Hamas, the UN Human Rights Council set up an independent fact-finding mission, headed by Richard Goldstone, to investigate human rights and humanitarian law violations in the Gaza war. (See Resolution A/HRC/S-9/L.1, point 14.)

Thirdly, international organizations can use inquiry to investigate matters concerning another international organization, although this is not common.

example

In 2007, the European Union called for an inquiry into why the African Union (AU) delayed paying its troops in Darfur, Sudan, despite the fact that the EU had given the AU money to that effect.

In a public statement ('EU Parliaments wants inquiry into pay delays to Darfur troops', *Sudan Tribune*, 12 July 2007, available at http://www.sudantribune.com/spip.php?article22817), it was written that:

> The European Parliament...stepped up pressure on the European Union to establish why African troops in Darfur have not been paid for months even though the EU has provided millions of dollars for the military force.... The AU mission to Sudan acknowledged in a statement that its soldiers have not been paid for four months, but called on the EU to simplify the paperwork necessary for the funds to be released. The EU said its financial experts were helping the AU at its headquarters in Addis Ababa, Ethiopia, to 'strengthen its financial management capacities'.

It must be noted that the use of inquiry by one organization to investigate the affairs of another, as we have just seen, is unique to relations between organizations. States do not use inquiry in this manner. Under international law, all States are equal and sovereign.

example

It is therefore impossible for Candoma to order an inquiry into whether Rutamu uses chemical weapons against its own people. Only Rutamu or an international organization to which it belongs can do so.

There are two exceptions to this rule.

example

(a) If Candoma consents to it, Rutamu can send an inquiry to investigate a matter within Candoma's territory.

(b) Under Chapter VII of the UN Charter (see our discussion in Chapter 11), the Security Council could authorize an inquiry in respect of any State whether or not the State is a UN member.

In reality, however, the Security Council will rarely send an inquiry into a State that has not consented to it despite the fact that, as a matter of law, the Security Council is empowered to do so.

thinking points

• *Are there any differences between how States and international organizations use inquiry?*

• *How widely used are the Bryan Treaties?*

14.3.3 Mediation and good offices

Often parties to a dispute may not wish to deal directly with each other, usually because one side, or both sides, feel(s) very passionate about the dispute. Causes of disputes between States are often very sensitive, because they may border on issues of territory, sovereignty, and so on. In those circumstances, negotiation is practically impossible. The first thing to do is to find a way for external parties to help to diffuse tension and to facilitate communication between disputing States.

Defining 'mediation'

According to Article 2 of the 1899 Hague Convention:

> In case of serious disagreement or conflict, before an appeal to arms, the Signatory Powers agree to have recourse, as far as circumstances allow, to the good offices or mediation of one or more friendly Powers.

In a dispute, parties are encouraged to allow mediation by other States. However, failure by disputing States to invite other States to mediate in the dispute does not bar such an intervention. According to Article 3 of the Convention:

> Independently of this recourse, the Signatory Powers recommend that one or more Powers, strangers to the dispute, should, on their own initiative, and as far as circumstances may allow, offer their good offices or mediation to the States at variance.

NOTE Article 3 does not impose an obligation on other States to mediate in a dispute, but merely encourages them to act of their own volition when parties to a dispute have not invited them. Nonetheless, such self-invitation requires the approval of the disputing States, otherwise mediation is impossible.

Regardless of how mediation comes about the role of the mediator, according to Article 4 of the 1899 Convention:

> consists in reconciling the opposing claims and appeasing the feelings of resentment which may have arisen between the States at variance.

Mediation and good offices: what distinction?

'Mediation' and 'good offices' are both mentioned in the 1899 and 1907 Hague Conventions, although 'good offices' is not in the UN Charter. However, the Hague Conventions do not distinguish between the two; rather, the terms are used interchangeably.

Sometimes academic writers distinguish between mediation and good offices. Thus John Merrills (2006, at p. 537, see section 14.1.2) says that, on the one hand:

> a mediator . . . is an active participant, authorized, and indeed expected, to advance fresh ideas and to interpret, as well as to transmit, each party's proposals to the other.

'Good offices', on the other hand, is to 'encourage the protagonists to resume negotiations, or simply acts as a channel of communication'.

This distinction is useful in theory, but is of little value in practice, because a good office holder can be as proactive as a mediator.

Nonetheless, we can differentiate between mediation and good offices in two ways.

- Mediation is often undertaken by States, but good offices are mostly discharged by individual persons, although States are not precluded from so acting.
- While mediating States are often friendly with both sides to the dispute, good office holders are appointed on the basis of their moral standing or international status. Hence, the Pope, or the UN Secretary-General, and eminent political figures such as Nelson Mandela, have all acted as good office holders in disputes amongst States.

Whereas treaties do not generally distinguish between 'mediation' and 'good offices', some do. An example is the 1948 American Treaty on Pacific Settlement (known as the 'Pact of Bogota').

According to Article IX of the 1948 Pact:

> The procedure of good *offices* consists in the attempt by one or more American Governments not parties to the controversy, or *by one or more eminent citizens of any American State* which is not a party to the controversy, to bring the parties together, so as to make it possible for them to reach an adequate solution between themselves. [Emphasis added]

Similarly, in the Manila Declaration on the Settlement of Disputes between States (A/RES/37/10, 15 November 1982), 'good offices' is directly mentioned in paragraph 5 as one of the various dispute settlement methods.

When does mediation take place?

Is there any particular point in a dispute at which mediation must take place?

There are two major views on this point, one of which is the proposition that mediation should start before disputing States resort to armed conflict: see, for example, F. Edmead, *Analysis and Prediction in International Mediation* (New York: UNITAR Study, 1971).

The opposing view states that mediation is best employed after a dispute has gone through many phases and parties show a willingness to talk: see F. S. Northedge and M. Donelan, *International Disputes: Political Aspects* (London: Europa, 1971).

It is difficult to lay down general rules about *when* or not to mediate. When mediation should take place depends on the circumstances of individual cases.

However, in practice, mediation tends to occur when:

- parties do not wish to communicate with each other directly;
- disputes have been protracted;
- individual efforts have reached stalemate and there seems no way out; and/or
- parties refuse to shift ground on their positions.

It is not necessary for all of these factors to be present before mediation can arise: mere refusal by parties to engage each other directly or to shift on their positions, for example, is enough to trigger mediation.

example

On 2 April 1982, Argentine forces invaded and occupied the Falkland Islands. The Islands had been the subject of a long dispute between the UK and Argentina. The UK did not immediately respond militarily, but chose instead to try to resolve the conflict diplomatically. US Secretary of State Haig attempted to use his good offices to resolve the dispute diplomatically. Both the UK and Argentina refused to shift ground on the question of sovereignty over the Islands, and with the failure of the UN to resolve the crisis, armed conflict followed, resulting in a British victory. This is a clear example of a case in which, although some of the previously mentioned conditions were present, the mediation did not work.

The principles of mediation and good offices

It is important that, in order to make the outcome of mediation acceptable to disputing parties, such mediation be based on certain core principles, as follows.

Confidence of all sides to the dispute

Where a mediator is appointed jointly by parties to a dispute, there is usually a higher probability that the mediator is fair. After all, a mediator is usually a State that is friendly to both parties to the dispute. However, where mediation takes place on the mediator's initiative, as clearly permitted by the Hague Conventions, there is a risk that a mediator may not inspire the confidence of one or both parties to the dispute. In this situation, the outcome of mediation may be unacceptable to one or both parties, and it is possible that the mediator will not enjoy the cooperation of one or both parties. This could be fatal to the process.

Impartiality of the mediator

Irrespective of how mediation comes about, it is vital that a mediator remains impartial at all times. Impartiality is the key to the success of mediation, and many mediation efforts have been ruined because of the perception that mediators were biased against certain parties.

Voluntariness

Mediation is voluntary and any party or the mediator may terminate at any time. It is important that parties are made to understand that they are under no obligation to mediate their dispute. This helps to make them more favourably disposed to a settlement. Imposition of mediation can be counterproductive.

As Jacob Bercovitch notes, in *Resolving International Conflicts: The Theory and Practice of Mediation* (Boulder, CO: Lynne Rienner, 1996), p. 4:

> It is important to bear in mind that neither mediator role nor mediator performance can be stipulated in advance. Generic principles promoting better outcomes must be viewed with caution, as mediation is a dynamic and flexible process and adaptability is its prized attribute and its key to success.

In the final analysis, mediation is what parties decide to make of it. Results cannot be imposed; neither can a mediator do more than the parties are ready to accept and allow. The core role of a mediator is to ease the tension between parties, to facilitate communication, to help them to identify common grounds, and to isolate contentious positions. After achieving these, all that remains is for the mediator to advance proposals to the parties towards settlement—but whether they will accept or not is a matter solely for them to decide.

14.3.4 Conciliation

The Institute of International Law (IIL), in Article 1 of its 1961 Regulations on the Procedure of International Conciliation, defines 'conciliation' as:

> a method of settlement of international disputes of any nature according to which a Commission set up by the Parties, either on a permanent or ad hoc basis to deal with a dispute proceeds to the impartial examination of the dispute and attempts to define the terms of a settlement susceptible of being accepted by them, or affording the Parties with a view to its settlement, such aid as they may have requested.

According to J.-P. Cot, a leading academic writer on the subject, in *International Conciliation* (London: Europa, 1972), p. 9, 'conciliation' is an:

> intervention in the settlement of an international dispute by a body having no political authority of its own, but enjoying the confidence of the parties to the dispute, with the task of investigating every aspect of the dispute and of proposing a solution which is not binding on the parties.

The nature and features of conciliation

Conciliation is similar to both inquiry and mediation in some respects. Like inquiry, conciliation is usually undertaken by commissions set up for that purpose, and involves investigating causes of disputes and other associated facts. Like mediation, conciliation always involves intervention by external parties.

While conciliation is often performed by commissions, there are instances in which single conciliators can be appointed.

example

Dr Victor Umbricht, an experienced Swiss diplomat, was appointed by the three former East African Community (EAC) States (Uganda, Kenya, and Tanzania) with the task of distributing the assets of the EAC among the States. Although the final mode of distribution of the assets of the dissolved organization departed from the recommendations of the conciliator in certain respects, there was no doubt that the conciliator's recommendations provided the basis for the distribution.

Another feature that conciliation shares with mediation is that it often arises when parties to a dispute refuse direct communication with each other. The account given by Dr Umbricht of his involvement in the EAC asset-sharing conciliation illustrates this point.

In his personal account, 'Pages From World Bank History: East African Mediation', 12 September 2003, available at http://web.worldbank.org/WBSITE/EXTERNAL/EXTABOUTUS/ EXTARCHIVES/0,,print:Y~isCURL:Y~contentMDK:20129168~pagePK:36726~piPK:36092~t heSitePK:29506,00.html, Dr Umbricht recounted what led to the breakdown of the EAC, and how its three State parties, Uganda, Tanzania, and Kenya, approached the World Bank for loans to bail them out of their difficulties. The Bank refused and, instead, asked the States to sort out their problems and discharge their existing liabilities to the Bank. In response:

> the governments informed the Bank that they *were no longer on speaking terms, and how can you settle a problem between us if you are unable to meet and to talk*. Therefore the Bank and the Fund suggested that if they could not talk directly to each other, they should talk to somebody in between, a Mediator. That is how the Mediation system came up. The proposal was made and the three countries accepted to have Mediation and asked the Bank to propose a Mediator. And the Bank proposed four or five names. Amongst those names was mine. So, I moved over to east Africa and I stayed there for nine years and three months. [Emphasis added]

Conciliation is not binding and a conciliator is always chosen by disputing parties.

Conciliation and treaties

The 1899 and 1907 Hague Conventions did not provide for conciliation. However, most multilateral treaties concluded after the First World War included conciliation, although this practice has now declined significantly.

The League of Nations, in particular, supported the use of conciliation commissions. On 22 September 1922, its Third Assembly adopted a resolution encouraging States to use conciliation commissions (see *League of Nations Records of the Third Assembly, Preliminary Meetings*, 1922, pp. 199–200).

One common feature of the conciliation commissions that emerged in the 1920s is that they were permanent—that is, all of these commissions had members that could always be drawn upon to provide conciliation services to needy States.

The role of conciliation commissions is usually stated in the treaty establishing them. As stated in Article 5 of the 1925 Treaty of Conciliation between Italy and Switzerland:

> the task of the Permanent Conciliation Commission shall be to further the settlement of disputes by an impartial and conscientious examination of the facts and by formulating proposals with a view to settling the case.

This and other 1920s treaties on conciliation are called the 'Locarno Treaties'. They were named after the place in Switzerland where they were negotiated, during 5–16 October 1925, although, they were signed in London on 1 December of that year.

Conciliation and international organizations

Despite the decline in the use of conciliation, modern treaties—especially those of international organizations—do regularly include it.

Article 284(1) of UNCLOS III states that:

> A State Party which is a party to a dispute concerning the interpretation or application of this Convention may invite the other party or parties to submit the dispute to conciliation in accordance with the procedure under Annex V, section 1, or another conciliation procedure.

Article 1 of the 1962 Protocol Instituting a Conciliation and Good Offices Commission to be Responsible for Seeking the Settlement of any Disputes which may Arise between States Parties to the Convention against Discrimination in Education (651 UNTS 632) states that:

> There shall be established under the auspices of the United Nations Educational, Scientific and Cultural Organization a Conciliation and Good Offices Commission, hereinafter referred to as the Commission, to be responsible for seeking the amicable settlement of disputes between States Parties to the Convention against Discrimination in Education, hereinafter referred to as the Convention, concerning the application or interpretation of the Convention.

Other examples include the 1948 Pact of Bogota, the 1957 European Convention for Peaceful Settlement of Disputes, and the 1969 Vienna Convention on the Law of Treaties (VCLT).

The use of the various conciliation commissions established by these treaties differs. For example, while conciliation commissions are frequently used to resolve trade disputes, the United Nations Educational, Scientific and Cultural Organization (UNESCO) Conciliation Commission on Discrimination has never been used to settle a dispute between its member States.

Conciliation may be used when direct negotiation between parties fails, as occurred in 1929 between Bolivia and Paraguay in what is known as the 'Chaco Dispute' (see L. H. Woolsey, 'The Chaco Dispute' (1932) 26(4) AJIL 796).

example

The dispute between Bolivia and Paraguay (1928–35) arose over ownership claims over the Gran Chaco territory, a territory that traditionally belonged to Bolivia, but over which an indigenous Paraguay tribe had exercised undisturbed rights. Matters heated up between the two countries after oil was discovered on the territory.

A conciliation commission of five neutral States was set up to help the parties to resolve the dispute. However, despite the efforts of the Commission, hostilities occurred and continued until 1953, when the parties respectively held on to their military gains.

What is important is that the Chaco conciliation did not settle the dispute between the parties; instead, it made its services available if direct negotiation between the parties failed, as was eventually the case.

It must be noted that a conciliation commission does not have to apply the rule of law, although nothing prevents it from recognizing such rules.

· ·

● **Conciliation Commission on the Continental Shelf between Iceland and Norway in the Area between Greenland and Jan Mayen** (1981) 27 RIAA 1

In this case, the Conciliation Commission stated (at 23) that it:

> shall not act as a court of law. Its function is to make recommendations to the two governments which in the unanimous opinion of the Commission will lead to acceptable and equitable solution of the problems involved.

Nonetheless, the Commission did consider State practice in its work, as well as in several 'decisions of courts including that of the ICJ in the *North Sea Continental Shelf* cases', according to Collier and Lowe (1999, see section 14.1.2), p. 31.

The future of conciliation

Conciliation is one of the least but widely used dispute settlement methods. Not only do international organizations regularly include it in their treaties, the UN General Assembly has also lent its support to conciliation.

In 1990, the General Assembly adopted and requested the UN Secretary-General to circulate the Draft Rules for the Conciliation of Disputes between States. Members were to comment on these rules as part of the UN International Law Decade. The revised rules were approved by the General Assembly in 1996 as Resolution A/50/50.

For commentary, see J. G. Merrills, *International Dispute Settlement* (Cambridge: Cambridge University Press, 2005), p. 82.

Arbitration

Arbitration is a method for settling disputes under which disputing parties submit their cases to an independent arbitrator agreed by them and whose decision they undertake to accept.

14.4.1 The origins of arbitration in modern international law

Arbitration is regarded as the oldest method for settling disputes among States. The earliest known treaty of arbitration was the 1794 Treaty of Amity, Commerce and Navigation (known as the 'Jay Treaty') between the USA and Great Britain.

The 1794 Jay Treaty

Named after its chief negotiator John Jay, the 1794 Jay Treaty sought to resolve trade disputes between the USA and Great Britain.

Article V of the Treaty sets out the rules governing the arbitral process. It identifies the dispute between the parties and requests that questions relating to the dispute:

> shall be referred to the final decision of commissioners to be appointed in the following man-ner…One commissioner shall be named by His Majesty, and one by the President of the United States, by and with the advice and consent of the Senate thereof, and the said two commissioners shall agree on the choice of a third; or if they cannot so agree, they shall each propose one person, and of the two names so proposed, one shall be drawn by lot in the presence of the two original Commissioners.
>
> And the three Commissioners so appointed shall be sworn, *impartially* to examine and decide the said question, according to such *evidence* as shall respectively be laid before them on the part of the British Government and of the United States. The said Commissioners shall meet at Halifax, and shall have power *to adjourn* to such other place or places as they shall think fit. They shall have power to appoint a Secretary, and to employ such surveyors or other persons as they shall judge necessary. The said Commissioners shall, by a declaration, under their hands and seals, decide what river is the river St. Croix, intended by the treaty. [Emphasis added]

KEY POINTS

• Arbitration is the oldest method of dispute settlement.

• The 1794 Jay Treaty was the first modern treaty to include arbitration. It deals with disputes between the USA and Great Britain.

14.4.2 The features of arbitration

It is obvious from the provisions of the Jay Treaty set out in the previous extract that arbitration is different, in several ways, from the other dispute settlement methods that we have discussed.

Arbitration is a quasi-judicial process

Arbitration consists of certain features of judicial processes. Article 5 of the Jay Treaty clearly intends the USA–Britain arbitration to have legal pedigrees. The treaty uses such legal phrases as 'adjournment' and 'judges', and it expects arbitral decisions to be based on 'evidence'.

Arbitration involves the participation of disputing parties

Unlike the other dispute settlement methods discussed earlier, parties to arbitrations nominate arbitrators. The entitlement to nominate arbitrators gives disputing parties some level of control over their own affairs.

Normally, each party to a dispute will nominate one arbitrator and the two will then nominate the chair of arbitration. The position of the chair of an arbitration panel or commission is crucial, especially if the votes of the two arbitrators do not tally.

Arbitral awards are legally binding on the parties

In our earlier discussion, we noted that the success of negotiation, mediation, inquiry, or conciliation depends much on the goodwill of disputing parties. Hence, refusal by a party to cooperate can adversely affect any of these methods. Also, the outcome of these processes is not binding on disputing parties.

An arbitral award is different in these respects. Once arbitration is constituted, parties are expected to cooperate with the commissioners. Also, only in cases of procedural irregularities or vitiating conditions (see later) will disputing parties not comply with the decision of an arbitrator.

Arbitration arises when diplomacy has failed

Arbitration does not promote negotiation, and it mostly arises after negotiation has failed. According to Article 38 of the 1907 Hague Convention:

> In questions of a legal nature, and especially in the interpretation or application of International Conventions, arbitration is recognized by the Contracting Powers as the most effective, and, at the same time, the most equitable means of settling disputes which *diplomacy has failed to settle*. [Emphasis added]

thinking points

- *Distinguish between arbitration and other dispute settlement methods.*
- *Why is arbitration regarded as quasi-judicial?*

14.4.3 The early practice of arbitration and unreasoned decisions

The 1794 Jay Treaty recommends that arbitral decisions should be based on evidence. However, this has not always been the case. Most arbitral awards decided during the first half of the nineteenth century were unreasoned. This was particularly the case in situations in which sovereigns, such as kings, or heads of State and government, served as arbitrators.

Let us consider a few examples of cases of unreasoned arbitral decisions.

● *France v. Great Britain* (1843) 1 Recueil Des Arbitrages Internationaux 512 (The *Portendick Claim*)

In a dispute between Great Britain and France, the arbitrator, the King of Prussia, gave his decision without stating any reason.

● *Italy v. Colombia* (1897) 2 Moore Arbitrations 2117; 11 UNRIAA 377 (The *Cerutti Claims*)

See 'Cerutti Claims settled', *The New York Times*, 11 March 1899.

The US President Grover Cleveland, who arbitrated this dispute, gave his decision, awarding substantial sums against Colombia. He, however, did not give any reason for his decision.

Other examples include the *De Cala Case* (Mexico Claims Commission, 1839) and the *Fabiani Case* (decided by the French–Venezuelan Commission under the 1902 Protocol), both of which are reviewed in Kazimierz Grzybowski, 'Interpretation of decisions of international tribunals' (1941) 35(3) AJIL 482.

KEY POINTS

- The 1794 Jay Treaty intends arbitral decisions to be reasoned and based on evidence.

- It is important to note that early arbitrators did not give reasons for their decisions. This was particularly so in cases in which sovereigns acted as arbitrators.

14.4.4 The rise of modern arbitration: the *Alabama Claim* (1872)

During the American Civil War, Great Britain, which was officially a neutral party, allowed several ships used by the confederates to be built in Britain, including the *CSS Alabama*, which did considerable damage to American maritime vessels. The USA claimed against Great Britain for the latter's violation of her neutrality. An arbitral tribunal made its award in favour of the USA.

However, it must be pointed out that the success of the 1872 *Alabama Claim* owes much to the 1871 Treaty of Washington, concluded by the USA and Great Britain, for the purpose of resolving disputes arising out of the American Civil War.

Remarkably, the *Alabama Claim* applied legal principles, and thus the arbitral award against Britain was reasoned and based on evidence.

The *Alabama* arbitration inspired many arbitration commissions to apply legal rules and to give reasoned decisions, as will be seen in the following examples.

. . . .

● *Great Britain v. USA* (1893) MOORE'S INTERNATIONAL ARBITRATION 755 (The *Bering Sea Arbitration*)

This dispute arose out of the USA's arrest of some British ocean liners inside the waters of Alaska, a region that the USA had bought from Russia. The resultant arbitral panel consisted of one US Supreme Court justice and the terms of reference of the panel were to determine serious legal questions. The tribunal decided in favour of Britain and gave reasons for the award.

. . . .

● *British Guiana v. Venezuela* (1899–1900) 92 BFSP 160 (The *British Guiana–Venezuela Boundary Arbitration*)

See Clifton J. Child, 'The British Guiana–Venezuela Boundary Arbitration 1899' (1950) 40(4) AJIL 682.

Great Britain had purchased British Guiana (now Guyana) from the Netherlands. Britain claimed that its lands included an area that Venezuela claimed as its own; Venezuela accused Britain of encroachment. Venezuela broke off diplomatic relations with Britain and appealed to the USA for assistance. The USA, eager to enforce the so-called Monroe Doctrine—a doctrine enunciated during the reign of US President Monroe, which sought to protect the Americas (Western hemisphere) from foreign invasions—invited Britain to submit the dispute to an American boundary commission functioning as an arbitration panel. Britain did so. In a reasoned judgment, the arbitral panel decided in favour of Great Britain.

14.4.5 Types of arbitration

Under international law, arbitration is mostly used to settle disputes between States. However, arbitration is sometimes used to settle disputes between States and non-State entities, such as multinational corporations (MNCs). This is called a 'mixed arbitration' and has become more frequently used in modern times.

However, the term 'mixed arbitration' can also be used to refer to an arbitration commission that consists of different nationalities and may be formed either through bilateral or multilateral instruments. An example of a mixed arbitration is the US–Iran Claims Tribunal, set up to resolve issues arising from the hostage crisis between those two countries. This arbitration consists of members from Italy, Belgium, the USA, and Iran. This was also a temporary arbitration, the panel of which would cease to exist once the specific objective for which it was established was realized.

Arbitration panels could also exist on a permanent basis and continue to exist as long as the treaty remains in force. The most prominent example of this category is the Permanent Court of Arbitration (PCA).

thinking points

• What does the Alabama Claim *contribute to the development of arbitration?*
• What are mixed arbitrations?

Arbitration

517

14.4.6 The Permanent Court of Arbitration

The PCA was established on a permanent basis by the 1899 and 1907 Hague Conventions as an institutional means of settling disputes through arbitration.

Article 41 of the 1907 Hague Convention states that:

> With the object of facilitating an immediate recourse to arbitration for international differences, which it has not been possible to settle by diplomacy, the Contracting Powers undertake to maintain the Permanent Court of Arbitration, as established by the First Peace Conference, accessible at all times, and operating, unless otherwise stipulated by the parties, in accordance with the rules of procedure inserted in the present Convention.

The PCA sits in The Hague, although parties may decide to locate the panel elsewhere (Article 60). The PCA is intended to be a permanent arbitration court and is competent to deal with all arbitration cases (Article 42), except if parties agree to institute a special tribunal (Article 42).

Features of the PCA

The Court has an international bureau (IB), which serves as its registry. The IB facilitates communication between State parties to the PCA, and deals with matters such as meetings and the record-keeping of the PCA. State parties provide the IB with details such as their laws, regulations, and documents relating to how they implement decisions of the PCA (Article 43).

Each party to the PCA nominates four members to be kept on the PCA's list to serve as arbitrators. They are regarded as members of the PCA and are usually persons of high moral calibre.

They are elected for six years, renewable, and the same person may be nominated by more than one country (Article 44).

To try a dispute, the IB identifies certain arbitrators from the list to serve on the case. However, if parties fail to agree on whom to select, then they themselves will nominate two arbitrators each, who will then nominate the fifth arbitrator to serve as the umpire (Article 45).

The IB then communicates the *compromis* to the parties. The *compromis* is a document in which the subject of the dispute in question, and the time, order, and form of arbitration are defined (Article 52).

KEY POINTS

- The PCA is permanent and is intended to function as a court.

- The PCA is established by a multilateral treaty and member States play an active part in its operation by nominating members to the Court.

The procedure of the PCA

Articles 51–85 of the 1907 Hague Convention deal with the procedure of the PCA. Articles 52–54 deal with the *compromis* in general, while more substantive issues such as the rules governing the arbitration, the language to be used, communications of pleadings, counsel to parties, the taking of evidence, and the serving of notices are all contained in Articles 55–78.

Reasoned decisions

Article 79 of the 1907 Convention provides that:

> the award must give reason on which it is based. It contains the names of the Arbitrators; it is signed by the President and Registrar or by the Secretary acting as Registrar.

As may be recalled from the earlier discussion, early arbitrations did not give reasons for their decisions. Thus the PCA improved the standard of arbitration in this regard and aligned it fully with a proper legal process.

. . . .

● *Guinea-Bissau v. Senegal* (1991) ICJ REP 53 (*Case Concerning Arbitral Award of 31 July 1989*)

Judge Weeramantry (dissenting at 164–165) underscored the importance of giving reasons for arbitral awards:

> The necessity for reasons in an arbitral award is of course obvious as it removes any appearance of arbitrariness in the Tribunal's decision. It is a long-established and well-respected rule ... There have been occasional instances of major international arbitrations in which no reasons have been given for the award, as for instance in the Portendick arbitration of 1843 between France and Great Britain in which the arbitrator was the King of Prussia. However, such award without reasons immediately attracted criticism from learned publicists even at that early stage in the evolution of international arbitral law. The Portendick arbitration was criticized by Fauchille, and in 1897 when President Cleveland failed to give reasons for his decision in the Cerruti arbitration between Colombia and Italy, this was criticized by Darras.

Sovereign arbitrators

Article 56 of the 1907 Hague Convention also provides that a head of State might serve as the arbitrator. Where this is the case, he or she decides the case.

Two issues arise from this provision. First, where arbitration under the PCA is decided by a sovereign, unlike in the early arbitrations already considered, he or she must give reasons for the resultant award. As far as giving reasons for awards is concerned, Article 79 makes no distinction between arbitration by arbitrators or by a sovereign.

Secondly, the appointment of a sovereign arbitrator means that parties to disputes do not have to nominate arbitrators, although they could nominate the sovereign by agreement or the IB could do so on their behalf.

The effect of a PCA arbitral award

An award made either by ordinary or sovereign arbitrators is binding on parties to the dispute, but not anyone else (Article 84). The award, which must be read in public (Article 80), is final and not appealable (Article 81). However, if disputes arise in relation to the award, such must be submitted only to the tribunal that decided it (Article 82). Parties are entitled to reserve in the *compromis* the right to demand that an award be revised (Article 83).

The use and decline of the PCA

The PCA enjoyed great success for a while and tried many cases, which include: *Venezuelan Preferential Claims* (1904) 9 RIAA 103; *Japanese House Tax* (1905) ICGJ 407, PCA; *Italy v. Peru* (1912) 11 RIAA 405 (the *Canevaro Case*); and *Russia v. Turkey* (1912) 11 RIAA 421 (the *Russian Indemnity Case*).

However, the creation of the PCIJ in 1923 affected the prospects of the PCA. States preferred recourse to the PCIJ for many reasons, including the following.

- There is no right of appeal in relation to PCA awards, and the fact that only the arbitral tribunal that decides may review such a case is very limiting. This does not bode well for an institution that was intended to act as a court of some sort.

- The use of sovereign arbitrators is also somewhat uninspiring. State parties to a dispute clearly prefer to have the opportunity of having representatives on an arbitral tribunal. Thus they may accept sovereign arbitrators for diplomatic reasons or as a result of pressure, whereas in reality they might prefer a fully composed arbitral tribunal.

It must be noted, however, that the PCA still functioned to some extent shortly after the PCIJ emerged. For example, it was used by the UK to decide the *Chevreau Case* (1931) 2 UNRIAA 1113, but has not been invoked since 1932, although it remains in existence.

Efforts to reinvigorate the PCA include the introduction, in 1962, of a mixed-arbitration model to its activities, so that non-State entities may benefit from its services. There is no doubt that the PCA is not in great demand today—but the fact that, in 1990, its IB was still engaged in devising means of modernizing the institution shows that it is too early to declare that the PCA is dead. In 1994, the PCA established the Financial Assistance Fund (FAF), which 'aims at helping developing countries meet part of the costs involved in international arbitration or other means of dispute settlement offered by the PCA' (available at http://www.pca-cpa.org/showpage.asp?pag_id=1179). Furthermore, on 22 July 2009, the PCA delivered an important judgment regarding the boundary dispute between Sudan and the Sudan People's Liberation Movement Army (SPLMA) (see PCA, 'ABYEI arbitration: final award rendered', Press release, 22 July 2009). These developments—especially the latest—show that the PCA may be on its way to greater relevance as a modern institution.

KEY POINTS

- An arbitral award is final and the decision cannot be appealed. However, if parties have so provided in their *compromis*, then they can apply for a revision of the decision, but only to the tribunal that made the award.

- This lack of appeal process undermined the attractiveness of the PCA.

Conclusion

The methods for peacefully settling international disputes are very useful tools in defusing tension among States, and in promoting international peace and security. As we have seen, the utility, effectiveness, and appeal of the methods differ, depending on the nature of disputes involved and, sometimes, on the purposes for which parties resort to them. Negotiation may be the most frequently used dispute settlement method, but there has been a rise also in the use of inquiry, and arbitration outside the PCA has indeed become as popular as mediation. Conciliation is useful, but has seen a slow decline. This is because the use of single conciliators is no longer as attractive as perhaps the use of good offices. In 2009, former US President Bill Clinton secured from North Korea the release of two American journalists imprisoned by that country on allegations of entering North Korea illegally. What was interesting in this episode was that not only had the two countries refused to communicate with each other directly, but that the diplomatic machinery of the USA, headed by its Secretary of State, Hillary Clinton, had also failed to secure the journalists. This shows the value of good offices, which work quietly away from the sometimes noisy machinery of State diplomacy.

? Questions

Self-test questions

1 What is a 'dispute'?

2 List the various methods for settling international disputes peacefully.

3 Define 'mediation' and 'commissions of inquiry'.

4 What is a *compromis* and in what context is it used?

5 What are 'good offices' and how do these differ from mediation?

6 What is 'good-faith negotiation'?

Discussion questions

1 'There is no obligation to reach an agreement in international law even if there is an obligation to negotiate.' Discuss.

2 'The Permanent Court of Arbitration is a court in all respects and does what a normal court of law will often do.' To what extent do you agree with this statement?

3 'The various methods for settling international disputes are not significantly different from one another. In fact, we can regard them as more of the same.' With reference to two methods of settling international disputes peacefully, examine the validity of this statement.

4 'Mediation and good offices are two sides of the same coin.' Discuss.

5 'Negotiation is an informal process. It can be conducted however the parties want and does not have to follow any process or principles.' To what extent is this assertion true of negotiation as a method for settling international disputes?

Assessment question

Candoma has accused Rutamu of developing nuclear weapons and threatened that if Rutamu does not put an end to this, it will be compelled to attack it. Rutamu argued that, as a State, it has a right to develop nuclear weapons, just as Candoma and all of its friends have. Tensions are continuing to rise between the two States and there seems no feasible solution. Recently, Candoma has moved some of its troops to international waters from which it could launch military attacks that would reach Rutamu in a matter of minutes. Rutamu sees this as a serious provocation. Fortunately, this action coincides with the presence in the region of Elder Eidon, the leader of the DiaDia order, a world-acknowledged moral/philosophical order, the members of which are famous for peace. Elder Eidon is visiting the DiaDia followers in the region. Both Candoma and Rutamu respect Elder Eidon and his DiaDia order, and immediately signify, through clandestine contacts, their readiness to allow him to intervene in the crisis.

As an independent researcher working with the Everlasting Peace Institute, you have been contacted by the foreign ministries of both countries to advise them on which course of action to take. Advise the parties regarding their choices.

🔑 Key cases

- *Great Britain v. Russia* (1908) 2 AJIL 931 (ICI Report of 26 February 1905) (the *Dogger Bank Case*)

- *Greece v. United Kingdom* (1924) PCIJ Ser. A, No. 2 (the *Mavrommatis Palestine Concessions*)

- *Pakistan v. India* (1973) ICJ Rep 347 (the *Trial of Pakistani Prisoners of War*)
- *Railway Traffic between Poland and Lithuania Advisory Opinion* (1931) PCIJ Ser. A/B, No. 42
- *United States of America v. Iran (United States Diplomatic and Consular Staff in Tehran)* (1980) ICJ Rep 3 (the *Hostages Case*)

 # Further reading

Collier, J. and Lowe, V., *The Settlement of Disputes in International Law* (Oxford: Oxford University Press, 1999)

Maluwa, T., 'The peaceful settlement of disputes among African States 1963–1983: some conceptual issues and practical trends' (1989) 38 ICLQ 299

Merrills, J. G., *International Dispute Settlement* (Cambridge: Cambridge University Press, 2005)

Merrills, J. G., 'The means of dispute settlement' in M. Evans (ed.), *International Law* (2nd edn, Oxford: Oxford University Press, 2006), p. 533

Northedge, F. S. and Donelan, M., *International Disputes: Political Aspects* (London: Europa, 1971)

Sven, M. G., *Diplomatic Dispute Settlement: The Use of Inter-State Conciliation* (The Hague: T. M. C. Asser Press, 2008)

15

The International Court of Justice

Learning objectives

This chapter will help you to:

- understand the role of the International Court of Justice in settling international disputes;
- appreciate the functioning of the Court;
- learn the various jurisdictions of the Court;
- understand the procedures for bringing cases to the Court; and
- recognize the importance of the Court and its relations to other organs of the United Nations.

Introduction

Article 92 of the Charter of the United Nations (UN Charter) describes the International Court of Justice (ICJ) as the 'principal judicial organ' of the United Nations. This makes the Court the main judicial body for the UN. The Court exercises contentious and advisory jurisdictions, and its decisions are final and cannot be appealed. As a judicial body, the ICJ has to coexist with political organs of the UN, such as the General Assembly and the Security Council. The Court's relationship with these organs has not always been free from challenges, just as the fact that its jurisdiction depends on the consent of UN members has had some limitation on its functioning. That notwithstanding, the Court has proved to be creative, resourceful, and continues to inspire confidence among States leading to a steady increase in the number of States using it to resolve their disputes. While most textbook writers often treat the ICJ within the chapter on 'settlement of international disputes', separately focusing on it allows for a detailed study of the various aspects of this pivotal institution than would have been possible in the last chapter.

 ## 15.1 A short history of the Court

The Permanent Court of International Justice (PCIJ) was established in 1922 under the League of Nations, as the first international court to settle disputes amongst States. During its existence, the PCIJ dealt with sixty-six contentious cases and twenty-two advisory opinions (the differences between which will be clarified later). Due to several factors, including non-participation by the world's superpowers, the USA and Soviet Union, and the fact that the Court was not an organ of the League, the PCIJ was unable to function effectively. Its authority was greatly undermined by States and its decisions were mostly unimplemented. The Second World War fatally affected the Court's operations. When Germany occupied the Netherlands, the seat of the Court, the Court was temporarily relocated to Geneva where, on 18 April 1946, it was formally dissolved by the UN General Assembly upon the inauguration of the ICJ the same day.

KEY POINTS

- The PCIJ preceded the ICJ, but unlike the role that the latter has played in the United Nations, the PCIJ was not the principal judicial organ of the League of Nations.

- The ICJ is the principal judicial organ of the United Nations.

15.2 The functions of the ICJ

According to Article 38(1) of the Statute of the International Court of Justice (the ICJ Statute), the Court is 'to decide in accordance with international law such disputes as are submitted to it'. And in doing so, the Court shall apply:

a. international conventions, whether general or particular, establishing rules expressly recognized by the contesting states;

b. international custom, as evidence of a general practice accepted as law;

c. the general principles of law recognized by civilized nations;

d. subject to the provisions of Article 59, judicial decisions and the teachings of the most highly qualified publicists of the various nations, as subsidiary means for the determination of rules of law.

Since we have already discussed these provisions in Chapter 2, we do not need revisit them here.

15.2.1 What constitutes a legal dispute for the purposes of the ICJ?

Article 38(1) states that the Court shall decide a case in accordance with *international law*. In the Chapter 14, one of the things we considered was when a dispute can be said to arise between parties to a case before the Court, as without a dispute the Court cannot try a case. The reference to 'international law' in Article 38(1) is thus the confirmation that the Court is concerned with legal and not political disputes. Therefore, we do not need to restate what constitutes a legal dispute here.

However, it is not only in contentious cases (that is, a case involving at least two States disagreeing on a point of law) that the ICJ may have to determine whether there is a legal dispute. In its practice, the Court has regularly determined the existence of a legal dispute before issuing its advisory opinions, notwithstanding that, unlike in contentious cases, in advisory opinions, as will be shown below, only one party addresses a request to the Court.

● ***Interpretation of Peace Treaties with Bulgaria, Hungary and Romania Advisory Opinion (First Phase)*** (1950) ICJ REP 74

In a case concerning a request for an advisory opinion, the Court stated that, after examining the diplomatic exchanges between the States concerned, 'the two sides hold clearly opposite views concerning the question of the performance or non-performance of certain treaty obligations', and concluded that a legal dispute had arisen.

● ***Applicability of the Obligation to Arbitrate under Section 21 of the United Nations Headquarters Agreement of 26 June 1947 Advisory Opinion*** (1988) ICJ REP 12

The General Assembly requested that the ICJ gives its opinion as to whether the USA had an obligation to arbitrate pursuant to Article 21 of the 1947 Headquarters Agreement between the UN and the USA. In determining the existence of a legal dispute, the Court said (at [35]), that it 'found that the opposing attitudes of the parties clearly established the existence of a dispute'.

It is for the court, and not the parties, to decide whether a legal dispute has arisen. As the Court said in *Interpretation of Peace Treaties with Bulgaria, Hungary and Romania* (above), 'whether there exists an international dispute is a matter for objective determination'.

....

● *Ethiopia v. South Africa; Liberia v. South Africa* (1962) ICJ REP 319 (The *South West Africa Cases*)

In this case, the Court made it clear (at 328) that:

> It is not sufficient for one party to a contentious case to assert that a dispute exists with the other party. A mere assertion is not sufficient to prove the existence of a dispute any more than a mere denial of the existence of the dispute proves its non-existence. Nor is it adequate to show that the interests of the two parties to such a case are in conflict. It must be shown that the claim of one party is positively opposed by the other.

Thus where one party alleges that an issue exists and the other party denies that issue, the ICJ has consistently held that a dispute arises.

15.3 Access to the Court

Only States can appear before the ICJ in contentious cases—that is, cases involving parties arguing legal points (Article 34 of the ICJ Statute). However, under Article 96, organs of the UN, such as the General Assembly and the Security Council, and UN specialized agencies, such as the World Health Organization (WHO), can seek advisory opinions from the Court. Unlike contentious cases, advisory opinions do not involve parties appearing to argue a point of law before the Court; rather, they involve situations in which a UN organ or a specialized agency seeks clarification from the Court, in writing, as to the meaning or interpretation of a word, phrase, or condition contained in a treaty or other legal instrument, on which there is a broad disagreement among States. We will return to this point later.

Thus, as a general rule, only States, UN organs, and UN specialized agencies may access the Court. However, the fact that only States may appear before the Court in contentious cases does not mean that *all* States can appear before the Court. As a matter of fact, only one class of States is able to access the Court automatically, while others can do so only after meeting certain conditions, making access to the ICJ either automatic or conditional.

15.3.1 Automatic access to the ICJ

Article 92 of the UN Charter states that the ICJ is the principal judicial organ of the UN, while Article 35(1) of the ICJ Statute provides that 'the Court shall be opened to the state parties to the present Statute'. Article 93(1) of the UN Charter states that all members of the UN are *automatically* parties to the Statue of the Court. Thus, membership of the UN means automatic membership of the ICJ.

However, acceptance of the ICJ Statute does not imply that the Court has jurisdiction over a State. Automatic access to the Court, guaranteed by membership of the UN, is not the same thing as automatic jurisdiction of the court.

....

● **Serbia and Montenegro v. Belgium (Preliminary Objections) (Judgment)** [2004] ICJ REP 295 (**Case Concerning the Legality of Use of Force**)

As the Court said in this case (at [36]):

> a distinction has to be made between a question of jurisdiction that relates to the consent of a party and the question of the right of a party to appear before the Court under the requirements of the Statute, which is not a matter of consent.

15.3.2 Conditional access to the ICJ

Under Article 93(2) of the ICJ Statute, a State that is not a member of the UN can access the Court if that State *becomes a party to the ICJ Statute* and accepts the conditions laid down by the General Assembly for that purpose, upon the recommendation of the UN Security Council.

On 26 October 1946, Switzerland requested the General Assembly to lay out the conditions upon which it may become a party to the ICJ Statute in accordance with Article 93(2). UN General Assembly Resolution 91(1), adopted on 11 December 1946, set out the following conditions:

1. Acceptance of the provisions of the Statute of the International Court of Justice;
2. Acceptance of all obligations of a Member of the United Nations under Article 94 of the Charter;
3. An undertaking to contribute to the expenses of the Court such equitable amount as the General Assembly shall, from time to time assess after consultation with the Swiss Government.

A State may also become party to the Statute based on conditions determined by the Security Council. According to Article 35(2) of the ICJ Statute:

> the conditions under which the Court shall be open to other states shall, subject to the special provisions contained in treaties in force, be laid down by the Security Council, but in no case shall such conditions place the parties in a position of inequality before the Court.

On 15 October 1946, the UN Security Council stated in Resolution 9 (1946), that:

> The International Court of Justice shall be open to a State which is not a party to the Statute of the International Court of Justice, upon the following conditions, namely, that such States shall previously have deposited with the Registrar of the Court a declaration by which it accepts the jurisdiction of the Court, in accordance with the Charter of the United Nations, and with the terms and subject to the conditions of the Statute and the Rules of the Court, and undertake to comply in good faith with the decision or decisions of the Court and to accept all the obligations of a Member of the United Nations under Article 94 of the UN Charter.

Furthermore, Article 35(2) of the ICJ Statute provides that a State may have access to the Court pursuant to 'special provisions contained in treaties in force'. The ICJ confirmed this route in the following case.

. . . .

● **Bosnia and Herzegovina v. Yugoslavia (Serbia and Montenegro) (Order, Provisional Measures)** [1993] ICJ REP 3 (The **Case Concerning the Application of the Convention on the Prevention and Punishment of the Crime of Genocide**, or the **Genocide Convention Case**)

The Court said (at [14]) that it:

> considers that proceedings may validly be instituted by a State against a State which is a party to such a special provision in a treaty in force, *but is not party to the Statute, and independently of the conditions laid down by the Security Council in its resolution 9 of 1946* ... whereas a compromissory clause in a multi-lateral convention, such as Article IX of the Genocide Convention relied on by Bosnia-Herzegovina in the present case, could, in the view of the Court, be regarded prima facie as a special provision contained in a treaty in force. [Emphasis added]

This particular route can, however, be highly problematic for two reasons. First, where the treaty concerned has been in force for one State that then dissolves or disintegrates into several States, the question always arises as to which of the surviving States succeeds to the obligations of the former State. In the *Genocide Convention Case*, the question was whether Serbia and Montenegro succeeded the former Socialist Federal Republic of Yugoslavia (SFRY).

Secondly, the uncertainty that often characterizes the determination of when a treaty is in *force* adds to the problem. In the *Case Concerning the Legality of Use of Force* (see section 15.3.1), the ICJ ruled that a treaty in force meant a treaty in force *as at the time when the Statute of the ICJ itself entered into force in 1945*. The implication of this is that a treaty that enters into force *after* that date cannot be a basis for granting access to a State under the route under consideration. Yet, in the *Genocide Convention Case*, the treaty concerned entered into force for those States *after* 1945. Thus there was a clear case of inconsistency in the way in which the Court dealt with the question of 'entry into force' in these two cases.

The Court corrected this anomaly when it eventually tried the *Genocide Case* on merit in 2007.

. . . .

● **Bosnia and Herzegovina v. Serbia and Montenegro** [2007] ICJ REP 43 (The **Case Concerning the Application of the Convention on the Prevention and Punishment of the Crime of Genocide**, or the **Bosnian Genocide Case**)

Particularly (at [134] and [135]), the Court not only restored its decision in the *Genocide Convention Case (Provisional Measures)* to the effect that there is no cut-off date for the entering into force of treaties, but also rejected the narrow interpretation that it adopted in the *Case Concerning the Legality of Use of Force*.

The Court justified its revision of the *Legality of Use of Force* position on the basis that that case did not constitute a *res judicata* for its future position, because it said (at [135]) that:

> the concern of the Court was not then with the scope of *res judicata* of the 1996 Judgment, since in any event such *res judicata* could not extend to the proceedings in the cases that were then before it, between different parties.

thinking points

- *What are the different ways in which a State can have access to the ICJ?*
- *Which approach to the interpretation of 'treaties in force' as seen in the* Genocide Convention Case (Provisional Measures) *and the* Case Concerning the Legality of Use of Force *(affirmed by the* Genocide Case*) do you find more attractive, and why?*

KEY POINTS

- A State that is a member of the United Nations has automatic access to the Court, but that does not mean that the Court can automatically try a case involving the State.

- Access to the Court can be automatic or conditional.

15.4 The composition, election, and retirement of judges of the ICJ

Article 2 of the ICJ Statute:

> The Court shall be composed of a body of independent judges, elected regardless of their nationality from among persons of high moral character, who possess the qualifications required in their respective countries for appointment to the highest judicial offices, or are jurisconsults of recognized competence in international law.

The Court is composed of fifteen judges drawn from across the globe, no two of whom may be nationals of the same State (Article 3). Where a judge, for example, holds dual nationality, then he or she will be deemed to be a national of the State 'in which he ordinarily exercises civil and political rights' (Article 3).

To elect judges into the ICJ, the Permanent Court of Arbitration (PCA) prepares a list of candidates nominated by its national groups. The UN General Assembly and the UN Security Council then elect judges from this list (Article 4), but each organ must do so separately (Article 8). However, where a State is not represented in the national group of the PCA, such a State shall appoint a national group of its own for the purpose of nominating candidates to the ICJ (Article 4).

Despite the fact that no provision of the ICJ Statute requires judges to come from particular States, the practice has developed whereby each permanent member of the Security Council is always represented by a judge at the ICJ at any given time.

However, only United Nations members (which are automatically members of the Court) may nominate judges to the ICJ. Non-UN members may nominate judges to the Court only if the General Assembly, acting upon recommendation of the Security Council, lays down conditions for such purpose (Article 4(3)). Judges are elected from persons of the highest moral values, and represent the main forms of civilization and the principal legal systems of the world (Article 9).

Upon election, each ICJ judge takes office for nine years subject to re-election (Article 13). However, in order to guarantee continuity and consistency in the Court's work, the expiration of the tenure of the first elected judges was distributed unevenly. Hence, of the first fifteen judges, the terms of only five expired after three years and another five at the end of six years. This arrangement left five of the inaugural judges in office for three more years, to be joined by the replacements of the retired ten. Those to be retired mandatorily after serving five and six years in office were drawn by lot by the UN Secretary-General (Article 13).

Judges are appointed in their own right and not as representatives of their countries, and the fact that a case involves a judge's country does not prevent the judge from sitting on the case (Article 31(1)). Unless there are other reasons outside nationality barring his or her involvement, a judge is expected to sit on all cases that come before the Court.

KEY POINTS

- ICJ judges are elected by the UN Security Council and the UN General Assembly, from nominations by national groups of the PCA.

- Permanent members of the Security Council have always been represented in the Court, although there is no formal rule to this effect.

- Normally, the ICJ is composed of fifteen judges for a nine-year term, subject to re-election.

15.4.1 The full Court, ad hoc judges, and the Special Chambers

Generally, a full Court is required to decide a case. A full Court comprises all fifteen members of the Court, but this number could rise to seventeen if one of the two parties to a case does not have a judge of its nationality in the Court. In that case, such a party is allowed to elect an ad hoc judge to sit on the case, as will be explained fully later.

Instead of a full Court, it is possible for the Court, on the basis of its own Rules of Procedure, to allow one or more judges to be rotated. This means that fewer than fifteen judges (or seventeen, as the case may be) may sit on a case, provided that there are at least eleven judges available in the Court. It only takes nine judges to achieve a quorum of the Court (Article 25).

This section will provide more information on the number of judges that it takes to sit on a case under different circumstances.

Special Chambers

Under Article 26 of the ICJ Statute, three or more judges may compose a Court for the purpose of trying specific cases. These are cases that are of a highly specialized nature and include cases concerning environmental matters, labour, and communication. It is for the Court to decide how many judges should compose a Special Chamber, but it is essential for parties to agree to this (Article 26(2)). A judgment given by a Special Chamber is considered to be a judgment rendered by the full Court (Article 27) and it is not necessary that the Chamber sit in The Hague (Article 29).

● **United States v. Canada** (1984) ICJ Rep 246 (**Case Concerning the Delimitation of the Maritime Boundary in the Gulf of Maine Area**)

The Special Chamber was first used in this case, which also underscores the significance of parties' consent to the composition of such Chambers as a condition for their participation. The USA and Canada threatened withdrawal from the case unless the Court complied with their wishes regarding the composition of the Chamber. The Court acceded to this eventually.

The use of Chambers has proved more popular in recent times and was used in several other cases, including *Burkina Faso v. Mali* (1986) ICJ Rep 3 (*Frontier Dispute*), *USA v. Italy* (1989) ICJ Rep 15 (*Elettronica Sicula*), and *Benin v. Niger* (2002) ICJ Rep 613 (*Frontier Dispute*).

Chambers are much quicker, more flexible, and give parties a greater choice in deciding which judges should hear and decide their case. Yet the fact that the selection of the Chamber judges usually reflects the wishes of the parties (as seen in *Gulf of Maine*) tends to undermine the independence of the Court, at least as far as perception is concerned.

Special Chambers are courts of summary procedure for which the Statute provides under Article 29. They are expected to be formed on an annual basis, only at the request of parties to a case, and deal with cases more quickly. The Special Chambers considered under Article 26 do not have such restrictions, because they can be formed at any time, are not dependent on request by parties, and are formed to deal mainly with specialized cases and not only for reasons of speed.

It is important to note that, to date, the Court has never activated the Chamber of Summary Procedures envisaged under Article 29.

531

KEY POINTS

- A full Court is composed of fifteen or seventeen judges.

- Only nine judges are required for the purpose of a quorum in the Court.

- Special Chambers deal with highly specialized cases and are composed of numbers determined by the Court.

Ad hoc judges

As mentioned earlier, ad hoc judges are appointed when one of the parties to a case has no judge of its nationality in the Court.

example

In a case between Candoma and Rutamu, Rutamu is entitled to nominate an ad hoc judge if there is a Candoman judge sitting on the case. However, if neither of the two States has a judge of its nationality in the Court, then there is no need for ad hoc judges.

According to Article 31 of the ICJ Statute, although any of the parties retains the right to provide a judge in accordance with Article 31(3) of the ICJ Statute:

If the Court includes upon the Bench a judge of the nationality of one of the parties, any other party may choose a person to sit as judge. Such person shall be chosen preferably from among those persons who have been nominated as candidates as provided in Articles 4 and 5.

The use of ad hoc judges can certainly be a boost to morale and can increase the use of the Court by member States, since such States are always guaranteed the presence of 'their own' judges in cases involving them.

The rationale for ad hoc judges was perhaps best explained in the views expressed by authoritative international lawyers and institutions, some of which date back to the time of the PCIJ, when the idea was first introduced.

In the *Fourth Annual Report of Permanent Court of International Justice* (1928) PCIJ Ser. E, No. 4, committee of the Court stated at p. 75, that:

> In the attempt to establish international courts of justice, the fundamental problem always has been, and probably always will be, that of the representation of the litigants in the constitution of the tribunal. Of all influences to which men are subject, none is more powerful, more pervasive, or more subtle, than the tie of allegiance that binds them to the land of their homes and kindred and to the great sources of the honours and preferments for which they are so ready to spend their fortunes and to risk their lives. This fact, known to all the world, the [Court's] Statute frankly recognises and deals with.

In *Procès-Verbaux of the Proceedings of the Advisory Committee of Jurists*, 24th Meeting, 14 July 1920, pp. 528–529, Lord Phillimore stated that:

> it would be necessary to make it possible for parties to be represented on the Court by a member of their nationality; or that at any rate it would be necessary to prevent one party being represented if the other party were not. There were several ways of obtaining this end; the judge of the nationality of one party might be excluded, or the judge of the nationality of the other might be included; but ... it would be preferable to give a national representative to both parties, *not only to protect their interests*, but to enable the Court *to understand certain questions* which require highly specialised knowledge and relate to differences between various legal systems. [Emphasis added]

Clearly, Lord Phillimore believed, as do many others, that ad hoc judges represent the national interests of their countries and could enrich the understanding of the Court in a particular case, since such judges are able to bring to bear specific understanding of the dynamics of the national context.

Arguing in the same vein on p. 538 of the *Procès-Verbaux*, Elihu Root noted:

> the instinctive mistrust felt by nations for a Court composed of foreign judges ... If they cannot be assured of representation of the Court it will prove impossible to obtain their assent. This assent will be still more difficult to obtain if a State is informed that any representative which it may have on the Court must give up his place when a case with which it is concerned is brought up for trial ... it must be possible to tell the masses that there will be at least one person upon the Court who is able to understand them ...

It is implied, in this statement, that the institution of ad hoc judges makes recourse to the ICJ more popular and attractive among States, and that governments find it easier to explain to their citizens why they exercise recourse to the Court if they have ad hoc judges sitting on their cases.

Nevertheless, the justifications put forward by the various views considered here raise fundamental questions about the place of ad hoc judges in the work of the ICJ.

(a) If judges are appointed to sit on the basis of the nationality of the parties to a case, then serious questions are raised about the independence of the Court.

(b) There is an issue arising about the confidentiality of information. Since ad hoc judges are part of the Court only for specific cases, there is no reason to expect that they will continue to treat with the required confidentiality information that they receive, or to which they have access, by the virtue of their temporary involvement with the Court. They may divulge such information either to their own governments or to third parties who may require such.

(c) Appointing ad hoc judges characteristically brings the status of the ICJ closer to arbitration than a judicial institution, since one of the distinguishing features of arbitration is the right of parties to choose judges that will sit on the case.

While these concerns seem to be well founded, practice shows that some of the concerns do not play out in reality. First, it is not necessarily true that ad hoc judges will be partial or biased towards, or always vote in favour of, their countries. Often, considerations such as morality and the general interest of the Court condition the manner in which ad hoc judges dispense their duties in the Court.

As Hersch Lauterpacht writes in *The Function of Law in the International Community* (Oxford: Clarendon Press, 1933), p. 215:

> Undoubtedly, the fact that a judge is a national of a State may influence him subconsciously and independently of his will ... However, although the subconscious factor cannot be entirely eliminated, it is to a large extent a function of the human will, of the individual sense of moral duty, and of the enlightened consideration of the paramount interest of peace and justice entrusted to the care of judges.

In practice, national judges have voted for their countries in many cases as they have also voted against their countries in a significant minority of cases.

KEY POINTS

- The inclusion of ad hoc judges to the Court depends on whether one of the parties to a case has a judge of its nationality sitting in the Court.

- Ad hoc judges are important, because they represent their national interest, and provide the Court with local knowledge and an understanding of context.

- The use of ad hoc judges increases the prospects of the Court and its resources being employed by its member States.

thinking points
- *What are the arguments for and against the institution of ad hoc judges?*
- *Do you agree with the view that ad hoc judges are necessary in order to make recourse to the Court more attractive to member States, and to enrich the Court's knowledge and understanding of the circumstances of cases?*

15.5   # The independence of the Court

The fact that the ICJ is the principal judicial organ of the UN does not imply that the Court is dependent on or influenced by the organization. The Court's Statute guarantees the independence of its judges of the Court through many protective measures. For example, judges are prohibited from undertaking any political, administrative, or professional job during their period of office (Article 16); they cannot act as agent, counsel, or advocate in any case (Article 17). Also, judges cannot participate in the decision of any case in which they have previously taken part as agent, counsel, or advocate for one of the parties, or as a member of a national or international court, or of a commission of inquiry, or in any other capacity. If there is a doubt on any of these points, the Court itself shall settle the doubt (Article 17).

● **_Malaysia v. Singapore_** (2003) ICJ Rep 12 (*Case Concerning Sovereignty over Pedra Branca, Pulau Batu Puteh, Middle Rocks and South Ledge*)

Judge Higgins (at [8]), referring to Article 17(2) of the ICJ Statute, recused herself from participating.

Care must be taken, however, not to confuse a judge who, in his or her previous involvement in a case, served merely as representative of his or her government with a judge who, in such a previous role, actively took part in the matters that relate to the subsequent case before the international Court.

● **_Ethiopia v. South Africa; Liberia v. South Africa (Preliminary Objections) (Second Phase)_** (1966) ICJ Rep 6 (The *South West Africa Cases*)

Judge Zaffrula Khan was excluded from sitting, on the basis of his previous involvement, as a member of the Pakistani delegation to the UN, in issues concerning South West Africa (now Namibia).

● **_The Namibia Advisory Opinion_** (1971) ICJ Rep 16

In this case, however, the ICJ rejected opposition to the involvement of certain judges (including Zaffrula Khan), and took the opportunity to clarify the meaning of Article 17(2) of its Statute.

The UN requested the ICJ's advisory opinion on the legal consequences of the continued presence of States within the territory of another State, despite a resolution of the Security Council to the contrary. South Africa objected to the participation of three judges in the case—namely, Judge Zaffrula Khan of Pakistan, Judge Morozov of the Soviet Union, and Judge Nervo of Mexico—on the basis of their previous involvement in matters affecting South West Africa.

The Court overruled all of the objections. The Court (at [9]):

> ...reached the conclusion that the participation of the Member concerned in his former capacity as *representative* of his Government ... did not attract the application of Article 17, paragraph 2, of the Statute of the Court ... Court took into consideration that the activities in United Nations organs of the Members concerned, prior to their election to the Court ... do not furnish grounds for treating these objections differently ... [Emphasis added]

Justifying its position, the Court noted that:

> account must also be taken in this respect of precedents established by the present Court and the Permanent Court wherein judges sat in certain cases even though they had taken part in the formulation of texts the Court was asked to interpret.

The precedents to which the ICJ referred include *United Kingdom v. Germany (Question of Intervention by Poland)* (1923) PCIJ Ser. A, No. 1 (the *SS Wimbledon Case*) and *Italy v. France* (1938) PCIJ Ser. C, No. 84 (the *Phosphates in Morocco Case*).

The salaries of the judges are fixed by the UN General Assembly and paid from the regular UN budget. Such salaries, while they may be increased, may never be decreased during the term of the judges in office (Article 32). This measure certainly protects the independence of judges against political organs of the UN, such as the General Assembly and the Security Council.

thinking points

- *What are the measures aimed at ensuring the independence of the ICJ judges?*
- *What are the circumstances under which a judge's previous engagement with a case or with the parties to the case may bar him or her from sitting on the case?*

15.6 The jurisdiction of the ICJ

The ICJ has two types of jurisdiction: contentious jurisdiction and advisory jurisdiction. Under its contentious jurisdiction, only States may appear before the Court to argue a case. With regard to the advisory jurisdiction of the Court, UN organs and specialized agencies are entitled formally to request the opinion of the ICJ regarding clarification of disputed words, phrases, or meanings contained usually in a legal instrument. This implies that States cannot seek an advisory opinion from the Court directly, but can do so through the organs of the UN or its specialized agencies, while the latter also cannot appear as parties to contentious cases before the Court.

15.6.1 The contentious jurisdiction of the Court

A State which is a member of the UN is automatically bound by the ICJ Statute. However, this does not imply that the State has therefore given its consent to the ICJ to try cases involving it. Consent for the purpose of the Court exercising jurisdiction is not the same as access of a State to the Court.

Article 36(1) and (2) of the ICJ Statute lays down the jurisdiction of the Court:

Article 36

....

1. The jurisdiction of the Court comprises all cases which the parties refer to it and all matters specially provided for in the Charter of the United Nations or in treaties and conventions in force.

2. The states parties to the present Statute may at any time declare that they recognize as compulsory ipso facto and without special agreement, in relation to any other state accepting the same obligation, the jurisdiction of the Court in all legal disputes concerning:

   a. the interpretation of a treaty;

   b. any question of international law;

   c. the existence of any fact which, if established, would constitute a breach of an international obligation;

   d. the nature or extent of the reparation to be made for the breach of an international obligation

Thus, under Article 36(1), States can confer jurisdiction on the ICJ either through:

- a special agreement to do so (*compromis*); or

- by advance agreement contained in the UN Charter or treaties and conventions in force.

The reference to the UN Charter in this provision is merely aspirational. It was envisaged in the original draft of the Charter that the Court would have compulsory jurisdiction over certain matters, which were to be listed in the Charter. Unfortunately, the UN Charter neither provides for such matters nor mentions anything about the Court's jurisdiction. The question therefore is: of what relevance is the provision concerning the Charter to the jurisdiction of the Court?

● **United Kingdom v. Albania (Preliminary Objections)** (1948) ICJ REP 15 (The *Corfu Channel Case*)

The UK argued that the provision entitled the UN Security Council to refer certain matters to the ICJ compulsorily. This was against the background that, on 9 April 1947, the Security Council adopted a resolution by which it made certain recommendations to the two States with regards to settling their dispute.

Although the Court did not pronounce on the point raised by the UK, seven judges emphatically rejected the argument in their separate opinion. In their separate opinion, Judges Basdevant, Alvarez, Winiarski, Zoričić, De Visscher, Badawi, and Krylov said (at 31) that:

In particular, having regard . . . to the normal meaning of the word recommendation . . . to the general structure of the Charter and of the Statute which founds the jurisdiction of the Court on the consent of States, and . . . to the terms used in Article 36, paragraph 3, of the Charter and to its object which is to remind the Security Council that legal disputes should normally be decided by judicial methods, *it appears impossible to us to accept an interpretation according to which this article, without explicitly saying so, has introduced more or less surreptitiously, a new case of compulsory jurisdiction.* [Emphasis added]

● **Pakistan v. India** (1999) ICJ REP 1 (*Case Concerning the Aerial Incident of 10 August 1999*)

Pakistan argued that the jurisdiction of the Court arose by virtue of reference to the Charter. Rejecting this argument, the Court said (at [48]) that:

the United Nations Charter contains no specific provision of itself conferring compulsory jurisdiction on the Court. In particular, there is no such provision in Articles 1, paragraph 1. 2, paragraphs 3 and 4, 33, 36, paragraph 3 and 92 of the Charter, relied on by Pakistan.

Special agreement (*compromis*) to submit dispute to the ICJ

There are two ways by which States can refer disputes to the ICJ under Article 36(1). First, both parties to a dispute can simply agree by virtue of a *compromis* to refer the case to the ICJ.

A special agreement, or *compromis*, will usually be concluded after a dispute has arisen. Thus once a dispute arises between two States, both parties can draw up an agreement to refer the matter to the ICJ. Typically, the *compromis* will identify the issues involved and the scope of the agreement to settle it. It will also make provision for such matters as the law applicable to the dispute (usually international law, as laid down in Article 38(1) of the ICJ Statute), the entry into force of the agreement (usually a date after the dispute has arisen), certain procedures to be followed in dealing with the case (for example, how to serve notices, etc.), and the effect of the decision of the Court (usually that it is final and binding on both parties). Therefore, due to its specificity, clarity on many issues, and the fact that it is drawn contemporaneously with, and not in speculation of, a dispute, the *compromis* is by far the most effective way in which States can confer ad hoc jurisdiction on the Court.

The ICJ has exercised jurisdiction in several cases on the basis of such special agreements:

- *France v. United Kingdom* (1953) ICJ Rep 53 (the *Minquiers and Ecrehos Case*);

- *Indonesia v. Malaysia* (2002) ICJ Rep 625 (the *Sovereignty over Pulau Ligitan and Pulau Sipadan Case*);

- *Malaysia v. Singapore* (2003) ICJ Rep 12 (the *Case Concerning Sovereignty over Pedra Branca/Pulau Batu Puteh, Middle Rocks and South Ledge*). and

- *Hungary v. Slovakia* (1997) ICJ Rep 7 (the *Case Concerning the Gabčikova-Nagymaros Project*)

Sometimes parties to a dispute may have no special agreement to refer it to the Court or only one party thereto has accepted the Court's jurisdiction through another means such as the optional clause (discussed later). This is problematic since the other party is under no obligation to take the dispute to the Court either by *compromis*, which does not exist, or by virtue of its consent under other category, which is also absent. In these circumstances, it is possible that such a party may decide to accept the jurisdiction of the Court unilaterally, as France has done in two cases.

● *Congo v. France (Provisional Measures)* (2003) ICJ REP 102 (The *Certain Criminal Proceedings in France Case*)

Some human rights organizations brought a case, before a French court, for human rights violations application against certain Congolese officials, including the country's president. France accepted the jurisdiction of the Court in this case unilaterally, under Article 38(5) of the ICJ Rules of the Court.

● *Djibouti v. France* (2008) ICJ REP 177 (*Case Concerning Certain Questions of Mutual Assistance in Criminal Matters*)

The death of a French diplomat in Djibouti occurred under circumstances that raised serious questions as to whether death occurred by suicide or murder. Both States disagreed on the level of access and assistance that they were each entitled to give to the other in respect of the investigation of the case. By the time the dispute broke out, Djibouti had already accepted the jurisdiction of the Court under the optional clause (Article 36(2) of the ICJ Statute), but France had not. There was no special agreement (*compromis*) to refer the case to the Court.

Djibouti, however, argued that:

> there is nothing to prevent consent to the jurisdiction of the Court from being effected by two separate and successive acts, *instead of jointly and beforehand by a special agreement*. [Emphasis added]

It cited the *Corfu Channel Case* (see earlier in this section) to support its view.

The Court held (at [48]) that consent to confer jurisdiction on the Court can be:

> expressed through a compromissory clause inserted in an international agreement, as was contended to be the case in *Armed Activities on the Territory of the Congo (New Application: 2002) (Democratic Republic of the Congo v. Rwanda)*, or through 'two separate and successive acts' (*Corfu Channel (United Kingdom v. Albania), Preliminary Objection, Judgment, 1948, I.C.J. Reports 1947–1948*, p. 28), as is the case here.

Whether there exists a *proper* agreement between parties to refer disputes to the Court is often the subject of controversy.

● *Qatar v. Bahrain* (1994) ICJ REP 112 (*Maritime Delimitation and Territorial Questions between Qatar and Bahrain, Jurisdiction and Admissibility*)

A territorial dispute arose between Qatar and Bahrain. During a Saudi-brokered negotiation, both States signed several documents, including two important ones in 1987 and 1990. The latter were the minutes of the consultation between the two States detailing what they had agreed, including some agreements that they had reached in 1987. Principal amongst those previous agreements was that if peaceful negotiation between them failed, either State may apply to the ICJ for settlement. Consequently, following the failure of the Saudi intervention, Qatar instituted a proceeding before the ICJ on 8 July 1991. Bahrain challenged the jurisdiction of the Court on the basis, inter alia, that the 1990 Minutes did not constitute a legally binding instrument.

The Court held (at 120) that:

international agreements may take a number of forms and be given a diversity of names...in a case concerning a joint communiqué, 'it knows of no rule of international law which might preclude a joint communiqué from constituting an international agreement to submit a dispute to arbitration or judicial settlement'.

KEY POINTS

- A *compromis* does not have to be in a specific format. The content of a *compromis* is more important than its form.

- Ad hoc consent is given after a dispute arises and only in relation to the dispute.

- Ad hoc consent is usually given by means of a *compromis*, which does not have to be in a particular form or format.

- A State party to a dispute may unilaterally accept the jurisdiction of the Court where the other party has already accepted that jurisdiction, and there is no special agreement between the parties to refer the dispute to the Court.

'Matters provided for in treaties and conventions in force'

The second basis for conferring jurisdiction on the ICJ under Article 36(1) is where conventions or treaties in force provide that parties shall submit their disputes to the Court. This mode is often described as the '*compulsory*' clause of the Court, given that it is consent given in advance by States, on a treaty basis.

Examples include the following:

● *Bosnia and Herzegovina v. Yugoslavia (Preliminary Objections)* [1996] ICJ REP 595
  (*Case Concerning the Application of the Convention on the Prevention and Punishment of Genocide*, or the *Genocide Convention Case*)

In this case, the jurisdiction of the ICJ was founded on Article IX of the 1948 UN Convention on the Prevention and Punishment of the Crime of Genocide (the Genocide Convention), which provides that:

> Disputes between the Contracting Parties relating to the interpretation, application or fulfilment of the present Convention, including those relating to the responsibility of a State for genocide or for any of the other acts enumerated in article III, shall be submitted to the International Court of Justice at the request of any of the parties to the dispute.

Similar provisions can be found in Article XXXI of the 1948 American Treaty on Pacific Settlement (the 'Pact of Bogota'), as well as the Optional Clause to the 1963 Vienna Convention on Consular Relations. Although all of the aforementioned treaties are multilateral in nature, special agreements can also be provided for in bilateral treaties—that is, treaties between two parties.

● *Libya v. Chad* [1994] ICJ REP 6 (The *Territorial Disputes Case*)

This case was, in fact, based on a bilateral treaty: the 1989 Framework Agreement (*Accord-Cadre*) on the Peaceful Settlement of the Territorial Dispute between the Great Socialist People's Libyan Arab Jamahiriya and the Republic of Chad.

Naturally, the ICJ will have jurisdiction over any dispute that a treaty provides shall be referred to the Court, provided that the treaty was concluded by parties after the ICJ Statute entered into force in 1946. However, several similar treaties existed before the establishment of the ICJ and conferred jurisdiction on the PCIJ. Thus, in order to save the substantive content of such treaties, Article 37 of the ICJ Statute states that:

> Whenever a treaty or convention in force provides for reference of a matter to a tribunal to have been instituted by the League of Nations, or to the Permanent Court of International Justice, the matter shall, as between the parties to the present Statute, be referred to the International Court of Justice.

However, it is important that those matters that the treaty refers to the ICJ could have been dealt with either by a tribunal instituted by the League of Nations or by the PCIJ. In short, the effect of Article 37 is to allow the ICJ to inherit all of those disputes that treaties in force during the PCIJ era referred to that earlier Court for resolution.

. . . .

● *Belgium v. Spain (Preliminary Objections) (Judgment)* (1964) ICJ REP 6 (The *Barcelona Traction Case*)

The full facts of the case were considered in Chapter 13.

Belgium founded the Court's jurisdiction on Article 17 of the 1927 Spain–Belgium Treaty of Conciliation, Judicial Settlement and Arbitration. This Article enjoins parties to the treaty to refer their dispute to the PCIJ. The PCIJ was dissolved in 1946 and Spain did not join the UN until 1955, nine years after the dissolution of the Court. Spain, therefore, claimed that since it only accepted the ICJ Statute in 1955, when it joined the UN, Article 17 of the 1927 Treaty had ceased to exist, and the ICJ did not have jurisdiction over the case.

Rejecting Spain's argument, the Court said (at 36) that:

> as regards the whole question of consent, the Court considers the case of the reactivation of a jurisdictional clause by virtue of Article 37 to be no more than a particular case of the familiar principle of consent given generally and in advance, in respect of a certain class of jurisdictional clause. Consent to an obligation of compulsory jurisdiction must be regarded as given *ipso facto* by joining an international organization, membership of which involves such an obligation, and irrespective of the date of joining. In consequence, States joining the United Nations or otherwise becoming parties to the Statute, at whatever date, knew in advance (or must be taken to have known) that, by reason of Article 37, one of the results of doing so would, as between themselves and other parties to the Statute, be the reactivation in relation to the present Court, of any jurisdictional clauses referring to the Permanent Court, in treaties still in force, by which they were bound.

Thus clearly, in this case, the Court considered that Article 37 of the ICJ Statute reactivated the jurisdictional clause related to the PCIJ.

KEY POINTS

- Jurisdiction based on 'conventions or treaties in force' is usually given in advance of disputes, and written into conventions and treaties. They are binding on parties to the treaty.

- Conventions and treaties in force can be either multilateral or bilateral.

- The treaties and conventions in force include those concluded after the entry into force of the ICJ Statute and those that were saved from the PCIJ era by virtue of Article 37 of the ICJ Statute.

- For the purpose of treaties in force, it does not matter when a State joins the UN (and thus accepts the ICJ Statute). Upon joining the UN, States are deemed to accept the jurisdiction of the Court over such of their disputes as might have been specifically referred to the PCIJ in the enabling treaty (see *Barcelona Traction*).

Given that the consent to refer disputes exists in treaty form, there is an element of compulsion on parties to accept the Court's jurisdiction. Nonetheless, it is overstretching to describe this as creating a compulsory jurisdiction for the Court and whether parties to such treaties will or will not accept the Court's jurisdiction when a dispute arises is often uncertain.

Conditions attaching to jurisdiction on the basis of conventions or treaties in force

The fact that a treaty or convention in force provides for referring a dispute to the ICJ does not necessarily mean that a dispute will, in fact, be so referred by States when it arises. Much will depend on whether, when the dispute arises, it fits into the scope determined by the treaty in question and whether the treaty itself can be said to be in 'force' at the relevant time.

'Dispute within the scope of treaty'

. . . .
● **Liechtenstein v. Germany** (2005) ICJ REP 6 (The **Certain Properties Case**)

In 2005, Liechtenstein brought an action against Germany for the latter's treating certain properties belonging to Liechtenstein nationals as German assets, having been seized for the purpose of reparation consequent to the Second World War. Liechtenstein relied on Article 1 of the 1957 European Convention for the Peaceful Settlement of Disputes, which entered into force between the parties in 1980.

The contention in this case was whether the dispute between the two States fell within the meaning of Article 27 of the 1957 Convention. Germany argued that the facts that gave rise to the dispute arose long before the Convention entered into force and so did not apply; Liechtenstein rejected this position.

The Court reviewed its jurisprudence on similar points in cases such as *Phosphates in Morocco* (see section 15.5), *Portugal v. India (Merit)* (1960) ICJ Rep 35 (the *Rights of Passage over Indian Territory Case*), and *Belgium v. Bulgaria* (1939) PCIJ Ser. A/B, No. 77 (the *Electricity Company in Sofia and Bulgaria Case*), and upheld the German position (see [52] in particular).

Thus, in this case, it was not in doubt that both Germany and Liechtenstein accepted the jurisdiction of the Court by means of a treaty in force. However, the treaty itself had delimited the scope of such disputes that the parties may submit to the Court under the treaty.

'Treaty in force'

What is the 'relevant date' for a treaty in force in dispute settlement? Is it the date when the crucial facts leading to the dispute arise or the date on which the dispute itself arises? As we have seen in the *Certain Properties Case*, the issue of the critical date of dispute has to do with whether the fundamental issues in the dispute arise before the treaty is adopted or not.

It was found in that case that this was not so, hence Liechtenstein could not bring an action against Germany.

Generally, whether a treaty or convention is *in force* can always be ascertained by making inquiries to the UN Secretariat for a register of all treaties. This should be a simple and straight-forward matter. However, problems may arise where, for example, although a treaty or convention is registered at a particular date, it is not clear whether it is still in operation. Thus the question of the date on which a treaty enters into force, for the purpose of conferring the Court with jurisdiction, deals with whether one of the parties to the dispute can be bound by the related treaty. This kind of problem can arise, for example, where a treaty is adopted by a particular international organization, which has then ceased to exist by the time the parties to a dispute decide to rely on the treaty for resolving their dispute.

● **Ethiopia v. South Africa; Liberia v. South Africa (Preliminary Objections)** (1962) ICJ REP 319 (The **South West Africa Cases**)

Under a League of Nations trusteeship, South Africa was entrusted with the administrative care of South West Africa in 1920. Liberia and Ethiopia brought an action against South Africa on the basis of Article 7 of the mandate. South Africa claimed (at 326–327) that since the League of Nations had been dissolved, the relevant mandate was no longer 'a treaty or convention in force' within the meaning of Article 37 of the ICJ Statute.

The Court, rejecting South Africa's claim, said (at 334) that 'the League of Nations in ending its own existence did not terminate the Mandates'.

In coming to this conclusion, the Court relied heavily on its *International Status of South West Africa Advisory Opinion* (1950) ICJ Rep 128, in which the opinion of the Court had been sought as to the status of South West Africa following the dissolution of the League of Nations. Consequently, in the present case, the Court followed its own opinion (at 138 of the 1950 case) and concluded that:

> Having regard to Article 37 of the Statute of the International Court of Justice, and Article 80, para-graph 1, of the Charter, the Court is of the opinion that this clause in the Mandate is still in force and that, therefore, the Union of South Africa is under an obligation to accept the compulsory jurisdic-tion of the Court according to those provisions.

thinking points

- *Do you think that conventions or treaties in force confer compulsory jurisdiction on the Court?*
- *What are the conditions that may affect acceptance of the jurisdiction of the Court despite reference of a dispute to the Court on the basis of a treaty or convention in force?*
- *Distinguish between jurisdictions on the basis of a special agreement (compromis) and on the basis of a convention or treaty in force.*

Consent by implication (*forum prorogatum*)

Although Article 36(1) enumerates some processes through which States can confer jurisdic-tion on the Court by their consent, there is no prescription as to how or when consent is to be given. While *compromis* and treaties and conventions exemplify some of these processes, it is possible for a State to give consent to the Court's jurisdiction inexplicitly and after another State has taken a matter to the Court.

Earlier, we considered a situation under Article 38(5) of the Rules of the Court whereby States that have not accepted the jurisdiction of the Court by the time a dispute arises may do so by notifying their acceptance of such jurisdiction unilaterally. We saw in the two cases discussed previously involving France (*Certain Criminal Proceedings in France* and *Certain Questions Concerning Mutual Assistance in Criminal Matters*) that France *explicitly* communicated its consent to the Court.

Forum prorogatum is yet another method by which States may accept the jurisdiction of the Court under Article 38(5) of the Rules of the Court. This method much resembles that considered earlier in the cases concerning the unilateral acceptance of jurisdiction by France. The difference between the latter and *forum prorogatum* is that, in the jurisdictional basis concerning unilateral acceptance already discussed under Article 35 (such as by France in those two cases), acceptance of the jurisdiction of the Court is explicit and mostly indicated by the consenting State; hence, France notified its acceptance to the Court following Djibouti's and Congo's applications to the Court. Under *forum prorogatum*, acceptance of jurisdiction is more implied than explicit, and it is often the applicant (that is, Djibouti or Congo) that must claim (and prove) that the defendant (France), by taking certain steps after receiving notice of the case against it in the Court, has accepted the jurisdiction of the Court.

● **Germany v. Poland** (1928) PCIJ Ser. A, No. 15 (The **Rights of Minorities in Polish Upper Silesia Case**)

Commenting in this case on the fact that consent can be expressed or implied, the PCIJ stated (at 23–24) that:

> The acceptance by a State of the Court's jurisdiction in a particular case is not, under the Statute, subordinated to the observance of certain forms . . . there seems to be no doubt that the consent of a State to the submission of a dispute to the Court may not only result from an express declaration, but may also be inferred from acts conclusively establishing it . . .

Let us now demonstrate the difference between unilateral acceptance of the ICJ jurisdiction under Article 38(5) of the Rules of the Court (such as that by France in the cases considered) and acceptance *forum prorogatum* under the same Article, which we will discuss fully later.

First, let us look at unilateral acceptance.

example

Candoma, which has already accepted the jurisdiction of the Court, brings an action against Rutamu, which has not accepted the Court's jurisdiction over the particular dispute. Nonetheless, upon receiving the notice of the case against it, Rutamu writes to the Court indicating that it accepts its jurisdiction under Article 38(5) of the Rules of the Court.

Thus, here, acceptance is explicit (by writing; although it could also be by any other explicit means). In addition, it is Rutamu itself, as the defendant in the case, which communicates its acceptance to the Court.

In comparison, acceptance *forum prorogatum* operates as follows.

example

Candoma, which has already accepted the jurisdiction of the Court, brings an action against Rutamu, which has not accepted the Court's jurisdiction over the particular dispute. Nonetheless, upon receiving the notice of the case against it, Rutamu writes to the Court to challenge Candoma's claims against it. It challenges the accuracy of some of the claims and provides the Court, in its response, with new details. It even attaches some evidence to its response to prove to the Court the inaccuracy of Candoma's claims.

In this scenario, Rutamu does not explicitly tell the Court that it accepts its jurisdiction. However, it is possible that, taking all of the measures that constitute its response together, the Court might infer from them consent by conduct (*forum prorogatum*). If Rutamu does not intend to accept the jurisdiction of the Court, why would it bother to refute Candoma's claim against it? Why would it supply the Court with evidential material?

thinking point

What are the main differences between the two modes of accepting the Court's jurisdiction on the basis of Article 38(5) of the Rules of the Court?

In many cases, the Court has expressed the view that consent can be express or implied.

● ***Greece v. United Kingdom*** (1925) PCIJ Ser. A, No. 5 (The ***Mavrommatis Jerusalem Concessions***)

The ICJ (at 6) accepted an extension of its jurisdiction over a matter over which it should not, under normal circumstances, have had such—but it did so on the basis of a tacit agreement of the parties to the dispute.

However, a State that intends to confer jurisdiction on the Court *forum prorogatum* must do so by taking some positive steps from which the Court can unequivocally infer acceptance of its jurisdiction.

● ***United Kingdom v. Albania (Preliminary Objections)*** (1948) ICJ Rep 15 (The ***Corfu Channel Case***)

The UK made a unilateral application to the Court in respect of its dispute with Albania following damage and death to a UK naval ship and its personnel, as a result of an explosion of mines in Albanian waters. The Court transmitted notice of the action of the UK to Albania, which the latter acknowledged by a letter to the Court. In the letter, Albania stated that the procedure adopted by the UK in bringing an action against it in the Court was irregular, because the UK had not complied with a UN Security Council recommendation that requested both parties to refer the matter to the ICJ 'in accordance with the provisions of the Statute of the Court' (at 18). Albania therefore argued that since it had not accepted the jurisdiction of the ICJ either by an optional clause or any other means, the UK should never have brought an action against it in the Court. Albania then challenged the jurisdiction of the Court on this basis.

In its judgment, the Court noted the irregularity inherent in the UK bringing a suit against Albania before the ICJ. However, the Court stated (at 23) that:

> The Government of Albania, after delivery of the United Kingdom Application, stated in its letter of July, 1947, that it fully accepted the recommendation of the Security Council, and that it was prepared to appear before the Court and to accept its jurisdiction in this case. This Albanian letter, coupled with the Resolution of the Security Council of 9th April, 1947, was accepted by the President of the Court as a document which satisfied the conditions laid down by the Security Council for the appearance before the Court of a State not party to the Statute.

Consequently, the Court held that:

> in these circumstances the jurisdiction of the Court to make the Order of 31st July, 1947 and to proceed with the trial of this dispute is fully established.

Evidently, the steps taken by the defendant must be clear and unambiguous, and cannot be interpreted in any other way than as an unequivocal acceptance of the Court's jurisdiction. Where steps taken by States occasion doubt or indicate a contrary intention, then the Court must decline jurisdiction.

● *United Kingdom v. Iran* (1952) ICJ REP 93 (The *Anglo-Iranian Oil Case*)

The UK brought this action against Iran in matters relating to a British oil company. Iran objected to the jurisdiction of the Court. However, in its objection it raised certain questions about the claims against it by the UK.

The UK argued that the Court had jurisdiction over Iran. The UK argued (at 113) that:

> the Iranian Government, having in its conclusions submitted to the Court for decision several questions which are not objections to the jurisdiction of the Court, and which could only be decided if the Court had jurisdiction, has by this action conferred jurisdiction upon the Court on the basis of the principle of *forum prorogatum*.

The Court noted, in accordance with the argument made by the UK, that, in its response, Iran had indeed raised some objections that did not deal with jurisdiction. However, the Court said that Iran had included these objections as measures of defence on which it would rely if *its main objection to the Court's jurisdiction were rejected*. The Court also found that Iran had consistently maintained its objection to its jurisdiction.

Consequently, the Court held (at 114) that:

> The principle of *forum prorogatum*, if it could be applied to the present case, would have to be based on some conduct or statement of the Government of Iran which involves an element of consent regarding the jurisdiction of the Court . . . Accordingly, the Court has arrived at the conclusion that it has no jurisdiction to deal with the case.

Here, it is clear that the Court was cautious not to confuse Iran's preparedness to argue its case, should the Court reject its objection to its jurisdiction, with an acceptance of the Court's jurisdiction. Obviously, in Iran's response, it combined its objection to the jurisdiction of the Court with objections to some of the points raised by the UK. It also consistently maintained its objection to the Court's jurisdiction. In these circumstances, it would have been incredulous if the Court had inferred its jurisdiction from the Iranian response.

KEY POINTS

- Jurisdiction *forum prorogatum* is based on an inference of consent from positive and unequivocal measures by the defendant State.

- Jurisdiction *forum prorogatum*, as with the other unilateral methods of accepting the jurisdiction of the ICJ, arises by virtue of the provisions of Article 38(5) of the Rules of the Court.

- The response of a State to the Court, to object to the jurisdiction of the latter, does not amount to acceptance by conduct unless it is coupled with clear and unequivocal steps towards that effect (see *Anglo-Iranian Oil*).

- Instances in which the Court established its jurisdiction *forum prorogatum* are very few. The comparative unpopularity of this method owes much to its extremely controversial nature. *Forum prorogatum* is a high-risk method of conferring jurisdiction on the Court.

Compulsory jurisdiction (optional clause)

As seen earlier, Article 36(2) of the ICJ Statute provides for the jurisdiction of the Court on the basis of a declaration to that effect by States, in respect of legal disputes concerning the interpretation of treaties, and so on.

The 'optional clause' is a method by which States accept the jurisdiction of the Court on an 'opt in, opt out' basis, with regard to whatever disputes they deem fit and for a period of time to be determined solely by that State. Under this mode, a State deposits with the UN Secretary-General a declaration to the effect that it is accepting the jurisdiction of the Court. The declaration will normally specify the types of dispute in respect of which the State accepts the Court's jurisdiction, the period for which the declaration will be operative, and whatever restrictions or limitations the State wishes to place on the Court's jurisdiction in such matters— otherwise known as 'reservations'.

Accepting the jurisdiction of the Court through the optional clause is the only mode that the ICJ Statute itself describes as compulsory. This is mainly because once a State deposits a declaration with the UN Secretary-General, that State is automatically bound to accept the Court's jurisdiction in respect of disputes concerning all other States that might have made similar declarations. Hence, upon a dispute arising, a State that has made a declaration can unilaterally bring a dispute to the Court against another State that has also made a declaration.

Having said that, it might appear overly generous to describe this method as 'compulsory'. First, only States that make declarations accept the jurisdiction of the Court. Secondly, a State that accepts jurisdiction under this method may withdraw its consent, provided that it follows the applicable procedure. Thirdly, jurisdiction is accepted only to the extent that the concerned dispute is covered by the declaration. It is therefore difficult to regard the jurisdiction of the Court as compulsory under this mode.

 15.7

The effects of a declaration under Article 36(2)

● ***Spain v. Canada*** (1998) ICJ Rep 4 (The ***Fisheries Jurisdiction Case***)

The Court said in this case (at [46]) that:

A declaration of acceptance of the compulsory jurisdiction of the Court, whether there are specified limits set to that acceptance or not, is a unilateral act of State sovereignty. At the same time, it establishes a consensual bond and the potential for a jurisdictional link with the other States which have made declarations pursuant to Article 36, paragraph 2, of the Statute, and makes a standing offer to the other States party to the Statute which have not yet deposited a declaration of acceptance.

15.7.1 The duration of a declaration and the relevant date of the Court's jurisdiction

A State may accept the jurisdiction of the Court for a fixed period or on a permanent basis. Once a State deposits its declaration, it is under a legal obligation to accept the Court's jurisdiction from that moment, regardless of the date on which the other party accepts the jurisdiction or that on which such acceptance is communicated to it.

example

If Candoma deposits its declaration on 1 January 2010, to remain in force for twenty years, and Rutamu accepts the Court's jurisdiction on 30 December 2015, Candoma shall be bound by the jurisdiction of the Court to settle a dispute that Rutamu takes to the Court on 1 January 2016. It is irrelevant that Candoma is not aware or notified of Rutamu's acceptance of the Court's jurisdiction before Rutamu takes the matter to the Court.

● *Portugal v. India (Preliminary Objections)* (1957) ICJ REP 125 (The *Rights of Passage over Indian Territory Case*)

A dispute arose between Portugal and India. India accepted the Court's jurisdiction by a declaration that it made in 1940. Portugal accepted the Court's jurisdiction on 19 December 1955 and, on 22 December 1955, brought an action against India. On 30 December 1955, India was notified of Portugal's acceptance of the Court's jurisdiction by declaration. India argued that the Court did not have jurisdiction to entertain the case on the basis, among others, that it was not notified of Portugal's declaration before it went to the Court.

The ICJ rejected this argument, and held (at 146) that:

The contractual relation between the Parties and the compulsory jurisdiction of the Court resulting therefrom are established . . . by the fact of the making of the Declaration. Accordingly, every State which makes a Declaration of Acceptance must be deemed to take into account the possibility that, under the Statute, it may at *any time find* itself subjected to the obligations of the Optional Clause in relation to a new Signatory as the result of the deposit by that Signatory of a Declaration of acceptance. A State accepting the jurisdiction of the Court *must expect that an Application may be filed against it before the Court by a new declarant State on the same day* on which that State deposits with the Secretary-General its Declaration of Acceptance. For it is *on that very day* that the consensual bond, which is the basis of the Optional Clause, comes into being between the States concerned. [Emphasis added]

The Court went ahead in eliminating any lingering doubt by further stating (at 147) that:

the Statute does not prescribe any interval between the deposit by a State of its Declaration of Acceptance and the filing of an Application by that State, and that the principle of reciprocity is not affected by any delay in the receipt of copies of the Declaration by the Parties to the Statute.

Clearly, if Portugal had notified India of its acceptance of the Court's jurisdiction before it brought the case against India, it is highly likely that India would have withdrawn its declaration or modified its declaration, as it had indeed done before. However, it would have been difficult for India to have taken either step, because a right of withdrawal of declaration is subject to reasonable notice to all other parties. Considering the closeness between the date on which Portugal declared for the Court (19 December 1955) and that on which it brought an action against India (22 December 1955), it might have proved difficult for India to satisfy the condition of 'reasonable notice'.

● **Cameroon v. Nigeria (Preliminary Objections)** (1998) ICJ REP 275 (**Land and Maritime Boundary between Cameroon and Nigeria Case**)

Nigeria accepted the jurisdiction of the Court on 14 August 1965, and Cameroon did the same on 3 March 1994. Cameroon brought an action against Nigeria on 29 March 1994. The Court notified all parties to the Statute after Cameroon brought the case against Nigeria. Nigeria argued that the Court did not have jurisdiction.

The Court rejected Nigeria's argument on the same basis as it had India's argument in *Right of Passage*. In addition to the reasoning in that case, the Court applied the principle of law of contract to reach the same conclusion, and stated (at 293) that:

> Any State party to the Statute, in adhering to the jurisdiction of the Court in accordance with Article 36, paragraph 2, accepts jurisdiction in its relations with States previously having adhered to that clause. At the same time, it makes a standing offer to the other States party to the Statute which have not yet deposited a declaration of acceptance. The day one of those States accepts that offer by depositing in its turn its declaration of acceptance, the consensual bond is established and no further condition needs to be fulfilled.

thinking points

- *Does a State's acceptance of the jurisdiction of the Court under the optional clause have to be notified to other States before the State that has newly accepted jurisdiction can bring an action before the ICJ? (In addition to* Right of Passage *and* Cameroon v. Nigeria, *see also the discussion of the* Nicaragua Case *in the following section.)*
- *Of what effect would States accepting the jurisdiction of the Court on one day and bringing an action against other States on the next be for the Court system?*

15.7.2 Modification and termination

Another important issue to consider regarding the optional clause method of accepting the jurisdiction of the Court is the modification and withdrawal of declarations. As a general principle, States are entitled to modify or withdraw their declarations, provided that they give reasonable notice to other States that have also accepted the jurisdiction of the ICJ by optional clause.

The effect of modifying a declaration is the same as terminating a declaration and, as such, the same rule of notice applies to both.

● *Portugal v. India (Preliminary Objections)* (1957) ICJ REP 125 (The *Rights of Passage over Indian Territory Case*)

As the Court said in this case (at 143):

> Under the existing [optional clause] system, Governments can rely upon being informed of any changes in the declarations in the same manner as they are informed of total denunciations of the Declarations.

It is irrelevant whether the declaration in question is in operation only for a specified period of time or ad infinitum, or whether the changes proposed to the declaration merely modify or completely terminate it. The Court has thus generally applied the same conditions of notice to parties that intend to modify their declarations as those that apply to parties that intend to terminate their declarations.

● *Nicaragua v. United States (Jurisdiction and Admissibility)* (1984) ICJ REP 421 (The *Military and Paramilitary Activities in and against Nicaragua Case*, or the *Nicaragua Case*)

Nicaragua brought an action against the USA. Both parties had accepted the jurisdiction of the Court by optional clause: the USA by a 1946 declaration; Nicaragua by a 1929 declaration to the PCIJ, which was incorporated by Article 36(5) of the ICJ Statute.

Three days before Nicaragua brought the action in 1984, the USA deposited with the UN Secretary-General a modification of its declaration, purportedly limiting, with immediate effect, the jurisdiction of the Court in matters involving the USA. The USA attempted to justify its position by arguing that:

(a) the '1984 notification' that it served on the Court was a modification and not a termination and, as such, did not require the same length of notice as the latter (in its 1946 declaration, the USA had specified a notice period of six months for termination);

(b) declarations made under Article 36(2) of ICJ Statute were not to be compared with treaties and therefore could not be subject to the same notice term as treaties; and

(c) Nicaragua's declaration of 1929 was for an unspecified duration and, as such, was liable to immediate termination, and might not rely on the six-month notice period provided for in the US declaration.

Had these arguments been accepted by the Court, it would have meant that different notice periods apply to modification and termination of declaration, and that modification and termination were of different effect for the purpose of the optional clause system.

However, the Court treated as irrelevant the question of whether the 1984 US notification constituted a modification or termination for the purpose of determining the applicable notice period (at [58]). While the Court agreed that States are entitled to accept its jurisdiction under the optional clause unilaterally, it nevertheless stated (at [59]) that:

> the unilateral nature of declarations does not signify that the State making the declaration is free to amend the scope and the contents of its solemn commitments as it pleases.

Furthermore, the Court stated (at [61]) that:

> although the United States retained the right to modify the contents of the 1946 Declaration or to terminate it, a power which is inherent in any unilateral act of a State, it has, nevertheless assumed an inescapable obligation towards other States accepting the Optional Clause, by stating formally and solemnly that any such change should take effect only after six months have elapsed as from the date of notice.

On the USA's argument that since Nicaragua's declaration did not contain a notice period, being one of an unlimited duration, it was liable to immediate termination and therefore that the USA was accordingly entitled to rely on it on the basis of reciprocity and terminate its own declaration without notice, the Court said (at [63]):

> the right of immediate termination of declarations with indefinite duration is far from established. It appears from the requirements of good faith that they should be treated, by analogy, according to the law of treaties, which requires a reasonable time for withdrawal from or termination of treaties that contain no provision regarding the duration of their validity.

KEY POINTS

The effects of the Court's judgment in *Nicaragua* on the question of modification and termination of declarations can be summarized thus.

- Modification and termination are of the same effect on declarations.

- Optional clause declarations are to be treated as treaties as far as the obligations that they create are concerned.

- Declarations that are not limited in duration and which do not specify a notice period are subject to the same notice period as those that are of limited duration. The notice period is a 'reasonable' time, except where a specific time is stipulated, as was the case in the 1946 US declaration.

- A State that has stipulated a notice period in its own declaration cannot rely on the non-stipulation of such notice in another State's declaration to circumvent its obligation to comply with the notice period.

15.7.3 The difference between the notices required for making and terminating declarations

One interesting question concerning declarations that has come to the Court is whether the same length of notice is required for the purpose of making a declaration as for modifying or terminating it.

● *Cameroon v. Nigeria (Preliminary Objections)* (1998) ICJ REP 275 (*Land and Maritime Boundary between Cameroon and Nigeria Case*)

The relevance of this question was brought before the Court by Nigeria.

It will be recalled that Nigeria had argued that the Court did not have jurisdiction since it (Nigeria) had not been notified of Cameroon's acceptance of the Court's jurisdiction prior to the latter bringing a suit before the ICJ. In support of this argument, Nigeria relied on the decision of the Court in the *Nicaragua Case* (in the previous extract) that it is required that a State wishing to terminate its declaration must give reasonable notice. Conversely, Nigeria argued that since the Court requires a reasonable notice for withdrawal purposes, the same should apply to depositing declarations, so that all parties needed to be given notice of the acceptance of the jurisdiction of the Court by Cameroon before it could bring a claim before the Court.

Although this argument seems logical, it was inapplicable to the optional clause system, and hence was rejected by the Court. In explaining the correct position, the Court distinguished between applicable notice periods for depositing and withdrawing declarations. The Court said (at [34]) that:

> withdrawal ends existing consensual bonds, while deposit establishes such bonds. The effect of withdrawal is therefore purely and simply to deprive other States which have already accepted the jurisdiction of the Court of the right they had to bring proceedings before it against the withdrawing State. In contrast, the deposit of a declaration does not deprive those States of any accrued right. Accordingly no time period is required for the establishment of a consensual bond following such a deposit.

Aside from the dissimilar effect that depositing and withdrawal of declaration carry, the Court also indicated another reason why different notice periods should apply to the two under the optional clause system. It said (at [35]) that:

> to require a reasonable time to elapse before a declaration can take effect would be to introduce an element of uncertainty into the operation of the Optional Clause system ... The Court cannot introduce into the Optional Clause an additional time requirement which is not there.

KEY POINTS

- Different notice periods apply to making a declaration and terminating it.

- The making and termination of declarations create different legal consequences on States and, as such, are subject to different obligations.

15.7.4 Modification or termination after the Court is seized of jurisdiction

Where the ICJ has, however, been seized of jurisdiction in a particular case, the modification or termination of a declaration by a party to the dispute is of no effect. The Court will still be seized of jurisdiction.

● *Liechtenstein v. Guatemala (Preliminary Objections)* [1953] ICJ Rep 111 (The *Nottebohm Case*)

On 17 December 1951, Liechtenstein brought a suit against Guatemala in the ICJ. At that date, both States had valid declarations. However, on 26 January 1952, Guatemala's declaration expired. Guatemala then claimed that the Court had no jurisdiction to deal with the case.

Distinguishing between a situation in which a declaration expires *prior* to and *after* a dispute has been brought before the Court, the Court said (at 121) that:

> There can be no doubt that an Application filed after the expiry of this period would not have the effect of legally seising the Court. But neither in its Declaration nor in any other way did Guatemala then indicate that the time-limit provided for in its Declaration meant that the expiry of the period would deprive the Court of jurisdiction to deal with cases of which it had been previously seised.

In *Nicaragua*, both the USA and Nicaragua accepted this interpretation (at [54], see section 15.7.2).

15.8 The conditions of declaration

The conditions upon which States may make declarations vary but, as a whole, they are designed to ensure that once a State deposits its declaration, a legal relationship is created between it and other States that make similar declarations; nevertheless, the State retains a right to make the kind of declaration with which it is comfortable. There are therefore two major conditions governing declarations: *reciprocity* and *reservations*.

15.8.1 Reciprocity

Article 36 of the ICJ Statute contains two conditions governing declarations. First, according to Article 36(2), a State accepts the Court's jurisdiction 'in relation to any other State accepting the *same* obligation'. This condition creates equality between States that accept the jurisdiction of the ICJ. This is called 'reciprocity', and it forms an integral part of Article 36(2) and applies automatically.

Typically, Candoma may accept the Court's jurisdiction over all disputes involving it except such matters arising in connection with terrorism. Rutamu may accept the ICJ's jurisdiction on all matters except those deriving from maritime activities. The operation of reciprocity here means that the Court cannot hear a case involving the two States that touch on either condition of their declarations.

● *Nicaragua v. United States (Jurisdiction and Admissibility)* [1984] ICJ REP 392 (The *Military and Paramilitary Activities in and against Nicaragua Case*, or the *Nicaragua Case*)

The Court highlighted the nature of the condition contained in Article 36(2) in this case, in which the USA argued that since Nicaragua's declaration was not limited in duration, Nicaragua would be able to terminate it without notice. Hence, the USA argued that it was thus entitled to rely on Nicaragua's declaration on the basis of reciprocity to modify its own declaration without notice.

Rejecting the argument, the Court said (at 419) that since Nicaragua's declaration did not contain any express restrictions, it was:

therefore clear that the United States is not in a position to invoke *reciprocity* as a basis for its action in making the 1984 notification which purported to modify the content of the 1946 Declaration. On the contrary it is Nicaragua that can invoke the six months' notice against the United States—not of course on the basis of reciprocity, but because it is an undertaking which is an integral part of the instrument that contains it. [Emphasis added]

Thus reciprocity forms an integral part of a declaration, unlike reservation (discussed in the following section), which is optional and does not form part of the declaration as such.

However, it must be noted that reciprocity under Article 36(2) does not mean that States have to define exhaustively the conditions of reciprocity for accepting the jurisdiction of the Court at the time of depositing their declaration.

● *Portugal v. India (Preliminary Objections)* (1957) ICJ REP 125 (The *Rights of Passage over Indian Territory Case*)

In this case, the Court said (at 144) that:

It is not necessary that the 'same obligation' should be irrevocably defined at the time of the deposit of the Declaration of acceptance for the entire period of its duration. That expression means no more than that, as between States adhering to the Optional Clause, each and all of them are bound by such identical obligations as may exist at any time during which the acceptance is mutually binding.

One important use that States can make of reciprocity is to prevent 'sharp practices' by States that accept the jurisdiction of the Court only in one case and then withdraw their declaration immediately afterwards. It will be recalled that in *Rights of Passage over Indian Territory* (see section 15.7.1), India faced a situation in which Portugal accepted the Court's jurisdiction just three days before it brought an action against India before the ICJ. Cameroon did the same when it accepted the jurisdiction of the Court less than four weeks before it sued Nigeria. These 'hit and run' uses of the optional clause system can be curtailed by the reciprocity principle. For example, the reservation in the UK declaration denies jurisdiction in respect of cases involving States that accept the Court's jurisdiction only for the specific dispute. The UK benefited from this hugely in the *Case Concerning the Legality of Use of Force* (see section 15.3.1), because while Yugoslavia was able to bring actions against other States, it could not bring an action against the UK.

15.8.2 Reservations

The second condition that governs declarations under Article 36 of the ICJ Statute is reservations. Reservations are provided for by Article 36(3), which enjoins States to make their declarations 'unconditionally or on condition of reciprocity on the part of several or certain States, or for a certain time'. This reciprocity clearly entitles States to reserve the operation of their declarations until certain States have accepted the Court's jurisdiction, or until a specified time.

example

Candoma may deposit a declaration and stipulate that it shall only be effective if Rutamu and other States make similar declarations. The effect is that no State can sue Candoma until Rutamu and the other named States have accepted the jurisdiction of the Court.

Reservations are indeed a very useful tool in the hands of States that accept the jurisdiction of the Court through the optional clause, because a reservation enables such a State to control, in advance, the nature of disputes involving it on which the Court may adjudicate.

It was believed—especially during the period of the PCIJ—that Article 36(3) permitted only reservations concerning named States and a specified time. This view was obviously inspired by the specific mention of those two elements in Article 36(3), but has been rejected repeatedly by the ICJ.

● *Pakistan v. India (Jurisdiction)* (2000) ICJ REP 12 (*Case Concerning the Aerial Incident of 10 August 1999*)

Pakistan brought an action against India over the destruction of an aircraft belonging to the former. India claimed that the Court did not have jurisdiction, because its declaration had contained some reservations that excluded from the Court's jurisdiction disputes involving (1) members of the Commonwealth, and (2) disputes concerning interpretation of treaties, unless all of the parties to those treaties were also parties to the dispute before the Court, or if India specially consented to the jurisdiction of the Court.

In response, Pakistan claimed (at [30]) that India's reservations were of no effect, because they were 'in excess of the conditions permitted under Article 36(3) of the Statute'. The Court rejected this argument and stated (at [37]) that:

> paragraph 3 of Article 36 of its Statute has never been regarded as laying down in an exhaustive manner the conditions under which declarations might be made. Moreover when the Statute of the present Court was being drafted, the right of a State to attach reservations to its declaration was confirmed, and it was indeed considered unnecessary to clarify the terms of Article 36, paragraph 3.

It is now accepted that reservations can be made in respect of any issues, ranging from time, to the type of disputes on which the Court can adjudicate, and so on.

The following are some examples of declarations with some typical reservations.

1998 Declaration by the Federal Republic of Nigeria

I have the honour, on behalf of the Government of the Federal Republic of Nigeria, to declare that the acceptance by the Government of the Federal Republic of Nigeria of the compulsory jurisdiction of the International Court of Justice by virtue of the Declaration made on 14th of August, 1965 under Article 36 of the Statute of the Court, is hereby amended so as to read as set out in the following paragraph;

In conformity with paragraph 2 of Article 36 of the statute, the Government of the Federal Republic of Nigeria accepts as compulsory ipso facto and without special agreement, in relation to any other State accepting the same obligation, that is to say, on condition of reciprocity, the jurisdiction of the Court over all legal disputes referred to in that paragraph of the Statute, other than:

(i) disputes in respect of which any party to the disputes has accepted the jurisdiction of the Court by a Declaration deposited less than Twelve Months prior to the filing of an Application bringing the dispute before the Court after the date of this Amended Declaration;

(ii) disputes in respect of which any party has filed an Application in substitution for or in lieu of all or any part of any Application to which sub-paragraph (i) refers;

(iii) disputes relating to matters which are essentially within the domestic jurisdiction of the Federal Republic of Nigeria;

(iv) in respect of which any party to the dispute has accepted the jurisdiction of the Court in relation to or for the purposes of the dispute;

(v) disputes in regard to which the parties have agreed or agree to have recourse to any other method of peaceful settlement;

(vi) disputes relating to or connected with facts or situations of hostilities or armed conflict, whether internal or international in character;

(vii) disputes with any State with which the Government of Nigeria does not have diplomatic relations;

(viii) disputes concerning the allocation, delimitation or demarcation of territory (whether land, maritime, lacustrine or super jacent air space) unless the Government of Nigeria specially agrees to such jurisdiction and within the limits of any such special agreement;

(ix) disputes in relation to matters which arose prior to the date of Nigeria's independence, including any dispute the causes, origins or bases of which arose prior to that date.

The Government of the Federal Republic of Nigeria further reserves the right at any time, by means of a notification addressed to the Secretary-General of the United Nations, and with effect from the moment of such notification, to add to, amend or withdraw this Declaration or the reservations contained therein or any that may hereafter be added.

Done at Abuja, this 29th day of April 1998.

(Signed) Chief Tom IKIMI,

Hon. Minister of Foreign Affairs,

Federal Republic of Nigeria.

2002 Declaration by Australia

WHEREAS on the first day of November one thousand nine hundred and forty-five Australia ratified the Charter of the United Nations, of which the Statute of the International Court of Justice is an integral part; and

WHEREAS the Government of Australia deposited for and on behalf of Australia on the first day of November one thousand nine hundred and forty-five its instrument of ratification to the Statute of the International Court of Justice done at San Francisco on the twenty-sixth day of June, one thousand nine hundred and forty-five; and

WHEREAS Australia made a declaration under paragraph 2 of Article 36 of the said Statute on the thirteenth day of March one thousand nine hundred and seventy-five effective until such time as notice may be given to withdraw that declaration;

THE GOVERNMENT OF AUSTRALIA, having considered the said declaration, hereby gives notice effective immediately of the WITHDRAWAL of that declaration and REPLACES the same with the following declaration:

The Government of Australia declares that it recognises as compulsory ipso facto and without special agreement, in relation to any other State accepting the same obligation, the jurisdiction of the International Court of Justice in conformity with paragraph 2 of Article 36 of the Statute of the Court, until such time as notice may be given to the Secretary-General of the United Nations withdrawing this declaration. This declaration is effective immediately.

This declaration does not apply to:

(a) any dispute in regard to which the parties thereto have agreed or shall agree to have recourse to some other method of peaceful settlement;

(b) any dispute concerning or relating to the delimitation of maritime zones, including the territorial sea, the exclusive economic zone and the continental shelf, or arising out of, concerning, or relating to the exploitation of any disputed area of or adjacent to any such maritime zone pending its delimitation;

(c) any dispute in respect of which any other party to the dispute has accepted the compulsory jurisdiction of the Court only in relation to or for the purpose of the dispute; or where the acceptance of the Court's compulsory jurisdiction on behalf of any other party to the dispute was deposited less than 12 months prior to the filing of the application bringing the dispute before the Court.

IN WITNESS WHEREOF, I, ALEXANDER JOHN GOSSE DOWNER, Minister for Foreign Affairs, have hereunto set my hand and affixed my seal.

DONE at Canberra this 21st day of March, two thousand and two.

(Signed) A.J.G. DOWNER,

Minister for Foreign Affairs of Australia.

The examples of declarations provided above are important, because they encompass a wide range of reservations, which demonstrate that Article 36(3) is now more widely construed than as argued by Pakistan in *Aerial Incident*. This shows that there are different types of reservation that a State may make to its declaration. But also—and perhaps more importantly—the examples (particularly of the Nigerian declaration) show a type of reservation known as the 'Connally reservation' that has generated considerable controversy and which therefore deserves to be given special attention.

15.9 Types of reservation

15.9.1 Reservation *ratione temporis*

Reservations can be made that limit the jurisdiction of the Court to disputes arising from certain times or periods. This is known as the reservation *ratione temporis*—that is, the reservation concerning time. States regularly insert this type of reservation in their declarations. As seen in reservations (i) and (c) of the Nigerian and Australian declarations in the previous section, respectively, both States bar the Court from adjudicating disputes involving them and other States that have not accepted the jurisdiction of the Court for at least twelve months prior to bringing the action before the Court. Clearly, like the UK reservation preventing a one-off acceptance of the Court's jurisdiction, the reservation *ratione temporis* can be very instrumental in averting abuse of the optional clause system by opportunistic States.

Reservations *ratione temporis* may contain clauses that limit the Court's jurisdiction only to matters arising from a specified date, as seen in the Nigerian and Australian reservations (the 'single-barrel *temporis*'), but may also contain clauses that, in addition to date of entry into force of the declaration, or any date, may address limits to the date on which facts giving rise to a dispute must have arisen (the 'double-barrel *temporis*'). The 2004 UK declaration provides a good example of a double-barrel reservation *temporis*, which limits the jurisdiction of the Court to both the date on which a dispute arises and that on which the material facts arise:

> The Government of the United Kingdom of Great Britain and Northern Ireland accept as compulsory ipso facto and without special convention, on condition of reciprocity, the jurisdiction of the International Court of Justice, in conformity with paragraph 2 of Article 36 of the Statute of the Court, until such time as notice may be given to terminate the acceptance, over all disputes arising after 1 January 1974, with regard to situations or facts subsequent to the same date...

Also, the 2007 Declaration by Japan states, inter alia, that the Court shall not have jurisdiction:

> over all disputes arising on and after 15 September 1958 with regard to situations or facts subsequent to the same date and being not settled by other means of peaceful settlement.

It is for the Court to determine when a dispute arises for the purpose of interpreting and applying the declarations of parties. As we have already seen earlier (see *Interpretation of Peace Treaties with Bulgaria, Hungary and Romania* and the *Certain Property Case*), the Court will have to consider the specific point at which a dispute can be said to have arisen, regardless of what the parties to the dispute subjectively believe or claim this to be.

· ·

● ***Italy v. France (Preliminary Objections)*** (1938) PCIJ Ser. A/B, no. 74 (The ***Phosphates in Morocco Case***)

In 1920, France proclaimed a monopoly over some phosphates in Morocco in violation of treaty obligations that gave an Italian licence over the sale items. In 1931, France accepted the jurisdiction of the Court in respect of all disputes arising after 1931. Although the Court found that the monopolization of the phosphates continued well beyond the day on which France accepted its jurisdiction, it held, however, that the facts leading to the dispute started much earlier than the acceptance date, and hence this precluded it from exercising jurisdiction.

15.9.2 Reservation *ratione materiae*

Reservations may define the subject matter of the Court's jurisdiction. Thus States may prevent the Court from exercising jurisdiction in disputes concerning land or maritime matters, over issues involving members of the Commonwealth (as we saw in section 15.8.2 in *Aerial Incident*), or over matters that the parties have agreed will be subject to arbitration or other dispute settlement mechanisms (as with the Australian reservation in section 15.8.2). Some more recent declarations contain reservations barring the Court from dealing with environment and debt-related matters.

The 1990 Declaration of the Republic of Poland entitles the Court to deal with disputes except, inter alia:

> ...
>
> (c) disputes with regard to pollution of the environment unless the jurisdiction of the International Court of Justice result from the treaty obligations of the Republic of Poland;
>
> (d) disputes with regard to foreign liabilities or debts...

(See Renata Szafarz, 'Poland accepts the optional clause of the ICJ Statute' (1991) 85 AJIL 374.)

States often insert many reservations in their declarations which sometimes leaves the Court with almost no jurisdiction. One prominent example is the 2005 Declaration by Djibouti—a small East African country—which includes twelve reservations excluding issues relating to the country's air space, territory (water, land, etc.), disputes subject to other settlement processes, disputes falling within Djibouti's domestic jurisdiction, disputes resulting from the use of force or self-defence measures, disputes concerning the application of bilateral or multilateral treaties, disputes concerning States with which Djibouti has diplomatic relations, and disputes involving non-sovereign States or entities, among others.

Multilateral treaty reservations (known as 'Vanderberg reservations') are reservations by which States limit the jurisdiction of the Court in respect of disputes arising from the interpretation of multilateral treaties to only those disputes in which *all of the* parties to the concerned treaty are involved.

● *Pakistan v. India (Jurisdiction)* (2000) ICJ REP 12 (*Case Concerning the Aerial Incident of 10 August 1999*)

India challenged the Court's jurisdiction on the basis of a reservation contained in its declaration to the effect that the Court shall not exercise jurisdiction in:

> disputes concerning the interpretation or application of a multilateral treaty unless all the parties to the treaty are also parties to the case before the Court or Government of India specially agree to jurisdiction.

The Court did not find it necessary to pronounce on the issue. This was because India succeeded in objecting to the jurisdiction of the Court on the basis that Pakistan is a member of the Commonwealth. One of India's reservations forbade the Court to deal with such matters, unless all members of the Commonwealth are parties to the dispute or India gave special consent to the dispute.

● *Nicaragua v. United States (Jurisdiction and Admissibility)* (1984) ICJ REP 421
(The *Military and Paramilitary Activities in and against Nicaragua Case*, or the *Nicaragua Case*)

The Court was confronted with interpreting another multilateral treaty, the UN Charter. The USA objected to the Court's jurisdiction on the basis that Costa Rica and El Salvador, both parties to the UN Charter and both involved in the dispute, were not before the Court.

Although the Court accepted that this reservation ousted its jurisdiction, it did, however, assert its jurisdiction in this case on the basis that the issue involved in the case (the use of force) also existed under customary international law.

Nonetheless, the fact that the Court was prepared to accept the Vandenberg reservation in this case, but for the customary international law venue, suggested that such reservations could be used to prevent the jurisdiction of the Court.

KEY POINTS

- Reservations can be made to set the date of disputes, or facts thereto, over which the Court will have jurisdiction (*ratione temporis*), or to limit the subject matter of the Court's jurisdiction (*ratione materiae*).

- Article 36(3) is not exhaustive and States are permitted to make any kind of reservations, insofar as they do not contradict the ICJ Statute.

- Vandenberg reservations prevent the jurisdiction of the Court, except where the issue involved is also covered by customary international law (*Nicaragua*).

15.9.3 Reservation against disputes within domestic jurisdiction

States include some reservations in their declaration that seek to bar the Court from adjudicating upon matters that they consider as falling within their domestic jurisdictions. The 1946 declaration by the USA was the first to contain this kind of reservation, which is known as a 'Connally reservation' and is named after its chief architect, Tom Connally, a US Senator.

The United Nations is forbidden to intervene in matters falling within the domestic jurisdiction of any member State (Article 2(7) of the UN Charter). Hence, being a UN organ, the ICJ is thus bound by this restraint. Therefore, in principle, there is nothing wrong with States barring the Court from adjudicating upon matters that fall within their domestic jurisdiction.

The problem with Connally reservations, however, is that in most cases it is the State that makes the reservation that ultimately decides what matters fall within its jurisdiction. The 2005 Declaration by Djibouti and the 1998 Declaration by Nigeria are examples of such declarations that do not empower these countries to decide when disputes fall within their domestic jurisdiction. This undermines the Court's responsibility to determine its own jurisdiction as its Statute empowers it to do. Hence, Connally reservations have been aptly described as 'self-judging' reservations. (See the *Norwegian Loans Case* (later in this section), *Switzerland v. USA* (the *Interhandel Case*), and other similar cases discussed in Chapter 3 on the Court's attitude to Connally reservations.) In *Interhandel*, Judge Lauterpacht said (at 34) that:

(a) the reservation in question, while constituting an essential part of the Declaration of Acceptance, is contrary to paragraph 6 of Article 36 of the Statute of the Court; it cannot, accordingly, be acted upon by the Court; which means that it is invalid;

(b) that, irrespective of its inconsistency with the Statute, that reservation by effectively conferring upon the Government of the United States the right to determine with finality whether in any particular case it is under an obligation to accept the jurisdiction of the Court, deprives the Declaration of Acceptance of the character of a legal instrument, cognizable before a judicial tribunal, expressing legal rights and obligations;

(c) that reservation, being an essential part of the Declaration of Acceptance, cannot be separated from it so as to remove from the Declaration the vitiating element of inconsistency with the Statute and of the absence of a legal obligation.

...Accordingly, there being before the Court no valid Declaration of Acceptance, the Court cannot act upon it in any way-even to the extent of examining objections to admissibility and jurisdiction other than that expressed in the automatic reservation.

. . . .

● *Nicaragua v. United States (Jurisdiction and Admissibility)* (1984) ICJ Rep 421
  (The *Military and Paramilitary Activities in and against Nicaragua Case*, or the
  Nicaragua Case)

Although the USA did not invoke the Connally reservation, Judge Schwebel took the opportunity, in his dissenting opinion (at 551) to deal with the Connally reservation. He agreed with
Judge Lauterpacht's conclusion that 'Connally reservations' rendered declarations completely
invalid and stated that this should have been the position of the Court in the present case,
insofar as the USA came to the Court via the offending declaration.

One point that needs to be emphasized is that, in all of these cases, the Court itself did not
go into the effect of Connally reservations, or the impact that any reservation, for that matter, has on the whole of a declaration, but simply held that such prevented it from exercising
jurisdiction.

. . . .

● *Spain v. Canada* (1998) ICJ Rep 4 (The *Fisheries Jurisdiction Case*)

Spain brought an action against Canada for unlawful arrest and harassment of a Spanish ship
in Canadian waters. Canada's declaration accepting the jurisdiction of the Court contained
a reservation precluding the Court from disputes 'arising out of or concerning conservation
and management measures taken by Canada with respect to vessels fishing in the NAFO
Regulatory Area' (reservation (d)). Spain argued that the said reservation was contrary to the
ICJ Statute and that the Court therefore had no jurisdiction.

The Court therefore had to determine whether a reservation forms an integral part of a
declaration.

The Court (at [47]), relying on its previous decisions in *Anglo-Iranian Oil* (see section 15.6.1)
and *France v. Norway* (1957) ICJ Rep 9 (the *Norwegian Loans Case*), concluded that:

> every declaration must be interpreted as it stands, having regard to the words actually used . . . dec-
> larations and reservations are to be read as a whole. Moreover, 'the Court cannot base itself on a
> purely grammatical interpretation of the text. It must seek the interpretation which is in harmony
> with a natural and reasonable way of reading the text.

Despite this statement, the Court recognized (at [49]) that the intention of the parties should
be reflected in construing the declaration:

> The Court will thus interpret the relevant words of a declaration *including a reservation* contained
> therein in a natural and reasonable way, having due regard to the *intention* of the State concerned
> at the time when it accepted the compulsory jurisdiction of the Court. The intention of a reserving
> State may be deduced *not only from the text of the relevant clause*, but also from *the context in which the
> clause is to be read*, and an examination of evidence regarding the circumstances of its preparation
> and the purposes intended to be served. [Emphasis added]

The Court concluded (at [59]):

> It follows that this reservation is not only an integral part of the current declaration but also an
> essential component of it, and hence of the acceptance by Canada of the Court's compulsory
> jurisdiction.

The Court appears to be saying that since reservations form an integral part of a declaration, and manifest the intention of the States making them, then an offending reservation forms an integral part of the declaration and cannot be removed from the declaration without destroying the declaration as a whole. This would certainly lead to the same conclusion reached by Lauterpacht and Schwebel.

However, given the absence of a categorical statement by the Court about whether reservations form an integral part of declarations and, considering that it is yet to make such a decision, the best approach is to regard the matter as being as yet unsettled.

It needs to be pointed out, however, that some judges do not believe that the effect of a Connally reservation is to render the pertinent declaration void as a whole. They believe that the offending reservation should be removed on its own, while the remaining parts of the declaration survive.

As Judge Klaestad reasoned in *Interhandel* ([at 78]), to completely reject jurisdiction on the basis of offending reservations is for the Court to find itself in exactly the same position as it would be if it were dealing with a State that has not accepted its jurisdiction.

thinking points

- *What is the basis upon which Judge Lauterpacht believed that Connally reservations completely invalidate declarations?*
- *What is your view about the approach of Klaestad et al. to the problem of Connally reservations?*
- *What is the purpose of Connally reservations?*

15.10 Interventions

Under certain circumstances, States which are not parties to a dispute may intervene in a dispute before the Court, either by right or because they have a legal interest in the dispute. Articles 62 and 63 of the ICJ Statute deal with such situations.

15.10.1 Article 62 interventions

According to Article 62 of the ICJ Statute:

> Should a state consider that it has an interest of a legal nature which may be affected by the decision in the case, it may submit a request to the Court to be permitted to intervene.

What constitutes 'interests of a legal nature' is, however, uncertain. In the past, the Court has given conflicting decisions on this issue.

. . . .

● *Ethiopia v. South Africa; Liberia v. South Africa (Second Phase)* (1966) ICJ REP 6 [The *South West Africa Cases*]

The Court adopted a narrow view of the term 'legal interest' in this case, saying that it must be personal and include 'rights and obligations which must be clothed in legal form' (at 34).

Thus a bare majority of the Court denied the application by Ethiopia and Liberia to intervene 'to take legal action in vindication of a public interest'. The approach of the Court was that there can be no legal interest of a general or public nature.

Interestingly—and quite contradictorily—in *Barcelona Traction* (see section 15.6.1), the Court was to hold (at 32) that some rights are so fundamental in nature that 'all States can be held to have a legal interest in their protection'.

In more recent cases, the Court has avoided characterizing 'interest of legal nature' in very specific terms as it did in *South West Africa* and *Barcelona Traction*.

● *Libya v. Malta* (1984) ICJ REP 9 (The ***Continental Shelf Case***)

In this case, the Court confirmed (at [13]) that it now sees 'interest of legal nature' as being:

> no more than an indication of the reasons which may impel a State to seek to intervene; but it is clear that the intention of the text is that the existence of such an interest is, objectively, a requirement for intervention.

thinking points

- *What does 'interest of a legal nature' mean?*
- *Between* South West Africa *and* Barcelona Traction, *which approach to interpreting 'legal interest' do you support and why?*

15.10.2 Conditions for intervention under Article 62

In addition to the provisions of Article 62 of the ICJ Statute, Article 81(1) of the Rules of the Court requires a State applying to intervene to do so 'as soon as possible, and not later than the closure of the written proceedings'. Furthermore, under Article 81(2) of the Rules, the State must set out in its application:

(a) the interest of a legal nature which the State applying to intervene considers may be affected by the decision in that case;

(b) the precise object of the intervention;

(c) any basis of jurisdiction which is claimed to exist as between the State applying to intervene and the parties to the case.

Whereas these requirements appear quite simple, it has proved considerably difficult for States to establish that they fulfil these conditions. Even in cases in which they do meet the conditions, the Court may yet reject their applications for inability to demonstrate that their intervention is necessary for the successful adjudication of the case.

● *Tunisia v. Libya* (1981) ICJ REP 3 (The ***Continental Shelf Case***)

Malta applied to intervene in a case between Tunisia and Libya, in order to 'submit its views to the Court on the issues raised in the pending case, before the Court has given its decision in that case' (at 9). Libya objected.

The Court said (at [19]):

> The interest of a legal nature invoked by Malta does not relate to any legal interest of its own directly in issue as between Tunisia and Libya in the present proceedings or as between itself and either one of those countries. It concerns rather the *potential implications of reasons* which the Court may give in its decision in the present case on matters in issue as between Tunisia and Libya with respect to the delimitation of their continental shelves for a subsequent delimitation of Malta's own continental shelf. [Emphasis added]

At [34] that:

> ...To allow such a form of 'intervention' would, in the particular circumstances of the present case, also leave the Parties quite uncertain as to whether and how far they should consider their own separate legal interests vis-à-vis Malta as in effect constituting part of the subject-matter of the present case. A State seeking to intervene under Article 62 of the Statute is, in the view of the Court, clearly not entitled to place the parties to the case in such a position, and this is the more so since it would not be submitting its own claims to decision by the Court nor be exposing itself to counterclaims.

From this case, it emerges that fear of an outcome cannot constitute the basis for making an application under Article 62 of the ICJ Statute. Also, in considering whether an application will or will not succeed, the Court must attempt to balance the interests of the applicant with those of the parties to the dispute. Where the interests of the intervener will dislocate or prejudice those of the parties to a dispute, then the Court may decline the application.

● ***Libya v. Malta*** (1984) ICJ REP 92 (The ***Continental Shelf Case***)

Libya brought an action against Malta. Italy applied to intervene under Article 62 of the ICJ Statute. Although the Court found that Italy complied with all of the conditions stipulated in Article 62 and the relevant provisions of the Rules of the Court, it nonetheless rejected its application.

According to the Court (at [43]), the interest that Italy sought to protect was already protected under Article 59 of the ICJ Statute, and it was the interest of the parties, not that of Italy, which would be affected by the absence of the latter's participation in the case.

● ***El Salvador v. Honduras*** (1992) ICJ REP 92 (***Land and Maritime Frontier Dispute Case***)

A Chamber of the Court permitted Nicaragua to intervene on certain aspects of the case, on the basis of Article 62 of the ICJ Statute. (See [85] and [92] in particular.)

This case is important for a reason other than being the first time that the Court granted an application for intervention; it also provided clarification by the Court of the requirements of an Article 62 application. The Court said (at [61]) that:

> it is clear, first, that it is for a State seeking to intervene to demonstrate convincingly what it asserts, and thus to bear the burden of proof; and, second, that it has only to show that its interest 'may' be affected, not that it will or must be affected. What needs to be shown by a State seeking permission to intervene can only be judged *in concreto* and in relation to all the circumstances of a particular case. It is for the State seeking to intervene to identify the interest of a legal nature which it considers may be affected by the decision in the case, and to show in what way that interest may be affected; it is not for the Court itself—or in the present case the Chamber—to substitute itself for the State in that respect.

It must be noted that it is for the Court, and not the State parties to the case, to consent to intervention. As the Court said (at [96]):

> The competence of the Court in this matter of intervention is not, like its competence to hear and determine the dispute referred to it, derived from the consent of the parties to the case, but from the consent given by them, in becoming parties to the Court's Statute, to the Court's exercise of its powers conferred by the Statute.

thinking points
- *What are the conditions governing intervention under Article 62 of the ICJ Statute?*
- *Distinguish the facts and the position of the Court in* Tunisia v. Libya *from those in* Land and Maritime Frontier Dispute.

15.10.3 Article 63 interventions

Unlike Article 62, intervention under Article 63 of the ICJ Statute is as of right. Thus:

> every state so notified has the right to intervene in the proceedings; but if a State intervenes under this rule, the construction given by the judgment will be equally binding upon it.

Intervention under Article 63 is permitted solely in respect of a dispute concerning the interpretation of a multilateral treaty to which the intervening State is a party.

States intervening under Article 63 must disclose in their application:

(a) particulars of the basis on which the declarant State considers itself a party to the convention;

(b) particular provisions of the convention, the construction of which it considers to be in question;

(c) a statement of the construction of those provisions for which it contends; and

(d) a list of the documents in support, which documents shall be attached.

Although intervention under Article 63 is a right, under Article 84 of the Rules of the Court, it is for the Court to decide whether the application is admissible.

● *United Kingdom v. Germany (Question of Intervention by Poland)* (1923) PCIJ Ser. A, No. 1 (The *SS Wimbledon Case*)

Britain, France, and Italy brought a suit to the Court in respect of a British vessel, *SS Wimbledon*, to which Germany had refused access to its port at Kiel. Poland, where the ship was heading, applied to intervene. The case involved the interpretation of Article 380 of the Treaty of Versailles, to which Poland is a party and in respect of which Poland alleged violation of its rights.

Accepting the Polish application, the Court said (at 13) that:

> It will suffice for the Court to note that in this case the interpretation of certain clauses of the Treaty of Versailles is involved and that the suit and that the Polish Republic is one of the States which are parties to this treaty.

● *Colombia v. Peru* (1951) ICJ Rep 71 (The *Haya de la Torre Case*)

Cuba applied to intervene in a dispute between Colombia and Peru. At issue here was the 1928 Havana Convention on Asylum, to which Cuba is a party and which country would potentially be affected by the interpretation of the treaty by the Court. Nevertheless, the Court rejected Cuba's application. The Court found that Cuba was using the treaty as a pretext to reopen a case (*Columbia v. Peru* (1950) ICJ Rep 266 (the *Asylum Case*)).

As seen in this case, Cuba clearly had a right to intervene under Article 63, but the Court was able to exercise its competence to decide whether the application was admissible. This demonstrates that possession of the right to intervene is not a guarantee that the application to intervene will succeed.

● *Cameroon v. Nigeria (Preliminary Objections)* (1998) ICJ Rep 275 (*Land and Maritime Boundary between Cameroon and Nigeria Case*)

In this case (discussed in section 15.7.1), the Court granted Equatorial Guinea's application to intervene.

While they are useful, interventions under Article 63 are uncommon. This perhaps flows from the fact that the Court's interpretation of the multilateral treaty in question would become binding not only on the parties to the dispute, but also on the intervener.

● *United Kingdom v. Germany (Question of Intervention by Poland)* (1923) PCIJ Ser. A, No. 1 (The *SS Wimbledon Case*)

As the Court said (at 12):

> When the object of the suit before the Court is the interpretation of an international convention, any State which is a party to this convention has, under Article 63 of the Statute, the right to intervene in the proceedings instituted by others and, should it make use of the right thus accorded, the construction given by the judgment of the Court will be equally binding upon it as upon the original parties.

KEY POINTS

- An intervention under Article 63 of the ICJ Statute is an intervention by right.

- The Court has the competence to decide the admissibility of Article 63 interventions.

- Any interpretation given by the Court in such a case is binding on all parties to the case, including the intervener.

15.11 Advisory opinions

As noted earlier, in addition to jurisdiction over contentious cases, the ICJ also has jurisdiction to render advisory opinions. Article 65 of the ICJ Statute empowers it to:

> give an advisory opinion on any legal question at the request of whatever body may be authorized by or in accordance with the Charter of the United Nations to make such a request.

Under Article 96 of the UN Charter, the UN Security Council, the UN General Assembly, and other organs of the UN, as well as specialized agencies, can request advisory opinions from the Court. What is important is that such other organs and specialized agencies are authorized by the General Assembly to do so.

Advisory opinions can be requested only in respect of legal questions and it is entirely within the competence of the Court to decline such a request.

15.11.1 Legal questions

● **Western Sahara Advisory Opinion** [1975] ICJ Rep 12

The Court construes 'legal question' as flexible and not restrictive (at 20), and that it may also consist of non-legal elements (at 19). The Court may decline a request for an advisory opinion, even if the question is of a legal character (at 21).

The Court's advisory opinion can be sought on a wide variety of subjects, such as the benefits of members of international organizations, the question of whether the construction of a wall by a State along its borders with an occupied territory State is legal, whether a territory is Stateless or ownerless, and whether the threat or use of nuclear weapons is legal, to mention but a few. Regardless of motives, it is important that the request for an advisory opinion concerns a legal question and falls within the scope of the requesting agency's activities.

● **Legality of the Threat or Use of Nuclear Weapons Advisory Opinion** [1996] ICJ Rep 90

The WHO requested the Court's opinion on the legality of the threat or use of nuclear weapons. The Court declined to admit the request on the basis that it was beyond the scope of the activities of the WHO.

However, mixing a legal question with political facts will not prevent the Court from entertaining a request for its advisory opinion.

● **Certain Expenses of the United Nations Advisory Opinion** [1962] ICJ Rep 151

The General Assembly requested the opinion of the Court as to whether certain expenses, authorized by the General Assembly in respect of some UN operations, constituted 'UN expenses' under Article 17(2) of the UN Charter. The political undercurrent of this request was that the said missions were authorized not by the Security Council, which the Charter explicitly empowers to do so, but by the General Assembly, which believed that it had residual responsibility to authorize such missions—especially when the Security Council is immobilized by the veto.

Despite the Court's awareness of this political tussle, it nonetheless admitted the request. The Court said (at 155) that it found:

> no 'compelling reason' why it should not give the advisory opinion which the General Assembly requested by its resolution 1731 (XVI). It has been argued that the question put to the Court is intertwined with political questions, and that for this reason the Court should refuse to give an opinion. It is true that most interpretations of the Charter of the United Nations will have political

significance, great or small. In the nature of things it could not be otherwise. The Court, however, cannot attribute a political character to a request which invites it to undertake an essentially judicial task, namely, the interpretation of a treaty provision.

(For a similar view, see also *Judgments of the Administrative Tribunal of the International Labour Organization [ILO] upon Complaints Made against the United Nations Educational, Scientific and Cultural Organization [UNESCO]* (1956) ICJ Rep 86.)

. . . .

● ***Conditions of Admission of a State to Membership of the United Nations Advisory Opinion*** (1948) ICJ Rep 57

In this case, the Court explained how it is able to give its opinion in a request that contains political elements. The Court said (at 61) that it:

cannot attribute a political character to a request which, framed in abstract terms, invites it to undertake an essentially judicial task, the interpretation of a treaty provision. It is not concerned with the motives which may have inspired this request, nor with the considerations which, in the concrete cases submitted for examination to the Security Council, formed the subject of the exchange of views which took place in that body. It is the duty of the Court to envisage the question submitted to it only in the abstract form which has been given to it.

The Court will also not decline requests for its opinions just because an opinion may touch on facts that relate to a dispute between the concerned States.

. . . .

● ***The Namibia Advisory Opinion*** (1971) ICJ Rep 16

South Africa objected to the request made to the ICJ about its continued presence in Namibia, despite a UN Security Council resolution to the contrary. South Africa claimed (at [30]) that the relevant legal question related to an existing dispute between it and other States.

The Court rejected this argument, stating (at [34]) that:

The fact that, in the course of its reasoning, and in order to answer the question submitted to it, the Court may have to pronounce on legal issues upon which radically divergent views exist between South Africa and the United Nations, does not convert the present case into a dispute nor bring it within the compass of Articles 82 and 83 of the Rules of Court . . .

At [40]:

the contingency that there may be factual issues underlying the question posed does not alter its character as a 'legal question' as envisaged in Article 96 of the Charter. The reference in this provision to legal questions cannot be interpreted as opposing legal to factual issues.

KEY POINTS

- Requests for the ICJ's advisory opinions must concern legal questions and fall within the activities of the requesting organ or agency.

- The presence of political components in the legal question will not automatically cause the Court to decline the request.

15.12 Consent and advisory opinion

Another important issue to consider is whether a State needs to give its consent before the Court can give an advisory opinion. As for its contentious jurisdiction, there is no doubt that the Court can adjudicate only disputes concerning States that have accepted its jurisdiction, regardless of how that acceptance is established.

However, neither the ICJ Statute nor the UN Charter requires that States must give their consent before the Court can give its advisory opinion. Once a State has become a member of the ICJ, by virtue of UN membership, such a State automatically accepts the jurisdiction of the Court to give advisory opinions. Thus, as a general rule, the Court will not decline a request for its opinion simply because a party to the dispute objects to, or is absent from, the proceedings.

Nonetheless, the Court's initial approach to requests for advisory opinions in cases in which one of the States has not accepted its consent was to decline admissibility.

• *Status of Eastern Carelia Advisory Opinion* (1923) PCIJ SER. B, NO. 5

The PCIJ was asked for its advisory opinion as to the status of Eastern Carelia, over which the Soviet Union and Finland were in dispute. The Soviet Union was neither a member of the Court nor of the League of Nations. The Court declined the request.

It must be noted, however, that aside from the non-membership status of the Soviet Union of both the League of Nations and the PCIJ, there were other reasons for the decision of the Court in this case. The Court said that, first, the issue between the parties was 'really one of fact' and that answering it would involve the duty of ascertaining what evidence might throw light upon the contentions of the parties. This would be difficult to achieve, given the status of the Soviet Union vis-à-vis the Court and the League.

As the Court said (at 28):

> The question put to the Court is not one of abstract law, but concerns directly the main point of the controversy between Finland and Russia, and can only be decided by an investigation into the facts underlying the case. Answering the question would be substantially equivalent to deciding the dispute between the parties.

It must always be borne in mind that *Eastern Carelia* was an exception to the general rule that the Court will not decline a request because of objection, absence, or opposition of a party to the dispute, based on the peculiar circumstances of that case, as already mentioned. Thus, where such circumstances are absent, the Court will not decline a request merely because one of the concerned States is neither a UN member nor a party to the ICJ Statute.

• *Proceedings Concerning the Interpretation of Peace Treaties with Bulgaria, Hungary and Romania (First Phase)* (1950) ICJ REP 65

The Court stated (at 71) that:

> the consent of States, parties to a dispute, is the basis of the Court's jurisdiction in contentious cases. The situation is different in regard to advisory proceedings even where the Request for an Opinion relates to a legal question actually pending between States. The Court's reply is only

of an advisory character: as such, it has no binding force. It follows that no State, whether a Member of the United Nations or not, can prevent the giving of an Advisory Opinion which the United Nations considers to be desirable in order to obtain enlightenment as to the course of action it should take. The Court's Opinion is given not to the States, but to the organ which is entitled to request it;

The Court distinguished this case from *Eastern Carelia* stating (at 72) that:

In the opinion of the Court, the circumstances of the present case are profoundly different from those which were before the Permanent Court of International Justice in the *Eastern Carelia* case . . . when that Court declined to give an Opinion because it found that the question put to it was directly related to the main point of a dispute actually pending between two States, so that answering the question would be substantially equivalent to deciding the dispute between the parties, and that at the same time it raised a question of fact which could not be elucidated without hearing both parties. As has been observed, the present Request for an Opinion is solely concerned with the applicability to certain disputes of the procedure for settlement instituted by the Peace Treaties, and it is justifiable to conclude that it in no way touches the merits of those disputes. Furthermore, the settlement of these disputes is entrusted solely to the Commissions provided for by the Peace Treaties.

● ***Western Sahara Advisory Opinion*** (1975) ICJ REP 12

In this case, the Court rendered an advisory opinion despite objection by Spain, which had relied heavily on *Eastern Carelia*. The Court made it very clear that what was in issue in the case was the nature of Moroccan and Mauritanian rights vis-à-vis the disputed territory, and not the dispute between Spain and Morocco.

● ***Legal Consequences of the Construction of a Wall in the Occupied Palestinian Territory Advisory Opinion*** (2004) ICJ REP 136 (The ***Palestinian Wall Case***)

The Court's opinion was asked on the legality of walls being constructed by Israel within the occupied Palestinian territory. Israel objected to the request, citing the *Interpretation of Peace Treaties with Bulgaria, Hungary and Romania* (earlier in this section). It argued (at 161) that:

the Court could not give an opinion on issues which raise questions of fact that cannot be elucidated without hearing all parties to the conflict. According to Israel, if the Court decided to give the requested opinion, it would be forced to speculate about essential facts and make assumptions about arguments of law.

The Court rejected Israel's argument and ruled that it had enough evidence at its disposal to deal with the case. In that way, the Court subtly distinguished the present case from *Interpretation of Peace Treaties*.

As a general principle, advisory opinions are not binding on States. However, there may be instances in which States may agree to be bound by advisory opinions. This is possible where the treaty or convention, the interpretation of which gives rise to the dispute between the States, specifically makes provisions to that effect.

● *Opinion on the Difference Relating to Immunity from Legal Process of a Special Rapporteur of the Commission of Human Rights* (1999) ICJ REP 62

The opinion of the Court was sought as to the interpretation of the 1946 Convention on the Privileges and Immunities of the United Nations. However, by Article 30 of this convention:

> ...if a difference arises between the United Nations on the one hand and a Member on the other hand, a request shall be made for an advisory opinion on any legal question involved in accordance with Article 96 of the Charter and Article 65 of the Statute of the Court. The *opinion given by the Court shall be accepted as decisive by the parties.* [Emphasis added]

KEY POINTS

• As a general rule, consent is not required for the Court to exercise its jurisdiction in advisory matters.

• Where the Court's advisory opinion will affect the rights of a State that is not party to the dispute, or has not accepted the Court's jurisdiction, then the Court may decline jurisdiction (*Eastern Carelia*).

15.13 The effects of ICJ judgments

According to Article 60 of the ICJ Statute, the judgments of the Court are final and without appeal. Therefore, if States decide to use the Court as a dispute settlement mechanism, then they *ipso facto* accept that there can be no appeal against whatever decision is reached by the Court. If there is a disagreement as to the meaning or scope of a judgment, then the Court can, at the request of either party to the case, interpret its own judgments.

Furthermore, the Court is not bound to follow its decision in a previous case. Under the common law system, the principle of *stare decisis* means that a court is bound by its previous decision until such a decision is overruled by a court of higher jurisdiction or by the Court itself. The ICJ does not follow this principle. Nonetheless, the Court constantly refers to its own reasoning in previous decisions as though they are binding. This has ensured a great deal of consistency in the jurisprudence of the Court.

15.13.1 The *Monetary Gold* principle

Where the Court is concerned that the right of a third State not party to a dispute might be affected by its decision (and if such a party has not applied for intervention), it may decline to give judgment on merit. This is known as the *Monetary Gold* principle, after the case in which it first emerged.

● *Italy v. France; United Kingdom v. United States* (1954) ICJ REP 19 (The *Monetary Gold Case*)

The Court had to decide a matter concerning some gold removed from Rome. Italy and Albania both claimed ownership, as did the UK, although for different reasons. Relevant to the issue at hand was that Italy, which accepted the Court's jurisdiction, claimed the gold as compensation for some injury that it claimed Albania caused it. Albania did not accept the jurisdiction of the Court.

The Court declined jurisdiction, and said (at 32) that:

> to adjudicate upon the international responsibility of Albania without her consent would run counter to a well-established principle of international law embodied in the Court's Statute, namely, that the Court can only exercise jurisdiction over a State with its consent.

Note that the fact that Albania could have intervened (but did not) did not affect the decision of the Court on this point.

● *Portugal v. Australia* (1995) ICJ REP 90 (The *East Timor Case*)

Portugal sued Australia over the legality of a treaty between the latter and Indonesia concerning East Timor, a former colony of Portugal relinquished to Indonesia. Indonesia was not party to the dispute. Australia objected to the jurisdiction of the Court on the ground that the Court could not adjudicate to determine the legality of the 1989 treaty between it and Indonesia without delving into how Indonesia entered into East Timor.

The Court agreed with this reasoning and held (at [29]) that it had no jurisdiction:

> The Court could not rule on the lawfulness of the conduct of a State when its judgment would imply an evaluation of the lawfulness of the conduct of another State which is not a party to the case. Where this is so, the Court cannot act, even if the right in question is a right *erga omnes*.

15.13.2 Revision of judgments

Under Article 61 of the ICJ Statute, a party to a dispute in which the Court has rendered its judgment may apply for a revision of the judgment if it discovers:

> some fact of such a nature as to be a decisive factor, which fact was, when the judgment was given, unknown to the Court and also to the party claiming revision, always provided that such ignorance was not due to negligence.

There have been two applications for revision of the Court's judgments, both of which were unsuccessful.

● *Application for Revision and Interpretation of the Judgment of 24 February 1982 in the Case Concerning the Continental Shelf (Tunisia v. Libya)* (1985) ICJ REP 182

Tunisia applied for a revision of the judgment of the Court to 'correct an error', among other reasons. The Court rejected the application by Tunisia (at [38]) on the basis that the newly discovered evidence did not affect the reasoning of the Court in reaching its decision.

● *Application for Revision of the Judgment of 11 July 1996 in the Case Concerning Application of the Convention on the Prevention and Punishment of the Crime of Genocide (Bosnia and Herzegovina v. Yugoslavia), Preliminary Objections (Yugoslavia v. Bosnia and Herzegovina)* (2003) ICJ REP 7

The Federal Republic of Yugoslavia (FRY) applied for a revision of the judgment of the Court on the basis that the admission of FRY to the United Nations on 1 November 2000 'is certainly a new fact' (at [17]). It claimed that the specific facts that had existed at the time of the 1996 judgment were 'that FRY *was* not party to the Statute' and that these facts were revealed by its admission to the United Nations in 2000.

Rejecting the argument by the FRY, the Court said (at [67]) that:

[U]nder the terms of Article 61, paragraph 1, of the Statute, an application for revision of a judgment may be made only when it is 'based upon the discovery' of some fact which, 'when the judgment was given', was unknown. These are the characteristics which the 'new' facts referred to in paragraph 2 of that Article must possess. Thus both paragraphs refer to a fact existing at the time when the judgment was given and discovered subsequently. A fact which occurs several years after a judgment has been given is not a 'new' fact within the meaning of Article 61, this remains the case irrespective of the legal consequences that such fact may have.

KEY POINTS

- The judgments of the ICJ are final and not appealable/not subject to appeal.

- The principle of *stare decisis* does not apply to the ICJ.

- The Court is able to interpret its judgments as to meaning and scope if there is disagreement and if either party to the dispute applies for interpretation.

- The Court may revise its decisions if a party discovers a new fact unknown to both it and the Court at the time of the judgment.

 # Conclusion

The ICJ is central to the settlement of disputes among States. However, the Court has a rather difficult task, given that its jurisdiction over disputes among States is subject to the consent of the latter. It is only in regard to its advisory opinions that the Court has a bit of leeway, since consent is not required. But, even then, circumstances may exist, as we see in *Eastern Carelia*, which may prevent the Court from entertaining a request for an advisory opinion.

The Court strives to be even and transparent in the way in which it handles disputes that come before it—but it does not always get it right. As was seen in the *South West Africa Case*, the Court declined to admit the application by Liberia and Ethiopia on the basis that they did not have a personal legal interest in the matter before the Court. Yet, in *Barcelona Traction* the Court accepted that legal interest could be of a general nature. This sort of contradiction may open the Court to all sorts of allegations and affect the way some States perceive the Court.

 # Questions

Self-test questions

1 What is the difference between the 'contentious' and 'advisory' jurisdiction of the ICJ?

2 What are the different ways in which a State can accept the jurisdiction of the ICJ?

3 What is the difference between 'intervention by right' and 'discretionary intervention'?

4 What are 'reservations' and how are they used?

5 When can a party to a case apply for revision of the Court's judgment?

6 What is the *Monetary Gold* principle?

Discussion questions

1 'Access to the Court is the same as the jurisdiction of the Court.' Is this statement true? Give reasons for your answer.

2 '*Forum prorogatum* is the most controversial way of accepting the ICJ's jurisdiction.' Discuss the validity of this statement.

3 'A State has a right to intervene in a dispute between other States before the ICJ.' Expand on this statement.

4 'Connally reservations are the most disruptive to the jurisdiction of the Court.' To what extent is this assertion true?

5 'Once a State has accepted the jurisdiction of the Court by exercising the optional clause, it is automatically bound by it and can never object to the Court's jurisdiction.' Is this statement true? Give reasons for your answer.

6 What are the ways in which the ICJ Statute enables the Court to revise its decisions and also to ensure that the rights of State parties are not affected?

Assessment question

Candoma and Rutamu are in dispute over an island that adjoins both States. Candoma has deposited a declaration with the Court's registrar under Article 36(2) of the ICJ Statute in which it accepts the jurisdiction of the Court. However, the declaration states that the Court shall have no jurisdiction over 'all matters concerning boundary questions, mortgages, and maritime activities in which Candoma is interested, because such matters are within its domestic jurisdiction'. Rutamu, which has not accepted the jurisdiction of the Court, writes a letter to the registrar of the Court stating that although it has not accepted the jurisdiction of the Court, it wishes to state categorically that the allegations contained in the Candoman application are entirely inaccurate and ridiculous, and that this will be demonstrated at trial. The Court has now named a date on which it will commence proceedings and Rutamu is refusing to appear on the basis that the Court has no jurisdiction.

Advise Candoma.

Key cases

- *El Salvador v. Honduras* (1992) ICJ Rep 92 (the *Land and Maritime Frontier Dispute Case*)
- *Ethiopia v. South Africa; Liberia v. South Africa (Second Phase)* (1966) ICJ Rep 6 (the *South West Africa Cases*)

- *Interpretation of Peace Treaties with Bulgaria, Hungary and Romania (First Phase)* (1950) ICJ Rep 74

- *Nicaragua v. United States of America* (1984) ICJ Rep 421 (the *Military and Paramilitary Activities in and against Nicaragua Case*, or the *Nicaragua Case*)

- *Pakistan v. India (Jurisdiction)* (2000) ICJ Rep 12 (the *Case Concerning the Aerial Incident of 10 August 1999*)

- *Status of Eastern Carelia Advisory Opinion* (1923) PCIJ Ser. B, No. 5 (the *Eastern Carelia Case*)

- *Switzerland v. USA* (1959) ICJ Rep 6 (the *Interhandel Case*)

- *Tunisia v. Libya* (1981) ICJ Rep 3 (the *Continental Shelf Case*)

Further reading

Chinkin, C. M., 'Third-party intervention before the International Court of Justice' (1986) AJIL 495

Evans, M., '*El Salvador v. Honduras*, the Nicaraguan intervention' (1992) 41 ICLQ 896

Franck, T., '*Nicaragua v. USA*: jurisdiction and admissibility' (1985) 79 AJIL 373

Kelly, P. J., 'The International Court of Justice: crisis and reformation' (1987) 12(2) Yale JIL 1

Lamm, V., 'The legal character of the optional clause system' (2001) 42(1–2) Acta Juridica Hungarica 25

Schwebel, S., 'Chambers of the ICJ formed for particular cases' in Y. Dinstein (ed.), *International Law at a Time of Perplexity* (The Hague: Martinus Nijhoff, 1989)

Stanimir, A., *Reservations in Unilateral Declarations: Accepting the Compulsory Jurisdiction of the International Court of Justice* (The Hague: Martinus Nijhoff, 1995)

16

International criminal law

Learning objectives

This chapter will help you to:

- learn about the development of international criminal law;

- understand the general principles of international criminal law;

- know what specific international crimes are and recognize their elements;

- understand how to apply international criminal law to practical situations; and

- appreciate current issues in international criminal law.

Introduction

International criminal law is the law that governs individual criminal responsibility, or liability, for international crimes, as opposed to State liability for crimes. As will be recalled from Chapter 1, international law has traditionally applied to States and not to individuals. Under classical international law, whenever a person committed a crime, he or she was punished by his or her State, and where a crime was committed against a person abroad, his or her State took up the case on his or her behalf before international tribunals. However, following the atrocities of the First and Second World Wars, international criminal law became applicable to individuals. Individuals, no matter how highly placed, are today held liable for crimes committed against their own citizens or foreigners living among them. It is no longer an excuse that a head of State or government, or another important official in the government of a State, committed the crime in the course of his or her official duties—although whether such officials can be brought to justice while still serving in their various countries remains a contentious question.

16.1 What is international criminal law and how did it develop?

While a concise definition of 'international criminal law' is rather elusive, it is possible to describe what the notion means with relevance to its main features.

M. Cherif Bassiouni, 'The penal characteristics of conventional international criminal law' (1983) 15 Case W Res JIL 27, describes international criminal law as:

> a product of the convergence of two different legal disciplines which have emerged and developed ostensibly along different paths to be complementary but co-extensive, and separate. These two disciplines are the criminal aspects of international law and the international aspects of national criminal law.

The development of international criminal law, in modern times, is generally considered to have started with the Nuremberg trials following the end of the Second World War; at the end of the First World War, numerous attempts were made to bring the German Kaiser to trial, but these met with little success. In 'World War I: "the war to end all wars" and the birth of a handicapped international criminal justice system' (2001–02) 30 Denv JIL & Pol'y 224, 250, Bassiouni suggests that:

> The factors that contributed to this demand to indict the Kaiser included the general public's aversion to the horrors of a protracted war, the success of newly developed wartime propaganda techniques, and the desire of Allied politicians to advance their public standing by acting

on their wartime pledges to bring to trial the Germans responsible for the war and those who committed war crimes.

Consequently, Article 227 of the 1919 Treaty of Versailles, which became known as the 'Kaiser Clause', provided that:

> The Allied and Associated Powers publicly arraigns William II of Hohenzollern, formerly German Emperor, for a supreme offence against international morality and the sanctity of treaties. A special tribunal will be constituted to try the accused, thereby assuring him the guarantees essential to the right to defence.

While the Kaiser was granted asylum in the Netherlands and thus never prosecuted, the importance of this albeit failed attempt is, according to Bassiouni (2001–02, above), at 267:

> for the first time in history, a treaty established the individual criminal responsibility of heads of states for initiating and conducting what was later called a war of aggression.

It was not until after the Second World War that international tribunals were established and used for the first time to hold individuals to account for the atrocities of a conflict. While there are criticisms of the Nuremberg International Military Tribunal (IMT)—mainly that it was a signifier of victor's justice and the application of *ex post facto* laws—one should not disregard its positive outcomes.

Michael Scharf, 'Have we really learned the lessons of Nuremberg?' (1995) 149 Mil L Rev 65, characterizes the Nuremberg IMT as:

> the first international criminal tribunal in modern times. It's Charter and Judgment are among the most significant developments in international law in this century.

What is perhaps most relevant when considering the shift in attitudes to invoking individual criminal responsibility was stated by Justice Robert Jackson at Nuremberg.

● *International Military Tribunal (Nuremberg),* (Judgment and Sentences, OCTOBER 1, 1946), REPRINTED IN (1947) 41 AJIL 172

In his opening speech for the prosecution, Jackson observed:

> that four great nations, flushed with victory and stung with injury, stay the hand of vengeance and voluntarily submit their captive enemies to the judgment of the law is one of the most significant tributes that Power has ever paid to reason.

Whether or not one considers this the most significant contribution to international law, it is indisputable that it represents a move towards accountability for international crimes.

● *Prosecutor v. Dusko Tadić (Interlocutory Appeal)* CASE NO. IT-94–1-AR72, ICTY APPEALS CHAMBER, 2 OCTOBER 1995

In this case, it was said (at [97]) that:

> A State-sovereignty-oriented approach has been gradually supplanted by a human-being-oriented approach . . . [I]nternational law, while of course duly safeguarding the legitimate interest of States, must gradually turn to the protection of human beings.

. . . .

● *Nuremberg IMT (Opinion and Judgment)* (1946), Reprinted in (1947) 41 AJIL 172

In this case, it was stated (at 221) that the rationale for international criminal law is the recognition that:

> Crimes against international law are committed by men, not abstract entities, and only by punishing individuals who commit such crimes can the provisions of international law be enforced . . . individuals have international duties which transcend the national obligations of obedience imposed by an individual state.

Nowadays, international criminal law is more substantive in nature and has developed over time to include treaties, agreements, conventions, and other measures. Bassiouni, in 'The history of the Draft Code of Crimes against the Peace and Security of Mankind' (1993) 27 Israel L Rev 247, 262, notes that:

> The principal reason for the codification of international law after Nuremberg and Tokyo was to eliminate the problems generated by the absence of clearly defined offenses, elements and sanctions.

KEY POINTS

- International criminal law concerns holding individuals, as opposed to States, accountable for international crimes.

- International criminal law was a product of the First and Second World Wars, although the latter was a much a greater catalyst in its evolution.

- Although the Nuremberg trial of Nazi war criminals was credited with being the first modern-day trial of individuals for international crimes, the pace was set by the immaterialized attempt to prosecute the German Kaiser after the First World War.

 16.2 # Sources, nature, and scope of international criminal law

The sources of international law discussed in Chapter 2 also make up the sources of international criminal law, since the latter is a component of the former.

However, it is difficult to consider international criminal law in isolation, because it encompasses elements of other areas of international law, such as human rights law. The development of Nuremberg was a result of the outrage felt by the public about the gross human rights violations of so many. While human rights had not developed into a distinct area of international law at that time, reactions to the Nazi crimes committed during the Second World War led to the emergence of the human rights movement and the agitation for the protection of lives through the promotion of human rights. It is no coincidence, therefore, that many international crimes contain elements of human rights, or are related to specific human rights. However, it must be borne in mind that the violation of human rights does not necessarily imply the commission of an international crime.

Furthermore, international humanitarian law and international criminal law are interlinked. War crimes relate to international humanitarian law insofar as the violation of international humanitarian law is likely to result in war crimes. Many of the same sources are used to establish whether a violation and a resulting crime have occurred.

16.3 The distinction between State and individual responsibility

As already mentioned previously, international criminal law is concerned with the acts of individuals and not those of States. This does not mean that the two are completely separate, only that the mechanisms for dealing with them are so.

● ***Prosecutor v. Anto Furundžija (Judgment)*** Case No. IT-95-17/1-T, ICTY Trial Chamber II, 10 December 1998

The International Criminal Tribunal for the former Yugoslavia (ICTY) noted that the same act may invoke both individual and State responsibility when it stated (at [142]) that:

> Under current international humanitarian law, in addition to individual criminal liability, State responsibility may ensue as a result of State officials engaging in torture or failing to prevent torture or to punish torturers.

579

thinking points
- Are there any differences between the sources of international law and those of international criminal law?
- What distinction exists between individual responsibility and State responsibility for international crimes?

16.4 General principles of international criminal law

Before discussing the specific international crimes, it is necessary to consider briefly certain principles that govern international criminal law. While most of these principles exist under customary international law, some have also been codified by international treaties, such as the Statute of the International Criminal Court (the ICC Statute).

16.4.1 *Nullum crimen sine lege*

The principle *nullum crimen sine lege* (that is, 'no crime without a law') prevents retroactive application of the law. This is especially important given the 1966 UN International Covenant on Civil and Political Rights (ICCPR), Article 15 of which requires that:

> No one shall be held guilty on account of any act or omission which did not constitute a criminal offence, under national or international law, at the time it was committed . . . nothing in this article shall prejudice the trial of any person for any act or omission which, at the time it was committed, was criminal according to the general principles of law recognised by the community of nations.

Both the Nuremberg International Military Tribunal (IMT), which predates the International Covenant on Civil and Political Rights (ICCPR), and the ICTY addressed this matter.

. . . .

● *Nuremberg IMT (Opinion and Judgment)* [1946], REPRINTED IN [1947] 41 AJIL 172

The Tribunal said (at 217) that:

> The maxim *nullum crimen sine lege* is not a limitation of sovereignty, but is in general a principle of justice. To assert that it is unjust to punish those who in defiance of treaties and assurances have attacked neighbouring States without warning is obviously untrue, for in such circumstances the attacker must know that he is doing wrong, and so far from it being unjust to punish him, it would be unjust if his wrong was allowed to go unpunished.

. . . .

● *Prosecutor v. Mitar Vasiljević* CASE NO. IT-98-32, ICTY TRIAL CHAMBER I, 29 NOVEMBER 2002

The ICTY said (at [193]) that:

> A criminal conviction should indeed never be based upon a norm which an accused could not reasonably have been aware of at the time of his acts, and this norm must make it sufficiently clear what act or omission could engage his criminal responsibility

During the drafting stages of the Statute of the International Criminal Tribunal for Yugoslavia (ICTY Statute), in his *Report of the Secretary-General Pursuant to Paragraph 2 of Security Council Resolution 808* (UN Doc. S/25704), the UN Secretary-General acknowledged the principle, addressing the criticisms that had followed Nuremberg regarding the retroactivity and lack of clarity of the laws applied. At paragraph 34 of the report, he said that:

> The application of the principle of *nullum crimen sine lege* requires that the international tribunal should apply rules of international humanitarian law which are beyond any doubt part of customary law so that the problem of adherence of some but not all states to specific conventions does not arise. This would appear to be particularly important in the context of an international tribunal prosecuting persons responsible for serious violations of international humanitarian law.

Article 22 of the ICC Statute provides for the principle thus:

> 1. A person shall not be criminally responsible under this Statute unless the conduct in question constitutes, at the time it takes place, a crime within the jurisdiction of the Court
>
> 2. The definition of a crime shall be strictly construed and shall not be extended by analogy. In the case of ambiguity, the definition shall be interpreted in favour of the person being investigated, prosecuted or convicted.

This has the ultimate effect of preventing the ICC from expanding the types of crime under its jurisdiction or under international criminal law as a whole; nevertheless, its jurisprudence will continue to be influential.

16.4.2 *Nulla poena sine lege*

The principle of *nulla poena sine lege* (that is, 'no penalty without a law') implies that there can be no punishment for an act that was not a crime at the time that it was committed and thus calls for defined penalties for crimes. In theory, this is not problematic; in practice, however, it has caused some problems in how international criminal sentences have been approached.

Article 24 of the ICTY Statute and Article 23 of that for the International Criminal Tribunal for Rwanda (ICTR) attempt to address this issue by spelling out the framework within which punishment may be prescribed:

> The penalty imposed by the Trial chamber shall be limited to imprisonment. In determining the terms of imprisonment, the Trial chambers shall have recourse to the general practice regarding prison sentences in the courts of [their respective states].

Article 23 of the ICC Statute also addresses the principle when it says that '[a] person convicted by the court may be punished only in accordance with this Statute'.

Customary international law does not prevent the use of the death penalty for international crimes.

● ***Trial of Kriminalassistent Karl-Hans Herman Klinge*** (1946) 3 LRTWC 1, Supreme Court of Norway

In this case, Judge Skau stated (at 3) that:

> According to the same laws and customs of war, war crimes could be punished by the most severe penalties, including the death sentence.

This presents problems, given the many international agreements that are aimed at abolishing the use of the death penalty.

KEY POINT There can be no crime without law (*nullum crimen sine lege*) and there can be no penalty without law (*nulla poena sine lege*).

16.5 International criminal tribunals

As said in the Introduction, the First and Second World Wars inspired the rapid development of international criminal law. However, it was not until 1993, following the war in the Balkans, and 1994, following the genocide in Rwanda, that the international community would establish its first postwar international criminal tribunals. The ICTY and the ICTR are very similar in nature and competence. Furthermore, as will be seen from the section on the core international crimes, both tribunals have been very influential in the development of the jurisprudence, as well as in defining and clarifying those crimes.

16.5.1 The International Criminal Tribunal for the former Yugoslavia (ICTY)

In May 1993, the UN Security Council adopted Resolution 827 (1993), which contained a supplementary document in the form of a statute establishing the ICTY. The competence of the Tribunal is set out in Article 1 of the ICTY Statute, which states that:

> The International Tribunal shall have the power to prosecute persons responsible for serious violations of international humanitarian law committed in the territory of the former Yugoslavia since 1991 in accordance with the provisions of the present Statute.

The tribunals have jurisdiction over grave breaches of the Geneva Conventions (Article 2), violations of the laws or customs of war (Article 3), genocide (Article 4), and crimes against humanity (Article 5).

The ICTY covers individual criminal responsibility and not that of the State (Article 7). The Statute specifically states that the official position of an individual does not prevent him or her being held individually liable (Article 7(2)) and that the defence of command responsibility is not available to anyone before the Tribunal (Article 7(3)).

The ICTY relies on cooperation from States in matters of investigation and prosecution. In addition, Article 29(2) requests that States 'comply without undue delay with any request for assistance or an order issued by a Trial Chamber'.

The ICTY is not governed by the traditional notion of complementarity and is, in fact, superior to national courts. This, however, did not mean that national courts were prevented from trying crimes that had occurred. According to Article 9:

> 1. The International Tribunal and national courts shall have concurrent jurisdiction to prosecute persons for serious violations of international humanitarian law committed in the territory of the former Yugoslavia since 1 January 1991.
> 2. The International Tribunal shall have primacy over national courts. At any stage of the procedure, the International Tribunal may formally request national courts to defer to the competence of the International Tribunal in accordance with the present Statute and the Rules of Procedure and Evidence of the International Tribunal.

Judge Gabrielle Kirk McDonald's *Sixth Annual Report of the International Tribunal for the Prosecution of Persons Responsible for Serious Violations of International Humanitarian Law Committed in the Former Yugoslavia since 1991* (UN GAOR, 54th Session, UN Doc. A/54/187, 1999) sums up the ICTY's accomplishments at paragraphs 205–212:

> The tribunal's decisions on both procedural and substantive matters are on the cutting edge of the development of international humanitarian law. Many of the legal issues adjudicated by the tribunal have either never been dealt with before, or have been dormant since the end of the Second World War ... [T]he experience of the tribunal has laid the foundation for the establishment of a practical and permanent system of international criminal justice.

Despite the success of the ICTY, there are notable shortcomings. As David Tolbert notes, in 'The International Criminal Tribunal for the former Yugoslavia: unforeseen successes and foreseeable shortcomings' (2002) 26 Fletcher Forum World Aff 7 at 15–16:

The authors of the tribunal Statute not only created as quite separate and apart from the region, with the local authorities legally obliged to defer to the tribunal Prosecutor, but also made no provision for creating sustainable links with the region. Therefore, the ICTY has no clearly stated obligation to support or build the judicial system in the region....

Approaches to war crimes in other post-conflict situations that have been addressed since the establishment of the ICTY seem to be more cognizant of the importance of developing the local systems.

One of the many criticisms levelled at the ICTY—and any tribunal, in fact—is the cost and length of duration of the trials, which is sometimes unjustified. As Antonio Cassese comments, in 'The ICTY: a living and vital reality' (2004) 2 JICJ 585, 594:

Many lament that the ICTY is cumbersome and costly, and that its trials are lengthy. It has also been observed that the defendants spend too much time in pre-trial detention. I submit that these criticisms, although not ill-founded, miss an important point: the unique features of international criminal proceedings. In short, the authors of these criticisms are blinded by the 'domestic analogy', in that they compare international trials with those that take place in their own countries.

Despite the criticisms, the role of the tribunal in developing the jurisprudence of international criminal law cannot be overemphasized. It has also contributed to other aspects of international law concerning armed conflict, the status of UN Security Council resolutions, and other aspects of international law, as evidenced by *Tadić*.

16.5.2 The International Criminal Tribunal for Rwanda (ICTR)

The ICTR was established not long after the ICTY and shares many similarities with it. In fact, the statutes of both are nearly identical in many respects. One of the key differences with regards to the type of conflict was that the Rwandan conflict and genocide had come to an end, and would be characterized as an internal conflict, whereas the conflict in the former Yugoslavia had elements of an international, as well as internal, conflict.

The ICTR has achieved many things, despite any flaws, and Erik Møse, 'Appraising the role of the ICTR: main achievements of the ICTR' (2005) 3 JICJ 920, 934, notes that 'ICTR case law provides abundant interpretative material on the legal nature and factual realities of [genocide]'.

Payam Akhavan tells us, in 'The International Criminal Tribunal for Rwanda: the politics and pragmatics of punishment' (1996) 90(3) AJIL 501, 505, that the Rwandese government wanted to secure an international tribunal because:

The Rwandese Government was convinced that, through the punishment of 'those responsible for the Rwandese tragedy', the Tribunal 'will help national reconciliation and the construction of a new society based on social justice and respect for the fundamental rights of the human person'.

The ICTR was established by Security Council Resolution 955 (1994), in which the UN Security Council:

> Decide[d] hereby, having received the request of the Government of Rwanda (S/1994/1115), to establish an international tribunal for the sole purpose of prosecuting persons responsible for genocide and other serious violations of international humanitarian law committed in the territory of Rwanda and Rwandan citizens responsible for genocide and other such violations committed in the territory of neighbouring States, between 1 January 1994 and 31 December 1994 and to this end to adopt the Statute of the International Criminal Tribunal for Rwanda.

As with the ICTY, the ICTR Statute sets out the competence of the Tribunal in Article 1:

> The International Tribunal for Rwanda shall have the power to prosecute persons responsible for serious violations of international humanitarian law committed in the territory of Rwanda and Rwandan citizens responsible for such violations committed in the territory of neighbouring States between 1 January 1994 and 31 December 1994, in accordance with the provisions of the present Statute.

The UN Security Council set out a clearly defined period during which the Tribunal could claim jurisdiction over the territory of Rwanda and over Rwandan citizens outside the territory of the country. This would seem to be a logical approach, given the internal nature of the conflict, but it has been criticized for taking such a limited time frame, especially since many of the acts that culminated in the 1994 genocide are considered to have started or taken place in 1993. Luc Reydams, 'The ICTR ten years on: back to the Nuremberg paradigm?' (2005) 3 JICJ 977, 980, argues that:

> By severely limiting the temporal jurisdiction and by accentuating genocide in the statute, the Security Council very much screened out the underlying conflict, which, after 1994, was exported to neighbouring countries, where it continues to this day.

The crimes that are covered by the ICTR Statute include: genocide (Article 2); crimes against humanity (Article 3); and violations of Common Article 3 of the Geneva Conventions and of Additional Protocol II (Article 4). The more limited scope of crimes covered by the ICTR Statute, as compared to that of the ICTY, is attributable to the type of conflict that occurred and the situation in which it occurred. War crimes would not be applicable, because this was a conflict that did not involve combatants strictly so called, but rather a civil conflict in which the civilian population—albeit a particular demographic or ethnic group—was targeted.

The ICTR covers individual criminal responsibility and not that of the State (Article 6). The Statute specifically states that the official position of an individual does not prevent him or her being held individually liable (Article 6(2)), and the defence of command responsibility is not available to anyone before the Tribunal (Article 6(3)).

As with the ICTY, the ICTR and Rwanda's national courts are to have concurrent jurisdiction subject to Article 8 of the Statute. The ICTR has supremacy, with the ability to request the national courts to refer any case to it (Article 8(2)).

As with all international criminal tribunals and mechanisms, the ICTR relies on the cooperation and judicial assistance of States to ensure its effective working (Article 28).

The ICTR has one major flaw, however, which is likely to scar its record and contribution to international criminal law. As Reydams (2005, see earlier in this section) notes:

> It has become more apparent that the International Criminal Tribunal for Rwanda will sit only in judgment of the genocide of Hutu against Tutsi.

This one-sided approach can be problematic in promoting reconciliation, because it ignores a whole aspect of the conflict, thus impacting on the historical record of the conflict provided by the trials.

16.5.3 Special tribunals: the Special Court for Sierra Leone (SCSL)

Following the civil war in Sierra Leone, the UN Security Council established the SCSL, a hybrid by Resolution 1315 (2000) with international, as well as national, elements.

As Laura Dickinson states in 'The promise of hybrid courts' (2003) 97(2) AJIL 295:

> Such courts are 'hybrid' because both the institutional apparatus and the applicable law consist of a blend of the international and the domestic.

The competence of the SCSL was agreed, in Article 1 of the Resolution, as follows:

1. The Special Court shall, except as provided in subparagraph (2), have the power to prosecute persons who bear the greatest responsibility for serious violations of international humanitarian law and Sierra Leonean law committed in the territory of Sierra Leone since 30 November 1996, including those leaders who, in committing such crimes, have threatened the establishment of and implementation of the peace process in Sierra Leone.

2. Any transgressions by peacekeepers and related personnel present in Sierra Leone pursuant to the Status of Mission Agreement in force between the United Nations and the Government of Sierra Leone or agreements between Sierra Leone and other Governments or regional organizations, or, in the absence of such agreement, provided that the peacekeeping operations were undertaken with the consent of the Government of Sierra Leone, shall be within the primary jurisdiction of the sending State.

3. In the event the sending State is unwilling or unable genuinely to carry out an investigation or prosecution, the Court may, if authorized by the Security Council on the proposal of any State, exercise jurisdiction over such persons.

Perhaps an achievement of the SCSL is its ability to consider transgressions of peacekeepers and other such personnel. But the extent to which this enables all sides to be brought to justice will require an analysis of the cases to see how balanced they were, which is beyond the remit of this chapter.

The SCSL jurisdiction comprises crimes against humanity (Article 2), violations of Article 3 common to the 1949 Geneva Conventions and of Additional Protocol II (Article 3), and other serious violations of international humanitarian law (Article 4), as well as crimes under Sierra Leonean domestic law. In this case, it also covers crimes that are committed against girls in violation of the Sierra Leonean Prevention of Cruelty to Children Act 1926 (Article 5(a)) and the wanton destruction of property under the Malicious Damage Act 1861 (Article 5(b)). Because the SCSL is not an international tribunal in the traditional sense, it was able to apply local criminal laws in addition to international criminal laws.

As with the ICTY and ICTR, the SCSL also has concurrent jurisdiction (Article 8) with national courts, and it enjoys primacy, with the ability to request referrals to it.

Due to the nature of the conflict in Sierra Leone and the prevalence of the use of child soldiers, an express provision (Article 7(1)) deals with the age of individuals who fall under the SCSL's competence:

> The Special Court shall have no jurisdiction over any person who was under the age of 15 at the time of the alleged commission of the crime. Should any person who was at the time of the alleged commission of the crime between 15 and 18 years of age come before the Court, he or she shall be treated with dignity and a sense of worth, taking into account his or her young age and the desirability of promoting his or her rehabilitation, reintegration into and assumption of a constructive role in society, and in accordance with international human rights standards, in particular the rights of the child.

While the SCSL Statute prohibits a Sierra Leonean national court from trying someone once the SCSL has already tried them, there are situations in which the SCSL can try an individual despite the national courts having already tried them. This, however, is subject to the following conditions (Article 9):

> a.   The act for which he or she was tried was characterized as an ordinary crime; or
>
> b.   The national court proceedings were not impartial or independent, were designed to shield the accused from international criminal responsibility or the case was not diligently prosecuted.

This has become common practice when considering the complementarity principle with regards to the ICC, a discussion of which takes place later.

One of the advantages of a hybrid court is its ability to help to develop the domestic legal infrastructure, through the inclusion of local staff in its processes, as well as developing their capacity and capability to apply international law principles in their legal system.

As Laura Dickinson notes (2003, see earlier in this section), at 307:

> The international humanitarian laws are thus more likely to penetrate into Sierra Leonean legal culture than norms applied in a remote tribunal by foreigners.

And at 306, she comments that 'Hybrid courts may offer at least partial responses to the problems of legitimacy, capacity, and non-penetration'.

William Schabas notes, in 'International criminal tribunals: a review of 2007' (2007–08) 6 Nw J Int'l HR 382, 387, that the SCSL has:

> Gone furthest in attempting a balanced approach to prosecutions, organizing three multiple-defendant trials, each of them focused on one of the warring parties in the civil war

However, there are also problems with such courts. As Dickinson (2003) writes, at 308:

> Hybrid courts were plagued with problems—such as perceived bias towards specific political or ethnic groups or excessive delay due to lack of resources—those problems might taint the entire international justice efforts. And turf battles between the two types of institutions, including disputes about evidence-sharing and the appropriate division of cases among the two institutions, might lead to difficulties.

The SCSL is concerned only with individual responsibility (Article 6) regardless of parties' official positions (Article 6(2)), and command responsibility and following orders are not a defence (Article 6(3) and (4)).

- The ICTY and the ICTR were established by the UN Security Council to deal with specific situations in the former Yugoslavia and Rwanda, respectively.

- The SCSL is a hybrid of national and international legal systems.

- Once the mandates of the ICTY and ICTR expire, their work will be taken over by the ICC.

The amnesty agreement and the SCSL

The government of Sierra Leone had reached an amnesty agreement after the initial end of the conflict. This would appear to be a barrier to the SCSL and its ability to prosecute. President Kabbah of Sierra Leone then claimed that the Revolutionary United Front (RUF) had reneged on the peace agreement and therefore the amnesty. But as William Schabas has noted, in 'Amnesty, the Sierra Leone Truth and Reconciliation Commission, and the Special Court for Sierra Leone' (2004–05) 11 UC Davis JIL & Pol'y 145, 160:

> The suggestion that an amnesty in a peace agreement becomes null and void, or that it is voidable, because some parties later violate the agreement does not seem to be sustainable.

The UN Security Council addressed, although in a very preliminary manner without expansion, the amnesty that was granted, and the need for an effective justice system to be developed to deal with the situation and crimes.

In its Preamble to Resolution 1315 (2000), it:

> *Recall[ed]* that the Special Representative of the Secretary-General appended to his signature of the Lomé Agreement a statement that the United Nations holds the understanding that the amnesty provisions of the Agreement shall not apply to international crimes of genocide, crimes against humanity, war crimes and other serious violations of international humanitarian law.
> *Recogniz[ed]* that, in the particular circumstances of Sierra Leone, a credible system of justice and accountability for the very serious crimes committed there would end impunity and would contribute to the process of national reconciliation and to the restoration and maintenance of peace.

Although the United Nations does recognize amnesties, it takes a strong position that amnesties cannot be provided for core international crimes.

As clarified in the *Report of the Secretary-General on the Establishment of a Special Court for Sierra Leone* (SC Res 915, UN SCOR 55th Session, 915th Meeting, UN Doc. S/2000/915, 2000), paragraph 22:

> Amnesty is an accepted legal concept and a gesture of peace and reconciliation at the end of a civil war or an internal armed conflict . . . the United Nations has consistently maintained the position that amnesty cannot be granted in respect of international crimes, such as genocide, crimes against humanity or other serious violations of international humanitarian law.

Furthermore, Article 10 of the SCSL Statute states that:

> An amnesty granted to any person falling within the jurisdiction of the Special Court in respect of the crimes referred to in Articles 2 to 4 of the present Statute shall not be a bar to prosecution.

● *Prosecutor v. Morris Kallon and Brima Buzzy Kamara (Decision on Challenge to Jurisdiction: Lome Accord Amnesty)* CASE NOS SCSL-2004-15-AR72(E) AND SCSL-2004-16-AR72(E), 13 MARCH 2004

The Appeals Chamber of the SCSL (at [71]) also addressed the amnesty issue:

> It is, therefore, not difficult to agree with the submission made on behalf of Redress that the amnesty granted by Sierra Leone cannot cover crimes under international law that are the subject of universal jurisdiction. In the first place, it stands to reason that a state cannot sweep such crimes into oblivion and forgetfulness which other States have jurisdiction to prosecute by reason of the fact that the obligation to protect human dignity is a peremptory norm and has assumed the nature of obligation *erga omnes*.

William Schabas (2004–05, see earlier in this section), at 168, has also noted that it is:

> quite correct to note that a grant of amnesty under one jurisdictional regime cannot deprive another of the authority to prosecute where universal jurisdiction exists.

One of the problems that has resulted from the decision of the Sierra Leonean government and the United Nations to go back on the agreed amnesty, as the Sierra Leone Truth and Reconciliation Commission stated in its 2004 final report (available at http://www.sierra-leone.org/TRCDocuments.html), vol. 3B, ch. 6, p. 3, is that:

> both the United Nations and the Government of Sierra Leone have sent an unfortunate message to combatants in future wars that they cannot trust peace agreements that contain amnesty clauses.

This is especially true when one takes into consideration Article 6(5) of Additional Protocol II to the 1949 Geneva Conventions:

> At the end of hostilities, the authorities in power shall endeavour to grant the broadest possible amnesty to persons who have participated in the armed conflict, or those deprived of their liberty for reasons related to the armed conflict, whether they are interned or detained.

We will discuss amnesties further in the next sections on the ICC and on problems with international criminal justice.

16.6 The International Criminal Court (ICC)

The ICC is the first permanent international criminal court. The Statute that established the court (the ICC Statute) was adopted in 1998 in Rome (hence, it is often also known as the 'Rome Statute'), but entered into force on 1 July 2002. The ICC constitutes a single international criminal court, and is expected to replace both the ICTY and ICTR once their mandates expire. As Antonio Cassese notes in 'The Statute of the International Criminal Court: some preliminary reflections' (1999) 10 EJIL 144, 145, there is no doubt that:

> this is a revolutionary institution that intrudes into state sovereignty by subjecting states' nationals to an international criminal jurisdiction.

Before going into the specifics of the Court, it is important first to consider its relationship with the domestic courts of its member States. After all, as will be recalled from Chapter 7, a State has adjudicatory jurisdiction over crimes committed by its nationals, or anyone for that matter, on its territory. Jurisdiction is also one of the principal features of sovereignty and, as such, it is important to understand how the ICC and courts of its member States are able to exercise their jurisdictions without creating tension.

16.6.1 The principle of complementarity

The ICC is a court of last resort—that is, a court of secondary jurisdiction that can act only as a complement to, not a replacement for, the national court of its member States. This principle, known as 'complementarity', is a decisive principle governing the admissibility of cases before the Court.

According to paragraph 10 of the Preamble to the ICC Statute, 'the International Criminal Court established under this Statute shall be complementary to national criminal jurisdictions'.

Thus Article 17(1)(a) provides that the Court cannot admit a case that:

> is being investigated or prosecuted by a State which has jurisdiction over it, unless the State is *unwilling* or *unable* genuinely to carry out the investigation or prosecution. [Emphasis added]

Hence, only where a member State of the ICC, which has primary jurisdiction over a case, is either 'unwilling' or 'unable' to exercise such jurisdiction may the Court take over the case.

According to El Zeidy, 'The principle of complementarity: a new machinery to implement international criminal law' (2001–02) 23 Mich JIL 869, 905:

> The principle of complementarity reconciles two competing features and jurisdictions. The first is State sovereignty, which claims national jurisdiction over its citizens or those crimes committed on its territory, even though these crimes are of an international character and may fall under the international jurisdiction. The second feature only functions in exceptional circumstance and gives an international tribunal jurisdiction over these heinous crimes.

And as Sascha Rolf Lüder notes, in 'The history of the prosecution of war crimes' (2003) 42 Mil L & L War Rev 395, 409, although the complementarity principle was a clear departure from the precedence set by the ICTY and ICTR:

> It should nevertheless be said that a conscious decision was made to turn away from the overruling jurisdiction of the International Criminal Tribunals for the former Yugoslavia and for Rwanda and to make the principle of complementarity a fundamental element of the ICC statute.

The rationale behind complementarity, according to Cassese (1999, see section 16.6), at 158, is that:

> national institutions are in the best position to do justice, for they normally constitute the *forum conveniens*, where both the evidence and the alleged culprit are to be found.

Article 17(2) of the ICC Statute considers the situation to be one of the unwillingness of a State when the proceedings are undertaken in such a manner as to shield the person from criminal responsibility, in which there have been unjustified delays that demonstrate a lack of intent to prosecute, and in which there has not been an independent and impartial trial.

The ability of a State to prosecute (Article 17(3)) is based upon a consideration of whether:

> due to a total or substantial collapse or unavailability of its national judicial system, the State is unable to obtain the accused or the necessary evidence and testimony or otherwise unable to carry out its proceedings.

Where a national court is prevented from exercising its jurisdiction due to a lack of inclusion in its domestic criminal law of relevant laws on the concerned crime, this can amount to inability to prosecute and the ICC can take over the case.

The argument has been made, however, that in determining whether a State is unwilling, the Court should not automatically disregard approaches other than criminal prosecutions.

As Daniel Nsereko has argued in 'The International Criminal Court: jurisdictional and related issues' (1999) 10 Crim L Forum 87, 119, a State does not have to disclose the reasons for declining to prosecute:

> But if it does, and says that it has done so in the interest of peace and national reconciliation, the Court will have to listen sympathetically. It should not dismiss out of hand the State's efforts at national reconciliation as unwillingness or inability to prosecute. Peace and national reconciliation are legitimate goals for any country to pursue.

Challenges to the jurisdiction of the Court are provided for in Article 19 and may be made by an accused or a subject of an arrest warrant, or a State claiming jurisdiction. Non-party States, not only the State parties, are able to challenge the jurisdiction of the ICC.

Article 20 covers the principle *ne bis in idem* under which (at Article 20(1)):

> except as provided in this Statute, no person shall be tried before the Court with respect to conduct which formed the basis of crimes for which the person has been convicted or acquitted by the Court.

And by Article 20(2), no person shall be:

> tried by another court for a crime referred to in article 5 for which that person has already been convicted or acquitted by the Court.

A problematic consequence of complementarity is that it gives States incentives to ensure that their domestic legislation provides for them to undermine the admissibility criteria.

According to Cassese (1999, see section 16.6), at 170:

> Instead of granting the Court greater authority over states, the draughtsmen have left too many loopholes permitting states to delay or even thwart the Court's proceedings.

16.6.2 Composition

The composition of the Court is set out in Part 4 of the Statute (Articles 34–52). The organs of the Court are: the presidency (Article 34(a)), which is in charge of the administration of the Court and other functions that the Statute confers (Article 38(3)); the Appeals, Trial, and Pre-Trial Divisions (Article 34(b)); the Office of the Prosecutor (Article 34(c)); and the Registry (Article 34(d)), which is 'responsible for the non-judicial aspects of the administration and servicing of the Court' (Article 43(1)).

The election of judges is subject to strict conditions. Article 36 sets out the requisite qualifications:

(a) The judges shall be chosen from among persons of high moral character, impartiality and integrity who possess the qualifications required in their respective States for appointment to the highest judicial offices.

(b) Every candidate for election to the Court shall:
  (i) Have established competence in criminal law and procedure, and the necessary relevant experience, whether as judge, prosecutor, advocate or in other similar capacity, in criminal proceedings; or
  (ii) Have established competence in relevant areas of international law such as international humanitarian law and the law of human rights, and extensive experience in a professional legal capacity which is of relevance to the judicial work of the Court; . . .

Geographical representation of the judges and the legal systems that they represent needs to be taken into account when voting, as well as the gender distribution of judges (Article 36(8)(a)).

There is also the possibility of the Assembly of States Parties deciding to 'Establish, if appropriate, an Advisory Committee on nominations' (Article 36(4)(c)).

16.6.3 Crimes under ICC jurisdiction

As stated earlier, the ICC has jurisdiction over genocide, crimes against humanity, war crimes, and aggression, which are commonly considered the most serious crimes of international concern (Article 5(1)). The last of these, however, is not technically under the Court's jurisdiction, because there has yet to be an agreed definition of 'aggression' (see section 16.7.1).

Unlike the Tribunals, the ICC has specifically defined the crimes under its jurisdiction, which are listed in Articles 5–8 as well as in the 2002 Elements of Crimes. According to Article 22(2):

The definition of a crime shall be strictly construed and shall not be extended by analogy. In case of ambiguity, the definition shall be interpreted in favour of the person being investigated, prosecuted or convicted.

Article 10 of the ICC Statute prevents the above from impacting negatively on the development of international criminal law generally:

Nothing in this Part shall be interpreted as limiting or prejudicing in any way existing or developing rules of international law for purposes other than this Statute.

However, the Statute makes no provision on the mental and material elements (*actus reus* and *mens rea*) of the crimes.

Other crimes

Article 123(1) of the ICJ Statute provides that:

Seven years after the entry into force of this Statute the Secretary-General of the United Nations shall convene a Review Conference to consider any amendments to this Statute. Such review may include, but is not limited to, the list of crimes contained in article 5. The Conference shall be open to those participating in the Assembly of States Parties and on the same conditions.

This was mainly a result of unsuccessful attempts at the Rome Conference to include other crimes, such as drug trafficking and enforced disappearance, for which many were lobbying. However, where an additional crime has, or additional crimes have, been added, it is not automatically applicable to every signatory State. Under Article 121(5):

> Any amendment to articles 5, 6, 7 and 8 of this Statute shall enter into force for those States Parties which have accepted the amendment one year after the deposit of their instruments of ratification or acceptance. In respect of a State Party which has not accepted the amendment, the Court shall not exercise its jurisdiction regarding a crime covered by the amendment when committed by that State Party's nationals or on its territory.

16.6.4 Exercise of jurisdiction by the Court

By virtue of Article 13, the ICC can exercise jurisdiction through three different means commonly referred to as 'trigger mechanisms':

> (a) A situation in which one or more of such crimes appears to have been committed is referred to the Prosecutor by a State Party in accordance with article 14;
>
> (b) A situation in which one or more of such crimes appears to have been committed is referred to the Prosecutor by the Security Council acting under Chapter VII of the Charter of the United Nations; or
>
> (c) The Prosecutor has initiated an investigation in respect of such a crime in accordance with article 15.

According to Article 12(2), the Court can exercise jurisdiction where one or more of the following are parties to the Statute or have temporarily accepted its jurisdiction under Article 13:

> (a) The State on the territory of which the conduct in question occurred or, if the crime was committed on board a vessel or aircraft, the State of registration of that vessel or aircraft;
>
> (b) The State of which the person accused of the crime is a national; . . .

A State that ratifies the Statute automatically accepts jurisdiction; under Article 124, a State can make a reservation for seven years to reject jurisdiction. This provision seems to be in conflict with Article 120, which provides that no reservations may be made to the Statute. However, as Cassese (1999, see section 16.6) notes at 146:

> Admittedly, these are reservations whose purpose and contents, as well as duration in time, are predetermined by the Treaty. The fact remains, however, that, on account of their object and scope, they cannot but be regarded as reservations proper.

The Court is able to hear cases only involving individuals over the age of 18 at the time of commission of the crime of which they are accused (Article 26), while the principle of non-retroactivity is also applied. Only crimes committed after 1 July 2002 (the date of entry into force of the Statute) are admissible (Article 11). Yet there is no statute of limitation imposed on the crimes over which the Court can exercise jurisdiction (Article 29).

thinking points
- Describe the jurisdiction of the ICC, especially with reference to non-State parties.
- To what extent does the complementarity principle serve the purpose of the ICC?
- List the conditions for the exercise of jurisdiction by the ICC.

16.6.5 The ICC and the UN Security Council

The ICC and the UN Security Council are separate institutions under international law. However, they have a cooperative relationship with each other, governed primarily by the 2004 Relationship Agreement between the United Nations and the International Criminal Court.

Article 3 of the agreement imposes an obligation of cooperation and coordination on the two institutions:

> The United Nations and the Court agree that, with a view to facilitating the effective discharge of their respective responsibilities, they shall cooperate closely, whenever appropriate, with each other and consult each other on matters of mutual interest pursuant to the provisions of the present Agreement and in conformity with the respective provisions of the Charter and the Statute.

The UN Security Council's relationship with the ICC is governed by Articles 13 and 16 of the ICC Statute. Article 13 entitles the Security Council to refer any situation to the ICC Prosecutor for investigation and possible trial. This provision has been considered as granting the ICC virtual universal jurisdiction insofar as it enables the ICC to exercise jurisdiction over a case regardless of whether the national State of the accused is a party to the ICC Statute or not.

Article 16 of the Statute permits deferral of situations before the ICC for a period of twelve months when the Security Council has adopted a resolution under Chapter VII. Arguments have been put forward that such a deferral can be applied for an indefinite period. However, this does not seem to be the case—especially since the Statute stipulates that it is for a twelve-month period.

Additionally, Article 16 requires 'that request may be renewed by the Council under the same conditions'. This would seem to imply there are conditions for the initial deferral that must be met, and subsequently must continue to be met should the deferral be extended, although it is also possible to take an opposite position.

16.6.6 Amnesty and the ICC

There is nothing in the ICC Statute that specifically states that amnesties are not to be used or accepted by the Court. This legal uncertainty is likely to be clarified when a situation or case concerning an agreed amnesty is investigated or prosecuted.

Carsten Stahn, 'Complementarity, amnesties and alternative forms of justice: some interpretative guidelines for the International Criminal Court' (2005) 3 JICJ 695, 718, argues that:

> The Statute does not strictly prescribe a zero tolerance policy towards amnesties for the core crimes. It leaves both the Prosecutor and the Judges of the Court some leeway to strike a balance between the needs of a society in transition and the requirements under universal and regional treaty instruments and customary international law. But this assessment must be made within the framework of specific statutory provisions, which pursue different rationales.

It has been postulated that amnesties that are accompanied by some form of justice, such as truth commissions, are more likely to be upheld. This is most likely to be considered when the Court is considering the 'unwilling' or 'unable' criterion. As Stahn (2005, above) notes, at 719:

> As it stands, the Statute leaves some room to recognize amnesties and pardons, where they are conditional and accompanied by alternative forms of justice which may lead to prosecution.

Nevertheless, amnesties have met with important opposition. In United Nations Human Rights Committee (HRC) General Comment No. 20 in relation to Article 7 of the ICCPR, the HRC said that:

> Amnesties are generally incompatible with the duty of States to investigate such acts; to guarantee freedom from such acts within their jurisdiction; and to ensure that they do not occur in the future. States may not deprive individuals of the right to an effective remedy including compensation and such full rehabilitation as may be possible.

16.6.7 Procedural concerns

Following the first judgment of the ICC concerns were raised over the method of collecting evidence used before the Court. The *Thomas Lubanga* case is concerned with the ongoing conflict in the Democratic Republic of Congo and as such there are a large number of security concerns and the ICC lacks a police force. Not to mention the fact the conflict is ongoing further hinders the ability of ICC personnel from being able to travel to the country and gather evidence and speak to witnesses. The Office of the Prosecutor decided to use intermediaries which collected evidence, interviewed witnesses, and acted as the go-between for the prosecution and the witnesses. However during the trial issues came to light as to the credibility of the witnesses and the admissibility of the evidence. It was claimed by the defence that the intermediaries had suborned the witnesses. While the ICC judges were understanding towards the need to use intermediaries, they were critical of the prosecution's level of reliance on them and concerned over-protection of already vulnerable child witnesses:

> The Chamber is of the view that the prosecution should not have delegated its investigative responsibilities to the intermediaries in the way set out above, notwithstanding the extensive security difficulties it faced. A series of witnesses have been called during this trial whose evidence, as a result of the essentially unsupervised actions of three of the principal intermediaries, cannot safely be relied on. The Chamber spent a considerable period of time investigating the circumstances of a substantial number of individuals whose evidence was, at least in part, inaccurate or dishonest. The prosecution's negligence in failing to verify and scrutinise this material sufficiently before it was introduced led to significant expenditure on the part of the Court. An additional consequence of the lack of proper oversight of the intermediaries is that they were potentially able to take advantage of the witnesses they contacted. Irrespective of the Chamber's conclusions regarding the credibility and reliability of these alleged former child soldiers, given their youth and likely exposure to conflict, they were vulnerable to manipulation. (*The Prosecutor v. Thomas Lubanga Dyilo (Judgment)* ICC-01/04-01/06, 14 March 2012, 482)

16.7 International crimes

While international criminal law covers a wide range of crimes that are international in nature, this chapter will be looking at the four crimes that have come to be regarded as the core international crimes: aggression; crimes against humanity; war crimes; and genocide. It must be noted, however, that these are not the *only* international crimes. Other international crimes include piracy, terrorism, and drug trafficking. However, unlike the four crimes discussed in this chapter, these other crimes are dealt with more effectively by national laws and mechanisms.

16.7.1 Aggression

Aggression is one of the most controversial core crimes in international criminal law. Numerous problems surround the actualization of the crime despite attempts, failed and realized, to include provisions in international documents, treaties, and court jurisdictions. Arguably the biggest concern is the lack of a definitive definition.

The crime of aggression has previously been known as the 'crime against peace'. Attempts at the prosecution of this crime date back to Nuremberg. At that time, 'aggression' was defined under Article 6(a) of the Statute of the Nuremberg IMT (the Nuremberg Statute) as:

> Planning, preparation, initiation or waging of a war of aggression, or a war in violation of treaties, agreements or assurances, or participation in a common plan or conspiracy for the accomplishing of any of the foregoing.

There were problems with Nuremberg, as well as the International Military Tribunal for the Far East (IMTFE), known as the Tokyo War Crimes Tribunal or Tokyo IMT, trying the crime of aggression. The Nuremberg IMT had previously declared the crime of aggression to be part of customary law and proceeded on that basis, without a clear definition.

● *Tokyo IMT Judgment*, 60–153, TRANSCRIPT 48

Judge Pal, in his dissenting opinion at 233, warned of the problems that this was creating for courts in resolving the definitional gap:

> ...in definition there is danger. But I do not agree that all danger is eliminated simply by leaving the term undefined and thus allowing it to remain chameleonic. It may be easy for every nation to determine for others what is aggression. Perhaps every nation will say that war against what it considers its interest is aggressive. No term is more elastic or more susceptible to interested interpretation, whether by individuals, or by groups, than aggression. But when a court is called upon to determine the question it may not always be so easy to come to a decision.

The next attempt at a definition was made by the UN General Assembly in Article 1 of the 1974 United Nations General Assembly Resolution 3314(XXIX):

> Aggression is the use of armed force by a State against the sovereignty, territorial integrity or political independence of another State, or in any other manner inconsistent with the Charter of the United Nations, as set out in this Definition.

This defines aggression generally and does not define the crime of aggression in the strictest terms, a criticism that has been made by observers such as Robert Cryer, in 'Aggression at the Court of Appeal' (2005) 10(2) J Conf & Sec L 209, 224:

> Many are critical of using the General Assembly's definition of aggression as a basis for a definition of the *crime* of aggression. There may be strong reasons for this. In particular, it was not drafted as a definition of the crime against peace.

Given the UN Security Council's power to determine acts of aggression committed by States, the implication of the approach that has developed in terms of aggression has made this area more of a political matter than a judicial one.

Bassiouni (1993, see section 16.1), at 258, notes that:

> The definition of aggression, which took more than 20 years in its formulation, was neither included in a multilateral convention nor even voted upon in the resolution that adopted it. The adoption of a Resolution by consensus indicated the view of the Member-State governments that aggression is a political and not a justiciable crime.

Aggression is one of the four crimes falling under the Court's jurisdiction in the ICC Statute. Nonetheless, the Statute's approach to aggression is rather vague and unhelpful in addressing the definitional gap. The ICC takes an extremely cautious approach in the matter, at Article 5(2):

> The Court shall exercise jurisdiction over the crime of aggression once a provision is adopted in accordance with Articles 121 and 123 defining the crime and setting out the conditions under which the Court shall exercise jurisdiction with respect to this crime. Such a provision shall be consistent with the relevant provisions of the Charter of the United Nations.

The ICC Review Conference of 2010, held in Uganda, adopted a definition of 'aggression'. This definition, and other amendments to the ICC Statute adopted at the Kampala Conference, are contained in Resolution RC/Res.6, adopted at the 13th Plenary Meeting, on 11 June 2010, by consensus. According to Article 8 *bis*:

> 1. For the purpose of this Statute, 'crime of aggression' means the planning, preparation, initiation or execution, by a person in a position effectively to exercise control over or to direct the political or military action of a State, of an act of aggression which, by its character, gravity and scale, constitutes a manifest violation of the Charter of the United Nations.

However, by virtue of Article 15 *bis*:

> The Court shall exercise jurisdiction over the crime of aggression in accordance with this article, subject to a decision to be taken after 1 January 2017 by the same majority of States Parties as is required for the adoption of an amendment to the Statute.

Whether or not the State parties will agree to activate the jurisdiction of the ICC over aggression remains conjectural, but for now there is at least a starting point for a definition of aggression. Part of the requirement, in addition to Article 15 *bis* above, for the provision on aggression coming into force is the ratification or acceptance of the amendments by thirty State Parties. To date, fourteen State parties have ratified the provision.

- There is no clear definition of aggression in international law and the hope that the 2010 review meeting in Uganda would produce one did not materialize.

- Currently, only the UN Security Council may determine the occurrence of aggression, thus making aggression a political rather than a legally ascertainable issue.

- The ICC can exercise jurisdiction over aggression, provided that there is a definition of the term and that such a definition conforms to the Charter of the United Nations (the UN Charter).

16.7.2 Crimes against humanity

'Crimes against humanity' are not as clearly provided for in international law as genocide and war crimes. This is a category of crime that has developed more recently and has been limited in applicability as international criminal law emerged.

Egon Schwelb, 'Crimes against humanity' (1946) 23 BYBIL 178, 195, states that:

> A crime against humanity is an offence against general principles of law which, in certain circumstances, become the concern of the international community, namely, if it has repercussions reaching across international frontiers, or if it passes 'in magnitude or savagery any limits of what is tolerable by modern civilisations'.

The position of the British government was outlined by the Attorney-General in *Speeches of the Chief Prosecutor at the Close of the Case against the Individual Defendants* (Cmd 6964, London: HMSO, 1946), at p. 63:

> International Law has in the past made some claim that there is a limit to the omnipotence of the State and that the individual human being, the ultimate unit of all law, is not disentitled to the protection of mankind when the State tramples upon his rights in a manner which outrages the conscience of mankind.

Under Article 6(c) of the Nuremberg Statute, crimes against humanity consisted of:

> murder, extermination, enslavement, deportation, and other inhumane acts committed against any civilian population, before or during the war; or persecutions on political, racial, or religious grounds in execution of or in connection with any crime within the jurisdiction of the Tribunal, whether or not in violation of the domestic law of the country where perpetrated.

Most important to note is that crimes against humanity apply only to civilians and do not cover combatants, acts against whom fall under other international crimes. It is important to note that this definition is context-specific to a degree, since the requirement that the act occur 'before or during the war' limited its coverage by the Nuremberg IMT. However, this was the first provision regarding the crime, hence Schwelb (1946, see earlier in this section) notes, at 178, that:

> The provisions relating to crimes against humanity have been acclaimed as a 'revolution in international criminal law.

According to Bassiouni, 'Crimes against humanity': the need for a specialized convention' (1993–94) 31 Colum J Transn'l L 457, 493:

> while various components of Article 6(c) found their way into later formulations, none of the other conventions have covered all the elements of the original Nuremberg definition.
>
> The criminalization of 'Crimes Against Humanity' was intended not only to punish World War II perpetrators but to deter future human depredations and to enhance the prospects of world peace. The subsequent historical record has not proven that to be the case.

The next major contribution to the development of crimes against humanity occurred with the establishment of the ICTY and ICTR. Both Statutes provided for the crime, listed inhumane acts, and stipulated the situations under which these crimes could be committed, although each has a different context for applicability.

The ICTY may prosecute under Article 5 if the crime was 'committed in armed conflict, whether international or internal in character, and directed against any civilian population', while the ICTR has jurisdiction under Article 3 over crimes:

> committed as part of a widespread or systematic attack against any civilian population on national, political, ethnic, racial or religious grounds.

The ICC takes a different approach to crimes against humanity. Article 7 of the ICC Statute provides for crimes committed as part of a widespread or systematic attack directed against any civilian population, with knowledge of the attack.

As Darryl Robinson said in 'Crimes against humanity' (1999) 93 AJIL 57:

> Article 7 of the ICC statute sets forth a modernized and clarified definition of crimes against humanity that should provide a sound basis for international criminal prosecution in the future.

thinking points

- *What are crimes against humanity and in what circumstances can they be committed?*
- *Against which category of peoples can crimes against humanity be committed?*

It is now appropriate to explore the different elements that make up crimes against humanity. This will be split into the *actus reus* components and the *mens rea*.

Material elements of crime against humanity

Crimes against humanity covers a wide range of acts including:

> murder, extermination, enslavement, deportation or forcible transfer of population, imprisonment, torture, rape, sexual slavery, enforced prostitution, forced pregnancy, enforced sterilization, persecution based on religious, political, and racial grounds, enforced disappearance, other inhumane acts, the crime of apartheid.

Each individual crime has its own specific *actus reus* elements, however there are some general and contextual elements which are common to all. It is these which are discussed in the following sections.

'Nexus to armed conflict'

As mentioned earlier, the ICTY Statute requires linkage between the crime and an armed conflict. However, it needs to be emphasized that there is no customary law basis for this requirement.

. . . .

● ***Prosecutor v. Dusko Tadić (Jurisdiction)*** Case No. IT-94-1-AR72, ICTY Appeals Chamber, 2 October 1995

It was stated *obiter*, (at 72) that:

> It is by now a settled rule of customary international law that crimes against humanity do not require a connection to international armed conflict. Indeed, as the Prosecutor points out, customary international law may not require a connection between crimes against humanity and any conflict at all. Thus, by requiring that crimes against humanity be committed in either internal or international armed conflict, the Security Council may have defined the crime in Article 5 more narrowly than necessary under international law.

. . . .

● ***Prosecutor v. Dragan Nikolić (Review of Indictment Pursuant to Rule 61)*** Case No. IT-94-2-R61, ICTY Trial Chamber, 20 October 1994

Furthermore, in this case the ICTY had held (at 14) that:

> Since the judgment at Nuremberg, the concept has taken on a certain autonomy as there is no longer any need to determine a link with a crime against the peace or a war crime.

'Discriminatory requirement'

The ICTR discriminatory clause contained in Article 3 (see previously) did not follow most of the precedents and authorities at the time. In addition, the ICTY, in *Tadić*, held that the discrimination requirement was not applicable to crimes against humanity.

. . . .

● ***Prosecutor v. Dusko Tadić*** Case No. IT-94-1-AR72, ICTY Appeals Chamber, 15 July 1999

The Tribunal stated (at [283]) that:

> ... The ordinary meaning of Article 5 makes it clear that this provision does not require all crimes against humanity to have been perpetrated with a discriminatory intent. Such intent is only made necessary for one sub-category of those crimes, namely 'persecutions' provided for in Article 5 (h) ...

It continued (at [283]–[295]):

> As rightly submitted by the Prosecution, the interpretation of Article 5 in the light of its object and purpose bears out the above propositions. The aim of those drafting the Statute was to make all crimes against humanity punishable, including those which, while fulfilling all the conditions required by the notion of such crimes, may not have been perpetrated on political, racial or religious grounds as specified in paragraph (h) of Article 5. In light of the humanitarian goals of the framers of the Statute, one fails to see why they should have seriously restricted the class of offences coming within the purview of 'crimes against humanity', thus leaving outside this class all the possible instances of serious and widespread or systematic crimes against civilians on account only of their lacking a discriminatory intent. For example, a discriminatory intent requirement would prevent the penalization of random and indiscriminate violence intended to spread terror among a civilian population as a crime against humanity.

It seems from the case law and practice that the requirement of discrimination is applicable only to the ICTR, based on Article 3 of the ICTR Statute.

'Any civilian population'

The use of the term 'any civilian population' follows the rationale of crimes against humanity—to protect civilians regardless of nationality or affiliation to victims.

● ***Prosecutor v. Dusko Tadić (Judgement)*** Case No. IT-94-1-T, ICTY Trial Chamber II, 7 May 1997

The Tribunal (at [935]) clarified the word 'any':

> The inclusion of the word 'any' makes it clear that crimes against humanity can be committed against civilians of the same nationality as the perpetrator or those who are stateless, as well as those of a different nationality.

● ***Prosecutor v. Dragoljub Kunarac*** Case No. IT-96-23, ICTY Trial Chamber II, 22 February 2001

In this case, the ICTY clarified the term 'civilian' (at [425]):

> The 'civilian population' comprises, as suggested by the Commentary to the two Additional Protocols of 1977 to the Geneva Conventions of 1949, all persons who are civilians as opposed to members of the armed forces and other legitimate combatants. The targeted population must be of a predominantly civilian nature. However, the presence of certain non-civilians in its midst does not change the character of the population.

However, the phrase can include a certain element of non-civilians.

● ***Prosecutor v. Dario Kordić*** Case No. IT-95-14, ICTY Trial Chamber III, 26 February 2001

The Tribunal held (at [180]) that:

> A population may be considered as 'civilian' even if certain non-civilians are present—it must simply be 'predominantly civilian in nature'. Moreover, a wide definition of what constitutes a civilian population was adopted. It was decided that individuals who at one time performed acts of resistance may in certain circumstances be victims of a crime against humanity.

● ***Prosecutor v. Dusko Tadić (Judgement)*** Case No. IT-94-1-T, ICTY Trial Chamber II, 7 May 1997

The Tribunal said (at [638]) that:

> ... It is clear that the targeted population must be of a predominantly civilian nature. The presence of certain non-civilians in their midst does not change the character of the population. The notion of population requires more than an isolated act.

There is a need for more than one individual to be targeted. Thus there is a collective notion behind the use of population.

● ***Prosecutor v. Dusko Tadić (Judgement)*** Case No. IT-94-1-T, ICTY Trial Chamber II, 7 May 1997

The Tribunal confirmed (at [644]) that:

'Widespread or systematic'

Widespread or systematic comprises two distinct elements, because it is regarded as being disjunctive rather than conjunctive.

. . . .

● **Prosecutor v. Jean-Paul Akayesu (Judgement)** CASE NO. ICTR-96-4-T, TRIAL CHAMBER I, 2 SEPTEMBER 1998

It was said (at [579]) that 'The act can be part of a widespread or systematic attack and need not be a part of both'.

The ICTR also explained (at [580]) what was meant by the terms 'widespread' and 'systematic':

The above is sometimes considered to be a high standard to meet, so *Kunarac* took a less stringent approach.

. . . .

● **Prosecutor v. Dragoljub Kunarac** CASE NO. IT-96-23, ICTY TRIAL CHAMBER II, 22 FEBRUARY 2001

It was said (at [428]) that:

'Policy requirement'

The policy requirement has been interpreted quite loosely.

● *Prosecutor v. Dusko Tadić (Judgement)* Case No. IT-94-1-T, ICTY Trial Chamber II, 7 May 1997

The ICTY (at [653]) notes the traditional approach taken:

> Traditionally this requirement was understood to mean that there must be some form of policy to commit these acts…Importantly, however, such a policy need not be formalized and can be deduced from the way in which the acts occur. Notably, if the acts occur on a widespread or systematic basis that demonstrates a policy to commit those acts, whether formalized or not. Although some doubt the necessity of such a policy the evidence in this case clearly establishes the existence of a policy.

● *Prosecutor v. Dragan Nikolić (Review of Indictment Pursuant to Rule 61)* Case No. IT-94-2-R61, ICTY Trial Chamber, 20 October 1994

The ICTY further expanded on this view, when it said (at [26]) that:

> Although they need not be related to a policy established at a State level, in the conventional sense of the term, they cannot be the work of isolated individuals alone.

● *Prosecutor v. Laurent Semanza* Case No. ICTR-97-20-T, ICTR Trial Chamber, 15 May 2003

In this case, the ICTR held (at [326]) that:

> A crime against humanity must have been committed as part of a widespread or systematic attack against any civilian population on discriminatory grounds. Although the act need not be committed at the same time and place as the attack or share all of the features of the attack, it must, by its characteristics, aims, nature, or consequence objectively form part of the discriminatory attack.

● *Prosecutor v. Dusko Tadić* Case No. IT-94-1-AR72, ICTY Appeals Chamber, 15 July 1999

In this case, the ICTY took the view (at [271]) that:

> to convict an accused of crimes against humanity, it must be proved that the crimes were related to the attack on a civilian population (occurring during an armed conflict) and that the accused knew that his crimes were so related.

● *Prosecutor v. Tihomir Blaškić* Case No. IT-95-14-A, ICTY Appeals Chamber, 29 July 2004

The Tribunal explained (at [101]) that:

> Only the attack, not the individual acts of the accused, must be widespread or systematic. The Appeals Chamber underscores that the acts of the accused need only be a part of this attack, and all other conditions being met, a single or limited number of acts on his or her part would qualify as a crime against humanity, unless those acts may be said to be isolated or random.

• *Prosecutor v. Tihomir Blaškić* Case No. UIT-95-14-T, ICTY Trial Chamber I, 3 March 2000

It was held (at [206]) that:

> A crime may be widespread or committed on a large-scale by the cumulative effect of a series of inhumane acts or the singular effect of an inhumane act of extraordinary magnitude.

Mens rea

A person can be found guilty of a crime against humanity only in circumstances in which they were aware of the context in which their conduct took place.

• *Prosecutor v. Dusko Tadić* Case No. IT-94-1-AR72, ICTY Appeals Chamber, 15 July 1999

In this case (at [248]) the Appeals Chamber:

> Agrees with the Prosecution that there is nothing in Article 5 to suggest that it contains a requirement that crimes against humanity cannot be committed for purely personal motives. The Appeals Chamber agrees that it may be inferred from the words 'directed against any civilian population' in Article 5 of the Statute that the acts of the accused must comprise part of a pattern of widespread or systematic crimes directed against a civilian population and that the accused must have known that his acts fit into such a pattern. There is nothing in the Statute, however, which mandates the imposition of a further condition that the acts in question must not be committed for purely personal reasons, except to the extent that this condition is a consequence or a re-statement of the other two conditions mentioned.

• *Prosecutor v. Laurent Semanza* Case No. ICTR-97-20-T, ICTR Trial Chamber, 15 May 2003

The ICTR took the position (at [322]) that:

> The accused must have acted with knowledge of the broader context of the attack and knowledge that his act formed part of the attack on the civilian population. However, the accused need not necessarily share the purpose or goals behind the broader attack. There is no requirement that the enumerated acts other than persecution be committed with discriminatory intent.

It should be pointed out that the purpose of the attack by the accused does not need to have the same aim as the general attack; all that is required is a knowledge of the context.

• *Prosecutor v. Dusko Tadić* Case No. IT-94-1-AR72, ICTY Appeals Chamber, 15 July 1999

The ICTY confirmed (at [271]–[272]) that:

> The Trial Chamber correctly recognised that crimes which are unrelated to widespread or systematic attacks on a civilian population should not be prosecuted as crimes against humanity. Crimes against humanity are crimes of a special nature to which a greater degree of moral turpitude

attaches than to an ordinary crime. Thus to convict an accused of crimes against humanity, it must be proved that the crimes were related to the attack on a civilian population (occurring during an armed conflict) and that the accused knew that his crimes were so related.

For the above reasons, however, the Appeals Chamber does not consider it necessary to further require, as a substantive element of mens rea, a nexus between the specific acts allegedly committed by the accused and the armed conflict, or to require proof of the accused's motives. Consequently, in the opinion of the Appeals Chamber, the requirement that an act must not have been carried out for the purely personal motives of the perpetrator does not form part of the prerequisites necessary for conduct to fall within the definition of a crime against humanity under Article 5 of the Tribunal's Statute.

It would seem a logical conclusion to require some knowledge of the context to which an individual assumed that their attacks were related. This is a vital element of what distinguishes a crime against humanity from a general criminal act. Darryl Robinson (1999, see earlier in this section), at 52, reasonably makes the point that:

> The connection to a widespread or systematic attack is the essential and central element that raises an 'ordinary' crime to one of the most serious crimes known to humanity. To convict a person of this most serious international crime, if the person was truly unaware of this essential and central element, would violate the principle *actus non facit reum nisi mens sit rea*.

The ICC's approach to crimes against humanity

The position of crimes against humanity in international criminal law generally has been noted earlier. This section will consider crimes against humanity under the jurisdiction of the ICC. One of the most important developments of the ICC is the clear and concise manner in which the term 'crimes against humanity' is laid out in the ICC Statute, Article 7 of which states that there needs to be an act 'committed as part of a widespread or systematic attack directed against any civilian population, with knowledge of the attack'.

According to Article 7(2)(a):

> 'Attack directed against any civilian population' means a course of conduct involving the multiple commission of acts referred to in paragraph 1 against any civilian population, pursuant to or in furtherance of a State or organizational policy to commit such attack.

From the wording of the ICC Statute, it is clear that there is no need for an act to be linked to an armed conflict. Further, the Statute makes no reference to the issue of discrimination. As Robinson (1999, see earlier in this section), at 56–57, notes:

> The negotiations in Rome produced agreement that a discriminatory motive is not an element required for all crimes against humanity. This approach avoids the imposition of an onerous and unnecessary burden on the prosecution. Moreover, the requirement of a discriminatory motive, particularly when coupled with a closed list of prohibited grounds, could have resulted in the inadvertent exclusion of some very serious crimes against humanity.

Article 7 lays out the acts that are to be considered crimes against humanity and then clarifies these in Article 7(2).

Overall, the ICC contribution to crimes against humanity can be seen in its ability to get a large number of States to come to consensus on the matter, defining terms and crimes to be accepted under the jurisdiction of a first permanent international criminal court—and that is no small feat.

thinking points

- List the elements of 'crimes against humanity'.
- What does the term mens rea *mean*?
- Of what relevance is the widespread or systematic nature of attacks to crimes against humanity, and how does this relate to the issue of 'policy'?
- Explain the approach of the ICC to crimes against humanity.

16.7.3 Genocide

There is no single definition of genocide, but several instruments have been adopted to help to define the crime.

According to Article 2 of the 1948 UN Convention on the Prevention and Punishment of the Crime of Genocide (the Genocide Convention):

> genocide means any of the following acts committed with intent to destroy, in whole or in part, a national, ethnical, racial or religious group, as such:
>
> (a) Killing members of the group;
>
> (b) Causing serious bodily or mental harm to members of the group;
>
> (c) Deliberately inflicting on the group conditions of life calculated to bring about its physical destruction in whole or in part;
>
> (d) Imposing measures intended to prevent births within the group;
>
> (e) Forcibly transferring children of the group to another group...

In UN General Assembly Resolution 96(1), 'genocide' is characterized as '[a] denial of the right of existence of entire human groups, as homicide is the denial of the right to live of individual human beings'.

....

● *Prosecutor v. Jean Kambanda* Case No. ICTR-97-23-S, ICTR Trial Chamber I, 4 September 1998

In this case (at [16]), genocide was called 'crime of crimes'.

Originally, genocide was linked to crimes against humanity.

....

● *Re Altstötter & ors* [1947] 14 Annual Digest 278 (The *Justice Trial*)

In this case (at 285), the Tribunal saw genocide as constituting:

> a prime illustration of a crime against humanity under Control Council Law 10, which by reason of its magnitude and its international repercussions has been recognized as a violation of common international law, we cite 'genocide', is nothing but the gravest type of 'crime against humanity'.

● **Prosecutor v. Clément Kayishema and Obed Ruzindana** Case No. ICTR-95-I-T, ICTR Trial Chamber, 21 May 1999

In this case (at [89]), the ICTR similarly stated that:

> the definition of the crime of genocide was based upon that of crimes against humanity, that is, a combination of 'extermination and persecutions on political, racial or religious grounds' and it was intended to cover '*the intentional destruction of groups in whole or in substantial part*'. The crime of genocide is a type of crime against humanity. Genocide, however, is different from other crimes against humanity. The essential difference is that genocide requires the aforementioned specific intent to exterminate a protected group (in whole or in part) while crimes against humanity require the civilian population to be targeted as part of a widespread or systematic attack. There are instances where the discriminatory grounds coincide and overlap. [Emphasis added]

However, this was not the approach taken by the drafters of the Genocide Convention. In 'The definition of genocide: joining the dots in the light of recent practice' (2000) 1 Int Crim L Rev 285, 287–288, Nina Jørgensen explains that:

> The drafters did not wish to limit the potential scope of the crime of genocide by identifying it with crimes against humanity and the corresponding requirement of a war nexus, and it certainly seems that genocide has since taken on a theoretical life of its own.

The ICTR, in particular, helped to develop this area of international criminal law substantially, which is not surprising given the nature of the crimes that it seeks to address.

In 'Statement by UN Secretary-General Kofi Annan on the Occasion of the Announcement of the First Judgment in a Case of Genocide by the International Criminal Tribunal for Rwanda' (UN Doc. PR/10/98/UNIC, 1998), UN Secretary-General Kofi-Annan described the case of *Akayesu* as:

> a landmark decision in the history of international criminal law ... [that] ... brings to life, for the first time, the ideals of the Genocide Convention adopted 50 years ago.

Genocide is one of the international crimes in which individual responsibility is applicable, as well as State responsibility. The case law of the tribunals on genocide highlights some of the important aspects.

● **Prosecutor v. Radislav Krštić** Case No. IT-98-33-A, ICTY Appeals Chamber, 19 April 2004

The Tribunal stated (at [36]) that:

> Among the grievous crimes this Tribunal has the duty to punish, the crime of genocide is singled out for special condemnation and opprobrium.

● **Prosecutor v. Jean Kambanda** Case No. ICTR-97-23-S, ICTR Trial Chamber I, 4 September 1998

The ICTR said (at [16]) that:

> The crime of genocide is unique because of its element of *dolus specialis* (special intent) which requires that the crime be committed with the intent 'to destroy in whole or in part, a national ethnic, racial or religious group as such; hence the Chamber is of the opinion that genocide constitutes the crime of crimes, which must be taken into account when deciding the sentence.

One major question about genocide is whether an individual who intends to destroy a group can commit genocide without any evidence of a wider context.

● *Prosecutor v. Goran Jelsić ('Brcko')* Case No. IT-95-01-T, ICTY Trial Chamber, 14 December 1999

In this case (at [100]), the ICTY ruled that, with regard to the material element of genocide:

> It is a priori possible to conceive that the accused harboured the plan to exterminate an entire group without this intent having been supported by any organisation in which other individuals participated. In this respect, the preparatory work of the Convention of 1948 brings out that premeditation was not selected as a legal ingredient of the crime of genocide, after having been mentioned by the ad hoc committee at the draft stage, on the grounds that it seemed superfluous given the special intention already required by the text and that such precision would only make the burden of proof even greater. It ensues from this omission that the drafters of the Convention did not deem the existence of an organisation or a system serving a genocidal objective as a legal ingredient of the crime. In so doing, they did not discount the possibility of a lone individual seeking to destroy a group as such.

KEY POINTS

- There is no universally acceptable definition of genocide.

- Genocide has been described as the 'crime of crimes', the most fundamentally debilitating of all crimes, and one directed towards the destruction of a people, in part or whole.

- There is no requirement of premeditation in genocide, nor is it important that genocidal acts must occur within or with knowledge of a wider plan to destroy or kill.

'Protected groups'

Within the definition provided by the Genocide Convention, ICTY and ICTR Statutes, and the ICC Statute, the act of 'genocide' is committed against an exhaustive list of protected groups, limited to 'national, ethnical, racial or religious groups'.

● *Prosecutor v. Goran Jelsić ('Brcko')* Case No. IT-95-01-T, ICTY Trial Chamber, 14 December 1999

It was stated (at [171]) that:

> A group may be stigmatised in this manner by way of positive or negative criteria. A 'positive approach' would consist of the perpetrators of the crime distinguishing a group by the characteristics which they deem to be particular to a national, ethnical, racial or religious group. A 'negative approach' would consist of identifying individuals as not being part of the group to which the perpetrators of the crime consider that they themselves belong and which to them displays specific national, ethnical, racial or religious characteristics. Thereby, all individuals thus rejected would, by exclusion, make up a distinct group. The Trial Chamber concurs here with the opinion already expressed by the Commission of Experts and deems that it is consonant with the object and the purpose of the Convention to consider that its provisions also protect groups defined by exclusion where they have been stigmatised by the perpetrators of the act in this way.

At [70], it had been said that:

> Although the objective determination of a religious group still remains possible, to attempt to define a national, ethnical or racial group today using objective and scientifically irreproachable criteria would be a perilous exercise whose result would not necessarily correspond to the perception of the persons concerned by such categorisation. Therefore, it is more appropriate to evaluate the status of a national, ethnical or racial group from the point of view of those persons who wish to single that group out from the rest of the community. The Trial Chamber consequently elects to evaluate membership in a national, ethnical or racial group using a subjective criterion. It is the stigmatisation of a group as a distinct national, ethnical or racial unit by the community which allows it to be determined whether a targeted population constitutes a national, ethnical or racial group in the eyes of the alleged perpetrators. This position corresponds to that adopted by the Trial Chamber in its Review of the Indictment Pursuant to Article 61 filed in the Nikolić case.

The ICTR ruled out the possibility of extending the category of protected groups.

● **Prosecutor v. Jean-Paul Akayesu (Judgement)** CASE NO. ICTR-96-4-T, TRIAL CHAMBER I, 2 SEPTEMBER 1998

The Tribunal said (at 516) that:

> The Chamber considered whether the groups protected by the Genocide Convention, echoed in Article 2 of the Statute, should be limited to only the four groups expressly mentioned and whether they should not also include any group which is stable and permanent like the said four groups. In other words, the question that arises is whether it would be impossible to punish the physical destruction of a group as such under the Genocide Convention, if the said group, although stable and membership is by birth, does not meet the definition of any one of the four groups expressly protected by the Genocide Convention. In the opinion of the Chamber, it is particularly important to respect the intention of the drafters of the Genocide Convention, which according to the travaux préparatoires, was patently to ensure the protection of any stable and permanent group.

Identifying the protected group

Whose opinion counts when considering whether the victims are part of a particular protected group? It seems that the opinion of the perpetrator of the crimes can be accepted, as well as that of others. This arguably makes the classification of these groups excessively broad, because self-identification is possible, which may be different from the perpetrators' intention.

● **Prosecutor v. Clément Kayishema and Obed Ruzindana** CASE NO. ICTR-95-I-T, ICTR TRIAL CHAMBER, 21 MAY 1999

In this case (at [98]), it was said that:

> An ethnic group is one whose members share a common language and culture; or, a group which distinguishes itself, as such (self identification); or, a group identified as such by others, including perpetrators of the crimes (identification by others). A racial group is based on hereditary physical traits often identified with geography. A religious group includes denomination or mode of worship or a group sharing common beliefs.

● **Prosecutor v. Georges Anderson Nderubumwe Rutaganda** CASE NO. ICTR-96-3, ICTR TRIAL CHAMBER I, 6 DECEMBER 1999

At [56]:

> The Chamber notes that ... for the purposes of applying the Genocide Convention, membership of a group is, in essence, a subjective rather than an objective concept. The victim is perceived by the perpetrator of genocide as belonging to a group slated for destruction. In some instances, the victim may perceive himself/herself as belonging to the said group.

Yet the Trial Chamber qualified this when it said (at [57]) that:

> a subjective definition alone is not enough to determine victim groups ... It appears, from a reading of the *travaux préparatoires* of the Genocide Convention, that certain groups, such as political and economic groups, have been excluded from the protected groups, because they are considered to be 'mobile groups' which one joins through individual, political commitment. That would seem to suggest *a contrario* that the Convention was presumably intended to cover relatively stable and permanent groups.

thinking points

- *Who are protected groups and why are they important to the crime of genocide?*
- *How may we identify 'protected groups' for the purpose of genocide?*
- *The class of 'protected groups' is thought not to be expandable. Why?*

Material elements of genocide: prohibited acts

Killing

This element requires the death of another, and as Claus Kreß notes in 'The crime of genocide under international law' (2006) 6 Int Crim L Rev 461, 480, 'Causing the death of one member of a protected group suffices'.

. . . .

● ***Prosecutor v. Clément Kayishema and Obed Ruzindana*** Case No. ICTR-95-1-A, ICTR Appeals Chamber, 1 June 2001

The ICTR addressed this matter when it stated (at [151]) that:

> The Appeals Chamber understands the Trial Chamber's reasoning to be that, if a doubt exists in the interpretation of a statute, the doubt must be interpreted in favour of the accused. The Trial Chamber considered that '*meurtre*' is not the same as 'killing'. However, having regard to the operative part of Article 2(2) of the Statute, it found that 'there is virtually no difference' between the two terms as the term 'killing' is linked to the intent to destroy in whole or in part. The Appeals Chamber accepts this view, but states that if the word 'virtually' is interpreted in a manner that suggests a difference, though minimal, between the two terms, it would construe them both as referring to intentional but not necessarily premeditated murder, this being, in its view, the meaning to be assigned to the word '*meurtre*'.

Causing serious bodily or mental harm

Genocide is not actually limited to death, because other acts can result in genocide.

● *Attorney-General of Israel v. Eichmann* (1968) 36 ILR 5 (DC) 340
(The *Eichmann Case*)

In this case, the District Court of Jerusalem held that serious bodily or mental harm could occur from:

> The enslavement, starvation, deportation and persecution of people … and by the detention in ghettos, transit camps and concentration camps in conditions which were designed to cause their degradation, deprivation of their rights as human beings and to suppress them and cause them inhumane suffering and torture.

The ICTR further extended this notion to include sexual violence and rape, which was later adopted by the 2002 ICC Elements of Crimes and Rules of Procedure.

● *Prosecutor v. Jean-Paul Akayesu (Judgement)* CASE NO. ICTR-96-4-T, TRIAL CHAMBER I,
2 SEPTEMBER 1998

The ICTR said (at [731]) that:

> With regard, particularly, to the acts described in paragraphs 12(A) and 12(B) of the Indictment, that is, rape and sexual violence, the Chamber wishes to underscore the fact that in its opinion, they constitute genocide in the same way as any other act as long as they were committed with the specific intent to destroy, in whole or in part, a particular group, targeted as such. Indeed, rape and sexual violence certainly constitute infliction of serious bodily and mental harm on the victims and are even, according to the Chamber, one of the worst ways of [sic] inflict harm on the victim as he or she suffers both bodily and mental harm.

However, there is no requirement that this harm, as well as any mental harm, needs to be permanent. As the Tribunal said (at [502]):

> Causing serious bodily or mental harm to members of the group does not necessarily mean that the harm is permanent and irremediable.

● *Prosecutor v. Clément Kayishema and Obed Ruzindana* CASE NO. ICTR-95-I-T, ICTR TRIAL
CHAMBER, 21 MAY 1999

Thus in this case (at [109]), the Tribunal said:

> It is the view of the Trial Chamber that, [sic] to large extent, 'causing serious bodily harm' is self-explanatory. This phrase could be construed to mean harm that seriously injures the health, causes disfigurement or causes any serious injury to the external, internal organs or senses.

It said (at [108]) that:

> In order to determine what constitutes serious physical and mental harm, the ICTR decided a case-by-case approach basis was best.

See [110] for a similar quote regarding mental harm being case by case.

Deliberately inflicting on the group conditions of life calculated to bring about its physical destruction in whole or in part

A difference between this act and the other elements provided for is the requirement that the 'conduct must be extended beyond one member of the protected group', as Claus Kreß notes (2006, see earlier in this section), at 481.

● **Prosecutor v. Jean-Paul Akayesu (Judgement)** CASE NO. ICTR-96-4-T, TRIAL CHAMBER I, 2 SEPTEMBER 1998

The ICTR Trial Chamber (at [505]) expressed its opinion that:

> the expression deliberately inflicting on the group conditions of life calculated to bring about its physical destruction in whole or in part, should be construed as the methods of destruction by which the perpetrator does not immediately kill the members of the group, but which, ultimately, seek their physical destruction.

The interpretational aspects of what acts are to be included, which incorporates a slow death within this meaning, has been explained by the Trial Chamber of the ICTR (at [506]) to mean that:

> For purposes of interpreting Article 2(2)(c) of the Statute, the Chamber is of the opinion that the means of [sic] deliberate inflicting on the group conditions of life calculated to bring about its physical destruction, in whole or part, include, inter alia, subjecting a group of people to a subsistence diet, systematic expulsion from homes and the reduction of essential medical services below minimum requirement.

● **Prosecutor v. Milomir Stakić** CASE NO. IT-9724-T, ICTY TRIAL CHAMBER II, 31 JULY 2003

In this case, it was said (at [519]) that:

> It does not suffice to deport a group or a part of a group. A clear distinction must be drawn between physical destruction and mere dissolution of a group. The expulsion of a group or part of a group does not in itself suffice for genocide.

Imposing measures intended to prevent births within the group

Given the nature of the Nazi practice of forced sterilization during, and before, the Second World War, the Genocide Convention attempted to address this matter by including the crime. The ICTR expanded this concept and justified the reasoning behind its chosen interpretation.

● **Prosecutor v. Jean-Paul Akayesu (Judgement)** CASE NO. ICTR-96-4-T, TRIAL CHAMBER I, 2 SEPTEMBER 1998

It was stated (at [507]) that:

> For purposes of interpreting Article 2(2)(d) of the Statute, the Chamber holds that the measures intended to prevent births within the group, should be construed as sexual mutilation, the practice of sterilization, forced birth control, separation of the sexes and prohibition of marriages. In patriarchal societies, where membership of a group is determined by the identity of the father, an example of a measure intended to prevent births within a group is the case where, during rape, a woman of the said group is deliberately impregnated by a man of another group, with the intent to have her give birth to a child who will consequently not belong to its mother's group

One should not confuse this element of the crime of genocide with the forced impregnation crime, which is used to change the ethnic composition of a particular group (as included in Article 7(2)(f) of the ICC Statute). As Payam Akhavan explains, in 'The crime of genocide in the ICTR jurisprudence' (2005) 3 JICJ 989, 1005:

> Preventing births as a form of genocide is conceptually different from forced impregnation intended to affect the ethnic composition of a group.

Forcibly transferring children of the group to another group

This is often considered as being similar to cultural genocide. However, the Genocide Convention does not explicitly mention cultural genocide and the ICTY has held that cultural genocide is not part of customary international law.

● **Prosecutor v. Radislav Krštić** CASE NO. IT-98-33-T, ICTY TRIAL CHAMBER I, 2 AUGUST 2001

The Tribunal stated (at [580]) that:

> The Trial Chamber is aware that it must interpret the Convention with due regard for the principle of *nullum crimen sine lege*. It therefore recognises that, despite recent developments, customary international law limits the definition of genocide to those acts seeking the physical or biological destruction of all or part of the group. Hence, an enterprise attacking only the cultural or sociological characteristics of a human group in order to annihilate these elements which give to that group its own identity distinct from the rest of the community would not fall under the definition of genocide. The Trial Chamber however points out that where there is physical or biological destruction there are often simultaneous attacks on the cultural and religious property and symbols of the targeted group as well, attacks which may legitimately be considered as evidence of an intent to physically destroy the group.

There is generally little case law on this matter.

● **Prosecutor v. Jean-Paul Akayesu (Judgement)** CASE NO. ICTR-96-4-T, TRIAL CHAMBER I, 2 SEPTEMBER 1998

In this case (at [509]), it was stated that:

> With respect to forcibly transferring children of the group to another group, the Chamber is of the opinion that, as in the case of measures intended to prevent births, the objective is not only to sanction a direct act of forcible physical transfer, but also to sanction acts of threats or trauma which would lead to the forcible transfer of children from one group to another.

The ICC Statute is the most developed in terms of stating elements of this aspect of the crime. It notes, in the 2002 Elements of Crimes, at note 5, that:

> The term 'forcibly' is not restricted to physical force, but may include threat of force or coercion, such as that caused by fear of violence, duress, detention, psychological oppression or abuse of power, against such person or persons or another person, or by taking advantage of a coercive environment.

Context of the act

The ICC has taken a different stance from that of the tribunal jurisprudence. Unlike in *Jelsić*, which provides that a single act of an individual may fall under the scope of genocide, the ICC is much more restrictive, requiring, under Article 6(a)(4) of the ICC Elements of Crimes, that:

> the conduct took place in the context of a manifest pattern of similar conduct directed against that group or was conduct that could itself effect such destruction.

● **Prosecutor v. Radislav Krštić** CASE No. IT-98-33-A, ICTY APPEALS CHAMBER, 19 APRIL 2004

However, the ICTY incorporated this into its reasoning in this case (at [224]):

> the Trial Chamber relied on the definition of genocide in the Elements of Crimes adopted by the ICC. This definition, stated the Trial Chamber, 'indicates clearly that genocide requires that "the conduct took place in the context of a manifest pattern of similar conduct".' The Trial Chamber's reliance on the definition of genocide given in the ICC's Elements of Crimes is inapposite. As already explained, the requirement that the prohibited conduct be part of a widespread or systematic attack does not appear in the Genocide Convention and was not mandated by customary international law. Because the definition adopted by the Elements of Crimes did not reflect customary law as it existed at the time Krstić committed his crimes, it cannot be used to support the Trial Chamber's conclusion.

KEY POINTS

- Not only death can lead to genocide; other acts, such as physical or biological destruction, rape, prevention of birth, etc., can also constitute genocide.

- Generally speaking, there can be lone genocides—that is, a genocidal act occurring on its own without a link to any policy or widespread practice.

Mental elements: *mens rea*

Intent

An important observation to make regarding genocide and the other core crimes is that rank or position in society has no effect on the individual guilt of a person, provided that they have the necessary intent.

● **Prosecutor v. Jean-Paul Akayesu (Judgement)** CASE No. ICTR-96-4-T, TRIAL CHAMBER I, 2 SEPTEMBER 1998

At [498]:

> Genocide is distinct from other crimes inasmuch as it embodies a special intent or dolus specialis. Special intent of a crime is the specific intention, required as a constitutive element of the crime, which demands that the perpetrator clearly seeks to produce the act charged. Thus, the special intent in the crime of genocide lies in 'the intent to destroy, in whole or in part, a national, ethnical, racial or religious group, as such'.

However, where a perpetrator does not have the specific desire to destroy any individuals, 'it merely excludes the categorization of the individual as a *principal* perpetrator' (Claus Kreß, 2006, at 493, see earlier in this section).

This idea was explained by the ICTY Appeals Chamber in the following way.

● *Prosecutor v. Radislav Krštić* Case No. IT-98-33-A, ICTY Appeals Chamber, 19 April 2004

At [134]:

> As has been demonstrated, all that the evidence can establish is that Krstić was aware of the intent to commit genocide on the part of some members of the VRS Main Staff, and with that knowledge, he did nothing to prevent the use of Drina Corps personnel and resources to facilitate those killings. This knowledge on his part alone cannot support an inference of genocidal intent. Genocide is one of the worst crimes known to humankind, and its gravity is reflected in the stringent requirement of specific intent. Convictions for genocide can be entered only where that intent has been unequivocally established. There was a demonstrable failure by the Trial Chamber to supply adequate proof that Radislav Krstić possessed the genocidal intent. Krstić, therefore, is not guilty of genocide as a principal perpetrator.

In order to establish whether there is this specific intent to destroy a particular group, one can deduce from circumstantial evidence that the intention existed. This is most often the case, because it is generally difficult to prove from direct evidence that there was such an intention.

● *Prosecutor v. Jean-Paul Akayesu (Judgement)* Case No. ICTR-96-4-T, Trial Chamber I, 2 September 1998

At [523]:

> On the issue of determining the offender's specific intent, the Chamber considers that intent is a mental factor which is difficult, even impossible, to determine. This is the reason why, in the absence of a confession from the accused, his intent can be inferred from a certain number of presumptions of fact. The Chamber considers that it is possible to deduce the genocidal intent inherent in a particular act charged from the general context of the perpetration of other culpable acts systematically directed against that same group, whether these acts were committed by the same offender or by others. Other factors, such as the scale of atrocities committed, their general nature, in a region or a country, or furthermore, the fact of deliberately and systematically targeting victims on account of their membership of a particular group, while excluding the members of other groups, can enable the Chamber to infer the genocidal intent of a particular act.

Furthermore, as the ICTR has established, in cases in which an individual should have been aware of a situation, intent can be deduced.

● *Prosecutor v. Jean-Paul Akayesu (Judgement)* Case No. ICTR-96-4-T, Trial Chamber I, 2 September 1998

In this case, the Tribunal established that genocide was committed against the Tutsi group in Rwanda in 1994, throughout the period covering the events alleged in the Indictment 180.

At [730]:

> Owing to the very high number of atrocities committed against the Tutsi, their widespread nature not only in the commune of Taba, but also throughout Rwanda, and to the fact that the victims were systematically and deliberately selected because they belonged to the Tutsi group, with persons belonging to other groups being excluded, the Chamber is also able to infer, beyond reasonable doubt, the genocidal intent of the accused in the commission of the above-mentioned crimes.

As for the concurrence of the *actus reus* and *mens rea*, the ICTR held as follows.

. . . .
● *Prosecutor v. Clément Kayishema and Obed Ruzindana* Case No. ICTR-95-I-T, ICTR Trial
   Chamber, 21 May 1999

The Tribunal held (at [91]) that:

> For the crime of genocide to occur, the *mens rea* must be formed prior to the commission of the
> genocidal acts. The individual acts themselves, however, do not require premeditation; the only
> consideration is that the act should be done in furtherance of the genocidal intent.

One must also distinguish between the individual and collective intent of the crime.

. . . .
● *Prosecutor v. Radislav Krštić* Case No. IT-98-33-T, ICTY Trial Chamber I, 2 August 2001

At [549]:

> the Chamber emphasises the need to distinguish between the individual intent of the accused and
> the intent involved in the conception and commission of the crime. The gravity and the scale of the
> crime of genocide ordinarily presume that several protagonists were involved in its perpetration.
> Although the motive of each participant may differ, the objective of the criminal enterprise remains
> the same. In such cases of joint participation, the intent to destroy, in whole or in part, a group as
> such must be discernible in the criminal act itself, apart from the intent of particular perpetrators.
> It is then necessary to establish whether the accused being prosecuted for genocide shared the
> intention that a genocide be carried out.

'To destroy'

As stated earlier, genocide can arise from acts other than death. But according to *Krštić*, only
physical or biological destruction counts, not cultural or sociological destruction.

. . . .
● *Prosecutor v. Radislav Krštić* Case No. IT-98-33-A, ICTY Appeals Chamber, 19 April 2004

The ICTY held (at [25]) that:

> The Genocide Convention, and customary international law in general, prohibit only the physical
> or biological destruction of a human group. The Trial Chamber expressly acknowledged this limi-
> tation, and eschewed any broader definition. The Chamber stated: '[C]ustomary international
> law limits the definition of genocide to those acts seeking the physical or biological destruction
> of all or part of the group. [A]n enterprise attacking only the cultural or sociological character-
> istics of a human group in order to annihilate these elements which give to that group its own
> identity distinct from the rest of the community would not fall under the definition of genocide.'

. . . .
● *Prosecutor v. Vidoje Blagojević and Dragan Jokić* Case No. IT-02-60-T, ICTY Trial Chamber I,
   17 January 2005

In this case, however, (at [666]) the Chamber clarified what destruction entails:

> The Trial Chamber finds in this respect that the physical or biological destruction of a group is
> not necessarily the death of the group members. While killing large numbers of a group may
> be the most direct means of destroying a group, other acts or series of acts, can also lead to

the destruction of the group. A group is comprised of its individuals, but also of its history, traditions, the relationship between its members, the relationship with other groups, the relationship with the land. The Trial Chamber finds that the physical or biological destruction of the group is the likely outcome of a forcible transfer of the population when this transfer is conducted in such a way that the group can no longer reconstitute itself—particularly when it involves the separation of its members. In such cases the Trial Chamber finds that the forcible transfer of individuals could lead to the material destruction of the group, since the group ceases to exist as a group, or at least as the group it was. *The Trial Chamber emphasises that its reasoning and conclusion are not an argument for the recognition of cultural genocide, but rather an attempt to clarify the meaning of physical or biological destruction.* [Emphasis added]

'In whole or in part'

Through inclusion of 'in part' in the definition, the intention does not need to be the complete destruction or elimination of the particular group. This can be seen through the historical example of the Nazi regime's attempt to destroy the Jewish population in Europe, as opposed to the world, as well as the attempt, in Rwanda alone, to destroy the Tutsis.

● ***Prosecutor v. Radislav Krštić*** Case No. IT-98-33-A, ICTY Appeals Chamber, 19 April 2004

The ICTY Appeals Chamber stated (at [23]) that:

> The historical examples of genocide also suggest that the area of the perpetrators' activity and control, as well as the possible extent of their reach, should be considered. Nazi Germany may have intended only to eliminate Jews within Europe alone; that ambition probably did not extend, even at the height of its power, to an undertaking of that enterprise on a global scale. Similarly, the perpetrators of genocide in Rwanda did not seriously contemplate the elimination of the Tutsi population beyond the country's borders. The intent to destroy formed by a perpetrator of genocide will always be limited by the opportunity presented to him.

There is also evidence that the number of people who are destroyed, or whom attempts are made to destroy, should make up a substantial part of that group.

● ***Prosecutor v. Radislav Krštić*** Case No. IT-98-33-A, ICTY Appeals Chamber, 19 April 2004

At [12]:

> The intent requirement of genocide under Article 4 of the Statute is therefore satisfied where evidence shows that the alleged perpetrator intended to destroy at least a substantial part of the protected group. The determination of when the targeted part is substantial enough to meet this requirement may involve a number of considerations. The numeric size of the targeted part of the group is the necessary and important starting point, though not in all cases the ending point of the inquiry. The number of individuals targeted should be evaluated not only in absolute terms, but also in relation to the overall size of the entire group. In addition to the numeric size of the targeted portion, its prominence within the group can be a useful consideration. If a specific part of the group is emblematic of the overall group, or is essential to its survival, that may support a finding that the part qualifies as substantial within the meaning of Article 4.

KEY POINTS

- To destroy in part or whole means that a genocidal act does not need to target an entire population or to seek to wipe out a targeted people in its entirety; the destruction of a substantial part suffices.

- There may be both individual and collective intent, but they do not have to be identical. Individual knowledge of the collective intent to destroy is enough to create liability.

- Destruction of a group is not accomplished only by death.

16.7.4 War crimes

War crimes are the violations of the laws and customs of war, otherwise known as 'international humanitarian law' (see chapter 12). War crimes have come under the jurisdiction of all modern attempts at international justice, including the Nuremberg and Tokyo IMTs, the ICTY and ICTR, the SCSL, and the ICC, as well as domestic trials. It is important to note that war crimes in international law are broader than those in the Tribunals' jurisprudence, because not all of the crimes were included in their jurisdiction.

The Nuremberg Charter defines 'war crimes' at Article 6(b) as:

namely, violations of the laws or customs of war. Such violations shall include, but not be limited to, murder, ill-treatment or deportation to slave labour or for any other purpose of civilian population of or in occupied territory, murder or ill-treatment of prisoners of war or persons on the seas, killing of hostages, plunder of public or private property, wanton destruction of cities, towns or villages, or devastation not justified by military necessity.

War crimes are governed both by treaties regulating international humanitarian law and customary international law.

● **Nuremberg IMT (Opinion and Judgment)** (1946), REPRINTED IN (1947) 41 AJIL 172

It was said at Nuremberg (at 218) that:

The Hague Convention of 1907 prohibited resort to certain methods of waging war. These included the inhumane treatment of prisoners, the employment of poisoned weapons, the improper use of flags of true, and similar matters. Many of these prohibitions had been enforced long before the date of the Convention; but since 1907 they have certainly been crimes, punishable as offenses against the law of war; yet the Hague Convention nowhere designates such practices as criminal, nor is any sentence prescribed, nor any mention made of a court to try and punish offenders. For many years past, however, military tribunals have tried and punished individuals guilty of violating the rules of land warfare laid down by this Convention.

Each tribunal has been granted jurisdiction over a limited set of war crimes: under Article 3 of the ICTY Statute specifically, and under Article 2 through the notion of grave breaches of the 1949 Geneva Conventions; under Article 4 of the ICTR Statute through violations of Common Article 3 of the Geneva Conventions and Additional Protocol II; and under Article 8 of the ICC Statute.

Traditionally, conflicts were considered only to occur between States, thus the natural consequence of this was that war crimes did not apply to internal conflicts. However, when the Geneva Conventions were being drafted, consideration was taken of the regulation of internal conflicts, despite these being considered an internal affair of the State. This resulted in Common Article 3, which applies to internal armed conflicts as well. Additional Protocol II expanded the protection—but this applies only to signatory States and does not cover all violations of international humanitarian law.

The ICC has also incorporated war crimes for internal armed conflicts in Article 8 of its Statute, but the list of acts that constitute war crimes is more limited than the case law of the ICTY and ICTR. Examples of war crimes, as adjudicated by the tribunals and the ICC include:

- crimes against non-combatants;
- attacks on prohibited targets;
- attacks that inflict excessive civilian damage;
- attacks against property;
- prohibited means and methods of warfare; and
- war crimes that attack other values—such as the drafting of child soldiers and transferring populations into occupied territory.

Elements of war crimes

Armed conflict

For a war crime to be committed, there must be armed conflict. What constitutes 'armed conflict' is a question of fact often left to the determination of tribunals; the official position taken by warring States is of less weight.

. . . .

● **Prosecutor v. Dusko Tadić** Case No. IT-94-1-AR72, ICTY Appeals Chamber, 2 October 1995

In this case, the Tribunal took a broad approach (at [70]), finding that 'an armed conflict exists whenever there is a resort to armed force between States'.

There has been some indication that a level of intensity is required as opposed to a mere generic resort to force. Also, conflict may exist even if there is no resistance by an occupied State (see Article 2 of the 1949 Geneva Convention for the Amelioration of the Condition of the Wounded and Sick in Armed Forces in the Field—that is, the First Geneva Convention).

For internal armed conflicts, there is a threshold of intensity that must be met. This is important in distinguishing between disturbances and riots, which are not governed under international humanitarian law. In reality, it is always difficult to make this distinction and judicial attitude has been incoherent.

. . . .

● **Prosecutor v. Dusko Tadić** Case No. IT-94-1-AR72, ICTY Appeals Chamber, 2 October 1995

According to the Tribunal in this case (at [70]), there must be:

> protracted armed violence between governmental authorities and organized armed groups or between such groups within a State.

. . . .

● **Prosecutor v. Dusko Tadić (Judgement)** Case No. IT-94-1-T, ICTY Trial Chamber II, 7 May 1997

It was said (at [562]) that:

> The test applied by the Appeals Chamber to the existence of an armed conflict for the purposes of the rules contained in Common Article 3 focuses on two aspects of a conflict; the intensity of the conflict and the organization of the parties to the conflict. In an armed conflict of an internal

or mixed character, these closely related criteria are used solely for the purpose, as a minimum, of distinguishing an armed conflict from banditry, unorganized and short-lived insurrections, or terrorist activities, which are not subject to international humanitarian law.

Additional Protocol II includes the requirement that one of the parties must be a government, unlike the ICC (Article 8(2)(f) of the ICC Statute) and the ICTY (*Tadić*), both of which recognize conflicts between armed groups. The ICC Statute refers to 'protracted armed conflict', unlike the ICTY's preference of 'violence'. However, when the French text of the ICC Statute is taken into consideration, it can be seen that the intention was to follow the established jurisprudence and to use 'protracted armed violence'.

● *Prosecutor v. Georges Anderson Nderubumwe Rutaganda* CASE No. ICTR-96-3, ICTR TRIAL CHAMBER I, 6 DECEMBER 1999

Also, in this case (at [92]) the ICTR said that:

it is clear that mere acts of banditry, internal disturbances and tensions, and unorganized and short-lived insurrections are to be ruled out. The International Committee of the Red Cross (the 'ICRC'), specifies further that conflicts referred to in Common Article 3 are armed conflicts with armed forces on either side engaged in hostilities: conflicts, in short, which are in many respects similar to an international conflict, but take place within the confines of a single country.

Nexus between the crime and conflict

For a particular crime to be considered a war crime, there needs to be a link between the criminal act and the conflict. There is a specific logic behind this, which the ICTR explains as follows.

● *Prosecutor v. Laurent Semanza* CASE No. ICTR-97-20-T, ICTR TRIAL CHAMBER, 15 MAY 2003

At [368]:

the Chamber must find that there existed a nexus between the alleged breach of Common Article 3 or Additional Protocol II and the underlying armed conflict. This requirement is best understood upon appreciation of the purpose of Common Article 3 and Additional Protocol II. The purpose of the said provisions is the protection of people as victims of internal armed conflicts, not the protection of people against crimes unrelated to the conflict, however reprehensible such crimes may be.

● *Prosecutor v. Dragoljub Kunarac* CASE No. IT-96-23/1-A, ICTY APPEALS CHAMBER, 12 JUNE 2002

The ICTY said in this case (at [58]) that:

What ultimately distinguishes a war crime from a purely domestic offence is that a war crime is shaped by or dependent upon the environment—the armed conflict—in which it is committed. It need not have been planned or supported by some form of policy. The armed conflict need not have been causal to the commission of the crime, but the existence of an armed conflict must, at a minimum, have played a substantial part in the perpetrator's ability to commit it, his decision to commit it, the manner in which it was committed or the purpose for which it was committed.

Crimes that occur during an armed conflict, but which are unrelated to the crime—such as killing an individual for reasons unrelated to the conflict—are not war crimes. The requirement of the conflict playing a 'substantial part' in the act, the 'decision to commit it, the manner' in which it was committed, and the 'purpose' of committing it are critical. However, nexus between conflict and crime does not mean geographical nexus.

● ***Prosecutor v. Dragoljub Kunarac*** Case No. IT-96 23/1-A, ICTY Appeals Chamber, 12 June 2002

The ICTY said (at [57]):

> As indicated by the Trial Chamber, the requirement that the acts of the accused must be closely related to the armed conflict would not be negated if the crimes were temporally and geographically remote from the actual fighting. It would be sufficient, for instance, for the purpose of this requirement, that the alleged crimes were closely related to hostilities occurring in other parts of the territories controlled by the parties to the conflict.

The perpetrator

War crimes cover more than military personnel and leaders.

● ***Prosecutor v. Jean-Paul Akayesu*** Case No. ICTR-96-4-A, Appeals Chamber, 1 June 2001

It was held (at [444]–[445]) that:

> 'The category of persons to be held accountable in this respect then, would in most cases be limited to commanders, combatants and other members of the armed forces'... In actuality authors of violations of common Article 3 will likely fall into one of these categories. This stems from the fact that common Article 3 requires a close nexus between violations and the armed conflict. This nexus between violations and the armed conflict implies that, in most cases, the perpetrator of the crime will probably have a special relationship with one party to the conflict. However, such a special relationship is not a condition precedent to the application of common Article 3 and, hence of Article 4 of the Statute.

The issue of the awareness of the perpetrator of the conflict situation has not been well explored, although the ICTY suggested in *Kordić* that it is relevant.

The ICC Elements of Crime require that the accused have knowledge of the conflict, by requiring, at Article 8(2)(a)(i), element 5, that 'The perpetrator was aware of factual circumstances that established the existence of an armed conflict', and at the introduction to Article 8 that:

> There is only a requirement for the awareness of the factual circumstances that established the existence of an armed conflict that is implicit in the terms 'took place in the context of and was associated with'.

Victim

Certain international treaties protect certain groups of people from war crimes (see Articles 4 and 147 of the 1949 Geneva Convention (IV), Article 8(2)(a) of the ICC Statute, and Article 2 of the ICTY Statute).

Common Article 3 of all the four Geneva Conventions covers:

> Persons no longer taking active part in hostilities, including members of the armed forces who have laid down their arms and those placed *hors de combat* by sickness, wounds, detention or other cause

● *Prosecutor v. Mladen Naletilić (aka 'Tuta') and Vinko Martinović (aka 'Stela')* Case No. IT-98-34-T, ICTY Trial Chamber II, 31 March 2003

The ICTY adopted a view (at [229]) of who can be classified as a victim that was more expansive than that provided for in the treaties:

> Common Article 3 imposes that victims be persons taking no active part in the hostilities. In view of the jurisprudence, this test extends to 'any individual not taking part in hostilities', and is therefore broader than that envisioned by Geneva Convention IV, under which the status of 'protected person' is only accorded in defined circumstances.

ICC Statute jurisdictional threshold

An anomaly with regard to jurisdiction appears in the ICC Statute as a requirement in Article 8(1):

> The Court shall have jurisdiction in respect of war crimes in particular when committed as part of a plan or policy or as part of a large-scale commission of such crimes.

The criterion of 'policy or large-scale commission' is not a usual requirement for war crimes. Unlike crimes against humanity, a war crime can be an isolated act. The reasoning for this inclusion in the ICC Statute may be due to the intended nature of the ICC, which is to deal with the highest level of individual responsibility, and also the ICC being a court of last resort. Arguably, the inclusion of 'in particular' denotes the recommendatory nature of the requirement.

The recent ICC judgment and its impact on the development of war crimes *actus reus* and *mens rea* elements

621

The ICC delivered its first judgment in March 2012 in *The Prosecutor v. Thomas Lubanga Dyilo*. The case relates to the situation in the Democratic Republic of Congo and Lubanga was found guilty as a co-perpetrator of conscripting and enlisting children (under fifteen years) into the Union of Congolese Patriots' (UPC) military wing, which he claimed to lead, and using them in the hostilities from September 2002 to 13 August 2003. The use of child soldiers, their conscription, and enlistment constitutes a war crime. The ICC clarified that:

> the offences of conscripting and enlisting are committed at the moment a child under the age of 15 is enrolled into or joins an armed force or group, with or without compulsion. In the circumstances of this case, conscription and enlistment are dealt with together, notwithstanding the Chamber's earlier conclusion that they constitute separate offences. These offences are continuous in nature. They end only when the child reaches 15 years of age or leaves the force or group. (*The Prosecutor v. Thomas Lubanga Dyilo [Judgment]* ICC-01/04-01/06, 14 March 2012, para [618])

The ICC also explored the requirement of 'active participation' in the conflict as part of the criteria for the crime. The judges did not lay down a generic definition for this term, preferring a case-by-case approach. However, they ruled that active participation is not limited to frontline roles by children, such as participating directly in hostilities, but could include situations in which the children play 'indirect' roles. The Court said that:

> The decisive factor . . . in deciding if an "indirect" role is to be treated as active participation in hostilities is whether the support provided by the child to the combatants exposed him or her to real danger

as a potential target. In the judgment of the Chamber these combined factors—the child's support and this level of consequential risk—mean that although absent from the immediate scene of the hostilities, the individual was nonetheless actively involved in them. Given the different types of roles that may be performed by children used by armed groups, the Chamber's determination of whether a particular activity constitutes "active participation" can only be made on a case-by-case basis. (*The Prosecutor v. Thomas Lubanga Dyilo (Judgement)* ICC-01/04-01/06, 14 March 2012, [628].)

In her dissenting opinion in the case, Judge Odito Benito criticized the Court's failure to define what constitutes 'active participation' instead of leaving it to a case-by-case treatment (ICC-01/04-01/06, 14 March 2012, 613/624, [15]).

With regard to the required level of knowledge (*mens rea*) for individual criminal responsibility, Article 25(3)(a) of the Rome Statute states that 'a person shall be criminally responsible and liable for punishment for a crime within the jurisdiction of the Court if that person: (a) Commits such a crime, whether as an individual, jointly with another or through another person, regardless of whether that other person is criminally responsible'.

The Court considered the implication of this provision and lay down the principles that, to determine *mens rea* for individual criminal responsibility, it must be proved that there is:

an agreement or common plan between accused and at least one other co-perpetrator, that, once implemented, will result in the commission of the relevant crime in the ordinary course of events; the accused provided an essential contribution to the common plan that resulted in the commission of the relevant *crime*; the accused meant to conscript, enlist or use children under the age of 15 to participate actively in hostilities or he was aware that by implementing the common plan these consequences 'will occur in the ordinary course of events'; the accused was aware that he provided an essential contribution to the implementation of the common plan; and . . . the accused was aware of the factual circumstances that established the existence of an armed conflict and the link between these circumstances and his conduct. (*The Prosecutor v. Thomas Lubanga Dyilo (Judgment)* ICC-01/04-01/06, 14 March 2012, [1018].)

 ## 16.8 Immunity

Another point of contention to which the relationship between the ICC and UN Security Council has led to is the issue of immunity for heads of States. The ICC explicitly rejects any immunity before the Court (Article 27). This is revolutionary in international law: it is the first time that States have agreed to prosecution regardless of immunities—although it must be questioned whether those States that have ratified the Treaty ever envisioned a situation in which a sitting head of State would be subject to prosecution.

Following the Security Council's referral of the situation within Darfur to the Court, the Prosecutor sought, and was granted, an arrest warrant for the Sudanese President Omar Al-Bashir. This was the first instance of an international court indicting a sitting head of State and, quite naturally, the incident caused waves amongst other States.

Reasons for the non-recognition of immunity by the ICC Statute are principally owed to the nature of crimes under the Court's jurisdiction. Because these crimes are the core international crimes and are, in many cases, perpetrated by State officials, the ICC formally recognizes the individual responsibility of those individuals who would otherwise be immune. Without this, the ICC would be prevented from exercising its function of trying those most responsible for such crimes.

As Dapo Akande notes in 'International law immunities and the International Criminal Court' (2004) 98 AJIL 407, 420:

> To the extent that an international rule establishes that the official himself ought to be held responsible for the act, that reason for immunity disappears. Secondly, by providing that the ICC Statute applies to state officials, Article 27(1) establishes that those officials are subject to prosecution by the ICC even when they acted in their official capacity.

thinking points

- *Explain the tension between peace and justice.*
- *What powers, if any, does the UN Security Council possess under the ICC Statute?*
- *Of what relevance are amnesty and immunity to the ICC Statute?*

Conclusion

International criminal law has helped to ensure the prosecution of many of those responsible for some of the most horrendous crimes committed over the last two centuries. However, further development in this area, which has seen much progress since the Second World War, remains to be seen. Undoubtedly, the ICC was a huge step forward towards an international homogenous criminal system, but whether the ICC survives or not will depend on a variety of factors. At one point, John Bolton tells us, in 'Courting danger: what's wrong with the International Criminal Court' (1998–9) 54 The National Interest 60, 71, the USA believed that:

> whether the ICC survives and flourishes depends in a large measure on the United States. We should therefore ignore it in our official posture, and attempt to isolate it though our diplomacy, in order to prevent it from acquiring any further legitimacy or resources.

Perhaps, as Charles Chernor Jalloh notes in 'Regionalizing international criminal law?' (2009) 9 ICLR 445, 464:

> Even more significant to the future of the ICC as a young institution was the political reaction within regional organizations.

However, the ICC Prosecutor argues in 'Paper on some policy issues before the Office of the Prosecutor' (September 2003, available at http://www.amicc.org/docs/OcampoPolicyPaper9_03.pdf), p. 4, that:

> the number of cases that reach the Court should not be a measure of its efficiency. On the contrary, the absence of trials before this Court, as a consequence of the regular functioning of national institutions, would be a major success.

But as Adam Branch has noted, in 'What the ICC Review Conference can't fix' (Oxford: OTJR Working Paper Series, 2010), p. 1:

> The first of these inherent problems stems from the fact that the ICC, like any international mechanism intended to promote or protect human rights, faces the impossible task of acting morally in a political world rent by power inequalities, domination, and violence.

? Questions

Self test questions

1 Define 'genocide'.

2 Outline the elements of genocide.

3 Explain *dolus specialis*.

4 What are the elements of crimes against humanity?

5 What is the complementarity principle?

6 Who are 'protected groups' and of what relevance are they to the crime of genocide?

7 Define 'war crimes' and explain what elements must be proved in the establishment of such crimes.

8 What is 'international criminal law'?

Discussion questions

1 With reference to decided cases, explain the requirement of grievous bodily harm in genocide cases.

2 To what extent can we distinguish between 'crime against humanity' and 'genocide'?

3 With reference to decided cases, discuss the jurisdiction of the ICTY and that of the ICTR.

4 Explain the relationship between the ICC and the UN Security Council.

5 Explain the principles *nullum crimen sine lege* and *nulla poena sine lege*, and the differences (if any) between the two.

Assessment question

Candoma and the Farara National Liberation Movement (FNLM), a rebel group based in the northern part of the country, which has prosecuted a guerrilla war against Candoma for twenty years, have signed a peace agreement. Under the agreement, all FNLM soldiers are to be granted amnesty for the crimes that they have committed against Candomans. Candoma is a signatory to the International Criminal Court. The ICC Prosecutor has investigated the crimes committed by FNLM members and decided to press ahead with their indictment. Candoma is concerned that such a step may lead to the rebel movement withdrawing from the agreement and renewing its campaign. Various pressure groups in Candoma have held public demonstrations, chanting 'We want peace!' and 'Down with criminal justice!'

As the Attorney General of Candoma, the President has asked you to draw up the pros and cons of Candoma sticking to the peace agreement and its amnesty, or complying with its ICC obligation to surrender the criminals. How will you advise him?

Key cases

- *Prosecutor v. Jean-Paul Akayesu (Judgment)* Case No. ICTR-96-4-T, Trial Chamber I, 2 September 1998
- *Prosecutor v. Tihomir Blaškić* Case No. IT-95-14-A, ICTY Appeals Chamber, 29 July 2004
- *Prosecutor v. Goran Jelsić ('Brcko')* Case No. IT-95-01-T, ICTY Trial Chamber, 14 December 1999
- *Prosecutor v. Jean Kambanda* Case No. ICTR-97-23-S, ICTR Trial Chamber I, 4 September 1998
- *Prosecutor v. Clément Kayishema and Obed Ruzindana* Case No. ICTR-95-I-T, ICTR Trial Chamber, 21 May 1999
- *Prosecutor v. Radislav Krštić* Case No. IT-98-33-A, ICTY Appeals Chamber, 19 April 2004
- *Prosecutor v. Georges Anderson Nderubumwe Rutaganda* Case No. ICTR-96-3, ICTR Trial Chamber I, 6 December 1999
- *Prosecutor v. Laurent Semanza* Case No. ICTR-97-20-T, ICTR Trial Chamber, 15 May 2003
- *Prosecutor v. Dusko Tadić* Case No. IT-94-1-AR72, ICTY Appeals Chamber, 2 October 1995

Further reading

Abass, A., 'The competence of the Security Council to terminate the jurisdiction of the International Criminal Court' (2005) 40 Texas Int'l LJ 263

Akande, D., 'International law immunities and the International Criminal Court' (2004) 98 AJIL 407

Akhavan, P., 'The International Criminal Tribunal for Rwanda: the politics and pragmatics of punishment' (1996) 90(3) AJIL 501

Bassiouni, M. C., 'Searching for peace and achieving justice: the need for accountability' (1996) 59 Law & Contemp Probs 9

Bassiouni, M. C., 'World War I: "the war to end all wars" and the birth of a handicapped international criminal justice system' (2001–02) 30 Denv J Int'l L & Pol'y 224

El Zeidy, M. M., 'The principle of complementarity: a new machinery to implement international criminal law' (2001–02) 23 Mich JIL 869

Robinson, D., 'Crimes against humanity' (1999) 93 AJIL 57

Schabas, W., 'International criminal tribunals: a review of 2007' (2007–08) 6 NW J Int'l HR 382

Stahn, C., 'Complementarity, amnesties and alternative forms of justice: some interpretative guidelines for the International Criminal Court' (2005) 3 J Int'l Crim Just 695

International environmental law

Learning objectives

This chapter will help you to:

- learn about the development of international environmental law;
- appreciate what principles govern international environmental law;
- understand the problems of compliance with and the enforcement of the international environmental legal regime; and
- anticipate the future of international environmental regulation.

Introduction

International environmental law is one of the more recent developments in international law. Unlike other areas of international law, the development of international environmental law has been painstakingly slow. Reasons for this include the complex nature of environmental regulation, and the problems associated with detecting environmental violations and impacts, as well as the question of what constitutes an appropriate remedy in a given situation. While a State is responsible for remedying breaches of international obligations (see Chapter 13), consequences of environmental breaches may not immediately be known—and may continue for generations to come—so that the question of what is an appropriate remedy becomes very difficult to tackle. Furthermore, international regulation of the environment has serious implications for the economic growth of States. In this chapter, we consider what international environmental law is, its development, and the various challenges confronting States vis-à-vis the development of an international environmental legal regime.

17.1 What is international environmental law?

'International environmental law' can be defined as the total sum of laws that govern the protection of the environment, broadly defined, and which aim at ensuring its preservation, both through conservation of its resources and the reduction of practices that are harmful to them.

Tseming Yang and Robert V. Percival, 'The emergence of global environmental law' (2009) 36 Ecology LQ 615, 616, define international environmental law as:

> a set of legal principles developed by national, international and transnational environment regulatory systems to protect the environment and manage natural resources. As a body of law, it is made up of a distinct set of substantive principles and procedural methods that are specifically important or unique to governance of the environment across the world.

According to Philippe Sands, *Principles of International Environmental Law* (2nd edn, Cambridge: Cambridge University Press, 2003), p. 15:

> International environmental law comprises those substantive, procedural and institutional rules of international law which have as their primary objective the protection of the environment.

From the above, it is clear that definitions of international environmental law often relate to specific aspects of the environment. It is impossible to find a single, all-encompassing definition of the environment or the laws that govern it. Nonetheless, it follows from these definitions that international environmental law includes not only *substantive* legal rules that govern the environment, but also the *procedural* methods adopted towards achieving the goals of environmental governance.

Most definitions of international environmental law include 'procedural methods' and what Philippe Sands (2003, see earlier in this section) called 'institutional rules'. Given that the quick pace of environmental occurrences and challenges is not always matched by the rather slow processes of international regulation, rules formulated by institutions are important mechanisms for coping with environmental exigencies.

As Paolo Contini and Peter H. Sand observe in 'Methods to expedite environment protection: international ecostandards' (1972) 66 AJIL 37, 38:

> Environmental problems characteristically require *expeditious and flexible* solutions, subject to current up-dating and amendments—*to meet rapidly changing situations and scientific-technological progress. In contrast, the classical procedures of multilateral treaty-making*, treaty acceptance and treaty amendment are notoriously slow and cumbersome. If international standards for environmental quality are to be set by diplomatic negotiations, the technical components of those standards may well be outdated by the time agreement is reached, and even more so by the time the agreement enters into force. [Emphasis added]

KEY POINTS

- It is impossible to ascribe a single, all-encompassing definition to international environmental law due to its extensive scope and the divergent nature of instruments that govern it.

- The international environmental legal regime includes substantive, procedural, and institutional rules, with the institutional rules making it possible for more expeditious regulation of the environment.

17.2 The development of international environmental law: a short history

As with the general field of international law, there was little or no serious attempt to develop international regulation of the environment during the classical period (see Chapter 1). The primacy of sovereignty during this time meant that whatever a State did within its territory was considered to be entirely its own province.

From the early nineteenth century, however, considerable advances in scientific knowledge began to make national regulation of the environment grossly inadequate. As we saw in Chapter 6 on the law of the sea, as States' exploratory capabilities increased, so did their ability to push their territorial seas beyond what was traditionally 'acceptable'. As already mentioned earlier, since the environment includes aquatic resources, there then began to emerge a need to balance the exploratory activities of one State against the conservation efforts of another.

Although most of the early international legal regimes of the environment had emerged in response to developments in the marine environment, it was in respect of an incident that occurred within Canada, with effects in the USA, that the international regulation of the environment commenced its development.

. . . .

● *United States v. Canada (Preliminary Decision)* (1938) 3 RIAA 1911 (The *Trail Smelter Case*)

Fumes from a privately owned smelting business in Canada caused damage to agricultural property in Washington in the USA. The question before an international tribunal was whether the Canadian trail smelter could be restrained from causing further damage and, if so, on what ground and to what extent.

The tribunal found that Canada was liable. In an important passage, it was said (at 65) that:

> Under the principles of international law, as well as of the law of the United States, no State has the right to use or permit the use of its territory in such a manner as to cause injury by fumes in or to the territory of another or the properties or persons therein, when the case is of serious consequence and the injury is established by clear and convincing evidence.

The *Trail Smelter Case* is of particular relevance to this chapter, because it summed up the international approach towards regulation of the environment in the first half of the twentieth century—that is, the prevention of environmental pollution, and the requirement of 'clear and convincing' evidence of injury caused by an action to warrant restriction.

While the *Trail Smelter Case* was pioneering, it had limited utility as a precedent for the development of international environmental regulation for two principal reasons. First, there was the need to prove that a culpable State had been negligent, which can prove difficult, especially since non-negligent or diligent use of one's environment may still cause serious harm or environmental damage to another.

Secondly, there was the requirement of 'clear and convincing evidence' of injury resulting to the other party before it could seek remedies against the culpable State. This requirement is particularly unsuitable for the purposes of protecting the environment.

In 'Technological challenge to the shared environment: United States practice' (1972) 66 AJIL 290, 294, Frederic L. Kirgis observes that:

> One may wonder whether a disinterested decision maker thirty years after *Trail Smelter*, in a world awakened to the existence of environmental deterioration, would find the 'clear and convincing' standard literally applicable when there are plausible consequences magnified far beyond those considered in that case. It would be consistent with the approach taken by the *Trail Smelter* tribunal to apply a reasonableness test, with potentially greater harm calling for abstention from conduct under a proportionately lesser showing that the harm will occur.

The second half of the twentieth century saw the evolution of several attempts to regulate certain aspects of the environment—especially the marine environment. The 1958 Geneva Convention on the High Seas, enjoins States, in Article 25(1), to 'take measures to prevent pollution of the seas from the dumping of radioactive waste', while the 1961 World Health Organization (WHO) Resolution WHA/14.56 required all members to prohibit all discharge of radioactive waste into watercourses or the sea, to the extent that the safety of such discharge has not been proved.

Similar efforts pursued at this time included the adoption of the 1954 International Convention for the Prevention of Pollution of the Sea by Oil. This convention was aimed at preventing environmental disasters, such as the Santa Barbara oil spill of 1969 in the USA. Although the huge oil spillage in Santa Barbara did not affect other countries, the international response to this disaster addressed the possibility of preventing such an occurrence.

In the 1970 United Nations General Assembly Declaration of Principles Governing the Seabed and the Ocean Floor, and the Subsoil thereof, beyond the Limits of National Jurisdiction, adopted under Resolution 2749, paragraph 11 states that:

> With respect to activities in the [seabed] area and acting in conformity with the international regime to be established, States shall take appropriate measures for and shall co-operate in the adoption and implementation of international rules, standards and procedures for, *inter alia*,: (a) The prevention of pollution and contamination, and other hazards to the marine environment, including the coastline, and of interference with the ecological balance of the marine environment; (b) The protection and conservation of the natural resources of the area and prevention of damage to the flora and fauna of the marine environment.

There was also some development in the area of space environment during the first half of the twentieth century. The USA's attempt to create a 'space mirror' through the implantation of 350 million tiny needles into orbit in 1963 provoked a series of international reactions leading to the adoption, in 1967, of the Treaty on Principles Governing the Activities of States in the Exploration and Use of Outer Space (the Outer Space Treaty), which prescribes certain standards for environmental conduct that is to be carried out in space.

Article IX of the Outer Space Treaty states that:

> In the exploration and use of outer space, including the Moon and other celestial bodies, States Parties to the Treaty shall be guided by the principle of co-operation and mutual assistance and shall conduct all their activities in outer space, including the Moon and other celestial bodies, with due regard to the corresponding interests of all other States Parties to the Treaty. States Parties to the Treaty shall pursue studies of outer space, including the Moon and other celestial bodies, and conduct exploration of them so as to avoid their harmful contamination and also adverse changes in the environment of the Earth resulting from the introduction of extraterrestrial matter and, where necessary, shall adopt appropriate measures for this purpose. If a State Party to the Treaty has reason to believe that an activity or experiment planned by it or its nationals in outer space, including the Moon and other celestial bodies, would cause potentially harmful interference with activities of other States Parties in the peaceful exploration and use of outer space, including the Moon and other celestial bodies, it shall undertake appropriate international consultations before proceeding with any such activity or experiment.

Obviously, the various international efforts restated previously were, much like the *Trail Smelter Case*, geared towards preventing environmental pollution. What makes the Outer Space Treaty pivotal is its reference to the fact that State parties shall undertake 'international consultation' before embarking on any space exploration that might affect the rights of other States. As the then US Secretary of State Rogers noted, in 'US foreign policy in a technological age' (1971) 64 Department of State Bulletin 198, 200–201:

> ...perhaps it is time for the international community to begin moving toward a consensus that nations have a right to be consulted before actions are taken which could affect their

environment or the international environment at large. This implies, of course, that nations contemplating such actions would be expected to consult in advance other states which could be affected.

The other significance of this provision, as noted by Kirgis (1972, see earlier in this section), at 316, is that:

> it uses the language of rights and obligations; it applies not just to the environment of individual states, but to the environment at large; and it contemplates a duty to consult states which merely 'could' be affected. The very suggestion by a United States Secretary of State that the international community move toward consensus in requiring consultations, much of the burden of which would fall on the United States, constitutes a significant step in the direction of a new binding norm.

But, by and large, the efforts adopted during this early developmental period of environmental regulation were inchoate and limited. As noted by Philippe Roch and Franz Xaver Perrez, 'International environmental governance: The strive towards a comprehensive, coherent, effective and efficient international environmental regime' (2005) 16 Colo J Int'l Env L & Pol'y 1, 24:

> The first international environmental treaties and agreements were enacted in the middle of the nineteenth century as a response to the need to limit the exploitation and destruction of natural resources, yet these early treaties provided for ad hoc solutions that were limited in scope and approach. As pressures on the environment have increased and the necessity for cooperative responses has become more obvious, international agreements for the protection of the environment have multiplied.

The move towards building an international consensus on environmental issues, which commenced with the Outer Space Treaty, influenced the adoption of several treaties on various aspects of the environment. Some of the reasons accounting for the dramatic increase in environmental regulation in the second half of the twentieth century include the growth in public awareness of environmental issues and challenges, the emergence of early evidence of the monumental impact of environmental disasters, and the increasing determination by the international community to tackle the various environmental concerns confronting the world.

ozone layer
An atmospheric layer that contains relatively high concentrations of ozone and which absorbs 97–99 per cent of the Sun's high-frequency ultraviolet rays, which are damaging to life on Earth.

However, it was not until the second half of the twentieth century that a decisive moment in the international regulation of the environment commenced. The first major occurrence, at this time, was the significant shift in States' approach towards the environment. Whereas, at the early stages, attention had been focused on the need to conserve the environment, the 1970s and later years witnessed the emergence of a more proactive regime—especially in relation to the protection of the **ozone layer** and the use of economic instruments, rather than direct legislative control, to influence States' behaviour. The end-product of this rethinking led to a series of international conferences, beginning in 1972 with the all-important conference in Stockholm.

thinking points
- What role did the realization that a State's activities on its territory, outer space, or the seabed might affect the rights of other States play in the historical evolution of international environmental law?

- What factors contributed to the development of international environmental law at the turn of the nineteenth century?
- How would you describe the approach by States to environmental issues in the period from the nineteenth century to the first half of the twentieth century, and how is this different from the trend started by such instruments as the Outer Space Treaty?
- Of what relevance is the standard of requiring clear and convincing evidence of injury caused by environmental disaster or pollution as a condition for international regulation? (Please read the Trail Smelter Case before answering this question.)

Sources of international environmental law

As with most other public international law disciplines, international environmental law derives principally from the sources of international law listed under Article 38(1) of the Statute of the International Court of Justice (the ICJ Statute), as outlined in Chapter 2. Although those sources include treaties, conventions, writings of jurists, and the judgments of the ICJ, only treaties and customs are discussed here, since it is only in these two aspects that many of the issues specifically related to environmental law arise.

17.3.1 Treaties and conventions

As seen from the brief summary of the historical development of environmental law, treaties and conventions play a crucial role as a source of what have so far emerged as obligations of States regarding the environment. A clear example is the duty to consult other States in cases in which one State's activities may impair or otherwise affect the rights of other States. Another important example is the 1998 Convention on Access to Information, Public Participation in Decision-Making and Access to Justice in Environmental Matters, adopted in Aarhus, Denmark, and hence known as the 'Aarhus Convention'.

Similarly, as will be seen in the discussion of the various international conferences and conventions, such as the Stockholm and the Rio Conferences, declarations, which are lesser agreements to the extent that they are not usually binding, play a crucial role in gently steering States towards ultimately accepting binding obligations towards the environment.

That treaties are the most popular source of international environmental law is clearly indicated by the fact of the exponential rate at which environmental treaties are concluded.

In 'Customary (and not so customary) international environmental law' (1995–96) 3 Ind J Global Legal Stud 105, 106, Daniel Bodansky notes that:

> Recent years have witnessed a proliferation of international environmental agreements. For each new environmental problem, a new treaty is negotiated: depletion of the atmospheric ozone layer, transboundary movements of hazardous wastes, climate change, the loss of biological diversity, desertification, and so on . . . most scholars consider treaties to be the preeminent method of international environmental lawmaking.

Similarly, Yang and Percival (2009, see section 17.1), at 646, state that:

> Between 1970 and 2000 the number of international treaties addressing environmental concerns more than quadrupled from 52 to 215 ... Such environmental agreements have contributed to the global acceptance and spread of international environmental legal norms, and has entrenched environmental norms, some as aspirational, others as legally binding.

Therefore, it is probably true to assert that it is in the area of environmental regulations that the use of treaties and convention has been most prolific in the last forty years or so.

17.3.2 Customary international environmental law

The view is widely held among international lawyers that customs constitute a source of international environmental law, just like any other branch of international law, although it should be pointed out that they are of less importance to international environmental law.

According to Rüdiger Wolfrum, 'Purposes and principles of international environmental law' (1990) 33 GYBIL, 303, 309:

> There is an agreement in international law that, in general, transfrontier damage is prohibited. This prohibition has essentially been developed under customary international law.

Similarly, Patricia Birnie and Alan Boyle, *International Environmental Law and the Environment* (Oxford: Clarendon Press, 1992), p. 89, state that:

> It is beyond serious argument that states are required by international law to take adequate steps to control and regulate sources of serious global environmental pollution or transboundary harm within their territory or subject to their jurisdiction.

For example, Peter Sand, 'International environmental law after Rio' (1993) 4 EJIL 377, 382, asserts that Principle 21 of the 1972 Declaration of the United Nations Conference on the Human Environment (the Stockholm Declaration) is widely regarded as 'having become a rule of customary international law'. Some writers even go as far as to argue that such customary international environmental law entitles animals to particular rights.

In 'Whales: their emerging right to life' (1991) 85 AJIL 21, 25, Anthony D'Amato and Sudhir K. Chopra, arguing vociferously for the right to life in favour of whales, contend that:

> Anyone who has watched a mammal in intense pain—a dog, a cat, a rabbit, a horse—knows that the animal is suffering and, moreover, that it is aware of its own suffering. When we consider whales, whose intelligence may be superior to our own, it is nearly impossible to avoid concluding that these majestic creatures are capable of a degree of suffering that we may not be able to fathom.

Similarly, in 'Has international law failed the elephant?' (1990) 84 AJIL 1, Michael J. Glennon lamented that:

> Although customary international law now requires states to protect endangered species, the norm has received virtually no attention, perhaps because of its acknowledged indeterminacy in application.

While customs constitute a source of international environmental law, their status as such, unlike treaties and conventions, is less assured. Despite opinions to the effect that there is customary international environmental law, as stated previously, there exists considerable doubt about customs as a source of international environmental law.

Those who oppose the view that there is customary international environmental law argue that there is a disconnect between what States say and what they in fact do. And since customary law can be established only by *opinio juris* and State practice, the fact that most States do the exact opposite of what is asserted to be customary international environmental law nullifies the proposition.

According to one of the arch opponents of customary international environmental law, Bodansky (1995–96, see section 17.3.1), at 115:

> In the environmental realm, however, verbal claims and physical behaviour diverge. States acknowledge a duty to prevent significant transboundary harm, but continue to cause such harm; they accept resolutions recommending assessment and notification, but seldom act accordingly . . .

Oscar Schachter has also cast serious doubt on the way in which customs are readily inferred in matters of environmental law. In 'The emergence of international environmental law' (1991) 44(2) J Int'l Aff 457, 463, he argues:

> To say that a state has no right to injure the environment of another seems quixotic in the face of the great variety of transborder environmental harms that occur every day. Many result from ordinary economic and social activity; others occur by accident, often unrelated to fault. No one expects that all these injurious activities can be eliminated by general legal fiat, but there is little doubt that international legal restraints can be an important part of the response.

Also, after considering the bases on which Principle 21 and other cogent principles of international environmental law developed after the Stockholm Conference (see section 17.4.1) are described as having become customary rules, Schachter (1991, above) notes, at 462, that:

> . . . to assert categorically that the principles have become customary law would require evidence of general state practice and [sic] opinio jurist Such evidence is only fragmentary. Principle 21 of the Stockholm declaration is, at best, a starting point. On its own terms, it has not become state practice: States generally do not 'ensure that the activities within their jurisdiction do not cause damage' to the environments of others. Nor have governments given any significant indication that they regard this far-reaching principle as binding customary law. Environmental treaties, though numerous, are limited in scope and in participation. On the whole, they are not accepted as expressions of customary law and are regarded as binding for the parties alone.

In his chapter 'The identification of international law' in Bin Cheng (ed.), *International Law: Teaching and Practice* (London: Stevens & Sons, 1982), p. 3, Sir Robert Jennings was both more scathing and forceful in his objection, at p. 5:

> Most of what we perversely persist in calling customary international law is not only *not* customary law; it does not even faintly resemble a customary law.

In 'What is international law and how do we know it when we see it?' (1981) 37 L'Annuaire Suisse de Droit International 59, 67, Sir Robert Jennings had surmised that:

> Perhaps it is time to face squarely the fact that the orthodox tests of custom—practice and *opinio juris*—are often not only inadequate but even irrelevant for the identification of much new law today.

Sir Robert Jennings's objections relate more to customary international law in general than they do to international environmental law. Nonetheless, they certainly reinforce the views expressed by both Bodansky and Schachter about the utility of customs as a source of international environmental law.

It should be noted, however, that those who oppose the view that there is customary international environmental law do not argue against that *possibility* in fact; rather, their objection is that there is a failure of the twin tests of ascertaining customs—*opinio juris* and State practice—in relation to norms that are claimed to have evolved into customary international environmental law.

One question that arises from this debate is whether there is any particular benefit to derive from an ascertainment of the legal status of environmental norms and principles. An attempt to determine definitively that legal status is fraught with many problems.

As Lluis Paradell-Trius, 'Principles of international environmental law: an overview' (2000) 9(2) RECIEL 93, 94, notes:

> It is difficult to give a general definition of the legal status of the principle of international environmental law. In addition, the precise legal status of specific principles is also the object of considerable uncertainty and disagreement. This uncertainty is mostly due to the fact that principles may be drawn from any source of international law, and in particular from soft law documents, the most traditional source of principles.

One major hindrance is the uncertainty of the legal effect of environmental norms and principles. Whereas environmental norms and principles are mostly viewed as 'soft law', meaning that they have no formal legal validity, many scholars do believe that such norms and principles are, in fact, not devoid of legal implications.

As noted by Alan Boyle in 'Some reflections on the relationship of treaties and soft law' (1999) 48 ICLQ 901, 902:

> While the legal effect of these different soft law instruments is not necessarily the same, it is characteristic of all of them that they are carefully negotiated, and often carefully drafted statements, which are in some cases intended to have some normative significance despite their non-binding non-treaty form.

When considering the legal significance of environmental principles, one crucial factor to bear in mind is the intention of the parties who adopt the principles.

● ***New Zealand v. France (Judgment)*** (1974) ICJ Rep 457 (The ***Nuclear Tests Case***)

The ICJ reflected this sentiment when, in an important passage, it stated (at [46]) that:

> It is well recognized that declarations made by way of unilateral acts, concerning legal or factual situations, may have the effect of creating legal obligations. Declarations of this kind may be, and often are, very specific. When it is the intention of the State making the declaration that it should become bound according to its terms, that intention confers on the declaration the character of a legal undertaking, the State being thenceforth legally required to follow a course of conduct consistent with the declaration. An undertaking of this kind, if given publicly, and with an intent to be bound, even though not made within the context of international negotiations, is binding. In these circumstances, nothing in the nature of a quid pro quo, nor any subsequent acceptance of the declaration, nor even any reply or reaction from other States, is required for the declaration to take

effect, since such a requirement would be inconsistent with the strictly unilateral nature of the juridical act by which the pronouncement by the State was made.

In addition, environmental principles, even if they are soft law, are of considerable utility in the process of treaty implementation.

Boyle states (1999, see earlier in this section), at 902, that:

> Given their explicit role as guidance and their explicitly softer formulation, the 'principles' in Article 3 [UN Climate Change Convention] are not necessarily binding rules which must be complied with or which entail responsibility for breach if not complied with; yet, despite all these limitations *they are not legally irrelevant*. At the very least Article 3 is relevant to interpretation and implementation of the Convention as well as creating expectations concerning matters which must be taken into account in good faith in the negotiation of further instruments. [Emphasis added]

The ICJ has upheld that principles can be used for aiding interpretation of treaties and obligations owed.

● *Hungary v. Slovakia* (1997) ICJ REP 7 (The *Gabčíkovo-Nagymaros Project Case*)

Speaking in relation to a treaty between Hungary and Slovakia that was the subject of dispute before the Court, the ICJ said (at [112]) that:

> On the other hand, the Court wishes to point out that newly developed norms of environmental law are relevant for the implementation of the Treaty and that the parties could, by agreement, incorporate them through the application of Articles 15, 19 and 20 of the Treaty. These articles do not contain specific obligations of performance but require the parties, in carrying out their obligations to ensure that the quality of water in the Danube is not impaired and that nature is protected, to take new environmental norms into consideration when agreeing upon the means to be specified in the Joint Contractual Plan.

The Court added (at [140]) that:

> new norms and standards have been developed, set forth in a great number of instruments during the last two decades. Such new norms have to be taken into consideration, and such new standards given proper weight.

It is far more important to understand the usefulness of environmental norms and principles than to seek a precise determination of their legal status in international law. As Bodansky observes (1995–96, see section 17.3.1), at 119:

> Whether the duty to prevent transboundary pollution or the precautionary principle are part of customary international law, they will set the terms of international discussions and serve as the framework for negotiations. If so, the current debates over the legal versus non-legal status of these norms are of little consequence...Rather than continue them, our time and efforts would be better spent attempting to translate the general norms of international environmental relations into concrete treaties and actions.

thinking points

- List the sources of international environmental law.
- Of what importance are treaties as a source of international environmental law?
- Summarize the arguments against the view that there is customary international environmental law. (Please read the entire articles of Schachter, Bodansky, and Sir Robert Jennings before answering this question.)

Having dealt with the sources of international environmental law, it is now necessary to consider the specific efforts of the international community to establish a strong, coherent, and robust regime of international environmental law.

17.4 Major international efforts towards international regulation of the environment

From the early 1970s, international efforts towards regulating the use of the environment grew phenomenally. In particular, the period from 1972 to 2009 witnessed unprecedented efforts by the international community to address increasing challenges to the environment. This momentum was due partly to the emergence, in this period, of scientific evidence to the effect that there were more urgent and compelling threats to the environment other than traditional environmental problems, such as pollution and the transboundary movement of hazardous waste. Evidence emerged that certain chemical agents produced by industrial activities—that is, chlorofluorocarbons (CFCs)—were causing serious damage to the ozone layer. There was also increased awareness about the shrinking of the populations of certain species, both on land and at sea. All of this evidence called for both conservationist and drastic efforts by the international community, to which the latter began to respond in 1972 with the first truly global conference on the environment. Although there are countless international efforts worth discussing, this section focuses only on the major ones.

17.4.1 The 1972 Stockholm Declaration on the Human Environment

In June 1972, the United Nations convened an international conference in Stockholm, Sweden, with representatives of 113 countries in attendance. The Stockholm Conference, the first major international conference to consider the relationship between the environment and development, adopted three crucial instruments: the Action Plan for the Human Environment, with 109 recommendations; the Stockholm Declaration; and a Recommendation on Institutional and Financial Arrangements. These instruments are non-binding and are generally referred to as 'soft law'. Nonetheless, as Roch and Perrez (2005, see section 17.2) note, at 7, 'the Stockholm Conference succeeded in putting the environment at the top of the global agenda'.

Of the three documents, the Stockholm Declaration was regarded as the most important. It embodies twenty-six Principles, which together have considerably influenced international environmental law. As Sands (2003, see section 17.1) has observed, at p. 36:

> the Conference was generally considered to have been successful, largely because the preparatory process had allowed agreement to be reached on most issues prior to the Conference.

It must be pointed out that, prior to the Stockholm Conference, there was no international organization specifically responsible for regulating the environment. The Recommendation on Institutional and Financial Arrangement proposed, among other things, the establishment of an intergovernmental governing council for environmental programmes, an environmental secretariat, and an environment fund, as well as an inter-agency environmental coordinating body. Consequently, the UN General Assembly adopted Resolution 2997 (XXVII) of 1972, which established the United Nations Environmental Programme (UNEP) with its headquarters in Nairobi, Kenya.

The Principles that are contained in the Stockholm Declaration reflect the compromise between those advocating for strict rules and procedures, on the one hand, and those who wished to use the conference merely to increase awareness of environmental issues, on the other.

Generally, the Principles that are considered of importance from a legal stance are Principle 21 (sovereign right to exploit a State's own resources without damaging other States' environments), Principle 22 (development of liability and compensation for victims), Principle 23 (considering a system of values in determining standards that may be different between advanced and developing countries), and Principle 24 (cooperation through multilateral and bilateral agreements). The rest of the Principles contained in the Stockholm Declaration use non-legal language, casting doubt over the possibility of legal enforcement.

Principle 21 has become one of the most important principles used in international environmental law. It states that:

> States have, in accordance with the Charter of the United Nations and the principles of international law, the sovereign right to exploit their own resources pursuant to their own environmental policies, and the responsibility to ensure that activities within their jurisdiction or control do not cause damage to the environment of other States or of areas beyond the limits of national jurisdiction.

Principle 21 incorporates international environmental norms, such as the principle laid down in the *Trail Smelter Case*, into the UN system by linking such norms to the Charter on the United Nations (the UN Charter), a move that was calculated to encourage many States to subscribe to those norms.

Principle 21 and its relevance to international environmental law

Principle 21 is often considered to be the foundation of international environmental law. Oscar Schachter noted (1991, see section 17.3.2), at 459–460, that:

> Principle 21, in a characteristic U.N. formulation asserted the competing principles of international responsibility and national authority within a general framework of international rights and obligations. The governments recognized, of course, that a specific body of law would

have to be developed to give effect to Principle 21. The declaration itself included Principle 22, which called on states 'to develop further the international law regarding liability and compensation for the victims of pollution and other environmental damage caused by activities within the jurisdiction or control of such states to areas beyond their jurisdiction ...

These principles are often cited as the starting point of international environmental law ...

Nonetheless, Schachter casts serious doubt on the pre-eminent status of Principle 21 as a foundation of international environmental law. According to him (ibid):

Though the term only came into wide usage after the Stockholm conference, international law took cognizance of transborder environmental injury in some cases long before the Stockholm declaration. Shared rivers and other watercourses gave rise to problems of pollution and inequitable use that were considered in an international legal framework. Oil spills on the High Seas, excessive fishing, transfrontier fumes and the transport of dangerous substances required legal answers before international environmental law was recognized as such ... The maxim *sic utere tuo ut alienum non laedas* (literally, use your own so as not to injure another), a principle also expressed in the concept of abuse of rights, provided a basis for restricting the use of territory in ways harmful to other states.

While the position of Principle 21 as the originator of international environmental law remains contentious, there is no doubt that the Stockholm Conference, which gave birth to that principle, significantly contributed to the development of international environmental law as a whole.

Furthermore, it appears that the huge momentum created by the Stockholm Conference was not matched with commensurate follow-up measures in the following years. As noted by Gill Seyfang, 'Environmental mega-conferences: from Stockholm to Johannesburg and beyond' (2003) 13 Global Environmental Change 223, 224:

the United Nations Conference on the Human Environment (UNCHE), was held in Stockholm in 1972. For the first time it brought together world leaders and scientists to discuss growing international environmental concerns such as trans-boundary air and water pollution. Although there was widespread support for the pledges and principles agreed at the meeting ... there has been little in the way of follow-up ...

On the whole, it can be said that the Stockholm Conference was a very important pacesetter in the international community's effort at establishing a decisive and strong regime of environmental regulation. However, as seen earlier, the principles agreed on by the Conference soon proved inadequate and insufficiently comprehensive to deal with the more fundamental challenges to the environment that lay beyond mere conservation efforts and which called instead for more proactive measures dealing with the environment.

KEY POINTS

- The Stockholm Conference was the first major international conference on environmental law, and it succeeded in focusing on how to prevent pollution and how to make States behave more responsibly towards the environment.

- There was evidence in the 1970s that, in addition to traditional environmental challenges such as pollution, significant damage was being done to the ozone layer by the use of chemicals like CFCs, therefore making more cogent the need to tackle environmental problems robustly.

- There was no international agency responsible for the regulation of the environment until after the Stockholm Conference, which led to the establishment of UNEP.

- Principle 21 of the Stockholm Declaration is considered to be the most fundamental outcome of the conference and is also thought of as an expression of an existing norm.

17.4.2 The 1992 Rio Declaration on Environment and Development

In 1992, the United Nations held its second major environmental conference—the Conference on Environment and Development (UNCED), also known as the 'Earth Summit', in Rio de Janeiro, Brazil. The Rio Conference adopted the Declaration on Environment and Development (the Rio Declaration), which brought 'developmental' issues and 'management' into global environmental discourse and approaches. Up until this conference, there had been little or no discussion about linking 'environment' and 'development', because both ideas were pursued independently. But, as Gill Seyfang notes (2003, see section 17.4.1), at 224:

> This meeting [Earth Summit in Rio] redefined the issues identified at Stockholm into the new language of sustainable development in the Rio Declaration, and took on a far broader agenda, covering social as well as environmental issues.

Similarly, Peter Sand (1993, see section 17.3.2) observed, at 378, that:

> What is worth noting at the outset, however, is a major paradigm shift at Rio, from international 'environmental law' to a new (and yet to be defined) 'law of sustainable development'... It may be seen as another incremental step in the evolution of international sources of law in the rapidly growing field.

The Rio Conference produced two sets of instruments. On the one hand are instruments that were negotiated by intergovernmental committees and presented for signature at Rio. Examples include the UN Framework Convention on Climate Change (the Climate Change Convention) and the Convention on Biological Diversity (the Biodiversity Convention). These instruments are classified as 'hard' law, because they were the product of bilateral or multilateral negotiation and were formally signed up to by governments. On the other hand are soft law instruments, such as the Rio Declaration on Environment and Development, consisting of twenty-one Principles, which were merely adopted by the conference and later approved by the UN General Assembly as unenforceable, declaratory principles.

The Rio Declaration is a remarkable improvement on its predecessor in many respects. In particular, Principle 2 of the Rio Declaration modified Principle 21 of the Stockholm Declaration by including in its focus 'developmental policies', in addition to the environmental policies contained in the Stockholm Declaration.

Principle 2 of the Rio Declaration states that:

States have, in accordance with the Charter of the United Nations and the principles of international law, the sovereign right to exploit their own resources pursuant to their own environmental and *developmental policies*, and the responsibility to ensure that activities within their jurisdiction or control do not cause damage to the environment of other States or of areas beyond the limits of national jurisdiction. [Emphasis added]

Under the Rio regime, the environment is considered to be of common concern to all States to ensure life and national interests.

According to Mukul Sanwal, 'Sustainable development, the Rio Declaration and multilateral cooperation' (1993) 4 Colo J Int'l Env L & Pol'y 45:

> The significance of Rio, in providing a base for multilateral cooperation, is the universal recognition that environmental quality as an essential life support system is a common concern that is not more important *than* national interests, but that is an important factor *to* national interests.
> [Emphasis original]

Aside from the inclusion of developmental issues, another remarkable contribution of the Rio Conference is its striking of a balance between the substantive requirements of development and the procedural requirements for implementing environmental protection. This balance is reflected in Principles 3 and 4 of the Rio Declaration, which state that:

3. The right to development must be filled so as to equitably meet developmental and environmental needs of present and future generations.

4. In order to achieve sustainable development, environmental protection shall constitute an integral part of the development process and cannot be considered in isolation from it.

. . . .

● *Hungary v. Slovakia* (1997) ICJ REP 7 (The *Gabčíkovo-Nagymaros Project Case*)

The Court alluded to the principle of sustainable development enunciated in Principles 3 and 4 of the Rio Conference in this case between Hungary and Slovakia. At [140] of its judgment, the ICJ stated that:

> Throughout the ages, mankind has, for economic and other reasons, constantly interfered with nature. In the past, this was often done without consideration of the effects upon the environment. Owing to new scientific insights and to a growing awareness of the risks for mankind for present and future generations—of pursuit of such interventions at an unconsidered and unabated pace, new norms and standards have been developed, set forth in a great number of instruments during the last two decades. *Such new norms have to be taken into consideration, and such new standards given proper weight, not only when States contemplate new activities but also when continuing with activities begun in the past. This need to reconcile economic development with protection of the environment is aptly expressed in the concept of sustainable development.* [Emphasis added]

KEY POINTS

- The Rio Conference was the first to introduce the theme of sustainable development into the discourse of international environmental law. By doing so, the Conference aimed to focus attention on ensuring an equitable use of environmental resources so that use by the present generation does not imperil or otherwise adversely affect future generations.

- The Rio Conference created two distinct sets of principles: those that created binding legal obligations; and those that were merely aspirational.

- Under the Rio regime, a balance is to be struck between environmental consideration and developmental consideration, with the former forming an integral part of the latter.

Some specific high points of the Rio Declaration

The introduction of substantial measures and innovative principles

More than its Stockholm counterpart, the Rio Declaration provides for substantial measures. It consists of several innovative principles that are envisaged eventually to lead to the creation of binding legal obligations for State parties. Moreover, it is also expected that these principles will contribute to the development not only of international environmental law but also to other related areas.

The inclusion of compensatory measures

As will be recalled from the previous discussion, one of the earliest environmental challenges was how to ensure that States would not use their environment in such a way as to affect the rights of others. This problem was manifested in the *Trail Smelter Case*.

Mukul Sanwal (1993, see earlier in this section) explains, at 50, thus:

> The Declaration also requires states to adopt certain procedures to ensure the environmental considerations are integrated into the decision-making process . . . For the first time in international environmental negotiations focusing on economic issues, elements of international cooperation for sustainable development are also laid out.

Compensation for transboundary pollution is now embodied by Principle 13 of the Rio Declaration, which provides that:

> States shall develop national law regarding liability and compensation for the victims of pollution and other environmental damage. States shall also cooperate in an expeditious and more determined manner to develop further international law regarding liability and compensation for adverse effects of environmental damage caused by activities within their jurisdiction or control to areas beyond their jurisdiction.

It should be pointed out that the scope of claims covered by Principle 13 of the Rio Declaration is much wider than those enunciated by the *Trail Smelter Case*, or which otherwise applied prior to Rio. Principle 13 not only covers injuries to persons and property, but it also covers environmental damage. Environmental damage may occur, for example, to the sea or the atmosphere, etc. which, obviously, are not owned by individuals in the affected society. It is generally believed that placing a price on pollution, as Principle 13 apparently does, will encourage States to pursue more effective preventive measures in their dealings with the environment.

Recognition of a special role for developed countries: the 'distinguished responsibility'

The Rio Declaration demonstrates the ability of developed and developing countries to reach agreement on the types of environmental goal towards which they should be working through cooperation. This was particularly manifest in the consensus found by these countries on crucial principles in the declaration, which are vital to environmental progress.

As Peter Sand has noted (1993, see section 17.3.2), at 381:

> As it stands, the Declaration represents a delicate balance of policy goals supported by developed and developing countries, reflected mainly in two sets of key principles without which the

compromise would have collapsed. They are, on the one hand, public participation, 'the precautionary approach' and the 'polluter pays' maxim (principles 10, 15 and 16) which are considered to be essential by the developed countries. On the other hand the developing countries insisted that the key principles include the 'right to development', poverty alleviation and the recognition of 'common but differentiated responsibilities' (principles 3, 5 and 7).

While we will consider the implications of these principles in detail later in this chapter, it suffices for now to underscore that Principle 7, concerning 'common but differentiated responsibilities', is of particular significance. It states that:

> States shall cooperate in a spirit of global partnership to conserve, protect and restore the health and integrity of the Earth's ecosystem. In view of the different contributions to the global environmental degradation, States have common but differentiated responsibilities. The developed countries acknowledge the responsibility that they bear in the international pursuit to sustainable development in view of the pressures their societies place on the global environment and of the technologies and financial resources they command.

This principle is vital for two reasons. First, it obligates States to cooperate in matters concerning the protection and restoration of the ecosystem. This is remarkably different from the hortatory pose of the Stockholm Declaration. Secondly, by virtue of this principle, developed countries acknowledge the special responsibility that they bear towards their developing counterparts concerning sustainable development. This is apparently due to the fact that the developed countries are said to contribute more to environmental degradation.

As a principle, 'differentiated responsibility' offers many benefits. These include an apparent equitable allocation of responsibility for environmental damage and the lessening of the financial burden of the developing countries, as well as discouraging the latter from adopting measures that might seriously harm the environment. Nonetheless, the principle is fraught with problems. While the problems of 'differentiated responsibilities' as an international environmental norm in general will be discussed fully later in this chapter, its specific application to the Rio Conference raises particular concerns.

To start with, it is not possible for differentiation *always* to be based on the classification of countries into developed and developing, with the presumption that the former will *always* be responsible for greater environmental degradation. Presently, certain developing countries, such as China and India, have shown as high a (if not a higher) propensity to impact on the environment through increased (and arguably unsustainable) use of environmental resources as have their developed counterparts. The differentiation formula adopted in Principle 7 of the Rio Declaration has also made future negotiations among States more difficult, as was the case with the Kyoto Conference (to be discussed in section 17.4.4). Peter Sand (1993, see section 17.3.2) underscores this point when he notes, at 388, that:

> the Rio Conference may have succeeded in averting—or at least postponing—a North-South showdown, the head-on confrontation between developed and developing countries which many had predicted. What it could not avoid or defer was a trend towards a further polarization, manifested not only in the constant balancing (based on parity or alternation) of 'Northern' and 'Southern' positions, on everything from meeting venues and committee chairmen to agenda priorities, but also in a distinct new bipolar pattern of negotiating and decision-making procedures.

Despite the laudable contributions of the Rio Conference, it must be noted that the Rio Declaration does not impose legal obligations on States as such, even if it consists of some robust measures in contrast to the Stockholm Declaration. On the contrary, it can be said that the Rio Conference actually increased the politicization of environmental issues. As noted by Sanwal (1993, see earlier in this section), at 67:

> The emphasis in framing issues on sustainable development has shifted from legal notions of 'common heritage' to political 'common concerns'.

What the Rio Conference was able to achieve at the very least, which is demonstrated by the principles of the Rio Declaration, is that the world can no longer plead ignorance and use development as an excuse to avoid responsibility for environmental damage. This sentiment was aptly captured by Indonesia's Minister of Population and Environment, who claimed that the Rio Conference was 'a loss of innocence' since no government can henceforth plead ignorance to the challenges that we face as a planet (cited by Sand, 1993, at 377, see section 17.3.2).

In conclusion, the Stockholm and Rio Declarations were important developments in international environmental law. They provide principles that governments have agreed to adopt and are part of the soft law in this field. This makes it easier for binding laws to be developed—or at least more likely that they will be developed—within international environmental law. This development cannot be ignored, because it has helped to shape the direction taken by international environmental law.

KEY POINTS

- The Rio Conference introduced several innovative principles, such as 'differentiated responsibility' and 'compensation', and adopted concrete measures towards dealing with environmental challenges. While these measures are not legally binding, they are important first steps.

- The compensation regime embraced by the Rio Declaration is much wider than that laid down in *Trail Smelter*, in that the former applies also to environmental damage.

- Although useful in many respects, 'differentiated responsibility' is fraught with many dangers that might prove to be its greatest undoing in future negotiations.

17.4.3 The 1992 United Nations Framework Convention on Climate Change (UNFCCC)

The UN Framework Convention on Climate Change (UNFCCC, or FCCC) was adopted during the Rio Conference in 1992. Article 2 of the Convention, which entered into force on 21 March 1994, outlines its aims as:

> to achieve in accordance with the relevant provisions of the Convention, stabilization of greenhouse gas concentrations in the atmosphere at a level that would prevent dangerous anthropogenic interference with the climate system ...

The UNFCCC was the first international treaty to deal specifically with greenhouse gases in an attempt to stabilize the levels in the atmosphere. It aims to tackle the menace of greenhouse gases through many measures, starting with imposing the obligation on State parties to, according to Article 4(1)(a):

> develop, periodically update, publish and make available to the Conference of the Parties, in accordance with Article 12, national inventories of anthropogenic emissions by sources and removals by sinks of all greenhouse gases not controlled by the Montreal Protocol, using comparable methodologies to be agreed upon by the Conference of the Parties.

Under Article 4(2)(a), the Convention obligates Annex I State parties—developed States and States from the former Soviet Union that were, at the relevant time, undergoing market economy reforms—to:

> adopt national policies and take corresponding measures on the mitigation of climate change, by limiting its anthropogenic emissions of greenhouse gases and protecting and enhancing its greenhouse gas sinks and reservoirs.

This provision reflects the principle of 'differentiated responsibility' which, like the Rio Declaration, the UNFCCC recognizes in Article 3(1), enjoining the parties to:

> protect the climate system for the benefit of present and future generations of humankind, on the basis of equity and in accordance with their common but differentiated responsibilities and respective capabilities. Accordingly, the developed country Parties should take the lead in combating climate change and the adverse effects thereof.

In 'The Kyoto Protocol to the United Nations Framework Convention on Climate Change' (1998) 92 AJIL 315, Clare Breidenich, Daniel Magraw, Anne Rowley, and James Rubin explain that:

> In general, the view of many of the developing countries, even before the negotiation of the FCCC, has been that it is the responsibility of the industrialized countries to adopt significant measures to reduce their GHG emissions before the developing countries might place their economic development at risk by adopting any similar measures.

The UNFCCC requires reporting and updates to the UN Conference of Parties, established under Article 7 of the Convention, regarding their emissions (Article 4(1)(a)). Additionally, under Article 4(1)(b), they are to:

> Formulate, implement, publish and regularly update national and, where appropriate, regional programmes containing measures to mitigate climate change by addressing anthropogenic emissions.

The UNFCCC also established a secretariat to oversee the implementation and working of the UNFCCC. The secretariat, which is based in Bonn, has the same name as the UNFCCC, and the Convention established the mandate of the secretariat.

The shortcomings of the UNFCCC

Despite the Convention establishing clear commitments and imposing obligations on State parties, the fact that it does not provide for enforcement mechanisms greatly undermines its efficacy. What the UNFCCC does call for, by way of implementing its provisions, is for the Conference of Parties to adopt protocols, pursuant to Article 17, to address the issue of anthropogenic emissions. These protocols will be applicable only to those States already party to the Convention (Article 17(4)).

The most well-known—and, indeed, the only—protocol that the UNFCCC Conference of Parties has adopted is the Kyoto Protocol, which was due to end in 2012 (see section 17.4.4).

It should be pointed out that the Rio Declaration and the UNFCCC were adopted during the same period, and were both results of the same UN Conference. These instruments clearly focus on developing countries, but in different ways. Sanwal (1993, see section 17.4.2) notes, at 55, that while the:

> Rio Declaration recognizes the 'right to development' while the Framework Convention on Climate Change acknowledges the right to sustainable development, and the 'specific needs and special circumstances' of developing countries.

thinking points

- What are the main contributions of the UNFCCC to the discussion on international environmental law?
- To what extent does the principle of differentiated responsibilities contained in the UNFCCC differ from that enunciated in the Rio Declaration, and of what relevance is this difference, if any?
- What is the single most significant weakness of the UNFCCC?

17.4.4 The 1997 Kyoto Protocol

Adopted on 11 December 1997 in Kyoto, Japan, pursuant to Article 17 of the UNFCCC, the Kyoto Protocol entered into force on 16 February 2005 and currently has 191 member States, thus making it one of the most widely ratified treaties. The Protocol was aimed at combating global warming—an increase in the average temperature of the earth's atmosphere, which itself is a consequence of the relentless release of greenhouses gases (GHGs) into the atmosphere. The Kyoto Protocol is unarguably one of the most highly developed mechanisms in international environmental law in terms of its objectives and its legal attributes. Parties are free to withdraw from the Protocol pursuant to Article 27, although this cannot be earlier than three years after the Protocol enters into force and can only be by written notification. Even then, the withdrawal is effective only one year after the written request. Additionally, where a State withdraws from the UNFCCC, it is also considered to have withdrawn from the Kyoto Protocol. It does seem that the procedural hurdles placed in the way of a party intending to withdraw from the Kyoto Protocol highlight the seriousness attached to the Protocol, because they serve to discourage parties from actually taking such steps.

Breidenich et al. (1998, see section 17.4.3) aptly summarize the tight structure of the Kyoto Protocol, at 319, thus:

> The fundamental architecture of the Kyoto Protocol is marked by several defining features. It provides legally binding emissions targets for Annex I countries, based on a five-year budget period. It makes allowance for flexibility with respect to the parties' national implementation of their commitments. It also allows for flexibility in the international context by providing for

the use of emissions trading and other market-based mechanisms, including a mechanism for cooperative projects between developed and developing countries. In addition, it takes a comprehensive approach by covering both GHG emissions and sequestration by sinks, and by including not only CO_2, methane and N_2O, but also the three synthetic GHGs.

The scheme of the Kyoto Protocol is that it commits the thirty-seven Annex I countries (see earlier) to take measures to reduce specific GHGs, adopting the 1990 emission level as benchmarks—that is, as the acceptable emission targets. They agree to reduce GHG emissions by 5 per cent from the 1990 level, although international aviation and shipping emissions are excluded from this target.

In practical terms, the Kyoto Protocol embodies five crucial strategies towards achieving its aims:

(a) it sets out clear targets for emissions (Article 3);

(b) it stipulates measures to be taken towards implementing the various commitments of State parties (Articles 2, 5, 6, and 7);

(c) it provides funds for developing countries to enable them to adapt to climate change (Article 11(2)(a));

(d) it establishes accountability, reporting, and review mechanisms for the Protocol (Articles 8, 9, 10, and 17); and

(e) it establishes a compliance regime (Article 18).

KEY POINTS

- The Kyoto Protocol was the first major international instrument to establish a binding regime of environmental regulation and it was adopted pursuant to the UNFCCC.

- The Kyoto Protocol specifically aims to combat global warming by regulating GHG emissions.

- The Kyoto Protocol is one of the most widely ratified treaties and can be regarded as the pioneer of a decisive international environmental law regime.

The high points of Kyoto

The Kyoto Protocol made several noble contributions—more than could be justifiably dealt with in this chapter—to the development of a strong and coherent regulation of the environment, especially with reference to global warming. Among these, a few stand out for particular attention for their innovation and for ushering in strict legal obligations.

A legally binding emission target

Unlike any efforts before it, the Kyoto Protocol established clear, legally binding emission targets for Annex I States. This singular achievement places the Protocol above any other international environmental law regime.

As stated in Article 3(1):

> The Parties included in Annex I shall, individually or jointly, ensure that their aggregate anthropogenic carbon dioxide equivalent emissions of the greenhouse gases listed in Annex A do not exceed their assigned amounts, calculated pursuant to their quantified emission limitation and reduction commitments inscribed in Annex B and in accordance with the provisions of this Article, with a view to reducing their overall emissions of such gases by at least 5 per cent below 1990 levels in the commitment period 2008 to 2012.

As noted by Breidenich et al. (1998, see section 17.4.3), at 327:

> The FCCC established an aspirational commitment ... [I]n contrast, the Kyoto Protocol establishes a clear, mandatory set of targets ... [as demonstrated by Article 3(1) in which] the obligation is clear and precise, objective assessment of compliance with targets is greatly facilitated and there is a legal consequence for exceeding the targets-noncompliance with the Protocol.

It should be emphasized that the period within which the Annex I States had to implement this obligation was 2008–12. In other words, the obligation does not exist ad infinitum.

The compliance regime

The Kyoto Protocol was the first international environmental legal regime to address comprehensively the issue of non-compliance. Non-compliance is often a serious problem of international law, especially with multilateral agreements. The problem is addressed by a rather awkward method: usually, when a State breaches an international obligation, non-breaching parties are entitled to suspend performance of their obligations vis-à-vis the breaching State. However, it is difficult to apply this method to environmental issues. This is because if, for example, all State parties to the Kyoto Protocol were to decide to suspend their emissions reduction obligation towards a State that was in breach, such steps could actually worsen the emissions level, since it would mean, in fact, that all other States would be free to breach their emissions level, just like the breaching State.

The Kyoto Protocol does not specifically establish a compliance regime; rather, it provides, in Article 18, that:

> the Conference of the Parties (COP) serving as the meeting of the Parties to this Protocol shall, at its first session, *approve appropriate and effective procedures and mechanisms to determine and to address cases of non-compliance with the provisions of this Protocol*, including through the development of an indicative list of consequences, taking into account the cause, type, degree and frequency of non-compliance. Any procedures and mechanisms under this Article entailing binding consequences shall be adopted by means of an amendment to this Protocol. [Emphasis added]

In 2001, at Marrakesh, the Conference of the Parties on the UNFCCC (COP 7) adopted detailed rules for the implementation of the Protocol, which are referred to as the 'Marrakesh Accords'. These 'Accords' were approved by the first session of the Conference of the Parties, serving as the meeting of the parties to the Kyoto Protocol (usually known as COP/MOP or simply COP11), as required by Article 18 of the Protocol (see Decision-/CMP.1, Annex; FCCC/CP/2005/1).

It must be emphasized that the non-compliance processes can be adopted and considered binding on State parties only if adopted through amendment of the Kyoto Protocol pursuant to Article 18. According to Breidenich et al. (1998, see section 17.4.3), at 330, this was:

> a compromise between those parties that wanted binding, but unspecified consequences, on the one hand, and those that were not willing to commit themselves to binding, but unspecified consequences, on the other hand.

Describing how the non-compliance regime of Kyoto fits with the overall structure of the Protocol, Breidenich et al. (ibid.), at 327, note that:

> Overall, the compliance provisions are designed to work together to form a logical progression of steps, beginning with reporting and review requirements and potentially culminating in consequences for noncompliance.

An emission trading system

A unique provision of the Kyoto Protocol is its provision for an emissions trading system. Simply put, this is a system that allows a State party to increase its emissions target by buying emissions credits from other States.

example

Suppose Candoma and Rutamu—developed and developing countries, respectively—were signatories to the Kyoto Protocol and were obliged to reduce emissions by 5 per cent over five years. Suppose, too, that Candoma discovers that complying with the obligation will seriously hamper its economic development, whereas Rutamu, even if it were to be manufacturing every day for those five years, would never reach that level anyway. In those circumstances, Candoma may not want to injure its economy by complying with the obligation, but also it may not want to breach its international obligation by exceeding its emission target. So what does it do?

Under the Kyoto Protocol, it is possible for Candoma to buy some of the emission credits off Rutamu, which will then allow Candoma to exceed its own emissions target, but without breaching its obligations.

It has been noted that the emissions trading system may actually be more attractive to States. According to David G. Victor, *The Collapse of the Kyoto Protocol and the Struggle to Slow Global Warming* (Princeton, NJ: Princeton University Press, 2001), p. 4:

> a trading system could allow U.S. firms to purchase emission credits overseas, which might be much cheaper than making all the needed emission controls at home

The Kyoto Protocol thus lightens the burden of States in this manner, by providing them with a variety of emissions credits. As Victor observes (ibid.):

> The Kyoto Protocol envisions three interrelated trading systems. One, known formally as emission trading, would allow an industrialized country to increase its emission cap by purchasing part of another industrialized nation's Kyoto allocation. A second system, known as joint implementation (JI), would allow industrialized countries to earn credits when they jointly implement specific projects that reduce emissions. A third System, known as the Clean Development Mechanism (CDM), allows industrialized nations to earn credits for projects implemented within developing nations.

The possibility of flexible implementation, note Breidenich et al. (1998, see section 17.4.3), at 327, such as that provided for by the emission trading process:

> will enhance implementation and compliance because it allows each party to design its own approach in light of its unique environmental, economic, social and political situation.

Common, but differentiated, responsibility

The Kyoto Protocol targets, and its provisions, impose different obligations on developed countries from those imposed on developing countries. The principle of common, but differentiated, responsibilities is firmly entrenched in the Protocol.

The developed countries, which are those considered to be industrialized, have been given specific targets, whereas less stringent obligations have been set for developing countries.

Annex I States (developed countries) are obliged not to exceed the Kyoto Protocol assigned limits, whereas Non-Annex I States (developing countries) are to reduce their overall emissions, without having a strict obligation placed upon them. The Kyoto Protocol also makes it possible for regional organizations to sign up, and imposes obligations on these organizations and their member States.

Article 24(2) provides that:

> Any regional economic integration organization which becomes a Party to this Protocol without any of its member States being a Party shall be bound by all the obligations under this Protocol. In the case of such organizations, one or more of whose member States is a Party to this Protocol, the organization and its member States shall decide on their respective responsibilities for the performance of their obligations under this Protocol. In such cases, the organization and the member States shall not be entitled to exercise rights under this Protocol concurrently.

thinking points

- *The Kyoto Protocol introduced a variety of measures, such as emissions trading, a process for achieving an effective compliance regime, and an articulated differentiated responsibility. How relevant are these measures in light of the relations of States to such instruments as the UNFCCC?*
- *What is the principal rationale behind the emissions trading system, and how realistic is it to achieve the stated objective?*
- *Do you think the best way in which to achieve equity between States concerning their capacity to pollute the environment through GHG emissions is by means of the 'differentiated responsibility' principle?*

The problems with Kyoto

While the Kyoto Protocol was a major step for international environmental law, the period after it has not proved to be as fruitful as its proponents had hoped.

The differentiated responsibilities, although welcomed in the beginning, have proved to be a hindrance. There are calls being made for a re-evaluation of the Non-Annex I States to take into account the changing circumstances of certain major developing countries, such as India and China, which are contributing heavily to the levels of emission and the amount of environmental damage caused.

However, the mistrust felt amongst developing States towards the developed States makes discussions difficult and prevents any progress being made. As will be seen later, this was one of the major challenges faced at the 2009 Copenhagen Summit, which was aimed at enhancing the Kyoto Protocol.

In 'Addressing the "post-Kyoto" stress disorder: reflections on the emerging legal architecture of the climate regime' (2009) 58 ICLQ 803, 805, Lavanya Rajamani observes that one of the hindrances is the:

> lack of trust amongst some developing countries that industrialized countries will, given current and past form, honour their commitments, and/or take the lead in the new climate agreement. Anxiety (and wariness) that industrial countries will talk the talk of equity, but in effect seek to shift the burden of responsibility to developing countries in the 'agreed outcome' at Copenhagen, is now palpable in the negotiations.

Some scholars have also pointed to the attempt to undermine the Kyoto Protocol by some countries. Gill Seyfang (2003, see section 17.4.1) notes, at 227, that:

> The cynical undermining of the UN and the Kyoto Protocol by the USA, and the lack of coherence among other nations, simply serves to highlight the urgent need for a strong international institution for global sustainability governance.

Amendment to the Kyoto Protocol (2013–20)

As noted previously, the first commitment period of the Kyoto Protocol was set to expire in 2012. On 8 December 2012, parties to the Kyoto Protocol, meeting at Doha, Qatar, adopted the Doha Amendment to the Kyoto Protocol, in accordance with Articles 20 and 21 of the Kyoto Protocol. (See decision 1/CMP.8 of the eighth session of the Conference of the Parties serving as the meeting of the Parties to the Kyoto Protocol.) The amendment set out new commitments for the member States, which include:

- new commitments for Annex I parties to the Kyoto Protocol who agreed to take on commitments in a second commitment period from 1 January 2013 to 31 December 2020;
- a revised list of GHGs to be reported on by parties in the second commitment period; and
- amendments to several Articles of the Kyoto Protocol which specifically referenced issues pertaining to the first commitment period and which needed to be updated for the second commitment period. See https://unfccc.int/kyoto_protocol/items/2830.php

One important change brought by the amendment is that unlike during the first period in which thirty-seven industrialized countries and the European Community committed to reduce GHG emissions to an average of 5 per cent against 1990 levels, in the second period parties committed to reduce GHG emissions by at least 18 per cent below 1990 levels in the eight-year period from 2013 to 2020. It should be noted, however, that the composition of parties in the second commitment period is different from the first.

Moreover, the amended protocol has not yet entered into force and will not do so until the nineteenth day after which the UN Secretary-General receives depository that not less than 144 parties (or three-quarters of members) to the Kyoto Protocol have accepted the amendment.

17.4.5 The 2002 World Summit on Sustainable Development

In 2002, the United Nations convened a World Summit on Sustainable Development (WSSD, or the 'Earth Summit' as it is sometimes called) in Johannesburg, South Africa, principally to discuss sustainable development. The notion of 'sustainable development' refers to the use of natural resources in a manner that does not imperil their availability for future generations. Simply put, the Summit was all about ensuring that the world's natural resources are used in the most judicious and conscionable manner with the utmost consideration for future generations.

The Johannesburg Declaration on Sustainable Development

The Earth Summit adopted the Johannesburg Declaration on Sustainable Development on 4 September 2002. The Declaration consists of wide-ranging provisions touching on several vital issues of concern to all peoples of the world. In paragraph 2 of the Declaration, participants commit themselves 'to building a humane, equitable and caring global society, cognizant of the need for human dignity for all', while in paragraph 5, they:

> assume a collective responsibility to advance and strengthen the interdependent and mutually reinforcing pillars of sustainable development—economic development, social development and environmental protection—at the local, national, regional and global levels.

The Declaration also calls on developed nations to effectuate the realization of 'internationally agreed levels of official development assistance' to developing countries (paragraph 22), and advocates paying special attention to the situation of small islands, developing States, and least developed countries (paragraph 24), among others.

The problems with the Earth Summit

The Earth Summit was more famous for what it did *not* achieve than for the few gains that it made. To start with, the USA did not participate in the Summit, with then President George W. Bush deciding to stay away. The most notable US presence at the Summit was the brief appearance of then US Secretary of State Colin Powell, who was recorded as having hastily declared the Summit closed while his aircraft taxied at the airport. Without doubt, the non-participation of the USA—the world's largest polluter of the environment and consumer of such natural resources as oil—considerably undermined the chances of success of the Summit.

Furthermore, the fact that the conference was not open to advocacy groups and individuals, whose early efforts put conservation on the global agenda, drew the ire of many critics.

Despite these and many other flaws, the Earth Summit was nonetheless another commendable step in the global search for an effective regime of environmental regulation. Clearly, the whole essence of the Earth Summit was to bring to the fore the serious threats that unsustainable utilization of natural resources pose to humankind as a whole. In this regard, one can say that the Summit achieved a modest success. At the very least, efforts are being made at various levels of human society towards achieving sustainable development.

KEY POINTS

- The World Summit on Sustainable Development (the Earth Summit) mainly concerned conservation and the equitable use of natural resources.

- The USA did not participate in the Summit and this significantly undermined its chances of success.

17.4.6 The 2009 Copenhagen Accord

From 7 to 19 December 2009 at Copenhagen, Denmark, the United Nations convened yet another summit, which, according to Leonardo Massai, 'The long way to the Copenhagen Accord: climate change negotiation in 2009' (2010) 19(1) RECIEL 104, was meant to provide:

> legal certainty and political guidance to the future of international climate regime after 2012 in accordance with the Bali Roadmap set in 2007.

The Copenhagen Summit was preceded by several initial efforts, including at Montreal, Canada, where the first meeting following the entry into force of the Kyoto Protocol was held, with the aim of amending Annex B to the Kyoto Protocol and establishing new commitments by Annex I parties. Another effort, in Bali, Indonesia, the so-called Bali Action Plan (BAP) on how to strengthen the implementation of the UNFCCC regime was agreed upon. The Roadmap set up by the BAP was based on, and further developed by, several meetings at Accra, Bangkok, Bonn and Poznan, and Barcelona, with the grand finale in Copenhagen.

In terms of specifics, the main tasks before the Copenhagen Summit could be summed up by the need to achieve concrete agreements on three issues: developed country mitigation; developing country mitigation; and financial and technological support, including for adaptation—that is, to adjust to a more efficient system.

'Developed country mitigation' implies that the Summit must find a way in which to accommodate and allow developed countries, such as the USA, to remain engaged effectively with the climate process, by such States subscribing to new emissions control commitments, if possible. This is particularly important given that the USA had already repudiated the Kyoto Protocol in 2001.

'Developing country mitigation' has to do with ways in which to manage the dynamics of this group, especially with regard to which States should remain in the group and whether the group should take on new commitments. All of these were made more complicated by the fact that the developing countries, which had always previously negotiated as a bloc, decided to negotiate their commitments to the process on an individual basis.

As regards financial and technological support, it was pertinent that Copenhagen reached a consensus on how to finance whatever mitigation measures were agreed on by developing countries.

KEY POINTS

- The Copenhagen Summit was aimed at creating legal certainty and political guidance for future environmental regulation, following the many problems of the Kyoto Protocol.

- The Copenhagen Summit was mainly aimed at achieving greater participation in the environmental process by developed States, especially the USA, encouraging developing States to take more responsibility, while providing them with the necessary funds and technological support required for such efforts.

Setbacks at Copenhagen

The Copenhagen Summit was not able to live up to all of its expectations for numerous reasons. Even before the Summit had taken place, there were considerable doubts that substantive decisions would be made.

As foreseen by Joanna Depledge, 'Crafting the Copenhagen Consensus: some reflections' (2008) 17(2) RECIEL 154, 165:

> The Copenhagen 'meta-negotiation' will be difficult, but it need not be insurmountable. A key message in this regard is the need to be realistic, both procedurally and substantively. Procedurally, the Copenhagen consensus can only be a *political deal*. Implementation guidelines and detailed provisions will have to be considered later, as will certain ideas that have no prospect of being agreed in time. [Emphasis in original]

Indeed, the most notable achievement of Copenhagen was the adoption of the so-called Copenhagen Accord, which Massai (2010, see earlier in this section), at 115, calls a 'document attached to a decision expressly rejected by several parties', indicating that it did not reflect consensus amongst the States.

Under the Accord, States are given the option to report periodically on the mitigation measures that they take. One improvement is that where developing countries do provide reports, this will be the first time that national reports will be provided by them under an international system agreement. There is, however, no mention of non-compliance and oversight procedures.

On a more positive note, the Copenhagen Accord establishes new institutions: the High Level Panel on Financing, the Copenhagen Green Climate Fund (CGCF); and a technology mechanism. However, there is no elaboration on how these new institutions will interact with existing institutions.

Despite many of the shortcomings of the Copenhagen Accord, it is not all negative, and it is arguably a political success in terms of the publicity and commitments that were agreed. Yet this is not necessarily enough to negate all of the elements that are lacking. As stated by David Hunter, 'Implications of the Copenhagen Accord for Global Climate Governance' (2009–10) Sustainable Dev & Pol'y 4, 8:

> The pledges under the Copenhagen Accord have been met with mixed response. On the one hand, some value must be attached to getting so many countries to commit publicly to addressing climate change—and many of these commitments are specific and significant. Overall, however, the aggregation of commitments does not appear to get the world close to the levels necessary to limit temperature increases to the 2 degree Celsius goal identified in the Accord.

Many criticisms were levelled at the Copenhagen Accord. Most centre on the lack of clarity and uncertainty created by the system. According to Massai (2010, see earlier in this section), at 120:

> The end result of the Copenhagen Summit has suffered from the lack of clarity on the mandate of the solution identified by parties and by the COP Presidency at the final stage of negotiations when the decision on how to unblock the process was not completely transparent and therefore did not meet the expectations of some parties.

The original aim of the Copenhagen Summit in helping to clear up some of the uncertainty over the future of the Kyoto Protocol is glaringly missing, which is undoubtedly a major failure. For example, as Massai (2010, above) notes, at 121:

the continuation of the Kyoto Protocol is not mentioned by the Copenhagen Accord, which does not refer to any legally binding reduction commitment for Annex I parties in the second commitment period of the Protocol.

In fact, as far as Hunter is concerned (2009–10, see earlier in this section), at 13:

> The Accord was seen as a new path separate from, and potentially dominant over, the UNFCCC process. It also revealed the weakness of the UN process, in which under the current rules of decision even a handful of oil-dependent states, for example, can continue to disrupt the overall progress. To some observers the UN process is too unwieldy and too easily held hostage by a small number of states to allow for effective negotiations. On the other hand, the heavy-handed approach by just a few states in negotiating and announcing the Accord also arguably undermines progress toward reaching a broad global consensus for long-term cooperative action.

The Copenhagen Accord clearly illustrates the lack of political consensus during the negotiations. However, it is worthwhile noting that one principal reason why no agreement on legal obligations could be reached at the Summit was the fact that many of the ad hoc and working groups responsible for individual issues suffered from serious time constraints.

Despite the Copenhagen Accord being an outcome of the Copenhagen Summit, it was not adopted by the Conference of Parties and its meeting (CMP), when the Accord was presented to it at the final plenary session.

In a sense, the several challenges encountered by the Copenhagen Summit—particularly the lack of consensus and the rabidly different positions of participating States—underscore the view that climate change is 'a diabolical policy problem … harder than any other issue of high importance that has come before our polity in living memory' (Ross Garnaut, 'Garnut Climate Change Review 2008', available at http://www.garnautreview.org.au, restated in Adrian Macey, 'Climate change: governance challenges for Copenhagen' (2009) 15 Global Governance 443).

However, one of the greatest achievements of international environmental law, arguably, is how it has impacted upon the national environmental policies and legal approaches developed by States for their individual application.

KEY POINTS

- The Copenhagen Summit was one of the most high-profile, well-attended, and ambitious international summits. However, it records one of the least encouraging outcomes ever and, more than any effort before it, undermined the efforts of the international community at strengthening international environmental regulation.

- The Copenhagen Accord does not create a legally binding regime and, despite the fact that it mainly consists of voluntary measures, it was not even adopted by the States.

- The Copenhagen Summit suffered from a lack of consensus amongst participating States, did not resolve the problem of the classification of developing countries, and failed to bind developed States, especially the USA, to any new emissions control agreement.

- The Copenhagen Accord provides for no certainty, contains no mechanisms for oversights, and does not spell out the relations of the new institutions that it creates with the existing ones; nor does it forecast or specify the fate of the Kyoto Protocol.

17.5 Enforcement of international environmental law

Having considered the several efforts made by the international community towards establishing international environmental law, let us now consider its enforcement. As hinted earlier, the enforcement of international law is generally one of the most difficult issues in international law and the field of environmental law is no exception. Of course, within its territory a State could use several methods to control and enforce its laws against environmental breaches. Some of the most popular domestic environmental control and enforcement measures include the self-explanatory 'polluter pays' principle (PPP), environmental taxes, penal sanctions, fines, and even imprisonment in grievous circumstances. For several reasons, some of these measures are not applicable to international environmental law. For a start, no one can jail a State, and a regime of fines or taxation in environmental breaches is no easy option either.

What we consider briefly in the following section therefore are some of the measures that have been *proposed* for enforcing international environmental law. It must always be borne in mind, however, that the main aim of enforcement of international environmental law is not to penalize States per se, much less to make them feel bad for their transgressions, but rather to encourage them towards a more effective, sustainable, and considerate use of the environment and its resources.

17.5.1 Why is international environmental law not enforced?

The nature of environmental breaches

As already noted, countermeasures are the most common and recognized means of enforcement of international law, but, as explained previously, the nature of environmental breaches makes this method wholly inapplicable to this field. A State may breach international environmental law by acts that occur entirely within its own territory and through no fault of anyone.

example

A recent example is the massive environmental disaster that hit Japan in March 2011. Following a huge earthquake and tsunami, some of Japan's nuclear facilities suffered an outage—a shutting down of the reactors—followed by a meltdown, in which radioactive material breached its containment, and released significant radiation into the atmosphere.

If nationals of other countries suffer as a result of this radiation, it will be hard to hold Japan responsible: although the act occurred within its territory, it was a result of what lawyers call *force majeure* (that is, a force or act of nature), a concept known to constitute a defence to culpability.

Moreover, States affected by environmental disasters in one State's territory may not be interested in bringing claims against responsible countries.

Following a major chemical disaster at Chernobyl in the former Soviet Union, many affected States chose not to bring claims, because they did not want to put additional pressure on the then Soviet leader, who was vigorously pursuing market reforms much clamoured for by the West.

Therefore the nature of environmental disasters, coupled with the intensely political nature of the relationships between States, makes it difficult to impose countermeasures, which may even be impossible in many instances in which there is a lack of active wrongdoing on the part of the State concerned.

Perceptions about enforcement in international law

According to Mary Ellen O'Connell, 'Enforcement and success of international environmental law' (1995) 3 Ind J Global Legal Stud 47, 52:

> Enforcement sits on the margins of international law, which remains a compliance-based, not an enforcement-based, system. International law governs a system more akin to an association of corporations than to a domestic system of individuals. Indeed, in this light, it is hard to understand why international law is labelled as a 'primitive system'. One can argue that a system based on enforcement is far more primitive than one based on compliance.

This statement suggests that, since international law as a whole is based on compliance, there is very little need for enforcement. Under international law, States, no matter how big or small, how rich or poor, are equal sovereigns. Hence, as equals, States are more amenable to *complying* with their international obligations than they are to having those obligations *enforced* against them. The very notion of enforcement makes States very uncomfortable, since they see it as a violation of their sovereignty by other States, which are equal to them in the eyes of international law.

The ambiguous nature of environmental violations

As is obvious from the previous discussion on the UNFCCC and Kyoto Protocol, most environmental obligations imposed on States are either outright ambiguous or, at the very least, unclear and uncertain. This often makes it difficult to establish whether a State has been in breach of its obligation. In other words, ambiguous obligations often beget ambiguous violations. Often, a State is party to a treaty which, in itself, does not contain obligations, but is not party to a protocol to that treaty which imposes obligations. Ellen O'Connell (1995, see earlier in this section) gives the example of the USA, which is party to the Long-Range Transboundary Air Pollution Treaty (LRTAP). The treaty does not contain any important obligations, which are instead provided for by various protocols. The USA is, however, not party to the supplementary protocol that requires a reduction of sulphur dioxide (SO_2) emissions into the atmosphere.

As O'Connell (ibid.) observes, at 54:

> Regardless of how much soft coal the United States burns, it has violated no treaty obligations, and no other state may take action to enforce the treaty against the United States.

A State may not necessarily be complying with desirable environmental standards, but yet not be clearly violating its international obligations. It is difficult to argue that a State that increases its manufacturing capacity in order to meet its obligations towards its citizens violates emission standards for using the most economic, even if more harmful, chemical substances in the process. The environmental desire to protect trees and prevent deforestation in Africa, for example, needs to be balanced against the affordability of modern cooking substitutes, such as gas cookers, etc., for the millions of people in the developing world who rely daily on firewood to survive. In that situation, arguing that an African State violates environmental obligations flies in the face of reality.

17.5.2 A case for enforcing international environmental law

Despite the considerations discussed earlier, several scholars have argued for the enforcement of international environmental law.

According to Andrew Watson Samaan, 'Enforcement of international environmental treaties: an analysis' (1993–94) 5 Fordham Envt LJ 261, 273:

> It is important to create an enforcement mechanism for this body of law, since without enforcement the law is but a shallow code riddled with dubious realizations.

Similarly, Martti Koskenniemi, 'Breach of treaty or non-compliance? Reflections on the enforcement of the Montreal Protocol' (1992) 3 YB Int'l Env L 123, 127–128, while supporting the fact that international law is compliance-based, argues that 'It is doubtful whether such [compliance] procedures suffice to deter or deal with serious or persistent breaches'.

In fact, the majority of international legal scholars subscribe to the view that there is need for the enforcement of international environmental law, since the preferred method of monitoring and reporting compliance and non-compliance with environmental obligations has not proved effective, as we saw earlier with regard to the UNFCCC and the Kyoto processes. The next question therefore is: how might international environmental law be enforced, given the hurdles identified in the previous discussion?

17.5.3 The means of enforcing international environmental law

Domestic mechanisms

There is a school of thought that canvasses the view that the best means of enforcing international environmental law is through domestic mechanisms and institutions. This view derives principally from the realization that, unlike typical State-to-State disputes, which are responsive to international settlement mechanisms, most environmental disputes among States usually occur through the activities of individuals and corporations within a State. Therefore it makes more sense for such disputes to be addressed before domestic institutions such as courts.

As O'Connell (1995, see section 17.5.1) states, at 57:

> Domestic courts already enforce a significant portion of international law. The idea of expanding the use of domestic courts for international environmental law against citizens and governments of other countries is a more recent and interesting concept ... The use of domestic courts

makes particular sense in the environmental area because domestic courts tend to focus on most common polluters—individuals and corporations. The courts' clear authority over assets and persons is necessary for successful enforcement. Most courts can issue injunctions which may prevent environmental damage before it occurs.

As will be recalled from Chapter 9, some States practise the monist doctrine of international law. This implies that international obligations of such States become automatically binding once they ratify the concerned treaties. Thus such States are able to enforce international law directly.

. . . .

● **The Paquette Habana** 175 US 677 (1900)

The US Navy arrested Cuban fishing ships during the Spanish–American war and auctioned the ships as war booty. The US Supreme Court held that it was long established under customary international law that fishing vessels could not be captured as war prizes. The Court ordered the proceeds of the sale and interests thereto to be returned to the shipowners.
The significance of *The Paquette Habana* lies in its integration of customary international law with US law, meaning that such obligations automatically became part of US domestic law.

Thus customary international environmental obligations automatically form part of the domestic law of monist States, such as the USA, making the domestic implementation and enforcement of such obligations much easier.

However, for countries that practise dualism (see Chapter 9), matters may not be so simple, because international obligations have to be transformed into domestic law before they can become binding. It is to be expected that most parliaments of such countries may want to ensure that they regulate the enforcement of international environmental law before their domestic courts. But this prospect does not undermine the merits of the domestic enforcement of international environmental law.

The use of non-governmental organizations (NGOs) and international agencies

NGOs, most of which are privately funded, are particularly effective at exerting pressure on governments. This relative financial independence makes them particularly suitable as a tool with which to enforce international environmental law.

As noted by Samaan (1993–94, see section 17.5.2), at 274:

> International agencies are neither shackled by international politics [*sic*] or influenced by political pressures, since, for the most part, they are generally privately funded. In addition by 'fostering an environmental ethics within State bureaucracies, these agencies can encourage assent to and implementation of international agreements'... For these reasons Intergovernmental Organizations (IGOs) are ideally suited for the task in the absence of unanimity or supranational authority by establishing procedures for adopting substantive standards in a way that raises the political costs of nonconformity.

Naming and shaming

One of the more popular means of pressuring States to comply with their international obligations is 'naming and shaming'. The role of the media in pressuring States to comply with environmental obligations can be significant, as with, for example, the international media scrutiny of US reluctance to conform to the several obligations of the Kyoto Protocol. However, this particular method is also prone to irritating States and can actually be counterproductive if not well managed. A State can easily become obstinate on a particular issue if it thinks that it has received an unjustifiable level of media attack.

Conclusion

International environmental law is undoubtedly one of the most important areas of international law. It is concerned with the regulation of the environment and its resources, and how to ensure that both are not used in a way that imperils the earth and causes harm to the atmosphere. An unbridled release of dangerous gases into the atmosphere seriously harms the ozone layer, just as deforestation constitutes a serious danger to the sustainable use of natural resources.

As has been seen, the international regulation of the environment is a particularly difficult and sensitive issue. The need to balance States' desires for economic advancement with sustainable environmental activities is not always easy to strike, just as the tension between international environmental law and State sovereignty often frustrates multilateral negotiations and agreements on environmental protection.

However, with increasing concern of the international community about the state of the environment and with growing evidence of global warming across the world, it is hoped that States and world leaders will become more engaged with finding abiding solutions to the world's environmental challenges sooner rather than later.

Questions

Self-test questions

1 What is 'international environmental law'?

2 List the sources of international environmental law.

3 What is the 'ozone layer'?

4 What does the principle of 'differentiated responsibilities' imply?

5 What is 'emissions trading'?

6 When were the UNFCCC and the Kyoto Protocol adopted?

7 List the major setbacks of the Copenhagen Summit.

8 Describe the enforcement of international environmental law.

Discussion questions

1 What are the main contributions of the UNFCCC? Do you think that the Convention addresses the responsibilities of developed and developing countries in the most effective manner?

2 To what extent does the Kyoto Protocol improve or detract from efforts to achieve more rigorous international environmental regulation?

3 What is international environmental law and from which sources does such law derive?

4 What is the 'differentiated responsibility principle' and of what relevance, if any, is it to the development of international environmental law?

5 Evaluate the achievement and failures of the Copenhagen Summit.

Assessment question

In preparation for the forthcoming Global Conference on Strengthening Compliance with International Environmental Regulation, the Rutamuan Environment Minister has contacted you, as a leading thinker on environmental matters, to help the government to draft a memorandum on how best to enforce environmental regulation. Having participated in several similar efforts previously, and being fully aware of the intricacies and sensitivity surrounding the enforcement of environmental regulation, you are particularly keen not to repeat past mistakes.

What will be your key proposals and will you favour an enforcement-based or a compliance-based approach to enforcing international environmental regulation? Why?

 # Key cases

- *Hungary v. Slovakia* (1997) ICJ Rep 7 (the *Gabčíkovo-Nagymaros Project Case*)
- *New Zealand v. France (Nuclear Tests)* (1974) ICJ Rep 457 (the *Nuclear Tests Case*)
- *Paquette Habana, The* 175 US 677 (1900)
- *United States v. Canada (Preliminary Decision)* (1938) 3 RIAA 1911 (the *Trail Smelter Case*)

 # Further reading

Birnie, P. and Boyle, A., *International Environmental Law and the Environment* (Oxford: Oxford University Press, 1992)

Birnie, P., Boyle, A., and Redgwell, C., *International Law and the Environment* (3rd edn, Oxford: Oxford University Press, 2009)

Bodansky, D., 'Customary (and not so customary) international environmental law' (1995–96) 3 Ind J Global Legal Stud 105

Bodansky, D., Brunée, J., and Hey, E., *Oxford Handbook of International Environmental Law* (Oxford: Oxford University Press, 2007)

Boyle, A., 'Some reflections on the relationship of treaties and soft law' (1999) 48 ICLQ 901

D'Amato, A., 'Whales: their emerging right to life' (1991) 85 AJIL 21

Fitzmaurice, M., Ong, D. M., and Merkouris, P. (eds), *Research Handbook on International Environmental Law* (Cheltenham: Edward Elgar, 2010)

O'Connell, M. E., 'Enforcement and success of international environmental law' (1995) 3 Ind J Global Legal Stud 47

Sanwal, M., 'Sustainable development, the Rio Declaration and multilateral cooperation' (1993) 4 Col J Int'l Env L & Pol'y 45

Schachter, O., 'The emergence of international environmental law' (1991) 44(2) J Int'l Aff 457

Wolfrum, R., 'Purposes and principles of international environmental law' (1990) 33 GYBIL 303

Yang, T. and Percival, R., 'The emergence of global environmental law' (2009) 36 Ecol LQ 615

18

International economic law

Learning objectives

This chapter will help you to:

- learn about the development of international economic law (IEL);

- understand the nature of IEL;

- appreciate the role of public international law in regulating economic relations among States; and

- study the role of the General Agreement on Tariffs and Trade (GATT) and the World Trade Organization (WTO), the International Monetary Fund (IMF), and the World Bank in regulating the international economy.

Introduction

International economic law (IEL) is a generic term used to describe the international regulation of economic relations amongst States. IEL governs not the 'economics' of individual States as such, but the economic *relations* of States. It regulates international trade by establishing common standards and rules towards ensuring the global economic health of nations. This chapter studies IEL as a distinct topic within public international law focusing mainly on the regulatory aspects of IEL, and its characteristics. The chapter discusses the institutions for regulating world economics, such as General Agreement on Trade and Tariffs (GATT) and the World Trade Organization (WTO), the International Monetary Fund (IMF), the rules of which—together with those of GATT/WTO—form the crux of IEL.

18.1 The origins and nature of international economic law

The international regulation of economics is a fairly recent phenomenon and emerged only after the Second World War. That does not mean, however, that there was no international trading before this period. Prior to the Second World War, States interacted with one another in matters of trade and economics; they conducted international commercial transactions and devised various mechanisms for engaging with one another commercially. Monies and various other forms of legal tender moved amongst States.

However, one major feature of this period was that individual States were wholly responsible for setting standards and rules that governed their commercial interactions with one another, although such rules were often negotiated and agreed between trading partners. In other words, most commercial rules at that time were bilateral in nature. There was neither international legal regulation of how States traded, nor any international regulating mechanisms for that matter.

In 'The international monetary system: a look back over seven decades' (2010) 13 J Int'l Econ L 575, 576, Andreas Lowenfeld notes that:

> It would not be accurate to say that before 1945 there was no international monetary system. States and their enterprises traded with one another, currencies were exchanged, and states held monetary reserves in gold, in silver, and in foreign currencies. But prior to the end of the World War II no international legal regime governed the conduct of states with respect to monetary affairs.

The absolute control that States had over the regulation of their economies and trading before the Second World War was facilitated by the common understanding of world economics by the major Western States. Countries, such as the UK, USA, Germany, and France, accepted gold as the universal commodity to which they linked their currencies. After all, crude oil, perhaps the most important natural resource today, had not yet acquired the status that it currently enjoys. Thus Western States fixed the price of gold and linked the fate of their national currencies to its well-being. The consequence of this was a stable and predictable market and international economy. In a world of great stability and relative economic prosperity, this economic system was highly desirable.

The Second World War devastated most Western economies and shattered their economic system. This compelled a rethinking of how to conduct global economy and trading. During the war many States—particularly Nazi Germany—pursued aggressive policies of fixing gold prices. This badly affected the stability of gold as a result of which all economies that depended on gold suffered greatly. Shortly before the war ended, other major Western States started to consider how better to regulate international trade. They primarily focused on establishing an effective international monetary system that would be shielded from the manipulations and misdeeds of individual States.

The result of several conferences and negotiations, which took place in 1944 at Bretton Woods, New Hampshire, in the USA, was the establishment of the International Monetary Fund (IMF), which was mainly concerned with regulating the international currency. It was not until 1947, two years after the creation of the United Nations, that GATT, the first international mechanism to regulate international trade, would emerge. GATT laid the foundation of IEL, which would be consolidated by the more inclusive and powerful WTO when it replaced GATT in 1995 (see later).

According to Curtis Reitz, 'Enforcement of the General Agreement on Tariffs and Trade' (1996) 17 U Penn J Int'l Econ L 555:

> An important new field of international law, known today as 'international economic law', has emerged and taken form. Although the fundamentals of international economic law have existed for at least half a century, the modern international law system stands at a critical juncture.

Generally speaking, IEL can broadly be divided into 'regulatory' and 'transactional' aspects. According to John Jackson, 'Global economics and international economic law' (1998) 1(I) J Int'l Econ L 1, 9:

> Transactional IEL refers to transactions carried out in the context of international trade or economic activities, and focuses on the way mostly private entrepreneurs or other parties carry out their activity...Regulatory IEL, however, emphasizes the role of government institutions (national, local, or international).

Both aspects of IEL are undoubtedly significant and merit considerable attention. However, as John Jackson has noted (ibid.):

> Although it can be argued that the 'international trade transactions is the most government regulated of all private economic transactions...in today's world the real challenges for understanding IEL and its impact on governments and private citizens' lives, suggests a focus on IEL as 'regulatory laws'.

KEY POINTS

- International trading existed before the Second World War, but there was no international regulation of such trading until after the war. Thus 'international economic law' properly so called only existed after the Second World War.

- The stark realization during the Second World War that entrusting individual States with the responsibility of regulating their economies was sufficient to safeguard the health of global economics and trading inspired the emergence of IEL.

- IEL can be categorized as transactional or regulatory. However, it is with the regulatory aspect of IEL that international law is mostly concerned.

18.2 International economic law and public international law

IEL is widely considered today as a public international law field, but its status as such has not been as long established as that of human rights, criminal law, or even environmental law. This was because for a long time international law did not concern itself with regulating economics. However, not only is IEL now a bona fide theme of public international law; it has also been said to belong to private international law—that is, the conflict of laws—in some regards.

Thomas Cottier, 'Challenges ahead in international economic law' (2009) 12(I) J Int'l Econ L 3, observes that:

> Since the conclusion of the Uruguay Round of multilateral trade negotiation and the entry into force of the WTO Agreements in 1995, international economic law has witnessed an unprecedented emphasis on trade regulation. The field has moved centre stage in public international law ... The many linkages to other fields, in particular, environmental law, human rights, culture and many others, have broadened perspectives and assisted in the process of bringing trade regulation fully into the realm of public international law.

In fact, John Jackson (1998, see section 18.1), at 8, has gone as far as to state that:

> Indeed, it is plausible to suggest that 90 per cent of international law work is in reality international economic law in some form or another.

The rationale for the ultimate engagement of public international law with IEL is to be found in the realization by States and scholars that the law—and in particular international law—has a special role to play in States' economic relations. Economists use theoretical postulations and forecasting to 'regulate' economics, but leaving international economics to be regulated solely by market forces is fraught with many dangers. Law, therefore brings to bear on economics concrete rules and regulation, which economic predictions and theories often lack.

Unlike economics, the particular strength of law derives from experience, not logic or predictions.

As the famous American judge, Oliver Wendell Holmes, once pronounced, in the first of the twelve Lowell lectures delivered on 23 November 1880 (available at http://www.infoplease.com/cig/supreme-court/oliver-wendell-holmes-1902-1932.html):

> The life of the law has not been logic; it has been experience. The felt necessities of the time, the prevalent moral and political theories, intuitions of public policy, avowed or unconscious, even the prejudices which judges share with their fellow men, have had a good deal more to do than the syllogism in determining the rules by which men should be governed. The law embodies the story of a nation's development through many centuries, and it cannot be dealt with as if it contained only the axioms and corollaries of a book of mathematics.

If we adapt this statement to the present subject matter, we can say that the regulation of international economics by international law is a *necessity* dictated today by the present realities of economic relations among States. The strength of such legal regime derives not from simple theoretical formulations or logic, but from the series of events, experiences, and activities, all of which affect the economic well-being of States and people.

The relationship of IEL with public international law can, however, be a very tricky one if not properly handled. There are notable structural differences between States' approach to commerce and international law's approach to regulation and these may often cause friction:

> The very structure of international law and particularly the normal rigidities of treaties and their formation, as well as the intricate links of treaty developments to many constitutional structures, will often create barriers to what some policy makers perceive to be the optimum solutions to problems. (John Jackson, 'International economic law in times that are interesting' (2000) 3 J' Int'l Econ L 3, 5)

It is necessary to balance the international law's regulation of IEL with the constitutional realities of States if we are to achieve the full benefits of international law regulation of economics. Since we have already dealt with the relationship between international law and municipal law in general in Chapter 9, we will not repeat this discussion here.

thinking points

- *What is the relationship between IEL and public international law?*
- *What is the distinction between the transactional aspect and regulatory aspect of IEL, and of what relevance, if any, is this difference as far as the international regulation of IEL is concerned?*
- *Why is public international law important in the regulation of IEL?*

Having dealt with some preliminary issues concerning IEL, let us now consider some specific mechanisms for regulating IEL. We focus here on GATT and the WTO, on the one hand, and the IMF and World Bank, on the other. The combination of GATT and the WTO is what is usually referred to as 'international trade law' (ITL), while the IMF/World Bank angle is known as 'international finance law' (IFL). However, since we discuss both these aspects as elements of IEL and not as trade or finance law per se, we will adopt the term 'institutional mechanisms for regulating IEL' generically for both.

18.3 Institutional mechanisms for regulating international economic law

As noted earlier, the backbone of IEL comprises the institutions established for the purpose of implementing the regime. There exist today several such mechanisms, and most regions of the world now have some kind of authorities and institutions that regulate and coordinate activities within those specific regions. Our focus here is, however, on global institutions as GATT and the WTO, which are the most important international economic regulatory bodies in existence in terms of their significance and status.

18.3.1 The General Agreement on Tariffs and Trade

As Curtis Reitz (1996, see section 18.1) has noted, at 555, 'The centrepiece of international economic law system is the General Agreement on Tariffs and Trade'.

The main reason for GATT is the desire to reduce governments' ability to impose measures, which either distort or restrain international trade.

As noted by William J. Davey, 'Dispute settlement in GATT' (1987–88) 11 Fordham Int'l LJ 51, 53:

> The basic goal of GATT is to promote free international trade by establishing rules that limit national impediments to trade.

Background

In order to understand how GATT developed, one needs first to appreciate the emergence of the International Trade Organization (ITO), which was originally proposed as the mechanism for regulating international trade. At the conferences that took place in New York, Geneva, and Havana in 1946, 1947, and 1948, respectively, it was proposed that GATT, which was drafted at those conferences, would establish the ITO as an organization to implement GATT. The Geneva Conference focused on three principal issues: the finalization of the ITO Charter; the negotiation of a multilateral agreement to reduce tariffs; and the drafting of 'general clauses' of obligations relating to tariffs.

However, the USA, which was one of the principal architects of GATT, had not intended the treaty to be implemented by an organization. Thus, for this and many other reasons, with which we need not be concerned here, the US Congress refused to pass the ITO Charter, but passed GATT provisionally by the Protocol of Provisional Application (PPA) in 1948. The fact that most of the agreements on tariffs and the 'general clauses' on obligations relating to tariffs were already well developed within the US system facilitated their incorporation into GATT and the latter's acceptance, even if provisionally, by the US Congress. Indeed GATT would remain a provisional agreement until 1995 when it was replaced by the WTO. However, as a multilateral treaty, it was a force to be reckoned with.

As John Jackson (1998, section 18.1), noted at 17:

> the GATT, which for reasons partly relating to the constitutional structure of the USA had come into 'provisional force', filled the gap left by the ITO failure, and became de facto the major trade treaty and institution for international trade relations and diplomacy.

Dispute resolution under GATT 1947

One of the most remarkable features of GATT was the development of its dispute resolution mechanism. Yet despite its featuring in GATT, dispute resolution is one of the least provided-for elements in the treaty, and those provisions that do exist are, at best, basic and ambiguous.

Article XXIII(1), which is the core of GATT dispute settlement, states that:

> If any contracting party should consider that any benefit accruing to it directly or indirectly under this Agreement is being nullified or impaired or that the attainment of any objective of the Agreement is being impeded as the result of

(a) the failure of another contracting party to carry out its obligations under this Agreement, or

(b) the application by another contracting party of any measure, whether or not it conflicts with the provisions of this Agreement, or

(c) the existence of any other situation,

the contracting party may, with a view to the satisfactory adjustment of the matter, make written representations or proposals to the other contracting party or parties which it considers to be concerned. Any contracting party thus approached shall give sympathetic consideration to the representations or proposals made to it.

Clearly, this provision does not entitle any party to GATT to bring a claim for dispute settlement merely on the ground that there has been a violation of GATT obligations; rather, an aggrieved party must show that benefits, which accrue to it under the treaty directly or indirectly, have been 'nullified' or 'impaired'—terms that the Article does not clarify.

The meaning of 'nullification' or 'impairment'

Despite the lack of clarity in Article XXIII(1), case law has shed light on what 'nullification' and 'impairment' mean in the context of GATT.

● *Report of the Working Party on the Australian Subsidy on Ammonium Sulphate* GATT/ CP.4/39, ADOPTED 3 APRIL 1950, BISD II/188

In 1949, Chile complained that Australia's discontinuance of a policy of parallel subsidies on two competing fertilizer products, as a result of which a subsidy on imported sodium nitrate was removed, whereas domestic ammonium sulphate continued to be subsidized, had nullified or impaired the tariff concession granted by Australia to Chile on sodium nitrate in 1947.

The GATT Working Party concluded:

> that no evidence had been presented to show that the Australian Government had failed to carry out its obligations under the Agreement.

However, the Working Party agreed that the injury that the government of Chile said that it had suffered constituted a nullification or impairment of a benefit accruing to Chile directly or indirectly under GATT Article XXIII:

> if the action of the Australian Government which resulted in upsetting the competitive relationship between sodium nitrate and ammonium sulphate *could not reasonably have been anticipated* by the Chilean Government, taking into consideration all pertinent circumstances and the provisions of the General Agreement, at the time it negotiated for the duty-free binding on sodium nitrate. [Emphasis added]

Clearly, a measure that one party complains constitutes nullification or impairment must not have been reasonably foreseeable by the other party.

● *Report of the GATT Panel on the Treatment by Germany of Imports of Sardines* G/26, ADOPTED 31 OCTOBER 1952, BISD 1S/53

The same approach was adopted in a dispute between Germany and Norway, in which the latter had complained, in 1952, that the former imposed tariffs rates, border taxes, and quantitative restrictions on certain types of trade in a manner that nullified or impaired benefits derivable by Norway.

The GATT Panel concluded that:

> no sufficient evidence had been presented to show that the German Government had failed to carry out its obligations under Article I:1 and Article XIII:1.

But the Panel agreed that nullification or impairment in terms of Article XXIII would exist:

> if the action of the German Government, which resulted in upsetting the competitive relationship . . . could not reasonably have been anticipated by the Norwegian Government at the time it negotiated for tariff reductions . . .

However, a change in attitude towards the interpretation of 'nullification' and 'impairment' was signalled in 1962 in a dispute involving Uruguay.

● **Report of the Panel on Uruguay an Recourse to Article XXIII** L/1923, ADOPTED 16
   NOVEMBER 1962, BISD 11S/95

Uruguay had complained that measures taken by some fifteen State parties to GATT, limited marketing opportunities available to them and the failure of the prices of their products to be maintained at a satisfactory level. The Panel considered whether the measures complained about nullified or impaired benefits that accrued to Uruguay under GATT. Following the well-established jurisprudence of the Panel, it held that measures that would constitute nullification or impairment must be seen to affect benefits accruing to parties.

However, in a groundbreaking move, the Panel also considered whether measures not thought to have affected benefits could constitute nullification or impairment.

The Panel held (at [15]) that:

> In cases where there is a clear infringement of the provisions of the General Agreement, or in other words, where measures are applied in conflict with the provisions of GATT and are not permitted under the terms of the relevant protocol under which the GATT is applied by the contracting party, the action would, *prima facie, constitute a case of nullification or impairment* and would *ipso facto require consideration of whether the circumstances are serious enough to justify the authorization of suspension of concessions or obligations . . . While it is not precluded that a prima facie case of nullification or impairment could arise even if there is no infringement of GATT provisions*, it would be in such cases *incumbent on the country invoking Article XXIII to demonstrate* the grounds and reasons of its invocation. [Emphasis added]

This was a remarkable departure from the previous decisions in many respects. First, it established the possibility of a measure constituting nullification or impairment by the simple fact of its violating the relevant GATT provisions, even if no benefits had been affected. Secondly, such a general violation could be sufficient for contracting parties to authorize the suspension of obligations. Thirdly, the onus is on the party alleging breach to prove grounds invoking Article XXIII. This line of reasoning has been followed by many subsequent decisions.

The procedure for dealing with disputes is provided for by Article XXIII(2) GATT. This Article states that:

If no satisfactory adjustment is effected between the contracting parties concerned within a reasonable time... the matter may be referred to the CONTRACTING PARTIES. The CONTRACTING PARTIES shall promptly investigate any matter so referred to them and shall make appropriate recommendations to the contracting parties which they consider to be concerned, or give a ruling on the matter, as appropriate. The CONTRACTING PARTIES may consult with contracting parties, with the Economic and Social Council of the United Nations and with any appropriate inter-governmental organization in cases where they consider such consultation necessary. If the CONTRACTING PARTIES consider that the circumstances are serious enough to justify such action, they may authorize a contracting party or parties to suspend the application to any other contracting party or parties of such concessions or other obligations under this Agreement as they determine to be appropriate in the circumstances. If the application to any contracting party of any concession or other obligation is in fact suspended, that contracting party shall then be free, not later than sixty days after such action is taken, to give written notice to the Executive Secretary to the CONTRACTING PARTIES of its intention to withdraw from this Agreement and such withdrawal shall take effect upon the sixtieth day following the day on which such notice is received by him.

This rather convoluted dispute settlement procedure generated a lot of debate. Some scholars have argued that the provision does not empower legally binding decisions to be taken against defaulting parties, while others argue against such a conclusion. Whatever may be the correct interpretation, it is interesting to note that whereas the provision of Article XXIII(2) empowers contracting parties to authorize the suspension of concessions or obligations against other parties (which would seem to suggest that the dispute settlement system is, in fact, legally binding), such a step was rarely taken.

KEY POINTS

- It is important that a party who wishes to bring a complaint for dispute settlement must show not only that the other party has breached GATT obligations, but also that such a breach has resulted in nullifying or impairing the benefits that accrue to the complainant under GATT.

- 'Nullification or impairment' is usually determined with reference to whether the wrongdoing party could have reasonably foreseen that its actions would have such effect on the complainant.

- In *Uruguay*, the Panel contemplated and established that it was possible for nullification or impairment to result from measures that merely breach GATT obligations. In other words, the complainant does not have to prove that it has suffered loss of benefits. This was a major improvement. But such a complainant must prove the ground for invoking Article XXIII against the other party.

- The whole process under Article XXIII(2) centres on the action of the contracting parties, who could authorize the suspension of obligations in a dispute.

Development in GATT 1947 dispute settlement procedure

Over the years, many developments arose in the GATT dispute settlement process. Initially, a plenary meeting of the contracting parties took place biannually, which considered the disputes submitted. This was later replaced by an intersessional committee made up of the contracting parties, after which a working party was established to look into disputes brought under GATT.

In 1955, a new approach was established whereby a panel of experts, established in their own right and not as representatives of their governments, began to deal with disputes.

The utility of Article XXIII GATT as a dispute settlement procedure has been criticized on many fronts. Although there are several such criticisms, the most serious was that the procedure does not establish formal procedures for handling disputes (William Davey, 1987–88, at 57, see earlier in this section).

Consequently, States and scholars began to advocate for a system that could produce judicial-type decisions despite the preference of others for a largely informal conciliatory process. This issue was to be addressed during the GATT Tokyo Round, which took place between 1973 and 1979.

The Tokyo Round culminated in the contracting parties adopting, in November 1979, an Understanding Regarding Notification, Consultation, Dispute Settlement and Surveillance (the Tokyo Understanding). Paragraph 7 of the Understanding provides that:

> The CONTRACTING PARTIES agree that the customary practice of the GATT in the field of dispute settlement, described in the Annex, should be continued in the future, with the improvements set out below. They recognize that the efficient functioning of the system depends on their will to abide by the present understanding. The CONTRACTING PARTIES *reaffirm that the customary practice* includes the procedures for the settlement of disputes between developed and less-developed countries adopted by the CONTRACTING PARTIES in 1966 and that these remain available to less-developed contracting parties wishing to use them. [Emphasis added]

What the Tokyo Understanding basically did was continue the practice of dispute settlement as had already been in existence, although it proposed some improvements. For example, it recognized the conciliation role of the Director General of GATT, even if this role was hardly ever used. The Understanding also improved upon the operation of the panels.

The Tokyo Round faced many problems. The legal status of the document was questioned, because it is neither a treaty of its own accord nor a waiver as provided for in Article XXV(5) GATT. By far the most insurmountable problem of the Tokyo Understanding was with the operation of the panels, especially with regard to the status of its reports on parties' disputes. Usually, the panels submitted their reports to the Council, which acted as a standing body of GATT. It must be pointed out that the Council was not a creation of GATT but rather emerged from practice and the contracting States. The Tokyo Understanding made it possible for the Council then to adopt the reports of the Council by consensus. Thus if one State brought a complaint against another State, the panel prepared a report on the dispute and referred this to the Council. The Council would then, by consensus, adopt the report—that is, it would accept the finding of the panel.

The problem, however, is that adoption of such reports was based on consensus. This means that the State that 'lost' in a dispute would then be able effectively to block the adoption of the panel's report, which would have made some recommendations against it. This was the greatest weakness of the Tokyo Understanding.

As observed by Davey (1987–88, see earlier in this section), at 60:

> A panel report in and of itself has no force. It must first be adopted by the Council on behalf of the contracting parties. Although the issue discussed in the report are not relitigated in the Council, the Council does not usually act absent consensus. Thus, the 'losing' party (at least an

important losing party) may hold up adoption of a panel report interminably while it purports to analyze it and to explore possible negotiated solutions with the prevailing party.

The wider implication of this system, as Davey further observes (ibid.), at 87, was that:

> The failure of the Council to adopt reports in these cases . . . undermines the system because it deprives the panel report of any precedential effect.

That notwithstanding, the Tokyo Understanding did recognize the responsibility that the contracting States have in taking action when it comes to panel reports. Paragraph 21 of the Understanding states that:

> Reports of panels and working parties should be given prompt consideration by the CONTRACTING PARTIES. The CONTRACTING PARTIES should take appropriate action on reports of panels and working parties within a reasonable period of time. If the case is one brought by a less-developed contracting party, such action should be taken in a specially convened meeting, if necessary. In such cases, in considering what appropriate action might be taken the CONTRACTING PARTIES shall take into account not only the trade coverage of measures complained of, but also their impact on the economy of less-developed contracting parties concerned.

The additional obligation that the Understanding imposes on contracting parties enhances this responsibility. Paragraph 22 provides that:

> The CONTRACTING PARTIES shall keep under surveillance any matter on which they have made recommendations or given rulings. If the CONTRACTING PARTIES' recommendations are not implemented within a reasonable period of time, the contracting party bringing the case may ask the CONTRACTING PARTIES to make suitable efforts with a view to finding an appropriate solution.

But despite GATT's progressiveness, none of the decisions that came out of the dispute settlement mechanisms were enforceable:

> Final decisions in favour of complainants are not self-enforcing in any legal system, but enforcement is a particular difficulty in GATT litigation. GATT plenary bodies lack power to enforce their rulings. Compliance or noncompliance is the choice of the nations against whom decisions have been rendered. (Curtis Reitz (1996, see section 18.1), at 570)

Over time, GATT became considerably weakened. Between 1959 and 1978, GATT's dispute settlement mechanism went mostly unused. Several of the criticisms that many States levelled against GATT were to do with its structural and procedural aspects. William Davey (1987–88, see earlier in this section), at 65, summarizes the main criticisms against GATT as being that it:

(a) was inappropriate and ill-conceived because it stressed judicial solutions to problems that were really resolvable only through negotiations;

(b) had become irrelevant because it was not used, except occasionally by the USA, and it was impractical to expand its usage;

(c) was inefficient because of long delays; and

(d) was ineffective because of its inability to ensure implementation of its decisions.

One major weakness of GATT was that it dealt only with trade in goods; it did not cover other economic transactions, which were left to alternative agreements made between States and other areas of IEL. Naturally, because GATT led to a substantial reduction in tariffs on trade—which was its main objective—greater attention became focused on non-tariff measures, which States still used to inhibit competition in trade. GATT did not provide for this and it was also unable to deal effectively with trade measures taken by several governments in respect of their agricultural products.

Consequently, in an attempt to address the failings or flaws of GATT, another round of multilateral trade negotiations was held. Known as the Uruguay Round, it started towards the end of 1986 and finished in 1994. As a treaty, GATT was reformed and, in addition, the WTO was established as its implementing institution.

thinking points

- *What are the most important improvements made by the Tokyo Understanding to GATT dispute settlement procedures?*
- *List the major weaknesses of GATT dispute settlement procedures.*
- *Explain what 'adoption by consensus' means in relation to the GATT dispute settlement process.*
- *Summarize the factors that weakened GATT as a whole.*

18.3.2 The World Trade Organization

Following the Uruguay Round of 1994, GATT came to be regarded as almost two distinct agreements. There is GATT 1947, the original GATT agreement, on which the discussion in the previous section focused, and there is GATT 1994, the product of the Uruguay Round, which substantially changed GATT's approach and framework to many issues. The terms 'GATT 1947' and 'GATT 1994' are commonly adopted in the literature in order to distinguish the two temporal senses in which GATT may be used.

Another major document adopted during the Uruguay Round was the 1994 Understanding on Rules and Procedures Governing the Settlement of Disputes (the Dispute Settlement Understanding, or DSU), which was adopted by an annex to the Agreement. This was to change the way in which the dispute settlement mechanism worked and will be discussed later in this section.

Furthermore, the 1994 Round produced the WTO as an institutional mechanism for the resolution of all disputes between member States of GATT. The WTO is a major force in the development of an international economy system in general and in international trade in particular.

Donald McRae, 'The WTO in international law: tradition continued or new frontier?' (2000) 3(I) J Int'l Econ L 27, 28, describes the WTO as:

> an international organization. Unlike the GATT, which was somewhat deficient institutionally, the WTO has a range of organs and responsibilities that make it a worthy study in the field of international organizations or international institutional law. Its constitution is a treaty and the legal obligations that apply to members are treaty obligations.

The WTO is governed by a Ministerial Conference and a General Council, which comprise member States. Pursuant to Article III of the Agreement, the WTO administers the 1994 DSU, and the General Council of the WTO is to act as the Dispute Settlement Body (DSB), with its own rules of procedure and chair.

18.3.3 Major improvements under GATT 1994

GATT 1994 improved upon several aspects of GATT 1947 and responded to the many weaknesses of the latter. These specifically relate to coverage and the creation of a more formal, robust, and effective dispute settlement procedure. It will be recalled that GATT 1947 dealt only with trade in goods; GATT 1994 broadened this and incorporated trade in services, intellectual property, and some aspects of foreign investments. The implication of this is that all such non-tariff measures that States previously used to inhibit trade, because GATT 1947 did not apply to such, now came under the coverage of GATT 1994. Naturally, this was to enhance the overarching goal of GATT: the constraint of measures taken by governments to inhibit trading.

Judith Hippler Bello, 'The WTO dispute settlement understanding: less is more' (1996) 90 AJIL 416, states that:

> The Agreement Establishing the World Trade Organization (WTO Agreement) dramatically expands and improves the trade rules of the predecessor General Agreement on Tariffs and Trade (GATT), thereby facilitating trade, economic growth and jobs in the increasingly interdependent global economy. Supporters of trade liberalization generally welcome these new rules, including in particular the dramatically improved procedures for settling disputes.

Another major weakness of GATT 1947 was that decisions of its panels regarding disputes were not self-enforcing. Much depended on the States themselves—that is, on whether they wanted to comply with such decisions—and such decisions could also be avoided where there was no consensus to adopt them. GATT 1994 provides for a system whereby the provisions of GATT can be interpreted at various levels. (We will discuss this further after considering the dispute settlement procedure brought about by GATT 1994.)

KEY POINTS

- GATT 1994 modified and strengthened GATT 1947, and established the WTO as its institutional mechanism.

- GATT 1994 made some improvements to the GATT 1947 regime, especially with regard to coverage and dispute settlement procedure. Thus non-tariff measures that previously escaped from GATT 1947 became subject to GATT 1994.

Dispute settlement procedure under GATT 1994

The dispute settlement mechanism under the WTO set out by GATT 1994 is meant to address the many shortcoming of GATT 1947. The mechanism is set out and clarified in the 1994 DSU; it provides for one unified system under both GATT and the WTO, which encompasses the new areas of services and intellectual property, as were agreed at the Uruguay Round, and establishes a new appellate procedure.

The new dispute settlement procedure does not disregard the 1947 mechanism and practice, which it evolved; in fact, the DSU incorporates it. Article III(I) of the 1994 DSU states that:

> Members affirm their adherence to the principles for the management of disputes heretofore applied under Article XXII and Article XXIII of GATT 1947, and the rules and procedures as further elaborated and modified therein.

This provision is important in two respects. First, it demonstrates clearly that GATT 1994 builds on GATT 1947 in all aspects of its functions. Thus GATT 1994 places a high premium on the customary practices of State parties under GATT 1947. Secondly, this reference to GATT 1947 provides some level of continuity to the GATT system, as well as assuring State parties that the new dispensation recognizes all of the hard work that went into the old regime.

For the first time, the DSU stated the *purpose* of the dispute settlement system. Article 3(2) states that:

> The dispute settlement system of the WTO is a central element in providing security and predictability to the multilateral trading system. The Members recognize that it serves to preserve the rights and obligations of Members under the covered agreements, and to clarify the existing provisions of those agreements in accordance with customary rules of interpretation of public international law. Recommendations and rulings of the DSB cannot add to or diminish the rights and obligations provided in the covered agreements.

Consequently, GATT 1994 maintains the panel system of GATT 1947, although with some modifications to how the panels now work. Whereas under the 1947 regime, the GATT Council established the panels, under the 1994 DSU panels are established by the DSB and the panels' main responsibility is to assist the DSB in its work. Also, unlike under GATT 1947 whereby each panel was responsible for setting up its own procedures, the 1994 DSU lays out default working procedures applicable to all panels (although a panel might decide not to use this procedure, according to Appendix 3 of the DSU). Furthermore, it was in 1994 that the qualifications to be possessed by panel members were laid down for the first time; such panellists act in their own regard, not as representatives of their governments. In fact, Article 8(9) DSU prohibits governments from influencing panellists' decisions in any way. Finally, unlike the 1947 panels, 1994 panels are not bound to apply information and arguments of disputing parties in coming to a decision. The panel is also able to receive information from outside parties and not only the States involved.

Article 13 DSU states that:

> 1. Each panel shall have the right to seek information and technical advice from any individual or body which it deems appropriate. However, before a panel seeks such information or advice from any individual or body within the jurisdiction of a Member it shall inform the authorities of that Member. A Member should respond promptly and fully to any request by a panel for such information as the panel considers necessary and appropriate. Confidential information which is provided shall not be revealed without formal authorization from the individual, body, or authorities of the Member providing the information.
> 2. Panels may seek information from any relevant source and may consult experts to obtain their opinion on certain aspects of the matter. With respect to a factual issue concerning a scientific or other technical matter raised by a party to a dispute, a panel may request an advisory report in writing from an expert review group. Rules for the establishment of such a group and its procedures are set forth in Appendix 4.

Although the DSU does not provide a list of where such extra information could be sought, this has been held to include from non-governmental organizations (NGOs).

● *Report of the Appellate Body on United States—Import Prohibition of Certain Shrimp and Shrimp Products* AB-1998-4, 12 OCTOBER 1998

The Appellate Body stated (at [110]) that:

> We find, and so hold, that the Panel erred in its legal interpretation that accepting non-requested information from non-governmental sources is incompatible with the provisions of the DSU. At the same time, we consider that the Panel acted within the scope of its authority under Articles 12 and 13 of the DSU in allowing any party to the dispute to attach the briefs by nongovernmental organizations, or any portion thereof, to its own submissions.

KEY POINTS

- By virtue of the 1994 DSU, panels are appointed by the DSB and assist the latter in its work. This differs from the 1947 regime under which the GATT Council established the panels.

- GATT 1994 maintains the dispute settlement system under GATT 1947, although it made some major alterations—especially in relation to the qualifications of the panels, the source of information that they could consider, and the source of their rules of procedures.

- GATT 1994 did not discard the dispute settlement procedure of the old GATT, but actually incorporated it—especially in relation to the customary way in which the old regime evolved its practice.

The Appellate Body

It may be said that the appellate system is the most profound addition that GATT 1994 made to the GATT dispute settlement process. The appeal process under GATT is arguably one of the most changed areas which, despite not imposing a court structure, acts in a very similar manner.

As Curtis Reitz (1996, see section 18.1) noted, at 583:

> The single most dramatic change in the 1994 Understanding is that it establishes an Appellate Body to review panel reports . . . The Understanding eschews designating this body as a court, but its organization and functions have many of the essential aspects of a judicial body.

An appeal can be brought only for claims against an issue of law. Article 17(6) DSU provides that 'An appeal shall be limited to issues of law covered in the panel report and legal interpretations developed by the panel.'

The Appellate Body has the power to 'uphold, modify or reverse the legal findings and conclusions of the panel' (Article 7(13) DSU).

One of the main improvements envisioned by the new Appellate Body's power is described by Curits Reitz (1996, see section 18.1), at 584:

> the Appellate Body should expound on the meaning of the agreements within its jurisdiction and create a corpus of decisions that will assure its jurisdiction and create a corpus of decisions that will assure consistency in GATT law and, hopefully, elevate the professional quality of the GATT dispute resolution mechanism. Growing respect for and confidence in the rulings of this professional body, even though not denominated a court, will advance international trade further into a stable regime that is governed by law and legal process.

The decision-making procedure is still that of consensus, but to prevent the GATT 1947 situation in which the 'losing' State has the ability to block a report from being adopted, a report is automatically considered adopted unless the DSB specifically chooses not to adopt it. The trade-off against consensus is the right of a losing party to appeal the decision. Where an appeal occurs, the decision is considered, not adopted. Under Article 16(4) DSU:

Within 60 days after the date of circulation of a panel report to the Members, the report shall be adopted at a DSB meeting unless a party to the dispute formally notifies the DSB of its decision to appeal or the DSB decides by consensus not to adopt the report. If a party has notified its decision to appeal, the report by the panel shall not be considered for adoption by the DSB until after completion of the appeal. This adoption procedure is without prejudice to the right of Members to express their views on a panel report.

Remedies

The remedies available are also set out in the 1994 DSU, as is clarification of what the aim of the remedies ought to be. Article 3(7) DSU states that:

Before bringing a case, a Member shall exercise its judgment as to whether action under these procedures would be fruitful. The aim of the dispute settlement mechanism is to secure a positive solution to a dispute. A solution mutually acceptable to the parties to a dispute and consistent with the covered agreements is clearly to be preferred. In the absence of a mutually agreed solution, the first objective of the dispute settlement mechanism is usually to secure the withdrawal of the measures concerned if these are found to be inconsistent with the provisions of any of the covered agreements. The provision of compensation should be resorted to only if the immediate withdrawal of the measure is impracticable and as a temporary measure pending the withdrawal of the measure which is inconsistent with a covered agreement. The last resort which this Understanding provides to the Member invoking the dispute settlement procedures is the possibility of suspending the application of concessions or other obligations under the covered agreements on a discriminatory basis vis-à-vis the other Member, subject to authorization by the DSB of such measures.

Clearly, the scheme of remedies under DSU is three-pronged, relating to compliance, compensation, and suspension of concessions or obligations. In terms of compliance, the aim is to ensure that the wrongdoer ceases or desists from the offending measures, as provided for by Article 19(1) DSU. Due to the fact that compliance may not always be achieved, especially since it implies cessation of the offending act, compensation and suspension are provided for, although these are temporary measures to be decided upon only where compliance is not achieved within a reasonable time after the ruling (Article 22(1) DSU).

It must be pointed out that suspension is not an easy option. Once a State brings an action for suspension before the DSB, the rule of consensus relating to adoption of decisions under GATT 1947 applies, not the GATT 1994 rule. The implication of this is that a losing party could effectively block a move towards suspension, because such a party is not disqualified or otherwise prevented from taking part in the DSB's discussion of suspension. However, despite this possibility, it is often the case that political pressure exacted on the losing party prevents it from blocking a suspension; instead, a referral to arbitration is encouraged.

The most that the DSB can do in terms of enforcement is to keep appraised of the matter by considering the implementation of the recommendations or rulings that are undertaken. Article 21(6) DSU states that:

The DSB shall keep under surveillance the implementation of adopted recommendations or rulings. The issue of implementation of the recommendations or rulings may be raised at the DSB by any Member at any time following their adoption. Unless the DSB decides otherwise, the issue of implementation of the recommendations or rulings shall be placed on the agenda of the DSB meeting after six months following the date of establishment of the reasonable period of time pursuant to paragraph 3 and shall remain on the DSB's agenda until the issue is resolved. At least

> 10 days prior to each such DSB meeting, the Member concerned shall provide the DSB with a status report in writing of its progress in the implementation of the recommendations or rulings.

The decision of the DSB arbitrator is considered to be final (Article 22(7) DSU), and the arbitrator can apply both the GATT agreement and, more importantly, non-WTO laws—a system that has been criticized.

For example, Joel P. Trachtman, 'The domain of WTO dispute resolution' (1999) 40 Harv Int'l LJ 333, 337, argues that:

> One persistent problem of the WTO legal system is the recognition and application of legal rules from outside the system.

thinking points

- *Explain the jurisdiction of the Appellate Body.*
- *What is the nature of decisions given by the Appellate Body?*
- *What difficulty is present in the use of the same consensus process under GATT 1947 for decisions as to whether a matter should be referred to an arbitrator under GATT 1994?*
- *When can compensation and suspension be resorted to as remedies under the 1994 DSU, and why?*

18.3.4 Weaknesses of GATT 1994/WTO system

There are several factors that undermine the strength of the GATT 1994/WTO system. It has been said (Curtis Reitz, 1996, at 599, see section 18.1) that, as a governmental institution, the WTO:

> lacks significant strength in legislative and executive function. The Director-General and the Secretariat cannot be expected to take strong initiatives in shaping the law.

Another criticism is that the GATT 1994/WTO system is unable to develop in the way in which GATT 1947 did through the incorporation of practice, and cannot easily react to the changing nature of trade due to its more defined institutional procedures and legal rule approach.

John H. Jackson, 'Dispute settlement and the WTO: emerging problems' (1998) 1(3) J Int'l Econ L 329, 347, suggests that:

> Thus the opportunity to evolve by experiment and trial and error, plus practice over times, seems considerably more constrained under the WTO than was the case under the very loose and ambiguous language of the GATT, with its minimalist institutional language.

Furthermore, the fact that a State's right to avail itself of one of the remedies (suspension) can be curtailed by the losing party's decision not to support suspension is detrimental to the process.

That notwithstanding, one of the most remarkable improvements that has occurred since 1994 and the reformation of the old GATT system is the increase in cases that are being brought before the DSU, by both developed and developing countries. This would imply that States are reacting favourably to the stricter structure and procedures that are imposed.

International finance law

The second leg of IEL is that which deals with the regulation of international finance, which is commonly known as international finance law (IFL). This section briefly looks at the IMF and the World Bank, the major pillars of this aspect.

18.4.1 The International Monetary Fund

The IMF came out of the United Nations Monetary and Financial Conference, more commonly known as the 'Bretton Woods Conference', held in July 1944. The results were agreements requiring the setting up of GATT, the International Bank for Reconstruction and Development (IBRD), and the IMF. The IMF sought to help to develop an international monetary system.

Following the Second World War, it was felt that, for a peaceful coexistence between States, trade and other international monetary aspects should be encouraged. The Bretton Woods Conference saw the adoption of the Articles of Agreement for an International Monetary Fund (the Articles of Agreement), which were based on the collaborative draft of John Maynard Keynes and Harry Dexter White. The Keynes and White proposal also envisioned the World Bank as a sister institution.

The IMF is composed of a board of governors, which represent the finance ministers or central bank governors of the member States, as well as a board of executive directors, with the president of the World Bank and the managing director of the IMF heading up the staff.

Andreas Lowenfeld (2010, see section 18.1), at 577, explains how tradition has come to play a major role in determining the appointment of the president and managing director:

> Under a tradition not stated in the Articles of Agreement of either institution, the President of the World Bank has always been an American, and the Managing Director of the IMF has always been a European.

The purposes of the IMF

The purpose of the IMF, as described by Article I of the Articles of Agreement, is:

(i) To promote international monetary cooperation through a permanent institution which provides the machinery for consultation and collaboration on international monetary problems.

(ii) To facilitate the expansion and balanced growth of international trade, and to contribute thereby to the promotion and maintenance of high levels of employment and real income and to the development of the productive resources of all members as primary objectives of economic policy.

(iii) To promote exchange stability, to maintain orderly exchange arrangements among members, and to avoid competitive exchange depreciation.

(iv) To assist in the establishment of a multilateral system of payments in respect of current transactions between members and in the elimination of foreign exchange restrictions which hamper the growth of world trade.

(v) To give confidence to members by making the general resources of the Fund temporarily available to them under adequate safeguards, thus providing them with opportunity to

> correct maladjustments in their balance of payments without resorting to measures destructive of national or international prosperity.
>
> (vi) In accordance with the above, to shorten the duration and lessen the degree of disequilibrium in the international balances of payments of members.

It will be recalled from the introduction to this chapter that the whole rationale for developing a coherent international economic and monetary system was against the backdrop of a fixed gold value in the early 1940s, which, in turn, created stability in the international market.

As Rosa Maria Lastra notes in 'The International Monetary Fund in historical perspective' (2000) 3 J Int'l Econ L 504, 513:

> The IMF's mandate was to maintain the good order of this predictable and 'stable' international monetary system, by enforcing rules about adjustment in international monetary relations and by providing temporary resources to deal with short-term balance of payments problems.

thinking points

- *Explain the mandate of the IMF.*
- *List the purposes of the IMF, and explain the link between these purposes and the historical background to the emergence of the IMF.*

The functions of the IMF

The IMF performs three essential functions: conducting surveillance; providing conditional financial support; and providing technical assistance (Lastra, 2000, at 514 *et seq*, see earlier in this section). Whereas surveillance entitles the IMF to undertake an assessment of a country's economic policies and prepare a report to advise the country accordingly, conditional financial support enables the Fund to provide loans to member States. Such loans can, however, be provided only on the basis of 'conditionality', which, according to Lastra (ibid., 516) is:

> The set of policies and procedures developed by the Fund to govern the access to and the use of its resources by member countries … The logic behind the conditionality requirements is that a country with external payment problems is spending more than it is taking in. Unless economic reform takes place, it will continue to spend more than it takes in.

It is through 'conditionality' that the IMF is able to determine how much a member State is able to borrow from the Fund, since such borrowing is usually linked to the amount contributed by the State upon joining the IMF. Conditionality, therefore, is the adoption and implementation by a member State of adjustment policies prescribed by the IMF. In this way, 'conditionality' looks more like collateral security, which a borrower in a domestic system is required to provide as a means of demonstrating his or her ability to repay. However, conditionality does more than serve as a substitute for collateral. As Lastra notes (ibid., 517):

> IMF conditionality can signal policy credibility to the market. The existence of an IMF program encourages private investment into the country. Being in arrears to the IMF brings a country into the status of an 'economic pariah'.

Thus, when countries take loans from the IMF, they are particularly careful not to default, because this sends the wrong signal to investors and can lead to an isolation of that State from the international economic community—known as 'pariah status'. It must be pointed out that the use of conditionality has been greatly reduced over the years as a result of the emergence of new facilities and procedures.

The IMF also provides technical assistance to its member States. This is extremely important when we consider that developing and least developed countries often lack the necessary technological know-how and capacity to acquire the sophisticated and expensive facilities required in today's global financial market. The IMF is thus able to provide training in several aspects of banking and financial services to staff of its member States.

In general, the IMF was meant to allow States that were unable to meet their obligations to seek financial help, as well as to enable those States having financial difficulties to receive help in order to establish equilibrium in the international monetary system.

The IMF established a pool of funds upon which its members would be able to draw. The funds were received from the member States in accordance with a specifically designed quota which, in theory, represented their economic importance. It also soon became a fact that not all currencies were to be used for international account settlements.

Lowenfeld (2010, see section 18.1), at 578–579, notes that:

> As it turned out, only a few members' currencies were generally acceptable convertible curren-cies. Typically, a member state needing resources to settle its accounts would draw US dollars from the Fund and use these to redeem its own currency ... held by a creditor country.

KEY POINTS

- The IMF performs a surveillance function and provides member States with loans (subject to conditionality), as well as technical assistance.

- Conditionality enables the IMF to prescribe programmes that States that intend to draw funds from it must implement. It enables the Fund to assess the repayment capability of the borrowing States and, to that extent, it resembles collateral security in the domestic banking system.

- The IMF funds are pooled from the contributions made by member States upon joining (usually called 'quotas'), which are often determined in accordance with the economic abilities of individual States.

Modality for drawing loans from the IMF

drawing rights
Supplementary foreign exchange reserve assets maintained by IMF mem-bers for the purpose of meeting shortfalls in their economies.

The IMF was subject to revision during the 1970s but, before this time, it was undecided, when a State had a **drawing right**, whether it was to be subject to specific conditions. Whereas the UK preferred a system whereby States had an automatic right to draw from the Fund—that is, to draw funds without preconditions—the USA took the line that any State wishing to receive funds had to satisfy conditions. It was this latter approach that was adopted.

A State had to provide evidence that it would be able to solve the problem with the funds and supply this in a letter of intent. Andreas Lowenfeld (2010, see section 18.1), at 580, describes the letter of intent:

> Although in the form a Letter of Intent is a unilateral declaration, in practice it is a document resulting from negotiation between the Fund and the applicant country. Letters of Intent are

considered binding on the country involved, even though they have not been submitted to its parliament and even when the administration in office has changed during the period of the drawing.

These letters used to be confidential, but they are now public and even published online.

Things worked relatively well for the IMF until 1967, at which time problems arose that impacted the IMF considerably and almost destroyed it. The UK devalued its currency, sterling, which was at that time used as a reserve; this impacted its commitments to the IMF. Even though the USA said that it would continue with its financial commitments, this was only a temporary fix: the country started experiencing its own problems in 1971, which presented a major hurdle for the IMF when then US President Nixon made the decision that the USA would no longer be converting US dollars held by foreigners to gold or other reserve assets, due to the USA's depleting reserves. These issues meant that it was no longer possible for the IMF to use its fixed-rate system. All of the major currencies were floating by 1973—that is, there were no governmental interventions in the financial market and the currency value was allowed to fluctuate according to the foreign exchange market.

Following these problems, the IMF was able to preserve only its structure, but not its substance. The new Articles of Agreement no longer imposed the former par value obligation; instead, they only obliged member States to refrain from manipulating the exchange rate (Article IV).

Despite the fact that member States were no longer obliged to follow the fixed exchange rate and currencies were allowed to float on the open market, the IMF did still retain some of its surveillance powers. Article IV(3) of the Articles of Agreement states that:

(a) The Fund shall oversee the international monetary system in order to ensure its effective operation, and shall oversee the compliance of each member with its obligations under Section 1 of this Article.

(b) In order to fulfill its functions under (a) above, the Fund shall exercise firm surveillance over the exchange rate policies of members, and shall adopt specific principles for the guidance of all members with respect to those policies. Each member shall provide the Fund with the information necessary for such surveillance, and, when requested by the Fund, shall consult with it on the member's exchange rate policies. The principles adopted by the Fund shall be consistent with cooperative arrangements by which members maintain the value of their currencies in relation to the value of the currency or currencies of other members, as well as with other exchange arrangements of a member's choice consistent with the purposes of the Fund and Section 1 of this Article. These principles shall respect the domestic social and political policies of members, and in applying these principles the Fund shall pay due regard to the circumstances of members.

After the 1970s, the IMF ceased to play an influential role in the international monetary and economic system. In fact, GATT, and then the WTO, took over some of the areas that the IMF had previously governed.

As Lowenfeld (2010, see section 18.1) notes, at 585–586:

Leadership in legislation concerning the international economy passed to the GATT and subsequently to the World Trade Organization (WTO) as new rules were being negotiated and drafted by trade ministries and not by finance ministries . . . De facto, the IMF became essentially a foreign aid agency.

The significance of the IMF in providing financial aid to developing countries has also continued to decrease over time, especially given the sensitivity inherent in the requirement that States wanting loans from the Fund should submit letters of intent. Also, there is now a proliferation of private loans and of loans provided by different groups of States outside the IMF framework. A prominent example is the so-called Paris Club, which now offers such facilities as debt restructuring, debt relief, and total debt cancellation.

Also, on 26 September 2009, a group of seven South American nations—Argentina, Bolivia, Brazil, Ecuador, Paraguay, Uruguay, and Venezuela—established the Bank of the South, with headquarters in Caracas, Venezuela. The Bank serves as an alternative to borrowing from the IMF. The founding States felt strongly that the IMF is dominated by Northern countries and claimed that this affected the IMF policies. Already, borrowing by Latin American countries from the IMF has fallen sharply, with many States such as Brazil refusing to borrow more from the Fund. The overall aim of the Bank is that all Latin American countries will become members—a move that will surely further whittle away the importance and relevance of the IMF in the long run.

thinking points

- *What approaches did the UK and USA prefer in terms of States drawing funds from the IMF, and which of these prevailed?*
- *What does 'surveillance' mean and why does the IMF carry out surveillance of its member States?*
- *Explain what is meant by a 'letter of intent'.*

18.4.2 The World Bank

The World Bank is another institution that emerged from the Bretton Woods Conference in response to the world wars. It originally comprised only the IBRD; it now includes the International Development Association (IDA).

Article I of the Articles of Agreement of the IBRD (amended in 1989) provides that the purposes of the Bank are:

(i) To assist in the reconstruction and development of territories of members by facilitating the investment of capital for productive purposes, including the restoration of economies destroyed or disrupted by war, the reconversion of productive facilities to peacetime needs and the encouragement of the development of productive facilities and resources in less developed countries.

(ii) To promote private foreign investment by means of guarantees or participations in loans and other investments made by private investors; and when private capital is not available on reasonable terms, to supplement private investment by providing, on suitable conditions, finance for productive purposes out of its own capital, funds raised by it and its other resources.

(iii) To promote the long-range balanced growth of international trade and the maintenance of equilibrium in balances of payments by encouraging international investment for the development of the productive resources of members, thereby assisting in raising productivity, the standard of living and conditions of labor in their territories.

(iv) To arrange the loans made or guaranteed by it in relation to international loans through other channels so that the more useful and urgent projects, large and small alike, will be dealt with first.

(v) To conduct its operations with due regard to the effect of international investment on business conditions in the territories of members and, in the immediate postwar years, to assist in bringing about a smooth transition from a wartime to a peacetime economy.

The World Bank discharges these responsibilities by providing low-interest loans, and interest-free credits and grants, to developing countries to address a wide range of issues and areas. Although most of its clients are invariably developing countries, the Bank's loan facilities are open to all member States; indeed, France was the first country to benefit from World Bank financial aid.

Under Article III(1) of the IBRD Articles of Agreement:

(a) The resources and the facilities of the Bank shall be used exclusively for the benefit of members with equitable consideration to projects for development and projects for reconstruction alike.

(b) For the purpose of facilitating the restoration and reconstruction of the economy of members whose metropolitan territories have suffered great devastation from enemy occupation or hostilities, the Bank, in determining the conditions and terms of loans made to such members, shall pay special regard to lightening the financial burden and expediting the completion of such restoration and reconstruction.

The IDA's purpose is set out in Article I of its Articles of Agreement:

The purposes of the Association are to promote economic development, increase productivity and thus raise standards of living in the less-developed areas of the world included within the Association's membership, in particular by providing finance to meet their important developmental requirements on terms which are more flexible and bear less heavily on the balance of payments than those of conventional loans, thereby furthering the developmental objectives of the International Bank for Reconstruction and Development (hereinafter called 'the Bank') and supplementing its activities.

KEY POINTS

- The World Bank is a Bretton Woods institution that exists to assist member States to undertake a wide range of activities, such as reconstruction and development.

- The World Bank provides low-interest loans and interest-free credit facilities to developing countries. However, developed countries can also benefit from World Bank loan facilities.

18.5 The World Bank's Inspection Panel

Established in 1993 by the World's Bank Board of Executive Directors, and commencing operations on 1 August 1994, the Inspection Panel is an independent body responsible for dealing with complaints over the World Bank's funded projects. As a major developmental bank, the World Bank funds numerous projects across the world. Some of these projects often generate tension between the beneficiaries of the projects, usually governments, and their citizens. Sources of discord have been known to include proposals to cultivate forests, which locals claimed served traditional purposes for them, or to build resources that are perceived to threaten the ecosystem or the people's traditional way of life. While the Bank itself does not have direct responsibility for such issues, the fact that it is providing funding for the project makes it a key player.

Where there are complaints that World Bank-funded projects will adversely affect people's lives, it is important to have independent mechanisms to deal with such complaints. This is the rationale behind the Inspection Panel.

18.5.1 Composition

The Inspection Panel consists of three members appointed by the Board of Executive Directors for a five-year, non-renewable term. Selection is based on the competence and ability of each Member 'to deal thoroughly and fairly with the complaints brought to them, their integrity and independence from Bank Management, and their exposure to developmental issues and living conditions in developing countries'. (See http://ewebapps. worldbank.org/apps/ip/Pages/AboutUs.aspx). The Panel also has a Secretariat, which supports its work, and is additionally serviced by experts and consultants which it hires from time to time.

18.5.2 Function

The Panel's main function is to serve as a watchdog to the World Bank to ensure that it complies with its operational policies and procedures. These include such issues as:

- adverse effects on people and livelihoods as a consequence of displacement and resettlement related to infrastructure projects, such as dams, roads, pipelines, mines, and landfills;
- risks to people and the environment related to dam safety, use of pesticides, and other indirect effects of investments;
- risks to indigenous peoples, their culture, traditions, lands tenure, and development rights;
- adverse effects on physical cultural heritage, including sacred places;
- adverse effects on natural habitats, including protected areas, such as wetlands, forests, and water bodies.

(See http://ewebapps.worldbank.org/apps/ip/Pages/AboutUs.aspx).

The Panel is therefore an accountability mechanism although, as will be seen in the evaluation of its process later, whether it lives up to this important billing is debatable.

thinking points
- *Explain the rationale for establishing the World Bank Inspection Panel.*
- *What are the criteria for selecting the members of the Panel, and what other criteria can you suggest?*

18.5.3 The Inspection Panel's review process

The Panel review process starts with it receiving a request for inspection from one or more persons called requesters. A request for inspection is an invitation, sent to the Panel by a member(s) of the community who fears that what the World Bank-funded project is doing will destroy or is destroying their means of livelihood or environment. Such complaints, if they are found to be true, are directly opposed to the values of the World Bank's policies and procedure which is to safeguard social welfare and the environment.

Upon receiving a request, the Panel registers the request, which kicks in the eligibility phase. This phase is to determine whether the request for inspection is or is not suitable to be admitted. The World Bank's management then has twenty-one days, from the date of registration of the request, within which it must provide the Panel with evidence that it complied or intended to comply with the Bank's relevant policies and procedures. The Panel also has twenty-one business days after receiving the response from the Bank's management, to determine the eligibility of the request.

A successful determination of eligibility of request is followed by the Panel reviewing the management's response after which the Panel may undertake a visit to the concerned project, following which it may then make recommendations to investigate the request. Up to this point, the Panel functions completely independently of the Bank's management, as it should as an oversight body. However, the picture changes once the Panel makes recommendations to investigate the request. A recommendation to investigate requires the approval of the Bank's Board of Executive Directors, and it is only after this is given that the Panel can progress to the second stage of its work, the investigation phase, in which it assesses the merits of the request. The task of the Panel in this phase includes visiting the place complained about, meeting with the local people, both those who originated the request and others whose views may be instrumental and useful to the Panel's investigation. The duration of the investigation depends on the nature of the issue at hand.

At the end of this phase, the Panel produces a report which it then submits to the Bank's management. The management will also prepare its recommendations, based on the report, which will then be considered along with the Panel report, by the Board of Executive Directors. The Board may or may not approve the recommendations.

From this, it seems overgenerous to describe the Inspection Panel as an 'independent body'. The Panel was set up to assess whether or not the Bank is following its own policies and procedures. Yet whether or not the Panel can investigate a complaint depends on the approval of the Bank management which may decide to withhold its approval. Furthermore, the final report of the Panel is submitted to the management which will consider it and write its own recommendations to be forwarded with the Panel's report to the Board. The Board's approval is given or withheld not to the Panel's report, but to the management's recommendations which do not have to agree with the Panel's report. If anything, this process is far from being independent.

thinking points
- *Describe the review process of the Inspection Panel and explain what benefits it confers for the World Bank.*
- *How far can one claim that the Inspection Panel is independent of the World Bank?*

 # Conclusion

IEL is undoubtedly a vital tool in ensuring the health of nations. The current financial crisis shows clearly why it is extremely important to put in place a strong regime of international economic regulation. However, in pursuing such an endeavour, there are various challenges to be expected, all of which will affect the future of IEL.

There are institutional-specific problems. The long-term sustainability of the funds available to such institutions as the IMF has been questioned. Also, there is an increasing perception, especially in the developing world, that rich and powerful countries are not always transparent, even in the way in which they engage with each other. For example, most WTO negotiations have been marred by bitter division between developed and developing worlds on a number of issues such as subsidies and so on.

In addition, States are often reluctant to cede authority over their economies to international institutions. Former British Prime Minister Margaret Thatcher once said 'No one is going to tell me how to run economic policy', while an official of the US Treasury responded 'We wouldn't want to have the IMF order us around' (both restated in Lowenfeld, 2010, at 584, see section 18.1). Yet, while the preservation of sovereignty is important, it must be noted that it is only by not allowing sovereignty to stand in the way of strong international economic regulation that States can actually be guaranteed peace and prosperity. Otherwise, States risk monumental economic meltdown, such as that which has now led many States, including Portugal, Greece, and Ireland, to seek huge financial bailouts from international institutions. Such action, in itself, cannot bode well for sovereignty.

 # Questions

Self test questions

1 What is 'international economic law'?

2 Explain what is meant by the 'Bretton Woods institutions'.

3 What is the relationship between international economic law and public international law?

4 Explain 'conditionality' in the context of the IMF.

5 What do 'nullification' and 'impairment' mean in the context of GATT?

6 Why was the Bank of the South established?

7 What is the IBRD?

8 Explain what is meant by 'surveillance'.

Discussion questions

1 Explain the functions of the IMF.

2 What are the major weaknesses of the GATT/WTO system?

3 To what extent does the dispute settlement system under GATT 1947 differ from that under GATT 1994?

4 Explain why public international law was slow to regulate international economics.

5 Which types of State can access the World Bank loan facilities?

Assessment question

'There is no real difference between the dispute settlement procedure under GATT 1947 and that under GATT 1994. In the final analysis, both deal with disputes in the same way, and use the same media and institutions. It is an exaggeration, and nothing more, to think that one is better than the other.'

Discuss.

Key cases

- *Report of the Working Party on the Australian Subsidy on Ammonium Sulphate* GATT/CP.4/39, adopted 3 April 1950, BISD II/188

- *Report of the Panel on Uruguay Recourse to Article XXIII* L/1923, adopted 16 November 1962, BISD 11S/95

- *Report of the GATT Panel on the Treatment by Germany of Imports of Sardines* G/26, adopted 31 October 1952, BISD 1S/53

Further reading

Cottier, T., 'Challenges ahead in international economic law' (2009) 12 J Int'l Econ L 3

Davey, W. J., 'Dispute settlement in GATT' (1987–88) 11 Fordham Int'l LJ 51

Jackson, J., 'Global economics and international economic law' (1998) 1(I) J Int'l Econ L 1

Jackson, J., 'International economic law in times that are interesting' (2000) 3 J Int'l Econ L 3

Lastra, R. M., 'The International Monetary Fund in historical perspective ' (2000) 3 J Int'l Econ L 504

Lowenfeld, A., 'The international monetary system: a look back over seven decades' (2010) 13 J Int'l Econ L 575

Reitz, C., 'Enforcement of the General Agreement on Tariffs and Trade' (1996) 17 U Penn J Int'l Econ L 555

Shihata, I., *The World Bank Inspection Panel: In Practice* (Oxford: Oxford University Press, 2000)

Trachtman, J. P., 'The domain of WTO dispute resolution' (1999) 40 Harv Int'l LJ 333

International human rights

Learning objectives

This chapter will help you to:

- understand what human rights are and learn about the emergence of human rights;
- understand what the international human rights regime is;
- comprehend how, and by what means, human rights are protected; and
- appreciate the enforcement of human rights.

Introduction

It is as impossible to find a single acceptable definition of 'human rights' as it is to locate their exact origin. Theories vary. Some regard human rights as inherent in human beings. It is said that human rights are born with human beings, so that, in a sense, they are simply the rights of humanity in general. Some believe that human rights are given by God or nature. In this chapter, we will consider what international human rights are, who has the responsibility to protect human rights, and vindicate them when they are violated. This chapter is not concerned with how individual States protect human rights within their systems, although the relations of States to human rights in general will be considered briefly; neither is it the intention to delve deeply into the history of the evolution of human rights.

19.1 States and human rights

It is well known that States can, and do, derogate from the fundamental rights of those present in their territory. The power of a State to derogate from or deny peoples their human rights derives principally from the fact that States are the arch-custodians of human rights. It is State institutions that are charged by the constitution or fundamental law of every country to protect the fundamental human rights of people. Furthermore, when these rights are violated, it is the same State institutions that must ensure that the law is enforced against violators, even if such be the State itself.

According to the 1993 Vienna Declaration and Programme of Action:

> Human rights derive from the dignity and worth inherent in the human person...the human person is the central subject of human rights and fundamental freedoms, and consequently should be the principal beneficiary and should participate actively in the realization of these rights and freedoms. Human rights and fundamental freedoms are the birthright of all human beings; their protection and promotion is the first responsibility of Governments.

Human rights, often expressed as 'fundamental freedoms', 'fundamental human rights', or 'fundamental rights' and usually guaranteed by the constitutions of most States, are many and vary widely in content. The most common rights include the right to life, freedom of movement, freedom of expression, the right to form and belong to associations, and freedom of religion, etc.

Despite their widespread recognition, for various reasons States often violate the fundamental human rights of people. Violations may be as a result of 'necessity', such as during national emergencies that may necessitate restrictions on certain freedoms, such as the freedom of movement or association. Sometimes, States may violate human rights on the basis of a mere suspicion that a certain individual is engaged in activities that are inimical to public or State interest. Whatever may account for such violation of human rights, it is important to ensure that States do not disregard, violate, or threaten fundamental human rights for no just cause.

When a State violates the rights of the people, redress is usually sought first before the courts of that State. However, whether a person is able to challenge the violation of their human rights effectively before the courts depends largely on the type of government in operation in the country in question. In most democratic societies, there is usually an effective process for seeking redress in the courts following human rights violations. However, in parts of the world in which other less participatory types of government exist, such as military regimes, absolute monarchies, or other forms of authoritarian government, national courts are often unable to deal freely with human rights violations. This is due to the fact that, under such political systems, the judiciary is usually under immense pressure not to upset the executive arm of the government, which is the arm that most frequently commits human rights violations, since it consists of, among others, the police, the military, and other law enforcement agencies in regular direct contact with the people.

KEY POINTS

- Human rights are inherent in humans since they are believed to accrue to human beings by virtue of their 'humanness'.

- States can permanently deny or temporarily withdraw the human rights of their people.

- Undemocratic governments, such as military regimes and monarchies, do not guarantee the protection of human rights as predictably as democratic societies.

19.2 The rise of international human rights

In the past, human rights were regarded as an exclusive matter for individual States, irrespective of the type of government in existence in that State. The issue belonged to the exclusive jurisdiction of States and this was especially so before the First World War. States dealt with their citizens, and all who lived within their territories, as they pleased. Where States violated the rights of foreigners, for example, such cases would normally be taken up by the countries of nationality of such foreigners. There were no specialized courts for that purpose, but rather such cases were taken to international tribunals to which the two States would agree.

In classical international law, the only means through which to exert pressure on States not to violate the rights of foreigners were diplomatic intervention, such as an exchange of notes, a regular exchange of views on States' international obligations, and so on. If the situation were particularly desperate, then it might require the use of force against the concerned States in what is known as a 'humanitarian intervention' (see Chapter 11). We will recall, however, that the doctrine of humanitarian intervention, which is still practised today, has always been very unpopular, precisely because it overrides a State's sovereignty to do as it pleases within its own territory, including how it deals with its people. Even then, humanitarian intervention does not give violated people justice; it only compels a State to stop violating its people's rights on a massive scale. Such violations could continue even after the intervention, provided that they are neither massive nor particularly gruesome.

The outbreak of the First World War and the extensive atrocities committed by States against peoples, especially minority groups, revealed that States could not be trusted always to protect peoples' human rights, let alone to ensure their vindication when they are violated. But nothing much was done to resolve this situation during the interwar period.

The human rights situation of the world worsened during the Second World War, as more atrocities were committed against people singled out on the basis of their race. As the world began to search for means of dealing with peace-breaching States such as Germany, Italy, and Japan, it realized that it must also start thinking about how to protect the human rights of people against violations by their own governments. (It must be recalled that most of the Jews who were persecuted and executed under the Nazi regime were actually German citizens.)

Early academic efforts concentrated on making human rights part and parcel of State obligations. There was no serious effort made to place human rights under international law as such, even if it was widely recognized that international law could be used to impose obligations on States to protect the rights of their citizens. Even Hersch Lauterpacht, one of the earliest scholars to propose that human rights be included in the constitutions of every State and that international law be used to sensitize States towards human rights protection, recognized the limits of international law on the recognition and enforcement of human rights when he said, in *An International Bill of Rights of Man* (New York: Columbia University Press, 1945), pp. 9–10, that:

> any attempt to translate the idea of an International Bill of the Rights of Man into a working rule of law is fraught with difficulties which disturb orthodox thought to the point of utter discouragement.

In (1946) 243 Ann Am Acad Polit Soc Sci 150, Edwin Borchard, reviewing Lauterpacht's *An International Bill of Rights of Man*, says of Lauterpacht that:

> His intention is undoubtedly praiseworthy, and he has seen, as have few scholars, the obstacles and hurdles in the path of assuring legal protection to the individual against his own states. Possibly logic compels him to analogize the guarantees of the bill of rights to the few instances of humanitarian intervention which we know.

thinking points

- *Why was it that only States could deal with human rights under classical international law?*
- *What is the rationale for arguing that human rights should be made the business of international law?*

19.3 The United Nations and human rights

In 1945, the United Nations was formed. The Preamble to the Charter establishing the United Nations (the UN Charter) states that:

> *We the people of the United Nations determined*
>
> to save succeeding generations from the scourge of war, which twice in our lifetime has brought untold sorrow to mankind, and to reaffirm faith in fundamental human rights, in the dignity and worth of the human person, in the equal rights of men and women and of nations large and small, and to establish conditions under which justice and respect for the obligations arising from treaties and other sources of international law can be maintained, and to promote social progress and better standards of life in larger freedom.

This was the first time that an international organization had so clearly included individuals in a discussion of international law and human rights, firmly entrenching the notion within international law. In Chapter IX, under the heading 'International Economic and Social Cooperation', Article 55 aims for:

> the creation of conditions of stability and well-being which are necessary for peaceful and friendly relations among nations based on respect for the principle of equal rights and self-determination of peoples.

And such objectives shall be promoted through the Article 55(c) provision for:

> universal respect for, and observance of, human rights and fundamental freedoms for all without distinction as to race, sex, language, or religion.

Article 61 creates the Economic and Social Council (ECOSOC), which, according to Article 62(2), has the power to:

> make recommendations for the purpose of promoting respect for, and observance of, human rights and fundamental freedoms for all.

ECOSOC established a commission for the protection of human rights, with a number of other complementary bodies. This body has now been replaced by the Human Rights Council.

Nevertheless, it must be stressed that the UN Charter did not establish a system of human rights protection, nor indeed did it say in 1945 that human rights belonged to the realm of international law. All that the Charter did was emphasize the world's faith in human rights, regardless of race and creed, and canvass for the promotion and encouragement of 'respect for human rights and for fundamental freedoms for all without distinction as to race, sex, language, or religion' (Article 1(3)).

Despite the UN Charter containing human rights terms and aims, there is no definition of what these human rights are and no system was put in place to deal comprehensively with the issue. Given the reluctance of some States, during the drafting phase of the UN Charter, to include human rights, this is perhaps the compromise that was reached. As Lauterpacht (1945, see section 19.2), p. 57 has noted (emphasis original):

> The vindication of human liberties did not begin with their complete and triumphant assertion at the very outset ... It commenced with recognizing them in *some* matters, to *some* extent, for *some* people, against *some* organ of the State.

Nonetheless, the idea of international protection of human rights began to gain momentum and popularity shortly after the emergence of the Charter.

There is no doubt that the Second World War had a profound impact on the development of a worldwide human rights system. According to Durward Sandifer, 'The international protection of human rights: the United Nations system' (1949) 43 AJIL 59, 60:

> The flagrant excesses of the Nazi and Fascist regimes preceding and during World War II shocked the conscience of mankind into a realization that there could be no assurance of stability and order in an international society which left man at the mercy of whatever government happened to be in control of its component states. From this sprung the conviction that there are fundamental human rights and freedoms which must be given international protection.

Therefore efforts to clarify the nature and means of establishing an international protection of human rights began in earnest. According to Moses Moskowitz, 'Is the UN's Bill of Human Rights dangerous?' (1949) ABA J 358:

> There is no such thing as recognized human rights in international common law. The idea of affording international protection of certain human rights and freedoms can be realized only within the framework of treaty provisions establishing the rights to be placed under international protection, defining their content, limitations and prohibitions.

Despite initial caution and reluctance, the UN has made tremendous progress in developing international human rights. It has led to, and encouraged the adoption of, various treaties and conventions, and it has helped to exert considerable political pressure on States and international organizations, as well as in developing a strong human rights culture. Most notable among UN efforts are:

- the 1948 Universal Declaration of Human Rights (UDHR);
- the 1966 International Covenant on Civil and Political Rights (ICCPR);
- the 1966 International Covenant on Economic, Social and Cultural Rights (ICESCR);
- the 1966 International Convention on the Elimination of Racial Discrimination (ICERD);
- the 1979 Convention on the Elimination of All Forms of Discrimination against Women (CEDAW);
- the 1984 Convention Against Torture and Other Cruel, Inhuman and Degrading Treatment (CAT); and
- the 1989 Convention on the Rights of the Child (CRC).

The UN, through the above treaties, established monitoring committees, which work with ECOSOC and the Secretary-General, and provide to these relevant reports on their work.

The approach adopted by the UN to set up these human rights bodies/monitoring committees has been both at a Charter- and treaty-based level. The differences primarily stem from their basis of establishment and scope. Charter-based bodies are established by UN Charter provisions, have mandates which cover a broad range of human rights issues, and apply to all States. In order for decisions to be taken there is a need for majority voting. The Human Rights Council, and the former Commission on Human Rights (the predecessor to the Human Rights Council), were established by UN principal organs; the Human Rights Council was established by UN General Assembly Resolution 60/215 on 15 March 2006, while the Commission on Human Rights was established by the Economic and Social Council Resolution 5(1) of 16 February 1946. Treaty-based bodies are established by specific international instruments and have narrow mandates related to the areas covered by the treaty only. In addition, their scope of application is more restricted as it is limited to the States that have ratified the treaty in question and require consensus to reach a decision. Examples of such include the Human Rights Committee (not to be confused with the Human Rights Council) which oversees the ICCPR and associated Optional Protocols as per Article 28 of the ICCPR; the Committee against Torture oversees the CAT pursuant to Article 17; and the Committee on Economic, Social and Cultural Rights has oversight of the ICESCR provided for by Economic and Social Council Resolution 1985/17 of 28 May 1985.

KEY POINTS

- The UN was the first international organization to make provision for human rights.

- The UN Charter did not establish a protection mechanism or demand that international law enforce respect for human rights, but only provided that people should be treated on an equal basis and with dignity.

- ECOSOC was principally tasked with making recommendations to the UN General Assembly on the promotion and respect for human rights.

19.3.1 The 1948 Universal Declaration of Human Rights

The UDHR was adopted by the UN General Assembly on 10 December 1948 by Resolution 217A (III), with forty-eight States in favour and eight abstaining. The UDHR is a non-binding instrument in international law and is not a treaty. It is a General Assembly recommendation to member States, which possesses moral and political influence over the signatories rather than any legally enforceable provisions. The UDHR falls into the class of legal instruments called 'soft law': they are 'laws' because they contain regulations and rules, but they are 'soft' because they are not enforceable against signatories. However, it is generally believed that most 'soft law' emerging from the General Assembly has a tendency to ripen into hardcore legal obligations in the future, given the huge number of States that usually accept them and the pervasiveness of State practice in that respect (see Chapter 2 on customary international law).

In 'The Universal Declaration of Human Rights' (1948) 25 BYBIL 354, Lauterpacht considers the nature of the obligations that States assume under the UDHR:

> The practical unanimity of the Members of the United Nations in stressing the importance of the Declaration was accompanied by an equally *general repudiation of the idea that the Declaration imposed upon them a legal obligation to respect the human rights and fundamental freedoms* which it proclaimed. [Emphasis added]

Nonetheless, the learned jurist believed strongly that the UDHR was little more than only a non-binding declaration. Consequently, he argued (ibid., 365–366) that:

> it may be said, and has been said, that although the Declaration in itself may not be a legal document involving legal obligations, it is of legal value inasmuch as it contains an authoritative interpretation of the 'human rights and of international freedoms' which do constitute an obligation, however imperfect, binding upon the Members of the United Nations ... To maintain that a

document contains an authoritative interpretation of a legally binding instrument is to assert that the former document itself is as legally binding and as important as the instrument which it is supposed to interpret.

Lauterpacht grounded his view on the rather ambiguous nature of the UDHR, noting (ibid.) that:

> It is not clear whether the Declaration is in the nature of a recommendation—a term which, in turn, bristles with a multiplicity of meanings...The Declaration of Human Rights is cast in the form of a Resolution. But the only operative part of the Resolution is to 'proclaim' the Declaration 'as a common standard of achievement for all peoples and nations'. Significantly it does not contain a recommendation to Members of the United Nations to observe its principles.

The opinion of the majority of States is that the UDHR is not a binding instrument. However, Henry Steiner, 'Securing human rights: the first half-century of the Universal Declaration, and beyond' (1998) Sep–Oct Harvard Magazine 45, has pointed out that the UDHR:

> Has retained its place of honor in the human rights movement. No other document has so caught the historical moment, achieved the same moral and rhetorical force, or exerted as much influence on the movement as a whole... [T]he Declaration expressed in lean, eloquent language the hopes and idealism of a world released from the grip of World War II.

In the years that followed the adoption of the UDHR, the UN intensified its efforts in the area of international human rights. Attempts were made to elevate some of the rights embodied in the UDHR.

In 1949, the UN convened its Conference on Freedom of Information and the Movement against International Propaganda. Writing on the importance of freedom of information, John B. Whitton, 'Conference on Freedom of Information and the Movement against International Propaganda' (1949) 43 AJIL 73, states that:

> The main emphasis during both the Conference and the extensive preparations that preceded it was definitely positive. The major objective was the improvement in the means of sending information across frontiers in accordance with the view, solemnly affirmed by the Conference, that freedom of information is a 'fundamental human right and...the touchstone of all the freedoms to which the United Nations is consecrated'.

The UDHR is wide in scope, covering rights, freedoms, and duties, and the instrument incorporates almost all of the areas understood as falling under the ambit of human rights at the time. The principle of universality and indivisibility is an important element of the UDHR, and is visible throughout the document. The original idea was for the UDHR to be a springboard for more comprehensive instruments that would create legal obligations for States. However, due to the Cold War, even the issues covered by the UDHR became highly contentious.

Despite the non-binding nature of the UDHR, it is often cited as an authority, and the provisions included have been incorporated into other treaties and legally binding instruments. Two of the most prominent resulting treaties are the ICCPR and the ICESCR, adopted in 1966 by UN General Assembly Resolution 2200A (XXI).

19.3.2 The United Nations Human Rights Council

The role of the United Nations Human Rights Council (HRC) is the promotion and protection of human rights while seeking to address human rights violations, of all kinds, through recommendations. The HRC was established in 2006 and replaced the United Nations Commission on Human Rights that was in existence from 1946 to 2006. The mandate of the HRC is not confined to any particular thematic area of human rights, and it can consider all situations which concern human rights. The General Assembly elects the forty-seven UN member States which make up the HRC and uses an equitable geographical distribution; thirteen seats given to African States, thirteen to Asia-Pacific States, eight to Latin American and Caribbean States, seven to Western Europe and other States, and six seats to Eastern European States. Each member of the HRC is elected for three years and can serve for up to two consecutive terms.

The HRC undertakes it role through the use of subsidiary bodies. The Universal Periodic Review Working Group considers the UN member States' human rights situations, which takes place three times a year with sixteen States' human rights records being reviewed at each session. The Advisory Committee's role is the provision of advice and expertise on thematic issues through eighteen experts serving in their personal capacity. Under the Special Procedures provision the HRC encompasses the work of special rapporteurs, special representatives, independent experts, and working groups for examining, monitoring, and providing advice and reporting on thematic human rights issues and situations.

19.3.3 The International Covenant on Civil and Political Rights

The ICCPR entered into force on 23 March 1976, following the thirty-fifth instrument of ratification, as required by Article 49. It is a legally binding instrument creating obligations for its signatories. It establishes a treaty body under Article 28—the Human Rights Committee (discussed in section 19.3.4). The ICCPR provisions are similar to those of the UDHR, but the former contains greater expansion and attempts at clarification. Furthermore, there have been two Optional Protocols to the ICCPR. The First Optional Protocol (adopted in 1966 and entered into force on 23 March 1976) covers procedural matters, while the Second Optional Protocol (adopted in 1989) is aimed at abolishing the death penalty.

The ICCPR generally covers individual rights as opposed to group rights. In other words, a person cannot bring a claim of violation of a group right, such as that environmental pollution affects all people in an area. Actions deriving from such claims are generally referred to as ***actio popularis***. The few exceptions to this are the right to self-determination contained in Article 1 and the Article 27 provision on survival of cultures. (On group rights, see Russel L. Barsh, 'Indigenous peoples: an emerging object of international law' (1986) 80 AJIL 369 and 'Evolving conceptions of group rights in international law' (1987) 13 Transnational Perspectives 1.)

The ICCPR focuses mainly on rights, paying little or no attention to duties. In general, States have the duty to ensure the protection of human rights, not individual rights. In fact, only in the Preamble to the ICCPR is an individual considered to have 'duties to other individuals and to the community to which he belongs'.

***actio popularis*
(popular action)**

An action by one or more persons to obtain remedy for collective interests.

The question remains how relevant the ICCPR is to the national human rights systems. In 'The United Nations Covenant on Civil and Political Rights and the European Convention on Human Rights' (1968) 43 BYBIL 25, Robertson observes that:

> The Covenant will not necessarily have a direct effect on the national legal systems. It is possible for States to ratify it without immediately complying with the obligations it contains, provided that they have the intention of doing so in the future; but there is no time-limit for doing so.

Unlike the UDHR, the ICCPR provides for a remedial structure under Article 2. The provision calls for rights to be recognized, an effective remedy to be made available, legislation adopted, or any other measures to ensure this, as well as requiring the enforcement of remedies by the competent authorities. This is possible only due to the binding nature of the ICCPR as distinct from the UDHR.

ICCPR State parties may derogate from their obligation under the treaty only in certain circumstances. Under Article 4(1):

> In time of public emergency which threatens the life of the nation and the existence of which is officially proclaimed, the States Parties to the present Covenant may take measures derogating from their obligations under the present Covenant to the extent strictly required by the exigencies of the situation, provided that such measures are not inconsistent with their other obligations under international law and do not involve discrimination solely on the ground of race, colour, sex, language, religions or social origin.

It must be noted that the sanctioned derogation is temporary, and subject to specific conditions and situations. It is not possible for a State to derogate whenever it so chooses.

Furthermore, a State may derogate from Articles 18 (freedom of thought, conscience, and religion) and 19 (the right to hold opinions without interference) when such derogations are (according to those two Articles):

> prescribed by law and are necessary to protect public safety, order, health, or morals or the fundamental rights and freedoms of others.

Further limitations are contained in Articles 21 (right of peaceful assembly) and 22 (freedom of association), which require the limitation to be 'necessary in a democratic society'.

While the ICCPR is a step forward for international human rights, divergences in the interpretations given by States have led to different implementations and disagreements over what the important basic provisions are. In turn, this can make enforcement difficult and complicated at the international level.

Unlike many other treaties, the ICCPR contains no provisions on the withdrawal of a State party, which provision would have the effect of terminating that particular State's obligations under the Convention. In 1997, the Human Rights Committee issued General Comment 26 regarding withdrawal, in which it stated thus:

3.   ...[I]t is clear that the Covenant is not the type of treaty which, by its nature, implies a right of denunciation. Together with the simultaneously prepared and adopted International Covenant on Economic, Social and Cultural Rights, the Covenant codifies in treaty form the universal human rights enshrined in the Universal Declaration of Human Rights, the three instruments together often being referred to as the 'International Bill of Human Rights'. As

such, the Covenant does not have a temporary character typical of treaties where a right of denunciation is deemed to be admitted, notwithstanding the absence of a specific provision to that effect.

4. The rights enshrined in the Covenant belong to the people living in the territory of the State party. The Human Rights Committee has consistently taken the view... that once the people are accorded the protection of the rights under the Covenant, such protection devolves with territory and continues to belong to them, notwithstanding change in government of the State party, including dismemberment in more than one State or State succession...

5. The Committee is therefore firmly of the view that international law does not permit a State which has ratified or acceded or succeeded to the Covenant to denounce it or withdraw from it.

KEY POINTS

- The ICCPR covers political and civil rights and, unlike the UDHR, it is binding on all State parties.

- There is no *actio popularis* under the ICCPR, thus actions brought to enforce the Covenant can be only individual, not group, actions.

- Derogation from the ICCPR is stringent and specific, and must comply with standards prescribed by the Covenant.

19.3.4 The Human Rights Committee

The Human Rights Committee (HR Committee), established by Article 28 ICCPR, is tasked with monitoring UN member States' compliance with the ICCPR, under Article 40(1), by means of receiving reports on a five-yearly basis from those States:

> on the measures they have adopted which give effect to the rights recognized herein and on the progress in the enjoyment of those rights.

These reports are submitted to the UN Secretary-General, who gives them to the HR Committee (Article 40(2)), and where the Secretary-General consults with the HR Committee, reports can be transmitted to specialized agencies when parts of such reports fall within their competencies. The HR Committee issues guidelines, which are non-binding, in relation to the reports, and is also able to request ad hoc reports from States (Article 40(1)(b)), but this latter capability has rarely been used.

The lack of specificity on the HR Committee powers in relation to reports has been commented on by Thomas Buergenthal, a HR Committee member until 1999, in 'The UN Human Rights Committee' (2001) 5 Max Planck YBUNL 341, 347, thus:

> The language of Article 40 indicates that those who drafted this provision did not wish to spell out very clearly what powers the Committee had in dealing with State reports.

Interstate complaints are possible, where a State claims another State party has not fulfilled its obligations, but the State party complained of must have accepted the competence of the Committee (Article 41). The claiming State must give written communication to the other State party about its claim and allowed that State time to reply (Article 41(1)(a)). Where six months have passed and the matter has not been satisfactorily dealt with, the matter can be referred to the HR Committee (Article 41(1)(b)). This is possible only when 'all available domestic remedies have been invoked and exhausted', but this requirement is not applicable when the 'application of the remedies is unreasonably prolonged' (Article 41(1)(c)).

Under the First Optional Protocol to the ICCPR, adopted 16 December 1966 and entered into force on 23 March 1976, the HR Committee can hear individual petitions once domestic remedies have been exhausted (Article 2). The complaint may also not be currently under examination by another international procedure (Article 5).

A weakness of the procedure is the lack of any legally binding decision taken by the HR Committee. Furthermore, the Protocol permits denunciation under Article 12, as has been the case in relation to Jamaica, and Trinidad and Tobago. However, where the HR Committee considers a matter and comes up with its concluding observations, as Buergenthal (2001, see earlier in this section) notes, at 347:

> the findings set out in concluding observations must be viewed as authoritative pronounce-ments on whether a particular state has or has not complied with its obligations under the Covenant. What we have here is a type of Committee 'jurisprudence', which provides some insights about the manner in which the Committee interprets the Covenant.

The HR Committee does not have the power to undertake independent fact-finding missions and relies on State parties to respond in full. The HR Committee can, pursuant to Article 40(4), give general comments 'as it may consider appropriate'. To date, the Committee has issued thirty-four general comments of a non-binding nature, covering numerous areas of ICCPR rights, internal procedures, and interpretational guidance.

Commenting on the value of general comments, Philip Alston, 'The historical origins of the concept of general comments in human rights law' in L. Boisson de Chazournes and V. Gowlland-Debbas (eds), *The International Legal System in Quest of Equity and Universality: Liber Amicorum Georges Abi-Saab* (The Hague: Martinus Nijhoff, 2001), p. 763, observes that:

> It would be more difficult to imagine a more oddly and even misleadingly named instrument than a 'General Comment'. What, after all, could be the jurisprudential value of a mere 'com-ment', and an explicitly 'general' one at that? Yet the adoption of such a statement is today one of the potentially most significant and influential tools available to each of the [then] six United Nations human rights treaty bodies.

Another power of the HR Committee is to impose interim measures under Rule 92 of the Committee's Rules of Procedure, where it considers that such measures are 'desirable to avoid irreparable damage to the victim of the alleged violation'. It should be noted that such meas-ures do 'not imply a determination of the merits of the communication'.

● *Piandiong et al. v. Philippines* COMMUNICATION NO. 869/1999, UN DOC. CCPR/ C/70/D/869/1999 (2000), UN HR Committee

The HR Committee considered the case of interim measures when a State—in this case, the Philippines—ignored a request from the HR Committee to refrain from imposing the death sentence on two individuals. At [5.4] of its comment, the HR Committee stated that:

As can be seen from the above, even in the face of such severe violations, the language of the Committee remains somewhat docile, and this may not augur well for actively promoting its kind of work. The HR Committee submits an annual report to the UN General Assembly detailing its activities and listing those States that have not submitted reports.

KEY POINTS

- The UN HR Committee was established under the ICCPR as an implementation mechanism of that Covenant.

- By virtue of the First Optional Protocol to the ICCPR, the HR Committee can hear complaints from individuals, provided that local remedies have been exhausted.

- Pronouncements of the HR Committee on ICCPR provisions are contained in its general comments, which are non-binding.

19.3.5 The International Covenant on Economic, Social and Cultural Rights

Adopted by UN General Assembly Resolution 2200A(XXI) on 16 December 1966 and entered into force in 1976, the ICESCR is considered to be, in theory, as important as the ICCPR. Yet, in practice, there are significant differences between the two instruments. The advent of the Cold War, and the increase in the understanding of economic and social rights, led to extensive debate in this area. For example, there has been controversy between communist and Western States, and between developed and the developing countries, as to whether there should have been two separate covenants. Underlining this controversy is often the difference in the perceptions among developed and developing countries of the importance of the different rights embodied by the two covenants. While most developed Western nations believe that the rights contained in the two covenants are equally important, many developing States view economic and social rights as a luxury that they cannot afford.

In 'Annotations on the text of the Draft International Covenant on Human Rights' (UN Doc. A/2929, 1955), it is noted that:

9. Those in favour of drafting two separate covenants argued that civil and political rights were enforceable, or justiciable, or of an 'absolute' character, while economic, social and cultural rights were not or might not be; that the former were immediately applicable, while the latter were to be progressively implemented; and that, generally speaking, the former were rights of the individual 'against' the States, that is, against unlawful and unjust action of the State, while the latter were rights which the State would have to take positive action to promote. Since the nature of civil and political rights and that of economic, social and cultural rights and the obligations of the State in respect thereof, were different, it was desirable that two separate instruments should be prepared.

10. ... Generally speaking, civil and political rights were thought to be 'legal' rights and could best be implemented by the creation of a good offices committee, while economic, social

and cultural rights were thought to be 'programme' rights and could best be implemented by the establishment of a system of periodic reports ...

11. ... it was argued that not in all countries and territories were all civil and political rights 'legal' rights, nor all economic, social and cultural rights 'programme' rights. A civil or political right might well be a 'programme' right under one régime, an economic, social or cultural right a 'legal' right under another.

The Economic, Social and Cultural Rights Committee

The Economic, Social and Cultural Rights (ESCR) Committee is a body established by the ICESCR, through a 1985 resolution of the Economic and Social Council, as a result of the failure of previous monitoring measures. The State parties are to submit reports to the ESCR Committee, which in turn can submit a report, or part of a report, to the HRC for general recommendations (Article 19 ICESCR).

The relatively lesser importance and attention paid to the ICESCR by States, in contrast with the ICCPR, was underscored by the ESCR Committee during the Vienna World Conference in 1993, when the Committee recognized (UN Doc. E/1993/22, Annex III, para. 5):

> the shocking reality ... that States and the international community as a whole continue to tolerate all too often breaches of economic, social and cultural rights which, if they occurred in relation to civil and political rights, would provoke expressions of horror and outrage and would lead to concerted calls for immediate remedial action. In effect, despite the rhetoric, violations of civil and political rights continue to be treated as though they were far more serious, and more patently intolerable, than massive and direct denials of economic, social and cultural rights.

A point of interest in the ICESCR is its ability to look beyond the State's capability to provide the conditions necessary for enjoyment of the rights contained therein. Pursuant to Article 2, every State party is to:

> take steps, individually and through international assistance and co-operation, especially economic and technical, *to the maximum of its available resources*, with a view to achieving progressively the full realization of the rights recognised ... *by all appropriate means*, including particularly the adoption of legislative measures. [Emphasis added]

Economic and social rights are commonly understood in terms of welfare rights. This leads to conflicting views amongst States as to their obligations and the ability of individuals to enforce these rights, as opposed to civil and political rights, which are arguably easier to ensure. As Aryeh Neier, 'Social and economic rights: a critique' (2006) 13 HR Brief 2, observes, 'rights only have meaning if it is possible to enforce them'—a point that the writer expands upon by expressing that his concern:

> with economic and social rights is when there are broad assertions ... of a right to shelter or housing, a right to education, a right to social security, a right to a job, a right to health care. There, I think, we get into territory that is unmanageable through the judicial process and that intrudes fundamentally into an area where the democratic process ought to prevail.

The limits of judicial enforcement mechanisms to address ICESCR rights and the ability of States to deliver these rights have to be taken into account. Where these are ignored, it will impact negatively on the ability to ensure that any forms of ICESCR rights are upheld. The wealth that a State possesses, in theory at least, will impact on its ability to deliver on its obligations.

The availability of a State's resources as a consideration in terms of its ability to discharge its obligation or duty under the ICESCR is addressed by Article 2, as well as by ECSR Committee General Comment 3 (UN Doc. E/1991/23, 1990), Annex III:

1. ... [W]hile the Covenant provides for progressive realization and acknowledges the constraints due to limits of available resources, it also imposes various obligations which are of immediate effect. Of these, two are of particular importance in understanding the precise nature of State Parties' obligations. One of these, ... is the 'undertaking to guarantee' that relevant rights 'will be exercised without discrimination ...'

10. ... In order for a State party to be able to attribute its failure to meet at least its minimum core obligations to a lack of available resources it must demonstrate that every effort has been made to use all resources that are at its disposition in an effort to satisfy, as a matter of priority, those minimum obligations.

In terms of a remedy, it is not always to be assumed that there is a need for a judicial remedy. As ECSR Committee General Comment 9 (UN Doc. E/1999/22, 1998), Annex IV, makes clear:

Administrative remedies will, in many cases, be adequate ... Any such administrative remedies should be accessible, affordable, timely and effective ... whenever a Covenant right cannot be made fully effective without some role for the judiciary, judicial remedies are necessary.

By and large, arguments against judicial involvement have centred on the claim that it is not for the judiciary to become involved in matters that are considered to be in the realm of government policies. Hence, General Comment 9 (ibid.) states that:

While the respective competences of the different branches of government must be respected, it is appropriate to acknowledge that courts are generally already involved in a considerable range of matters which have important resource implications. The adoption of a rigid classification of economic, social and cultural rights which puts them, by definition, beyond the reach of the courts would thus be arbitrary and incompatible with the principle that the two sets of human rights are invisible and interdependent. It would also drastically curtail the capacity of the courts to protect the rights of the most vulnerable and disadvantaged groups in society.

The above quotes basically allude to the fact that State parties to the ICESCR must at least guarantee economic, social, and cultural rights, and provide a means of accessing those rights, whether judicial or other. Therefore it is not compulsory that the only recourse that citizens have for the protection of their rights is to the courts. Nevertheless, State parties are not expected to restrict or bar access to the courts for the protection of these rights. In line with this view, courts of many States have indeed taken an active role in adjudicating matters relating to ICESCR rights. In some countries, one innovative way through which courts have done this is by dealing with the otherwise unjusticiable ICESCR matters within what are known as 'directive principles of State policies'. Matters usually contained in this section of a country's constitution are not enforceable by courts, but they constitute guidelines that are considered fundamental in the governance of the country, making it the duty of the State to apply these principles in making laws in order to establish a just society.

● *Olga Tellis v. Bombay Municipal Corporation* 1986 AIR 180, Indian Supreme Court

Certain pavement dwellers in Bombay city claimed before the court that they could not be moved by the municipality unless they were provided with alternative accommodation. The issue for determination before the court turned on whether Article 21 of the Indian Constitution, which provides that 'No person shall be deprived of his life or personal liberty except according to procedure established by law', can be extended to include right to livelihood, which is a directive principle of State policy under the Indian Constitution.

The Indian Supreme Court applied the directive principle, as opposed to a constitutional right, to affirm that the applicants were so entitled.

A similar judgment was given by the Indian Supreme Court in *Ahmedabad Municipal Corporation v. Nawab Khan Gulab Khan and ors* 1997 AIR SC 152, the facts of which are similar to those of *Olga Telis*.

However, some States, such as South Africa, give full constitutional recognition to social rights and do not treat them as merely directive principles. The South African approach and jurisprudence has impacted significantly on the economic and social rights debate.

● *Soobramoney v. Minister of Health (Kwazulu-Natal)* Case CCT 32/97, 27 November 1997, Constitutional Court of South Africa

In a case that concerned access to health care, the appellant was a diabetic who suffered from ischaemic heart disease and cerebrovascular disease. His kidneys failed in 1996 and his condition was diagnosed as irreversible. He asked to be admitted to the dialysis programme of the Addington Hospital (a State hospital). He was informed that he did not qualify for admission. Addington Hospital, like many State hospitals, has a severe shortage of dialysis machines and trained nursing staff. Owing to limited resources, the hospital adopted a policy of admitting only those patients who could be cured within a short period and those with chronic renal failure who were eligible for a kidney transplant. Mr Soobramoney did not fulfil either of these conditions.

The court held that the responsibility for making the difficult decisions of fixing the health budget and deciding upon the priorities that needed to be met lay with political organs and the medical authorities, and added that the court would be slow to interfere with such decisions if they were rational and taken in good faith. The court concluded that it had not been shown that the State's failure to provide renal dialysis facilities for all persons suffering from chronic renal failure constituted a breach of its constitutional obligation.

See http://www.saflii.org/za/cases/ZACC/1997/17media.pdf for media summary of the case.

● *Treatment Action Campaign v. Minister of Health* Case CCT 8/02, 5 July 2002, Constitutional Court of South Africa

In another health care-related case, this time involving HIV/AIDS, an appeal was brought to reverse a High Court order against the government because of perceived shortcomings in its response to an aspect of the HIV/AIDS challenge. As part of its response to the HIV/AIDS pandemic, the government devised a programme to deal with mother-to-child transmission of HIV at birth and identified nevirapine as its drug of choice for this purpose. The programme imposed restrictions on the availability of nevirapine in the public health sector. The applicants argued that these restrictions were unreasonable, because they were inconsistent with the Constitution, which obligates the State and all of its organs to give effect to the rights guaranteed by the Bill of Rights.

It was held that the government had not reasonably addressed the need to reduce the risk of HIV-positive mothers transmitting the disease to their babies at birth. More specifically, the finding (at [2]) was that the government had acted unreasonably in:

(a) refusing to make an antiretroviral drug called nevirapine available in the public health sector, where the attending doctor considered it medically indicated; and

(b) not setting out a time frame for a national programme to prevent mother-to-child transmission of HIV.

. . . .

● **_Government of South Africa v. Grootboom_** CASE CCT 11/00, 4 OCTOBER 2000, CONSTITUTIONAL COURT OF SOUTH AFRICA

This case relating to the right to shelter was brought by Mrs Irene Grootboom and other respondents, who were all rendered homeless as a result of their eviction from their informal homes situated on private land earmarked for formal low-cost housing. They applied for an order compelling the government to provide them with adequate basic shelter or housing until they obtained permanent accommodation.

The order was granted. The judgment provisionally concluded that 'tents, portable latrines and a regular supply of water (albeit transported) would constitute the bare minimum'.

KEY POINTS

- The ICESCR covers economic, social, and cultural rights, and, like the ICCPR, but unlike the UDHR, is binding on State parties.

- Implementation of the ICESCR has varied tremendously, and is often determined by resources, ability, and capacity of an individual country, as well as the ideological leanings of the State.

- Generally speaking, ICESCR rights are non-justiciable, which means that they cannot be entertained or adjudicated upon by the courts. In such countries as South Africa and India, however, courts have demonstrated a considerably proactive approach towards adjudicating such rights.

19.3.6 The Convention on the Elimination of All Forms of Discrimination against Women and the CEDAW Committee

CEDAW was adopted by the UN General Assembly in 1979. The Convention focuses on tackling discrimination against women and improving their equality with men, while being attentive specifically to women's particular experiences that need to be addressed. CEDAW Article 17 established a monitoring committee, known as the CEDAW Committee, which is very active in its work.

Article 1 of CEDAW provides a clear definition of discrimination against women:

> [it] shall mean any distinction, exclusion or restriction made on the basis of sex which has the effect or purpose of impairing or nullifying the recognition, enjoyment or exercise by women, irrespective of their marital status, on a basis of equality of men and women, of human rights and fundamental freedoms in the political, economic, social, cultural, civil or any other field.

This definition encompasses a wide range of discriminatory acts, including direct and indirect, deliberate and unintended discrimination. This extensiveness is possibly one of the strongest outcomes of CEDAW in terms of its clear definition of what 'discrimination' is.

CEDAW applies to more than only the public sphere of women's lives. Article 2(e) calls for discrimination by 'any person, organization or enterprise' to be eliminated, while Article 2(f) calls for 'all appropriate measures, including legislation, to modify or abolish existing laws, regulations, customs and practices' that discriminate. Articles 3, 5, and 6 are further examples of the varied forms and areas of discrimination that CEDAW attempts to address.

The CEDAW Committee has further clarified the wide scope of CEDAW provisions in its General Recommendation 19 (HRI/GEN/1/Rev.9 (Vol. II) 331, 2008), paragraph 9, thus:

> It is emphasized, however, that discrimination under the Convention is not restricted to action by or on behalf of Governments (see Articles 2(e), 2(f) and 5) ... Under general international law and specific human rights covenants, States may also be responsible for private acts if they fail to act with due diligence to prevent violations of rights or to investigate and punish acts of violence, and for providing compensation.

CEDAW advocates non-identical treatment between the sexes when it is aimed at addressing situations in which women are disadvantaged. Yet there is a clear distinction between temporary and permanent measures that are used to achieve this aim. Article 4(1) covers temporary provisions, provided that they do not continue unequal treatment or promote separate standards, and should be discontinued once their aim has been achieved. CEDAW specifically addresses this in terms of education under Article 10.

CEDAW attempts to address the social, religious, and cultural traditions that discriminate against women. Article 5(a) puts the obligation on the State to attempt to eliminate prejudices and 'practices which are based on the idea of inferiority or the superiority of either of the sexes or on stereotyped roles'.

Article 15(3) goes even further with its obligation that:

> States Parties agree that all contracts and all other private instruments of any kind with a legal effect which is directed at restricting the legal capacity of women shall be deemed null and void.

Despite CEDAW's progressive approach to tackling discrimination against women, there are weaknesses. CEDAW's approach of comparing women with men neglects a whole category of rights that women require that do not necessarily concern men, such as reproductive rights. Another shortcoming is the absence of a reference to violence against women. It must be noted, however, that the CEDAW Committee, in its General Recommendation 19, does include violence against women and considers gender-based violence a form of discrimination in paragraphs 1 and 6:

Gender-based violence is a form of discrimination that seriously inhibits women's ability to enjoy rights and freedoms on a basis of equality with men. . . .

The Convention in Article 1 defines discrimination against women. The definition of discrimination includes gender-based violence, that is, violence that is directed against a woman because she is a woman or that affects women disproportionately. It includes acts that inflict physical, mental or sexual harm or suffering, threats of such acts, coercion and other deprivations of liberty. Gender-based violence may breach specific provisions of the Convention, regardless of whether those provisions expressly mention violence.

Another shortcoming is that CEDAW approaches family life from the perspective of heterosexual marriage. This automatically excludes non-married heterosexual women, as well as homosexual women. However, given the very divergent views of States on homosexuality, this provision may have been a compromise in order to ensure that States ratified CEDAW. The CEDAW Committee, however, addressed this issue indirectly in its General Recommendation 21 (HRI/GEN/1/Rev.9 (Vol. II) 337, 2008), paragraph 22, with its referral to 'spouse or partner'.

Furthermore, CEDAW treats women as one homogenous group, failing to recognize that different groups of women experience different forms of discrimination. Once again, it has been the CEDAW Committee that has expanded the concept through its distinction between rural and urban women, as well as interpreting 'rural' to include issues such as age, ethnicity, and caste. General Recommendation 24 (HRI/GEN/1/Rev.9 (Vol. II) 358, 2008), paragraph 6, highlights the special attention required for 'vulnerable and disadvantaged groups' of women in terms of health:

> While biological differences between women and men may lead to differences in health status, there are social factors which are determinative of the health status of women and men and which can vary among women themselves. For that reason, special attention should be given to the health needs and rights of women belonging to vulnerable and disadvantaged groups, such as migrant women, refugee and internally displaced women, the girl child and older women, women in prostitution, indigenous women and women with physical and mental disabilities.

CEDAW has, however, the highest number of reservations among all human rights conventions—a finding that is not surprising considering the different attitudes among the States and society towards women worldwide.

thinking points

- *What are the main differences between the ICCPR and ICESCR, and how do these two covenants differ from the UDHR?*
- *What is the nature of the obligation of States towards protecting women's rights, and how does this compare to the ICCPR and ICESCR?*
- *What are some of the shortcomings of CEDAW and how have they been addressed?*

19.3.7 The Convention against Torture and Other Cruel, Inhuman or Degrading Treatment or Punishment

CAT, as the Convention is commonly called, was adopted in 1984. Although it was not the first international attempt at addressing the issue of torture, it is by far the most comprehensive. For example, although the term is mentioned in the UDHR and the ICCPR, no definition of 'torture' is given in either instrument.

Article 1 CAT defines 'torture' as:

> any act which severe pain or suffering, whether physical or mental, is intentionally inflicted on a person for such purposes as obtaining from him or a third person information or a confession, punishing him for an act he or a third person has committed or is suspected of having committed, or intimidating or coercing him or a third person, or for any reason based on discrimination of any kind when pain or suffering is inflicted by or at the instigation of or with the consent or acquiescence of a public official or other person acting in an official capacity.

What this definition provided by CAT makes clear is that torture is committed by public or State officials, or persons acting under the authority of a State. It would appear that acts committed by an individual, unconnected to any public capacity, would not fall under the scope of the Convention.

Under the Convention, there are no exceptional circumstances in which torture can be justified (Article 2(2)), with torture being made a criminal offence under the national law of all State parties (Article 4(1)). In addition, CAT requires the prevention of any form of cruel, inhuman, or degrading treatment, or punishment that does not constitute torture (Article 16).

A State's obligation to prevent torture is not restricted to the act being committed on its territory or a territory that it controls, but also applies to the possibility of such acts being committed as a result of **extradition treaties** against extraditable people on its territory (Article 3):

> no State party shall expel, return or extradite a person to another State where there are substantial grounds for believing that he would be in danger of being subjected to torture.

. . . .

extradition treaties

Bilateral or multilateral agreements between two or more States to send back nationals of contracting parties who may be resident in another contracting State to face prosecution for crimes. A fugitive from one State living in another State is an extraditable person provided that there is an extradition agreement between the two States.

. . . .

The UN HR Committee has considered such cases of possible torture resulting from extradition and held that any such extradition would violate CAT, in *Mutombo v. Switzerland* Communication No. 13/1993 (UN Doc. A/49/44, 1994) and *Khan v. Canada* Communication No. 15/1994 (UN Doc. A/50/44, 1994).

CAT has been invoked in cases of the death penalty, and the UN HR Committee has concluded that gas asphyxiation as a means of execution is cruel and inhuman treatment.

. . . .

● ***Charles Chitat Ng v. Canada*** COMMUNICATION No. 469/1991, UN DOC. CCPR/C/49/D/469/1991 (1994), UN HR Committee

The Committee stated (at [16.4]) that:

> execution by gas asphyxiation, should the death penalty be imposed on the author, would not meet the test of 'least possible physical and mental suffering', and constitutes cruel and inhuman treatment, in violation of article 7 of the Covenant. Accordingly, Canada, which could reasonably foresee that Mr. Ng, if sentenced to death, would be executed in a way that amounts to a violation of article 7, failed to comply with its obligations under the Covenant, by extraditing Mr. Ng without having sought and received assurances that he would not be executed.

The Committee Against Torture

The Committee Against Torture is established by Article 17 of CAT for the purposes of monitoring implementation of CAT. State parties submit a report a year after acceding to CAT and subsequently every four years, with the Committee Against Torture adopting 'concluding observations' in which they raise their concerns and recommendations, adopted during their biannual sessions. It is also possible for individuals to raise complaints or communications, subject to Article 22. In particular Article 22(1) stipulates that the State in question must have provided for individual complaints/communications:

> A State Party to this Convention may at any time declare under this article that it recognizes the competence of the Committee to receive and consider communications from or on behalf of individuals subject to its jurisdiction who claim to be victims of a violation by a State Party of the provisions of the Convention. No communication shall be received by the Committee if it concerns a State Party which has not made such a declaration, which prevents the submission from being anonymous, or abuses the complaints procedure.

Article 21 enables interstate complaints to be heard, while pursuant to Article 20 CAT:

> If the Committee receives reliable information which appears to it to contain well-founded indications that torture is being systematically practised in the territory of a State Party, the Committee shall invite that State Party to co-operate in the examination of the information and to this end to submit observations with regard to the information concerned.

However, this is subject to consent from the suspected violating State, which hampers the effectiveness of any such investigation.

The Committee Against Torture's general comments are authoritative in their interpretation of CAT provisions. The Optional Protocol to CAT provides for a UN Subcommittee on Prevention of Torture (SPT) that can visit detention facilities in order to prevent acts of torture; additionally, the Committee Against Torture can help States to improve their detention facilities.

19.3.8 The Convention on the Rights of the Child

The CRC covers civil and political, as well as economic, social, and cultural, rights—the first binding international instrument to do so. The vulnerability of children is recognized worldwide and the CRC attempts to address many of the issues that could negatively affect children. All children under the age of 18 are covered by this Convention. The CRC focuses on the concept of the child's best interests as a deciding factor (Article 3), yet it has also recognized the child's ability to participate, through the notion of 'evolving capacities' (Article 5).

The CRC aims to protect children from such harms as discrimination (Article 2), to ensure their right to a family life (Articles 9 and 10), and to prevent the trafficking of children and their sexual exploitation (Articles 11 and 34, respectively). These protections have been extended, with the Optional Protocol on the Involvement of Children in Armed Conflict, which primarily addresses the issue of child soldiers and child participation in hostilities.

The CRC provides for the basic needs of children, noting that it is a State's obligation to ensure the 'survival and development of the child' (Article 6). The provision of health care for children is addressed by Article 24, which extends to pre-natal, as well as post-natal, care, highlighting the importance of child protection and the provision of needs from the earliest possible moment. While all children are granted rights under the CRC, special consideration is to be made for refugee children or those seeking refuge (Article 22), as well as those who are mentally or physically disabled (Article 23).

Article 27(2) provides that:

> The parent(s) or others responsible for the child have the primary responsibility to secure, within their abilities and financial capacities, the conditions of living necessary for the child's development.

This Article, while identifying those responsible, acknowledges and accepts that parents and other carers of children can be limited in their abilities to provide for children due to financial constraints, as well as other abilities. Article 27(3) CRC therefore provides that:

> States Parties, in accordance with national conditions and within their means, shall take appropriate measures to assist parents and others responsible for the child to implement this right and shall in case of need provide material assistance and support programmes, particularly with regard to nutrition, clothing and housing.

The Committee on the Rights of the Child

The Committee on the Rights of the Child was established by Article 43 CRC and is the monitoring body of the CRC and its Optional Protocols' implementation. CRC State parties submit reports every five years to the Committee on the Rights of the Child, which then adopts 'concluding observations'. Like the other treaty-based bodies, the Committee on the Rights of the Child publishes its 'general comments' on CRC interpretational matters. As of April 2014, the Committee on the Rights of the Child will be able to receive individual complaints by children as the Optional Protocol to the Convention on the Rights of the Child on a Communications Procedure has received ten ratifications, the number required for the Protocol to come into force.

thinking points

- *Define 'torture'.*
- *Is there a territorial limit to States' obligations to prevent torture?*

19.4 Regional human rights systems

In the section below, we discuss regional human rights systems with particular focus on the African, European, and American systems. As is well known, there is no well-developed regional human rights system in Asia, the Far East, or the Middle East to warrant a discussion of any such systems in this section.

19.4.1 The African Charter on Human and Peoples' Rights

The African Charter on Human and Peoples' Rights (also known as the 'Banjul Charter', after the capital city of The Gambia, where it was adopted in 1981) entered into force in 1986. The

Banjul Charter is the most recent of the three major regional human rights systems (the other two being the European and the Inter-American) and the least developed in terms of practical application. It is also regarded as perhaps the most progressive human rights system, at least in theory. Remarkably, the Charter includes 'peoples' rights', in addition to 'human rights', which implies a distinction between the two terms. The Charter does not define what it means by 'peoples' but the inclusion was deliberate and guided by a distinct African conception of society.

As observed by the Report of the Organization of African Unity (OAU) Rapporteur on the drafting process (OAU Doc. CM/1149(XXXVII), 1981), Annex 1, p. 4, paragraph 14:

> Noting that in Africa, Man is part and parcel of the group, some delegations concluded that individual rights could be explained and justified only by the rights of the community. Consequently, they wished that the draft charter made room for the peoples' rights.

According to Fatsah Ouguergouz, *The African Charter on Human and Peoples' Rights: A Comprehensive Agenda for Human Dignity and Sustainable Democracy in Africa* (The Hague: Martinus Nijhoff, 2003), p. 203:

> 'peoples' encompasses at least four categories: the 'people-state', meaning all the nationals of a state; the population of a state; peoples under colonial or racial domination; and 'people-ethnic group', meaning the different peoples integrated into one state.

The Charter's inclusion of not only individual, but also collective, rights (Articles 19–24) explains the inclusion of such collective rights as environmental rights and those relating to natural resources.

● *Social and Economic Rights Action Center & Center for Economic and Social Rights v. Nigeria* Communication No. 155/96 (2001), African Commission on Human and Peoples' Rights

The communication alleged that the military government of Nigeria was guilty of, amongst other things, violations of the right to health, the right to dispose of wealth and natural resources, the right to a clean environment, and family rights, due to its condoning and facilitating the operations of oil corporations in Ogoniland.

The Commission ruled that the Ogoni people had suffered violations of their right to health (Article 16) and to a general satisfactory environment favourable to development (Article 24), due to the government's failure to prevent pollution and ecological degradation. It held further that the State's failure to monitor oil activities and to involve local communities in decisions violated the right of the Ogoni people to dispose freely of their wealth and natural resources (Article 21), although it did not provide a definition of a 'people'.

The Commission commended the inclusion of 'collective rights' in the Banjul Charter when, in expressing its thanks to the non-governmental organizations (NGOs), it stated (at [49]) that:

> Such is a demonstration of the usefulness to the Commission and individuals of *actio popularis*, which is wisely allowed under the African Charter.

Aside from incorporating peoples' rights, the African Charter is also distinguishable from other regional systems in its provisions for individual and group duties that are owed to the State, as well as the inability of States to derogate from the provisions even in times of emergency. Nonetheless, some of the duties imposed by the Banjul Charter do seem to be counterproductive.

As Olusola Ojo and Amadu Sesay, 'The OAU and human rights: prospects for the 1980s and beyond' (1986) 8 HRQ 89, 99, have rightly pointed out:

> Some of the provisions are not only vague but also unrealistic, if not retrogressive. At best, they are pious hopes which would have no practical effect. Article 29(1) for instance, imposes on the individual the duty to 'preserve the harmonious development of the family and to work for the cohesion and respect of the family, to respect his parents at all times, to maintain them in case of need'. At worst, the provisions are oppressive and in fact, could be used by states to curtail human and peoples' rights.

The Preamble to the African Charter underscores the belief of the OAU, the organization under the auspices of which the treaty was adopted, in the right to development. It states that:

> ...it is henceforth essential to pay a particular attention to the right to development and that civil and political rights cannot be dissociated from economic, social and cultural rights in their conception as well as universality and that the satisfaction of economic, social and cultural rights is a guarantee for the enjoyment of civil and political rights.

The right to development is one of the progressive rights included in the African Charter under Article 22, as well as the environmental link to development provided for in Article 24, even though, at the relevant time, it was thought to be a new right in international law.

According to U. O. Umozurike, 'The African Charter on Human and Peoples' Rights' (1983) 77 AJIL 902, 906–907:

> The right to development, if indeed it is a right in international law, is new. It was first enunciated by the President of the Senegal Supreme Court, Keba M'baye, in an address to the Institute of International Human Rights in Strasbourg in 1972. He suggested that all rights are intertwined with the right of existence, with a progressively higher standard of living, and therefore with development. He referred to Articles 55–56 of the UN Charter and 22–27 of the Universal Declaration of Human Rights, and to statutes of the specialized agencies in which international cooperation and solidarity are important. In 1978, as President of the International Commission of Jurists, he further adumbrated on the right at the Darkar Conference on the Development of the Law of Human Rights. At the request of the Commission of Human Rights, the UN Secretary-General made a study in which he concluded that a large number of principles based on the UN Charter and human rights texts and declarations confirm the existence of the right in law. This conclusion was later confirmed by the General Assembly.

The colonial experiences of Africa are clearly seen in the Charter, as evidenced by Articles 19, 20(2) and (3), and 21(5), as well as Article 12(5). The Banjul Charter prohibits mass expulsion of foreign nationals; however, this does not include illegal immigrants.

KEY POINTS

- The African Charter contains far-reaching human rights provisions, such as the inclusion of peoples' rights, and it also recognizes *actio popularis*.

- The African Charter is arguably the most developed of its kind, reflecting a deeply African notion of society, and embodying provisions that recognize Africa's colonial past and experiences.

- The provisions of the African Charter are influenced by a distinct African under-standing of the individual's role in society. Examples of such provisions include those concerning the duties of the individual to society.

19.4.1.1 The African Commission on Human and Peoples' Rights

The African Commission on Human and Peoples' Rights was established in 1987, pursuant to Article 30 of the African Charter. The Commission's mandate is detailed in Article 45, and covers the promotion of human and peoples' rights, and ensures the protection of these rights. The Commission interprets all provisions when requested by a State party, OAU and now African Union (AU) institutions, or any institution recognized by the AU, as well as undertakes any other tasks that the Assembly of Heads of State and Government ask of it.

The investigative powers of the African Commission appear to be wide, with Article 46 provid-ing for 'any appropriate method of investigation'. States are meant to provide reports to the African Commission every two years (Article 62). The African Commission is able to receive communications from States (Article 47) as long as the State against which a claim is brought is given time to answer the claim (Article 48). This is subject to exhaustion of local remedies 'unless it is obvious to the Commission that the procedure of achieving these remedies would be unduly prolonged' (Article 50).

As noted by Christof Heyns and Magnus Killander, 'The African regional human rights system' in F. Gomez Isa and K. De Feyter (eds), *International Protection of Human Rights: Achievements and Challenges* (Bilbao: University of Deusto, 2006), p. 524, section 5.2.2:

> the Commission has stated that for a case not to be admissible local remedies must be avail-able, effective, sufficient and not unduly prolonged.

In 'So far, so fair: the local remedies rule in the jurisprudence of the African Commission on Human and Peoples' Rights' (2003) 1 AJIL 1, 16, Nsongurua J. Udombana underscores the problem with the exhaustion of local remedies in Africa. He notes that the state of the judici-ary in most African countries, where the executive arm of government frequently impairs the independence of the judiciary:

> contrasts with that of Europe, for example, whose highly functioning domestic legal systems allow the rule of law to blossom. This difference plausibly explains why a higher percentage of cases filed with the European Court of Human Rights are declared inadmissible on exhaus-tion grounds. For if the domestic courts are performing their functions as they should perform them, logic suggests that supranational institutions should interfere with them as little as pos-sible. But in Africa most domestic courts are not able to serve as defenders of human rights. The problem is compounded by the difficulty encountered by the 'small man', in some places and at certain times, in getting his case heard, unless he has the wherewithal to bribe the judge. If such a complainant cannot afford to 'oil the palm' of the judge, then his case may not be heard on time or at all. As a result, hundreds of thousands of Africans who have been stripped of their human dignity often do not have redress, though they have the right entirely on their side, at least in theory.

Individual complaints, as well as those from NGOs, are admissible before the African Commission, despite ambiguity in the African Charter in this regard.

According to Christof Heyns and Magnus Killander (2006, see earlier in this section), p. 524, section 5.2.2:

> the so-called individual communication or complaints procedure is not clearly provided for in the African Charter. One reading of the Charter is that communications could be considered only where 'serious or massive violations' are at stake, which then triggers the rather futile Article 58 procedure . . . However, the African Commission has accepted from the start that it has the power to deal with complaints about any human rights violations under the charter even if 'serious or massive' violations are not at stake, provided the admissibility criteria are met.
>
> The Charter is silent on the question who can bring such complaints, but the Commission practice is that complaints from individuals as well as NGOs are accepted. From the case law of the Commission it is clear that the complainant does not need to be a victim or a family member of a victim.

The African Commission is not without its problems. According to Chidi Odinkalu, 'The individual complaints procedures of the African Commission on Human and Peoples' Rights: a preliminary assessment' (1998) 8 Transn'l L & Contemp Probs 359, 365:

> Foremost among the problems that the Commission has encountered is the very text of the African Charter itself, which, like the Rules of Procedure, is opaque and difficult to interpret . . . Another set of problems is found in what a former member of the Commission has bluntly described as 'a lack of money, lack of funds, lack of ability to act'. The resource and personnel problems of the Commission are endemic . . .

Nonetheless, Odinkalu (ibid.) emphasizes that:

> on its interpretation of the Charter, the Commission has been mostly positive and sometimes even innovative . . . In cases where it has proceeded to the merits, it has interpreted the rights in the Charter effectively, although its application of the principles thus established has not always been consistent.

thinking points

- *What is the main function of the African Commission on Human and Peoples' Rights?*
- *What are the major weaknesses of the African Commission?*
- *Can NGOs and non-State entities or individuals bring complaints before the African Commission?*

19.4.2 The American Convention on Human Rights

The first human rights declaration, the American Declaration of the Rights and Duties of Man, came from the Organization of American States (OAS) in 1948, seven months before the UDHR. The American Declaration is similar to the UDHR, except for the inclusion of Articles in the former setting out citizens' duties. It was not until 1959 that the Inter-American Commission on Human Rights was created, as an autonomous organ of the OAS (itself established in 1948). In 1969, the American Convention on Human Rights was adopted, and it entered into force in 1978. It is interesting to note that while the USA signed the American Convention in 1977, it has not yet ratified it.

The rights provided for in the American Convention are similar to ICCPR rights, but only one Article covers economic, social, and cultural rights. Article 26 provides that:

> The States Parties undertake to adopt measures, both internally and through international cooperation, especially those of an economic and technical nature, with a view to achieving progressively, by legislation or other appropriate means, the full realization of the rights implicit in the economic, social, educational, scientific, and cultural standards set forth in the Charter of the Organization of American States as amended by the Protocol of Buenos Aires.

In 1988, the OAS adopted the Additional Protocol to the American Convention on Human Rights in the Area of Economic, Social and Cultural Rights, which is similar to the ICESCR, but only sixteen States are parties to it to date.

According to Philip Alston, Henry J. Steiner, and Ryan Goodman, *International Human Rights in Context: Law, Politics, Morals* (4th edn, Oxford: Oxford University Press, 2013), p. 1038:

> Domestic implementation of the Convention remains highly unsatisfactory in the Americas. For the most part, states have failed to take effective measures to promote domestic implementation of the standards contained in the American Convention, even when these nominally enjoy superior status within the domestic legal order. The result is that while many states indicate that international standards are applicable within their domestic legal systems, those standards are rarely invoked and even more rarely given effect by the courts.

David Harris and Stephen Livingstone, 'Regional protection of human rights: the Inter-American achievement', in their edited book *The Inter-American System of Human Rights* (Oxford: Clarendon Press, 1998), p. 1, describe the Inter-American system as:

> More complex than that of the European Convention in that it is based upon two overlapping instruments, namely the American Declaration on the Rights and Duties of Man and the American Convention . . . It also has more than one dimension in that the Inter American Commission not only hears petitions but also conducts *in loco* visits, leading to the adoption of country reports on the human rights situation in OAS member states. This second, very important dimension to the Inter-American Commission's work has no counterpart in the European system . . . A final difference exists at the stage of enforcing final decisions and judgments. The inter-American system provides no counterpart to the supervisory role of the Committee of Ministers of the Council of Europe. Related to this is the fact that the outcome of proceedings in the inter-American system is not necessarily a legally binding decision. The judgments of the Inter-American Court are legally binding upon the parties.

The Inter-American Commission on Human Rights

The Inter-American Commission on Human Rights (IACHR) was established in 1959 to promote and protect human rights. It carries out on-site visits to investigate specific situations or general human rights observance, culminating in country reports. The IACHR's role is divided into three functions; individual petitions, monitoring, and consideration of thematic issues. Since 1965 the IACHR has the authority to consider complaints or petitions regarding specific human rights violations.

Under Article 44 of the American Convention:

> any person or group of persons, or any nongovernmental entity legally recognized in one or more member States of the Organization, may lodge petitions with the Commission containing denunciations or complaints of violation of this Convention by a State Party.

Despite the ability of the Inter-American Commission to consider individual complaints as well as interstate complaints (Articles 45–51), compliance with decisions of the Inter-American Commission has produced mixed results. Moreover, the interstate complaints 'procedures have proved unpopular with governments' (Alston et al., 2013, at p. 1038, see earlier in this section).

As with other regional systems, local remedies have to be exhausted (Article 46) subject to exceptions under Article 46(2)—that is, when legislation does not offer protection (Article 46(2)(a)), or where there has been a denial of access (Article 46(2)(b)) and an unwarranted delay (Article 46(2)(c)).

Unlike the African system, there are no provisions detailing the need for reports to be submitted. Instead, member States submit annual reports to the Inter-American Council for Integral Development Executive Committee, which sends copies to the American Commission (Article 42).

KEY POINTS

- The American Charter is the oldest Charter and the most complicated, insofar as it deals with two systems—namely, the American Declaration on the Rights and Duties of Man, and the American Convention on Human Rights.

- The Commission entertains complaints from individuals and NGOs, as well as States.

- The Commission makes no provision for submission of reports, unlike the African system.

19.4.3 The European Convention on the Protection of Human Rights and Fundamental Freedoms

The European Convention on the Protection of Human Rights and Fundamental Freedoms (usually called the European Convention on Human Rights, or ECHR) was adopted in 1950 and entered into force in 1953. This was the first international treaty that comprehensively dealt with human rights. The first international complaints procedure and international court were created under the ECHR. It is important to note that this was done under the Council of Europe, which was founded in 1949 to work towards European integration.

The rights contained in the ECHR mostly follow the first half of the UDHR—that is, they are predominantly civil and political rights. But these rights have been expanded upon and amended through protocols, most of which are optional, except in the case of protocols dealing with implementation and institutional processes, such as Protocol 11.

Interference with and limitations on Convention rights are subject to what is 'necessary in a democratic society' (Articles 8–11), and under Article 15 derogation is allowed only in 'public emergency threatening the life of the nation', although derogation from the right to life guaranteed under Article 2 can be made only for lawful acts of war, while no derogation is permitted to the prohibition of torture under Article 3, and slavery and forced labour under Article 4.

The European Commission on Human Rights

The 1997 Summit of Heads of State and Government approved the position of a European Commission on Human Rights and such a body was created in 1999. The Commission was to promote human rights education and raise awareness within member States, and to identify legal and practical shortcomings. The Commission was tasked with receiving complaints and deciding on the issue of admissibility, as well as providing non-binding opinions for the European Court of Human Rights (ECtHR). Following the entry into force of Protocol 11 in 1998, the European Commission on Human Rights was abolished, with its roles now being undertaken by the ECtHR.

KEY POINTS

- The European Convention is the first regional instrument to deal comprehensively with human rights.

- The Commission dealt with complaints, but has now been replaced by the ECtHR, following the adoption of Protocol 11 in 1998.

- The first international human rights court was established under the European Convention.

Having considered the various regional human right treaties and the commissions established to monitor compliance with them, we now turn to an appreciation of the regional human rights courts established for vindicating human rights violations.

19.5 Regional human rights courts

19.5.1 The African Court of Justice and Human Rights

In 1998, the Protocol establishing the African Court on Human and Peoples' Rights (ACHPR) was adopted by the OAU, and it entered into force on 25 January 2004. The introduction of the Court was due to the lack of enforcement powers of the African Commission on Human and Peoples' Rights (the African Commission), decisions of which were not binding on States. The Human Rights Court was to 'complement the protective mandate' of the African Commission (Article 2 of the Protocol on the Human Rights Court).

However, Article 18 of the Constitutive Act of the African Union (the AU Act), adopted in 2001, establishes another court: the African Court of Justice. While the court established by the 1998 Protocol had only jurisdiction over human rights matters, Article 18 of the AU Act makes no reference to human rights. That means that there are two distinct regional courts in Africa: one established under the 1998 Protocol, with jurisdiction over human rights; the other established under Article 18 of the AU Act with other jurisdictions not including human rights.

How should this be resolved?

On 1 July 2008, the AU adopted the Protocol on the Statute of the African Court of Justice and Human Rights, which effectively merged the two separate courts. The merged court is now known as the African Court of Justice and Human Rights (the African Court). Thus, instead of the pre-existing two courts with two different jurisdictions, the merger Protocol established a single court with two different jurisdictions organized under the Human Rights Section and the General Affairs Section of that Court (Article 16 of the Statute of the African Court).

Despite that the 2008 Protocol has not yet entered into force, in May 2012 a meeting of African Ministers for Justice and Attorney Generals adopted the Draft Protocol on Amendments to Protocol on the Statute of the African Court of Justice and Human Rights, which extended the jurisdiction of the African Court to international crimes. This Protocol makes it possible for the African Court to prosecute traditional international crimes such as war crimes, crimes against humanity and genocide, and less accustomed ones including corruption, unconstitutional changes of governments, illicit flow of capital, and so on.

Article 2(1) of the Statute of the Court, annexed to the 2008 (Merger) Protocol, describes the African Court as the 'principal judicial organ of the African Union'—language reminiscent of Article 91 of the UN Charter regarding the status of the International Court of Justice (ICJ). This means that once an AU member State ratifies the Protocol it *automatically* accepts the Court's jurisdiction (Article 8(1) of the Protocol). The question then is: since the merging Protocol has not yet entered into force, what becomes of the 1998 Court?

Pending the entry into force of the merger Protocol, and hence the Statute of the African Court, the 1998 Court—the ACHPR—which became operational in 2004, will continue to function on the basis of several transitional provisions contained in the merging Protocol. Its judges were elected at the Eighth Ordinary Session of the Executive Council of the African Union, and its seat was set up in Arusha, Tanzania. The ACHPR delivered its first judgment on 15 December 2009, finding an application against Senegal inadmissible. Cases pending before the ACHPR will be transferred to the merged court upon the entry into force of the latter, and the 1998 court will remain operational for no longer than one year, or any such term as may otherwise be decided by the AU Assembly, after the merging Protocol enters into force.

The competence of the African Court of Justice and Human Rights

Instead of two courts with two different jurisdictions, which existed until 2008, what now exists in Africa is one court with two different jurisdictions. The African Court now combines the jurisdictions of the 1998 Court (human rights) and the Article 18 Court (general matters). The human rights jurisdiction of the 1998 Court, and the *general* jurisdiction of the Article 18 Court are now found in the Human Rights and General Affairs Sections of the Statute of the African Court, respectively (Article 16).

The Court has both contentious and advisory jurisdiction. Under Article 28 of its Statute, the African Court has jurisdiction over a wide expanse of treaties of a general nature, or specifically on human rights, including all treaties adopted by the OAU/AU, the African Charter on the Rights and Welfare of the Child, all other human rights treaties entered into by AU member States, and many more. However, Article 17(2) specifically confers the Human Rights Section of the Court with competence to hear all cases relating to human and/or peoples' rights.

Article 53 of the Statute provides that:

1. The Court may give an advisory opinion on any legal question at the request of the Assembly, the Parliament, the Executive Council, the Peace and Security Council, the Economic, Social and Cultural Council (ECOSOCC), the Financial Institutions or any other organ of the Union as may be authorized by the Assembly.

2. A request for an advisory opinion shall be in writing and shall contain an exact statement of the question upon which the opinion is required and shall be accompanied by all relevant documents.

3. A request for an advisory opinion must not be related to a pending application before the African Commission or the African Committee of Experts.

According to Articles 29 and 30 of the Statute, two different groups of applicants can bring complaints before the Court. Under Article 29, State parties to the Protocol, the AU Assembly, the Parliament, and other organs of the Union authorized by the Assembly can bring any action listed under Article 28 of the Statute.

Gino Naldi, 'The role of the Human and Peoples' Rights Section of the African Court of Justice and Human Rights' in Ademola Abass (ed.), *Protecting Human Security in Africa* (Oxford: Oxford University Press, 2010), p. 296, refers to this group as 'privileged applicants', since the fact that Article 28 covers non-human rights matters means that they can bring applications on matters not confined to human rights. The second class of applicants are, according to Article 30, State parties to the Protocol, the African Commission on Human and Peoples' Rights, the African Committee of Experts on the Rights and Welfare of the Child, African intergovernmental organizations accredited to the Union or its organs, and African national human rights institutions. This group can bring applications relating only to human rights violations.

Also, under Article 35(1) of the Statute, the Court, either *proprio motu* (on its own volition) or on application by the parties, may indicate provisional measures that ought to be taken to preserve the respective rights of the parties if it considers that circumstances so require.

Decisions of the African Court are final and binding on parties, except where a party against whom judgment is given objects under Article 41(3) of the Statute. Upon failure by a party to comply with a judgment, the Court shall refer the matter to the Assembly, which shall decide upon measures to be taken to give effect to that judgment.

One conspicuous omission in the Statute was the lack of a provision on whether a State, whose application to a section of the Court has been rejected, can appeal to the full Court. It may be that the Court will develop such matters through its procedural rules at a later stage.

KEY POINTS

- The African Court of Justice and Human Rights (the African Court) was established as an amalgamation of the African Court on Human and Peoples' Rights established by the 1998 Protocol, and the African Court of Justice, established pursuant to the AU Act.

- The African Court has both adjudicatory and advisory roles, and can take complaints from individuals, States, and a wide range of other entities.

- Pending the entry into force of the 2008 Protocol that established the African Court, the African Court on Human and Peoples' Rights established in 1998 remains in force.

19.5.2 The Inter-American Court of Human Rights

Pursuant to Article 1 of the Statute of the IACHR, the Court is:

> An autonomous judicial institution whose purpose is the application and interpretation of the American Convention on Human Rights.

The Court comprises seven judges serving in a personal capacity (Article 52), who are elected by the General Assembly for a renewable term of six years (Article 54). Pursuant to Article 55, a State party involved in a case can appoint an ad hoc judge to serve during the case. The IACHR was modelled on the ECtHR, but developed its own procedures after its inception. Since December 2003, once a case before the IACHR involves a violation of the American Convention, *locus standi* is given to the alleged victim(s) and their next of kin and/or appointed representatives.

IACHR jurisdiction is advisory and adjudicatory, and States decide whether they accept the IACHR's jurisdiction when they ratify the American Convention or at any other time after that.

Interim measures are permitted, under Article 64(2):

> in cases of extreme gravity and urgency, and when necessary to avoid irreparable damage to persons, the Court shall adopt such provisional measures as it deems pertinent in matters it has under consideration. With respect to a case not yet submitted to the Court, it may act at the request of the Commission.

The IACHR may impose remedies and compensation.

. . . .

● ***Velásquez Rodríguez v. Honduras*** (1988) IACHR Ser. C, No. 4

In this case, it was stated (at [189]) that:

> the Court cannot order that the victim be guaranteed the enjoyment of the right or liberty violated. The Court, however, can rule that the consequences of the breach of the rights be remedied and rule that just compensation be paid.

There will be allowances made in instances in which the Court believes an agreement on damages can be reached between the parties. Otherwise, as noted at [191]:

> If an agreement cannot be reached, the Court shall award an amount. The case shall, therefore, remain open for that purpose. The Court reserves the right to approve the agreement and, in the event no agreement is reached, to set the amount and order the payment.

. . . .

● ***Sawhoyamaxa Indigenous Community v. Paraguay*** (2006) IACHR Ser. C, No. 146

This case concerned indigenous peoples' right to property (Article 21), the right to life (Article 4), and the right to judicial personality (Article 3).

With regard to reparation, the IACHR ordered (at [210]):

> The State [to] adopt all legislative, administrative or other type of measure necessary to guarantee the members of the Community ownership rights over their traditional lands, and consequently the right to use and enjoy those lands.

The IACHR required the State to put money into a fund to be used to improve the community's conditions through ensuring access to other rights (at [224]), and the IACHR ordered (at [226]):

> the State to pay compensation in the amount of US$ 20,000.00…to each of the 17 members of the Community who died as a result of the events in the instant case.

Indigenous peoples' rights, as well as enforced disappearance, are common issues in Latin American States, which make up most of the member States of the IACHR and the Inter-American system.

thinking points
- *What is the nature of the IACHR's competence?*
- *What is the composition of the IACHR and in what capacity are judges appointed?*

19.5.3 The European Court of Human Rights

The ECtHR was established by the ECHR and previously worked together with the European Commission on Human Rights; after the coming into force of Protocol 11, the Commission ceased to exist.

Under the current Article 22 ECHR, judges are elected for six years, which will be extended to nine years after Protocol 14 comes into force (upon ratification by Russia). The number of judges is determined by the number of high contracting parties (Article 20). As with the other regional courts, judges serve in an independent personal capacity and do not represent their State of nationality (Article 21). The Court is subject to its own rules of procedure and is composed of four sections: the Committee; the Chamber; the Grand Chamber; and the Committee of Ministers. These sections are further divided into committees, which comprise three judges, serving for a duration of twelve months. The committees undertake some of the work previously handled by the European Commission on Human Rights.

The Chamber and Grand Chamber, when hearing a case, include an *ex officio* judge from the State party concerned, who is to provide expert advice on the position in domestic law (Article 27(2)). When the Chamber has decided a case, there is a three-month period in which one of the parties to the case can refer that matter to the Grand Chamber. The Grand Chamber decides, by a five-judge panel, whether it will accept or reject the case (Article 43). Pursuant to Article 44(1), all Grand Chamber judgments are considered final, whereas Chamber judgments are final in instances in which a referral to the Grand Chamber has not been requested or taken within three months (Article 44(2)(a) and (b)), or once the Grand Chamber panel has rejected the referral (Article 44(2)(c)). All judges are to give reasons for their decisions and separate opinions are permitted when a decision is not unanimous (Article 45).

Under Article 32, the jurisdiction of the ECtHR shall:

> extend to all matters concerning the interpretation and application of the Convention and the protocols thereto which are referred to it as provided in Article 33, 34 and 47.

Various ECtHR decisions have addressed the issue of jurisdiction when it has involved a contracting State, but the violation has occurred outside its territory.

. . . .

● *Banković & ors v. Belgium & ors* APPLICATION No. 52207/99, ECtHR GRAND CHAMBER, 12 DECEMBER 2001

The ECtHR had to decide on a case concerning a North Atlantic Treaty Organization (NATO) missile launch from within the territory of a contracting State that caused damage outside its territory to a non-contracting State—in this case, Yugoslavia. The ECtHR considered its previous decision in *Soering v. United Kingdom* (1989) 11 EHRR 439 and ruled (at [86]) that:

> Article 1 sets a limit, notably territorial, on the reach of the Convention. In particular, the engagement undertaken by a Contracting State is confined to 'securing' the listed rights and freedoms to persons within its own 'jurisdiction'. Further, the Convention does not govern the actions of States not Parties to it, nor does it purport to be a means of requiring the Contracting States to impose Convention standards on other States.

The Court took the view (at [70]) that when a State is exercising extraterritorial control over another:

> bearing in mind the object and purpose of the Convention, the responsibility of a Contracting Party was capable of being engaged when as a consequence of military action (lawful or unlawful) it exercised effective control of an area outside its national territory. The obligation to secure, in such an area, the Convention rights and freedoms was found to derive from the fact of such control whether it was exercised directly, through the respondent State's armed forces, or through a subordinate local administration.

This case reveals the territorial limitation of the Convention, as well as the jurisdiction of the Court. This limitation would not apply, however, where a State is in control of a particular territory that is not part of its own territory. For example, in the case of a military occupation by a contracting State, such State will be liable for the acts of its soldiers within the occupied territory. Control may be administrative, or based on an agreement, but whatever the case, the Court will be able to exercise jurisdiction over the acts of such a contracting State in such a territory.

The ECtHR is able to receive individual complaints under Article 34. Protocol 11 made obligatory the individual complaints process for all contracting States; whereas previously States could decide whether they accepted the Court's jurisdiction. Protocol 14 will attempt to establish a process whereby applications that raise no substantial Convention issue can be struck off, in order to address the large number of cases being brought before the ECtHR. Under Article 34, individual applications are possible from:

> any person, non-governmental organisation or group of individuals claiming to be the victim of a violation by one of the High Contracting Parties of the rights set forth in the Convention or the protocols thereto. The High Contracting Parties undertake not to hinder in any way the effective exercise of this right.

Interstate complaints are also possible under Article 33, thus:

> any High Contracting Party may refer to the Court any alleged breach of the provisions of the Convention and the protocols thereto by another High Contracting Party.

To date, there have been only four judgments related to interstate complaints:

- *Ireland v. United Kingdom* Application No. 5310/71 (1978) 2 EHRR 25;
- *Denmark v. Turkey* Application No. 34382/97 [2000] ECHR 149;
- *Cyprus v. Turkey* Application No. 25781/94 (2002) 35 EHRR 30; and
- *Georgia v. Russia* Application No. 13255/07 (2009), unreported.

● **Ireland v. United Kingdom** Application No. 5310/71 (1978) 2 EHRR 25

In this case, the ECtHR held (at [154]) that:

> The Court's judgments in fact serve not only to decide those cases brought before the Court, but, more generally, to explain, safeguard and develop the rules instituted by the Convention, thereby contributing to the observance by the States of the engagements undertaken by them as Contracting Parties.

Some of the more controversial areas that the ECtHR has addressed relate to the issue of sexuality and military service, and the right to privacy.

● **Handyside v. United Kingdom** Application No. 5493/72 (1979) 1 EHRR 737

The UK had prevented the translation of the Danish book *The Little Red Schoolbook* from being distributed with its full content, due to the presence of sections dealing with sexuality, on the basis of protecting the public good. The ECtHR held that no breach of Article 10 had occurred while also addressing the concept of the margin of appreciation (that is, the doctrine that entitles parties to the ECHR to interpret the Convention differently, and according to their varied circumstances).

The Court said (at [48]) that:

> By reason of their direct and continuous contact with the vital forces of their countries, State authorities are in principle in a better position than the international judge to give an opinion on the exact content of these requirements as well as on the 'necessity' of a 'restriction' or 'penalty' intended to meet them ... [I]t is for the national authorities to make the initial assessment of the reality of the pressing social need implied by the notion of 'necessity' in this context. Consequently, Article 10(2) leaves the Contracting States a margin of appreciation. This margin is given both to the domestic legislator ('prescribed by law') and to the bodies, judicial amongst others, that are called upon to interpret and apply the laws in force.

In contrast, when national laws prove detrimental to society or a group within society, the ECtHR looks differently on the matter.

● **Norris v. Ireland** Application No. 10581/83 (1988) 13 EHRR 186

At [46]:

> The Court is of the opinion that such justifications as there are for retaining the law in force unamended are outweighed by the detrimental effects which the very existence of the legislative provisions in question can have on the life of a person of homosexual orientation.

In terms of military personnel being discharged due to their sexual orientation, the ECtHR has considered the defence of national security.

● **Lustig-Prean and Beckett v. United Kingdom** APPLICATION NOS 31417/96 AND 32377/96
    (1999) 29 EHRR 548

The Court said (at [82]) that:

> when the core of the national security aim pursued is the operational effectiveness of the armed forces, it is accepted that each State is competent to organise its own system of military discipline and enjoys a certain margin of appreciation in this respect. The Court also considers that it is open to the State to impose restrictions on an individual's right to respect for his private life where there is a real threat to the armed forces operational effectiveness, as the proper functioning of an army is hardly imaginable without legal rules designed to prevent service personnel from undermining it.

Another issue at which the ECtHR has looked concerns rights related to democracy and political participation.

● **United Communist Party of Turkey v. Turkey** APPLICATION NO. 133/1996/752/951, ECtHR
    GRAND CHAMBER, 30 JANUARY 1998

The United Communist Party of Turkey (TBKP) was formed on 4 June 1990 and, on the same day, submitted its constitution and programme to the Turkish Constitutional Court for assessment of their compatibility with the Constitution and Law 2820 on the Regulation of Political Parties. The principal State counsel applied to the Court to have the TBKP dissolved. The application alleged, among other things, that the Party had infringed the Constitution by seeking to establish the domination of one social class over the others. This was because the Party had included the term 'communist' in its name (contrary to section 96(3) of Law 2820), and also because it advocated the establishment of a Kurdish nation, which the counsel claimed was contrary to the territorial integrity of Turkey.

The Constitutional Court found in favour of the application on both grounds and thus dissolved the TBKP.

In its appeal to the Commission, the TBKP complained that the dissolution of the Party infringed its right to freedom of association, as guaranteed by Article 11 ECHR.

Upholding the application, the ECtHR held (at [27]):

> that (1) in view of the importance of democracy within the Convention system, there could be no doubt that political parties came within the scope of Art.11. An association was not excluded from the protection afforded by the Convention simply because its activities were regarded by the national authorities as undermining the constitutional structures of the State, *Open Door Counselling Ltd v. Ireland* (A/246) (1993) 15 E.H.R.R. 244 applied.

● **Refah Partisi (the Welfare Party) & ors v. Turkey** APPLICATION NOS 41340/98, 41342/98,
    41343/98 AND 41344/98, ECtHR GRAND CHAMBER, 13 FEBRUARY 2003

The Turkish Constitutional Court dissolved Refah Partisi (RP), a political party that advocated the imposition of Sharia law. The Court's dissolution order was on the basis that RP's activities were contrary to democratic principles and conflicted with the secular nature of the State.

The Party appealed.

The ECtHR refused to uphold the complaint by four votes to three, finding (at [42]) that:

> that there had been no violation of Art.11. Given the importance of the democratic system in Turkey, RP's dissolution satisfied the legitimate aims of maintaining national security and public safety, preventing crime and disorder and the protection of the rights and freedoms of others. The interests of democracy and the need to uphold the rule of law were closely linked and Art.11 had to be considered in light of Art.10, which protected the freedom to express differing opinions in a democracy. The dissolution of RP was therefore proportionate to the legitimate aim pursued.

From these cases, it is obvious that the Court will interpret the provisions of the Convention and their applicability to national domestic situations based on the circumstances of the case, and with due regard to public safety and security in the territory of the contracting State.

In terms of the implementation of Convention provisions, the Committee on Legal Affairs and Human Rights of the Parliamentary Assembly of the Council of Europe released a draft report on 'Member States' Duty to Cooperate with the European Court of Human Rights' (Doc. 11183, 9 February 2007), which addressed the issue of States not adhering to their obligation to refrain from hindering effective exercise of the right to individual application under Article 34. The Committee noted that it was:

> ... deeply worried about the fact that a number of cases involving the alleged killing, disappearance, beating or threatening of applicant initiating cases before the Court have still have not been fully and effectively investigated by the competent authorities. On the contrary, in a significant number of cases there are clear signs of lack of willingness to effectively investigate the allegations and in some cases the intention of whitewashing is clearly apparent.
>
> Illicit pressure has also been brought to bear on lawyers who defend applicants before the Court, and who assist victims of human rights violations in exhausting national remedies before applying to the Court.
>
> It also encourages the Court to continue taking an assertive stand in counteracting pressure on applicants and their lawyers, as well as on lawyers working on the exhaustion of internal remedies, including by an increased use of interim measures, and the granting of priority to relevant cases. As regards the lack of co-operation of member states in the establishments of facts, concrete measures proposed by the Committee include increased recourse, in appropriate cases, to factual inferences and the reversal of the burden of proof.

KEY POINTS

- The ECtHR is the oldest international human rights court in existence and perhaps the most active.

- The Court adjudicates on individual and State applications, and has decided many important cases of varied interests.

- The Court recognizes the doctrine of margin of appreciation by which member States interpret and apply Convention rights differently.

- Individuals can appear before the ECtHR.

Current issues in international human rights law

19.6.1 Terrorism and human rights

Terrorism, due to its nature, has proved difficult to define, because there is a lack of consensus. However, Article 2(1)(b) of the 1999 International Convention for the Suppression of the Financing of Terrorism defines the term as:

> Any other act intended to cause death or serious bodily injury to a civilian, or to any other person not taking an active part in the hostilities in a situation of armed conflict, when the purpose of such act, by its nature or context is to intimidate a population, or to compel a Government or an international organization to do or abstain from doing any act.

Some States have made reservations when ratifying the Convention. Jordan, for example, said that its government:

> does not consider acts of national armed struggle and fighting foreign occupation in the exercise of people's right to self-determination as terrorist within the context of paragraph 1(b) of Article 2 of the Convention.

In paragraph 3 of the 2004 UN Security Council Resolution 1566 (S/RES/1566), the UN Security Council, acting under Chapter VII of the UN Charter:

> *Recall[ed]* that criminal acts, including against civilians, committed with the intent to cause death or serious bodily injury, or taking of hostages, with the purpose to provoke a state of terror in the general public or in a group of persons or particular persons, intimidate a population or compel a government or an international organization to do or to abstain from doing any act, and all other acts which constitute offences within the scope of and as defined in the international conventions and protocols relating to terrorism, are under no circumstance justifiable by considerations of political, philosophical, ideological, racial, ethnic, religious or other similar nature.

This clearly is a general description, rather than a definition, of 'terrorism'. The responsibility of individuals, organizations, and governments alike is also vague with regard to terrorism and the relevant international provisions. At paragraph 2, the Security Council:

> *Call[ed] upon* States to cooperate fully in the fight against terrorism, especially with those States where or against whose citizens terrorist acts are committed, in accordance with their obligations under international law, in order to find, deny safe haven and bring to justice, on the basis of the principle to extradite or prosecute, any person who supports, facilitates, participates or attempts to participate in the financing, planning, preparation or commission of terrorist acts or provides safe havens.

Amnesty International, *United Nations: Proposed Anti-Terrorism Resolution Undermines Human Rights* (London: Amnesty International, 2004), criticized the vagueness of this provision on the basis that the:

> Language casts the net so wide that people, including human rights advocates or peaceful political activists can easily and unintentionally fall victim to the measures advocated in the

resolution. The resolution does not even require that act contributing to 'terrorists acts', such as unknowingly providing lodging, have to be intentional or done with the knowledge that they will assist the crime. In resorting to such exceptionally broad language, the resolution would call for measures which do not even permit individuals to foresee whether their acts will be lawful or not, a basic requirement in international law.

Following the 11 September 2001 attacks on the USA (the '9/11 attacks'), some States have taken a tougher stance on terrorism, and this has meant that States and NGOs have increased their focus on issues pertinent to terrorism. The effect of this is that even those who have no proper understanding of the issues make and implement important decisions, which usually inevitably affect many of the human rights espoused by domestic and international instruments.

In 'Sources and trends in post-9/11 anti-terrorism laws' in Benjamin Goold and Liora Lazarus (eds), *Security and Human Rights* (Oxford: Hart Publishing, 2007), pp. 227 *et seq*, Kent Roach notes that:

> in the five years since the terrorist attacks on the United States, a staggering array of new anti-terrorism laws have been enacted throughout the world... [I]nternational and domestic organizations often draft anti-terrorism initiatives on the fly, engaging in bricolage with what is at hand, but with limited information about the effects of various measures on security or human rights... there has been a faddish aspect to post 9/11 anti-terrorism laws with a number of countries following trends established by a small number of influential international and domestic instruments.
>
> Many countries have followed the lead of the Security Council and used immigration law as anti-terrorism law. This has had adverse effects on various human rights because immigration proceedings typically offer less procedural protections for detainees than criminal proceedings and because a number of countries are re-evaluating the right not to be deported to torture. The focus on immigration law also has had adverse effects on security as it has encouraged some western states to focus anti-terrorism efforts on non-citizens even though, as the London bombings tragically confirm, citizens also commit acts of terrorism...
>
> Broad definitions of terrorism could have adverse effect on security, as well as human rights, if they result in a misallocation of limited law enforcement and security intelligence resources

thinking points

- *Define 'terrorism'.*
- *What are the shortcomings of UN Security Council Resolution 1566 on terrorism?*

Arrest and detention of terror suspects: the use of control orders in the UK

The issue of detention and its regulation has been affected by terrorism laws and practices. Prior to the 9/11 attacks, the UK passed the Terrorism Act 2000. After 9/11, it passed the Anti-Terrorism, Crime and Security Act 2001, granting wide powers of detention of non-nationals, where deportation is not viable, due to the threat of torture or lack of agreement with the home country.

Section 23(1) of the 2001 Act provides that:

> A suspected international terrorist may be detained...despite the fact that his removal or departure from the United Kingdom is prevented (whether temporarily or indefinitely) by—
>
> (a) a point of law which wholly or partly relates to an international agreement, or
>
> (b) a practical consideration.

. . . .

● *A & ors v. Secretary of State for the Home Department* [2004] UKHL 56

The 2001 Act was declared to be incompatible with certain provisions of the Human Rights Act 1998, since the former permitted discrimination against suspected terrorists, particularly on the grounds of nationality and immigration status.

The House of Lords, per Lord Bingham at [9], recalled the case of *Chahal v. United Kingdom* Application No. 70/1995/576/662 (1996) ECtHR, 15 November 1996. His lordship quoted the ECtHR, which states in para 113 of *Chahal* case, that:

> any deprivation of liberty under Article 5(1)(f) will be justified only for as long as deportation proceedings are in progress...But a non-national who faces the prospect of torture or inhuman treatment if returned to his own country, and who cannot be deported to any third country and is not charged with any crime, may not under Article 5(1)(f) of the convention and Schedule 3 to the Immigration Act 1971 be detained here even if judged to be a threat to national security.

The UK government then passed the Prevention of Terrorism Act 2005, which provides, under section 1, for 'control orders', defined in section 1(1) as:

> an order against an individual that imposes obligations on him for purposes connected with protecting members of the public from a risk of terrorism.

Section 1(2)(a) and (b) outlines exceptions to the ability to issue control orders when they relate to a situation that would be:

> (a) imposing obligations that are *incompatible with the individual's right to liberty* under Article 5 of the Human Rights Convention, by the Secretary of State; or
>
> (b) in the case of an order imposing obligations that are or include derogating obligations, by the court on an application by the Secretary of State. [Emphasis added]

There is an extensive list of obligations that can be imposed on an individual detailed under section 4(a)–(p).

In 'Anti-terrorism control order: liberty and security still in the balance' (2009) 29 Legal Stud 99, 99–100, Ed Bates described control orders as the UK government's:

> response to the Law Lords' condemnation of s 23 of the Anti-Terrorism Crime and Security Act 2001 (ATCSA) in the *Belmarsh* detainees' case. The new orders were presented as a non-discriminatory and proportionate anti-terrorism tool that would manage the risk posed by those identified by the government as a terrorist *threat*, yet who could neither be prosecuted nor deported.

Bates (ibid., 110) has also considered the lack of criminal trials and the related fair trials procedure that control orders lack, noting the UK case *Belmarsh (A, X and Y & ors) v. Secretary of State* [2004] QB 335, the House of Lord addressed the issue:

> He [Lord Bingham] noted too that previous domestic case-law had made a distinction between preventive measures and those which had 'a more punitive, retributive and deterrent object'. That case-law did not involve measures the impact of which was anything like as serious as control orders and, as Lord Bingham noted, it has been strongly criticised. Nonetheless, he held that, 'on balance', control order hearings were not the determination of a criminal charge. It is surely telling that he added that Parliament had gone 'to some lengths to avoid a procedure which crosses the criminal boundary'. It had carefully drafted the PTA so as to ensure that control orders were preventive in nature and specifically avoided the criminal law.

This quote shows that the issue of control orders lies somewhere between bringing an actual criminal charge against a person and pursuing an investigation against the person, while the person remains freely within the community. They lie somewhere between prevention, which Parliament seemed to pursue, and punishment.

The UK House of Lords considered numerous cases regarding the legality of control order conditions.

. . . .

● **Secretary of State for the Home Department v. JJ & ors** [2007] UKHL 45

The defendants, who were all foreign nationals and under various permissions to stay in the UK, were put under control orders by the Secretary of State pursuant to the Prevention of Terrorism Act 2005. In the order, the six of them were confined to a single bedroom, they had limited contact with the outside world, and they were placed under a stringent visitation regime, among many other things. It was generally agreed that none of the instances of the defendants fell under the exemption clauses in Article 5(1)(a)–(f) ECHR.

The High Court quashed the order, prompting the Secretary of State to appeal to the Court of Appeal, which upheld the High Court's decision. The Secretary of State then appealed to the House of Lords in the present suit claiming (at [4]), as in the Court of Appeal, the:

> imperative duty of democratic governments to do what could lawfully be done to protect the public against the grave threat presented by the criminal activity of terrorists; and that even if the court had been correct to find that the control orders wrongly deprived defendants of their liberty, s.3[12] of the Act supported a view that only some of the individual obligations ought to have been quashed, rather than the entire control order.

The Law Lords, summing up (at [11] *et seq*), held that a non-derogating control order that, inter alia, imposed an eighteen-hour curfew and forbade social contact with anybody except as may be authorized by the Home Office, amounted to a deprivation of liberty. The House of Lords also stated that the High Court had not erred in quashing the order rather than opposing or amending it, as the Secretary of State had argued. According to their Lordships, the defects in such an order could not be cured by amending specific obligations and it would be contrary in principle to decline to quash an order made without power to make it, which had unlawfully deprived a person of his or her liberty.

• **Secretary of State for the Home Department v. MB; Secretary of State for the Home Department v. AF** [2007] UKHL 46

This was an appeal to the House of Lords.

In these two separate, but joined, cases, M and F were placed under a non-derogating order. In both cases, the Secretary of State's application for the order was based on open and closed statements, not generally accessible to the public. The principal issue before the House of Lords was whether the procedures provided for by section 3 of the Act and Part 76 of the Criminal Procedure Rules (CPR) were compatible with Article 6 ECHR in circumstances in which they resulted in the cases being made against M and F being entirely undisclosed to them, with no specific allegation of terrorism-related activity contained in open material.

It was held that:

> Where the justification for the making of a non-derogating control order, as was in the present case, was based entirely on closed material that could not be disclosed to the controlled person, then the Prevention of Terrorism Act 2005 Sch.1 para.4(3)(d) had to be read and given effect 'except where to do so would be incompatible with the right of the controlled person to a fair trial'.

The ECtHR has addressed the deprivation of liberty that detention measures can violate and under which control orders are likely to fall. Given the nature of control orders and their use by the UK authorities, concerns have been raised. As Bates (2009, see earlier in this section) notes, at 102:

> The Strasbourg Court has held that there is a deprivation of liberty for house arrest for 24 hours a day, for detention in an open prison, and even for non-consensual confinement in a particular restricted space for a not negligible length of time. Nonetheless, and in apparent contradiction to this last statement, it has determined that there is no deprivation of liberty in cases where suspected criminals have been subjected to 12-hour curfews and mere restrictions on their general movements. Here, the court usually finds there to be an interference with the right to freedom of movement, which is protected by Art 2 of Protocol 4 to the ECHR, which the UK has not ratified. The control orders . . . which included substantial curfews coupled with other severe restrictions, therefore required a searching examination of the Art 5 jurisprudence in order to see whether they effected a deprivation of liberty.

While control orders are a controversial topic that the UK government and authorities have attempted to ensure remains out of the scope of human rights protection, as much as possible, the problem of terrorism has resulted in a varied response to these measures. As Clive Walker, 'Clamping down on terrorism in the United Kingdom' (2006) 4 JICJ 1137, 1145, advocates:

> It is evident that measures such as detention without trial and control orders do not reflect the ideal. Whenever invoked, it would be better to signal their extraordinary nature by derogation which would create an impetus to find alternatives—especially prosecution through the use of electronic surveillance evidence.

And as Ed Bates (2009, see earlier in this section) observes, at 120:

> the risk of terrorism today may provide a legitimate basis for having a preventive scheme like control orders, consistent with the duty states have to protect everyone from terrorism. The latter is identified in the *Guidelines on Human Rights and the Fight Against Terrorism* promulgated by the

Committee of Ministers of the Council of Europe. But the *Guidelines* insist that measures taken restricting human rights 'must be defined as precisely as possible and be necessary and proportionate to the aim pursued'... Control orders set aside normal, criminal law fair trial standards on the basis of security considerations benefiting the majority. Whilst there may be doubt as to that benefit (the controlee is, after all, only suspected of terrorism-related activity), the cost to the innocent individual is certainly very high: potentially severe restrictions on liberty *and* no chance to establish his innocence under the terms of a criminal fair trial.

At 125–6, he continues:

...any assessment of the human rights compatibility of control orders should appreciate the limited protection afforded by Arts 5 and (in the criminal law sphere) 6 of the ECHR. It should also be appreciated that positive human rights protection in the UK is deficient in that the right to freedom of movement is not protected. The protection of this right would not necessarily lead to the abolition of control orders; indeed, as a last resort, they *may* have a legitimate place as part of the government's anti-terrorism agenda. However, the right to freedom of movement would help to ensure that in individual cases control orders remain in place on a legitimate and proportionate basis.

KEY POINTS

- Control orders are granted against foreign nationals in the UK when there is no option of extraditing such nationals to their home countries.

- Control orders are subject to some exceptions. They cannot impose obligations that violate the controlled person's right to liberty under Article 5 ECHR or where they are, or include, a derogation of the concerned State from its Convention obligations.

- Where a control order was made unlawfully, quashing of such an order, not amendment, is a reasonable cause of action by the court (*Secretary of State for the Home Department v. JJ & ors*).

19.6.2 Torture

Numerous international treaties address torture and its prohibition, including the UDHR, ICCPR, and CAT (discussed earlier). There are, however, different interpretations of what acts constitute 'torture', as well as cruel, inhuman, or degrading treatment. Some of the regional as well as domestic courts have addressed claims of torture.

● *Ireland v. United Kingdom* APPLICATION No. 5310/71 (1978) 2 EHRR 25

In this case, Ireland alleged that the UK's detention of Irish Republican Army (IRA) suspects, involving such treatments as wall-standing, hooding, and deprivation of sleep and food, infringed Article 3 ECHR as well as Article 5. It also claimed that the acts did not constitute a 'public emergency' under Article 15 and that it was discriminatory under Article 14, since it singled out one group (the IRA).

The ECtHR held that although the detention without trial violated Article 5(1)–(4), it was exempted under the area of public emergency (Article 15). The Court also held that the acts were not discriminatory under Article 14, but that the five interrogation techniques amounted to inhuman or degrading treatment, thereby violating Article 3.

The above case also distinguishes between torture and the lesser considered 'cruel, inhuman, and degrading treatment'. It is important to highlight that, regardless of whether this is considered a 'lesser' crime, both acts are illegal.

As previously discussed in the earlier section on the CAT, torture is confined to acts of public officials. The ability of a State to condone or sanction the use of techniques that could be construed as torture or other cruel, inhuman, or degrading treatment has been targeted.

. . . .

● ***Public Committee against Torture in Israel v. State of Israel*** (1999) HC 5100/94, HCJ 769/02/, Israeli Supreme Court

The Israeli Supreme Court recognized the effect that terrorism has on a State's security and the methods of interrogation that Israel employs, and considered (at [35]) that the State authorizes the use of techniques that could be considered as torture:

> According to the existing state of the law, neither the government nor the heads of security services possess the authority to establish directives and bestow authorization regarding the use of liberty infringing physical means during the interrogation of suspects of hostile terrorist activities, beyond the general directives which can be inferred from the very concept of an interrogation. Similarly, the individual GSS investigator—like any police officer—does not possess the authority to employ physical means which infringe upon a suspect's liberty during the interrogation, unless these means are inherently necessary to the very essence of an interrogation and are both fair and reasonable.

The Supreme Court addressed the difficulties that the reality of such a situation presents when faced with the laws of a State (at [39]):

> This decision opens with a description of the difficult reality in which Israel finds herself security wise. We shall conclude this judgment by re-addressing that harsh reality. We are aware that this decision does not ease dealing with that reality. This is the destiny of democracy, as not all means are acceptable to it, and not all practices employed by its enemies are open before it ... If it will nonetheless be decided that it is appropriate for Israel, in light of its security difficulties to sanction physical means in interrogations ... , this is an issue that must be decided by the legislative branch which represents the people ... It is there that the required legislation may be passed, provided of course, that a law infringing upon a suspect's liberty 'befitting the values of the State of Israel', is enacted for a proper purpose, and to an extent no greater than is required.

Following the situations and massive human rights violations that were exposed in the Guantánamo Bay and Abu Ghraib detention camps, the USA, in particular, has come under criticism for its alleged acts of torture. In response, the US Department of Justice issued numerous memoranda. One of the most controversial was the memorandum from Jay Bybee, Assistant Attorney General, to Alberto Gonzales, Counsel to the President, of 1 August 2002, which reiterated the availability of measures to be taken under §2340A of the US Torture Act:

> whoever outside the United States commits or attempts to commit torture shall be fined under this title or imprisoned not more than 20 years, or both, and if death results to any person from conduct prohibited by this subsection, shall be punished by death or imprisoned for any term of years or for life.

The memo considered what degree of activity would be considered as 'severe', as required by the US Torture Act, and claimed that such act:

> must rise to a similarly high level—the level that would ordinarily be associated with a sufficiently serious physical condition or injury such as death, organ failure, or serious impairment of body function—in order to constitute torture.

The memo went further, stating that:

> Each component of the definition emphasizes that torture is not the mere infliction of pain or suffering on another, but is instead a step well removed. The victim must experience intense pain or suffering of the kind that is equivalent to the pain that would be associated with serious physical injury so severe that death, organ failure, or permanent damage resulting in a loss of significant body function will likely result. If the pain or suffering is psychological, that suffering must result from one of the acts set forth in the statute. In addition, these acts must cause long-term mental harm.

It is sometimes advocated by States, as in the case of the USA, that during times of armed conflict human rights laws do not apply—in particular those relating to torture and cruel, inhumane, and degrading treatment. The idea that the CAT is not applicable in times of armed conflict was addressed by the Committee against Torture in its Conclusion and Recommendations of Committee against Torture Relating to Report Submitted by the United States (CAT/C/USA/CO/2, 25 July 2006):

> The Committee regrets the State party's opinion that the Convention is not applicable in times and in the context of armed conflict, on the basis of the argument that the 'law of armed conflict' is the exclusive *lex specialis* applicable, and that the Convention's application 'would result in an overlap of the different treaties which would undermine the objective of eradicating torture'. The State party should recognize and ensure that the Convention applies at all times, whether in peace, war or armed conflict, in any territory under its jurisdiction and that the application of the Convention's provisions are without prejudice to the provisions of any other international instrument.

KEY POINTS

- States often try to preclude the application of the CAT during armed conflicts, but the Committee against Torture has consistently pronounced against this.

- Although torture is usually considered more severe than inhuman and degrading treatment, both are illegal.

19.6.3 Conflicts between human rights and culture, tradition, and related practices

Human rights are meant to be universal, but this has proved problematic to implement due to various States and regions claiming that the protection of certain human rights are incompatible with their cultures, traditions, or practices. Often, these terms are used indiscriminately and without clear understanding or consensus as to their meaning.

As Sally Engle Merry observes in *Human Rights and Gender Violence: Translating International Law into Local Justice* (Chicago, IL: University of Chicago Press, 2005), p. 2:

> although culture is a term on everyone's lips, people rarely talk about what they mean by it. The term has many meanings in the contemporary world. It is often seen as the basis of national, ethnic, or religious identities. Culture is sometimes romanticized as the opposite of globalization, resolutely local and distinct ... In international human rights meetings, culture often refers to traditions and customs: ways of doing things that are justified by their roots in the past.

Tracy Higgins, 'Anti-essentialism, relativism, and human rights' (1996) 19 Harv Women's LJ 86, 89, has also raised the point that:

> treating culture as monolithic fails to respect relevant intra-cultural differences just as the assumption of the universality of human rights standards fails to respect cross-cultural difference. Cultural differences that may be relevant to assessing human rights claims are neither uniform nor static. Rather, they are constantly created, challenged, and renegotiated by individuals living within inevitably overlapping cultural communities.
>
> This oversimplification of culture may lead relativists to accept too readily a cultural defense articulated by state actors or other elites on the international level, actors that tend not to be women. Yet, it seems unlikely that a cultural defense offered by the state will adequately reflect the dynamic, evolving, and possibly conflicting cultural concerns of its citizens ... culture has been selectively and perhaps cynically invoked to justify oppressive practices.

The freedom to express and/or practise one's religion has, at times, been seen as conflicting with human rights. As Dinah Shelton and Alexandre Kiss have noted in their chapter 'A draft model law on freedom of religion' in Johan van der Vyer and J. Witte, Jr (eds), *Religious Human Rights in Global Perspective* (The Hague: Martinus Nijhoff, 1996), p. 572:

> The freedom to have a religion means that the government does not prescribe orthodoxy or prohibit particular religions or beliefs. In practice, this is not always the case ...
>
> The constitutions of some states establish the primacy of a religion over the state, granting privileges that are incompatible with religious liberty and non-discrimination.

It must be pointed out, however, that the fact that a State adopts a particular religion does not mean that it contradicts the freedom of religion or that it does not permit the practice of other religions.

example

The Iranian Constitution affords a considerable degree of religious freedom. The recognized religion of the State is Islam (Article 12 of the Constitution), but religious minorities—specifically Zoroastrian, Jewish, and Christian Iranians—are recognized (Article 13) and non-Muslim rights are protected in Article 14, as well as the freedom of beliefs (Article 23). Under Chapter III of the Iranian Constitution, the principle of non-discrimination applies (Articles 19 and 20) and women's rights are provided for (Article 21); however, these are subject to conformity with Islamic criteria. Conflicts sometimes occur in relation to human rights in the interpretation and limiting of rights to Islamic criteria, as subject to the current interpretation in Iran. Furthermore, the interpretation of the ordinary laws is given to the Islam Consultative Assembly (Article 73) and any review is undertaken by the Guardian Council, which, according to Article 91, is established to:

safeguard the Islamic ordinances and the Constitution, in order to examine the compatibility of the legislations passed by the Islamic Consultative Assembly with Islam.

The Guardian Council also possesses the authoritative interpretation of the Constitution (Article 98). This demonstrates that while, obviously, the Constitution is progressive and contains many guarantees, tension can arise between certain provisions of the Constitution and tenets of Islam, due to the interpretative preferences of the Guardian Council and Islam Consultative Assembly. But such divergent views should not be automatically read to mean the subversion of the Constitution; after all, divergent views are possible even in secular States.

The UN HR Committee's General Comment 22 on the ICCPR (HRI/GEN/1/Rev.1, 1994) states, at paragraph 2, that:

> Article 18 protects theistic, non-theistic and atheistic beliefs, as well as the right not to profess any religion or belief. The terms 'belief' and 'religion' are to be broadly construed. Article 18 is not limited in its application to traditional religions or to religions and beliefs with institutional characteristics or practices analogous to those of traditional religions.

While the right to express and practise the religion of choice is espoused by the Convention and other human rights instruments, as shown previously, it should be noted that there are also restrictions allowed on the freedom to manifest one's religion or belief. Paragraph 8 of UN HR Committee General Comment 20 (HRI/GEN/1/Rev.1, 1994) provides that:

> If limitations are prescribed by law and are necessary to protect public safety, order, health or morals, or the fundamental rights and freedoms of others. The freedom from coercion to have or to adopt a religion or belief and the liberty of parents and guardians to ensure religious and moral education cannot be restricted. In interpreting the scope of permissible limitation clauses... limitations may be applied only for those purposes for which they were prescribed and must be directly related and proportionate to the specific need on which they are predicated.

On the tension between Islam, as well as other religions, and human rights, Abdullah Ahmed An-Na'im, 'Human rights in the Muslim world: socio-political conditions and scriptural imperatives' (1990) 3 Harv HRJ 13, 14–15, reflects that:

> Shari'a influences individual and collective behaviour in Muslim countries through its role in the socialization processes of such nations regardless of its status in their formal legal systems. For example, the status and rights of women in the Muslim world have always been significantly influenced by Shari'a, regardless of the degree of Islamization in public life. Of course, Shari'a is not the sole determinant of human behaviour nor the only formative force behind social and political institutions in Muslim countries...
>
> I conclude that human rights advocates in the Muslim world must work within the framework of Islam to be effective. They need not be confined, however, to the particular historical interpretations of Islam known as Shari'a. Muslims are obliged, as a matter of faith, to conduct their private and public affairs in accordance with the dictates of Islam, but there is room for legitimate disagreement over the precise nature of these dictates in the modern context.

On improving relations between Islam and human rights, An-Na'im (ibid., 46–47) contends that:

> Based on the work of the late Sudanese Muslim reformer Ustadh Mahmoud Mohamed Taha,... the Shari'a reflects a historically-conditioned interpretation of Islamic scriptures in the

sense that the founding jurists had to understand those sources in accordance with their own social, economic, and political circumstances. In relation to the status and rights of women, for example, equality between men and women in the eighth and ninth centuries in the Middle East, or anywhere else at the time, would have been inconceivable and impracticable. It was therefore natural and indeed inevitable that Muslim jurists would understand the relevant texts of the Qur'an and Sunna as confirming rather than repudiating the realities of the day . . .

Working with the same primary sources, modern Muslim jurists might shift emphasis from one class of texts to the other, and interpret the previously enacted texts in ways consistent with a new understanding of what is believed to be the intent and purpose of the sources. This new understanding would be informed by contemporary social, economic, and political circumstances in the same way that the 'old' understanding on which Shari'a jurists acted was informed by the then prevailing circumstances.

Most importantly, An-Na'im (ibid., 47–48) draws on the texts of the Qur'an, which are similar to or in line with human rights standards:

in numerous verses the Qur'an speaks of honor and dignity for 'humankind' and 'children of Adam', without distinction as to race, color, gender, or religion' . . . [S]imilarly, numerous verses of the Qur'an provide for freedom of choice and non-compulsion in religious belief and conscience. These verses have been either de-emphasized as having been 'overruled' by other verses which were understood to legitimize coercion, or 'interpreted' in ways which permitted such coercion.

Judicial decisions about what is or is not reasonable, as far as religious practices are concerned, vary and often depend on the individual attitudes of States towards the issue and various domestic legislations on the subject matter.

The ECtHR has confronted the issue of dress and symbolism, and their relation to human rights.

. . . .

● *Sahin v. Turkey* APPLICATION No. 44774/98 (2005) 41 EHRR 8

Sahin, a Turkish national, alleged that the university rules that prohibited the wearing of Islamic headscarves violated her rights under Articles 8, 9, 10, and 14 ECHR and Article 2 of Protocol 1. Despite the university rule, Sahin continued to wear her headscarf, and was subsequently denied access to lectures and examinations. She unsuccessfully applied to have the rule set aside and disciplinary proceedings were brought against her. Sahin left her university in Istanbul to pursue her studies in Vienna and brought a complaint to the ECtHR.

The Chamber ruled that the interference with Sahin's rights under Article 9 was justified in principle, proportionate, and necessary in a democratic society. Sahin appealed to the Grand Chamber.

It was held, dismissing the complaint (Tulkens J dissenting), that while there had been an interference with Sahin's rights under Article 9 since she wore a headscarf for religious reasons, the interference was permitted under Turkish law. The Grand Chamber also ruled that the consequences of Sahin's actions were foreseeable, since it would have been clear to her on entering Istanbul University that there were restrictions on wearing the headscarf. (The Chamber applied *Gorzelik v. Poland* Application No. 44158/98 (2005) 40 EHRR 4.) It was also said that the interference pursued the legitimate aim of protecting the rights and freedoms of others, and protecting public order in a secular State. Hence, it was therefore reasonable that the university would want to preserve the secular nature of the institution and restrict the wearing of religious attire. Article 9 was not an absolute guarantee of the right to behave in a manner governed by religious belief and it did not allow those who professed such beliefs to disregard rules that were otherwise justifiable.

The Canadian Supreme Court also considered a similar issue.

....

● **Multani v. Commission Scolaire Marguerite-Bourgeoys** [2006] 1 SCR 256, CANADIAN SUPREME COURT

On 2 March 2006, the Supreme Court of Canada ruled, first, that a total ban on wearing to school a kirpan (a ceremonial sword or dagger carried by orthodox Sikhs) violated an individual's freedom of religion protected by Article 2(a) of the Canadian Charter of Rights and Freedoms and, secondly, that this ban on religious expression was not reasonable or justifiable.

....

● **Goldman v. Weinberger** 475 US 503 (1986), US SUPREME COURT

In this case, the US Supreme Court considered a case in which the petitioner, an Orthodox Jew and ordained rabbi, was ordered not to wear a yarmulke (a cloth-made skullcap often worn by Jewish men) while on duty and in uniform as a commissioned officer in the US Air Force at March Air Force Base, pursuant to an Air Force regulation that provides that authorized headgear may be worn out of doors, but that indoors 'Headgear [may] not be worn . . . except by armed security police in the performance of their the duties'.

The petitioner first brought an action in the Federal District Court, claiming that the application of the regulation to prevent him from wearing his yarmulke infringed upon his First Amendment freedom to exercise his religious beliefs. The District Court permanently enjoined the Air Force from enforcing the regulation against the petitioner.

The Court of Appeals reversed the decision, which reversal was affirmed by the Supreme Court, holding (at 506–510) that:

> The First Amendment does not prohibit the challenged regulation from being applied to petitioner, even though its effect is to restrict the wearing of the headgear required by his religious beliefs. That Amendment does not require the military to accommodate such practices as wearing a yarmulke in the face of its view that they would detract from the uniformity sought by dress regulations. Here, the Air Force has drawn the line essentially between religious apparel that is visible and that which is not, and the challenged regulation reasonably and evenhandedly regulates dress in the interest of the military's perceived need for uniformity.

thinking points

- What is 'culture' and how has the term been used in relation to human rights?
- Do religion and human rights necessarily clash?
- In what principal areas do culture and human rights conflict?

The relationship between the UN Security Council and international organizations and the protection of human rights

The UN Security Council has adopted several resolutions under Chapter VII of the UN Charter (see Chapter 11) in response to terrorism. These resolutions provide for sanctions to be implemented by UN member States against people and entities placed on the Security Council Sanction List. The implementation of such measures by States and regional organizations has impacted on the protection of human rights, and has brought tension in the relationship between UN and regional organizations. In particular, the sanctions regime has been called into question due to the alleged violation of individuals human rights in terms of the right to a fair hearing. While individuals and entities placed on the UN Sanction Committee's list are unable to challenge their inclusion in such lists, challenging domestic implementation of sanctions imposed against them before national and regional courts raises the question of whether decisions of the UN Security Council can be reviewed.

The jurisprudence of the ECtHR and the European Court of Justice (ECJ) recent decisions in cases arising from the UN Sanction List seems to indicate that national or regional implementation of Security Council decisions does not prevent reviewing the consistency of such decisions with human rights obligations of UN member States.

In *Kadi & Al Barakaat International Foundation v. Council and Commission* the ECJ had to determine whether it was able to review European Council Regulation 881/2002, enacted to implement Security Council Resolutions 1267 (1999) and 1333 (2000). Resolution 1333 (2000) granted the Sanction Committee the role of maintaining a list of individuals and entities, which were to be subject to economic sanctions based upon their association with Osama bin Laden, and called on States to freeze the funds and assets of the named individuals and entities. Regulation 881/2002 put this into effect by requiring European Council member States to freeze funds and assets of named individuals. Mr Kadi and the Al Barakaat International Foundation brought a claim based on the grounds that their right to be heard, right to an effective judicial review, and respect for property had been breached, and sought annulment of the Regulation. The issue of contention here was that if the ECJ decided that the EC Regulation violated the specified human rights it would indirectly also be determining the validity of a Security Council resolution, as this was the basis of the EC Regulation.

The ECJ held that the matter was not immune from review despite being a Security Council Resolution. It stated that:

> The Community judicature must . . . ensure the review, in principle the full review, of the lawfulness of all Community acts in the light of the fundamental rights forming an integral part of the general principles of Community law, including review of Community measures which, like the contested regulation, are designed to give effect to the resolutions adopted by the Security Council under Chapter VII of the Charter of the United Nations (*Kadi & Al Barakaat International Foundation v. Council and Commission* (2008) 3 CMLR 41, 326)

Similarly, in *Nada v Switzerland* Mr Nada found himself subject to UN sanctions as a listed individual by the Sanctions Committee and brought his case before the Swiss national courts. The Swiss government, a non-EU member, had autonomously enacted UN Security Council Resolution 1267 (1999) and Mr Nada sought a review of the decision to include him in the list. The Swiss Federal Tribunal found Mr Nada's right to a fair hearing was suspended by Resolution 1967 (1999), which Mr Nada appealed before the ECtHR. The ECtHR focused on whether Switzerland had done all it could in its power to limit the conflict between the UN Security Council Resolution and the ECHR obligations. The ECtHR found Switzerland had not done this. Furthermore, the ECtHR held that Switzerland did not provide Mr Nada with the opportunity for judicial review at the domestic level and Resolution 1267 (1999) itself did not prevent judicial review, as in line with:

the finding of the [ECJ] that 'it is not a consequence of the principles governing the international legal order under the United Nations that any judicial review of the internal lawfulness of the contested regulation in the light of fundamental freedoms is excluded by virtue of the fact that that measure is intended to give effect to a resolution of the Security Council adopted under Chapter VII of the Charter of the United Nations' (see the Kadi judgment of the [ECJ], § 299). The Court is of the opinion that the same reasoning must be applied, mutatis mutandis, to the present case, more specifically to the review by the Swiss authorities of the conformity of the Taliban Ordinance with the Convention. It further finds that there was nothing in the Security Council resolutions to prevent the Swiss authorities from introducing mechanisms to verify the measures taken at national level pursuant to those resolutions. (*Nada v. Switzerland* Application No. 10593/08, ECtHR [Judgment] [Grand Chamber], 12 September 2012, [212].)

From these two decisions, it is clear that the ECJ and ECtHR confirm that:

(a) neither national or regional implementation of UN Security Council resolutions prevents the review of the lawfulness of such resolutions with human rights obligations of UN member States;

(b) reviewing the consistency of UN Security Council resolutions with UN member States' obligations does not amount to reviewing the legality of the Security Council decisions in general.

The ECtHR/ECJ approach of not regarding Security Council resolutions as subverting human rights obligations is commendable. Nonetheless, it can hardly be doubted that reviewing the lawfulness of the Security Council resolutions under domestic or regional law raises serious questions for international law.

Conclusion

International human rights are undoubtedly one of the most important contributions made by international law in the last sixty years or so. From the various case law and scholastic opinions examined in this chapter, human rights are clearly a contentious issue, the observation, promotion, and implementation of which are often subject to the whim of governments. Numerous reasons account for why human rights are often derogated from or abrogated. While it would be idealistic to wish to see a society in which human rights reign freely at all times, regardless of the interest of States and the protection of general interests, it is equally dangerous to reduce human rights to poor cousins of State interests. Human rights and national interests, such as State security, will often diverge; what is important for the health of nations and peoples is how to accommodate these two without damaging either.

Questions

Self-test questions

1 What are 'international human rights'?

2 Explain the difference, if any, between 'civil and political' and 'social, cultural, and economic' rights.

3 List the jurisdictional competences of the African Court of Justice and Human Rights.

4 What is the main function of the UN Human Rights Committee and of what effect are its comments?

5 In what major way does ECHR Protocol 11 affect the European human rights system?

6 Identify one major weakness of the Inter-American Convention on Human Rights.

7 Explain the term 'control order'.

Discussion questions

1 With reference to decided cases, critically examine the assertion that human rights and cultural practices are unavoidably incompatible.

2 'Terrorism is what a given State regards as terrorism and cannot be subject to an international definition.' Discuss.

3 'In the final analysis, a State that claims that it has not committed torture is free to claim that those against whom the acts were committed were caught in situations of armed conflict.' Briefly consider this statement in light of the US position regarding the torture of Guantánamo Bay and Abu Ghraib detainees.

4 Discuss the jurisdiction of the African Court of Justice and Human Rights.

5 What functions does the Human Rights Committee perform and to what extent have its comments influenced or affected States' implementation of the ICCPR?

Assessment question

'The rights enshrined in the ICESCR are fundamentally different from those that are contained in the ICCPR, yet both are expressed to be for the benefit of people. Nonetheless, while the rights contained in the ICCPR can be adjudicated upon, the rights contained in the ICESCR are non-justiciable.'

Critically analyse this statement, with reference to decided cases.

 # Key cases

- *Ireland v. United Kingdom* Application No. 5310/71 (1978) 2 EHRR 25
- *Olga Tellis v. Bombay Municipal Corporation* 1986 AIR 180, Indian Supreme Court
- *Sawhoyamaxa Indigenous Community v. Paraguay* (2006) IACHR Ser. C, No. 146
- *Social and Economic Rights Action Center & Center for Economic and Social Rights v. Nigeria* Communication No. 155/96 (2001), African Commission on Human and Peoples' Rights
- *Soobramoney v. Minister of Health (Kwazulu-Natal)* Case CCT 32/97, 27 November 1997, Constitutional Court of South Africa

Further reading

Alston, P. and Robinson, M. (eds), *Human Rights and Development: Towards Mutual Reinforcement* (Oxford: Oxford University Press, 2005)

Alston, P., Steiner H.J., and Goodman, R., *International Human Rights in Context: Law, Politics, Morals* (4th edn, Oxford: Oxford University Press, 2013)

An Na'im, A., 'Human rights in the Muslim world: socio-political conditions and scriptural imperatives' (1990) 3 Harv HRJ 13

Baderin, M. and Ssenyonjo, M. (eds), *International Human Rights Law: Six Decades after the UDHR and Beyond* (Aldershot: Ashgate Publishing, 2010)

Lauterpacht, H., *An International Bill of Rights of Man* (New York: Columbia University Press, 1945)

Lauterpacht, H., 'The Universal Declaration of Human Rights' (1948) 25 BYBIL 354

Osiatyński, W., *Human Rights and Their Limits* (Cambridge: Cambridge University Press, 2009)

Sandifer, D., 'The international protection of human rights: the United Nations system' (1949) 43 AJIL 59

Shelton, D. L., *Regional Protection of Human Rights* (Oxford: Oxford University Press, 2010)

Walker, C., 'Clamping down on terrorism in the United Kingdom' (2006) 4 J Int'l Crim Just 1137

Index

Index

complete: law solution

Reading and making sense of original case extracts is a vital part of understanding how law works. But how do you know which sections of which cases to read?

Books in the **complete** series combine extracts from a wide range of primary materials with clear explanatory text to provide students with a complete introductory resource.

Each author carefully unfolds the complexities of the subject, exposing the reader to relevant case extracts and supporting them with illuminating commentary. Helpful learning features are clearly presented and effectively employed, ensuring each **complete** title provides students with a stimulating introduction to the subject.

complete
series

For further details about titles in the series, visit

www.oxfordtextbooks.co.uk/law/complete